TRANSNATIONAL COMMERCIAL LAW

INTERNATIONAL INSTRUMENTS & COMMENTARY

TRANSNATIONAL COMMERCIAL LAW

INTERNATIONAL INSTRUMENTS AND COMMENTARY

Roy Goode

*Emeritus Professor of Law, University of Oxford, and
Emeritus Fellow of St. John's College, Oxford*

Herbert Kronke

*Secretary-General UNIDROIT, Rome, and
Professor of Law at the University of Heidelberg*

Ewan McKendrick

*Professor of English Private Law, University of Oxford,
and Professorial Fellow, Lady Margaret Hall, Oxford*

Jeffrey Wool

Partner, Perkins Coie, Washington

OXFORD
UNIVERSITY PRESS

OXFORD

UNIVERSITY PRESS

Great Clarendon Street, Oxford OX2 6DP

Oxford University Press is a department of the University of Oxford.
It furthers the University's objective of excellence in research, scholarship,
and education by publishing worldwide in

Oxford New York

Auckland Bangkok Buenos Aires Cape Town Chennai
Dar es Salaam Delhi Hong Kong Istanbul Karachi Kolkata
Kuala Lumpur Madrid Melbourne Mexico City Mumbai Nairobi
São Paulo Shanghai Taipei Tokyo Toronto

Oxford is a registered trade mark of Oxford University Press
in the UK and in certain other countries

Published in the United States
by Oxford University Press Inc., New York

British Library Cataloguing in Publication Data

Data available

Library of Congress Cataloging in Publication Data

Data available

ISBN 0-19-925167-3

1 3 5 7 9 10 8 6 4 2

Typeset by Newgen Imaging Systems (P) Ltd., Chennai, India
Printed in Great Britain
on acid-free paper by
Biddles Ltd., King's Lynn

PREFACE

The past two decades have witnessed an explosion in the growth of transnational commercial law, which represents the product of work to harmonize national laws and create international law affecting domestic and cross-border transactions. Diverse instruments have been used to advance this process: international and regional conventions, model laws, EC directives and regulations, uniform rules produced by bodies such as the International Chamber of Commerce, and international and European restatements of contract law by scholars.

For the busy practitioner, the search for international and regional commercial law instruments can be frustrating and time-consuming. So too is the effort to synthesize these texts, identifying their key feature, and seeing their relationship with other international instruments addressing the same topic. This new compilation, consisting of some 60 instruments of the various kinds described above, is designed to provide the reader with immediate access to the main primary materials relating to cross-border commercial contracts and structured financing transactions, and to related matters such as electronic commerce, dispute resolution and insolvency, as well as the principal source of treaty law, the Vienna Convention on Treaties.

Among the relatively few such collections currently on the market this volume possesses a number of distinctive features:

- It is comprehensive and fully up-to-date, including, for example, the 2004 UNIDROIT Principles of International Commercial Contracts.
- The materials are organized into groups of instruments distributed over 12 chapters, each containing a linking commentary which provides the context, identifies key issues, and explains the major provisions of each instrument and the general development of the law in the relevant field.
- The *complete text* of each international convention is reproduced, including the preamble, which is important for interpretation, and the final clauses, which nowadays are far from standard.
- Each convention is followed by a list of states signing and/or ratifying the convention, with dates of signature, ratification and entry into force for each state.
- For ease of reference each instrument is headed by an internal table of contents showing the page number of every Article.

v

- Other reading aids include an overall table of contents, tables of national legislation, international treaties and other instruments, and a detailed index.

We hope that this volume will be found useful by all those with an interest in transnational commercial law, whether as practising lawyers, judges, arbitrators, academics or legislators.

In the preparation of this volume we have been greatly assisted by Adam Kramer, Katherine Worthington and Oren Bigos, who verified sources, obtained documents and assisted in the checking of proofs. Their help is deeply appreciated.

We should also like to thank all those institutions which have given permission to reproduce their materials and which are listed separately. We are also indebted to Oxford University Press for its meticulous preparation of this volume, and in particular to Rachel Mullaly, the commissioning editor, Michelle Thompson, the production editor, Sarah Nattrass, the proofreader, and Michael Hayes, who compiled the index.

Roy Goode	Herbert Kronke	Jeffrey Wool
Ewan McKendrick	Rome	Washington
Oxford		

August 2004

CONTENTS

TABLE OF CASES

TABLE OF NATIONAL LEGISLATION

Page numbers in **bold** indicate where the legislation is reproduced in part or in full.

TABLE OF INTERNATIONAL TREATIES
AND CONVENTIONS AND MODEL LAWS

Page numbers in **bold** indicate where the legislation is reproduced in part or in full.

TABLE OF EUROPEAN CONVENTIONS
AND LEGISLATION

TABLE OF OTHER INSTRUMENTS

Page numbers in **bold** indicate where the instrument is reproduced in part or in full.

1

TREATY LAW

A. Introductory Text

1. Vienna Convention on the Law of Treaties, 1969

Much transnational commercial law is developed through treaties. While these texts, grouped by some as *international private law* instruments, confer rights to and among parties to private transactions (transaction-parties), their legal status is firmly rooted in treaty law, which deals with the rights and obligations of States (States-parties). In that field, no formal distinction exists between international public and private law. Norms and leading jurisprudence are common to both treaty types. A trend towards varying practices, however, is emerging where function dictates.

The Vienna Convention on the Law of Treaties, 1969 (Vienna 1969) is the principal authoritative source of treaty law. It largely codified existing law but developed it further in certain areas. A large number of States are parties to Vienna 1969.[1] Certain others, while not parties, follow all or most of its rules and otherwise consider it authoritative,[2] treating it as reflecting customary law,[3] which, not coincidentally, is expressly retained by Vienna 1969 as operative to address questions not governed by the text.[4]

Treaty practice is an important vehicle supplementing and developing the rules in Vienna 1969, and that is increasingly the case in the context of transaction-focused

---

[1] As of September 2003, 96 States are parties to Vienna 1969.

[2] See, e.g., U.S. Department of State's statement, in 1971, that it is 'already recognised as the authoritative guide to current treaty law and practice'. S.Exec. Doc.L., 92d Cong. 1st Sess. (1971), p.1.

[3] See Art 38 of the Treaty.   [4] See the final clause of the preamble.

international private law treaties, where transaction-parties, rather than States-parties, are the key actors.

Vienna 1969, as a stand-alone instrument, is outside the scope of this volume. Rather, select features of particular import to transnational private commercial law treaties are addressed.

Treaties and domestic law

Every treaty binds its States-parties,[5] and provisions of domestic law may not be invoked as a justification for failure to perform a treaty.[6] Yet international law and domestic law operate on different planes. A treaty may well be in force for a State-party without being the domestic law of that State. In such circumstances, while State-party to State-party liability may exist, the terms of the treaty may not be relied upon by transaction-parties as enforceable legal rules.

Domestic law, usually constitutional in nature, determines whether and the extent to which a treaty needs to be incorporated or otherwise transformed into domestic law by further act. Vienna 1969 does not address that fundamental question. The label *monism* has come to refer to States in which a treaty may become domestic law without legislation (sometimes, although not always, as a self-executing instrument) upon its entering into force for that State,[7] and *dualism* to States where legislation is required. Most States actually have elements of both, and these categories should be viewed as a continuum.

Where legislation is required, a challenge is to ensure its conformity with the source treaty and fit with domestic law, superseding all items inconsistent with the source treaty. As many modern commercial law treaties cut across a wide range of otherwise applicable domestic law, particular care is required.

Interpretation of treaties

The general rule of treaty interpretation set out in Article 31 of Vienna 1969 is that a treaty shall be interpreted in good faith 'in accordance with the ordinary meaning to be given to the terms of the treaty in their context and in the light of its object and purpose'. This is a single rule with three elements: the text (provisions), context (including preamble and annexes and other materials surrounding the conclusion of the treaty, such as agreements in a final act),[8] and object and purpose (often seen in the preamble as well). In addition to context, subsequent agreement (on

---

[5] Article 26.   [6] Article 27; see Art 46 for a restricted exception to the rule.

[7] A treaty is in force for a State upon satisfaction of the last of two conditions. First, it must have expressed its 'consent to be bound', by (among other acts) ratification, acceptance, approval, or accession, in accordance with the treaty's terms (for simplicity, hereinafter 'ratification'): Arts 2(1)(b) and 11–17. Secondly, the treaty must either be in force or come into force upon that State's ratification: Art 24.

[8] Article 31(2). Also included are instruments made by a State-party at the conclusion of the treaty and accepted by the others.

interpretation or application) and practice (in application which established agreement on interpretation) shall also be taken into account.[9]

A secondary rule permits recourse to supplementary materials, including the preparatory work of the treaty (*travaux preparatoires*), to 'confirm' the meaning resulting from the application of Article 31 or to determine the meaning when the interpretation according to that Article leaves the meaning ambiguous or obscure or leads to a result which is manifestly absurd or unreasonable.[10] This secondary rule follows from the basic *pacta sunt servanda* rule,[11] requiring good faith performance of a treaty, as interpretation is part of performance.

These rules, which seek to balance purely textual and teleological approaches, with initial emphasis on the former, find parallelism in international private law treaty practice. The standard treaty provision calls for interpretation having regard to (a) a treaty's 'purpose', often with specific reference to the preamble, (b) its 'international character', and (c) the need to promote uniformity. Certain texts, tracking Vienna 1969, also refer to 'good faith' interpretation. Others add the need to ensure interpretation that promotes 'predictability'. An additional provision typically refers to the 'general principles' underlying the instrument as a means to fill textual gaps. Once again, the preamble is the common starting point for determining such principles.

More generally, there is a trend in the modern commercial law treaties to provide detailed materials in aid of uniform interpretation. These include official commentaries and explanatory reports. In certain cases, these commentaries and reports might constitute 'context' under the general rule of interpretation. This trend reflects the needs for commercial predictability, and has been assisted by greater reliance on rule-based drafting techniques.

Most modern commercial law treaties are multilingual in the sense of being authenticated in more than one language. Many are authenticated in all official UN languages. Where this occurs, each text is 'equally authoritative'.[12] If a comparison of the texts reveal a 'difference of meaning', the general and supplemental rules are employed to resolve the matter (unless the treaty or States-parties have agreed on a prevailing text). Failing resolution, a meaning that best reconciles the texts having regard to the treaty's object and purposes will be adopted.[13]

Declarations and reservations

International private law treaty practice, particularly that associated with commercial law, is basic to the topic of declarations and reservations. While Vienna 1969 deals at length with reservations ('any unilateral statement made by a State', at

---

[9] Article 31(3).
[10] Article 32. Vienna 1969 does not specify what constitutes preparatory work. All drafts and conference records will usually constitute part of the *travaux*, and uncontested interpretative statements by the chairman of a drafting committee may also do so.   [11] Article 26.
[12] Article 33(1).   [13] Article 33(4).

signing or ratifying, that 'purports to exclude or modify the legal effect of certain provisions of the treaty in their application to that State'[14]), it does not provide detailed provisions on what we will label 'contemplated declarations'.

Contemplated declarations are declarations that States are expressly invited to make by the treaty's terms. They may permit a State to opt into (or 'apply') or opt out of (or 'disapply') a provision or otherwise make legally operative statements (e.g., which courts have jurisdiction or to which of its territorial units a treaty applies). Provision for declarations is increasingly common in transnational commercial law treaties. Treaty practice confirms that contemplated declarations made pursuant to such a provision may not be 'reservations' for certain purposes of Vienna 1969, avoiding the myriad implications of the contrary conclusion.

Nor are many simple 'interpretative declarations' necessarily disguised reservations, although they (and other 'understandings' and similar statements) may be.

Should an actual reservation be made, Vienna 1969 provides specific rules that answer many, though not all, questions.[15] The main features of these rules are as follows. A reservation may be made unless (a) the reservation is prohibited by the treaty, or (b) the treaty provides that only specified reservations, which do not include the reservation in question, may be made, or (c) the reservation is incompatible with the objects and purpose of the treaty.[16] A reservation expressly authorized does not require acceptance by other States-parties (unless the treaty otherwise provides),[17] but otherwise it takes effect only vis-à-vis States that accept it,[18] and this is so whether or not it is prohibited. Such a reservation does not modify obligations in respect of the subject provision for other States-parties *inter se*.[19] Different rules apply to a restricted multilateral treaty (e.g. a treaty between EC Member States), where unanimity on all provisions is essential.[20]

Dispute resolution and remedies for breach

International private law treaties are principally concerned with creating rights and obligations among transaction-parties and other private parties (including State entities engaged in commercial activities), enforceable by them in courts with jurisdiction under that treaty, if applicable, or otherwise under the rules of private international law. However, States, as States-parties to international private law treaties, undertake obligations that may have an impact on transaction-parties. In the context of commercial law treaties, a State-party's non-performance of such obligations may result in significant financial loss to transaction-parties.

---

[14] Article 1(d).

[15] The International Law Commission has been working on the topic of reservations to treaties since 1993. Its work, including a Guide to Practice, will assist in further harmonization of reservation practice. This important work is ongoing. (See the Eighth Report on Reservations to Treaties, ILC 55th Session (2003)A/CN 4/535. [16] Article 19

[17] Article 20(1).   [18] Articles 20(4)(a), 21.   [19] Article 21(2).

[20] Article 20(2).

In very broad terms, however, a State-party's obligations under a treaty enure to the benefit of other States-parties, not transaction-parties. While there may be special exceptions to this rule, and matters are further complicated where a transaction-party seeks redress under domestic law for non-performance of a treaty-derived obligation, Vienna 1969 provides no direct rights for transaction-parties. It simply provides that a 'material breach'[21] of a multilateral treaty by a State-party entitles affected States-parties to invoke the breach as a ground for suspending operation of the treaty in their relation with the defaulting State.[22] It also confirms that its provisions do not 'prejudge' any question that may arise relating to a treaty from the 'international responsibility of a State',[23] a topic being continuously developed by the international legal community.[24] Customary international law addresses these items.[25]

In equally broad terms, customary international law in this field also focuses on the State-party to State-party legal consequences arising from breach,[26] although developments in non-commercial law fields of international law may gradually affect this principle. While remedies, or, in the parlance, 'reparations for injury', are in theory fairly broad,[27] they generally must be pursued through soft consultative diplomatic channels,[28] as a practical matter,[29] where a treaty does not contemplate meaningful dispute resolution or enforcement,[30] which is the case in the commercial law context.[31]

---

[21] Article 60(3) (a non-sanctioned repudiation or violation of a provision 'essential to the accomplishment of the object or purpose of the treaty').   [22] Article 60(1)–(2).

[23] Article 73.

[24] The International Law Commission has undertaken work on this topic, resulting in the adoption in 2001 of draft articles on *Responsibility of States for Internationally Wrongful Acts* (ILC, State Responsibility). See Report of the International Law Commission on the work of its Fifty-sixth session, *Official Records of the General Assembly, Fifty-sixth session, Supplement No. 10* (A/56/10), chp.IV.E.1   [25] As retained in the final clause of the preamble.

[26] Compare ILC, State Responsibility, above note 24, at Art 33 (the text, rather than specifying rights in favour of private parties, is 'without prejudice to any right, arising from the international responsibility of a State, which may accrue directly to any person or entity other than a State').

[27] See ibid. at ch 2. Forms of reparations are compensation (most common), restitution, and satisfaction. In addition, 'proportional' countermeasures may be taken by a State (to induce treaty compliance, not penalize).

[28] Historically, concepts of nationality have been central to actions of this kind taken by States-parties. States-parties will consider acting for their citizens, including their corporate citizens. Yet, matters are becoming more complex in the commercial law field, even beyond the implications of international corporate groupings. One reason, not yet fully assessed, relates to the gradual loosening of the traditional 'internationality' feature in commercial law treaties that required transaction parties to be located in different Contracting States.

[29] The settlement of international disputes of this kind (through negotiations and consultations, possibly conciliation and mediation) is voluntary, consent being required for compulsory settlement (i.e. arbitration or judicial settlement).

[30] Compare the field of international economic law, where a central feature of the WTO regime is compulsory States-parties dispute resolution and elaborate enforcement mechanisms.

[31] Only one such treaty contained in this volume, the International Convention Relating to the Arrest of Sea-Going Ships, 1952 (see p. 504 below), contains a provision on compulsory States-parties

Withdrawal from a treaty

All modern commercial law treaties are of indefinite duration with broad rights in favour of States-parties to withdraw from the treaty. Typically all that is required is notice to the depositary followed by the passage of a specified period of time. That act, technically a 'denunciation' (unilateral act by which a State terminates its participation in a treaty), may affect transaction-parties that have relied upon the treaty provisions in entering into and structuring their contracts.

Vienna 1969, following the treaty-as-contract paradigm, endorses treaty provisions permitting denunciation.[32] As to the consequences of withdrawal, it states that, unless a treaty otherwise provides, denunciation (a) releases that withdrawing State from any further obligation to perform the treaty, and (b) 'does not affect any right, obligation or legal situation *of the parties* created through the execution of the treaty prior to its termination' (emphasis added).[33] As 'parties' means States-parties, the italicized words, underscoring that the provision does not protect vested interests of transaction-parties, have given rise to commercial law treaty provisions that expressly provide such protection. The same issues, and the same express treaty provisions, apply to the related concept of the effect of future declarations or modifications of existing declarations.

Vienna 1969 endorses clear treaty provisions, which are common, addressing the relationship between successive treaties relating to the same subject matter.[34]

Treaties and non-Contracting States

Treaties neither impose obligations or confer rights on a third State without its consent.[35] A 'third State' is a State that is not a party to the treaty, including one whose ratification has not yet taken effect.[36] While Vienna 1969 addresses cases where a third State may be affected by a treaty, in particular, where the States-parties intend to confer a right or impose an obligation on a third State and that State accepts (obligation) or assents (rights), and modifications thereto,[37] these circumstances have not been seen in the commercial law treaty context. The same is true of a treaty's terms becoming binding on a third State as a customary rule of international law.[38]

As noted above, many commercial law treaties apply notwithstanding certain transaction-parties being located in non-Contracting States (non-States-parties).

---

dispute resolution (arbitration). While that context—the arrest of ships—naturally raises special concerns, no such provision is included in the more recent shipping arrest convention, the International Convention on Arrest of Ships, 1999 (see p. 520 below). Nor is one contained in the aircraft treaties.

[32] Article 42(2).   [33] Article 70.   [34] Article 30.

[35] Article 34. There are certain treaties valid *erga omnes*—for the world—but they are outside these provisions in Vienna 1969. Treaties dealing with activities in outer space are examples. See Treaty on the Principles Governing the Activities of States in the Exploration and Use of Outer Space Including the Moon and Other Celestial Bodies, 610 U.N.T.S. (1967).   [36] Article 2(1)(h).

[37] Articles 35–7.   [38] Article 38.

Complex issues may arise in that circumstance where, in the context of a treaty dispute, a third State engages in consultations with a State-party on behalf of its nations.

Effect of treaties prior to entry into force

Certain technical provisions in a treaty 'regulating matters arising necessarily before the entry into force of the treaty' apply from the time of adoption of the treaty.[39] These include provisions regarding the authentication of the text, ratification and declaration procedures, and the functions of the depositary, discussed below.[40] Recently and increasingly, this treaty rule has been employed to authorize the work of a preparatory commission to establish items (such as commercial registries) needed for the treaty's effectiveness. It that context, express treaty provisions determine the rights and responsibilities of negotiating or signing States.

Vienna 1969 also contains a provision, which may have ventured beyond then customary international law, to the effect that a signing State is obliged to 'refrain from acts which would defeat' the object and purpose of a treaty 'until it shall have made its intention clear not to become a party to the treaty'.[41] The same applies to a ratifying State prior to entry into force provided that time is not 'unduly delayed'.[42] There is little precedent and practice in this area, and none in the context of modern commercial law treaties. Nonetheless, this a very light obligation, and neither requires action consistent with the treaty nor prevents action inconsistent with the treaty.

Role of depositary

Vienna 1969 contains several provisions dealing with the identity, nature, and function of treaty depositaries. A depositary may be a State, an international organization (e.g. UNIDROIT), or the chief administrative officer of such an organization (e.g. the Secretary General of the UN)[43]. For modern transnational commercial treaties, States are less likely to serve in this role. A depositary's functions are 'international in nature', and, above all, it has an obligation to 'act impartially',[44] that issue being more acute if it is a State. Its particular duties generally relate to (a) custody of documents relating to the treaty and the participation therein of States-parties, (b) examination of the form of such document, (c) notifications to and communications with States and others, and (d) registration and publication of the treaty.[45] A depositary also has certain responsibilities regarding the correction of errors after authentication of the text.[46] A treaty may and generally does modify, refine, and elaborate upon these functions and add other responsibilities.

---

[39] Article 24(4).　[40] See pp. 7-8 below.　[41] Article 18(a).
[42] Article 18(b).　[43] Article 76(1).　[44] Article 76(2).
[45] Articles 77 and 80.　[46] Article 79.

The role of the depositary of increasingly complex transnational commercial law treaties is quite important. Such texts may require or permit the making of a number of contemplated declarations, many of which may be highly technical, both in terms of underlying legal content and conformity with the treaty text. In addition, modern depositaries are called upon to interact with a large number transaction-parties. In many cases, the depositary performs invaluable education and promotional functions, including the preparation of explanatory materials and the construction and maintenance of websites. Its skill and effort have a material impact on the success of a treaty.

B. Instruments

(i) VIENNA CONVENTION ON THE LAW OF TREATIES*

---

* The United Nations is the author of the original material.

PREAMBLE

The States Parties to the present Convention,

Considering the fundamental role of treaties in the history of international relations,

Recognizing the ever-increasing importance of treaties as a source of international law and as a means of developing peaceful co-operation among nations, whatever their constitutional and social systems,

Noting that the principles of free consent and of good faith and the *pacta sunt servanda* rule are universally recognized,

Affirming that disputes concerning treaties, like other international disputes, should be settled by peaceful means and in conformity with the principles of justice and international law,

Recalling the determination of the peoples of the United Nations to establish conditions under which justice and respect for the obligations arising from treaties can be maintained,

Having in mind the principles of international law embodied in the Charter of the United Nations, such as the principles of the equal rights and self-determination of peoples, of the sovereign equality and independence of all States, of non-interference in the domestic affairs of States, of the prohibition of the threat or use of force and of universal respect for, and observance of, human rights and fundamental freedoms for all,

Believing that the codification and progressive development of the law of treaties achieved in the present Convention will promote the purposes of the United Nations set forth in the Charter, namely, the maintenance of international peace and security, the development of friendly relations and the achievement of co-operation among nations,

Affirming that the rules of customary international law will continue to govern questions not regulated by the provisions of the present Convention,

Have agreed as follows:

PART I
INTRODUCTION

Article 1
Scope of the present Convention

The present Convention applies to treaties between States.

Article 2
Use of terms

1. For the purposes of the present Convention:
   (a) 'treaty' means an international agreement concluded between States in written form and governed by international law, whether embodied in a single instrument or in two or more related instruments and whatever its particular designation;
   (b) 'ratification', 'acceptance', 'approval' and 'accession' mean in each case the international act so named whereby a State establishes on the international plane its consent to be bound by a treaty;
   (c) 'full powers' means a document emanating from the competent authority of a State designating a person or persons to represent the State for negotiating, adopting or authenticating the text of a treaty, for expressing the consent of the State to be bound by a treaty, or for accomplishing any other act with respect to a treaty;
   (d) 'reservation' means a unilateral statement, however phrased or named, made by a State, when signing, ratifying, accepting, approving or acceding to a treaty, whereby it purports to exclude or to modify the legal effect of certain provisions of the treaty in their application to that State;
   (e) 'negotiating State' means a State which took part in the drawing up and adoption of the text of the treaty;
   (f) 'contracting State' means a State which has consented to be bound by the treaty, whether or not the treaty has entered into force;
   (g) 'party' means a State which has consented to be bound by the treaty and for which the treaty is in force;
   (h) 'third State' means a State not a party to the treaty;
   (i) 'international organization' means an intergovernmental organization.
2. The provisions of paragraph 1 regarding the use of terms in the present Convention are without prejudice to the use of those terms or to the meanings which may be given to them in the internal law of any State.

Article 3
International agreements not within the scope of the present Convention

The fact that the present Convention does not apply to international agreements concluded between States and other subjects of international law or between such other subjects of international law, or to international agreements not in written form, shall not affect:
   (a) the legal force of such agreements;

(b) the application to them of any of the rules set forth in the present Convention to which they would be subject under international law independently of the Convention;

(c) the application of the Convention to the relations of States as between themselves under international agreements to which other subjects of international law are also parties.

Article 4
Non-retroactivity of the present Convention

Without prejudice to the application of any rules set forth in the present Convention to which treaties would be subject under international law independently of the Convention, the Convention applies only to treaties which are concluded by States after the entry into force of the present Convention with regard to such States.

Article 5
Treaties constituting international organizations and treaties adopted within an international organization

The present Convention applies to any treaty which is the constituent instrument of an international organization and to any treaty adopted within an international organization without prejudice to any relevant rules of the organization.

PART II
CONCLUSION AND ENTRY INTO FORCE OF TREATIES

SECTION I
CONCLUSION OF TREATIES

Article 6
Capacity of States to conclude treaties

Every State possesses capacity to conclude treaties.

Article 7
Full powers

1. A person is considered as representing a State for the purpose of adopting or authenticating the text of a treaty or for the purpose of expressing the consent of the State to be bound by a treaty if:

   (a) he produces appropriate full powers; or

   (b) it appears from the practice of the States concerned or from other circumstances that their intention was to consider that person as representing the State for such purposes and to dispense with full powers.

2. In virtue of their functions and without having to produce full powers, the following are considered as representing their State:

   (a) Heads of State, Heads of Government and Ministers for Foreign Affairs, for the purpose of performing all acts relating to the conclusion of a treaty;

   (b) heads of diplomatic missions, for the purpose of adopting the text of a treaty between the accrediting State and the State to which they are accredited;

(c) representatives accredited by States to an international conference or to an international organization or one of its organs, for the purpose of adopting the text of a treaty in that conference, organization or organ.

Article 8
Subsequent confirmation of an act performed without authorization

An act relating to the conclusion of a treaty performed by a person who cannot be considered under article 7 as authorized to represent a State for that purpose is without legal effect unless afterwards confirmed by that State.

Article 9
Adoption of the text

1. The adoption of the text of a treaty takes place by the consent of all the States participating in its drawing up except as provided in paragraph 2.
2. The adoption of the text of a treaty at an international conference takes place by the vote of two-thirds of the States present and voting, unless by the same majority they shall decide to apply a different rule.

Article 10
Authentication of the text

The text of a treaty is established as authentic and definitive:
   (a) by such procedure as may be provided for in the text or agreed upon by the States participating in its drawing up; or
   (b) failing such procedure, by the signature, signature *ad referendum* or initialling by the representatives of those States of the text of the treaty or of the Final Act of a conference incorporating the text.

Article 11
Means of expressing consent to be bound by a treaty

The consent of a State to be bound by a treaty may be expressed by signature, exchange of instruments constituting a treaty, ratification, acceptance, approval or accession, or by any other means if so agreed.

Article 12
Consent to be bound by a treaty expressed by signature

1. The consent of a State to be bound by a treaty is expressed by the signature of its representative when:
   (a) the treaty provides that signature shall have that effect;
   (b) it is otherwise established that the negotiating States were agreed that signature should have that effect; or
   (c) the intention of the State to give that effect to the signature appears from the full powers of its representative or was expressed during the negotiation.
2. For the purposes of paragraph 1:
   (a) the initialling of a text constitutes a signature of the treaty when it is established that the negotiating States so agreed;

(b) the signature *ad referendum* of a treaty by a representative, if confirmed by his State, constitutes a full signature of the treaty.

Article 13
Consent to be bound by a treaty expressed by an exchange of instruments constituting a treaty

The consent of States to be bound by a treaty constituted by instruments exchanged between them is expressed by that exchange when:
   (a) the instruments provide that their exchange shall have that effect; or
   (b) it is otherwise established that those States were agreed that the exchange of instruments should have that effect.

Article 14
Consent to be bound by a treaty expressed by ratification, acceptance or approval

1. The consent of a State to be bound by a treaty is expressed by ratification when:
   (a) the treaty provides for such consent to be expressed by means of ratification;
   (b) it is otherwise established that the negotiating States were agreed that ratification should be required;
   (c) the representative of the State has signed the treaty subject to ratification; or
   (d) the intention of the State to sign the treaty subject to ratification appears from the full powers of its representative or was expressed during the negotiation.
2. The consent of a State to be bound by a treaty is expressed by acceptance or approval under conditions similar to those which apply to ratification.

Article 15
Consent to be bound by a treaty expressed by accession

The consent of a State to be bound by a treaty is expressed by accession when:
   (a) the treaty provides that such consent may be expressed by that State by means of accession;
   (b) it is otherwise established that the negotiating States were agreed that such consent may be expressed by that State by means of accession; or
   (c) all the parties have subsequently agreed that such consent may be expressed by that State by means of accession.

Article 16
Exchange or deposit of instruments of ratification, acceptance, approval or accession

Unless the treaty otherwise provides, instruments of ratification, acceptance, approval or accession establish the consent of a State to be bound by a treaty upon:
   (a) their exchange between the contracting States;
   (b) their deposit with the depositary; or
   (c) their notification to the contracting States or to the depositary, if so agreed.

15

Article 17
Consent to be bound by part of a treaty and choice of differing provisions

1. Without prejudice to articles 19 to 23, the consent of a State to be bound by part of a treaty is effective only if the treaty so permits or the other contracting States so agree.
2. The consent of a State to be bound by a treaty which permits a choice between differing provisions is effective only if it is made clear to which of the provisions the consent relates.

Article 18
Obligation not to defeat the object and purpose of a treaty prior to its entry into force

A State is obliged to refrain from acts which would defeat the object and purpose of a treaty when:
   (a) it has signed the treaty or has exchanged instruments constituting the treaty subject to ratification, acceptance or approval, until it shall have made its intention clear not to become a party to the treaty; or
   (b) it has expressed its consent to be bound by the treaty, pending the entry into force of the treaty and provided that such entry into force is not unduly delayed.

SECTION 2

RESERVATIONS

Article 19
Formulation of reservations

A State may, when signing, ratifying, accepting, approving or acceding to a treaty, formulate a reservation unless:
   (a) the reservation is prohibited by the treaty;
   (b) the treaty provides that only specified reservations, which do not include the reservation in question, may be made; or
   (c) in cases not falling under sub-paragraphs (a) and (b), the reservation is incompatible with the object and purpose of the treaty.

Article 20
Acceptance of and objection to reservations

1. A reservation expressly authorized by a treaty does not require any subsequent acceptance by the other contracting States unless the treaty so provides.
2. When it appears from the limited number of the negotiating States and the object and purpose of a treaty that the application of the treaty in its entirety between all the parties is an essential condition of the consent of each one to be bound by the treaty, a reservation requires acceptance by all the parties.
3. When a treaty is a constituent instrument of an international organization and unless it otherwise provides, a reservation requires the acceptance of the competent organ of that organization.

4. In cases not falling under the preceding paragraphs and unless the treaty otherwise provides:
   (a) acceptance by another contracting State of a reservation constitutes the reserving State a party to the treaty in relation to that other State if or when the treaty is in force for those States;
   (b) an objection by another contracting State to a reservation does not preclude the entry into force of the treaty as between the objecting and reserving States unless a contrary intention is definitely expressed by the objecting State;
   (c) an act expressing a State's consent to be bound by the treaty and containing a reservation is effective as soon as at least one other contracting State has accepted the reservation.
5. For the purposes of paragraphs 2 and 4 and unless the treaty otherwise provides, a reservation is considered to have been accepted by a State if it shall have raised no objection to the reservation by the end of a period of twelve months after it was notified of the reservation or by the date on which it expressed its consent to be bound by the treaty, whichever is later.

Article 21
Legal effects of reservations and of objections to reservations

1. A reservation established with regard to another party in accordance with articles 19, 20 and 23:
   (a) modifies for the reserving State in its relations with that other party the provisions of the treaty to which the reservation relates to the extent of the reservation; and
   (b) modifies those provisions to the same extent for that other party in its relations with the reserving State.
2. The reservation does not modify the provisions of the treaty for the other parties to the treaty *inter se*.
3. When a State objecting to a reservation has not opposed the entry into force of the treaty between itself and the reserving State, the provisions to which the reservation relates do not apply as between the two States to the extent of the reservation.

Article 22
Withdrawal of reservations and of objections to reservations

1. Unless the treaty otherwise provides, a reservation may be withdrawn at any time and the consent of a State which has accepted the reservation is not required for its withdrawal.
2. Unless the treaty otherwise provides, an objection to a reservation may be withdrawn at any time.
3. Unless the treaty otherwise provides, or it is otherwise agreed:
   (a) the withdrawal of a reservation becomes operative in relation to another contracting State only when notice of it has been received by that State;
   (b) the withdrawal of an objection to a reservation becomes operative only when notice of it has been received by the State which formulated the reservation.

Article 23
Procedure regarding reservations

1. A reservation, an express acceptance of a reservation and an objection to a reservation must be formulated in writing and communicated to the contracting States and other States entitled to become parties to the treaty.

2. If formulated when signing the treaty subject to ratification, acceptance or approval, a reservation must be formally confirmed by the reserving State when expressing its consent to be bound by the treaty. In such a case the reservation shall be considered as having been made on the date of its confirmation.

3. An express acceptance of, or an objection to, a reservation made previously to confirmation of the reservation does not itself require confirmation.

4. The withdrawal of a reservation or of an objection to a reservation must be formulated in writing.

SECTION 3

ENTRY INTO FORCE AND PROVISIONAL APPLICATION OF TREATIES

Article 24
Entry into force

1. A treaty enters into force in such manner and upon such date as it may provide or as the negotiating States may agree.

2. Failing any such provision or agreement, a treaty enters into force as soon as consent to be bound by the treaty has been established for all the negotiating States.

3. When the consent of a State to be bound by a treaty is established on a date after the treaty has come into force, the treaty enters into force for that State on that date, unless the treaty otherwise provides.

4. The provisions of a treaty regulating the authentication of its text, the establishment of the consent of States to be bound by the treaty, the manner or date of its entry into force, reservations, the functions of the depositary and other matters arising necessarily before the entry into force of the treaty apply from the time of the adoption of its text.

Article 25
Provisional application

1. A treaty or a part of a treaty is applied provisionally pending its entry into force if:
   (a) the treaty itself so provides; or
   (b) the negotiating States have in some other manner so agreed.

2. Unless the treaty otherwise provides or the negotiating States have otherwise agreed, the provisional application of a treaty or a part of a treaty with respect to a State shall be terminated if that State notifies the other States between which the treaty is being applied provisionally of its intention not to become a party to the treaty.

PART III
OBSERVANCE, APPLICATION AND
INTERPRETATION OF TREATIES

SECTION I

OBSERVANCE OF TREATIES

Article 26
Pacta sunt servanda

Every treaty in force is binding upon the parties to it and must be performed by them in good faith.

18

Article 27
Internal law and observance of treaties

A party may not invoke the provisions of its internal law as justification for its failure to perform a treaty. This rule is without prejudice to article 46.

Article 28
Non-retroactivity of treaties

Unless a different intention appears from the treaty or is otherwise established, its provisions do not bind a party in relation to any act or fact which took place or any situation which ceased to exist before the date of the entry into force of the treaty with respect to that party.

Article 29
Territorial scope of treaties

Unless a different intention appears from the treaty or is otherwise established, a treaty is binding upon each party in respect of its entire territory.

Article 30
Application of successive treaties relating to the same subject-matter

1. Subject to Article 103 of the Charter of the United Nations, the rights and obligations of States parties to successive treaties relating to the same subject-matter shall be determined in accordance with the following paragraphs.
2. When a treaty specifies that it is subject to, or that it is not to be considered as incompatible with, an earlier or later treaty, the provisions of that other treaty prevail.
3. When all the parties to the earlier treaty are parties also to the later treaty but the earlier treaty is not terminated or suspended in operation under article 59, the earlier treaty applies only to the extent that its provisions are compatible with those of the latter treaty.
4. When the parties to the later treaty do not include all the parties to the earlier one:
   (a) as between States parties to both treaties the same rule applies as in paragraph 3;
   (b) as between a State party to both treaties and a State party to only one of the treaties, the treaty to which both States are parties governs their mutual rights and obligations.
5. Paragraph 4 is without prejudice to article 41, or to any question of the termination or suspension of the operation of a treaty under article 60 or to any question of responsibility which may arise for a State from the conclusion or application of a treaty the provisions of which are incompatible with its obligations towards another State under another treaty.

Article 31
General rule of interpretation

1. A treaty shall be interpreted in good faith in accordance with the ordinary meaning to be given to the terms of the treaty in their context and in the light of its object and purpose.

2. The context for the purpose of the interpretation of a treaty shall comprise, in addition to the text, including its preamble and annexes:
   (a) any agreement relating to the treaty which was made between all the parties in connection with the conclusion of the treaty;
   (b) any instrument which was made by one or more parties in connection with the conclusion of the treaty and accepted by the other parties as an instrument related to the treaty.
3. There shall be taken into account, together with the context:
   (a) any subsequent agreement between the parties regarding the interpretation of the treaty or the application of its provisions;
   (b) any subsequent practice in the application of the treaty which establishes the agreement of the parties regarding its interpretation;
   (c) any relevant rules of international law applicable in the relations between the parties.
4. A special meaning shall be given to a term if it is established that the parties so intended.

Article 32
Supplementary means of interpretation

Recourse may be had to supplementary means of interpretation, including the preparatory work of the treaty and the circumstances of its conclusion, in order to confirm the meaning resulting from the application of article 31, or to determine the meaning when the interpretation according to article 31:
   (a) leaves the meaning ambiguous or obscure; or
   (b) leads to a result which is manifestly absurd or unreasonable.

Article 33
Interpretation of treaties authenticated in two or more languages

1. When a treaty has been authenticated in two or more languages, the text is equally authoritative in each language, unless the treaty provides or the parties agree that, in case of divergence, a particular text shall prevail.
2. A version of the treaty in a language other than one of those in which the text was authenticated shall be considered an authentic text only if the treaty so provides or the parties so agree.
3. The terms of the treaty are presumed to have the same meaning in each authentic text.
4. Except where a particular text prevails in accordance with paragraph 1, when a comparison of the authentic texts discloses a difference of meaning which the application of articles 31 and 32 does not remove, the meaning which best reconciles the texts, having regard to the object and purpose of the treaty, shall be adopted.

SECTION 4

TREATIES AND THIRD STATES

Article 34
General rule regarding third States

A treaty does not create either obligations or rights for a third State without its consent.

Article 35
Treaties providing for obligations for third States

An obligation arises for a third State from a provision of a treaty if the parties to the treaty intend the provision to be the means of establishing the obligation and the third State expressly accepts that obligation in writing.

Article 36
Treaties providing for rights for third States

1. A right arises for a third State from a provision of a treaty if the parties to the treaty intend the provision to accord that right either to the third State, or to a group of States to which it belongs, or to all States, and the third State assents thereto. Its assent shall be presumed so long as the contrary is not indicated, unless the treaty otherwise provides.
2. A State exercising a right in accordance with paragraph 1 shall comply with the conditions for its exercise provided for in the treaty or established in conformity with the treaty.

Article 37
Revocation or modification of obligations or rights of third States

1. When an obligation has arisen for a third State in conformity with article 35, the obligation may be revoked or modified only with the consent of the parties to the treaty and of the third State, unless it is established that they had otherwise agreed.
2. When a right has arisen for a third State in conformity with article 36, the right may not be revoked or modified by the parties if it is established that the right was intended not to be revocable or subject to modification without the consent of the third State.

Article 38
Rules in a treaty becoming binding on third States through international custom

Nothing in articles 34 to 37 precludes a rule set forth in a treaty from becoming binding upon a third State as a customary rule of international law, recognized as such.

PART IV
AMENDMENT AND MODIFICATION OF TREATIES

Article 39
General rule regarding the amendment of treaties

A treaty may be amended by agreement between the parties. The rules laid down in Part II apply to such an agreement except in so far as the treaty may otherwise provide.

Article 40
Amendment of multilateral treaties

1. Unless the treaty otherwise provides, the amendment of multilateral treaties shall be governed by the following paragraphs.

2. Any proposal to amend a multilateral treaty as between all the parties must be notified to all the contracting States, each one of which shall have the right to take part in:
   (a) the decision as to the action to be taken in regard to such proposal;
   (b) the negotiation and conclusion of any agreement for the amendment of the treaty.
3. Every State entitled to become a party to the treaty shall also be entitled to become a party to the treaty as amended.
4. The amending agreement does not bind any State already a party to the treaty which does not become a party to the amending agreement; article 30, paragraph 4(b), applies in relation to such State.
5. Any State which becomes a party to the treaty after the entry into force of the amending agreement shall, failing an expression of a different intention by that State:
   (a) be considered as a party to the treaty as amended; and
   (b) be considered as a party to the unamended treaty in relation to any party to the treaty not bound by the amending agreement.

Article 41
Agreements to modify multilateral treaties between certain of the parties only

1. Two or more of the parties to a multilateral treaty may conclude an agreement to modify the treaty as between themselves alone if:
   (a) the possibility of such a modification is provided for by the treaty; or
   (b) the modification in question is not prohibited by the treaty and:
      (i) does not affect the enjoyment by the other parties of their rights under the treaty or the performance of their obligations;
      (ii) does not relate to a provision, derogation from which is incompatible with the effective execution of the object and purpose of the treaty as a whole.
2. Unless in a case falling under paragraph 1(a) the treaty otherwise provides, the parties in question shall notify the other parties of their intention to conclude the agreement and of the modification to the treaty for which it provides.

PART V
INVALIDITY, TERMINATION AND SUSPENSION OF THE OPERATION OF TREATIES

SECTION I
GENERAL PROVISIONS

Article 42
Validity and continuance in force of treaties

1. The validity of a treaty or of the consent of a State to be bound by a treaty may be impeached only through the application of the present Convention.
2. The termination of a treaty, its denunciation or the withdrawal of a party, may take place only as a result of the application of the provisions of the treaty or of the present Convention. The same rule applies to suspension of the operation of a treaty.

Article 43
Obligations imposed by international law independently of a treaty

The invalidity, termination or denunciation of a treaty, the withdrawal of a party from it, or the suspension of its operation, as a result of the application of the present Convention or of the provisions of the treaty, shall not in any way impair the duty of any State to fulfil any obligation embodied in the treaty to which it would be subject under international law independently of the treaty.

Article 44
Separability of treaty provisions

1. A right of a party, provided for in a treaty or arising under article 56, to denounce, withdraw from or suspend the operation of the treaty may be exercised only with respect to the whole treaty unless the treaty otherwise provides or the parties otherwise agree.
2. A ground for invalidating, terminating, withdrawing from or suspending the operation of a treaty recognized in the present Convention may be invoked only with respect to the whole treaty except as provided in the following paragraphs or in article 60.
3. If the ground relates solely to particular clauses, it may be invoked only with respect to those clauses where:
   (a) the said clauses are separable from the remainder of the treaty with regard to their application;
   (b) it appears from the treaty or is otherwise established that acceptance of those clauses was not an essential basis of the consent of the other party or parties to be bound by the treaty as a whole; and
   (c) continued performance of the remainder of the treaty would not be unjust.
4. In cases falling under articles 49 and 50 the State entitled to invoke the fraud or corruption may do so with respect either to the whole treaty or, subject to paragraph 3, to the particular clauses alone.
5. In cases falling under articles 51, 52 and 53, no separation of the provisions of the treaty is permitted.

Article 45
Loss of a right to invoke a ground for invalidating, terminating, withdrawing from or suspending the operation of a treaty

A State may no longer invoke a ground for invalidating, terminating, withdrawing from or suspending the operation of a treaty under articles 46 to 50 or articles 60 and 62 if, after becoming aware of the facts:
   (a) it shall have expressly agreed that the treaty is valid or remains in force or continues in operation, as the case may be; or
   (b) it must by reason of its conduct be considered as having acquiesced in the validity of the treaty or in its maintenance in force or in operation, as the case may be.

Article 46
Provisions of internal law regarding competence to conclude treaties

1. A State may not invoke the fact that its consent to be bound by a treaty has been expressed in violation of a provision of its internal law regarding competence to conclude treaties as invalidating its consent unless that violation was manifest and concerned a rule of its internal law of fundamental importance.
2. A violation is manifest if it would be objectively evident to any State conducting itself in the matter in accordance with normal practice and in good faith.

Article 47
Specific restrictions on authority to express the consent of a State

If the authority of a representative to express the consent of a State to be bound by a particular treaty has been made subject to a specific restriction, his omission to observe that restriction may not be invoked as invalidating the consent expressed by him unless the restriction was notified to the other negotiating States prior to his expressing such consent.

Article 48
Error

1. A State may invoke an error in a treaty as invalidating its consent to be bound by the treaty if the error relates to a fact or situation which was assumed by that State to exist at the time when the treaty was concluded and formed an essential basis of its consent to be bound by the treaty.
2. Paragraph 1 shall not apply if the State in question contributed by its own conduct to the error or if the circumstances were such as to put that State on notice of a possible error.
3. An error relating only to the wording of the text of a treaty does not affect its validity; article 79 then applies.

Article 49
Fraud

If a State has been induced to conclude a treaty by the fraudulent conduct of another negotiating State, the State may invoke the fraud as invalidating its consent to be bound by the treaty.

Article 50
Corruption of a representative of a State

If the expression of a State's consent to be bound by a treaty has been procured through the corruption of its representative directly or indirectly by another negotiating State, the State may invoke such corruption as invalidating its consent to be bound by the treaty.

Article 51
Coercion of a representative of a State

The expression of a State's consent to be bound by a treaty which has been procured by the coercion of its representative through acts or threats directed against him shall be without any legal effect.

Article 52
Coercion of a State by the threat or use of force

A treaty is void if its conclusion has been procured by the threat or use of force in violation of the principles of international law embodied in the Charter of the United Nations.

Article 53
Treaties conflicting with a peremptory norm
of general international law (*jus cogens*)

A treaty is void if, at the time of its conclusion, it conflicts with a peremptory norm of general international law. For the purposes of the present Convention, a peremptory norm of general international law is a norm accepted and recognized by the international community of States as a whole as a norm from which no derogation is permitted and which can be modified only by a subsequent norm of general international law having the same character.

SECTION 3
TERMINATION AND SUSPENSION OF THE OPERATION OF TREATIES

Article 54
Termination of or withdrawal from a treaty under its
provisions or by consent of the parties

The termination of a treaty or the withdrawal of a party may take place:
(a) in conformity with the provisions of the treaty; or
(b) at any time by consent of all the parties after consultation with the other contracting States.

Article 55
Reduction of the parties to a multilateral treaty below
the number necessary for its entry into force

Unless the treaty otherwise provides, a multilateral treaty does not terminate by reason only of the fact that the number of the parties falls below the number necessary for its entry into force.

Article 56
Denunciation of or withdrawal from a treaty containing no
provision regarding termination, denunciation or withdrawal

1. A treaty which contains no provision regarding its termination and which does not provide for denunciation or withdrawal is not subject to denunciation or withdrawal unless:
   (a) it is established that the parties intended to admit the possibility of denunciation or withdrawal; or
   (b) a right of denunciation or withdrawal may be implied by the nature of the treaty.
2. A party shall give not less than twelve months' notice of its intention to denounce or withdraw from a treaty under paragraph 1.

Article 57
Suspension of the operation of a treaty under its provisions or by consent of the parties

The operation of a treaty in regard to all the parties or to a particular party may be suspended:
(a) in conformity with the provisions of the treaty; or
(b) at any time by consent of all the parties after consultation with the other contracting States.

Article 58
Suspension of the operation of a multilateral treaty by agreement between certain of the parties only

1. Two or more parties to a multilateral treaty may conclude an agreement to suspend the operation of provisions of the treaty, temporarily and as between themselves alone, if:
(a) the possibility of such a suspension is provided for by the treaty; or
(b) the suspension in question is not prohibited by the treaty and:
   (i) does not affect the enjoyment by the other parties of their rights under the treaty or the performance of their obligations;
   (ii) is not incompatible with the object and purpose of the treaty.
2. Unless in a case falling under paragraph 1(a) the treaty otherwise provides, the parties in question shall notify the other parties of their intention to conclude the agreement and of those provisions of the treaty the operation of which they intend to suspend.

Article 59
Termination or suspension of the operation of a treaty implied by conclusion of a later treaty

1. A treaty shall be considered as terminated if all the parties to it conclude a later treaty relating to the same subject-matter and:
(a) it appears from the later treaty or is otherwise established that the parties intended that the matter should be governed by that treaty; or
(b) the provisions of the later treaty are so far incompatible with those of the earlier one that the two treaties are not capable of being applied at the same time.
2. The earlier treaty shall be considered as only suspended in operation if it appears from the later treaty or is otherwise established that such was the intention of the parties.

Article 60
Termination or suspension of the operation of a treaty as a consequence of its breach

1. A material breach of a bilateral treaty by one of the parties entitles the other to invoke the breach as a ground for terminating the treaty or suspending its operation in whole or in part
2. A material breach of a multilateral treaty by one of the parties entitles:
(a) the other parties by unanimous agreement to suspend the operation of the treaty in whole or in part or to terminate it either:
   (i) in the relations between themselves and the defaulting State, or
   (ii) as between all the parties;

(b) a party specially affected by the breach to invoke it as a ground for suspending the operation of the treaty in whole or in part in the relations between itself and the defaulting State;

(c) any party other than the defaulting State to invoke the breach as a ground for suspending the operation of the treaty in whole or in part with respect to itself if the treaty is of such a character that a material breach of its provisions by one party radically changes the position of every party with respect to the further performance of its obligations under the treaty.

3. A material breach of a treaty, for the purposes of this article, consists in:

(a) a repudiation of the treaty not sanctioned by the present Convention; or

(b) the violation of a provision essential to the accomplishment of the object or purpose of the treaty.

4. The foregoing paragraphs are without prejudice to any provision in the treaty applicable in the event of a breach.

5. Paragraphs 1 to 3 do not apply to provisions relating to the protection of the human person contained in treaties of a humanitarian character, in particular to provisions prohibiting any form of reprisals against persons protected by such treaties.

Article 61
Supervening impossibility of performance

1. A party may invoke the impossibility of performing a treaty as a ground for terminating or withdrawing from it if the impossibility results from the permanent disappearance or destruction of an object indispensable for the execution of the treaty. If the impossibility is temporary, it may be invoked only as a ground for suspending the operation of the treaty.

2. Impossibility of performance may not be invoked by a party as a ground for terminating, withdrawing from or suspending the operation of a treaty if the impossibility is the result of a breach by that party either of an obligation under the treaty or of any other international obligation owed to any other party to the treaty.

Article 62
Fundamental change of circumstances

1. A fundamental change of circumstances which has occurred with regard to those existing at the time of the conclusion of a treaty, and which was not foreseen by the parties, may not be invoked as a ground for terminating or withdrawing from the treaty unless:

(a) the existence of those circumstances constituted an essential basis of the consent of the parties to be bound by the treaty; and

(b) the effect of the change is radically to transform the extent of obligations still to be performed under the treaty.

2. A fundamental change of circumstances may not be invoked as a ground for terminating or withdrawing from a treaty:

(a) if the treaty establishes a boundary; or

(b) if the fundamental change is the result of a breach by the party invoking it either of an obligation under the treaty or of any other international obligation owed to any other party to the treaty.

3. If, under the foregoing paragraphs, a party may invoke a fundamental change of circumstances as a ground for terminating or withdrawing from a treaty it may also invoke the change as a ground for suspending the operation of the treaty.

Article 63
Severance of diplomatic or consular relations

The severance of diplomatic or consular relations between parties to a treaty does not affect the legal relations established between them by the treaty except in so far as the existence of diplomatic or consular relations is indispensable for the application of the treaty.

Article 64
Emergence of a new peremptory norm of general international law (*jus cogens*)

If a new peremptory norm of general international law emerges, any existing treaty which is in conflict with that norm becomes void and terminates.

SECTION 4

PROCEDURE

Article 65
Procedure to be followed with respect to invalidity, termination, withdrawal from or suspension of the operation of a treaty

1. A party which, under the provisions of the present Convention, invokes either a defect in its consent to be bound by a treaty or a ground for impeaching the validity of a treaty, terminating it, withdrawing from it or suspending its operation, must notify the other parties of its claim. The notification shall indicate the measure proposed to be taken with respect to the treaty and the reasons therefor.
2. If, after the expiry of a period which, except in cases of special urgency, shall not be less than three months after the receipt of the notification, no party has raised any objection, the party making the notification may carry out in the manner provided in article 67 the measure which it has proposed.
3. If, however, objection has been raised by any other party, the parties shall seek a solution through the means indicated in article 33 of the Charter of the United Nations.
4. Nothing in the foregoing paragraphs shall affect the rights or obligations of the parties under any provisions in force binding the parties with regard to the settlement of disputes.
5. Without prejudice to article 45, the fact that a State has not previously made the notification prescribed in paragraph 1 shall not prevent it from making such notification in answer to another party claiming performance of the treaty or alleging its violation.

Article 66
Procedures for judicial settlement, arbitration and conciliation

If, under paragraph 3 of article 65, no solution has been reached within a period of 12 months following the date on which the objection was raised, the following procedures shall be followed:
(a) any one of the parties to a dispute concerning the application or the interpretation of articles 53 or 64 may, by a written application, submit it to the International

Court of Justice for a decision unless the parties by common consent agree to submit the dispute to arbitration;

(b) any one of the parties to a dispute concerning the application or the interpretation of any of the other articles in Part V of the present Convention may set in motion the procedure specified in the Annex to the Convention by submitting a request to that effect to the Secretary-General of the United Nations.

Article 67
Instruments for declaring invalid, terminating, withdrawing from or suspending the operation of a treaty

1. The notification provided for under article 65 paragraph 1 must be made in writing.
2. Any act declaring invalid, terminating, withdrawing from or suspending the operation of a treaty pursuant to the provisions of the treaty or of paragraphs 2 or 3 of article 65 shall be carried out through an instrument communicated to the other parties. If the instrument is not signed by the Head of State, Head of Government or Minister for Foreign Affairs, the representative of the State communicating it may be called upon to produce full powers.

Article 68
Revocation of notifications and instruments provided for in articles 65 and 67

A notification or instrument provided for in articles 65 or 67 may be revoked at any time before it takes effect.

SECTION 5
CONSEQUENCES OF THE INVALIDITY, TERMINATION
OR SUSPENSION OF THE OPERATION OF A TREATY

Article 69
Consequences of the invalidity of a treaty

1. A treaty the invalidity of which is established under the present Convention is void. The provisions of a void treaty have no legal force.
2. If acts have nevertheless been performed in reliance on such a treaty:
   (a) each party may require any other party to establish as far as possible in their mutual relations the position that would have existed if the acts had not been performed;
   (b) acts performed in good faith before the invalidity was invoked are not rendered unlawful by reason only of the invalidity of the treaty.
3. In cases falling under articles 49, 50, 51 or 52, paragraph 2 does not apply with respect to the party to which the fraud, the act of corruption or the coercion is imputable.
4. In the case of the invalidity of a particular State's consent to be bound by a multilateral treaty, the foregoing rules apply in the relations between that State and the parties to the treaty.

Article 70
Consequences of the termination of a treaty

1. Unless the treaty otherwise provides or the parties otherwise agree, the termination of a treaty under its provisions or in accordance with the present Convention:
   (a) releases the parties from any obligation further to perform the treaty;

(b) does not affect any right, obligation or legal situation of the parties created through the execution of the treaty prior to its termination.

2. If a State denounces or withdraws from a multilateral treaty, paragraph 1 applies in the relations between that State and each of the other parties to the treaty from the date when such denunciation or withdrawal takes effect.

Article 71
Consequences of the invalidity of a treaty which conflict with a peremptory norm of general international law

1. In the case of a treaty which is void under article 53 the parties shall:
    (a) eliminate as far as possible the consequences of any act performed in reliance on any provision which conflicts with the peremptory norm of general international law; and
    (b) bring their mutual relations into conformity with the peremptory norm of general international law.
2. In the case of a treaty which becomes void and terminates under article 64, the termination of the treaty:
    (a) releases the parties from any obligation further to perform the treaty;
    (b) does not affect any right, obligation or legal situation of the parties created through the execution of the treaty prior to its termination; provided that those rights, obligations or situations may thereafter be maintained only to the extent that their maintenance is not in itself in conflict with the new peremptory norm of general international law.

Article 72
Consequences of the suspension of the operation of a treaty

1. Unless the treaty otherwise provides or the parties otherwise agree, the suspension of the operation of a treaty under its provisions or in accordance with the present Convention:
    (a) releases the parties between which the operation of the treaty is suspended from the obligation to perform the treaty in their mutual relations during the period of the suspension;
    (b) does not otherwise affect the legal relations between the parties established by the treaty.
2. During the period of the suspension the parties shall refrain from acts tending to obstruct the resumption of the operation of the treaty.

PART VI
MISCELLANEOUS PROVISIONS

Article 73
Cases of State succession, State responsibility and outbreak of hostilities

The provisions of the present Convention shall not prejudge any question that may arise in regard to a treaty from a succession of States or from the international responsibility of a State or from the outbreak of hostilities between States.

Article 74
Diplomatic and consular relations and the conclusion of treaties

The severance or absence of diplomatic or consular relations between two or more States does not prevent the conclusion of treaties between those States. The conclusion of a treaty does not in itself affect the situation in regard to diplomatic or consular relations.

Article 75
Case of an aggressor State

The provisions of the present Convention are without prejudice to any obligation in relation to a treaty which may arise for an aggressor State in consequence of measures taken in conformity with the Charter of the United Nations with reference to that State's aggression.

PART VII
DEPOSITARIES, NOTIFICATIONS, CORRECTIONS AND REGISTRATION

Article 76
Depositaries of treaties

1. The designation of the depositary of a treaty may be made by the negotiating States, either in the treaty itself or in some other manner. The depositary may be one or more States, an international organization or the chief administrative officer of the organization.
2. The functions of the depositary of a treaty are international in character and the depositary is under an obligation to act impartially in their performance. In particular, the fact that a treaty has not entered into force between certain of the parties or that a difference has appeared between a State and a depositary with regard to the performance of the latter's functions shall not affect that obligation.

Article 77
Functions of depositaries

1. The functions of a depositary, unless otherwise provided in the treaty or agreed by the contracting States, comprise in particular:
   (a) keeping custody of the original text of the treaty and of any full powers delivered to the depositary;
   (b) preparing certified copies of the original text and preparing any further text of the treaty in such additional languages as may be required by the treaty and transmitting them to the parties and to the States entitled to become parties to the treaty;
   (c) receiving any signatures to the treaty and receiving and keeping custody of any instruments, notifications and communications relating to it;
   (d) examining whether the signature or any instrument, notification or communication relating to the treaty is in due and proper form and, if need be, bringing the matter to the attention of the State in question;
   (e) informing the parties and the States entitled to become parties to the treaty of acts, notifications and communications relating to the treaty;

31

(f) informing the States entitled to become parties to the treaty when the number of signatures or of instruments of ratification, acceptance, approval or accession required for the entry into force of the treaty has been received or deposited;

(g) registering the treaty with the Secretariat of the United Nations;

(h) performing the functions specified in other provisions of the present Convention.

2. In the event of any difference appearing between a State and the depositary as to the performance of the latter's functions, the depositary shall bring the question to the attention of the signatory States and the contracting States or, where appropriate, of the competent organ of the international organization concerned.

Article 78
Notifications and communications

Except as the treaty or the present Convention otherwise provide, any notification or communication to be made by any State under the present Convention shall:

(a) if there is no depositary, be transmitted direct to the States for which it is intended, or if there is a depositary, to the latter;

(b) be considered as having been made by the State in question only upon its receipt by the State to which it was transmitted or, as the case may be, upon its receipt by the depositary;

(c) if transmitted to a depositary, be considered as received by the State for which it was intended only when the latter State has been informed by the depositary in accordance with article 77, paragraph 1 (e).

Article 79
Correction of errors in texts or in certified copies of treaties

1. Where, after the authentication of the text of a treaty, the signatory States and the contracting States are agreed that it contains an error, the error shall, unless they decide upon some other means of correction, be corrected:

(a) by having the appropriate correction made in the text and causing the correction to be initialled by duly authorized representatives;

(b) by executing or exchanging an instrument or instruments setting out the correction which it has been agreed to make; or

(c) by executing a corrected text of the whole treaty by the same procedure as in the case of the original text.

2. Where the treaty is one for which there is a depositary, the latter shall notify the signatory States and the contracting States of the error and of the proposal to correct it and shall specify an appropriate time-limit within which objection to the proposed correction may be raised. If, on the expiry of the time-limit:

(a) no objection has been raised, the depositary shall make and initial the correction in the text and shall execute a *procès-verbal* of the rectification of the text and communicate a copy of it to the parties and to the States entitled to become parties to the treaty;

(b) an objection has been raised, the depositary shall communicate the objection to the signatory States and to the contracting States.

3. The rules in paragraphs 1 and 2 apply also where the text has been authenticated in two or more languages and it appears that there is a lack of concordance which the signatory States and the contracting States agree should be corrected.

4. The corrected text replaces the defective text *ab initio,* unless the signatory States and the contracting States otherwise decide.
5. The correction of the text of a treaty that has been registered shall be notified to the Secretariat of the United Nations.
6. Where an error is discovered in a certified copy of a treaty, the depositary shall execute a *procés-verbal* specifying the rectification and communicate a copy of it to the signatory States and to the contracting States.

Article 80
Registration and publication of treaties

1. Treaties shall, after their entry into force, be transmitted to the Secretariat of the United Nations for registration or filing and recording, as the case may be, and for publication.
2. The designation of a depositary shall constitute authorization for it to perform the acts specified in the preceding paragraph.

PART VIII
FINAL PROVISIONS

Article 81
Signature

The present Convention shall be open for signature by all States Members of the United Nations or of any of the specialized agencies or of the International Atomic Energy Agency or parties to the Statute of the International Court of Justice, and by any other State invited by the General Assembly of the United Nations to become a party to the Convention, as follows: until 30 November 1969, at the Federal Ministry for Foreign Affairs of the Republic of Austria, and subsequently, until 30 April 1970, at United Nations Headquarters, New York.

Article 82
Ratification

The present Convention is subject to ratification. The instruments of ratification shall be deposited with the Secretary-General of the United Nations.

Article 83
Accession

The present Convention shall remain open for accession by any State belonging to any of the categories mentioned in article 81. The instruments of accession shall be deposited with the Secretary-General of the United Nations.

Article 84
Entry into force

1. The present Convention shall enter into force on the thirtieth day following the date of deposit of the thirty-fifth instrument of ratification or accession.

2. For each State ratifying or acceding to the Convention after the deposit of the thirty-fifth instrument of ratification or accession, the Convention shall enter into force on the thirtieth day after deposit by such State of its instrument of ratification or accession.

Article 85
Authentic texts

The original of the present Convention, of which the Chinese, English, French, Russian and Spanish texts are equally authentic, shall be deposited with the Secretary-General of the United Nations.

In witness whereof the undersigned Plenipotentiaries, being duly authorized thereto by their respective Governments, have signed the present Convention.

Done at Vienna, this twenty-third day of May, one thousand nine hundred and sixty-nine.

ANNEX

1. A list of conciliators consisting of qualified jurists shall be drawn up and maintained by the Secretary-General of the United Nations. To this end, every State which is a Member of the United Nations or a party to the present Convention shall be invited to nominate two conciliators, and the names of the persons so nominated shall constitute the list. The term of a conciliator, including that of any conciliator nominated to fill a casual vacancy, shall be five years and may be renewed. A conciliator whose term expires shall continue to fulfil any function for which he shall have been chosen under the following paragraph.

2. When a request has been made to the Secretary-General under article 66, the Secretary-General shall bring the dispute before a conciliation commission constituted as follows:

The State or States constituting one of the parties to the dispute shall appoint:
   (a) one conciliator of the nationality of that State or of one of those States, who may or may not be chosen from the list referred to in paragraph 1; and
   (b) one conciliator not of the nationality of that State or of any of those States, who shall be chosen from the list.

The State or States constituting the other party to the dispute shall appoint two conciliators in the same way. The four conciliators chosen by the parties shall be appointed within sixty days following the date on which the Secretary-General receives the request.

The four conciliators shall, within sixty days following the date of the last of their own appointments, appoint a fifth conciliator chosen from the list, who shall be chairman.

If the appointment of the chairman or of any of the other conciliators has not been made within the period prescribed above for such appointment, it shall be made by the Secretary-General within sixty days following the expiry of that period. The appointment of the chairman may be made by the Secretary-General either from the list or from the membership of the International Law Commission. Any of the periods within which appointments must be made may be extended by agreement between the parties to the dispute.

Any vacancy shall be filled in the manner prescribed for the initial appointment.

3. The Conciliation Commission shall decide its own procedure. The Commission, with the consent of the parties to the dispute, may invite any party to the treaty to submit to it its views orally or in writing. Decisions and recommendations of the Commission shall be made by a majority vote of the five members.

4. The Commission may draw the attention of the parties to the dispute to any measures which might facilitate an amicable settlement.

5. The Commission shall hear the parties, examine the claims and objections, and make proposals to the parties with a view to reaching an amicable settlement of the dispute.

6. The Commission shall report within twelve months of its constitution. Its report shall be deposited with the Secretary-General and transmitted to the parties to the dispute. The report of the Commission, including any conclusions stated therein regarding the facts or questions of law, shall not be binding upon the parties and it shall have no other character than that of recommendations submitted for the consideration of the parties in order to facilitate an amicable settlement of the dispute.

7. The Secretary-General shall provide the Commission with such assistance and facilities as it may require. The expenses of the Commission shall be borne by the United Nations.

TABLE OF STATE RATIFICATIONS

Entry into force: 27 January 1980, in accordance with article 84 (1).
Registration: 27 January 1980, No. 18232.
Status: Signatories: 45, Parties: 96.
Text: United Nations, *Treaty Series,* vol. 1155, p. 331.

Note: The Convention was adopted on 22 May 1969 and opened for signature on 23 May 1969 by the United Nations Conference on the Law of Treaties. The Conference was convened pursuant to General Assembly resolutions 2166 (XXI)[1] of 5 December 1966 and 2287 (XXII)[2] of 6 December 1967. The Conference held two sessions, both at the Neue Hofburg in Vienna, the first session from 26 March to 24 May 1968 and the second session from 9 April to 22 May 1969. In addition to the Convention, the Conference adopted the Final Act and certain declarations and resolutions, which are annexed to that Act. By unanimous decision of the Conference, the original of the Final Act was deposited in the archives of the Federal Ministry for Foreign Affairs of Austria. The text of the Final Act is included in document A/CONF.39/11/Add.2.

PARTICIPANTS AND RATIFICATIONS

Participant	Signature	Ratification, Accession (a), Succession (d)
Afghanistan	23 May 1969	
Albania		27 Jun 2001 a
Algeria		8 Nov 1988 a
Argentina	23 May 1969	5 Dec 1972
Australia		13 Jun 1974 a

[1] Official Records of the General Assembly, Twenty-first Session, Supplement No. 16 (A/6316), p. 95.
[2] Ibid., Twenty-second Session, Supplement No. 16 (A/6716), p. 80.

Participant	Signature	Ratification, Accession (a), Succession (d)
Austria		30 Apr 1979 a
Barbados	23 May 1969	24 Jun 1971
Belarus		1 May 1986 a
Belgium		1 Sep 1992 a
Bolivia	23 May 1969	
Bosnia and Herzegovina		1 Sep 1993 d
Brazil	23 May 1969	
Bulgaria		21 Apr 1987 a
Cambodia	23 May 1969	
Cameroon		23 Oct 1991 a
Canada		14 Oct 1970 a
Central African Republic		10 Dec 1971 a
Chile	23 May 1969	9 Apr 1981
China		3 Sep 1997 a
Colombia	23 May 1969	10 Apr 1985
Congo	23 May 1969	12 Apr 1982
Costa Rica	23 May 1969	22 Nov 1996
Côte d'Ivoire	23 Jul 1969	
Croatia		12 Oct 1992 d
Cuba		9 Sep 1998 a
Cyprus		28 Dec 1976 a
Czech Republic		22 Feb 1993 d
Democratic Republic of the Congo		25 Jul 1977 a
Denmark	18 Apr 1970	1 Jun 1976
Ecuador	23 May 1969	
Egypt		11 Feb 1982 a
El Salvador	16 Feb 1970	
Estonia		21 Oct 1991 a
Ethiopia	30 Apr 1970	
Finland	23 May 1969	19 Aug 1977
Georgia		8 Jun 1995 a
Germany	30 Apr 1970	21 Jul 1987
Ghana	23 May 1969	
Greece		30 Oct 1974 a
Guatemala	23 May 1969	21 Jul 1997
Guyana	23 May 1969	
Haiti		25 Aug 1980 a
Holy See	30 Sep 1969	25 Feb 1977
Honduras	23 May 1969	20 Sep 1979
Hungary		19 Jun 1987 a
Iran (Islamic Republic of)	23 May 1969	
Italy	22 Apr 1970	25 Jul 1974
Jamaica	23 May 1969	28 Jul 1970
Japan		2 Jul 1981 a
Kazakhstan		5 Jan 1994 a
Kenya	23 May 1969	
Kuwait		11 Nov 1975 a
Kyrgyzstan		11 May 1999 a
Lao People's Democratic Republic		31 Mar 1998 a
Latvia		4 May 1993 a
Lesotho		3 Mar 1972 a

Participant	Signature	Ratification, Accession (a), Succession (d)
Liberia	23 May 1969	29 Aug 1985
Liechtenstein		8 Feb 1990 a
Lithuania		15 Jan 1992 a
Luxembourg	4 Sep 1969	23 May 2003
Madagascar	23 May 1969	
Malawi		23 Aug 1983 a
Malaysia		27 Jul 1994 a
Mali		31 Aug 1998 a
Mauritius		18 Jan 1973 a
Mexico	23 May 1969	25 Sep 1974
Mongolia		16 May 1988 a
Morocco	23 May 1969	26 Sep 1972
Mozambique		8 May 2001 a
Myanmar		16 Sep 1998 a
Nauru		5 May 1978 a
Nepal	23 May 1969	
Netherlands		9 Apr 1985 a
New Zealand	29 Apr 1970	4 Aug 1971
Niger		27 Oct 1971 a
Nigeria	23 May 1969	31 Jul 1969
Oman		18 Oct 1990 a
Pakistan	29 Apr 1970	
Panama		28 Jul 1980 a
Paraguay		3 Feb 1972 a
Peru	23 May 1969	14 Sep 2000
Philippines	23 May 1969	15 Nov 1972
Poland		2 Jul 1990 a
Republic of Korea	27 Nov 1969	27 Apr 1977
Republic of Moldova		26 Jan 1993 a
Russian Federation		29 Apr 1986 a
Rwanda		3 Jan 1980 a
Saint Vincent and the Grenadines		27 Apr 1999 a
Saudi Arabia		14 Apr 2003 a
Senegal		11 Apr 1986 a
Serbia and Montenegro		12 Mar 2001 d
Slovakia		28 May 1993 d
Slovenia		6 Jul 1992 d
Solomon Islands		9 Aug 1989 a
Spain		16 May 1972 a
Sudan	23 May 1969	18 Apr 1990
Suriname		31 Jan 1991 a
Sweden	23 Apr 1970	4 Feb 1975
Switzerland		7 May 1990 a
Syrian Arab Republic		2 Oct 1970 a
Tajikistan		6 May 1996 a
The Former Yugoslav Republic of Macedonia		8 Jul 1999 d
Togo		28 Dec 1979 a
Trinidad and Tobago	23 May 1969	
Tunisia		23 Jun 1971 a
Turkmenistan		4 Jan 1996 a
Ukraine		14 May 1986 a

Participant	Signature	Ratification, Accession (a), Succession (d)
United Kingdom of Great Britain and Northern Ireland	20 Apr 1970	25 Jun 1971
United Republic of Tanzania		12 Apr 1976 a
United States of America	24 Apr 1970	
Uruguay	23 May 1969	5 Mar 1982
Uzbekistan		12 Jul 1995 a
Viet Nam		10 Oct 2001 a
Zambia	23 May 1969	

Note. A list of reservations and declarations made by States has not been included in the text. These can be obtained from http://www.un.org/law/ilc/texts/treatfra.htm.

2

INTERNATIONAL AND EUROPEAN RESTATEMENTS OF CONTRACT LAW

A. Introductory Text

The scholarly restatement of principles of a given field of law as a means of promoting harmonization of the laws of different jurisdictions originated in the United States with the series of Restatements published by the American Law Institute. Of course, the term 'restatement' is used in a rather loose sense, since the process necessarily involves departures from at least some of the rules from which the restatement is drawn, not only because these differ from each other but also because of a concern to produce best solutions to typical problems in the light of experience.

In the field of contract law the restatement concept has crossed national boundaries. Two separate projects have now been completed, the *Principles of International Commercial Contracts* ('the UNIDROIT Principles'), produced by a group of international scholars and practitioners under the direction of Professor Joachim Bonell and adopted by the Governing Council of UNIDROIT, and the *Principles of European Contract Law*, prepared by scholars drawn from every Member State of the European Community under the chairmanship of Professor Ole Lando ('the PECL').[1] The two groups had a degree of commonality of membership.

---

[1] In addition, the preliminary draft of a European Contract Code has been produced by the Academy of European Private Lawyers (the Pavia Group) under the direction of Professor Giuseppe Gandolfi. The European Commission had contemplated the preparation of a binding European Contract Code but for the time being seems to have moved away from this idea, though it has not

Part 1 of the UNIDROIT Principles was published in 1994 and the consolidated Part I and II in 2004. The PECL were published in three phases. Part I was published in 1995 and was re-published with Part II (and re-numbered) in 1999, while Part III was published in 2003. The PECL will in due course be supplemented by rules for specific contracts prepared by the Study Group on a European Civil Code under the direction of Professor Christian von Bar.

Though the UNIDROIT Principles are directed at international commercial contracts and the PECL at all types of contract within the European Community, whether cross-border or domestic and whether commercial or consumer, they cover much the same ground and for the most part arrive at similar solutions.

Nature and purposes

Neither set of Principles is a legally operative instrument. The Commission on European Contract Law was a private group of scholars; UNIDROIT is an international, intergovernmental organization but governments were not involved in the UNIDROIT Principles. Moreover, since the Principles do not constitute laws of a national legal system they cannot, under traditional conflict of laws rules, be selected as the law to govern the contract,[2] though they could be incorporated as contract terms, in which case they would take effect subject to any applicable mandatory rules. But in arbitration proceedings under a *lex arbitri* which recognizes the freedom of parties to choose 'rules of law' not necessarily forming part of a national legal system, selection of one of the two sets of Principles would enable the arbitral tribunal to apply them and to override purely domestic mandatory rules (rules applicable despite any agreement to the contrary on the assumption that the relevant domestic law applied), though not overriding super-mandatory rules (rules applicable whatever the governing law).

The Principles have several stated purposes in common. Both may be used to identify 'general principles of law' or the *lex mercatoria* relating to contracts, to fill gaps in national law, and to provide models or guidelines for national courts and legislatures. The UNIDROIT Principles, being international, may also be used to interpret or supplement international conventions, such as the UN Convention on Contracts for the International Sale of Goods ('the CISG'),[3] while the PECL include among their purposes the facilitation of cross-border transactions within Europe, the strengthening of the Single European Market and the provision of an infrastructure for Community laws governing contracts. The PECL are also

been abandoned. See Communication from the Commission to the European Parliament and the Council: A More Coherent European Contract Law—An Action Plan, COM(2003) 68 final, 12.2.2003.

[2] There is, however, a minority view to the contrary. See *post* p. 727.

[3] For example, Art 78 of CISG (see p. 233 below) has a provision on interest but does not state how this is to be calculated. Article 7.4.9 of the UNIDROIT Principles and Art 9:508 of PECL have detailed provisions for this, which can be used to supplement Art 78.

designed to bridge the gap between civil law and common law systems in the field of contract law. Both Principles have been heavily influenced by CISG.

The Principles cover the whole spectrum of contract law, from formation, representation, validity, and interpretation through performance and remedies for non-performance to assignment, novation, set-off, and prescription. A number of the rules are common to many national legal systems; some are closer to one legal family or system than to others; and a few are *de lege ferenda* and are designed to advance legal thinking beyond what any legal system currently provides, for example, the duty of the parties to renegotiate in the event of a fundamental change of circumstances. Key features common to the Principles are set out in the following paragraphs.

Freedom of contract

The Principles adopt the near-universal approach of general contract law in their insistence on party autonomy[4] (including the freedom to derogate from or vary the Principles themselves[5]), subject only to some interesting provisions on mandatory rules discussed below and to the overriding requirement of good faith.

Pacta sunt servanda

Likewise the Principles adhere strongly to the concept *pacta sunt servanda*[6] and provide that in the absence of one party's own failure of performance, only exceptional circumstances excuse performance by the other party, namely impediments outside a party's control[7] or a fundamental change in the burden of performance or the economic equilibrium of the contract.[8]

Mandatory rules

In those cases where choice of the Principles as the applicable law is valid[9] they will override domestic mandatory rules, which cannot be excluded by contract but operate only where that law is the governing law and may thus be excluded by a choice of foreign law. By contrast, the Principles always take effect subject to internationally mandatory rules, that is those mandatory rules which apply regardless of the governing law.[10]

As well as providing for deferment to external mandatory rules, the Principles contain mandatory rules of their own. At first sight it seems odd that Principles which do not themselves have the force of law should incorporate mandatory rules of any kind. But this is not as strange as it seems. In the first place, under a legal regime

---

[4] UNIDROIT Principles, Art 1.1; PECL, Art 1:102.
[5] UNIDROIT Principles, Art 1.5; PECL, Art 1:102(2).
[6] Expressly stated in the UNIDROIT Principles, Art 1.3
[7] UNIDROIT Principles, Art 7.1.7; PECL, Art 8:108. Both formulations closely follow Art 79 of CISG.
[8] UNIDROIT Principles, Arts 6.2.2, 6.2.3; PECL, Art 6.111.   [9] See above.
[10] UNIDROIT Principles, Art 1.4; PECL, Art 1:103. The UNIDROIT Principles are intentionally silent on the applicability of domestic mandatory rules.

which allows the parties to choose the Principles as the applicable law the exclusion of domestic mandatory rules of a national legal system follows established conflict of laws principles. Secondly, in stating what provisions are to be considered mandatory the Principles send a signal to courts and arbitrators that such provisions are of a kind that ought to be considered incapable of exclusion by the parties. Thirdly, even where the Principles take effect only by incorporation as terms of the contract, rather than being selected as the applicable law, their adoption will signify an intention on the part of the parties that the rest of the contract should, as far as possible, be construed so as to be consistent with the provisions expressed to be mandatory.

Provisions of the Principles which are mandatory in the sense that where the Principles apply such provisions cannot be excluded or varied by agreement include the duty of good faith,[11] the substitution of a reasonable price or term for a grossly unreasonable determination by a party empowered to determine that price or term,[12] reduction of a grossly excessive stipulated payment for non-performance,[13] and curbs on contractual provisions excluding or limiting liability.[14]

Good faith

Article 1:201 of the PECL requires the parties to act in accordance with good faith and fair dealing. This is buttressed by specific rules imposing a duty to co-operate in order to give full effect to the contract[15] and requiring negotiations to be conducted in good faith[16] and confidential information not to be disclosed,[17] and specifying fraud[18] and the taking of unfair advantage[19] as grounds for avoiding a contract. But these specific rules, so far as requiring the exercise of good faith, must always be read in conjunction with Article 1:201, for this is a mandatory rule, whereas the specific rules are not so designated and derive their mandatory force solely from Article 1:201. Quite apart from these specific cases, Article 1:201 exercises a pervasive influence on the Principles as a whole, so that termination of a contract for a trivial breach could be held contrary to good faith even if technically constituting a fundamental non-performance.[20] The PECL do not define good faith. In some systems good faith means no more than subjective honesty in fact, while in others it extends to objective fair dealing and in yet others is considered breached by conduct which does not involve dishonesty or sharp practice but is simply a failure to act reasonably. The addition of the words 'and fair dealing' in the PECL shows that an objective test is to be applied, and this will no doubt pick up at least some forms of honest but unreasonable behaviour. It does not, however, follow that every failure to act in a reasonable manner constitutes a breach of the duty of good faith and fair dealing.

---

[11] UNIDROIT Principles, Art 1.7; PECL, Art 1:201.
[12] UNIDROIT Principles, Art 5.1.7; PECL, Art 6:105.
[13] UNIDROIT Principles, Art 7.4.13; PECL, Art 9:509(2).
[14] UNIDROIT Principles, Art 7.1.6; PECL, Art 8:109.   [15] Article 1:202.
[16] Article 2:301.   [17] Article 2:302.   [18] Article 4:107.   [19] Article 4:109.
[20] *Principles of European Contract Law, Parts I and II* (ed. Lando and Beale), Comment B to Art 1:201.

Article 1:7 of the UNIDROIT Principles also embodies a requirement of good faith and fair dealing but adds the word 'in international trade' to signify that the standards to be applied are those adopted internationally.[21] Again, the concept of good faith is given a very broad interpretation.[22]

Interpretation

The principles applied by courts and arbitral tribunals when interpreting contract terms are of enormous significance in practice, given that so many cases raise issues of interpretation. Both Principles emphasize the importance of the 'common intention' of the parties in the interpretative process and, at least in the case of PECL, attach less weight to the literal meaning of the words used by the parties.[23] When interpreting the contract, courts and arbitral tribunals can draw on a wide range of materials,[24] including preliminary negotiations between the parties, conduct subsequent to the making of the contract, usages and, in the case of PECL, good faith and fair dealing. This list is broader than the range of materials traditionally admissible in evidence in common law jurisdictions but there have been signs recently that common law courts may be prepared to adopt a more liberal approach to the admissibility of such evidence and the Principles may, possibly, encourage them to take further steps down this road.

Adequate assurance of performance

There may be cases where, though a party has not expressed his inability or unwillingness to perform, his conduct or other circumstances have generated a reasonable belief by the other party that there will be a fundamental non-performance by the first party. Under Article 7.3.4 of the UNIDROIT Principles the other party may demand adequate assurance of performance and if this is not forthcoming within a reasonable time he may terminate the contract. There is a similar provision in Article 8:105 of PECL. Though inspired by §2-609 of the American Uniform Commercial Code, the UNIDROIT and PECL solutions are more restricted, requiring a reasonable belief that there *will be* a fundamental non-performance, whereas §2-609 imposes on a party the duty to ensure that the other party's expectation of receiving due performance will not be impaired and confers the right to demand adequate assurance of due performance when reasonable grounds for insecurity of performance arise.

Specific performance as a primary remedy

Departing from the common law tradition, in which the primary remedy for non-performance is debt or damages, the Principles adopt the civil law rule by which

---

[21] *The UNIDROIT Principles in Practice* (ed. Bonell), Comment 2 to Art 1:7.
[22] See the long list of Articles referred to in the above work, in Comment 1 to Art 1:7, as constituting a direct or indirect application of the principle of good faith and fair dealing.
[23] PECL, Art 5:101(1); UNIDROIT Principles, Art 4.1.1.
[24] PECL, Art 5:102; UNIDROIT Principles, Art 4.3.

specific performance is a primary remedy.[25] However, this is cut down by exceptions which exclude the remedy where, *inter alia*, it would cause the debtor unreasonable effort or expense or where the aggrieved party may reasonably obtain performance from another source,[26] for example, by buying equivalent goods on the market.

Other remedies

Apart from the normal remedies of damages, termination, and the like, the Principles give a party whose non-conforming tender is rejected an opportunity to cure the default by a fresh and conforming tender;[27] and where the non-conforming tender is accepted then in lieu of damages the innocent party is given by PECL a claim to a reduction in price proportionate to the reduction in the value of the promised performance,[28] so that if, for example, the performance should have been worth £150,000 but by reason of the breach is only worth £100,000, and the price was £180,000, then instead of claiming damages of £50,000 the innocent party can claim a price reduction of one-third, i.e. £60,000. This *actio quanti minoris* is not available under the UNIDROIT Principles.

Impediment to performance

The common law and the civil law are equally reluctant to excuse performance because one party finds it difficult or impossible to perform his obligation. But in exceptional cases where performance is impeded without fault on either side relief may be given. Legal systems differ, however, in the form of such relief. In common law countries, in which *force majeure* is not a legal concept at all, simply a matter of contractual provision,[29] the contract is said to be frustrated and comes to an end automatically by force of law. In civil law countries the doctrine of *force majeure* comes into play. This has the effect of suspending the duty to perform and of absolving the non-performing party from liability for damages but leaves intact other remedies, such as termination for fundamental non-performance or, if the impediment to performance was purely temporary, specific performance. The Principles follow Article 79 of CISG[30] in adopting the *force majeure* approach.

Hardship; change of circumstances

The most innovative provisions of the Principles are those relating to the effect of an adverse change of circumstances on a party's duty to perform. In the UNIDROIT

---

[25] PECL, Art 9:102; UNIDROIT Principles, Art 7.2.2.   [26] Ibid.
[27] PECL, Art 8:104; UNIDROIT Principles, Art 7.1.4.   [28] PECL, Art 9:401.
[29] For a recommended *force majeure* clause, see the ICC Force Majeure Clause 2003 (No. 650).
[30] See further p. 212 below.

Principles this is labelled hardship, and involves a fundamental change in the equilbrium of the contract because of an increase in the cost of performance or diminution in the value of the performance received.[31] The PECL equivalent is labelled 'change of circumstances'[32] and refers to performance becoming 'excessively onerous', but the concept is the same. It is clear from the comments to both provisions that only in exceptional circumstances will a party be able to invoke these provisions.[33] The mere fact that a contract has become unprofitable for one party does not suffice. Where the provisions do apply, then under the PECL the parties come under a duty to enter into negotiations with a view to adapting the contract or ending it,[34] while under the UNIDROIT Principles the disadvantaged party may request negotiations. On the parties' failure to reach agreement within a reasonable time the court is empowered to terminate the contract or to adapt it in order to reflect the change of circumstances.[35] Though most systems have rules for dealing with the effect of a radical change of circumstances, the duty to negotiate goes further than is required by most legal systems.

Assignment and novation

Both Principles contain rules on assignment and novation.[36] These do not require comment except to note that, in line with the rule adopted in certain international conventions,[37] assignments of accounts are, in general, effective despite a no-assignment clause in the assigned contract.[38] The purpose of this rule is to avoid the impediments to receivables financing that would otherwise arise.

Agency

Both principles contain rules relating to the external aspects of agency,[39] that is to say, the extent of an agent's authority to bind his principal in relation to a contract with a third party. Agency is discussed in more detail in Chapter 5 of this work.

---

[31] Article 6.2.2.   [32] Article 6:111.

[33] It is, of course, open to the parties to make provision in their contract for its adjustment through change of circumstances. See in that connection the ICC Hardship Clause 2003 (No. 650).

[34] Article 6:111(2).   [35] UNIDROIT Principles, Art 6.2.3; PECL, Art 6:111(3).

[36] UNIDROIT Principles, Ch 9; PECL, Ch 11.

[37] The 1988 UNIDROIT Convention on International Factoring; the 2001 UN Convention on the Assignment of Receivables in International Trade, Art 9(1). Both of these provisions drew their inspiration from what is now §9-406(d) of the Uniform Commercial Code.

[38] UNIDROIT Principles, Art 9.1.9; PECL, Art, 11:301, which, however, is limited to the three cases there mentioned.

[39] UNIDROIT Principles, Art 2.2.1 et seq PECL, Ch 3.

B. Instruments

(i) 2004 UNIDROIT PRINCIPLES OF INTERNATIONAL COMMERCIAL CONTRACTS[(i)]*

[(i)] The reader is reminded that the complete version of the UNIDROIT Principles contains not only the black-letter rules reproduced hereunder, but also detailed comments on each article and, where appropriate, illustrations. The volume may be ordered from UNIDROIT at www.unidroit.org.

For an update of international case law and bibliography relating to the Principles see <http://www.unilex.info>.

* Reproduced with the kind permission of UNIDROIT.

47

These Principles set forth general rules for international commercial contracts.

They shall be applied when the parties have agreed that their contract be governed by them.[*]

They may be applied when the parties have agreed that their contract be governed by general principles of law, the *lex mercatoria* or the like.

They may be applied when the parties have not chosen any law to govern their contract.

They may be used to interpret or supplement international uniform law instruments.

They may be used to interpret or supplement domestic law.

They may serve as a model for national and international legislators.

CHAPTER 1
GENERAL PROVISIONS

Article 1.1
Freedom of contract

The parties are free to enter into a contract and to determine its content.

Article 1.2
No form required

Nothing in these Principles requires a contract, statement or any other act to be made in or evidenced by a particular form. It may be proved by any means, including witnesses.

Article 1.3
Binding character of contract

A contract validly entered into is binding upon the parties. It can only be modified or terminated in accordance with its terms or by agreement or as otherwise provided in these Principles.

Article 1.4
Mandatory rules

Nothing in these Principles shall restrict the application of mandatory rules, whether of national, international or supranational origin, which are applicable in accordance with the relevant rules of private international law.

(*) Parties wishing to provide that their agreement be governed by the Principles might use the following words, adding any desired exceptions or modifications:

'This contract shall be governed by the UNIDROIT Principles (2004) [except as to Articles ...]'.

Parties wishing to provide in addition for the application of the law of a particular jurisdiction might use the following words:

'This contract shall be governed by the UNIDROIT Principles (2004) [except as to Articles ...], supplemented when necessary by the law of [jurisdiction X]'.

Article 1.5
Exclusion or modification by the parties

The parties may exclude the application of these Principles or derogate from or vary the effect of any of their provisions, except as otherwise provided in the Principles.

Article 1.6
Interpretation and supplementation of the Principles

(1) In the interpretation of these Principles, regard is to be had to their international character and to their purposes including the need to promote uniformity in their application.
(2) Issues within the scope of these Principles but not expressly settled by them are as far as possible to be settled in accordance with their underlying general principles.

Article 1.7
Good faith and fair dealing

(1) Each party must act in accordance with good faith and fair dealing in international trade.
(2) The parties may not exclude or limit this duty.

Article 1.8
Inconsistent behaviour

A party cannot act inconsistently with an understanding it has caused the other party to have and upon which that other party reasonably has acted in reliance to its detriment.

Article 1.9
Usages and practices

(1) The parties are bound by any usage to which they have agreed and by any practices which they have established between themselves.
(2) The parties are bound by a usage that is widely known to and regularly observed in international trade by parties in the particular trade concerned except where the application of such a usage would be unreasonable.

Article 1.10
Notice

(1) Where notice is required it may be given by any means appropriate to the circumstances.
(2) A notice is effective when it reaches the person to whom it is given.
(3) For the purpose of paragraph (2) a notice 'reaches' a person when given to that person orally or delivered at that person's place of business or mailing address.
(4) For the purpose of this article 'notice' includes a declaration, demand, request or any other communication of intention.

50

Article 1.11
Definitions

In these Principles
—'court' includes an arbitral tribunal;
—where a party has more than one place of business the relevant 'place of business' is that which has the closest relationship to the contract and its performance, having regard to the circumstances known to or contemplated by the parties at any time before or at the conclusion of the contract;
—'obligor' refers to the party who is to perform an obligation and 'obligee' refers to the party who is entitled to performance of that obligation.
—'writing' means any mode of communication that preserves a record of the information contained therein and is capable of being reproduced in tangible form.

Article 1.12
Computation of time set by parties

(1) Official holidays or non-business days occurring during a period set by parties for an act to be done are included in calculating the period.
(2) However, if the last day of the period is an official holiday or a non-business day at the place of business of the party to do the act, the period is extended until the first business day which follows, unless the circumstances indicate otherwise.
(3) The relevant time zone is that of the place of business of the party setting the time, unless the circumstances indicate otherwise.

CHAPTER 2
FORMATION AND AUTHORITY OF AGENTS

SECTION I

FORMATION

Article 2.1.1
Manner of formation

A contract may be concluded either by the acceptance of an offer or by conduct of the parties that is sufficient to show agreement.

Article 2.1.2
Definition of offer

A proposal for concluding a contract constitutes an offer if it is sufficiently definite and indicates the intention of the offeror to be bound in case of acceptance.

Article 2.1.3
Withdrawal of offer

(1) An offer becomes effective when it reaches the offeree.
(2) An offer, even if it is irrevocable, may be withdrawn if the withdrawal reaches the offeree before or at the same time as the offer.

Article 2.1.4
Revocation of offer

(1) Until a contract is concluded an offer may be revoked if the revocation reaches the offeree before it has dispatched an acceptance.
(2) However, an offer cannot be revoked
    (a) if it indicates, whether by stating a fixed time for acceptance or otherwise, that it is irrevocable; or
    (b) if it was reasonable for the offeree to rely on the offer as being irrevocable and the offeree has acted in reliance on the offer.

Article 2.1.5
Rejection of offer

An offer is terminated when a rejection reaches the offeror.

Article 2.1.6
Mode of acceptance

(1) A statement made by or other conduct of the offeree indicating assent to an offer is an acceptance. Silence or inactivity does not in itself amount to acceptance.
(2) An acceptance of an offer becomes effective when the indication of assent reaches the offeror.
(3) However, if, by virtue of the offer or as a result of practices which the parties have established between themselves or of usage, the offeree may indicate assent by performing an act without notice to the offeror, the acceptance is effective when the act is performed.

Article 2.1.7
Time of acceptance

An offer must be accepted within the time the offeror has fixed or, if no time is fixed, within a reasonable time having regard to the circumstances, including the rapidity of the means of communication employed by the offeror. An oral offer must be accepted immediately unless the circumstances indicate otherwise.

Article 2.1.8
Acceptance within a fixed period of time

A period of acceptance fixed by the offeror begins to run from the time that the offer is dispatched. A time indicated in the offer is deemed to be the time of dispatch unless the circumstances indicate otherwise.

Article 2.1.9
Late acceptance. Delay in acceptance

(1) A late acceptance is nevertheless effective as an acceptance if without undue delay the offeror so informs the offeree or gives notice to that effect.
(2) If a communication containing a late acceptance shows that it has been sent in such circumstances that if its transmission had been normal it would have reached the offeror in due time, the late acceptance is effective as an acceptance unless, without undue delay, the offeror informs the offeree that it considers the offer as having lapsed.

Article 2.1.10
Withdrawal of acceptance

An acceptance may be withdrawn if the withdrawal reaches the offeror before or at the same time as the acceptance would have become effective.

Article 2.1.11
Modified acceptance

(1) A reply to an offer which purports to be an acceptance but contains additions, limitations or other modifications is a rejection of the offer and constitutes a counter-offer.
(2) However, a reply to an offer which purports to be an acceptance but contains additional or different terms which do not materially alter the terms of the offer constitutes an acceptance, unless the offeror, without undue delay, objects to the discrepancy. If the offeror does not object, the terms of the contract are the terms of the offer with the modifications contained in the acceptance.

Article 2.1.12
Writings in confirmation

If a writing which is sent within a reasonable time after the conclusion of the contract and which purports to be a confirmation of the contract contains additional or different terms, such terms become part of the contract, unless they materially alter the contract or the recipient, without undue delay, objects to the discrepancy.

Article 2.1.13
Conclusion of contract dependent on agreement on specific matters or in particular form

Where in the course of negotiations one of the parties insists that the contract is not concluded until there is agreement on specific matters or in a particular form, no contract is concluded before agreement is reached on those matters or in that form.

Article 2.1.14
Contract with terms deliberately left open

(1) If the parties intend to conclude a contract, the fact that they intentionally leave a term to be agreed upon in further negotiations or to be determined by a third person does not prevent a contract from coming into existence.
(2) The existence of the contract is not affected by the fact that subsequently
    (a) the parties reach no agreement on the term; or
    (b) the third person does not determine the term,
    (c) provided that there is an alternative means of rendering the term definite that is reasonable in the circumstances, having regard to the intention of the parties.

Article 2.1.15
Negotiations in bad faith

(1) A party is free to negotiate and is not liable for failure to reach an agreement.
(2) However, a party who negotiates or breaks off negotiations in bad faith is liable for the losses caused to the other party.
(3) It is bad faith, in particular, for a party to enter into or continue negotiations when intending not to reach an agreement with the other party.

Article 2.1.16
Duty of confidentiality

Where information is given as confidential by one party in the course of negotiations, the other party is under a duty not to disclose that information or to use it improperly for its own purposes, whether or not a contract is subsequently concluded. Where appropriate, the remedy for breach of that duty may include compensation based on the benefit received by the other party.

Article 2.1.17
Merger clauses

A contract in writing which contains a clause indicating that the writing completely embodies the terms on which the parties have agreed cannot be contradicted or supplemented by evidence of prior statements or agreements. However, such statements or agreements may be used to interpret the writing.

Article 2.1.18
Modification in particular form

A contract in writing which contains a clause requiring any modification or termination by agreement to be in a particular form may not be otherwise modified or terminated. However, a party may be precluded by its conduct from asserting such a clause to the extent that the other party has acted in reliance on that conduct Article 2.1.19.

Article 2.1.19
Contracting under standard terms

(1) Where one party or both parties use standard terms in concluding a contract, the general rules on formation apply, subject to Articles 2.1.20–2.1.22.
(2) Standard terms are provisions which are prepared in advance for general and repeated use by one party and which are actually used without negotiation with the other party.

Article 2.1.20
Surprising terms

(1) No term contained in standard terms which is of such a character that the other party could not reasonably have expected it, is effective unless it has been expressly accepted by that party.
(2) In determining whether a term is of such a character regard is to be had to its content, language and presentation.

Article 2.1.21
Conflict between standard terms and non-standard terms

In case of conflict between a standard term and a term which is not a standard term the latter prevails.

Article 2.1.22
Battle of forms

Where both parties use standard terms and reach agreement except on those terms, a contract is concluded on the basis of the agreed terms and of any standard terms which are common in substance unless one party clearly indicates in advance, or later and without undue delay informs the other party, that it does not intend to be bound by such a contract.

SECTION 2

AUTHORITY OF AGENTS

Article 2.2.1
Scope of the Section

(1) This Section governs the authority of a person, the agent, to affect the legal relations of another person, the principal, by or with respect to a contract with a third party, whether the agent acts in its own name or in that of the principal.

(2) It governs only the relations between the principal or the agent on the one hand, and the third party on the other.

(3) It does not govern an agent's authority conferred by law or the authority of an agent appointed by a public or judicial authority.

Article 2.2.2
Establishment and scope of the authority of the agent

(1) The principal's grant of authority to an agent may be express or implied.

(2) The agent has authority to perform all acts necessary in the circumstances to achieve the purposes for which the authority was granted.

Article 2.2.3
Agency disclosed

(1) Where an agent acts within the scope of its authority and the third party knew or ought to have known that the agent was acting as an agent, the acts of the agent shall directly affect the legal relations between the principal and the third party and no legal relation is created between the agent and the third party.

(2) However, the acts of the agent shall affect only the relations between the agent and the third party, where the agent with the consent of the principal undertakes to become the party to the contract.

Article 2.2.4
Agency undisclosed

(1) Where an agent acts within the scope of its authority and the third party neither knew nor ought to have known that the agent was acting as an agent, the acts of the agent shall affect only the relations between the agent and the third party.

(2) However, where such an agent, when contracting with the third party on behalf of a business, represents itself to be the owner of that business, the third party, upon discovery of the real owner of the business, may exercise also against the latter the rights it has against the agent.

Article 2.2.5
Agent acting without or exceeding its authority

(1) Where an agent acts without authority or exceeds its authority, its acts do not affect the legal relations between the principal and the third party.

55

(2) However, where the principal causes the third party reasonably to believe that the agent has authority to act on behalf of the principal and that the agent is acting within the scope of that authority, the principal may not invoke against the third party the lack of authority of the agent.

Article 2.2.6
Liability of agent acting without or exceeding its authority

(1) An agent that acts without authority or exceeds its authority is, failing ratification by the principal, liable for damages that will put the third party in the same position as if the agent had acted with authority and not exceeded its authority.
(2) However, the agent is not liable if the third party knew or ought to have known that the agent had no authority or was exceeding its authority.

Article 2.2.7
Conflict of interests

(1) If a contract concluded by an agent involves the agent in a conflict of interests with the principal of which the third party knew or ought to have known, the principal may avoid the contract. The right to avoid is subject to Articles 3.12 and 3.14 to 3.17.
(2) However, the principal may not avoid the contract
   (a) if the principal had consented to, or knew or ought to have known, the agent's involvement in the conflict of interests; or
   (b) if the agent had disclosed the conflict of interests to the principal and it had not objected within a reasonable time.

Article 2.2.8
Subagency

An agent has implied authority to appoint a subagent to perform acts which it is not reasonable to expect the agent to perform itself. The rules of this chapter apply to the subagency.

Article 2.2.9
Ratification

(1) An act by an agent that acts without authority or exceeds its authority may be ratified by the principal. On ratification the act produces the same effects as if it had initially been carried out with authority.
(2) The third party may by notice to the principal specify a reasonable period of time for ratification. If the principal does not ratify within that period it can no longer do so.
(3) Where, at the time of the agent's act, the third party neither knew nor ought to have known of the lack of authority, it may, at any time before ratification, by notice to the principal indicate its refusal to become bound by a ratification.

Article 2.2.10
Termination of authority

(1) Termination of authority is not effective in relation to the third party unless the third party knew or ought to have known of it.
(2) Notwithstanding the termination of its authority, an agent remains authorised to perform the acts that are necessary to prevent harm to the principal's interests.

CHAPTER 3
VALIDITY

Article 3.1
Matters not covered

These Principles do not deal with invalidity arising from
(a) lack of capacity;
(b) immorality or illegality.

Article 3.2
Validity of mere agreement

A contract is concluded, modified or terminated by the mere agreement of the parties, without any further requirement.

Article 3.3
Initial impossibility

(1) The mere fact that at the time of the conclusion of the contract the performance of the obligation assumed was impossible does not affect the validity of the contract.
(2) The mere fact that at the time of the conclusion of the contract a party was not entitled to dispose of the assets to which the contract relates does not affect the validity of the contract.

Article 3.4
Definition of mistake

Mistake is an erroneous assumption relating to facts or to law existing when the contract was concluded.

Article 3.5
Relevant mistake

(1) A party may only avoid the contract for mistake if, when the contract was concluded, the mistake was of such importance that a reasonable person in the same situation as the party in error would only have concluded the contract on materially different terms or would not have concluded it at all if the true state of affairs had been known, and
(a) the other party made the same mistake, or caused the mistake, or knew or ought to have known of the mistake and it was contrary to reasonable commercial standards of fair dealing to leave the mistaken party in error; or
(b) the other party had not at the time of avoidance reasonably acted in reliance on the contract.
(2) However, a party may not avoid the contract if
(a) it was grossly negligent in committing the mistake; or
(b) the mistake relates to a matter in regard to which the risk of mistake was assumed or, having regard to the circumstances, should be borne by the mistaken party.

Article 3.6
Error in expression or transmission

An error occurring in the expression or transmission of a declaration is considered to be a mistake of the person from whom the declaration emanated.

Article 3.7
Remedies for non-performance

A party is not entitled to avoid the contract on the ground of mistake if the circumstances on which that party relies afford, or could have afforded, a remedy for non-performance.

Article 3.8
Fraud

A party may avoid the contract when it has been led to conclude the contract by the other party's fraudulent representation, including language or practices, or fraudulent non-disclosure of circumstances which, according to reasonable commercial standards of fair dealing, the latter party should have disclosed.

Article 3.9
Threat

A party may avoid the contract when it has been led to conclude the contract by the other party's unjustified threat which, having regard to the circumstances, is so imminent and serious as to leave the first party no reasonable alternative. In particular, a threat is unjustified if the act or omission with which a party has been threatened is wrongful in itself, or it is wrongful to use it as a means to obtain the conclusion of the contract.

Article 3.10
Gross disparity

(1) A party may avoid the contract or an individual term of it if, at the time of the conclusion of the contract, the contract or term unjustifiably gave the other party an excessive advantage. Regard is to be had, among other factors, to
  (a) the fact that the other party has taken unfair advantage of the first party's dependence, economic distress or urgent needs, or of its improvidence, ignorance, inexperience or lack of bargaining skill; and
  (b) the nature and purpose of the contract.
(2) Upon the request of the party entitled to avoidance, a court may adapt the contract or term in order to make it accord with reasonable commercial standards of fair dealing.
(3) A court may also adapt the contract or term upon the request of the party receiving notice of avoidance, provided that that party informs the other party of its request promptly after receiving such notice and before the other party has reasonably acted in reliance on it. The provisions of Article 3.13(2) apply accordingly.

Article 3.11
Third persons

(1) Where fraud, threat, gross disparity or a party's mistake is imputable to, or is known or ought to be known by, a third person for whose acts the other party is responsible,

the contract may be avoided under the same conditions as if the behaviour or knowledge had been that of the party itself.

(2) Where fraud, threat or gross disparity is imputable to a third person for whose acts the other party is not responsible, the contract may be avoided if that party knew or ought to have known of the fraud, threat or gross disparity, or has not at the time of avoidance reasonably acted in reliance on the contract.

Article 3.12
Confirmation

If the party entitled to avoid the contract expressly or impliedly confirms the contract after the period of time for giving notice of avoidance has begun to run, avoidance of the contract is excluded.

Article 3.13
Loss of right to avoid

(1) If a party is entitled to avoid the contract for mistake but the other party declares itself willing to perform or performs the contract as it was understood by the party entitled to avoidance, the contract is considered to have been concluded as the latter party understood it. The other party must make such a declaration or render such performance promptly after having been informed of the manner in which the party entitled to avoidance had understood the contract and before that party has reasonably acted in reliance on a notice of avoidance.

(2) After such a declaration or performance the right to avoidance is lost and any earlier notice of avoidance is ineffective.

Article 3.14
Notice of avoidance

The right of a party to avoid the contract is exercised by notice to the other party.

Article 3.15
Time limits

(1) Notice of avoidance shall be given within a reasonable time, having regard to the circumstances, after the avoiding party knew or could not have been unaware of the relevant facts or became capable of acting freely.

(2) Where an individual term of the contract may be avoided by a party under Article 3.10, the period of time for giving notice of avoidance begins to run when that term is asserted by the other party.

Article 3.16
Partial avoidance

Where a ground of avoidance affects only individual terms of the contract, the effect of avoidance is limited to those terms unless, having regard to the circumstances, it is unreasonable to uphold the remaining contract.

Article 3.17
Retroactive effect of avoidance

(1) Avoidance takes effect retroactively.
(2) On avoidance either party may claim restitution of whatever it has supplied under the contract or the part of it avoided, provided that it concurrently makes restitution of whatever it has received under the contract or the part of it avoided or, if it cannot make restitution in kind, it makes an allowance for what it has received.

Article 3.18
Damages

Irrespective of whether or not the contract has been avoided, the party who knew or ought to have known of the ground for avoidance is liable for damages so as to put the other party in the same position in which it would have been if it had not concluded the contract.

Article 3.19
Mandatory character of the provisions

The provisions of this Chapter are mandatory, except insofar as they relate to the binding force of mere agreement, initial impossibility or mistake.

Article 3.20
Unilateral declarations

The provisions of this Chapter apply with appropriate adaptations to any communication of intention addressed by one party to the other.

CHAPTER 4
INTERPRETATION

Article 4.1
Intention of the parties

(1) A contract shall be interpreted according to the common intention of the parties.
(2) If such an intention cannot be established, the contract shall be interpreted according to the meaning that reasonable persons of the same kind as the parties would give to it in the same circumstances.

Article 4.2
Interpretation of statements and other conduct

(1) The statements and other conduct of a party shall be interpreted according to that party's intention if the other party knew or could not have been unaware of that intention.
(2) If the preceding paragraph is not applicable, such statements and other conduct shall be interpreted according to the meaning that a reasonable person of the same kind as the other party would give to it in the same circumstances.

Article 4.3
Relevant circumstances

In applying Articles 4.1 and 4.2, regard shall be had to all the circumstances, including
    (a) preliminary negotiations between the parties;
    (b) practices which the parties have established between themselves;
    (c) the conduct of the parties subsequent to the conclusion of the contract;
    (d) the nature and purpose of the contract;
    (e) the meaning commonly given to terms and expressions in the trade concerned;
    (f) usages.

Article 4.4
Reference to contract or statement as a whole

Terms and expressions shall be interpreted in the light of the whole contract or statement in which they appear.

Article 4.5
All terms to be given effect

Contract terms shall be interpreted so as to give effect to all the terms rather than to deprive some of them of effect.

Article 4.6
Contra proferentem rule

If contract terms supplied by one party are unclear, an interpretation against that party is preferred.

Article 4.7
Linguistic discrepancies

Where a contract is drawn up in two or more language versions which are equally authoritative there is, in case of discrepancy between the versions, a preference for the interpretation according to a version in which the contract was originally drawn up.

Article 4.8
Supplying an omitted term

(1) Where the parties to a contract have not agreed with respect to a term which is important for a determination of their rights and duties, a term which is appropriate in the circumstances shall be supplied.
(2) In determining what is an appropriate term regard shall be had, among other factors, to
    (a) the intention of the parties;
    (b) the nature and purpose of the contract;
    (c) good faith and fair dealing;
    (d) reasonableness.

CHAPTER 5
CONTENT AND THIRD PARTY RIGHTS

SECTION I

CONTENT

Article 5.1.1
Express and implied obligations

The contractual obligations of the parties may be express or implied.

Article 5.1.2
Implied obligations

Implied obligations stem from
(a) the nature and purpose of the contract;
(b) practices established between the parties and usages;
(c) good faith and fair dealing;
(d) reasonableness.

Article 5.1.3
Co-operation between the parties

Each party shall co-operate with the other party when such co-operation may reasonably be expected for the performance of that party's obligations.

Article 5.1.4
Duty to achieve a specific result
Duty of best efforts

(1) To the extent that an obligation of a party involves a duty to achieve a specific result, that party is bound to achieve that result.
(2) To the extent that an obligation of a party involves a duty of best efforts in the performance of an activity, that party is bound to make such efforts as would be made by a reasonable person of the same kind in the same circumstances.

Article 5.1.5
Determination of kind of duty involved

In determining the extent to which an obligation of a party involves a duty of best efforts in the performance of an activity or a duty to achieve a specific result, regard shall be had, among other factors, to
(a) the way in which the obligation is expressed in the contract;
(b) the contractual price and other terms of the contract;
(c) the degree of risk normally involved in achieving the expected result;
(d) the ability of the other party to influence the performance of the obligation.

Article 5.1.6
Determination of quality of performance

Where the quality of performance is neither fixed by, nor determinable from, the contract a party is bound to render a performance of a quality that is reasonable and not less than average in the circumstances.

Article 5.1.7
Price determination

(1) Where a contract does not fix or make provision for determining the price, the parties are considered, in the absence of any indication to the contrary, to have made reference to the price generally charged at the time of the conclusion of the contract for such performance in comparable circumstances in the trade concerned or, if no such price is available, to a reasonable price.
(2) Where the price is to be determined by one party and that determination is manifestly unreasonable, a reasonable price shall be substituted notwithstanding any contract term to the contrary.
(3) Where the price is to be fixed by a third person, and that person cannot or will not do so, the price shall be a reasonable price.
(4) Where the price is to be fixed by reference to factors which do not exist or have ceased to exist or to be accessible, the nearest equivalent factor shall be treated as a substitute.

Article 5.1.8
Contract for an indefinite period

A contract for an indefinite period may be ended by either party by giving notice a reasonable time in advance.

Article 5.1.9
Release by agreement

(1) An obligee may release its rights by agreement with the obligor.
(2) An offer to release a right gratuitously shall be deemed accepted if the obligor does not reject the offer without delay after having become aware of it.

SECTION 2

THIRD PARTY RIGHTS

Article 5.2.1
Contracts in favour of third parties

(1) Parties (the 'promisor' and the 'promisee') may confer by express or implied agreement a right on a third party (the 'beneficiary').
(2) The existence and content of the beneficiary's right against the promisor are determined by the agreement of the parties and are subject to any conditions or other limitations under the agreement.

Article 5.2.2
Third party identifiable

The beneficiary must be identifiable with adequate certainty by the contract but need not be in existence at the time the contract is made.

Article 5.2.3
Exclusion and limitation clauses

The conferment of rights in the beneficiary includes the right to invoke a clause in the contract which excludes or limits the liability of the beneficiary.

Article 5.2.4
Defences

The promisor may assert against the beneficiary all defences which the promisor could assert against the promisee.

Article 5.2.5
Revocation

The contracting parties may modify or revoke the rights conferred by the contract on the beneficiary until the beneficiary has accepted them or reasonably acted in reliance on them.

Article 5.2.6
Renunciation

The beneficiary may renounce a right conferred on it.

CHAPTER 6
PERFORMANCE

SECTION 1
PERFORMANCE IN GENERAL

Article 6.1.1
Time of performance

A party must perform its obligations:
   (a) if a time is fixed by or determinable from the contract, at that time;
   (b) if a period of time is fixed by or determinable from the contract, at any time within that period unless circumstances indicate that the other party is to choose a time;
   (c) in any other case, within a reasonable time after the conclusion of the contract.

Article 6.1.2
Performance at one time or in instalments

In cases under Article 6.1.1(b) or (c), a party must perform its obligations at one time if that performance can be rendered at one time and the circumstances do not indicate otherwise.

Article 6.1.3
Partial performance

(1) The obligee may reject an offer to perform in part at the time performance is due, whether or not such offer is coupled with an assurance as to the balance of the performance, unless the obligee has no legitimate interest in so doing.

(2) Additional expenses caused to the obligee by partial performance are to be borne by the obligor without prejudice to any other remedy.

Article 6.1.4
Order of performance

(1) To the extent that the performances of the parties can be rendered simultaneously, the parties are bound to render them simultaneously unless the circumstances indicate otherwise.

(2) To the extent that the performance of only one party requires a period of time, that party is bound to render its performance first, unless the circumstances indicate otherwise.

Article 6.1.5
Earlier performance

(1) The obligee may reject an earlier performance unless it has no legitimate interest in so doing.

(2) Acceptance by a party of an earlier performance does not affect the time for the performance of its own obligations if that time has been fixed irrespective of the performance of the other party's obligations.

(3) Additional expenses caused to the obligee by earlier performance are to be borne by the obligor, without prejudice to any other remedy.

Article 6.1.6
Place of performance

(1) If the place of performance is neither fixed by, nor determinable from, the contract, a party is to perform:
   (a) a monetary obligation, at the obligee's place of business;
   (b) any other obligation, at its own place of business.

(2) A party must bear any increase in the expenses incidental to performance which is caused by a change in its place of business subsequent to the conclusion of the contract.

Article 6.1.7
Payment by cheque or other instrument

(1) Payment may be made in any form used in the ordinary course of business at the place for payment.

(2) However, an obligee who accepts, either by virtue of paragraph (1) or voluntarily, a cheque, any other order to pay or a promise to pay, is presumed to do so only on condition that it will be honoured.

Article 6.1.8
Payment by funds transfer

(1) Unless the obligee has indicated a particular account, payment may be made by a transfer to any of the financial institutions in which the obligee has made it known that it has an account.
(2) In case of payment by a transfer the obligation of the obligor is discharged when the transfer to the obligee's financial institution becomes effective.

Article 6.1.9
Currency of payment

(1) If a monetary obligation is expressed in a currency other than that of the place for payment, it may be paid by the obligor in the currency of the place for payment unless
    (a) that currency is not freely convertible; or
    (b) the parties have agreed that payment should be made only in the currency in which the monetary obligation is expressed.
(2) If it is impossible for the obligor to make payment in the currency in which the monetary obligation is expressed, the obligee may require payment in the currency of the place for payment, even in the case referred to in paragraph (1)(b).
(3) Payment in the currency of the place for payment is to be made according to the applicable rate of exchange prevailing there when payment is due.
(4) However, if the obligor has not paid at the time when payment is due, the obligee may require payment according to the applicable rate of exchange prevailing either when payment is due or at the time of actual payment.

Article 6.1.10
Currency not expressed

Where a monetary obligation is not expressed in a particular currency, payment must be made in the currency of the place where payment is to be made.

Article 6.1.11
Costs of performance

Each party shall bear the costs of performance of its obligations.

Article 6.1.12
Imputation of payments

(1) An obligor owing several monetary obligations to the same obligee may specify at the time of payment the debt to which it intends the payment to be applied. However, the payment discharges first any expenses, then interest due and finally the principal.
(2) If the obligor makes no such specification, the obligee may, within a reasonable time after payment, declare to the obligor the obligation to which it imputes the payment, provided that the obligation is due and undisputed.
(3) In the absence of imputation under paragraphs (1) or (2), payment is imputed to that obligation which satisfies one of the following criteria and in the order indicated:
    (a) an obligation which is due or which is the first to fall due;
    (b) the obligation for which the obligee has least security;

(c) the obligation which is the most burdensome for the obligor;

(d) the obligation which has arisen first.

If none of the preceding criteria applies, payment is imputed to all the obligations proportionally.

Article 6.1.13
Imputation of non-monetary obligations

Article 6.1.12 applies with appropriate adaptations to the imputation of performance of non-monetary obligations.

Article 6.1.14
Application for public permission

Where the law of a State requires a public permission affecting the validity of the contract or its performance and neither that law nor the circumstances indicate otherwise

(a) if only one party has its place of business in that State, that party shall take the measures necessary to obtain the permission;

(b) in any other case the party whose performance requires permission shall take the necessary measures.

Article 6.1.15
Procedure in applying for permission

(1) The party required to take the measures necessary to obtain the permission shall do so without undue delay and shall bear any expenses incurred.

(2) That party shall whenever appropriate give the other party notice of the grant or refusal of such permission without undue delay.

Article 6.1.16
Permission neither granted nor refused

(1) If, notwithstanding the fact that the party responsible has taken all measures required, permission is neither granted nor refused within an agreed period or, where no period has been agreed, within a reasonable time from the conclusion of the contract, either party is entitled to terminate the contract.

(2) Where the permission affects some terms only, paragraph (1) does not apply if, having regard to the circumstances, it is reasonable to uphold the remaining contract even if the permission is refused.

Article 6.1.17
Permission refused

(1) The refusal of a permission affecting the validity of the contract renders the contract void. If the refusal affects the validity of some terms only, only such terms are void if, having regard to the circumstances, it is reasonable to uphold the remaining contract.

(2) Where the refusal of a permission renders the performance of the contract impossible in whole or in part, the rules on non-performance apply.

SECTION 2

HARDSHIP

Article 6.2.1
Contract to be observed

Where the performance of a contract becomes more onerous for one of the parties, that party is nevertheless bound to perform its obligations subject to the following provisions on hardship.

Article 6.2.2
Definition of hardship

There is hardship where the occurrence of events fundamentally alters the equilibrium of the contract either because the cost of a party's performance has increased or because the value of the performance a party receives has diminished, and
  (a) the events occur or become known to the disadvantaged party after the conclusion of the contract;
  (b) the events could not reasonably have been taken into account by the disadvantaged party at the time of the conclusion of the contract;
  (c) the events are beyond the control of the disadvantaged party; and
  (d) the risk of the events was not assumed by the disadvantaged party.

Article 6.2.3
Effects of hardship

(1) In case of hardship the disadvantaged party is entitled to request renegotiations. The request shall be made without undue delay and shall indicate the grounds on which it is based.
(2) The request for renegotiation does not in itself entitle the disadvantaged party to withhold performance.
(3) Upon failure to reach agreement within a reasonable time either party may resort to the court.
(4) If the court finds hardship it may, if reasonable,
  (a) terminate the contract at a date and on terms to be fixed; or
  (b) adapt the contract with a view to restoring its equilibrium.

CHAPTER 7
NON-PERFORMANCE

SECTION I

NON-PERFORMANCE IN GENERAL

Article 7.1.1
Non-performance defined

Non-performance is failure by a party to perform any of its obligations under the contract, including defective performance or late performance.

Article 7.1.2
Interference by the other party

A party may not rely on the non-performance of the other party to the extent that such non-performance was caused by the first party's act or omission or by another event as to which the first party bears the risk.

Article 7.1.3
Withholding performance

(1) Where the parties are to perform simultaneously, either party may withhold performance until the other party tenders its performance.

(2) Where the parties are to perform consecutively, the party that is to perform later may withhold its performance until the first party has performed.

Article 7.1.4
Cure by non-performing party

(1) The non-performing party may, at its own expense, cure any non-performance, provided that
   (a) without undue delay, it gives notice indicating the proposed manner and timing of the cure;
   (b) cure is appropriate in the circumstances;
   (c) the aggrieved party has no legitimate interest in refusing cure; and
   (d) cure is effected promptly.

(2) The right to cure is not precluded by notice of termination.

(3) Upon effective notice of cure, rights of the aggrieved party that are inconsistent with the non-performing party's performance are suspended until the time for cure has expired.

(4) The aggrieved party may withhold performance pending cure.

(5) Notwithstanding cure, the aggrieved party retains the right to claim damages for delay as well as for any harm caused or not prevented by the cure.

Article 7.1.5
Additional period for performance

(1) In a case of non-performance the aggrieved party may by notice to the other party allow an additional period of time for performance.

(2) During the additional period the aggrieved party may withhold performance of its own reciprocal obligations and may claim damages but may not resort to any other remedy. If it receives notice from the other party that the latter will not perform within that period, or if upon expiry of that period due performance has not been made, the aggrieved party may resort to any of the remedies that may be available under this Chapter.

(3) Where in a case of delay in performance which is not fundamental the aggrieved party has given notice allowing an additional period of time of reasonable length, it may terminate the contract at the end of that period. If the additional period allowed is not of reasonable length it shall be extended to a reasonable length. The aggrieved party may in its notice provide that if the other party fails to perform within the period allowed by the notice the contract shall automatically terminate.

(4) Paragraph (3) does not apply where the obligation which has not been performed is only a minor part of the contractual obligation of the non-performing party.

Article 7.1.6
Exemption clauses

A clause which limits or excludes one party's liability for non-performance or which permits one party to render performance substantially different from what the other party reasonably expected may not be invoked if it would be grossly unfair to do so, having regard to the purpose of the contract.

Article 7.1.7
Force majeure

(1) Non-performance by a party is excused if that party proves that the non-performance was due to an impediment beyond its control and that it could not reasonably be expected to have taken the impediment into account at the time of the conclusion of the contract or to have avoided or overcome it or its consequences.
(2) When the impediment is only temporary, the excuse shall have effect for such period as is reasonable having regard to the effect of the impediment on the performance of the contract.
(3) The party who fails to perform must give notice to the other party of the impediment and its effect on its ability to perform. If the notice is not received by the other party within a reasonable time after the party who fails to perform knew or ought to have known of the impediment, it is liable for damages resulting from such non-receipt.
(4) Nothing in this article prevents a party from exercising a right to terminate the contract or to withhold performance or request interest on money due.

SECTION 2
RIGHT TO PERFORMANCE

Article 7.2.1
Performance of monetary obligation

Where a party who is obliged to pay money does not do so, the other party may require payment.

Article 7.2.2
Performance of non-monetary obligation

Where a party who owes an obligation other than one to pay money does not perform, the other party may require performance, unless
  (a) performance is impossible in law or in fact;
  (b) performance or, where relevant, enforcement is unreasonably burdensome or expensive;
  (c) the party entitled to performance may reasonably obtain performance from another source;
  (d) performance is of an exclusively personal character; or
  (e) the party entitled to performance does not require performance within a reasonable time after it has, or ought to have, become aware of the non-performance.

Article 7.2.3
Repair and replacement of defective performance

The right to performance includes in appropriate cases the right to require repair, replacement, or other cure of defective performance. The provisions of Articles 7.2.1 and 7.2.2 apply accordingly.

Article 7.2.4
Judicial penalty

(1) Where the court orders a party to perform, it may also direct that this party pay a penalty if it does not comply with the order.

(2) The penalty shall be paid to the aggrieved party unless mandatory provisions of the law of the forum provide otherwise. Payment of the penalty to the aggrieved party does not exclude any claim for damages.

Article 7.2.5
Change of remedy

(1) An aggrieved party who has required performance of a non-monetary obligation and who has not received performance within a period fixed or otherwise within a reasonable period of time may invoke any other remedy.

(2) Where the decision of a court for performance of a non-monetary obligation cannot be enforced, the aggrieved party may invoke any other remedy.

SECTION 3

TERMINATION

Article 7.3.1
Right to terminate the contract

(1) A party may terminate the contract where the failure of the other party to perform an obligation under the contract amounts to a fundamental non-performance.

(2) In determining whether a failure to perform an obligation amounts to a fundamental non-performance regard shall be had, in particular, to whether

(a) the non-performance substantially deprives the aggrieved party of what it was entitled to expect under the contract unless the other party did not foresee and could not reasonably have foreseen such result;

(b) strict compliance with the obligation which has not been performed is of essence under the contract;

(c) the non-performance is intentional or reckless;

(d) the non-performance gives the aggrieved party reason to believe that it cannot rely on the other party's future performance;

(e) the non-performing party will suffer disproportionate loss as a result of the preparation or performance if the contract is terminated.

(3) In the case of delay the aggrieved party may also terminate the contract if the other party fails to perform before the time allowed it under Article 7.1.5 has expired.

Article 7.3.2
Notice of termination

(1) The right of a party to terminate the contract is exercised by notice to the other party.

(2) If performance has been offered late or otherwise does not conform to the contract the aggrieved party will lose its right to terminate the contract unless it gives notice to the other party within a reasonable time after it has or ought to have become aware of the offer or of the non-conforming performance.

Article 7.3.3
Anticipatory non-performance

Where prior to the date for performance by one of the parties it is clear that there will be a fundamental non-performance by that party, the other party may terminate the contract.

Article 7.3.4
Adequate assurance of due performance

A party who reasonably believes that there will be a fundamental non-performance by the other party may demand adequate assurance of due performance and may meanwhile withhold its own performance. Where this assurance is not provided within a reasonable time the party demanding it may terminate the contract.

Article 7.3.5
Effects of termination in general

(1) Termination of the contract releases both parties from their obligation to effect and to receive future performance.

(2) Termination does not preclude a claim for damages for non-performance.

(3) Termination does not affect any provision in the contract for the settlement of disputes or any other term of the contract which is to operate even after termination.

Article 7.3.6
Restitution

(1) On termination of the contract either party may claim restitution of whatever it has supplied, provided that such party concurrently makes restitution of whatever it has received. If restitution in kind is not possible or appropriate allowance should be made in money whenever reasonable.

(2) However, if performance of the contract has extended over a period of time and the contract is divisible, such restitution can only be claimed for the period after termination has taken effect.

SECTION 4
DAMAGES

Article 7.4.1
Right to damages

Any non-performance gives the aggrieved party a right to damages either exclusively or in conjunction with any other remedies except where the non-performance is excused under these Principles.

Article 7.4.2
Full compensation

(1) The aggrieved party is entitled to full compensation for harm sustained as a result of the non-performance. Such harm includes both any loss which it suffered and any gain of which it was deprived, taking into account any gain to the aggrieved party resulting from its avoidance of cost or harm.

(2) Such harm may be non-pecuniary and includes, for instance, physical suffering or emotional distress.

Article 7.4.3
Certainty of harm

(1) Compensation is due only for harm, including future harm, that is established with a reasonable degree of certainty.

(2) Compensation may be due for the loss of a chance in proportion to the probability of its occurrence.

(3) Where the amount of damages cannot be established with a sufficient degree of certainty, the assessment is at the discretion of the court.

Article 7.4.4
Foreseeability of harm

The non-performing party is liable only for harm which it foresaw or could reasonably have foreseen at the time of the conclusion of the contract as being likely to result from its non-performance.

Article 7.4.5
Proof of harm in case of replacement transaction

Where the aggrieved party has terminated the contract and has made a replacement transaction within a reasonable time and in a reasonable manner it may recover the difference between the contract price and the price of the replacement transaction as well as damages for any further harm.

Article 7.4.6
Proof of harm by current price

(1) Where the aggrieved party has terminated the contract and has not made a replacement transaction but there is a current price for the performance contracted for, it may recover the difference between the contract price and the price current at the time the contract is terminated as well as damages for any further harm.

(2) Current price is the price generally charged for goods delivered or services rendered in comparable circumstances at the place where the contract should have been performed or, if there is no current price at that place, the current price at such other place that appears reasonable to take as a reference.

Article 7.4.7
Harm due in part to aggrieved party

Where the harm is due in part to an act or omission of the aggrieved party or to another event as to which that party bears the risk, the amount of damages shall be reduced to the extent that these factors have contributed to the harm, having regard to the conduct of each of the parties.

Article 7.4.8
Mitigation of harm

(1) The non-performing party is not liable for harm suffered by the aggrieved party to the extent that the harm could have been reduced by the latter party's taking reasonable steps.
(2) The aggrieved party is entitled to recover any expenses reasonably incurred in attempting to reduce the harm.

Article 7.4.9
Interest for failure to pay money

(1) If a party does not pay a sum of money when it falls due the aggrieved party is entitled to interest upon that sum from the time when payment is due to the time of payment whether or not the non-payment is excused.
(2) The rate of interest shall be the average bank short-term lending rate to prime borrowers prevailing for the currency of payment at the place for payment, or where no such rate exists at that place, then the same rate in the State of the currency of payment. In the absence of such a rate at either place the rate of interest shall be the appropriate rate fixed by the law of the State of the currency of payment.
(3) The aggrieved party is entitled to additional damages if the non-payment caused it a greater harm.

Article 7.4.10
Interest on damages

Unless otherwise agreed, interest on damages for non-performance of non-monetary obligations accrues as from the time of non-performance.

Article 7.4.11
Manner of monetary redress

(1) Damages are to be paid in a lump sum. However, they may be payable in instalments where the nature of the harm makes this appropriate.
(2) Damages to be paid in instalments may be indexed.

Article 7.4.12
Currency in which to assess damages

Damages are to be assessed either in the currency in which the monetary obligation was expressed or in the currency in which the harm was suffered, whichever is more appropriate.

Article 7.4.13
Agreed payment for non-performance

(1) Where the contract provides that a party who does not perform is to pay a specified sum to the aggrieved party for such non-performance, the aggrieved party is entitled to that sum irrespective of its actual harm.

(2) However, notwithstanding any agreement to the contrary the specified sum may be reduced to a reasonable amount where it is grossly excessive in relation to the harm resulting from the non-performance and to the other circumstances.

CHAPTER 8
SET-OFF

Article 8.1
Conditions of set-off

(1) Where two parties owe each other money or other performances of the same kind, either of them ('the first party') may set off its obligation against that of its obligee ('the other party') if at the time of set-off
    (a) the first party is entitled to perform its obligation,
    (b) the other party's obligation is ascertained as to its existence and amount and performance is due.
(2) If the obligations of both parties arise from the same contract, the first party may also set off its obligation against an obligation of the other party which is not ascertained as to its existence or to its amount.

Article 8.2
Foreign currency set-off

Where the obligations are to pay money in different currencies, the right of set-off may be exercised, provided that both currencies are freely convertible and the parties have not agreed that the first party shall pay only in a specified currency.

Article 8.3
Set-off by notice

The right of set-off is exercised by notice to the other party.

Article 8.4
Content of notice

(1) The notice must specify the obligations to which it relates.
(2) If the notice does not specify the obligation against which set-off is exercised, then the other party may, within a reasonable time, declare to the first party the obligation to which the set-off relates, or, if no such declaration is made, the set-off will relate to all the obligations proportionally.

Article 8.5
Effect of set-off

(1) Set-off discharges the obligations.
(2) If obligations differ in amount, set-off discharges the obligations up to the amount of the lesser obligation.
(3) Set-off takes effect as from the time of notice.

CHAPTER 9
ASSIGNMENT OF RIGHTS, TRANSFER OF OBLIGATIONS, ASSIGNMENT OF CONTRACTS

SECTION 1
ASSIGNMENT OF RIGHTS

Article 9.1.1
Definitions

'Assignment of a right' means the transfer by agreement from one person ('the assignor') to another person ('the assignee'), including transfer by way of security, of the assignor's right to payment of a monetary sum or other performance from a third person ('the obligor').

Article 9.1.2
Exclusions

This Section does not apply to transfers made under the special rules governing the transfer:
(a) of instruments such as negotiable instruments, documents of title and financial instruments, or
(b) of rights in the course of transferring a business.

Article 9.1.3
Assignability of non-monetary rights

A right to non-monetary performance may be assigned only if the assignment does not render the obligation significantly more burdensome.

Article 9.1.4
Partial assignment

(1) A right to payment of a monetary sum may be assigned partially.
(2) A right to other performance may be assigned partially only if it is divisible, and the assignment does not render the obligation significantly more burdensome.

Article 9.1.5
Future rights

A future right is deemed to be transferred at the time of the agreement, provided the right, when it comes into existence, can be identified as the right to which the assignment relates.

Article 9.1.6
Rights assigned without individual specification

A number of rights may be assigned without individual specification provided such rights can be identified as rights to which the assignment relates at the time of the assignment or when they come into existence.

Article 9.1.7
Agreement between assignor and assignee sufficient

(1) A right is assigned by mere agreement between assignor and assignee, without notice to the obligor.
(2) The consent of the obligor is not required, unless the obligation, in the circumstances, is of an essentially personal character.

Article 9.1.8
Obligor's additional costs

The obligor has a right to be compensated by the assignor or the assignee for any additional costs caused by the assignment.

Article 9.1.9
Non-assignment clauses

(1) Assignment of a right to payment of a monetary sum is effective notwithstanding an agreement between the assignor and the obligor limiting or prohibiting such assignment. However, the assignor may be liable to the obligor for breach of contract.
(2) Assignment of a right to other performance is ineffective, if it is contrary to an agreement between the assignor and the obligor limiting or prohibiting the assignment. Nevertheless, the assignment is effective if the assignee, at the time of assignment, neither knew nor ought to have known of the agreement; the assignor may then be liable to the obligor for breach of contract.

Article 9.1.10
Notice to the obligor

(1) Until receiving a notice of the assignment, from either the assignor or the assignee, the obligor is discharged by paying the assignor.
(2) After receiving such a notice, the obligor is discharged only by paying the assignee.

Article 9.1.11
Successive assignments

If the same right has been assigned by the same assignor to two or more successive assignees, the obligor is discharged by paying according to the order in which the notices were received.

Article 9.1.12
Adequate proof of assignment

(1) If notice of the assignment is given by the assignee, the obligor may request the assignee to provide within a reasonable time adequate proof that the assignment has been made.
(2) Until adequate proof is provided, the obligor may withhold payment.
(3) Unless adequate proof is provided, notice is not effective.
(4) Adequate proof includes, but is not limited to, any writing emanating from the assignor and indicating that the assignment has taken place.

Article 9.1.13
Defences and rights of set-off

(1) The obligor may assert against the assignee all defences which the obligor could assert against the assignor.
(2) The obligor may exercise against the assignee any right of set-off available to the obligor against the assignor up to the time notice of assignment was received.

Article 9.1.14
Rights related to the claim assigned

Assignment of a right transfers to the assignee :
  (a) all the assignor's rights to payment or other performance under the contract in respect of the rights assigned, and
  (b) all rights securing performance of the rights assigned.

Article 9.1.15
Assignor's undertakings

The assignor undertakes towards the assignee, except as otherwise disclosed to the assignee, that :
  (a) the assigned right exists at the time of the assignment, unless the right is a future right;
  (b) the assignor is entitled to assign the right;
  (c) the right has not been previously assigned to another assignee, and it is free from any right or claim from a third party;
  (d) the obligor does not have any defences;
  (e) neither the obligor nor the assignor has given notice of set-off concerning the assigned right and will not give any such notice;
  (f) the assignor will reimburse the assignee for any payment received from the obligor before notice of the assignment was given.

SECTION 2

TRANSFER OF OBLIGATIONS

Article 9.2.1
Modes of transfer

An obligation to pay money or render other performance may be transferred from one person ('the original obligor') to another person ('the new obligor') either
  (a) by an agreement between the original obligor and the new obligor subject to Article 9.2.3, or
  (b) by an agreement between the obligee and the new obligor, by which the new obligor assumes the obligation.

Article 9.2.2
Exclusion

This Section does not apply to transfers of obligations made under the special rules governing transfers of obligations in the course of transferring a business.

Article 9.2.3
Requirement of obligee's consent to transfer

Transfer of an obligation by an agreement between the original and the new obligor requires the consent of the obligee.

Article 9.2.4
Advance consent of obligee

(1) The obligee may give its consent in advance.
(2) The transfer of the obligation becomes effective when notice of the transfer is given to the obligee or when the obligee acknowledges it.

Article 9.2.5
Discharge of old obligor

(1) The obligee may discharge the original obligor.
(2) The obligee may also retain the original obligor as an obligor in case the new obligor does not perform properly.
(3) Otherwise the original obligor remains as an obligor, jointly and severally with the new obligor.

Article 9.2.6
Third party performance

(1) Without the obligee's consent, the obligor may contract with another person that this person will perform the obligation in place of the obligor, unless the obligation, in the circumstances, has an essentially personal character.
(2) The obligee retains its claim against the obligor.

Article 9.2.7
Defences and rights of set-off

(1) The new obligor may assert against the obligee all defences which the original obligor could assert against the obligee.
(2) The new obligor may not exercise against the obligee any right of set-off available to the original obligor against the obligee

Article 9.2.8
Rights related to the obligation transferred

(1) The obligee may assert against the new obligor all its rights to payment or other performance under the contract in respect of the obligation transferred.
(2) If the original obligor is discharged under Article 9.2.5 (1), a security granted by any person other than the new obligor for the performance of the obligation is discharged, unless that other person agrees that it should continue to be available to the obligee.
(3) Discharge of the original obligor also extends to any security of the original obligor given to the obligee for the performance of the obligation, unless the security is over an asset which is transferred as part of a transaction between the original and the new obligor.

SECTION 3
ASSIGNMENT OF CONTRACTS

Article 9.3.1
Definitions

'Assignment of a contract' means the transfer by agreement from one person ('the assignor') to another person ('the assignee') of the assignor's rights and obligations arising out of a contract with another person ('the other party').

Article 9.3.2
Exclusion

This Section does not apply to assignment of contracts made under the special rules governing transfers of contracts in the course of transferring a business.

Article 9.3.3
Request of consent of the other party

Assignment of a contract requires the consent of the other party.

Article 9.3.4
Advance consent of the other party

(1) The other party may give its consent in advance.
(2) The assignment of the contract becomes effective when notice of the assignment is given to the other party or when the other party acknowledges it.

Article 9.3.5
Discharge of the assignor

(1) The other party may discharge the assignor.
(2) The other party may also retain the assignor as an obligor in case the assignee does not perform properly.
(3) Otherwise the assignor remains as the other party's obligor, jointly and severally with the assignee.

Article 9.3.6
Defences and rights of set-off

(1) To the extent that assignment of a contract involves an assignment of rights, Article 9.1.13 applies accordingly.
(2) To the extent that assignment of a contract involves a transfer of obligations, Article 9.2.7 applies accordingly.

Article 9.3.7
Rights transferred with the contract

(1) To the extent that assignment of a contract involves an assignment of rights, Article 9.1.14 applies accordingly.
(2) To the extent that assignment of a contract involves a transfer of obligations, Article 9.2.8 applies accordingly.

CHAPTER 10
LIMITATION PERIODS

Article 10.1
Scope of the chapter

(1) The exercise of rights governed by these Principles is barred by expiration of a period of time, referred to as 'limitation period', according to the rules of this chapter.

(2) This chapter does not govern the time within which one party is required under these Principles, as a condition for the acquisition or exercise of its right, to give notice to the other party or perform any act other than the institution of legal proceedings.

Article 10.2
Limitation periods

(1) The general limitation period is three years beginning on the day after the day the obligee knows or ought to know the facts as a result of which the obligee's right can be exercised.

(2) In any event, the maximum limitation period is ten years beginning on the day after the day the right can be exercised.

Article 10.3
Modification of limitation periods by the parties

(1) The parties may modify the limitation periods.

(2) However they may not
    (a) shorten the general limitation period to less than one year;
    (b) shorten the maximum limitation period to less than 4 years;
    (c) extend the maximum limitation period to more than 15 years.

Article 10.4
New limitation period by acknowledgement

(1) Where the obligor, before the expiration of the general limitation period, acknowledges the right of the obligee, a new general limitation period begins on the day after the day of the acknowledgement.

(2) The maximum limitation period does not begin to run again, but may be exceeded by the beginning of a new general limitation period under Art. 10.2 (1).

Article 10.5
Suspension by judicial proceedings

(1) The running of the limitation period is suspended
    (a) when the obligee performs any act, by commencing judicial proceedings or in judicial proceedings already instituted, that is recognised by the law of the court as asserting the obligee's right against the obligor;
    (b) in the case of the obligor's insolvency when the obligee has asserted its rights in the insolvency proceedings; or
    (c) in the case of proceedings for dissolution of the entity which is the obligor when the obligee has asserted its rights in the dissolution proceedings.

(2) Suspension lasts until the proceedings have been terminated by a final decision of the court or otherwise.

81

Article 10.6
Suspension by arbitral proceedings

(1) The running of the limitation period is suspended when the obligee performs any act, by commencing arbitral proceedings or in arbitral proceedings already instituted, that is recognised by the law of the arbitral tribunal as asserting the obligee's right against the obligor. In the absence of regulations for arbitral proceedings or provisions determining the exact date of the commencement of arbitral proceedings, the proceedings are deemed to commence on the date on which a request that the right in dispute should be adjudicated reaches the obligor.
(2) Suspension lasts until the proceedings have been terminated by a binding decision of the arbitral tribunal or otherwise.

Article 10.7
Alternative dispute resolution

The provisions of Arts. 10.5 and 10.6 apply with appropriate modifications to other proceedings whereby parties request a third person to assist them in their attempt to reach an amicable settlement of their dispute.

Article 10.8
Suspension in case of force majeure, death or incapacity

(1) Where the obligee has been prevented by an impediment that is beyond its control and that it could neither avoid nor overcome, from causing a limitation period to cease to run under the preceding articles, the general limitation period is suspended so as not to expire before one year after the relevant impediment has ceased to exist.
(2) Where the impediment consists of the incapacity or death of the obligee or obligor, suspension ceases when a representative for the incapacitated or deceased party or its estate has been appointed or a successor inherited the respective party's position; the additional one-year period under para. 1 applies respectively.

Article 10.9
The effects of expiration of limitation period

(1) The expiration of the limitation period does not extinguish the right.
(2) For the expiration of the limitation period to have effect, the obligor must assert it as a defence.
(3) A right may still be relied on as a defence even though the expiration of the limitation period for that right has been asserted.

Article 10.10
Exercise of set-off after expiration of the limitation period

The obligee may exercise the right of set-off until the obligor has asserted the expiration of the limitation period.

Article 10.11
Restitution

Where there has been performance in order to discharge an obligation, there is no right to restitution merely because the period of limitation had expired.

(ii) THE PRINCIPLES OF EUROPEAN CONTRACT LAW*
Prepared by the Commission on European Contract Law

---

* Reproduced with the kind permission of the Commission on European Contract Law.

CHAPTER 1
GENERAL PROVISIONS

SECTION I
SCOPE OF THE PRINCIPLES

Article 1:101
Application of the Principles

(1) These Principles are intended to be applied as general rules of contract law in the European Union.

(2) These Principles will apply when the parties have agreed to incorporate them into their contract or that their contract is to be governed by them.

(3) These Principles may be applied when the parties:
    (a) have agreed that their contract is to be governed by 'general principles of law', the 'lex mercatoria' or the like; or
    (b) have not chosen any system or rules of law to govern their contract.
(4) These Principles may provide a solution to the issue raised where the system or rules of law applicable do not do so.

Article 1:102
Freedom of contract

(1) Parties are free to enter into a contract and to determine its contents, subject to the requirements of good faith and fair dealing, and the mandatory rules established by these Principles.
(2) The parties may exclude the application of any of the Principles or derogate from or vary their effects, except as otherwise provided by these Principles.

Article 1:103
Mandatory law

(1) Where the law otherwise applicable so allows, the parties may choose to have their contract governed by the Principles, with the effect that national mandatory rules are not applicable.
(2) Effect should nevertheless be given to those mandatory rules of national, supranational and international law which, according to the relevant rules of private international law, are applicable irrespective of the law governing the contract.

Article 1:104
Application to questions of consent

(1) The existence and validity of the agreement of the parties to adopt or incorporate these Principles shall be determined by these Principles.
(2) Nevertheless, a party may rely upon the law of the country in which it has its habitual residence to establish that it did not consent if it appears from the circumstances that it would not be reasonable to determine the effect of the party's conduct in accordance with these Principles.

Article 1:105
Usages and practices

(1) The parties are bound by any usage to which they have agreed and by any practice they have established between themselves.
(2) The parties are bound by a usage which would be considered generally applicable by persons in the same situation as the parties, except where the application of such usage would be unreasonable.

Article 1:106
Interpretation and supplementation

(1) These Principles should be interpreted and developed in accordance with their purposes. In particular, regard should be had to the need to promote good faith and fair dealing, certainty in contractual relationships and uniformity of application.

87

(2) Issues within the scope of these Principles but not expressly settled by them are so far as possible to be settled in accordance with the ideas underlying the Principles. Failing this, the legal system applicable by virtue of the rules of private international law is to be applied.

Article 1:107
Application of the principles by way of analogy

These Principles apply with appropriate modifications to agreements to modify or end a contract, to unilateral promises and other statements and conduct indicating intention.

SECTION 2

GENERAL DUTIES

Article 1:201
Good faith and fair dealing

(1) Each party must act in accordance with good faith and fair dealing.
(2) The parties may not exclude or limit this duty.

Article 1:202
Duty to co-operate

Each party owes to the other a duty to co-operate in order to give full effect to the contract.

SECTION 3

TERMINOLOGY AND OTHER PROVISIONS

Article 1:301
Meaning of terms

In these Principles, except where the context otherwise requires:
(1) 'act' includes omission;
(2) 'court' includes arbitral tribunal;
(3) an 'intentional' act includes an act done recklessly;
(4) 'non-performance' denotes any failure to perform an obligation under the contract, whether or not excused, and includes delayed performance, defective performance and failure to co-operate in order to give full effect to the contract.
(5) a matter is 'material' if it is one which a reasonable person in the same situation as one party ought to have known would influence the other party in its decision whether to contract on the proposed terms or to contract at all;
(6) 'written' statements include communications made by telegram, telex, telefax and electronic mail and other means of communication capable of providing a readable record of the statement on both sides.

Article 1:302
Reasonableness

Under these Principles reasonableness is to be judged by what persons acting in good faith and in the same situation as the parties would consider to be reasonable. In particular, in assessing what is reasonable the nature and purpose of the contract, the circumstances of the case, and the usages and practices of the trades or professions involved should be taken into account.

Article 1:303
Notice

(1) Any notice may be given by any means, whether in writing or otherwise, appropriate to the circumstances.
(2) Subject to paragraphs (4) and (5), any notice becomes effective when it reaches the addressee.
(3) A notice reaches the addressee when it is delivered to it or to its place of business or mailing address, or, if it does not have a place of business or mailing address, to its habitual residence.
(4) If one party gives notice to the other because of the other's non-performance or because such non-performance is reasonably anticipated by the first party, and the notice is properly dispatched or given, a delay or inaccuracy in the transmission of the notice or its failure to arrive does not prevent it from having effect. The notice shall have effect from the time at which it would have arrived in normal circumstances.
(5) A notice has no effect if a withdrawal of it reaches the addressee before or at the same time as the notice.
(6) In this Article, 'notice' includes the communication of a promise, statement, offer, acceptance, demand, request or other declaration.

Article 1:304
Computation of time

(1) A period of time set by a party in a written document for the addressee to reply or take other action begins to run from the date stated as the date of the document. If no date is shown, the period begins to run from the moment the document reaches the addressee.
(2) Official holidays and official non-working days occurring during the period are included in calculating the period. However, if the last day of the period is an official holiday or official non-working day at the address of the addressee, or at the place where a prescribed act is to be performed, the period is extended until the first following working day in that place.
(3) Periods of time expressed in days, weeks, months or years shall begin at 00.00 on the next day and shall end at 24.00 on the last day of the period; but any reply that has to reach the party who set the period must arrive, or any other act which is to be done must be completed, by the normal close of business in the relevant place on the last day of the period.

Article 1:305
Imputed knowledge and intention

If any person who with a party's assent was involved in making a contract, or who was entrusted with performance by a party or performed with its assent:
    (a) knew or foresaw a fact, or ought to have known or foreseen it; or
    (b) acted intentionally or with gross negligence, or not in accordance with good faith and fair dealing,
this knowledge, foresight or behaviour is imputed to the party itself.

CHAPTER 2
FORMATION

Article 2:101
Conditions for the conclusion of a contract

(1) A contract is concluded if:
    (a) the parties intend to be legally bound, and
    (b) they reach a sufficient agreement
without any further requirement.
(2) A contract need not be concluded or evidenced in writing nor is it subject to any other requirement as to form. The contract may be proved by any means, including witnesses.

Article 2:102
Intention

The intention of a party to be legally bound by contract is to be determined from the party's statements or conduct as they were reasonably understood by the other party.

Article 2:103
Sufficient agreement

(1) There is sufficient agreement if the terms:
    (a) have been sufficiently defined by the parties so that the contract can be enforced, or
    (b) can be determined under these Principles.
(2) However, if one of the parties refuses to conclude a contract unless the parties have agreed on some specific matter, there is no contract unless agreement on that matter has been reached.

Article 2:104
Terms not individually negotiated

(1) Contract terms which have not been individually negotiated may be invoked against a party who did not know of them only if the party invoking them took reasonable steps to bring them to the other party's attention before or when the contract was concluded.
(2) Terms are not brought appropriately to a party's attention by a mere reference to them in a contract document, even if that party signs the document.

Article 2:105
Merger clause

(1) If a written contract contains an individually negotiated clause stating that the writing embodies all the terms of the contract (a merger clause), any prior statements, undertakings or agreements which are not embodied in the writing do not form part of the contract.

(2) If the merger clause is not individually negotiated it will only establish a presumption that the parties intended that their prior statements, undertakings or agreements were not to form part of the contract. This rule may not be excluded or restricted.

(3) The parties' prior statements may be used to interpret the contract. This rule may not be excluded or restricted except by an individually negotiated clause.

(4) A party may by its statements or conduct be precluded from asserting a merger clause to the extent that the other party has reasonably relied on them.

Article 2:106
Written modification only

(1) A clause in a written contract requiring any modification or ending by agreement to be made in writing establishes only a presumption that an agreement to modify or end the contract is not intended to be legally binding unless it is in writing.

(2) A party may by its statements or conduct be precluded from asserting such a clause to the extent that the other party has reasonably relied on them.

Article 2:107
Promises binding without acceptance

A promise which is intended to be legally binding without acceptance is binding.

SECTION 2
OFFER AND ACCEPTANCE

Article 2:201
Offer

(1) A proposal amounts to an offer if:
  (a) it is intended to result in a contract if the other party accepts it, and
  (b) it contains sufficiently definite terms to form a contract.

(2) An offer may be made to one or more specific persons or to the public.

(3) A proposal to supply goods or services at stated prices made by a professional supplier in a public advertisement or a catalogue, or by a display of goods, is presumed to be an offer to sell or supply at that price until the stock of goods, or the supplier's capacity to supply the service, is exhausted.

Article 2:202
Revocation of an offer

(1) An offer may be revoked if the revocation reaches the offeree before it has dispatched its acceptance or, in cases of acceptance by conduct, before the contract has been concluded under Article 2:205(2) or (3).

(2) An offer made to the public can be revoked by the same means as were used to make the offer.

(3) However, a revocation of an offer is ineffective if:
  (a) the offer indicates that it is irrevocable; or
  (b) it states a fixed time for its acceptance; or
  (c) it was reasonable for the offeree to rely on the offer as being irrevocable and the offeree has acted in reliance on the offer.

Article 2:203
Rejection

When a rejection of an offer reaches the offeror, the offer lapses.

Article 2:204
Acceptance

(1) Any form of statement or conduct by the offeree is an acceptance if it indicates assent to the offer.
(2) Silence or inactivity does not in itself amount to acceptance.

Article 2:205
Time of conclusion of the contract

(1) If an acceptance has been dispatched by the offeree the contract is concluded when the acceptance reaches the offeror.
(2) In case of acceptance by conduct, the contract is concluded when notice of the conduct reaches the offeror.
(3) If by virtue of the offer, of practices which the parties have established between them selves, or of a usage, the offeree may accept the offer by performing an act without notice to the offeror, the contract is concluded when the performance of the act begins.

Article 2:206
Time limit for acceptance

(1) In order to be effective, acceptance of an offer must reach the offeror within the time fixed by it.
(2) If no time has been fixed by the offeror acceptance must reach it within a reasonable time.
(3) In the case of an acceptance by an act of performance under art. 2:205 (3), that act must be performed within the time for acceptance fixed by the offeror or, if no such time is fixed, within a reasonable time.

Article 2:207
Late acceptance

(1) A late acceptance is nonetheless effective as an acceptance if without delay the offeror informs the offeree that he treats it as such.
(2) If a letter or other writing containing a late acceptance shows that it has been sent in such circumstances that if its transmission had been normal it would have reached the offeror in due time, the late acceptance is effective as an acceptance unless, without delay, the offeror informs the offeree that it considers its offer as having lapsed.

Article 2:208
Modified acceptance

(1) A reply by the offeree which states or implies additional or different terms which would materially alter the terms of the offer is a rejection and a new offer.
(2) A reply which gives a definite assent to an offer operates as an acceptance even if it states or implies additional or different terms, provided these do not materially alter

the terms of the offer. The additional or different terms then become part of the contract.

(3) However, such a reply will be treated as a rejection of the offer if:

    (a) the offer expressly limits acceptance to the terms of the offer; or

    (b) the offeror objects to the additional or different terms without delay; or

    (c) the offeree makes its acceptance conditional upon the offeror's assent to the additional or different terms, and the assent does not reach the offeree within a reasonable time.

Article 2:209
Conflicting general conditions

(1) If the parties have reached agreement except that the offer and acceptance refer to conflicting general conditions of contract, a contract is nonetheless formed. The general conditions form part of the contract to the extent that they are common in substance.

(2) However, no contract is formed if one party:

    (a) has indicated in advance, explicitly, and not by way of general conditions, that it does not intend to be bound by a contract on the basis of paragraph (1); or

    (b) without delay, informs the other party that it does not intend to be bound by such contract.

(3) General conditions of contract are terms which have been formulated in advance for an indefinite number of contracts of a certain nature, and which have not been individually negotiated between the parties.

Article 2:210
Professional's written confirmation

If professionals have concluded a contract but have not embodied it in a final document, and one without delay sends the other a writing which purports to be a confirmation of the contract but which contains additional or different terms, such terms will become part of the contract unless:

    (a) the terms materially alter the terms of the contract, or

    (b) the addressee objects to them without delay.

Article 2:211
Contracts not concluded through offer and acceptance

The rules in this section apply with appropriate adaptations even though the process of conclusion of a contract cannot be analysed into offer and acceptance.

SECTION 3
LIABILITY FOR NEGOTIATIONS

Article 2:301
Negotiations contrary to good faith

(1) A party is free to negotiate and is not liable for failure to reach an agreement.

(2) However, a party who has negotiated or broken off negotiations contrary to good faith and fair dealing is liable for the losses caused to the other party.

(3) It is contrary to good faith and fair dealing, in particular, for a party to enter into or continue negotiations with no real intention of reaching an agreement with the other party.

Article 2:302
Breach of confidentiality

If confidential information is given by one party in the course of negotiations, the other party is under a duty not to disclose that information or use it for its own purposes whether or not a contract is subsequently concluded. The remedy for breach of this duty may include compensation for loss suffered and restitution of the benefit received by the other party.

CHAPTER 3
AUTHORITY OF AGENTS

SECTION I
GENERAL PROVISIONS

Article 3:101
Scope of the Chapter

(1) This Chapter governs the authority of an agent or other intermediary to bind its principal in relation to a contract with a third party.
(2) This Chapter does not govern an agent's authority bestowed by law or the authority of an agent appointed by a public or judicial authority.
(3) This Chapter does not govern the internal relationship between the agent or intermediary and its principal.

Article 3:102
Categories of representation

(1) Where an agent acts in the name of a principal, the rules on direct representation apply (Section 2). It is irrelevant whether the principal's identity is revealed at the time the agent acts or is to be revealed later.
(2) Where an intermediary acts on instructions and on behalf of, but not in the name of, a principal, or where the third party neither knows nor has reason to know that the intermediary acts as an agent, the rules on indirect representation apply (Section 3).

SECTION 2
DIRECT REPRESENTATION

Article 3:201
Express, implied and apparent authority

(1) The principal's grant of authority to an agent to act in its name may be express or may be implied from the circumstances.
(2) The agent has authority to perform all acts necessary in the circumstances to achieve the purposes for which the authority was granted.

(3) A person is to be treated as having granted authority to an apparent agent if the person's statements or conduct induce the third party reasonably and in good faith to believe that the apparent agent has been granted authority for the act performed by it.

Article 3:202
Agent acting in exercise of its authority

Where an agent is acting within its authority as defined by article 3: 201, its acts bind the principal and the third party directly to each other. The agent itself is not bound to the third party.

Article 3:203
Unidentified principal

If an agent enters into a contract in the name of a principal whose identity is to be revealed later, but fails to reveal that identity within a reasonable time after a request by the third party, the agent itself is bound by the contract.

Article 3:204
Agent acting without or outside its authority

(1) Where a person acting as an agent acts without authority or outside the scope of its authority, its acts are not binding upon the principal and the third party.
(2) Failing ratification by the principal according to article 3:207, the agent is liable to pay the third party such damages as will place the third party in the same position as if the agent had acted with authority. This does not apply if the third party knew or could not have been unaware of the agent's lack of authority.

Article 3:205
Conflict of interest

(1) If a contract concluded by an agent involves the agent in a conflict of interest of which the third party knew or could not have been unaware, the principal may avoid the contract according to the provisions of articles 4:112 to 4:116.
(2) There is presumed to be a conflict of interest where:
    (a) the agent also acted as agent for the third party; or
    (b) the contract was with itself in its personal capacity.
(3) However, the principal may not avoid the contract:
    (a) if it had consented to, or could not have been unaware of, the agent's so acting; or
    (b) if the agent had disclosed the conflict of interest to it and it had not objected within a reasonable time.

Article 3:206
Subagency

An agent has implied authority to appoint a subagent to carry out tasks which are not of a personal character and which it is not reasonable to expect the agent to carry out itself. The rules of this Section apply to the subagency; acts of the subagent which are within its and the agent's authority bind the principal and the third party directly to each other.

Article 3:207
Ratification by principal

(1) Where a person acting as an agent acts without authority or outside its authority, the principal may ratify the agent's acts.
(2) Upon ratification, the agent's acts are considered as having been authorised, without prejudice to the rights of other persons.

Article 3:208
Third party's right with respect to confirmation of authority

Where the statements or conduct of the principal gave the third party reason to believe that an act performed by the agent was authorised, but the third party is in doubt about the authorisation, it may send a written confirmation to the principal or request ratification from it. If the principal does not object or answer the request without delay, the agent's act is treated as having been authorised.

Article 3:209
Duration of authority

(1) An agent's authority continues until the third party knows or ought to know that:
    (a) the agent's authority has been brought to an end by the principal, the agent, or both; or
    (b) the acts for which the authority had been granted have been completed, or the time for which it had been granted has expired; or
    (c) the agent has become insolvent or, where a natural person, has died or become incapacitated; or
    (d) the principal has become insolvent.
(2) The third party is considered to know that the agent's authority has been brought to an end under paragraph (1)(a) above if this has been communicated or publicised in the same manner in which the authority was originally communicated or publicised.
(3) However, the agent remains authorised for a reasonable time to perform those acts which are necessary to protect the interests of the principal or its successors.

SECTION 3
INDIRECT REPRESENTATION

Article 3:301
Intermediaries not acting in the name of a principal

(1) Where an intermediary acts:
    (a) on instructions and on behalf, but not in the name, of a principal, or
    (b) on instructions from a principal but the third party does not know and has no reason to know this,
the intermediary and the third party are bound to each other.
(2) The principal and the third party are bound to each other only under the conditions set out in Articles 3:302 to 3:304.

96

Article 3:302
Intermediary's insolvency or fundamental non-performance to principal

If the intermediary becomes insolvent, or if it commits a fundamental non-performance towards the principal, or if prior to the time for performance it is clear that there will be a fundamental non-performance:

(a) on the principal's demand, the intermediary shall communicate the name and address of the third party to the principal; and

(b) the principal may exercise against the third party the rights acquired on the principal's behalf by the intermediary, subject to any defences which the third party may set up against the intermediary.

Article 3:303
Intermediary's insolvency or fundamental non-performance to third party

If the intermediary becomes insolvent, or if it commits a fundamental non-performance towards the third party, or if prior to the time for performance it is clear that there will be a fundamental non-performance:

(a) on the third party's demand, the intermediary shall communicate the name and address of the principal to the third party; and

(b) the third party may exercise against the principal the rights which the third party has against the intermediary, subject to any defences which the intermediary may set up against the third party and those which the principal may set up against the intermediary.

Article 3:304
Requirement of notice

The rights under Articles 3:302 and 3:303 may be exercised only if notice of intention to exercise them is given to the intermediary and to the third party or principal, respectively. Upon receipt of the notice, the third party or the principal is no longer entitled to render performance to the intermediary.

CHAPTER 4
VALIDITY

Article 4:101
Matters not covered

This chapter does not deal with invalidity arising from illegality, immorality or lack of capacity.

Article 4:102
Initial impossibility

A contract is not invalid merely because at the time it was concluded performance of the obligation assumed was impossible, or because a party was not entitled to dispose of the assets to which the contract relates.

Article 4:103
Fundamental mistake as to facts or law

(1) A party may avoid a contract for mistake of fact or law existing when the contract was concluded if:
    (a) (i)   the mistake was caused by information given by the other party; or
        (ii) the other party knew or ought to have known of the mistake and it was contrary to good faith and fair dealing to leave the mistaken party in error; or
        (iii) the other party made the same mistake,
    and
    (b) the other party knew or ought to have known that the mistaken party, had it known the truth, would not have entered the contract or would have done so only on fundamentally different terms.
(2) However a party may not avoid the contract if:
    (a) in the circumstances its mistake was inexcusable, or
    (b) the risk of the mistake was assumed, or in the circumstances should be borne, by it.

Article 4:104
Inaccuracy in communication

An inaccuracy in the expression or transmission of a statement is to be treated as a mistake of the person who made or sent the statement and Article 4:103 applies.

Article 4:105
Adaptation of contract

(1) If a party is entitled to avoid the contract for mistake but the other party indicates that it is willing to perform, or actually does perform, the contract as it was understood by the party entitled to avoid it, the contract is to be treated as if it had been concluded as the that party understood it. The other party must indicate its willingness to perform, or render such performance, promptly after being informed of the manner in which the party entitled to avoid it understood the contract and before that party acts in reliance on any notice of avoidance.
(2) After such indication or performance the right to avoid is lost and any earlier notice of avoidance is ineffective.
(3) Where both parties have made the same mistake, the court may at the request of either party bring the contract into accordance with what might reasonably have been agreed had the mistake not occurred.

Article 4:106
Incorrect information

A party which has concluded a contract relying on incorrect information given it by the other party may recover damages in accordance with Article 4:117(2) and (3) even if the information does not give rise to a fundamental mistake under Article 4:103, unless the party who gave the information had reason to believe that the information was correct.

Article 4:107
Fraud

(1) A party may avoid a contract when it has been led to conclude it by the other party's fraudulent representation, whether by words or conduct, or fraudulent non-disclosure of any information which in accordance with good faith and fair dealing it should have disclosed.

(2) A party's representation or non-disclosure is fraudulent if it was intended to deceive.

(3) In determining whether good faith and fair dealing required that a party disclose particular information, regard should be had to all the circumstances, including:

(a) whether the party had special expertise;

(b) the cost to it of acquiring the relevant information;

(c) whether the other party could reasonably acquire the information for itself; and

(d) the apparent importance of the information to the other party.

Article 4:108
Threats

A party may avoid a contract when it has been led to conclude it by the other party's imminent and serious threat of an act:

(a) which is wrongful in itself, or

(b) which it is wrongful to use as a means to obtain the conclusion of the contract,

unless in the circumstances the first party had a reasonable alternative.

Article 4:109
Excessive benefit or unfair advantage

(1) A party may avoid a contract if, at the time of the conclusion of the contract:

(a) it was dependent on or had a relationship of trust with the other party, was in economic distress or had urgent needs, was improvident, ignorant, inexperienced or lacking in bargaining skill, and

(b) the other party knew or ought to have known of this and, given the circumstances and purpose of the contract, took advantage of the first party's situation in a way which was grossly unfair or took an excessive benefit.

(2) Upon the request of the party entitled to avoidance, a court may if it is appropriate adapt the contract in order to bring it into accordance with what might have been agreed had the requirements of good faith and fair dealing been followed.

(3) A court may similarly adapt the contract upon the request of a party receiving notice of avoidance for excessive benefit or unfair advantage, provided that this party informs the party who gave the notice promptly after receiving it and before that party has acted in reliance on it.

Article 4:110
Unfair terms not individually negotiated

(1) A party may avoid a term which has not been individually negotiated if, contrary to the requirements of good faith and fair dealing, it causes a significant imbalance in the parties' rights and obligations arising under the contract to the detriment of that party, taking into account the nature of the performance to be rendered under

the contract, all the other terms of the contract and the circumstances at the time the contract was concluded.

(2) This Article does not apply to:
  (a) a term which defines the main subject matter of the contract, provided the term is in plain and intelligible language; or to
  (b) the adequacy in value of one party's obligations compared to the value of the obligations of the other party.

Article 4:111
Third persons

(1) Where a third person for whose acts a party is responsible, or who with a party's assent is involved in the making of a contract:
  (a) causes a mistake by giving information, or knows of or ought to have known of a mistake,
  (b) gives incorrect information,
  (c) commits fraud,
  (d) makes a threat, or
  (e) takes excessive benefit or unfair advantage,

remedies under this Chapter will be available under the same conditions as if the behaviour or knowledge had been that of the party itself.

(2) Where any other third person:
  (a) gives incorrect information,
  (b) commits fraud,
  (c) makes a threat, or
  (d) takes excessive benefit or unfair advantage,

remedies under this Chapter will be available if the party knew or ought to have known of the relevant facts, or at the time of avoidance it has not acted in reliance on the contract.

Article 4:112
Notice of avoidance

Avoidance must be by notice to the other party.

Article 4:113
Time limits

(1) Notice of avoidance must be given within a reasonable time, with due regard to the circumstances, after the avoiding party knew or ought to have known of the relevant facts or became capable of acting freely.

(2) However, a party may avoid an individual term under Article 4:110 if it gives notice of avoidance within a reasonable time after the other party has invoked the term.

Article 4:114
Confirmation

If the party who is entitled to avoid a contract confirms it, expressly or impliedly, after it knows of the ground for avoidance, or becomes capable of acting freely, avoidance of the contract is excluded.

Article 4:115
Effect of avoidance

On avoidance either party may claim restitution of whatever it has supplied under the contract, provided it makes concurrent restitution of whatever it has received. If restitution cannot be made in kind for any reason, a reasonable sum must be paid for what has been received.

Article 4:116
Partial avoidance

If a ground of avoidance affects only particular terms of a contract, the effect of an avoidance is limited to those terms unless, giving due consideration to all the circumstances of the case, it is unreasonable to uphold the remaining contract.

Article 4:117
Damages

(1) A party who avoids a contract under this Chapter may recover from the other party damages so as to put the avoiding party as nearly as possible into the same position as if it had not concluded the contract, provided that the other party knew or ought to have known of the mistake, fraud, threat or taking of excessive benefit or unfair advantage.

(2) If a party has the right to avoid a contract under this Chapter, but does not exercise its right or has lost its right under the provisions of Articles 4:113 or 4:114, it may recover, subject to paragraph (1), damages limited to the loss caused to it by the mistake, fraud, threat or taking of excessive benefit or unfair advantage. The same measure of damages shall apply when the party was misled by incorrect information in the sense of Article 4:106.

(3) In other respects, the damages shall be in accordance with the relevant provisions of Chapter 9, Section 5, with appropriate adaptations.

Article 4:118
Exclusion or restriction of remedies

(1) Remedies for fraud, threats and excessive benefit or unfair advantage-taking, and the right to avoid an unfair term which has not been individually negotiated, cannot be excluded or restricted.

(2) Remedies for mistake and incorrect information may be excluded or restricted unless the exclusion or restriction is contrary to good faith and fair dealing.

Article 4:119
Remedies for non-performance

A party who is entitled to a remedy under this Chapter in circumstances which afford that party a remedy for non-performance may pursue either remedy.

CHAPTER 5
INTERPRETATION

Article 5:101
General rules of interpretation

(1) A contract is to be interpreted according to the common intention of the parties even if this differs from the literal meaning of the words.
(2) If it is established that one party intended the contract to have a particular meaning, and at the time of the conclusion of the contract the other party could not have been unaware of the first party's intention, the contract is to be interpreted in the way intended by the first party.
(3) If an intention cannot be established according to (1) or (2), the contract is to be interpreted according to the meaning that reasonable persons of the same kind as the parties would give to it in the same circumstances.

Article 5:102
Relevant circumstances

In interpreting the contract, regard shall be had, in particular, to:
  (a) the circumstances in which it was concluded, including the preliminary negotiations;
  (b) the conduct of the parties, even subsequent to the conclusion of the contract;
  (c) the nature and purpose of the contract;
  (d) the interpretation which has already been given to similar clauses by the parties and the practices they have established between themselves;
  (e) the meaning commonly given to terms and expressions in the branch of activity concerned and the interpretation similar clauses may already have received;
  (f) usages; and
  (g) good faith and fair dealing.

Article 5:103
Contra proferentem rule

Where there is doubt about the meaning of a contract term not individually negotiated, an interpretation of the term against the party who supplied it is to be preferred.

Article 5:104
Preference to negotiated terms

Terms which have been individually negotiated take preference over those which are not.

Article 5:105
Reference to contract as a whole

Terms are to be interpreted in the light of the whole contract in which they appear.

Article 5:106
Terms to be given effect

An interpretation which renders the terms of the contract lawful, or effective, is to be preferred to one which would not.

Article 5:107
Linguistic discrepancies

Where a contract is drawn up in two or more language versions none of which is stated to be authoritative, there is, in case of discrepancy between the versions, a preference for the interpretation according to the version in which the contract was originally drawn up.

CHAPTER 6
CONTENTS AND EFFECTS

Article 6:101
Statements giving rise to contractual obligations

(1) A statement made by one party before or when the contract is concluded is to be treated as giving rise to a contractual obligation if that is how the other party reasonably understood it in the circumstances, taking into account:
   (a) the apparent importance of the statement to the other party;
   (b) whether the party was making the statement in the course of business; and
   (c) the relative expertise of the parties.
(2) If one of the parties is a professional supplier which gives information about the quality or use of services or goods or other property when marketing or advertising them or otherwise before the contract for them is concluded, the statement is to be treated as giving rise to a contractual obligation unless it is shown that the other party knew or could not have been unaware that the statement was incorrect.
(3) Such information and other undertakings given by a person advertising or marketing services, goods or other property for the professional supplier, or by a person in earlier links of the business chain, are to be treated as giving rise to a contractual obligation on the part of the professional supplier unless it did not know and had no reason to know of the information or undertaking.

Article 6:102
Implied terms

In addition to the express terms, a contract may contain implied terms which stem from:
   (a) the intention of the parties,
   (b) the nature and purpose of the contract, and
   (c) good faith and fair dealing.

Article 6:103
Simulation

When the parties have concluded an apparent contract which was not intended to reflect their true agreement, as between the parties the true agreement prevails.

Article 6:104
Determination of price

Where the contract does not fix the price or the method of determining it, the parties are to be treated as having agreed on a reasonable price.

Article 6:105
Unilateral determination by a party

Where the price or any other contractual term is to be determined by one party and that party's determination is grossly unreasonable, then notwithstanding any provision to the contrary, a reasonable price or other term shall be substituted.

Article 6:106
Determination by a third person

(1) Where the price or any other contractual term is to be determined by a third person, and it cannot or will not do so, the parties are presumed to have empowered the court to appoint another person to determine it.
(2) If a price or other term fixed by a third person is grossly unreasonable, a reasonable price or term shall be substituted.

Article 6:107
Reference to a non existent factor

Where the price or any other contractual term is to be determined by reference to a factor which does not exist or has ceased to exist or to be accessible, the nearest equivalent factor shall be substituted.

Article 6:108
Quality of performance

If the contract does not specify the quality, a party must tender performance of at least average quality.

Article 6:109
Contract for an indefinite period

A contract for an indefinite period may be ended by either party by giving notice of reasonable length.

Article 6:110
Stipulation in favour of a third party

(1) A third party may require performance of a contractual obligation when its right to do so has been expressly agreed upon between the promisor and the promisee, or when such agreement is to be inferred from the purpose of the contract or the circumstances of the case. The third party need not be identified at the time the agreement is concluded.
(2) If the third party renounces the right to performance the right is treated as never having accrued to it.

(3) The promisee may by notice to the promisor deprive the third party of the right to performance unless:

    (a) the third party has received notice from the promisee that the right has been made irrevocable, or

    (b) the promisor or the promisee has received notice from the third party that the latter accepts the right.

Article 6:111
Change of circumstances

(1) A party is bound to fulfil its obligations even if performance has become more onerous, whether because the cost of performance has increased or because the value of the performance it receives has diminished.

(2) If, however, performance of the contract becomes excessively onerous because of a change of circumstances, the parties are bound to enter into negotiations with a view to adapting the contract or terminating it, provided that:

    (a) the change of circumstances occurred after the time of conclusion of the contract,

    (b) the possibility of a change of circumstances was not one which could reasonably have been taken into account at the time of conclusion of the contract, and

    (c) the risk of the change of circumstances is not one which, according to the contract, the party affected should be required to bear.

(3) If the parties fail to reach agreement within a reasonable period, the court may:

    (a) end the contract at a date and on terms to be determined by the court ; or

    (b) adapt the contract in order to distribute between the parties in a just and equitable manner the losses and gains resulting from the change of circumstances.

In either case, the court may award damages for the loss suffered through a party refusing to negotiate or breaking off negotiations contrary to good faith and fair dealing.

CHAPTER 7
PERFORMANCE

Article 7:101
Place of performance

(1) If the place of performance of a contractual obligation is not fixed by or determinable from the contract it shall be:

    (a) in the case of an obligation to pay money, the creditor's place of business at the time of the conclusion of the contract;

    (b) in the case of an obligation other than to pay money, the debtor's place of business at the time of conclusion of the contract.

(2) If a party has more than one place of business, the place of business for the purpose of the preceding paragraph is that which has the closest relationship to the contract, having regard to the circumstances known to or contemplated by the parties at the time of conclusion of the contract.

(3) If a party does not have a place of business its habitual residence is to be treated as its place of business.

Article 7:102
Time of performance

A party has to effect its performance:
(1) if a time is fixed by or determinable from the contract, at that time;
(2) if a period of time is fixed by or determinable from the contract, at any time within that period unless the circumstances of the case indicate that the other party is to choose the time;
(3) in any other case, within a reasonable time after the conclusion of the contract.

Article 7:103
Early performance

(1) A party may decline a tender of performance made before it is due except where acceptance of the tender would not unreasonably prejudice its interests.
(2) A party's acceptance of early performance does not affect the time fixed for the performance of its own obligation.

Article 7:104
Order of performance

To the extent that the performances of the parties can be rendered simultaneously, the parties are bound to render them simultaneously unless the circumstances indicate otherwise.

Article 7:105
Alternative performance

(1) Where an obligation may be discharged by one of alternative performances, the choice belongs to the party who is to perform, unless the circumstances indicate otherwise.
(2) If the party who is to make the choice fails to do so by the time required by the contract, then:
    (a) if the delay in choosing is fundamental, the right to choose passes to the other party;
    (b) if the delay is not fundamental, the other party may give a notice fixing an additional period of reasonable length in which the party to choose must do so. If the latter fails to do so, the right to choose passes to the other party.

Article 7:106
Performance by a third person

(1) Except where the contract requires personal performance the creditor cannot refuse performance by a third person if:
    (a) the third person acts with the assent of the debtor; or
    (b) the third person has a legitimate interest in performance and the debtor has failed to perform or it is clear that it will not perform at the time performance is due.
(2) Performance by the third person in accordance with paragraph (1) discharges the debtor.

106

Article 7:107
Form of payment

(1) Payment of money due may be made in any form used in the ordinary course of business.

(2) A creditor which, pursuant to the contract or voluntarily, accepts a cheque or other order to pay or a promise to pay is presumed to do so only on condition that it will be honoured. The creditor may not enforce the original obligation to pay unless the order or promise is not honoured.

Article 7:108
Currency of payment

(1) The parties may agree that payment shall be made only in a specified currency.

(2) In the absence of such agreement, a sum of money expressed in a currency other than that of the place where payment is due may be paid in the currency of that place according to the rate of exchange prevailing there at the time when payment is due.

(3) If, in a case falling within the preceding paragraph, the debtor has not paid at the time when payment is due, the creditor may require payment in the currency of the place where payment is due according to the rate of exchange prevailing there either at the time when payment is due or at the time of actual payment.

Article 7:109
Appropriation of performance

(1) Where a party has to perform several obligations of the same nature and the performance tendered does not suffice to discharge all of the obligations, then subject to paragraph (4) the party may at the time of its performance declare to which obligation the performance is to be appropriated.

(2) If the performing party does not make such a declaration, the other party may within a reasonable time appropriate the performance to such obligation as it chooses. It shall inform the performing party of the choice. However, any such appropriation to an obligation which:
(a) is not yet due, or
(b) is illegal, or
(c) is disputed,
is invalid.

(3) In the absence of an appropriation by either party, and subject to paragraph (4), the performance is appropriated to that obligation which satisfies one of the following criteria in the sequence indicated:
(a) the obligation which is due or is the first to fall due;
(b) the obligation for which the creditor has the least security;
(c) the obligation which is the most burdensome for the debtor
(d) the obligation which has arisen first.
If none of the preceding criteria applies, the performance is appropriated proportionately to all obligations.

(4) In the case of a monetary obligation, a payment by the debtor is to be appropriated, first, to expenses, secondly, to interest, and thirdly, to principal, unless the creditor makes a different appropriation.

Article 7:110
Property not accepted

(1) A party which is left in possession of tangible property other than money because of the other party's failure to accept or retake the property must take reasonable steps to protect and preserve the property.
(2) The party left in possession may discharge its duty to deliver or return:
  (a) by depositing the property on reasonable terms with a third person to be held to the order of the other party, and notifying the other party of this; or
  (b) by selling the property on reasonable terms after notice to the other party, and paying the net proceeds to that party.
(3) Where, however, the property is liable to rapid deterioration or its preservation is unreasonably expensive, the party must take reasonable steps to dispose of it. It may discharge its duty to deliver or return by paying the net proceeds to the other party.
(4) The party left in possession is entitled to be reimbursed or to retain out of the proceeds of sale any expenses reasonably incurred.

Article 7:111
Money not accepted

Where a party fails to accept money properly tendered by the other party, that party may after notice to the first party discharge its obligation to pay by depositing the money to the order of the first party in accordance with the law of the place where payment is due.

Article 7:112
Costs of performance

Each party shall bear the costs of performance of its obligations.

CHAPTER 8
NON-PERFORMANCE AND REMEDIES IN GENERAL

Article 8:101
Remedies available

(1) Whenever a party does not perform an obligation under the contract and the non-performance is not excused under Article 8:108, the aggrieved party may resort to any of the remedies set out in Chapter 9.
(2) Where a party's non-performance is excused under Article 8:108, the aggrieved party may resort to any of the remedies set out in Chapter 9 except claiming performance and damages.
(3) A party may not resort to any of the remedies set out in Chapter 9 to the extent that its own act caused the other party's non-performance.

Article 8:102
Cumulation of remedies

Remedies which are not incompatible may be cumulated. In particular, a party is not deprived of its right to damages by exercising its right to any other remedy.

Article 8:103
Fundamental non-performance

A non-performance of an obligation is fundamental to the contract if:
   (a) strict compliance with the obligation is of the essence of the contract; or
   (b) the non-performance substantially deprives the aggrieved party of what it was entitled to expect under the contract, unless the other party did not foresee and could not reasonably have foreseen that result; or
   (c) the non-performance is intentional and gives the aggrieved party reason to believe that it cannot rely on the other party's future performance.

Article 8:104
Cure by non-performing rarty

A party whose tender of performance is not accepted by the other party because it does not conform to the contract may make a new and conforming tender where the time for performance has not yet arrived or the delay would not be such as to constitute a fundamental non-performance.

Article 8:105
Assurance of performance

(1) A party who reasonably believes that there will be a fundamental non-performance by the other party may demand adequate assurance of due performance and meanwhile may withhold performance of its own obligations so long as such reasonable belief continues.
(2) Where this assurance is not provided within a reasonable time, the party demanding it may terminate the contract if it still reasonably believes that there will be a fundamental non-performance by the other party and gives notice of termination without delay.

Article 8:106
Notice fixing additional period for performance

(1) In any case of non-performance the aggrieved party may by notice to the other party allow an additional period of time for performance.
(2) During the additional period the aggrieved party may withhold performance of its own reciprocal obligations and may claim damages, but it may not resort to any other remedy. If it receives notice from the other party that the latter will not perform within that period, or if upon expiry of that period due performance has not been made, the aggrieved party may resort to any of the remedies that may be available under Chapter 9.
(3) If in a case of delay in performance which is not fundamental the aggrieved party has given a notice fixing an additional period of time of reasonable length, it may terminate the contract at the end of the period of notice. The aggrieved party may in its notice provide that if the other party does not perform within the period fixed by the notice the contract shall terminate automatically. If the period stated is too short, the aggrieved party may terminate, or, as the case may be, the contract shall terminate automatically, only after a reasonable period from the time of the notice.

Article 8:107
Performance entrusted to another

A party who entrusts performance of the contract to another person remains responsible for performance.

Article 8:108
Excuse due to an impediment

(1) A party's non-performance is excused if it proves that it is due to an impediment beyond its control and that it could not reasonably have been expected to take the impediment into account at the time of the conclusion of the contract, or to have avoided or overcome the impediment or its consequences.
(2) Where the impediment is only temporary the excuse provided by this Article has effect for the period during which the impediment exists. However, if the delay amounts to a fundamental non-performance, the creditor may treat it as such.
(3) The non-performing party must ensure that notice of the impediment and of its effect on its ability to perform is received by the other party within a reasonable time after the non-performing party knew or ought to have known of these circumstances. The other party is entitled to damages for any loss resulting from the non-receipt of such notice.

Article 8:109
Clause excluding or restricting remedies

Remedies for non-performance may be excluded or restricted unless it would be contrary to good faith and fair dealing to invoke the exclusion or restriction.

CHAPTER 9
PARTICULAR REMEDIES FOR NON-PERFORMANCE

SECTION I
RIGHT TO PERFORMANCE

Article 9:101
Monetary obligations

(1) The creditor is entitled to recover money which is due.
(2) Where the creditor has not yet performed its obligation and it is clear that the debtor will be unwilling to receive performance, the creditor may nonetheless proceed with its performance and may recover any sum due under the contract unless:
  (a) it could have made a reasonable substitute transaction without significant effort or expense; or
  (b) performance would be unreasonable in the circumstances.

Article 9:102
Non-monetary obligations

(1) The aggrieved party is entitled to specific performance of an obligation other than one to pay money, including the remedying of a defective performance.

(2) Specific performance cannot, however, be obtained where:
  (a) performance would be unlawful or impossible; or
  (b) performance would cause the debtor unreasonable effort or expense; or
  (c) the performance consists in the provision of services or work of a personal character or depends upon a personal relationship, or
  (d) the aggrieved party may reasonably obtain performance from another source.
(3) The aggrieved party will lose the right to specific performance if it fails to seek it within a reasonable time after it has or ought to have become aware of the non-performance.

Article 9:103
Damages not precluded

The fact that a right to performance is excluded under this Section does not preclude a claim for damages.

SECTION 2

WITHHOLDING PERFORMANCE

Article 9:201
Right to withhold performance

(1) A party which is to perform simultaneously with or after the other party may withhold performance until the other has tendered performance or has performed. The first party may withhold the whole of its performance or a part of it as may be reasonable in the circumstances.
(2) A party may similarly withhold performance for as long as it is clear that there will be a non-performance by the other party when the other party's performance becomes due.

SECTION 3

TERMINATION OF THE CONTRACT

Article 9:301
Right to terminate the contract

(1) A party may terminate the contract if the other party's non-performance is fundamental.
(2) In the case of delay the aggrieved party may also terminate the contract under Article 8:106 (3).

Article 9:302
Contract to be performed in parts

If the contract is to be performed in separate parts and in relation to a part to which a counter-performance can be apportioned, there is a fundamental non-performance, the aggrieved party may exercise its right to terminate under this Section in relation to the part concerned. It may terminate the contract as a whole only if the non-performance is fundamental to the contract as a whole.

111

Article 9:303
Notice of termination

(1) A party's right to terminate the contract is to be exercised by notice to the other party.

(2) The aggrieved party loses its right to terminate the contract unless it gives notice within a reasonable time after it has or ought to have become aware of the non-performance.

(3) (a) When performance has not been tendered by the time it was due, the aggrieved party need not give notice of termination before a tender has been made. If a tender is later made it loses its right to terminate if it does not give such notice within a reasonable time after it has or ought to have become aware of the tender.

 (b) If, however, the aggrieved party knows or has reason to know that the other party still intends to tender within a reasonable time, and the aggrieved party unreasonably fails to notify the other party that it will not accept performance, it loses its right to terminate if the other party in fact tenders within a reasonable time.

(4) If a party is excused under Article 8:108 through an impediment which is total and permanent, the contract is terminated automatically and without notice at the time the impediment arises.

Article 9:304
Anticipatory non-performance

Where prior to the time for performance by a party it is clear that there will be a fundamental non-performance by it, the other party may terminate the contract.

Article 9:305
Effects of termination in general

(1) Termination of the contract releases both parties from their obligation to effect and to receive future performance, but, subject to Articles 9:306 to 9:308, does not affect the rights and liabilities that have accrued up to the time of termination.

(2) Termination does not affect any provision of the contract for the settlement of disputes or any other provision which is to operate even after termination.

Article 9:306
Property reduced in value

A party which terminates the contract may reject property previously received from the other party if its value to the first party has been fundamentally reduced as a result of the other party's non-performance.

Article 9:307
Recovery of money paid

On termination of the contract a party may recover money paid for a performance which it did not receive or which it properly rejected.

Article 9:308
Recovery of property

On termination of the contract a party which has supplied property which can be returned and for which it has not received payment or other counter-performance may recover the property.

Article 9:309
Recovery for performance that cannot be returned

On termination of the contract a party who has rendered a performance which cannot be returned and for which it has not received payment or other counter-performance may recover a reasonable amount for the value of the performance to the other party.

SECTION 4
PRICE REDUCTION

Article 9:401
Right to reduce price

(1) A party which accepts a tender of performance not conforming to the contract may reduce the price. This reduction shall be proportionate to the decrease in the value of the performance at the time this was tendered compared to the value which a conforming tender would have had at that time.
(2) A party which is entitled to reduce the price under the preceding paragraph and which has already paid a sum exceeding the reduced price may recover the excess from the other party.
(3) A party which reduces the price cannot also recover damages for reduction in the value of the performance but remains entitled to damages for any further loss it has suffered so far as these are recoverable under Section 5 of this Chapter.

SECTION 5
DAMAGES AND INTEREST

Article 9:501
Right to damages

(1) The aggrieved party is entitled to damages for loss caused by the other party's non-performance which is not excused under Article 8:108.
(2) The loss for which damages are recoverable includes:
   (a) non-pecuniary loss; and
   (b) future loss which is reasonably likely to occur.

Article 9:502
General measure of damages

The general measure of damages is such sum as will put the aggrieved party as nearly as possible into the position in which it would have been if the contract had been duly performed. Such damages cover the loss which the aggrieved party has suffered and the gain of which it has been deprived.

Article 9:503
Foreseeability

The non-performing party is liable only for loss which it foresaw or could reasonably have foreseen at the time of conclusion of the contract as a likely result of its non-performance, unless the non-performance was intentional or grossly negligent.

Article 9:504
Loss attributable to aggrieved party

The non-performing party is not liable for loss suffered by the aggrieved party to the extent that the aggrieved party contributed to the non-performance or its effects.

Article 9:505
Reduction of loss

(1) The non-performing party is not liable for loss suffered by the aggrieved party to the extent that the aggrieved party could have reduced the loss by taking reasonable steps.
(2) The aggrieved party is entitled to recover any expenses reasonably incurred in attempting to reduce the loss.

Article 9:506
Substitute transaction

Where the aggrieved party has terminated the contract and has made a substitute transaction within a reasonable time and in a reasonable manner, it may recover the difference between the contract price and the price of the substitute transaction as well as damages for any further loss so far as these are recoverable under this Section.

Article 9:507
Current Price

Where the aggrieved party has terminated the contract and has not made a substitute transaction but there is a current price for the performance contracted for, it may recover the difference between the contract price and the price current at the time the contract is terminated as well as damages for any further loss so far as these are recoverable under this Section.

Article 9:508
Delay in payment of money

(1) If payment of a sum of money is delayed, the aggrieved party is entitled to interest on that sum from the time when payment is due to the time of payment at the average commercial bank short-term lending rate to prime borrowers prevailing for the contractual currency of payment at the place where payment is due.
(2) The aggrieved party may in addition recover damages for any further loss so far as these are recoverable under this Section.

Article 9:509
Agreed payment for non-performance

(1) Where the contract provides that a party which fails to perform is to pay a specified sum to the aggrieved party for such non-performance, the aggrieved party shall be awarded that sum irrespective of its actual loss.

(2) However, despite any agreement to the contrary the specified sum may be reduced to a reasonable amount where it is grossly excessive in relation to the loss resulting from the non-performance and the other circumstances.

Article 9:510
Currency by which damages to be measured

Damages are to be measured by the currency which most appropriately reflects the aggrieved party's loss.

CHAPTER 10
PLURALITY OF PARTIES

SECTION I
PLURALITY OF DEBTORS

Article 10:101
Solidary, separate and communal obligations

(1) Obligations are solidary when all the debtors are bound to render one and the same performance and the creditor may require it from any one of them until full performance has been received.

(2) Obligations are separate when each debtor is bound to render only part of the performance and the creditor may require from each debtor only that debtor's part.

(3) An obligation is communal when all the debtors are bound to render the performance together and the creditor may require it only from all of them.

Article 10:102
When solidary obligations arise

(1) If several debtors are bound to render one and the same performance to a creditor under the same contract, they are solidarily liable, unless the contract or the law provides otherwise.

(2) Solidary obligations also arise where several persons are liable for the same damage.

(3) The fact that the debtors are not liable on the same terms does not prevent their obligations from being solidary.

Article 10:103
Liability under separate obligations

Debtors bound by separate obligations are liable in equal shares unless the contract or the law provides otherwise.

Article 10:104
Communal obligations: special rule when money claimed for non-performance

Notwithstanding Article 10:101(3), when money is claimed for non-performance of a communal obligation, the debtors are solidarily liable for payment to the creditor.

Article 10:105
Apportionment between solidary debtors

(1) As between themselves, solidary debtors are liable in equal shares unless the contract or the law provides otherwise.
(2) If two or more debtors are liable for the same damage under Article 10:102(2), their share of liability as between themselves is determined according to the law governing the event which gave rise to the liability.

Article 10:106
Recourse between solidary debtors

(1) A solidary debtor who has performed more than that debtor's share may claim the excess from any of the other debtors to the extent of each debtor's unperformed share, together with a share of any costs reasonably incurred.
(2) A solidary debtor to whom paragraph (1) applies may also, subject to any prior right and interest of the creditor, exercise the rights and actions of the creditor, including accessory securities, to recover the excess from any of the other debtors to the extent of each debtor's unperformed share.
(3) If a solidary debtor who has performed more than that debtor's share is unable, despite all reasonable efforts, to recover contribution from another solidary debtor, the share of the others, including the one who has performed, is increased proportionally.

Article 10:107
Performance, set-off and merger in solidary obligations

(1) Performance or set-off by a solidary debtor or set-off by the creditor against one solidary debtor discharges the other debtors in relation to the creditor to the extent of the performance or set-off.
(2) Merger of debts between a solidary debtor and the creditor discharges the other debtors only for the share of the debtor concerned.

Article 10:108
Release or settlement in solidary obligations

(1) When the creditor releases, or reaches a settlement with, one solidary debtor, the other debtors are discharged of liability for the share of that debtor.
(2) The debtors are totally discharged by the release or settlement if it so provides.
(3) As between solidary debtors, the debtor who is discharged from that debtor's share is discharged only to the extent of the share at the time of the discharge and not from any supplementary share for which that debtor may subsequently become liable under Article 10:106(3).

Article 10:109
Effect of judgment in solidary obligations

A decision by a court as to the liability to the creditor of one solidary debtor does not affect:

(a) the liability to the creditor of the other solidary debtors; or

(b) the rights of recourse between the solidary debtors under Article 10:106.

Article 10:110
Prescription in solidary obligations

Prescription of the creditor's right to performance ('claim') against one solidary debtor does not affect:

(a) the liability to the creditor of the other solidary debtors; or

(b) the rights of recourse between the solidary debtors under Article 10:106.

Article 10:111
Opposability of other defences in solidary obligations

(1) A solidary debtor may invoke against the creditor any defence which another solidary debtor can invoke, other than a defence personal to that other debtor. Invoking the defence has no effect with regard to the other solidary debtors.

(2) A debtor from whom contribution is claimed may invoke against the claimant any personal defence that that debtor could have invoked against the creditor.

SECTION 2
PLURALITY OF CREDITORS

Article 10:201
Solidary, separate and communal claims

(1) Claims are solidary when any of the creditors may require full performance from the debtor and when the debtor may render performance to any of the creditors.

(2) Claims are separate when the debtor owes each creditor only that creditor's share of the claim and each creditor may require performance only of that creditor's share.

(3) A claim is communal when the debtor must perform to all the creditors and any creditor may require performance only for the benefit of all.

Article 10:202
Apportionment of separate claims

Separate creditors are entitled to equal shares unless the contract or the law provides otherwise.

Article 10:203
Difficulties of executing a communal claim

If one of the creditors in a communal claim refuses, or is unable to receive, the performance, the debtor may discharge the obligation to perform by depositing the property or money with a third party according to Articles 7:110 or 7:111 of the Principles.

Article 10:204
Apportionment of solidary claims

(1) Solidary creditors are entitled to equal shares unless the contract or the law provides otherwise.
(2) A creditor who has received more than that creditor's share must transfer the excess to the other creditors to the extent of their respective shares.

Article 10:205
Regime of solidary claims

(1) A release granted to the debtor by one of the solidary creditors has no effect on the other solidary creditors.
(2) The rules of Articles 10:107, 10:109, 10:110 and 10:111(1) apply, with appropriate adaptations, to solidary claims.

CHAPTER 11
ASSIGNMENT OF CLAIMS

SECTION I
GENERAL PRINCIPLES

Article 11:101
Scope of Chapter

(1) This Chapter applies to the assignment by agreement of a right to performance ('claim') under an existing or future contract.
(2) Except where otherwise stated or the context otherwise requires, this Chapter also applies to the assignment by agreement of other transferable claims.
(3) This Chapter does not apply:
   (a) to the transfer of a financial instrument or investment security where, under the law otherwise applicable, such transfer must be by entry in a register maintained by or for the issuer; or
   (b) to the transfer of a bill of exchange or other negotiable instrument or of a negotiable security or a document of title to goods where, under the law otherwise applicable, such transfer must be by delivery (with any necessary endorsement).
(4) In this Chapter 'assignment' includes an assignment by way of security.
(5) This Chapter also applies, with appropriate adaptations, to the granting by agreement of a right in security over a claim otherwise than by assignment.

Article 11:102
Contractual claims generally assignable

(1) Subject to Articles 11:301 and 11:302, a party to a contract may assign a claim under it.
(2) A future claim arising under an existing or future contract may be assigned if at the time when it comes into existence, or at such other time as the parties agree, it can be identified as the claim to which the assignment relates.

118

Article 11:103
Partial assignment

A claim which is divisible may be assigned in part, but the assignor is liable to the debtor for any increased costs which the debtor thereby incurs.

Article 11:104
Form of assignment

An assignment need not be in writing and is not subject to any other requirement as to form. It may be proved by any means, including witnesses.

SECTION 2

EFFECTS OF ASSIGNMENT AS BETWEEN ASSIGNOR AND ASSIGNEE

Article 11:201
Rights transferred to assignee

(1) The assignment of a claim transfers to the assignee:
    (a) all the assignor's rights to performance in respect of the claim assigned; and
    (b) all accessory rights securing such performance.
(2) Where the assignment of a claim under a contract is associated with the substitution of the assignee as debtor in respect of any obligation owed by the assignor under the same contract, this Article takes effect subject to Article 12:201.

Article 11:202
When assignment takes effect

(1) An assignment of an existing claim takes effect at the time of the agreement to assign or such later time as the assignor and assignee agree.
(2) An assignment of a future claim is dependent upon the assigned claim coming into existence but thereupon takes effect from the time of the agreement to assign or such later time as the assignor and assignee agree.

Article 11:203
Preservation of assignee's tights against assignor

An assignment is effective as between the assignor and assignee, and entitles the assignee to whatever the assignor receives from the debtor, even if it is ineffective against the debtor under Article 11:301 or 11:302.

Article 11:204
Undertakings by assignor

By assigning or purporting to assign a claim the assignor undertakes to the assignee that:
    (a) at the time when the assignment is to take effect the following conditions will be satisfied except as otherwise disclosed to the assignee:
        (i) the assignor has the right to assign the claim;
        (ii) the claim exists and the assignee's rights are not affected by any defences or rights (including any right of set-off) which the debtor might have against the assignor; and

(iii) the claim is not subject to any prior assignment or right in security in favour of any other party or to any other incumbrance;

(b) the claim and any contract under which it arises will not be modified without the consent of the assignee unless the modification is provided for in the assignment agreement or is one which is made in good faith and is of a nature to which the assignee could not reasonably object; and

(c) the assignor will transfer to the assignee all transferable rights intended to secure performance which are not accessory rights.

SECTION 3

EFFECTS OF ASSIGNMENT AS BETWEEN ASSIGNEE AND DEBTOR

Article 11:301
Contractual prohibition of assignment

(1) An assignment which is prohibited by or is otherwise not in conformity with the contract under which the assigned claim arises is not effective against the debtor unless:

(a) the debtor has consented to it; or

(b) the assignee neither knew nor ought to have known of the non-conformity; or

(c) the assignment is made under a contract for the assignment of future rights to payment of money.

(2) Nothing in the preceding paragraph affects the assignor's liability for the non-conformity.

Article 11:302
Other ineffective assignments

An assignment to which the debtor has not consented is ineffective against the debtor so far as it relates to a performance which the debtor, by reason of the nature of the performance or the relationship of the debtor and the assignor, could not reasonably be required to render to anyone xcept the assignor.

Article 11:303
Effect on debtor's obligation

(1) Subject to Articles 11:301, 11:302, 11:307 and 11:308, the debtor is bound to perform in favour of the assignee if and only if the debtor has received a notice in writing from the assignor or the assignee which reasonably identifies the claim which has been assigned and requires the debtor to give performance to the assignee.

(2) However, if such notice is given by the assignee, the debtor may within a reasonable time request the assignee to provide reliable evidence of the assignment pending which the debtor may withhold performance.

(3) Where the debtor has acquired knowledge of the assignment otherwise than by a notice conforming to paragraph (1), the debtor may either withhold performance from or give performance to the assignee.

(4) Where the debtor gives performance to the assignor, the debtor is discharged if and only if the performance is given without knowledge of the assignment.

Article 11:304
Protection of debtor

A debtor who performs in favour of a person identified as assignee in a notice of assignment under Article 11:303 is discharged unless the debtor could not have been unaware that such person was not the person entitled to performance.

Article 11:305
Competing demands

A debtor who has received notice of two or more competing demands for performance may discharge liability by conforming to the law of the due place of performance, or, if the performances are due in different places, the law applicable to the claim.

Article 11:306
Place of performance

(1) Where the assigned claim relates to an obligation to pay money at a particular place, the assignee may require payment at any place within the same country or, if that country is a Member State of the European Union, at any place within the European Union, but the assignor is liable to the debtor for any increased costs which the debtor incurs by reason of any change in the place of performance.
(2) Where the assigned claim relates to a non-monetary obligation to be performed at a particular place, the assignee may not require performance at any other place.

Article 11:307
Defences and rights of set-off

(1) The debtor may set up against the assignee all substantive and procedural defences to the assigned claim which the debtor could have used against the assignor.
(2) The debtor may also assert against the assignee all rights of set-off which would have been available against the assignor under Chapter 13 in respect of any claim against the assignor:
   (a) existing at the time when a notice of assignment, whether or not conforming to Article 11:303(1), reaches the debtor; or
   (b) closely connected with the assigned claim.

Article 11:308
Unauthorised modification not binding on assignee

A modification of the claim made by agreement between the assignor and the debtor, without the consent of the assignee, after a notice of assignment, whether or not conforming to Article 11:303(1), reaches the debtor does not affect the rights of the assignee against the debtor unless the modification is provided for in the assignment agreement or is one which is made in good faith and is of a nature to which the assignee could not reasonably object.

SECTION 4
ORDER OF PRIORITY BETWEEN ASSIGNEE AND
COMPETING CLAIMANTS

Article 11:401
Priorities

(1) Where there are successive assignments of the same claim, the assignee whose assignment is first notified to the debtor has priority over any earlier assignee if at the time of the later assignment the assignee under that assignment neither knew nor ought to have known of the earlier assignment.

(2) Subject to paragraph (1), the priority of successive assignments, whether of existing or future claims, is determined by the order in which they are made.

(3) The assignee's interest in the assigned claim has priority over the interest of a creditor of the assignor who attaches that claim, whether by judicial process or otherwise, after the time the assignment has taken effect under Article 11:202.

(4) In the event of the assignor's bankruptcy, the assignee's interest in the assigned claim has priority over the interest of the assignor's insolvency administrator and creditors, subject to any rules of the law applicable to the bankruptcy relating to:
   (a) publicity required as a condition of such priority;
   (b) the ranking of claims; or
   (c) the avoidance or ineffectiveness of transactions in the bankruptcy proceedings.

CHAPTER 12
SUBSTITUTION OF NEW DEBTOR: TRANSFER OF CONTRACT

SECTION I
SUBSTITUTION OF NEW DEBTOR

Article 12:101
Substitution: General rules

(1) A third person may undertake with the agreement of the debtor and the creditor to be substituted as debtor, with the effect that the original debtor is discharged.

(2) A creditor may agree in advance to a future substitution. In such a case the substitution takes effect only when the creditor is given notice by the new debtor of the agreement between the new and the original debtor.

Article 12:102
Effects of substitution on defences and securities

(1) The new debtor cannot invoke against the creditor any rights or defences arising from the relationship between the new debtor and the original debtor.

(2) The discharge of the original debtor also extends to any security of the original debtor given to the creditor for the performance of the obligation, unless the security is over an asset which is transferred to the new debtor as part of a transaction between the original and the new debtor.

(3) Upon discharge of the original debtor, a security granted by any person other than the new debtor for the performance of the obligation is released, unless that other person agrees that it should continue to be available to the creditor.

(4) The new debtor may invoke against the creditor all defences which the original debtor could have invoked against the creditor.

SECTION 2

TRANSFER OF CONTRACT

Article 12:201
Transfer of contract

(1) A party to a contract may agree with a third person that that person is to be substituted as the contracting party. In such a case the substitution takes effect only where, as a result of the other party's assent, the first party is discharged.

(2) To the extent that the substitution of the third person as a contracting party involves a transfer of rights to performance ('claims'), the provisions of Chapter 11 apply; to the extent that obligations are transferred, the provisions of Section 1 of this Chapter apply.

CHAPTER 13
SET-OFF

Article 13:101
Requirements for set-off

If two parties owe each other obligations of the same kind, either party may set off that party's right to performance ('claim') against the other party's claim, if and to the extent that, at the time of set-off, the first party:
  (a) is entitled to effect performance; and
  (b) may demand the other party's performance.

Article 13:102
Unascertained claims

  (a) A debtor may not set off a claim which is unascertained as to its existence or value unless the set-off will not prejudice the interests of the other party.
  (b) Where the claims of both parties arise from the same legal relationship it is presumed that the other party's interests will not be prejudiced.

Article 13:103
Foreign currency set-off

Where parties owe each other money in different currencies, each party may set off that party's claim against the other party's claim, unless the parties have agreed that the party declaring set-off is to pay exclusively in a specified currency.

Article 13:104
Notice of set-off

The right of set-off is exercised by notice to the other party.

Article 13:105
Plurality of claims and obligations

(1) Where the party giving notice of set-off has two or more claims against the other party, the notice is effective only if it identifies the claim to which it relates.
(2) Where the party giving notice of set-off has to perform two or more obligations towards the other party, the rules in Article 7:109 apply with appropriate adaptations.

Article 13:106
Effect of set-off

Set-off discharges the obligations, as far as they are coextensive, as from the time of notice.

Article 13:107
Exclusion of right of set-off

Set-off cannot be effected:
    (a) where it is excluded by agreement;
    (b) against a claim to the extent that that claim is not capable of attachment; and
    (c) against a claim arising from a deliberate wrongful act.

CHAPTER 14
PRESCRIPTION

SECTION I
GENERAL PROVISION

Article 14:101
Claims subject to prescription

A right to performance of an obligation ('claim') is subject to prescription by the expiry of a period of time in accordance with these Principles.

SECTION 2
PERIODS OF PRESCRIPTION AND THEIR COMMENCEMENT

Article 14:201
General period

The general period of prescription is three years.

Article 14:202
Period for a claim established by legal proceedings

(1) The period of prescription for a claim established by judgment is ten years.
(2) The same applies to a claim established by an arbitral award or other instrument which is enforceable as if it were a judgment.

Article 14:203
Commencement

(1) The general period of prescription begins to run from the time when the debtor has to effect performance or, in the case of a right to damages, from the time of the act which gives rise to the claim.

(2) Where the debtor is under a continuing obligation to do or refrain from doing something, the general period of prescription begins to run with each breach of the obligation.

(3) The period of prescription set out in Article 14:202 begins to run from the time when the judgment or arbitral award obtains the effect of res judicata, or the other instrument becomes enforceable, though not before the debtor has to effect performance.

SECTION 3

EXTENSION OF PERIOD

Article 14:301
Suspension in case of ignorance

The running of the period of prescription is suspended as long as the creditor does not know of, and could not reasonably know of:

(a) the identity of the debtor; or
(b) the facts giving rise to the claim including, in the case of a right to damages, the type of damage.

Article 14:302
Suspension in case of judicial and other proceedings

(1) The running of the period of prescription is suspended from the time when judicial proceedings on the claim are begun.

(2) Suspension lasts until a decision has been made which has the effect of res judicata, or until the case has been otherwise disposed of.

(3) These provisions apply, with appropriate adaptations, to arbitration proceedings and to all other proceedings initiated with the aim of obtaining an instrument which is enforceable as if it were a judgment.

Article 14:303
Suspension in case of impediment beyond creditor's control

(1) The running of the period of prescription is suspended as long as the creditor is prevented from pursuing the claim by an impediment which is beyond the creditor's control and which the creditor could not reasonably have been expected to avoid or overcome.

(2) Paragraph (1) applies only if the impediment arises, or subsists, within the last six months of the prescription period.

Article 14:304
Postponement of expiry in case of negotiations

If the parties negotiate about the claim, or about circumstances from which a claim might arise, the period of prescription does not expire before one year has passed since the last communication made in the negotiations.

Article 14:305
Postponement of expiry in case of incapacity

(1) If a person subject to an incapacity is without a representative, the period of prescription of a claim held by or against that person does not expire before one year has passed after either the incapacity has ended or a representative has been appointed.

(2) The period of prescription of claims between a person subject to an incapacity and that person's representative does not expire before one year has passed after either the incapacity has ended or a new representative has been appointed.

Article 14:306
Postponement of expiry: deceased's estate

Where the creditor or debtor has died, the period of prescription of a claim held by or against the deceased's estate does not expire before one year has passed after the claim can be enforced by or against an heir, or by or against a representative of the estate.

Article 14:307
Maximum length of period

The period of prescription cannot be extended, by suspension of its running or postponement of its expiry under these Principles, to more than ten years or, in case of claims for personal injuries, to more than thirty years. This does not apply to suspension under Article 14:302.

SECTION 4
RENEWAL OF PERIODS

Article 14:401
Renewal by acknowledgement

(1) If the debtor acknowledges the claim, vis-à-vis the creditor, by part payment, payment of interest, giving of security, or in any other manner, a new period of prescription begins to run.

(2) The new period is the general period of prescription, regardless of whether the claim was originally subject to the general period of prescription or the ten year period under Article 14:202. In the latter case, however, this Article does not operate so as to shorten the ten year period.

Article 14:402
Renewal by attempted execution

The ten year period of prescription laid down in Article 14:202 begins to run again with each reasonable attempt at execution undertaken by the creditor.

SECTION 5
EFFECTS OF PRESCRIPTION

Article 14:501
General effect

(1) After expiry of the period of prescription the debtor is entitled to refuse performance.
(2) Whatever has been performed in order to discharge a claim may not be reclaimed merely because the period of prescription had expired.

Article 14:502
Effect on ancillary claims

The period of prescription for a right to payment of interest, and other claims of an ancillary nature, expires not later than the period for the principal claim.

Article 14:503
Effect on set-off

A claim in relation to which the period of prescription has expired may nonetheless be set off, unless the debtor has invoked prescription previously or does so within two months of notification of set-off.

SECTION 6
MODICATION BY AGREEMENT

Article 14:601
Agreements concerning prescription

(1) The requirements for prescription may be modified by agreement between the parties, in particular by either shortening or lengthening the periods of prescription.
(2) The period of prescription may not, however, be reduced to less than one year or extended to more than thirty years after the time of commencement set out in Article 14:203.

CHAPTER 15
ILLEGALITY

Article 15:101
Contracts contrary to fundamental principles

A contract is of no effect to the extent that it is contrary to principles recognised as fundamental in the laws of the Member States of the European Union.

Article 15:102
Contracts infringing mandatory rules

(1) Where a contract infringes a mandatory rule of law applicable under Article 1:103 of these Principles, the effects of that infringement upon the contract are the effects, if any, expressly prescribed by that mandatory rule.

(2) Where the mandatory rule does not expressly prescribe the effects of an infringement upon a contract, the contract may be declared to have full effect, to have some effect, to have no effect, or to be subject to modification.

(3) A decision reached under paragraph (2) must be an appropriate and proportional response to the infringement, having regard to all relevant circumstances, including:
   (a) the purpose of the rule which has been infringed;
   (b) the category of persons for whose protection the rule exists;
   (c) any sanction that may be imposed under the rule infringed;
   (d) the seriousness of the infringement;
   (e) whether the infringement was intentional; and
   (f) the closeness of the relationship between the infringement and the contract.

Article 15:103
Partial ineffectiveness

(1) If only part of a contract is rendered ineffective under Articles 15:101 or 15:102, the remaining part continues in effect unless, giving due consideration to all the circumstances of the case, it is unreasonable to uphold it.

(2) Articles 15:104 and 15:105 apply, with appropriate adaptations, to a case of partial ineffectiveness.

Article 15:104
Restitution

(1) When a contract is rendered ineffective under Articles 15:101 or 15:102, either party may claim restitution of whatever that party has supplied under the contract, provided that, where appropriate, concurrent restitution is made of whatever has been received.

(2) When considering whether to grant restitution under paragraph (1), and what concurrent restitution, if any, would be appropriate, regard must be had to the factors referred to in Article 15:102(3).

(3) An award of restitution may be refused to a party who knew or ought to have known of the reason for the ineffectiveness.

(4) If restitution cannot be made in kind for any reason, a reasonable sum must be paid for what has been received.

Article 15:105
Damages

(1) A party to a contract which is rendered ineffective under Articles 15:101 or 15:102 may recover from the other party damages putting the first party as nearly as possible into the same position as if the contract had not been concluded, provided that the other party knew or ought to have known of the reason for the ineffectiveness.

(2) When considering whether to award damages under paragraph (1), regard must be had to the factors referred to in Article 15:102(3).

(3) An award of damages may be refused where the first party knew or ought to have known of the reason for the ineffectiveness.

CHAPTER 16
CONDITIONS

Article 16:101
Types of condition

A contractual obligation may be made conditional upon the occurrence of an uncertain future event, so that the obligation takes effect only if the event occurs (suspensive condition) or comes to an end if the event occurs (resolutive condition).

Article 16:102
Interference with conditions

(1) If fulfilment of a condition is prevented by a party, contrary to duties of good faith and fair dealing or co-operation, and if fulfilment would have operated to that party's disadvantage, the condition is deemed to be fulfilled.
(2) If fulfilment of a condition is brought about by a party, contrary to duties of good faith and fair dealing or co-operation, and if fulfilment operates to that party's advantage, the condition is deemed not to be fulfilled.

Article 16:103
Effect of conditions

(1) Upon fulfilment of a suspensive condition, the relevant obligation takes effect unless the parties otherwise agree.
(2) Upon fulfilment of a resolutive condition, the relevant obligation comes to an end unless the parties otherwise agree.

CHAPTER 17
CAPITALISATION OF INTEREST

Article 17:101
When interest to be added to capital

(1) Interest payable according to Article 9:508(1) is added to the outstanding capital every 12 months.
(2) Paragraph (1) of this Article does not apply if the parties have provided for interest upon delay in payment.

3

ELECTRONIC COMMERCE

A. Introductory Text

Exponential advances in information technology have provided the commercial and financial communities with efficient alternatives to paper-based contracting. These alternative modes of contracting, swept under the rubric of electronic commerce, put pressure on traditional legal rules containing rigid or formalistic contract requirements. Electronic commerce also exposes the incompleteness of legal rules applicable with geographical limits to which technology is impervious.

For these reasons among others, transnational commercial law is increasingly concerned with rules addressing electronic commerce. Characteristically responding to the needs of mercantile practices, these developing rules share the common element of seeking to promote these efficient contract practices, as they may develop, while respecting the fundamental policy objectives underlying traditional contract rules, most of which are equally relevant to electronic commerce. This is a balance with far-reaching legal, commercial, and technological implications. An overarching question in striking this balance is whether rules with technological content should be of a generalized or specific character, the former providing greater flexibility and adaptability, the latter greater clarity and legal predictability.

Not surprisingly given the broad implications of electronic commerce, and the differing contexts in which such transactions arise, various approaches have been undertaken, and, it is fair to say, other supplementing and differing efforts are anticipated in the medium term. We shall highlight the two groundbreaking works of the United Nations Commission on International Trade Law (UNCITRAL), one on electronic commerce, the other on electronic signatures, and two key regional instruments, European directives on the same subjects. We then summarize, by way of example, one set of private rules, available as a basis for contract, namely, the rules of the Comité Maritime International (CMI) on electronic bills of lading. We shall conclude with a short description of another set of private rules, the Bolero rules, which provide for the issue of bills of lading, and the carrying out of transfers, electronically through a central registry.

Beyond these instruments, modern commercial law treaties must now address certain electronic commerce issues. Most common in that context are expanded definitions of 'writing', as seen is the most recent treaties addressing equipment financing,[1] receivables financing,[2] and securities held with an intermediary.[3]

1. UNCITRAL Model Law on Electronic Commerce, 1996

The UNCITRAL Model Law on Electronic Commerce (UNCITRAL E-Commerce) was adopted by the Commission in 1996, and an additional provision Article 5 *bis* was inserted in 1998. As a model law, it is not a legally operative instrument and is not open to ratification. States are free to reject it, to enact it in its entirety, or to select, amend or add to particular provisions. An accompanying and detailed Guide to Enactment of the model law was also published by UNCITRAL (Guide-EC).[4]

UNCITRAL E-Commerce was the first major international effort of a general nature[5] in this field, and in varying degrees has influenced all subsequent

---

[1] See Convention on International Interests in Mobile Equipment (see further below, p. 550), Art 1(nn) ('writing' means a 'record of information (including information communicated by teletransmission) which is in tangible or other form and is capable of being reproduced in tangible form on a subsequent occasion and which indicates by reasonable means a person's approval of the record').

[2] See UN Convention on the Assignment of Receivables in International Trade (see further below p. 604), Art 5(c) ('writing' means 'any form of information that is accessible so as to be usable for subsequent reference ... [a writing requirement] is met, if, by generally accepted means or a procedure agreed to by the person whose signature is required, the writing identifies that person and indicates that person's approval of the information contained in the writing').

[3] See Hague Convention on the Law Applicable to Certain Rights Securities in respect of Securities held with an Intermediary (see further below p. 775), Art 1(n) ('writing' and 'written' mean 'a record of information (including information communicated by teletransmission) which is in tangible or other form and is capable of being reproduced in tangible form on a subsequent occasion').

[4] *UNCITRAL Model Law on Electronic Commerce with Guide to Enactment* (1996).

[5] Specialized texts with electronic commerce aspects include the *UNCITRAL Model Law on International Credit Transfers* (1992) and *The Legal Guide on Electronic Funds Transfers* (1987).

harmonizing work on electronic commerce. The principal objective of the model law is to remove legal obstacles to the use of electronic commerce, such as those that prescribe the use of 'written', 'signed', or 'original documents', thereby promoting equality of treatment between paper-based and electronic contracting.[6]

Scope of application

The model law contains no definition of electronic commerce. Rather, it applies broadly to 'any kind of data message used in the context of commercial activities'.[7] 'Data message' is an equally wide concept, comprising 'electronic data interchange',[8] electronic mail, fax[9] and telex, and any other 'information generated, sent, received or stored by electronic, optical or similar means'.[10] These definitions seek to cover future comparable technologies and to provide legal neutrality among them, on a functional basis, as discussed below.

Annotations to the model law invite certain scope modifications,[11] and state expressly that the text does not override any consumer protection law.

The model law embodies the principle of party autonomy[12] as regards matters *inter se* between contracting parties, including interchange agreement or 'system rules', that is, general terms provided by communication networks and certain specific contracting rules that may be included in an agreement.[13] On these matters, the model law provides default rules in Chapter III that may be included in or excluded from an agreement, or may be available to fill contractual gaps or omissions.

Functional equivalent approach

Rather than seeking to expand the scope of legal form requirements applicable to paper documents (written, signed, and original documents), as has been done in the past,[14] the model law takes the 'functional equivalent approach'.[15] It identifies the purposes and functions of traditional paper-based requirements and, based thereon, provides validity criteria applicable to data messages. To the extent that a data

---

[6] See Guide-EC, para 43 for a fuller statement of the general principles on which the model law are based, relevant for purposes of interpretation, Art 3(2).

[7] Article 1; Guide-EC, paras 7–9.

[8] Article 2(b) (defined as the electronic transfer from computer to computer of information 'using an agreed standard to structure information'); Guide-EC, para 33–4.

[9] Fax (and telex) are covered for two reasons. First, certain national laws do not contain clear contract rules in these contexts. Secondly, digitalized information initially sent in the form of a data message may well, in the chain between sender and recipient, be forwarded by fax or telex (which themselves may be computer-generated).

[10] Article 2(a); Guide-EC, paras 30–1. Computer-generated records and revocations or amendments (by means of a data message) are included in the concept.

[11] Alternative wording has been provided which would restrict the law to international electronic commerce. The law may be expanded beyond the commercial sphere, e.g. to the relation between users of electronic commerce and public authorities.

[12] Article 4; Guide-EC, paras 19–21.   [13] Article 11–15.

[14] See, e.g., UN Convention on Contracts for the International Sale of Goods, Article 13 (p. 219 below) and UNCITRAL Model Law on International Commercial Arbitration, Art 7 (p. 917 below).

[15] Guide-EC, paras 15–18.

message meets those criteria, it enjoys the same level of legal recognition as corresponding paper documents performing the same function.

Legal form requirements—written, signed and original documents

The threshold concept in the model law is that information shall 'not be denied legal effect, validity or enforceability solely on the grounds' that it is a data message.[16] This reflects the fundamental principle of equal treatment of data messages and paper documents. This provision does not, however, establish the legal validity of data messages. That is provided for elsewhere, in the specific contexts of requirements for written, signed, original documents, with an internal hierarchy reflecting differing levels of reliability, traceability and unalterability.

(i) Written documents   Where the law requires writing that requirement is met by a data message under the model law if the information contained therein is 'accessible so as to be usable for subsequent reference'.[17] This is a baseline requirement, and is not meant to subsume requirements derived from traditional concepts relating to signatures and original documents (although a number of legal systems combine such elements of each function) including those that seek to identify the time and place of the writing. In enacting the law, a State may exclude specified legal or factual situations, for example, product warning requirements.[18]

The Guide-EC contains a list of the functions traditionally performed by various types of writing,[19] yet seeks to avoid excessive complexity or overlap with functions more logically linked to the requirements underpinning signed and original documents. It thus distils matters to this objective test: is the information 'accessible' (in a form a computer can read and understand, possibly with the aid of necessary software) 'so as to be usable for subsequent reference'?[20]

(ii) Signed documents   Where the law requires the signature of a person, that requirement is met in relation to a data message under the model law if a method is used (a) to identify that person, and (b) to indicate that person's approval of the information contained in the message.[21] The standard for a qualifying method is determined by facts and content: it must be 'as reliable as was appropriate for the purpose for which it was generated or communicated in light of all circumstances,

---

[16] Article 5; Guide-EC, para 46. Article 5(b) establishes the same principles in respect to information incorporated by reference in a data message. [17] Article 6(1)–(2).

[18] Article 6(3).

[19] Guide-EC, para 48. These functions include: tangible evidence of the existence and nature of the intent of parties to bind themselves, including finalization of that intent; a form through which information could be authenticated by means of a signature; aid in awareness of the consequences of contracting; legibility to third parties and in a form acceptable to public authorities and courts; a permanent unaltered record of a transaction, which parties may retain in custody and reproduce; to facilitate regulatory control (e.g. audit and taxation); and as a step in the creation of legal rights and obligation where writing is a condition to validity.

[20] More objective than 'readable' or 'intelligible', but less stringent than 'durable' or 'non-alterable': Guide-EC, para 50. [21] Article 7(1)(a)–(b).

including any relevant agreement'.[22] This standard is more stringent than that required to satisfy writing requirements, yet less stringent than that required for original document requirements. In enacting the law, a State may wish to exclude specified legal or factual situations.[23] The UNCITRAL Model Law on Electronic Signatures supplements the current model law on this item.[24]

While noting the common functions of handwritten signature requirements[25] and certain additional elements in that context,[26] the model law avoids specific rules as to what constitutes an electronic signature. Instead, and in line with its overarching philosophy, it sets out functional equivalents of signature requirements for application in the context of data messages. This 'flexible' approach focuses on the core point of use of a reliable method to identify the sender of the message (originator[27]) and to establish that the originator approved the content of the message.[28]

A number of factors may be taken into account when deciding whether the method is 'appropriately reliable under all circumstances'.[29] While flexible, this approach lacks commercial predictability. The model law does not distinguish situations where a prior electronic contracting relationship exists between the parties,[30] but the Guide-EC encourages methods used in any such relations to be taken into account, whether they are bilateral, multilateral or involve intermediaries[31] such as networks.[32]

As a handwritten signature on a document is not necessarily sufficient to establish legal rights, so also with a functional equivalent on a data message. The conditions necessary to create legally valid rights or obligations are left to the applicable law.[33]

(iii) Original documents   Many commercial disputes centre on whether a document should be treated as an original document. That problem has become more acute as a result of computerized methods for transmitting data. The question is particularly important in relation to negotiable instruments and documents of title

---

[22] Article 7(2).   [23] Article 7(3) below.

[24] See UNCITRAL Model Law-ES, below notes 3, 49–52 and text.

[25] Guide-EC, para 53–4. Three are identified: (i) to identify a person; (ii) to link the personal involvement of that person to the act of signature; (iii) to associate that person with the contents of the document.

[26] Guide-EC, para 53–4. Such as evidence of an intent (i) to be bound, (ii) to endorse authorship of a text; or (iii) of a person to be associated with the contents of a document written by another. It may also provide evidence of fact that a person was in a specific place at a specific time.

[27] 'Originator' of a data message means the person by whom, or on whose behalf, the data message purports to have been sent or generated (prior to any storage and excluding any intermediary). Article 2(c). An 'addressee' of a data message means the person who is intended by the originator to receive the data message. Article 2(d).   [28] Article 7(1).

[29] Guide-EC, para 58. These functions include the sophistication of the equipment and capacity of communication systems; the nature, size, and frequency of the transactions and the importance of the information in the data message; the function of signatures in the regulatory environment; the range of authentication procedures offered by intermediaries and compliance therewith; the availability of insurance coverage for unauthorized use; trade practices; and the availability and cost of other methods of identification.   [30] Guide-EC, para 59.

[31] 'Intermediary' means a person who, on behalf of another person, sends, receives, or stores a data message or provides services with respect thereto. Art 2(e).   [32] Guide-EC, para 60.

[33] Guide-EC, para 61.

(the essence of which are the existence and transfer of unique originals) but can also arise in many other areas of commerce.[34]

Where the law requires an original document, that requirement is met under the model law if (a) there exists a 'reliable assurance' as to the 'integrity of the information' from the time is was first generated in its final form (which could be when composed as a paper document), and (b) where presentation to a person is required, the information is capable of being displayed to that person.[35] The criteria for assessing integrity are whether the information has remained 'complete and unaltered', apart from any endorsement or change in the normal course of communication, storage, and display.[36] The standard of reliability, as in the case of signature equivalencies, is to be assessed in light of the purpose for which the information was generated and all relevant circumstances.[37] Given its function, this standard is the most stringent one in the model law. In enacting the law, a State may exclude specified legal or factual situations.[38]

There are various technical means to certify the contents of a data message as original, and the requirements in the model law, aimed essentially at a suitable method of authentication under all facts and circumstances, set out the minimum acceptable standard.[39]

Evidential weight and legal retention of data messages

The model law provides rules on admissibility of data messages as evidence and their evidential value. It overrides otherwise applicable rules of evidence that would deny the admissibility of a data message *per se* or where it is the best evidence reasonably available, given no original paper document.[40] It also speaks in affirmative terms requiring that information in the form of data messages shall be given 'due evidential weight', taking into account, *inter alia*, the reliability of data generation, maintenance, storage, and communication.[41]

The model law also addresses data messages in the context of legal requirements that documents, records, or information be retained.[42]

Additional contracting formalities

Chapter III of the model law, the provisions of which may be varied by the parties *inter se*,[43] covers a range of matters relating to the communication of data messages. It consists of rules on the formation and validity of contracts,[44]

---

[34] Such as real estate, technical trade and inspection, and insurance, as well as chattel security, and other areas where it is necessary or advisable to transfer or otherwise deal with documents in their original form. Many legal systems impose notarisation or registration requirements in these contexts.
[35] Article 8(1).   [36] Article 8(3)(a).   [37] Article 8(3)(b).   [38] Article 8(4).
[39] Guide-EC, paras 63–4.
[40] Article 9(1); Guide-EC, para 70 (noting, in particular, that the concept of 'best evidence', a common law concept, may be unknown and problematic in other systems, thus justifying its omission in such States).   [41] Article 9(2); Guide-EC, para 71.
[42] Article 10; Guide-EC, paras 72–5.   [43] Article 4.
[44] Article 11; Guide-EC, paras 76–80. Rules are provided in relation to the conclusion of contracts by electronic means, and on the form in which an offer and acceptance may be expressed.

recognition by parties of data messages,[45] attribution of data messages,[46] acknowledgement of receipt,[47] and time and place of dispatch and receipt of data messages.[48] These default rules would apply absent contractual agreement or to fill in contractual gaps.

2. UNCITRAL Model Law on Electronic Signatures, 2001

In 2001 UNCITRAL adopted a Model Law on Electronic Signatures (UNCI-TRAL E-Signature). An accompanying and detailed Guide to Enactment of the model law was also published by UNCITRAL (Guide-ES).

The text focused on the issues associated with electronic signatures since they appeared to many to be primary impediments to the accelerated use of electronic commerce.

Basic regime

A main provision of this model law, designed to address the perceived shortcomings of Article 7 of UNCITRAL E-Commerce, is Article 6(3) and its adjunct, Article 7. Taken together, these provisions provide a mechanism, in effect a safe-harbour, for establishing an electronic signature deemed sufficiently reliable to satisfy the function equivalency standard.

The model law starts with a definition of 'electronic signature'[49] and a substantive rule,[50] each consistent with UNCITRAL E-Commerce, Article 7, and restates the basic principle of equal treatment of differing technologies (although the text has been criticized for the predominant role played by public-key cryptography technology).[51] Users of electronic signatures may operate under one or other of two distinct regimes. The first is that of UNCITRAL E-Commerce, Article 7, supplemented by additional reliability criteria (while terminology is changing

---

[45] Article 12; Guide-EC, paras 81–82. Non-discrimination against electronic commerce in the context of performance of certain contractual obligations is the basic topic.

[46] Article 13; Guide-EC, paras 83–92. This provision deals primarily with issues arising in connection with a message sent by a person not indicated as the originator, for example, a fraudulent message by someone with access to authentication codes. It creates a presumption—applicable in most but not all cases that a data message was sent by the originator. The presumption may be rebutted where the addressee knew or should have known that the originator did not send the message.

[47] Article 14; Guide-EC paras 93–100. A number of issues arising in the context of acknowledgement of receipts (ranging from receipt of an unspecified message to an agreement with a specified message) are addressed, but without establishing a comprehensive system. It focuses primarily on core aspects relating to the receipt of a data message.

[48] Article 15; Guide-EC, paras 100–7.

[49] Article 2(a); Guide-ES, paras 93–4. An electronic signature, linked to a text message, must (a) identify the signatory, and (b) indicate the signatory's approval of content. This is the same as E-Commerce, Art 7(1)(a).

[50] Article 6(1)–(2); Guide-ES, paras 115–31. This is the same as E-Commerce, Art 7(1)(b) and (2).

[51] Cf paras 14, 19, 20, 28, and 32.

rapidly, such criteria focus on what are relatively more 'secure' or 'enhanced' signing devices).[52] Transacting parties employ a signing method which they believe will meet the test of functional equivalence to handwritten signatures. To ensure validity, however, they may need to establish that the method was 'appropriate under all circumstances'. The second option—use of a safe haven—permits users to seek pre-approval of their method by a public authority or accredited private entity specified by the State.[53] That approach would provide *ex ante* assurances as to the legal effects of an electronic signature.

Provisions relating to conduct of parties

UNCITRAL E-signature contains provisions relating to the conduct of the principal parties involved in transactions involving electronic signatures—the signatory,[54] a 'party relying',[55] and (revealing the influence of public key infrastructure technology concepts and terminology in the model law) a certification service provider.[56] No attempt is made to set out a detailed or comprehensive liability regime, yet general criteria are established for use in assessing the conduct of these parties.

Select additional provisions

The model law contains a provision prohibiting discrimination against foreign electronic signatures and certificates.[57]

The principle of party autonomy is respected, as parties are free to derogate from (exclude) or vary the terms of the law, unless prohibited from doing so under the applicable law.[58]

---

[52] Article 6(3); Guide, paras 115–31. This adds substantive elements to UNCITRAL E-Commerce, namely that an electronic signature is appropriately reliable if (a) the signature creation data (i) are linked to the signatory and to no other person, and (ii) were at the time of signing under the control of the signatory and no other person, and (b) any alterations to the electronic signature or information (where a legal signature is for the purpose of providing assurances as to integrity of that information) are detectable.

[53] Article 7; Guide–ES, paras 132–6. The sanctioning authority must act with reference to the criteria specified in Art 6.

[54] Article 8; Guide-ES, paras 137–41. The signatory must take reasonable precautions, and must advise others relating to the unauthorized use of an electronic signature.

[55] Article 2(f) and 11; Guide-ES, paras 148–51. The relying party must take reasonable steps to verify the reliability of an electronic signature.

[56] Article 2(e), 9, and 10; Guide-ES, paras 142–7. A certification service provider—an entity that issues certificates and performs services relating to electronic signatures—must (a) employ trustworthy procedures and systems (including financial, human resources, and auditing aspects), (b) make material representations and act in accordance with them, (c) make a number of declarations relating to the establishment and purposes of the electronic signature, including identification methods.

[57] Article 12; Guide-ES, paras 152–60. 'No regard' shall be had to the geographic locations of the signatory or certificate issuer as regards legal effectiveness. National and foreign certificates of a 'substantially equivalent level of reliability' shall have the same legal effect. [58] Article 5.

3. EC Directive on Electronic Commerce, 2000

The EC Directive on electronic commerce of 2000 (EC E-Commerce)[59] covers a range of topics in the wider field of electronic commerce, including internal European market and regulatory aspects, which fall outside the scope of the present chapter. From the vantage point of transactional commercial law, its central provision relates to the treatment of contracts. A number of its other provisions which set the general regulatory framework for electronic commerce are also worthy of note.

As a European directive, EC E-commerce is mandatory, and must be implemented by all Member States. It affects parties in non-Member States where the law of a Member State is applicable to a matter within its scope.

Treatment of contracts

The approach taken is that of articulating general principles, requiring implementation at the national level, rather than setting out harmonizing rules. Member States are required to ensure that 'their legal system allows contracts to be concluded by electronic means'.[60] In particular, national legal requirements applicable to the contract process may 'neither create obstacles for the use of electronic contracts nor result in such contracts being deprived of legal effectiveness and validity on account of their having been made by electronic means'.[61] This obligation is not limited to the conclusion of the contract. It extends to all aspects of the electronic contracting process.[62]

Member States may impose requirements in relation to the electronic contract process,[63] and may restrict the use of electronic contracting in four specific areas.[64]

Member States must also ensure that service providers make advance disclosures relating to electronic contracting. Prior to the time of contracting, a service provider must 'clearly, comprehensively and unambiguously' provide basic information to the recipients of its services.[65] EC E-Commerce also contains rules relating to receipts and the acknowledgement thereof (except for electronic mail transactions)[66] and the time at which the order and acknowledgement are deemed to have been received.[67] These rules may be modified by the parties *inter se* in non-consumer transactions.[68]

---

[59] Directive 2000/31/EC of the European Parliament and of the Council of 8 June 2000 on certain legal aspects of information society services, in particular electronic commerce, in the Internal Market, 2000 OJ L 178.   [60] Article 9(1).

[61] Ibid.   [62] Recital 34.   [63] Recital 35.

[64] Article 9(2); see also Recital 36. These are (i) transfers of real estate (but not rentals), (ii) family law, (iii) contracts requiring by law the involvement of public authorities or professionals exercising public authority (e.g. notaries), and (iv) contracts of surety granted and on collateral securities furnished by a person acting for purposes outside their trade, business, or profession.

[65] Article 10. The information includes (i) the technical steps to follow to conclude the contract, (ii) whether the contract will be filed and accessible, (iii) means for identifying and correcting input prior to finalization of the contract, (iv) the languages offered for conclusion of the contract, (v) codes of conduct, and (vi) general conditions.   [66] Article 11(1).

[67] Ibid.   [68] Ibid.

Additional framework provisions

The framework provisions, with the treatment of contracts, form the basic structure within which electronic commerce and its related services may develop. As such, it is seen as contributing to the 'proper functioning of the internal market' by ensuring the 'free movement of information society services'[69] between Member States.[70]

A basic principle is that any person may provide information society services (be a 'service provider') throughout the EU provided they comply with laws related to such services (broadly defined 'coordinated field') of the Member States in which they are established,[71] without the need for prior authorization.[72] In addition, EC E-Commerce provides transparency requirements for 'commercial communications',[73] liability rules for intermediary service providers,[74] and online dispute settlement[75] and the availability of judicial redress for electronic commerce activities.[76]

Member States are encouraged to have the commercial and financial communities draw up codes of conduct,[77] and the Directive will be re-examined every two years,[78] which may lead to deeper harmonization in this field.

4. EC Directive on Electronic Signatures, 1999

The EC Directive on Electronic Signatures of 1999 (EC E-Signature)[79] covers a wide range of topics, including those addressed in UNCITRAL E-signature. Its core provisions address the characteristics of electronic signatures and their effect. Other provisions cover related regulatory and implementation aspects.

Characteristics of electronic signatures and their legal effect

The Directive makes a distinction between an 'electronic signature'[80] and an 'advanced electronic signature'.[81] The latter, based upon a 'qualifying certificate',[82] and created by a 'secure-signature-creation device', is given higher legal recognition

---

[69] Defined in Art 1(2) of Directive 98/34/EC, as amended by Directive 98/48/EC.
[70] Article 1(1).
[71] Article 3; see also Art 2(b) (service provider) and (h) (coordinated field).
[72] Article 4.   [73] Article 6; see also Art 2(f) (commercial communication).
[74] Article 12.   [75] Article 17.   [76] Article 18.   [77] Article 16.
[78] Article 21.
[79] Directive 1999/93/EC of the European Parliament and of the Council of 13 December 1999 on a Community framework for electronic signatures, 2000 OJ L 13 p.12.
[80] Article 2(1). A simple electronic signature is linked to electronic data and 'serves as a method of authentication'.
[81] Article 2(2). An enhanced electronic signature is an electronic signature which is: (a) uniquely linked to and capable of identifying the signatory, (b) created using means that the signatory can maintain under his sole control, and (c) linked to its related data such that any subsequent change of that data is detectable.
[82] Article 2(10). The requirements for qualified certificates are contained in Annex I. Requirements for certificate-service-issuing qualified certificates are contained in Annex II. As 'secure signature-creation devices', see Art 2(6), are needed for qualifying advanced electronic signatures, Annexes III (requirements for secure signature-creation devices) and IV (recommendations for secure signature verification) are also relevant.

than the former.[83] Member States must ensure that advanced electronic signatures (a) satisfy legal requirements in relation to data in electronic form in the same manner as a handwritten signature on a paper document, and (b) are admissible as evidence.[84] In contrast, the rule for simple electronic signatures is only that Member States may not deny their legal effectiveness and admissibility solely on the ground that they are in electronic form or they are not advanced electronic signatures.[85]

Regulatory and implementation aspects

Provisions relating to the liability of providers of qualifying certificates augment the regime. In exchange for the right to provide such certificates, issuers accept a higher liability.[86] This is intended to strengthen general confidence in the system, thereby encouraging use of advanced techniques. With a view towards greater convergence, EC E-signature also creates a committee,[87] whose tasks are, *inter alia*, to clarify the requirements for enhanced electronic signatures and procedures which qualify as such.[88]

The Directive recognizes the importance of international aspects, meaning transactions with parties outside the Community, in facilitating the use of advanced electronic signature technology. It mandates the European Commission to make international proposals seeking cross-border harmonization.[89]

5. CMI Rules for Electronic Bills of Lading, 1990

Where it is envisaged that the buyer of goods that are being shipped may wish to sell or pledge them in transit, the conventional instrument to facilitate this is the bill of lading, a document of title issued by the carrier which gives the holder constructive possession of the goods and the right to take delivery at the port of destination in exchange for the bill of lading. This right may be transferred by delivery of the bill of lading with any necessary endorsement, the carrier's obligation being to sur-render the goods to whoever is the holder and present the bill of lading on their arrival. However, paper bills of lading suffer from a number of disadvantages. Their preparation involves time and expense, they are subject to fraudulent alteration and to theft, and frequently the bill of lading has to pass down a long chain of buyers and sub-buyers, not infrequently reaching the ultimate buyer after the goods have arrived. In recent years there has been a significant move towards the use of sea waybills as importers came to realize that there is no need for a bill of lading if it is not intended to deal with the goods in transit.

Various attempts have been made to surmount problems with paper-based of bills of lading through the use of electronic systems. Among the first of these was

---

[83] Article 5.   [84] Article 5(1).   [85] Article 5(2).
[86] Article 6. The basic standard is that of negligence.
[87] Articles 3(4)–(6), 9, 11, and 12.   [88] Article 10.   [89] Article 7.

the SeaDocs experiment, in which a paper bill of lading would be issued and signed in the ordinary way but would then be immobilized in a central registry, appointed agent for all relevant parties to record transfer instructions and acceptances, so that all transfers would be electronic and the bill of lading would be released only to the ultimate transferee. But this system did not gain acceptance. In 1990 the CMI issued Rules for an Electronic Bill of Lading (CMI Rules). These dispense with paper-based bills altogether and so no longer conform with international shipping conventions which predicate a document and a signature. Nevertheless they have been found useful in a variety of ways. A later development, which may in part have taken its inspiration from SeaDocs but has proved rather more successful is Bolero.net. This system, described below, also involves the issue of an electronic bill of lading, distinguishing it from SeaDocs, but in addition provides a Title Registry function not dissimilar to that of SeaDocs.

Probably not a true bill of lading

The CMI Rules serve some but not all of these functions. In particular, the provisions on transfer are based on the notion of attornment by the carrier to each new holder of the electronic bill.[90] It is therefore probable that the CMI bill of lading is neither a document of title nor a true bill of lading within the Hague and Hague-Visby Rules, which will thus be inapplicable unless incorporated into the contract of carriage by a clause paramount.

Binding agreement on writing equivalence

Yet there are many efficiencies. By adopting the CMI Rules, the parties agree *inter se* that all requirements for written and signed documents are satisfied by the transmitted and confirmed electronic data.[91] The parties further agree to waive any defences based on the absence of paper documents.[92] These agreements would not override mandatory rules under the *lex fori* that may require signature and prevent electronic signature, although the spread of mercantile legal concepts (including those related to electronic commerce noted in this chapter) have reduced the number of jurisdictions in which issues of this type would arise. Such agreements permit use of the advanced electronic contracting techniques,[93] which lower transaction costs.

6. The Bolero Bill of Lading

The Bolero[94] project was established as a joint venture by the Through Transport Mutual Insurance Association (the TT Club) and the Society for Worldwide Inter Bank Financial Telecommunications (SWIFT) and represents part of the Bolero.net

---

[90] Articles 7 and 9. [91] Article 11. [92] Ibid.
[93] Such as use of electronic data interchange (EDI) and public key infrastructure (PKI) technology. See Art 2–5, 7, and 9.
[94] An acronym for the Bill of Lading Electronic Registration Organization.

system, operated through the joint venture company Bolero International Limited. The Bolero bill of lading is a bill of lading sent by the carrier in electronic form, and authenticated by a digital signature, to the Bolero Title Registry. The message must identify the holder to whom the bill of lading is issued and designate an order party or consignee or contain an endorsement in blank. Each holder gives instructions to the Registry electronically using public-private encryption keys. The bill of lading is transferred by instructions to the Registry and attornment of the Registry[95] to the new holder. Each transfer results in a novation, the transferee replacing the transferor as party to the contract of carriage with the carrier. On arrival of the goods the final holder of the bill of lading instructs the Registry to surrender the bill of lading and issues a delivery order to the carrier.

Those wishing to use the Bolero system must first become members of the Bolero Association. Each member agrees to appoint Bolero Association Limited (BAL) as its agent to conclude contracts with other users. All users also agree to abide by the Bolero Rule Book governing use of the system, and in so doing bind themselves not to challenge the validity of Bolero messages and digital signatures. Whether an electronic bill of lading satisfies the requirements of the Hague and Hague-Visby Rules is doubtful, but users of the Bolero system can make effective contracts under the Bolero rules governing relations between themselves and their transferees.

7. The eUCP

A further initiative is the publication by the International Chamber of Commerce of rules supplementing the Uniform Customs and Practice for Documentary Credits so as to govern the electronic presentation of documents under a documentary credit.[96]

---

[95] By acknowledgment to the new holder that the Registry now holds the bill of lading for that holder.   [96] See p. 337 and, for the text of the eUCP, p. 379.

B. Instruments

(i) UNITED NATIONS COMMISSION ON INTERNATIONAL TRADE LAW
MODEL LAW ON ELECTRONIC COMMERCE WITH GUIDE TO ENACTMENT
1996*
with additional article 5 bis as adopted in 1998

RESOLUTION ADOPTED BY THE GENERAL ASSEMBLY

[on the report of the Sixth Committee (A/51/628)]
51/162 Model Law on Electronic Commerce Adopted by the United Nations Commission on International Trade Law

The General Assembly,

Recalling its resolution 2205 (XXI) of 17 December 1966, by which it created the United Nations Commission on International Trade Law, with a mandate to further the progressive harmonization and unification of the law of international trade and in that

---

* Reproduced with the kind permission of UNCITRAL.

respect to bear in mind the interests of all peoples, in particular those of developing countries, in the extensive development of international trade,

Noting that an increasing number of transactions in international trade are carried out by means of electronic data interchange and other means of communication, commonly referred to as 'electronic commerce', which involve the use of alternatives to paper-based methods of communication and storage of information,

Recalling the recommendation on the legal value of computer records adopted by the Commission at its eighteenth session, in 1985, and paragraph 5(b) of General Assembly resolution 40/71 of 11 December 1985, in which the Assembly called upon Governments and international organizations to take action, where appropriate, in conformity with the recommendation of the Commission, so as to ensure legal security in the context of the widest possible use of automated data processing in international trade,

Convinced that the establishment of a model law facilitating the use of electronic commerce that is acceptable to States with different legal, social and economic systems, could contribute significantly to the development of harmonious international economic relations,

Noting that the Model Law on Electronic Commerce was adopted by the Commission at its twenty-ninth session after consideration of the observations of Governments and interested organizations,

Believing that the adoption of the Model Law on Electronic Commerce by the Commission will assist all States significantly in enhancing their legislation governing the use of alternatives to paper-based methods of communication and storage of information and in formulating such legislation where none currently exists,

1. *Expresses* its appreciation to the United Nations Commission on International Trade Law for completing and adopting the Model Law on Electronic Commerce contained in the annex to the present resolution and for preparing the Guide to Enactment of the Model Law;
2. *Recommends* that all States give favourable consideration to the Model Law when they enact or revise their laws, in view of the need for uniformity of the law applicable to alternatives to paper-based methods of communication and storage of information;
3. *Recommends* also that all efforts be made to ensure that the Model Law, together with the Guide, become generally known and available.

85th plenary meeting
16 December 1996

145

PART ONE
ELECTRONIC COMMERCE IN GENERAL

CHAPTER I
GENERAL PROVISIONS

Article 1
Sphere of application *

This Law** applies to any kind of information in the form of a data message used in the context***of commercial**** activities.

Article 2
Definitions

For the purposes of this Law:

(a) 'Data message' means information generated, sent, received or stored by electronic, optical or similar means including, but not limited to, electronic data interchange (EDI), electronic mail, telegram, telex or telecopy;

(b) 'Electronic data interchange (EDI)' means the electronic transfer from computer to computer of information using an agreed standard to structure the information;

(c) 'Originator' of a data message means a person by whom, or on whose behalf, the data message purports to have been sent or generated prior to storage, if any, but it does not include a person acting as an intermediary with respect to that data message;

(d) 'Addressee' of a data message means a person who is intended by the originator to receive the data message, but does not include a person acting as an intermediary with respect to that data message;

(e) 'Intermediary', with respect to a particular data message, means a person who, on behalf of another person, sends, receives or stores that data message or provides other services with respect to that data message;

(f) 'Information system' means a system for generating, sending, receiving, storing or otherwise processing data messages.

---

* The Commission suggests the following text for States that might wish to limit the applicability of this Law to international data messages: 'This Law applies to a data message as defined in paragraph (1) of article 2 where the data message relates to international commerce.'

** This Law does not override any rule of law intended for the protection of consumers.

*** The Commission suggests the following text for States that might wish to extend the applicability of this Law: 'This Law applies to any kind of information in the form of a data message, except in the following situations: [. . .].'

**** The term 'commercial' should be given a wide interpretation so as to cover matters arising from all relationships of a commercial nature, whether contractual or not. Relationships of a commercial nature include, but are not limited to, the following transactions: any trade transaction for the supply or exchange of goods or services; distribution agreement; commercial representation or agency; factoring; leasing; construction of works; consulting; engineering; licensing; investment; financing; banking; insurance; exploitation agreement or concession; joint venture and other forms of industrial or business cooperation; carriage of goods or passengers by air, sea, rail or road.

Article 3
Interpretation

(1) In the interpretation of this Law, regard is to be had to its international origin and to the need to promote uniformity in its application and the observance of good faith.

(2) Questions concerning matters governed by this Law which are not expressly settled in it are to be settled in conformity with the general principles on which this Law is based.

Article 4
Variation by agreement

(1) As between parties involved in generating, sending, receiving, storing or otherwise processing data messages, and except as otherwise provided, the provisions of chapter III may be varied by agreement.

(2) Paragraph (1) does not affect any right that may exist to modify by agreement any rule of law referred to in chapter II.

CHAPTER II
APPLICATION OF LEGAL REQUIREMENTS TO DATA MESSAGES

Article 5
Legal recognition of data messages

Information shall not be denied legal effect, validity or enforceability solely on the grounds that it is in the form of a data message.

Article 5
bis Incorporation by reference
(as adopted by the Commission at its thirty-first session, in June 1998)

Information shall not be denied legal effect, validity or enforceability solely on the grounds that it is not contained in the data message purporting to give rise to such legal effect, but is merely referred to in that data message.

Article 6
Writing

(1) Where the law requires information to be in writing, that requirement is met by a data message if the information contained therein is accessible so as to be usable for subsequent reference.

(2) Paragraph (1) applies whether the requirement therein is in the form of an obligation or whether the law simply provides consequences for the information not being in writing.

(3) The provisions of this article do not apply to the following: [. . .].

Article 7
Signature

(1) Where the law requires a signature of a person, that requirement is met in relation to a data message if:

    (a) a method is used to identify that person and to indicate that person's approval of the information contained in the data message; and

    (b) that method is as reliable as was appropriate for the purpose for which the data message was generated or communicated, in the light of all the circumstances, including any relevant agreement.

(2) Paragraph (1) applies whether the requirement therein is in the form of an obligation or whether the law simply provides consequences for the absence of a signature.

(3) The provisions of this article do not apply to the following: [. . .].

Article 8
Original

(1) Where the law requires information to be presented or retained in its original form, that requirement is met by a data message if:

    (a) there exists a reliable assurance as to the integrity of the information from the time when it was first generated in its final form, as a data message or otherwise; and

    (b) where it is required that information be presented, that information is capable of being displayed to the person to whom it is to be presented.

(2) Paragraph (1) applies whether the requirement therein is in the form of an obligation or whether the law simply provides consequences for the information not being presented or retained in its original form.

(3) For the purposes of subparagraph (a) of paragraph (1):

    (a) the criteria for assessing integrity shall be whether the information has remained complete and unaltered, apart from the addition of any endorsement and any change which arises in the normal course of communication, storage and display; and

    (b) the standard of reliability required shall be assessed in the light of the purpose for which the information was generated and in the light of all the relevant circumstances.

(4) The provisions of this article do not apply to the following: [. . .].

Article 9
Admissibility and evidential weight of data messages

(1) In any legal proceedings, nothing in the application of the rules of evidence shall apply so as to deny the admissibility of a data message in evidence:

    (a) on the sole ground that it is a data message; or,

    (b) if it is the best evidence that the person adducing it could reasonably be expected to obtain, on the grounds that it is not in its original form.

(2) Information in the form of a data message shall be given due evidential weight. In assessing the evidential weight of a data message, regard shall be had to the reliability of the manner in which the data message was generated, stored or communicated, to the reliability of the manner in which the integrity of the information was maintained, to the manner in which its originator was identified, and to any other relevant factor.

Article 10
Retention of data messages

(1) Where the law requires that certain documents, records or information be retained, that requirement is met by retaining data messages, provided that the following conditions are satisfied:

    (a) the information contained therein is accessible so as to be usable for subsequent reference; and

    (b) the data message is retained in the format in which it was generated, sent or received, or in a format which can be demonstrated to represent accurately the information generated, sent or received; and

    (c) such information, if any, is retained as enables the identification of the origin and destination of a data message and the date and time when it was sent or received.

(2) An obligation to retain documents, records or information in accordance with paragraph (1) does not extend to any information the sole purpose of which is to enable the message to be sent or received.

(3) A person may satisfy the requirement referred to in paragraph (1) by using the services of any other person, provided that the conditions set forth in subparagraphs (a), (b) and (c) of paragraph (1) are met.

CHAPTER III
COMMUNICATION OF DATA MESSAGES

Article 11
Formation and validity of contracts

(1) In the context of contract formation, unless otherwise agreed by the parties, an offer and the acceptance of an offer may be expressed by means of data messages. Where a data message is used in the formation of a contract, that contract shall not be denied validity or enforceability on the sole ground that a data message was used for that purpose.

(2) The provisions of this article do not apply to the following: [. . .].

Article 12
Recognition by parties of data messages

(1) As between the originator and the addressee of a data message, a declaration of will or other statement shall not be denied legal effect, validity or enforceability solely on the grounds that it is in the form of a data message.

(2) The provisions of this article do not apply to the following: [. . .].

Article 13
Attribution of data messages

(1) A data message is that of the originator if it was sent by the originator itself.

(2) As between the originator and the addressee, a data message is deemed to be that of the originator if it was sent:

    (a) by a person who had the authority to act on behalf of the originator in respect of that data message; or

    (b) by an information system programmed by, or on behalf of, the originator to operate automatically.

(3) As between the originator and the addressee, an addressee is entitled to regard a data message as being that of the originator, and to act on that assumption, if:

   (a) in order to as certain whether the data message was that of the originator, the addressee properly applied a procedure previously agreed to by the originator for that purpose; or

   (b) the data message as received by the addressee resulted from the actions of a person whose relationship with the originator or with any agent of the originator enabled that person to gain access to a method used by the originator to identify data messages as its own.

(4) Paragraph (3) does not apply:

   (a) as of the time when the addressee has both received notice from the originator that the data message is not that of the originator, and had reasonable time to act accordingly; or

   (b) in a case within paragraph (3)(b), at any time when the addressee knew or should have known, had it exercised reasonable care or used any agreed procedure, that the data message was not that of the originator.

(5) Where a data message is that of the originator or is deemed to be that of the originator, or the addressee is entitled to act on that assumption, then, as between the originator and the addressee, the addressee is entitled to regard the data message as received as being what the originator intended to send, and to act on that assumption. The addressee is not so entitled when it knew or should have known, had it exercised reasonable care or used any agreed procedure, that the transmission resulted in any error in the data message as received.

(6) The addressee is entitled to regard each data message received as a separate data message and to act on that assumption, except to the extent that it duplicates another data message and the addressee knew or should have known, had it exercised reasonable care or used any agreed procedure, that the data message was a duplicate.

Article 14
Acknowledgement of receipt

(1) Paragraphs (2) to (4) of this article apply where, on or before sending a data message, or by means of that data message, the originator has requested or has agreed with the addressee that receipt of the data message be acknowledged.

(2) Where the originator has not agreed with the addressee that the acknowledgement be given in a particular form or by a particular method, an acknowledgement may be given by

   (a) any communication by the addressee, automated or otherwise, or

   (b) any conduct of the addressee,

sufficient to indicate to the originator that the data message has been received.

(3) Where the originator has stated that the data message is conditional on receipt of the acknowledgement, the data message is treated as though it has never been sent, until the acknowledgement is received.

(4) Where the originator has not stated that the data message is conditional on receipt of the acknowledgement, and the acknowledgement has not been received by the originator within the time specified or agreed or, if no time has been specified or agreed, within a reasonable time, the originator:

(a) may give notice to the addressee stating that no acknowledgement has been received and specifying a reasonable time by which the acknowledgement must be received; and

(b) if the acknowledgement is not received within the time specified in subparagraph (a), may, upon notice to the addressee, treat the data message as though it had never been sent, or exercise any other rights it may have.

(5) Where the originator receives the addressee's acknowledgement of receipt, it is presumed that the related data message was received by the addressee. That presumption does not imply that the data message corresponds to the message received.

(6) Where the received acknowledgement states that the related data message met technical requirements, either agreed upon or set forth in applicable standards, it is presumed that those requirements have been met.

(7) Except in so far as it relates to the sending or receipt of the data message, this article is not intended to deal with the legal consequences that may flow either from that data message or from the acknowledgement of its receipt.

Article 15
Time and place of dispatch and receipt of data messages

(1) Unless otherwise agreed between the originator and the addressee, the dispatch of a data message occurs when it enters an information system outside the control of the originator or of the person who sent the data message on behalf of the originator.

(2) Unless otherwise agreed between the originator and the addressee, the time of receipt of a data message is determined as follows:

(a) if the addressee has designated an information system for the purpose of receiving data messages, receipt occurs:

(i)   at the time when the data message enters the designated information system; or

(ii) if the data message is sent to an information system of the addressee that is not the designated information system, at the time when the data message is retrieved by the addressee;

(b) if the addressee has not designated an information system, receipt occurs when the data message enters an information system of the addressee.

(3) Paragraph (2) applies notwithstanding that the place where the information system is located may be different from the place where the data message is deemed to be received under paragraph (4).

(4) Unless otherwise agreed between the originator and the addressee, a data message is deemed to be dispatched at the place where the originator has its place of business, and is deemed to be received at the place where the addressee has its place of business. For the purposes of this paragraph:

(a) if the originator or the addressee has more than one place of business, the place of business is that which has the closest relationship to the underlying transaction or, where there is no underlying transaction, the principal place of business;

(b) if the originator or the addressee does not have a place of business, reference is to be made to its habitual residence.

(5) The provisions of this article do not apply to the following: [. . .].

PART TWO
ELECTRONIC COMMERCE IN SPECIFIC AREAS

CHAPTER I
CARRIAGE OF GOODS

Article 16
Actions related to contracts of carriage of goods

Without derogating from the provisions of part one of this Law, this chapter applies to any action in connection with, or in pursuance of, a contract of carriage of goods, including but not limited to:

(a) (i)   furnishing the marks, number, quantity or weight of goods;
    (ii) stating or declaring the nature or value of goods;
    (iii) issuing a receipt for goods;
    (iv) confirming that goods have been loaded;

(b) (i)   notifying a person of terms and conditions of the contract;
    (ii) giving instructions to a carrier;

(c) (i)   claiming delivery of goods;
    (ii) authorizing release of goods;
    (iii) giving notice of loss of, or damage to, goods;

(d) giving any other notice or statement in connection with the performance of the contract;

(e) undertaking to deliver goods to a named person or a person authorized to claim delivery;

(f) granting, acquiring, renouncing, surrendering, transferring or negotiating rights in goods;

(g) acquiring or transferring rights and obligations under the contract.

Article 17
Transport documents

(1) Subject to paragraph (3), where the law requires that any action referred to in article 16 be carried out in writing or by using a paper document, that requirement is met if the action is carried out by using one or more data messages.

(2) Paragraph (1) applies whether the requirement therein is in the form of an obligation or whether the law simply provides consequences for failing either to carry out the action in writing or to use a paper document.

(3) If a right is to be granted to, or an obligation is to be acquired by, one person and no other person, and if the law requires that, in order to effect this, the right or obligation must be conveyed to that person by the transfer, or use of, a paper document, that requirement is met if the right or obligation is conveyed by using one or more data messages, provided that a reliable method is used to render such data message or messages unique.

(4) For the purposes of paragraph (3), the standard of reliability required shall be assessed in the light of the purpose for which the right or obligation was conveyed and in the light of all the circumstances, including any relevant agreement.

(5) Where one or more data messages are used to effect any action in subparagraphs (f) and (g) of article 16, no paper document used to effect any such action is valid unless the use of data messages has been terminated and replaced by the use of paper documents. A paper document issued in these circumstances shall contain a statement of such termination. The replacement of data messages by paper documents shall not affect the rights or obligations of the parties involved.

(6) If a rule of law is compulsorily applicable to a contract of carriage of goods which is in, or is evidenced by, a paper document, that rule shall not be inapplicable to such a contract of carriage of goods which is evidenced by one or more data messages by reason of the fact that the contract is evidenced by such data message or messages instead of by a paper document.

(7) The provisions of this article do not apply to the following: [. . .].

LEGISLATION IMPLEMENTING THE MODEL LAW

Legislation implementing provisions of the Model Law has been adopted in:

1998	1999	2000	2001	2002
Singapore	Australia	France	Panama	Dominican Republic
			Jordan	Ecuador
	Bermuda	India*	Venezuela	New Zealand
	Colombia	Ireland		Pakistan
	Republic of Korea	Mexico		Thailand
		Philippines		South Africa*
		Slovenia		
		Mauritius		

* Except for the provisions on certification and electronic signatures.

The Model Law has also been adopted in:

1998	1999	2000	2001	2002
	Bermuda	Bailiwick of Guernsey		
		Bailiwick of Jersey		
		Cayman Islands		
		Isle of Man		
		All Crown Dependencies of the		
		United Kingdom of Great		
		Britain and Northern Ireland		
		Turks and Caicos Islands		
		Overseas territories of the		
		United Kingdom of Great		
		Britain and Northern Ireland		
		Hong Kong Special		
		Administrative Region of China		

Uniform legislation influenced by the Model Law and the principles on which it is based has been prepared in the United States (Uniform Electronic Transactions Act, adopted in

1999 by the National Conference of Commissioners on Uniform State Law) and enacted by the States of:

1999	2000	2001	2002	2003
California	Arizona	Alabama	Colorado	Missouri
Pennsylvania	Delaware	Arkansas	Connecticut	Vermont
	Florida	Louisiana		
	Hawaii	Mississippi		
	Idaho	Montana		
	Indiana	Nevada		
	Iowa	New Hampshire		
	Kansas	New Mexico		
	Kentucky	North Dakota		
	Maine	Oregon		
	Maryland	Tennessee		
	Michigan	Texas		
	Minnesota	West Virginia		
	Nebraska	Wyoming		
	New Jersey	District of Columbia		
	North Carolina			
	Ohio			
	Oklahoma			
	Rhode Island			
	South Dakota			
	Utah			
	Virginia			

The State of Illinois had already enacted the Model Law in 1998.

Uniform legislation influenced by the Model Law and the principles on which it is based has also been prepared in Canada (Uniform Electronic Commerce Act, adopted in 1999 by the Uniform Law Conference of Canada) and enacted in a number of Provinces and Territories, including:

1999	2000	2001	2002	2003
	Manitoba	British Columbia		
	Nova Scotia	New Brunswick		
	Saskatchewan	Newfoundland and Labrador		
	Yukon	Ontario		
		Prince Edward Island		

Legislation influenced by the Model Law and the principles on which it is based has also been adopted in the Province of Quebec (2001).

(ii) UNCITRAL MODEL LAW ON ELECTRONIC SIGNATURES (2001)*

RESOLUTION ADOPTED BY THE GENERAL ASSEMBLY

[on the report of the Sixth Committee (A/56/588)]
56/80 Model Law on Electronic Signatures
adopted by the United Nations Commission on International
Trade Law The General Assembly]

Recalling its resolution 2205 (XXI) of 17 December 1966, by which it established the United Nations Commission on International Trade Law, with a mandate to further the progressive harmonization and unification of the law of international trade and in that respect to bear in mind the interests of all peoples, and particularly those of developing countries, in the extensive development of international trade,

Noting that an increasing number of transactions in international trade are carried out by means of communication commonly referred to as electronic commerce, which involves the use of alternatives to paper-based forms of communication, storage and authentication of information,

Recalling the recommendation on the legal value of computer records adopted by the Commission at its eighteenth session, in 1985, and paragraph 5(b) of General Assembly resolution 40/71 of 11 December 1985, in which the Assembly called upon Governments and international organizations to take action, where appropriate, in conformity with the recommendation of the Commission,[1] so as to ensure legal security in the context of the widest possible use of automated data processing in international trade,

Recalling also the Model Law on Electronic Commerce adopted by the Commission at its twenty-ninth session, in 1996,[2] complemented by an additional article 5 bis adopted by

---

* Reproduced with the kind permission of UNCITRAL.
[1] *Official Records of the General Assembly, Fortieth Session, Supplement No. 17(A/40/17)*, Ch VI, sect. B.
[2] Ibid., Fifty-first Session, Supplement No. 17 (A/51/17), para 209.

the Commission at its thirty-first session, in 1998,[3] and paragraph 2 of General Assembly resolution 51/162 of 16 December 1996, in which the Assembly recommended that all States should give favourable consideration to the Model Law when enacting or revising their laws, in view of the need for uniformity of the law applicable to alternatives to paper-based methods of communication and storage of information,

Convinced that the Model Law on Electronic Commerce is of significant assistance to States in enabling or facilitating the use of electronic commerce, as demonstrated by the enactment of that Model Law in a number of countries and its universal recognition as an essential reference in the field of electronic commerce legislation,

Mindful of the great utility of new technologies used for personal identification in electronic commerce and commonly referred to as electronic signatures,

Desiring to build on the fundamental principles underlying article 7 of the Model Law on Electronic Commerce[4] with respect to the fulfillment of the signature function in an electronic environment, with a view to promoting reliance on electronic signatures for producing legal effect where such electronic signatures are functionally equivalent to handwritten signatures,

Convinced that legal certainty in electronic commerce will be enhanced by the harmonization of certain rules on the legal recognition of electronic signatures on a technologically neutral basis and by the establishment of a method to assess in a technologically neutral manner the practical reliability and the commercial adequacy of electronic signature techniques,

Believing that the Model Law on Electronic Signatures will constitute a useful addition to the Model Law on Electronic Commerce and significantly assist States in enhancing their legislation governing the use of modem authentication techniques and in formulating such legislation where none currently exists,

Being of the opinion that the establishment of model legislation to facilitate the use of electronic signatures in a manner acceptable to States with different legal, social and economic systems could contribute to the development of harmonious international economic relations,

1. *Expresses its appreciation* to the United Nations Commission on International Trade Law for completing and adopting the Model Law on Electronic Signatures contained in the annex to the present resolution, and for preparing the Guide to Enactment of the Model Law;

2. *Recommends* that all States give favourable consideration to the Model Law on Electronic Signatures, together with the Model Law on Electronic Commerce adopted in 1996 and complemented in 1998, when they enact or revise their laws, in view of the need for uniformity of the law applicable to alternatives to paper-based forms of communication, storage and authentication of information;

3. *Recommends* also that all efforts be made to ensure that the Model Law on Electronic Commerce and the Model Law on Electronic Signatures, together with their respective Guides to Enactment, become generally known and available.

---

[3] *Official Records of the General Assembly, Fortieth Session, Supplement No. 17 (A/40/17)*, Ch III, sect. B, Fifty-third Session, Supplement No. 17 (A/53/17), Ch III, B.

[4] General Assembly resolution 51/162, annex.

Article 1
Sphere of application

This Law applies where electronic signatures are used in the context* of commercial** activities. It does not override any rule of law intended for the protection of consumers.

Article 2
Definitions

For the purposes of this Law:
    (a) 'Electronic signature' means data in electronic form in, affixed to or logically associated with, a data message, which may be used to identify the signatory in relation to the data message and to indicate the signatory's approval of the information contained in the data message;

    (b) 'Certificate' means a data message or other record confirming the link between a signatory and signature creation data;

    (c) 'Data message' means information generated, sent, received or stored by electronic, optical or similar means including, but not limited to, electronic data interchange (EDI), electronic mail, telegram, telex or telecopy; and acts either on its own behalf or on behalf of the person it represents;

    (d) 'Signatory' means a person that holds signature creation data and acts either on its own behalf or on behalf of the person it represents;

    (e) 'Certification service provider' means a person that issues certificates and may provide other services related to electronic signatures;

    (f) 'Relying party' means a person that may act on the basis of a certificate or an electronic signature.

Article 3
Equal treatment of signature technologies

Nothing in this Law, except article 5, shall be applied so as to exclude, restrict or deprive of legal effect any method of creating an electronic signature that satisfies the requirements referred to in article 6, paragraph 1, or otherwise meets the requirements of applicable law.

Article 4
Interpretation

1. In the interpretation of this Law, regard is to be had to its international origin and to the need to promote uniformity in its application and the observance of good faith.

---

    * The Commission suggests the following text for States that might wish to extend the applicability of this Law: 'This Law applies where electronic signatures are used, except in the following situations: [. . .],'.

    ** The term 'commercial' should be given a wide interpretation so as to cover matters arising from all relationships of a commercial nature, whether contractual or not. Relationships of a commercial nature include, but are not limited to, the following transactions: any trade transaction for the supply or exchange of goods or services; distribution agreement; commercial representation or agency; factoring; leasing; construction of works; consulting; engineering; licensing; investment; financing; banking; insurance; exploitation agreement or concession; joint venture and other forms of industrial or business cooperation; carriage of goods or passengers by air, sea, rail or road.

2. Questions concerning matters governed by this Law which are not expressly settled in it are to be settled in conformity with the general principles on which this Law is based.

Article 5
Variation by agreement

The provisions of this Law may be derogated from or their effect may be varied by agreement, unless that agreement would not be valid or effective under applicable law.

Article 6
Compliance with a requirement for a signature

1. Where the law requires a signature of a person, that requirement is met in relation to a data message if an electronic signature is used that is as reliable as was appropriate for the purpose for which the data message was generated or communicated, in the light of all the circumstances, including any relevant agreement.
2. Paragraph 1 applies whether the requirement referred to therein is in the form of an obligation or whether the law simply provides consequences for the absence of a signature.
3. An electronic signature is considered to be reliable for the purpose of satisfying the requirement referred to in paragraph 1 if:
   (a) The signature creation data are, within the context in which they are used, linked to the signatory and to no other person;
   (b) The signature creation data were, at the time of signing, under the control of the signatory and of no other person;
   (c) Any alteration to the electronic signature, made after the time of signing, is detectable; and
   (d) Where a purpose of the legal requirement for a signature is to provide assurance as to the integrity of the information to which it relates, any alteration made to that information after the time of signing is detectable.
4. Paragraph 3 does not limit the ability of any person:
   (a) To establish in any other way, for the purpose of satisfying the requirement referred to in paragraph 1, the reliability of an electronic signature; or
   (b) To adduce evidence of the non-reliability of an electronic signature.
5. The provisions of this article do not apply to the following: [. . .].

Article 7
Satisfaction of article 6

1. [*Any person, organ or authority, whether public or private, specified by the enacting State as competent*] may determine which electronic signatures satisfy the provisions of article 6 of this Law.
2. Any determination made under paragraph 1 shall be consistent with recognized international standards.
3. Nothing in this article affects the operation of the rules of private international law.

Article 8
Conduct of the signatory

1. Where signature creation data can be used to create a signature that has legal effect, each signatory shall:

   (a) Exercise reasonable care to avoid unauthorized use of its signature creation data;

   (b) Without undue delay, utilize means made available by the certification service provider pursuant to article 9 of this Law, or otherwise use reasonable efforts, to notify any person that may reasonably be expected by the signatory to rely on or to provide services in support of the electronic signature if:

      (i) The signatory knows that the signature creation data have been compromised; or

      (ii) The circumstances known to the signatory give rise to a substantial risk that the signature creation data may have been compromised;

   (c) Where a certificate is used to support the electronic signature, exercise reasonable care to ensure the accuracy and completeness of all material representations made by the signatory that are relevant to the certificate throughout its life cycle or that are to be included in the certificate.

2. A signatory shall bear the legal consequences of its failure to satisfy the requirements of paragraph 1.

Article 9
Conduct of the certification service provider

1. Where a certification service provider provides services to support an electronic signature that may be used for legal effect as a signature, that certification service provider shall:

   (a) Act in accordance with representations made by it with respect to its policies and practices;

   (b) Exercise reasonable care to ensure the accuracy and completeness of all material representations made by it that are relevant to the certificate throughout its life cycle or that are included in the certificate;

   (c) Provide reasonably accessible means that enable a relying party to ascertain from the certificate:

      (i) The identity of the certification service provider;

      (ii) That the signatory that is identified in the certificate had control of the signature creation data at the time when the certificate was issued;

      (iii) That signature creation data were valid at or before the time when the certificate was issued;

   (d) Provide reasonably accessible means that enable a relying party to ascertain, where relevant, from the certificate or otherwise:

      (i) The method used to identify the signatory;

      (ii) Any limitation on the purpose or value for which the signature creation data or the certificate may be used;

      (iii) That the signature creation data are valid and have not been compromised;

      (iv) Any limitation on the scope or extent of liability stipulated by the certification service provider;

    (v) Whether means exist for the signatory to give notice pursuant to article 8, paragraph 1 (b), of this Law;

    (vi) Whether a timely revocation service is offered;

  (e) Where services under subparagraph (d) (v) are offered, provide a means for a signatory to give notice pursuant to article 8, paragraph 1 (b), of this Law and, where services under subparagraph (d) (vi) are offered, ensure the availability of a timely revocation service;

  (f) Utilize trustworthy systems, procedures and human resources in performing its services.

2. A certification service provider shall bear the legal consequences of its failure to satisfy the requirements of paragraph 1.

Article 10
Trustworthiness

For the purposes of article 9, paragraph 1 (f), of this Law in determining whether, or to what extent, any systems, procedures and human resources utilized by a certification service provider are trustworthy, regard may be had to the following factors:

(a) Financial and human resources, including existence of assets;

(b) Quality of hardware and software systems;

(c) Procedures for processing of certificates and applications for certificates and retention of records;

(d) Availability of information to signatories identified in certificates and to potential relying parties;

(e) Regularity and extent of audit by an independent body;

(f) The existence of a declaration by the State, an accreditation body or the certification service provider regarding compliance with or existence of the foregoing; or

(g) Any other relevant factor.

Article 11
Conduct of the relying party

A relying party shall bear the legal consequences of its failure:

  (a) To take reasonable steps to verify the reliability of an electronic signature; or

  (b) Where an electronic signature is supported by a certificate, to take reasonable steps:

    (i) To verify the validity, suspension or revocation of the certificate; and

    (ii) To observe any limitation with respect to the certificate.

Article 12
Recognition of foreign certificates and electronic signatures

1. In determining whether, or to what extent, a certificate or an electronic signature is legally effective, no regard shall be had:

  (a) To the geographic location where the certificate is issued or the electronic signature created or used; or

  (b) To the geographic location of the place of business of the issuer or signatory.

2. A certificate issued outside *[the enacting State]* shall have the same legal effect in *[the enacting State]* as a certificate issued in *[the enacting State]* if it offers a substantially equivalent level of reliability.

3. An electronic signature created or used outside *[the enacting State]* shall have the same legal effect in *[the enacting State]* as an electronic signature created or used in *[the enacting State]* if it offers a substantially equivalent level of reliability.

4. In determining whether a certificate or an electronic signature offers a substantially equivalent level of reliability for the purposes of paragraph 2 or 3, regard shall be had to recognized international standards and to any other relevant factors.

5. Where, notwithstanding paragraphs 2, 3 and 4, parties agree, as between themselves, to the use of certain types of electronic signatures or certificates, that agreement shall be recognized as sufficient for the purposes of cross-border recognition, unless that agreement would not be valid or effective under applicable law.

LEGISLATION IMPLEMENTING THE MODEL LAW

Legislation based on the UNCITRAL Model Law on Electronic Signatures has been adopted in Thailand and Mexico (2003).

(iii) DIRECTIVE 2000/1/EC OF THE EUROPEAN PARLIAMENT AND OF THE COUNCIL OF 8 JUNE 2000 ON CERTAIN LEGAL ASPECTS OF INFORMATION SOCIETY SERVICES, IN PARTICULAR ELECTRONIC COMMERCE, IN THE INTERNAL MARKET (DIRECTIVE ON ELECTRONIC COMMERCE)

PREAMBLE

THE EUROPEAN PARLIAMENT AND THE COUNCIL OF THE EUROPEAN UNION,

Having regard to the Treaty establishing the European Community, and in particular Articles 47(2), 55 and 95 thereof,

Having regard to the proposal from the Commission,[1]

Having regard to the opinion of the Economic and Social Committee,[2]

---

[1] OJ C 30, 5.2.1999, p. 4.   [2] OJ C 169, 16.6.1999, p. 36.

Acting in accordance with the procedure laid down in Article 251 of the Treaty,[3]

Whereas:

(1) The European Union is seeking to forge ever closer links between the States and peoples of Europe, to ensure economic and social progress; in accordance with Article 14(2) of the Treaty, the internal market comprises an area without internal frontiers in which the free movements of goods, services and the freedom of establishment are ensured; the development of information society services within the area without internal frontiers is vital to eliminating the barriers which divide the European peoples.

(2) The development of electronic commerce within the information society offers significant employment opportunities in the Community, particularly in small and medium-sized enterprises, and will stimulate economic growth and investment in innovation by European companies, and can also enhance the competitiveness of European industry, provided that everyone has access to the Internet.

(3) Community law and the characteristics of the Community legal order are a vital asset to enable European citizens and operators to take full advantage, without consideration of borders, of the opportunities afforded by electronic commerce; this Directive therefore has the purpose of ensuring a high level of Community legal integration in order to establish a real area without internal borders for information society services.

(4) It is important to ensure that electronic commerce could fully benefit from the internal market and therefore that, as with Council Directive 89/552/EEC of 3 October 1989 on the coordination of certain provisions laid down by law, regulation or administrative action in Member States concerning the pursuit of television broadcasting activities,[4] a high level of Community integration is achieved.

(5) The development of information society services within the Community is hampered by a number of legal obstacles to the proper functioning of the internal market which make less attractive the exercise of the freedom of establishment and the freedom to provide services; these obstacles arise from divergences in legislation and from the legal uncertainty as to which national rules apply to such services; in the absence of coordination and adjustment of legislation in the relevant areas, obstacles might be justified in the light of the case-law of the Court of Justice of the European Communities; legal uncertainty exists with regard to the extent to which Member States may control services originating from another Member State.

(6) In the light of Community objectives, of Articles 43 and 49 of the Treaty and of secondary Community law, these obstacles should be eliminated by coordinating certain national laws and by clarifying certain legal concepts at Community level to the extent necessary for the proper functioning of the internal market; by dealing only with certain specific matters which give rise to problems for the internal market, this Directive is fully consistent with the need to respect the principle of subsidiarity as set out in Article 5 of the Treaty.

---

[3] Opinion of the European Parliament of 6 May 1999 (OJ C 279, 1.10.1999, p. 389), Council common position of 28 February 2000 (OJ C 128, 8.5.2000, p. 32) and Decision of the European Parliament of 4 May 2000 (not yet published in the Official Journal).

[4] OJ L 298, 17.10.1989, p. 23. Directive as amended by Directive 97/36/EC of the European Parliament and of the Council (OJ L 202, 30.7.1997, p. 60).

(7)   In order to ensure legal certainty and consumer confidence, this Directive must lay down a clear and general framework to cover certain legal aspects of electronic commerce in the internal market.

(8)   The objective of this Directive is to create a legal framework to ensure the free movement of information society services between Member States and not to harmonise the field of criminal law as such.

(9)   The free movement of information society services can in many cases be a specific reflection in Community law of a more general principle, namely freedom of expression as enshrined in Article 10(1) of the Convention for the Protection of Human Rights and Fundamental Freedoms, which has been ratified by all the Member States; for this reason, directives covering the supply of information society services must ensure that this activity may be engaged in freely in the light of that Article, subject only to the restrictions laid down in paragraph 2 of that Article and in Article 46(1) of the Treaty; this Directive is not intended to affect national fundamental rules and principles relating to freedom of expression.

(10)   In accordance with the principle of proportionality, the measures provided for in this Directive are strictly limited to the minimum needed to achieve the objective of the proper functioning of the internal market; where action at Community level is necessary, and in order to guarantee an area which is truly without internal frontiers as far as electronic commerce is concerned, the Directive must ensure a high level of protection of objectives of general interest, in particular the protection of minors and human dignity, consumer protection and the protection of public health; according to Article 152 of the Treaty, the protection of public health is an essential component of other Community policies.

(11)   This Directive is without prejudice to the level of protection for, in particular, public health and consumer interests, as established by Community acts; amongst others, Council Directive 93/13/EEC of 5 April 1993 on unfair terms in consumer contracts[5] and Directive 97/7/EC of the European Parliament and of the Council of 20 May 1997 on the protection of consumers in respect of distance contracts[6] form a vital element for protecting consumers in contractual matters; those Directives also apply in their entirety to information society services; that same Community acquis, which is fully applicable to information society services, also embraces in particular Council Directive 84/450/EEC of 10 September 1984 concerning misleading and comparative advertising,[7] Council Directive 87/102/EEC of 22 December 1986 for the approximation of the laws, regulations and administrative provisions of the Member States concerning consumer credit,[8] Council Directive 93/22/EEC of 10 May 1993 on investment services in the securities field,[9] Council Directive 90/314/EEC of 13 June 1990 on package travel, package holidays and package tours,[10] Directive 98/6/EC of the European

---

[5] OJ L 95, 21.4.1993, p. 29.   [6] OJ L 144, 4.6.1999, p. 19.

[7] OJ L 250, 19.9.1984, p. 17. Directive as amended by Directive 97/55/EC of the European Parliament and of the Council (OJ L 290, 23.10.1997, p. 18).

[8] OJ L 42, 12.2.1987, p. 48. Directive as last amended by Directive 98/7/EC of the European Parliament and of the Council (OJ L 101, 1.4.1998, p. 17).

[9] OJ L 141, 11.6.1993, p. 27. Directive as last amended by Directive 97/9/EC of the European Parliament and of the Council (OJ L 84, 26.3.1997, p. 22).

[10] OJ L 158, 23.6.1990, p. 59.

Parliament and of the Council of 16 February 1998 on consumer production in the indication of prices of products offered to consumers,[11] Council Directive 92/59/ EEC of 29 June 1992 on general product safety,[12] Directive 94/47/EC of the European Parliament and of the Council of 26 October 1994 on the protection of purchasers in respect of certain aspects on contracts relating to the purchase of the right to use immovable properties on a timeshare basis,[13] Directive 98/27/EC of the European Parliament and of the Council of 19 May 1998 on injunctions for the protection of consumers' interests,[14] Council Directive 85/374/EEC of 25 July 1985 on the approximation of the laws, regulations and administrative provisions concerning liability for defective products,[15] Directive 1999/44/EC of the European Parliament and of the Council of 25 May 1999 on certain aspects of the sale of consumer goods and associated guarantees,[16] the future Directive of the European Parliament and of the Council concerning the distance marketing of consumer financial services and Council Directive 92/28/EEC of 31 March 1992 on the advertising of medicinal products;[17] this Directive should be without prejudice to Directive 98/43/EC of the European Parliament and of the Council of 6 July 1998 on the approximation of the laws, regulations and administrative provisions of the Member States relating to the advertising and sponsorship of tobacco products[18] adopted within the framework of the internal market, or to directives on the protection of public health; this Directive complements information requirements established by the abovementioned Directives and in particular Directive 97/7/EC.

(12) It is necessary to exclude certain activities from the scope of this Directive, on the grounds that the freedom to provide services in these fields cannot, at this stage, be guaranteed under the Treaty or existing secondary legislation; excluding these activities does not preclude any instruments which might prove necessary for the proper functioning of the internal market; taxation, particularly value added tax imposed on a large number of the services covered by this Directive, must be excluded form the scope of this Directive.

(13) This Directive does not aim to establish rules on fiscal obligations nor does it pre-empt the drawing up of Community instruments concerning fiscal aspects of electronic commerce.

(14) The protection of individuals with regard to the processing of personal data is solely governed by Directive 95/46/EC of the European Parliament and of the Council of 24 October 1995 on the protection of individuals with regard to the processing of personal data and on the free movement of such data[19] and Directive 97/66/EC of the European Parliament and of the Council of 15 December 1997 concerning the processing of personal data and the protection of privacy in the telecommunications sector[20] which are fully applicable to information society services; these Directives already establish a Community legal framework in the field of personal

---

[11] OJ L 80, 18.3.1998, p. 27.   [12] OJ L 228, 11.8.1992, p. 24.
[13] OJ L 280, 29.10.1994, p. 83.
[14] OJ L 166, 11.6.1998, p. 51. Directive as amended by Directive 1999/44/EC (OJ L 171, 7.7.1999, p. 12).
[15] OJ L 210, 7.8.1985, p. 29. Directive as amended by Directive 1999/34/EC (OJ L 141, 4.6.1999, p. 20).   [16] OJ L 171, 7.7.1999, p. 12.
[17] OJ L 113, 30.4.1992, p. 13.   [18] OJ L 213, 30.7.1998, p. 9.
[19] OJ L 281, 23.11.1995, p. 31.   [20] OJ L 24, 30.1.1998, p. 1.

data and therefore it is not necessary to cover this issue in this Directive in order to ensure the smooth functioning of the internal market, in particular the free movement of personal data between Member States; the implementation and application of this Directive should be made in full compliance with the principles relating to the protection of personal data, in particular as regards unsolicited commercial communication and the liability of intermediaries; this Directive cannot prevent the anonymous use of open networks such as the Internet.

(15) The confidentiality of communications is guaranteed by Article 5 Directive 97/66/EC; in accordance with that Directive, Member States must prohibit any kind of interception or surveillance of such communications by others than the senders and receivers, except when legally authorised.

(16) The exclusion of gambling activities from the scope of application of this Directive covers only games of chance, lotteries and betting transactions, which involve wagering a stake with monetary value; this does not cover promotional competitions or games where the purpose is to encourage the sale of goods or services and where payments, if they arise, serve only to acquire the promoted goods or services.

(17) The definition of information society services already exists in Community law in Directive 98/34/EC of the European Parliament and of the Council of 22 June 1998 laying down a procedure for the provision of information in the field of technical standards and regulations and of rules on information society services[21] and in Directive 98/84/EC of the European Parliament and of the Council of 20 November 1998 on the legal protection of services based on, or consisting of, conditional access;[22] this definition covers any service normally provided for remuneration, at a distance, by means of electronic equipment for the processing (including digital compression) and storage of data, and at the individual request of a recipient of a service; those services referred to in the indicative list in Annex V to Directive 98/34/EC which do not imply data processing and storage are not covered by this definition.

(18) Information society services span a wide range of economic activities which take place on-line; these activities can, in particular, consist of selling goods on-line; activities such as the delivery of goods as such or the provision of services off-line are not covered; information society services are not solely restricted to services giving rise to on-line contracting but also, in so far as they represent an economic activity, extend to services which are not remunerated by those who receive them, such as those offering on-line information or commercial communications, or those providing tools allowing for search, access and retrieval of data; information society services also include services consisting of the transmission of information via a communication network, in providing access to a communication network or in hosting information provided by a recipient of the service; television broadcasting within the meaning of Directive EEC/89/552 and radio broadcasting are not information society services because they are not provided at individual request; by contrast, services which are transmitted point to point, such as video-on-demand or the provision of commercial communications by electronic mail are information

---

[21] OJ L 204, 21.7.1998, p. 37. Directive as amended by Directive 98/48/EC (OJ L 217, 5.8.1998, p. 18).   [22] OJ L 320, 28.11.1998, p. 54.

society services; the use of electronic mail or equivalent individual communications for instance by natural persons acting outside their trade, business or profession including their use for the conclusion of contracts between such persons is not an information society service; the contractual relationship between an employee and his employer is not an information society service; activities which by their very nature cannot be carried out at a distance and by electronic means, such as the statutory auditing of company accounts or medical advice requiring the physical examination of a patient are not information society services.

(19) The place at which a service provider is established should be determined in conformity with the case-law of the Court of Justice according to which the concept of establishment involves the actual pursuit of an economic activity through a fixed establishment for an indefinite period; this requirement is also fulfilled where a company is constituted for a given period; the place of establishment of a company providing services via an Internet website is not the place at which the technology supporting its website is located or the place at which its website is accessible but the place where it pursues its economic activity; in cases where a provider has several places of establishment it is important to determine from which place of establishment the service concerned is provided; in cases where it is difficult to determine from which of several places of establishment a given service is provided, this is the place where the provider has the centre of his activities relating to this particular service.

(20) The definition of 'recipient of a service' covers all types of usage of information society services, both by persons who provide information on open networks such as the Internet and by persons who seek information on the Internet for private or professional reasons.

(21) The scope of the coordinated field is without prejudice to future Community harmonisation relating to information society services and to future legislation adopted at national level in accordance with Community law; the coordinated field covers only requirements relating to on-line activities such as on-line information, on-line advertising, on-line shopping, on-line contracting and does not concern Member States' legal requirements relating to goods such as safety standards, labelling obligations, or liability for goods, or Member States' requirements relating to the delivery or the transport of goods, including the distribution of medicinal products; the coordinated field does not cover the exercise of rights of pre-emption by public authorities concerning certain goods such as works of Art.

(22) Information society services should be supervised at the source of the activity, in order to ensure an effective protection of public interest objectives; to that end, it is necessary to ensure that the competent authority provides such protection not only for the citizens of its own country but for all Community citizens; in order to improve mutual trust between Member States, it is essential to state clearly this responsibility on the part of the Member State where the services originate; moreover, in order to effectively guarantee freedom to provide services and legal certainty for suppliers and recipients of services, such information society services should in principle be subject to the law of the Member State in which the service provider is established.

(23) This Directive neither aims to establish additional rules on private international law relating to conflicts of law nor does it deal with the jurisdiction of Courts;

provisions of the applicable law designated by rules of private international law must not restrict the freedom to provide information society services as established in this Directive.

(24) In the context of this Directive, notwithstanding the rule on the control at source of information society services, it is legitimate under the conditions established in this Directive for Member States to take measures to restrict the free movement of information society services.

(25) National courts, including civil courts, dealing with private law disputes can take measures to derogate from the freedom to provide information society services in conformity with conditions established in this Directive.

(26) Member States, in conformity with conditions established in this Directive, may apply their national rules on criminal law and criminal proceedings with a view to taking all investigative and other measures necessary for the detection and prosecution of criminal offences, without there being a need to notify such measures to the Commission.

(27) This Directive, together with the future Directive of the European Parliament and of the Council concerning the distance marketing of consumer financial services, contributes to the creating of a legal framework for the on-line provision of financial services; this Directive does not pre-empt future initiatives in the area of financial services in particular with regard to the harmonisation of rules of conduct in this field; the possibility for Member States, established in this Directive, under certain circumstances of restricting the freedom to provide information society services in order to protect consumers also covers measures in the area of financial services in particular measures aiming at protecting investors.

(28) The Member States' obligation not to subject access to the activity of an information society service provider to prior authorisation does not concern postal services covered by Directive 97/67/EC of the European Parliament and of the Council of 15 December 1997 on common rules for the development of the internal market of Community postal services and the improvement of quality of service[23] consisting of the physical delivery of a printed electronic mail message and does not affect voluntary accreditation systems, in particular for providers of electronic signature certification service.

(29) Commercial communications are essential for the financing of information society services and for developing a wide variety of new, charge-free services; in the interests of consumer protection and fair trading, commercial communications, including discounts, promotional offers and promotional competitions or games, must meet a number of transparency requirements; these requirements are without prejudice to Directive 97/7/EC; this Directive should not affect existing Directives on commercial communications, in particular Directive 98/43/EC.

(30) The sending of unsolicited commercial communications by electronic mail may be undesirable for consumers and information society service providers and may disrupt the smooth functioning of interactive networks; the question of consent by recipient of certain forms of unsolicited commercial communications is not addressed by this Directive, but has already been addressed, in particular, by Directive 97/7/EC and by Directive 97/66/EC; in Member States which authorise

---

[23] OJ L 15, 21.1.1998, p. 14.

unsolicited commercial communications by electronic mail, the setting up of appropriate industry filtering initiatives should be encouraged and facilitated; in addition it is necessary that in any event unsolicited commercial communities are clearly identifiable as such in order to improve transparency and to facilitate the functioning of such industry initiatives; unsolicited commercial communications by electronic mail should not result in additional communication costs for the recipient.

(31) Member States which allow the sending of unsolicited commercial communications by electronic mail without prior consent of the recipient by service providers established in their territory have to ensure that the service providers consult regularly and respect the opt-out registers in which natural persons not wishing to receive such commercial communications can register themselves.

(32) In order to remove barriers to the development of cross-border services within the Community which members of the regulated professions might offer on the Internet, it is necessary that compliance be guaranteed at Community level with professional rules aiming, in particular, to protect consumers or public health; codes of conduct at Community level would be the best means of determining the rules on professional ethics applicable to commercial communication; the drawing-up or, where appropriate, the adaptation of such rules should be encouraged without prejudice to the autonomy of professional bodies and associations.

(33) This Directive complements Community law and national law relating to regulated professions maintaining a coherent set of applicable rules in this field.

(34) Each Member State is to amend its legislation containing requirements, and in particular requirements as to form, which are likely to curb the use of contracts by electronic means; the examination of the legislation requiring such adjustment should be systematic and should cover all the necessary stages and acts of the contractual process, including the filing of the contract; the result of this amendment should be to make contracts concluded electronically workable; the legal effect of electronic signatures is dealt with by Directive 1999/93/EC of the European Parliament and of the Council of 13 December 1999 on a Community framework for electronic signatures;[24] the acknowledgement of receipt by a service provider may take the form of the on-line provision of the service paid for.

(35) This Directive does not affect Member States' possibility of maintaining or establishing general or specific legal requirements for contracts which can be fulfilled by electronic means, in particular requirements concerning secure electronic signatures.

(36) Member States may maintain restrictions for the use of electronic contracts with regard to contracts requiring by law the involvement of courts, public authorities, or professions exercising public authority; this possibility also covers contracts which require the involvement of courts, public authorities, or professions exercising public authority in order to have an effect with regard to third parties as well as contracts requiring by law certification or attestation by a notary.

(37) Member States' obligation to remove obstacles to the use of electronic contracts concerns only obstacles resulting from legal requirements and not practical obstacles resulting from the impossibility of using electronic means in certain cases.

---

[24] OJ L 13, 19.1.2000, p. 12.

(38) Member States' obligation to remove obstacles to the use of electronic contracts is to be implemented in conformity with legal requirements for contracts enshrined in Community law.

(39) The exceptions to the provisions concerning the contracts concluded exclusively by electronic mail or by equivalent individual communications provided for by this Directive, in relation to information to be provided and the placing of orders, should not enable, as a result, the by-passing of those provisions by providers of information society services.

(40) Both existing and emerging disparities in Member States' legislation and case-law concerning liability of service providers acting as intermediaries prevent the smooth functioning of the internal market, in particular by impairing the development of cross-border services and producing distortions of competition; service providers have a duty to act, under certain circumstances, with a view to preventing or stopping illegal activities; this Directive should constitute the appropriate basis for the development of rapid and reliable procedures for removing and disabling access to illegal information; such mechanisms could be developed on the basis of voluntary agreements between all parties concerned and should be encouraged by Member States; it is in the interest of all parties involved in the provision of information society services to adopt and implement such procedures; the provisions of this Directive relating to liability should not preclude the development and effective operation, by the different interested parties, of technical systems of protection and identification and of technical surveillance instruments made possible by digital technology within the limits laid down by Directives 95/46/EC and 97/66/EC.

(41) This Directive strikes a balance between the different interests at stake and establishes principles upon which industry agreements and standards can be based.

(42) The exemptions from liability established in this Directive cover only cases where the activity of the information society service provider is limited to the technical process of operating and giving access to a communication network over which information made available by third parties is transmitted or temporarily stored, for the sole purpose of making the transmission more efficient; this activity is of a mere technical, automatic and passive nature, which implies that the information society service provider has neither knowledge of nor control over the information which is transmitted or stored.

(43) A service provider can benefit from the exemptions for 'mere conduit' and for 'caching' when he is in no way involved with the information transmitted; this requires among other things that he does not modify the information that he transmits; this requirement does not cover manipulations of a technical nature which take place in the course of the transmission as they do not alter the integrity of the information contained in the transmission.

(44) A service provider who deliberately collaborates with one of the recipients of his service in order to undertake illegal acts goes beyond the activities of 'mere conduit' or 'caching' and as a result cannot benefit from the liability exemptions established for these activities.

(45) The limitations of the liability of intermediary service providers established in this Directive do not affect the possibility of injunctions of different kinds; such injunctions can in particular consist of orders by courts or administrative authorities

requiring the termination or prevention of any infringement, including the removal of illegal information or the disabling of access to it.

(46) In order to benefit from a limitation of liability, the provider of an information society service, consisting of the storage of information, upon obtaining actual knowledge or awareness of illegal activities has to act expeditiously to remove or to disable access to the information concerned; the removal or disabling of access has to be undertaken in the observance of the principle of freedom of expression and of procedures established for this purpose at national level; this Directive does not affect Member States' possibility of establishing specific requirements which must be fulfilled expeditiously prior to the removal or disabling of information.

(47) Member States are prevented from imposing a monitoring obligation on service providers only with respect to obligations of a general nature; this does not concern monitoring obligations in a specific case and, in particular, does not affect orders by national authorities in accordance with national legislation.

(48) This Directive does not affect the possibility for Member States of requiring service providers, who host information provided by recipients of their service, to apply duties of care, which can reasonably be expected from them and which are specified by national law, in order to detect and prevent certain types of illegal activities.

(49) Member States and the Commission are to encourage the drawing-up of codes of conduct; this is not to impair the voluntary nature of such codes and the possibility for interested parties of deciding freely whether to adhere to such codes.

(50) It is important that the proposed directive on the harmonisation of certain aspects of copyright and related rights in the information society and this Directive come into force within a similar time scale with a view to establishing a clear framework of rules relevant to the issue of liability of intermediaries for copyright and relating rights infringements at Community level.

(51) Each Member State should be required, where necessary, to amend any legislation which is liable to hamper the use of schemes for the out-of-court settlement of disputes through electronic channels; the result of this amendment must be to make the functioning of such schemes genuinely and effectively possible in law and in practice, even across borders.

(52) The effective exercise of the freedoms of the internal market makes it necessary to guarantee victims effective access to means of settling disputes; damage which may arise in connection with information society services is characterised both by its rapidity and by its geographical extent; in view of this specific character and the need to ensure that national authorities do not endanger the mutual confidence which they should have in one another, this Directive requests Member States to ensure that appropriate court actions are available; Member States should examine the need to provide access to judicial procedures by appropriate electronic means.

(53) Directive 98/27/EC, which is applicable to information society services, provides a mechanism relating to actions for an injunction aimed at the protection of the collective interests of consumers; this mechanism will contribute to the free movement of information society services by ensuring a high level of consumer protection.

(54) The sanctions provided for under this Directive are without prejudice to any other sanction or remedy provided under national law; Member States are not obliged to provide criminal sanctions for infringement of national provisions adopted pursuant to this Directive.

(55) This Directive does not affect the law applicable to contractual obligations relating to consumer contracts; accordingly, this Directive cannot have the result of depriving the consumer of the protection afforded to him by the mandatory rules relating to contractual obligations of the law of the Member State in which he has his habitual residence.

(56) As regards the derogation contained in this Directive regarding contractual obligations concerning contracts concluded by consumers, those obligations should be interpreted as including information on the essential elements of the content of the contract, including consumer rights, which have a determining influence on the decision to contract.

(57) The Court of Justice has consistently held that a Member State retains the right to take measures against a service provider that is established in another Member State but directs all or most of his activity to the territory of the first Member State if the choice of establishment was made with a view to evading the legislation that would have applied to the provider had he been established on the territory of the first Member State.

(58) This Directive should not apply to services supplied by service providers established in a third country; in view of the global dimension of electronic commerce, it is, however, appropriate to ensure that the Community rules are consistent with international rules; this Directive is without prejudice to the results of discussions within international organisations (amongst others WTO, OECD, Uncitral) on legal issues.

(59) Despite the global nature of electronic communications, coordination of national regulatory measures at European Union level is necessary in order to avoid fragmentation of the internal market, and for the establishment of an appropriate European regulatory framework; such coordination should also contribute to the establishment of a common and strong negotiating position in international forums.

(60) In order to allow the unhampered development of electronic commerce, the legal framework must be clear and simple, predictable and consistent with the rules applicable at international level so that it does not adversely affect the competitiveness of European industry or impede innovation in that sector.

(61) If the market is actually to operate by electronic means in the context of globalisation, the European Union and the major non-European areas need to consult each other with a view to making laws and procedures compatible.

(62) Cooperation with third countries should be strengthened in the area of electronic commerce, in particular with applicant countries, the developing countries and the European Union's other trading partners.

(63) The adoption of this Directive will not prevent the Member States from taking into account the various social, societal and cultural implications which are inherent in the advent of the information society; in particular it should not hinder measures which Member States might adopt in conformity with Community law to achieve social, cultural and democratic goals taking into account their linguistic diversity, national and regional specificities as well as their cultural heritage, and to ensure and maintain public access to the widest possible range of information society services; in any case, the development of the information society is to ensure that Community citizens can have access to the cultural European heritage provided in the digital environment.

(64) Electronic communication offers the Member States an excellent means of providing public services in the cultural, educational and linguistic fields.

(65) The Council, in its resolution of 19 January 1999 on the consumer dimension of the information society,[25] stressed that the protection of consumers deserved special attention in this field; the Commission will examine the degree to which existing consumer protection rules provide insufficient protection in the context of the information society and will identify, where necessary, the deficiencies of this legislation and those issues which could require additional measures; if need be, the Commission should make specific additional proposals to resolve such deficiencies that will thereby have been identified,

HAVE ADOPTED THIS DIRECTIVE:

CHAPTER I
GENERAL PROVISIONS

Article 1
Objective and scope

1. This Directive seeks to contribute to the proper functioning of the internal market by ensuring the free movement of information society services between the Member States.

2. This Directive approximates, to the extent necessary for the achievement of the objective set out in paragraph 1, certain national provisions on information society services relating to the internal market, the establishment of service providers, commercial communications, electronic contracts, the liability of intermediaries, codes of conduct, out-of-court dispute settlements, court actions and cooperation between Member States.

3. This Directive complements Community law applicable to information society services without prejudice to the level of protection for, in particular, public health and consumer interests, as established by Community acts and national legislation implementing them in so far as this does not restrict the freedom to provide information society services.

4. This Directive does not establish additional rules on private international law nor does it deal with the jurisdiction of Courts.

5. This Directive shall not apply to:
   (a) the field of taxation;
   (b) questions relating to information society services covered by Directives 95/46/EC and 97/66/EC;
   (c) questions relating to agreements or practices governed by cartel law;
   (d) the following activities of information society services:
       —the activities of notaries or equivalent professions to the extent that they involve a direct and specific connection with the exercise of public authority,
       —the representation of a client and defence of his interests before the courts,

---

[25] OJ C 23, 28.1.1999, p. 1.

—gambling activities which involve wagering a stake with monetary value in games of chance, including lotteries and betting transactions.

6. This Directive does not affect measures taken at Community or national level, in the respect of Community law, in order to promote cultural and linguistic diversity and to ensure the defence of pluralism.

Article 2
Definitions

For the purpose of this Directive, the following terms shall bear the following meanings:

(a) 'information society services': services within the meaning of Article 1(2) of Directive 98/34/EC as amended by Directive 98/48/EC;

(b) 'service provider': any natural or legal person providing an information society service;

(c) 'established service provider': a service provider who effectively pursues an economic activity using a fixed establishment for an indefinite period. The presence and use of the technical means and technologies required to provide the service do not, in themselves, constitute an establishment of the provider;

(d) 'recipient of the service': any natural or legal person who, for professional ends or otherwise, uses an information society service, in particular for the purposes of seeking information or making it accessible;

(e) 'consumer': any natural person who is acting for purposes which are outside his or her trade, business or profession;

(f) 'commercial communication': any form of communication designed to promote, directly or indirectly, the goods, services or image of a company, organisation or person pursuing a commercial, industrial or craft activity or exercising a regulated profession. The following do not in themselves constitute commercial communications:

— information allowing direct access to the activity of the company, organisation or person, in particular a domain name or an electronic-mail address,

— communications relating to the goods, services or image of the company, organisation or person compiled in an independent manner, particularly when this is without financial consideration;

(g) 'regulated profession': any profession within the meaning of either Article 1(d) of Council Directive 89/48/EEC of 21 December 1988 on a general system for the recognition of higher-education diplomas awarded on completion of professional education and training of at least three-years' duration[26] or of Article 1(f) of Council Directive 92/51/EEC of 18 June 1992 on a second general system for the recognition of professional education and training to supplement Directive 89/48/EEC;[27]

(h) 'coordinated field': requirements laid down in Member States' legal systems applicable to information society service providers or information society services, regardless of whether they are of a general nature or specifically designed for them.

---

[26] OJ L 19, 24.1.1989, p. 16.

[27] OJ L 209, 24.7.1992, p. 25. Directive as last amended by Commission Directive 97/38/EC (OJ L 184, 12.7.1997, p. 31).

(i) The coordinated field concerns requirements with which the service provider has to comply in respect of:

—the taking up of the activity of an information society service, such as requirements concerning qualifications, authorisation or notification,

—the pursuit of the activity of an information society service, such as requirements concerning the behaviour of the service provider, requirements regarding the quality or content of the service including those applicable to advertising and contracts, or requirements concerning the liability of the service provider;

(ii) The coordinated field does not cover requirements such as:

—requirements applicable to goods as such,

—requirements applicable to the delivery of goods,

—requirements applicable to services not provided by electronic means.

Article 3
Internal market

1. Each Member State shall ensure that the information society services provided by a service provider established on its territory comply with the national provisions applicable in the Member State in question which fall within the coordinated field.

2. Member States may not, for reasons falling within the coordinated field, restrict the freedom to provide information society services from another Member State.

3. Paragraphs 1 and 2 shall not apply to the fields referred to in the Annex.

4. Member States may take measures to derogate from paragraph 2 in respect of a given information society service if the following conditions are fulfilled:

(a) the measures shall be:

(i) necessary for one of the following reasons:

—public policy, in particular the prevention, investigation, detection and prosecution of criminal offences, including the protection of minors and the fight against any incitement to hatred on grounds of race, sex, religion or nationality, and violations of human dignity concerning individual persons,

—the protection of public health,

—public security, including the safeguarding of national security and defence,

—the protection of consumers, including investors;

(ii) taken against a given information society service which prejudices the objectives referred to in point (i) or which presents a serious and grave risk of prejudice to those objectives;

(iii) proportionate to those objectives;

(b) before taking the measures in question and without prejudice to court proceedings, including preliminary proceedings and acts carried out in the framework of a criminal investigation, the Member State has:

—asked the Member State referred to in paragraph 1 to take measures and the latter did not take such measures, or they were inadequate,

—notified the Commission and the Member State referred to in paragraph 1 of its intention to take such measures.

5. Member States may, in the case of urgency, derogate from the conditions stipulated in paragraph 4(b). Where this is the case, the measures shall be notified in the shortest possible time to the Commission and to the Member State referred to in paragraph 1, indicating the reasons for which the Member State considers that there is urgency.

6. Without prejudice to the Member State's possibility of proceeding with the measures in question, the Commission shall examine the compatibility of the notified measures with Community law in the shortest possible time; where it comes to the conclusion that the measure is incompatible with Community law, the Commission shall ask the Member State in question to refrain from taking any proposed measures or urgently to put an end to the measures in question.

CHAPTER II
PRINCIPLES

SECTION I
ESTABLISHMENT AND INFORMATION REQUIREMENTS

Article 4
Principle excluding prior authorization

1. Member States shall ensure that the taking up and pursuit of the activity of an information society service provider may not be made subject to prior authorisation or any other requirement having equivalent effect.

2. Paragraph 1 shall be without prejudice to authorisation schemes which are not specifically and exclusively targeted at information society services, or which are covered by Directive 97/13/EC of the European Parliament and of the Council of 10 April 1997 on a common framework for general authorisations and individual licences in the field of telecommunications services.[28]

Article 5
General information to be provided

1. In addition to other information requirements established by Community law, Member States shall ensure that the service provider shall render easily, directly and permanently accessible to the recipients of the service and competent authorities, at least the following information:
   (a) the name of the service provider;
   (b) the geographic address at which the service provider is established;
   (c) the details of the service provider, including his electronic mail address, which allow him to be contacted rapidly and communicated with in a direct and effective manner;

---

[28] OJ L 117, 7.5.1997, p. 15.

(d) where the service provider is registered in a trade or similar public register, the trade register in which the service provider is entered and his registration number, or equivalent means of identification in that register;

(e) where the activity is subject to an authorisation scheme, the particulars of the relevant supervisory authority;

(f) as concerns the regulated professions:

—any professional body or similar institution with which the service provider is registered,

—the professional title and the Member State where it has been granted,

—a reference to the applicable professional rules in the Member State of establishment and the means to access them;

(g) where the service provider undertakes an activity that is subject to VAT, the identification number referred to in Article 22(1) of the sixth Council Directive 77/388/EEC of 17 May 1977 on the harmonisation of the laws of the Member States relating to turnover taxes—Common system of value added tax: uniform basis of assessment.[29]

2. In addition to other information requirements established by Community law, Member States shall at least ensure that, where information society services refer to prices, these are to be indicated clearly and unambiguously and, in particular, must indicate whether they are inclusive of tax and delivery costs.

SECTION 2
COMMERCIAL COMMUNICATIONS

Article 6
Information to be provided

In addition to other information requirements established by Community law, Member States shall ensure that commercial communications which are part of, or constitute, an information society service comply at least with the following conditions:

(a) the commercial communication shall be clearly identifiable as such;

(b) the natural or legal person on whose behalf the commercial communication is made shall be clearly identifiable;

(c) promotional offers, such as discounts, premiums and gifts, where permitted in the Member State where the service provider is established, shall be clearly identifiable as such, and the conditions which are to be met to qualify for them shall be easily accessible and be presented clearly and unambiguously;

(d) promotional competitions or games, where permitted in the Member State where the service provider is established, shall be clearly identifiable as such, and the conditions for participation shall be easily accessible and be presented clearly and unambiguously.

---

[29] OJ L 145, 13.6.1977, p. 1. Directive as last amended by Directive 1999/85/EC (OJ L 277, 28.10.1999, p. 34).

Article 7
Unsolicited commercial communication

1. In addition to other requirements established by Community law, Member States which permit unsolicited commercial communication by electronic mail shall ensure that such commercial communication by a service provider established in their territory shall be identifiable clearly and unambiguously as such as soon as it is received by the recipient.
2. Without prejudice to Directive 97/7/EC and Directive 97/66/EC, Member States shall take measures to ensure that service providers undertaking unsolicited commercial communications by electronic mail consult regularly and respect the opt-out registers in which natural persons not wishing to receive such commercial communications can register themselves.

Article 8
Regulated professions

1. Member States shall ensure that the use of commercial communications which are part of, or constitute, an information society service provided by a member of a regulated profession is permitted subject to compliance with the professional rules regarding, in particular, the independence, dignity and honour of the profession, professional secrecy and fairness towards clients and other members of the profession.
2. Without prejudice to the autonomy of professional bodies and associations, Member States and the Commission shall encourage professional associations and bodies to establish codes of conduct at Community level in order to determine the types of information that can be given for the purposes of commercial communication in conformity with the rules referred to in paragraph 1.
3. When drawing up proposals for Community initiatives which may become necessary to ensure the proper functioning of the Internal Market with regard to the information referred to in paragraph 2, the Commission shall take due account of codes of conduct applicable at Community level and shall act in close cooperation with the relevant professional associations and bodies.
4. This Directive shall apply in addition to Community Directives concerning access to, and the exercise of, activities of the regulated professions.

SECTION 3
CONTRACTS CONCLUDED BY ELECTRONIC MEANS

Article 9
Treatment of contracts

1. Member States shall ensure that their legal system allows contracts to be concluded by electronic means. Member States shall in particular ensure that the legal requirements applicable to the contractual process neither create obstacles for the use of electronic contracts nor result in such contracts being deprived of legal effectiveness and validity on account of their having been made by electronic means.

2. Member States may lay down that paragraph 1 shall not apply to all or certain contracts falling into one of the following categories:
   (a) contracts that create or transfer rights in real estate, except for rental rights;
   (b) contracts requiring by law the involvement of courts, public authorities or professions exercising public authority;
   (c) contracts of suretyship granted and on collateral securities furnished by persons acting for purposes outside their trade, business or profession;
   (d) contracts governed by family law or by the law of succession.
3. Member States shall indicate to the Commission the categories referred to in paragraph 2 to which they do not apply paragraph 1. Member States shall submit to the Commission every five years a report on the application of paragraph 2 explaining the reasons why they consider it necessary to maintain the category referred to in paragraph 2(b) to which they do not apply paragraph 1.

Article 10

Information to be provided

1. In addition to other information requirements established by Community law, Member States shall ensure, except when otherwise agreed by parties who are not consumers, that at least the following information is given by the service provider clearly, comprehensibly and unambiguously and prior to the order being placed by the recipient of the service:
   (a) the different technical steps to follow to conclude the contract;
   (b) whether or not the concluded contract will be filed by the service provider and whether it will be accessible;
   (c) the technical means for identifying and correcting input errors prior to the placing of the order;
   (d) the languages offered for the conclusion of the contract.
2. Member States shall ensure that, except when otherwise agreed by parties who are not consumers, the service provider indicates any relevant codes of conduct to which he subscribes and information on how those codes can be consulted electronically.
3. Contract terms and general conditions provided to the recipient must be made available in a way that allows him to store and reproduce them.
4. Paragraphs 1 and 2 shall not apply to contracts concluded exclusively by exchange of electronic mail or by equivalent individual communications.

Article 11
Placing of the order

1. Member States shall ensure, except when otherwise agreed by parties who are not consumers, that in cases where the recipient of the service places his order through technological means, the following principles apply:
   —the service provider has to acknowledge the receipt of the recipient's order without undue delay and by electronic means,
   —the order and the acknowledgement of receipt are deemed to be received when the parties to whom they are addressed are able to access them.

2. Member States shall ensure that, except when otherwise agreed by parties who are not consumers, the service provider makes available to the recipient of the service appropriate, effective and accessible technical means allowing him to identify and correct input errors, prior to the placing of the order.

3. Paragraph 1, first indent, and paragraph 2 shall not apply to contracts concluded exclusively by exchange of electronic mail or by equivalent individual communications.

SECTION 4
LIABILITY OF INTERMEDIARY SERVICE PROVIDERS

Article 12
'Mere conduit'

1. Where an information society service is provided that consists of the transmission in a communication network of information provided by a recipient of the service, or the provision of access to a communication network, Member States shall ensure that the service provider is not liable for the information transmitted, on condition that the provider:
   (a) does not initiate the transmission;
   (b) does not select the receiver of the transmission; and
   (c) does not select or modify the information contained in the transmission.

2. The acts of transmission and of provision of access referred to in paragraph 1 include the automatic, intermediate and transient storage of the information transmitted in so far as this takes place for the sole purpose of carrying out the transmission in the communication network, and provided that the information is not stored for any period longer than is reasonably necessary for the transmission.

3. This Article shall not affect the possibility for a court or administrative authority, in accordance with Member States' legal systems, of requiring the service provider to terminate or prevent an infringement.

Article 13
'Caching'

1. Where an information society service is provided that consists of the transmission in a communication network of information provided by a recipient of the service, Member States shall ensure that the service provider is not liable for the automatic, intermediate and temporary storage of that information, performed for the sole purpose of making more efficient the information's onward transmission to other recipients of the service upon their request, on condition that:
   (a) the provider does not modify the information;
   (b) the provider complies with conditions on access to the information;
   (c) the provider complies with rules regarding the updating of the information, specified in a manner widely recognised and used by industry;
   (d) the provider does not interfere with the lawful use of technology, widely recognised and used by industry, to obtain data on the use of the information; and
   (e) the provider acts expeditiously to remove or to disable access to the information it has stored upon obtaining actual knowledge of the fact that the information at the initial source of the transmission has been removed from the network, or access to

it has been disabled, or that a court or an administrative authority has ordered such removal or disablement.

2. This Article shall not affect the possibility for a court or administrative authority, in accordance with Member States' legal systems, of requiring the service provider to terminate or prevent an infringement.

Article 14
Hosting

1. Where an information society service is provided that consists of the storage of information provided by a recipient of the service, Member States shall ensure that the service provider is not liable for the information stored at the request of a recipient of the service, on condition that:
   (a) the provider does not have actual knowledge of illegal activity or information and, as regards claims for damages, is not aware of facts or circumstances from which the illegal activity or information is apparent; or
   (b) the provider, upon obtaining such knowledge or awareness, acts expeditiously to remove or to disable access to the information.

2. Paragraph 1 shall not apply when the recipient of the service is acting under the authority or the control of the provider.

3. This Article shall not affect the possibility for a court or administrative authority, in accordance with Member States' legal systems, of requiring the service provider to terminate or prevent an infringement, nor does it affect the possibility for Member States of establishing procedures governing the removal or disabling of access to information.

Article 15
No general obligation to monitor

1. Member States shall not impose a general obligation on providers, when providing the services covered by Articles 12, 13 and 14, to monitor the information which they transmit or store, nor a general obligation actively to seek facts or circumstances indicating illegal activity.

2. Member States may establish obligations for information society service providers promptly to inform the competent public authorities of alleged illegal activities undertaken or information provided by recipients of their service or obligations to communicate to the competent authorities, at their request, information enabling the identification of recipients of their service with whom they have storage agreements.

CHAPTER III
IMPLEMENTATION

Article 16
Codes of conduct

1. Member States and the Commission shall encourage:
   (a) the drawing up of codes of conduct at Community level, by trade, professional and consumer associations or organisations, designed to contribute to the proper implementation of Articles 5 to 15;

(b) the voluntary transmission of draft codes of conduct at national or Community level to the Commission;

(c) the accessibility of these codes of conduct in the Community languages by electronic means;

(d) the communication to the Member States and the Commission, by trade, professional and consumer associations or organisations, of their assessment of the application of their codes of conduct and their impact upon practices, habits or customs relating to electronic commerce;

(e) the drawing up of codes of conduct regarding the protection of minors and human dignity.

2. Member States and the Commission shall encourage the involvement of associations or organisations representing consumers in the drafting and implementation of codes of conduct affecting their interests and drawn up in accordance with paragraph 1(a). Where appropriate, to take account of their specific needs, associations representing the visually impaired and disabled should be consulted.

Article 17
Out-of-court dispute settlement

1. Member States shall ensure that, in the event of disagreement between an information society service provider and the recipient of the service, their legislation does not hamper the use of out-of-court schemes, available under national law, for dispute settlement, including appropriate electronic means.

2. Member States shall encourage bodies responsible for the out-of-court settlement of, in particular, consumer disputes to operate in a way which provides adequate procedural guarantees for the parties concerned.

3. Member States shall encourage bodies responsible for out-of-court dispute settlement to inform the Commission of the significant decisions they take regarding information society services and to transmit any other information on the practices, usages or customs relating to electronic commerce.

Article 18
Court actions

1. Member States shall ensure that court actions available under national law concerning information society services' activities allow for the rapid adoption of measures, including interim measures, designed to terminate any alleged infringement and to prevent any further impairment of the interests involved.

2. The Annex to Directive 98/27/EC shall be supplemented as follows:
   '11. Directive 2000/31/EC of the European Parliament and of the Council of 8 June 2000 on certain legal aspects on information society services, in particular electronic commerce, in the internal market (Directive on electronic commerce) (OJ L 178, 17.7.2000, p. 1).'

Article 19
Cooperation

1. Member States shall have adequate means of supervision and investigation necessary to implement this Directive effectively and shall ensure that service providers supply them with the requisite information.

2. Member States shall cooperate with other Member States; they shall, to that end, appoint one or several contact points, whose details they shall communicate to the other Member States and to the Commission.

3. Member States shall, as quickly as possible, and in conformity with national law, provide the assistance and information requested by other Member States or by the Commission, including by appropriate electronic means.

4. Member States shall establish contact points which shall be accessible at least by electronic means and from which recipients and service providers may:

  (a) obtain general information on contractual rights and obligations as well as on the complaint and redress mechanisms available in the event of disputes, including practical aspects involved in the use of such mechanisms;

  (b) obtain the details of authorities, associations or organisations from which they may obtain further information or practical assistance.

5. Member States shall encourage the communication to the Commission of any significant administrative or judicial decisions taken in their territory regarding disputes relating to information society services and practices, usages and customs relating to electronic commerce. The Commission shall communicate these decisions to the other Member States.

Article 20
Sanctions

Member States shall determine the sanctions applicable to infringements of national provisions adopted pursuant to this Directive and shall take all measures necessary to ensure that they are enforced. The sanctions they provide for shall be effective, proportionate and dissuasive.

CHAPTER IV
FINAL PROVISIONS

Article 21
Re-examination

1. Before 17 July 2003, and thereafter every two years, the Commission shall submit to the European Parliament, the Council and the Economic and Social Committee a report on the application of this Directive, accompanied, where necessary, by proposals for adapting it to legal, technical and economic developments in the field of information society services, in particular with respect to crime prevention, the protection of minors, consumer protection and to the proper functioning of the internal market.

2. In examining the need for an adaptation of this Directive, the report shall in particular analyse the need for proposals concerning the liability of providers of hyperlinks and location tool services, 'notice and take down' procedures and the attribution of liability following the taking down of content. The report shall also analyse the need for additional conditions for the exemption from liability, provided for in Articles 12 and 13, in the light of technical developments, and the possibility of applying the internal market principles to unsolicited commercial communications by electronic mail.

Article 22
Transposition

1. Member States shall bring into force the laws, regulations and administrative provisions necessary to comply with this Directive before 17 January 2002. They shall forthwith inform the Commission thereof.
2. When Member States adopt the measures referred to in paragraph 1, these shall contain a reference to this Directive or shall be accompanied by such reference at the time of their official publication. The methods of making such reference shall be laid down by Member States.

Article 23
Entry into force

This Directive shall enter into force on the day of its publication in the Official Journal of the European Communities.

Article 24
Addressees

This Directive is addressed to the Member States.

Done at Luxemburg, 8 June 2000.

For the European Parliament
The President
N. Fontaine

For the Council
The President
G. d'Oliveira Martins

ANNEX
DEROGATIONS FROM ARTICLE 3

As provided for in Article 3(3), Article 3(1) and (2) do not apply to:
—copyright, neighbouring rights, rights referred to in Directive 87/54/EEC[1] and Directive 96/9/EC[2] as well as industrial property rights,
—the emission of electronic money by institutions in respect of which Member States have applied one of the derogations provided for in Article 8(1) of Directive 2000/46/EC,[3]
—Article 44(2) of Directive 85/611/EEC,[4]

---

[1] OJ L 24, 27.1.1987, p. 36.   [2] OJ L 77, 27.3.1996, p. 20.
[3] Not yet published in the Official Journal.
[4] OJ L 375, 31.12.1985, p. 3. Directive as last amended by Directive 95/26/EC (OJ L 168, 18.7.1995, p. 7).

—Article 30 and Title IV of Directive 92/49/EEC,[5] Title IV of Directive 92/96/EEC,[6] Articles 7 and 8 of Directive 88/357/EEC[7] and Article 4 of Directive 90/619/EEC,[8]

—the freedom of the parties to choose the law applicable to their contract,

—contractual obligations concerning consumer contacts,

—formal validity of contracts creating or transferring rights in real estate where such contracts are subject to mandatory formal requirements of the law of the Member State where the real estate is situated,

—the permissibility of unsolicited commercial communications by electronic mail.

---

[5] OJ L 228, 11.8.1992, p. 1. Directive as last amended by Directive 95/26/EC.
[6] OJ L 360, 9.12.1992, p. 2. Directive as last amended by Directive 95/26/EC.
[7] OJ L 172, 4.7.1988, p. 1. Directive as last amended by Directive 92/49/EC.
[8] OJ L 330, 29.11.1990, p. 50. Directive as last amended by Directive 92/96/EC.

(iv) DIRECTIVE 1999/93/EC OF THE EUROPEAN PARLIAMENT AND OF THE COUNCIL OF 13 DECEMBER 1999 ON A COMMUNITY FRAMEWORK FOR ELECTRONIC SIGNATURES

PREAMBLE

THE EUROPEAN PARLIAMENT AND THE COUNCIL OF THE
EUROPEAN UNION,

Having regard to the Treaty establishing the European Community, and in particular Articles 47(2), 55 and 95 thereof,

Having regard to the proposal from the Commission,[1]

Having regard to the opinion of the Economic and Social Committee,[2]

Having regard to the opinion of the Committee of the Regions,[3]

Acting in accordance with the procedure laid down in Article 251 of the Treaty,[4]

Whereas:

(1) On 16 April 1997 the Commission presented to the European Parliament, the Council, the Economic and Social Committee and the Committee of the Regions a Communication on a European Initiative in Electronic Commerce;

(2) On 8 October 1997 the Commission presented to the European Parliament, the Council, the Economic and Social Committee and the Committee of the Regions a Communication on ensuring security and trust in electronic communication—towards a European framework for digital signatures and encryption;

---

[1] OJ C 325, 23.10.1998, p. 5.   [2] OJ C 40, 15.2.1999, p. 29.
[3] OJ C 93, 6.4.1999, p. 33.
[4] Opinion of the European Parliament of 13 January 1999 (OJ C 104, 14.4.1999, p. 49), Council Common Position of 28 June 1999 (OJ C 243, 27.8.1999, p. 33) and Decision of the European Parliament of 27 October 1999 (not yet published in the Official Journal). Council Decision of 30 November 1999.

(3)   On 1 December 1997 the Council invited the Commission to submit as soon as possible a proposal for a Directive of the European Parliament and of the Council on digital signatures;

(4)   Electronic communication and commerce necessitate 'electronic signatures' and related services allowing data authentication; divergent rules with respect to legal recognition of electronic signatures and the accreditation of certification-service providers in the Member States may create a significant barrier to the use of electronic communications and electronic commerce; on the other hand, a clear Community framework regarding the conditions applying to electronic signatures will strengthen confidence in, and general acceptance of, the new technologies; legislation in the Member States should not hinder the free movement of goods and services in the internal market;

(5)   The interoperability of electronic-signature products should be promoted; in accordance with Article 14 of the Treaty, the internal market comprises an area without internal frontiers in which the free movement of goods is ensured; essential requirements specific to electronic-signature products must be met in order to ensure free movement within the internal market and to build trust in electronic signatures, without prejudice to Council Regulation (EC) No 3381/94 of 19 December 1994 setting up a Community regime for the control of exports of dual-use goods[5] and Council Decision 94/942/CFSP of 19 December 1994 on the joint action adopted by the Council concerning the control of exports of dual-use goods;[6]

(6)   This Directive does not harmonise the provision of services with respect to the confidentiality of information where they are covered by national provisions concerned with public policy or public security;

(7)   The internal market ensures the free movement of persons, as a result of which citizens and residents of the European Union increasingly need to deal with authorities in Member States other than the one in which they reside; the availability of electronic communication could be of great service in this respect;

(8)   Rapid technological development and the global character of the Internet necessitate an approach which is open to various technologies and services capable of authenticating data electronically;

(9)   Electronic signatures will be used in a large variety of circumstances and applications, resulting in a wide range of new services and products related to or using electronic signatures; the definition of such products and services should not be limited to the issuance and management of certificates, but should also encompass any other service and product using, or ancillary to, electronic signatures, such as registration services, time-stamping services, directory services, computing services or consultancy services related to electronic signatures;

(10) The internal market enables certification-service-providers to develop their cross-border activities with a view to increasing their competitiveness, and thus to offer consumers and businesses new opportunities to exchange information and trade electronically in a secure way, regardless of frontiers; in order to stimulate the

---

[5] OJ L 367, 31.12.1994, p. 1. Regulation as amended by Regulation (EC) No 837/95 (OJ L 90, 21.4.1995, p. 1).

[6] OJ L 367, 31.12.1994, p. 8. Decision as last amended by Decision 99/193/CFSP (OJ L 73, 19.3.1999, p. 1).

Community-wide provision of certification services over open networks, certification-service-providers should be free to provide their services without prior authorisation; prior authorisation means not only any permission whereby the certification-service-provider concerned has to obtain a decision by national authorities before being allowed to provide its certification services, but also any other measures having the same effect;

(11) Voluntary accreditation schemes aiming at an enhanced level of service-provision may offer certification-service-providers the appropriate framework for developing further their services towards the levels of trust, security and quality demanded by the evolving market; such schemes should encourage the development of best practice among certification-service-providers; certification-service-providers should be left free to adhere to and benefit from such accreditation schemes;

(12) Certification services can be offered either by a public entity or a legal or natural person, when it is established in accordance with the national law; whereas Member States should not prohibit certification-service-providers from operating outside voluntary accreditation schemes; it should be ensured that such accreditation schemes do not reduce competition for certification services;

(13) Member States may decide how they ensure the supervision of compliance with the provisions laid down in this Directive; this Directive does not preclude the establishment of private-sector-based supervision systems; this Directive does not oblige certification-service-providers to apply to be supervised under any applicable accreditation scheme;

(14) It is important to strike a balance between consumer and business needs;

(15) Annex III covers requirements for secure signature-creation devices to ensure the functionality of advanced electronic signatures; it does not cover the entire system environment in which such devices operate; the functioning of the internal market requires the Commission and the Member States to act swiftly to enable the bodies charged with the conformity assessment of secure signature devices with Annex III to be designated; in order to meet market needs conformity assessment must be timely and efficient;

(16) This Directive contributes to the use and legal recognition of electronic signatures within the Community; a regulatory framework is not needed for electronic signatures exclusively used within systems, which are based on voluntary agreements under private law between a specified number of participants; the freedom of parties to agree among themselves the terms and conditions under which they accept electronically signed data should be respected to the extent allowed by national law; the legal effectiveness of electronic signatures used in such systems and their admissibility as evidence in legal proceedings should be recognised;

(17) This Directive does not seek to harmonise national rules concerning contract law, particularly the formation and performance of contracts, or other formalities of a non-contractual nature concerning signatures; for this reason the provisions concerning the legal effect of electronic signatures should be without prejudice to requirements regarding form laid down in national law with regard to the conclusion of contracts or the rules determining where a contract is concluded;

(18) The storage and copying of signature-creation data could cause a threat to the legal validity of electronic signatures;

(19) Electronic signatures will be used in the public sector within national and Community administrations and in communications between such administrations and with citizens and economic operators, for example in the public procurement, taxation, social security, health and justice systems;

(20) Harmonised criteria relating to the legal effects of electronic signatures will preserve a coherent legal framework across the Community; national law lays down different requirements for the legal validity of hand-written signatures; whereas certificates can be used to confirm the identity of a person signing electronically; advanced electronic signatures based on qualified certificates aim at a higher level of security; advanced electronic signatures which are based on a qualified certificate and which are created by a secure-signature-creation device can be regarded as legally equivalent to hand-written signatures only if the requirements for hand-written signatures are fulfilled;

(21) In order to contribute to the general acceptance of electronic authentication methods it has to be ensured that electronic signatures can be used as evidence in legal proceedings in all Member States; the legal recognition of electronic signatures should be based upon objective criteria and not be linked to authorisation of the certification-service-provider involved; national law governs the legal spheres in which electronic documents and electronic signatures may be used; this Directive is without prejudice to the power of a national court to make a ruling regarding conformity with the requirements of this Directive and does not affect national rules regarding the unfettered judicial consideration of evidence;

(22) Certification-service-providers providing certification-services to the public are subject to national rules regarding liability;

(23) The development of international electronic commerce requires cross-border arrangements involving third countries; in order to ensure interoperability at a global level, agreements on multilateral rules with third countries on mutual recognition of certification services could be beneficial;

(24) In order to increase user confidence in electronic communication and electronic commerce, certification-service-providers must observe data protection legislation and individual privacy;

(25) Provisions on the use of pseudonyms in certificates should not prevent Member States from requiring identification of persons pursuant to Community or national law;

(26) The measures necessary for the implementation of this Directive are to be adopted in accordance with Council Decision 1999/468/EC of 28 June 1999 laying down the procedures for the exercise of implementing powers conferred on the Commission;[7]

(27) Two years after its implementation the Commission will carry out a review of this Directive so as, inter alia, to ensure that the advance of technology or changes in the legal environment have not created barriers to achieving the aims stated in this Directive; it should examine the implications of associated technical areas and submit a report to the European Parliament and the Council on this subject;

(28) In accordance with the principles of subsidiarity and proportionality as set out in Article 5 of the Treaty, the objective of creating a harmonised legal framework for

---

[7] OJ L 184, 17.7.1999, p. 23.

the provision of electronic signatures and related services cannot be sufficiently achieved by the Member States and can therefore be better achieved by the Community; this Directive does not go beyond what is necessary to achieve that objective,

HAVE ADOPTED THIS DIRECTIVE:

Article 1
Scope

The purpose of this Directive is to facilitate the use of electronic signatures and to contribute to their legal recognition. It establishes a legal framework for electronic signatures and certain certification-services in order to ensure the proper functioning of the internal market.

It does not cover aspects related to the conclusion and validity of contracts or other legal obligations where there are requirements as regards form prescribed by national or Community law nor does it affect rules and limits, contained in national or Community law, governing the use of documents.

Article 2
Definitions

For the purpose of this Directive:
1. 'electronic signature' means data in electronic form which are attached to or logically associated with other electronic data and which serve as a method of authentication;
2. 'advanced electronic signature' means an electronic signature which meets the following requirements:
   (a) it is uniquely linked to the signatory;
   (b) it is capable of identifying the signatory;
   (c) it is created using means that the signatory can maintain under his sole control; and
   (d) it is linked to the data to which it relates in such a manner that any subsequent change of the data is detectable;
3. 'signatory' means a person who holds a signature-creation device and acts either on his own behalf or on behalf of the natural or legal person or entity he represents;
4. 'signature-creation data' means unique data, such as codes or private cryptographic keys, which are used by the signatory to create an electronic signature;
5. 'signature-creation device' means configured software or hardware used to implement the signature-creation data;
6. 'secure-signature-creation device' means a signature-creation device which meets the requirements laid down in Annex III;
7. 'signature-verification-data' means data, such as codes or public cryptographic keys, which are used for the purpose of verifying an electronic signature;
8. 'signature-verification device' means configured software or hardware used to implement the signature-verification-data;
9. 'certificate' means an electronic attestation which links signature-verification data to a person and confirms the identity of that person;

10. 'qualified certificate' means a certificate which meets the requirements laid down in Annex I and is provided by a certification-service-provider who fulfils the requirements laid down in Annex II;

11. 'certification-service-provider' means an entity or a legal or natural person who issues certificates or provides other services related to electronic signatures;

12. 'electronic-signature product' means hardware or software, or relevant components thereof, which are intended to be used by a certification-service-provider for the provision of electronic-signature services or are intended to be used for the creation or verification of electronic signatures;

13. 'voluntary accreditation' means any permission, setting out rights and obligations specific to the provision of certification services, to be granted upon request by the certification-service-provider concerned, by the public or private body charged with the elaboration of, and supervision of compliance with, such rights and obligations, where the certification-service-provider is not entitled to exercise the rights stemming from the permission until it has received the decision by the body.

Article 3
Market access

1. Member States shall not make the provision of certification services subject to prior authorisation.

2. Without prejudice to the provisions of paragraph 1, Member States may introduce or maintain voluntary accreditation schemes aiming at enhanced levels of certification-service provision. All conditions related to such schemes must be objective, transparent, proportionate and non-discriminatory. Member States may not limit the number of accredited certification-service-providers for reasons which fall within the scope of this Directive.

3. Each Member State shall ensure the establishment of an appropriate system that allows for supervision of certification-service-providers which are established on its territory and issue qualified certificates to the public.

4. The conformity of secure signature-creation-devices with the requirements laid down in Annex III shall be determined by appropriate public or private bodies designated by Member States. The Commission shall, pursuant to the procedure laid down in Article 9, establish criteria for Member States to determine whether a body should be designated.

   A determination of conformity with the requirements laid down in Annex III made by the bodies referred to in the first subparagraph shall be recognised by all Member States.

5. The Commission may, in accordance with the procedure laid down in Article 9, establish and publish reference numbers of generally recognised standards for electronic-signature products in the Official Journal of the European Communities. Member States shall presume that there is compliance with the requirements laid down in Annex II, point (f), and Annex III when an electronic signature product meets those standards.

6. Member States and the Commission shall work together to promote the development and use of signature-verification devices in the light of the recommendations for secure signature-verification laid down in Annex IV and in the interests of the consumer.

7. Member States may make the use of electronic signatures in the public sector subject to possible additional requirements. Such requirements shall be objective, transparent,

proportionate and non-discriminatory and shall relate only to the specific characteristics of the application concerned. Such requirements may not constitute an obstacle to cross-border services for citizens.

Article 4
Internal market principles

1. Each Member State shall apply the national provisions which it adopts pursuant to this Directive to certification-service-providers established on its territory and to the services which they provide. Member States may not restrict the provision of certification-services originating in another Member State in the fields covered by this Directive.
2. Member States shall ensure that electronic-signature products which comply with this Directive are permitted to circulate freely in the internal market.

Article 5
Legal effects of electronic signatures

1. Member States shall ensure that advanced electronic signatures which are based on a qualified certificate and which are created by a secure-signature-creation device:
    (a) satisfy the legal requirements of a signature in relation to data in electronic form in the same manner as a handwritten signature satisfies those requirements in relation to paper-based data; and
    (b) are admissible as evidence in legal proceedings.
2. Member States shall ensure that an electronic signature is not denied legal effectiveness and admissibility as evidence in legal proceedings solely on the grounds that it is:
    —in electronic form, or
    —not based upon a qualified certificate, or
    —not based upon a qualified certificate issued by an accredited certification-service-provider, or
    —not created by a secure signature-creation device.

Article 6
Liability

1. As a minimum, Member States shall ensure that by issuing a certificate as a qualified certificate to the public or by guaranteeing such a certificate to the public a certification-service-provider is liable for damage caused to any entity or legal or natural person who reasonably relies on that certificate:
    (a) as regards the accuracy at the time of issuance of all information contained in the qualified certificate and as regards the fact that the certificate contains all the details prescribed for a qualified certificate;
    (b) for assurance that at the time of the issuance of the certificate, the signatory identified in the qualified certificate held the signature-creation data corresponding to the signature-verification data given or identified in the certificate;
    (c) for assurance that the signature-creation data and the signature-verification data can be used in a complementary manner in cases where the certification-service-provider generates them both;

unless the certification-service-provider proves that he has not acted negligently.

2. As a minimum Member States shall ensure that a certification-service-provider who has issued a certificate as a qualified certificate to the public is liable for damage caused to any entity or legal or natural person who reasonably relies on the certificate for failure to register revocation of the certificate unless the certification-service-provider proves that he has not acted negligently.

3. Member States shall ensure that a certification-service-provider may indicate in a qualified certificate limitations on the use of that certificate. Provided that the limitations are recognisable to third parties. The certification-service-provider shall not be liable for damage arising from use of a qualified certificate which exceeds the limitations placed on it.

4. Member States shall ensure that a certification-service-provider may indicate in the qualified certificate a limit on the value of transactions for which the certificate can be used, provided that the limit is recognisable to third parties.

5. The certification-service-provider shall not be liable for damage resulting from this maximum limit being exceeded.

6. The provisions of paragraphs 1 to 4 shall be without prejudice to Council Directive 93/13/EEC of 5 April 1993 on unfair terms in consumer contracts.[8]

Article 7
International aspects

1. Member States shall ensure that certificates which are issued as qualified certificates to the public by a certification-service-provider established in a third country are recognised as legally equivalent to certificates issued by a certification-service-provider established within the Community if:

    (a) the certification-service-provider fulfils the requirements laid down in this Directive and has been accredited under a voluntary accreditation scheme established in a Member State; or

    (b) a certification-service-provider established within the Community which fulfils the requirements laid down in this Directive guarantees the certificate; or

    (c) the certificate or the certification-service-provider is recognised under a bilateral or multilateral agreement between the Community and third countries or international organisations.

2. In order to facilitate cross-border certification services with third countries and legal recognition of advanced electronic signatures originating in third countries, the Commission shall make proposals, where appropriate, to achieve the effective implementation of standards and international agreements applicable to certification services. In particular, and where necessary, it shall submit proposals to the Council for appropriate mandates for the negotiation of bilateral and multilateral agreements with third countries and international organisations. The Council shall decide by qualified majority.

3. Whenever the Commission is informed of any difficulties encountered by Community undertakings with respect to market access in third countries, it may, if necessary, submit proposals to the Council for an appropriate mandate for the

---

[8] OJ L 95, 21.4.1993, p. 29.

negotiation of comparable rights for Community undertakings in these third countries. The Council shall decide by qualified majority.

Measures taken pursuant to this paragraph shall be without prejudice to the obligations of the Community and of the Member States under relevant international agreements.

Article 8
Data protection

1. Member States shall ensure that certification-service-providers and national bodies responsible for accreditation or supervision comply with the requirements laid down in Directive 95/46/EC of the European Parliament and of the Council of 24 October 1995 on tile protection of individuals with regard to the processing of personal data and on the free movement of such data.[9]
2. Member States shall ensure that a certification-service-provider which issues certificates to the public may collect personal data only directly from the data subject, or after the explicit consent of the data subject, and only insofar as it is necessary for the purposes of issuing and maintaining the certificate. The data may not be collected or processed for any other purposes without the explicit consent of the data subject.
3. Without prejudice to the legal effect given to pseudonyms under national law, Member States shall not prevent certification service providers from indicating in the certificate a pseudonym instead of the signatory's name.

Article 9
Committee

1. The Commission shall be assisted by an 'Electronic-Signature Committee', hereinafter referred to as 'the committee'.
2. Where reference is made to this paragraph, Articles 4 and 7 of Decision 1999/468/EC shall apply, having regard to the provisions of Article 8 thereof. The period laid down in Article 4(3) of Decision 1999/468/EC shall be set at three months.
3. The Committee shall adopt its own rules of procedure.

Article 10
Tasks of the committee

The committee shall clarify the requirements laid down in the Annexes of this Directive, the criteria referred to in Article 3(4) and the generally recognised standards for electronic signature products established and published pursuant to Article 3(5), in accordance with the procedure laid down in Article 9(2).

Article 11
Notification

1. Member States shall notify to the Commission and the other Member States the following:
   (a) information on national voluntary accreditation schemes, including any additional requirements pursuant to Article 3(7);

---

[9] OJ L 281, 23.11.1995, p. 31.

(b) the names and addresses of the national bodies responsible for accreditation and supervision as well as of the bodies referred to in Article 3(4);

(c) the names and addresses of all accredited national certification service providers.

2. Any information supplied under paragraph 1 and changes in respect of that information shall be notified by the Member States as soon as possible.

Article 12
Review

1. The Commission shall review the operation of this Directive and report thereon to the European Parliament and to the Council by 19 July 2003 at the latest.

2. The review shall inter alia assess whether the scope of this Directive should be modified, taking account of technological, market and legal developments. The report shall in particular include an assessment, on the basis of experience gained, of aspects of harmonisation. The report shall be accompanied, where appropriate, by legislative proposals.

Article 13
Implementation

1. Member States shall bring into force the laws, regulations and administrative provisions necessary to comply with this Directive before 19 July 2001. They shall forthwith inform the Commission thereof.

   When Member States adopt these measures, they shall contain a reference to this Directive or shall be accompanied by such a reference on the occasion of their official publication. The methods of making such reference shall be laid down by the Member States.

2. Member States shall communicate to the Commission the text of the main provisions of domestic law which they adopt in the field governed by this Directive.

Article 14
Entry into force

This Directive shall enter into force on the day of its publication in the Official Journal of the European Communities.

Article 15
Addressees

This Directive is addressed to the Member States.

Done at Brussels, 13 December 1999.

For the European Parliament
The President
N. Fontaine
For the Council
The President
S. Hassi

ANNEX I
REQUIREMENTS FOR QUALIFIED CERTIFICATES

Qualified certificates must contain:
  (a) an indication that the certificate is issued as a qualified certificate;
  (b) the identification of the certification-service-provider and the State in which it is established;
  (c) the name of the signatory or a pseudonym, which shall be identified as such;
  (d) provision for a specific attribute of the signatory to be included if relevant, depending on the purpose for which the certificate is intended;
  (e) signature-verification data which correspond to signature-creation data under the control of the signatory;
  (f) an indication of the beginning and end of the period of validity of the certificate;
  (g) the identity code of the certificate;
  (h) the advanced electronic signature of the certification-service-provider issuing it;
  (i) limitations on the scope of use of the certificate, if applicable; and
  (j) limits on the value of transactions for which the certificate can be used, if applicable.

ANNEX II
REQUIREMENTS FOR CERTIFICATION-SERVICE-PROVIDERS ISSUING QUALIFIED CERTIFICATES

Certification-service-providers must:
  (a) demonstrate the reliability necessary for providing certification services;
  (b) ensure the operation of a prompt and secure directory and a secure and immediate revocation service;
  (c) ensure that the date and time when a certificate is issued or revoked can be determined precisely;
  (d) verify, by appropriate means in accordance with national law, the identity and, if applicable, any specific attributes of the person to which a qualified certificate is issued;
  (e) employ personnel who possess the expert knowledge, experience, and qualifications necessary for the services provided, in particular competence at managerial level, expertise in electronic signature techology and familiarity with proper security procedures; they must also apply administrative and management procedures which are adequate and correspond to recognised standards;
  (f) use trustworthy systems and products which are protected against modification and ensure the technical and cryptographic security of the process supported by them;
  (g) take measures against forgery of certificates, and, in cases where the certification-service-provider generates signature-creation data, guarantee confidentiality during the process of generating such data;

(h) maintain sufficient financial resources to operate in conformity with the requirements laid down in the Directive, in particular to bear the risk of liability for damages, for example, by obtaining appropriate insurance;

(i) record all relevant information concerning a qualified certificate for an appropriate period of time, in particular for the purpose of providing evidence of certification for the purposes of legal proceedings. Such recording may be done electronically;

(j) not store or copy signature-creation data of the person to whom the certification-service-provider provided key management services;

(k) before entering into a contractual relationship with a person seeking a certificate to support his electronic signature inform that person by a durable means of communication of the precise terms and conditions regarding the use of the certificate, including any limitations on its use, the existence of a voluntary accreditation scheme and procedures for complaints and dispute settlement. Such information, which may be transmitted electronically, must be in writing and in readily understandable language. Relevant parts of this information must also be made available on request to third-parties relying on the certificate;

(l) use trustworthy systems to store certificates in a verifiable form so that:
—only authorised persons can make entries and changes,
—information can be checked for authenticity,
—certificates are publicly available for retrieval in only those cases for which the certificate-holder's consent has been obtained, and
—any technical changes compromising these security requirements are apparent to the operator.

ANNEX III
REQUIREMENTS FOR SECURE SIGNATURE-CREATION DEVICES

1. Secure signature-creation devices must, by appropriate technical and procedural means, ensure at the least that:
   (a) the signature-creation-data used for signature generation can practically occur only once, and that their secrecy is reasonably assured;
   (b) the signature-creation-data used for signature generation cannot, with reasonable assurance, be derived and the signature is protected against forgery using currently available technology;
   (c) the signature-creation-data used for signature generation can be reliably protected by the legitimate signatory against the use of others.

2. Secure signature-creation devices must not alter the data to be signed or prevent such data from being presented to the signatory prior to the signature process.

ANNEX IV
RECOMMENDATIONS FOR SECURE SIGNATURE VERIFICATION

During the signature-verification process it should be ensured with reasonable certainty that:

(a) the data used for verifying the signature correspond to the data displayed to the verifier;

(b) the signature is reliably verified and the result of that verification is correctly displayed;

(c) the verifier can, as necessary, reliably establish the contents of the signed data;

(d) the authenticity and validity of the certificate required at the time of signature verification are reliably verified;

(e) the result of verification and the signatory's identity are correctly displayed;

(f) the use of a pseudonym is clearly indicated; and

(g) any security-relevant changes can be detected.

(v) CMI RULES FOR ELECTRONIC BILLS OF LADING*

1. Scope of Application

These Rules shall apply whenever the parties so agree.

2. Definitions

(a) 'Contract of Carriage' means any agreement to carry goods wholly or partly by sea.

(b) 'EDI' means Electronic Data Interchange, i.e. the interchange of trade data effected by teletransmission.

(c) 'UN/EDIFACT' means the United Nations Rules for Electronic Data Interchange for Administration, Commerce and Transport.

(d) 'Transmission' means one or more messages electronically sent together as one unit of dispatch which includes heading and terminating data.

(e) 'Confirmation' means a Transmission which advises that the content of a Transmission appears to be complete and correct, without prejudice to any subsequent consideration or action that the content may warrant.

(f) 'Private Key' means any technically appropriate form, such as a combination of numbers and/or letters, which the parties may agree for securing the authenticity and integrity of a Transmission.

(g) 'Holder' means the party who is entitled to the rights described in Article 7(a) by virtue of its possession of a valid Private Key.

(h) 'Electronic Monitoring System' means the device by which a computer system can be examined for the transactions that it recorded, such as a Trade Data Log or an Audit Trail.

(i) 'Electronic Storage' means any temporary, intermediate or permanent storage of electronic data including the primary and the back-up storage of such data.

3. Rules of procedure

(a) When not in conflict with these Rules, the Uniform Rules of Conduct for Interchange of Trade Data by Teletransmission, 1987 (UNCID) shall govern the conduct between the parties.

(b) The EDI under these Rules should conform with the relevant UN/EDIFACT standards. However, the parties may use any other method of trade data interchange acceptable to all of the users.

(c) Unless otherwise agreed, the document format for the Contract of Carriage shall conform to the UN Layout Key or compatible national standard for bills of lading.

---

* Reproduced with the kind permission of Comité Maritime International.

199

(d) Unless otherwise agreed, a recipient of a Transmission is not authorised to act on a Transmission unless he has sent a Confirmation.

(e) In the event of a dispute arising between the parties as to the data actually transmitted, an Electronic Monitoring System may be used to verify the data received. Data concerning other transactions not related to the data in dispute are to be considered as trade secrets and thus not available for examination. If such data are unavoidably revealed as part of the examination of the Electronic Monitoring System, they must be treated as confidential and not released to any outside party or used for any other purpose.

(f) Any transfer of rights to the goods shall be considered to be private information, and shall not be released to any outside party not connected to the transport or clearance of the goods.

4. Form and content of the receipt message

(a) The carrier, upon receiving the goods from the shipper, shall give notice of the receipt of the goods to the shipper by a message at the electronic address specified by the shipper.

(b) This receipt message shall include:
   (i)   the name of the shipper;
   (ii) the description of the goods, with any representations and reservations, in the same tenor as would be required if a paper bill of lading were issued;
   (iii) the date and place of the receipt of the goods;
   (iv) a reference to the carrier's terms and conditions of carriage; and
   (v)   the Private Key to be used in subsequent Transmissions.

The shipper must confirm this receipt message to the carrier, upon which Confirmation the shipper shall be the Holder.

(c) Upon demand of the Holder, the receipt message shall be updated with the date and place of shipment as soon as the goods have been loaded on board.

(d) The information contained in (ii), (iii) and (iv) of paragraph (b) above including the date and place of shipment if updated in accordance with paragraph (c) of this Rule, shall have the same force and effect as if the receipt message were contained in a paper bill of lading.

5. Terms and conditions of the Contract of Carriage

(a) It is agreed and understood that whenever the carrier makes a reference to its terms and conditions of carriage, these terms and conditions shall form part of the Contract of Carriage.

(b) Such terms and conditions must be readily available to the parties to the Contract of Carriage.

(c) In the event of any conflict or inconsistency between such terms and conditions and these Rules, these Rules shall prevail.

6. Applicable law

The Contract of Carriage shall be subject to any international convention or national law which would have been compulsorily applicable if a paper bill of lading had been issued.

7. Right of Control and Transfer

(a) The Holder is the only party who may, as against the carrier:
    (1) claim delivery of the goods;
    (2) nominate the consignee or substitute a nominated consignee for any other party, including itself;
    (3) transfer the Right of Control and Transfer to another party;
    (4) instruct the carrier on any other subject concerning the goods, in accordance with the terms and conditions of the Contract of Carriage, as if he were the holder of a paper bill of lading.

(b) A transfer of the Right of Control and Transfer shall be effected: (i) by notification of the current Holder to the carrier of its intention to transfer its Right of Control and Transfer to a proposed new Holder, and (ii) confirmation by the carrier of such notification message, whereupon (iii) the carrier shall transmit the information as referred to in article 4 (except for the Private Key) to the proposed new Holder, whereafter (iv) the proposed new Holder shall advise the carrier of its acceptance of the Right of Control and Transfer, whereupon (v) the carrier shall cancel the current Private Key and issue a new Private Key to the new Holder.

(c) If the proposed new Holder advises the carrier that it does not accept the Right of Control and Transfer or fails to advise the carrier of such acceptance within a reasonable time, the proposed transfer of the Right of Control and Transfer shall not take place. The carrier shall notify the current Holder accordingly and the current Private Key shall retain its validity.

(d) The transfer of the Right of Control and Transfer in the manner described above shall have the same effects as the transfer of such rights under a paper bill of lading.

8. The Private Key

(a) The Private Key is unique to each successive Holder. It is not transferable by the Holder. The carrier and the Holder shall each maintain the security of the Private Key.

(b) The carrier shall only be obliged to send a Confirmation of an electronic message to the last Holder to whom it issued a Private Key, when such Holder secures the Transmission containing such electronic message by the use of the Private Key.

(c) The Private Key must be separate and distinct from any means used to identify the Contract of Carriage, and any security password or identification used to access the computer network.

9. Delivery

(a) The carrier shall notify the Holder of the place and date of intended delivery of the goods. Upon such notification the Holder has a duty to nominate a consignee and to give adequate delivery instructions to the carrier with verification by the Private Key. In the absence of such nomination, the Holder will be deemed to be the consignee.

(b) The carrier shall deliver the goods to the consignee upon production of proper identification in accordance with the delivery instructions specified in paragraph (a) above; such delivery shall automatically cancel the Private Key.

(c) The carrier shall be under no liability for misdelivery if it can prove that it exercised reasonable care to ascertain that the party who claimed to be the consignee was in fact that party.

10. Option to receive a paper document

(a) The Holder has the option at any time prior to delivery of the goods to demand from the carrier a paper bill of lading. Such document shall be made available at a location to be determined by the Holder, provided that no carrier shall be obliged to make such document available at a place where it has no facilities and in such instance the carrier shall only be obliged to make the document available at the facility nearest to the location determined by the Holder. The carrier shall not be responsible for delays in delivering the goods resulting from the Holder exercising the above option.

(b) The carrier has the option at any time prior to delivery of the goods to issue to the Holder a paper bill of lading unless the exercise of such option could result in undue delay or disrupts the delivery of the goods.

(c) A bill of lading issued under Rules 10(a) or (b) shall include: the information set out in the receipt message referred to in Rule 4 (except for the Private Key); and (ii) a statement to the effect that the bill of lading has been issued upon termination of the procedures for EDI under the CMI Rules for Electronic Bills of Lading. The aforementioned bill of lading shall be issued at the option of the Holder either to the order of the Holder whose name for this purpose shall then be inserted in the bill of lading or 'to bearer'.

(d) The issuance of a paper bill of lading under Rule 10(a) or (b) shall cancel the Private Key and terminate the procedures for EDI under these Rules. Termination of these procedures by the Holder or the carrier will not relieve any of the parties to the Contract of Carriage of their rights, obligations or liabilities while performing under the present Rules nor of their rights, obligations or liabilities under the Contract of Carriage.

(e) The Holder may demand at any time the issuance of a print-out of the receipt message referred to in Rule 4 (except for the Private Key) marked as 'non-negotiable copy'. The issuance of such a print-out shall not cancel the Private Key nor terminate the procedures for EDI.

11. Electronic data is equivalent to writing

The carrier and the shipper and all subsequent parties utilizing these procedures agree that any national or local law, custom or practice requiring the Contract of Carriage to be evidenced in writing and signed, is satisfied by the transmitted and confirmed electronic data residing on computer data storage media displayable in human language on a video screen or as printed out by a computer. In agreeing to adopt these Rules, the parties shall be taken to have agreed not to raise the defence that this contract is not in writing.

4

INTERNATIONAL SALES

A. Introductory Text

The contract of sale is one of the most important contracts in commercial law. It can assume many different forms. It can be domestic or international, consumer or commercial and it can take the form either of a sale confined to the goods themselves or of a documentary sale, in which the seller also undertakes to transfer to the buyer agreed transport and trade documents, the essential documents being a bill of lading, a policy or certificate of marine insurance, and a commercial invoice. Documentary sales are particularly prevalent where the goods are to be shipped to or from another country. Not all contracts of sale are of significance for this book. Purely domestic sales are beyond its scope on the basis that they are made and performed within one jurisdiction by parties within that jurisdiction. Consumer sales (that is to say, contracts of sale concluded between a business and a private person who is not acting in the course of his or her business) also lie largely outside its scope.[1]

Our concern is with international sales. Two documents assume particular significance in this context. The first is the Vienna Convention on Contracts for the International Sale of Goods ('CISG') and the second consists of a set of standard trade terms, sponsored by the International Chamber of Commerce, known as Incoterms.[2] The two documents assume very different legal forms. CISG is a legally operative instrument which has been ratified by many of the major trading nations of the world.[3] The Incoterms, by contrast, do not have the force of law as such. Rather, they derive their legal effect from their incorporation, either expressly or impliedly, into contracts of sale. Incoterms are widely used in export sales. Their function is to define (or to assist in the definition of) the price and delivery terms of the contract of sale. The most important instrument is, however, CISG and it is to its provisions that we must first turn.

1. The Vienna Convention on Contracts for the International Sale of Goods, 1980

The CISG was agreed at Vienna in 1980 and came into effect on 1 January 1988 after it had been ratified by 10 States. It has now been ratified by 63 States[4] and is in force in many of the major trading nations of the world. The Convention was the product of many years of work and it is built upon a foundation laid by academics and practitioners. The starting point was the work of Professor Ernst Rabel beginning in the late 1920s. That work did not bear fruit immediately. However it did lead eventually to the ratification of two Conventions after the Second World War, namely the Uniform Law on the Formation of Contracts for the International Sale of Goods 1964 and the Uniform Law on the International Sale of Goods 1964. These Conventions were not, however, successful. They were ratified by only nine States[5] and were viewed with suspicion by a number of developing nations. But it

---

[1] Although in the case of consumer contracts concluded within the European Union, a significant degree of harmonization has been introduced as a result of the Directive on Certain Aspects of the Sale of Consumer Goods and Associated Guarantees (1999/44/EC (25 May 1999), 1999 OJ L 171 p.12). The case for a greater degree of harmonization of consumer sales may increase in future years as consumers make greater use of the Internet, thus reducing the practical significance of jurisdictional boundaries.   [2] ICC Publication No. 560 (2000).

[3] The CISG has also had a considerable impact on the law of contract more generally. Thus the provisions of CISG provided the foundation for the drafting of the Principles of International Commercial Contracts (see p. 46 above) and the Principles of European Contract Law (see p. 83 above) and they have also had an impact on the reform of contract law and sales law within nation States.

[4] A list of the States that have ratified CISG at the date of publication is provided at p. 239 below. The list is kept up to date at http://www.uncitral.org/en-index.htm.

[5] Namely, the United Kingdom, Belgium, West Germany, Italy, Luxemburg, Netherlands, San Marino, Israel, and Gambia. It was possible to ratify the Conventions on an 'opt-in' basis, that is to

would be a mistake to conclude from this that these Conventions are therefore devoid of significance. Their prime significance lies in the fact that they formed the starting point for the work of those responsible for framing the text of CISG and the CISG has been said to be a radically revised version of the Hague Uniform Laws.

The CISG is divided into four parts and these parts are in turn divided into various chapters.

Sphere of application

Part I deals with the sphere of application of the Convention and also contains some general provisions. In terms of the sphere of application of the Convention, Article 1 has proved to be a provision of some controversy. Article 1(1)(a) is relatively straightforward in so far as it provides that the Convention applies to contracts for the sale of goods between parties whose places of business are in different States when the States are Contracting States.[6] Much more difficult has been Article 1(1)(b) which extends the sphere of application of the Convention so that it applies when the rules of private international law lead to the application of the law of a Contracting State. The controversy that lurks behind this provision is reflected in Article 95 which entitles a State, at the time of ratification, acceptance, approval, or accession, to declare that it will not be bound by Article 1(1)(b). A number of States have entered an Article 95 reservation.[7] The balancing act conducted by Article 1(1)(b) is a difficult one. On the one hand, it enables the sphere of application of the Convention to be extended so that it does not only apply as between parties both of whom have their place of business in Contracting States. As a result of Article 1(1)(b) the Convention can apply to a contract concluded between a party which has its place of business in a Contracting State and a party that has its place of business in a non-Contracting State. Yet it is this extension which is the source of the problem because its effect is that where the rules of private international law of the forum State lead to the application of the law of a non-Contracting State then that State's law will govern the contract but where those rules lead to the application of the law of a Contracting State, the law applicable will be CISG and not the domestic law of that Contracting State. The consequence

---

say, the Conventions were only applicable if the parties expressly or, perhaps, impliedly incorporated the Conventions into their contract. The United Kingdom ratified the Conventions on this basis (see the Uniform Laws on International Sales Act 1967). It is not possible to ratify CISG on an 'opt-in' basis. While it is generally open to the parties to exclude the operation of the Convention, either in whole or in part, the onus is put upon the parties to exclude the operation of the convention in the case of a contract of sale which falls within the sphere of application of the Convention.

[6] It should be noted that the test of internationality adopted by CISG relates to the identity of the contracting parties and not to the movement of the goods between different jurisdictions. Thus it is the fact that the parties have their places of business (as defined in Art 10) in different States that is decisive in terms of the application of the Convention.

[7] A list of the States that have entered an Article 95 reservation can be obtained at http://www.uncitral.org/en-index.htm.

of Article 1(1)(b) is therefore to diminish the significance of the domestic law of a Contracting State in favour of CISG. For some States this was a step too far. While they were prepared to accept the displacement of their own domestic law in contracts concluded between businesses in Contracting States, they were not willing to accept the same displacement of their domestic law in contracts concluded with businesses in non-Contracting States. The price paid for the compromise to be found in Article 95 has proved to be a high one, in the sense that it has given rise to a very complex body of law.[8] That said, the significance of this debate is likely to diminish in the future. As the number of States ratifying the Convention increases, the consequence will be that more and more cases will fall within the scope of Article 1(1)(a) and the controversy associated with the application of Article 1(1)(b), and its relationship with Article 95, will gradually fade away.

Definitions and exclusions

The Convention does not purport to define a contract of sale. Instead, it excludes certain contracts from its scope. Thus Articles 2 and 3 exclude consumer sales from the scope of CISG, attempt to distinguish a contract for the sale of goods from a contract for services (or a contract for work and materials), and they provide a partial definition of goods.

Also excluded from the scope of the Convention are matters relating to the validity of the contract and the effect which the contract may have on the property in the goods sold. At first sight, it seems strange to exclude from the Convention matters relating to the validity of the contract and the passing of property, given that sale is a contract under which property in goods passes from the seller to the buyer. The reason for their exclusion is essentially a pragmatic one. The law relating to the validity of contracts and the passing of property differs sharply as between different nation States and the task of producing a uniform set of rules on these intractable topics would have been a formidable one. Pragmatic considerations therefore dictated a narrower sphere of application of the Convention so that it applies, in essence, to the formation of a contract of sale, the rights and obligations of buyers and sellers, and the remedial consequences that flow from non-performance of one or more of these obligations.

Article 5 is also an exclusionary provision in that it excludes from the scope of the Convention the liability of the seller for death or personal injury caused by the goods of any person.

Article 6 is also significant, in so far as it provides that, subject to Article 12, the parties to a contract of sale are entitled to exclude the application of the

---

[8] For example, whether a judge in a forum State which is a Contracting State is bound to respect the reservation which has been entered by the State whose law is found to be the governing law as a consequence of the application of the rules of private international law or whether on the other hand the judge should apply CISG on the ground that only a reservation made by the forum State is relevant.

Convention. This is an important point. The Convention is not mandatory in the sense that it is not open to the parties to contract out of it.[9] Parties can contract out of it, or parts of it, but the onus is put on the parties to do so; unless they do so they will be bound by the terms of the Convention. This is a relatively straightforward matter where the parties expressly exclude the application of CISG. More difficult is the case where it is submitted that the parties have impliedly excluded CISG. For example, does the incorporation of the Incoterms operate to displace the application of CISG? It is very unlikely that the Incoterms will operate to displace it in its entirety because the Incoterms do not purport to be comprehensive. They therefore leave room for CISG to operate but, where a particular Incoterm is inconsistent with a provision in CISG which would otherwise have governed the issue, the provision in CISG will give way to the term of the contract (unless the term of the contract and the relevant provision in CISG can be read together in an harmonious fashion). Again, the parties' choice of the law of a non-Contracting Sate by implication excludes CISG.

Interpretation and good faith

Article 7 deals with a number of issues of significance. The first relates to the direction that, in the interpretation of the Convention, regard is to be had to its international character and to the need to promote uniformity in its application. The aim of this provision is clear; it is to ensure that, as far as possible, the Convention is interpreted in the same way in different jurisdictions. In this respect the Convention is to have an autonomous interpretation. The problem is the obvious one, namely what practical steps can be taken in order to ensure that the text of the Convention is given an autonomous interpretation? Two important steps have been taken. The first is the provision of information. Databases now exist which contain the text of many court decisions and arbitral awards relating to the Convention. The most important databases are CLOUT[10] and Unilex.[11] Other good websites exist.[12] A court or arbitration panel that wishes to discover the interpretation that has previously been placed upon a provision of the Convention can now take steps in order to do so. The weight to be given to these precedents is not an entirely straightforward matter. A court or arbitrator is not bound to follow previous decisions. It may have 'regard' to them, but is not bound by them. The second step relates to the existence of academic commentaries on the Convention.[13]

---

[9] The exception is Art 12 which expressly states that the parties may not derogate from or vary its effect.   [10] See http://www.uncitral.org/english/clout/.

[11] See http://www.unilex.info/dynasite.cfm

[12] See, for example, PACE (www.cisg.law.pace.edu) and University of Freiburg (http://www.cisg-online.ch/).

[13] See, for example, P. Schlechtriem, *Commentary on the UN Convention on the International Sale of Goods* (Oxford, 1998); J. Honnold, *Uniform Law for International Sales under the 1980 United Nations Convention* (2nd edn, 1991) and C. M. Bianca and M. G. Bonell, *Commentary on the International Sales Law* (1987).

These commentaries may help to achieve a more harmonious interpretation of the Convention. A further step has been taken with the formation of a private body, the International Sales Convention Advisory Council ('CISG—AC'). It consists of a panel of experts whose declared function is to support the understanding of CISG and to assist in the promotion of a uniform interpretation of CISG. It will do so through, *inter alia,* the preparation of opinions on issues which have been the subject of divergent interpretations in national courts and arbitral tribunals. The difficulty is that these opinions and commentaries lack official status. However, in the long run, they may help to iron out inconsistencies in the interpretation of the Convention.

The second problem with Article 7 relates to the role of good faith. This is a vexed issue which has divided civil law and common law jurisdictions. The text is a compromise between the different views and, as such, has given rise to interpretative difficulties. Three different views are possible. The first is that the Convention does not impose a duty of good faith on the parties to the contract of sale. Rather, good faith is a principle that is to be applied by judges and arbitrators only in the interpretation of the Convention. This construction gains support from the fact that the good faith obligation is located in an article the subject-matter of which is the interpretation of the Convention. The second view is that the Article does impose a duty of good faith on the parties to the contract. In favour of this view is the proposition that it is not possible to draw a clear line of distinction between a good faith duty that is directed at the interpretation of the Convention and a duty that is directed at the interpretation and enforcement of the contract of sale itself. Interpretation does not exist in the abstract; it inevitably impacts on the rights and duties of the parties that are the subject of the interpretative exercise. The difficulty with this argument is the obvious one, namely that it appears to undermine the compromise supposedly created by Article 7. The third view is that Article 7(1) does not impose a duty of good faith on the parties but that this duty is one of the 'general principles' on which the Convention is based with the result that the duty is imposed on the parties by Article 7(2) rather than 7(1). Whether such a general principle can be extracted from the various other provisions of the Convention depends very much on how broadly the concept of good faith is to be understood. While many legal systems in the world recognize the existence of a doctrine of good faith and fair dealing, their conception of good faith is not homogenous: significant differences exist in relation to the scope and the content of the doctrine of good faith. The existence of these different views as to the scope and content of the duty of good faith recognized in Article 7 serves to underline the difficulties inherent in any compromise. A text which is deliberately drafted in ambiguous terms in order to secure agreement will almost inevitably give rise to interpretative difficulties in the future. The appearance of agreement only postpones the time at which the issue of principle has to be decided.

Article 7(2) also directs courts and arbitrators to have regard to the general principles on which the Convention is based. But it does so only where the matter is 'governed by' the Convention but the Convention does not expressly answer the problem that has arisen on the facts of the case. In such a case the court or arbitrator is to resolve the problem by reference to the general principles on which the Convention is based and only to revert to national law as a last resort. However, where the matter is not governed by the Convention then it must be regulated by the otherwise applicable domestic law. The problem is that the distinction between matters governed by the Convention and those not so governed may cause considerable difficulty in individual cases. Yet, the distinction is a vital one in terms of the scope of the Convention. The UNIDROIT Principles for International Commercial Contracts[14] may also have a role to play as a gap-filler.[15]

Usage

The parties are bound by any usage to which they have agreed and by any practices which they have established between themselves.[16] This agreement need not be express; it can be implied. Incoterms can be incorporated into a contract of sale in this way. As has been noted, the Incoterms do not themselves have the force of law; they must be incorporated into the contract.[17] The most obvious method of incorporation is usage.

Formalities

The general rule is clear: contracts of sale need not be made in writing, nor are they subject to other requirements of form.[18] This provision proved to be a controversial one for some jurisdictions at the time of the negotiation of the Convention[19] and the result is Article 96 which entitles a State to enter a reservation so as to preserve requirements of form.[20]

Formation

Part II of the Convention deals with the formation of a contract of sale. This part was also a source of some controversy, in particular for Scandinavian countries. As a

---

[14] See further pp. 212–213 below.

[15] For example, in relation to Art 78 of CISG which is discussed in note 51 below.

[16] Article 9(1). See also the elaboration of this test in Art 9(2) which sets up a rebuttable presumption that certain usages, which are widely known and observed in international trade, are applicable to the contract.

[17] The test applied by the courts when deciding whether or not to incorporate the Incoterms into the contract may vary between States. In some countries the courts may be very willing to find that the Incoterms have been incorporated into the contract, while in other cases, the courts may require more by way of evidence to establish that the Incoterms have been incorporated into the contract.

[18] Article 11.

[19] It is less significant today, given the prevalence of electronic forms of communication, on which see pp. 131–143 above.

[20] The States that have entered a reservation can be found at http://www.uncitral.org/en-index.htm.

consequence, Article 92 makes it possible for a State to make a declaration that it will not be bound by Part II.[21] The framework adopted by the Convention is the offer and acceptance framework,[22] with appropriate modifications.[23] The Convention provides answers to old problems, in particular the time at which a contract is concluded when the parties make use of the post,[24] the battle of the forms,[25] and the revocability of offers.[26]

The rights and duties of the parties

Part III of the Convention is, in many ways, the heart of the Convention. It consists of 64 Articles. It is divided into five chapters and these chapters are often split into sections. A State can enter a declaration that it will not be bound by Part III.[27]

Breach and fundamental breach

Chapter I deals with general provisions. Two issues stand out. The first is the definition of fundamental breach in Article 25. The word 'breach' is not defined in the Convention. However it is clear that it encompasses not only an unexcused failure in performance (the sense in which English law uses the word breach) but any failure to perform, whether that failure to perform is excused or not.[28] The word 'fundamental' is also important. From the perspective of a common lawyer, particularly the perspective of an English commercial lawyer, the definition appears to be a narrow one in that it is an objective test which appears to deny to the parties the ability to decide for themselves which breaches shall, and which shall not, constitute a fundamental breach.[29] In other words, it is for the court or the arbitrator to decide whether or not a breach is fundamental and, in so deciding, the court or arbitrator is to have regard to the matters referred to in Article 25.

Specific performance

The second point of importance which emerges from Chapter I relates to the remedy of specific performance. Here again we encounter the divide between common law and civil law jurisdictions because specific performance is traditionally a primary remedy in the latter jurisdictions, but only a secondary role in the former. Article 28 does not attempt to resolve this problem; rather it relegates the issue to national law.

---

[21] A list of the States that have made such a reservation can be found at http://www.uncitral.org/en-index.htm.

[22] Articles 14–17 define and regulate offers, while Art 18–22 regulate the acceptance.

[23] For example, in the case of the battle of the forms: see Art 19.

[24] Articles 16(2), 18(2), 21(2), and 24. The time chosen is the time at which the acceptance reaches the offeror, and not the time of posting. [25] Article 19.

[26] Article 16.

[27] Article 92. A list of the States that have made such a reservation can be found at http://www.uncitral.org/en-index.htm.

[28] The fact that the word breach is used in this wider sense becomes apparent from an examination of Art 79, on which see p. 212 below.

[29] Contrast in this respect Art 8:103(a) of the Principles of European Contract Law (p. 109 above).

The obligations of the seller

Chapter II sets out the obligations of the sellers and is, in turn, divided into three sections. The first section[30] regulates the delivery obligations of the seller (and delivery here extends to the delivery of documents). The second section[31] deals with the obligations of the seller in relation to the conformity of the goods and claims by third parties. This section has generated numerous interpretative difficulties, particularly in relation to the notification obligations of the buyer.[32]

Remedies of the buyer

The third section of Chapter II deals with the remedies for breach of contract by the seller. The section contains within it a multiplicity of remedies, including delivery by the seller of substitute goods,[33] repair of the goods,[34] avoidance of the contract,[35] the fixture of an additional period of time of reasonable length for performance by the seller of its obligations (followed by avoidance in the case of non-compliance by the seller),[36] cure by the seller (either before or, in certain cases after, the time for performance),[37] price reduction,[38] and damages.[39] Viewed from the perspective of a common law lawyer, a striking feature of the remedial regime is its complexity. It provides for a broader range of remedies than that found in many common law jurisdictions. A second feature is that termination (or, in the language of CISG, avoidance) appears to play a subsidiary role. The philosophy underpinning the Convention appears to be that the law should encourage the parties to the contract of sale to stick together and to work out their difficulties. The response should not be to encourage parties to walk away from the transaction at the first sign of difficulty, via a wide right of termination.

The obligations of the buyer and the remedies of the seller

Chapter III regulates the obligations of the buyer. The obligations of the buyer are to pay the price[40] and to take delivery of the goods.[41] The remedies for breach of contract by the buyer[42] in many ways mirror the remedies available to the buyer in the event of a failure by the seller to perform its obligations under the contract. Thus we find that the seller may be entitled to require the buyer to pay the price, take delivery or perform his other obligations under the contract.[43] Alternatively the seller may fix an additional period of time of reasonable length for performance by the buyer of his obligations,[44] and in default of such performance may avoid the contract[45] and/or claim damages.[46]

---

[30] Articles 31–4. [31] Articles 35–4. [32] Article 39 and, albeit to a lesser extent, Art 43.
[33] Article 46(1) and (2). [34] Article 46(3).
[35] Article 49. The effects of avoidance are set out in Art 81–4. Avoidance releases both parties from their obligations to perform under the contract (subject to any damages claim which may arise) but, crucially, a party who has performed his obligations under the contract, is entitled to restitution from the other party. [36] Article 47.
[37] Article 48. [38] Article 50. [39] Article 45(1)(b) and Art 74–7.
[40] Articles 54–9. [41] Article 60. [42] Articles 61–5. [43] Article 62.
[44] Article 63. [45] Article 64. [46] Articles 61(1)(b), 63(2) and 74–7.

Risk

Chapter IV deals with the passing of risk. This is a notoriously difficult subject and in many cases will be regulated expressly by the terms of the contract of sale. The default rule adopted by CISG is that risk passes with control or custody of the goods.[47] Particular provision is made for contracts of sale which involve the carriage of the goods[48] and for goods sold while in transit.[49] The link between risk and control is not, however, an automatic one. In the case of c.i.f. contracts, the passage of risk is frequently backdated to the time of shipment. This is reflected in the second sentence of Article 68 which provides that risk can pass with retrospective effect where the goods are handed over to a carrier who issues documents embodying the contract of carriage.

Anticipatory breach, damages, and interest

Chapter V deals with matters which are stated to be 'common to the obligations of the seller and of the buyer'. A miscellany of issues fall within the scope of this Chapter. Firstly, the Convention recognizes the concept of anticipatory breach and the right to suspend performance of the contract.[50] Secondly, the principles governing the assessment of damages are located in Articles 74–7, which fixes the basic measure of recovery, the remoteness rule applicable, and recognises the existence of an obligation to mitigate. The entitlement of a party to recover interest is regulated by Article 78. However, the regulation is only partial. The Article says nothing about the rate of interest, nor the date from which interest is payable. In the absence of answers in the text of the Convention, courts and arbitrators have had to look elsewhere for answers to these questions (answers have been found either in Article 7.4.9 of the UNIDROIT Principles for International Commercial Contracts[51] or in the otherwise applicable national law).

Force majeure

Article 79 deals with a difficult issue. It is headed 'exemption' but deals with what, in civilian terms, may be called 'force majeure.' There is no direct equivalent in common law systems. The doctrine of frustration operates in a very different manner in the common law, largely because the effect of the operation of the doctrine is to bring the contract between the parties to an end. The nearest equivalent of the doctrine of force majeure in common law systems is probably in the force majeure clauses that are to be found in many modern commercial contracts. However, the content of Article 79 does not reflect the doctrine of force majeure in any one legal system. In this respect, the provision is a compromise. From the perspective of a common lawyer, a striking feature of the Article is that it

---

[47] Article 69. This is a better rule than one which links risk to the passing of property.
[48] Article 67.   [49] Article 68.   [50] Articles 71–3.
[51] See p. 46 above. This is an example of the supplementary role that the UNIDROIT Principles can play in relation to CISG.

shields a party from liability in damages but purports to leave all other remedies intact.[52] The existence of an entitlement to terminate is not regulated by Article 79 but by the general provisions of Part III dealing with avoidance for non-performance. Article 79 also raises a number of interpretative difficulties; the principal difficulty is probably the meaning of the word 'impediment'. It clearly encompasses events which make it physically impossible to perform in accordance with the terms of the contract but the position is less clear in relation to events which do not physically prevent performance from taking place but, instead, make it economically more difficult to perform. The predominant view is that economic difficulties do not, except possibly in extreme cases, amount to an impediment. Article 79 is less innovative than the corresponding provisions to be found in both the UNIDROIT Principles and the Principles of European Contract Law. The latter instruments also contain provisions the effect of which is to impose upon the parties a duty to enter into negotiations with a view to adapting or ending the contract in cases of 'hardship'[53] or 'change of circumstances'.[54] This is an area in which it may be possible for a court or an arbitral tribunal to resort to the UNIDROIT Principles or to PECL for the purpose of supplementing Article 79.

Final provisions

Part IV deals with a number of important issues relating to matters such as ratifications and reservations. A complete list of accessions together with all the reservations can be found on the UNICITRAL website.[55]

2. Incoterms, 2000

As has been noted,[56] the Incoterms are a set of trade terms, sponsored by the International Chamber of Commerce, which are designed for incorporation into export sale contracts. They are widely used in practice. Their primary function is to define the obligations of buyers and sellers in relation to matters such as delivery, payment, insurance, export and import licences, and the transfer of risk. It is important to note this definitional role of the Incoterms. They do not purport to deal with the remedial consequences of a breach of any of these obligations. These must be regulated by the law applicable to the contract of sale. To this extent, the Incoterms can only bring about partial harmonization of the law relating to export sales.

Incoterms can be divided into four broad groups. These are arranged in ascending order; that is to say, the obligations of the seller increase in scope as we move from the first group through to the fourth and final group. First there is an

---

[52] Including specific performance. This qualification is not as strange as it might appear because an impediment may be temporary in nature.

[53] UNIDROIT Principles, Art 6.2.2 and 6.2.3, on which see p. 45 above.

[54] PECL, Art 6:111(3), on which see p. 45 above.   [55] http://www.unicitral.org/en-index.htm.

[56] See p. 209 above.

E-term (ex works) where the delivery point is stated to be the seller's premises and the seller has no responsibility for delivery to the carrier nor to load the goods on to any vehicle provided by the buyer. Secondly, there are the F-terms (FCA, FAS, and FOB) under which the seller assumes an obligation to deliver the goods to the carrier but the buyer remains responsible for payment for the freight for the carriage of the goods. Thirdly, there are the C-terms (CFR, CIF, CPT, and CIP) under which the seller assumes the further obligation to arrange and pay for the carriage of the goods. Finally, there are the D-terms (DAF, DES, DEQ, DDU, and DDP) which are arrival contracts under which the seller is required to deliver the goods to the buyer at an agreed delivery point, usually in the buyer's country.

B. Instruments

(i) UNITED NATIONS CONVENTION ON CONTRACTS FOR THE INTERNATIONAL SALE OF GOODS (1980)*

* Reproduced with the kind permission of UNCITRAL.

PREAMBLE

The States Parties to this Convention,

Bearing in mind the broad objectives in the resolutions adopted by the sixth special session of the General Assembly of the United Nations on the establishment of a New International Economic Order,

Considering that the development of international trade on the basis of equality and mutual benefit is an important element in promoting friendly relations among States,

Being of the opinion that the adoption of uniform rules which govern contracts for the international sale of goods and take into account the different social, economic and legal systems would contribute to the removal of legal barriers in international trade and promote the development of international trade,

Have agreed as follows:

PART I
SPHERE OF APPLICATION AND
GENERAL PROVISIONS

CHAPTER 1
SPHERE OF APPLICATION

Article 1

(1) This Convention applies to contracts of sale of goods between parties whose places of business are in different States:
(a) when the States are Contracting States; or
(b) when the rules of private international law lead to the application of the law of a Contracting State.
(2) The fact that the parties have their places of business in different States is to be disregarded whenever this fact does not appear either from the contract or from any dealings between, or from information disclosed by, the parties at any time before or at the conclusion of the contract.
(3) Neither the nationality of the parties nor the civil or commercial character of the parties or of the contract is to be taken into consideration in determining the application of this Convention.

Article 2

This Convention does not apply to sales:
(a) of goods bought for personal, family or household use, unless the seller, at any time before or at the conclusion of the contract, neither knew nor ought to have known that the goods were bought for any such use;
(b) by auction;
(c) on execution or otherwise by authority of law;
(d) of stocks, shares, investment securities, negotiable instruments or money;
(e) of ships, vessels, hovercraft or aircraft;
(f) of electricity.

Article 3

(1) Contracts for the supply of goods to be manufactured or produced are to be considered sales unless the party who orders the goods undertakes to supply a substantial part of the materials necessary for such manufacture or production.
(2) This Convention does not apply to contracts in which the preponderant part of the obligations of the party who furnishes the goods consists in the supply of labour or other services.

Article 4

This Convention governs only the formation of the contract of sale and the rights and obligations of the seller and the buyer arising from such a contract. In particular, except as otherwise expressly provided in this Convention, it is not concerned with:

    (a) the validity of the contract or of any of its provisions or of any usage;

    (b) the effect which the contract may have on the property in the goods sold.

Article 5

This Convention does not apply to the liability of the seller for death or personal injury caused by the goods to any person.

Article 6

The parties may exclude the application of this Convention or, subject to article 12, derogate from or vary the effect of any of its provisions.

CHAPTER II
GENERAL PROVISIONS

Article 7

(1) In the interpretation of this Convention, regard is to be had to its international character and to the need to promote uniformity in its application and the observance of good faith in international trade.

(2) Questions concerning matters governed by this Convention which are not expressly settled in it are to be settled in conformity with the general principles on which it is based or, in the absence of such principles, in conformity with the law applicable by virtue of the rules of private international law.

Article 8

(1) For the purposes of this Convention statements made by and other conduct of a party are to be interpreted according to his intent where the other party knew or could not have been unaware what that intent was.

(2) If the preceding paragraph is not applicable, statements made by and other conduct of a party are to be interpreted according to the understanding that a reasonable person of the same kind as the other party would have had in the same circumstances.

(3) In determining the intent of a party or the understanding a reasonable person would have had, due consideration is to be given to all relevant circumstances of the case including the negotiations, any practices which the parties have established between themselves, usages and any subsequent conduct of the parties.

Article 9

(1) The parties are bound by any usage to which they have agreed and by any practices which they have established between themselves.

(2) The parties are considered, unless otherwise agreed, to have impliedly made applicable to their contract or its formation a usage of which the parties knew or ought to have known and which in international trade is widely known to, and regularly observed by, parties to contracts of the type involved in the particular trade concerned.

Article 10

For the purposes of this Convention:
(a) if a party has more than one place of business, the place of business is that which has the closest relationship to the contract and its performance, having regard to the circumstances known to or contemplated by the parties at any time before or at the conclusion of the contract;
(b) if a party does not have a place of business, reference is to be made to his habitual residence.

Article 11

A contract of sale need not be concluded in or evidenced by writing and is not subject to any other requirement as to form. It may be proved by any means, including witnesses.

Article 12

Any provision of article 11, article 29 or Part II of this Convention that allows a contract of sale or its modification or termination by agreement or any offer, acceptance or other indication of intention to be made in any form other than in writing does not apply where any party has his place of business in a Contracting State which has made a declaration under article 96 of this Convention. The parties may not derogate from or vary the effect of this article.

Article 13

For the purposes of this Convention 'writing' includes telegram and telex.

PART II
FORMATION OF THE CONTRACT

Article 14

(1) A proposal for concluding a contract addressed to one or more specific persons constitutes an offer if it is sufficiently definite and indicates the intention of the offeror to be bound in case of acceptance. A proposal is sufficiently definite if it indicates the goods and expressly or implicitly fixes or makes provision for determining the quantity and the price.
(2) A proposal other than one addressed to one or more specific persons is to be considered merely as an invitation to make offers, unless the contrary is clearly indicated by the person making the proposal.

Article 15

(1) An offer becomes effective when it reaches the offeree.
(2) An offer, even if it is irrevocable, may be withdrawn if the withdrawal reaches the offeree before or at the same time as the offer.

Article 16

(1) Until a contract is concluded an offer may be revoked if the revocation reaches the offeree before he has dispatched an acceptance.

(2) However, an offer cannot be revoked:
  (a) if it indicates, whether by stating a fixed time for acceptance or otherwise, that it is irrevocable; or
  (b) if it was reasonable for the offeree to rely on the offer as being irrevocable and the offeree has acted in reliance on the offer.

Article 17

An offer, even if it is irrevocable, is terminated when a rejection reaches the offeror.

Article 18

(1) A statement made by or other conduct of the offeree indicating assent to an offer is an acceptance. Silence or inactivity does not in itself amount to acceptance.
(2) An acceptance of an offer becomes effective at the moment the indication of assent reaches the offeror. An acceptance is not effective if the indication of assent does not reach the offeror within the time he has fixed or, if no time is fixed, within a reasonable time, due account being taken of the circumstances of the transaction, including the rapidity of the means of communication employed by the offeror. An oral offer must be accepted immediately unless the circumstances indicate otherwise.
(3) However, if, by virtue of the offer or as a result of practices which the parties have established between themselves or of usage, the offeree may indicate assent by performing an act, such as one relating to the dispatch of the goods or payment of the price, without notice to the offeror, the acceptance is effective at the moment the act is performed, provided that the act is performed within the period of time laid down in the preceding paragraph.

Article 19

(1) A reply to an offer which purports to be an acceptance but contains additions, limitations or other modifications is a rejection of the offer and constitutes a counteroffer.
(2) However, a reply to an offer which purports to be an acceptance but contains additional or different terms which do not materially alter the terms of the offer constitutes an acceptance, unless the offeror, without undue delay, objects orally to the discrepancy or dispatches a notice to that effect. If he does not so object, the terms of the contract are the terms of the offer with the modifications contained in the acceptance.
(3) Additional or different terms relating, among other things, to the price, payment, quality and quantity of the goods, place and time of delivery, extent of one party's liability to the other or the settlement of disputes are considered to alter the terms of the offer materially.

Article 20

(1) A period of time of acceptance fixed by the offeror in a telegram or a letter begins to run from the moment the telegram is handed in for dispatch or from the date shown on the letter or, if no such date is shown, from the date shown on the envelope. A period of time for acceptance fixed by the offeror by telephone, telex or other means of instantaneous communication, begins to run from the moment that the offer reaches the offeree.

(2) Official holidays or non-business days occurring during the period for acceptance are included in calculating the period. However, if a notice of acceptance cannot be delivered at the address of the offeror on the last day of the period because that day falls on an official holiday or a non-business day at the place of business of the offeror, the period is extended until the first business day which follows.

Article 21

(1) A late acceptance is nevertheless effective as an acceptance if without delay the offeror orally so informs the offeree or dispatches a notice to that effect.
(2) If a letter or other writing containing a late acceptance shows that it has been sent in such circumstances that if its transmission had been normal it would have reached the offeror in due time, the late acceptance is effective as an acceptance unless, without delay, the offeror orally informs the offeree that he considers his offer as having lapsed or dispatches a notice to that effect.

Article 22

An acceptance may be withdrawn if the withdrawal reaches the offeror before or at the same time as the acceptance would have become effective.

Article 23

A contract is concluded at the moment when an acceptance of an offer becomes effective in accordance with the provisions of this Convention.

Article 24

For the purposes of this Part of the Convention, an offer, declaration of acceptance or any other indication of intention 'reaches' the addressee when it is made orally to him or delivered by any other means to him personally, to his place of business or mailing address or, if he does not have a place of business or mailing address, to his habitual residence.

PART III
SALE OF GOODS

CHAPTER I
GENERAL PROVISIONS

Article 25

A breach of contract committed by one of the parties is fundamental if it results in such detriment to the other party as substantially to deprive him of what he is entitled to expect under the contract, unless the party in breach did not foresee and a reasonable person of the same kind in the same circumstances would not have foreseen such a result.

Article 26

A declaration of avoidance of the contract is effective only if made by notice to the other party.

Article 27

Unless otherwise expressly provided in this Part of the Convention, if any notice, request or other communication is given or made by a party in accordance with this Part and by means appropriate in the circumstances, a delay or error in the transmission of the communication or its failure to arrive does not deprive that party of the right to rely on the communication.

Article 28

If, in accordance with the provisions of this Convention, one party is entitled to require performance of any obligation by the other party, a court is not bound to enter a judgement for specific performance unless the court would do so under its own law in respect of similar contracts of sale not governed by this Convention.

Article 29

(1) A contract may be modified or terminated by the mere agreement of the parties.
(2) A contract in writing which contains a provision requiring any modification or termination by agreement to be in writing may not be otherwise modified or terminated by agreement. However, a party may be precluded by his conduct from asserting such a provision to the extent that the other party has relied on that conduct.

CHAPTER II
OBLIGATIONS OF THE SELLER

Article 30

The seller must deliver the goods, hand over any documents relating to them and transfer the property in the goods, as required by the contract and this Convention.

SECTION I
DELIVERY OF THE GOODS AND HANDING OVER OF DOCUMENTS

Article 31

If the seller is not bound to deliver the goods at any other particular place, his obligation to deliver consists:
(a) if the contract of sale involves carriage of the goods—in handing the goods over to the first carrier for transmission to the buyer;
(b) if, in cases not within the preceding subparagraph, the contract relates to specific goods, or unidentified goods to be drawn from a specific stock or to be manufactured or produced, and at the time of the conclusion of the contract the parties knew that the goods were at, or were to be manufactured or produced at, a particular place—in placing the goods at the buyer's disposal at that place;
(c) in other cases—in placing the goods at the buyer's disposal at the place where the seller had his place of business at the time of the conclusion of the contract.

Article 32

(1) If the seller, in accordance with the contract or this Convention, hands the goods over to a carrier and if the goods are not dearly identified to the contract by markings on the goods, by shipping documents or otherwise, the seller must give the buyer notice of the consignment specifying the goods.

(2) If the seller is bound to arrange for carriage of the goods, he must make such contracts as are necessary for carriage to the place fixed by means of transportation appropriate in the circumstances and according to the usual terms for such transportation.

(3) If the seller is not bound to effect insurance in respect of the carriage of the goods, he must, at the buyer's request, provide him with all available information necessary to enable him to effect such insurance.

Article 33

The seller must deliver the goods:
   (a) if a date is fixed by or determinable from the contract, on that date;
   (b) if a period of time is fixed by or determinable from the contract, at any time within that period unless circumstances indicate that the buyer is to choose a date; or
   (c) in any other case, within a reasonable time after the conclusion of the contract.

Article 34

If the seller is bound to hand over documents relating to the goods, he must hand them over at the time and place and in the form required by the contract. If the seller has handed over documents before that time, he may, up to that time, cure any lack of conformity in the documents, if the exercise of this right does not cause the buyer unreasonable inconvenience or unreasonable expense. However, the buyer retains any right to claim damages as provided for in this Convention.

SECTION II

CONFORMITY OF THE GOODS AND THIRD PARTY CLAIMS

Article 35

(1) The seller must deliver goods which are of the quantity, quality and description required by the contract and which are contained or packaged in the manner required by the contract.

(2) Except where the parties have agreed otherwise, the goods do not conform with the contract unless they:
   (a) are fit for the purposes for which goods of the same description would ordinarily be used;
   (b) are fit for any particular purpose expressly or impliedly made known to the seller at the time of the conclusion of the contract, except where the circumstances show that the buyer did not rely, or that it was unreasonable for him to rely, on the seller's skill and judgement;
   (c) possess the qualities of goods which the seller has held out to the buyer as a sample or model;

(d) are contained or packaged in the manner usual for such goods or, where there is no such manner, in a manner adequate to preserve and protect the goods.

(3) The seller is not liable under subparagraphs (a) to (d) of the preceding paragraph for any lack of conformity of the goods if at the time of the conclusion of the contract the buyer knew or could not have been unaware of such lack of conformity.

Article 36

(1) The seller is liable in accordance with the contract and this Convention for any lack of conformity which exists at the time when the risk passes to the buyer, even though the lack of conformity becomes apparent only after that time.

(2) The seller is also liable for any lack of conformity which occurs after the time indicated in the preceding paragraph and which is due to a breach of any of his obligations, including a breach of any guarantee that for a period of time the goods will remain fit for their ordinary purpose or for some particular purpose or will retain specified qualities or characteristics.

Article 37

If the seller has delivered goods before the date for delivery, he may, up to that date, deliver any missing part or make up any deficiency in the quantity of the goods delivered, or deliver goods in replacement of any non-conforming goods delivered or remedy any lack of conformity in the goods delivered, provided that the exercise of this right does not cause the buyer unreasonable inconvenience or unreasonable expense. However, the buyer retains any right to claim damages as provided for in this Convention.

Article 38

(1) The buyer must examine the goods, or cause them to be examined, within as short a period as is practicable in the circumstances.

(2) If the contract involves carriage of the goods, examination may be deferred until after the goods have arrived at their destination.

(3) If the goods are redirected in transit or redispatched by the buyer without a reasonable opportunity for examination by him and at the time of the conclusion of the contract the seller knew or ought to have known of the possibility of such redirection or redispatch, examination may be deferred until after the goods have arrived at the new destination.

Article 39

(1) The buyer loses the right to rely on a lack of conformity of the goods if he does not give notice to the seller specifying the nature of the lack of conformity within a reasonable time after he has discovered it or ought to have discovered it.

(2) In any event, the buyer loses the right to rely on a lack of conformity of the goods if he does not give the seller notice thereof at the latest within a period of two years from the date on which the goods were actually handed over to the buyer, unless this time-limit is inconsistent with a contractual period of guarantee.

Article 40

The seller is not entitled to rely on the provisions of articles 38 and 39 if the lack of conformity relates to facts of which he knew or could not have been unaware and which he did not disclose to the buyer.

Article 41

The seller must deliver goods which are free from any right or claim of a third party, unless the buyer agreed to take the goods subject to that right or claim. However, if such right or claim is based on industrial property or other intellectual property, the seller's obligation is governed by article 42.

Article 42

(1) The seller must deliver goods which are free from any right or claim of a third party based on industrial property or other intellectual property, of which at the time of the conclusion of the contract the seller knew or could not have been unaware, provided that the right or claim is based on industrial property or other intellectual property:
   (a) under the law of the State where the goods will be resold or otherwise used, if it was contemplated by the parties at the time of the conclusion of the contract that the goods would be resold or otherwise used in that State; or
   (b) in any other case, under the law of the State where the buyer has his place of business.
(2) The obligation of the seller under the preceding paragraph does not extend to cases where:
   (a) at the time of the conclusion of the contract the buyer knew or could not have been unaware of the right or claim; or
   (b) the right or claim results from the seller's compliance with technical drawings, designs, formulae or other such specifications furnished by the buyer.

Article 43

(1) The buyer loses the right to rely on the provisions of article 41 or article 42 if he does not give notice to the seller specifying the nature of the right or claim of the third party within a reasonable time after he has become aware or ought to have become aware of the right or claim.
(2) The seller is not entitled to rely on the provisions of the preceding paragraph if he knew of the right or claim of the third party and the nature of it.

Article 44

Notwithstanding the provisions of paragraph (1) of article 39 and paragraph (1) of article 43, the buyer may reduce the price in accordance with article 50 or claim damages, except for loss of profit, if he has a reasonable excuse for his failure to give the required notice.

SECTION III
REMEDIES FOR BREACH OF CONTRACT BY THE SELLER

Article 45

(1) If the seller fails to perform any of his obligations under the contract or this Convention, the buyer may:
   (a) exercise the rights provided in articles 46 to 52;

(b) claim damages as provided in articles 74 to 77.

(2) The buyer is not deprived of any right he may have to claim damages by exercising his right to other remedies.

(3) No period of grace may be granted to the seller by a court or arbitral tribunal when the buyer resorts to a remedy for breach of contract.

Article 46

(1) The buyer may require performance by the seller of his obligations unless the buyer has resorted to a remedy which is inconsistent with this requirement.

(2) If the goods do not conform with the contract, the buyer may require delivery of substitute goods only if the lack of conformity constitutes a fundamental breach of contract and a request for substitute goods is made either in conjunction with notice given under article 39 or within a reasonable time thereafter.

(3) If the goods do not conform with the contract, the buyer may require the seller to remedy the lack of conformity by repair, unless this is unreasonable having regard to all the circumstances. A request for repair must be made either in conjunction with notice given under article 39 or within a reasonable time thereafter.

Article 47

(1) The buyer may fix an additional period of time of reasonable length for performance by the seller of his obligations.

(2) Unless the buyer has received notice from the seller that he will not perform within the period so fixed, the buyer may not, during that period, resort to any remedy for breach of contract. However, the buyer is not deprived thereby of any right he may have to claim damages for delay in performance.

Article 48

(1) Subject to article 49, the seller may, even after the date for delivery, remedy at his own expense any failure to perform his obligations, if he can do so without unreasonable delay and without causing the buyer unreasonable inconvenience or uncertainty of reimbursement by the seller of expenses advanced by the buyer. However, the buyer retains any right to claim damages as provided for in this Convention.

(2) If the seller requests the buyer to make known whether he will accept performance and the buyer does not comply with the request within a reasonable time, the seller may perform within the time indicated in his request. The buyer may not, during that period of time, resort to any remedy which is inconsistent with performance by the seller.

(3) A notice by the seller that he will perform within a specified period of time is assumed to include a request, under the preceding paragraph, that the buyer make known his decision.

(4) A request or notice by the seller under paragraph (2) or (3) of this article is not effective unless received by the buyer.

Article 49

(1) The buyer may declare the contract avoided:
    (a) if the failure by the seller to perform any of his obligations under the contract or this Convention amounts to a fundamental breach of contract; or

(b) in case of non-delivery, if the seller does not deliver the goods within the additional period of time fixed by the buyer in accordance with paragraph (1) of article 47 or declares that he will not deliver within the period so fixed.

(2) However, in cases where the seller has delivered the goods, the buyer loses the right to declare the contract avoided unless he does so:

(a) in respect of late delivery, within a reasonable time after he has become aware that delivery has been made;

(b) in respect of any breach other than late delivery, within a reasonable time:

    (i) after he knew or ought to have known of the breach;

    (ii) after the expiration of any additional period of time fixed by the buyer in accordance with paragraph (1) of article 47, or after the seller has declared that he will not perform his obligations within such an additional period; or

    (iii) after the expiration of any additional period of time indicated by the seller in accordance with paragraph (2) of article 48, or after the buyer has declared that he will not accept performances.

Article 50

If the goods do not conform with the contract and whether or not the price has already been paid, the buyer may reduce the price in the same proportion as the value that the goods actually delivered had at the time of the delivery bears to the value that conforming goods would have had at that time. However, if the seller remedies any failure to perform his obligations in accordance with article 37 or article 48 or if the buyer refuses to accept performance by the seller in accordance with those articles, the buyer may not reduce the price.

Article 51

(1) If the seller delivers only a part of the goods or if only a part of the goods delivered is in conformity with the contract, articles 46 to 50 apply in respect of the part which is missing or which does not conform.

(2) The buyer may declare the contract avoided in its entirety only if the failure to make delivery completely or in conformity with the contract amounts to a fundamental breach of the contract.

Article 52

(1) If the seller delivers the goods before the date fixed, the buyer may take delivery or refuse to take delivery.

(2) If the seller delivers a quantity of goods greater than that provided for in the contract, the buyer may take delivery or refuse to take delivery of the excess quantity. If the buyer takes delivery of all or part of the excess quantity, he must pay for it at the contract rate.

CHAPTER III
OBLIGATIONS OF THE BUYER

Article 53

The buyer must pay the price for the goods and take delivery of them as required by the contract and this Convention.

Article 54

The buyer's obligation to pay the price includes taking such steps and complying with such formalities as may be required under the contract or any laws and regulations to enable payment to be made.

Article 55

Where a contract has been validly concluded but does not expressly or implicitly fix or make provision for determining the price, the parties are considered, in the absence of any indication to the contrary, to have impliedly made reference to the price generally charged at the time of the conclusion of the contract for such goods sold under comparable circumstances in the trade concerned.

Article 56

If the price is fixed according to the weight of the goods, in case of doubt it is to be determined by the net weight.

Article 57

(1) If the buyer is not bound to pay the price at any other particular place, he must pay it to the seller:
   (a) at the seller's place of business; or
   (b) if the payment is to be made against the handing over of the goods or of documents, at the place where the handing over takes place.
(2) The seller must bear any increase in the expenses incidental to payment which is caused by a change in his place of business subsequent to the conclusion of the contract.

Article 58

(1) If the buyer is not bound to pay the price at any other specific time, he must pay it when the seller places either the goods or documents controlling their disposition at the buyer's disposal in accordance with the contract and this Convention. The seller may make such payment a condition for handing over the goods or documents.
(2) If the contract involves carriage of the goods, the seller may dispatch the goods on terms whereby the goods, or documents controlling their disposition, will not be handed over to the buyer except against payment of the price.
(3) The buyer is not bound to pay the price until he has had an opportunity to examine the goods, unless the procedures for delivery or payment agreed upon by the parties are inconsistent with his having such an opportunity.

Article 59

The buyer must pay the price on the date fixed by or determinable from the contract and this Convention without the need for any request or compliance with any formality on the part of the seller.

228

Article 60

The buyer's obligation to take delivery consists:

(a) in doing all the acts which could reasonably be expected of him in order to enable the seller to make delivery; and

(b) in taking over the goods.

SECTION III

REMEDIES FOR BREACH OF CONTRACT BY THE BUYER

Article 61

(1) If the buyer fails to perform any of his obligations under the contract or this Convention, the seller may:

(a) exercise the rights provided in articles 62 to 65;

(b) claim damages as provided in articles 74 to 77.

(2) The seller is not deprived of any right he may have to claim damages by exercising his right to other remedies.

(3) No period of grace may be granted to the buyer by a court or arbitral tribunal when the seller resorts to a remedy for breach of contract.

Article 62

The seller may require the buyer to pay the price, take delivery or perform his other obligations, unless the seller has resorted to a remedy which is inconsistent with this requirement.

Article 63

(1) The seller may fix an additional period of time of reasonable length for performance by the buyer of his obligations.

(2) Unless the seller has received notice from the buyer that he will not perform within the period so fixed, the seller may not, during that period, resort to any remedy for breach of contract. However, the seller is not deprived thereby of any right he may have to claim damages for delay in performance.

Article 64

(1) The seller may declare the contract avoided:

(a) if the failure by the buyer to perform any of his obligations under the contract or this Convention amounts to a fundamental breach of contract; or

(b) if the buyer does not, within the additional period of time fixed by the seller in accordance with paragraph (1) of article 63, perform his obligation to pay the price or take delivery of the goods, or if he declares that he will not do so within the period so fixed;

229

(2) However, in cases where the buyer has paid the price, the seller loses the right to declare the contract avoided unless he does so:
   (a) in respect of late performance by the buyer, before the seller has become aware that performance has been rendered; or
   (b) in respect of any breach other than late performance by the buyer, within a reasonable time:
      (i) after the seller knew or ought to have known of the breach; or
      (ii) after the expiration of any additional period of time fixed by the seller in accordance with paragraph (1) of article 63, or after the buyer has declared that he will not perform his obligations within such an additional period.

Article 65

(1) If under the contract the buyer is to specify the form, measurement or other features of the goods and he fails to make such specification either on the date agreed upon or within a reasonable time after receipt of a request from the seller, the seller may, without prejudice to any other rights he may have, make the specification himself in accordance with the requirements of the buyer that may be known to him.
(2) If the seller makes the specification himself, he must inform the buyer of the details thereof and must fix a reasonable time within which the buyer may make a different specification. If, after receipt of such a communication, the buyer fails to do so within the time so fixed, the specification made by the seller is binding.

CHAPTER IV
PASSING OF RISK

Article 66

Loss of or damage to the goods after the risk has passed to the buyer does not discharge him from his obligation to pay the price, unless the loss or damage is due to an act or omission of the seller.

Article 67

(1) If the contract of sale involves carriage of the goods and the seller is not bound to hand them over at a particular place, the risk passes to the buyer when the goods are handed over to the first carrier for transmission to the buyer in accordance with the contract of sale. If the seller is bound to hand the goods over to a carrier at a particular place, the risk does not pass to the buyer until the goods are handed over to the carrier at that place. The fact that the seller is authorized to retain documents controlling the disposition of the goods does not affect the passage of the risk.
(2) Nevertheless, the risk does not pass to the buyer until the goods are clearly identified to the contract, whether by markings on the goods, by shipping documents, by notice given to the buyer or otherwise.

Article 68

The risk in respect of goods sold in transit passes to the buyer from the time of the conclusion of the contract. However, if the circumstances so indicate, the risk is assumed by the buyer from the time the goods were handed over to the carrier who issued the documents embodying the contract of carriage. Nevertheless, if at the time of the conclusion of the contract of sale the seller knew or ought to have known that the goods had been lost or damaged and did not disclose this to the buyer, the loss or damage is at the risk of the seller.

Article 69

(1) In cases not within articles 67 and 68, the risk passes to the buyer when he takes over the goods or, if he does not do so in due time, from the time when the goods are placed at his disposal and he commits a breach of contract by failing to take delivery.

(2) However, if the buyer is bound to take over the goods at a place other than a place of business of the seller, the risk passes when delivery is due and the buyer is aware of the fact that the goods are placed at his disposal at that place.

(3) If the contract relates to goods not then identified, the goods are considered not to be placed at the disposal of the buyer until they are clearly identified to the contract.

Article 70

If the seller has committed a fundamental breach of contract, articles 67, 68 and 69 do not impair the remedies available to the buyer on account of the breach.

CHAPTER V
PROVISIONS COMMON TO THE OBLIGATIONS OF THE
SELLER AND OF THE BUYER

SECTION I
ANTICIPATORY BREACH AND INSTALMENT CONTRACTS

Article 71

(1) A party may suspend the performance of his obligations if, after the conclusion of the contract, it becomes apparent that the other party will not perform a substantial part of his obligations as a result of:
(a) a serious deficiency in his ability of perform or in his creditworthiness; or
(b) his conduct in preparing to perform or in performing the contract.

(2) If the seller has already dispatched the goods before the grounds described in the preceding paragraph become evident, he may prevent the handing over of the goods to the buyer even though the buyer holds a document which entitles him to obtain them. The present paragraph relates only to the rights in the goods as between the buyer and the seller.

(3) A party suspending performance, whether before or after dispatch of the goods, must immediately give notice of the suspension to the other party and must continue with performance if the other party provides adequate assurance of his performance.

Article 72

(1) If prior to the date for performance of the contract it is clear that one of the parties will commit a fundamental breach of contract, the other party may declare the contract avoided.

(2) If time allows, the party intending to declare the contract avoided must give reasonable notice to the other party in order to permit him to provide adequate assurance of his performance.

(3) The requirements of the preceding paragraph do not apply if the other party has declared that he will not perform his obligations.

Article 73

(1) In the case of a contract for delivery of goods by instalments, if the failure of one party to perform any of his obligations in respect of any instalment constitutes a fundamental breach of contract with respect to that instalment, the other party may declare the contract avoided with respect to that instalment.

(2) If one party's failure to perform any of his obligations in respect of any instalment gives the other party good grounds to conclude that a fundamental breach of contract will occur with respect to future installments, he may declare the contract avoided for the future, provided that he does so within a reasonable time.

(3) A buyer who declares the contract avoided in respect of any delivery may, at the same time, declare it avoided in respect of deliveries already made or of future deliveries if, by reason of their interdependence, those deliveries could not be used for the purpose contemplated by the parties at the time of the conclusion of the contract.

SECTION II
DAMAGES

Article 74

Damages for breach of contract by one party consist of a sum equal to the loss, including loss of profit, suffered by the other party as a consequence of the breach. Such damages may not exceed the loss which the party in breach foresaw or ought to have foreseen at the time of the conclusion of the contract, in the light of the facts and matters of which he then knew or ought to have known, as a possible consequence of the breach of contract.

Article 75

If the contract is avoided and if, in a reasonable manner and within a reasonable time after avoidance, the buyer has bought goods in replacement or the seller has resold the goods, the party claiming damages may recover the difference between the contract price and the price in the substitute transaction as well as any further damages recoverable under article 74.

Article 76

(1) If the contract is avoided and there is a current price for the goods, the party claiming damages may, if he has not made a purchase or resale under article 75, recover the difference between the price fixed by the contract and the current price at the time of avoidance as well as any further damages recoverable under article 74. If, however, the party claiming damages has avoided the contract after taking over the goods, the current price at the time of such taking over shall be applied instead of the current price at the time of avoidance.

(2) For the purposes of the preceding paragraph, the current price is the price prevailing at the place where delivery of the goods should have been made or, if there is no current price at that place, the price at such other place as serves as a reasonable substitute, making due allowance for differences in the cost of transporting the goods.

Article 77

A party who relies on a breach of contract must take such measures as are reasonable in the circumstances to mitigate the loss, including loss of profit, resulting from the breach. If he fails to take such measures, the party in breach may claim a reduction in the damages in the amount by which the loss should have been mitigated.

SECTION III

INTEREST

Article 78

If a party fails to pay the price or any other sum that is in arrears, the other party is entitled to interest on it, without prejudice to any claim for damages recoverable under article 74.

SECTION IV

EXEMPTION

Article 79

(1) A party is not liable for a failure to perform any of his obligations if he proves that the failure was due to an impediment beyond his control and that he could not reasonably be expected to have taken the impediment into account at the time of the conclusion of the contract or to have avoided or overcome it or its consequences.

(2) If the party's failure is due to the failure by a third person whom he has engaged to perform the whole or a part of the contract, that party is exempt from liability only if:
    (a) he is exempt under the preceding paragraph; and
    (b) the person whom he has so engaged would be so exempt if the provisions of that paragraph were applied to him.

(3) The exemption provided by this article has effect for the period during which the impediment exists.

(4) The party who fails to perform must give notice to the other party of the impediment and its effect on his ability to perform. If the notice is not received by the other party within a reasonable time after the party who fails to perform knew or ought to have known of the impediment, he is liable for damages resulting from such non-receipt.

(5) Nothing in this article prevents either party from exercising any right other than to claim damages under this Convention.

Article 80

A party may not rely on a failure of the other party to perform, to the extent that such failure was caused by the first party's act or omission.

SECTION V
EFFECTS OF AVOIDANCE

Article 81

(1) Avoidance of the contract releases both parties from their obligations under it, subject to any damages which may be due. Avoidance does not affect any provision of the contract for the settlement of disputes or any other provision of the contract governing the rights and obligations of the parties consequent upon the avoidance of the contract.

(2) A party who has performed the contract either wholly or in part may claim restitution from the other party of whatever the first party has supplied or paid under the contract. If both parties are bound to make restitution, they must do so concurrently.

Article 82

(1) The buyer loses the right to declare the contract avoided or to require the seller to deliver substitute goods if it is impossible for him to make restitution of the goods substantially in the condition in which he received them.

(2) The preceding paragraph does not apply:
  (a) if the impossibility of making restitution of the goods or of making restitution of the goods substantially in the condition in which the buyer received them is not due to his act or omission;
  (b) the goods or part of the goods have perished or deteriorated as a result of the examination provided for in article 38; or
  (c) if the goods or part of the goods have been sold in the normal course of business or have been consumed or transformed by the buyer in the course of normal use before he discovered or ought to have discovered the lack of conformity.

Article 83

A buyer who has lost the right to declare the contract avoided or to require the seller to deliver substitute goods in accordance with article 82 retains all other remedies under the contract and this Convention.

Article 84

(1) If the seller is bound to refund the price, he must also pay interest on it, from the date on which the price was paid.

(2) The buyer must account to the seller for all benefits which he has derived from the goods or part of them:
  (a) if he must make restitution of the goods or part of them; or
  (b) if it is impossible for him to make restitution of all or part of the goods or to make restitution of all or part of the goods substantially in the condition in which he received them, but he has nevertheless declared the contract avoided or required the seller to deliver substitute goods.

SECTION VI
PRESERVATION OF THE GOODS

Article 85

If the buyer is in delay in taking delivery of the goods or, where payment of the price and delivery of the goods are to be made concurrently, if he fails to pay the price, and the seller is either in possession of the goods or otherwise able to control their disposition, the seller must take such steps as are reasonable in the circumstances to preserve them. He is entitled to retain them until he has been reimbursed his reasonable expenses by the buyer.

Article 86

(1) If the buyer has received the goods and intends to exercise any right under the contract or this Convention to reject them, he must take such steps to preserve them as are reasonable in the circumstances. He is entitled to retain them until he has been reimbursed his reasonable expenses by the seller.

(2) If goods dispatched to the buyer have been placed at his disposal at their destination and he exercises the right to reject them, he must take possession of them on behalf of the seller, provided that this can be done without payment of the price and without unreasonable inconvenience or unreasonable expense. This provision does not apply if the seller or a person authorized to take charge of the goods on his behalf is present at the destination. If the buyer takes possession of the goods under this paragraph, his rights and obligations are governed by the preceding paragraph.

Article 87

A party who is bound to take steps to preserve the goods may deposit them in a warehouse of a third person at the expense of the other party provided that the expense incurred is not unreasonable.

Article 88

(1) A party who is bound to preserve the goods in accordance with article 85 or 86 may sell them by any appropriate means if there has been an unreasonable delay by the other party in taking possession of the goods or in taking them back or in paying the price or the cost of preservation, provided that reasonable notice of the intention to sell has been given to the other party.

(2) If the goods are subject to rapid deterioration or their preservation would involve unreasonable expense, a party who is bound to preserve the goods in accordance with article 85 or 86 must take reasonable measures to sell them. To the extent possible he must give notice to the other party of his intention to sell.

(3) A party selling the goods has the right to retain out of the proceeds of sale an amount equal to the reasonable expenses of preserving the goods and of selling them. He must account to the other party for the balance.

235

PART IV
FINAL PROVISIONS

Article 89

The Secretary-General of the United Nations is hereby designated as the depositary for this Convention.

Article 90

This Convention does not prevail over any international agreement which has already been or may be entered into and which contains provisions concerning the matters governed by this Convention, provided that the parties have their places of business in States parties, to such agreement.

Article 91

(1) This Convention is open for signature at the concluding meeting of the United Nations Conference on Contracts for the International Sale of Goods and will remain open for signature by all States at the Headquarters of the United Nations, New York until 30 September 1981.
(2) This Convention is subject to ratification, acceptance or approval by the signatory States.
(3) This Convention is open for accession by all States which are not signatory States as from the date it is open for signature.
(4) Instruments of ratification, acceptance, approval and accession are to be deposited with the Secretary-General of the United Nations.

Article 92

(1) A Contracting State may declare at the time of signature, ratification, acceptance, approval or accession that it will not be bound by Part II of this Convention or that it will not be bound by Part III of this Convention.
(2) A Contracting State which makes a declaration in accordance with the preceding paragraph in respect of Part II or Part III of this Convention is not to be considered a Contracting State within paragraph (1) of article 1 of this Convention in respect of matters governed by the Part to which the declaration applies.

Article 93

(1) If a Contracting State has two or more territorial units in which, according to its constitution, different systems of law are applicable in relation to the matters dealt with in this Convention, it may, at the time of signature, ratification, acceptance, approval or accession, declare that this Convention is to extend to all its territorial units or only to one or more of them, and may amend its declaration by submitting another declaration at any time.
(2) These declarations are to be notified to the depositary and are to state expressly the territorial units to which the Convention extends.

(3) If, by virtue of a declaration under this article, this Convention extends to one or more but not all of the territorial units of a Contracting State, and if the place of business of a party is located in that State, this place of business, for the purposes of this Convention, is considered not to be in a Contracting State, unless it is in a territorial unit to which the Convention extends.

(4) If a Contracting State makes no declaration under paragraph (1) of this article, the Convention is to extend to all territorial units of that State.

Article 94

(1) Two or more Contracting States which have the same or closely related legal rules on matters governed by this Convention may at any time declare that the Convention is not to apply to contracts of sale or to their formation where the parties have their places of business in those States. Such declarations may be made jointly or by reciprocal unilateral declarations.

(2) A Contracting State which has the same or closely related legal rules on matters governed by this Convention as one or more non-Contracting States may at any time declare that the Convention is not to apply to contracts of sale or to their formation where the parties have their places of business in those States.

(3) If a State which is the object of a declaration under the preceding paragraph subsequently becomes a Contracting State, the declaration made will, as from the date on which the Convention enters into force in respect of the new Contracting State, have the effect of a declaration made under paragraph (1), provided that the new Contracting State joins in such declaration or makes a reciprocal unilateral declaration.

Article 95

Any State may declare at the time of the deposit of its instrument of ratification, acceptance, approval or accession that it will not be bound by subparagraph (1) (b) of article 1 of this Convention.

Article 96

A Contracting State whose legislation requires contracts of sale to be concluded in or evidenced by writing may at any time make a declaration in accordance with article 12 that any provision of article 11, article 29, or Part II of this Convention, that allows a contract of sale or its modification or termination by agreement or any offer, acceptance, or other indication of intention to be made in any form other than in writing, does not apply where any party has his place of business in that State.

Article 97

(1) Declarations made under this Convention at the time of signature are subject to confirmation upon ratification, acceptance or approval.

(2) Declarations and confirmations of declarations are to be in writing and be formally notified to the depositary.

(3) A declaration takes effect simultaneously with the entry into force of this Convention in respect of the State concerned. However, a declaration of which the depositary receives formal notification after such entry into force takes effect on the first day of

the month following the expiration of six months after the date of its receipt by the depositary. Reciprocal unilateral declarations under article 94 take effect on the first day of the month following the expiration of six months after the receipt of the latest declaration by the depositary.

(4) Any State which makes a declaration under this Convention may withdraw it at any time by a formal notification in writing addressed to the depositary. Such withdrawal is to take effect on the first day of the month following the expiration of six months after the date of the receipt of the notification by the depositary.

(5) A withdrawal of a declaration made under article 94 renders inoperative, as from the date on which the withdrawal takes effect, any reciprocal declaration made by another State under that article.

Article 98

No reservations are permitted except those expressly authorized in this Convention.

Article 99

(1) This Convention enters into force, subject to the provisions of paragraph (6) of this article, on the first day of the month following the expiration of twelve months after the date of deposit of the tenth instrument of ratification, acceptance, approval or accession, including an instrument which contains a declaration made under article 92.

(2) When a State ratifies, accepts, approves or accedes to this Convention after the deposit of the tenth instrument of ratification, acceptance, approval or accession, this Convention, with the exception of the Part excluded, enters into force in respect of that State, subject to the provisions of paragraph (6) of this article, on the first day of the month following the expiration of twelve months after the date of the deposit of its instrument of ratification, acceptance, approval or accession.

(3) A State which ratifies, accepts, approves or accedes to this Convention and is a party to either or both the Convention relating to a Uniform Law on the Formation of Contracts for the International Sale of Goods done at The Hague on 1 July 1964 (1964 Hague Formation Convention) and the Convention relating to a Uniform Law on the International Sale of Goods done at The Hague on 1 July 1964 (1964 Hague Sales Convention) shall at the same time denounce, as the case may be, either or both the 1964 Hague Sales Convention and the 1964 Hague Formation Convention by notifying the Government of the Netherlands to that effect.

(4) A State party to the 1964 Hague Sales Convention which ratifies, accepts, approves or accedes to the present Convention and declares or has declared under article 92 that it will not be bound by Part II of this Convention shall at the time of ratification, acceptance, approval or accession denounce the 1964 Hague Sales Convention by notifying the Government of the Netherlands to that effect.

(5) A State party to the 1964 Hague Formation Convention which ratifies, accepts, approves or accedes to the present Convention and declares or has declared under article 92 that it will not be bound by Part III of this Convention shall at the time of ratification, acceptance, approval or accession denounce the 1964 Hague Formation Convention by notifying the Government of the Netherlands to that effect.

(6) For the purpose of this article, ratifications, acceptances, approvals and accessions in respect of this Convention by States parties to the 1964 Hague Formation Convention or to the 1964 Hague Sales Convention shall not be effective until such denunciations as may be required on the part of those States in respect of the latter two Conventions have themselves become effective. The depositary of this Convention shall consult with the Government of the Netherlands, as the depositary of the 1964 Conventions, so as to ensure necessary co-ordination in this respect.

Article 100

(1) This Convention applies to the formation of a contract only when the proposal for concluding the contract is made on or after the date when the Convention enters into force in respect of the Contracting States referred to in subparagraph (1) (a) or the Contracting State referred to in subparagraph (1) *(b)* of article 1.

(2) This Convention applies only to contracts concluded on or after the date when the Convention enters into force in respect of the Contracting States referred to in subparagraph (1)(a) or the Contracting State referred to in subparagraph (1)(b) of article 1.

Article 101

(1) A Contracting State may denounce this Convention, or Part II or Part III of the Convention, by a formal notification in writing addressed to the depositary.

(2) The denunciation takes effect on the first day of the month following the expiration of twelve months after the notification is received by the depositary. Where a longer period for the denunciation to take effect is specified in the notification, the denunciation takes effect upon the expiration of such longer period after the notification is received by the depositary.

Done at Vienna, this day of eleventh day of April, one thousand nine hundred and eighty, in a single original, of which the Arabic, Chinese, English, French, Russian and Spanish texts are equally authentic.

In witness whereof the undersigned plenipotentiaries, being duly authorized by their respective Governments, have signed this Convention.

TABLE OF STATE RATIFICATIONS

State	Signature	Ratification, Accession (a), Approval (AA), Acceptance (A), succession (d)	Entry into force
Argentina	–	19 July 1983 a	1 January 1988
Australia	–	17 March 1988 a	1 April 1989
Austria	11 April 1980	29 December 1987	1 January 1989
Belarus	–	9 October 1989 a	1 November 1990
Belgium	–	31 October 1996 a	1 November 1997
Bosnia and Herzegovina	–	12 January 1994 d	6 March 1992
Bulgaria	–	9 July 1990 a	1 August 1991
Burundi	–	4 September 1998 a	1 October 1999

State	Signature	Ratification, Accession (a), Approval (AA), Acceptance (A), succession (d)	Entry into force
Canada	–	23 April 1991 a	1 May 1992
Chile	11 April 1980	7 February 1990	1 March 1991
China	30 September 1981	11 December 1986 AA	1 January 1988
Colombia		10 July 2001 a	1 August 2002
Croatia	–	8 June 1998 d	8 October 1991
Cuba	–	2 November 1994 a	1 December 1995
Czech Republic	–	30 September 1993 d	1 January 1993
Denmark	26 May 1981	14 February 1989	1 March 1990
Ecuador	–	27 January 1992 a	1 February 1993
Egypt	–	6 December 1982 a	1 January 1988
Estonia	–	20 September 1993 a	1 October 1994
Finland	26 May 1981	15 December 1987	1 January 1989
France	27 August 1981	6 August 1982 AA	1 January 1988
Georgia	–	16 August 1994 a	1 September 1995
Germany	26 May 1981	21 December 1989	1 January 1991
Ghana	11 April 1980	–	–
Greece	–	12 January 1998 a	1 February 1999
Guinea	–	23 January 1991 a	1 February 1992
Honduras	–	10 October 2002 a	1 November 2003
Hungary	11 April 1980	16 June 1983	1 January 1988
Iceland		10 May 2001 a	1 June 2002
Iraq	–	5 March 1990 a	1 April 1991
Israel	–	22 January 2002 a	1 February 2003
Italy	30 September 1981	11 December 1986	1 January 1988
Kyrgyzstan	–	11 May 1999 a	1 June 2000
Latvia	–	31 July 1997 a	1 August 1998
Lesotho	18 June 1981	18 June 1981	1 January 1988
Lithuania	–	18 January 1995 a	1 February 1996
Luxembourg	–	30 January 1997 a	1 February 1998
Mauritania	–	20 August 1999 a	1 September 2000
Mexico	–	29 December 1987 a	1 January 1989
Mongolia	–	31 December 1997 a	1 January 1999
Netherlands	29 May 1981	13 December 1990 A	1 January 1992
New Zealand	–	22 September 1994 a	1 October 1995
Norway	26 May 1981	20 July 1988	1 August 1989
Peru	–	25 March 1999 a	1 April 2000
Poland	28 September 1981	19 May 1995	1 June 1996
Republic of Korea	–	17 February 2004 a	1 March 2005
Republic of Moldova	–	13 October 1994 a	1 November 1995
Romania	–	22 May 1991 a	1 June 1992
Russian Federation	–	16 August 1990 a	1 September 1991
Saint Vincent and the Grenadines	–	12 September 2000 a	1 October 2001
Serbia and Montenegro	–	12 March 2001 d	27 April 1992
Singapore	11 April 1980	16 February 1995	1 March 1996
Slovakia	–	28 May 1993 d	1 January 1993
Slovenia	–	7 January 1994 d	25 June 1991
Spain	–	24 July 1990 a	1 August 1991
Sweden	26 May 1981	15 December 1987	1 January 1989
Switzerland	–	21 February 1990 a	1 March 1991

State	Signature	Ratification, Accession (a), Approval (AA), Acceptance (A), succession (d)	Entry into force
Syrian Arab Republic	–	19 October 1982 a	1 January 1988
Uganda	–	12 February 1992 a	1 March 1993
Ukraine	–	3 January 1990 a	1 February 1991
United States of America	31 August 1981	11 December 1986	1 January 1988
Uruguay	–	25 January 1999 a	1 February 2000
Uzbekistan	–	27 November 1996 a	1 December 1997
Venezuela	28 September 1981	–	–
Zambia	–	6 June 1986 a	1 January 1988

Parties: 63

Note: A list of reservations and declarations made by States has not been included in the text. These can be obtained from http://www.uncitral.org/en-index.htm.

(ii) ICC OFFICIAL RULES FOR THE INTERPRETATION OF TRADE TERMS: INCOTERMS 2000*

EXW
EX WORKS

(...named place)

'Ex works' means that the seller delivers when he places the goods at the disposal of the buyer at the seller's premises or another named place (i.e. works, factory, warehouse, etc.) not cleared for export and not loaded on any collecting vehicle.

This term thus represents the minimum obligation for the seller, and the buyer has to bear all costs and risks involved in taking the goods from the seller's premises.

However, if the parties wish the seller to be responsible for the loading of the goods on departure and to bear the risks and all the costs of such loading, this should be made clear by adding explicit wording to this effect in the contract of sale[1]. This term should not be used when the buyer cannot carry out the export formalities directly or indirectly. In such circumstances, the FCA term should be used, provided the seller agrees that he will load at his cost and risk.

A THE SELLER'S OBLIGATIONS	B THE BUYER'S OBLIGATIONS
A1 Provision of goods in conformity with the contract	**B1 Payment of the price**
The seller must provide the goods and the commercial invoice, or its equivalent electronic message, in conformity with the contract of sale and any other evidence of conformity which may be required by the contract.	The buyer must pay the price as provided in the contract of sale.

* ICC Publication No. 560(E)–ISBN 92.842.1199.9. Published in its official English version by the International Chamber of Commerce, Paris. Copyright ©1999–International Chamber of Commerce (ICC).

A2 Licences, authorizations and formalities

The seller must render the buyer, at the latter's request, risk and expense, every assistance in obtaining, where applicable, any export licence or other official authorization necessary for the export of the goods.

A3 Contracts of carriage and insurance

a) Contract of carriage
No obligation.

b) Contract of insurance
No obligation.

A4 Delivery

The seller must place the goods at the disposal of the buyer at the named place of delivery, not loaded on any collecting vehicle, on the date or within the period agreed or, if no such time is agreed, at the usual time for delivery of such goods. If no specific point has been agreed within the named place, and if there are several points available, the seller may select the point at the place of delivery which best suits his purpose.

A5 Transfer of risks

The seller must, subject to the provisions of B5, bear all risks of loss of or damage to the goods until such time as they have been delivered in accordance with A4.

B2 Licences, authorizations and formalities

The buyer must obtain at his own risk and expense any export and import licence or other official authorization and carry out, where applicable, all customs formalities for the export of the goods.

B3 Contracts of carriage and insurance

a) Contract of carriage
No obligation.

b) Contract of insurance
No obligation.

B4 Taking delivery

The buyer must take delivery of the goods when they have been delivered in accordance with A4 and A7/B7.

B5 Transfer of risks

The buyer must bear all risks of loss of or damage to the goods
- from the time they have been delivered in accordance with A4; and
- from the agreed date or the expiry date of any period fixed for taking delivery which arise because he fails to give notice in accordance with B7, provided, however, that the goods have been duly appropriated to the contract, that is to say clearly set aside or otherwise identified as the contract goods.

A6 Division of costs

The seller must, subject to the provisions of B6, pay all costs relating to the goods until such time as they have been delivered in accordance with A4.

B6 Division of costs

The buyer must pay
- all costs relating to the goods from the time they have been delivered in accordance with A4; and
- any additional costs incurred by failing either to take delivery of the goods when they have been placed at his disposal, or to give appropriate notice in accordance with B7 provided, however, that the goods have been duly appropriated to the contract, that is to say, clearly set aside or otherwise identified as the contract goods; and
- where applicable, all duties, taxes and other charges as well as the costs of carrying out customs formalities payable upon export.

  The buyer must reimburse all cost and charges incurred by the seller in rendering assistance in accordance with A2.

A7 Notice to the buyer

The seller must give the buyer sufficient notice as to when and where the goods will be placed at his disposal.

B7 Notice to the seller

The buyer must, whenever he is entitled to determine the time within an agreed period and/or the place of taking delivery, give the seller sufficient notice thereof.

A8 Proof of delivery, transport document or equivalent electronic message

No obligation.

B8 Proof of delivery, transport document or equivalent electronic message

The buyer must provide the seller with appropriate evidence of having taken delivery.

A9 Checking—packaging—marking

The seller must pay the costs of those checking operations (such as checking quality, measuring, weighing, counting) which are necessary for the purpose of placing the goods at the buyer's disposal.

The seller must provide at his own expense packaging (unless it is usual for the particular trade to make the goods of the contract description available unpacked) which is required for the transport of the goods, to the extent that the circumstances relating to the transport (for example modalities, destination) are made known to the seller before the contract of sale is concluded. Packaging is to be marked appropriately.

B9 Inspection of goods

The buyer must pay the costs of any pre-shipment inspection, including inspection mandated by the authorities of the country of export.

A10 Other obligations	B10 Other obligations

The seller must render the buyer at the latter's request, risk and expense, every assistance in obtaining any documents or equivalent electronic messages issued or transmitted in the country of delivery and/or of origin which the buyer may require for the export and/or import of the goods and, where necessary, for their transit through any country.

The seller must provide the buyer, upon request, with the necessary information for procuring insurance.

The buyer must pay all costs and charges incurred in obtaining the document or equivalent electronic messages mentioned in A10 and reimburse those incurred by the seller in rendering his assistance in accordance therewith.

FCA
FREE CARRIER

(... named place)

'Free Carrier' means that the seller delivers the goods, cleared for export, to the carrier nominated by the buyer at the named place. It should be noted that the chosen place of delivery has an impact on the obligations of loading and unloading the goods at that place. If delivery occurs at the seller's premises, the seller is responsible for loading. If delivery occurs at any other place, the seller is not responsible for unloading.

This term may be used irrespective of the mode of transport, including multimodal transport.

'Carrier' means any person who, in a contract of carriage, undertakes to perform or to procure the performance of transport by rail, road, air, sea, inland waterway or by a combination of such modes.

If the buyer nominates a person other than a carrier to receive the goods the seller is deemed to have fulfilled his obligation to deliver the goods when they are delivered to that person.

A THE SELLER'S OBLIGATIONS	B THE BUYER'S OBLIGATIONS

A1 Provision of goods in conformity with the contract

The seller must provide the goods and the commercial invoice, or its equivalent electronic message, in conformity with the contract of sale and any other evidence of conformity which may be required by the contract.

B1 Payment of the price

The buyer must pay the price as provided in the contract of sale.

A2 Licences, authorizations and formalities

The seller must obtain at his own risk and expense any export licence or other official authorization and carry out, where applicable, all customs formalities necessary for the export of the goods.

B2 Licences, authorizations and formalities

The buyer must obtain at his own risk and expense any import licence or other official authorization and carry out, where applicable, all customs formalities for the import of the goods and for their transit through any country.

A3 Contracts of carriage and insurance

a) Contract of carriage
No obligations. However, if requested by the buyer or if it is commercial practice and the buyer does not give an instruction to the contrary in due time, the seller may contract for carriage on usual terms at the buyer's risk and expense. In either case, the seller may decline to make the contract and, if he does, shall promptly notify the buyer accordingly.

b) Contract of insurance
No obligation.

B3 Contracts of carriage and insurance

a) Contract of carriage
The buyer must contract at his own expense for the carriage of the goods from the named place, except when the contract of carriage is made by the seller as provided for in A3 a).

b) Contract of insurance
No obligation.

A4 Delivery

The seller mus deliver the goods to the carrier or another person nominated bu the buyer, or chosen by the seller in accordance with A3 a), at the named place on the date or within the period agreed for delivery.

Delivery is completed;
a) if the named place is the seller's premises, when the goods have been loaded on the means of transport provided by the carrier nominated by the buyer or another person action on his hebalf

b) If the named place is anywhere other than
a), when the goods are placed at the disposal of the carrier or another person nominated by the buyer, or chosen by the seller in accordance with A3 a) on the seller's means of transport not unloaded

If no specific point has been agreed within the named place, and if there are sevel points available, the seller may select the point at the placee of delivery which best suits his purpose

Failing precise instrucions from the buyer, the seller may deliver tge goods for carriage in such a manner as the transport mode and/or the quantity and/or nature of the goods may require

B4 Taking delivery

The buyer must take delivery of the goods when they have been delivered in accordance with A4.

A5 Transfer of risks

The seller must, subject to the provisions of B5, bear all risks of loss of or damage to the goods until such time as they have been delivered in accordance with A4.

B5 Transfer of risks

The buyer must bear all risks of loss of or damage to the goods

- from the time they have been delivered in accordance with A4; and
- from the agreed date or the expiry date of any agreed period for delivery which arise either because he fails to nominate the carrier or another person in accordance with A4, or because the carrier or the party nominated by the buyer fails to take the goods into his charge at the agreed time, or because the buyer fails to give appropriate notice in accordance with B7, provided, however, that the goods have been duly appropriated to the contract, that is to say, clearly set aside or otherwise identified as the contract goods.

A6 Division of costs

The seller must, subject to the provisions of B6, pay

- all costs relating to the goods until such time as they have been delivered in accordance with A4; and
- where applicable, the cost of customs formalities as well as all duties, taxes, and other charges payable upon export.

B6 Division of costs

The buyer must pay

- all costs relating to the goods from the time they have been delivered in accordance with A4; and
- any additional costs incurred, either because he fails to nominate the carrier or another person in accordance with A4 or because the party nominated by the buyer fails to take the goods into his charge at the agreed time, or because he has failed to give appropriate notice in accordance with B7, provided, however, that the goods have been duly appropriated to the contract, that is to say, clearly set aside or otherwise identified as the contract goods; and
- where applicable, all duties, taxes and other charges as well as the costs of carrying out customs formalities payable upon import of the goods and for their transit through any country.

A7 Notice to the buyer

The seller must give the buyer sufficient notice that the goods have been delivered in accordance with A4. Should the carrier fail to take delivery in accordance with A4 at the time agreed, the seller notify the buyer accordingly.

B7 Notice to the seller

The buyer must give the seller sufficient notice of the name of the party designated in A4 and, where necessary, specify the mode of transport, as well as the date or period for delivering the goods to him and, as the case may be, the point within the place where the goods should be delivered to that party.

A8 Proof of delivery, transport document or equivalent electronic message

The seller must provide the buyer at the seller's expense with the usual proof of delivery of the goods in accordance with A4.

Unless the document referred to in the preceding paragraph is the transport document, the seller must render the buyer at the latter's request, risk and expense, every assistance in obtaining a transport document for the contract of carriage (for example a negotiable bill of lading, a non-negotiable sea waybill, an inland waterway document, an air waybill, a raliway consignment note, a road consignment note, or a multimodal transport document).

When the seller and the buyer have agreed to communicate electronically, the document referred to in the preceding paragraph may be replaced by an equivalent electronic data interchange (EDI) message.

B8 Proof of delivery, transport document or equivalent electronic message

The buyer must accept the proof of delivery in accordance with A8.

A9 Checking—packaging—marking

The seller must pay the costs of those checking operations (such as checking quality, measuring, weighing, counting) which are necessary for the purpose of delivering the goods in accordance with A4.

The seller must provide at his own expense packaging (unless it is usual for the particular trade to send the goods of the contract description unpacked) which is required for the transport of the goods, to the extent that the circumstances relating to the transport (for example modalities, destination) are made known to the seller before the contract of sale is concluded. Packaging is to be marked appropriately.

B9 Inspection of goods

The buyer must pay the costs of any pre-shipment inspection except when such inspection is mandated by the authorities of the county of export.

A10 Other obligations	B10 Other obligations
The seller must render the buyer at the latter's request, risk and expense, every assistance in obtaining any documents or equivalent electronic messages (other than those mentioned in A8) issued or transmitted in the country of delivery and/or of origin which the buyer may require for the import of the goods and, where necessary, for their transit through any country.	The buyer must pay all costs and charges incurred in obtaining the documents or equivalent electronic messages mentioned in A10 and reimburse those incurred by the seller in rendering his assistance in accordance therewith and in contracting for carriage in accordance with A3 a).
The seller must provide the buyer, upon request, with the necessary information for procuring insurance.	The buyer must give the seller appropriate instructions whenever the seller's assistance in contracting for carriage is required in accordance with A3 a).

FAS
FREE ALONGSIDE SHIP

(. . . named port of shipment)

'Free Alongside Ship' means that the seller delivers when the goods are placed alongside the vessel at the named port of shipment. This means that the buyer has to bear all costs and risks of loss of or damage to the goods from that moment.

The FAS term requires the seller to clear the goods for export. THIS IS A REVERSAL FROM PREVIOUS INCOTERMS VERSIONS WHICH REQUIRED THE BUYER TO ARRANGE FOR EXPORT CLEARANCE.

However, if the parties wish the buyer to clear the goods for export, this should be made clear by adding explicit wording to this effect in the contract of sale.

This term can be used only for sea or inland waterway transport.

A THE SELLER'S OBLIGATIONS	B THE BUYER'S OBLIGATIONS
A1 Provision of goods in conformity with the contract	**B1 Payment of the price**
The seller must provide the goods and the commercial invoice, or its equivalent electronic message, in conformity with the contract of sale and any other evidence of conformity which may be required by the contract.	The buyer must pay the price as provided in the contract of sale.
A2 Licences, authorizations and formalities	**B2 Licences, authorizations and formalities**
The seller must obtain at his own risk and expense any export licence or other official authorization and carry out, where applicable, all customs formalities necessary for the export of the goods.	The buyer must obtain at his own risk and expense any import licence or other official authorization and carry out, where applicable, all customs formalities for the import of the goods and for their transit through any country.

A3 Contracts of carriage and insurance

a) Contract of carriage
No obligations.

b) Contract of insurance
No obligations.

A4 Delivery

The seller must place the goods alongside the vessel nominated by the buyer at the loading place named by the buyer at the named port of shipment on the date or within the agreed period and in the manner customary at the port.

A5 Transfer of risks

The seller must, subject to the provisions of B5, bear all risks of loss of or damage to the goods until such time as they have been delivered in accordance with A4.

A6 Division of costs

The seller must, subject to the provisions of B6, pay
- all costs relating to the goods until such time as they have been delivered in accordance with A4; and
- where applicable, the costs of customs formalities as well as all duties, taxes, and other charges payable upon export.

B3 Contracts of carriage and insurance

a) Contract of carriage
The buyer must contract at his own expense for the carriage of the goods from the named port of shipment.

b) Contract of insurance
No obligation.

B4 Taking delivery

The buyer must take delivery of the goods when they have been delivered in accordance with A4.

B5 Transfer of risks

The buyer must bear all risks of loss of or damage to the goods
- from the time they have been delivered in accordance with A4; and
- from the agreed date or the expiry date of the agreed period for delivery which arise because he fails to give notice in accordance with B7, or because the vessel nominated by him fails to arrive on time, or is unable to take the goods, or closes for cargo earlier than the time notified in accordance with B7, provided, however, that the goods have been duly appropriated to the contract, that is to say, clearly set aside or otherwise identified as the contract goods.

B6 Division of costs

The buyer must pay
- all costs relating to the goods from the time they have been delivered in accordance with A4; and
- any additional costs incurred, either because the vessel nominated by him has failed to arrive on time, or is unable to take the goods, or closes for cargo earlier than the time notified in accordance with B7, or because the buyer has failed to give appropriate notice in accordance with B7 provided, however, that the goods have been duly appropriated to the contract, that is to say, clearly set aside or otherwise identified as the contract goods; and
- where applicable, all duties, taxes and other charges as well as the costs of carrying out customs formalities payable upon import of the goods and for their transit through any country.

A7 Notice to the buyer

The seller must give the buyer sufficient notice that the goods have been delivered alongside the nominated vessel.

A8 Proof of delivery, transport document or equivalent electronic message

The seller must provide the buyer at the seller's expense with the usual proof of delivery of the goods in accordance with A4.

Unless the document referred to in the preceding paragraph is the transport document, the seller must render the buyer at the latter's request, risk and expense, every assistance in obtaining a transport document (for example a negotiable bill of lading, a non-negotiable sea waybill, an inland waterway document).

When the seller and the buyer have agreed to communicate electronically, the document referred to in the preceding paragraphs may be replaced by an equivalent electronic data interchange (EDI) message.

A9 Checking—packaging—marking

The seller must pay the costs of those checking operations (such as checking quality, measuring, weighing, counting) which are necessary for the purpose of delivering the goods in accordance with A4.

The seller must provide at his own expense packaging (unless it is usual for the particular trade to ship the goods of the contract description unpacked) which is required for the transport of the goods, to the extent that the circumstances relating to the transport (for example modalities, destination) are made known to the seller before the contract of sale is concluded. Packaging is to be marked appropriately.

B7 Notice to the seller

The buyer must give the seller sufficient notice of the vessel name, loading point and required delivered time.

B8 Proof of delivery, transport document or equivalent electronic message

The buyer must accept the proof of delivery in accordance with A8.

B9 Inspection of goods

The buyer must pay the costs of any pre-shipment inspection, except with such inspection is mandated by the authorities of the county of export.

A10 Other obligations

The seller must render the buyer at the latter's request, risk and expense, every assistance in obtaining any documents or equivalent electronic messages (other than those mentioned in A8) issued or transmitted in the country of shipment and/or of origin which the buyer may require for the import of the goods and, where necessary for their transit through any country.

The seller must provide the buyer, upon request, with the necessary information for procuring insurance.

B10 Other obligations

The buyer must pay all costs and charges incurred in obtaining the documents or equivalent electronic messages mentioned in A10 and reimburse those incurred by the seller in rendering his assistance in accordance therewith.

FOB
FREE ON BOARD

(. . . named port of shipment)

'Free on Board' means that the seller delivers when the goods pass the ship's rail at the named port of shipment. This means that the buyer has to bear all costs and risks of loss of or damage to the goods from that point. The FOB term requires the seller to clear the goods for export. This term can be used only for sea or inland waterway transport. If the parties do not intend to deliver the goods across the ship's rail, the FCA term should be used.

A THE SELLER'S OBLIGATIONS

A1 Provision of goods in conformity with the contract

The seller must provide the goods and the commercial invoice, or its equivalent electronic message, in conformity with the contract of sale and any other evidence of conformity which may be required by the contract.

A2 Licenses, authorizations and formalities

The seller must obtain at his own risk and expense any export licence or other official authorization and carry out, where applicable, all customs formalities necessary for the export of the goods.

B THE BUYER'S OBLIGATIONS

B1 Payment of the price

The buyer must pay the price as provided in the contract of sale.

B2 Licences, authorizations and formalities

The buyer must obtain at his own risk and expense any import licence or other official authorization and carry out, where applicable, all customs formalities for the import of the goods and, where necessary, for their transit through any country.

A3 Contracts of carriage and insurance

a) Contract of carriage
No obligation.

b) Contract of insurance
No obligation.

A4 Delivery

The seller must deliver the goods on the date or within the agreed period at the named port of shipment and in the manner customary at the port on board the vessel nominated by the buyer.

A5 Transfer of risks

The seller must, subject to the provisions of B5, bear all risks of loss of or damage to the goods until such time as they have passed the ship's rail at the named port of shipment.

B3 Contracts of carriage and insurance

a) Contract of carriage
The buyer must contract at his own expense for the carriage of the goods from the named port of shipment.

b) Contract of insurance
No obligation.

B4 Taking delivery

The buyer must take delivery of the goods when they have been delivered in accordance with A4.

B5 Transfer of risks

The buyer must bear all risks of loss of or damage to the goods
- from the time they have been passed the ship's rail at the named port of shipment; and
- from the agreed date or the expiry date of the agreed period for delivery which arise because he fails to give notice in accordance with B7, or because the vessel nominated by him fails to arrive on time, or is unable to take the goods, or closes for cargo earlier than the time notified in accordance with B7, provided, however, that the goods have been duly appropriated to the contract, that is to say, clearly set aside or otherwise identified as the contract goods.

A6 Division of costs

The seller must, subject to the provisions of B6, pay

- all costs relating to the goods until such time as they have passed the ship's rail at the named port of shipment; and
- where applicable, the costs of customs formalities necessary for export as well as all duties, taxes and other charges payable upon export.

B6 Division of costs

The buyer must pay

- all costs relating to the goods from the time they have passed the ship's rail at the named port of shipment, and
- any additional costs incurred, either because the vessel nominated by him has failed to arrive on time, or is unable to take the goods, or closes for cargo earlier than the time notified accordance with B7, or because the buyer has failed to give appropriate notice in accordance with B7 provided, however, that the goods have been duly appropriated to the contract, that is to say, clearly set aside or otherwise identified as the contract goods; and
- where applicable, all duties, taxes and other charges as well as the costs of carrying out customs formalities payable upon import of the goods and for their transit through any country.

A7 Notice to the buyer

The seller must give the buyer sufficient notice that the goods have been delivered in accordance with A4.

B7 Notice to the seller

The buyer must give the seller sufficient notice of the vessel name, loading point and required delivered time.

A8 Proof of delivery, transport document or equivalent electronic message

The seller must provide the buyer at the seller's expense with the usual proof of delivery in accordance with A4.

Unless the document referred to in the preceding paragraph is the transport document, the seller must render the buyer, at the latter's request, risk and expense, every assistance in obtaining a transport document for the contract of carriage (for example, a negotiable bill of lading, a non-negotiable sea waybill, an inland waterway document, or a multimodal transport document).

Where the seller and the buyer have agreed to communicate electronically, the document referred to in the preceding paragraph may be replaced by and equivalent electronic data interchange (EDI) message.

B8 Proof of delivery, transport document or equivalent electronic message

The buyer must accept the proof of delivery in accordance with A8.

A9 Checking—packaging—marking

The seller must pay the costs of those checking operations (such as checking quality, measuring, weighing, counting) which are necessary for the purpose of delivering the goods in accordance with A4.

The seller must provide at his own expense packaging (unless it is usual for the particular trade to ship the goods of the contract description unpacked) which is required for the transport of the goods, to the extent that the circumstances relating to the transport (for example modalities, destination) are made known to the seller before the contract of sale is concluded. Packaging is to be marked appropriately.

B9 Inspection of goods

The buyer must pay the costs of any pre-shipment inspection, except when such inspection is mandated by the authorities of the country of export.

A10 Other obligations

The seller must render the buyer at the latter's request, risk and expense, every assistance in obtaining any documents or equivalent electronic messages (other than those mentioned in A8) issued or transmitted in the country of shipment and/or of origin which the buyer may require for the import of the goods and, where necessary, for their transit through any country.

The seller must provide the buyer, upon request, with the necessary information for procuring insurance.

B10 Other obligations

The buyer must pay all costs and charges incurred in obtaining the document or equivalent electronic messages mentioned in A10 and reimburse those incurred by the seller in rendering his assistance in accordance therewith.

CFR
COST AND FREIGHT

(. . . named port of destination)

'Cost and Freight' means that the seller delivers when the goods pass the ship's rail in the port of shipment.

The seller must pay the costs and freight necessary to bring the goods to the named port of destination BUT the risk of loss of or damage to the goods, as well as any additional costs due to events occurring after the time of delivery, are transferred from the seller to the buyer.

The CFR term requires the seller to clear the goods for export.

This term can be used only for sea and inland waterway transport. If the parties do not intend to deliver the goods across the ship's rail, the CPT term should be used.

A THE SELLER'S OBLIGATIONS

A1 Provision of goods in conformity with the contract

The seller must provide the goods and the commercial invoice, or its equivalent electronic message, in conformity with the contract of sale and any other evidence of conformity which may be required by the contract.

A2 Licenses, authorizations and formalities

The seller must obtain at his own risk and expense any export licence or other official authorization and carry out, where applicable, all customs formalities necessary for the export of the goods.

A3 Contracts of carnage and insurance

a) Contract of carriage
The Seller must contract on usual terms at his own expense for the carriage of the goods to the named port of destination by the usual route in a seagoing vessel (or inland waterway vessel as the case may be) of the type normally used for the transport of goods of the contract description.

b) Contract of insurance
No Obligation.

A4 Delivery

The seller must deliver the goods on board the vessel at the port of shipment on the date or within the agreed period.

A5 Transfer of risks

The seller must, subject to the provisions of B5, bear all risks of loss of or damage to the goods until such time as they have passed the ship's rail at the named port of shipment.

B THE BUYER'S OBLIGATIONS

B1 Payment of the price

The buyer must pay the price as provided in the contract of sale.

B2 Licences, authorizations and formalities

The buyer must obtain at his own risk and expense any import licence or other official authorization and carry out, where applicable, all customs formalities for the import of the goods and, for their transit through any country.

B3 Contracts of carriage and insurance

a) Contract of carriage
No Obligation.

b) Contract of insurance
No obligation.

B4 Taking delivery

The buyer must take delivery of the goods when they have been delivered in accordance with A4 and receive them from the carrier at the named port of destination.

B5 Transfer of risks

The buyer must bear all risks of loss of or damage to the goods from the time they have passed the ship's rail at the port of shipment.

The buyer must, should be fail to give notice in accordance with B7, bear all risks of loss of or damage to the goods from the agreed date or the expiry date of the period fixed for shipment provided, however, that the goods have been duly appropriated to the contract, that is to say, clearly set aside or otherwise identified as the contract goods.

A6 Division of costs

The seller must, subject to the provisions of B6, pay

- all costs relating to the goods until such time as they have been delivered in accordance with A4; and
- the freight and all other costs resulting from A3 a), including the costs of loading the goods on board and any charges for unloading at the agreed port of discharge which were for the seller's account under the contract of carriage; and
- where applicable, the costs of customs formalities necessary for export as well as all duties, taxes and other charges payable upon export, and for their transit through any country if they were for the seller's account under the contract of carriage

B6 Division of costs

The buyer must, subject to the provisions of A3 a), pay

- all costs relating to the goods from the time they have been delivered in accordance with A4; and
- all costs and charges relating to the goods whilst in transit until their arrival at the port of destination, unless such costs and charges were for the seller's account under the contract of carriage; and
- unloading costs including lightrage and wharfage charges, unless such costs and charges were for the seller's account under the contract of carriage; and
- all additional costs incurred if he fails to give notice in accordance with B7, for the goods from the agreed date or the expiry date of the period fixed for shipment, provided, however, that the goods have been duly appropriated to the contract, that is to say, clearly set aside or otherwise identified as the contract goods; and
- where applicable, all duties, taxes and other charges as well as the costs of carrying out customs formalities payable upon import of the goods and, where necessary, for their transit through any country unless included within the cost of the contract of carriage.

A7 Notice to the buyer

The seller must give the buyer sufficient notice that the goods have been delivered in accordance with A4 as well as any other notice required in order to allow the buyer to take measures which are normally necessary to enable him to take the goods.

B7 Notice to the seller

The buyer must, whenever he is entitled to determine the time for shipping the goods and/or the port of destination, give the seller sufficient notice thereof.

A8 Proof of delivery, transport document or equivalent electronic message

The seller must at his own expense provide the buyer without delay with the usual transport document for the agreed port of destination.

This document (for example a negotiable bill of lading, a non-negotiable sea waybill or an inland waterway document) must cover the contract goods, be dated within the period agreed for shipment, enable the buyer to claim the goods from the carrier at the port of destination and, unless otherwise agreed, enable the buyer to sell the goods in transit by the transfer of the document to a subsequent buyer (the negotiable bill of lading) or by notification to the carrier.

When such a transport document is issued in several originals, a full set of originals must be presented to the buyer.

Where the seller and the buyer have agreed to communicate electronically, the document referred to in the preceding paragraph may be replaced by and equivalent electronic data interchange (EDI) message.

A9 Checking—packaging—marking

The seller must pay the costs of those checking operations (such as checking quality, measuring, weighing, counting) which are necessary for the purpose of delivering the goods in accordance with A4.

The seller must provide at his own expense packaging (unless it is usual for the particular trade to ship the goods of the contract description unpacked) which is required for the transport of the goods arranged by him. Packaging is to be marked appropriately.

A10 Other obligations

The seller must render the buyer at the latter's request, risk and expense, every assistance in obtaining any documents or equivalent electronic messages (other than those mentioned in A8) issued or transmitted in the country of shipment and/or of origin which the buyer may require for the import of the goods and, where necessary, for their transit through any country.

The seller must provide the buyer, upon request, with the necessary information for procuring insurance.

B8 Proof of delivery, transport document or equivalent electronic message

The buyer must accept the transport document in accordance with A8 if it is in conformity with the contract.

B9 Inspection of goods

The buyer must pay the costs of any pre-shipment inspection except when such inspections is mandated by the authorities of the country of export.

B10 Other obligations

The buyer must pay all costs and charges incurred in obtaining the documents or equivalent electronic messages mentioned in A10 and reimburse those incurred by the seller in rendering his assistance in accordance therewith.

258

CIF
COST INSURANCE AND FREIGHT

(... named port of destination)

'Cost, Insurance and Freight' means that the seller delivers when the goods pass the ship's rail in the port of shipment.

The seller must pay the costs and freight necessary to bring the goods to the named port of destination BUT the risk of loss of or damage to the goods, as well as any additional costs due to events occurring after the time of delivery, are transferred from the seller to the buyer. However, in CIF the seller also has to procure marine insurance against the buyer's risk of loss of or damage to the goods during the carriage.

Consequently, the seller contracts for insurance and pays the insurance premium. The buyer should note that under the CIF term the seller is required to obtain insurance only on minimum cover. Should the buyer wish to have the protection of greater cover, he would either need to agree as much expressly with the seller or to make his own extra insurance arrangements.

The CIF term requires the seller to clear the goods for export.

This term can be used only for sea and inland waterway transport. If the parties do not intend to deliver the goods across the ship's rail, the CIP term should be used.

A THE SELLER'S OBLIGATIONS

A1 Provision of goods in conformity with the contract

The seller must provide the goods and the commercial invoice, or its equivalent electronic message, in conformity with the contract of sale and any other evidence of conformity which may be required by the contract.

A2 Licences, authorizations and formalities

The seller must obtain at his own risk and expense any export licence or other official authorization and carry out, where applicable, all customs formalities necessary for the export of the goods.

B THE BUYER'S OBLIGATIONS

B1 Payment of the price

The buyer must pay the price as provided in the contract of sale.

B2 Licences, authorizations and formalities

The buyer must obtain at his own risk and expense any import licence or other official authorization and carry out, where applicable, all customs formalities for the import of the goods and, for their transit through any country.

A3 Contracts of carriage and insurance

a) Contract of carriage

The seller must contract on usual terms at his own expense for the carriage of the goods to the named port of destination by the usual route in a seagoing vessel (or inland waterway vessel as the case may be) of the type normally used for the transport of goods of the contract description.

b) Contract of insurance

The seller must obtain at his own expense cargo insurance as agreed in the contract, such that the buyer, or any other person having an insurable interest in the goods, shall be entitled to claim directly from the insurer and provide the buyer with the insurance policy or other evidence of insurance cover.

The insurance shall be contracted with underwriters or an insurance company of good repute and, failing express agreement to the contrary, be in accordance with minimum cover of the Institute Cargo Clauses (Institute of London Underwriters) or any similar set of clauses. The duration of insurance cover shall be in accordance with B5 and B4. When required by the buyer, the seller shall provide at the buyer's expense war, strikes, riots and civil commotion risk insurances if procurable. The minimum insurance shall cover the price provided in the contract plus ten per cent (i.e. 110%) and shall be provided in the currency of the contract.

B3 Contracts of carriage and insurance

a) Contract of carriage
No Obligation.

b) Contract of insurance
No Obligation.

A4 Delivery

The seller must deliver the goods on board the vessel at the port of shipment on the date or within the agreed period.

B4 Taking delivery

The buyer must accept delivery of the goods when they have been delivered in accordance with A4 and receive them from the carrier at the named port of destination.

A5 Transfer of risks

The seller must, subject to the provisions of B5, bear all risks of loss of or damage to the goods until such time as they have passed the ship's rail at the port of shipment.

B5 Transfer of risks

The buyer must bear all risks of loss of or damage to the goods from the time they have passed the ship's rail at the port of shipment.

The buyer must, should he fail to give notice in accordance with B7, bear all risks of loss of or damage to the goods from the agreed date or the expiry date of the period fixed for shipment provided, however, that the goods have been duly appropriated to the contract, that is to say, clearly set aside or otherwise identified as the contract goods.

A6 Division of costs

The seller must, subject to the provisions of B6, pay

- all costs relating to the goods until such time as they have been delivered in accordance with A4; and
- the freight and all other costs resulting from A3 a), including the costs of loading the goods on board; and
- the cost of insurance resulting from A3 b); and
- any charges for unloading at the agreed port of discharge which were for the seller's account under the contract of carriage; and
- where applicable, the costs of customs formalities necessary for export as well as all duties, taxes and other charges payable upon export, and for their transit through any country if they were for the seller's account under the contract of carriage.

B6 Division of costs

The buyer must, subject to the provisions of A3, pay

- all costs relating to the goods from the time they have been delivered in accordance with A4; and
- all costs and charges relating to the goods whilst in transit until their arrival at the port of destination, unless such costs and charges were for the seller's account under the contract of carriage; and
- unloading costs including lighterage and wharfage charges, unless such costs and charges were for the seller's account under the contract of carriage; and
- all additional costs incurred if he fails to give notice in accordance with B7, for the goods from the agreed date or the expiry date of the period fixed for shipment, provided, however, that the goods have been duly appropriated to the contract, that is to say, clearly set aside or otherwise identified as the contract goods; and
- where applicable, all duties, taxes and other charges as well as the costs of carrying out customs formalities payable upon import of the goods and, where necessary, for their transit through any country unless included within the cost of the contract of carriage.

A7 Notice to the buyer

The seller must give the buyer sufficient notice that the goods have been delivered in accordance with A4 as well as any other notice required in order to allow the buyer to take measures which are normally necessary to enable him to take the goods.

B7 Notice to the seller

The buyer must, whenever he is entitled to determine the time for shipping the goods and/or the port of destination, give the seller sufficient notice thereof.

A8 Proof of delivery, transport document or equivalent electronic message

The seller must at his own expense provide the buyer without delay with the usual transport document for the agreed port of destination.

This document (for example a negotiable bill of lading, a non-negotiable sea waybill or an inland waterway document) must cover the contract goods, be dated within the period agreed for shipment, enable the buyer to claim the goods from the carrier at the port of destination and, unless otherwise agreed, enable the buyer to sell the goods in transit by the transfer of the document to a subsequent buyer (the negotiable bill of lading) or by notification to the carrier.

When such a transport document is issued in several originals, a full set of originals must be presented to the buyer.

Where the seller and the buyer have agreed to communicate electronically, the document referred to in the preceding paragraphs may be replaced by an equivalent electronic data interchange (EDI) message.

A9 Checking—packaging—marking

The seller must pay the costs of those checking operations (such as checking quality, measuring, weighing, counting) which are necessary for the purpose of delivering the goods in accordance with A4.

The seller must provide at his own expense packaging (unless it is usual for the particular trade to ship the goods of the contract description unpacked) which is required for the transport of the goods arranged by him. Packaging is to be marked appropriately.

A10 Other obligations

The seller must render the buyer at the latter's request, risk and expense, every assistance in obtaining any documents or equivalent electronic messages (other than those mentioned in A8) issued or transmitted in the country of shipment and/or of origin which the buyer may require for the import of the goods and, where necessary, for their transit through any country.

The seller must provide the buyer, upon request, with the necessary information for procuring any additional insurance.

B8 Proof of delivery, transport document or equivalent electronic message

The buyer must accept the transport document in accordance with A8 if it is in conformity with the contract.

B9 Inspection of goods

The buyer must pay the costs of any pre-shipment inspection except when such inspection is mandated by the authorities of the country of export.

B10 Other obligations

The buyer must pay all costs and charges incurred in obtaining the documents or equivalent electronic messages mentioned in A10 and reimburse those incurred by the seller in rendering his assistance in accordance therewith.

The buyer must provide the seller, upon request, with the necessary information for procuring insurance.

CPT
CARRIAGE PAID TO

(... named place of destination)

'Carriage paid to ...' means that the seller delivers the goods to the carrier nominated by him but the seller must in addition pay the cost of carriage necessary to bring the goods to the named destination. This means that the buyer bears all risks and any other costs occurring after the goods have been so delivered.

'Carrier' means any person who, in a contract of carriage, undertakes to perform or to procure the performance of transport, by rail, road, air, sea, inland waterway or by a combination of such modes.

If subsequent carriers are used for the carriage to the agreed destination, the risk passes when the goods have been delivered to the first carrier.

The CPT term requires the seller to clear the goods for export.

This term may be used irrespective of the mode of transport including multimodal transport.

A THE SELLER'S OBLIGATIONS

A1 Provision of goods in conformity with the contract

The seller must provide the goods and the commercial invoice, or its equivalent electronic message, in conformity with the contract of sale and any other evidence of conformity which may be required by the contract.

A2 Licences, authorizations and formalities

The seller must obtain at his own risk and expense any export license or other official authorization and carry out, where applicable, all customs formalities for the export of the goods.

A3 Contracts of carriage and insurance

a) Contract of carriage
The seller must contract on usual terms at his own expense for the carriage of the goods to the named port of destination by the usual route and in a customary manner. If a point is not agreed or is not determined by practice, the seller may select the point at the named place of destination which best suits his purpose.

b) Contract of insurance
No obligation.

B THE BUYER'S OBLIGATIONS

B1 Payment of the price

The buyer must pay the price as provided in the contract of sale.

B2 Licences authorizations and formalities

The buyer must obtain at his own risk and expense any import licence or other official authorization and carry out, where applicable, all customs formalities for the import of the goods and for their transit through any country.

B3 Contracts of carriage and insurance

a) Contract of carriage
No obligation.

b) Contract of insurance
No obligation.

263

A4 Delivery

The seller must deliver the goods to the carrier contracted in accordance with A3 or, if there are subsequent carriers to the first carrier, for transport to the agreed point at the named place on the date or within the agreed period.

B4 Taking delivery

The buyer must accept delivery of the goods when they have been delivered in accordance with A4 and receive them from the carrier at the named place.

A5 Transfer of risks

The seller must, subject to the provisions of B5, bear all risks of loss of or damage to the goods until such time as they have been delivered in accordance with A4.

B5 Transfer of risks

The buyer must bear all risks of loss of or damage to the goods from the time they have been delivered in accordance with A4.

The buyer must, should he fail to give notice in accordance with B7, bear all risks of or the goods from the agreed date or the expiry date of the period fixed for delivery provided, however, that the goods have been duly appropriated to the contract, that is to say, clearly set aside or otherwise identified as the contract goods.

A6 Division of costs

The seller must, subject to the provisions of B6, pay
- all costs relating to the goods until such time as they have been delivered in accordance with A4; as well as the freight and all other costs resulting from A3 a), including the costs of loading the goods and any charges for unloading at the place of distination which were for the seller's account under the contract of carriage; and
- where applicable, the costs of customs formalities necessary for export as well as all duties, taxes and other charges payable upon export, and for their transit through any country if they were for the seller's account under the contract of carriage.

B6 Division of costs

The buyer must, subject to the provisions of A3 a), pay
- all costs relating to the goods from the time they have been delivered in accordance with A4; and
- all costs and charges relating to the goods whilst in transit until their arrival at the agreed place of destination, unless such costs and charges were for the seller's account under the contract of carriage; and
- unloading costs, unless such costs and charges were for the seller's account under the contract of carriage; and
- all additional costs incurred if he fails to give notice in accordance with B7, for the goods from the agreed date or the expiry date of the period fixed for dispatch, provided, however, that the goods have been duly appropriated to the contract, that is to say, clearly set aside or otherwise identified as the contract goods; and
- where applicable, all duties, taxes and other charges as well as the costs of carrying out customs formalities payable upon import of the goods and, for their transit through any country unless included within the cost of the contract of carriage.

264

A7 Notice to the buyer

The seller must give the buyer sufficient notice that the goods have been delivered in accordance with A4 as well as any other notice required in order to allow the buyer to take measures which are normally necessary to enable him to take the goods.

A8 Proof of delivery, transport document or equivalent electronic message

The seller must provide the buyer at the seller's expense, if customary, with the usual transport document or documents (for example a negotiable bill of lading, a non-negotiable sea waybill, an inland waterway document, an air waybill, a railway consignment note, a road consignment note, or a multimodal transport document) for the transport contracted in accordance with A3.

Where the seller and the buyer have agreed to comminicate electronically, the document referred to in the preceding paragraph may be replaced by an equivalent electronic data interchange (EDI) message.

A9 Checking—packaging—marking

The seller must pay the costs of those checking operations (such as checking quality, measuring, weighing, counting) which are necessary for the purpose of delivering the goods in accordance with A4.

The seller must provide at his own expense packaging (unless it is usual for the particular trade to send the goods of the contract description unpacked) which is required for the transport of the goods arranged by him. Packaging is to be marked appropriately.

A10 Other obiigations

The seller must render the buyer at the latter's request, risk and expense, every assistance in obtaining any documents or equivalent electronic messages (other than those mentioned in A8) issued or transmitted in the country of dispatch and/or of origin which the buyer may require for the import of the goods and, for their transit through any country.

The seller must provide the buyer, upon request, with the necessary information for procuring insurance.

B7 Notice to the seller

The buyer must, whenever he is entitled to determine the time for dispatching the goods and/or the destination, give the seller sufficient notice thereof.

B8 Proof of delivery, transport document or equivalent electronic message

The buyer must accept the transport document in accordance with A8 if it is in conformity with the contract.

B9 Inspection of goods

The buyer must pay the costs of any pre-shipment inspection except when such inspection is mandated by the authorities of the country of export.

B10 Other obligations

The buyer must pay all costs and charges incurred in obtaining the documents or equivalent electronic messages mentioned in A10 and reimburse those incurred by the seller in rendering his assistance in accordance therewith.

CIP
CARRIAGE AND INSURANCE PAID TO

(named place of destination)

'Carriage and Insurance paid to' means that the seller delivers the goods to the carrier nominated by him, but the seller must in addition pay the cost of carriage necessary to bring the goods to the named destination. This means that the buyer bears all risks and any additional costs occurring after the goods have been so delivered. However, in CIP the seller also has to procure insurance against the buyer's risk of loss of or damage to the goods during the carriage.

Consequently, the seller contracts for insurance and pays the insurance premium.

The buyer should note that under the CIP term the seller is required to obtain insurance only on minimum cover. Should the buyer wish to have the protection of greater cover, he would either need to agree as much expressly with the seller or to make his own extra insurance arrangements.

'Carrier' means any person who, in a contract of carriage, undertakes to perform or to procure the performance of transport, by rail, road, air, sea, inland waterway or by a combination of such modes.

If subsequent carriers are used for the carriage to the agreed destination, the risk passes when the goods have been delivered to the first carrier.

The CIP term requires the seller to clear the goods for export.

This term may be used irrespective of the mode of transport, including multimodal transport.

A THE SELLER'S OBLIGATIONS

A1 Provision of goods in conformity with the contract

The seller must provide the goods and the commercial invoice, or its equivalent electronic message, in conformity with the contract of sale and any other evidence of conformity which may be required by the contract.

A2 Licences, authorizations and formalities

The seller must obtain at his own risk and expense any export license or other official authorization and carry out, where applicable, all customs formalities necessary for the export of the goods.

B THE BUYER' OBLIGATIONS

B1 Payment of the price

The buyer must pay the price as provided in the contract of sale.

B2 Licences, authorizations and formalities

The buyer must obtain at his own risk and expense any import licence or other official authorization and carry out, where applicable, all customs formalities for the import of the goods and for their transit through any country.

266

A3 Contracts of carriage and insurance

a) Control of carriage

The seller must contract on usual terms at his own expense for the carriage of the goods to the agreed point at the named place of destination by the usual route and in a customary manner. If a point is not agreed or is not determined by practice, the seller may select the point at the named place of destination which best suits his purpose.

b) Contract of insurance

The seller must obtain at his own expense cargo insurance as agreed in the contract, such that the buyer, or any other person having an insurable interest in the goods, shall be entitled to claim directly from the insurer and provide the buyer with the insurance policy or other evidence of insurance cover.

The insurance shall be contracted with underwriters or an insurance company of good repute and, failing express agreement to the contrary, be in accordance with minimum cover of the Institute Cargo Clauses (Institute of London Underwriters) or any similar set of clauses. The duration of insurance cover shall be in accordance with B5 and B4. When required by the buyer, the seller shall provide at the buyer's expense war, strikes, riots and civil commotion risk insurances if procurable. The minimum insurance shall cover the price provided in the contract plus ten per cent (i.e. 110%) and shall be provided in the currency of the contract.

A4 Delivery

The seller must deliver the goods to the carrier contracted in accordance with A3 or, if there are subsequent carriers to the first carrier, for transport to the agreed point at the named place on the date or within the agreed period.

B3 Contracts of carriage and insurance

a) Contract of carriage
No obligation.

b) Contract of insurance
No obligation.

B4 Taking delivery

The buyer must accept delivery of the goods when they have been delivered in accordance with A4 and receive them from the carrier at the named place.

A5 Transfer of risks

The seller must, subject to the provisions of B5, bear all risks of loss of or damage to the goods until such time as they have been delivered in accordance with A4.

B5 Transfer of risks

The buyer must bear all risks of loss of or damage to the goods from the time they have been delivered in accordance with A4.

The buyer must, should he fail to give notice in accordance with B7, bear all risks of the goods from the agreed date or the expiry date of the period fixed for delivery provided, however, that the goods have been duly appropriated to the contract, that is to say clearly set aside or otherwise indentified as the contract goods.

A6 Division of costs

The seller must, subject to the provisions of B6, pay
- all costs relating to the goods until such time as they have been delivered in accordance with A4 as well as the freight and all other costs resulting from A3 a), including the costs of loading the goods and any charges for unloading at the place of destination which were for the seller's account under the contract of carriage; and
- the costs of insurance resulting from A3 b); and
- where applicable, the costs of customs formalities necessary for export as well as all duties, taxes or other charges payable upon export, and for their transit through any country if they were for the seller's account under the contract of carriage.

B6 Division of costs

The buyer must, subject to the provisions of A3 a), pay
- all costs relating to the goods from the time they have been delivered in accordance with A4; and
- all cost and charges relating to the goods whilst in transit until their arrival at the agreed place of destination, unless such costs and charges were for the seller's account under the contract of carriage; and
- unloading costs unless such costs and charges were for the seller's account under the contract of carriage; and
- all additional costs incurred if he fails to give notice in accordance with B7, for the goods from the agreed date or the expiry date of the period fixed for dispatch, provided, however, that the goods have been duly appropriated to the contract, that is to say, clearly set aside or otherwise identified as the contract goods; and
- where applicable, all duties, taxes and other charges as well as the costs of carrying out customs formalities payable upon import of the goods and for their transit through any country unless included within the cost of the contract of carriage.

A7 Notice to the buyer

The seller must give the buyer sufficient notice that the goods have been delivered in accordance with A4, as well as any other notice required in order to allow the buyer to take measures which are normally necessary to enable him to take the goods.

B7 Notice to the seller

The buyer must, whenever, he is entitled to determine the time for dispatching the goods and/or the destination, give the seller sufficient notice thereof.

A8 Proof of delivery, transport document or equivalent electronic message

The seller must provide the buyer at the seller's expense, if customary, with the usual transport document or documents (for example a negotiable bill of lading, a non-negotiable sea waybill, an inland waterway document, an air waybill, a railway consignment note, a road consignment note, or a multimodal transport document) for the transport contracted in accordance with A3.

Where the seller and the buyer have agreed to communicate electronically, the document referred to in the preceding paragraph may be replaced by an equivalent electronic data interchange (EDI) message.

A9 Checking—packaging—marking

The seller must pay the costs of those checking operations (such as checking quality, measuring, weighing, counting) which are necessary for the purpose of delivering the goods in accordance with A4.

The seller must provide at his own expense packaging (unless it is usual for the particular trade to ship the goods of the contract description unpacked) which is required for the transport of the goods arranged by him. Packaging is to be marked appropriately.

A10 Other obligations

The seller must render the buyer at the latter's request, risk and expense, every assistance in obtaining any documents or equivalent electronic messages (other than those mentioned in A8) issued or transmitted in the country of dispatch and/or of origin which the buyer may require for the import of the goods and for their transit through any country.

The seller must provide the buyer, upon request, with the necessary information for procuring any additional insurance.

B8 Proof of delivery, transport document or equivalent electronic message

The buyer must accept the transport document in accordance with A8 if it is in conformity with the contract.

B9 Inspection of goods

The buyer must pay the costs of any pre-shipment inspection except when such inspection is mandated by the authorities of the country of export.

B10 Other obligations

The buyer must pay all costs and charges incurred in obtaining the documents or equivalent electronic messages mentioned in A10 and reimburse those incurred by the seller in rendering his assistance in accordance therewith.

The buyer must provide the seller, upon request, with the necessary information for procuring any additional insurance.

DAF
DELIVERED AT FRONTIER

(. . . named place)

'Delivered at Frontier' means that the seller delivers when the goods are placed at the disposal of the buyer on the arriving means of transport not unloaded, cleared for export, but not cleared for import at the named point and place at the frontier, but before the customs border of the adjoining country. The term 'frontier' may be used for any frontier including that of the country of export. Therefore, it is of vital importance that the frontier in question be defined precisely by always naming the point and place in the term.

However, if the parties wish the seller to be responsible for the unloading of the goods from the arriving means of transport and to bear the risks and costs of unloading, this should be made clear by adding explicit wording to this effect in the contract of sale.

This term may be used irrespective of the mode of transport when goods are to be delivered at a land frontier. When delivery is to take place in the port of destination, on board a vessel or on the quay (wharf), the DES or DEQ terms should be used.

A THE SELLER'S OBLIGATIONS

A1 Provision of goods in conformity with the contract

The seller must provide the goods and the commercial invoice, or its equivalent electronic message, in conformity with the contract of sale and any other evidence of conformity which may be required by the contract.

A2 Licences, authorizations and formalities

The seller must obtain at his own risk and expense any export licence or other official authorization or other document necessary for placing the goods at the buyer's disposal.

The seller must carry out, where applicable, all customs formalities necessary for the export of the goods to the named place of delivery at the frontier and for their transit through any country.

B THE BUYER'S OBLIGATIONS

B1 Payment of the price

The buyer must pay the price as provided in the contract of sale.

B2 Licences, authorizations and formalities

The buyer must obtain at his own risk and expense any import licence or other official authorization and carry out, where applicable all customs formalities necessary for the import of the goods, and for their subsequent transport.

A3 Contracts of carriage and insurance

a) Contract of carriage
i) The seller must contract at his own expense for the carriage of the goods to the named point, if any, at the place of delivery at the frontier. If a point at the named place of delivery at the frontier is not agreed or is not determined by practice, the seller may select the point at the named place of delivery which best suits his purpose.

ii) However, if requested by the buyer, the seller may agree to contract on usual terms at the buyer's risk and expense for the on-going carriage of the goods beyond the named place at the frontier to the final destination in the country of import named by the buyer. The seller may decline to make the contract and, if he does, shall promptly notify the buyer accordingly.

b) Contract of insurance
No obligation.

A4 Delivery

The seller must place the goods at the disposal of the buyer on the arriving means of transport not unloaded at the named place of delivery at the frontier on the date or within the agreed period.

A5 Transfer of risks

The seller must, subject to the provisions of B5, bear all risks of loss of or damage to the goods until such time as they have been delivered in accordance with A4.

B3 Contracts of carriage and insurance

a) Contract of carriage
No obligation.

b) Contract of insurance
No obligation.

B4 Taking delivery

The buyer must take delivery of the goods when they have been delivered in accordance with A4.

B5 Transfer of risks

The buyer must bear all risks of loss of or damage to the goods from the time they have been delivered in accordance with A4.

The buyer must, should he fail to give notice in accordance with B7, bear all risks of loss of or damage to the goods from the agreed date or the expiry date of the agreed period for delivery provided, however, that the goods have been duly appropriated to the contract, that is to say, clearly set aside or otherwise identified as the contract goods.

A6 Division of costs

The seller must, subject to the provisions of B6, pay

- in addition to the costs resulting from A3 a), all costs relating to the goods until such time as they have been delivered in accordance with A4; and
- where applicable, the costs of customs formalities necessary for export as well as all duties, taxes and other charges payable upon export of the goods and for their transit through any country prior to delivery in accordance with A4.

B6 Division of costs

The buyer must pay

- all costs relating to the goods from the time they have been delivered in accordance with A4, including the expenses of unloading necessary to take delivery of the goods from the arriving means of transport at the named place of delivery at the frontier; and
- all additional costs incurred if he fails to take delivery of the goods when they have been delivered in accordance with A4, or to give notice in accordance with B7, provided, however, that the goods have been appropriated to the contract, that is to say, clearly set aside or otherwise identified as the contract goods; and
- where applicable, the cost of customs formalities as well as all duties, taxes and other charges payable upon import of the goods and for their subsequent transport.

A7 Notice to the buyer

The seller must give the buyer sufficient notice of the dispatch of the goods to the named place at the frontier as well as any other notice required in order to allow the buyer to take measures which are normally necessary to enable him to take delivery of the goods.

B7 Notice to the seller

The buyer must, whenever he is entitled to determine the time within an agreed period and/or the point of taking delivery in the named place, give the seller sufficient notice thereof.

A8 Proof of delivery, transport document or equivalent electronic message

i) The seller must provide the buyer at the seller's expense with the usual document or other evidence of the delivery of the goods at the named place at the frontier in accordance with A3 a) i).

ii) The seller must, should the parties agree on on-going carriage beyond the frontier in accordance with A3 a) ii), provide the buyer at the latter's request, risk and expense, with the through document of transport normally obtained in the country of dispatch covering on usual terms the transport of the goods from the point of dispatch in that country to the place of final destination in the country of import named by the buyer.

Where the seller and the buyer have agreed to communicate electronically, the document referred to in the preceding paragraph may be replaced by an equivalent electronic data interchange (EDI) message.

B8 Proof of delivery, transport document or equivalent electronic message

The buyer must accept transport document and/or other evidence of delivery in accordance with A8.

A9 Checking—packaging—marking

The seller must pay the costs of those checking operations (such as checking quality, measuring, weighing, counting) which are necessary for the purpose of delivering the goods in accordance with A4.

The seller must provide at his own expense packaging (unless it is agreed or usual for the particular trade to deliver the goods of the contract description unpacked) which is required for the delivery of the goods at the frontier and for the subsequent transport to the extent that the circumstances (for example modalities, destination) are made known to the seller before the contract of sale is concluded. Packaging is to be marked appropriately.

B9 Inspection of goods

The buyer must pay the costs of any pre-shipment inspection except when such inspection is mandated by the authorities of the country of export.

A10 Other obligations

The seller must render the buyer at the latter's request, risk and expense, every assistance in obtaining any documents or equivalent electronic messages (other than those mentioned in A8) issued or transmitted in the country of dispatch and/or origin which the buyer may require for the import of the goods and, where necessary, for their transit through any country.

The seller must provide the buyer, upon request, with the necessary information for procuring insurance.

B10 Other obligations

The buyer must pay all costs and charges incurred in obtaining the documents or equivalent electronic messages mentioned in A10 and reimburse those incurred by the seller in rendering his assistance in accordance therewith.

If necessary, according to A3 a) ii), the buyer must provide the seller at his request and the buyer's risk and expense with the exchange control authorization, permits, other documents or certified copies thereof, or with the address of the final destination of the goods in the country of import for the purpose of obtaining the through document of transport or any other document contemplated in A8 ii).

DES
DELIVERED EX SHIP

(. . . named port of destination)

'Delivered Ex Ship' means that the seller delivers when the goods are placed at the disposal of the buyer on board the ship not cleared for import at the named port of destination. The seller has to bear all the costs and risks involved in bringing the goods to the named port of destination before discharging. If the parties wish the seller to bear the costs and risks of discharging the goods, then the DEQ term should be used.

This term can be used only when the goods are to be delivered by sea or inland waterway or multimodal transport on a vessel in the port of destination.

A THE SELLER'S OBLIGATIONS

A1 Provision of goods in conformity with the contract

The seller must provide the goods and the commercial invoice, or its equivalent electronic message, in conformity with the contract of sale and any other evidence of conformity which may be required by the contract.

A2 Licences, authorizations and formalities

The seller must obtain at his own risk and expense any export licence or other official authorization or other documents and carry out, where applicable, all customs formalities necessary for the export of the goods and for their transit through any country.

A3 Contracts of carriage and insurance

a) Contract of carriage
The seller must contract at his own expense for the carriage of the goods to the named point, if any, at the named port of destination. If a point is not agreed or is not determined by practice, the seller may select the point at the named port of destination which best suits his purpose.

b) Contract of insurance
No obligation.

A4 Delivery

The seller must place the goods at the disposal of the buyer on board the vessel at the unloading point referred to in A3 a), in the named port of destination on the date or within the agreed period, in such a way as to enable them to be removed from the vessel by unloading equipment appropriate to the nature of the goods.

B THE BUYER'S OBLIGATIONS

B1 Payment of the price

The buyer must pay the price as provided in the contract of sale.

B2 Licences, authorizations and formalities

The buyer must obtain at his own risk and expense any import licence or other official authorization and carry out, where applicable, all customs formalities necessary for the import of the goods.

B3 Contracts of carriage and insurance

a) Contract of carriage
No obligation.

b) Contract of insurance
No obligation.

B4 Taking delivery

The buyer must take delivery of the goods when they have been delivered in accordance with A4.

274

A5 Transfer of risks

The seller must, subject to the provisions of B5, bear all risks of loss of or damage to the goods until such time as they have been delivered in accordance with A4.

A6 Division of costs

The seller must, subject to the provisions of B6, pay

- in addition to costs resulting from A3 a), all costs relating to the goods until such time as they have been delivered in accordance with A4; and
- where applicable, the costs of customs formalities necessary for export as well as all duties, taxes or other charges payable upon export of the goods and for their transit through any country prior to delivery in accordance with A4.

A7 Notice to the buyer

The seller must give the buyer sufficient notice of the estimated time of arrival of the nominated vessel in accordance with A4 as well as any other notice required in order to allow the buyer to take measures which are normally necessary to enable him to take delivery of the goods.

B5 Transfer of risks

The buyer must bear all risks of loss of or damage to the goods from the time they have been delivered in accordance with A4.

The buyer must, should he fail to give notice in accordance with B7, bear all risks of loss of or damage to the goods from the agreed date or the expiry date of the agreed period for delivery provided, however, that the goods have been duly appropriated to the contract, that is to say, clearly set aside or otherwise identified as the contract goods.

B6 Division of costs

The buyer must pay

- all costs relating to the goods from the time they have been delivered in accordance with A4, including the expenses of discharge operations necesary to take delivery of the goods from the vessel; and
- all additional costs incurred if he fails to take delivery of the goods when they have been placed at his disposal in accordance with A4, or to give notice in accordance with B7, provided, however, that the goods have been appropriated to the contract, that is to say, clearly set aside or otherwise identified as the contract goods; and
- where applicable, the costs of customs formalities as well as all duties, taxes and other charges payable upon import of the goods.

B7 Notice to the seller

The buyer must, whenever he is entitled to determine the time within an agreed period and/or the point of taking delivery in the named port of destination, give the seller sufficient notice thereof.

A8 Proof of delivery, transport document or equivalent electronic message

The seller must provide the buyer at the seller's expense with the delivery order and/or the usual transport document (for example a negotiable bill of lading, a non-negotiable sea waybill, an inland waterway document, or a multimodal transport document) to enable the buyer to claim the goods from the carrier at the port of destination.

Where the seller and the buyer have agreed to communicate electronically, the document referred to in the preceding paragraph may be replaced by an equivalent electronic data interchange (EDI) message.

A9 Checking—packaging—marking

The seller must pay the costs of those checking operations (such as checking quality, measuring, weighing, counting) which are necessary for the purpose of delivering the goods in accordance with A4.

The seller must provide at his own expense packaging (unless it is usual for the particular trade to deliver the goods of the contract description unpacked) which is required for the delivery of the goods. Packaging is to be marked appropriately.

A10 Other obligations

The seller must render the buyer at the latter's request, risk and expense, every assistance in obtaining any documents or equivalent electronic messages (other than those mentioned in A8) issued or transmitted in the country of shipment and/or of origin which the buyer may require for the import of the goods and, where necessary, for their transit through any country.

The seller must provide the buyer, upon request, with the necessary information for procuring insurance.

B8 Proof of delivery, transport document or equivalent electronic message

The buyer must accept the delivery order or transport document in accordance with A8.

B9 Inspection of goods

The buyer must pay the costs of any pre-shipment inspection except when such inspection is mandated by the authorities of the country of export.

B10 Other obligations

The buyer must pay all costs and charges incurred in obtaining the documents or equivalent electronic messages mentioned in A10 and reimburse those incurred by the seller in rendering his assistance in accordance therewith.

DEQ
DELIVERED EX QUAY

(... named port of destination)

'Delivered Ex Quay' means that the seller delivers when the goods are placed at the disposal of the buyer not cleared for import on the quay (wharf) at the named port of destination. The seller has to bear costs and risks involved in bringing the goods to the named port of destination and discharging the goods on the quay (wharf). The DEQ term requires the buyer to clear the goods for import and to pay for all formalities, duties, taxes and other charges upon import.

THIS IS A REVERSAL FROM PREVIOUS INCOTERMS VERSIONS WHICH REQUIRED THE SELLER TO ARRANGE FOR IMPORT CLEARANCE.

If the parties wish to include in the seller's obligations all or part of the costs payable upon import of the goods, this should be made clear by adding explicit wording to this effect in the contract of sale.

This term can be used only when the goods are to be delivered by sea or inland waterway or multimodal transport on discharging from a vessel onto the quay (wharf) in the port of destination. However if the parties wish to include in the seller's obligations the risks and costs of the handling of the goods from the quay to another place (warehouse, terminal, transport station, etc.) in or outside the port, the DDU or DDP terms should be used.

A THE SELLER'S OBLIGATIONS

A1 Provision of goods in conformity with the contract

The seller must provide the goods and the commercial invoice, or its equivalent electronic message, in conformity with the contract of sale and any other evidence of conformity which may be required by the contract.

A2 Licences, authorizations and formalities

The seller must obtain at his own risk and expense any export licence or other official authorization or other documents and carry out, where applicable, all customs formalities necessary for the export of the goods, and for their transit through any country.

A3 Contracts of carriage and insurance

a) Contract of carriage
The seller must contract at his own expense for the carriage of the goods to the named quay (wharf) at the named port of destination. If a specific quay (wharf) is not agreed or is not determined by practice, the seller may select the quay (wharf) at the named port of destination which best suits his purpose.

b) Contract of insurance
No obligation.

B THE BUYER'S OBLIGATIONS

B1 Payment of the price

The buyer must pay the price as provided in the contract of sale.

B2 Licences, authorizations and formalities

The buyer must obtain at his own risk and expense any import licence or other official authorization or other documents and carry out, where applicable, all customs formalities necessary for the import of the goods.

B3 Contracts of carriage and insurance

a) Contract of carriage
No obligation.

b) Contract of insurance
No obligation.

277

A4 Delivery

The seller must place the goods at the disposal of the buyer on the quay (wharf) referred to in A3 a), on the date or within the agreed period.

B4 Taking delivery

The buyer must take delivery of the goods when they have been delivered in accordance with A4.

A5 Transfer of risks

The seller must, subject to the provisions of B5, bear all risks of loss of or damage to the goods until such time as they have been delivered in accordance with A4.

B5 Transfer of risks

The buyer must bear all risks of loss of or damage to the goods from the time they have been delivered in accordance with A4.

The buyer must, should he fail to give notice in accordance with B7, bear all risks of loss of or damage to the goods from the agreed date or the expiry date of the agreed period for delivery provided, however, that the goods have been duly appropriated to the contract, that is to say, clearly set aside or otherwise identified as the contract goods.

A6 Division of costs

The seller must, subject to the provisions of B6, pay
- in addition to costs resulting from A3 a), all costs relating to the goods until such time as they are delivered on the quay (wharf) in accordance with A4; and
- where applicable, the costs of customs formalities necessary for export as well as all duties, taxes or other charges payable upon export of the goods and for their transit through any country prior to delivery.

B6 Division of costs

The buyer must pay
- all costs relating to the goods from the time they have been delivered in accordance with A4, including any costs of handling the goods in the port for subsequent transport or storage in warehouse or terminal; and
- all additional costs incurred if he fails to take delivery of the goods when they have been delivered in accordance with A4, or to give notice in accordance with B7, provided, however, that the goods have been appropriated to the contract, that is to say, clearly set aside or otherwise identified as the contract goods; and
- where applicable, the costs of customs formalities as well as all duties, taxes and other charges payable upon import of the goods and for their subsequent transport.

A7 Notice to the buyer

The seller must give the buyer sufficient notice of the estimated time of arrival of the nominated vessel in accordance with A4, as well as any other notice required in order to allow the buyer to take measures which are normally necessary to enable him to take delivery of the goods.

B7 Notice to the seller

The buyer must, whenever he is entitled to determine the time within an agreed period and/or the point of taking delivery in the named port of destination, give the seller sufficient notice thereof.

A8 Proof of delivery, transport document or equivalent electronic message

The seller must provide the buyer at the seller's expense with the delivery order and/or the usual transport document (for example a negotiable bill of lading, a non-negotiable sea waybill, an inland waterway document, or a multimodal transport document) to enable him to take the goods and remove them from the quay (wharf).

Where the seller and the buyer have agreed to communicate electronically, the document referred to in the preceding paragraph may be replaced by an equivalent electronic data interchange (EDI) message.

B8 Proof of delivery, transport document or equivalent electronic message

The buyer must accept the appropriate delivery order or transport document in accordance with A8.

A9 Checking—packaging—marking

The seller must pay the costs of those checking operations (such as checking quality, measuring, weighing, counting) which are necessary for the purpose of delivering the goods in accordance with A4.

The seller must provide at his own expense packaging (unless it is usual for the particular trade to deliver the goods of the contract description unpacked) which is required for the delivery of the goods. Packaging is to be marked appropriately.

B9 Inspection of goods

The buyer must pay the costs of any pre-shipment inspection except when such inspection is mandated by the authorities of the country of export.

A10 Other obligations

The seller must render the buyer at the latter's request, risk and expense, every assistance in obtaining any documents or equivalent electronic messages (other than those mentioned in A8) issued or transmitted in the country of dispatch and/or origin which the buyer may require for the import of the goods.

The seller must provide the buyer, upon request, with the necessary information for procuring insurance.

B10 Other obligations

The buyer must pay all costs and charges incurred in obtaining the documents or equivalent electronic messages mentioned in A10 and reimburse those incurred by the seller in rendering his assistance in accordance therewith.

DDU
DELIVERED DUTY UNPAID

(. . . named place of destination)

'Delivered duty unpaid' means that the seller delivers the goods to the buyer, not cleared for import, and not unloaded from any arriving means of transport at the named place of destination. The seller has to bear the costs and risks involved in bringing the goods thereto, other than, where applicable, and 'duty' (which term includes the responsibility for and the risks of the carrying out of customs formalities, and the payment of formalities, customs duties, taxes and other charges) for import in the country of destination. Such "duty" has to be borne by the buyer as well as any costs and risks caused by his failure to clear the goods for import in time.

However, if the parties wish the seller to carry out customs formalities and bear the costs and risks resulting therefrom as well as some of the costs payable upon import of the goods, this should be made clear by adding explicit wording to this effect in the contract of sale.

This term may be used irrespective of the mode of transport but when delivery is to take place in the port of destination on board the vessel or on the quay (wharf), the DES or DEQ terms should be used.

A THE SELLER'S OBLIGATIONS	B THE BUYER'S OBLIGATIONS
A1 Provision of the goods in conformity with the contract	**B1 Payment of the price**
The seller must provide the goods and the commercial invoice, or its equivalent electronic message, in conformity with the contract of sale and any other evidence of conformity which may be required by the contract.	The buyer must pay the price as provided in the contract of sale.
A2 Licences, authorizations and formalities	**B2 Licences, authorizations and formalities**
The seller must obtain at his own risk and expense any export licence or other official authorization or other documents and carry out, where applicable, all customs formalities necessary for the export of the goods and for their transit through any country.	The buyer must obtain at his own risk and expense any import licence or other official authorization or other documents and carry out, where applicable, all customs formalities necessary for the import of the goods.
A3 Contracts of carriage and insurance	**B3 Contracts of carriage and insurance**
a) Contract of carriage The seller must contract at his own expense for the carriage of the goods to the named place of destination. If a specific point is not agreed or is not determined by practice, the seller may select the point at the named place of destination which best suits his purpose. b) Contract of insurance No obligation.	a) Contract of carriage No obligation. b) Contract of insurance No obligation.

A4 Delivery

The seller must place the goods at the disposal of the buyer, or at that of another person named by the buyer, on any arriving means of transport not unloaded, at the named place of destination on the date or within the period agreed for delivery.

A5 Transfer of risks

The seller must, subject to the provisions of B5, bear all risks of loss of or damage to the goods until such time as they have been delivered in accordance with A4.

A6 Division of costs

The seller must, subject to the provisions of B6, pay
- in addition to costs resulting from A3 a), all costs relating to the goods until such time as they have been delivered in accordance with A4; and
- where applicable, the costs of customs formalities necessary for export as well as all duties, taxes or other charges payable upon export and for their transit through any country prior to delivery in accordance with A4.

A7 Notice to the buyer

The seller must give the buyer sufficient notice of the dispatch of the goods as well as any other notice required in order to allow the buyer to take measures which are normally necessary to enable him to take delivery of the goods.

B4 Taking delivery

The buyer must take delivery of the goods when they have been delivered in accordance with A4.

B5 Transfer of risks

The buyer must bear all risks of loss of or damage to the goods from the time they have been delivered in accordance with A4.

The buyer must, should he fail to fulfil his obligations in accordance with B2, bear all additional risks of loss of or damage to the goods incurred thereby.

The buyer must, should he fail to give notice in accordance with B7, bear all risks of loss of or damage to the goods from the agreed date or the expiry date of the agreed period for delivery provided, however, that the goods have been duly appropriated to the contract, that is to say, clearly set aside or otherwise identified as the contract goods.

B6 Division of costs

The buyer must pay
- all costs relating to the goods from the time they have been delivered in accordance with A4; and
- all additional costs incurred if he fails to fulfill his obligations in accordance with B2, or to give notice in accordance with B7, provided, however, that the goods have been duly appropriated to the contract, that is to say, clearly set aside or otherwise identified as the contract goods; and
- where applicable, the costs of customs formalities as well as all duties, taxes and other charges payable upon import of the goods.

B7 Notice to the seller

The buyer must, whenever he is entitled to determine the time within an agreed period and/or the point of taking delivery at the named place, give the seller sufficient notice thereof.

A8 Proof of delivery, transport document or equivalent electronic message

The seller must provide the buyer at the seller's expense the delivery order and/or the usual transport document (for example a negotiable bill of lading, a non-negotiable sea waybill, an inland waterway document, an air waybill, a railway consignment note, a road consignment note, or a multimodal transport document) which the buyer may require to take delivery of the goods in accordance with A4/B4.

Where the seller and the buyer have agreed to communicate electronically, the document referred to in the preceding paragraph may be replaced by an equivalent electronic data interchange (EDI) message.

A9 Checking—packaging—marking

The seller must pay the costs of those checking operations (such as checking quality, measuring, weighing, counting) which are necessary for the purpose of delivering the goods in accordance with A4.

The seller must provide at his own expense packaging (unless it is usual for the particular trade to deliver the goods of the contract description unpacked) which is required for the delivery of the goods. Packaging is to be marked appropriately.

A10 Other obligations

The seller must render the buyer at the latter's request, risk and expense, every assistance in obtaining any documents or equivalent electronic messages (other than those mentioned in A8) issued or transmitted in the country of dispatch and/or of origin which the buyer may require for the import of the goods.

The seller must provide the buyer, upon request, with the necessary information for procuring insurance.

B8 Proof of delivery, transport document or equivalent electronic message

The buyer must accept the appropriate delivery order or transport document in accordance with A8.

B9 Inspection of goods

The buyer must pay the costs of any pre-shipment inspection except when such inspection is mandated by the authorities of the country of export.

B10 Other obligations

The buyer must pay all costs and charges incurred in obtaining the documents or equivalent electronic messages mentioned in A10 and reimburse those incurred by the seller in rendering his assistance in accordance therewith.

DDP
DELIVERED DUTY PAID

(. . . named place of destination)

'Delivered duty paid' means that the seller delivers the goods to the buyer, cleared for import, and not unloaded from any arriving means of transport at the named place of destination. The seller has to bear all the costs and risks involved in bringing the goods thereto including, where applicable, any 'duty' (which term includes the responsibility for and the risks of the carrying out of customs formalities and the payment of formalities, customs duties, taxes and other charges) for import in the country of destination.

Whilst the EXW term represents the minimum obligation for the seller, DDP represents the maximum obligation.

This term should not be used if the seller is unable directly or indirectly to obtain the import licence.

However, if the parties wish to exclude from the seller's obligations some of the costs payable upon import of the goods (such as value-added tax: VAT), this should be made clear by adding explicit wording to this effect in the contract of sale.

If the parties wish the buyer to bear all risks and costs of the import, the DDU term should be used.

This term may be used irrespective of the mode of transport but when delivery is to take place in the port of destination on board the vessel or on the quay (wharf), the DES or DEQ terms should be used.

A THE SELLER'S OBLIGATIONS

A1 Provision of the goods in conformity with the contract

The seller must provide the goods and the commercial invoice, or its equivalent electronic message, in conformity with the contract of sale and any other evidence of conformity which may be required by the contract.

A2 Licences, authorizations and formalities

The seller must obtain at his own risk and expense any export and import licence and other official authorization or other documents and carry out, where applicable, all customs formalities necessary for the export of the goods, for their transit through any country and for their import.

B THE BUYER'S OBLIGATIONS

B1 Payment of the price

The buyer must pay the price as provided in the contract of sale.

B2 Licences, authorizations and formalities

The buyer must render the seller at the latter's request, risk and expense, every assistance in obtaining, where applicable, any import licence or other official authorization necessary for the import of the goods.

A3 Contracts of carriage and insurance

a) Contract of carriage

The seller must contract at his own expense for the carriage of the goods to the named place of destination. If a specific point is not agreed or is not determined by practice, the seller may select the point at the named place of destination which best suits his purpose.

b) Contract of insurance
No obligation.

A4 Delivery

The seller must place the goods at the disposal of the buyer, or at that of another person named by the buyer, on any arriving means of transport not unloaded at the named place of destination on the date or within the period agreed for delivery.

A5 Transfer of risks

The seller must, subject to the provisions of B5, bear all risks of loss of or damage to the goods until such time as they have been delivered in accordance with A4.

A6 Division of costs

The seller must, subject to the provisions of B6, pay
• in addition to costs resulting from A3 a), all costs relating to the goods until such time as they have been delivered in accordance with A4; and
• where applicable, the costs of customs formalities necessary for export as well as all duties, taxes or other charges payable upon export of the goods and for their transit through any country prior to delivery in accordance with A4.

B3 Contracts of carriage and insurance

a) Contract of carriage
No obligation.

b) Contract of insurance
No obligation.

B4 Taking delivery

The buyer must take delivery of the goods when they have been delivered in accordance with A4.

B5 Transfer of risks

The buyer must bear all risks of loss of or damage to the goods from the time they have been delivered in accordance with A4.

The buyer must, should he fail to fulfil his obligations in accordance with B2, bear all additional risks of loss of or damage to the goods incurred thereby.

The buyer must, should he fail to give notice in accordance with B7, bear all risks of loss of or damage to the goods from the agreed date or the expiry date of the agreed period for delivery provided, however, that the goods have been duly appropriated to the contract, that is to say, clearly set aside or otherwise identified as the contract goods.

B6 Division of costs

The buyer must pay
• all costs relating to the goods from the time they have been delivered in accordance with A4; and
• all additional costs incurred if he fails to fulfil his obligations in accordance with B2, or to give notice in accordance with B7, provided, however, that the goods have been duly appropriated to the contract, that is to say, clearly set aside or otherwise identified as the contract goods.

A7 Notice to the buyer

The seller must give the buyer sufficient notice of the dispatch of the goods as well as any other notice required in order to allow the buyer to take measures which are normally necessary to enable him to take delivery of the goods.

A8 Proof of delivery, transport document or equivalent electronic message

The seller must provide the buyer at the seller's expense with the delivery order and/or the usual transport document (for example a negotiable bill of lading, a non-negotiable sea waybill, an inland waterway document, an air waybill, a railway consignment note, a road consignment note, or a multimodal transport document) which the buyer may require to take delivery of the goods in accordance with A4/B4.

Where the seller and the buyer have agreed to communicate electronically, the document referred to in the preceding paragraph may be replaced by an equivalent electronic data interchange (EDI) message.

A9 Checking—packaging—marking

The seller must pay the costs of those checking operations (such as checking quality, measuring, weighing, counting) which are necessary for the purpose of delivering the goods in accordance with A4.

The seller must provide at his own expense packaging (unless it is usual for the particular trade to deliver the goods of the contract description unpacked) which is required for the delivery of the goods. Packaging is to be marked appropriately.

A10 Other obligations

The seller must pay all costs and charges incurred in obtaining the documents or equivalent electronic messages mentioned in B10 and reimburse those incurred by the buyer in rendering his assistance herewith.

The seller must provide the buyer, upon request, with the necessary information for procuring insurance.

B7 Notice to the seller

The buyer must, whenever he is entitled to determine the time within an agreed period and/or the point of taking delivery at the named place, give the seller sufficient notice thereof.

B8 Proof of delivery, transport document or equivalent electronic message

The buyer must accept the appropriate delivery order or transport document in accordance with A8.

B9 Inspection of goods

The buyer must pay the costs of any pre-shipment inspection except when such inspection is mandated by the authorities of the country of export.

B10 Other obligations

The buyer must render the seller, at the latter's request, risk and expense, every assistance in obtaining any documents or equivalent electronic messages issued or transmitted in the country of import which the seller may require for the purpose of making the goods available to the buyer in accordance therewith.

5

AGENCY AND DISTRIBUTION

A. Introductory Text

Agency and distribution have proved to be extremely difficult subjects to regulate at transnational level. The reason for this lies largely in the complexity of the topics. This complexity arises in part out of the number of parties involved. Agency provides us with a convenient example. Agency involves three parties namely the principal, the agent, and the third party. The three relationships thus generated (between principal and third party, agent and third party, here referred to as the 'external' aspect of agency, and between principal and agent, here referred to as the 'internal' aspect of agency) give rise to a diverse range of issues. Agency relationships can arise in a wide variety of contexts; for example, financial services, insurance, the sale of land, the sale of goods, partnerships, and, in some jurisdictions, the organization of companies. Agency relationships are often contractual in nature, but need not be: they can arise gratuitously or as a matter of law. Agency also touches on many other areas of law. Certain agents may benefit from employment protection legislation enacted in nation states and so trigger questions of labour law. All of these factors have conspired to make agency law a subject of some difficulty and complexity.

Similar issues can arise in the context of distribution agreements. These agreements are often part of a complex web of contractual relations and the agreements themselves contain provisions which deal with a wide range of legal issues, from purely contractual issues through to issues such as intellectual property and trade secrets.

Two consequences have followed from this complexity. The first is that the success rate of instruments, the aim of which has been to bring about a greater degree of harmonization, has been limited. An example of this is provided by the UNIDROIT Convention on Agency in the International Sale of Goods 1983,[1] which, notwithstanding the passage of 20 years since its conclusion, has failed to secure the necessary ten ratifications required in order to bring it into force. Secondly, attempts at harmonization have generally been partial in nature; that is to say, they have not attempted to deal with all aspects of agency law or of distribution agreements but have chosen to concentrate on particular aspects. Thus the UNIDROIT Convention deals with the external aspects of agency but does not regulate its internal aspects.[2] Conversely, the EC Directive on Self-Employed Commercial Agents 1986 regulates the internal aspects of agency but not its external aspects. The UNIDROIT Model Franchise Disclosure law deals with the franchisor's duty to disclose material information to the franchisee but does not deal with other aspects of distribution agreements.

While it has not been possible to draft a Convention or a Model Law which has enjoyed widespread acceptance and been implemented in practice, it has been possible to secure a measure of agreement through the formulation of standard contract terms which regulate particular aspects of agency or distribution agreements. Two documents are worthy of note here, although neither is reproduced in this volume. The first is the International Chamber of Commerce Agency Model Contract, now in its second edition,[3] which consists of a set of contract terms designed to regulate the relationship between a principal and an agent. It therefore deals with the internal but not the external aspects of agency. The model form has been prepared on the assumption that it will apply to international agency agreements involving self-employed commercial agents acting in connection with transactions for the sale of goods. The aim of the model form is to strike a fair balance between the respective interests of the agent and the principal. While the contract as a whole seeks to balance the rights and duties of the parties in a fair and equitable manner, the balance is not of course binding on the parties who remain free to depart from its terms as they see fit (or as bargaining power dictates). Secondly, in the context of distribution agreements, UNIDROIT has published a 'Guide to International Master Franchise Agreements' and the International Chamber of Commerce has also published an International Franchising Model Contract, both of which are mentioned later in this chapter.[4]

---

[1] See p. 312 below.   [2] Article 1(3).
[3] Published in June 2002: ICC Publication No. 644 E.   [4] See p. 295 below.

The instruments contained in this section can be divided into three broad categories. One consists of regional instruments. Two such instruments are included, both from the EEC. The first is the First Company Directive which deals in part with the capacity of agents of a company, in particular its directors, to bind the company. The other is the Directive on the coordination of the laws relating to self-employed commercial agents which has proved to be a significant instrument in practice in Europe as Member States have implemented the Directive into their own law. The second category consists of an international convention, namely the 1983 UNIDROIT Convention on Agency in the International Sale of Goods. This was intended as a legally operative instrument but it has failed, thus far, to achieve the necessary ratifications to bring it into force. The third consists of a model law, namely the UNIDROIT Model Franchise Disclosure Law.

One further point which should be made in this introductory section is that Chapter 3 of the Principles of European Contract Law[5] and Chapter 2 Section 2 of the recently completed UNIDROIT Principles for International Commercial Contracts[6] have provisions which deal with the external aspects of agency law but not the purely internal aspects. Neither set of Principles is a legally operative instrument and so the rules do not, of themselves, have the force of law. Nevertheless, the provisions to be found in both sets of Principles are of interest in the present context in that they build on the foundation laid in the 1983 UNIDROIT Convention and they also represent a further attempt to bridge the divide between civil law and common law jurisdictions.

1. The First Company Directive (EEC)[7]

Introduction

The first company law directive was a milestone in the history of the EEC in that it was the first instrument dealing with commercial law designed to achieve the policy objectives of this regional economic integration organization. Of the three problem areas addressed by the Directive, only one, namely the validity of obligations entered into by a company, is relevant in this context.

Principle of unlimited authority of organs to bind company

Under the key provision[8] of the Directive acts done by the organs, i.e. mainly the directors, of the company are binding upon it even if those acts are not within the objects of the company unless such acts exceed the powers conferred upon them by *law*. Domestic law may provide, however, that the company is not bound by such acts if the company proves that the third party knew or ought to have known that

---

[5] See pp. 94–97 above. [6] See pp. 55–56 above.
[7] EC Directive on co-ordination of safeguards which, for the protection of the interests of members and others, are required by Member States of companies: 1968 OJ L 65.
[8] Article 9(1).

they were outside the company's objects. Internally fixed limits on the organs' authority—be it in the articles of incorporation, the statute, or limits set by decisions of its organs—are never sufficient to escape from being bound, even if they had been disclosed.[9]

One exception to the general rule is provided for. Where domestic law provides that authority to represent a company may, in derogation from the legal rules, be conferred by articles or statute on a single person or several persons acting jointly, such a limit may be relied on if it relates to the general power of representation and if it has been publicized.[10]

Actions on the company's behalf before its having acquired legal personality

In respect of such acts the acting persons are liable without any limit unless the company assumes the obligations arising from such action.[11] Irregularities in the appointment of a person as an organ of the company, after completion of the disclosure formalities, may not be relied on as against third parties.[12] They may be relied upon, however, if the company proves that the third party had knowledge of those irregularities.

2. The EEC Directive on Commercial Agents[13]

Introduction

This Directive addresses key issues regarding the internal relationship between the *agent* and the *principal*[14]. It reflects the tradition in certain domestic laws of reflecting the economic value which the principal derives from an agent's activity in his interest. In certain respects this acknowledgement assumes connotations of the protection usually afforded to employees.

Scope of application

The Directive applies to self-employed intermediaries who have continuing authority to negotiate—or to negotiate and conclude—the sale or the purchase of goods on behalf and in the name[15] of a principal.

Rights and obligations

(i) General—Remuneration Both parties owe each other a duty to act in good faith.[16] While the agent is obliged to make the necessary efforts in the interest of the principal, to keep the latter fully informed and to follow his instructions,[17] the

---

[9] Article 9 (2).   [10] Article 9 (3); Art 3.   [11] Article 7.   [12] Article 8.
[13] Council Directive on the co-ordination of the laws of the Member States relating to self-employed commercial agents (86/653/EEC), 1986 OJ L 382, p.17.
[14] The Directive has no provisions relating to the rights of third parties.
[15] Article 1 (2). There are specific exclusions in Art 1(3) and 3.
[16] Article 3(1) and 4(1).   [17] Article 3(2).

principal must provide the agent with the necessary documentation and other relevant information.[18] All these are mandatory and may not be derogated from.

There are very detailed provisions on the remuneration to which the agent is entitled.[19]

(ii) Conclusion and termination of the agency contract   The parties are entitled to receive from each other a document setting out the terms of the agency contract including any subsequent amendments. This right cannot be waived.[20]

The Directive regulates in detail the requirements for making the termination of an agency contract effective.[21] Most strikingly for many domestic legal systems, the Directive provides for an indemnity to be paid by the principal to the agent if the agent's activities have brought the principal new customers or has otherwise increased the volume of business and if the principal continues to derive benefit therefrom.[22] Again, the parties may not derogate from these provisions.[23]

3. The UNIDROIT Convention on Agency in the International Sale of Goods

The UNIDROIT Convention on Agency in the International Sale of Goods was concluded in Geneva in 1983. It has not as yet come into force. Ten ratifications are required before it can do so but, as at 31 July 2003, it had been ratified by only five nation states.[24] The impact of the Convention has been, at best, muted.

The origins of the Convention can be traced back to work commenced by UNIDROIT in the 1930s. But the work made slow and difficult progress. The divide between common law and civil law jurisdictions proved to be particularly troublesome. Broadly speaking, civil law countries distinguish between direct and indirect representation. Agency is direct where the principal and the agent agree that the agent shall act in the principal's name and on his behalf when dealing with a third party. Agency is indirect where the principal authorizes the agent to carry out transactions on his behalf in his (the agent's) own name so that the agent, and not the principal, assumes contractual responsibility towards the third party, but the agent nevertheless remains accountable as an agent to his principal. The paradigm example of indirect agency is the commission agent, an institution which is not explicitly recognized in common law countries. In common law countries the most significant distinction is between disclosed and undisclosed agency. Disclosed agency in many respects parallels direct agency but undisclosed agency differs in a very important respect from indirect agency in that the undisclosed principal can, within limits, both sue and be sued by the third party. In this respect, the legal effects of the doctrine of undisclosed agency more closely resemble direct agency

---

[18] Article 4(2), (3).   [19] Article 6 to 12.   [20] Article 13(1).
[21] Article 15 and 16.   [22] Article 17 and 18.   [23] Article 19.
[24] A list of the States that have ratified the Convention is given below at pp. 320–321.

than indirect agency. These differences between indirect agency and undisclosed agency have been at the root of many of the problems faced by those seeking to introduce greater uniformity into this area of law.

Notwithstanding these difficulties, two draft uniform rules were produced in the 1960s[25] but they failed to secure agreement because they were thought to be a reflection of civil law rather than common law principles. The work stumbled through the 1970s but, once the decision was made by the Governing Council of UNIDROIT to adopt a less ambitious approach and to confine the scope of the Convention to the external aspects of agency law, it became possible to secure a sufficient consensus to enable agreement to be reached on the content of the Convention. This led to a diplomatic conference in Geneva in 1983, attended by delegates from 58 countries, at which the final text of the Convention was approved. Notwithstanding the unanimous approval of delegates the Convention has not been a success. The Convention nevertheless remains a document which is worthy of further study. A number of points can be noted.

The relationship with CISG

The first point relates to the link between this Convention and the Vienna Convention on Contracts for the International Sale of Goods ('CISG').[26] The Geneva Convention deals with agency in the context of international sale contracts and expressly refers to CISG in its Preamble. The two Conventions share a number of common techniques and rules. Thus there are similar provisions relating to the approach to be adopted in the interpretation of the Convention,[27] the role of usages,[28] and the definition of place of business.[29] The test of internationality and the rules relating to the sphere of application of the Convention are similar, albeit that the rules are slightly more complex in the case of the Agency Convention as a result of the fact that there are three actors, not two.

Sphere of Application

This leads us into the second point which relates to the sphere of application of the Convention. The test of internationality is based on the place of business of the principal and the third party[30] (not the place of business of the agent). Given that the aim of the Convention is to regulate the external aspects of agency law, the decision to focus attention on the position of the principal and the third party seems a sensible one given that this is the more important of the two external relations. It will also result in the greatest degree of overlap with CISG because, where the principal (seller) and the third party (buyer) have their places of business in different States, CISG may

---

[25] UNIDROIT Draft Convention providing a Uniform Law on Agency in Private Law Relations of an International Character and the UNIDROIT Draft Convention Providing a Uniform Law on the Contract of the Commission Agent on the International Sale or Purchase of Goods.
[26] See p. 215 above.   [27] See Art 6 and compare it with Art 7 of CISG.
[28] See Art 7 and compare it with Art 9 of CISG.
[29] See Art 8 and compare it with Art 10 of CISG.   [30] Article 2(1).

also regulate the contract of sale. However, in terms of the connecting factor with a Contracting State, it is the place of business of the agent that is crucial.[31] The proposal that it sufficed for the principal, the agent, **or** the third party to have his place of business in a Contracting State was rejected on the ground that it was too liberal. The place of business of the agent was chosen as the connecting factor because it provided an objective standard, in the sense that the principal and the third party are most likely to be aware of the place of business of the agent. As in the case of CISG, the Convention contains an alternative connecting factor, namely that the rules of private international law lead to the application of the law of a Contracting State. This provision was as controversial as the equivalent provision in CISG[32] and, consequently, States may declare at the time of signature, ratification, acceptance, approval, or accession that they will not be bound by this provision.[33]

The legal effect of the acts of the agent

The most important provisions in the Convention are Articles 12–16 and they have been described as a 'serious attempt to bridge the gap between the Common law and the Civil Law systems.'[34] Article 12 is relatively straightforward in so far as it provides that, where an agent acts within the scope of his authority and the third party knew or ought to have known that the agent was acting as an agent, the consequence that generally follows is the creation of a direct contractual relationship between the principal and the third party. In essence this is an extended form of direct representation in so far as it removes the need for the agent to represent that he is acting in the name of a principal and replaces it by a test which focuses on the knowledge of the third party as to the capacity in which the agent is acting. More difficult is the case where the third party neither knew nor ought to have known that the agent was acting as an agent or where the third party knows that the undertaking of the agent is to bind himself only. This situation is governed by Article 13 which attempts to strike a delicate balance between common law and civil law jurisdictions. Article 13 draws from civil law jurisdictions in so far as its starting point is that the acts of the agent in such a case shall 'bind only the agent and the third party'[35] but then gives something to the common law systems in so far as it provides that, where the agent fails to fulfil his obligations to the principal or the third party, these two may, within limits, sue each other directly.[36] While this compromise (or, if one prefers, balancing act) was sufficient to secure agreement in Geneva in 1983, it has not proved to be sufficient to turn that initial consensus into subsequent ratifications.

---

[31] Article 2(1)(a). [32] Article 1(1)(b), on which see p. 205 above.
[33] Article 28.
[34] M Evans, *Explanatory Report on the Convention on Agency in the International Sale of Goods* p.119. [35] Article 13.
[36] Article 13(2)–(6).

In the case where the agent acts without authority or outside the scope of his authority, the general rule is that his acts do not bind the principal and the third party to each other.[37] This rule is subject to an exception where the principal conducts himself in a such a way as to lead the third party reasonably and in good faith to believe that the party acting as an agent did in fact have authority and was acting within the scope of that authority.[38] Further, a principal can, within limits, ratify an unauthorized act of his agent and the effect of the ratification may be to give the principal rights enforceable against the third party.[39]

Termination of the agent's authority

Chapter IV deals with the termination of the agent's authority. This Chapter occupies an uneasy position within the structure of the Convention as a whole because it begins to stray into internal aspects of agency, that is to say, the relationship between the principal and the agent. At this point we see that the internal aspects of agency cannot be cleanly separated from its external aspects in that the authority of the agent to bind the principal in his relations with a third party is in large part derived from the relationship between the principal and the agent. This being the case, it was agreed that some minimum provision should be made for the termination of the agent's authority. Article 17 contains grounds of termination which are recognized by almost all legal systems and therefore excite little controversy (with the possible exception of sub-paragraph (c)). Article 18 further provides a supplement to these generally accepted rules by reference to the grounds of termination recognized by the applicable law.

Assessment

The fact that the Convention has thus far only secured five ratifications is a major disappointment in the light of the optimism that was apparent immediately after agreement was reached in Geneva in 1983. While the bridge between the common law and the civil law was spanned for the purpose of securing agreement in Geneva, the consensus, compromise, or balancing act (depending on one's point of view) has failed to translate itself into ratifications. It would, however, be a mistake to write off the Convention as an instrument devoid of consequence. While it has not yet attained the force of law, it has, nevertheless, been influential on subsequent developments, in particular the content of the relevant provisions in the Principles of European Contract Law and the UNIDROIT Principles for International Commercial Contracts. While the latter instruments depart from the Geneva Convention at various points, it is nevertheless clear that the Convention constituted an influential starting point for their work.

---

[37] Article 14(1).   [38] Article 14(2).   [39] Article 15.

4. UNIDROIT Model Franchise Disclosure Law

Introduction

International franchising is playing an ever greater role in refining 'distribution' in the widest sense in that it introduces commercial know-how into countries and markets where the goods or services had not been originally developed. The countries which stand to gain the most in terms of accelerated build-up of such know-how are arguably developing countries and countries with economies in transition. Legislative activity at the domestic level can be observed around the globe.

At the international level, two documents deserve mention. First, the UNI-DROIT 'Guide to International Master Franchise Arrangements'[40], prepared by a UNIDROIT Study Group and the publication of which was authorized by the Governing Council of UNIDROIT. While devoted particularly to the top-tier franchise agreement, i.e. the agreement between a franchisor and its partner, the sub-franchisor in a different country, it may be referred to as a compendium of high-level information regarding all problem areas, starting with the analysis of fundamental concepts of franchise arrangements, including a description of rights and duties of the parties, financial issues, issues of intellectual property, trade secrets, liability, and insurance through to regulatory problems and issues of conflict of laws. Secondly, the International Chamber of Commerce has published an International Franchising Model Contract.[41]

The document reproduced in this volume is devoted to the franchisor's duties to disclose material information to the franchisee. The UNIDROIT Model Franchise Disclosure Law focuses on this aspect because there is evidence that a significant part of litigation between franchisees and franchisors is about whether the franchisee was able to make informed decisions when he entered into the contractual relationship with the franchisor. The Model Law deliberately refrains from covering issues of general contract law. In this respect parties may wish to refer to one of the two restatements of contract law, i.e. the UNIDROIT Principles for International Commercial Contracts or the Principles of European Contract Law.[42]

The implementation,[43] interpretation, and application of the Model Law is facilitated by an official Explanatory Report.[44]

---

[40] (Rome 1998).

[41] International Chamber of Commerce (ed.), *The ICC Model International Franchising Contract* (Paris 2000).   [42] Above, ch 2.

[43] As a model law, the document places its rules at the disposal of national legislators who may adopt it as it is or modified so as to accommodate their specific needs. In any event it needs implementation.

[44] Available at http://www.unidroit.org/english/franchising/modellaw/modellaw-e.pdf or in *Uniform Law Review* 2002, pp. 1076–139.

Scope of application

The law[45] applies, as mentioned, only to a limited aspect of a franchise granted or renewed. Except as otherwise expressly provided it is not concerned with the validity of the franchise agreement or any of its provisions.[46]

Delivery of disclosure document

A franchisor must give every prospective franchisee a disclosure document, to which the proposed franchise agreement must be attached. The document must be updated regularly.[47] In certain circumstances, no disclosure document is required.[48]

Information to be disclosed

The Model Law's core provision[49] lists in great detail the items of information which the franchisor is required to provide. This ranges from identification of the franchisor, its affiliates, and officers, to their business, financial, and criminal record, other franchisees of interest for the party negotiating for a new franchise, intellectual property rights, the goods or services that the franchisee is required to purchase or lease, financial matters, including estimates of the prospective franchisee's investment, description of the relevant market, training, and limitations imposed on the franchisee, etc.

Acknowledgement of receipt

At the franchisor's request, the prospective franchisee must acknowledge in writing the receipt of the disclosure document.[50]

Remedies

If the disclosure document or notice of material change has not been duly delivered or contains a misrepresentation of a material fact, the franchisee may terminate the franchise agreement and/or claim damages.[51] These rights do not derogate from any other right the franchisee may have under the applicable law.[52] This is a reference to the conflict-of-laws rules[53] of the forum which will identify the law governing these matters.

No waivers

Any waiver by a franchisee of a right given by the law is void.[54]

---

[45] The document refers to itself as 'the law'. However, in light of its nature (cf. previous note), this has to be read as a reference to 'the national law implementing the Model Law'.   [46] Article 1.
[47] Article 3 and 4.   [48] Article 5.   [49] Article 6.
[50] Article 7.   [51] Article 8(1), (2).   [52] Artilce 8(3), (4).
[53] For particularly illustrative conflict-of-laws conventions, see below, Ch 10.
[54] Article 10.

B. Instruments

(i) FIRST COUNCIL DIRECTIVE OF 9 MARCH 1968 ON CO-ORDINATION OF SAFEGUARDS WHICH, FOR THE PROTECTION OF THE INTERESTS OF MEMBERS AND OTHERS, ARE REQUIRED BY MEMBER STATES OF COMPANIES WITHIN THE MEANING OF THE SECOND PARAGRAPH OF ARTICLE 58 OF THE TREATY, WITH A VIEW TO MAKING SUCH SAFEGUARDS EQUIVALENT THROUGHOUT THE COMMUNITY (68/151/EEC)

PREAMBLE

THE COUNCIL OF THE EUROPEAN COMMUNITIES,

Having regard to the Treaty establishing the European Economic Community, and in particular Article 54(3)(g) thereof;

Having regard to the General Programme for the abolition of restrictions on freedom of establishment,[1] and in particular Title VI thereof;

Having regard to the proposal from the Commission;

Having regard to the Opinion of the European Parliament;[2]

Having regard to the Opinion of the Economic and Social Committee;[3]

Whereas the co-ordination provided for in Article 54(3)(g) and in the General Programme for the abolition of restrictions on freedom of establishment is a matter of urgency, especially in regard to companies limited by shares or otherwise having limited liability, since the activities of such companies often extend beyond the frontiers of national territories;

Whereas the co-ordination of national provisions concerning disclosure, the validity of obligations entered into by, and the nullity of, such companies is of special importance,

---

[1] OJ No. 2, 15.1.1962, p. 36/62.　　[2] OJ No. 96, 28.5.1966, p. 1519/66.
[3] OJ No. 194, 27.11.1964, p. 3248/64.

particularly for the purpose of protecting the interests of third parties; Whereas in these matters Community provisions must be adopted in respect of such companies simultaneously, since the only safeguards they offer to third parties are their assets;

Whereas the basic documents of the company should be disclosed in order that third parties may be able to ascertain their contents and other information concerning the company, especially particulars of the persons who are authorised to bind the company; Whereas the protection of third parties must be ensured by provisions which restrict to the greatest possible extent the grounds on which obligations entered into in the name of the company are not valid;

Whereas it is necessary, in order to ensure certainty in the law as regards relations between the company and third parties, and also between members, to limit the cases in which nullity can arise and the retroactive effect of a declaration of nullity, and to fix a short time limit within which third parties may enter objection to any such declaration;

HAS ADOPTED THIS DIRECTIVE:

Article 1

The co-ordination measures prescribed by this Directive shall apply to the laws, regulations and administrative provisions of the Member States relating to the following types of company:
—In Germany:
—die Aktiengesellschaft, die Kommanditgesellschaft auf Aktien, die Gesellschaft mit beschränkter Haftung;
—In Belgium:
—de naamloze vennootschap, la société anonyme,
—In France:
—la société anonyme, la société en commandite par actions, la société à responsabilité limitée;
—In Italy:
—società per azioni, società in accomandita per azioni, società a responsabilità limitata;
—In Luxembourg:
—la société anonyme, la société en commandite par actions, la société à responsabilité limitée;
—In the Netherlands:
—de naamloze vennootschap, de commanditaire vennootschap op aandelen.

SECTION I
DISCLOSURE

Article 2

1. Member States shall take the measures required to ensure compulsory disclosure by companies of at least the following documents and particulars:
   (a) The instrument of constitution, and the statutes if they are contained in a separate instrument;
   (b) Any amendments to the instruments mentioned in (a), including any extension of the duration of the company;

(c) After every amendment of the instrument of constitution or of the statutes, the complete text of the instrument or statutes as amended to date;

(d) The appointment, termination of office and particulars of the persons who either as a body constituted pursuant to law or as members of any such body:

    (i) are authorised to represent the company in dealings with third parties and in legal proceedings;

    (ii) take part in the administration, supervision or control of the company.

It must appear from the disclosure whether the persons authorised to represent the company may do so alone or must act jointly;

(e) At least once a year, the amount of the capital subscribed, where the instrument of constitution or the statutes mention an authorised capital, unless any increase in the capital subscribed necessitates an amendment of the statutes;

(f) The balance sheet and the profit and loss account for each financial year. The document containing the balance sheet shall give particulars of the persons who are required by law to certify it.

However, in respect of the Gesellschaft mit beschränkter Haftung, société de personnes à responsabilité limitée, personenvennootschap met beperkte aansprakelijkheid, société à responsabilité limitée and società a responsabilità limitata under German, Belgian, French, Italian or Luxembourg law, referred to in Article 1, and the besloten naamloze vennootschap under Netherlands law, the compulsory application of this provision shall he postponed until the date of implementation of a Directive concerning co-ordination of the contents of balance sheets and of profit and loss accounts and concerning exemption of such of those companies whose balance sheet total is less than specified in the Directive from the obligation to make disclosure, in full or in part, of the said documents. The Council will adopt such a Directive within two years following the adoption of the present Directive;

(g) Any transfer of the seat of the company;

(h) The winding up of the company;

(i) Any declaration of nullity of the company by the courts;

(j) The appointment of liquidators, particulars concerning them, and their respective powers, unless such powers are expressly and exclusively derived from law or from the statutes of the company;

(k) The termination of the liquidation and, in Member States where striking off the register entails legal consequences, the fact of any such striking off.

2. For purposes of paragraph 1 (f), companies which fulfil the following conditions shall be considered as besloten naamloze vennootschappen:

(a) They cannot issue bearer shares;

(b) No bearer certificate of registered shares within the meaning of Article 42 (c) of the Netherlands Commercial Code can be issued by any person whatsoever;

(c) Their shares cannot be quoted on a stock exchange;

(d) Their statutes contain a clause requiring approval by the company before the transfer of shares to third parties, except in the case of transfer in the event of death and, if the statutes so provide, in the case of transfer to a spouse, forebears or issue; transfers shall not be in blank, but otherwise each transfer shall be in writing under hand, signed by the transferor and transferee or by notarial act;

(e) Their statutes specify that the company is a besloten naamloze vennootschap; the name of the company includes the words 'Besloten Naamloze Vennootschap' or the initials 'BNV'.

Article 3

1. In each Member State a file shall be opened in a central register, commercial register or companies register, for each of the companies registered therein.
2. All documents and particulars which must be disclosed in pursuance of Article 2 shall be kept in the file or entered in the register; the subject matter of the entries in the register must in every case appear in the file.
3. A copy of the whole or any part of the documents or particulars referred to in Article 2 must be obtainable by application in writing at a price not exceeding the administrative cost thereof.
   Copies supplied shall be certified as 'true copies', unless the applicant dispenses with such certification.
4. Disclosure of the documents and particulars referred to in paragraph 2 shall be effected by publication in the national gazette appointed for that purpose by the Member State, either of the full or partial text, or by means of a reference to the document which has been deposited in the file or entered in the register.
5. The documents and particulars may be relied on by the company as against third parties only after they have been published in accordance with paragraph 4, unless the company proves that the third parties had knowledge thereof. However, with regard to transactions taking place before the sixteenth day following the publication, the documents and particulars shall not be relied on as against third parties who prove that it was impossible for them to have had knowledge thereof.
6. Member States shall take the necessary measures to avoid any discrepancy between what is disclosed by publication in the press and what appears in the register or file. However, in cases of discrepancy, the text published in the press may not be relied on as against third parties; the latter may nevertheless rely thereon, unless the company proves that they had knowledge of the texts deposited in the file or entered in the register.
7. Third parties may, moreover, always rely on any documents and particulars in respect of which the disclosure formalities have not yet been completed, save where non-disclosure causes them not to have effect.

Article 4

Member States shall prescribe that letters and order forms shall state the following particulars:
—the register in which the file mentioned in Article 3 is kept, together with the number of the company in that register;
—the legal form of the company, the location of its scat and, where appropriate, the fact that the company is being wound up.
Where in these documents mention is made of the capital of the company, the reference shall be to the capital subscribed and paid up.

Article 5

Each Member State shall determine by which persons the disclosure formalities are to be carried out.

Article 6

Member States shall provide for appropriate penalties in case of:

—failure to disclose the balance sheet and profit and loss account as required by Article 2 (1) (f);

—omission from commercial documents of the compulsory particulars provided for in Article 4.

SECTION II
VALIDITY OF OBLIGATIONS ENTERED INTO BY A COMPANY

Article 7

If, before a company being formed has acquired legal personality, action has been carried out in its name and the company does not assume the obligations arising from such action, the persons who acted shall, without limit, be jointly and severally liable therefor, unless otherwise agreed.

Article 8

Completion of the formalities of disclosure of the particulars concerning the persons who, as an organ of the company, are authorised to represent it shall constitute a bar to any irregularity in their appointment being relied upon as against third parties unless the company proves that such third parties had knowledge thereof.

Article 9

1. Acts done by the organs of the company shall be binding upon it even if those acts are not within the objects of the company, unless such acts exceed the powers that the law confers or allows to be conferred on those organs. However, Member States may provide that the company shall not be bound where such acts are outside the objects of the company, if it proves that the third party knew that the act was outside those objects or could not in view of the circumstances have been unaware of it; disclosure of the statutes shall not of itself be sufficient proof thereof.
2. The limits on the powers of the organs of the company, arising under the statutes or from a decision of the competent organs, may never be relied on as against third parties, even if they have been disclosed.
3. If the national law provides that authority to represent a company may, in derogation from the legal rules governing the subject, be conferred by the statutes on a single person or on several persons acting jointly, that law may provide that such a provision in the statutes may be relied on as against third parties on condition that it relates to the general power of representation; the question whether such a provision in the statutes can be relied on as against third parties shall be governed by Article 3.

SECTION III
NULLITY OF THE COMPANY

Article 10

In all Member States whose laws do not provide for preventive control, administrative or judicial, at the time of formation of a company, the instrument of constitution, the company statutes and any amendments to those documents shall be drawn up and certified in due legal form.

Article 11

The laws of the Member States may not provide for the nullity of companies otherwise than in accordance with the following provisions:
1. Nullity must be ordered by decision of a court of law;
2. Nullity may be ordered only on the following grounds:
    (a) that no instrument of constitution was executed or that the rules of preventive control or the requisite legal formalities were not complied with;
    (b) that the objects of the company are unlawful or contrary to public policy;
    (c) that the instrument of constitution or the statutes do not state the name of the company, the amount of the individual subscriptions of capital, the total amount of the capital subscribed or the objects of the company;
    (d) failure to comply with the provisions of the national law concerning the minimum amount of capital to be paid up;
    (e) the incapacity of all the founder members;
    (f) that, contrary to the national law governing the company, the number of founder members is less than two.
Apart from the foregoing grounds of nullity, a company shall not be subject to any cause of non-existence, nullity absolute, nullity relative or declaration of nullity.

Article 12

1. The question whether a decision of nullity pronounced by a court of law may be relied on as against third parties shall be governed by Article 3. Where the national law entitles a third party to challenge the decision, he may do so only within six months of public notice of the decision of the court being given.
2. Nullity shall entail the winding up of the company, as may dissolution.
3. Nullity shall not of itself affect the validity of any commitments entered into by or with the company, without prejudice to the consequences of the company's being wound up.
4. The laws of each Member State may make provision for the consequences of nullity as between members of the company.
5. Holders of shares in the capital shall remain obliged to pay up the capital agreed to be subscribed by them but which has not been paid up, to the extent that commitments entered into with creditors so require.

SECTION IV
GENERAL PROVISIONS

Article 13

Member States shall put into force, within eighteen months following notification of this Directive, all amendments to their laws, regulations or administrative provisions required in order to comply with provisions of this Directive and shall forthwith inform the Commission thereof.

The obligation of disclosure provided for in Article 2(1)(f) shall not enter into force until thirty months after notification of this Directive in respect of naamloze vennootschappen under Netherlands law other than those referred to in the present Article 42 (c) of the Netherlands Commercial Code.

Member States may provide that initial disclosure of the full text of the statutes as amended since the formation of the company shall not be required until the statutes are next amended or until 31 December 1970, whichever shall be the earlier.

Member States shall ensure that they communicate to the Commission the text of the main provisions of national law which they adopt in the field covered by this Directive.

Article 14

This Directive is addressed to the Member States.

Done at Brussels, 9 March 1968.

For the Council
The President
M. Couve de Murville

(ii) COUNCIL DIRECTIVE OF 18 DECEMBER 1986 ON THE COORDINATION OF THE LAWS OF THE MEMBER STATE RELATING TO SELF-EMPLOYED COMMERCIAL AGENTS (86/653/EEC)

PREAMBLE

THE COUNCIL OF THE EUROPEAN COMMUNITIES,

Having regard to the Treaty establishing the European Economic Community, and in particular Articles 57(2) and 100 thereof,

Having regard to the proposal from the Commission,[1]

Having regard to the opinion of the European Parliament,[2]

Having regard to the opinion of the Economic and Social Committee,[3]

Whereas the restrictions on the freedom of establishment and the freedom to provide services in respect of activities of intermediaries in commerce, industry and small craft industries were abolished by Directive 64/224/EEC;[4]

Whereas the differences in national laws concerning commercial representation substantially affect the conditions of competition and the carrying-on of that activity within the Community and are detrimental both to the protection available to commercial agents vis-à-vis their principals and to the security of commercial transactions; whereas moreover those differences are such as to inhibit substantially the conclusion and operation of commerical representation contracts where principal and commercial agents are established in different Member States;

[1] OJ No. C 13, 18.1.1977, p. 2; OJ No. C 56, 2.3.1979, p. 5.
[2] OJ No. C 239, 9.10.1978, p. 17.   [3] OJ No. C 59, 8.03.1978, p. 31.
[4] OJ No. 56, 4.4.1964, p. 869/64.

Whereas trade in goods between Member States should be carried on under conditions which are similar to those of a single market, and this necessitates approximation of the legal systems of the Member States to the extent required for the proper functioning of the common market; whereas in this regard the rules concerning conflict of laws do not, in the matter of commercial representation, remove the inconsistencies referred to above, nor would they even if they were made uniform, and accordingly the proposed harmonization is necessary notwithstanding the existence of those rules;

Whereas in this regard the legal relationship between commercial agent and principal must be given priority;

Whereas it is appropriate to be guided by the principles of Article 117 of the Treaty and to maintain improvementsalready made, when harmonizing the laws of the Member States relating to commercial agents;

Whereas additional transitional periods should be allowed for certain Member States which have to make a particular effort to adapt their regulations, especially those concerning indemnity for termination of contract between the principal and the commercial agent, to the requirements of this Directive,

HAS ADOPTED THIS DIRECTIVE:

CHAPTER I
SCOPE

Article 1

1. The harmonization measures prescribed by this Directive shall apply to the laws, regulations and administrative provisions of the Member States governing the relations between commercial agents and their principals.
2. For the purposes of this Directive, 'commercial agent' shall mean a self-employed intermediary who has continuing authority to negotiate the sale or the purchase of goods on behalf of another person, hereinafter called the 'principal', or to negotiate and conclude such transactions on behalf of and in the name of that principal.
3. A commercial agent shall be understood within the meaning of this Directive as not including in particular:
   —a person who, in his capacity as an officer, is empowered to enter into commitments binding on a company or association,
   —a parter who is lawfully authorized to enter into commitments binding on his partners,
   —a receiver, a receiver and manager, a liquidator or a trustee in bankruptcy.

Article 2

1. This Directive shall not apply to:
   —commercial agents whose activities are unpaid,
   —commercial agents when they operate on commodity exchanges or in the commodity market, or
   —the body known is the Crown Agents for Overseas Governments and Administrations, as set up under the Crown Agents Act 1979 in the United Kingdom, or its subsidiaries.

305

2. Each of the Member States shall have the right to provide that the Directive shall not apply to those persons whose activities as commercial agents are considered secondary by the law of that Member State.

CHAPTER II
RIGHTS AND OBLIGATIONS

Article 3

1. In performing has activities a commercial agent must look after his principal's interests and act dutifully and in good faith.
2. In particular, a commercial agent must:
   (a) make proper efforts to negotiate and, where appropriate, conclude the transactions he is instructed to take care of;
   (b) communicate to his principal all the necessary information available to him;
   (c) comply with reasonable instructions given by his principal.

Article 4

1. In his relations with his commercial agent a principal must act dutifully and in good faith.
2. A principal must in particular:
   (a) provide his commercial agent with the necessary documentation relating to the goods concerned;
   (b) obtain for his commercial agent the information necessary for the performance of the agency contract, and in particular notify the commercial agent within a reasonable period once he anticipates that the volume of commercial transactions will be significantly lower than that which the commercial agent could normally have expected.
3. A principal must, in addition, inform the commercial agent within a reasonable period of his acceptance, refusal, and of any non-execution of a commercial transaction which the commercial agent has procured for the principal.

Article 5

The parties may not derogate from the provisions of Articles 3 and 4.

CHAPTER III
REMUNERATION

Article 6

1. In the absence of any agreement on this matter between the parties, and without prejudice to the application of the compulsory provisions of the Member States concerning the level of remuneration, a commercial agent shall be entitled to the remuneration that commercial agents appointed for the goods forming the subject of his agency contract are customarily allowed in the place where he carries on his activities. If there is no such customary practice a commercial agent shall be entitled to reasonable remuneration taking into account all the aspects of the transaction.
2. Any part of the remuneration which varies with the number or value of business transactions shall be deemed to be commission within the meaning of this Directive.

3. Articles 7 to 12 shall not apply if the commercial agent is not remunerated wholly or in part by commission.

Article 7

1. A commercial agent shall be entitled to commission on commercial transactions concluded during the period covered by the agency contract:
   (a) where the transaction has been concluded as a result of his action; or
   (b) where the transaction is concluded with a third party whom he has previously acquired as a customer for transactions of the same kind.
2. A commercial agent shall also be entitled to commission on transactions concluded during the period covered by the agency contract:
   —either where he is entrusted with a specific geographical area or group of customers,
   —or where he has an exclusive right to a specific geographical area or group of customers,

and where the transaction has been entered into with a customer belonging to that area or group.

Member State shall include in their legislation one of the possibilities referred to in the above two indents.

Article 8

A commercial agent shall be entitled to commission on commercial transactions concluded after the agency contract has terminated:
   (a) if the transaction is mainly attributable to the commercial agent's efforts during the period covered by the agency contract and if the transaction was entered into within a reasonable period after that contract terminated; or
   (b) if, in accordance with the conditions mentioned in Article 7, the order of the third party reached the principal or the commercial agent before the agency contract terminated.

Article 9

A commercial agent shall not be entitled to the commission referred to in Article 7, if that commission is payable, pursuant to Article 8, to the previous commercial agent, unless it is equitable because of the circumstances for the commission to be shared between the commercial agents.

Article 10

1. The commission shall become due as soon as and to the extent that one of the following circumstances obtains:
   (a) the principal has executed the transaction; or
   (b) the principal should, according to his agreement with the third party, have executed the transaction; or
   (c) the third party has executed the transaction.
2. The commission shall become due at the latest when the third party has executed his part of the transaction or should have done so if the principal had executed his part of the transaction, as he should have.

3. The commission shall be paid not later than on the last day of the month following the quarter in which it became due.
4. Agreements to derogate from paragraphs 2 and 3 to the detriment of the commercial agent shall not be permitted.

Article 11

1. The right to commission can be extinguished only if and to the extent that:
   —it is established that the contract between the third party and the principal will not be executed, and
   —that face is due to a reason for which the principal is not to blame.
2. Any commission which the commercial agent has already received shall be refunded if the right to it is extinguished.
3. Agreements to derogate from paragraph 1 to the detriment of the commercial agent shall not be permitted.

Article 12

1. The principal shall supply his commercial agent with a statement of the commission due, not later than the last day of the month following the quarter in which the commission has become due. This statement shall set out the main components used in calculating the amount of commission.
2. A commercial agent shall be entitled to demand that he be provided with all the information, and in particular an extract from the books, which is available to his principal and which he needs in order to check the amount of the commission due to him.
3. Agreements to derogate from paragraphs 1 and 2 to the detriment of the commercial agent shall not be permitted.
4. This Directive shall not conflict with the internal provisions of Member States which recognize the right of a commercial agent to inspect a principal's books.

CHAPTER IV
CONCLUSION AND TERMINATION OF
THE AGENCY CONTRACT

Article 13

1. Each party shall be entitled to receive from the other on request a signed written document setting out the terms of the agency contract including any terms subsequently agreed. Waiver of this right shall not be permitted.
2. Notwithstanding paragraph 1 a Member State may provide that an agency contract shall not be valid unless evidenced in writing.

Article 14

An agency contract for a fixed period which continues to be performed by both parties after that period has expired shall be deemed to be converted into an agency contract for an indefinite period.

Article 15

1. Where an agency contract is concluded for an indefinite period either party may terminate it by notice.

2. The period of notice shall be one month for the first year of the contract, two months for the second year commenced, and three months for the third year commenced and subsequent years. The parties may not agree on shorter periods of notice.
3. Member States may fix the period of notice at four months for the fourth year of the contract, five months for the fifth year and six months for the sixth and subsequent years. They may decide that the parties may not agree to shorter periods.
4. If the parties agree on longer periods than those laid down in paragraphs 2 and 3, the period of notice to be observed by the principal must not be shorter than that to be observed by the commercial agent.
5. Unless otherwise agreed by the parties, the end of the period of notice must coincide with the end of a calendar month.
6. The provision of this Article shall apply to an agency contract for a fixed period where it is converted under Article 14 into an agency contract for an indefinite period, subject to the proviso that the earlier fixed period must be taken into account in the calculation of the period of notice.

Article 16

Nothing in this Directive shall affect the application of the law of the Member States where the latter provides for the immediate termination of the agency contract:
    (a) because of the failure of one party to carry out all or part of his obligations;
    (b) where exceptional circumstances arise.

Article 17

1. Member States shall take the measures necessary to ensure that the commercial agent is, after termination of the agency contract, indemnified in accordance with paragraph 2 or compensated for damage in accordance with paragraph 3.
2. (a) The commercial agent shall be entitled to an indemnity if and to the extent that:
    —he has brought the principal new customers or has significantly increased the volume of business with existing customers and the principal continues to derive substantial benefits from the business with such customers, and
    —the payment of this indemnity is equitable having regard to all the circumstances and, in particular, the commission lost by the commercial agent on the business transacted with such customers. Member States may provide for such circumstances also to include the application or otherwise of a restraint of trade clause, within the meaning of Article 20;
  (b) The amount of the indemnity may not exceed a figure equivalent to an indemnity for one year calculated from the commercial agent's average annual remuneration over the preceding five years and if the contract goes back less than five years the indemnity shall be calculated on the average for the period in question;
  (c) The grant of such an indemnity shall not prevent the commercial agent from seeking damages.
3. The commercial agent shall be entitled to compensation for the damage he suffers as a result of the termination of his relations with the principal. Such damage shall be deemed to occur particularly when the termination takes place in circumstances:
    —depriving the commercial agent of the commission which proper performance of the agency contract would have procured him whilst providing the principal with substantial benefits linked to the commercial agent's activities,

309

—and/or which have not enabled the commercial agent to amortize the costs and expenses that he had incurred for the performance of the agency contract on the principal's advice.

4. Entitlement to the indemnity as provided for in paragraph 2 or to compensation for damage as provided for under paragraph 3, shall also arise where the agency contract is terminated as a result of the commercial agent's death.

5. The commercial agent shall lose his entitlement to the indemnity in the instances provided for in paragraph 2 or to compensation for damage in the instances provided for in paragraph 3, if within one year following termination of the contract he has not notified the principal that he intends pursuing his entitlement.

6. The Commission shall submit to the Council, within eight years following the date of notification of this Directive, a report on the implementation of this Article, and shall if necessary submit to it proposals for amendments.

Article 18

The indemnity or compensation referred to in Article 17 shall not be payable:
   (a) where the principal has terminated the agency contract because of default attributable to the commercial agent which would justify immediate termination of the agency contract under national law;
   (b) where the commercial agent has terminated the agency contract, unless such termination is justified by circumstances attributable to the principal or on grounds of age, infirmity or illness of the commercial agent in consequence of which he cannot reasonably be required to continue his activities;
   (c) where, with the agreement of the principal, the commercial agent assigns his rights and duties under the agency contract to another person.

Article 19

The parties may not derogate from Articles 17 and 18 to the detriment of the commercial agent before the agency contract expires.

Article 20

1. For the purposes of this Directive an agreement restricting the business activities of a commercial agent following termination of the agency contract is hereinafter referred to as a restraint of trade clause.

2. A restraint of trade clause shall be valid only if and to the extent that:
   (a) it is concluded in writing; and
   (b) it relates to the geographical area or the group of customers and the geographical area entrusted to the commercial agent and to the kind of goods covered by his agency under the contract.

3. A restraint of trade clause shall be valid for not more than two years after termination of the agency contract.

4. This Article shall not affect provisions of national law which impose other restrictions on the validity or enforceability of restraint of trade clauses or which enable the courts to reduce the obligations on the parties resulting from such an agreement.

CHAPTER V
GENERAL AND FINAL PROVISIONS

Article 21

Nothing in this Directive shall require a Member State to provide for the disclosure of information where such disclosure would be contrary to public policy.

Article 22

1. Member States shall bring into force the provisions necessary to comply with this Directive before 1 January 1990. They shall for with inform the Commission thereof. Such provisions shall apply at least to contracts concluded after their entry into force. They shall apply to contracts in operation by 1 January 1994 at the latest.
2. As from the notification of this Directive, Member States shall communicate to the Commission the main laws, regulations and administrative provisions which they adopt in the field governed by this Directive.
3. However, with regard to Ireland and the United Kingdom, 1 January 1990 referred to in paragraph 1 shall be replaced by 1 January 1994. With regard to Italy, 1 January 1990 shall be replaced by 1 January 1993 in the case of the obligations deriving from Article 17.

Article 23

This Directive is addressed to the Member States.

Done et Brussels, 18 December 1986.

For the Council
The President
M. Jopling

(iii) UNIDROIT CONVENTION ON AGENCY IN THE INTERNATIONAL SALE OF GOODS*

(Geneva, 17 February 1983)

PREAMBLE

The States parties to this Convention, Desiring to establish common provisions concerning agency in the international sale of goods,

Bearing in mind the objectives of the United Nations Convention on Contracts for the International Sale of Goods,

Considering that the development of international trade on the basis of equality and mutual benefit is an important element in promoting friendly relations among States, bearing in mind the New International Economic Order,

Being of the opinion that the adoption of uniform rules which govern agency in the international sale of goods and take into account the different social, economic and legal systems would contribute to the removal of legal barriers in international trade and promote the development of international trade,

* Reproduced with the kind permission of UNIDROIT.

Have agreed as follows:

CHAPTER I
SPHERE OF APPLICATION AND GENERAL PROVISIONS

Article 1

(1) This Convention applies where one person, the agent, has authority or purports to have authority on behalf of another person, the principal, to conclude a contract of sale of goods with a third party.

(2) It governs not only the conclusion of such a contract by the agent but also any act undertaken by him for the purpose of concluding that contract or in relation to its performance.

(3) It is concerned only with relations between the principal or the agent on the one hand, and the third party on the other.

(4) It applies irrespective of whether the agent acts in his own name or in that of the principal.

Article 2

(1) This Convention applies only where the principal and the third party have their places of business in different States and:
   (a) the agent has his place of business in a Contracting State, or
   (b) the rules of private international law lead to the application of the law of a Contracting State.

(2) Where, at the time of contracting, the third party neither knew nor ought to have known that the agent was acting as an agent, the Convention only applies if the agent and the third party had their places of business in different States and if the requirements of paragraph 1 are satisfied.

(3) Neither the nationality of the parties nor the civil or commercial character of the parties or of the contract of sale is to be taken into consideration in determining the application of this Convention.

Article 3

(1) This Convention does not apply to:
   (a) the agency of a dealer on a stock, commodity or other exchange;
   (b) the agency of an auctioneer;
   (c) agency by operation of law in family law, in the law of matrimonial property, or in the law of succession;
   (d) agency arising from statutory or judicial authorisation to act for a person without capacity to act;
   (e) agency by virtue of a decision of a judicial or quasi-judicial authority or subject to the direct control of such an authority.

(2) Nothing in this Convention affects any rule of law for the protection of consumers.

Article 4

For the purposes of this Convention:
   (a) an organ, officer or partner of a corporation, association, partnership or other entity, whether or not possessing legal personality, shall not be regarded as the agent of that

entity in so far as, in the exercise of his functions as such, he acts by virtue of an authority conferred by law or by the constitutive documents of that entity;

(b) a trustee shall not be regarded as an agent of the trust, of the person who has created the trust, or of the beneficiaries.

Article 5

The principal, or an agent acting in accordance with the express or implied instructions of the principal, may agree with the third party to exclude the application of this Convention or, subject to Article 11, to derogate from or vary the effect of any of its provisions.

Article 6

(1) In the interpretation of this Convention, regard is to be had to its international character and to the need to promote uniformity in its application and the observance of good faith in international trade.

(2) Questions concerning matters governed by this Convention which are not expressly settled in it are to be settled in conformity with the general principles on which it is based or, in the absence of such principles, in conformity with the law applicable by virtue of the rules of private international law.

Article 7

(1) The principal or the agent on the one hand and the third party on the other are bound by any usage to which they have agreed and by any practices which they have established between themselves.

(2) They are considered, unless otherwise agreed, to have impliedly made applicable to their relations any usage of which they knew or ought to have known and which in international trade is widely known to, and regularly observed by, parties to agency relations of the type involved in the particular trade concerned.

Article 8

For the purposes of this Convention:

(a) if a party has more than one place of business, the place of business is that which has the closest relationship to the contract of sale, having regard to the circumstances known to or contemplated by the parties at the time of contracting;

(b) if a party does not have a place of business, reference is to be made to his habitual residence.

CHAPTER II
ESTABLISHMENT AND SCOPE OF THE AUTHORITY
OF THE AGENT

Article 9

(1) The authorisation of the agent by the principal may be express or implied.

(2) The agent has authority to perform all acts necessary in the circumstances to achieve the purposes for which the authorisation was given.

Article 10

The authorisation need not be given in or evidenced by writing and is not subject to any other requirement as to form. It may be proved by any means, including witnesses.

Article 11

Any provision of Article 10, Article 15 of Chapter IV which allows an authorization, a ratification or a termination of authority to be made in any form other than in writing does not apply where the principal or the agent has his place of business in a Contracting State which has made a declaration under Article 27. The parties may not derogate from or vary the effect of this paragraph.

CHAPTER III
LEGAL EFFECTS OF ACTS CARRIED OUT BY THE AGENT

Article 12

Where an agent acts on behalf of a principal within the scope of his authority and the third party knew or ought to have known that the agent was acting as an agent, the acts of the agent shall directly bind the principal and the third party to each other, unless it follows from the circumstances of the case, for example, by a reference to a contract of commission, that the agent undertakes to bind himself only.

Article 13

(1) Where the agent acts on behalf of a principal within the scope of his authority, his acts shall bind only the agent and the third party if:
  (a) the third party neither knew nor ought to have known that the agent was acting as an agent, or
  (b) it follows from the circumstances of the case, for example by a reference to a contract of commission, that the agent undertakes to bind himself only.
(2) Nevertheless:
  (a) where the agent, whether by reason of the third party's failure of performance or for any other reason, fails to fulfil or is not in a position to fulfil his obligations to the principal, the principal may exercise against the third party the rights acquired on the principal's behalf by the agent, subject to any defences which the third party may set up against the agent;
  (b) where the agent fails to fulfil or is not in a position to fulfil his obligations to the third party, the third party may exercise against the principal the rights which the third party has against the agent, subject to any defences which the agent may set up against the third party and which the principal may set up against the agent.
(3) The rights under paragraph 2 may be exercised only if notice of intention to exercise them is given to the agent and the third party or principal, as the case may be. As soon as the third party or principal has received such notice, he may no longer free himself from his obligations by dealing with the agent.
(4) Where the agent fails to fulfil or is not in a position to fulfil his obligations to the third party because of the principal's failure of performance, the agent shall communicate the name of the principal to the third party.

(5) Where the third party fails to fulfil his obligations under the contract to the agent, the agent shall communicate the name of the third party to the principal.

(6) The principal may not exercise against the third party the rights acquired on his behalf by the agent if it appears from the circumstances of the case that the third party, had he known the principal's identity, would not have entered into the contract.

(7) An agent may, in accordance with the express or implied instructions of the principal, agree with the third party to derogate from or vary the effect of paragraph 2.

Article 14

(1) Where an agent acts without authority or acts outside the scope of his authority, his acts do not bind the principal and the third party to each other.

(2) Nevertheless, where the conduct of the principal causes the third party reasonably and in good faith to believe that the agent has authority to act on behalf of the principal and that the agent is acting within the scope of that authority, the principal may not invoke against the third party the lack of authority of the agent.

Article 15

(1) An act by an agent who acts without authority or who acts outside the scope of his authority may be ratified by the principal. On ratification the act produces the same effects as if it had initially been carried out with authority.

(2) Where, at the time of the agent's act, the third party neither knew nor ought to have known of the lack of authority, he shall not be liable to the principal if, at any time before ratification, he gives notice of his refusal to become bound by a ratification. Where the principal ratifies but does not do so within a reasonable time, the third party may refuse to be bound by the ratification if he promptly notifies the principal.

(3) Where, however, the third party knew or ought to have known of the lack of authority of the agent, the third party may not refuse to become bound by a ratification before the expiration of any time agreed for ratification or, failing agreement, such reasonable time as the third party may specify.

(4) The third party may refuse to accept a partial ratification.

(5) Ratification shall take effect when notice of it reaches the third party or the ratification otherwise comes to his attention. Once effective, it may not be revoked.

(6) Ratification is effective notwithstanding that the act itself could not have been effectively carried out at the time of ratification.

(7) Where the act has been carried out on behalf of a corporation or other legal person before its creation, ratification is effective only if allowed by the law of the State governing its creation.

(8) Ratification is subject to no requirements as to form. It may be express or may be inferred from the conduct of the principal.

Article 16

(1) An agent who acts without authority or who acts outside the scope of his authority shall, failing ratification, be liable to pay the third party such compensation as will place the third party in the same position as he would have been in if the agent had acted with authority and within the scope of his authority.

(2) The agent shall not be liable, however, if the third party knew or ought to have known that the agent had no authority or was acting outside the scope of his authority.

CHAPTER IV
TERMINATION OF THE AUTHORITY OF THE AGENT

Article 17

The authority of the agent is terminated:
    (a) when this follows from any agreement between the principal and the agent;
    (b) on completion of the transaction or transactions for which the authority was created;
    (c) on revocation by the principal or renunciation by the agent, whether or not this is consistent with the terms of their agreement.

Article 18

The authority of the agent is also terminated when the applicable law so provides.

Article 19

The termination of the authority shall not affect the third party unless he knew or ought to have known of the termination or the facts which caused it.

Article 20

Notwithstanding the termination of his authority, the agent remains authorised to perform on behalf of the principal or his successors the acts which are necessary to prevent damage to their interests.

CHAPTER V
FINAL PROVISIONS

Article 21

The Government of Switzerland is hereby designated as the depositary for this Convention.

Article 22

(1) This Convention is open for signature at the concluding meeting of the Diplomatic Conference on Agency in the International Sale of Goods and will remain open for signature by all States at Berne until 31 December 1984.
(2) This Convention is subject to ratification, acceptance or approval by the signatory States.
(3) This Convention is open for accession by all States which are not signatory States as from the date it is open for signature.
(4) Instruments of ratification, acceptance, approval and accession are to be deposited with the Government of Switzerland.

Article 23

This Convention does not prevail over any international agreement which has already been or may be entered into and which contains provisions of substantive law concerning the matters governed by this Convention, provided that the principal and the third party or, in the case referred to in Article 2, paragraph 2, the agent and the third party have their places of business in States parties to such agreement.

Article 24

(1) If a Contracting State has two or more territorial units in which different systems of law are applicable in relation to the matters dealt with in this Convention, it may, at the time of signature, ratification, acceptance, approval or accession, declare that this Convention is to extend to all its territorial units or only to one or more of them, and may amend its declaration by submitting another declaration at any time.
(2) These declarations are to be notified to the depositary and are to state expressly the territorial units to which the Convention extends.
(3) If, by virtue of a declaration under this Article, this Convention extends to one or more but not all of the territorial units of a Contracting State, and if the place of business of a party is located in that State, this place of business, for the purposes of this Convention, is considered not to be in a Contracting State, unless it is in a territorial unit to which the Convention extends.
(4) If a Contracting State makes no declaration under paragraph 1 of this Article, the Convention is to extend to all territorial units of that State.

Article 25

Where a Contracting State has a system of government under which executive, judicial and legislative powers are distributed between central and other authorities within that State, its signature or ratification, acceptance or approval of, or accession to this Convention, or its making of any declaration in terms of Article 24 shall carry no implication as to the internal distribution of powers within that State.

Article 26

(1) Two or more Contracting States which have the same or closely related legal rules on matters governed by this Convention may at any time declare that the Convention is not to apply where the principal and the third party or, in the case referred to in Article 2, paragraph 2, the agent and the third party have their places of business in those States. Such declarations may be made jointly or by reciprocal unilateral declarations.
(2) A Contracting State which has the same or closely related legal rules on matters governed by this Convention as one or more non-Contracting States may at any time declare that the Convention is not to apply where the principal and the third party or, in the case referred to in Article 2, paragraph 2, the agent and the third party have their places of business in those States.
(3) If a State which is the object of a declaration under the preceding paragraph subsequently becomes a Contracting State, the declaration made will, as from the date on which the Convention enters into force in respect of the new Contracting

State, have the effect of a declaration made under paragraph 1, provided that the new Contracting State joins in such declaration or makes a reciprocal unilateral declaration.

Article 27

A Contracting State whose legislation requires an authorization, ratification or termination of authority to be made in or evidenced by writing in all cases governed by this Convention may at any time make a declaration in accordance with Article 11 that any provision of Article 10, Article 15 or Chapter IV which allows an authorization, ratification or termination of authority to be other than in writing, does not apply where the principal or the agent has his place of business in that State.

Article 28

A Contracting State may declare at the time of signature, ratification, acceptance, approval or accession that it will not be bound by Article 2, paragraph 1 (b).

Article 29

A Contracting State, the whole or specific parts of the foreign trade of which are carried on exclusively by specially authorized organisations, may at any time declare that, in cases where such organisations act either as buyers or sellers in foreign trade, all these organisations or the organisations specified in the declaration shall not be considered, for the purposes of Article 13, paragraphs 2 (b) and 4, as agents in their relations with other organizations having their place of business in the same State.

Article 30

(1) A Contracting State may at any time declare that it will apply the provisions of this Convention to specified cases falling outside its sphere of application.
(2) Such declaration may, for example, provide that the Convention shall apply to:
    (a) contracts other than contracts of sale of goods;
    (b) cases where the places of business mentioned in Article 2, paragraph 1, are not situated in Contracting States.

Article 31

(1) Declarations made under this Convention at the time of signature are subject to confirmation upon ratification, acceptance or approval.
(2) Declarations and confirmations of declarations are to be in writing and to be formally notified to the depositary.
(3) A declaration takes effect simultaneously with the entry into force of this Convention in respect of the State concerned. However, a declaration of which the depositary receives formal notification after such entry into force takes effect on the first day of the month following the expiration of six months after the date of its receipt by the depositary. Reciprocal unilateral declarations under Article 26 take effect on the first day of the month following the expiration of six months after the receipt of the latest declaration by the depositary.

(4) Any State which makes a declaration under this Convention may withdraw it at any time by a formal notification in writing addressed to the depositary. Such withdrawal is to take effect on the first day of the month following the expiration of six months after the date of the receipt of the notification by the depositary.

(5) A withdrawal of a declaration made under Article 26 renders inoperative, as from the date on which the withdrawal takes effect, any reciprocal declaration made by another State under that Article.

Article 32

No reservations are permitted except those expressly authorised in this Convention.

Article 33

(1) This Convention enters into force on the first day of the month following the expiration of twelve months after the date of deposit of the tenth instrument of ratification, acceptance, approval or accession.

(2) When a State ratifies, accepts, approves or accedes to this Convention after the deposit of the tenth instrument of ratification, acceptance, approval or accession, this Convention enters into force in respect of that State on the first day of the month following the expiration of twelve months after the date of the deposit of its instrument of ratification, acceptance, approval or accession.

Article 34

This Convention applies when the agent offers to sell or purchase or accepts an offer of sale or purchase on or after the date when the Convention enters into force in respect of the Contracting State referred to in Article 2, paragraph 1.

Article 35

(1) A Contracting State may denounce this Convention by a formal notification in writing to the depositary.

(2) The denunciation takes effect on the first day of the month following the expiration of twelve months after the notification is received by the depositary. Where a longer period for the denunciation to take effect is specified in the notification, the denunciation takes effect upon the expiration of such longer period after the notification is received by the depositary.

In witness whereof the undersigned plenipotentiaries, being duly authorized by their respective Governments, have signed this Convention.

Done at Geneva this seventeenth day of February, one thousand nine hundred and eighty-three, in a single original, of which the English and French texts are equally authentic.

TABLE OF STATE RATIFICATIONS

Total number of signatures not followed by ratifications:	4
Total number of ratifications/accessions:	5

State	Signature	Ratification	By	Entry Into Force
Chile	17 February 1983			
France	25 October 1984	7 August 1987		
Holy See	17 February 1983			
Italy	9 April 1984	16 June 1986		
Mexico		22 December 1987	Accession	
Morocco	17 February 1983			
Netherlands*		2 February 1994	Accession	
South Africa		27 January 1986	Accession	
Switzerland	17 February 1983			

* The Netherlands extended the application of the Convention to Aruba (by declaration deposited 2 February 1995).

Note: Mexico made a declaration when it acceded to the Convention. The text of the declaration is available at http://www.unidroit.org/english/implement/i-83.htm.

(iv) UNIDROIT MODEL FRANCHISE DISCLOSURE LAW*

PREAMBLE

The International Institute for the Unification of Private Law (UNIDROIT),

Recognising that franchising is playing an ever greater role in a wide range of national economies,

Being mindful of the fact that in the legislative process, State legislators may wish to consider a number of different elements, including

- whether it is clear that there is a problem, what its nature is, and what action, if any, is necessary;
- whether prospective investors are more likely to protect themselves against fraud if they have access to truthful, important information in advance of their assent to any franchise agreement;
- whether the nation's economic and social interests are best served by legally requiring a balance of information between the parties to a franchise agreement;
- whether there is a pattern of abusive conduct, or whether this conduct is isolated or limited to particular industries;
- the nature of the evidence of abuse;
- whether existing laws address the concerns and whether they are adequately applied;
- whether an effective system of self-regulation exists;
- the financial burden the new legislation will place upon franchisors and investors as compared to the benefits of legally-required disclosure;
- whether the proposed legislation inhibits or facilitates entry to franchisors, and its effect on job-creation and investment; and
- the views of interested organisations, including national franchise associations;

Recalling that State legislators may want to adapt suggested provisions, especially with regard to the enumerated disclosure items, in response to specific circumstances of, or established methods of legislation in, each State;

Recalling that the text of the Model Law is accompanied by an Explanatory Report which, with a view to assisting legislators, explains the purpose of the provisions;

Finding that experiences with disclosure legislation has on the whole been positive;

---

* Reproduced with the kind permission of UNIDROIT.

is pleased to place the *Model Franchise Disclosure Law* and the Explanatory Report thereto presented in this document and prepared by a Committee of Governmental Experts convened by UNIDROIT at the disposal of the international community as an example that is not compulsory for States legislators and as an instrument intended to be a recommendation for States that have decided to adopt franchise specific legislation.

Article 1
Scope of Application

(1) This law applies to franchises to be granted or renewed for the operation of one or more franchised businesses within the [State adopting this law].
(2) Except as otherwise expressly provided in this law it is not concerned with the validity of the franchise agreement or any of its provisions.

Article 2
Definitions

For the purposes of this law:

affiliate of the franchisee means a natural or legal person who directly or indirectly controls or is controlled by the franchisee, or is controlled by another party who controls the franchisee;

affiliate of the franchisor means a natural or legal person who directly or indirectly controls or is controlled by the franchisor, or is controlled by another party who controls the franchisor;

development agreement means an agreement under which a franchisor in exchange for direct or indirect financial compensation grants to another party the right to acquire more than one franchise of the same franchise system;

disclosure document means a document containing the information required under this law;

franchise means the rights granted by a party (the franchisor) authorising and requiring another party (the franchisee), in exchange for direct or indirect financial compensation, to engage in the business of selling goods or services on its own behalf under a system designated by the franchisor which includes know-how and assistance, prescribes in substantial part the manner in which the franchised business is to be operated, includes significant and continuing operational control by the franchisor, and is substantially associated with a trademark, service mark, trade name or logotype designated by the franchisor. It includes:
   (A) the rights granted by a franchisor to a sub-franchisor under a master franchise agreement;
   (B) the rights granted by a sub-franchisor to a sub-franchisee under a sub-franchise agreement;
   (C) the rights granted by a franchisor to a party under a development agreement.
For the purposes of this definition 'direct or indirect financial compensation' shall not include the payment of a bona fide wholesale price for goods intended for resale;

franchise agreement means the agreement under which a franchise is granted;

franchised business means the business conducted by the franchisee under a franchise agreement;

franchisee includes a sub-franchisee in its relationship with the sub-franchisor and the sub-franchisor in its relationship with the franchisor;

franchisor includes the sub-franchisor in its relationship with its sub-franchisees;

master franchise means the right granted by a franchisor to another party (the sub-franchisor) to grant franchises to third parties (the sub-franchisees);

material change in the information required to be disclosed means a change which can reasonably be expected to have a significant effect on the prospective franchisee's decision to acquire the franchise;

material fact means any information that can reasonably be expected to have a significant effect on the prospective franchisee's decision to acquire the franchise;

misrepresentation means a statement of fact that the person making the statement knew or ought to have known to be untrue at the time the statement was made;

omission means the failure to state a fact of which the person making the statement was aware at the time the statement ought to have been made;

State includes the territorial units making up a State which has two or more territorial units, whether or not possessing different systems of law applicable in relation to the matters dealt with in this law;
and

sub-franchise agreement means a franchise agreement concluded by a sub-franchisor and a sub-franchisee pursuant to a master franchise.

Article 3
Delivery of Disclosure Document

(1) A franchisor must give every prospective franchisee a disclosure document, to which the proposed franchise agreement must be attached, at least fourteen days before the earlier of
   (A) the signing by the prospective franchisee of any agreement relating to the franchise, with the exception of agreements relating to confidentiality of information delivered or to be delivered by the franchisor; or
   (B) the payment to the franchisor or an affiliate of the franchisor by the prospective franchisee of any fees relating to the acquisition of a franchise that are not refundable or the refunding of which is subject to such conditions as to render them not refundable, with the exception of a security (bond or deposit) given on the conclusion of a confidentiality agreement.

(2) The disclosure document must be updated within [X] days of the end of the franchisor's fiscal year. Where there has been a material change in the information required to be disclosed under Article 6, notice in writing of such change should be delivered to the prospective franchisee as soon as practicable before either of the events described in Sub-Paragraphs (1)(A) or (1)(B) has occurred.

Article 4
Format of Disclosure Document

(1) Disclosure must be provided in writing.
(2) The franchisor may use any format for the disclosure document, provided that the information contained therein is presented as a single document at one time and meets the requirements imposed by this law.

Article 5
Exemptions from Obligation to Disclose

No disclosure document is required:

(A) in case of the grant of a franchise to a person who has been an officer or director of the franchisor or of an affiliate of the franchisor for at least one year immediately before the signing of the franchise agreement;

(B) in case of the assignment or other transfer of a franchisee's rights and obligations under an existing franchise agreement, where the assignee or transferee is bound by substantially the same terms as the assignor or transferor, and the franchisor has not had a significant role in the transaction other than approval of the transfer.

(C) in case of the grant of a franchise to sell goods or services to a natural or legal person who has been engaged in the same or a similar business for the previous two years, if the sales of the franchise, as reasonably anticipated by the parties at the time the franchise agreement is entered into, will not during the first year of the relationship exceed 20% of the total aggregate sales of the combined business of the franchisee and its affiliates;

(D) in case of the grant of a franchise pursuant to which the prospective franchisee commits to a total financial requirement under the franchise agreement in excess of [X];

(E) in case of the grant of a franchise to a prospective franchisee who together with its affiliates has a net worth in excess of [Y] or turnover in excess of [Z]; or

(F) in case of the renewal or extension of a franchise on the same conditions.

Article 6
Information to be Disclosed

(1) In the disclosure document the franchisor shall provide the following information:

(A) the legal name, legal form and legal address of the franchisor and the address of the principal place of business of the franchisor;

(B) the trademark, trade name, business name or similar name, under which the franchisor carries on or intends to carry on business in the State in which the prospective franchisee will operate the franchise business;

(C) the address of the franchisor's principal place of business in the State where the prospective franchisee is located;

(D) a description of the franchise to be operated by the prospective franchisee;

(E) a description of the business experience of the franchisor and its affiliates granting franchises under substantially the same trade name, including:
  (i) the length of time during which each has run a business of the type to be operated by the prospective franchisee; and
  (ii) the length of time during which each has granted franchises for the same type of business as that to be operated by the prospective franchisee;

(F) the names, business addresses, positions held, and business experience of any person who has senior management responsibilities for the franchisor's business operations in relation to the franchise;

(G) any criminal convictions or any finding of liability in a civil action or arbitration involving franchises or other businesses relating to fraud, misrepresentation,

325

or similar acts or practices of:

(i) the franchisor; and

(ii) any affiliate of the franchisor who is engaged in franchising

for the previous five years, and whether any such action is pending against the franchisor or its subsidiary, and the court or other citation of any of the above;

(H) any bankruptcy, insolvency or comparable proceeding involving the franchisor and its affiliate(s) for the previous five years and the court citation thereof;

(I) the total number of franchisees and company-owned outlets of the franchisor and of affiliates of the franchisor granting franchises under substantially the same trade name;

(J) the names, business addresses and business phone numbers of the franchisees, and of the franchisees of any affiliates of the franchisor which are granting franchises under substantially the same trade name whose outlets are located nearest to the proposed outlet of the prospective franchisee, but in any event of not more than [X] franchisees, in the State of the franchisee and/or contiguous States, or, if there are no contiguous States, the State of the franchisor;

(K) information about the franchisees of the franchisor and about franchisees of affiliates of the franchisor that grant franchises under substantially the same trade name that have ceased to be franchisees during the three fiscal years before the one during which the franchise agreement is entered into, with an indication of the reasons for which the franchisees have ceased to be franchisees of the franchisor;

(L) the following information regarding the franchisor's intellectual property to be licensed to the franchisee, in particular trademarks, patents, copyright and software:

(i) the registration and/or the application for registration, if any,

(ii) the name of the owner of the intellectual property rights and/or the name of the applicant, if any;

(iii) the date on which the registration of the intellectual property rights licensed expires; and

(iv) litigation or other legal proceedings, if any, which could have a material effect on the franchisee's legal right, exclusive or non-exclusive, to use the intellectual property under the franchise agreement

in the State in which the franchised business is to be operated;

(M) information on the categories of goods and/or services that the franchisee is required to purchase or lease, indicating

(i) whether any of these have to be purchased or leased from the franchisor, affiliates of the franchisor or from a supplier designated by the franchisor;

(ii) whether the franchisee has the right to recommend other suppliers for approval by the franchisor; and

(iii) whether any revenue or other benefit that may be directly or indirectly received by the franchisor or any of the affiliates of the franchisor from any supplier of goods and/or services to the franchisee, such as rebates, bonuses, or incentives with regard to those goods and/or services, shall be passed on to the prospective franchisee or, if not, whether a price mark-up will be made by the franchisor or the supplier recommended by the franchisor;

(N) financial matters, including:
    (i) (a) an estimate of the prospective franchisee's total initial investment;
        (b) financing offered or arranged by the franchisor, if any;
        (c) the financial statements of the franchisor and when available audited or otherwise independently verified financial statements, including balance sheets and statements of profit and loss, for the previous three years. Franchisors, the creation of which goes back less than three years, are under an obligation to disclose the same documents prepared since they began their activity;
    (ii) (a) If information is provided to the prospectivefranchisee by or on behalf of the franchisor concerning the historical or projected financial performance of outlets owned by the franchisor, its affiliates or franchisees, the information must:
        (aa) have a reasonable basis at the time it is made;
        (bb) include the material assumptions underlying its preparation and presentation;
        (cc) state whether it is based on actual results of existing outlets;
        (dd) state whether it is based on franchisor-owned and/or franchisee-owned outlets; and
        (ee) indicate the percentage of those outlets that meet or exceed each range or result.
        (b) If the financial information referred to in the preceding sub-paragraph is provided, the franchisor must state that the levels of performance of the prospective franchisee's outlet may differ from those contained in the information provided by the franchisor.

(O) a description of:
    (i) the state of the general market of the products or services that are the subject of the contract;
    (ii) the state of the local market of the products or services that are the subject of the contract;
    (iii) the prospects for development of the market; and

(P) anything else necessary to prevent any statement in the document from being misleading to a reasonable prospective franchisee.

(2) The following information shall also be included in the disclosure document. However, where the information is contained in the franchise agreement, the franchisor may in the disclosure document merely make reference to the relevant section of the franchise agreement. Where the following items of information are not included in the proposed franchise agreement, that fact shall be stated in the disclosure document :

(A) the term and conditions of renewal of the franchise, if any;

(B) a description of the initial and on-going training programmes;

(C) the extent of exclusive rights to be granted, if any, including exclusive rights relating to territory and/or to customers and also information on any reservation by the franchisor of the right
    (i) to use, or to license the use of, the trademarks covered by the franchise agreement;
    (ii) to sell or distribute the goods and/or services authorised for sale by the franchisee directly or indirectly through the same or any other channel of

distribution, whether under the trademarks covered by the agreement or any other trademark;

(D) the conditions under which the franchise agreement may be terminated by the franchisor and the effects of such termination;

(E) the conditions under which the franchise agreement may be terminated by the franchisee and the effects of such termination;

(F) the limitations imposed on the franchisee, if any, in relation to territory and/or to customers;

(G) in-term and post-term non-compete covenants;

(H) the initial franchise fee, whether any portion of the fee is refundable, and the terms and conditions under which a refund will be granted;

(I) other fees and payments, including any gross-up of royalties imposed by the franchisor in order to offset withholding tax;

(J) restrictions or conditions imposed on the franchisee in relation to the goods and/or services that the franchisee may sell;

(K) the conditions for the assignment or other transfer of the franchise; and

(L) any forum selection or choice of law provisions, and any selected dispute resolution processes.

(3) Where the franchise is a master franchise, the sub-franchisor must, in addition to the items specified in paragraphs (1) and (2), disclose to the prospective sub-franchisee the information on the franchisor that it has received under paragraphs (1)(A), (E), (H), and (2)(C) and (F) of this article, as well as inform the prospective sub-franchisee of the situation of the sub-franchise agreements in case of termination of the master franchise agreement and of the content of the master franchise agreement.

Article 7
Acknowledgement of Receipt of Disclosure Document

The prospective franchisee shall at the request of the franchisor acknowledge in writing the receipt of the disclosure document.

Article 8
Remedies

(1) If the disclosure document or notice of material change:

(A) has not been delivered within the period of time established in Article 3;

(B) contains a misrepresentation of a material fact; or

(C) makes an omission of a material fact;

then the franchisee may on 30 days prior written notice to the franchisor terminate the franchise agreement and/or claim against the franchisor for damages suffered from the conduct described in (A), (B) and (C), unless the franchisee had the information required to be disclosed through other means, did not rely on the misrepresentation, or termination is a disproportionate remedy in the circumstances.

(2) The remedies granted to the franchisee pursuant to this article must be exercised no later than the earlier of:

(A) one year after the act or omission constituting the breach upon which the right to terminate is based;

(B) three years after the act or omission constituting the breach upon which the right to claim for damages suffered is based;

(C) one year after the franchisee becomes aware of facts or circumstances reasonably indicating that it may have a right to claim for damages suffered; or

(D) within 90 days of the delivery to the franchisee of a written notice providing details of the breach accompanied by the franchisor's then current disclosure document.

(3) The rights provided by paragraph (1) of this Article do not derogate from any other right the franchisee may have under the applicable law.

(4) All matters regarding termination and damages, which have not been expressly regulated in this article, shall be governed by the applicable law.

Article 9
Temporal Scope of Application

This law applies whenever a franchise agreement is entered into or renewed after the law enters into force.

Article 10
Waivers

Any waiver by a franchisee of a right given by this law is void.

6

INTERNATIONAL CREDIT TRANSFERS AND BANK PAYMENT UNDERTAKINGS

A. Introductory Text

The materials in this section relate principally to rules governing international credit transfers and payment undertakings by banks and insurance companies to support obligations of their customers arising under cross-border transactions.

Credit transfers are funds transfers originated by the paying party, who by giving a payment order procures the push of funds to the beneficiary through the banking system. Credit transfers are to be contrasted with debit transfers in which it is the beneficiary who initiates the funds transfer by steps to collect payment, that is, by pulling funds from the paying party through the banking system, for example, by collection of bills of exchange or cheques or by direct debit. UNCITRAL published a Model Law on International Credit Transfers in 1992. This does not cover debit transfers.

Banks regularly assume payment obligations on behalf of customers to support cross-border transactions. These may take one of three forms. In the first, exemplified by the documentary credit, the bank undertakes to make payment (typically covering the price of goods which its customer is importing) on presentation of specified documents. The bank is the first port of call for payment, and the seller is not entitled to resort to the buyer unless the credit is dishonoured. In the second, exemplified by the demand guarantee and the standby letter of credit, the bank's payment obligation is, as before, triggered by the presentation of documents (often only a written demand is required) but while its duty to pay is not dependent on default a beneficiary making a demand knowing that there has been no default acts improperly and in breach of its duty to the account party. So in this type of undertaking resort to the bank is intended only as a fall-back, though this does not affect the documentary character of the guarantee as between bank and beneficiary. In the third form, the bank is merely a surety, so that its duty to pay is dependent on actual default by the account party and its liability is limited to that of the principal debtor.

Documentary credits are governed by the ICC's Uniform Customs and Practice for Documentary Credits (UCP), of which the current version is ICC 500, published in 1993 (as supplemented for electronic credits by the eUCP, published in 2002) and now in course of revision and the 2003 International Standard Banking Practice (ISBP) for the examination of documents under documentary credits. Demand guarantees are regulated by the 1992 ICC Uniform Rules for Demand Guarantees (URDG), published by the ICC in 1992; standby credits (which from a legal viewpoint are a form of demand guarantee), by the International Standby Practices (ISP98); and both forms of guarantee by the 1995 UN Convention on Independent Guarantees and Standby Letters of Credit. Finally, there are conditional (or suretyship) bonds under which the payment obligation is triggered by actual default. Such bonds are typically given by insurance companies to guarantee the obligations of contractors under construction contracts. A particular form of conditional bond is the contract bond, regulated by the 1993 ICC Uniform Rules for Contract Bonds (UCB), which is distinctive in that under the rules default is deemed to have been established, even without a judgment or award, by the issue of a certificate of default. The UCP, eUCP, URDG, ISP, and UCB take effect primarily by way of express incorporation into contracts,[1] though they could apply in other ways also, e.g. by usage or course of dealing.

---

[1] A credit subject to eUCP is also subject to the UCP without express incorporation (eUCP, Art e2).

1. International Credit Transfers

The most significant instrument on the subject of international credit transfers is the UNCITRAL Model Law on International Credit Transfers 1992. The aim of the Model Law is to influence the development of national practices and laws governing international credit transfers. While the Model Law may have had some success in stabilizing the terminology used to describe the parties to credit transfers,[2] it has not been a conspicuous success in terms of adoption by national legislatures. It was, however, influential in the drafting of the EC Directive on cross-border credit transfers.[3] While electronic transfers of funds provided the impetus for the creation of the Model Law, it is not restricted in its application to electronic transfers. It can apply to paper-based payment orders.

The critical factor in terms of application of the model law is that the credit transfer must be 'international' in character. A credit transfer is 'international' for this purpose where any sending bank and any receiving bank in the credit transfer are in different States.[4] Once there is a sending and a receiving bank in different States, every aspect of the credit transfer is within the scope of the Model Law. A 'credit transfer' is defined[5] as 'the series of operations, beginning with the originator's[6] payment order,[7] made for the purpose of placing funds[8] at the disposal of a beneficiary'.[9]

The Model Law does not contain a conflict of laws provision. However, Article Y, contained in a footnote to Article 1, is a conflicts provision which is available for adoption. It gives to the parties the freedom to choose the applicable law but provides that, in the absence of party choice, the law applicable to the rights and obligations arising out of the payment order shall be the law of the State of the receiving bank, except in relation to the determination of which law governs the question whether the actual sender of the payment order had the authority to bind the purported sender. This provision deals only with the rights and obligations arising out of the payment order; it does not purport to deal with the relationship between the beneficiary and the beneficiary's bank. Nor does it permit choice of law by reference to a credit-transfer-system rule (or a 'funds-transfer system rule'), that is to say, a rule which binds all participants to a credit transfer who have notice that the credit transfer system

---

[2] It has not been wholly successful even in its aim of producing a common terminology. In some jurisdictions a 'credit transfer' is known as a 'funds transfer'.

[3] Directive 97/5/EC of 27 January 1997. It is also the case that many of the concepts and definitions to be found in Art 4A of the Uniform Commercial Code can be traced back to the Model Law.   [4] Article 1.

[5] In Art 2(a).   [6] Defined in Art 2(c).

[7] Defined in Art 2(b). While the payment order must generally take the form of an unconditional instruction by a sender to a receiving bank, the Model Law does apply to conditional payment orders in the case where the bank executes the sender's conditional order 'by issuing an unconditional payment order' (Art 3).   [8] Defined in Art 2(h).

[9] Defined in Art 2(d).

might be used in the credit transfer and of the choice of law made by the system.

The rules are not mandatory in nature[10] and govern matters such as the obligations of the parties to the credit transfer,[11] the consequences of failed, erroneous, or delayed credit transfers,[12] and completion of the credit transfer.[13] A credit transfer is completed when the beneficiary's bank accepts a payment order for the benefit of the beneficiary.[14] Acceptance is broadly defined in the Model Law and may assume a number of different forms depending on whether the acceptance is made by the beneficiary's bank[15] or by a receiving bank other than the beneficiary's bank.[16] As between the beneficiary and the beneficiary's bank, the Model Law does not make any provision for the 'finality' of the payment to the beneficiary; that is to say, it does not contain a provision the effect of which is to make payment by the beneficiary's bank to the beneficiary 'final' and not conditional upon receipt of funds from the sender.[17]

2. International Bank Payment Undertakings

(a) The UCP and eUCP

The UCP

Most documentary credits issued in connection with international transactions are expressed to be governed by UCP 500. In essence, a documentary credit is an undertaking by a bank to make payment of a specified amount against presentation of specified documents, of which the key documents are a transport document (e.g. a bill of lading), an insurance document (e.g. a policy or certificate of insurance) and a commercial invoice, with others being furnished as required by the underlying contract, e.g. a certificate of origin, a certificate of quality, and a weight certificate. Once issued, a letter of credit is presumed to be irrevocable unless otherwise stated.[18] In contrast to a document against payment arrangement, a letter of credit gives the beneficiary the issuing bank's assurance of payment before the beneficiary has commenced performance of the underlying contract.

The opening of a credit is almost always advised by a bank other than the issuing bank—usually, the latter's correspondent in the beneficiary's country, the credit calling for presentation of documents to the advising bank. The latter does not itself incur any obligation to the beneficiary to honour the credit unless it adds its own separate undertaking (confirmation), in which case the credit becomes a confirmed

---

[10] Article 4. [11] Articles 5–12. [12] Articles 13–18.
[13] Article 19. [14] Article 19(1).
[15] Article 9 lists eight different forms of acceptance and acceptance takes place at the earliest point in time at which one of these methods is satisfied.
[16] Article 7. The definition of acceptance to be found in Art 7 is a broad one.
[17] Such a provision is to be found in Art 4A-405(c) of the Uniform Commercial Code.
[18] Article 6(c).

credit. An advising bank may also add its confirmation without the issuing bank's authority—the so-called 'silent confirmation'—but this falls outside the UCP and, while committing the 'confirming' bank to the beneficiary, does not entitle it to reimbursement by the issuing bank unless it had been authorized to pay the credit.

Classification of credits by payment method

Article 10 of the UCP requires that all credits clearly indicate whether they are available by sight payment, deferred payment, acceptance or negotiation. A sight payment credit entitles the beneficiary to payment on presentation of the documents. A deferred payment credit, now very common, is one under which payment is to be made at the end of a specified period after a stated date or event,[19] so that typically payment will not be made until some time after the documents have been presented, though a bank may be willing to negotiate the beneficiary's draft and/or documents, e.g. against its own obligation as confirming bank. An acceptance credit is one which entitles the beneficiary to call for acceptance of a draft by the issuing bank or other bank named in the credit. When the draft has been accepted, the purpose of the credit is completed and thereafter the beneficiary's rights stem from the draft, which must be presented at maturity. A credit which is available only to the named beneficiary is known as a straight credit. It is to be contrasted with a negotiation credit, which extends the payment promise to cover a bank that purchases or otherwise gives value for the draft and/or other documents. The negotiation credit authorizes a named bank, or in the case of a freely negotiable credit any bank, to negotiate drafts drawn by the beneficiary on the party stated in the credit, and/or other documents, without recourse to drawers or indorsers and entitles the negotiating bank to present the draft/documents at maturity and collect payment.[20]

Principles of documentary credits law

The UCP incorporate certain fundamental principles of documentary credit transactions:

(i) Autonomy of the credit Credits are separate transactions from the sales or other contracts on which they are based.[21] It follows that in the absence of fraud the beneficiary's breach of the underlying transaction does not entitle the bank to withhold payment of a credit, for the letter of credit engagement is between different parties and the payment obligation is conditioned only on tender of the relevant documents within the period of the credit and in conformity with its terms.[22] Fraud by the beneficiary or its agent is everywhere accepted as a ground for

---

[19] For example, 180 days after the date of the bill of lading or 90 days after presentation of the documents.

[20] Article 9(a)(iv).   [21] Article 3(a).

[22] Ibid. Similarly confirmation of a credit sets up a direct relationship between the confirming bank and the beneficiary which is separate from the relationship between the latter and the issuing bank.

non-payment, though this is a rule of law and is not to be found in the UCP. Legal systems differ as to whether the fraud must be in the documents or whether fraud in the underlying transaction suffices, and whether a beneficiary acting in good faith is entitled to be paid if the documents appear to be in order even if, without the beneficiary's knowledge, they are forged or otherwise fraudulent.

(ii) Documentary character of the credit   A corollary of the first principle is that all parties concerned deal with documents, and not with goods, services, or other performances.[23] Banks have to decide within a very short time—a maximum of seven days from presentation[24]—whether to accept the documents and an examination of goods or investigation of facts is incompatible with the need for a speedy payment mechanism. Accordingly banks have to concern themselves only with whether the documents appear on their face to conform to the credit.[25] The loose practice of specifying non-documentary conditions was thought to undermine the letter of credit mechanism, and Article 13(c) therefore provides that if a credit contains non-documentary conditions these are to be treated as not stated and disregarded.

(iii) Banks are concerned only with the apparent good order of the documents   The duty of a bank is to examine the documents presented to it with reasonable care to ascertain whether they appear on their face to conform to the credit.[26] Documents which are considered to be non-conforming appear on their face to be inconsistent with one another.[27] Compliance is to be determined by international standard banking practice as reflected in the UCP[28] and elaborated in the ISBP. Where on reasonable examination the documents appear to be in order, the bank is entitled to pay and to be indemnified by the applicant for the credit, even if a document or signature is forged.

(iv) Banks deal as principals, not as agents   A bank issuing a letter of credit assumes a payment liability as principal, not as agent for the account party, who cannot be sued on the credit, though if it is dishonoured he may be sued under the original contract. It follows from the fact that banks act as principals and from the autonomy of the credit that a bank's duty to pay against conforming documents is not dependent on its customer's consent and that, absent compelling evidence of fraud, the bank must refuse to accept its customer's instruction to withhold payment if the documents are in order.

(v) The terms of a credit must be strictly complied with   The general rule is that the documents must conform strictly to the terms of the credit and be presented within

---

[23] Article 4.   [24] Article 13(b).   [25] See below.

[26] Article 13(a).

[27] Ibid. This does not require that the data be identical (for example, the bill of lading may not contain all the data in the commercial invoice), merely that they are consistent (ISBP, para 24).

[28] Ibid.

the credit period. The fact that the non-conformity is minor or that the credit is presented only a day late does not entitle the beneficiary to claim payment. However, the principle of strict compliance is to be applied in a commercially sensible fashion. So misspellings or typing errors that do not affect the meaning of the word or sentence in which it occurred do not make a document discrepant.[29] Unless otherwise stated, documents to be presented under a credit must be originals.[30] What constitutes an original document has given rise to much debate and a number of court decisions. The position has now been helpfully clarified by an ICC Banking Commission Decision.[31]

(vi) A credit is not transferable unless expressly designated as such and even if transferring bank consents The general rule is that only the named beneficiary or its agent has the right to present documents under the credit and collect payment. A credit is not transferable unless it is designated as such[32] and even then it is transferable only to the extent and in the manner expressly consented to by the transferring bank.[33] In banking practice the form of transfer is not an assignment but a novation, the transferee replacing the transferor as beneficiary to the extent of the transfer. The fact that a credit is not stated to be transferable does not affect the beneficiary's right to assign the proceeds.[34]

The eUCP

The eUCP are a supplement to the UCP. They do not deal with the electronic issue of letters of credit, a well-established practice calling for no particular rules, but are directed to the presentation of electronic records, either alone or with paper-based documents. When fully developed, a system of electronic presentation embodying a standardized electronic format will have many advantages. In particular, it will enable presentation by the beneficiary direct to the issuer rather than to an advising or confirming bank and, more importantly, will provide an automated mechanism for checking the conformity of presented data with the terms of the credit, thus substantially reducing the currently high percentage of non-conforming presentations and enabling such presentations to be rapidly identified and rectified.

The definition of an electronic record embodies three distinct elements. The first describes the concept of an electronic record, namely the creation, generation, dispatch, communication, receipt, or storage of data by electronic means. The second is that the electronic record is capable of being authenticated as to the apparent identity of the sender and the apparent source of the data and as to

---

[29] ISBP, para 28.
[30] Though the UCP refer only to transport and insurance documents (Arts 23–7 and 34), documentary credit practice requires originals for all documents unless otherwise stated.
[31] *The Determination of an "Original" Document in the Context of UCP 500 Sub-Article 2c(b) : A Decision Prepared by the ICC Commission on Banking Technique and Practice* (1992). See also ISBP, paras 31–5 and see below as to electronic credits.   [32] Article 48(b).
[33] Article 48(c).   [34] Article 49.

whether it has remained complete and unaltered. The third is that it is capable of being examined for compliance with the terms of the eUCP credit.[35]

An eUCP credit must specify the formats in which electronic records are to be presented, and if it does not then presentation may be made in any format. The credit must state a place for presentation of the electronic record and, if the presentation is to be partly by paper documents, a place for their presentation.[36] However, a presentation under an eUCP credit is considered not received unless and until the beneficiary has provided a notice to the bank to which the presentation is made signifying when the presentation is complete.[37] The time of receipt of the notice of completeness marks the commencement of the period allowed for the examination of documents.[38]

(b) The URDG

Purpose of the URDG

The Uniform Rules for Demand Guarantees ('URDG') are designed to provide a set of rules for demand guarantees that are more in keeping with international practice than the 1978 Uniform Rules for Contract Guarantees. The latter made payment conditional on the production of a judgment or arbitral award or the principal's written approval of the claim. Though technically documentary in character, these requirements made demand guarantees almost indistinguishable from suretyship guarantees. The URDG, by contrast, recognize the practice of issuing guarantees payable on first written demand without need for further documents, though Article 20 imposes an additional requirement in the form of a statement of breach.[39] Technically the URDG are applicable to standby letters of credit, which do not differ in legal concept, only in the breadth and diversity of their business application and the adoption of a number of practices used in relation to documentary credits. However, the ISP are specifically designed for standbys and it is these rather than the URDG that are incorporated into standbys.

Guarantee structures

Demand guarantees are typically issued in favour of employers under construction contracts and buyers under contracts of sale, the purpose being to secure proper performance of obligations that are usually non-monetary in character. The URDG apply both to direct (three-party) guarantees and to indirect (four-party) guarantees. In a three-party guarantee the principal (the contractor, seller, etc.) instructs its bank (the guarantor), which is usually in the same country as the principal, to issue a guarantee directly in favour of the beneficiary, who is usually a foreign party. A four-party guarantee is issued where the beneficiary requires the assurance of payment from a bank in its own country and the principal

---

[35] Article E3(b)(i). Compare rule 1.09(c) of the ISP.   [36] Article E5(a).
[37] Article E5(c), (d).   [38] Article E7(a)(i).   [39] See below.

does not have an account with such a bank. The principal then instructs its own bank (which in this situation is designated 'the instructing party') to request a local bank in the beneficiary's country to issue a guarantee against a counter-guarantee (or counter-indemnity) by the instructing party, which thus has no relationship with the beneficiary.

Fundamental principles

Many of the principles governing documentary credits apply with equal force to demand guarantees. These are documentary in character, they are separate from the underlying transaction and from internal mandates between the same parties, the beneficiary is entitled to payment only on presentation of the relevant documents and the guarantor's duty is limited to exercising reasonable care to ensure that the documents appear to be in conformity with the guarantee. But the documents are usually much simpler (typically, a written demand and, if Article 20 is not excluded, a statement of breach), and whereas in the case of a documentary credit the bank is the first port of call for payment, a demand guarantee is intended as a fall-back position in the event of the principal's default, though such default is not a condition of payment as between guarantor and beneficiary.

Irrevocability and coming into effect

Like a documentary credit, a demand guarantee becomes irrevocable on issue[40] and takes effect from the same time unless otherwise provided.[41]

The demand for payment

The requirements for the demand under the guarantee contain a feature unique to the URDG. The demand must be in writing (which includes electronic data interchange)[42] and must be presented on or before the expiry date and before the expiry event[43] and in conformity with the requirements of the guarantee, together with such other documents (if any) as the guarantee may specify. But Article 20 also requires an additional document to be presented, whether or not specified in the guarantee, namely a statement (whether in the demand itself or in a separate document accompanying the demand and referred to in it) stating that the principal is in breach of his obligations under the underlying contract or in the case of a tender guarantee the tender conditions and the respect in which the principal is in breach.[44] The requirements for a demand under a counter-guarantee are simpler still. The demand must be accompanied by a written statement that the guarantor has received a demand for payment under the guarantee in accordance with its terms and with Article 20.[45]

---

[40] Article 5.   [41] Article 6.   [42] Article 2(a) (d).

[43] An expiry event means the presentation of a document specified for the purpose of expiry (Art 22), for example, an architect's certificate of completion, the presentation of which results in expiry of the guarantee.

[44] The statement of breach can be quite general, e.g. that the contract was not completed by the due date.   [45] Article 20(b).

Extend or pay demands

Article 26 deals with the extend or pay (alternatively pay or extend) demand, that is, a demand to extend the period of the guarantee or if not then to pay it. Such a demand is not necessarily improper, for there may in fact have been a breach or the beneficiary may believe a breach to have occurred. When such a demand is made the guarantor must inform the principal and suspend payment for such period as is reasonable to enable the beneficiary and the principal to reach agreement. If an extension is agreed, it takes effect on issue of the requisite amendment to the guarantee by the guarantor. If the extension is refused, the guarantor must pay, and the same is the case if nego-tiations are still current when the reasonable time elapses. But expiry of the guarantee before then does not affect the beneficiary's right to payment, since all that is required is that the demand should have been made before expiry of the guarantee.

Termination of the guarantee

The guarantee ends on payment,[46] on expiry,[47] on cancellation,[48] or by force of law. Termination is not dependent on return of the guarantee except where this act is itself relied on as an act of cancellation.[49]

Governing law and jurisdiction

Unless otherwise provided, the law governing the guarantee is that of the place of the business of the guarantor, while the law governing a counter-guarantee is that of the place of business of the instructing party.[50] Similarly, unless otherwise provided it is the competent court of the same place that has jurisdiction.[51]

(c) The ISP

UCP 500 is expressed to apply to standby credits as well as documentary credits,[52] which was a mistake in that most of the provisions are geared to presentation to the bank as the first port of call for payment and are thus wholly unsuited to standbys. The URDG were thus more appropriate, since from a legal perspective demand guarantees and standbys are indistinguishable. However, as stated earlier, standbys are used for a much wider variety of purposes and involve a number of techniques also used in documentary credit operations, so that what was required was a set of rules which utilized those aspects of the UCP that could be applied to standbys but were otherwise specifically geared to the nature of a standby as a fall-back recourse for the beneficiary. This is what the International Standby Practices ('ISP') are designed to provide.

Like the UCP and the URDG, the ISP embody the concepts of irrevocability, independence of the credit from the underlying transaction, and documentary

---

[46] Article 18.   [47] Articles 19, 22.   [48] Article 23.   [49] Article 22.
[50] Article 27.   [51] Article 28.   [52] Article 1.

character.[53] They also provide for electronic presentation where so permitted by the credit.[54] As with the URDG there is a specific rule for extend or pay demands[55] but it is differently structured. There is no suspension of the duty to pay; the issuer is allowed the maximum period of seven days to complete its examination of the documents and has a discretion whether to consult the applicant as to the extension or to pay if the demand is compliant. This is logical because an extension involves increased risk for the issuer, and since an amendment to the credit can only be effected with the issuer's consent there is no point in requiring the issuer to go through the consultation process if it has anyway decided not to grant the extension. If an amendment granting the extension is issued (which needs to be done within the seven days allowed for examination of the documents) the beneficiary is considered to have retracted its demand.

The ISP contain a number of other rules reflecting standby practice, including provisions for nomination of a person to advise, receive a presentation, effect a transfer, confirm, etc.,[56] transfer of drawing rights,[57] and syndication of and participation in the issuer's rights.[58]

(d) The UN Convention on Independent Guarantees and Stand-By Letters of Credit

The UN Convention on Independent Guarantees and Stand-By Letters of Credit results from a project by UNCITRAL to harmonize the law governing cross-border independent guarantees and standby letters of credit. For the Convention to apply the internationality requirement must be satisfied[59] and there must be the requisite connection to a Contracting State.[60] The Convention is limited to independent undertakings (standbys, demand guarantees, counter-guarantees) and does not apply to suretyship guarantees. It can also be applied to international letters of credit.[61] At first sight this seems as inappropriate as the inclusion of standby letters of credit in the UCP; but whereas the UCP takes effect by contractual incorporation the Convention, on coming into force and being brought into effect in Contracting States, becomes a legally operative instrument and contains useful provisions on defences to payment and on provisional court measures[62] that could not have been inserted into the UCP and give useful support to the latter.

---

[53] Rules 1.06 and 1.07. As under the UCP, non-documentary terms or conditions are to be disregarded (rule 4.11).   [54] Rules 3.06(d), 1.09.

[55] Rule 3.09.   [56] Rule 2.04.   [57] Rule 6.   [58] Rule 10.

[59] I.e. the places of business, as specified in the undertaking, of any two of the following persons are in different States, guarantor/issuer, beneficiary, principal/applicant, instructing party, confirmer (Art 4(1)).

[60] That is, either the place of business of the guarantor/issuer at which the undertaking is issued must be in a Contracting State or the rules of private international law lead to the application of the law of a Contracting State (Art 1(1)). Cf. CISG, Art 1 (p. 217 above).   [61] Article 1(2).

[62] Articles 19 and 20.

In general, the provisions track those of a kind contained in the UCP and URDG. Distinctive are the rules governing exceptions to the payment obligation and the ordering of provisional measures. Article 19(1) entitles the guarantor/issuer, acting in good faith,[63] to withhold payment from the beneficiary if 'it is manifest and clear that (a) any document is not genuine or has been falsified, (b) no payment is due on the basis asserted in the demand and the supporting documents, or (c) judging by the type and purpose of the undertaking, the demand has no conceivable basis'. Article 19(2) provides a list of situation types in which a demand has no conceivable basis. These include the beneficiary's wilful misconduct in preventing fulfilment of the underlying obligation. In any case in which the guarantor/issuer is entitled to withhold payment the principal/applicant or the instructing party may apply to the court, on the basis of immediately available strong evidence, for an order preventing the beneficiary from receiving payment or blocking the process paid to the beneficiary.[64] The choice of law rule is the same as under the URDG.[65]

(e) The UCB

The ICC Uniform Rules for Contract Bonds ('UCB') differ from the URDG in that the beneficiary must establish that there has been a default by the contractor (or 'principal' to use the language of the rules) before it is entitled to payment from the guarantor: it does not suffice for the beneficiary to issue a demand for payment accompanied only by a statement that the principal is in breach and the respect in which he is in breach. In this respect the contract bond partakes of the nature of a traditional suretyship bond; that is to say, the liability of the guarantor is an accessory liability, dependent upon a prior breach of one of his obligations by the contractor. However, it differs from an ordinary suretyship bond in that, for the purposes of the rules, default may be established not only by a judgment or award but also by the issue of a certificate as described below. The UCB are a set of contract terms and depend for their effect on incorporation by the parties into their contracts. In this respect, the rules depend for their use upon the operation of the market. The rules are most likely to be used in the construction industry, where an insurance company issues to the employer a contract bond under which the insurance company agrees to guarantee the obligations of the contractor under the building contract. But the rules are not confined in their scope to the construction industry. They can be incorporated to any contract where the parties so choose.

---

[63] It is not clear in what circumstances a guarantor/issuer invoking Art 19 could ever be said not to be acting in good faith.

[64] Article 20(1). The court may require the applicant for the order to furnish such security as the court deems appropriate, e.g. to cover the cost of compensating the beneficiary establishing its claim for loss suffered as the result of the order.

[65] Article 22 of the Convention.

Default

The obligation of the guarantor to honour the guarantee given is dependent upon the occurrence of a 'default'.[66] A default is deemed to have been established for the purposes of the rules (i) upon issue of a certificate of default by a third party if the bond so provides, (ii) if the bond does not provide for the issue of a certificate by a third party, upon the issue of a certificate of default by the guarantor or (iii) by the final judgment, order, or award of a court or tribunal of competent jurisdiction.[67] These rules provide substantial protection for the guarantor and, accordingly, it was not necessary to incorporate into the rules provisions protecting the guarantor against unfair or abusive calls.

Governing law and jurisdiction

In the absence of a choice of law by the parties, the law applicable to the bond is the law applicable to the contract between the principal (contractor) and the beneficiary.[68] This presumptive link to the underlying contract between the principal and the beneficiary, illustrates the closeness of the link between the obligation to pay under the bond and the liability of the principal to the beneficiary.

Further, the rules provide that all disputes arising between the beneficiary, the principal, and the guarantor in relation to a bond governed by the rules shall, unless otherwise agreed, be 'finally settled under the Rules of Conciliation and Arbitration' of the ICC.[69] The parties remain free to exclude the application of the ICC rules of conciliation and arbitration and to make their own provision for the determination of any dispute. Where they exclude the application of the ICC rules but do not make their own provision for the determination of disputes, any dispute shall be determined by a competent court of the guarantor's principal place of business or, at the option of the beneficiary, the competent court of the country in which the branch of the guarantor that issued the bond is situated.

---

[66] Article 7(i). Default is defined in Art 2.

[67] Article 7(j). In the case of (i) and (ii) the parties retain the right to require the determination of any dispute or difference arising under the contract or the bond or the review of any certificate of default or payment made pursuant thereto by a court or tribunal of competent jurisdiction.

[68] Article 8(a).

[69] In 1998, several years after the publication of the UCB, the ICC Rules of Arbitration were split off from the Rules of Conciliation and reissued in revised form.

B. Instruments

(i) UNCITRAL MODEL LAW ON INTERNATIONAL CREDIT TRANSFERS*

CHAPTER I
GENERAL PROVISIONS[1]

Article 1
Sphere of application[2]

(1) This law applies to credit transfers where any sending bank and its receiving bank are in different States.

(2) This law applies to other entities that as an ordinary part of their business engage in executing payment orders in the same manner as it applies to banks.

---

* Reproduced with the kind permission of UNCITRAL.

[1] The Commission suggests the following text for States that might wish to adopt it:

Article Y
Conflict of laws

(1) The rights and obligations arising out of a payment order shall be governed by the law chosen by the parties. In the absence of agreement, the law of the State of the receiving bank shall apply.

(2) The second sentence of paragraph (1) shall not affect the determination of which law governs the question whether the actual sender of the payment order had the authority to bind the purported sender.

(3) For the purposes of this article:
    (a) where a State comprises several territorial units having different rules of law, each territorial unit shall be considered to be a separate State;
    (b) branches and separate offices of a bank in different States are separate banks.

[2] This law does not deal with issues related to the protection of consumers.

(3) For the purpose of determining the sphere of application of this law, branches and separate offices of a bank in different States are separate banks.

Article 2
Definitions

For the purposes of this law:

(a) 'Credit transfer' means the series of operations, beginning with the originator's payment order, made for the purpose of placing funds at the disposal of a beneficiary. The term includes any payment order issued by the originator's bank or any intermediary bank intended to carry out the originator's payment order. A payment order issued for the purpose of effecting payment for such an order is considered to be part of a different credit transfer;

(b) 'Payment order' means an unconditional instruction, in any form, by a sender to a receiving bank to place at the disposal of a beneficiary a fixed or determinable amount of money if

　(i) the receiving bank is to be reimbursed by debiting an account of, or otherwise receiving payment from, the sender, and

　(ii) the instruction does not provide that payment is to be made at the request of the beneficiary.

Nothing in this paragraph prevents an instruction from being a payment order merely because it directs the beneficiary's bank to hold, until the beneficiary requests payment, funds for a beneficiary that does not maintain an account with it;

(c) 'Originator' means the issuer of the first payment order in a credit transfer;

(d) 'Beneficiary' means the person designated in the originator's payment order to receive funds as a result of the credit transfer;

(e) 'Sender' means the person who issues a payment order, including the originator and any sending bank;

(f) 'Receiving bank' means a bank that receives a payment order;

(g) 'Intermediary bank' means any receiving bank other than the originator's bank and the beneficiary's bank;

(h) 'Funds' or 'money' includes credit in an account kept by a bank and includes credit denominated in a monetary unit of account that is established by an intergovernmental institution or by agreement of two or more States, provided that this law shall apply without prejudice to the rules of the intergovernmental institution or the stipulations of the agreement;

(i) 'Authentication' means a procedure established by agreement to determine whether a payment order or an amendment or revocation of a payment order was issued by the person indicated as the sender;

(j) 'Banking day' means that part of a day during which the bank performs the type of action in question;

(k) 'Execution period' means the period of one or two days beginning on the first day that a payment order may be executed under article 11(1) and ending on the last day on which it may be executed under that article;

(l) 'Execution', in so far as it applies to a receiving bank other than the beneficiary's bank, means the issue of a payment order intended to carry out the payment order received by the receiving bank;

(m) 'Interest' means the time value of the funds or money involved, which, unless otherwise agreed, is calculated at the rate and on the basis customarily accepted by the banking community for the funds or money involved.

Article 3
Conditional instructions

(1) When an instruction is not a payment order because it is subject to a condition but a bank that has received the instruction executes it by issuing an unconditional payment order, thereafter the sender of the instruction has the same rights and obligations under this law as the sender of a payment order and the beneficiary designated in the instruction shall be treated as the beneficiary of a payment order.

(2) This law does not govern the time of execution of a conditional instruction received by a bank, nor does it affect any right or obligation of the sender of a conditional instruction that depends on whether the condition has been satisfied.

Article 4
Variation by agreement

Except as otherwise provided in this law, the rights and obligations of parties to a credit transfer may be varied by their agreement.

CHAPTER II
OBLIGATIONS OF THE PARTIES

Article 5
Obligations of sender

(1) A sender is bound by a payment order or an amendment or revocation of a payment order if it was issued by the sender or by another person who had the authority to bind the sender.

(2) When a payment order or an amendment or revocation of a payment order is subject to authentication other than by means of a mere comparison of signature, a purported sender who is not bound under paragraph (1) is nevertheless bound if
  (a) the authentication is in the circumstances a commercially reasonable method of security against unauthorized payment orders, and
  (b) the receiving bank complied with the authentication.

(3) The parties are not permitted to agree that a purported sender is bound under paragraph (2) if the authentication is not commercially reasonable in the circumstances.

(4) A purported sender is, however, not bound under paragraph (2) if it proves that the payment order as received by the receiving bank resulted from the actions of a person other than
  (a) a present or former employee of the purported sender, or
  (b) a person whose relationship with the purported sender enabled that person to gain access to the authentication procedure.
  The preceding sentence does not apply if the receiving bank proves that the payment order resulted from the actions of a person who had gained access to the authentication procedure through the fault of the purported sender.

(5) A sender who is bound by a payment order is bound by the terms of the order as received by the receiving bank. However, the sender is not bound by an erroneous duplicate of, or an error or discrepancy in, a payment order if

(a) the sender and the receiving bank have agreed upon a procedure for detecting erroneous duplicates, errors or discrepancies in a payment order, and

(b) use of the procedure by the receiving bank revealed or would have revealed the erroneous duplicate, error or discrepancy.

If the error or discrepancy that the bank would have detected was that the sender instructed payment of an amount greater than the amount intended by the sender, the sender is bound only to the extent of the amount that was intended. Paragraph (5) applies to an error or discrepancy in an amendment or a revocation order as it applies to an error or discrepancy in a payment order.

(6) A sender becomes obligated to pay the receiving bank for the payment order when the receiving bank accepts it, but payment is not due until the beginning of the execution period.

Article 6
Payment to receiving bank

For the purposes of this law, payment of the sender's obligation under article 5(6) to pay the receiving bank occurs

(a) if the receiving bank debits an account of the sender with the receiving bank, when the debit is made; or

(b) if the sender is a bank and subparagraph (a) does not apply,

(i) when a credit that the sender causes to be entered to an account of the receiving bank with the sender is used or, if not used, on the banking day following the day on which the credit is available for use and the receiving bank learns of that fact, or

(ii) when a credit that the sender causes to be entered to an account of the receiving bank in another bank is used or, if not used, on the banking day following the day on which the credit is available for use and the receiving bank learns of that fact, or

(iii) when final settlement is made in favour of the receiving bank at a central bank at which the receiving bank maintains an account, or

(iv) when final settlement is made in favour of the receiving bank in accordance with

a. provides for the settlement of obligations among participants either bilaterally or the rules of a funds transfer system that multilaterally, or

b. a bilateral netting agreement with the sender; or

(c) if neither subparagraph (a) nor (b) applies, as otherwise provided by law.

Article 7
Acceptance or rejection of a payment order by receiving bank other than the beneficiary's bank

(1) The provisions of this article apply to a receiving bank other than the beneficiary's bank.

347

(2) A receiving bank accepts the sender's payment order at the earliest of the following times:

    (a) when the bank receives the payment order, provided that the sender and the bank have agreed that the bank will execute payment orders from the sender upon receipt;

    (b) when the bank gives notice to the sender of acceptance;

    (c) when the bank issues a payment order intended to carry out the payment order received;

    (d) when the bank debits an account of the sender with the bank as payment for the payment order; or

    (e) when the time for giving notice of rejection under paragraph (3) has elapsed without notice having been given.

(3) A receiving bank that does not accept a payment order is required to give notice of rejection no later than on the banking day following the end of the execution period, unless:

    (a) where payment is to be made by debiting an account of the sender with the receiving bank, there are insufficient funds available in the account to pay for the payment order;

    (b) where payment is to be made by other means, payment has not been made;or

    (c) there is insufficient information to identify the sender.

(4) A payment order ceases to have effect if it is neither accepted nor rejected under this article before the close of business on the fifth banking day following the end of the execution period.

Article 8
Obligations of receiving bank other than the beneficiary's bank

(1) The provisions of this article apply to a receiving bank other than the beneficiary's bank.

(2) A receiving bank that accepts a payment order is obligated under that payment order to issue a payment order, within the time required by article 11, either to the beneficiary's bank or to an intermediary bank, that is consistent with the contents of the payment order received by the receiving bank and that contains the instructions necessary to implement the credit transfer in an appropriate manner.

(3) A receiving bank that determines that it is not feasible to follow an instruction of the sender specifying an intermediary bank or funds transfer system to be used in carrying out the credit transfer, or that following such an instruction would cause excessive costs or delay in completing the credit transfer, shall be taken to have complied with paragraph (2) if, before the end of the execution period, it inquires of the sender what further actions it should take.

(4) When an instruction is received that appears to be intended to be a payment order but does not contain sufficient data to be a payment order, or being a payment order it cannot be executed because of insufficient data, but the sender can be identified, the receiving bank shall give notice to the sender of the insufficiency, within the time required by article 11.

(5) When a receiving bank detects that there is an inconsistency in the information relating to the amount of money to be transferred, it shall, within the time required by article 11, give notice to the sender of the inconsistency, if the sender can be

identified. Any interest payable under article 17(4) for failing to give the notice required by this paragraph shall be deducted from any interest payable under article 17(1) for failing to comply with paragraph (2) of this article.

(6) For the purposes of this article, branches and separate offices of a bank, even if located in the same State, are separate banks.

Article 9
Acceptance or rejection of a payment order by beneficiary's bank

(1) The beneficiary's bank accepts a payment order at the earliest of the following times:

(a) when the bank receives the payment order, provided that the sender and the bank have agreed that the bank will execute payment orders from the sender upon receipt;

(b) when the bank gives notice to the sender of acceptance;

(c) when the bank debits an account of the sender with the bank as payment for the payment order;

(d) when the bank credits the beneficiary's account or otherwise places the funds at the disposal of the beneficiary;

(e) when the bank gives notice to the beneficiary that it has the right to withdraw the funds or use the credit;

(f) when the bank otherwise applies the credit as instructed in the payment order;

(g) when the bank applies the credit to a debt of the beneficiary owed to it or applies it in conformity with an order of a court or other competent authority; or

(h) when the time for giving notice of rejection under paragraph (2) has elapsed without notice having been given.

(2) A beneficiary's bank that does not accept a payment order is required to give notice of rejection no later than on the banking day following the end of the execution period, unless:

(a) where payment is to be made by debiting an account of the sender with the beneficiary's bank, there are insufficient funds available in the account to pay for the payment order;

(b) where payment is to be made by other means, payment has not been made; or

(c) there is insufficient information to identify the sender.

(3) A payment order ceases to have effect if it is neither accepted nor rejected under this article before the close of business on the fifth banking day following the end of the execution period.

Article 10
Obligations of beneficiary's bank

(1) The beneficiary's bank is, upon acceptance of a payment order, obligated to place the funds at the disposal of the beneficiary, or otherwise to apply the credit, in accordance with the payment order and the law governing the relationship between the bank and the beneficiary.

(2) When an instruction is received that appears to be intended to be a payment order but does not contain sufficient data to be a payment order, or being a payment order it cannot be executed because of insufficient data, but the sender can be identified, the

beneficiary's bank shall give notice to the sender of the insufficiency, within the time required by article 11.

(3) When the beneficiary's bank detects that there is an inconsistency in the information relating to the amount of money to be transferred, it shall, within the time required by article 11, give notice to the sender of the inconsistency if the sender can be identified.

(4) When the beneficiary's bank detects that there is an inconsistency in the information intended to identify the beneficiary, it shall, within the time required by article 11, give notice to the sender of the inconsistency if the sender can be identified.

(5) Unless the payment order states otherwise, the beneficiary's bank shall, within the time required for execution under article 11, give notice to a beneficiary who does not maintain an account at the bank that it is holding funds for its benefit, if the bank has sufficient information to give such notice.

Article 11
Time for receiving bank to execute payment order and give notices

(1) In principle, a receiving bank that is obligated to execute a payment order is obligated to do so on the banking day it is received. If it does not, it shall do so on the banking day after the order is received. Nevertheless, if
  (a) a later date is specified in the payment order, the payment order shall be executed on that date, or
  (b) the payment order specifies a date when the funds are to be placed at the disposal of the beneficiary and that date indicates that later execution is appropriate in order for the beneficiary's bank to accept a payment order and execute it on that date, the order shall be executed on that date.

(2) If the receiving bank executes the payment order on the banking day after it is received, except when complying with subparagraph (a) or (b) of paragraph (1), the receiving bank must execute for value as of the day of receipt.

(3) A receiving bank that becomes obligated to execute a payment order by virtue of accepting a payment order under article 7(2)(e) must execute for value as of the later of the day on which the payment order is received and the day on which
  (a) where payment is to be made by debiting an account of the sender with the receiving bank, there are sufficient funds available in the account to pay for the payment order, or
  (b) where payment is to be made by other means, payment has been made.

(4) A notice required to be given under article 8(4) or (5) or article 10(2), (3) or (4) shall be given on or before the banking day following the end of the execution period.

(5) A receiving bank that receives a payment order after the receiving bank's cut-off time for that type of payment order is entitled to treat the order as having been received on the next day the bank executes that type of payment order.

(6) If a receiving bank is required to perform an action on a day when it does not perform that type of action, it must perform the required action on the next day it performs that type of action.

(7) For the purposes of this article, branches and separate offices of a bank, even if located in the same State, are separate banks.

Article 12
Revocation

(1) A payment order may not be revoked by the sender unless the revocation order is received by a receiving bank other than the beneficiary's bank at a time and in a manner sufficient to afford the receiving bank a reasonable opportunity to act before the later of the actual time of execution and the beginning of the day on which the payment order ought to have been executed under subparagraph (a) or (b) of article 11(1).

(2) A payment order may not be revoked by the sender unless the revocation order is received by the beneficiary's bank at a time and in a manner sufficient to afford the bank a reasonable opportunity to act before the later of the time the credit transfer is completed and the beginning of the day when the funds are to be placed at the disposal of the beneficiary.

(3) Notwithstanding the provisions of paragraphs (1) and (2), the sender and the receiving bank may agree that payment orders issued by the sender to the receiving bank are to be irrevocable or that a revocation order is effective only if it is received earlier than the time specified in paragraph (1) or (2).

(4) A revocation order must be authenticated.

(5) A receiving bank other than the beneficiary's bank that executes, or a beneficiary's bank that accepts, a payment order in respect of which an effective revocation order has been or is subsequently received is not entitled to payment for that payment order. If the credit transfer is completed, the bank shall refund any payment received by it.

(6) If the recipient of a refund is not the originator of the credit transfer, it shall pass on the refund to its sender.

(7) A bank that is obligated to make a refund to its sender is discharged from that obligation to the extent that it makes the refund direct to a prior sender. Any bank subsequent to that prior sender is discharged to the same extent.

(8) An originator entitled to a refund under this article may recover from any bank obligated to make a refund hereunder to the extent that the bank has not previously refunded. A bank that is obligated to make a refund is discharged from that obligation to the extent that it makes the refund direct to the originator. Any other bank that is obligated is discharged to the same extent.

(9) Paragraphs (7) and (8) do not apply to a bank if they would affect the bank's rights or obligations under any agreement or any rule of a funds transfer system.

(10) If the credit transfer is completed but a receiving bank executes a payment order in respect of which an effective revocation order has been or is subsequently received, the receiving bank has such rights to recover from the beneficiary the amount of the credit transfer as may otherwise be provided by law.

(11) The death, insolvency, bankruptcy or incapacity of either the sender or the originator does not of itself operate to revoke a payment order or terminate the authority of the sender.

(12) The principles contained in this article apply to an amendment of a payment order.

(13) For the purposes of this article, branches and separate offices of a bank, even if located in the same State, are separate banks.

CHAPTER III
CONSEQUENCES OF FAILED, ERRONEOUS
OR DELAYED CREDIT TRANSFERS

Article 13
Assistance

Until the credit transfer is completed, each receiving bank is requested to assist the originator and each subsequent sending bank, and to seek the assistance of the next receiving bank, in completing the banking procedures of the credit transfer.

Article 14
Refund

(1) If the credit transfer is not completed, the originator's bank is obligated to refund to the originator any payment received from it, with interest from the day of payment to the day of refund. The originator's bank and each subsequent receiving bank is entitled to the return of any funds it has paid to its receiving bank, with interest from the day of payment to the day of refund.

(2) The provisions of paragraph (1) may not be varied by agreement except when a prudent originator's bank would not have otherwise accepted a particular payment order because of a significant risk involved in the credit transfer.

(3) A receiving bank is not required to make a refund under paragraph (1) if it is unable to obtain a refund because an intermediary bank through which it was directed to effect the credit transfer has suspended payment or is prevented by law from making the refund. A receiving bank is not considered to have been directed to use the intermediary bank unless the receiving bank proves that it does not systematically seek such directions in similar cases. The sender that first specified the use of that intermediary bank has the right to obtain the refund from the intermediary bank.

(4) A bank that is obligated to make a refund to its sender is discharged from that obligation to the extent that it makes the refund direct to a prior sender. Any bank subsequent to that prior sender is discharged to the same extent.

(5) An originator entitled to a refund under this article may recover from any bank obligated to make a refund hereunder to the extent that the bank has not previously refunded. A bank that is obligated to make a refund is discharged from that obligation to the extent that it makes the refund direct to the originator. Any other bank that is obligated is discharged to the same extent.

(6) Paragraphs (4) and (5) do not apply to a bank if they would affect the bank's rights or obligations under any agreement or any rule of a funds transfer system.

Article 15
Correction of underpayment

If the amount of the payment order executed by a receiving bank is less than the amount of the payment order it accepted, other than as a result of the deduction of its charges, it is obligated to issue a payment order for the difference.

Article 16
Restitution of overpayment

If the credit transfer is completed, but the amount of the payment order executed by a receiving bank is greater than the amount of the payment order it accepted, it has such rights to recover the difference from the beneficiary as may otherwise be provided by law.

Article 17
Liability for interest

(1) A receiving bank that does not comply with its obligations under article 8(2) is liable to the beneficiary if the credit transfer is completed. The liability of the receiving bank is to pay interest on the amount of the payment order for the period of delay caused by the receiving bank's non-compliance. If the delay concerns only part of the amount of the payment order, the liability shall be to pay interest on the amount that has been delayed.

(2) The liability of a receiving bank under paragraph (1) may be discharged by payment to its receiving bank or by direct payment to the beneficiary. If a receiving bank receives such payment but is not the beneficiary, the receiving bank shall pass on the benefit of the interest to the next receiving bank or, if it is the beneficiary's bank, to the beneficiary.

(3) An originator may recover the interest the beneficiary would have been entitled to, but did not, receive in accordance with paragraphs (1) and (2) to the extent the originator has paid interest to the beneficiary on account of a delay in the completion of the credit transfer. The originator's bank and each subsequent receiving bank that is not the bank liable under paragraph (1) may recover interest paid to its sender from its receiving bank or from the bank liable under paragraph (1).

(4) A receiving bank that does not give a notice required under article 8(4) or (5) shall pay interest to the sender on any payment that it has received from the sender under article 5(6) for the period during which it retains the payment.

(5) A beneficiary's bank that does not give a notice required under article 10(2), (3) or (4) shall pay interest to the sender on any payment that it has received from the sender under article 5(6), from the day of payment until the day that it provides the required notice.

(6) The beneficiary's bank is liable to the beneficiary to the extent provided by the law governing the relationship between the beneficiary and the bank for its failure to perform one of the obligations under article 10(1) or(5).

(7) The provisions of this article may be varied by agreement to the extent that the liability of one bank to another bank is increased or reduced. Such an agreement to reduce liability may be contained in a bank's standard terms of dealing. A bank may agree to increase its liability to an originator or beneficiary that is not a bank, but may not reduce its liability to such an originator or beneficiary. In particular, it may not reduce its liability by an agreement fixing the rate of interest.

Article 18
Exclusivity of remedies

The remedies in article 17 shall be exclusive, and no other remedy arising out of other doctrines of law shall be available in respect of non-compliance with articles 8 or 10, except any remedy that may exist when a bank has improperly executed, or failed to execute, a payment order (a) with the specific intent to cause loss, or (b) recklessly and with actual knowledge that loss would be likely to result.

CHAPTER IV
COMPLETION OF CREDIT TRANSFER

Article 19
Completion of credit transfer[3]

(1) A credit transfer is completed when the beneficiary's bank accepts a payment order for the benefit of the beneficiary. When the credit transfer is completed, the beneficiary's bank becomes indebted to the beneficiary to the extent of the payment order accepted by it. Completion does not otherwise affect the relationship between the beneficiary and the beneficiary's bank.

(2) A credit transfer is completed notwithstanding that the amount of the payment order accepted by the beneficiary's bank is less than the amount of the originator's payment order because one or more receiving banks have deducted charges. The completion of the credit transfer shall not prejudice any right of the beneficiary under the applicable law governing the underlying obligation to recover the amount of those charges from the originator.

---

[3] The Commission suggests the following text for States that might wish to adopt it:
   If a credit transfer was for the purpose of discharging an obligation of the originator to the beneficiary that can be discharged by credit transfer to the account indicated by the originator, the obligation is discharged when the beneficiary's bank accepts the payment order and to the extent that it would be discharged by payment of the same amount in cash.

(ii) ICC UNIFORM CUSTOMS & PRACTICE FOR DOCUMENTARY CREDITS (1993 REVISION—UCP 500)*

* ICC Publication No. 500–ISBN 92.842.1155.7. Published in its official English version by the International Chamber of Commerce. Copyright ©1993–International Chamber of Commerce (ICC), Paris.

A. GENERAL PROVISIONS AND DEFINITIONS

Article 1
Application of UCP

The Uniform Customs and Practice for Documentary Credits, 1993 Revision, ICC Publication No. 500, shall apply to all Documentary Credits (including to the extent to which they may be applicable, Standby Letter(s) of Credit) where they are incorporated into the text of the Credit. They are binding on all parties thereto, unless otherwise expressly stipulated in the Credit.

Article 2
Meaning of Credit

For the purposes of these Articles, the expressions 'Documentary Credit(s)' and 'Standby Letter(s) of Credit' (hereinafter referred to as 'Credit(s)'), mean any arrangement, however named or described, whereby a bank (the 'Issuing Bank') acting at the request and on the instructions of a customer (the 'Applicant') or on its own behalf,

   (i)   is to make a payment to or to the order of a third party (the 'Beneficiary'), or is to accept and pay bills of exchange (Draft(s)) drawn by the Beneficiary, or

  (ii) authorises another bank to effect such payment, or to accept and pay such bills of exchange (Draft(s)), or

 (iii) authorises another bank to negotiate,

against stipulated document(s),provided that the terms and conditions of the Credit are complied with.

For the purposes of these Articles, branches of a bank in different countries are considered another bank.

Article 3
Credits v. Contracts

(a) Credits, by their nature, are separate transactions from the sales or other contract(s) on which they may be based and banks are in no way concerned with or bound by such contract(s), even if any reference whatsoever to such contract(s) is included in the Credit. Consequently, the undertaking of a bank to pay, accept and pay Draft(s) or negotiate and/or to fulfil any other obligation under the Credit, is not subject to claims or defences by the Applicant resulting from his relationships with the Issuing Bank or the Beneficiary.

(b) A Beneficiary can in no case avail himself of the contractual relationships existing between the banks or between the Applicant and the Issuing Bank.

Article 4
Documents v. Goods/Services/Performances

In Credit operations all parties concerned deal with documents, and not with goods, services and/or other performances to which the documents may relate.

Article 5
Instructions to Issue/Amend Credits

(a) Instructions for the issuance of a Credit, the Credit itself, instructions for an amendment thereto, and the amendment itself, must be complete and precise.

In order to guard against confusion and misunderstanding, banks should discourage any attempt:

(i) to include excessive detail in the Credit or in any amendment thereto;

(ii) to give instructions to issue, advise or confirm a Credit by reference to a Credit previously issued (similar Credit) where such previous Credit has been subject to accepted amendment(s), and/or unaccepted amendment(s).

(b) All instructions for the issuance of a Credit and the Credit itself and, where applicable, all instructions for an amendment thereto and the amendment itself, must state precisely the document(s) against which payment, acceptance or negotiation is to be made.

B. FORM AND NOTIFICATION OF CREDITS

Article 6
Revocable v. Irrevocable Credits

(a) A Credit may be either
(i) revocable, or
(ii) irrevocable.

(b) The Credit, therefore, should clearly indicate whether it is revocable or irrevocable.

(c) In the absence of such indication the Credit shall be deemed to be irrevocable.

Article 7
Advising Bank's Liability

(a) A Credit may be advised to a Beneficiary through another bank (the 'Advising Bank') without engagement on the part of the Advising Bank, but that bank, if it elects to advise the Credit, shall take reasonable care to check the apparent authenticity of the Credit which it advises. If the bank elects not to advise the Credit, it must so inform the Issuing Bank without delay.

(b) If the Advising Bank cannot establish such apparent authenticity it must inform, without delay, the bank from which the instructions appear to have been received that it has been unable to establish the authenticity of the Credit and if it elects nonetheless to advise the Credit it must inform the Beneficiary that it has not been able to establish the authenticity of the Credit.

Article 8
Revocation of a Credit

(a) A revocable Credit may be amended or cancelled by the Issuing Bank at any moment and without prior notice to the Beneficiary.

(b) However, the Issuing Bank must:
  (i) reimburse another bank with which a revocable Credit has been made available for sight payment, acceptance or negotiation—for any payment, acceptance or negotiation made by such bank—prior to receipt by it of notice of amendment or cancellation, against documents which appear on their face to be in compliance with the terms and conditions of the Credit;
  (ii) reimburse another bank with which a revocable Credit has been made available for deferred payment, if such a bank has, prior to receipt by it of notice of amendment or cancellation, taken up documents which appear on their face to be in compliance with the terms and conditions of the Credit.

Article 9
Liability of Issuing and Confirming Banks

(a) An irrevocable Credit constitutes a definite undertaking of the Issuing Bank, provided that the stipulated documents are presented to the Nominated Bank or to the Issuing Bank and that the terms and conditions of the Credit are complied with:
  (i) If the Credit provides for sight payment—to pay at sight;
  (ii) If the Credit provides for deferred payment to pay on the maturity date(s) determinable in accordance with the stipulations of the Credit;
  (iii) If the Credit provides for acceptance:
    (a) by the Issuing Bank—to accept Draft(s) drawn by the Beneficiary on the Issuing Bank and pay them at maturity, or
    (b) by another drawee bank—to accept and pay at maturity Draft(s) drawn by the Beneficiary on the Issuing Bank in the event the drawee bank stipulated in the Credit does not accept Draft(s) drawn on it, or to pay Draft(s) accepted but not paid by such drawee bank at maturity;
  (iv) if the Credit provides for negotiation—to pay without recourse to drawers and/ or bona fide holders, Draft(s) drawn by the Beneficiary and/or document(s) presented under the Credit. A Credit should not be issued available by Draft(s) on the Applicant. If the Credit nevertheless calls for Draft(s) on the Applicant, banks will consider such Draft(s) as an additional document(s).
(b) A confirmation of an irrevocable Credit by another bank (the 'Confirming Bank') upon the authorisation or request of the Issuing Bank, constitutes a definite undertaking of the Confirming Bank, in addition to that of the Issuing Bank, provided that the stipulated documents are presented to the Confirming Bank or to any other Nominated Bank and that the terms and conditions of the Credit are complied with:
  (i) if the Credit provides for sight payment—to pay at sight;
  (ii) if the Credit provides for deferred payment—to pay on the maturity date(s) determinable in accordance with the stipulations of the Credit;
  (iii) if the Credit provides for acceptance:
    (a) by the Confirming Bank—to accept Draft(s) drawn by the Beneficiary on the Confirming Bank and pay them at maturity, or
    (b) by another drawee bank—to accept and pay at maturity Draft(s) drawn by the Beneficiary on the Confirming Bank, in the event the drawee bank stipulated in the Credit does not accept Draft(s) drawn on it, or to pay Draft(s) accepted but not paid by such drawee bank at maturity;

(iv) if the Credit provides for negotiation—to negotiate without recourse to drawers and/or bona fide holders, Draft(s) drawn by the Beneficiary and/or document(s) presented under the Credit. A Credit should not be issued available by Draft(s) on the Applicant. If the Credit nevertheless calls for Draft(s) on the Applicant, banks will consider such Draft(s) as an additional document(s).

(c) (i) If another bank is authorised or requested by the Issuing Bank to add its confirmation to a Credit but is not prepared to do so, it must so inform the Issuing Bank without delay.

(ii) Unless the Issuing Bank specifies otherwise in its authorisation or request to add confirmation, the Advising Bank may advise the Credit to the Beneficiary without adding its confirmation.

(d) (i) Except as otherwise provided by Article 48, an irrevocable Credit can neither be amended nor cancelled without the agreement of the Issuing Bank, the Confirming Bank, if any, and the Beneficiary.

(ii) The Issuing Bank shall be irrevocably bound by an amendment(s) issued by it from the time of the issuance of such amendment(s). A Confirming Bank may extend its confirmation to an amendment and shall be irrevocably bound as of the time of its advice of the amendment. A Confirming Bank may, however, choose to advise an amendment to the Beneficiary without extending its confirmation and if so, must inform the Issuing Bank and the Beneficiary without delay.

(iii) The terms of the original Credit (or a Credit incorporating previously accepted amendment(s)) will remain in force for the Beneficiary until the Beneficiary communicates his acceptance of the amendment to the bank that advised such amendment. The Beneficiary should give notification of acceptance or rejection of amendment(s). If the Beneficiary fails to give such notification, the tender of documents to the Nominated Bank or Issuing Bank, that conform to the Credit and to not yet accepted amendment(s), will be deemed to be notification of acceptance by the Beneficiary of such amendment(s) and as of that moment the Credit will be amended.

(iv) Partial acceptance of amendments contained in one and the same advice of amendment is not allowed and consequently will not be given any effect.

Article 10
Types of Credit

(a) All Credits must clearly indicate whether they are available by sight payment, by deferred payment, by acceptance or by negotiation.

(b) (i) Unless the Credit stipulates that it is available only with the Issuing Bank, all Credits must nominate the bank (the 'Nominated Bank') which is authorised to pay, to incur a deferred payment undertaking, to accept Draft(s) or to negotiate. In a freely negotiable Credit, any bank is a Nominated Bank.
Presentation of documents must be made to the Issuing Bank or the Confirming Bank, if any, or any other Nominated Bank.

(ii) Negotiation means the giving of value for Draft(s) and/or document(s) by the bank authorised to negotiate. Mere examination of the documents without giving of value does not constitute a negotiation.

(c) Unless the Nominated Bank is the Confirming Bank, nomination by the Issuing Bank does not constitute any undertaking by the Nominated Bank to pay, to incur a deferred payment undertaking, to accept Draft(s), or to negotiate. Except where expressly agreed to by the Nominated Bank and so communicated to the Beneficiary, the Nominated Bank's receipt of and/or examination and/or forwarding of the documents does not make that bank liable to pay, to incur a deferred payment undertaking, to accept Draft(s), or to negotiate.

(d) By nominating another bank, or by allowing for negotiation by any bank, or by authorising or requesting another bank to add its confirmation, the Issuing Bank authorises such bank to pay, accept Draft(s) or negotiate as the case may be, against documents which appear on their face to be in compliance with the terms and conditions of the Credit and undertakes to reimburse such bank in accordance with the provisions of these Articles.

Article 11
Teletransmitted and Pre-Advised Credits

(a) (i) When an Issuing Bank instructs an Advising Bank by an authenticated teletransmission to advise a Credit or an amendment to a Credit, the teletransmission will be deemed to be the operative Credit instrument or the operative amendment, and no mail confirmation should be sent. Should a mail confirmation nevertheless be sent, it will have no effect and the Advising Bank will have no obligation to check such mail confirmation against the operative Credit instrument or the operative amendment received by teletransmission.

(ii) If the teletransmission states full details to follow (or words of similar effect) or states that the mail confirmation is to be the operative Credit instrument or the operative amendment, then the teletransmission will not be deemed to be the operative Credit instrument or the operative amendment. The Issuing Bank must forward the operative Credit instrument or the operative amendment to such Advising Bank without delay.

(b) If a bank uses the services of an Advising Bank to have the Credit advised to the Beneficiary, it must also use the services of the same bank for advising an amendment(s).

(c) A preliminary advice of the issuance or amendment of an irrevocable Credit (pre-advice), shall only be given by an Issuing Bank if such bank is prepared to issue the operative Credit instrument or the operative amendment thereto. Unless otherwise stated in such preliminary advice by the Issuing Bank, an Issuing Bank having given such pre-advice shall be irrevocably committed to issue or amend the Credit, in terms not inconsistent with the pre-advice, without delay.

Article 12
Incomplete or Unclear Instructions

If incomplete or unclear instructions are received to advise, confirm or amend a Credit, the bank requested to act on such instructions may give preliminary notification to the Beneficiary for information only and without responsibility. This preliminary notification should state clearly that the notification is provided for information only and without the responsibility of the Advising Bank. In any event, the Advising Bank must inform the Issuing Bank of the action taken and request it to provide the necessary information.

The Issuing Bank must provide the necessary information without delay. The Credit will be advised, confirmed or amended, only when complete and clear instructions have been received and if the Advising Bank is then prepared to act on the instructions.

C. LIABILITIES AND RESPONSIBILITIES

Article 13
Standard for Examination of Documents

(a) Banks must examine all documents stipulated in the Credit with reasonable care, to ascertain whether or not they appear, on their face, to be in compliance with the terms and conditions of the Credit. Compliance of the stipulated documents on their face with the terms and conditions of the Credit, shall be determined by international standard banking practice as reflected in these Articles. Documents which appear on their face to be inconsistent with one another will be considered as not appearing on their face to be in compliance with the terms and conditions of the Credit.

Documents not stipulated in the Credit will not be examined by banks. If they receive such documents, they shall return them to the presenter or pass them on without responsibility.

(b) The Issuing Bank, the Confirming Bank, if any, or a Nominated Bank acting on their behalf, shall each have a reasonable time, not to exceed seven banking days following the day of receipt of the documents, to examine the documents and determine whether to take up or refuse the documents and to inform the party from which it received the documents accordingly.

(c) If a Credit contains conditions without stating the document(s) to be presented in compliance therewith, banks will deem such conditions as not stated and will disregard them.

Article 14
Discrepant Documents and Notice

(a) When the Issuing Bank authorises another bank to pay, incur a deferred payment undertaking, accept Draft(s), or negotiate against documents which appear on their face to be in compliance with the terms and conditions of the Credit, the Issuing Bank and the Confirming Bank, if any, are bound:
 (i) to reimburse the Nominated Bank which has paid, incurred a deferred payment undertaking, accepted Draft(s), or negotiated,
 (ii) to take up the documents.

(b) Upon receipt of the documents the Issuing Bank and /or Confirming Bank, if any, or a Nominated Bank acting on their behalf, must determine on the basis of the documents alone whether or not they appear on their face to be in compliance with the terms and conditions of the Credit. If the documents appear on their face not to be in compliance with the terms and conditions of the Credit, such banks may refuse to take up the documents.

(c) If the Issuing Bank determines that the documents appear on their face not to be in compliance with the terms and conditions of the Credit, it may in its sole judgment approach the Applicant for a waiver of the discrepancy(ies). This does not, however, extend the period mentioned in sub-Article 13 (b).

(d) (i) If the Issuing Bank and/or Confirming Bank, if any, or a Nominated Bank acting on their behalf, decides to refuse the documents, it must give notice to that effect by telecommunication or, if that is not possible, by other expeditious means, without delay but no later than the close of the seventh banking day following the day of receipt of the documents. Such notice shall be given to the bank from which it received the documents, or to the Beneficiary, if it received the documents directly from him.

(ii) Such notice must state all discrepancies in respect of which the bank refuses the documents and must also state whether it is holding the documents at the disposal of, or is returning them to, the presenter.

(iii) The Issuing Bank and/or Confirming Bank, if any, shall then be entitled to claim from the remitting bank refund, with interest, of any reimbursement which has been made to that bank.

(e) If the Issuing Bank and/or Confirming Bank, if any, fails to act in accordance with the provisions of this Article and/or fails to hold the documents at the disposal of, or return them to the presenter, the Issuing Bank and/or Confirming Bank, if any, shall be precluded from Claiming that the documents are not in compliance with the terms and conditions of the Credit.

(f) If the remitting bank draws the attention of the Issuing Bank and/or Confirming Bank, if any, to any discrepancy(ies) in the document(s) or advises such banks that it has paid, incurred a deferred payment undertaking, accepted Draft(s) or negotiated under reserve or against an indemnity in respect of such discrepancy(ies), the Issuing Bank and/or Confirming Bank, if any, shall not be thereby relieved from any of their obligations under any provision of this Article. Such reserve or indemnity concerns only the relations between the remitting bank and the party towards whom the reserve was made, or from whom, or on whose behalf, the indemnity was obtained.

Article 15
Disclaimer on Effectiveness of Documents

Banks assume no liability or responsibility for the form, sufficiency, accuracy, genuineness, falsification or legal effect of any document(s), or for the general and/or particular conditions stipulated in the document(s) or superimposed thereon; nor do they assume any liability or responsibility for the description, quantity, weight, quality, condition, packing, delivery, value or existence of the goods represented by any document(s), or for the good faith or acts and/or omissions, solvency, performance or standing of the consignors, the carriers, the forwarders, the consignees or the insurers of the goods, or any other person whomsoever.

Article 16
Disclaimer on the Transmission of Messages

Banks assume no liability or responsibility for the consequences arising out of delay and/or loss in transit of any message(s), letter(s) or document(s), or for delay, mutilation or other error(s) arising in the transmission of any telecommunication. Banks assume no liability or responsibility for errors in translation and/or interpretation of technical terms, and reserve the right to transmit Credit terms without translating them.

Article 17
Force Majeure

Banks assume no liability or responsibility for the consequences arising out of the interruption of their business by Acts of God, riots, civil commotions, insurrections, wars or any other causes beyond their control, or by any strikes or lockouts. Unless specifically authorised, banks will not, upon resumption of their business, pay, incur a deferred payment undertaking, accept Draft(s) or negotiate under Credits which expired during such interruption of their business.

Article 18
Disclaimer for Acts of an Instructed Party

(a) Banks utilizing the services of another bank or other banks for the purpose of giving effect to the instructions of the Applicant do so for the account and at the risk of such Applicant.

(b) Banks assume no liability or responsibility should the instructions they transmit not be carried out, even if they have themselves taken the initiative in the choice of such other bank(s).

(c) (i) A party instructing another party to perform services is liable for any charges, including commissions, fees, costs or expenses incurred by the instructed party in connection with its instructions

    (ii) Where a Credit stipulates that such charges are, for the account of a party other than the instructing party, and charges cannot be collected, the instructing party remains ultimately liable for the payment thereof.

(d) The Applicant shall be bound by and liable to indemnify the banks against all obligations and responsibilities imposed by foreign laws and usages.

Article 19
Bank-to-Bank Reimbursement Arrangements

(a) If an Issuing Bank intends that the reimbursement to which a paying, accepting or negotiating bank is entitled, shall be obtained by such bank (the 'Claiming Bank'), claiming on another party (the 'Reimbursing Bank'), it shall provide such Reimbursing Bank in good time with the proper instructions or authorisation to honour such reimbursement claims.

(b) Issuing Banks shall not require a Claiming Bank to supply a certificate of compliance with the terms and conditions of the Credit to the Reimbursing Bank.

(c) An Issuing Bank shall not be relieved from any of its obligations to provide reimbursement if and when reimbursement is not received by the Claiming Bank from the Reimbursing Bank.

(d) The Issuing Bank shall be responsible to the Claiming Bank for any loss of interest if reimbursement is not provided by the Reimbursing Bank on first demand, or as otherwise specified in the Credit, or mutually agreed, as the case may be.

(e) The Reimbursing Bank's charges should be for the account of the Issuing Bank. However, in cases where the charges are for the account of another party, it is the responsibility of the Issuing Bank to so indicate in the original Credit and in the reimbursement authorisation. In cases where the Reimbursing Bank's Charges are for the account of another party they shall be collected from the Claiming Bank when the

Credit is drawn under. In cases where the Credit is not drawn under, the Reimbursing Bank's charges remain the obligation of the Issuing Bank.

D. DOCUMENTS

Article 20
Ambiguity as to the Issuers of Documents

(a) Terms such as 'first class', 'well known', 'qualified', 'independent', 'official', 'competent', 'local' and the like, shall not be used to describe the issuers of any document(s) to be presented under a Credit. If such terms are incorporated in the Credit, banks will accept the relative document(s) as presented, provided that it appears on its face to be in compliance with the other terms and conditions of the Credit and not to have been issued by the Beneficiary.

(b) Unless otherwise stipulated in the Credit, banks will also accept as an original document(s), a document(s) produced or appearing to have been produced:
  (i) by reprographic, automated or computerized systems;
  (ii) as carbon copies;
     provided that it is marked as original and, where necessary, appears to be signed. A document may be signed by handwriting, by facsimile signature, by perforated signature, by stamp, by symbol, or by any other mechanical or electronic method of authentication.

(c) (i) Unless otherwise stipulated in the Credit, banks will accept as a copy(ies) a document(s) either labelled copy or not marked as an original—a copy(ies) need not be signed.
  (ii) Credits that require multiple document(s) such as 'duplicate', 'two fold', 'two Copies' and the like, will be satisfied by the presentation of one original and the remaining number in copies except where the document itself indicates otherwise.

(d) Unless otherwise stipulated in the Credit, a condition under a Credit calling for a document to be authenticated, validated, legalised, visaed, certified or indicating a similar requirement, will be satisfied by any signature, mark, stamp or label on such document that on its face appears to satisfy the above condition.

Article 21
Unspecified Issuers or Contents of Documents

When documents other than transport documents, insurance documents and commercial invoices are called for, the Credit should stipulate by whom such documents are to be issued and their wording or data content. If the Credit does not so stipulate, banks will accept such documents as presented, provided that their data content is not inconsistent with any other stipulated document presented.

Article 22
Issuance Date of Documents v. Credit Date

Unless otherwise stipulated in the Credit, banks will accept a document bearing a date of issuance prior to that of the Credit, subject to such document being presented within the time limits set out in the Credit and in these Articles.

Article 23
Marine/Ocean Bill of Lading

(a) If a Credit calls for a bill of lading covering a port-to-port shipment, banks will, unless otherwise stipulated in the Credit, accept a document, however named, which:

   (i) appears on its face to indicate the name of the carrier and to have been signed or otherwise authenticated by:

   —the carrier or a named agent for or on behalf of the carrier, or

   —the master or a named agent for or on behalf of the master.

   Any signature or authentication of the carrier or master must be identified carrier or master, as the case may be. An agent signing or authenticating for the carrier or master must also indicate the name and the capacity of the party, i.e. carrier or master, on whose behalf that agent is acting,

   and

   (ii) indicates that the goods have been loaded on board, or shipped on a named vessel.

   Loading on board or shipment on a named vessel may be indicated by pre-printed wording on the bill of lading that the goods have been loaded on board a named vessel or shipped on a named vessel, in which case the date of issuance of the bill of lading will be deemed to be the date of loading on board and the date of shipment.

   In all other cases loading on board a named vessel must be evidenced by a notation on the bill of lading which gives the date on which the goods have been loaded on board, in which case the date of the on board notation will be deemed to be the date of shipment.

   If the bill of lading contains the indication 'intended vessel', or similar qualification in relation to the vessel, loading on board a named vessel must be evidenced by an on board notation on the bill of lading which, in addition to the date on which the goods have been loaded on board, also includes the name of the vessel on which the goods have been loaded, even if they have been loaded on the vessel named as the 'intended vessel'.

   If the bill of lading indicates a place of receipt or taking in charge different from the port of loading, the on board notation must also include the port of loading stipulated in the Credit and the name of the vessel on which the goods have been loaded, even if they have been loaded on the vessel named in the bill of lading. This provision also applies whenever loading on board the vessel is indicated by pre-printed wording on the bill of lading, and

   (iii) indicates the port of loading and the port of discharge stipulated in the Credit, notwithstanding that it:

   (a) indicates a place of taking in charge different from the port of loading, and/or a place of final destination different from the port of discharge, and/or

   (b) contains the indication 'intended' or similar qualification in relation to the port of loading and/or port of discharge, as long as the document also states the ports of loading and/or discharge stipulated in the Credit, and

   (iv) consists of a sole original bill of lading or, if issued in more than one original, the full set as so issued, and

   (v) appears to contain all of the terms and conditions of carriage, or some of such terms and conditions by reference to a source or document other than the bill of lading (short form/ blank back bill of lading); banks will not examine the contents of such terms and conditions, and

(vi) contains no indication that it is subject to a charter party and/or no indication that the carrying vessel is propelled by sail only,

(vii) in all other respects meets the stipulations of the Credit.

(b) For the purpose of this Article, transhipment means unloading and reloading from one vessel to another vessel during the course of ocean carriage from the port of loading to the port of discharge stipulated in the Credit.

(c) Unless transhipment is prohibited by the terms of the Credit, banks will accept a bill of lading which indicates that the goods will be transhipped, provided that the entire ocean carriage is covered by one and the same bill of lading.

(d) Even if the Credit prohibits transhipment, banks will accept a bill of lading which:

(i) indicates that transhipment will take place as long as the relevant cargo is shipped in Container(s), Trailer(s) and/or 'LASH' barge(s) as evidenced by the bill of lading, provided that the entire ocean carriage is covered by one and the same bill of lading, and/or

(ii) incorporates clauses stating that the carrier reserves the right to tranship.

Article 24
Non-Negotiable Sea Waybill

(a) If a Credit calls for a non-negotiable sea waybill covering a port-to-port shipment, banks will, unless otherwise stipulated in the Credit, accept a document, however named, which:

(i) appears on its face to indicate the name of the carrier and to have been signed or otherwise authenticated by:
—the carrier or a named agent for or on behalf of the carrier, or
—the master or a named agent for or on behalf of the master,
Any signature or authentication of the carrier or master must be identified as carrier or master, as the case may be. An agent signing or authenticating for the carrier or master must also indicate the name and the capacity of the party, i.e. carrier or master, on whose behalf that agent is acting, and

(ii) indicates that the goods have been loaded on board, or shipped on a named vessel.

Loading on board or shipment on a named vessel may be indicated by pre-printed wording on the non-negotiable sea waybill that the goods have been loaded on board a named vessel or shipped on a named vessel, in which case the date of issuance of the non-negotiable sea waybill will be deemed to be the date of loading on board and the date of shipment.

In all other cases loading on board a named vessel must be evidenced by a notation on the non-negotiable sea waybill which gives the date on which the goods have been loaded on board, in which case the date of the on board notation will be deemed to be the date of shipment.

If the non-negotiable sea waybill contains the indication 'intended vessel', or similar qualification in relation to the vessel, loading on board a named vessel must be evidenced by an on board notation on the non-negotiable sea waybill which, in addition to the date on which the goods have been loaded on board, includes the name of the vessel on which the goods have been loaded, even if they have been loaded on the vessel named as the 'intended vessel'.

If the non-negotiable sea waybill indicates a place of receipt or taking in charge different from the port of loading, the on board notation must also include the port of loading stipulated in the Credit and the name of the vessel on which the goods have been loaded, even if they have been loaded on a vessel named in the non-negotiable sea waybill. This provision also applies whenever loading on board the vessel is indicated by pre-printed wording on the non-negotiable sea waybill, and

(iii) indicates the port of loading and the port of discharge stipulated in the Credit, notwithstanding that it:

    (a) indicates a place of taking in charge different from the port of loading, and/or a place of final destination different from the port of discharge, and/or

    (b) contains the indication 'intended' or similar qualification in relation to the port of loading and/or port of discharge, as long as the document also states the ports of loading and/or discharge stipulated in the Credit, and

(iv) consists of a sole original non-negotiable sea waybill, or if issued in more than one original, the full set as so issued, and

(v) appears to contain all or the terms and conditions of carriage, or some of such terms and conditions by reference to a source or document other than the non-negotiable sea waybill (short form/blank back non-negotiable sea waybill); banks will not examine the contents of such terms and conditions, and

(vi) contains no indication that it is subject to a charter party and/or no indication that the carrying vessel is propelled by sail only, and

(vii) in all other respects meets the stipulations of the Credit.

(b) For the purpose of this Article, transhipment means unloading and reloading from one vessel to another vessel during the course of ocean carriage from the port of loading to the port of discharge stipulated in the Credit.

(c) Unless transhipment is prohibited by the terms of the Credit, banks will accept a non-negotiable sea waybill which indicates that the goods will be transhipped, provided that the entire ocean carriage is covered by one and the same non-negotiable sea waybill.

(d) Even if the Credit prohibits transhipment, banks will accept a non-negotiable sea waybill which:

(i) indicates that transhipment will take place as long as the relevant cargo is shipped in Container(s), Trailer(s) and/or 'LASH' barge(s) as evidenced by the non-negotiable sea waybill, provided that the entire ocean carriage is covered by one and the same non-negotiable sea waybill, and/or

(ii) incorporates clauses stating that the carrier reserves the right to tranship.

Article 25
Charter Party Bill of Lading

(a) If a Credit calls for or permits a charter party bill of lading, banks will, unless otherwise stipulated in the Credit, accept a document, however named, which:

(i) contains any indication that it is subject to a charter party, and

(ii) appears on its face to have been signed or otherwise authenticated by:

    —the master or a named agent for or on behalf of the master, or

—the owner or a named agent for or on behalf of the owner.

Any signature or authentication of the master or owner must be identified as master or owner as the case may be. An agent signing or authenticating for the master or owner must also indicate the name and the capacity of the party, i.e. master or owner, on whose behalf that agent is acting, and

(iii) does or does not indicate the name of the Carrier, and

(iv) indicates that the goods have been loaded on board or shipped on a named vessel. Loading on board or shipment on a named vessel may be indicated by pre-printed wording on the bill of lading that the goods have been loaded on board a named vessel or shipped on a named vessel, in which case the date of issuance of the bill of lading will be deemed to be the date of loading on board and the date of shipment.

In all other cases loading on board a named vessel must be evidenced by a notation on the bill of lading which gives the date on which the goods have been loaded on board, in which case the date of the on board notation will be deemed to be the date of shipment, and

(v) indicates the port of loading and the port of discharge stipulated in the Credit, and

(vi) consists of a sole original bill of lading or, if issued in more than one original, the full set as so issued, and

(vii) contains no indication that the carrying vessel is propelled by sail only, and

(viii) in all other respects meets the stipulations of the Credit.

(b) Even if the Credit requires the presentation of a charter party contract in connection with a charter party bill of lading, banks will not examine such charter party contract, but will pass it on without responsibility on their part.

Article 26
Multimodal Transport Document

(a) If a Credit calls for a transport document Covering at least two different modes of transport (multimodal transport), banks will, unless otherwise stipulated in the Credit, accept a document, however named, which:

(i) appears on its face to indicate the name of the carrier or multimodal transport operator and to have been signed or otherwise authenticated by:

—the carrier or multimodal transport operator or a named agent for or on behalf of the carrier or multimodal transport operator, or

—the master or a named agent for or on behalf of the master.

Any signature or authentication of the carrier, multimodal transport operator or master must be identified as carrier, multimodal transport operator or master, as the case may be. An agent signing or authenticating for the carrier, multimodal transport operator or master must also indicate the name and the capacity of the party, i.e. carrier, multimodal transport operator or master, on whose behalf that agent is acting,

(ii) indicates that the goods have been dispatched, taken in charge or loaded on board.

Dispatch, taking in charge or loading on board may be indicated by wording to that effect on the multimodal transport document and the date of issuance will be deemed to be the date of dispatch, taking in charge or loading on board and the date of shipment. However, if the document indicates, by stamp or otherwise, a date of dispatch, taking in charge or loading on board, such date will be deemed to be the date of shipment, and

(iii) (a) indicates the place of taking in charge stipulated in the Credit which may be different from the port, airport or place of loading, and the place of final destination stipulated in the Credit which may be different from the port, airport or place of discharge, and/or

(b) contains the indication 'intended' or similar qualification in relation to the vessel and/or port of loading and/or port of discharge, and

(iv) consists of a sole original multimodal transport document or, if issued in more than one original, the full set as so issued, and

(v) appears to contain all of the terms and conditions of carriage, or some of such terms and conditions by reference to a source or document other than the multimodal transport document (short form/blank back multimodal transport document); banks will not examine the contents of such terms and conditions, and

(vi) contains no indication that it is subject to a charter party and/or no indication that the carrying vessel is propelled by sail only, and

(vii) in all other respects meets the stipulations of the Credit.

(b) Even if the Credit prohibits transhipment, banks will accept a multimodal transport document which indicates that transhipment will or may take place, provided that the entire carriage is covered by one and the same multimodal transport document.

Article 27
Air Transport Document

(a) If a Credit calls for an air transport document, banks will, unless otherwise stipulated in the Credit, accept a document, however named, which:

(i) appears on its face to indicate the name of the carrier and to have been signed or otherwise authenticated by:

(ii) indicates that the goods have been accepted for carriage, and
—the carrier, or
—a named agent for or on behalf of the carrier.

Any signature or authentication of the carrier must be identified as carrier. An agent signing or authenticating for the carrier must also indicate the name and the capacity of the party, i.e. carrier, on whose behalf that agent is acting, and

(iii) where the Credit calls for an actual date of dispatch, indicates a specific notation of such date, the date of dispatch so indicated on the airtransport document will be deemed to be the date of shipment.

For the purpose of this Article, the information appearing in the box on the air transport document (marked 'For Carrier Use Only' or similar expression) relative to the flight number and date will not be considered as a specific notation of such date of dispatch.

In all other cases, the date of issuance of the air transport document will be deemed to be the date of shipment, and

(iv) indicates the airport of departure and the airport of destination stipulated in the Credit, and

(v) appears to be the original for consignor/shipper even if the Credit stipulates a full set of originals, or similar expressions, and

(vi) appears to contain all of the terms and conditions of carriage, or some of such terms and Conditions, by reference to a source or document other than the air transport document; banks will not examine the contents of such terms and conditions, and

(vii) in all other respects meets the stipulations of the Credit.

(b) For the purpose of this Article, transhipment means unloading and reloading from one aircraft to another aircraft during the course of carriage from the airport of departure to the airport of destination stipulated in the Credit.

(c) Even if the Credit prohibits transhipment, banks will accept an air transport document which indicates that transhipment will or may take place, provided that the entire carriage is covered by one and the same air transport document

Article 28
Road, Rail or Inland Waterway Transport Documents

(a) If a Credit calls for a road, rail, or inland waterway transport document, banks will, unless otherwise stipulated in the Credit, accept a document of the type called for, however named, which:

(i) appears on its face to indicate the name of the carrier and to have been signed or otherwise authenticated by the carrier or a named agent for or on behalf of the carrier and/or to bear a reception stamp or other indication of receipt by the carrier or a named agent for or on behalf of the carrier.

Any signature, authentication, reception stamp or other indication of receipt of the carrier, must be identified on its face as that of the carrier. An agent signing or authenticating for the carrier, must also indicate the name and the capacity of the party, i.e. carrier, on whose behalf that agent is acting, and

(ii) indicates that the goods have been received for shipment, dispatch or carriage or wording to this effect. The date of issuance will be deemed to be the date of shipment unless the transport document Contains a reception stamp, in which case the date of the reception stamp will be deemed to be the date of shipment, and

(iii) indicates the place of shipment and the place of destination stipulated in the Credit, and

(iv) in all other respects meets the stipulations of the Credit.

(b) In the absence of any indication on the transport document as to the numbers issued, banks will accept the transport document(s) presented as constituting a full set. Banks will accept as original(s) the transport document(s) whether marked as original(s) or not.

(c) For the purpose of this Article, transhipment means unloading and reloading from one means of conveyance to another means of Conveyance, in different modes of transport, during the course of Carriage from the place of shipment to the place of destination stipulated in the Credit.

(d) Even if the Credit prohibits transhipment, banks will accept a road, rail, or inland waterway transport document which indicates that transhipment will or may take place, provided that the entire carriage is covered by one and the same transport document and within the same mode of transport.

Article 29
Courier and Post Receipts

(a) If a Credit calls for a post receipt or certificate of posting, banks will, unless otherwise stipulated in the Credit, accept a post receipt or certificate of posting which:

    (i) appears on its face to have been stamped or otherwise authenticated and dated in the place from which the Credit stipulates the goods are to be shipped or dispatched and such date will be deemed to be the date of shipment or dispatch, and

    (ii) in all other respects meets the stipulations of the Credit.

(b) If a Credit calls for a document issued by a courier or expedited delivery service evidencing receipt of the goods for delivery, banks will, unless otherwise stipulated in the Credit, accept a document, however named, which:

    (i) appears on its face to indicate the name of the courier/service, and to have been stamped, signed or otherwise authenticated by such named Courier/ service (unless the Credit specifically calls for a document issued by a named Courier/Service, banks will accept a document issued by any Courier/ Service), and

    (ii) indicates a date of pick-up or of receipt or wording to this effect, such date being deemed to be the date of shipment or dispatch, and

    (iii) in all other respects meets the stipulations of the Credit.

Article 30
Transport Documents issued by Freight Forwarders

Unless otherwise authorised in the Credit, banks will only accept a transport document issued by a freight forwarder if it appears on its face to indicate:

(i) the name of the freight forwarder as a carrier or multimodal transport operator and to have been signed or otherwise authenticated by the freight forwarder as carrier or multimodal transport operator, or

(ii) the name of the carrier or multimodal transport operator and to have been signed or otherwise authenticated by the freight forwarder as a named agent for or on behalf of the carrier or multimodal transport operator.

Article 31
'On Deck', 'Shipper's Load and Count', Name of Consignor

Unless otherwise stipulated in the Credit, banks will accept a transport document which:

(i) does not indicate, in the case of carriage by sea or by more than one means of conveyance including carriage by sea, that the goods are or will be loaded on deck. Nevertheless, banks will accept a transport document which contains a provision that the goods may be carried on deck, provided that it does not specifically state that they are or will be loaded on deck, and/or

(ii) bears a clause on the face thereof such as 'shipper's load and count' or 'said by shipper to contain' or words of similar effect, and/or

(iii) indicates as the consignor of the goods a party other than the Beneficiary of the Credit.

Article 32
Clean Transport Documents

(a) A clean transport document is one which bears no clause or notation which expressly declares a defective condition of the goods and/or the packaging.

(b) Banks will not accept transport documents bearing such clauses or notations unless the Credit expressly stipulates the clauses or notations which may be accepted.

(c) Banks will regard a requirement in a Credit for a transport document to bear the clause 'clean on board' as complied with if such transport document meets the requirements of this Article and of Articles 23, 24, 25, 26, 27, 28 or 30.

Article 33
Freight Payable/prepaid Transport Documents

(a) Unless otherwise stipulated in the Credit, or inconsistent with any of the documents presented under the Credit, banks will accept transport documents stating that freight or transportation charges (hereafter referred to as 'freight') have still to be paid.

(b) If a Credit stipulates that the transport document has to indicate that freight has been paid or prepaid, banks will accept a transport document on which words clearly indicating payment or prepayment of freight appear by stamp or otherwise, or on which payment or prepayment of freight is indicated by other means. If the Credit requires courier charges to be paid or prepaid banks will also accept a transport document issued by a courier or expedited delivery service evidencing that courier charges are for the account of a party other than the consignee.

(c) The words 'freight prepayable' or 'freight to be prepaid' or words of similar effect, if appearing on transport documents, will not be accepted as constituting evidence of the payment of freight.

(d) Banks will accept transport documents bearing reference by stamp or otherwise to costs additional to the freight, such as costs of, or disbursements incurred in connection with, loading, unloading or similar operations, unless the conditions of the Credit specifically prohibit such reference.

Article 34
Insurance Documents

(a) Insurance documents must appear on their face to be issued and signed by insurance companies or underwriters or their agents.

(b) If the insurance document indicates that it has been issued in more than one original, all the originals must be presented unless otherwise authorised in the Credit.

(c) Cover notes issued by brokers will not be accepted, unless specifically authorised in the Credit.

(d) Unless otherwise stipulated in the Credit, banks will accept an insurance certificate or a declaration under an open cover pre-signed by insurance companies or underwriters or their agents. If a Credit specifically calls for an insurance certificate or a declaration under an open cover, banks will accept, in lieu thereof, an insurance policy.

(e) Unless otherwise stipulated in the Credit, or unless it appears from the insurance document that the cover is effective at the latest from the date of loading on board or dispatch or taking in charge of the goods, banks will not accept an insurance document which bears a date of issuance later than the date of loading on board or dispatch or taking in charge as indicated in such transport document.

(f) (i) Unless otherwise stipulated in the Credit, the insurance document must be expressed in the same currency as the Credit.

(ii) Unless otherwise stipulated in the Credit, the minimum amount for which the insurance document must indicate the insurance cover to have been effected is the CIF (cost, insurance and freight (. . . 'named port of destination')) or CIP (carriage and insurance paid to (. . . 'named place of destination')) value of the goods, as the case may be, plus 10%, but only when the CIF or CIP value can be determined from the documents on their face. Otherwise, banks will accept as such minimum amount 110% of the amount for which payment, acceptance or negotiation is requested under the Credit, or 110% of the gross amount of the invoice, whichever is the greater.

Article 35
Type of Insurance Cover

(a) Credits should stipulate the type of insurance required and, if any, the additional risks which are to be covered. Imprecise terms such as 'usual risks' or 'customary risks' shall not be used; if they are used, banks will accept insurance documents as presented, without responsibility for any risks not being covered.

(b) Failing specific stipulations in the Credit, banks will accept insurance documents as presented, without responsibility for any risks not being covered.

(c) Unless otherwise stipulated in the Credit, banks will accept an insurance document which indicates that the cover is subject to a franchise or an excess (deductible).

Article 36
All Risks Insurance Cover

Where a Credit stipulates 'insurance against all risks', banks will accept an insurance document which contains any 'all risks' notation or clause, whether or not bearing the heading 'all risks', even if the insurance document indicates that certain risks are excluded, without responsibility for any risk(s) not being covered.

Article 37
Commercial Invoices

(a) Unless otherwise stipulated in the Credit, commercial invoices:
  (i) must appear on their face to be issued by the Beneficiary named in the Credit (except as provided in Article 48), and
  (ii) must be made out in the name of the Applicant (except as provided in sub-Article 48 (h)), and
  (iii) need not be signed

(b) Unless otherwise stipulated in the Credit, banks may refuse commercial invoices issued for amounts in excess of the amount permitted by the Credit. Nevertheless, if a bank authorised to pay, incur a deferred payment undertaking, accept Draft(s), or negotiate under a Credit accepts such invoices, its decision will be binding upon all parties, provided that such bank has not paid, incurred a deferred payment undertaking, accepted Draft(s) or negotiated for an amount in excess of that permitted by the Credit.

(c) The description of the goods in the commercial invoice must correspond with the description in the Credit. In all other documents, the goods may be described in general terms not inconsistent with the description of the goods in the Credit.

Article 38
Other Documents

If a Credit calls for an attestation or certification of weight in the case of transport other than by sea, banks will accept a weight stamp or declaration of weight which appears to have been superimposed on the transport document by the carrier or his agent unless the Credit specifically stipulates that the attestation or certification of weight must be by means of a separate document.

E. MISCELLANEOUS PROVISIONS

Article 39
Allowances in Credit Amount, Quantity and Unit Price

(a) The words 'about', 'approximately', 'circa' or similar expressions used in connection with the amount of the Credit or the quantity or the unit price stated in the Credit are to be construed as allowing a difference not to exceed 10% more or 10% less than the amount or the quantity or the unit price to which they refer.
(b) Unless a Credit stipulates that the quantity of the goods specified must not be exceeded or reduced, a tolerance of 5% more or 5% less will be permissible, always provided that the amount of the drawings does not exceed the amount of the Credit. This tolerance does not apply when the Credit stipulates the quantity in terms of a stated number of packing units or individual items.
(c) Unless a Credit which prohibits partial shipments stipulates otherwise, or unless sub-Article (b) above is applicable, a tolerance of 5% less in the amount of the drawing will be permissible, provided that if the Credit stipulates the quantity of the goods, such quantity of goods is shipped in full, and if the Credit stipulates a unit price, such price is not reduced. This provision does not apply when expressions referred to in sub-Article (a) above are used in the Credit.

Article 40
Partial Shipments/Drawings

(a) Partial drawings and/or shipments are allowed, unless the Credit stipulates otherwise.
(b) Transport documents which appear on their face to indicate that shipment has been made on the same means of conveyance and for the same journey, provided they indicate the same destination, will not be regarded as covering partial shipments, even if the transport documents indicate different dates of shipment and/or different ports of loading, places of taking in charge, or despatch.
(c) Shipments made by post or by courier will not be regarded as partial shipments if the post receipts or certificates of posting or courier's receipts or dispatch notes appear to have been stamped, signed or otherwise authenticated in the place from which the Credit stipulates the goods are to be dispatched, and on the same date.

Article 41
Instalment Shipments/Drawings

If drawings and/or shipments by instalments within given periods are stipulated in the Credit and any instalment is not drawn and/or shipped within the period allowed for that instalment, the Credit ceases to be available for that and any subsequent instalments, unless otherwise stipulated in the Credit.

Article 42
Expiry Date and Place for Presentation of Documents

(a) All Credits must stipulate an expiry date and a place for presentation of documents for payment, acceptance, or with the exception of freely negotiable Credits, a place for presentation of documents for negotiation An expiry date stipulated for payment, acceptance or negotiation will be construed to express an expiry date for presentation of documents.

(b) Except as provided in sub-Article 44(a), documents must be presented on or before such expiry date.

(c) If an Issuing Bank states that the Credit is to be available 'for one month', 'for six months', or the like, but does not specify the date from which the time is to run, the date of issuance of the Credit by the Issuing Bank will be deemed to be the first day from which such time is to run. Banks should discourage indication of the expiry date of the Credit in this manner.

Article 43
Limitation on the Expiry Date

(a) In addition to stipulating an expiry date for presentation of documents, every Credit which calls for a transport document(s) should also stipulate a specified period of time after the date of shipment during which presentation must be made in compliance with the terms and conditions of the Credit. If no such period of time is stipulated, banks will not accept documents presented to them later than 21 days after the date of shipment. In any event, documents must be presented not later than the expiry date of the Credit.

(b) In cases in which sub-Article 40(b) applies, the date of shipment will be considered to be the latest shipment date on any of the transport documents presented.

Article 44
Extension of Expiry Date

(a) If the expiry date of the Credit and/or the last day of the period of time for presentation of documents stipulated by the Credit or applicable by virtue of Article 43 falls on a day on which the bank to which presentation has to be made is closed for reasons other than those referred to in Article 17, the stipulated expiry date and/or the last day of the period of time after the date of shipment for presentation of documents, as the case may be, shall be extended to the first following day on which such bank is open.

(b) The latest date for shipment shall not be extended by reason of the extension of the expiry date and/or the period of time after the date of shipment for presentation of documents in accordance with sub-Article (a) above. If no such latest date for shipment is stipulated in the Credit or amendments thereto, banks will not accept transport documents indicating a date of shipment later than the expiry date stipulated in the Credit or amendments thereto.

(c) The bank to which presentation is made on such first following business day must provide a statement that the documents were presented within the time limits extended in accordance with sub-Article 44(a) of the Uniform Customs and Practice for Documentary Credits, 1993 Revision, ICC Publication No. 500.

Article 45
Hours of Presentation

Banks are under no obligation to accept presentation of documents outside their banking hours.

Article 46
General Expressions as to Dates for Shipment

(a) Unless otherwise stipulated in the Credit, the expression 'shipment' used in stipulating an earliest and/or a latest date for shipment will be understood to include expressions such as, loading on board', 'dispatch', 'accepted for carriage', 'date of post receipt', 'date of pick-up', and the like, and in the case of a Credit calling for a multimodal transport document the expression 'taking in charge'.

(b) Expressions such as 'prompt' 'immediately', 'as soon as possible'and the like should not be used. If they are used bank will disregard them.

(c) If the expression on or about or similar expressions are used, banks will interpret them as a stipulation that shipment is to be made during the period from five days before to five days after the specified date, both end days included.

Article 47
Date Terminology for Periods of Shipment

(a) The words 'to', 'until', 'till', 'from' and words of similar import applying to any date or period in the Credit referring to shipment will be understood to include the date mentioned.

(b) The word after' will be understood to exclude the date mentioned.

(c) The terms first half, 'second half' of a month shall be construed respectively as the 1st to the 15th, and the 15th to the last day of such month, all dates inclusive.

(d) The terms 'beginning', 'middle', or 'end' of a month shall be construed respectively as the 1st to the 10th, the 11th to the 20th, and the 21st to the last day of such month, all dates inclusive.

F. TRANSFERABLE CREDIT

Article 48
Transferable Credit

(a) A transferable Credit is a Credit under which the Beneficiary (First Beneficiary) may request the bank authorised to pay, incur a deferred payment undertaking, accept or negotiate (the 'Transferring Bank'), or in the case of a freely negotiable Credit, the bank specifically authorised in the Credit as a Transferring Bank, to make the Credit available in whole or in part to one or more other Beneficiary(ies) (Second Beneficiary(ies)).

(b) A Credit can be transferred only if it is expressly designated as 'transferable' by the Issuing Bank. Terms such as 'divisible', 'fractionable', 'assignable', and 'transmissible' do not render the Credit transferable. If such terms are used they shall be disregarded.

(c) The Transferring Bank shall be under no obligation to effect such transfer except to the extent and in the manner expressly consented to by such bank.

(d) At the time of making a request for transfer and prior to transfer of the Credit, the First Beneficiary must irrevocably instruct the Transferring Bank whether or not he retains the right to refuse to allow the Transferring Bank to advise amendments to the Second Beneficiary(ies). If the Transferring Bank consents to the transfer under these conditions, it must, at the time of transfer, advise the Second Beneficiary(ies) of the First Beneficiary's instructions regarding amendments.

(e) If a Credit is transferred to more than one Second Beneficiary(ies), refusal of an amendment by one or more Second Beneficiary(ies) does not invalidate the acceptance(s) by the other Second Beneficiary(ies) with respect to whom the Credit will be amended accordingly. With respect to the Second Beneficiary(ies) who rejected the amendment, the Credit will remain unamended.

(f) Transferring Bank charges in respect of transfers including commissions, fees, costs or expenses are payable by the First Beneficiary, unless otherwise agreed. If the Transferring Bank agrees to transfer the Credit it shall be under no obligation to effect the transfer until such charges are paid.

(g) Unless otherwise stated in the Credit, a transferable Credit can be transferred once only. Consequently, the Credit cannot be transferred at the request of the Second Beneficiary to any subsequent Third Beneficiary. For the purpose of this Article, a retransfer to the First Beneficiary does not Constitute a prohibited transfer.

Fractions of a transferable Credit (not exceeding in the aggregate the amount of the Credit) can be transferred separately, provided partial shipments/drawings are not prohibited, and the aggregate of such transfers will be considered as Constituting only one transfer of the Credit.

(h) The Credit can be transferred only on the terms and conditions specified in the original Credit, with the exception of:
—the amount of the Credit,
—any unit price stated therein,
—the expiry date,
—the last date for presentation of documents in accordance with Article 43,
—the period for shipment,
any or all of which may be reduced or curtailed.

The percentage for which insurance cover must be effected may be increased in such a way as to provide the amount of cover stipulated in the original Credit, or these Articles.

In addition, the name of the First Beneficiary can be substituted for that of the Applicant, but if the name of the Applicant is specifically required by the original Credit to appear in any document(s) other than the invoice, such requirement must be fulfilled.

(i) The First Beneficiary has the right to substitute his own invoice(s) (and Draft(s)) for those of the Second Beneficiary(ies), for amounts not in excess of the original amount stipulated in the Credit and for the original unit prices if stipulated in the Credit, and upon such substitution of invoice(s) and Draft(s) the First Beneficiary can draw under the Credit for the difference, if any, between his invoice and the Second Beneficiary's(ies') invoice(s).

When a Credit has been transferred and the First Beneficiary is to supply his own invoice(s) (and Draft(s)) in exchange for the Second Beneficiary's(ies') invoice(s) (and Draft(s)) but fails to do so on first demand, the Transferring Bank has the right to deliver to the Issuing Bank the documents received under the transferred Credit, including the Second Beneficiary's(ies') invoice(s) (and Draft(s)) without further responsibility to the First Beneficiary.

(j) The First Beneficiary may request that payment or negotiation be effected to the Second Beneficiary(ies) at the place to which the Credit has been transferred up to and including the expiry date of the Credit, unless the original Credit expressly states that it may not be made available for payment or negotiation at a place other than that stipulated in the Credit. This is without prejudice to the First Beneficiary's right to ... subsequently his own invoice(s) (and Draft(s)) for those of the Second Beneficiary(ies) and to claim any difference due to him.

Article 49
Assignment of Proceeds

The fact that a Credit is not stated to be transferable shall not affect the Beneficiary's right to assign any proceeds to which he may be, or may become, entitled under such Credit, in accordance with the provisions of the applicable law. This Article relates only to the assignment of proceeds and not to the assignment of the right to perform under the Credit itself.

(iii) SUPPLEMENT TO UCP 500 FOR ELECTRONIC PRESENTATION (eUCP)—VERSION 1.0*

Article e1
Scope of the eUCP

a. The Supplement to the Uniform Customs and Practice for Documentary Credits for Electronic Presentation ('eUCP') supplements the Uniform Customs and Practice for Documentary Credits (1993 Revision ICC Publication No. 500,) ('UCP') in order to accommodate presentation of electronic records alone or in combination with paper documents.

b. The eUCP shall apply as a supplement to the UCP where the Credit indicates that it is subject to eUCP.

c. This version is Version 1.0. A Credit must indicate the applicable version of the eUCP. If it does not do so, it is subject to the version in effect on the date the Credit is issued or, if made subject to eUCP by an amendment accepted by the Beneficiary, on the date of that amendment.

Article e2
Relationship of the eUCP to the UCP

a. A Credit subject to the eUCP ('eUCP Credit') is also subject to the UCP without express incorporation of the UCP.

b. Where the eUCP applies, its provisions shall prevail to the extent that they would produce a result different from the application of the UCP.

c. If an eUCP Credit allows the Beneficiary to choose between presentation of paper documents or electronic records and it chooses to present only paper documents, the UCP alone shall apply to that presentation. If only paper documents are permitted under an eUCP Credit, the UCP alone shall apply.

Article e3
Definitions

a. Where the following terms are used in the UCP, for the purposes of applying the UCP to an electronic record presented under an eUCP Credit, the term:
   i. 'appears on its face' and the like shall apply to examination of the data content of an electronic record.

---

* ICC Publication No. 500/3–ISBN 92.842.1307.X(E). Published in its original English version by the International Chamber of Commerce. Copyright ©2002–International Chamber of Commerce (ICC), Paris.

   ii. 'document' shall include an electronic record.

   iii. 'place for presentation' of electronic records means an electronic address.

   iv. 'sign' and the like shall include an electronic signature.

   v. 'superimposed', 'notation' or ' stamped' means data content whose supplementary character is apparent in an electronic record.

b. The following terms used in the eUCP shall have the following meanings:

   i. 'electronic record' means

- data created, generated, sent, communicated, received, or stored by electronic means
- that is capable of being authenticated as to the apparent identity of a sender and the apparent source of the data contained in it, and as to whether it has remained complete and unaltered, and
- is capable of being examined for compliance with the terms and conditions of the eUCP Credit.

   ii. 'electronic signature' means a data process attached to or logically associated with an electronic record and executed or adopted by a person in order to identify that person and to indicate that person's authentication of the electronic record.

   iii. 'format' means the data organisation in which the electronic record is expressed or to which it refers.

   iv. 'paper document' means a document in a traditional paper form.

   v. 'received' means the time when an electronic record enters the information system of the applicable recipient in a form capable of being accepted by that system. Any acknowledgement of receipt does not imply acceptance or refusal of the electronic record under an eUCP Credit.

Article e4
Format

An eUCP Credit must specify the formats in which electronic records are to be presented. If the format of the electronic record is not so specified, it may be presented in any format.

Article e5
Presentation

a. An eUCP Credit allowing presentation of:

   i. electronic records must state a place for presentation of the electronic records.

   ii. both electronic records and paper documents must also state a place for presentation of the paper documents.

b. Electronic records may be presented separately and need not be presented at the same time.

c. If an eUCP Credit allows for presentation of one or more electronic records, the Beneficiary is responsible for providing a notice to the Bank to which presentation is made signifying when the presentation is complete. The notice of completeness may be given as an electronic record or paper document and must identify the eUCP Credit to which it relates. Presentation is deemed not to have been made if the Beneficiary's notice is not received.

d. i. Each presentation of an electronic record and the presentation of paper documents under an eUCP Credit must identify the eUCP Credit under which it is presented.

   ii. A presentation not so identified may be treated as not received.

e. If the Bank to which presentation is to be made is open but its system is unable to receive a transmitted electronic record on the stipulated expiry date and/or the last day of the period of time after the date of shipment for presentation, as the case may be, the Bank will be deemed to be closed and the date for presentation and/or the expiry date shall be extended to the first following banking day on which such Bank is able to receive an electronic record. If the only electronic record remaining to be presented is the notice of completeness, it may be given by telecommunications or by paper document and will be deemed timely, provided that it is sent before the bank is able to receive an electronic record.

f. An electronic record that cannot be authenticated is deemed not to have been presented.

Article e6
Examination

a. If an electronic record contains a hyperlink to an external system or a presentation indicates that the electronic record may be examined by reference to an external system, the electronic record at the hyperlink or the referenced system shall be deemed to be the electronic record to be examined. The failure of the indicated system to provide access to the required electronic record at the time of examination shall constitute a discrepancy.

b. The forwarding of electronic records by a Nominated Bank pursuant to its nomination signifies that it has checked the apparent authenticity of the electronic records.

c. The inability of the Issuing Bank, or Confirming Bank, if any, to examine an electronic record in a format required by the eUCP Credit or, if no format is required, to examine it in the format presented is not a basis for refusal.

Article e7
Notice of Refusal

a. i. The time period for the examination of documents commences on the banking day following the banking day on which the Beneficiary's notice of completeness is received.

   ii. If the time for presentation of documents or the notice of completeness is extended, the time for the examination of documents commences on the first following banking day on which the bank to which presentation is to be made is able to receive the notice of completeness.

b. If an Issuing Bank, the Confirming Bank, if any, or a Nominated Bank acting on their behalf, provides a notice of refusal of a presentation which includes electronic records and does not receive instructions from the party to which notice of refusal is given within 30 calendar days from the date the notice of refusal is given for the disposition of the electronic records, the Bank shall return any paper documents not previously returned to the presenter but may dispose of the electronic records in any manner deemed appropriate without any responsibility.

Article e8
Originals and Copies

Any requirement of the UCP or an eUCP Credit for presentation of one or more originals or copies of an electronic record is satisfied by the presentation of one electronic record.

Article e9
Date of Issuance

Unless an electronic record contains a specific date of issuance, the date on which it appears to have been sent by the issuer is deemed to be the date of issuance. The date of receipt will be deemed to be the date it was sent if no other date is apparent.

Article e10
Transport

If an electronic record evidencing transport does not indicate a date of shipment or dispatch, the date of issuance of the electronic record will be deemed to be the date of shipment or dispatch. However, if the electronic record bears a notation that evidences the date of shipment or dispatch, the date of the notation will be deemed to be the date of shipment or dispatch. A notation showing additional data content need not be separately signed or otherwise authenticated.

Article e11
Corruption of an Electronic Record after Presentation

a. If an electronic record that has been received by the Issuing Bank, Confirming Bank, or another Nominated Bank appears to have been corrupted, the Bank may inform the presenter and may request that the electronic record be re-presented.
b. If the Bank requests that an electronic record be re-presented:
   i. the time for examination is suspended and resumes when the presenter re-presents the electronic record; and
   ii. if the Nominated Bank is not the Confirming Bank, it must provide the Issuing Bank and any Confirming Bank with notice of the request for re-presentation and inform it of the suspension; but
   iii. if the same electronic record is not re-presented within thirty (30) calendar days, the Bank may treat the electronic record as not presented, and
   iv. any deadlines are not extended.

Article e12
Additional Disclaimer of Liability for Presentation of Electronic Records under eUCP

By checking the apparent authenticity of an electronic record, Banks assume no liability for the identity of the sender, source of the information, or its complete and unaltered character other than that which is apparent in the electronic record received by the use of a commercially acceptable data process for the receipt, authentication, and identification of electronic records.

(iv) THE ICC UNIFORM RULES FOR DEMAND GUARANTEES 1992*

A. SCOPE AND APPLICATION OF THE RULES

Article 1

These Rules apply to any demand guarantee and amendment thereto which a Guarantor (as hereinafter described) has been instructed to issue and which states that it is subject to the Uniform Rules for Demand Guarantees of the international Chamber of Commerce (Publication No. 458) and are binding on all parties thereto except as otherwise expressly staled in the Guarantee or any amendment thereto.

B. DEFINITIONS AND GENERAL PROVISIONS

Article 2

(a) For the purpose of these Rules, a demand guarantee (hereinafter referred to as 'Guarantee') means any guarantee, bond or other payment undertaking, however named or described, by a bank, insurance company or other body or person (hereinafter called 'the Guarantor') given in writing for the payment of money on presentation in conformity with the terms of the undertaking of a written demand for payment and such other document(s) (for example, a certificate by an architect or

---

* ICC Publication No. 458(E)–ISBN 92.842.1094.1. Published in its official English version by the International Chamber of Commerce. Copyright ©1992–International Chamber of Commerce (ICC), Paris.

engineer, a judgment or an arbitral award) as may be specified in the Guarantee, such undertaking being given
  i. at the request or on the instructions and under the liability of a party (hereinafter called 'the Principal'); or
  ii. at the request or on the instructions and under the liability of a bank, insurance company or any other body or person (hereinafter 'the Instructing Party') acting on the instructions of a Principal to another party (hereinafter the 'Beneficiary').
(b) Guarantees by their nature are separate transactions from the contract(s) or tender conditions on which they may be based, and Guarantors are in no way concerned with or bound by such contract(s), or tender conditions, despite the inclusion of a reference to them in the Guarantee. The duty of a Guarantor under a Guarantee is to pay the sum or sums therein stated on the presentation of a written demand for payment and other documents specified in the Guarantee which appear on their face to be in accordance with the terms of the Guarantee.
(c) For the purpose of these Rules, 'Counter-Guarantee' means any guarantee, bond or other payment undertaking of the Instructing Party, however named or described, given in writing for the payment of money to the Guarantor on presentation in conformity with the terms of the undertaking of a written demand for payment and other documents specified in the Counter-Guarantee which appear on their face to be in accordance with the terms of the Counter-Guarantee. Counter-Guarantees are by their nature separate transactions from the Guarantees to which they relate and from any underlying contract(s) or tender conditions, and Instructing Parties are in no way concerned with or bound by such Guarantees, contract(s) or tender conditions, despite the inclusion of a reference to them in the Counter-Guarantee.
(d) The expressions 'writing' and 'written' shall include an authenticated teletransmission or tested electronic data interchange ('EDI') message equivalent thereto.

Article 3

All instructions for the issue of Guarantees and amendments thereto and Guarantees and amendments themselves should be clear and precise and should avoid excessive detail. Accordingly, all Guarantees should stipulate:
  (a) the Principal;
  (b) the Beneficiary;
  (c) the Guarantor;
  (d) the underlying transaction requiring the issue of the Guarantee;
  (e) the maximum amount payable and the currency in which it is payable;
  (f) the Expiry Date and/or Expiry Event of the Guarantee;
  (g) the terms for demanding payment;
  (h) any provision for reduction of the guarantee amount.

Article 4

The Beneficiary's right to make a demand under a Guarantee is not assignable unless expressly stated in the Guarantee or in an amendment thereto.
  This Article shall not, however, affect the Beneficiary's right to assign any proceeds to which he may be, or may become, entitled under the Guarantee.

Article 5

All Guarantees and Counter-Guarantees are irrevocable unless otherwise indicated.

Article 6

A Guarantee enters into effect as from the dale of its issue unless its terms expressly provide that such entry into effect is to be at a later date or is to be subject to conditions specified in the Guarantee and determinable by the Guarantor on the basis of any documents therein specified.

Article 7

(a) Where a Guarantor has been given instructions for the issue of a Guarantee hut the instructions are such that, if they were to be carried out, the Guarantor would by reason of law or regulation in the country of issue be unable to fulfil the terms of the Guarantee, the instructions shall not be executed and the Guarantor shall immediately inform the party who gave the Guarantor his instructions by telecommunication, or, it that is not possible, by other expeditious means, of the reasons for such inability and request appropriate instructions from that party.
(b) Nothing in this Article shall oblige the Guarantor to issue a Guarantee where the Guarantor has not agreed to do so.

Article 8

A Guarantee may contain express provision for reduction by a specified or determinable amount or amounts on a specified date or dates or upon presentation to the Guarantor of the document(s) specified for this purpose in the Guarantee.

C. LIABILITIES AND RESPONSIBILITIES

Article 9

All documents specified and presented under a Guarantee, including the demand, shall be examined by the Guarantor with reasonable care to ascertain whether or not they appear on their face to conform with the terms of the Guarantee. Where such documents do not appear so to conform or appear on their face to be inconsistent with one another, they shall be refused.

Article 10

(a) A Guarantor shall have a reasonable time within which to examine a demand under a Guarantee and to decide whether to pay or to refuse the demand.
(b) If the Guarantor decides to refuse a demand, he shall immediately give notice thereof to the Beneficiary by teletransmission, or, it that is not possible, by other expeditious means. Any documents presented under the Guarantee shall be held at the disposal of the Beneficiary.

Article 11

Guarantors and Instructing Parties assume no liability or responsibility for the form, sufficiency, accuracy, genuineness, falsification, or legal effect of any document presented to them or for the general and/or particular statements made therein, nor for the good faith or acts or omissions of any person whomsoever.

Article 12

Guarantors and Instructing Parties assume no liability or responsibility for the consequences arising out of delay and/or loss in transit of any messages, letters, demands or documents, or for delay, mutilation or other errors arising in the transmission of any telecommunication. Guarantors and Instructing Parties assume no liability for errors in translation or interpretation of technical terms and reserve the right to transmit Guarantee texts or any parts thereof without translating them.

Article 13

Guarantors and Instructing Parties assume no liability or responsibility for consequences arising out of the interruption of their business by acts of God, riots, civil commotions, insurrections, wars or any other causes beyond their control or by strikes, lock-outs or industrial actions of whatever nature.

Article 14

(a) Guarantors and Instructing Parties utilising the services of another party for the purpose of giving effect to the instructions of a Principal do so for the account and at the risk of that Principal.
(b) Guarantors and Instructing Parties assume no liability or responsibility should the instructions they transmit not be carried out even if they have themselves taken the initiative in the choice of such other party.
(c) The Principal shall be liable to indemnify the Guarantor or the Instructing Party, as the case may be, against all obligations and responsibilities imposed by foreign laws and usages.

Article 15

Guarantors and Instructing Parties shall not be excluded from liability or responsibility under the terms of Articles 11, 12, and 14 above for their failure to act in good faith and with reasonable care.

Article 16

A Guarantor is liable to the Beneficiary only in accordance with the terms, specified in the Guarantee and any amendment(s) thereto and in these Rules, and up to an amount not exceeding that slated in the Guarantee and any amendment(s) thereto.

D. DEMANDS

Article 17

Without prejudice to the terms of Article 10, in the event of a demand the Guarantor shall without delay so inform the Principal or, where applicable, his Instructing Party, and in that case the Instructing Party shall so inform the Principal.

Article 18

The amount payable under a Guarantee shaft be reduced by the amount of any payment made by the Guarantor in satisfaction of a demand in respect thereof and, where the maximum amount payable under a Guarantee has been satisfied by payment and/or reduction, the Guarantee shall thereupon terminate whether or not the Guarantee and any amendment(s) thereto are returned.

Article 19

A demand shall be made in accordance with the terms of the Guarantee before its expiry, that is, on or before its Expiry Date and before any Expiry Event as defined in Article 22. In particular, all documents specified in the Guarantee for the purpose of the demand, and any statement required by Article 20, shall be presented to the Guarantor before its expiry at its place of issue; otherwise the demand shall be refused by the Guarantor.

Article 20

(a) Any demand for payment under the Guarantee shall be in writing and shall (in addition to such other documents as may be specified in the Guarantee) be supported by a written statement (whether in the demand itself or in a separate document or documents accompanying the demand and referred to in it) stating:
   i. that the Principal is in breach of his obligation(s) under the underlying contract(s) or, in the case of a tender guarantee, the tender conditions; and
   ii. the respect in which the Principal is in breach.
(b) Any demand under the Counter-Guarantee shall be supported by a written statement that the Guarantor has received a demand for payment under the Guarantee in accordance with its terms and with this Article.
(c) Paragraph (a) of this Article applies except to the extent that it is expressly excluded by the terms of the Guarantee. Paragraph (b) of this Article applies except to the extent that it is expressly excluded by the terms of the Counter-Guarantee.
(d) Nothing in this Article affects the application of Articles 2(b) and 2(c), 9 and 11.

Article 21

The Guarantor shall without delay transmit the Beneficiary's demand and any related documents to the Principal or, where applicable, to the Instructing Party for transmission to the Principal.

E. EXPIRY PROVISIONS

Article 22

Expiry of the time specified in a Guarantee for the presentation of demands shall be upon a specified calendar date ('Expiry Date') or upon presentation to the Guarantor of the document(s) specified for the purpose of expiry ('Expiry Event'). If both an Expiry Date and an Expiry Event are specified in a Guarantee, the Guarantee shall expire on whichever of the Expiry Date or Expiry Event occurs first, whether or not the Guarantee and any amendment(s) thereto are returned.

Article 23

Irrespective of any expiry provision contained therein, a Guarantee shall be cancelled on presentation to the Guarantor of the Guarantor itself or the Beneficiary's written statement of release from liability under the Guarantee, whether or not, in the latter case, the Guarantee or any amendments thereto are returned.

Article 24

Where a Guarantee has terminated by payment, expiry, cancellation or otherwise, retention of the Guarantee or of any amendments thereto shall not preserve any rights of the Beneficiary under the Guarantee.

Article 25

Where to the knowledge of the Guarantor the Guarantee has terminated by payment, expiry, cancellation or otherwise, or these has been a reduction of the total amount payable thereunder, the Guarantor shall without delay so notify the Principal or, where applicable, the Instructing Party and, in that case, the Instructing Party shall so notify the Principal.

Article 26

If the Beneficiary requests an extension of the validity of the Guarantee as an alternative to a demand for payment submitted in accordance with the terms and conditions of the Guarantee and these Rules, the Guarantor shall without delay so inform the party who gave the Guarantor his instructions. The Guarantor shall then suspend payment of the demand for such time as is reasonable to permit the Principal and the Beneficiary to reach agreement on the granting of such extension, and for the Principal to arrange for such extension to be issued.

Unless an extension is granted within the time provided by the preceding paragraph, the Guarantor is obliged to pay the Beneficiary's conforming demand without requiring any further action on the Beneficiary's part. The guarantor shall incur no liability (for interest or otherwise) should any payment to the Beneficiary be delayed as a result of the above-mentioned procedure.

Even if the Principal agrees to or requests such extension, it shall not be granted unless the Guarantor and the Instructing Party or Parties also agree thereto.

F. GOVERNING LAW AND JURISDICTION

Article 27

Unless otherwise provided in the Guarantee or Counter-Guarantee, its governing law shall be that of the place of business of the Guarantor or Instructing Party (as the case may be), or, if the Guarantor or Instructing Party has more than one place of business, that of the branch that issued the Guarantee or Counter-Guarantee.

Article 28

Unless otherwise provided in the Guarantee or Counter-Guarantee, any dispute between the Guarantor and the Beneficiary relating to the Guarantee or between the instructing

Party and the Guarantor relating to the Counter-Guarantee shall be settled exclusively by the competent court of the country of the place of business of the Guarantor or Instructing Party (as the case may be), or, if the Guarantor or Instructing Party has more than one place of business, by the competent court of the country of the branch which issued the Guarantee or Counter-Guarantee.

(v) INTERNATIONAL STANDBY PRACTICES (ISP 98)*

RULE 1
GENERAL PROVISIONS

SCOPE, APPLICATION, DEFINITIONS, AND INTERPRETATION OF THESE RULES

1.01 Scope and Application

a. These Rules are intended to be applied to standby letters of credit (including performance, financial, and direct pay standby letters of credit).

b. A standby letter of credit or other similar undertaking, however named or described, whether for domestic or international use, may be made subject to these Rules by express reference to them.

c. An undertaking subject to these Rules may expressly modify or exclude their application.

d. An undertaking subject to these Rules is hereinafter referred to as a 'standby'.

1.02 Relationship to Law and Other Rules

a. These Rules supplement the applicable law to the extent not prohibited by that law.

b. These Rules supersede conflicting provisions in any other rules of practice to which a standby letter of credit is also made subject.

1.03 Interpretative Principles

These Rules shall be interpreted as mercantile usage with regard for:
  a. integrity of standbys as reliable and efficient undertakings to pay;
  b. practice and terminology of banks and businesses in day-to-day transactions;
  c. consistency within the worldwide system of banking operations and commerce; and
  d. worldwide uniformity in their interpretation and application.

1.04 Effect of the Rules

Unless the context otherwise requires, or unless expressly modified or excluded, these Rules apply as terms and conditions incorporated into a standby, confirmation, advice, nomination, amendment, transfer, request for issuance, or other agreement of:
  i. the issuer;
  ii. the beneficiary to the extent it uses the standby;
  iii. any advisor;
  iv. any confirmer;
  v. any person nominated in the standby who acts or agrees to act; and
  vi. the applicant who authorises issuance of the standby or otherwise agrees to the application of these Rules.

1.05 Exclusion of Matters Related to Due Issuance and Fraudulent or Abusive Drawing

These Rules do not define or otherwise provide for:
  a. power or authority to issue a standby;
  b. formal requirements for execution of a standby (e.g. a signed writing); or
  c. defenses to honour based on fraud, abuse, or similar matters.
These matters are left to applicable law.

GENERAL PRINCIPLES

1.06 Nature of Standbys

a. A standby is an irrevocable, independent, documentary, and binding undertaking when issued and need not so state.
b. Because a standby is irrevocable, an issuer's obligations under a standby cannot be amended or cancelled by the issuer except as provided in the standby or as consented to by the person against whom the amendment or cancellation is asserted.
c. Because a standby is independent, the enforceability of an issuer's obligations under a standby does not depend on:
  i. the issuer's right or ability to obtain reimbursement from the applicant;
  ii. the beneficiary's right to obtain payment from the applicant;
  iii. a reference in the standby to any reimbursement agreement or underlying transaction; or
  iv. the issuer's knowledge of performance or breach of any reimbursement agreement or underlying transaction.
d. Because a standby is documentary, an issuer's obligations depend on the presentation of documents and an examination of required documents on their face.

e. Because a standby or amendment is binding when issued, it is enforceable against an issuer whether or not the applicant authorised its issuance, the issuer received a fee, or the beneficiary received or relied on the standby or the amendment.

1.07 Independence of the Issuer-Beneficiary Relationship

An issuer's obligations toward the beneficiary are not affected by the issuer's rights and obligations toward the applicant under any applicable agreement, practice, or law.

1.08 Limits to Responsibilities

An issuer is not responsible for:
   a. performance or breach of any underlying transaction;
   b. accuracy, genuineness, or effect of any document presented under the standby;
   c. action or omission of others even if the other person is chosen by the issuer or nominated person; or
   d. observance of law or practice other than that chosen in the standby or applicable at the place of issuance.

TERMINOLOGY

1.09 Defined Terms

In addition to the meanings given in standard banking practice and applicable law, the following terms have or include the meanings indicated below:
   a. Definitions
   'Applicant' is a person who applies for issuance of a standby or for whose account it is issued, and includes (i) a person applying in its own name but for the account of another person or (ii) an issuer acting for its own account.
   'Beneficiary' is a named person who is entitled to draw under a standby. See Rule 1.11(c)(ii).
   'Business Day' means a day on which the place of business at which the relevant act is to be performed is regularly open; and 'Banking Day' means a day on which the relevant bank is regularly open at the place at which the relevant act is to be performed.
   'Confirmer' is a person who, upon an issuer's nomination to do so, adds to the issuer's undertaking its own undertaking to honour a standby. See Rule 1.11(c)(i).
   'Demand' means, depending on the context, either a request to honour a standby or a document that makes such request.
   'Document' means a draft, demand, document of title, investment security, invoice, certificate of default, or any other representation of fact, law, right, or opinion, that upon presentation (whether in a paper or electronic medium), is capable of being examined for compliance with the terms and conditions of a standby.
   'Drawing' means, depending on the context, either a demand presented or a demand honoured.
   'Expiration Date' means the latest day for a complying presentation provided in a standby.
   'Person' includes a natural person, partnership, corporation, limited liability company, government agency, bank, trustee, and any other legal or commercial association or entity.

'Presentation' means, depending on the context, either the act of delivering documents for examination under a standby or the documents so delivered.

'Presenter' is a person who makes a presentation as or on behalf of a beneficiary or nominated person.

'Signature' includes any symbol executed or adopted by a person with a present intent to authenticate a document.

b. Cross References

'Amendment'—Rule 2.06

'Advice'—Rule 2.05

'Approximately' ('About' or 'Circa')—Rule 3.08(f)

'Assignment of Proceeds'—Rule 6.06

'Automatic Amendment'—Rule 2.06(a)

'Copy'—Rule 4.15(d)

'Cover Instructions'—Rule 5.08

'Honour'—Rule 2.01

'Issuer'—Rule 2.01

'Multiple Presentations'—Rule 3.08(b)

'Nominated Person'—Rule 2.04

'Non-documentary Conditions'—Rule 4.11

'Original'—Rule 4.15(b) & (c)

'Partial Drawing'—Rule 3.08(a)

'Standby'—Rule 1.01(d)

'Transfer'—Rule 6.01

'Transferee Beneficiary'—Rule 1.11(c)(ii)

'Transfer by Operation of Law'—Rule 6.11

c. Electronic Presentations

The following terms in a standby providing for or permitting electronic presentation shall have the following meanings unless the context otherwise requires:

'Electronic Record' means:

i.   a record (information that is inscribed on a tangible medium or that is stored in an electronic or other medium and is retrievable in perceivable form);

ii. communicated by electronic means to a system for receiving, storing, re-transmitting, or otherwise processing information (data, text, images, sounds, codes, computer programs, software, databases, and the like); and

iii. capable of being authenticated and then examined for compliance with the terms and conditions of the standby.

'Authenticate' means to verify an electronic record by generally accepted procedure or methodology in commercial practice:

i.   the identity of a sender or source, and

ii. the integrity of or errors in the transmission of information content.

The criteria for assessing the integrity of information in an electronic record is whether the information has remained complete and unaltered, apart from the addition of any endorsement and any change which arises in the normal course of communication, storage, and display.

'Electronic signature' means letters, characters, numbers, or other symbols in electronic form, attached to or logically associated with an electronic record that are executed or adopted by a party with present intent to authenticate an electronic record.

'Receipt' occurs when:

i. an electronic record enters in a form capable of being processed by the information system designated in the standby, or

ii. an issuer retrieves an electronic record sent to an information system other than that designated by the issuer.

1.10 Redundant or Otherwise Undesirable Terms

a. A standby should not or need not state that it is:

 i. unconditional or abstract (if it does, it signifies merely that payment under it is conditioned solely on presentation of specified documents);

 ii. absolute (if it does, it signifies merely that it is irrevocable);

 iii. primary (if it does, it signifies merely that it is the independent obligation of the issuer);

 iv. payable from the issuer's own funds (if it does, it signifies merely that payment under it does not depend on the availability of applicant funds and is made to satisfy the issuer's own independent obligation);

 v. clean or payable on demand (if it does, it signifies merely that it is payable upon presentation of a written demand or other documents specified in the standby).

b. A standby should not use the term 'and/or' (if it does it means either or both).

c. The following terms have no single accepted meaning:

 i. and shall be disregarded:

 'callable',

 'divisible',

 'fractionable',

 'indivisible', and

 'transmissible'.

 ii. and shall be disregarded unless their context gives them meaning:

 'assignable',

 'evergreen',

 'reinstate', and

 'revolving'.

1.11 Interpretation of these Rules

a. These Rules are to be interpreted in the context of applicable standard practice.

b. In these Rules, 'standby letter of credit' refers to the type of independent undertaking for which these Rules were intended, whereas 'standby' refers to an undertaking subjected to these Rules.

c. Unless the context otherwise requires:

 i. 'Issuer' includes a 'confirmer' as if the confirmer were a separate issuer and its confirmation were a separate standby issued for the account of the issuer;

 ii. 'Beneficiary' includes a person to whom the named beneficiary has effectively transferred drawing rights ('transferee beneficiary');

 iii. 'Including' means 'including but not limited to';

 iv. 'A or B' means 'A or B or both'; 'either A or B' means 'A or B, but not both' and 'A and B' means 'both A and B';

     v.   Words in the singular number include the plural, and in the plural include the singular; and

     vi. Words of the neuter gender include any gender.

d. i.   Use of the phrase 'unless a standby otherwise states' or the like in a rule emphasizes that the text of the standby controls over the rule;

    ii. Absence of such a phrase in other rules does not imply that other rules have priority over the text of the standby;

    iii. Addition of the term 'expressly' or 'clearly' to the phrase 'unless a standby otherwise states' or the like emphasizes that the rule should be excluded or modified only by wording in the standby that is specific and unambiguous; and

    iv. While the effect of all of these Rules may be varied by the text of the standby, variations of the effect of some of these Rules may disqualify the standby as an independent undertaking under applicable law.

e. The phrase 'stated in the standby' or the like refers to the actual text of a standby (whether as issued or effectively amended) whereas the phrase 'provided in the standby' or the like refers to both the text of the standby and these Rules as incorporated.

RULE 2 OBLIGATIONS

2.01 Undertaking to Honour by Issuer and Any Confirmer to Beneficiary

a. An issuer undertakes to the beneficiary to honour a presentation that appears on its face to comply with the terms and conditions of the standby in accordance with these Rules supplemented by standard standby practice.

b. An issuer honours a complying presentation made to it by paying the amount demanded of it at sight, unless the standby provides for honour:

    i.   by acceptance of a draft drawn by the beneficiary on the issuer, in which case the issuer honours by:

       (a) timely accepting the draft; and

       (b) thereafter paying the holder of the draft on presentation of the accepted draft on or after its maturity.

    ii. by deferred payment of a demand made by the beneficiary on the issuer, in which case the issuer honours by:

       (i) timely incurring a deferred payment obligation; and

       (ii) thereafter paying at maturity.

    iii. by negotiation, in which case the issuer honours by paying the amount demanded at sight without recourse.

c. An issuer acts in a timely manner if it pays at sight, accepts a draft, or undertakes a deferred payment obligation (or if it gives notice of dishonour) within the time permitted for examining the presentation and giving notice of dishonour.

d. i.   A confirmer undertakes to honour a complying presentation made to it by paying the amount demanded of it at sight or, if the standby so states, by another method of honour consistent with the issuer's undertaking.

    ii. If the confirmation permits presentation to the issuer, then the confirmer undertakes also to honour upon the issuer's wrongful dishonour by performing as if the presentation had been made to the confirmer.

   iii. If the standby permits presentation to the confirmer, then the issuer undertakes also to honour upon the confirmer's wrongful dishonour by performing as if the presentation had been made to the issuer.

e. An issuer honours by paying in immediately available funds in the currency designated in the standby unless the standby states it is payable by:

   i. payment of a monetary unit of account, in which case the undertaking is to pay in that unit of account; or

   ii. 'delivery of other items of value, in which case the undertaking is to deliver those items.

2.02 Obligation of Different Branches, Agencies, or Other Offices

For the purposes of these Rules, an issuer's branch, agency, or other office acting or undertaking to act under a standby in a capacity other than as issuer is obligated in that capacity only and shall be treated as a different person.

2.03 Conditions to Issuance

A standby is issued when it leaves an issuer's control unless it clearly specifies that it is not then 'issued' or 'enforceable'. Statements that a standby is not 'available', 'operative', 'effective', or the like do not affect its irrevocable and binding nature at the time it leaves the issuer's control.

2.04 Nomination

a. A standby may nominate a person to advise, receive a presentation, effect a transfer, confirm, pay, negotiate, incur a deferred payment obligation, or accept a draft.

b. Nomination does not obligate the nominated person to act except to the extent that the nominated person undertakes to act.

c. A nominated person is not authorised to bind the person making the nomination.

2.05 Advice of Standby or Amendment

a. Unless an advice states otherwise, it signifies that:

   i. the advisor has checked the apparent authenticity of the advised message in accordance with standard letter of credit practice; and

   ii. the advice accurately reflects what has been received.

b. A person who is requested to advise a standby and decides not to do so should notify the requesting party.

2.06 When an Amendment is Authorised and Binding

a. If a standby expressly states that it is subject to 'automatic amendment' by an increase or decrease in the amount available, an extension of the expiration date, or the like, the amendment is effective automatically without any further notification or consent beyond that expressly provided for in the standby. (Such an amendment may also be referred to as becoming effective 'without amendment'.)

b. If there is no provision for automatic amendment, an amendment binds:

   i. the issuer when it leaves the issuer's control; and

   ii. the confirmer when it leaves the confirmer's control, unless the confirmer indicates that it does not confirm the amendment.

c. If there is no provision for automatic amendment:
   i. the beneficiary must consent to the amendment for it to be binding;
   ii. the beneficiary's consent must be made by an express communication to the person advising the amendment unless the beneficiary presents documents which comply with the standby as amended and which would not comply with the standby prior to such amendment; and
   iii. an amendment does not require the applicant's consent to be binding on the issuer, the confirmer, or the beneficiary.
d. Consent to only part of an amendment is a rejection of the entire amendment.

2.07 Routing of Amendments

a. An issuer using another person to advise a standby must advise all amendments to that person.
b. An amendment or cancellation of a standby does not affect the issuer's obligation to a nominated person that has acted within the scope of its nomination before receipt of notice of the amendment or cancellation.
c. Non-extension of an automatically extendable (renewable) standby does not affect an issuer's obligation to a nominated person who has acted within the scope of its nomination before receipt of a notice of non-extension.

RULE 3: PRESENTATION

3.01 Complying Presentation under a Standby

A standby should indicate the time, place and location within that place, person to whom, and medium in which presentation should be made. If so, presentation must be so made in order to comply. To the extent that a standby does not so indicate, presentation must be made in accordance with these Rules in order to be complying.

3.02 What Constitutes a Presentation

The receipt of a document required by and presented under a standby constitutes a presentation requiring examination for compliance with the terms and conditions of the standby even if not all of the required documents have been presented.

3.03 Identification of Standby

a. A presentation must identify the standby under which the presentation is made.
b. A presentation may identify the standby by stating the complete reference number of the standby and the name and location of the issuer or by attaching the original or a copy of the standby.
c. If the issuer cannot determine from the face of a document received that it should be processed under a standby or cannot identify the standby to which it relates, presentation is deemed to have been made on the date of identification.

3.04 Where and to Whom Complying Presentation Made

a. To comply, a presentation must be made at the place and any location at that place indicated in the standby or provided in these Rules.

b. If no place of presentation to the issuer is indicated in the standby, presentation to the issuer must be made at the place of business from which the standby was issued.

c. If a standby is confirmed, but no place for presentation is indicated in the confirmation, presentation for the purpose of obligating the confirmer (and the issuer) must be made at the place of business of the confirmer from which the confirmation was issued or to the issuer.

d. If no location at a place of presentation is indicated (such as department, floor, room, station, mail stop, post office box, or other location), presentation may be made to:
   i.   the general postal address indicated in the standby;
   ii. any location at the place designated to receive deliveries of mail or documents; or
   iii. any person at the place of presentation actually or apparently authorised to receive it.

3.05 When Timely Presentation Made

a. A presentation is timely if made at any time after issuance and before expiry on the expiration date.

b. A presentation made after the close of business at the place of presentation is deemed to have been made on the next business day.

3.06 Complying Medium of Presentation

a. To comply, a document must be presented in the medium indicated in the standby.

b. Where no medium is indicated, to comply a document must be presented as a paper document, unless only a demand is required, in which case:
   i. a demand that is presented via S.W.I.F.T., tested telex, or other similar authenticated means by a beneficiary that is a S.W.I.F.T. participant or a bank complies; otherwise
   ii. a demand that is not presented as a paper document does not comply unless the issuer permits, in its sole discretion, the use of that medium.

c. A document is not presented as a paper document if it is communicated by electronic means even if the issuer or nominated person receiving it generates a paper document from it.

d. Where presentation in an electronic medium is indicated, to comply a document must be presented as an electronic record capable of being authenticated by the issuer or nominated person to whom it is presented.

3.07 Separateness of Each Presentation

a. Making a non-complying presentation, withdrawing a presentation, or failing to make any one of a number of scheduled or permitted presentations does not waive or otherwise prejudice the right to make another timely presentation or a timely re-presentation whether or not the standby prohibits partial or multiple drawings or presentations.

b. Wrongful dishonour of a complying presentation does not constitute dishonour of any other presentation under a standby or repudiation of the standby.

c. Honour of a non-complying presentation, with or without notice of its non-compliance, does not waive requirements of a standby for other presentations.

3.08 Partial Drawing and Multiple Presentations; Amount of Drawings

a. A presentation may be made for less than the full amount available ('partial drawing').

b. More than one presentation ('multiple presentations') may be made.

c. The statement 'partial drawings prohibited' or a similar expression means that a presentation must be for the full amount available.

d. The statement 'multiple drawings prohibited' or a similar expression means that only one presentation may be made and honoured but that it may be for less than the full amount available.

e. If a demand exceeds the amount available under the standby, the drawing is discrepant. Any document other than the demand stating an amount in excess of the amount demanded is not discrepant for that reason.

f. Use of 'approximately', 'about', 'circa', or a similar word permits a tolerance not to exceed 10% more or 10% less of the amount to which such word refers.

3.09 Extend or Pay

A beneficiary's request to extend the expiration date of the standby or, alternatively, to pay the amount available under it:

a. is a presentation demanding payment under the standby, to be examined as such in accordance with these Rules; and

b. implies that the beneficiary:

   i. consents to the amendment to extend the expiry date to the date requested;

   ii. requests the issuer to exercise its discretion to seek the approval of the applicant and to issue that amendment;

   iii. upon issuance of that amendment, retracts its demand for payment; and

   iv. consents to the maximum time available under these Rules for examination and notice of dishonour.

3.10 No Notice of Receipt of Presentation

An issuer is not required to notify the applicant of receipt of a presentation under the standby.

3.11 Issuer Waiver and Applicant Consent to Waiver of Presentation Rules

In addition to other discretionary provisions in a standby or these Rules, an issuer may, in its sole discretion, without notice to or consent of the applicant and without effect on the applicant's obligations to the issuer, waive

a. the following Rules and any similar terms stated in the standby which are primarily for the issuer's benefit or operational convenience:

   i. treatment of documents received, at the request of the presenter, as having been presented at a later date (Rule 3.02);

   i. identification of a presentation to the standby under which it is presented (Rule 3.03(a));

   iii. where and to whom presentation is made (Rule 3.04(b), (c), and (d)), except the country of presentation stated in the standby; or

   iv. treatment of a presentation made after the close of business as if it were made on the next business day (Rule 3.05(b)).

b. the following Rule but not similar terms stated in the standby:
   i. a required document dated after the date of its stated presentation (Rule 4.06); or
   ii. the requirement that a document issued by the beneficiary be in the language of the standby (Rule 4.04).
c. the following Rule relating to the operational integrity of the standby only in so far as the bank is in fact dealing with the true beneficiary: acceptance of a demand in an electronic medium (Rule 3.06(b)).

Waiver by the confirmer requires the consent of the issuer with respect to paragraphs (b) and (c) of this Rule.

3.12 Original Standby Lost, Stolen, Mutilated, or Destroyed

a. If an original standby is lost, stolen, mutilated, or destroyed, the issuer need not replace it or waive any requirement that the original be presented under the standby.
b. If the issuer agrees to replace an original standby or to waive a requirement for its presentation, it may provide a replacement or copy to the beneficiary without affecting the applicant's obligations to the issuer to reimburse, but, if it does so, the issuer must mark the replacement or copy as such. The issuer may, in its sole discretion, require indemnities satisfactory to it from the beneficiary and assurances from nominated persons that no payment has been made.

CLOSURE ON EXPIRY DATE

3.13 Expiration Date on a Non-Business Day

a. If the last day for presentation stated in a standby (whether stated to be the expiration date or the date by which documents must be received) is not a business day of the issuer or nominated person where presentation is to be made, then presentation made there on the first following business day shall be deemed timely.
b. A nominated person to whom such a presentation is made must so notify the issuer.

3.14 Closure on a Business Day and Authorization of Another Reasonable Place for Presentation

a. If on the last business day for presentation the place for presentation stated in a standby is for any reason closed and presentation is not timely made because of the closure, then the last day for presentation is automatically extended to the day occurring thirty calender days after the place for presentation re-opens for business, unless the standby otherwise provides.
b. Upon or in anticipation of closure of the place of presentation, an issuer may authorise another reasonable place for presentation in the standby or in a communication received by the beneficiary. If it does so, then
   i. presentation must be made at that reasonable place; and
   ii. if the communication is received fewer than thirty calender days before the last day for presentation and for that reason presentation is not timely made, the last day for presentation is automatically extended to the day occurring thirty calender days after the last day for presentation.

RULE 4
EXAMINATION

4.01 Examination for Compliance

a. Demands for honour of a standby must comply with the terms and conditions of the standby.
b. Whether a presentation appears to comply is determined by examining the presentation on its face against the terms and conditions stated in the standby as interpreted and supplemented by these Rules which are to be read in the context of standard standby practice.

4.02 Non-Examination of Extraneous Documents

Documents presented which are not required by the standby need not be examined and, in any event, shall be disregarded for purposes of determining compliance of the presentation. They may without responsibility be returned to the presenter or passed on with the other documents presented.

4.03 Examination for Inconsistency

An issuer or nominated person is required to examine documents for inconsistency with each other only to the extent provided in the standby.

4.04 Language of Documents

The language of all documents issued by the beneficiary is to be that of the standby.

4.05 Issuer of Documents

Any required document must be issued by the beneficiary unless the standby indicates that the document is to be issued by a third person or the document is of a type that standard standby practice requires to be issued by a third person.

4.06 Date of Documents

The issuance date of a required document may be earlier but not later than the date of its presentation.

4.07 Required Signature on a Document

a. A required document need not be signed unless the standby indicates that the document must be signed or the document is of a type that standard standby practice requires be signed.
b. A required signature may be made in any manner that corresponds to the medium in which the signed document is presented.
c. Unless a standby specifies:
   i. the name of a person who must sign a document, any signature or authentication will be regarded as a complying signature.
   ii. the status of a person who must sign, no indication of status is necessary.

d. If a standby specifies that a signature must be made by:
  i. a named natural person without requiring that the signer's status be identified, a signature complies that appears to be that of the named person;
  ii. a named legal person or government agency without identifying who is to sign on its behalf or its status, any signature complies that appears to have been made on behalf of the named legal person or government agency; or
  iii. a named natural person, legal person, or government agency requiring the status of the signer be indicated, a signature complies which appears to be that of the named natural person, legal person, or government agency and indicates its status.

4.08 Demand Document Implied

If a standby does not specify any required document, it will still be deemed to require a documentary demand for payment.

4.09 Identical Wording and Quotation Marks

If a standby requires:
  a. a statement without specifying precise wording, then the wording in the document presented must appear to convey the same meaning as that required by the standby;
  b. specified wording by the use of quotation marks, blocked wording, or an attached exhibit or form, then typographical errors in spelling, punctuation, spacing, or the like that are apparent when read in context are not required to be duplicated and blank lines or spaces for data may be completed in any manner not inconsistent with the standby; or
  c. specified wording by the use of quotation marks, blocked wording, or an attached exhibit or form, and also provides that the specified wording be 'exact' or 'identical' then the wording in the documents presented must duplicate the specified wording, including typographical errors in spelling, punctuation, spacing and the like, as well as blank lines and spaces for data must be exactly reproduced.

4.10 Applicant Approval

A standby should not specify that a required document be issued, signed, or countersigned by the applicant. However, if the standby includes such a requirement, the issuer may not waive the requirement and is not responsible for the applicant's withholding of the document or signature.

4.11 Non-Documentary Terms or Conditions

a. A standby term or condition which is non-documentary must be disregarded whether or not it affects the issuer's obligation to treat a presentation as complying or to treat the standby as issued, amended, or terminated.
b. Terms or conditions are non-documentary if the standby does not require presentation of a document in which they are to be evidenced and if their fulfillment cannot be determined by the issuer from the issuer's own records or within the issuer's normal operations.
c. Determinations from the issuer's own records or within the issuer's normal operations include determinations of:
  i. when, where, and how documents are presented or otherwise delivered to the issuer;

    ii. when, where, and how communications affecting the standby are sent or received by the issuer, beneficiary, or any nominated person;

    iii. amounts transferred into or out of accounts with the issuer; and

    iv. amounts determinable from a published index (e.g., if a standby provides for determining amounts of interest accruing according to published interest rates).

d. An issuer need not re-compute a beneficiary's computations under a formula stated or referenced in a standby except to the extent that the standby so provides.

4.12 Formality of Statements in Documents

a. A required statement need not be accompanied by a solemnity, officialization, or any other formality.

b. If a standby provides for the addition of a formality to a required statement by the person making it without specifying form or content, the statement complies if it indicates that it was declared, averred, warranted, attested, sworn under oath, affirmed, certified, or the like.

c. If a standby provides for a statement to be witnessed by another person without specifying form or content, the witnessed statement complies if it appears to contain a signature of a person other than the beneficiary with an indication that the person is acting as a witness.

d. If a standby provides for a statement to be counter-signed, legalized, visaed, or the like by a person other than the beneficiary acting in a governmental, judicial, corporate, or other representative capacity without specifying form or content, the statement complies if it contains the signature of a person other than the beneficiary and includes an indication of that person's representative capacity and the organization on whose behalf the person has acted.

4.13 No Responsibility to Identify Beneficiary

Except to the extent that a standby requires presentation of an electronic record:

a. a person honouring a presentation has no obligation to the applicant to ascertain the identity of any person making a presentation or any assignee of proceeds:

b. payment to a named beneficiary, transferee, an acknowledged assignee, successor by operation of law, to an account or account number stated in the standby or in a cover instruction from the beneficiary or nominated person fulfills the obligation under the standby to effect payment.

4.14 Name of Acquired or Merged Issuer or Confirmer

If the issuer or confirmer is reorganized, merged, or changes its name, any required reference by name to the issuer or confirmer in the documents presented may be to it or its successor.

4.15 Original, Copy, and Multiple Documents

a. A presented document must be an original.

b. Presentation of an electronic record, where an electronic presentation is permitted or required, is deemed to be an 'original'.

c. i. A presented document is deemed to be an original unless it appears on its face to have been reproduced from an original.

    ii. A document which appears to have been reproduced from an original is deemed to be an original if the signature or authentication appears to be original.

d. A standby that requires presentation of a 'copy' permits presentation of either an original or copy unless the standby states that only a copy be presented or otherwise addresses the disposition of all originals.

e. If multiples of the same document are requested, only one must be an original unless:

    i. 'duplicate originals' or 'multiple originals' are requested in which case all must be originals; or

    ii. 'two copies', 'two-fold', or the like are requested in which case either originals or copies may be presented.

STANDBY DOCUMENT TYPES

4.16 Demand for Payment

a. A demand for payment need not be separate from the beneficiary's statement or other required document.

b. If a separate demand is required, it must contain:

    i. a demand for payment from the beneficiary directed to the issuer or nominated person;

    ii. a date indicating when the demand was issued;

    iii. the amount demanded; and

    iv. the beneficiary's signature.

c. A demand may be in the form of a draft or other instruction, order, or request to pay. If a standby requires presentation of a 'draft' or 'bill of exchange', that draft or bill of exchange need not be in negotiable form unless the standby so states.

4.17 Statement of Default or Other Drawing Event

If a standby requires a statement, certificate, or other recital of a default or other drawing event and does not specify content, the document complies if it contains:

a. a representation to the effect that payment is due because a drawing event described in the standby has occurred;

b. a date indicating when it was issued; and

c. the beneficiary's signature.

4.18 Negotiable Documents

If a standby requires presentation of a document that is transferable by endorsement and delivery without stating whether, how, or to whom endorsement must be made, then the document may be presented without endorsement, or, if endorsed, the endorsement may be in blank and, in any event, the document may be issued or negotiated with or without recourse.

4.19 Legal or Judicial Documents

If a standby requires presentation of a government-issued document, a court order, an arbitration award, or the like, a document or a copy is deemed to comply if it appears to be:

    i. issued by a government agency, court, tribunal, or the like;

    ii. suitably titled or named;

    iii. signed;

iv. dated; and

v. originally certified or authenticated by an official of a government agency, court, tribunal, or the like.

4.20 Other Documents

a. If a standby requires a document other than one whose content is specified in these Rules without specifying the issuer, data content, or wording, a document complies if it appears to be appropriately titled or to serve the function of that type of document under standard standby practice.

b. A document presented under a standby is to be examined in the context of standby practice under these Rules even if the document is of a type (such as a commercial invoice, transport documents, insurance documents or the like) for which the Uniform Customs and Practice for Documentary Credits contains detailed rules.

4.21 Request to Issue Separate Undertaking

If a standby requests that the beneficiary of the standby issue its own separate undertaking to another (whether or not the standby recites the text of that undertaking):

a. the beneficiary receives no rights other than its rights to draw under the standby even if the issuer pays a fee to the beneficiary for issuing the separate undertaking;

b. neither the separate undertaking nor any documents presented under it need be presented to the issuer; and

c. if originals or copies of the separate undertaking or documents presented under it are received by the issuer although not required to be presented as a condition to honour of the standby:

i. the issuer need not examine, and, in any event, shall disregard their compliance or consistency with the standby, with the beneficiary's demand under the standby, or with the beneficiary's separate undertaking; and

ii. the issuer may without responsibility return them to the presenter or forward them to the applicant with the presentation.

RULE 5
NOTICE, PRECLUSION, AND DISPOSITION OF DOCUMENTS

5.01 Timely Notice of Dishonour

a. Notice of dishonour must be given within a time after presentation of documents which is not unreasonable.

i. Notice given within three business days is deemed to be not unreasonable and beyond seven business days is deemed to be unreasonable.

ii. Whether the time within which notice is given is unreasonable does not depend upon an imminent deadline for presentation.

iii. The time for calculating when notice of dishonour must be given begins on the business day following the business day of presentation.

iv. Unless a standby otherwise expressly states a shortened time within which notice of dishonour must be given, the issuer has no obligation to accelerate its examination of a presentation.

b. i. The means by which a notice of dishonour is to be given is by telecommunication, if available, and, if not, by another available means which allows for prompt notice.

    ii. If notice of dishonour is received within the time permitted for giving the notice, then it is deemed to have been given by prompt means.

c. Notice of dishonour must be given to the person from whom the documents were received (whether the beneficiary, nominated person, or person other than a delivery person) except as otherwise requested by the presenter.

5.02 Statement of Grounds for Dishonour

A notice of dishonour shall state all discrepancies upon which dishonour is based.

5.03 Failure to Give Timely Notice of Dishonour

a. Failure to give notice of a discrepancy in a notice of dishonour within the time and by the means specified in the standby or these rules precludes assertion of that discrepancy in any document containing the discrepancy that is retained or re-presented, but does not preclude assertion of that discrepancy in any different presentation under the same or a separate standby.

b. Failure to give notice of dishonour or acceptance or acknowledgment that a deferred payment undertaking has been incurred obligates the issuer to pay at maturity.

5.04 Notice of Expiry

Failure to give notice that a presentation was made after the expiration date does not preclude dishonour for that reason.

5.05 Issuer Request for Applicant Waiver without Request by Presenter

If the issuer decides that a presentation does not comply and if the presenter does not otherwise instruct, the issuer may, in its sole discretion, request the applicant to waive non-compliance or otherwise to authorise honour within the time available for giving notice of dishonour but without extending it. Obtaining the applicant's waiver does not obligate the issuer to waive non-compliance.

5.06 Issuer Request for Applicant Waiver upon Request of Presenter

If, after receipt of notice of dishonour, a presenter requests that the presented documents be forwarded to the issuer or that the issuer seek the applicant's waiver:

a. no person is obligated to forward the discrepant documents or seek the applicant's waiver;

b. the presentation to the issuer remains subject to these Rules unless departure from them is expressly consented to by the presenter; and

c. if the documents are forwarded or if a waiver is sought:

    i. the presenter is precluded from objecting to the discrepancies notified to it by the issuer;

    ii. the issuer is not relieved from examining the presentation under these Rules;

    iii. the issuer is not obligated to waive the discrepancy even if the applicant waives it; and

iv. the issuer must hold the documents until it receives a response from the applicant or is requested by the presenter to return the documents, and if the issuer receives no such response or request within ten business days of its notice of dishonour, it may return the documents to the presenter.

5.07 Disposition of Documents

Dishonored documents must be returned, held, or disposed of as reasonably instructed by the presenter. Failure to give notice of the disposition of documents in the notice of dishonour does not preclude the issuer from asserting any defense otherwise available to it against honour.

5.08 Cover Instructions/Transmittal Letter

a. Instructions accompanying a presentation made under a standby may be relied on to the extent that they are not contrary to the terms or conditions of the standby, the demand, or these Rules.
b. Representations made by a nominated person accompanying a presentation may be relied upon to the extent that they are not contrary to the terms or conditions of a standby or these Rules.
c. Notwithstanding receipt of instructions, an issuer or nominated person may pay, give notice, return the documents, or otherwise deal directly with the presenter.
d. A statement in the cover letter that the documents are discrepant does not relieve the issuer from examining the presentation for compliance.

5.09 Applicant Notice of Objection

a. An applicant must timely object to an issuer's honour of a noncomplying presentation by giving timely notice by prompt means.
b. An applicant acts timely if it objects to discrepancies by sending a notice to the issuer stating the discrepancies on which the objection is based within a time after the applicant's receipt of the documents which is not unreasonable.
c. Failure to give a timely notice of objection by prompt means precludes assertion by the applicant against the issuer of any discrepancy or other matter apparent on the face of the documents received by the applicant, but does not preclude assertion of that objection to any different presentation under the same or a different standby.

RULE 6
TRANSFER, ASSIGNMENT, AND TRANSFER BY OPERATION OF LAW

TRANSFER OF DRAWING RIGHTS

6.01 Request to Transfer Drawing Rights

Where a beneficiary requests that an issuer or nominated person honour a drawing from another person as if that person were the beneficiary, these Rules on transfer of drawing rights ('transfer') apply.

6.02 When Drawing Rights are Transferable

a. A standby is not transferable unless it so states.
b. A standby that states that it is transferable without further provision means that drawing rights:
   i.   may be transferred in their entirety more than once;
   ii. may not be partially transferred; and
   iii. may not be transferred unless the issuer (including the confirmer) or another person specifically nominated in the standby agrees to and effects the transfer requested by the beneficiary.

6.03 Conditions to Transfer

An issuer of a transferable standby or a nominated person need not effect a transfer unless:
a. it is satisfied as to the existence and authenticity of the original standby; and
b. the beneficiary submits or fulfills:
   i.   a request in a form acceptable to the issuer or nominated person including the effective date of the transfer and the name and address of the transferee;
   ii. the original standby;
   iii. verification of the signature of the person signing for the beneficiary;
   iv. verification of the authority of the person signing for the beneficiary;
   v. payment of the transfer fee; and
   vi. any other reasonable requirements.

6.04 Effect of Transfer on Required Documents

Where there has been a transfer of drawing rights in their entirety:
  a. a draft or demand must be signed by the transferee beneficiary; and
  b. the name of the transferee beneficiary may be used in place of the name of the transferor beneficiary in any other required document.

6.05 Reimbursement for Payment Based on a Transfer

An issuer or nominated person paying under a transfer pursuant to Rule 6.03(a), (b)(i), and (b)(ii) is entitled to reimbursement as if it had made payment to the beneficiary.

ACKNOWLEDGMENT OF ASSIGNMENT OF PROCEEDS

6.06 Assignment of Proceeds

Where an issuer or nominated person is asked to acknowledge a beneficiary's request to pay an assignee all or part of any proceeds of the beneficiary's drawing under the standby, these Rules on acknowledgment of an assignment of proceeds apply except where applicable law otherwise requires.

6.07 Request for Acknowledgment

a. Unless applicable law otherwise requires, an issuer or nominated person
   i. is not obligated to give effect to an assignment of proceeds which it has not acknowledged; and
   ii. is not obligated to acknowledge the assignment.

b. If an assignment is acknowledged:
   i.   the acknowledgment confers no rights with respect to the standby to the assignee who is only entitled to the proceeds assigned, if any, and whose rights may be affected by amendment or cancellation; and
  ii. the rights of the assignee are subject to:
      (a) the existence of any net proceeds payable to the beneficiary by the person making the acknowledgment;
      (b) rights of nominated persons and transferee beneficiaries;
      (c) rights of other acknowledged assignees; and
      (d) any other rights or interests that may have priority under applicable law.

6.08 Conditions to Acknowledgment of Assignment of Proceeds

An issuer or nominated person may condition its acknowledgment on receipt of:
  a. the original standby for examination or notation;
  b. verification of the signature of the person signing for the beneficiary;
  c. verification of the authority of the person signing for the beneficiary;
  d. an irrevocable request signed by the eneficiary for acknowledgment of the assignment that includes statements, covenants, indemnities, and other provisions which may be contained in the issuer's or nominated person's required form requesting acknowledgment of assignment, such as:
      i.   the identity of the affected drawings if the standby permits multiple drawings;
      ii. the full name, legal form, location, and mailing address of the beneficiary and the assignee;
     iii. details of any request affecting the method of payment or delivery of the standby proceeds;
     iv. limitation on partial assignments and prohibition of successive assignments;
     v.   statements regarding the legality and relative priority of the assignment; or
     vi. right of recovery by the issuer or nominated person of any proceeds received by the assignee that are recoverable from the beneficiary;
  e. payment of a fee for the acknowledgment; and
  f. fulfillment of other reasonable requirements.

6.09 Conflicting Claims to Proceeds

If there are conflicting claims to proceeds, then payment to an acknowledged assignee may be suspended pending resolution of the conflict.

6.10 Reimbursement for Payment Based on an Assignment

An issuer or nominated person paying under an acknowledged assignment pursuant to Rule 6.08(a) and (b) is entitled to reimbursement as if it had made payment to the beneficiary. If the beneficiary is a bank, the acknowledgment may be based solely upon an authenticated communication.

6.11 Transferee by Operation of Law

Where an heir, personal representative, liquidator, trustee, receiver, successor corporation, or similar person who claims to be designated by law to succeed to the interests of a beneficiary presents documents in its own name as if it were the authorised transferee of the beneficiary, these Rules on transfer by operation of law apply.

6.12 Additional Document in Event of Drawing in Successor's Name

A claimed successor may be treated as if it were an authorised transferee of a beneficiary's drawing rights in their entirety if it presents an additional document or documents which appear to be issued by a public official or representative (including a judicial officer) and indicate:

a. that the claimed successor is the survivor of a merger, consolidation, or similar action of a corporation, limited liability company, or other similar organization;

b. that the claimed successor is authorised or appointed to act on behalf of the named beneficiary or its estate because of an insolvency proceeding;

c. that the claimed successor is authorised or appointed to act on behalf of the named beneficiary because of death or incapacity; or

d. that the name of the named beneficiary has been changed to that of the claimed successor.

6.13 Suspension of Obligations upon Presentation by Successor

An issuer or nominated person which receives a presentation from a claimed successor which complies in all respects except for the name of the beneficiary:

a. may request in a manner satisfactory as to form and substance:
   i. a legal opinion;
   ii. an additional document referred to in Rule 6.12 (Additional Document in Event of Drawing in Successor's Name) from a public official;
   iii. statements, covenants, and indemnities regarding the status of the claimed successor as successor by operation of law;
   iv. payment of fees reasonably related to these determinations; and
   v. anything which may be required for a transfer under Rule 6.03 (Conditions to Transfer) or an acknowledgment of assignment of proceeds under Rule 6.08 (Conditions to Acknowledgment of Assignment of Proceeds);

   but such documentation shall not constitute a required document for purposes of expiry of the standby.

b. Until the issuer or nominated person receives the requested documentation, its obligation to honour or give notice of dishonour is suspended, but any deadline for presentation of required documents is not thereby extended.

6.14 Reimbursement for Payment Based on a Transfer by Operation of Law

An issuer or nominated person paying under a transfer by operation of law pursuant to Rule 6.12 (Additional Document in Event of Drawing in Successor's Name) is entitled to reimbursement as if it had made payment to the beneficiary.

411

RULE 7
CANCELLATION

7.01 When an Irrevocable Standby is Cancelled or Terminated

A beneficiary's rights under a standby may not be cancelled without its consent. Consent may be evidenced in writing or by an action such as return of the original standby in a manner which implies that the beneficiary consents to cancellation. A beneficiary's consent to cancellation is irrevocable when communicated to the issuer.

7.02 Issuer's Discretion Regarding a Decision to Cancel

Before acceding to a beneficiary's authorization to cancel and treating the standby as cancelled for all purposes, an issuer may require in a manner satisfactory as to form and substance:

    a. the original standby;
    b. verification of the signature of the person signing for the beneficiary;
    c. verification of the authorization of the person signing for the beneficiary;
    d. a legal opinion;
    e. an irrevocable authority signed by the beneficiary for cancellation that includes statements, covenants, indemnities, and similar provisions contained in a required form;
    f. satisfaction that the obligation of any confirmer has been cancelled;
    g. satisfaction that there has not been a transfer or payment any nominated person; and
    h. any other reasonable measure.

RULE 8
REIMBURSEMENT OBLIGATIONS

8.01 Right to Reimbursement

    a. Where payment is made against a complying presentation in accordance with these Rules, reimbursement must be made by:
        i. an applicant to an issuer requested to issue a standby; and
        ii. an issuer to a person nominated to honour or otherwise give value.
    b. An applicant must indemnify the issuer against all claims, obligations, and responsibilities (including attorney's fees) arising out of:
        i. the imposition of law or practice other than that chosen in the standby or applicable at the place of issuance;
        ii. the fraud, forgery, or illegal action of others; or
        iii. the issuer's performance of the obligations of a confirmer that wrongfully dishonours a confirmation.
    c. This Rule supplements any applicable agreement, course of dealing, practice, custom or usage providing for reimbursement or indemnification on lesser or other grounds.

8.02 Charges for Fees and Costs

a. An applicant must pay the issuer's charges and reimburse the issuer for any charges that the issuer is obligated to pay to persons nominated with the applicant's consent to advise, confirm, honour, negotiate, transfer, or to issue a separate undertaking.
b. An issuer is obligated to pay the charges of other persons:
    i. if they are payable in accordance with the terms of the standby; or
    ii. if they are the reasonable and customary fees and expenses of a person requested by the issuer to advise, honour, negotiate, transfer, or to issue a separate undertaking, and they are unrecovered and unrecoverable from the beneficiary or other presenter because no demand is made under the standby.

8.03 Refund of Reimbursement

A nominated person that obtains reimbursement before the issuer timely dishonours the presentation must refund the reimbursement with interest if the issuer dishonours. The refund does not preclude the nominated person's wrongful dishonour claims.

8.04 Bank-to-Bank Reimbursement

Any instruction or authorization to obtain reimbursement from another bank is subject to the International Chamber of Commerce standard rules for bank-to-bank reimbursements.

RULE 9
TIMING

9.01 Duration of Standby

A standby must:
    a. contain an expiry date; or
    b. permit the issuer to terminate the standby upon reasonable prior notice or payment.

9.02 Effect of Expiration on Nominated Person

The rights of a nominated person that acts within the scope of its nomination are not affected by the subsequent expiry of the standby.

9.03 Calculation of Time

a. A period of time within which an action must be taken under these Rules begins to run on the first business day following the business day when the action could have been undertaken at the place where the action should have been undertaken.
b. An extension period starts on the calendar day following the stated expiry date even if either day falls on a day when the issuer is closed.

9.04 Time of Day of Expiration

If no time of day is stated for expiration, it occurs at the close of business at the place of presentation.

413

9.05 Retention of Standby

Retention of the original standby does not preserve any rights under the standby after the right to demand payment ceases.

RULE 10
SYNDICATION/PARTICIPATION

10.01 Syndication

If a standby with more than one issuer does not state to whom presentation may be made, presentation may be made to any issuer with binding effect on all issuers.

10.02 Participation

a. Unless otherwise agreed between an applicant and an issuer, the issuer may sell participations in the issuer's rights against the applicant and any presenter and may disclose relevant applicant information in confidence to potential participants.
b. An issuer's sale of participations does not affect the obligations of the issuer under the standby or create any rights or obligations between the beneficiary and any participant.

(vi) UNITED NATIONS CONVENTION ON INDEPENDENT GUARANTEES AND STAND-BY LETTERS OF CREDIT*

CHAPTER I
SCOPE OF APPLICATION

Article 1
Scope of application

(1) This Convention applies to an international undertaking referred to in article 2:
  (a) If the place of business of the guarantor/issuer at which the undertaking is issued is in a Contracting State, or
  (b) If the rules of private international law lead to the application of the law of a Contracting State,
unless the undertaking excludes the application of the Convention.
(2) This Convention applies also the to an international letter of credit not falling within article 2 if it expressly states that it is subject to this Convention.
(3) The provisions of articles 21 and 22 apply to international undertakings referred to in article 2 independently of paragraph (1) of this article.

---

* Reproduced with the kind permission of UNCITRAL.

Article 2
Undertaking

(1) For the purposes of this Convention, an undertaking is an independent commitment, known in international practice as an independent guarantee or as a stand-by letter of credit, given by a bank or other institution or person ('guarantor/issuer') to pay to the beneficiary a certain or determinable amount upon simple demand or upon demand accompanied by other documents, in conformity with the terms and any documentary conditions of the undertaking, indicating, or from which it is to be inferred, that payment is due because of a default in the performance of an obligation, or because of another contingency, or for money borrowed or advanced, or on account of any mature indebtedness undertaken by the principal/applicant or another person.

(2) The undertaking may be given:
  (a) At the request or on the instruction of the customer ('principal/applicant') of the guarantor/issuer;
  (b) On the instruction of another bank, institution or person ('instructing party') that acts at the request of the customer ('principal/applicant') of that instructing party; or
  (c) On behalf of the guarantor/issuer itself.

(3) Payment may be stipulated in the undertaking to be made in any form, including:
  (a) Payment in a specified currency or unit of account;
  (b) Acceptance of a bill of exchange (draft);
  (c) Payment on a deferred basis;
  (d) Supply of a specified item of value.

(4) The undertaking may stipulate that the guarantor/issuer itself is the beneficiary when acting in favour of another person.

Article 3
Independence of undertaking

For the purposes of this Convention, an undertaking is independent where the guarantor/issuer's obligation to the beneficiary is not:
  (a) Dependent upon the existence or validity of any underlying transaction, or upon any other undertaking (including stand-by letters of credit or independent guarantees to which confirmations or counter-guarantees relate); or
  (b) Subject to any term or condition not appearing in the undertaking, or to any future, uncertain act or event except presentation of documents or another such act or event within a guarantor/issuer's sphere of operations.

Article 4
Internationality of undertaking

(1) An undertaking is international if the places of business, as specified in the undertaking, of any two of the following persons are in different States: guarantor/issuer, beneficiary, principal/applicant, instructing party, confirmer.

(2) For the purposes of the preceding paragraph:
  (1) If the undertaking lists more than one place of business for a given person, the relevant place of business is that which has the closest relationship to the undertaking;

(2) If the undertaking does not specify a place of business for a given person but specifies its habitual residence, that residence is relevant for determining the international character of the undertaking.

CHAPTER II
INTERPRETATION

Article 5
Principles of interpretation

In the interpretation of this Convention, regard is to be had to its international character and to the need to promote uniformity in its application and the observance of good faith in the international practice of independent guarantees and stand-by letters of credit.

Article 6
Definitions

For the purposes of this Convention and unless otherwise indicated in a provision of this Convention or required by the context:

(a) 'Undertaking' includes 'counter-guarantee' and 'confirmation of an undertaking';

(b) 'Guarantor/issuer' includes 'counter-guarantor' and 'confirmer';

(c) 'Counter-guarantee' means an undertaking given to the guarantor/issuer of another undertaking by its instructing party and providing for payment upon simple demand or upon demand accompanied by other documents, in conformity with the terms and any documentary conditions of the undertaking, indicating, or from which it is to be inferred, that payment under that other undertaking has been demanded from, or made by, the person issuing that other undertaking;

(d) 'Counter-guarantor' means the person issuing a counter-guarantee;

(e) 'Confirmation' of an undertaking means an undertaking added to that of the guarantor/issuer, and authorized by the guarantor/issuer, providing the beneficiary with the option of demanding payment from the confirmer instead of from the guarantor/issuer, upon simple demand or upon demand accompanied by other documents, in conformity with the terms and any documentary conditions of the confirmed undertaking, without prejudice to the beneficiary's right to demand payment from the guarantor/issuer;

(f) 'Confirmer' means the person adding a confirmation to an undertaking;

(g) 'Document' means a communication made in a form that provides a complete record thereof.

CHAPTER III
FORM AND CONTENT OF UNDERTAKING

Article 7
Issuance, form and irrevocability of undertaking

(1) Issuance of an undertaking occurs when and where the undertaking leaves the sphere of control of the guarantor/issuer concerned.

(2) An undertaking may be issued in any form which preserves a complete record of the text of the undertaking and provides authentication of its source by generally accepted means or by a procedure agreed upon by the guarantor/issuer and the beneficiary.

(3) From the time of issuance of an undertaking, a demand for payment may be made in accordance with the terms and conditions of the undertaking, unless the undertaking stipulates a different time.

(4) An undertaking is irrevocable upon issuance, unless it stipulates that it is revocable.

Article 8
Amendment

(1) An undertaking may not be amended except in the form stipulated in the undertaking or, failing such stipulation, in a form referred to in paragraph (2) of article 7.

(2) Unless otherwise stipulated in the undertaking or elsewhere agreed by the guarantor/issuer and the beneficiary, an undertaking is amended upon issuance of the amendment if the amendment has previously been authorized by the beneficiary.

(3) Unless otherwise stipulated in the undertaking or elsewhere agreed by the guarantor/issuer and the beneficiary, where any amendment has not previously been authorized by the beneficiary, the undertaking is amended only when the guarantor/issuer receives a notice of acceptance of the amendment by the beneficiary in a form referred to in paragraph (2) of article 7.

(4) An amendment of an undertaking has no effect on the rights and obligations of the principal/applicant (or an instructing party) or of a confirmer of the undertaking unless such person consents to the amendment.

Article 9
Transfer of beneficiary's right to demand payment

(1) The beneficiary's right to demand payment may be transferred only if authorized in the undertaking, and only to the extent and in the manner authorized in the undertaking.

(2) If an undertaking is designated as transferable without specifying whether or not the consent of the guarantor/issuer or another authorized person is required for the actual transfer, neither the guarantor/issuer nor any other authorized person is obliged to effect the transfer except to the extent and in the manner expressly consented to by it.

Article 10
Assignment of proceeds

(1) Unless otherwise stipulated in the undertaking or elsewhere agreed by the guarantor/issuer and the beneficiary, the beneficiary may assign to another person any proceeds to which it may be, or may become, entitled under the undertaking.

(2) If the guarantor/issuer or another person obliged to effect payment has received a notice originating from the beneficiary, in a form referred to in paragraph (2) of

article 7, of the beneficiary's irrevocable assignment, payment to the assignee discharges the obligor, to the extent of its payment, from its liability under the undertaking.

Article 11
Cessation of right to demand payment

(1) The right of the beneficiary to demand payment under the undertaking ceases when:
   (a) The guarantor/issuer has received a statement by the beneficiary of release from liability in a form referred to in paragraph (2) of article 7;
   (b) The beneficiary and the guarantor/issuer have agreed on the termination of the undertaking in the form stipulated in the undertaking or, failing such stipulation, in a form referred to in paragraph (2) of article 7;
   (c) The amount available under the undertaking has been paid, unless the undertaking provides for the automatic renewal or for an automatic increase of the amount available or otherwise provides for continuation of the undertaking;
   (d) The validity period of the undertaking expires in accordance with the provisions of article 12.

(2) The undertaking may stipulate, or the guarantor/issuer and the beneficiary may agree elsewhere, that return of the document embodying the undertaking to the guarantor/ issuer, or a procedure functionally equivalent to the return of the document in the case of the issuance of the undertaking in non-paper form, is required for the cessation of the right to demand payment, either alone or in conjunction with one of the events referred to in subparagraphs (a) and (b) of paragraph (1) of this article. However, in no case shall retention of any such document by the beneficiary after the right to demand payment ceases in accordance with subparagraph (c) or (d) of paragraph (1) of this article preserve any rights of the beneficiary under the undertaking.

Article 12
Expiry

The validity period of the undertaking expires:
(a) At the expiry date, which may be a specified calendar date or the last day of a fixed period of time stipulated in the undertaking, provided that, if the expiry date is not a business day at the place of business of the guarantor/issuer at which the undertaking is issued, or of another person or at another place stipulated in the undertaking for presentation of the demand for payment, expiry occurs on the first business day which follows;
(b) If expiry depends according to the undertaking on the occurrence of an act or event not within the guarantor/issuer's sphere of operations, when the guarantor/issuer is advised that the act or event has occurred by presentation of the document specified for that purpose in the undertaking or, if no such document is specified, of a certification by the beneficiary of the occurrence of the act or event;
(c) If the undertaking does not state an expiry date, or if the act or event on which expiry is stated to depend has not yet been established by presentation of the required

document and an expiry date has not been stated in addition, when six years have elapsed from the date of issuance of the undertaking.

CHAPTER IV
RIGHTS, OBLIGATIONS AND DEFENCES

Article 13
Determination of rights and obligations

(1) The rights and obligations of the guarantor/issuer and the beneficiary arising from the undertaking are determined by the terms and conditions set forth in the undertaking, including any rules, general conditions or usages specifically referred to therein, and by the provisions of this Convention.

(2) In interpreting terms and conditions of the undertaking and in settling questions that are not addressed by the terms and conditions of the undertaking or by the provisions of this Convention, regard shall be had to generally accepted international rules and usages of independent guarantee or stand-by letter of credit practice.

Article 14
Standard of conduct and liability of guarantor/issuer

(1) In discharging its obligations under the undertaking and this Convention, the guarantor/issuer shall act in good faith and exercise reasonable care having due regard to generally accepted standards of international practice of independent guarantees or stand-by letters of credit.

(2) A guarantor/issuer may not be exempted from liability for its failure to act in good faith or for any grossly negligent conduct.

Article 15
Demand

(1) Any demand for payment under the undertaking shall be made in a form referred to in paragraph (2) of article 7 and in conformity with the terms and conditions of the undertaking.

(2) Unless otherwise stipulated in the undertaking, the demand and any certification or other document required by the undertaking shall be presented, within the time that a demand for payment may be made, to the guarantor/issuer at the place where the undertaking was issued.

(3) The beneficiary, when demanding payment, is deemed to certify that the demand is not in bad faith and that none of the elements referred to in subparagraphs (a), (b) and (c) of paragraph (1) of article 19 are present.

Article 16
Examination of demand and accompanying documents

(1) The guarantor/issuer shall examine the demand and any accompanying documents in accordance with the standard of conduct referred to in paragraph (1) of article 14. In determining whether documents are in facial conformity with the terms and

conditions of the undertaking, and are consistent with one another, the guarantor/ issuer shall have due regard to the applicable international standard of independent guarantee or stand-by letter of credit practice.

(2) Unless otherwise stipulated in the undertaking or elsewhere agreed by the guarantor/ issuer and the beneficiary, the guarantor/issuer shall have reasonable time, but not more than seven business days following the day of receipt of the demand and any accompanying documents, in which to:

(a) Examine the demand and any accompanying documents;

(b) Decide whether or not to pay;

(c) If the decision is not to pay, issue notice thereof to the beneficiary.

The notice referred to in subparagraph (c) above shall, unless otherwise stipulated in the undertaking or elsewhere agreed by the guarantor/issuer and the beneficiary, be made by teletransmission or, if that is not possible, by other expeditious means and indicate the reason for the decision not to pay.

Article 17
Payment

(1) Subject to article 19, the guarantor/issuer shall pay against a demand made in accordance with the provisions of article 15. Following a determination that a demand for payment so conforms, payment shall be made promptly, unless the undertaking stipulates payment on a deferred basis, in which case payment shall be made at the stipulated time.

(2) Any payment against a demand that is not in accordance with the provisions of article 15 does not prejudice the rights of the principal/applicant.

Article 18
Set-off

Unless otherwise stipulated in the undertaking or elsewhere agreed by the guarantor/ issuer and the beneficiary, the guarantor/issuer may discharge the payment obligation under the undertaking by availing itself of a right of set-off, except with any claim assigned to it by the principal/applicant or the instructing party.

Article 19
Exception to payment obligation

(1) If it is manifest and clear that:

(a) Any document is not genuine or has been falsified;

(b) No payment is due on the basis asserted in the demand and the supporting documents; or

(c) Judging by the type and purpose of the undertaking, the demand has no conceivable basis,

the guarantor/issuer, acting in good faith, has a right, as against the beneficiary, to withhold payment.

(2) For the purposes of subparagraph (c) of paragraph (1) of this article, the following are types of situations in which a demand has no conceivable basis:

(a) The contingency or risk against which the undertaking was designed to secure the beneficiary has undoubtedly not materialized;

(b) The underlying obligation of the principal/applicant has been declared invalid by a court or arbitral tribunal, unless the undertaking indicates that such contingency falls within the risk to be covered by the undertaking;

(c) The underlying obligation has undoubtedly been fulfilled to the satisfaction of the beneficiary;

(d) Fulfilment of the underlying obligation has clearly been prevented by wilful misconduct of the beneficiary;

(e) In the case of a demand under a counter-guarantee, the beneficiary of the counter-guarantee has made payment in bad faith as guarantor/issuer of the undertaking to which the counter-guarantee relates.

(3) In the circumstances set out in subparagraphs (a), (b) and (c) of paragraph (1) of this article, the principal/applicant is entitled to provisional court measures in accordance with article 20.

CHAPTER V
PROVISIONAL COURT MEASURES

Article 20
Provisional court measures

(1) Where, on an application by the principal/applicant or the instructing party, it is shown that there is a high probability that, with regard to a demand made, or expected to be made, by the beneficiary, one of the circumstances referred to in subparagraphs (a), (b) and (c) of paragraph (1) of article 19 is present, the court, on the basis of immediately available strong evidence, may:

(a) Issue a provisional order to the effect that the beneficiary does not receive payment, including an order that the guarantor/issuer hold the amount of the undertaking, or

(b) Issue a provisional order to the effect that the proceeds of the undertaking paid to the beneficiary are blocked, taking into account whether in the absence of such an order the principal/applicant would be likely to suffer serious harm.

(2) The court, when issuing a provisional order referred to in paragraph (1) of this article, may require the person applying therefor to furnish such form of security as the court deems appropriate.

(3) The court may not issue a provisional order of the kind referred to in paragraph (1) of this article based on any objection to payment other than those referred to in subparagraphs (a), (b) and (c) of paragraph (1) of article 19, or use of the undertaking for a criminal purpose.

CHAPTER VI
CONFLICT OF LAWS

Article 21
Choice of applicable law

The undertaking is governed by the law the choice of which is:

(a) Stipulated in the undertaking or demonstrated by the terms and conditions of the undertaking; or

(b) Agreed elsewhere by the guarantor/issuer and the beneficiary.

Article 22
Determination of applicable law

Failing a choice of law in accordance with article 21, the undertaking is governed by the law of the State where the guarantor/issuer has that place of business at which the undertaking was issued.

CHAPTER VII
FINAL CLAUSES

Article 23
Depositary

The Secretary-General of the United Nations is the depositary of this Convention.

Article 24
Signature, ratification, acceptance, approval, accession

(1) This Convention is open for signature by all States at the Headquarters of the United Nations, New York, until 11 December 1997.
(2) This Convention is subject to ratification, acceptance or approval by the signatory States.
(3) This Convention is open to accession by all States which are not signatory States as from the date it is open for signature.
(4) Instruments of ratification, acceptance, approval and accession are to be deposited with the Secretary-General of the United Nations.

Article 25
Application to territorial units

(1) If a State has two or more territorial units in which different systems of law are applicable in relation to the matters dealt with in this Convention, it may, at the time of signature, ratification, acceptance, approval or accession, declare that this Convention is to extend to all its territorial units or only one or more of them, and may at any time substitute another declaration for its earlier declaration.
(2) These declarations are to state expressly the territorial units to which the Convention extends.
(3) If, by virtue of a declaration under this article, this Convention does not extend to all territorial units of a State and the place of business of the guarantor/issuer or of the beneficiary is located in a territorial unit to which the Convention does not extend, this place of business is considered not to be in a Contracting State.
(4) If a State makes no declaration under paragraph (1) of this article, the Convention is to extend to all territorial units of that State.

Article 26
Effect of declaration

(1) Declarations made under article 25 at the time of signature are subject to confirmation upon ratification, acceptance or approval.

(2) Declarations and confirmations of declarations are to be in writing and to be formally notified to the depositary.

(3) A declaration takes effect simultaneously with the entry into force of this Convention in respect of the State concerned. However, a declaration of which the depositary receives formal notification after such entry into force takes effect on the first day of the month following the expiration of six months after the date of its receipt by the depositary.

(4) Any State which makes a declaration under article 25 may withdraw it at any time by a formal notification in writing addressed to the depositary. Such withdrawal takes effect on the first day of the month following the expiration of six months after the date of the receipt of the notification of the depositary.

Article 27
Reservations

No reservations may be made to this Convention.

Article 28
Entry into force

(1) This Convention enters into force on the first day of the month following the expiration of one year from the date of the deposit of the fifth instrument of ratification, acceptance, approval or accession.

(2) For each State which becomes a Contracting State to this Convention after the date of the deposit of the fifth instrument of ratification, acceptance, approval or accession, this Convention enters into force on the first day of the month following the expiration of one year after the date of the deposit of the appropriate instrument on behalf of that State.

(3) This Convention applies only to undertakings issued on or after the date when the Convention enters into force in respect of the Contracting State referred to in subparagraph (a) or the Contracting State referred to in subparagraph (b) of paragraph (1) of article 1.

Article 29
Denunciation

(1) A Contracting State may denounce this Convention at any time by means of a notification in writing addressed to the depositary.

(2) The denunciation takes effect on the first day of the month following the expiration of one year after the notification is received by the depositary. Where a longer period is specified in the notification, the denunciation takes effect upon the expiration of such longer period after the notification is received by the depositary.

DONE at New York, this eleventh day of December one thousand nine hundred and ninety-five, in a single original, of which the Arabic, Chinese, English, French, Russian and Spanish texts are equally authentic.

IN WITNESS WHEREOF the undersigned plenipotentiaries, being duly authorized by their respective Governments, have signed the present Convention.

TABLE OF STATE RATIFICATIONS

Total number of signatures not followed by ratifications: 1
Total number of ratifications/accessions: 6

State	Signature	Ratification	By	Entry into force
Belarus	3 December 1996	23 January 2002		1 February 2003
Ecuador		18 June 1997	Accession	1 January 2000
El Salvador	5 September 1997	31 July 1998		1 January 2000
Kuwait		28 October 1998	Accession	1 January 2000
Panama	9 July 1997	21 May 1998		1 January 2000
Tunisia		8 December 1998	Accession	1 January 2000
United States of America	11 December 1997			

Entered into force: 1 January 2000
(Condition: 5 ratifications)

(vii) ICC UNIFORM RULES FOR CONTRACT BONDS*

Article 1
Scope and Application

(a) These Rules shall be blown as the 'Uniform Rules for Contract Bonds' and shall apply to any Bond which states that these Rules shall apply, or otherwise incorporates these Rules by reference and, for such purposes, it shall suffice that the Bond incorporates a reference to these Rules and the publication number.

(b) If there shall be any conflict in the construction or operation of the obligations of any parties under a Bond, between the provisions of these Rules and such Bond, or mandatory provisions of the Applicable Law regulating the same, the provisions of the Bond or, as the case may be, the mandatory provisions of the Applicable Law shall prevail.

Article 2
Definitions

In these Rules, words or expressions shall bear the meanings set out below and be construed accordingly.

ADVANCE PAYMENT BOND

A Bond given by the Guarantor in favour of the Beneficiary to secure the repayment of any sum or sums advanced by the Beneficiary to the Principal under or for the purposes of the Contract, where such sum or sums is or are advanced before the carrying cut of works, the performance of services or the supply or provision of any goods pursuant to such Contract.

BENECIARY

The party in whose favour a Bond is issued or provided.

BOND

Any bond, guarantee or other instrument in writing issued or executed by the Guarantor in favour of the Beneficiary pursuant to which the Guarantor undertakes on Default, either:

(i) to pay or satisfy any claim or entitlement to payment of damages, compensation or other financial relief up to the Bond Amount; or

---

* ICC Publication No. 524(E)–ISBN 92.842.1164.6. Published in its official English version by the International Chamber of Commerce. Copyright ©1993–International Chamber of Commerce (ICC), Paris.

(ii) to pay or satisfy such claim or entitlement up to the Bond Amount or at the Guarantor's option to perform or execute the Contractor any Contractual Obligation.

In either case where the liability of the Guarantor shall be accessory to the liability of the Principal under the Contract or such Contractual Obligation and such expression shall without limitation include Advance Payment Bonds, Maintenance Bonds, Performance Bonds, Retention Bonds and Tender Bonds.

BOND AMOUNT

The sum inserted in tile Bond as the maximum aggregate liability of the Guarantor as amended, varied or reduced from time to time or, following the payment of any amount in satisfaction or partial satisfaction of a claim under any Bond, such lesser sum as shall be calculated by deducting from the sum inserted in the Bond the amount of such payment.

CONTRACT

Any written agreement between the Principal and the Beneficiary for the carrying out of works, the performance of services or the supply or provision of any goods.

CONTRACTUAL OBLIGATION

Any duty, obligation or requirement imposed by a clause, paragraph, section, term, condition, provision or stipulation contained in or forming part of a Contract or tender.

DEFAULT

Any breach, default or failure to perform any Contractual Obligation which shall give rise to a claim for performance, damages, compensation or other financial remedy by the Beneficiary and which is established pursuant to paragraph (j) of Article 7.

EXPIRY DATE

Either (a) the date fixed or the date of the event on which the obligations of the Guarantor under the Bond are expressed to expire or (b) if no such date is stipulated, the date determined in accordance with Article 4.

GUARANTOR

Any Person who shall issue or execute a Bond on behalf of a Principal.

MAINTENANCE BOND

A Bond to secure Contractual Obligations relating to the maintenance of works or goods following the physical completion of the provision thereof, pursuant to a Contract.

PERFORMANCE BOND

A Bond to secure the performance of any Contract or Contractual Obligation.

PERSON

Any company, corporation, firm' association, body, individual or any legal entity whatsoever.

PRINCIPAL

Any Person who (i) either (a) submits a tender for the purpose of entering into a Contract with the Beneficiary or (b) enters into a Contract with (the Beneficiary and (ii) assumes primary liability for all Contractual Obligations thereunder.

427

RETENTION BOND

A Bond to secure the payment of any sum or sums paid or released to the Principal by the Beneficiary before the date for payment or release thereof contained in the Contract.

TENDER BOND

A Bond in respect of a tender to secure the payment of any loss or damage suffered or incurred by the Beneficiary arising out of the failure by the Principal to enter into a Contract or provide a Performance Bond or other Bond pursuant to such tender.

WRITING AND WRITTEN

Shall include any authenticated tele-transmissions or tested electronic data interchange ('EDI') message equivalent thereto.

Article 3
Form of Bond and Liability of the Guarantor to the Beneficiary

(a) The Bond should stipulate:
    i.   The Principal.
    ii.   The Beneficiary.
    iii. The Guarantor.
    iv. The Contract.
    v.   Where the Bond does not extend to the whole of the Contract, the precise Contractual Obligation or Obligations to which the Bond relates.
    vi. The Bond Amount.
    vii. Any provisions for the reduction of the Bond Amount.
    viii. The date when the Bond becomes effective (defined in these rules as the 'Effective Date').
    ix. Whether the Guarantor shall be entitled at its option to perform or execute the Contract or any Contractual Obligation.
    x.   The Expiry Date.
    xi. The names, addresses, telex and/or telefax.numbers and contact references of the Beneficiary, the Guarantor and the Principal.
    xii. Whether sub-paragraph (i) of Article 7(j) is to apply and the name of the third party to be nominated thereunder for the purpose of Article 7 below (claims procedure).
    xiii. How disputes or differences between the Beneficiary, the Principal and the Guarantor in relation to the Bond are to be settled.

(b) The liability of the Guarantor to the Beneficiary under the Bond is accessory to the liability of the Principal to the Beneficiary under the Contract and shall arise upon Default. The Contract is deemed to be incorporated into and form part of the Bond, The liability of the Guarantor shall not exceed the Bond Amount.

(c) Save for any reduction of the Bond Amount under the terms of the Bond or the Contract and subject to Article 4, the liability of the Guarantor shall not be reduced or discharged by reason of any partial performance of the Contract or any Contractual Obligation.

(d) All defences, remedies, cross claims, counter-claims and other rights or entitlements to relief which the Principal may have against the Beneficiary under the Contract, or which may otherwise be available to the Principal in respect of the subject matter thereof, shall be available to the Guarantor in respect of any Default in addition to and without limiting any defence under or arising out of the Bond.

Article 4
Release and Discharge of Guarantor

(a) Subject to any contrary provision in the Bond and the provisions of paragraph (b) of this Article 4, the Expiry Date shall be six months from the latest date for the performance of the Contract or the relevant Contractual Obligations thereunder, as the case may be.

(b) Subject to any contrary provision of the Bond, the Expiry Date for the purposes of an Advance Payment Bond, a Maintenance Bond, a Retention Bond and a Tender Bond shall be as follows:

   i. In the case of an Advance Payment Bond the date on which the Principal shall have carried out works, supplied goods or services or otherwise performed Contractual Obligations having a value as certified or otherwise determined pursuant to the Contract equal to or exceeding the Bond Amount.

   ii. In the case of a Maintenance Bond, six months after either the date stipulated by the Contract or, if no date has been specified for the termination of the Principal's maintenance obligations, the last day of the applicable warranty period or defects liability period under the Contract.

   iii. In the case of a Retention Bond, six months after the date stipulated by the Contract for the payment, repayment or release of any retention monies.

   iv. In the case of a Tender Bond, six months after the latest date set out in the tender documents or conditions for the submission of tenders.

(c) Where the Expiry Date falls on a day which is not a Business Day, the Expiry Date shall be the first following Business Day. For the purpose of these Rules 'Business Day' shall mean any day on which the offices of the Guarantor shall ordinarily be open for business.

(d) A Bond shall terminate and without prejudice to any term, provision, agreement or stipulation of the Bond, any other agreement or the Applicable Law providing for earlier release or discharge, the liability of the Guarantor shall be discharged absolutely and the Guarantor shall be released upon the Expiry Date whether or not the Bond shall be returned to the Guarantor, save in respect of any claim served in accordance with Article 7.

(e) Notwithstanding the provisions of paragraph (d) of this Article 4, the Bond may be cancelled at any time by the return of the Bond itself to the Guarantor or by the service upon and delivery or transmission to the Guarantor of a release in writing duly signed by an authorised representative of the Beneficiary whether or not accompanied by the Bond and/or any amendment or amendments thereto.

(f) The Guarantor shall promptly inform the Principal of any payment made under or pursuant to the Bond and of the cancellation, release or discharge thereof or any reduction in the Bond Amount where the same shall not already have been communicated.

Article 5
Return of the Bond

The Bond shall immediately after release or discharge under these Rules be returned to the Guarantor, and the retention or possession of the Bond following such release or discharge shall not of itself operate to confer any right or entitlement the thereunder upon the Beneficiary.

Article 6
Amendments and Variations to and of the Contract and the Bond and Extensions of Time

(a) The Bond shall, subject to the Bond Amount and the Expiry Date, apply to the Contract as amended or varied by the Principal and the Beneficiary from time to time.

(b) A Tender Bond shall be valid only in respect of the works and contract particulars set out or described in the tender documents at the Effective Date, and shall not apply beyond the Expiry Date or in any case where there shall be any substantial or material variation of or amendment to the original tender after the Effective Date, unless the Guarantor shall confirm, in the same manner as set out in paragraph (c) of this Article 6, that the Tender Bond so applies or the Expiry Date has been extended.

(c) Any amendment to a Bond, including without limitation the increase of the Bond Amount or the alteration of the Expiry Date, shall be in writing duly signed or executed by authorised representatives of each of the Beneficiary, the Principal and the Guarantor.

Article 7
Submission of Claims and Claims Procedure

(a) A claim under a Bond shall be in writing and shall be served upon the Guarantor on or before the Expiry Date and by no later than the close of the Business Day at the Guarantor's principal place of business set out in the Bond, on the Expiry Date.

(b) A claim submitted by authenticated tele-transmission, EDI, telex or other means of telefax facsimile or electronic transmission shall be deemed to be received on the arrival of such transmission.

(c) A claim delivered to the Guarantor's principal place of business set out in the Bond shall, subject to proof of delivery, be deemed to be served on the date of such delivery.

(d) A claim served or transmitted by post, shall, subject to satisfactory proof of delivery by the beneficiary, be deemed to be served upon actual receipt thereof by the Guarantor.

(e) The Beneficiary shall when giving notice of any claim by telefax or other tele-transmission or EDI, also send a copy of such claim by post.

(f) Any claim shall state brief details of the Contract to identify the same, state that there has been a breach or default and set out the circumstances of such breach or default and any request for payment, performance or execution.

(g) Upon receipt of a claim from the Beneficiary, the Guarantor shall send notice in writing to the Principal of such claim as soon as reasonably practicable and before either
   i. making any payment in satisfaction or partial satisfaction of the same or,
   ii. performing the Contract or any part thereof pursuant to a Contractual Obligation.

(h) The Beneficiary shall, upon written request by the Guarantor, supply to the Guarantor such further information as the Guarantor may reasonably request to enable it to consider the claim, and shall provide copies or any correspondence or other documents relating to the Contract or the performance of any Contractual Obligations and allow the Guarantor, its employees, agents or representatives to inspect any works, goods or services carried out or supplied by the Principal.

(i) A Claim shall not be honoured unless
   i. A Default has occurred; and
   ii. The claim has been made and served in accordance with the provisions of paragraphs (a)–(f) of Article 7 on or before the Expiry Date.

(j) Notwithstanding any dispute or difference between the Principal and the Beneficiary in relation to the performance of the Contract or any Contractual Obligation, a Default shall be deemed to be established for the purposes of these Rules:
   i. upon issue of a certificate of Default by a third party (who may without limitation be an independent architect or engineer or a Pre-Arbitral referee of the ICC) if the Bond so provides and the service of such certificate or a certified copy thereof upon the Guarantor, or
   ii. if the Bond does not provide for the issue of a certificate by a third party, upon the issue of a certificate of Default by the Guarantor, or
   iii. by the final judgment, order or award of a court or tribunal of competent jurisdiction, and the issue of a certificate of Default under paragraph (i) or (ii) Shall not restrict the right of thc parties to seek or require the determination of any dispute or difference arising under the Contract or the Bond or the review of any certificate of Default or payment made pursuant thereto by a court or tribunal of competent jurisdiction.

(k) A copy of any certificate of Default issued under (j)(i) or (ii) shall be given by the Guarantor to the Principal and the Beneficiary forthwith.

(l) The Guarantor shall consider any claim expeditiously and, if such claim is rejected, shall immediately give notice thereof to the Beneficiary by authenticated tele-transmission or other telefax, facsimile transmission, telex, cable or EDI, confirming the same by letter, setting out the grounds for such refusal including any defences or other matters raised under paragraph (d) of Article 3.

Article 8
Jurisdiction and Settlement of Disputes

(a) The Applicable Law shall be the law of the country selected by the parties to govern the operation of the Bond and, in the absence of any express choice of law, shall be the law governing the Contract and any dispute or difference arising under these Rules in relation to a Bond shall be determined in accordance with the Applicable Law.

(b) All disputes arising between the Beneficiary, the Principal and the Guarantor or any of them in relation to a Bond governed by these Rules shall, unless otherwise agreed, be finally settled under the Rules of Conciliation and Arbitration of the International Chamber of Commerce by one or more arbitrators appointed in accordance with the said Rules.

(c) If the Bond shall exclude the operation of the arbitration provisions of this Article 8, any dispute between the parties to the Bond shall be determining by the courts of the country nominated in the Bond, or, if there is no such nomination, the competent court of the Guarantor's principal place of business or, at the option of the Beneficiary, the competent court of the country in which the branch of the Guarantor which issued the Bond is situated.

431

7

INTERNATIONAL SECURED TRANSACTIONS

A. Introductory Text

Secured transactions, debt backed by collateral, are efficient forms of credit extension. They permit the granting of credit to borrowers unable or unwilling to finance solely on terms reflecting their commercial capacity to repay. The essence of secured financing is that the risk of loss to the creditor in the event of default by its debtor is reduced by access to the value of collateral.

For a variety of reasons, rules embodied in many national legal system are inadequate to facilitate secured financing. Two reasons are paramount. First, such rules may not reflect the core principles underlying this transaction type. These principles include transparency of competing claims against collateral (priority), the ability promptly to realize the value of collateral upon default (prompt enforcement), and the reliability and enforceability of security in the insolvency context (insolvency rights). Secondly, problems arise from the nature of certain types of collateral, given extant legal rules. Notable in this regard are interests in mobile equipment, viewed against the traditional *lex rei sitae* rule. That rule is not workable in relation to equipment which is constantly moving from one State to another in the course of business. Difficulties also arise in taking security over intangible property, viewed against traditional rules that seek to fix the location of security based on criteria analogous to tangible property.

Characterization of interests is an additional complicating factor under the law applicable to secured financing. Different types of structures—financial and operational leases, conditional sales, and other title retention devices—are employed, to maximize legal protections. Yet these interests may be characterized differently in different legal systems. Such differences may be a source of significant legal risk and lack of predictability, or, alternatively, may be arbitraged, for example, to maximize taxation advantage.

The competition between secured financing interests and other interests in collateral arising by law (non-consensual interests), and the latter's rights to physically seize collateral, have been historically significant. That has particularly been the case in the maritime and aviation contexts, where operational practicalities and other policy objectives have combined to produce strong rights in favour of holders of non-consensual interests, such as taxing authorities and repairers. From a secured financier's perspective, non-consensual interests are often problematic—as they may be non-transparent, in effect, secret competing liens.

1. Secured Transactions in General

There are no international conventions or model laws laying down general rules for the creation, perfection, and priority of security interests. There are, however, two important model laws of a regional character, the 1994 EBRD Model Law on

Secured Transactions, prepared by the European Bank for Reconstruction and Development, and the 2002 Model Inter-American Law on Secured Transactions, concluded at a plenary conference hosted by the Organization of American States and referred to hereafter as the OAS Model Law.

(a) The EBRD Model Law

Nature and purposes

While designed principally to assist in the development of secured credit in the former communist bloc, the EBRD Model Law is a seminal text. It represents the first successful attempt to embody modern secured transaction rules in a major international text. It is both concise and comprehensive.

As a model law, it is not a legally operative instrument and is not open to ratification. States are free to reject it, to enact it in its entirety or to select, amend, or add to particular provisions. A number of States have done just that.[1]

The text seeks to strike a fair balance between the interests of debtors ('chargors') and creditors ('chargeholders'), but, importantly, does so in line with established principles underlying secured credit. Its express objective is the promotion of efficient secured transactions. Save for its reluctance specifically to address enforcement in the insolvency context[2]—the acid test of secured credit—the EBRD Model Law has provided inspiration for all subsequent efforts to modernize secured transactions law.

Single in rem security right over any property

The EBRD Model Law sets out a single security right, *in rem* in nature ('charge'),[3] over any type of property, including after-acquired property ('charged property').[4] The charge may be granted by and to any person. It may secure any debt (provided it is a business credit), including future debt ('secured debt').[5] It sweeps away formal distinctions between types of security, property, and parties eligible for secured transactions. Formalities and thus costs required to create security are kept to a minimum.[6] To facilitate the foregoing, the EBRD Model Law employs simple, inclusive terminology.

Creation, registration, and ranking of the charge

Non-possessory charges, other than an unpaid vendor's charge, must be registered in a public registry.[7] Somewhat unusually, this is required not merely to preserve the effectiveness of the charge against third parties but also to create the charge. It follows that while priority between competing charges is in general determined

---

[1] EBRD maintains current information on the use of the model law.
[2] See Article 31 setting out 'insolvency principles', rather than specific rules.
[3] Article 1.   [4] Article 5.8–5.9.   [5] Article 4.3.4–4.4.   [6] Article 6–7.
[7] Articles 6.2 and 8.

by the order of their creation,[8] in substance this means the order of registration.[9] By ensuring effective publicity, the system avoids the dual risks of 'false wealth' attributed to the debtor and secret liens in favour of creditors. On the other hand, the effect of requiring registration as a necessary element in the creation of the charge means that an unregistered charge is not enforceable even against the debtor.

Broad and speedy enforcement of security

Broad enforcement remedies are made available on a reasonably timely basis by virtue of non-judicial action, self-help.[10] A high degree of autonomy is given to the parties in establishing contractual remedies. Debtor protections are included, in particular the right to receive an 'enforcement notice', which must be registered. That mechanism, in effect, gives a debtor a 60 day grace period in respect of final disposition remedies.[11] Court action and damages are available to debtors and other parties suffering loss as a result of wrongful enforcement.[12]

(b) The OAS Model Law

This is a highly-developed Model Law running to no fewer than 72 articles. In contrast to the EBRD Model Law, the OAS Model Law distinguishes between the requirements for creation of an interest and those for its perfection. All that is required for the creation of a security interest is an agreement, which in the case of a non-possessory security interest must be in writing and contain various items of information, including the maximum amount secured.[13] To be effective against third parties, the security interest must be publicized, by registration or by delivery of possession or control to the creditor or a third person on its behalf.[14] A security interest in inventory may be publicized by a single filing.[15] The OAS Model Law contains detailed rules on enforcement[16] and on priorities,[17] and, like the EBRD Model Law, requires the creditor who intends to commence enforcement to register an enforcement form in the Registry and deliver copies to the debtor and certain other persons.[18] The basic rule is that priority is determined by the order in which publicity is effected,[19] with a special priority in favour of a possessory security

---

[8] Article 17.2.

[9] Article 6.7 and 17(2). Exceptions relate to unpaid vendor charges (Art 6.7.2) and possessory charges (Art 6.7.3). [10] Article 22–4.

[11] Ibid., particularly Art 24.1 (60 day requirement). [12] Article 30.

[13] Articles 5–7. Interestingly, Art 7(a) of the 2001 Cape Town Convention on International Interests in Mobile Equipment, while likewise requiring that the agreement enable the secured obligation to be determined, provides that it is not necessary to state the sum or maximum sum secured. There were two reasons for this. First, the requirement would merely encourage the secured creditor to play safe by stating a sum wildly in excess of the amount likely to be advanced. Secondly, the information would anyway be of limited value to a third party as it would not show the amount outstanding at any particular time.

[14] Articles 10 and 47. The secured creditor may hold the property through a third person, in which case the security interest is considered publicized only from the time that the person receives evidence in writing of the security interest (Art 30). [15] Article 31.

[16] Title VI. [17] Title V. [18] Article 54. [19] Article 48.

interest in a document of title or negotiable instrument.[20] Finally, the OAS Model Law adopts the *lex rei sitae* conflicts rule for cases where a security interest has contacts with more than one State, supplemented by a rule to deal with the case where the collateral is moved to a different State.[21]

2. Mobile Equipment Financing Transactions

In historical terms, ship and aircraft financing transactions have led the development of international commercial laws and conflict of laws, on the one hand, and advanced secured financing techniques, on the other. The expense, mobility, and national importance of these types of transport equipment have so demanded. Law and financing practices for other types of high value equipment, such as railway rolling stock and space assets, and certain forms of international project financing, have been significantly influenced by ship and aircraft financing.

Principal themes in these contexts that have been addressed and developed over time include (a) the criteria for creating or recognizing consensual security, (b) the relationship between financing and non-consensual creditors (including historical classes of liens and government preferences), and (c) the extent and limits of arrest and detention rights. Priority among competing creditors, based on recordation with flag registries, has also been important. Until recently, less attention was given to the other substantive aspects of security, namely prompt enforcement and insolvency rights.

(a) Maritime Conventions

Brussels Convention on Maritime Liens and Mortgages, 1926

The Brussels Convention on Maritime Liens and Mortgages (Brussels 1926)[22] established two fundamental principles that, taken together, were the starting point for the further development of much international secured financing law.

First, Contracting States must 'regard as valid and respect' consensual security 'duly effected in accordance with the laws of the contracting State to which the vessel belongs' provided such security was registered in a public register in the latter State.[23] This is a classic recognition of rights approach. A clear conflicts rule avoids choice of law and *lex rei sitae* problems. The use of shipping nationality, a flag, well grounded in historical conflicts thinking (*lex registri*), was safely employed. That approach, however, does not address substantive elements of security. This, as with all approaches which merely address the conflict of laws, produces a financing environment that is only as sound as the underlying rules of the applicable law. Many major shipping States have well-developed, commercially oriented, laws. Financing practices have centred on such States, and the liberal use of flag financing.

---

[20] Article 52.   [21] Article 69.
[22] International Convention for the Unification of Certain Rules of Law Relating to Maritime Liens and Mortgages, 1926.   [23] Article 1.

Secondly, Brussels 1926 sets out powerful rules in favour of lienholders—in our terminology, holders of non-consensual interests. In the case of conflict, broadly speaking, non-consensual creditors prevail over the holders of consensual security.[24] Non-consensual interests include supplier and repairer type liens, claims relating to contracts entered into by a ship's master, liens in favour of use-related services (e.g. pilotage and harbour dues), assistance and salvage claims, and indemnities for collisions or personal injury.[25] Such claims follow the vessel in the hands of third parties,[26] and subsequent lienholders prevail over prior lienholders.[27] In the signing protocol to Brussels 1926, States reserved the right to create other non-consensual priorities, for example, liens in favour of government claims ('safeguarding the interests of the treasury') and its administering authorities.

Brussels 1926 does lay down one criterion for the creation of consensual security. National laws must prescribe the nature and form of security documents carried on board the vessel. In other key areas, such as the jurisdictional and enforcement procedures, national laws are preserved.

Brussels Convention on Arrest of Sea-Going Ships, 1952

Arrest and related jurisdictional procedures, particularly in respect of prejudgment attachment, are of central importance in secured transactions involving inherently mobile ship collateral. Obtaining possession upon default, by attachment or otherwise, is naturally an essential first requisite in the realization of asset value through enforcement. Historically, significant differences between civil law and common law approaches to prejudgment arrest produced much uncertainty. Many civil law systems permitted, at a court's discretion, *saiise conservatoire* type orders. Such are court controlled. They are exclusively conservatory in nature, and do not include sale and final remedies. Common law systems, by contrast, were more inclined to permit non-judicial arrest, and, where contractually agreed, broader prejudgment remedies.

The Brussels Convention on Arrest of Sea-Going Ships, 1952 (Brussels 1952)[28] was a first attempt at harmonizing arrest rules. It met with partial success on substantive grounds, although material differences in its interpretation remain. It has not been widely accepted. Its core concept is that a ship flying the flag of one Contracting State may be 'arrested' in respect of any 'maritime claim' (but no other claim) in any other Contracting State.[29] Arrest means detention by court procedures, but excludes seizure in execution or satisfaction of a judgment.[30] Maritime claim is broadly defined to include, beyond classic shipping non-consensual liens, consensual security, as well as claims arising through disputes involving title, ownership, or possession.[31]

---

[24] Article 3.   [25] Article 2.   [26] Article 8.   [27] Article 6.
[28] International Convention Relating to the Arrest of Sea-Going Ships, 1952.   [29] Article 2.
[30] Article 1(2).
[31] Article 1(1) (general definition) and 10(b) (permitted reservation relating to consensual security).

Brussels 1952 contains other important subsidiary rules. The extent to which other ships owned by the vessel owner or charterer (a 'sister ship') can be arrested is addressed,[32] as are limitations on multiple arrest in different jurisdictions.[33] Brussels 1952 sets out jurisdiction rules regarding litigation on the merits[34] and the role of security (here typically meaning bonds and other financial undertakings) between arrest and final resolution[35] and liability for improper arrest.[36] Nothing in the text affects government arrest and detention rights,[37] the procedural rules of the place of arrest,[38] and arrest in respect of wholly national claims.[39]

The Brussels Convention 1967 and the Geneva Convention 1993

Between Brussels 1926 and the most recent attempt to modernize maritime lien and mortgage law, the Geneva Convention on Maritime Liens and Mortgages, 1993 (Geneva 1993),[40] a failed attempt was made. Nonetheless, that effort, the Brussels Convention on Maritime Liens and Mortgages, 1967 (Brussels 1967),[41] contained several important developments which have had an impact on the future course of the law.

While Brussels 1967, like Brussels 1926, was principally a conflict of laws instrument, eschewing many currently important substantive aspects, it was innovative, indeed too innovative, for its day. As many of its points were reflected in Geneva 1993, they are addressed below. The text rests on the shelf, with little chance of entering into force. Accordingly, Brussels 1967 is not reproduced in this volume.

It is too early to determine whether Geneva 1993 will sail or sink. It too is principally a conflicts text.[42] Following the thinking in Brussels 1967, it contains more stringent requirements for recognition of foreign security interests ('charges'), principally focusing on increased publicity.[43] It sets out a relatively high priority for consensual security vis-à-vis non-consensual creditors, although the specified classes of maritime liens continue to prevail over charges.[44] It contains an exhaustive list of preferred non-consensual creditors, permitting States to add junior ranking liens.[45] It includes stronger rights of retention in favour of construction financiers and repairers in possession.[46]

Of particular note, Geneva 1993 sharpens the focus on priorities among competing charges by setting out prohibitions against (a) the change of a ship from one register to another without adequate protection of creditors,[47] and (b) parallel registration in more than one State.[48] While remaining within a conflicts framework, and focusing on rules of national law, these registration points (undoubtedly

---

[32] Articles 3(1) (general rule) and 4(4) (special rules for charter by demise). [33] Article 3(3).
[34] Article 7. [35] Article 5. [36] Article 6. [37] Article 2. [38] Article 6.
[39] Article 8(4). [40] International Convention on Maritime Liens and Mortgages, 1993.
[41] International Convention for the Unification of Certain Rules Relating to Maritime Liens and Mortgages, 1967. [42] Article 2.
[43] Article 1. [44] Article 5. [45] Article 6. [46] Article 7. [47] Article 3(1).
[48] Article 3(2).

influenced by similar thinking in earlier aviation instruments, discussed below) reflect a movement towards greater predictability as regards priorities.

The approach to remedies is conservative, rooted in traditional shipping concepts. While the conflicts rule, applying the *lex registri*, speaks to effects of consensual security on third parties, 'all matters relating to the procedure for enforcement' are governed by the place where remedies are exercised.[49] The lines between substantive and procedural rules are not addressed. The sole mention of remedies is to the concept of a 'forced sale' through State-regulated procedures.[50] Unlike trends in other areas of modern secured transactions law, the obligations on States is high. They undertake to 'ensure' notice of a forced sale is given to a wide range of parties (including holders of all registered security and the vessel's owner)[51] and that proceeds from the sale are 'actually available and freely transferable'.[52] These undertakings are driven by the facts surrounding the position of non-consensual creditors, rather than those of consensual security, who are otherwise able to minimize these regulatory risks.

Geneva Convention on Arrest of Ships, 1999

The Geneva Convention on Arrest of Ships, 1999 (Geneva 1999) builds upon Brussels 1952.[53] While elegantly drafted and reflective of developments in the field, it does not make fundamental changes to Brussels 1952 as regards basic principles that materially affect security financing. Geneva 1999, like the other shipping conventions discussed in this chapter, is noteworthy for its highly advanced treatment of classic private international law issues, which stands in contrast with the relative generality of its treatment of secured financing issues.

Geneva 1999 expands the list of 'maritime claims', most notably to include environmental claims,[54] but retains an exhaustive, closed list.[55] It retains the basic arrest rules,[56] yet contains more elaborate and complex rules on jurisdiction[57] and (financial) security.[58] It also maintains the conceptualization of the arrest action as *in rem* in nature, with basic procedures determined under the *lex fori*.[59] Like Brussels 1952, the 'sister ship' provision is limited, thus, in effect, restricting arrest rights to ships of the principal debtor (notwithstanding the proliferation since 1952 of single-ship companies).[60]

(b) Aviation Conventions

Rome Convention on Precautionary Attachment of Aircraft, 1933

Paralleling the ship arrest conventions, the subject of the Rome Convention for the Unification of Certain Rules relating to the Precautionary Attachment of Aircraft, 1933 (Rome 1933) is the prejudgment arrest of aircraft. Driven by policy objectives,

---

[49] Article 2.   [50] Articles 11–12.   [51] Article 11(1).   [52] Article 12(6).
[53] International Convention on Arrests of Ships, 1999.   [54] Article 1, particularly clause (d).
[55] Article 2(2).   [56] Articles 2, 3, and 5.   [57] Article 7.   [58] Article 4.
[59] Article 2(4).   [60] Article 6.

Rome 1933 takes a much more restrictive approach than its shipping counterparts. It flatly prevents the prejudgment arrest of aircraft that would disrupt commercial aviation traffic or the provision of State aviation services.[61] The restriction does not apply to post-judgment execution. Relatively few States have become and remain party to Rome 1933.

The basic principle of Rome 1933, preventing arrest, is in tension with the prompt enforcement aspect of modern secured financing. Admittedly, advanced aircraft financing techniques were not employed in 1933. Subject to a permitted reservation for parties to that instrument, the Cape Town Convention (discussed below) will supersede Rome 1933.

Geneva Convention on Recognition of Rights in Aircraft, 1948

The Geneva Convention on Recognition of Rights in Aircraft, 1948 (Geneva 1948)[62] is an important text. It has served the aviation sector well. In 1948, it embodied best thinking and was forward-looking. However, it is primarily a recognition of rights instrument, with limited substantive law features. Moreover, such substantive elements do not reflect the principles underlying modern asset-based financing and thus no longer suit the needs of the highly sophisticated aviation sector. These facts gave rise to the strong sector support for the Cape Town Convention, which, for transactions within its scope, expressly supersedes Geneva 1948.

(i) Recognition of rights and its limitations Geneva 1948 is conceptually similar to its shipping counterpart, Brussels 1926. It requires Contracting States to 'recognize' consensual security and certain other property rights in aircraft 'constituted in accordance' with the *lex registri* which are 'regularly recorded in a public record' of the flag State (the State of aircraft nationality).[63] This is a conflicts rule—aimed squarely at the *lex rei sitae* problem—linked, on fairness grounds, to the notion of publicity as regards priority. It is not a substantive or validating rule. The security rights must be valid and recordable under the law of the State of nationality. To underscore the point, Contracting States 'may prohibit the recording of any right which cannot validly be constituted according to its national law'.[64] While not express, and subject to differing views, *the lex registri* is the substantive law of the State of registry, without reference to conflicts rules.

The foregoing has been interpreted to require application of the *lex registri* to determine the validity of a form of security. The majority view is that Contracting States must also recognize the position of the State of registry on the formalities to create that security. More contentious is the assertion that the *lex registri* determines certain other concepts such as the availability of security over after-acquired property or in respect of future advances.

---

[61] Article 2 (definition of precautionary arrest) and 3 (general rule).
[62] Convention on the International Recognition of Rights in Aircraft, 1948.
[63] Article I.   [64] Article II (3).   [65] Article II (2).

Similarly, Geneva 1948 addresses the 'effects of recording' with respect to third parties by reference to the *lex registri*.[65] This unquestionably includes basic priorities among consensual creditors. It should (with the above noted recognition rule) also ensure that a valid form of security will not be rendered invalid upon insolvency (not addressing, however, anti-preference rules). The priority regime is strengthened by restrictions on deregistration ('transfer of an aircraft from a nationality register') of an aircraft from a national registry, since that act would call into question the ranking of interests therein.[66] This is the problem first taken up in the shipping context in Brussels 1967.

In broader terms, while Geneva 1948 may satisfactorily address the priorities aspect of secured financing (except in respect of engines, discussed below), it does not provide rules relating to (a) prompt enforcement of remedies, or (b) enforcement in the insolvency context. These two elements are central to a modern system of secured financing.

(ii) Non-consensual creditors   Geneva 1948 implicitly limits the priority of traditional classes of preferred non-consensual creditors. Three classes which expressly retain their priority are costs incurred in the 'common interest of creditors', extraordinary asset preservation costs, and, with limits, tort claimants.[67] Air navigation and State claims for certain illegal activity may also be preferred depending on national law.[68] There are differences of opinion as to the priority of other classes of non-consensual creditors (e.g. tax claims, possessory liens, claims by employees to recover wages, etc.); one is that they are subordinated to recorded interests. In certain cases, this matter is clarified by the terms of national legislation implementing Geneva 1948.

(iii) Judicial Sale   The sole enforcement remedy set out in Geneva 1948 is that of judicial sale.[69] Thus, the range of customary mortgage and leasing remedies fall outside of Geneva 1948. Their availability is determined by the otherwise applicable law. Moreover, there are mandatory notice periods in connection with the contemplated judicial sale, which, in effect, amount to minimum grace periods (in general, six weeks).[70] For a range of reasons, including the mobility of aircraft, this is inadequate. The law of the State where the sale takes place governs other procedural elements relating to a judicial sale.

(iv) Aircraft engines and other spare parts and accession   Aircraft engines comprise a significant part of the value of an aircraft and are at times separately financed. They are often removed from and installed on different aircraft, and may encounter title problems under (often differing) national accession laws when so removed or installed. For these reasons, clear security rules addressing engines are needed.

---

[66] Article IX.   [67] Articles IV and VII.   [68] Article XII.
[69] Articles VI–VIII.   [70] Article VII (2).

Geneva 1948 made a first attempt at providing rules for security over spare parts, such as engines, but the rules fall far short of what is required.[71] Geneva 1948 includes a limited recognition rule where spare parts are separately stored (and thus cannot be profitably used) provided some form of 'appropriate public notice', the contours of which are unclear, is given. The recorded aircraft security document must note that spare parts are included in the security. Above all, recognition is only required if the *lex registri* extends recorded security rights to such spare parts, which often is not the case.

(c) Other Equipment Financing Conventions

UNIDROIT Convention on International Financial Leasing, 1988

The UNIDROIT Convention on International Financial Leasing, 1998 (UNIDROIT Leasing 1988) represents the first modern international convention specifically designed to facilitate a form of equipment financing, the financial lease. While it contains select conflicts elements, it is also the first modern substantive law treaty in this field. It also breaks new ground by creating a *sui generis* legal relation, not dependent upon or derived from national law. The Cape Town Convention, a more elaborate text, carries this concept further, actually creating, through its provisions, a *sui generis* property interest derived from the instrument itself.

Many of its substantive elements regarding legal relations and liabilities are advanced, reflecting best practices and broad party autonomy, checked by fairness-based mandatory provisions. However, viewed against the principles underlying secured financing—priority, prompt enforcement, and insolvency rights— UNIDROIT Leasing 1998 should be seen as a limited, if positive, initial step. While addressing a distinctive transaction type, it does not (a) set out substantive criteria for the creation of rights, (b) definitively deal with priorities,[72] or (c) address *in rem* enforcement, whether in or outside of insolvency proceedings.

(i) Scope of application UNIDROIT Leasing 1998 governs a 'financial leasing transaction', which is, in effect, two intimately related contracts, a supply agreement (supplier-lessor) and leasing agreement (lessor-lessee).[73] To fall within the Convention, the lessee, rather than the lessor, must be the principal party dealing with the supplier as regards the equipment.[74] The lessor is a financier, and the financial terms of the lease reflect that fact (rent is calculated so as to amortise the whole or a substantial part of the acquisition cost).[75]

The connecting factor provisions invite a wide application. The Convention applies when the lessor and the lessee are in different States and either (a) those States and the supplier's State are Contracting States, or (b) the laws governing each of the two contracts are those of Contracting States.[76] Thus, through the latter

---

[71] Article X.   [72] Article 7(5)(a).   [73] Article 1(1).
[74] Article 1(1)(a) and (2)(a)–(b).   [75] Article 1(2)(c).   [76] Article 3(1).

limb, transaction parties (from different States) can activate the Convention by their contractual choices of law, if valid under the *lex fori*. The party autonomy principle also permits exclusion of the Convention. If all three parties agree to exclude the Convention, it does not apply.[77]

(ii) Lessor's real rights   A lessor's 'real rights' in the equipment are 'valid' in the lessee's insolvency and against creditors generally.[78] Where the applicable law, as precisely defined in the Convention, requires publicity of such rights as a condition to that validity, public notice is then required under the Convention.[79] While not defined, validity should mean recognition of a property interest and (in the insolvency context) its effectiveness against other creditors. It does not mean that a lessor will necessarily be able to enforce its interest, nor will it prevent the insolvency trustee from seeking to restructure the related financial undertakings pursuant to the applicable insolvency law. The Convention makes clear that these rules do not affect recognition of rights provisions under other treaties (e.g. Brussels 1926 and Geneva 1948).[80]

(iii) Reflecting the triangular relationship   A basic problem set up by the triangular relationship in a financial lease (supplier-lessor-lessee) is that, although it is the lessee who selects the supplier and who negotiates the specifications of the equipment, price, and delivery terms, and the like, the supplier's contract is with the lessor. Even if the lessor can be regarded as entering into the contract for the benefit of the lessee as well as itself, the lessee can only sue the supplier in jurisdictions which recognize the rights of third-party beneficiaries. Leasing agreements usually contain an undertaking by the lessor to enforce the supply agreement for the lessee's benefit, but in principle the lessor can recover only for its own loss, not that of the lessee. Moreover, if the equipment is defective the lessee's remedy is against the lessor, not against the party responsible for the defect. Article 10(1) of the Convention offers a neat solution to these problems by providing that the duties of the supplier under the supply agreement are also owed to the lessee as if it were a party to the agreement and as if the equipment were to be supplied directly to the lessee. The lessor's financial type obligations are correspondingly diminished, being limited to repayment of any sums paid in advance should the lessee exercise a right to reject the equipment and terminate the lease. [81] Reflecting the primacy of the supplier-lessee relation regarding the equipment, a lessor's legal liability to a lessee is also limited,[82] and, correspondingly, the duties of a supplier under the supply contract are owed to a lessee as if the equipment were supplied directly by the

---

[77] Article 5(1).

[78] Article 7(1). This has been the subject of criticism on the ground that it lacks sufficient detail. It should mean, at the very least, that the proprietary interest will be recognized, thus precluding subordination to the interests of creditors generally.   [79] Article 7(2)–(3).

[80] Article 7(4).   [81] Article 12.   [82] Article 8(1)(a).

former to the latter.[83] A lessor may not adversely affect a lessee's rights under the supply agreement without a lessee's consent. [84]

(iv) Lessee default and damages provisions The text contains useful, detailed provisions on the effect of a lessee's default, including damages calculation rules and equipment recovery. Where the 'default' is 'substantial' (although neither concept is defined), accelerated payment of future rentals may be required.[85] Alternatively, a lessor may terminate the leasing agreement, recover possession (although timing and procedural aspects are not addressed) and recover damages calculated (with reference to the parties' agreement) to provide an expectation measure of damages.[86] A lessor must provide the lessee with a reasonable opportunity to remedy the default and also has a mitigation obligation.[87]

(v) Other additional substantive provisions A lessor warrants a lessee's 'quiet possession'—the right to undisturbed use of the equipment—unless the reason for the disruption relates to an act or omission of lessee.[88] There are limits on the parties' ability to derogate from that provision,[89] which are further augmented by a permitted State reservation that would apply domestic law relating to liability exclusions.[90] A lessee has responsibility to use the equipment in a reasonable manner and return it (assuming no exercised purchase option) in the conditioned delivered, fair wear and tear excepted, and as otherwise agreed.[91] A lessor, in that capacity, is not liable for death or damage caused to third parties by the equipment.[92]

Convention on International Interests in Mobile Equipment and the Aircraft Protocol thereto, 2001

In 2001, the Convention on International Interests in Mobile Equipment (Convention) and the Aircraft Protocol thereto (Aircraft Protocol) were concluded (together, Cape Town 2001).[93] The Convention establishes a comprehensive, international legal regime for the creation, enforcement, perfection, and priority of interests in aircraft objects, railway rolling stock, and space assets granted to a financier under a security agreement or reserved to a conditional seller or lessor under a title reservation or leasing agreement. With the Aircraft Protocol, it addresses insolvency aspects, thus forging the deepest substantive harmonization to date. Cape Town 2001 was specifically designed significantly to facilitate the financing of mobile equipment. Its guiding principles were those that underlie asset-based financing and leasing, summarized in the introduction to this chapter.

---

[83] Article 10(1).   [84] Article 11.   [85] Article 13(2).
[86] Article 13(2)(b) and 3(a) (general rule), and 13(3)(b) (minor limit on method of calculation). The latter provision is mandatory, preventing contractual variance: Art 5(2).
[87] Article 13(5)–(6).   [88] Article 8(2).   [89] Article 8(3); see also Art 5(2).
[90] Article 20.   [91] Article 9.   [92] Article 8(1)(b)–(c).
[93] For overviews and a detailed article-by-article analysis, see the *Official Commentary*, by Professor Sir Roy Goode.

(i) The international interest The Convention creates a *sui generis* property interest, an 'international interest'. An interest that satisfies the requirements of the Convention[94] constitutes an international interest, whether or not it would be recognized as such by national law, provided that, at the time of conclusion of the agreement, the debtor is situated in a Contracting State.[95]

(ii) Basic and expedited default remedies Chapter III of the Convention provides the creditor with a set of basic default remedies.[96] These vary according to whether the creditor is a chargee under a security agreement or a conditional seller or lessor. The primary remedies of the chargee, which are provided only to the extent agreed by the chargor, are: to take possession or control of any object charged, to sell or grant a lease of such an object, and to collect or receive any income or profits arising from its management or use.[97] The chargee may also, with the agreement of the debtor and other interested persons or on an order of the court, have the object vested in it in total or partial satisfaction of its claim.[98] In addition, there is a useful provision entitling a creditor who adduces evidence of default to obtain various forms of relief pending final determination of his claim within such period as the relevant Contracting State may specify in its declaration.[99]

(iii) Registration and priorities In order to make it effective against third parties, the international interest must be registered in the international registry which will be designed as a high-technology, electronic registry in which registrations may be effected, searches made and search certificates issued electronically without the need for human intervention. Registration is effected against an identified object, not against a debtor, which is why the Convention is confined to uniquely identifiable objects. The registration system is based on 'notice filing' in that the agreement itself is not filed, merely brief particulars which will enable an interested third person to obtain further information from the parties.[100] Registration confers priority over subsequently registered interests and over unregistered interests,[101] even if these are not registrable[102] and even if the registering creditor has knowledge

---

[94] Articles 2 and 7. These require that the interest (i) relate to an object of a category specified by the Convention as indicated above and designated in and identifiable in accordance with the relevant Protocol, (ii) be embodied in an agreement in writing which is a security agreement, a title reservation agreement or a leasing agreement, (iii) relate to an object of which the chargor, conditional seller, or lessor has power to dispose and (iv), in the case of a security agreement, enable the secured obligation to be determined, but without the need to state the maximum sum secured.

[95] Article 3. As to when a debtor is to be considered so situated, see Art 4.

[96] Articles 8–10. With the agreement of the relevant parties these remedies may be exercised without a court order except in a Contracting State that has made a contrary declaration under Art 54.

[97] Article 8(1).   [98] Article 9.   [99] Article 13; and see Protocol, Article 18.

[100] However, since the registration system is asset-based, it is not possible to provide one of the other advantages of a notice filing system, namely the ability to file one document to cover all existing and future transactions.   [101] Article 29(1).

[102] See the definition of 'unregistered interest' in Art 1(mm). There are exceptions in favour of an outright buyer (Art 29(3)), a conditional buyer or lessee, who can shelter under the registration of his

of them.[103] Further, the priority extends to value given by the holder of the registered interest even after knowledge of a subsequent interest and even if the latter has been registered.[104] A person intending to acquire an international interest in an identified object can register a prospective international interest.[105] When this develops into an actual international interest it automatically ranks for priority as from the time of registration of the prospective international interest[106] without the need for any further registration, provided that the registered particulars are sufficient.[107] Priorities may be varied by agreement but the creditor in whose favour a subordination is made should register the subordination, otherwise it will be ineffective against an assignee from the subordinated creditor.[108]

An interest registered prior to the opening of insolvency proceedings is effective in those proceedings—by which is meant that it must be recognized as proprietary in character and as giving priority over unsecured creditors—but takes effect subject to any rules of insolvency law relating to the avoidance of a transaction as a preference or a transfer in fraud of creditors.[109] It is also subject to any rules of procedure relating to the enforcement of rights of property under the control or supervision of the insolvency administrator,[110] for example, rules imposing an automatic stay on the enforcement of rights in an insolvency proceeding designed to facilitate a corporate reorganization. An elective provision in the Aircraft Protocol significantly modifies restrictions on enforcement in the context of insolvency.[111]

(iv) Treatment of associated rights   Chapter IX deals with the assignment of associated rights and international interests. Associated rights are defined as 'all rights to payment or other performance by a debtor under an agreement that is secured by or associated with the object'.[112] Except as otherwise agreed, an assignment of associated rights transfers to the assignee the related international interest and all the interests and priorities of the assignor under the Convention.[113] In a competition between competing assignees of different interests in the same item of equipment, each assignee takes the priority position of its assignor.[114] Where the competition is between assignees of associated rights related to the same international interest,

---

conditional seller or lessor (Art 29(4)(b)) and the holder of a non-consensual right or interest having priority by virtue of a declaration by a Contracting State under Art 39.

[103] This rule is designed to give certainty and to avoid factual disputes as to whether a person did or did not have knowledge.   [104] Article 29(2)(b).

[105] Article 16(1)(a).   [106] Article 19(4).

[107] Article 18(3). To enable this to happen without a searcher being misled, Art 22(3) requires that search certificates state merely that the creditor named has acquired or intends to acquire an interest in the object without stating whether what is registered is an international interest or merely a prospective international interest. The searcher is expected to make enquiry of the registrant.

[108] Article 29(5).   [109] Article 30(3)(a).   [110] Article 30(3)(b).

[111] Article XI, particularly Alternative A thereof.

[112] Article 1(c). Rights are 'secured by' a security agreement and 'associated with' a title reservation or leasing agreement.

[113] Article 31(1). Associated rights assigned in isolation from the related international interest are outside the scope of the Convention (Art 32(3)).   [114] Article 35.

priority is in principle given to the assignee whose assignment was registered first.[115] This is subject to the two limitations imposed by Article 36, which (1) requires that the contract under which the associated rights arise states that it is secured by or associated with the object,[116] and (2) restricts the priority to associated rights relating to the financing or leasing transaction.[117]

(v) Non-consensual rights and interests The Convention also has provisions allowing a Contracting State to make declarations enabling non-consensual rights or interest to be registered as if they were international interests[118] and specifying the categories of non-consensual right or interest which under its law have priority over an interest equivalent to that of the holder of an international interest and are to have priority over a registered international interest.[119] In this way the Convention responds to the differing policy issues of different States in regard to the priority of non-consensual rights and interests while providing flexibility.

(vi) Other substantive provisions There are important provisions as to jurisdiction, the most important of which endorses forum selection clauses.[120] The final clauses address transition, particularly as regards priority, and the effect of a State subsequently withdrawing from the Convention or modifying its declaration, the common import of which is to protect vested interests.[121]

The Aircraft Protocol

One of the unique features of the Convention is that its provisions take effect subject to the provisions of the relevant Protocol.[122] The Aircraft Protocol is finely tailored to the practical needs of the aviation financing sector. It extends the registration and priority provisions of the Convention to outright purchases of aircraft objects,[123] provides an alternative connecting factor,[124] adds the remedies of deregistration and export,[125] endorses contract choice of law clauses,[126] enforces waivers of sovereign immunity,[127] and, for transactions within its scope, supersedes the Geneva Convention 1948.[128] Most importantly, it strengthens the interim remedies regime,[129] adds judicial timetables,[130] and specifically addresses a range of

---

[115] This is the effect of Art 35(1).

[116] This is intended to cover the case where the initial agreement secures not only obligations under that agreement but also those under future agreements. If the creditor were then to make a separate advance under a new agreement, this would not need to state that it was secured (since it would already be secured under the initial agreement), and an assignee would then not know of the existence of the security interest. [117] See the *Official Commentary* (note 93 above), pp. 19–22, 128–134.

[118] Article 40. [119] Article 39. [120] Articles 42–44.

[121] Article 60 (transition) and Art 57(3), 58(2) and 59(3) (each subsequent State action).

[122] Article 49(1)(b).

[123] Article III, for which Art 41 of the Convention made provision. The default provisions do not, of course, apply because there is an outright transfer of title, but the priority rules do.

[124] Article IV. The Convention applies, in respect of an airframe, if the related aircraft is registered for nationality purposes in a Contracting State. [125] Article IX.

[126] Article VIII. [127] Article XXII. [128] Article XXIII.

[129] Article X. [130] Ibid.

insolvency issues aimed at enhancing enforceability of an international interest in that context.[131] A number of these provisions permit declarations.[132]

3. International Receivables Financing Transactions

The supplier of goods or services does not necessarily wish to tie up his capital while awaiting payment. Receivables financing, by which the supplier can sell its receivables to a factoring company or charge them to a bank, thus provides a useful source of liquidity, as well as other facilities referred to below. Despite these advantages most legal systems have historically displayed hostility towards security over or transfers of streams of contract debts. This may be seen in (a) restrictions on the assignment of future receivables, (b) the concept of specificity—the impractical requirement of specifying each assigned contract, and (c) the imposition of other requirements, such as notification to the debtor as a condition of creation of the security interest.

Over the past 20 years, some of these legal systems have modified these rules in order to facilitate receivables financing. However, much of this financing is international in nature and this trend will continue in the future. That has given rise to the need to address the legal impediments to receivables financing at the international level.

(a) UNIDROIT Convention on International Factoring, 1988

The first major development is this field, under UNIDROIT sponsorship, was the Convention on International Factoring, 1988 (UNIDROIT Factoring 1988). This instrument addresses 'notification factoring', where the obligor on the assigned receivable receives notice of the assignment. Notification factoring is often, although not always, non-recourse to the assignor, meaning that the factor takes the credit risk of the contract obligors, the quantum of that risk being spread over all or part of the customer base. This is subject to the assignor (the supplier) fulfilling its warranties and other obligations.

Like UNIDROIT Leasing 1988, this instrument is a groundbreaking, initial step. It addresses the threshold issues faced in this transaction type with the express objective of its facilitation. It does not, however, settle a number of difficult issues, including priorities, effects of insolvency, and the characterization of the interest (sale or security and its implications), which, in this context, are of particular significance.

(i) *Scope of application* The Convention governs 'factoring contracts' (factor-supplier) where the supplier assigns commercial receivables payable to it by its customers (debtors).[133] To fall within the scope of the instrument, the agreement must be one under which the factor is to perform at least two of four designated

---

[131] Article XI.   [132] Article XXX.   [133] Article 1(1) and (2)(a).

functions (finance to the supplier,[134] maintenance of accounts (ledgering), collection of receivables, and protection against debtor default) and notice of the assignment is to be given to the debtor. [135]

Like UNIDROIT Leasing 1998, the connecting factor provisions invite a wide application. The Convention applies when the supplier and a debtor are in different States and either (a) those States and the factor's State are Contracting States, or (b) the law governing the contract of sale of goods and the factoring contract are those of Contracting States.[136] Thus, through the latter limb, transaction parties (from different States) can activate the Convention by their contractual choices of law, if valid under the *lex fori*. Party autonomy is also present on exclusion of the Convention. If both parties to the factoring contract or the sales contract agree to exclude the Convention, it does not apply.[137]

(ii) Identifiability rather than specificity   The Convention overrides the specificity rule. An assignment of future receivables is not rendered invalid by lack of specificity if, at the time of contracting or when they come into existence, the receivables can be identified to the contract.[138] A contractual provision covering future receivables transfers each such receivable, when it arises, without the need for any new act of transfer.[139]

(iii) Prohibitions on assignment   Underlying contracts for the sale of goods may contain provisions expressed to prohibit assignment. A receivable financier, however, is not in a position to review all contracts for such provisions. To allow debtors to invoke non-assignment clauses against assignees would pose a serious impediment to receivables financing. As between the supplier and the factor, assignments are effective under the Convention notwithstanding an anti-assignment clause.[140] They are also effective against debtors unless a debtor's State makes a permitted declaration.[141] Whether or not such a declaration is made, a supplier assigning receivables in violation of an anti-assignment clause remains liable to the debtor for that breach, if liable under the applicable law.[142]

(iv) Debtor discharge, defences, and recourse   A debtor without knowledge of another party's superior right has a duty to pay a factor provided notice of assignment (a) was given by or under the authority of the debtor, (b) reasonably identifies the assigned receivables and the factor, and (c) relates to a receivable existing prior to the time of notice.[143] Under such circumstances, and without limiting other grounds for discharge, a debtor paying a factor receives a good discharge. A debtor retains and may assert the same defences against a factor that it has against the

---

[134] By allowing the supplier to draw on its account for the price before the assigned receivables mature.   [135] Articles 2(b), 1(3), and 1(4).
[136] Article 2(1).   [137] Article 3.   [138] Article 5.   [139] Ibid.
[140] Article 6(1).   [141] Ibid.; see also Articles 6(2) and 18.
[142] Article 6(3).   [143] Article 8.

supplier, and may set off against the factor all claims that 'arose and are available' against the supplier at the time of the notice of assignment. [144] Rules also address the situation where a debtor has recourse against the supplier.[145]

(b) UN Convention on the Assignment of Receivables in International Trade, 2001

In 2001, the United Nations Convention on the Assignment of Receivables in International Trade (UN Receivables 2001) was adopted by the UN General Assembly. It will enter into force after five States ratify or accede to the instrument. UN Receivables 2001, like Cape Town 2001, is highly sophisticated and specifically designed to facilitate transactions within its broad scope. It is complex—as it must be, given its subject matter. It covers a much wider range of topics than does UNIDROIT Factoring 1988 (which it supersedes, except in respect of certain debtor provisions), including, beyond factoring, aspects of asset-based financing, securitization, and project financing.

The Convention is a mixture of substantive and conflicts rules. The substantive rules seek deep harmonization. The conflicts rules, most notably the selection of the law of the assignor's location regarding priority issues, are employed where substantive rules were thought to be impractical or undesirable.

(i) Scope of application   The Convention covers an 'international assignment', an assignment of 'receivables' (assignor's contractual right to payment) where the assignor and assignee are in different States.[146] It also covers an 'assignment of an international receivable', an assignment of a receivable arising from a contract (an 'original contract') between an assignor (as original creditor) and a debtor located in a different State.[147] The latter was necessary to ensure a comprehensive approach to all priority issues. In either case, the connecting factor is whether the assignor is located in a Contracting State,[148] except as regards debtor aspects, where the debtor too must be located in a Contracting State or the law of such a State must govern the original contract.[149] The Convention even affects a domestic assignment of a domestic receivable, as regards certain priority conflicts particulary those related to a subsequent assignments.

(ii) Ensuring the effectiveness of the assignment

As with UNIDROIT Factoring 1988, the Convention's primary object is to ensure the effectiveness of assignments of receivables, doing away with historical impediments to the assignment of future receivables, such as the doctrine of specificity.[150] It replaces the specificity requirement with that of identifiability.[151] Beyond these legal impediments, the Convention also validates—as between assignor-assignee—an assignment made in the face of a no-assignment provision in the

---

[144] Article 9.   [145] Article 10.   [146] Articles 1–3 and 5(a).   [147] Ibid.
[148] Article 1(1).   [149] Article 1(3).
[150] Article 8 (general rule); see also Art 5(b) (definition of future receivable).
[151] Article 8(1).

original contract.[152] However, the assignor remains liable to the debtor for breach of a no-assignment clause.[153] In addition, consumer protection is not affected by the Convention,[154] and States may make a reservation which is more debtor protective.[155]

A conflicts rule is provided on validity of an assignment for property law purposes.[156] Security rights, as an accessory, transfer with the assigned receivable without the need for a further act.[157] That rule, however, defers to other more specific conventions, such as Cape Town 2001, on transactions within their scope.[158]

(iii) Position of the debtor   Beyond the above-noted provisions on anti-assignment clauses, Article 17 of the Convention provides precise rules on discharge. A debtor who receives a notice of assignment from two or more assignees is discharged by paying in accordance with the first notification.[159] A debtor may seek 'adequate proof' of assignments and resulting payment obligations.[160] That concept, however, is not clearly defined.

The defences and set-off provisions are substantially similar to UNIDROIT Factoring 1988. A debtor retains all defences under the original and related contract and may set-off such claims as well as those under unrelated contracts arising prior to notification.[161] However, the Convention expressly permits waiver of defences and set-off rights, with narrow restrictions.[162]

(iv) Assignor-assignee relations   The Convention appropriately provides assignor and assignee wide latitude in contractual aspects of their legal relation, though their agreement has no effect on third parties.[163]

(v) The priority regime   The Convention provides a clear conflicts rule on priorities disputes among an assignee and competing claimants, broadly defined.[164] The governing law is the law of the State in which the assignor is located,[165] that is, its place of business, or, if more than one, then the place where its central administration is exercised.[166] This is a material simplification of the law in this field, where a number of difficult rules might otherwise be applicable. There were some that wished to venture further still and provide substantive harmonization. For those States wishing to do so, the Convention permits a declaration linked to a set of optional substantive priority rules, including ones that contemplate registration as

---

[152] Article 9(1).   [153] Article 9(2).   [154] Article 4(4)   [155] Article 40.
[156] Article 27.   [157] Article 10.   [158] Article 38(1).   [159] Article 17(4).
[160] Article 17(7).
[161] Article 18. In contrast to the UNIDROIT Convention, Art 18(1) permits set-off of cross-claims arising under the same contract or transaction as the claim even if these arise after the notice of assignment.   [162] Article 19.
[163] Article 6 (an historical first reference to 'party autonomy' as a provision heading). This principle applies equally contracts with debtors. Ibid.   [164] Article 5(m).
[165] Article 22.   [166] Article 5(h).

the means of determining priorities.[167] The Convention also contains a limited proceeds rule (where applicable, priorities in proceeds follow priority in the receivable).[168] The Convention provides that none of the provisions relating to the form of the assignment or the applicable law is to affect mandatory rules that apply regardless of the applicable law.[169] The public policy rules of the forum State are also preserved in narrowly defined circumstances.[170]

---

[167] Article 42 and the Annex to the Convention.   [168] Article 24.
[169] Article 31.   [170] Article 32.

B. Instruments

(i) General

(a) ERBD MODEL LAW ON SECURED TRANSACTIONS*

PART 1
GENERAL PROVISIONS

Article 1
Nature of a Charge

1.1 Things and rights may be encumbered by the owner with a security right (called a charge) in order to grant security for a debt.

1.2 This law does not prevent a security right arising

    1.2.1 by operation of law or by judicial or administrative act; or

    1.2.2 pursuant to [*specific exceptions to be determined separately for each jurisdiction*].

---

* Reproduced with the kind permission of the European Bank for Reconstruction and Development.

Article 2
Person Giving a Charge

Any person may grant a charge over his things and rights except that a natural person may grant a charge only as part of his business activity and only over things and rights used for that activity at the time of creation of the charge pursuant to Article 6.7. The person granting the charge is called the chargor.

Article 3
Person Receiving a Charge

3.1 A charge may be granted to any person or persons to whom the debt or any of the debts being secured is owed. The person receiving the charge or to whom it is transferred is called the chargeholder.

3.2 The chargeholder may appoint another person (called a charge manager) to act in his place in relation to a charge pursuant to Article 16.

Article 4
Secured Debt

4.1 A charge may secure one or more debts (called a secured debt).

4.2 For the charge to be valid the secured debt must be capable of expression in money terms whether in national or foreign currency or monetary units of account or any combination of these. A charge securing an obligation which is not yet translated into a money obligation is not enforceable until this translation occurs.

4.3 A secured debt may be
  4.3.1 owed by any person or persons who need not be the chargor;
  4.3.2 identified specifically or generally;
  4.3.3 governed by national or foreign law;
  4.3.4 conditional or future.

4.4 A debt which is created after the date of the charging instrument will be included in the secured debt if that debt is identified in the charging instrument.

4.5 The amount of the debt secured by a charge is limited to the maximum shown on the registration statement pursuant to Article 8.4.3 or, in the case of a possessory charge, in the charging instrument pursuant to Article 7.3.3 plus any additional amounts included pursuant to Article 4.6.

4.6 The following additional amounts are included in the secured debt unless otherwise agreed between the chargor and the chargeholder
  4.6.1 interest on the secured debt to the extent contractually payable from the time at which the charge is created or deemed to be created pursuant to Article 6.7 or 6.8 until the date of payment; and
  4.6.2 interest on the secured debt payable by operation of law; and
  4.6.3 reasonable costs properly incurred by the chargeholder in preserving and maintaining the charged property and in enforcing the charge; and
  4.6.4 damages for any breach of the contract under which the secured debt arises up to twenty per cent
    4.6.4.1 of themaximum amount of the secured debt included in the registration statement pursuant to Article 8.4.3 or the charging instrument pursuant to Article 7.3.3; or

4.6.4.2 in the case of an unpaid vendor's charge, of the unpaid part of the purchase price referred to in Article 9.2.1.

Article 5
Charged Property

5.1 A charge may encumber one or more things or rights (called charged property).

5.2 Charged property may comprise anything capable of being owned, in the public sector or in the private sector, whether rights or movable or immovable things, and including debts due from the chargeholder to the chargor. The charged property includes any thing or right which, at the time of creation of the charge or subsequently, is attached or related to the charged property and which on a transfer of ownership of the charged property as described in the charging instrument would be included with the charged property by operation of law.

5.3 Things or rights which are not capable in law of being transferred separately cannot be charged separately.

5.4 A charge is valid notwithstanding any agreement entered into by the chargor not to charge things or rights except

    5.4.1 where the charged property is a contractual obligation which is not a debt for money; or

    5.4.2 as provided under Article 12.6.

An agreement that a contractual right which is not a debt for money is not transferable is deemed unless otherwise provided to be an agreement that the right cannot be charged.

5.5 Charged property may be identified specifically (in which case the charge is a specific charge) or generally (in which case the charge is a class charge).

5.6 Where a class charge covers

    5.6.1 all the things and rights used in an enterprise which is capable of operating as a going concern; or

    5.6.2 such part of the things and rights of an enterprise as needs to be transferred to enable an acquirer to continue the enterprise as a going concern;

    the charge may be registered as an enterprise charge pursuant to Article 8.4.5.

5.7 Charged property may be situated within or outside the jurisdiction.

5.8 A charge may be expressed to cover things and rights not owned by the chargor at the time at which the charge is deemed to be created pursuant to Article 6.8.

5.9 A charge extends to things and rights which become owned by the chargor after the charge is deemed to be created pursuant to Article 6.8 if they are identified in the charging instrument.

5.10 The charged property automatically extends to any rights of the chargor under any insurance policy which covers loss or reduction in value of the charged property.

PART 2
CREATION OF A CHARGE

Article 6
General Rules for the Creation of a Charge

6.1 A charge may be only

    6.1.1 a registered charge; or

    6.1.2 an unpaid vendor's charge; or

6.1.3 a possessory charge.

6.2 A registered charge is created by

6.2.1 the chargor and the chargeholder entering into a charging instrument pursuant to Article 7; and

6.2.2 registration of the charge pursuant to Article 8.

6.3 An unpaid vendor's charge is created pursuant to Article 9.1.

6.4 A possessory charge is created by

6.4.1 the chargor and the chargeholder entering into a charging instrument pursuant to Article 7; and

6.4.2 possession of the charged property being given pursuant to Article 10.1.

6.5 A charge is created only if

6.5.1 the chargor as referred to in Article 2 is the owner of the charged property; and

6.5.2 the chargor has the power to grant the charge at the time the charge is created or deemed to be created pursuant to Article 6.7 or 6.8; and

6.5.3 the charge secures a debt as referred to in Article 4.2.

6.6 An enterprise charge may only be created by a [*company*].

6.7 The time at which a charge over things or rights owned by the chargor is created is

6.7.1 in the case of a registered charge, the time of registration of the charge pursuant to Article 34.4 unless the charge was initially created as an unpaid vendor's charge or a possessory charge in which case it is the time of initial creation in accordance with Article 6.7.2 or 6.7.3;

6.7.2 in the case of an unpaid vendor's charge, the time at which title to the charged property is transferred to the purchaser pursuant to Article 9.1;

6.7.3 in the case of a possessory charge, the later of possession of the charged property being given pursuant to Article 10.1 and the date of signature of the charging instrument by or on behalf of the chargor.

6.8 Where a registered charge is granted over things or rights not yet owned by the chargor the charge is deemed to have been created at the time provided under Article 6.7.1.

6.9 An unpaid vendor's charge or a possessory charge is converted into a registered charge upon registration in accordance with Article 8.2.

6.10 A chargor and a chargeholder may agree to add to the debt secured by a charge, to increase the maximum amount of the secured debt pursuant to Article 4.5, to add to the charged property or to convert a charge as described in Article 5.6 into an enterprise charge. Such addition, increase or conversion is treated as the creation of a new charge and is accordingly subject to all the provisions of this law.

Article 7
Charging Instrument

7.1 The chargor and the chargeholder must enter into an agreement (called a charging instrument) except in the case of an unpaid vendor's charge. One charging instrument may relate to one or more charges.

7.2 The charging instrument may be in the form set out in schedule 1.

7.3 In order to be valid the charging instrument must be in writing and include

7.3.1 identification of the chargor, the person owing the secured debt (if not the chargor) and the chargeholder; and

7.3.2 specific or general identification of the secured debt; and

7.3.3 in the case of a possessory charge, the maximum amount of the secured debt expressed in national or foreign currency or monetary units of account or any combination of these; and

7.3.4 specific or general identification of the charged property; and

7.3.5 signatures by or on behalf of

    7.3.5.1 the chargor; and

    7.3.5.2 the chargeholder; and

7.3.6 the date of the charging instrument being the date of signature by or on behalf of the chargor.

7.4 A charge is not valid unless the charging instrument contains a statement that the purpose of the document is to create a charge or such purpose is implied from the instrument.

7.5 The charging instrument may include such other matters as the parties agree and, subject to Article 6.10, may subsequently be amended by the parties. In order for an amendment to be of effect against third parties it must be registered pursuant to Article 33.1.1.

7.6 If a charging instrument is signed by a person acting on behalf of the chargor the charge is valid only if that person is independent of the chargeholder.

Article 8
Registered Charge

8.1 In order to obtain registration of a registered charge as referred to in Article 6.2 a registration statement must be presented at the charges' registry not later than 30 days after the date of the charging instrument as defined in Article 7.3.6. If a registration statement is not presented by that date the charge is not created.

8.2 In order to convert an unpaid vendor's charge or a possessory charge into a registered charge a registration statement must be presented at the charges' registry during the time provided in Article 9.3 or Article 10.2.

8.3 The registration statement may be in the form set out in schedule 2.

8.4 In order for a registered charge to be valid the registration statement must include

8.4.1 identification of the chargor, the person owing the secured debt (if not the chargor), the chargeholder and the charge manager (if appointed); and

8.4.2 specific or general identification of the secured debt; and

8.4.3 the maximum amount of the secured debt expressed in national or foreign currency or monetary units of account or any combination of these; and

8.4.4 specific or general identification of the charged property; and

8.4.5 in the case of an enterprise charge, a statement that the charge is an enterprise charge; and

8.4.6 signature by or on behalf of

    8.4.6.1 the chargor and the charge manager (if appointed); or

    8.4.6.2 in the case of a registration statement pursuant to Article 8.2, the chargeholder; and

8.4.7 the date of the charging instrument except where an unpaid vendor's charge is converted into a registered charge; and

8.4.8 any additional information required pursuant to Article 8.5 or 8.6.

8.5 Where an unpaid vendor's charge is being converted into a registered charge the registration statement must in addition to the information required under Article 8.4 include

    8.5.1 a statement that the unpaid vendor's charge is being converted into a registered charge; and

    8.5.2 the date on which title to the charged property was transferred to the chargeholder as referred to in Article 9.1; and

    8.5.3 the date and identification of the written agreement referred to in Article 9.1.

8.6 Where a possessory charge is being converted into a registered charge the registration statement must in addition to the information required under Article 8.4 include

    8.6.1 a statement that the possessory charge is being converted into a registered charge; and

    8.6.2 the date on which possession of the charged property was given pursuant to Article 10.1 if given after the date of the charging instrument.

8.7 Where there is more than one chargor a separate registration statement must be presented for each chargor.

8.8 If a registration statement is signed by a person acting on behalf of the chargor the charge is valid only if that person is independent of the chargeholder.

8.9 The time of registration is as provided in Article 34.4.

Article 9
Unpaid Vendor's Charge

9.1 Where at or before the time of transfer of title by way of sale of a movable thing there is written agreement between the vendor and the purchaser that the vendor retains title or obtains a security right in the thing until payment of the purchase price

    9.1.1 title to the thing is not retained by the vendor but is transferred to the purchaser as if such agreement does not exist; and

    9.1.2 the vendor simultaneously receives a charge over the thing unless the parties otherwise agree without any requirement for a charging instrument or registration.

9.2 A charge created pursuant to Article 9.1 only secures

    9.2.1 any part of the purchase price of the charged property that remains unpaid at the time the charge is created; and

    9.2.2 additional amounts included pursuant to Article 4.6.

9.3 At any time within six months of the date on which an unpaid vendor's charge is created it may be converted into a registered charge by registration in accordance with Article 8.2.

9.4 An unpaid vendor's charge terminates

    9.4.1 six months after the date on which it was created unless an enforcement notice has been delivered in respect of the charge or any other charge over the same charged property pursuant to Article 22.2; or

    9.4.2 in the other events provided under Article 32.

Article 10
Possessory Charge

10.1 Where the charged property is capable of transfer by delivery the chargeholder or a person nominated by the chargeholder or a person holding on terms agreed between the chargeholder and the chargor may before or after the date of the charging instrument be given possession of the charged property by the chargor in which case registration pursuant to Article 8 is not required.

10.2 At any time while possession as referred to in Article 10.1 continues a possessory charge may be converted into a registered charge by registration in accordance with Article 8.2.

Article 11
Additional Registration

11.1 Where additional registration of a charge is required pursuant to this Article 11 a charge created pursuant to Article 6 cannot be enforced until such registration has been made.

11.2 [*Add specific requirements for additional registration to be determined separately for each jurisdiction.*]

Article 12
Charge of a Debt

12.1 Where the charged property is a debt for money the person owing the charged debt may satisfy it in a manner agreed with the chargor unless the chargeholder notifies that person pursuant to Article 12.2.

12.2 The chargeholder may at any time notify the person owing the charged debt that the charge exists. In that event

12.2.1 the charged debt can be satisfied only by payment to the chargeholder or to such person as the chargeholder nominates unless the chargeholder otherwise agrees; and

12.2.2 the chargeholder may directly pursue the person owing the charged debt for that debt.

12.3 For a notice given pursuant to Article 12.2 to be valid it must

12.3.1 be in writing; and

12.3.2 identify the chargor; and

12.3.3 describe the charged debt either specifically or generally in a manner which enables the person owing the charged debt to identify it; and

12.3.4 include clear instructions as to the person to whom the charged debt is to be paid.

12.4 The instructions given pursuant to Article 12.3.4 may be amended by a subsequent notice in accordance with Article 12.3.

12.5 Upon a charged debt being satisfied the charge terminates pursuant to Article 32.1.3.

12.6 Where the charged property is a secured debt the charge over the secured debt extends to the charge given in respect of that debt unless otherwise provided in the charging instrument for either charge. Where the charged property is described as the charge given in respect of a secured debt it is deemed to include that debt.

Article 13
Charge of a Contractual Obligation other than a Debt

Where the charged property is a contractual obligation which is not a debt for money the person owing the contractual obligation may satisfy it in the manner agreed with the chargor unless

13.1 the person owing the contractual obligation has received notice from the chargeholder pursuant to Article 23.3; and

13.2 the chargeholder exercises the chargor's rights pursuant to Article 23.3.3.

Article 14
Rights and Defences

14.1 A chargeholder may only claim rights arising out of a charge if the charge has been created pursuant to Article 6 and has not been terminated pursuant to Article 32.

14.2 A chargeholder may only claim rights arising out of a charge in relation to a debt if the charge extends to that debt.

14.3 A chargeholder may only claim rights arising out of a charge in relation to charged property if the charge extends to that property.

14.4 A charge is valid and enforceable only to the extent that the secured debt is valid and enforceable.

14.5 In any proceedings brought by the chargeholder claiming rights arising out of the charge

    14.5.1 the chargeholder must prove that the charge has been created; and

    14.5.2 the chargor or other party must prove that the charge has terminated or that any defences which he claims apply.

14.5 A chargor, any other chargeholder with a charge over the same charged property or any other party claiming rights in the charged property who disputes the creation or validity of the charge or claims that a charge has been terminated may apply to the court for a declaration that the charge is not created, is invalid or has been terminated.

Article 15
Rights and Obligations of Chargor and Chargeholder

15.1 The chargor and the chargeholder are free to determine the rights and obligations of each of them except as otherwise provided by law.

15.2 The chargor is under an obligation not to deal in the charged property except under a licence pursuant to Article 19 or Article 20 and is liable to the chargeholder for any loss suffered as a result of breach of this obligation.

15.3 The chargor has, except in the case of a possessory charge and unless otherwise agreed, the right

    15.3.1 to make use of or apply the charged property including to combine the charged property with any other thing or right, to apply the charged property in any manufacturing process and, where the charged property has been acquired for consumption, to consume the charged property; and

    15.3.2 to receive any fruits arising out of the charged property.

    Rights arising pursuant to this Article 15.3 terminate upon an enforcement notice being delivered pursuant to Article 22.2.

15.4 The chargor and the chargeholder have unless they otherwise agree the following further rights and obligations

    15.4.1 except in the case of a possessory charge, the chargor must preserve and maintain the charged property subject to his right to use it pursuant to Article 15.3.1. Where possession of the charged property is passed to a third party the chargor remains under an obligation to ensure that the charged property is preserved and maintained; and

15.4.2 in the case of a possessory charge, the chargeholder must preserve and maintain the charged property; and

15.4.3 the party not in possession of the charged property has a right to inspect; and

15.4.4 the chargor must insure the charged property against such risks as are habitually insured against by a prudent person owning similar things or rights.

Article 16
Charge Manager

16.1 The chargeholder may at any time appoint a charge manager for a registered charge either in the charging instrument or in a separate document.

16.2 The charge manager may be a chargeholder or a third party. Where a charge is granted to more than one chargeholder the appointment of the charge manager and any termination of that appointment must in order to be valid be made by or on behalf of all the chargeholders.

16.3 The powers and obligations of the charge manager are as provided in this Article 16 and any agreement relating to those powers and obligations is of effect only between the parties to that agreement.

16.4 Immediately upon a charge manager being registered pursuant to Article 8.4.1 or 33.1.2

16.4.1 the charge manager becomes entitled to exercise in the place of the chargeholder all the rights of the chargeholder arising under the charge including but not limited to the right to take enforcement proceedings pursuant to Articles 22 to 25 but excluding any right to transfer the secured debt;

16.4.2 the chargeholder ceases to be entitled to exercise such rights while the charge manager is appointed;

16.4.3 the charge manager becomes liable to perform all the obligations of the chargeholder to third parties arising out of the charge notwithstanding the continuing liability of the chargeholder.

16.5 When a person is registered as a charge manager pursuant to Article 8.4.1 or 33.1.2, any act of that person as charge manager is binding on the chargeholder even if the appointment of the charge manager is invalid except where the person claiming against the chargeholder has actual knowledge at the time of the act of the invalidity of the appointment.

16.6 The appointment of a charge manager can be terminated by the chargeholder or the charge manager at any time subject to any agreement between them. The termination becomes effective against a third party at the time when he has actual knowledge of the termination or, if he does not have such knowledge, at the time when the termination is registered pursuant to Article 33.1.3.

16.7 Upon any transfer by a chargeholder of the secured debt extending to the charge the powers and obligations of a charge manager pursuant to this Article 16 continue and the charge manager acts in the place of the new chargeholder.

PART 3
INVOLVEMENT OF THIRD PARTIES

Article 17
Priorities between chargeholders

17.1 A chargor may grant more than one charge over the same right or thing.

17.2 The priority between different charges over the same charged property is determined in accordance with the time at which they were created or deemed to be created pursuant to Articles 6.7 or 6.8 except as otherwise provided in this Article 17. Where title to a thing or right is acquired subject to a charge that charge will have priority over any charge granted by the acquirer.

17.3 An unpaid vendor's charge takes priority over any other charge granted by the purchaser over the thing transferred.

17.4 A possessory charge over negotiable instruments or negotiable documents takes priority over any prior charge.

17.5 The priority of a charge over a thing or right to which additional registration under Article 11 applies is determined by the later of the time of its creation or deemed creation pursuant to Articles 6.7 or 6.8 and the time at which such additional registration is made.

17.6 A security right arising by operation of law for money due for services in relation to a thing or right held takes priority over any prior charge.

17.7 [*Specific exceptions to be determined separately for each jurisdiction to cover charges under other laws*].

17.8 The priority of a charge may be changed at any time by written agreement between chargeholders or between the chargor and a chargeholder. An agreement to change the priority of a charge is valid only upon written consent being obtained from

　17.8.1 the chargeholder of any other charge which would cease to have priority over that charge as a result of the change; and

　17.8.2 the chargeholder of any other charge which as a result of the change

　　17.8.2.1 would cease to have the same priority as that charge; and

　　17.8.2.2 would not acquire priority over that charge.

Article 18
Transfer of a secured debt

18.1 A transfer of a secured debt by the chargeholder extends to the charge given in respect of that debt unless otherwise provided in the charging instrument or agreed between the parties to the transfer. An agreement which provides for the transfer of a charge is deemed to be a transfer of the debt secured by that charge. The charge terminates pursuant to Article 32.1.9 if the secured debt is transferred without the charge.

18.2 In the case of a transfer of a debt secured by a possessory charge, the transfer extends to the charge only if at the time of the transfer

　18.2.1 the transferor passes possession of the charged property to the new chargeholder or a person nominated by the new chargeholder; or

　18.2.2 the transferor agrees to hold the charged property on behalf of the new chargeholder.

18.3 Where a secured debt which extends to a registered charge has been transferred the charge is not enforceable unless

    18.3.1 the transfer is registered pursuant to Article 33.1.4; or

    18.3.2 a charge manager is registered in respect of the charge pursuant to Article 8.4.1 or 33.1.2.

18.4 The chargor may claim any defences which he has against the transferor also against the new chargeholder.

18.5 A transfer of a secured debt which extends to the charge automatically extends also to all rights of the chargeholder under the charging instrument unless otherwise provided in the charging instrument or agreed between the parties to the transfer.

18.6 Where only part of a secured debt and a charge is transferred the new chargeholder becomes entitled to the charge and any transferred rights under the charging instrument jointly with the transferring chargeholder up to the amount of the secured debt transferred.

18.7 A transfer of a secured debt by operation of law extends to the charge given in respect of that debt.

Article 19
Legal licence to transfer charged property

19.1 The chargor has a licence to transfer title to the charged property by way of sale free from the charge in the terms set out in this Article 19 except in the case of a possessory charge.

19.2 The chargor may transfer title to items of his charged trading stock by way of sale in the ordinary course of his trading activity.

19.3 The chargor may transfer title to other charged property by way of sale in the ordinary course of his business provided that the thing or right transferred is of a kind that is habitually transferred by him in the ordinary course of his business.

19.4 In the case of an enterprise charge the chargor may transfer title by way of sale in any charged property in respect of which applicable additional registration as provided in Article 11 has not been made.

19.5 The licence to transfer title by way of sale pursuant to this Article 19 is suspended automatically

    19.5.1 upon possession of the charged property being given pursuant to Article 10.1 until the time when such possession ceases; or

    19.5.2 upon an enforcement notice in respect of the charge being delivered pursuant to Article 22.2 until enforcement proceedings may no longer be continued pursuant to Article 22.4.

19.6 Any agreement between the chargor and the chargeholder restricting or terminating the licence pursuant to this Article 19 is of effect only between the parties.

Article 20
Contractual licence to deal in charged property

20.1 The chargeholder may, except in the case of a possessory charge, grant the chargor a contractual licence to transfer title to the charged property free from the charge in addition to the legal licence pursuant to Article 19.

20.2 In any contractual licence granted pursuant to Article 20.1 the charged property may be identified specifically or generally and the licence may be granted on such terms as the chargor and chargeholder may agree.

20.3 The grant of a contractual licence pursuant to Article 20.1 may be included in the charging instrument and in that event a person dealing with the chargor acquires charged property free from the charge pursuant to Article 21.2.3 without being under an obligation to make further enquiries.

20.4 A contractual licence granted pursuant to Article 20.1 is suspended automatically in the events as provided in Article 19.5 and may subject to Article 20.3 be terminated at any time by the chargeholder or in accordance with its terms.

Article 21
Third parties acquiring charged property

21.1 Any person acquiring title to charged property will acquire subject to the charge except as provided in Article 21.2.

21.2 If a person acquires title to charged property he acquires it free from the charge

   21.2.1 where the chargor transfers title to the charged property by way of sale under the licence granted pursuant to Article 19; or

   21.2.2 while the licence granted pursuant to Article 19 is suspended where the transfer of title by the chargor by way of sale if made prior to suspension would have been under the licence and where either

      21.2.2.1 the purchaser does not have actual knowledge at the time of the transfer of the existence of the charge; or

      21.2.2.2 the purchaser believes in good faith at the time of the transfer that the licence exists;

or

   21.2.3 where the chargor transfers title to the charged property under a contractual licence granted pursuant to Article 20.1; or

   21.2.4 while a contractual licence granted pursuant to Article 20.1 is suspended or after it is terminated where the transfer of title by the chargor if made prior to suspension or termination would have been under the licence and where the acquirer believes in good faith at the time of the transfer that the licence exists. Except where a contractual licence is contained in the charging instrument the acquirer is under an obligation to enquire of the chargeholder; or

   21.2.5 where the price paid for the charged property is less than [*amount*] and where the purchaser believes in good faith at the time of the transfer that no charge exists; or

   21.2.6 where the charged property is

      21.2.6.1 a negotiable instrument or negotiable document; or

      21.2.6.2 a share or debt instrument or a contract quoted on a recognised exchange or habitually traded in a recognised market; or

   21.2.7 where the charge is to an unpaid vendor pursuant to Article 9 unless

      21.2.7.1 a purpose of the chargor is to terminate the unpaid vendor's charge; and

      21.2.7.2 the acquirer has actual knowledge at the time of the transfer of that purpose or circumstances exist which should make him aware of that purpose.

21.3 For the purposes of Articles 21.2.2.2 and 21.2.4 a purchaser or an acquirer believes in good faith that a licence exists if

21.3.1 he does not have actual knowledge of the termination of the licence; and

21.3.2 there do not exist circumstances which should make him aware of the termination of the licence.

21.4 For the purposes of Article 21.2.5 a purchaser believes in good faith that no charge exists if

21.4.1 he does not have actual knowledge of the existence of the charge; and

21.4.2 there do not exist circumstances which should make him aware of the existence of the charge.

21.5 For the purposes of Articles 21.2.2, 21.2.4 and 21.2.5 the purchaser or acquirer is not under an obligation to search the charges' register unless the particular circumstances are abnormal and such as to make a search of the charges' register prudent.

21.6 Where a person acquires title to charged property subject to a registered charge the chargeholder may at any time register the charge against the name of such person pursuant to Article 33.1.5.

PART 4
ENFORCEMENT AND TERMINATION

Article 22
General rules on enforcement

22.1 A charge becomes immediately enforceable if there is a failure to pay the secured debt and it remains immediately enforceable until

22.1.1 the chargeholder agrees that the charge is no longer immediately enforceable; or

22.1.2 the secured debt is satisfied in full or otherwise ceases to exist; or

22.1.3 the charge terminates for any other reason.

22.2 The chargeholder of a charge which has become immediately enforceable may commence enforcement proceedings by delivering an enforcement notice to the chargor containing the information set out in Article 22.7.

22.3 When a chargeholder has delivered an enforcement notice pursuant to Article 22.2 he has the right to take protective measures pursuant to Article 23 and to realise the charge pursuant to Article 24 or, in the case of an enterprise charge, to have the charge enforced pursuant to Article 25.

22.4 Enforcement proceedings cannot be continued if

22.4.1 a supplementary registration statement in respect of the enforcement notice delivered pursuant to Article 22.2 has not been presented at the charges' registry pursuant to Article 33.1.6 within seven days of delivery to the chargor; or

22.4.2 the enforcement notice is declared invalid by the court; or

22.4.3 the charge ceases to be immediately enforceable in accordance with Article 22.1.

22.5 In the event of the chargeholder failing to register the enforcement notice as required by Article 22.4.1 the chargeholder is liable to the chargor, any other chargeholder with a charge over the same property and any other party claiming rights in the charged property for any loss suffered by any of them as a result of the protective measures. This does not apply where the charge ceases to be immediately enforceable in accordance with Article 22.1 within seven days of delivery of the enforcement notice to the chargor and where the protective measures were taken while the charge was immediately enforceable.

22.6 The chargeholder may at any time request deregistration of the enforcement notice pursuant to Article 33.1.11 and is under an obligation to do so in the events referred to in Article 22.4.2 and 22.4.3.

22.7 An enforcement notice delivered pursuant to Article 22.2 must in order to be valid be in writing and

    22.7.1 identify the charge in respect of which enforcement proceedings are being commenced

        22.7.1.1 in the case of a registered charge, by reference to the charges' register and the date of registration; or

        22.7.1.2 in the case of an unpaid vendor's charge or a possessory charge, by reference to the information required to register such a charge pursuant to Articles 8.4 to 8.6; and

    22.7.2 dentify the debt in respect of which enforcement proceedings are being commenced which may be the secured debt or any part of that debt; and

    22.7.3 contain a statement that the charge has become immediately enforceable; and

    22.7.4 where the chargeholder elects for a charged enterprise to be transferred as a going concern pursuant to Article 25.3 state that such election is being made and identify the person appointed as enterprise administrator; and

    22.7.5 be signed by or on behalf of the chargeholder and, where Article 22.7.4 applies, the enterprise administrator; and

    22.7.6 in the case of an enterprise charge, be signed by or on behalf of the chargeholder of any prior ranking enterprise charge.

Article 23
Measures for protection of charged property

23.1 When an enforcement notice has been delivered pursuant to Article 22.2 the chargeholder has the right to possession of charged property which is in the form of movable things.

23.2 Where taking possession of charged property referred to in Article 23.1 is impracticable or is disputed by a third party in possession of the charged property the chargeholder may take such steps as are necessary to immobilise the charged property, to prevent the chargor or a third party using it and to prevent the chargor transferring title to it.

23.3 Where an enforcement notice has been delivered pursuant to Article 22.2 in respect of charged property which is a contractual obligation other than a debt for money the chargeholder may notify the person owing the charged obligation that it is subject to a charge and that enforcement proceedings have been commenced. Upon such notification

    23.3.1 the chargor cannot modify the contractual obligation without the agreement of the chargeholder; and

23.3.2 the chargor cannot take any steps to exercise his rights in respect of the contractual obligation without the agreement of the chargeholder; and

23.3.3 the chargeholder may exercise the chargor's rights in respect of the contractual obligation but in such case the chargeholder must comply with any corresponding obligation owed by the chargor.

23.4 Where an enforcement notice has been delivered pursuant to Article 22.2 the chargeholder may take reasonable steps

23.4.1 to preserve, maintain and insure the charged property; and

23.4.2 with a view to increasing the sale price or reducing the sale costs including enhancing the charged property or renting it on commercially prudent terms to a third party.

23.5 Upon application by the chargeholder the court may make an order for other appropriate measures to protect the charged property after the enforcement notice has been registered as required by Article 22.4.1.

23.6 The chargeholder at any time may take protective measures as agreed with the chargor.

23.7 If in order to obtain possession as referred to in Article 23.1 or to take other steps as provided in Article 23.2 the chargeholder does not have the right to enter upon the site where the charged property is situated or where any such rights are refused to the chargeholder he may appoint a [*bailiff*] for such purpose. The [*bailiff*] may on the chargeholder's behalf take the protective measures to which the chargeholder is entitled provided

23.7.1 he is satisfied that the charge is registered or, in the case of an unpaid vendor's charge or a possessory charge, the enforcement notice is registered; and

23.7.2 he receives from the chargeholder a copy of the enforcement notice delivered pursuant to Article 22.2.

Article 24
Measures for realisation of charged property

24.1 When at least 60 days have elapsed since delivery of an enforcement notice pursuant to Article 22.2 the chargeholder has the right to transfer title to the charged property by way of sale in order to have the proceeds of sale applied towards satisfaction of the secured debt.

24.2 Any agreement entered into prior to delivery of an enforcement notice pursuant to Article 22.2 which provides for the transfer of title to charged property by way of sale by or to the chargeholder after delivery of the enforcement notice is invalid.

24.3 The chargeholder must

24.3.1 endeavour to realise a fair price for the charged property; and

24.3.2 advise the purchaser that he is transferring title to charged property in the capacity of chargeholder and that the proceeds of sale must be paid directly to a proceeds depositary appointed pursuant to Article 27.1.

24.4 The chargeholder may subject to the obligation under Article 24.3.1 transfer title to the charged property by way of sale in such manner as he considers appropriate which may include transfer by private agreement on the open market or at public or private auction. The chargeholder may appoint a person to act on his behalf for the transfer or for any matter connected with it.

24.5 A chargeholder is treated as having fulfilled his obligation under Article 24.3.1 if he can demonstrate that

 24.5.1 in the case of charged property of a kind for which there is a recognised market, he acted in the manner of a prudent person operating in that market; or

 24.5.2 in all other cases, he took such steps to realise a fair price as could be expected in the circumstances of a prudent person.

Article 25
Enterprise charge administration

25.1 An enterprise charge may be enforced pursuant to Articles 23 and 24 or pursuant to this Article 25.

25.2 Any agreement entered into prior to delivery of an enforcement notice pursuant to Article 22.2 which provides for the transfer of title to the charged enterprise by way of sale by or to the chargeholder after delivery of the enforcement notice is invalid.

25.3 A chargeholder of an enterprise charge who delivers an enforcement notice pursuant to Article 22.2 may elect for the enterprise to be transferred as a going concern pursuant to this Article 25 and in that case the enforcement notice must comply with the requirements of Articles 22.7.4, 22.7.5 and 22.7.6.

25.4 A chargeholder may only make an election under Article 25.3 if he believes that the enterprise is capable of being transferred as a going concern.

25.5 When an election is made pursuant to Article 25.3

 25.5.1 the chargeholder must appoint a person (called an enterprise administrator) who has the powers and obligations set out in this Article 25; and

 25.5.2 the chargeholder may not, except as provided under Article 25.20, exercise any rights pursuant to Articles 23 and 24 unless the election is rescinded.

25.6 In order for the appointment of the enterprise administrator to be valid

 25.6.1 he must be a [*qualified accountant or lawyer*]; and

 25.6.2 he must not be a chargeholder or the charge manager; and

 25.6.3 a statement of his appointment must be presented at the [*registry where the chargor is registered*] within seven days of delivery of the enforcement notice pursuant to Article 22.2.

25.7 Where an election is made pursuant to Article 25.3

 25.7.1 the powers of the persons authorised by law or by the chargor's constitution to administer the enterprise and to deal in the charged property cease upon delivery of the enforcement notice; and

 25.7.2 such powers are immediately vested in the enterprise administrator.

25.8 Each of the persons whose powers cease pursuant to Article 25.7.1 is under an obligation to give all necessary information and assistance to the enterprise administrator to enable him to manage the enterprise and to carry out his functions and may in addition be given such powers in relation to the enterprise as may be agreed with the enterprise administrator.

25.9 Each of the persons whose powers cease pursuant to Article 25.7.1 is liable for any loss suffered by the chargor or any third party as a result of any exercise by that person of any of his former powers after he has actual knowledge that his powers have ceased.

25.10 The enterprise administrator must

    25.10.1 fulfil all those obligations that are provided by law for the persons whose powers are vested in him pursuant to Article 25.7.2 (but not including the obligation under Article 15.2); and

    25.10.2 continue the enterprise as a going concern; and

    25.10.3 advise the chargeholder promptly if he believes that the enterprise is not capable of being transferred as a going concern; and

    25.10.4 endeavour to transfer the enterprise as a going concern and to realise a fair price; and

    25.10.5 advise the purchaser that he is transferring title to charged property in the capacity of enterprise administrator and that the proceeds of sale must be paid directly to a proceeds depositary appointed pursuant to Article 27.1.

25.11 The appointment of an enterprise administrator terminates upon

    25.11.1 his death; or

    25.11.2 his becoming incapable of performing his obligations; or

    25.11.3 his resignation; or

    25.11.4 his being removed by the chargeholder; or

    25.11.5 his being removed by the court; or

    25.11.6 the transfer of the enterprise by way of sale; or

    25.11.7 the administration of the enterprise ceasing pursuant to Article 25.22 or 25.23.

25.12 When the appointment of an enterprise administrator is terminated pursuant to Articles 25.11.1 to 25.11.5 a new enterprise administrator must be appointed

    25.12.1 in the case of Articles 25.11.1, 25.11.2 or 25.11.3, by the chargeholder within seven days of the occurrence of the death, incapacity or resignation;

    25.12.2 in the case of Article 25.11.4, by the chargeholder at the time of the removal of the previous enterprise administrator;

    25.12.3 in the case of Article 25.11.5, by the court at the time of his removal and in such case the court may, if appropriate, appoint a new enterprise administrator nominated by the chargeholder.

25.13 If the chargeholder fails to appoint a new enterprise administrator

    25.13.1 within seven days as provided in Article 25.12.1 the court may appoint a new enterprise administrator or rescind the election to have the enterprise transferred as a going concern pursuant to Article 25.3;

    25.13.2 at the time of the removal by him of the previous enterprise administrator as referred to in Article 25.11.4 the removal is not valid.

25.14 The appointment of a new enterprise administrator after the seven days as provided in Article 25.12.1 is valid but the chargeholder is liable to the chargor, any other chargeholder with a charge over the same charged property and any other party claiming rights in the charged property for any loss suffered by reason of any delay in the appointment caused by the chargeholder.

25.15 The chargeholder is under an obligation to present at the charges' registry pursuant to Article 33.1.7 or 33.1.8 and at [*the registry where the chargor is registered*] a request for registration of any termination of the appointment of an enterprise administrator or any appointment of a new enterprise administrator within seven days of the termination or appointment.

25.16 Within 60 days of delivery of an enforcement notice pursuant to Article 22.2 the enterprise administrator may renounce any contract to which the chargor is party and which imposes continuing obligations on the chargor.

25.17 Where a contract imposes continuing obligations on the chargor the other party may serve a notice on the enterprise administrator at any time within the 60 day period requiring the enterprise administrator to state whether or not he will be exercising his right under Article 25.16. Until the enterprise administrator replies to that notice the obligation of the other party to perform is suspended.

25.18 When at least 60 days have elapsed since delivery of an enforcement notice pursuant to Article 22.2 the enterprise administrator has the right to transfer the enterprise by way of sale in order to have the proceeds of sale applied towards satisfaction of the secured debt.

25.19 The enterprise administrator may subject to the obligation under Article 25.10.4 transfer the enterprise as a going concern by way of sale in such a manner as he considers appropriate which may include transfer by private agreement, on the open market or at public or private auction. The enterprise administrator may appoint a person to act on his behalf for the transfer or for any matter connected with it.

25.20 If the enterprise administrator determines that any part of the charged property can be transferred separately from the enterprise without preventing the transfer of the enterprise as a going concern he may agree with the chargeholder that such property is transferred by the chargeholder pursuant to Article 24.

25.21 An enterprise administrator is treated as having fulfilled his obligation under Article 25.10.4 if he can demonstrate that he took such steps as could be expected in the circumstances of a prudent person transferring an enterprise of that nature.

25.22 The election to have the enterprise transferred as a going concern pursuant to Article 25.3 must be rescinded by the chargeholder if he determines that the enterprise is no longer capable of being transferred as a going concern.

25.23 The election to have the enterprise transferred as a going concern pursuant to Article 25.3 may be rescinded

    25.23.1 by the chargeholder if he determines that to do so is in the interests of other creditors of the chargor; or

    25.23.2 by the court pursuant to Article 25.13.1 or 29.

25.24 In the event of the election being rescinded pursuant to Article 25.22 or 25.23 the charge may be enforced pursuant to Articles 23 and 24.

Article 26
Purchaser from chargeholder or enterprise administrator

26.1 If a person acquires title to charged property from the chargeholder pursuant to Article 24 or from the enterprise administrator pursuant to Article 25 he acquires it free from any charge if

    26.1.1 the enforcement notice and, in the case of a transfer pursuant to Article 25, the enterprise administrator remain registered on the charges' register until at least the third day (excluding weekends and public holidays) before the date of the transfer and no interim order remains registered pursuant to Article 33.1.9 at such time; and

    26.1.2 the sale price is paid to a proceeds depositary appointed by the chargeholder pursuant to Article 27.

26.2 A purchaser will not acquire title free from any charge if he has actual knowledge at the time of the purchase that

26.2.1 the charge being enforced is not created, invalid or unenforceable; or

26.2.2 the charge has ceased to be immediately enforceable in accordance with Article 22.1; or

26.2.3 the enforcement notice has been declared invalid by a court; or

26.2.4 an order made by the court pursuant to Article 29.3 is still outstanding; or

26.2.5 in the case of transfer of an enterprise pursuant to Article 25, the election made pursuant to Article 25.3 has been rescinded.

26.3 The purchaser has no obligation to enquire as to the creation, validity and enforceability of the charge or as to the powers of the enterprise administrator registered on the charges' register.

Article 27
Proceeds depositary

27.1 Prior to the day on which any proceeds of sale under Articles 24 or 25 become payable the chargeholder must appoint a person to receive the proceeds of sale (called a proceeds depositary). Such appointment may be made at any time after delivery of an enforcement notice pursuant to Article 22.2.

27.2 In order for the appointment of the proceeds depositary to be valid

27.2.1 he must be a [*qualified accountant or recognised bank*]; and

27.2.2 he cannot be the chargor, a chargeholder, the charge manager or the enterprise administrator.

27.3 The chargeholder or the enterprise administrator must cause the proceeds of sale to be paid to the proceeds depositary.

27.4 The proceeds depositary must place all amounts received by him on deposit on commercial terms with a prime bank in a segregated account.

27.5 Promptly after his appointment the proceeds depositary must establish a list setting out

27.5.1 the persons entitled to the proceeds of sale; and

27.5.2 the amount of the entitlement of each; and

27.5.3 the priority of the entitlement of each.

27.6 In order to establish the list pursuant to Article 27.5 the proceeds depositary

27.6.1 must examine the charges' register; and

27.6.2 must enquire of the chargor and the enterprise administrator; and

27.6.3 where the charged property includes a movable thing which may be subject to an unpaid vendor's charge, must determine the date of acquisition and, if appropriate, enquire of the vendor; and

27.6.4 must take note of any claim directly addressed to him; and

27.6.5 may but is not obliged to make other appropriate enquiries.

27.7 The proceeds depositary may exclude from the list any person who fails to provide information necessary to establish the list referred to in Article 27.5 if

27.7.1 the proceeds depositary has delivered two notices to that person requesting information as to his entitlement; and

27.7.2 there are at least 15 days between delivery of the first and of the second notice; and

27.7.3 both notices state that the information is needed for establishing the list and that any failure to provide the required information may cause loss of entitlement to proceeds of sale held by the proceeds depositary; and

27.7.4 the required information has not been received within 15 days of delivery of the second notice.

27.8 When the list is established pursuant to Article 27.5 the proceeds depositary must deliver a copy to the chargeholder, the enterprise administrator, the chargor, any chargeholder shown on the charges' register with a charge over the same charged property and any other person who, to the proceeds depositary's actual knowledge, has or claims to have a right in the charged property.

27.9 Any person who claims entitlement to the proceeds of sale and does not agree with the list as established by the proceeds depositary may within 21 days of delivery of the list pursuant to Article 27.8 notify the proceeds depositary of his disagreement. In this case the proceeds depositary must deliver to the persons referred to in Article 27.8 either an amended list or a statement that a disagreement has been notified but that the list remains unchanged.

27.10 Where establishment of a definitive list is delayed for any reason, the proceeds depositary may establish a provisional list making full reserve for any undetermined or disputed amounts.

Article 28
Distribution of proceeds of sale

28.1 The proceeds depositary must, subject to any order made by the court pursuant to Article 29, distribute the proceeds of sale promptly upon 30 days elapsing after the latest of

28.1.1 receipt by the proceeds depositary of the proceeds of sale; or

28.1.2 delivery of the list pursuant to Article 27.8; or

28.1.3 delivery of the list or statement pursuant to Article 27.9.

28.2 The proceeds depositary may make an initial distribution of proceeds of sale on the basis of a provisional list established pursuant to Article 27.10.

28.3 The proceeds depositary must distribute the proceeds of sale as follows

28.3.1 first, in payment of his fees and costs up to [*amount*];

28.3.2 second, where an election has been made pursuant to Article 25.3, in payment of the liabilities referred to in Article 28.4.1;

28.3.3 third, where an election has been made pursuant to Article 25.3, in payment of the liabilities referred to in Articles 28.4.2 and 28.4.3;

28.3.4 fourth, to chargeholders of charges over the charged property transferred in accordance with the priorities of their respective charges;

28.3.5 fifth, to other persons with rights in the charged property which entitle them to the proceeds of sale; and

28.3.6 sixth, to the chargor.

28.4 Where an election has been made pursuant to Article 25.3 the following liabilities have priority in any distribution of the proceeds of sale

28.4.1 reasonable remuneration of the enterprise administrator for continuing the enterprise as a going concern but excluding any remuneration or costs in respect of the transfer of the enterprise and any amounts due to an enterprise administrator by reason of termination of his appointment; and

28.4.2 liabilities incurred by the enterprise administrator in continuing the enterprise as a going concern; and

28.4.3 liabilities becoming due under contracts renounced pursuant to Article 25.16 after delivery of the enforcement notice pursuant to Article 22.2 and prior to renunciation excluding any liability arising by reason of such renunciation.

28.5 Where any amount payable by the proceeds depositary pursuant to this Article 28 is payable in a currency other than the currency held by the proceeds depositary he must purchase the necessary amount of that currency to make the payment.

28.6 The proceeds depositary must continue to hold the amount of the proceeds of sale attributable to any secured debt until it becomes payable.

28.7 The secured debt is satisfied to the extent that the proceeds depositary pays proceeds of sale to a chargeholder.

28.8 Any payment by the proceeds depositary to a non-resident chargeholder is treated for the purpose of currency exchange regulations as a payment of the secured debt by the debtor.

Article 29
Court remedies on enforcement

29.1 If at any time after delivery of an enforcement notice pursuant to Article 22.2 a chargor, any other chargeholder with a charge over the same charged property or any other party claiming rights in the charged property disputes the creation, validity or enforceability of the charge or claims termination of the charge he may apply to the court to have the enforcement notice declared invalid. Any application under this Article 29.1 must be treated by the court as urgent business [*state time limit for decision*]. Notwithstanding such application until the enforcement notice is declared invalid and subject to any order made by the court pursuant to Articles 29.3 to 29.5

29.1.1 the chargeholder may continue to take protective measures pursuant to Article 23; and

29.1.2 the chargeholder may continue to realise the charge pursuant to Article 24; and

29.1.3 where an election has been made pursuant to Article 25.3 the enterprise administrator may continue to operate the enterprise as a going concern and to realise the charge pursuant to Article 25.

29.2 If the court declares the enforcement notice invalid the chargor or the party who applied to the court may require the chargeholder to present at the charges' registry a request for deregistration of the enforcement notice pursuant to Article 33.1.11.

29.3 If upon an application being made pursuant to Article 29.1 the court is

29.3.1 unable to give its final decision within 60 days of the enforcement notice being delivered pursuant to Article 22.2; and

29.3.2 satisfied that there are reasonable grounds on which to claim that the charge is not created, invalid, or not enforceable or that it has been terminated; and

29.3.3 satisfied that, after taking into account the interests of all the parties, it is appropriate to make an order pursuant to this Article 29.3; the court may if so requested by the applicant make an interim order that the charged property may not be transferred pursuant to Article 24 or 25 until the court has rendered its final decision. The applicant is under an obligation to present at the charges' registry pursuant to Article 33.1.9 a request for registration of the interim order within seven days of it being made and pursuant to Article 33.1.12 a request for deregistration of the order within seven days of it being terminated. The applicant is liable to third parties for any loss suffered as a result of breach of this obligation.

29.4 A chargor, any other chargeholder with a charge over the same charged property or any other party claiming rights in the charged property who alleges that the chargeholder, the enterprise administrator or the proceeds depositary has failed to comply with the requirements of Articles 22 to 28 may apply to the court for an order

    29.4.1 to declare any measure taken which was not in compliance with the requirements of Articles 22 to 28 invalid subject to Article 26;

    29.4.2 requiring the chargeholder, the enterprise administrator or the proceeds depositary to comply with those requirements;

    29.4.3 for such other matter as the court considers appropriate.

29.5 A chargor, any other chargeholder with a charge over the same charged property or any other party claiming rights in the charged property who alleges that the chargeholder, the enterprise administrator or the proceeds depositary has taken in relation to enforcement of a charge measures to which he is not entitled may apply to the court for an order

    29.5.1 to declare the measures to which the application relates invalid subject to Article 26;

    29.5.2 requiring the chargeholder, the enterprise administrator or the proceeds depositary to refrain from taking any further measures to which he is not entitled;

    29.5.3 for such other matter as the court considers appropriate.

Article 30
Damages

A chargor, any other chargeholder with a charge over the same charged property or any other party claiming rights in the charged property has an action in damages

30.1 in the case of an enforcement notice declared invalid by the court pursuant to Article 29.1, for any loss suffered by any of them as a result of enforcement; and

30.2 for any loss suffered as a result of any failure by a chargeholder, charge manager, enterprise administrator or proceeds depositary to comply with the requirements of Articles 22 to 28 or as a result of any measure taken by any such person in relation to enforcement of a charge to which he is not entitled.

Article 31
Insolvency principles

The provisions to be included to cover the event of the insolvency of the chargor have to be drafted jurisdiction by jurisdiction to take into account local insolvency rules. The following basic principles must be respected:

1. The charge remains valid notwithstanding insolvency.

2. Any right to set aside a charge as an act in the period immediately prior to insolvency is in the same terms as for other pre-insolvency acts.
3. Either the charge remains enforceable by the chargeholder separately from insolvency proceedings or the liquidator is under an obligation to sell the charged property rapidly at a fair price and to satisfy the chargeholder's claim out of the proceeds of sale.
4. The creditors who may rank ahead of the chargeholder in respect of the proceeds of sale are limitatively defined.

Article 32
Termination of a charge

32.1 A charge terminates if and to the extent that
   32.1.1 the chargor and the chargeholder so agree; or
   32.1.2 the secured debt is satisfied or otherwise ceases to exist; or
   32.1.3 the charged property ceases to exist; or
   32.1.4 the charged property is changed or incorporated with another thing or right in such a manner that it ceases to exist in identifiable or separable form; or
   32.1.5 the charged property becomes part of another thing or right in such manner that the charged property and the other thing or right are transferable as a single item; or
   32.1.6 the charged property becomes owned by the chargeholder; or
   32.1.7 in the case of an unpaid vendor's charge, as provided in Article 9.4; or
   32.1.8 in the case of a possessory charge pursuant to Article 10, if possession of charged property ceases; or
   32.1.9 the secured debt is transferred and the transfer does not extend to the charge; or
   32.1.10 a third party acquires title to charged property free from the charge pursuant to Article 21.2; or
   32.1.11 a person acquires title to charged property free from any charge pursuant to Article 26.1.
32.2 A charge also terminates if the chargor or another chargeholder with a charge over the same charged property
   32.2.1 deposits a sum equal to 130 per cent. of the maximum amount of the secured debt referred to in Article 4.5 or, in the case of an unpaid vendor's charge, of the unpaid part of the purchase price referred to in Article 9.2.1 and in the same currency as the secured debt with a prime bank on terms agreed with the chargeholder or failing agreement on commercial terms then prevailing for similar sums in that currency; and
   32.2.2 grants to the chargeholder whose charge is being terminated a registered charge over the sum deposited pursuant to Article 32.2.1 in order to secure the debt previously secured by the charge that is terminated.
32.3 Upon termination of a charge the chargeholder must
   32.3.1 in the case of a registered charge, register the termination of the charge pursuant to Article 33.1.10; or
   32.3.2 in the case of a possessory charge, return the charged property to the chargor unless otherwise agreed between chargor and chargeholder.

PART 5
REGISTRATION

Article 33
Supplementary registration statement

33.1 In order to obtain registration of
    33.1.1 an amendment to a charging instrument; or
    33.1.2 the subsequent appointment of a charge manager; or
    33.1.3 the termination of the appointment of a charge manager; or
    33.1.4 the transfer of a secured debt extending to a charge; or
    33.1.5 a charge against the name of a person who has acquired title to charged property; or
    33.1.6 an enforcement notice; or
    33.1.7 the termination of the appointment of an enterprise administrator; or
    33.1.8 the appointment of a new enterprise administrator; or
    33.1.9 an interim order made under Article 29.3; or
    33.1.10 the termination of a registered charge; or in order to obtain deregistration of
    33.1.11 an enforcement notice; or
    33.1.12 an interim order made under Article 29.3;
    a supplementary registration statement must be presented at the charges' registry.
33.2 A supplementary registration statement presented pursuant to Article 33.1 must
    33.2.1 identify the charge by reference to the chargor, the date of registration (in the case of a registered charge) and other information as necessary; and
    33.2.2 state the purpose of the supplementary registration statement; and
    33.2.3 comply with the requirements of Article 33.3.
33.3 A supplementary registration statement presented pursuant to Article 33.1 must also include
    33.3.1 in the case of an amendment to a charging instrument pursuant to Article 7.5
        33.3.1.1 the date of the charging instrument; and
        33.3.1.2 the date of the amendment; and
        33.3.1.3 signatures by or on behalf of the chargor and the chargeholder; or
    33.3.2 in the case of the subsequent appointment of a charge manager pursuant to Article 16
        33.3.2.1 identification of the charge manager; and
        33.3.2.2 signatures by or on behalf of the chargeholder and the charge manager; or
    33.3.3 in the case of the termination of the appointment of a charge manager pursuant to Article 16
        33.3.3.1 identification of the charge manager; and
        33.3.3.2 signature by or on behalf of the chargeholder or the charge manager; or
    33.3.4 in the case of the transfer of a secured debt extending to a charge pursuant to Article 18.1
        33.3.4.1 identification of the transferor and the new chargeholder; and
        33.3.4.2 signatures by or on behalf of the transferring chargeholder and the new chargeholder;

or

33.3.5 in the case of registration of a charge against the name of a person who has acquired title to charged property as referred to in Article 21.6

    33.3.5.1 identification of the person who has acquired title; and

    33.3.5.2 signature by or on behalf of the chargeholder; or

33.3.6 in the case of an enforcement notice delivered pursuant to Article 22.2

    33.3.6.1 the date of delivery of the enforcement notice; and

    33.3.6.2 where the enforcement notice relates to an unpaid vendor's charge or a possessory charge the information required to register such a charge pursuant to Articles 8.4 to 8.6; and

    33.3.6.3 where an election has been made pursuant to Article 25.3, a statement that this is the case; and

    33.3.6.4 signature by or on behalf of the chargeholder; or

33.3.7 in the case of termination of the appointment of an enterprise administrator pursuant to Article 25.11

    33.3.7.1 identification of the enterprise administrator; and

    33.3.7.2 signature by or on behalf of the chargeholder; or

33.3.8 in the case of appointment of a new enterprise administrator pursuant to Article 25.12

    33.3.8.1 identification of the enterprise administrator; and

    33.3.8.2 signatures by or on behalf of the chargeholder and the enterprise administrator; or

33.3.9 in the case of an interim order made under Article 29.3

    33.3.9.1 a description of the interim order; and

    33.3.9.2 identification of the person who applied for the order; and

    33.3.9.3 signature by or on behalf of the person who applied for the order; or

33.3.10 in the case of the termination of a registered charge pursuant to Article 32, signature by or on behalf of the chargeholder; or

33.3.11 in the case of deregistration of an enforcement notice pursuant to Article 22.6

    33.3.11.1 the date of delivery of the enforcement notice; and

    33.3.11.2 signature by or on behalf of the chargeholder; or

33.3.12 in the case of deregistration of an interim order made under Article 29.3

    33.3.12.1 a description of the interim order; and

    33.3.12.2 signature by or on behalf of the person who applied for the order.

33.4 Where there is more than one chargor a separate supplementary registration statement must be presented for each chargor.

Article 34
Registration procedure

34.1 The registrar may accept a registration statement pursuant to Article 8 or a supplementary registration statement pursuant to Article 33 in such form as he deems fit and can only refuse to register

    34.1.1 if the registration statement or supplementary registration statement does not comply with the requirements of Article 8 or 33; or

    34.1.2 if the required registration fee is not paid.

34.2 Upon acceptance of a registration statement or a supplementary registration statement the registrar must immediately

    34.2.1 mark the time and date of presentation and the stamp of the registration office on the registration statement or supplementary registration statement and, if supplied, on a copy; and

    34.2.2 place the registration statement or supplementary registration statement on the register against the name of the chargor and hand the copy, if supplied, to the presenter.

34.3 If the registrar refuses to accept a registration statement or a supplementary registration statement for one of the reasons in Article 34.1 he must at the same time notify the person presenting the registration statement or supplementary registration statement in writing of the reasons for his refusal and that person may present

    34.3.1 a new registration statement within the 30 day period pursuant to Article 8.1 or, if later, within 15 days of such notification; or

    34.3.2 a new supplementary registration statement within seven days in the cases referred to in Articles 33.1.6 to 33.1.9 or at any time in any other case.

34.4 The time of registration is the time when the registration statement or supplementary registration statement is presented at the charges' registry or, where Article 34.3 applies, the time when the new registration statement or new supplementary registration statement is presented at the charges' registry.

Article 35
Access to the Register

Any person may against payment of the required fee have access to the register and receive a copy of any entry on it.

SCHEDULE 1
CHARGING INSTRUMENT (ARTICLE 7.2)

CHARGING INSTRUMENT

1. [*Name of chargor*]
   [*Address of chargor*]
   [*Other identification of chargor as necessary*]
   agrees to grant to
   [*Name of chargeholder*]
   [*Address of chargeholder*]
   [*Other identification of chargeholder as necessary*]
   a charge of the things and rights described below to secure the debt described below.
2. The debt secured by the charge is [*describe secured debt*].
   [*Include identification of person owing the secured debt if not chargor. For a possessory charge state maximum amount of secured debt*]
3. The things and rights charged are [*describe charged property*].
4. [*Other matters pursuant to Article 7.5*]

   Signature of chargor and date of signature

   Signature of chargeholder

SCHEDULE 2
REGISTRATION STATEMENT (ARTICLE 8.3)

REGISTRATION STATEMENT

1. [*Name, address and other identification as necessary of chargor*]
2. [*Name, address and other identification as necessary of person owing the secured debt* [if not the chargor]]
3. [*Name, address and other identification as necessary of chargeholder*]
4. [*Name address and other identification as necessary of charge manager* [if appointed]]
5. [*Identification of the secured debt*]
6. [*Maximum amount of the secured debt*]
7. [*Identification of the charged property*]
8. [*If appropriate*] The charge is an enterprise charge.
9. [*Date of the charging instrument*] [*Except where an unpaid vendor's charge is being converted into a registered charge*]
10. [*Where an unpaid vendor's charge is being converted into a registered charge*]
    10.1 This registration statement is for the conversion of an unpaid vendor's charge into a registered charge.
    10.2 [*Date on which charged property was transferred to the chargor*]
    10.3 [*Date and identification of the written agreement giving rise to the unpaid vendor's charge*]
11. [*Where a possessory charge is being converted into a registered charge*]
    11.1 This registration statement is for the conversion of a possessory charge into a registered charge.
    11.2 [*If later than the date of the charging instrument*] [*Date on which possession of the charged property was given*]

Signature of chargor

Signature of charge manager [*if appointed*]

Or [*Where an unpaid vendor's charge or a possessory charge is being converted into a registered charge*]

Signature of chargeholder

(b) MODEL INTER-AMERICAN LAW ON SECURED TRANSACTIONS, 2002*

* Reproduced with the kind permission of the Organization of American States.

TITLE I
SCOPE AND GENERAL APPLICATION

Article 1

The objective of the Model Inter-American Law on Secured Transactions (hereinafter, the 'Law') is to regulate security interest in movable property securing the performance of any obligations whatsoever, of any nature, present or future, determined or determinable.

A State may declare that this Law does not apply to the types of collateral expressly specified in this text.

A State adopting this Law shall create a unitary and uniform registration system applicable to all existing movable property security devices in the local legal framework, in order to give effect to this Law.

Article 2

The security interests to which this Law refers are created contractually over one or several specific items of movable property, on generic categories of movable property, or on all of the secured debtor's movable property, whether present or future, corporeal or incorporeal, susceptible to pecuniary valuation at the time of creation or thereafter, with the objective of securing the fulfillment of one or more present or future obligations regardless of the form of the transaction and regardless of whether ownership of the property is held by the secured creditor or the secured debtor.

When a security interest is publicized in accordance with this Law, the secured creditor has the preferential right to payment from the proceeds of the sale of the collateral.

Article 3

For purposes of this law, the following terms mean:
I. Registry: is the Registry of Movable Property Security Interests.
II. Secured Debtor: the person, whether the principal debtor or a third party, who creates a security interest over movable property in accordance with this Law.
III. Secured Creditor: the person in whose favor a security interest is created, possessory or non-possessory, whether for its own benefit or for the benefit of other persons.
IV. Buyer [or transferee] in the Ordinary Course of Business: a third party who, with or without knowledge of the fact that the transaction covers collateral subject to a security interest, gives value to acquire such collateral from a person who deals in property of that nature.

V. Movable Property Collateral: any movable property, including receivables and other kinds of incorporeal property, such as intellectual property, or specific or general categories of movable property, including attributable movable property, that serves to secure the fulfillment of a secured obligation according to the terms of the security contract.

The security interest in the collateral extends to, regardless of any mention in the security contract or in the registration form, the right to be indemnified for any loss or damage affecting the collateral during the course of the security interest, as well as to receive the product of an insurance policy or certificate that covers the value of such property.

VI. Attributable Movable Property: the movable property that can be identified as derived from the originally encumbered property, such as fruits, or property resulting from its sale, substitution or transformation.

VII. Registration Form: the form provided by the Registry referred to in Article 3.1, to register a security interest, and which will include at least the data prescribed by the regulations necessary to identify the applicant, the secured creditor, the secured debtor, the collateral, the maximum amount secured by the security interest, and the termination date of registration.

VIII. Inventory: movable property held by a person for sale or lease in the ordinary course of that person's business operations. Inventory does not include movable property held by the secured debtor for its on-going use.

IX. Acquisition Security Interest Movable property: a security interest granted in favor of a creditor—including a supplier—who finances the acquisition by the debtor of the moveable corporeal property over which the security interest is granted. Such security interest may secure the acquisition of present or subsequently acquired movable property so financed.

X. Receivable: the secured debtor's right (contractual or extra-contractual) to claim or receive payment of any monetary sum, currently or thereafter due, from a third party, including accounts receivable.

Article 4

The secured obligation, in addition to the principal debt may consist in:

I. Ordinary and default interests generated by the principal sum of the secured obligation calculated according to what is stated in the security contract, with the understanding that, if no rate has been stated, said interest will be calculated at the legal rate applicable at the time of default;

II. The commissions which must be paid to the secured creditor as provided in the Security contract;

III. Reasonable expenses incurred by the secured creditor for the maintenance and custody of the secured property;

IV. Reasonable expenses incurred by the secured debtor, generated by the acts necessary to effectuate the enforcement of the security interest;

V. Damages caused by the breach of the security contract as determined by a court, arbitration award or private settlement;

VI. The liquidated damages, if any, when these have been established.

TITLE II
CREATION

Article 5

A security interest is created by contract between the secured debtor and secured creditor.

Article 6

If the security interest is non-possessory, the contract creating the security must be in writing and the security interest takes effect between the parties from the moment of the execution of the writing, unless the parties otherwise agree.

However, a security interest in future or after-acquired property encumbers the secured debtor's rights (personal or real) in such property only from the moment the secured debtor acquires such rights.

Article 7

The written security contract must contain, as a minimum:
    I. Date of execution;
    II. Information to identify the secured debtor and the secured creditor, as well as the written or electronic signature of the secured debtor;
    III. The maximum amount secured by the security interest;
    IV. A description of the collateral, in the understanding that such description may be generic or specific;
    V. An express indication that the movable property described is to serve as collateral to a secured obligation; and,
    VI. A generic or specific description of the secured obligations.
The writing may be manifested by any method that leaves a permanent record of the consent of the parties to the creation of the security interest, including telex, telefax, electronic data interchange, electronic mail, and any other optical or similar method, according to the applicable norms on this matter and taking into account the resolution of this Conference attached to this Model Law (CIDIP-VI/RES. 6/02).

Article 8

If the security interest is possessory, it takes effect from the moment the secure debtor delivers possession or control of the collateral to the secured creditor or a third person designated on its behalf, unless the parties otherwise agree.

Article 9

If the security interest is non-possessory, the secured debtor or any person that acquires the collateral subject to the security interest, unless otherwise agreed, has the following rights and obligations:
    I. The right to use and dispose of the collateral and any proceeds derived from the original collateral in the ordinary course of the debtor's business;
    II. The obligation to discontinue the exercise of such right when the secured creditor notifies the secured debtor of its intention to enforce the security interest in the collateral under the terms of this Law;

III. The obligation to prevent damage and loss of the collateral and do what ever is necessary for such purpose;

IV. The obligation to allow the secured creditor to inspect the collateral to verify its quantity, quality and state of conservation; and

V. The obligation to adequately insure the collateral against destruction, loss or damage.

TITLE III
PUBLICITY

CHAPTER I
GENERAL RULES

Article 10

The rights conferred by the security interest take effect against third parties only when the security interest is publicized. A security interest may be publicized by registration in accordance with this Title and Title IV or by delivery of possession or control of the collateral to the secured creditor or to a third person on its behalf in accordance with this Title.

A security interest in any type of collateral may be publicized by registration, except as provided in Article 23. A security interest may be publicized by delivery of possession or control only if the nature of the collateral so permits or delivery is effected in the manner contemplated by this Title.

A security interest publicized by one method may later be publicized by another method and, provided there is no intermediate lapse without publicity, it will be considered that the security interest was continuously publicized for the purposes of this Law.

Article 11

A security interest may cover attributable movable property if this consequence is mentioned in the registration form.

CHAPTER II
ACQUISITION SECURITY INTEREST

Article 12

An acquisition security interest must be publicized by filing of a registration form that refers to the special character of this security interest and that describes the collateral thereby encumbered.

CHAPTER III
RECEIVABLES

Article 13

The provisions of this Law concerning security interests over receivables are applicable to every type of assignment of receivables. If the assignment is not for security it must comply only with the publicity provisions of this Law; if it fails to so comply, it will be subject to the priority rules of this Law.

Article 14

A security interest granted by the secured debtor in receivables owed to the secured debtor is publicized by registration.

Article 15

Except as otherwise provided in this Law, a security interest granted in receivables shall not modify the underlying legal standing nor increase the obligations of the account debtor without this party's consent.

Article 16

The account debtor of a receivable assigned in security has the rights and is subject to the obligations stated in this Chapter.

Article 17

The account debtor of the assigned receivable may discharge its obligation by paying the secured debtor or the assignor as the case may be. However, any outstanding amount owed to the secured debtor or assignor at the time or after the account debtor of the assigned receivable receives notice from the secured creditor to make payment to the secured creditor, the outstanding amount must be paid to the secured creditor. The account debtor may request the secured creditor to provide reasonable proof of the existence of the security interest, and, if reasonable proof is not provided within a reasonable time, the account debtor may make payment to the secured debtor.

The notice to the account debtor may be given by any generally accepted means of communication. In order for such notice to be effective, it must identify the receivable in respect of which payment is requested, and include sufficient payment instructions to enable the account debtor to comply. Unless otherwise agreed, the secured creditor shall not deliver such notice before the occurrence of an event of default that entitles the secured creditor to enforce the security interest.

Article 18

If an account debtor receives notice of more than one security interest of the same receivable, the account debtor shall make payment of the obligation in conformity with the payment instructions contained in the first notification received. Any actions between secured creditors designed to give effect to the priority provisions of Title V of the Law are preserved.

Article 19

A security interest in a receivable other than a claim under a letter of credit, is effective notwithstanding any agreement between the account debtor and the secured debtor limiting the right of the secured debtor to grant security in or assign the receivable. Nothing in this Article affects any liability of the secured debtor to pay damages to the account debtor for breach of any such agreement.

Article 20

The account debtor may raise against the secured creditor all defenses and rights of set-off arising from the original contract, or any other contract that was part of the same transaction, that the account debtor could raise against the secured debtor.

The account debtor may raise against the secured creditor any other right of set-off, provided that it was available to the account debtor when notification of the security interest was received by the account debtor.

The account debtor may agree with the secured debtor or assignor in a writing not to raise against the secured creditor the defenses and rights of set-off that the account debtor could raise pursuant to the first two paragraphs of this Article. Such an agreement precludes the account debtor from raising those defenses and rights of set-off.

The account debtor may not waive the following defenses:

I. Those arising from fraudulent acts on the part of the secured creditor or assignee; or

II. Those based on the account debtor's incapacity.

CHAPTER IV
NON-MONETARY CLAIMS

Article 21

A security interest granted by the secured debtor in a claim that is a non-monetary obligation, owed to the secured debtor, is publicized by registration.

Article 22

When the collateral is a claim that is a non-monetary obligation, the secured creditor has the right to notify the person obligated on the claim to render performance of the obligation to or for the benefit of the secured creditor and to otherwise enforce the obligation to the extent that the nature of the obligation permits. The person obligated on the claim may refuse only based on reasonable cause.

CHAPTER V
LETTERS OF CREDIT

Article 23

A security interest in a letter of credit the terms and conditions of which require that it be presented in order to obtain payment shall be publicized by the beneficiary's (secured debtor's) delivery of the letter of credit to the secured creditor, provided that such a letter of credit does not forbid its delivery to a party other than the paying bank. Unless the letter of credit has been amended to permit the secured creditor's draw, the delivery to the secured creditor does not entitle the latter to draw on the letter of credit and solely prevents the beneficiary's (secured debtor's) presentment of the letter of credit to the paying or negotiating bank.

Article 24

A beneficiary (secured debtor) may transfer or assign its right to draw on a letter of credit to a secured creditor by obtaining the issuance of a credit transferable to the name of the secured creditor as a transferee-beneficiary. The validity and effect upon third parties of such a transfer is governed by the applicable provisions of the prevailing version, at the moment in which it takes place, of the Uniform Customs and Practices for Documentary Credits of the International Chamber of Commerce.

Article 25

The existence of a security interest in the proceeds of a letter of credit is conditioned upon the beneficiary complying with the terms and conditions of the letter of credit thereby becoming entitled to payment thereon. To be publicized, such a security interest must be filed in the registry but not be enforceable against the issuing or confirming bank until the date and time on which this party accepts, under the terms and conditions governing the payment of the letter of credit.

Article 26

If the secured obligation consists of a future extension of credit or the giving of value in the future to the beneficiary (secured debtor), the secured creditor must extend such credit or value no later than 30 days from the date on which the issuing or confirming bank accepts the terms and conditions of the security interest in the proceeds of the letter of credit, unless otherwise agreed. If such credit is not extended or value is not given within this period, the security interest terminates, its registration, if any, may be cancelled, and the secured creditor must execute a signed release to the issuing or confirming bank allowing them to pay the beneficiary (secured debtor) according to its original terms and conditions.

CHAPTER VI
INSTRUMENTS AND DOCUMENTS

Article 27

Where the collateral is an instrument or document, the title to which is negotiable by endorsement and delivery, or delivery alone, the security interest may be publicized by delivery of possession of the instrument or document with any necessary endorsement.

Article 28

When the transfer or a pledge of a document of title has taken place in an electronic format, or its transfer or pledge has been effectuated in an electronic registry, the special rules governing such electronic registry shall apply.

Article 29

If the secured creditor publicizes its security interest by possession and endorsement of the document but subsequently delivers it to the secured debtor for any purpose including withdrawing, warehousing, manufacturing, shipping or selling the movable property represented by the document, the secured creditor must register its security interest before the document is returned to the secured debtor in accordance with Article 10 of this Law.

When the movable property represented by a document is in the possession of a third party depository or a bailee, the security interest may be publicized by the delivery of a written notice to the third party.

CHAPTER VII
PROPERTY IN POSSESSION OF A THIRD PARTY

Article 30

The secured creditor, with the consent of the secured debtor, may hold the property through a third person; detention by the third person effects publicity only from the time the third person receives evidence in writing of the security interest. The third person must at the request of any interested person disclose forthwith whether or not it has received notice of a security interest covering property in its possession.

CHAPTER VIII
INVENTORY

Article 31

A security interest over inventory, comprised of present and future property, and its attributable movable property, or any part thereof, may be publicized by a single registration.

CHAPTER IX
INTELLECTUAL PROPERTY RIGHTS

Article 32

A security interest in intellectual property rights, such as patents, trademarks, trade-names, goodwill, royalties and other attributable movable property derived therefrom, is governed by this Law, including Article 37.

CHAPTER X
OBLIGATIONS OF A CREDITOR IN
POSSESSION OF COLLATERAL

Article 33

A creditor in possession of the collateral:
  I. Shall exercise reasonable care in the custody and preservation of the collateral. Unless otherwise agreed, reasonable care implies the obligation to take the necessary steps to preserve the value of the collateral and the rights derived therefrom.
  II. Shall maintain the collateral in such a way that it remains identifiable, unless it is fungible.
  III. May use the collateral only as provided in the security contract.

Article 34

A possessory security interest may be converted into a non-possessory security interest and retain its priority provided that the security interest is publicized by registration before the collateral is returned to the secured debtor, in accordance with Article 10.

TITLE IV
REGISTRY AND RELATED MATTERS

Article 35

The security interest publicized by registration takes effect against third parties from the moment of its registration.

Article 36

Any person may effect a registration authorized by the secured creditor and the secured debtor, and any person may register a continuation of an existing registration with the authorization of the secured creditor.

Article 37

Where another law or an applicable international convention requires title to movable property to be registered in a special registry, and contains provisions relating to security interests created over such property, such provisions shall have precedence over this Law, to the extent of any inconsistency between the two.

Article 38

The registration form shall be in the standard form and medium prescribed by regulation. Such form shall provide for entry of the following data:
    I. The name and address of the secured debtor;
    II. The name and address of the secured creditor;
    III. The maximum amount secured by the security interest;
    IV. The description of the collateral, which can be generic or specific.
When there is more than one secured debtor granting a security interest over the same movable property, all secured debtors must be separately identified in the registration form

Article 39

The registration in the Registry will be valid for a term of five years, renewable for three-year terms, preserving the original priority.

Article 40

In order for an acquisition security interest to be publicized and have priority over previously perfected security interests over property of the same type, the secured creditor must comply with the following requirements, before the debtor takes possession of such property:
    I. Register in the registration form a notation that indicates the special character of the acquisition security interest; and,
    II. Notify the holders of previously perfected security interests over property of the same kind that the secured creditor has or expects to acquire an acquisition security interest in the collateral described in the notice.

Article 41

The registration data may be amended at any time by the registration of an amendment form; the amendment shall take effect only from the time of its registration.

Article 42

The secured creditor may cancel the original registration by filing a cancellation form.

If a cancellation is made in error or in a fraudulent manner, the secured creditor may reregister the registration form in substitution of the cancelled form. Such secured creditor retains its priority in relation to other secured creditors that registered a security interest during the time of validity of the erroneously cancelled registration form, but not against secured creditors who registered their security after the date of cancellation and before the date of reregistration.

Article 43

The entity designated by the State will operate and administrate the Registry, which will be public and automated and in which there will be an electronic folio, which will be indexed by the name of the secured debtor.

Article 44

The Registry will have a central database constituted by the registration records of the security interests inscribed in the State.

Article 45

For the registration and searches of information, the Registry will authorize remote and electronic access to users who so request.

Article 46

The users will have a confidential key to access the Registry system in order to register security interests by sending the registration form via electronic means or via any other method authorized by the legislation of this State, as well as in order to conduct the searches that are requested.

TITLE V
PRIORITY RULES

Article 47

The right conferred by a security interest in respect of the collateral is effective against third persons only when the publicity requirements have been fulfilled.

Article 48

The priority of a secured interest is determined by the time of its publicity.

A security interest confers on the secured creditor the right to follow the collateral in order to exercise its rights under the security.

Article 49

Nevertheless, a buyer or transferee of collateral in the ordinary course of the transferor's business takes free of any security interest in the collateral.

The secured creditor cannot interfere with the rights of a lessee or a licensee under a lease or a license granted in the ordinary course of the lessor's or licensor's business after the publication of the security interest.

Article 50

The priority of a security interest can be modified by written agreement between the secured creditors involved, unless it affects the rights of third parties or is prohibited by law.

Article 51

An acquisition security interest will have priority over a previous security interest that encumbers future movable property of the secured debtor, as long as it is created according to the provisions of this law and even when it was publicized after the previous security interest. The acquisition security interest will cover exclusively the specific movable property acquired with it and the cash proceeds attributable to their sale, provided the secured creditor has complied with the conditions set out in Article 40.

Article 52

I. A possessory security interest in a document of title has priority over a security interest in the property covered by such document of title if the latter is publicized after the document of title is issued.

II. The holder of money or a transferee of negotiable instruments who takes possession with any necessary endorsement in the ordinary course of the transferor's business takes free of any security interests.

III. The secured creditor who received notice of acceptance by the issuing or confirming bank, of its publicized security interest over the proceeds of a letter of credit, has priority over any security interest over such proceeds, regardless of the time of its publicity, obtained by another secured creditor who did not receive such acceptance or who received it at a later date. Where the security interest covers the proceeds of a letter of credit, the ordinary rule of priority set out in this Law applies.

IV. A publicized security interest in a movable that is affixed to an immovable, without losing its identity as a movable, has priority over security interests in the relevant immovable, provided the security interest over the movables has been registered in the immovable registry before affixation.

Article 53

The secured creditor may authorize the secured debtor to dispose of the collateral free of encumbrance, subject to any terms and conditions agreed to by the parties.

TITLE VI
ENFORCEMENT

Article 54

A secured creditor who intends to commence enforcement, in case of default of the secured debtor, shall register an enforcement form in the Registry and deliver a copy to the secured debtor, to the principal debtor of the secured obligation, to the person in possession of the collateral and to any person who has publicized a security interest in the same collateral.

The enforcement form shall contain:

I. A brief description of the default by the secured debtor;

II. A description of the collateral;

III. A statement of the amount required to satisfy the secured obligation and to pay the secured creditor's enforcement expenses as reasonably estimated;

IV. A statement of the rights provided by this Title to the recipient of the enforcement form; and

V. A statement of the nature of the remedies provided by this Title that the secured creditor intends to exercise.

Article 55

In case of default on the secured obligation, the secured creditor shall require the payment from the secured debtor. Notice of this requirement shall be issued in a notarized or judicial form, at the creditor's option, to the debtor's address as indicated in the registration form. In the requirement or notification process, the debtor shall be given a copy of the enforcement form filed at the registry.

Article 56

The debtor shall have a period of three days from the day following receipt of the enforcement form to object by giving evidence to the Judge or the Notary involved that full payment of the amount and its accessories has been made. No exception or defense, other than full payment, will be admitted.

Article 57

In case of a non-possessory security interest over corporeal property, once the period indicated in the previous Article has elapsed, the secured creditor may ask the Judge to issue an order of repossession, which shall be enforced forthwith, without granting a hearing to the debtor. In accordance with a Judge's order the collateral shall be delivered to the secured creditor, or to a third party at the request of the secured creditor. Any exception or defense that the debtor wishes to make against such order, other than that indicated in the previous Article, shall be initiated through an independent judicial action, as provided for in local procedural law; such independent judicial action shall not prevent the secured creditor from exercising its enforcement rights against the collateral.

Article 58

At any time before the secured creditor disposes of the collateral, the secured debtor, as well as any other interested person, has the right to terminate the enforcement proceedings by:

I. Paying the full amount owed to the secured creditor, as well as the reasonable enforcement costs of the secured creditor; or

II. If the secured obligations are installment obligations, reinstating the security contract by paying the amounts actually in arrears together with the secured creditor's reasonable enforcement expenses and remedying any other act of default.

Article 59

With respect to a possessory security interest, or with respect to a non-possessory security interest in incorporeal property, or with respect to a non-possessory security interest in corporeal property after repossession:

I. If the collateral is movable property that is customarily priced in the market in the State where enforcement takes place, it may be sold directly by the secured creditor at a price in accord with such market.

II. If the collateral consists of receivables, the secured creditor has the right to collect or enforce the receivables against the third person obligated on the receivable in accordance with the provisions of Title III of this Law.

III. If the collateral consists of stocks, bonds or similar types of property, the secured creditor has the right to exercise the secured debtor's rights in relation to the collateral, including redemption rights, rights to draw, voting rights and rights to collect dividends or other revenues derived from the collateral.

IV. The collateral may be sold privately, or taken in payment against the debt, provided that it has been previously appraised by an single qualified appraiser designated by the secured creditor, for the price of the appraisal. The secured creditor may elect to sell the collateral in a public auction previously announced in two daily publications of major circulation, at least five days before the sale, without minimun bid, to the highest bidder.

Article 60

The proceeds of the sale or auction will be applied in the following manner:

I. The costs of enforcement, storage, repair, insurance, preservation, sale or auction, and any other reasonable cost incurred by the creditor;

II. The payment of any outstanding taxes owing by the secured debtor if they are secured by a lien on the collateral provided by operation of law;

III. The payment of the outstanding amount of the secured obligation;

IV. The payment of secured obligations stemming from security interests with a secondary priority; and

V. Any remainder will be returned to the debtor.

If the outstanding loan amount owed by the secured debtor exceeds the proceeds of the disposition of the collateral, the secured creditor shall have the right to demand payment for any deficiency from the debtor of the obligation.

Article 61

The possible appeals of any judicial decision mentioned in this Title will not have suspensive effect.

Article 62

At any time, before or during the enforcement proceeding, the debtor may reach an agreement with the creditor on terms other than those previously established, either for the delivery of the goods, the terms of the sale or auction, or any other matter, provided that said agreement does not affect other secured creditors or buyers in the ordinary course of business.

Article 63

In any event, the debtor will retain the right to claim damages for the abuse of his rights by the creditor.

Article 64

Any subsequent secured creditor may subrogate the rights of a preceding secured creditor by paying the secured obligation of the secured debtor.

Article 65

The secured debtor's right to sell or transfer collateral in the ordinary course of business operations is suspended from the moment the secured debtor receives notice of the commencement of enforcement proceedings against the secured debtor, pursuant to the enforcement rules of this Law. This suspension will continue until the completion of the enforcement proceedings, unless the secured creditor otherwise agrees.

Article 66

Secured creditors are entitled to exercise their enforcement rights and to assume control of the collateral in the order of their priority rank.

Article 67

A person who purchases the collateral at a sale or auction, takes the property subject to the real rights with which it is encumbered, with the exception of the security interest of the creditor who sold the property and the security interests or claims which were subordinate to such security interest.

TITLE VII
ARBITRATION

Article 68

Any controversy arising out of the interpretation and fulfillment of a security interest may be submitted to arbitration by the parties, acting by mutual agreement and according to the legislation applicable in this State.

TITLE VIII
CONFLICT OF LAWS AND TERRITORIAL
SCOPE OF APPLICATION

Article 69

In cases where a security interest has contacts to more than one State, the law of the State where the collateral is located at the time the security interest is created shall govern issues relating to the validity, publicity and priority of:

  I. A security interest in corporeal movable property other than movable property of the kind referred to in the next Article; and

  II. A possessory security interest in incorporeal movable property.

If the collateral is moved to a different State than that in which the security interest was previously publicized, the law of the State to which the collateral has been moved governs issues relating to the publicity and priority of the security interest as against unsecured creditors and third persons who acquire rights in the collateral after the relocation. However, the priority of the security interest acquired under the law of the previous location of the collateral is preserved if the security interest is publicized in accordance with the law of the State of the new location within 90 days after the relocation of the property.

Article 70

In cases where a secured transaction has contacts to more than one State, the law of the State in which the secured debtor is located when the security interest is created governs issues relating to the validity, publicity and priority of:

  I. A non-possessory security interest in incorporeal property; and

  II. A security interest in movable corporeal property if the property is held by the secured debtor as equipment for use in the secured debtor's business, or as inventory for lease.

If the secured debtor changes its location to a different State than that in which the security interest was previously publicized, the law of the State of the secured debtor's new location governs issues relating to the publicity and priority of the security interest as against unsecured creditors and third persons who acquire rights in the collateral after the relocation. However, the priority of the security interest acquired under the law of the previous location of the secured debtor is preserved if the security interest is publicized in accordance with the law of the State of the secured debtor's new location within 90 days after the relocation of the debtor.

Article 71

The priority of a non-possessory security interest in negotiable incorporeal property as against third persons who acquire a possessory interest in the property is governed by the law of the State where the collateral is located when the possessory interest is acquired.

Article 72

For the purposes of applying Article 70, a secured debtor is considered located in the State where the secured debtor maintains the central administration of its business.

If the secured debtor does not operate a business or does not have a place of business, the secured debtor is considered located in the State of its habitual residence.

(ii) Equipment Financing Transactions

(a) INTERNATIONAL CONVENTION FOR THE UNIFICATION OF CERTAIN RULES RELATING TO MARITIME LIENS AND MORTGAGES*

*(Brussels, April 10, 1926)***

PREAMBLE

The President of the German Reich, the President of the Argentine Republic, ... etc.

Having recognized the desirability of determining by agreement certain uniform rules relating to maritime liens and mortgages, have decided to conclude a convention to that effect and have designated as their Plenipotentiaries, namely:

(Follows the list of Plenipotentiaries)

Who, duly authorized therefor, have agreed as follows:

Article 1

Mortgages, hypothecations, and other similar charges upon vessels, duly effected in accordance with the law of the contracting State to which the vessel belongs, and registered in a public register either at the port of the vessel's registry of at a central office, shall be regarded as valid and respected in all the other contracting countries.

Article 2

The following give rise to maritime liens on a vessel, on the freight for the voyage during which the claim giving rise to the lien arises, and on the accessories of the vessel and freight accrued since the commencement of the voyage:

1. Law costs due to the State, and expenses incurred in the common interest of the creditors in order to preserve the vessel or to procure its sale and the distribution of the

---

* Reproduced with the kind permission of the United Nations.

** *This Convention shall be abrogated in respect of the relations between States which ratify (or accede to) the International Convention for the unification of certain rules relating to maritime liens and mortgages, done at Brussels on May 27th, 1967.*

proceeds of sale; tonnage dues, light or harbor dues, and other public taxes and charges of the same character; pilotage dues, the cost of watching and preservation from the time of the entry of the vessel into the last port;

2. Claims arising out of the contract of engagement of the master, crew, and other persons hired on board;

3. Remuneration for assistance and salvage, and the contribution of the vessel in general average;

4. Indemnities for collisions or other accident of navigation, as also for damage caused to works forming part of harbors, docks, and navigable ways; indemnities for personal injury to passengers or crew; indemnities for loss of or damage to cargo or baggage:

5. Claims resulting from contracts entered into or acts done by the master, acting within the scope of his authority, away from the vessel's home port, where such contracts of acts are necessary for the preservation of the vessel or the continuation of its voyage, whether the master is or is not at the same time owner of the vessel, and whether the claim is his own or that of shipchandlers, repairers, lenders, or other contractual creditors.

Article 3

The mortgages, hypothecations, and other charges on vessels referred to in Article 1 rank immediately after the secured claims referred to in the preceding Article.

National laws may grant a lien in respect of claims other than those referred to in the said last-mentioned Article, so, however, as not to modify the ranking of claims secured by mortgages, hypothecations, and other similar charges, or by the liens taking precedence thereof.

Article 4

The accessories of the vessel and the freight mentioned in Article 2, mean:

1. Compensation due to the owner for material damage sustained by the vessel and not repaired, or for loss of freight;

2. General average contributions due to the owner, in respect of material damage sustained by the vessel and not repaired, or in respect of loss of freight;

3. Remuneration due to the owner for assistance and salvage services rendered at any time before the end of the voyage, any sums allotted to the master or other persons in the service of the vessel being deducted.

The provisions as to freight apply also the passage money, and, in the last resort, to the sums due under. Article 4 of the Convention on the limitation of shipowner's liability.

Payments made or due to the owner on policies of insurance, as well as bounties, subventions, and other national subsidies are not deemed to be accessories of the vessel or of the freight.

Notwithstanding anything in the opening words of Article 2, 2, the lien in favor of persons in the service of the vessel extends, to the total amount of freight due for all voyagers made during the subsistence of the same contract of engagement.

Article 5

Claims secured by a lien and relating to the same voyage rank in the order in which they are set out in Article 2. Claims included under any one heading share concurrently and retably in the event of the fund available being insufficient to pay the claims in full.

The claims mentioned under nrs 3 and 5 in that article rank, in each of the two categories, in the inverse order of the dates on which they came into existence.

Claims arising from one and the same occurrence are deemed to have come into existence at the same time.

Article 6

Claims secured a lien and attaching to the last voyage have priority over those attaching to previous voyage.

Provided that claims, arising on one and the same contract of engagement extending over several voyages, all rank with claims attaching to the last voyage.

Article 7

As regards the distribution of the sum resulting from the sale of the property subject to a lien, the creditors whose claims are secured by a lien have the right to put forward their claims in full, without any deduction on account of the rules relating to limitation of liability; provided, however, that the sum apportioned to them may not exceed the sum due having regard to the said rules.

Article 8

Claims secured by a lien follow the vessel into whatever hands it may pass.

Article 9

The liens cease to exist, apart from other cases provided for by national laws, at the expiration of one year, and in the case of liens for supplies mentioned in nr 5 of Article 2, shall continue in force for not more than six months.

The periods for which the lien remains in force in the case of liens securing claims in respect of assistance and salvage runs from the day when the services terminated, in the case of liens securing claims in respect of collision and other accidents and in respect of bodily injuries from the day when the damage was caused; in the case of liens for the loss of or damage to cargo or baggage from the day of the delivery of the cargo or baggage or from the day when they should have been delivered; for repairs and supplies and other cases mentioned in nr 5 of Article 2 from the day the claim originated. In all the other cases the period runs from the enforcibility of the claim.

The fact that any of the persons employed on board, mentioned in nr 2 of Article 2 has a right to any payment in advance or an account does not render his claim enforcible.

As respects the cases provided for in the national laws in which a lien is extinguished, a sale shall extinguish a lien only if accompagnied by formalities of publicity which shall be laid down by the national laws. These formalities shall include a notice given in such form and within such time as the national laws may prescribe to the authority charged with keeping the registers referred to in Article 1 of this Convention.

The grounds upon which the above periods may be interrupted and determined by the law of the court where the case is tried.

The High Contracting Parties reserve to themselves the right to provide by legislation in their respective countries, that the said periods shall be extended in cases where it has not been possible to arrest the vessel to which a lien attaches in the territorial waters of the State in which the claimant has his domicile or his principal place of business, provided that the extended period shall not exceed three years from the time when the claim originated.

Article 10

A lien on freight may be enforced so long as the freight is still due or the amount of the freight is still in the hands o the master or the agent of the owner. The same principle applies to a lien on accessories.

Article 11

Subject to the provisions of this Conventions, liens established by the preceding provisions are subject to no formality and to no special condition of proof.

    This provision does not affect the right of any. State to maintain in the legislation provisions requiring the master of a vessel to fulfil special formalities in the case of certain loans raised on the security of the vessel, or in the case of the sale of its cargo.

Article 12

National laws must prescribe the nature and the form of documents to be carried on board the vessel which entry must be made of the mortgages, hypothecations, and other charges referred to in Article 1; so, however, that the mortgages requiring such entry in the said form be not held responsible for any omission, mistake, or delay in inscribing the same on the said documents.

Article 13

The foregoing provisions apply to vessels under the management of a person who operates them without owing them of to the principal charterer, except in cases where the owner has been dispossessed by an illegal act or where the claimant is not a *bona fide* claimant.

Article 14

The provisions of this Convention shall be applied in each contracting State in cases in which the vessel to which the claim relates belongs to a contracting State, as well as in any other cases provided for by the national laws.

    Nevertheless the principle formulated in the preceding paragraph does not affect the right of the contracting States not to apply the provisions of this Conventions in favor of the nationals of a non-contracting State.

Article 15

This Convention does not apply to vessels of war, nor to government vessels appropriated exclusively to the public service.

Article 16

Nothing in the foregoing provisions shall be deemed to affect in any way the competence of tribunals, modes of procedure or methods of execution authorized by the national law.

Article 17

After an interval of not more than two years from the day on which the Conventions is signed, the Belgian Government shall place itself in communication with the Governments of the High Contracting Parties which have declared themselves prepared to ratify the Convention, with a view to deciding whether it shall be put into force.

The ratifications shall be deposited at Brussels at a date to be fixed by agreement among the said Governments. The first deposit of ratifications shall be recorded in a proces-verbal signed by the representatives of the Powers which take part therein and by the Belgian Minister for Foreign Affairs.

The subsequent deposits of ratifications shall be made by means of a written notification, addressed to the Belgian Government, and accompanied by the instrument of ratification.

A duly certified copy of the proces-verbal relating to the first deposit of ratifications, of the notifications referred to in the previous paragraph, and also of the instruments of ratification accompanying them, shall be immediately sent by the Belgian Government through the diplomatic channel to the Powers who have signed this Convention of who have acceded to it. In the cases contemplated in the preceding paragraph the said Government shall inform them at the same time of the date on which it received the notification.

Article 18

Non-signatory States may accede to the present Convention whether or not they have been represented at the international Conference at Brussels.

A State which desires to accede shall notify its intention in writing to the Belgian Government, forwarding to it the document of accession which shall be deposited in the archives of the said Government.

The Belgian Government shall immediately forward to all the States which have signed or acceded to the Convention a duly certified copy of the notification and of the act of accession, mentioning the date on which it received the notification.

Article 19

The High Contracting Parties may at the time of signature, ratification, or accession declare that their acceptance of the present Convention does not include any or all of the self-governing dominions, or of the colonies, overseas possessions, protectorates, or territories under their sovereignty or authority, and they may subsequently accede separately on behalf of any self-governing dominion, colony, overseas possession, protectorate or territory excluded in their declaration. They may also denounce the Convention separately in accordance with its provision in respect of any self-governing dominion, or any colony, overseas possession, protectorate, or territory under their sovereignty or authority.

Article 20

The present Convention shall take effect, in the case of the States which have taken part in the first deposit of ratifications one year after the date of the proces-verbal recording such deposit. As respects the States which ratify subsequently, or which accede, and also in case in which the convention is subsequently put into effect in accordance with Article 19, it shall take effect six months after the notifications specified in Article 17, § 2, and Article 18 § 2, have been received by the Belgian Government.

Article 21

In the event of one of the Contracting States wishing to denounce the present Convention, the denunciation shall be notified in writing to the Belgian Government, which shall immediately communicate a duly certified copy of the notification to all the other States informing them of the date on which it was received.

The denunciation shall only operate in respect of the State which made the notification, and on the expiration of one year after the notification has reached the Belgian Government.

Article 22

Any one of the Contracting States shall have the right to call for a new conference with a view to considering possible amendments.

A State which would exercise this right should give one year advance notice of its intention to the other States through the Belgian Government, which would make arrangements for convening the conference.

PROTOCOL OF SIGNATURE

In proceeding to the signature of the International Convention for the unification of certain rules relating to maritime liens and mortgages, the undersigned Plenipotentiaries have adopted the present Protocol, which will have the same force and the same value as if the provisions were inserted in the text of the Convention to which it relates:

I. It is understood that the legislation of each State remains free
1. to establish among the claims mentioned in nr 1 of Article 2, a definite order of priority with a view to safeguarding the interests of the Treasury;
2. To confer on the authorities administering harbors, docks, lighthouses, and navigable ways, who have caused a wreck or other obstruction to navigation to be removed, or who are creditors in respect of harbor dues, or for damage caused by the fault of a vessel, the right, in case of non-payment, to detain the vessel, wreck, or other property, to sell the same, and to indemnity themselves out of the proceed in priority to other claimants, and
3. to determine the rank of the claimants for damages done to works otherwise than as stated in Article 5 and in Article 6.

II There is no impairment of the provisions in the national laws of the contracting States conferring a lien upon public insurance associations in respect of claims arising out of the insurance of the personnel of vessels.

Done at Brussels, in a single copy, April 10th, 1926.

(Follow the signatures)

TABLE OF STATE RATIFICATIONS

Total number of signatures not followed by ratifications: 0
Total number of ratifications/accessions: 26

Brussels, 10 April 1926
Entered into force: 2 June 1931

State	Signature	Ratification	By	Entry into force
Algeria		13 April 1964	Accession	13 October 1964
Argentina		19 April 1961	Accession	19 October 1961
Belgium		2 June 1930	Ratification	2 June 1931
Brazil		28 April 1931	Ratification	28 October 1931
Cuba		21 November 1983	Accession	21 May 1983
Denmark (denunciation—1 March 1965)			Ratification	
Estonia		2 June 1930	Ratification	2 June 1931
Finland (denunciation—1 March 1965)		12 July 1934	Accession	
France		23 August 1935	Ratification	23 February 1936
Haiti		19 March 1965	Accession	19 September 1965
Hungary		2 June 1930	Ratification	2 June 1931
Iran		8 September 1966	Accession	8 March 1967
Italy		7 December 1949	Ratification	7 June 1950
Lebanon		18 March 1969	Accession	18 September 1969
Luxembourg		18 February 1991	Accession	18 August 1991
Madagascar		23 August 1935	Ratification	23 February 1936
Monaco		15 May 1931	Accession	15 November 1931
Norway (denunciation—1 March 1965)		10 October 1933	Ratification	10 April 1934
Poland		26 October 1936	Ratification	26 April 1937
Portugal		24 December 1931	Accession	24 June 1932
Romania		4 August 1937	Ratification	4 February 1938
Spain		2 June 1930	Ratification	2 June 1931
Sweden (denunciation—1 March 1965)		1 July 1938	Ratification	1 January 1939
Switzerland		28 May 1954	Accession	28 November 1954
Syrian Arab Republic		14 February 1951	Accession	14 August 1951
Turkey		4 July 1955	Accession	4 January 1956
Uruguay		15 September 1970	Accession	15 March 1971
Zaire		17 July 1967	Accession	17 January 1968

Note. A list of reservations and declarations made by States has not been included in this volume. These can be obtained from http://www.comitemaritime.org/.

(b) INTERNATIONAL CONVENTION RELATING TO THE ARREST OF SEA-GOING SHIPS*

(Brussels, May 10, 1952)

PREAMBLE

The High Contracting Parties,

Having recognized the desirability of determining by agreement certain uniform rules of law relating to the arrest of sea-going ships,

Have decided to conclude a convention for this purpose and thereto have agreed as follows:

Article 1

In this Convention the following words shall have the meanings hereby assigned to them:
(1) 'Maritime Claim' means a claim arising out of one or more of the following:
    (a) damage caused by any ship either in collision or otherwise;
    (b) loss of life or personal injury caused by any ship or occurring in connexion with the operation of any ship;
    (c) salvage;
    (d) agreement relating to the use or hire of any ship whether by charterparty or otherwise;
    (e) agreement relating to the carriage of goods in any ship whether by charterparty or otherwise;
    (f) loss of or damage to goods including baggage carried in any ship;
    (g) general average;
    (h) bottomry;
    (i) towage;
    (j) pilotage;
    (k) goods or materials wherever supplied to a ship for her operation or maintenance;
    (l) construction, repair or equipment of any ship or dock charges and dues;
    (m) wages of Masters, Officers, or crew;
    (n) Master's disbursements, including disbursements made by shippers, charterers or agent on behalf of a ship or her owner;

---

* The United Nations is the author of the original material.

(o) disputes as to the title to or ownership of any ship;

(p) disputes between co-owners of any ship as to the ownership, possession, employment, or earnings of that ship;

(q) the mortgage or hypothecation of any ship.

(2) 'Arrest' means the detention of a ship by judicial process to secure a maritime claim, but does not include the seizure of a ship in execution or satisfaction of a judgment.

(3) 'Person' includes individuals, partnerships and bodies corporate, Governments, their Departments, and Public Authorities.

(4) 'Claimant' means a person who alleges that a maritime claim exists in his favour.

Article 2

A ship flying the flag of one of the Contracting States may be arrested in the jurisdiction of any of the Contracting States in respect of any maritime claim, but in respect of no other claim; but nothing in this Convention shall be deemed to extend or restrict any right or powers vested in any governments or their departments, public authorities, or dock or habour authorities under their existing domestic laws or regulations to arrest, detain or otherwise prevent the sailing of vessels within their jurisdiction.

Article 3

(1) Subject to the provisions of para. (4) of this article and of article 10, a claimant may arrest either the particular ship in respect of which the maritime claim arose, or any other ship which is owned by the person who was, at the time when the maritime claim arose, the owner of the particular ship, even though the ship arrested be ready to sail; but no ship, other than the particular ship in respect of which the claim arose, may be arrested in respect of any of the maritime claims enumerated in article 1, (o), (p) or (q).

(2) Ships shall be deemed to be in the same ownership when all the shares therein are owned by the same person or persons.

(3) A ship shall not be arrested, nor shall bail or other security be given more than once in any one or more of the jurisdictions of any of the Contracting States in respect of the same maritime claim by the same claimant: and, if a ship has been arrested in any of such jurisdictions, or bail or other security has been given in such jurisdiction either to release the ship or to avoid a threatened arrest, any subsequent arrest of the ship or of any ship in the same ownership by the same claimant for the maritime claim shall be set aside, and the ship released by the Court or other appropriate judicial authority of that State, unless the claimant can satisfy the Court or other appropriate judicial authority that the bail or other security had been finally released before the subsequent arrest or that there is other good cause for maintaining that arrest.

(4) When in the case of a charter by demise of a ship the charterer and not the registered owner is liable in respect of a maritime claim relating to that ship, the claimant may arrest such ship or any other ship in the ownership of the charterer by demise, subject to the provisions of this Convention, but no other ship in the ownership of the registered owner shall be liable to arrest in respect of such maritime claim. The provisions of this paragraph shall apply to any case in which a person other than the registered owner of a ship is liable in respect of a maritime claim relating to that ship.

Article 4

A ship may only be arrested under the authority of a Court or of the appropriate judicial authority of the contracting State in which the arrest is made.

Article 5

The Court or other appropriate judicial authority within whose jurisdiction the ship has been arrested shall permit the release of the ship upon sufficient bail or other security being furnished, save in cases in which a ship has been arrested in respect of any of the maritime claims enumerated in article 1, (o) and (p). In such cases the Court or other appropriate judicial authority may permit the person in possession of the ship to continue trading the ship, upon such person furnishing sufficient bail or other security, or may otherwise deal with the operation of the ship during the period of the arrest. In default of agreement between the parties as to the sufficiency of the bail or other security, the Court or other appropriate judicial authority shall determine the nature and amount thereof. The request to release the ship against such security shall not be construed as an acknowledgment of liability or as a waiver of the benefit of the legal limitations of liability of the owner of the ship.

Article 6

All questions whether in any case the claimant is liable in damages for the arrest of a ship or for the costs of the bail or other security furnished to release or prevent the arrest of a ship, shalt be determined by the taw of the Contracting State in whose jurisdiction the arrest was made or applied for.

The rules of procedure relating to the arrest of a ship, to the application for obtaining the authority referred to in Article 4, and to all matters of procedure which the arrest may entail, shalt be governed by the taw of the Contracting State in which the arrest was made or applied for.

Article 7

(1) The Courts of the country in which the arrest was made shall have jurisdiction to determine the case upon its merits if the domestic law of the country in which the arrest is made gives jurisdiction to such Courts, or in any of the following cases namely:
  (a) if the claimant has his habitual residence or principal place of business in the country in which the arrest was made;
  (b) if the claim arose in the country in which the arrest was made;
  (c) if the claim concerns the voyage of the ship during which the arrest was made;
  (d) if the claim arose out of a collision or in circumstances covered by article 13 of the International Convention for the unification of certain rules of law with respect to collisions between vessels, signed at Brussels on 23rd September 1910;
  (e) if the claim is for salvage;
  (f) if the claim is upon a mortgage or hypothecation of the ship arrested.
(2) If the Court within whose jurisdiction the ship was arrested has not jurisdiction to decide upon the merits, the bail or other security given in accordance with article 5 to procure the release of the ship shall specifically provide that it is given as security for the satisfaction of any judgment which may eventually be pronounced by

a Court having jurisdiction so to decide; and the Court or other appropriate judicial authority of the country in which the claimant shall bring an action before a Court having such jurisdiction.

(3) If the parties have agreed to submit the dispute to the jurisdiction of a particular Court other than that within whose jurisdiction the arrest was made or to arbitration, the Court or other appropriate judicial authority within whose jurisdiction the arrest was made may fix the time within which the claimant shall bring proceedings.

(4) If, in any of the cases mentioned in the two preceding paragraphs, the action or proceeding is not brought within the time so fixed, the defendant may apply for the release of the ship or of the bail or other security.

(5) This article shall not apply in cases covered by the provisions of the revised Rhine Navigation Convention of 17 October 1868.

Article 8

(1) The provisions of this Convention shall apply to any vessel flying the flag of a Contracting State in the jurisdiction of any Contracting State.

(2) A ship flying the flag of a non-Contracting State may be arrested in the jurisdiction of any Contracting State in respect of any of the maritime claims enumerated in article 1 or of any other claim for which the law of the Contracting State permits arrest.

(3) Nevertheless any Contracting State shall be entitled wholly or partly to exclude from the benefits of this convention any government of a non-Contracting State or any person who has not, at the time of the arrest, his habitual residence or principal place of business in one of the Contracting States.

(4) Nothing in this Convention shall modify or affect the rules of law in force in the respective Contracting States relating to the arrest of any ship within the jurisdiction of the State of her flag by a person who has his habitual residence or principal place of business in that State.

(5) When a maritime claim is asserted by a third party other than the original claimant, whether by subrogation, assignment or other-wise, such third party shall, for the purpose of this Convention, be deemed to have the same habitual residence or principal place of business as the original claimant.

Article 9

Nothing in this Convention shall be construed as creating a right of action, which, apart from the provisions of this Convention, would not arise under the law applied by the Court which was seized of the case, nor as creating any maritime liens which do not exist under such law or under the Convention on maritime mortgages and liens, if the latter is applicable.

Article 10

The High Contracting Parties may at the time of signature, deposit or ratification or accession, reserve:

(a) the right not to apply this Convention to the arrest of a ship for any of the claims enumerated in paragraphs (o) and (p) of article 1, but to apply their domestic laws to such claims;

(b) the right not to apply the first paragraph of article 3 to the arrest of a ship within their jurisdiction for claims set out in article 1 paragraph (q).

Article 11

The High Contracting Parties undertake to submit to arbitration any disputes between States arising out of the interpretation or application of this Convention, but this shall be without prejudice to the obligations of those High Contracting Parties who have agreed to submit their disputes to the International Court of Justice.

Article 12

This Convention shall be open for signature by the States represented at the Ninth Diplomatic Conference on Maritime Law. The protocol of signature shall be drawn up through the good offices of the Belgian Ministry of Foreign Affairs.

Article 13

This Convention shall be ratified and the instruments of ratification shall be deposited with the Belgian Ministry of Foreign Affairs which shall notify all signatory and acceding States of the deposit of any such instruments.

Article 14

(a) This Convention shall come into force between the two States which first ratify it, six months after the date of the deposit of the second instrument of ratification.
(b) This Convention shall come into force in respect of each signatory State which ratifies it after the deposit of the second instrument of ratification six months after the date of the deposit of the instrument of ratification of that State.

Article 15

Any State not represented at the Ninth Diplomatic Conference on Maritime Law may accede to this Convention.

The accession of any State shall be notified to the Belgian Ministry of Foreign Affairs which shall inform through diplomatic channels all signatory and acceding States of such notification.

The Convention shall come into force in respect of the acceding State six months after the date of the receipt of such notification but not before the Convention has come into force in accordance with the provisions of Article 14(a).

Article 16

Any High Contracting Party may three years after coming into force of this Convention in respect of such High Contracting Party or at any time thereafter request that a conference be convened in order to consider amendments to the Convention.

Any High Contracting Party proposing to avail itself of this right shall notify the Belgian Government which shall convene the conference within six months thereafter.

Article 17

Any High Contracting Party shall have the right to denounce this Convention at any time after the coming into force thereof in respect of such High Contracting Party. This denunciation shall take effect one year after the date on which notification thereof has been received by the Belgian Government which shall inform through diplomatic channels all the other High Contracting Parties of such notification.

Article 18

(a) Any High Contracting Party may at the time of its ratification of or accession to this Convention or at any time thereafter declare by written notification to the Belgian Ministry of Foreign Affairs that the Convention shall extend to any of the territories for whose international relations it is responsible. The Convention shall six months after the date of the receipt of such notification by the Belgian Ministry of Foreign Affairs extend to the territories named therein, but not before the date of the coming into force of the Convention in respect of such High Contracting Party.

(b) A High Contracting Party which has made a declaration under paragraph (a) of this Article extending the Convention to any territory for whose international relations it is responsible may at any time thereafter declare by notification given to the Belgian Ministry of Foreign Affairs that the Convention shall cease to extend to such territory and the Convention shall one year after the receipt of the notification by the Belgian Ministry of Foreign Affairs cease to extend thereto.

(c) The Belgian Ministry of Foreign Affairs shall inform through diplomatic channels all signatory and acceding States of any notification received by it under this Article.

DONE in Brussels, on May 10, 1952, in the French and English languages, the two texts being equally authentic.

TABLE OF STATE RATIFICATIONS

Total number of signatures not followed by ratifications: 0
Total number of ratifications/accessions: 77

Brussels, 10th May 1952
Entered into force: 24 February 1956
(Condition: 2 ratifications)

State	Signature	Ratification	By	Entry into force
Algeria		18 August 1964	Accession	18 February 1965
Antigua and Barbuda		12 May 1965	Accession	12 November 1965
Bahamas		12 May 1965	Accession	12 November 1965
Belgium		10 April 1961	Ratification	10 October 1961
Belize		21 September 1965	Accession	21 March 1966
Benin		23 April 1958	Accession	23 October 1958
Burkina Faso		23 April 1958	Accession	23 October 1958
Cameroon		23 April 1958	Accession	23 October 1958
Central African Republic		23 April 1958	Accession	23 October 1958
Comoros		23 April 1958	Accession	23 October 1958
Congo		23 April 1958	Accession	23 October 1958
Costa Rica		13 July 1955	Accession	24 January 1956
Côte d'Ivoire		23 April 1958	Accession	23 October 1958
Croatia		8 October 1991	Ratification	8 April 1992
Cuba		21 November 1983	Accession	21 May 1984
Denmark		2 May 1989	Ratification	2 November 1989

State	Signature	Ratification	By	Entry into force
Djibouti		23 April 1958	Accession	23 October 1958
Dominica, Republic of		12 May 1965	Accession	12 November 1965
Egypt		24 August 1955	Ratification	24 February 1956
Fiji		29 March 1963	Accession	29 September 1963
Finland		21 December 1995	Ratification	21 June 1996
France		25 May 1957	Ratification	25 November 1957
Overseas Territories		23 April 1958	Accession	23 October 1958
Gabon		23 April 1958	Accession	23 October 1958
Germany		6 October 1972	Ratification	6 April 1973
Greece		27 February 1967	Ratification	27 August 1967
Grenada		12 May 1965	Accession	12 November 1965
Guyana		29 March 1963	Accession	29 September 1963
Guinea		12 December 1994	Accession	12 June 1995
Haiti		4 November 1954	Accession	24 February 1956
Haute-Volta		23 April 1958	Accession	23 October 1958
Holy Seat		10 August 1956	Ratification	10 February 1957
Ireland		17 October 1989	Accession	17 April 1990
Italy		9 November 1979	Ratification	9 May 1980
Khmere Republic		12 November 1956	Accession	12 May 1957
Kiribati		21 September 1965	Accession	21 March 1966
Latvia		17 May 1993	Accession	17 November 1993
Luxembourg		18 February 1991	Accession	18 August 1991
Madagascar		23 April 1958	Accession	23 October 1958
Morocco		11 July 1990	Accession	11 January 1991
Mauritania		23 April 1958	Accession	23 October 1958
Mauritius		29 March 1963	Accession	29 September 1963
Netherlands		20 January 1983	Ratification	20 July 1983
Niger		23 April 1958	Accession	23 October 1958
Nigeria		7 November 1963	Accession	7 May 1964
North Borneo		29 March 1963	Accession	29 September 1963
Norway		1 November 1994	Ratification	1 May 1995
Paraguay		22 November 1967	Accession	22 May 1968
Poland		16 July 1976	Accession	16 January 1977
Portugal		4 May 1957	Ratification	4 November 1957
Romania		28 November 1995	Accession	28 May 1996
St Kitts and Nevis		12 May 1965	Accession	12 November 1965
St Lucia		12 May 1965	Accession	12 November 1965
St Vincent and the Grenadines		12 May 1965	Accession	12 November 1965
Sarawak		28 August 1962	Accession	28 February 1963
Senegal		23 April 1958	Accession	23 October 1958
Seychelles		29 March 1963	Accession	29 September 1963
Slovenia		13 October 1993	Accession	13 April 1994
Solomon Islands		21 September 1965	Accession	21 March 1966
Spain		8 December 1953	Ratification	24 February 1956
Sudan		23 April 1958	Accession	23 October 1958
Sweden		30 April 1993	Accession	30 October 1993
Switzerland		28 May 1954	Accession	24 February 1956
Syrian Arab Republic		3 February 1972	Accession	3 August 1972
Tchad		23 April 1958	Accession	23 October 1958
Togo		23 April 1958	Accession	23 October 1958
Tonga		13 June 1978	Accession	13 December 1978

State	Signature	Ratification	By	Entry into force
Turks Isles and Caicos		21 September 1965	Accession	21 March 1966
Tuvalu		21 September 1965	Accession	21 March 1966
United Kingdom of Great Britain and Northern Ireland		18 March 1959	Ratification	18 September 1959
United Kingdom (Overseas Territories)				
Gibraltar, Hong Kong		29 March 1963	Accession	29 September 1963
British Virgin Islands		29 May 1963	Accession	29 November 1963
Bermuda		30 May 1963	Accession	30 November 1963
Anguilla, Cayman Islands, Montserrat, St Helena		12 May 1965	Accession	12 November 1965
Guernsey		8 December 1966	Accession	8 June 1967
Falkland Islands and dependencies		17 October 1969	Accession	17 April 1970
Zaire		17 July 1967	Accession	17 January 1968

Note. A list of reservations and declarations made by States has not been included in this volume. These can be obtained from http://www.comitemaritime.org/

(c) INTERNATIONAL CONVENTION ON MARITIME LIENS AND MORTGAGES*

(Geneva, 6 May 1993)

PREAMBLE

The States parties to this convention,

Conscious of the need to improve conditions for ship financing and the development of national merchant fleets,

Recognizing the desirability of international uniformity in the field of maritime liens and mortgages, and therefore

Convinced of the necessity for an international legal instrument governing maritime liens and mortgages,

Have decided to conclude a Convention for this purpose and have therefore agreed as follows:

Article 1

Recognition and enforcement of mortgages, 'hypothèques' and charges

Mortgages, 'hypothèques' and registrable charges of the same nature, which registrable charges of the same nature will be referred to hereinafter as 'charges', effected on seagoing vessels shall be recognized and enforceable in States Parties provided that:

(a) Such mortgages, 'hypothèques' and charges have been effected and registered in accordance with the law of the State in which the vessel is registered;

(b) The register and any instruments required to be deposited with the registrar in accordance with the law of the State in which the vessel is registered are open to public inspection, and that extracts from the register and copies of such instruments are obtainable from the registrar; and

(c) Either the register or any instruments referred to in subparagraph (b) specifies at least the name and address of the person in whose favour the mortgage, 'hypothèque' or charge has been effected or that it has been issued to bearer, the maximum amount secured, if that is a requirement of the law of the State of

---

* The United Nations is the author of the original material.

registration or if that amount is specified in the instrument creating the mortgage, 'hypothèque' or charge, and the date and other particulars which, according to the law of the State of registration, determine the ranking in relation to other registered mortgages, 'hypothèques' and charges.

Article 2
Ranking and effects of mortgages, 'hypothèques' and charges

The ranking of registered mortgages, 'hypothèques' or charges as between themselves and, without prejudice to the provisions of this Convention, their effect in regard to third parties shall be determined by the law of the State of registration; however, without prejudice to the provisions of this Convention, all matters relating to the procedure of enforcement shall be regulated by the law of the State where enforcement takes place.

Article 3
Change of ownership or registration

1. With the exception of the cases provided for in articles 11 and 12, in all other cases that entail the deregistration of the vessel from the register of a State Party, such State Party shall not permit the owner to deregister the vessel unless all registered mortgages, 'hypothèques' or charges are previously deleted or the written consent of all holders of such mortgages, 'hypothèques' or charges is obtained. However, where the deregistration of the vessel is obligatory in accordance with the law of a State Party, otherwise than as a result of a voluntary sale, the holders of registered mortgages, 'hypothèques' or charges shall be notified of the pending deregistration in order to enable such holders to take appropriate action to protect their interests; unless the holders consent, the deregistration shall not be implemented earlier than after a lapse of a reasonable period of time which shall be not less than three months after the relevant notification to such holders.

2. Without prejudice to article 12, paragraph 5, a vessel which is or has been registered in a State Party shall not be eligible for registration in another State Party unless either:
   (a) A certificate has been issued by the former State to the effect that the vessel has been deregistered; or
   (b) A certificate has been issued by the former State to the effect that the vessel will be deregistered with immediate effect, at such time as the new registration is effected. The date of deregistration shall be the date of the new registration of the vessel.

Article 4
Maritime liens

1. Each of the following claims against the owner, demise charterer, manager or operator of the vessel shall be secured by a maritime lien on the vessel:
   (a) Claims for wages and other sums due to the master, officers and other members of the vessel's complement in respect of their employment on the vessel, including costs of repatriation and social insurance contributions payable on their behalf;
   (b) Claims in respect of loss of life or personal injury occurring, whether on land or on water, in direct connection with the operation of the vessel;
   (c) Claims for reward for the salvage of the vessel;
   (d) Claims for port, canal, and other waterway dues and pilotage dues;

(e) Claims based on tort arising out of physical loss or damage caused by the operation of the vessel other than loss of or damage to cargo, containers and passengers' effects carried on the vessel.

(2) No maritime lien shall attach to a vessel to secure claims as set out in subparagraphs
(b) and (e) of paragraph 1 which arise out of or result from:

(a) Damage in connection with the carriage of oil or other hazardous or noxious substances by sea for which compensation is payable to the claimants pursuant to international conventions or national law providing for strict liability and compulsory insurance or other means of securing the claims; or

(b) The radioactive properties or a combination of radioactive properties with toxic, explosive or other hazardous properties of nuclear fuel or of radioactive products or waste.

Article 5
Priority of maritime liens

1. The maritime liens set out in article 4 shall take priority over registered mortgages, 'hypothèques' and charges, and no other claim shall take priority over such maritime liens or over such mortgages, 'hypothèques' or charges which comply with the requirements of article 1, except as provided in paragraphs 3 and 4 of article 12.
2. The maritime liens set out in article 4 shall rank in the order listed, provided however that maritime liens securing claims for reward for the salvage of the vessel shall take priority over all other maritime liens which have attached to the vessel prior to the time when the operations giving rise to the said liens were performed.
3. The maritime liens set out in each of subparagraphs (a), (b), (d) and (e) of paragraph 1 of article 4 shall rank pari passu as between themselves.
4. The maritime liens securing claims for reward for the salvage of the vessel shall rank in the inverse order of the time when the claims secured thereby accrued. Such claims shall be deemed to have accrued on the date on which each salvage operation was terminated.

Article 6
Other maritime liens

Each State Party may, under its law, grant other maritime liens on a vessel to secure claims, other than those referred to in article 4, against the owner, demise charterer, manager or operator of the vessel, provided that such liens:

(a) Shall be subject to the provisions of articles g, 10 and 12;

(b) Shall be extinguished

(i) after a period of 6 months, from the time when the claims secured thereby arose unless, prior to the expiry of such period, the vessel has been arrested or seized, such arrest or seizure leading to a forced sale; or

(ii) at the end of a period of 60 days following a sale to a *bona fide* purchaser of the vessel, such period to commence on the date on which the sate is registered in accordance with the law of the State in which the vessel is registered following the sale;

whichever period expires first; and

(c) Shall rank after the maritime liens set out in article 4 and also after registered mortgages, 'hypothèques' or charges which comply with the provisions of article 1.

Article 7
Rights of retention

1. Each State Party may grant under its law a right of retention in respect of a vessel in the possession of either:
   (a) A shipbuilder, to secure claims for the building of the vessel; or
   (b) A ship repairer, to secure claims for repair, including reconstruction of the vessel, effected during such possession.
2. Such right of retention shall be extinguished when the vessel ceases to be in the possession of the shipbuilder or shiprepairer, otherwise than in consequence of an arrest or seizure.

Article 8
Characteristics of maritime liens

Subject to the provisions of article 12, the maritime liens follow the vessel, notwithstanding any change of ownership or of registration or of flag.

Article 9
Extinction of maritime liens by lapse of time

1. The maritime liens set out in article 4 shall be extinguished after a period of one year unless, prior to the expiry of such period, the vessel has been arrested or seized, such arrest or seizure leading to a forced sale.
2. The one-year period referred to in paragraph 1 shall commence:
   (a) With respect to the maritime lien set out in article 4, paragraph 1(a), upon the claimant's discharge from the vessel;
   (b) With respect to the maritime liens set out in article 4, paragraph 1(b) to (e), when the claims secured thereby arise;
and shall not be subject to suspension or interruption, provided, however, that time shall not run during the period that the arrest or seizure of the vessel is not permitted by law.

Article 10
Assignment and subrogation

1. The assignment of or subrogation to a claim secured by a maritime lien entails the simultaneous assignment of or subrogation to such a maritime lien.
2. Claimants holding maritime liens may not be subrogated to the compensation payable to the owner of the vessel under an insurance contract.

Article 11
Notice of forced sale

1. Prior to the forced sale of a vessel in a State Party, the competent authority in such State Party shall ensure that notice in accordance with this article is provided to:
   (a) The authority in charge of the register in the State of registration;
   (b) All holders of registered mortgages, 'hypothèques' or charges which have not been issued to bearer;
   (c) All holders of registered mortgages, 'hypothèques' or charges issued to bearer and all holders of the maritime liens set out in article 4, provided that the competent authority conducting the forced sale receives notice of their respective claims; and
   (d) The registered owner of the vessel.

2. Such notice shall be provided at least 30 days prior to the forced sale and shall contain either:
    (a) The time and place of the forced sale and such particulars concerning the forced sale or the proceedings leading to the forced sale as the authority in a State Party conducting the proceedings shall determine is sufficient to protect the interests of persons entitled to notice; or,
    (b) If the time and place of the forced sale cannot be determined with certainty, the approximate time and anticipated place of the forced sale and such particulars concerning the forced sale as the authority in a State Party conducting the proceedings shall determine is sufficient to protect the interests of persons entitled to notice.

If notice is provided in accordance with subparagraph (b), additional notice of the actual time and place of the forced sale shall be provided when known but, in any event, not less than seven days prior to the forced sale.

3. The notice specified in paragraph 2 of this article shall be in writing and either given by registered mail, or given by any electronic or other appropriate means which provide confirmation of receipt, to the persons interested as specified in paragraph t, if known. In addition, the notice shall be given by press announcement in the State where the forced sale is conducted and, if deemed appropriate by the authority conducting the forced sale, in other publications.

Article 12
Effects of forced sale

1. In the event of the forced sale of the vessel in a State Party, all registered mortgages, 'hypothèques' or charges, except those assumed by the purchaser with the consent of the holders, and all liens and other encumbrances of whatsoever nature, shall cease to attach to the vessel, provided that:
    (a) At the time of the sate, the vessel is in the area of the jurisdiction of such State; and
    (b) The sale has been effected in accordance with the law of the said State and the provisions of article 11 and this article.
2. The costs and expenses arising out of the arrest or seizure and subsequent sale of the vessel shall be paid first out of the proceeds of sate. Such costs and expenses include, *inter alia*, the costs for the upkeep of the vessel and the crew as well as wages, other sums and costs referred to in article 4, paragraph 1(a), incurred from the time of arrest or seizure. The balance of the proceeds shall be distributed in accordance with the provisions of this Convention, to the extent necessary to satisfy the respective claims. Upon satisfaction of all claimants, the residue of the proceeds, if any, shall be paid to the owner and it shall be freely transferable.
3. A State Party may provide in its law that, in the event of the forced sale of a stranded or sunken vessel following its removal by a public authority in the interest of safe navigation or the protection of the marine environment, the costs of such removal shall be paid out of the proceeds of the sale, before all other claims secured by a maritime lien on the vessel.
4. If at the time of the forced sale the vessel is in the possession of a shipbuilder or of a shiprepairer who under the law of the State Party in which the sale takes place enjoys a right of retention, such shipbuilder or shiprepairer must surrender possession of the vessel to the purchaser but is entitled to obtain satisfaction of his claim out of the

proceeds of sate after the satisfaction of the claims of holders of maritime liens mentioned in article 4.

5. When a vessel registered in a State Party has been the object of a forced sale in any State Party, the competent authority shall, at the request of the purchaser, issue a certificate to the effect that the vessel is sold free of all registered mortgages, 'hypothèques' or charges, except those assumed by the purchaser, and of alt liens and other encumbrances, provided that the requirements set out in paragraph l (a) and (b) have been complied with. Upon production of such certificate, the registrar shall be bound to delete all registered mortgages, 'hypothèques' or charges except those assumed by the purchaser, and to register the vessel in the name of the purchaser or to issue a certificate of deregistration for the purpose of new registration, as the case may be.

6. States Parties shall ensure that any proceeds of a forced sale are actually available and freely transferable.

Article 13
Scope of application

1. Unless otherwise provided in this Convention, its provisions shall apply to all seagoing vessels registered in a State Party or in a State which is not a State Party, provided that the latter's vessels are subject to the jurisdiction of the State Party.

2. Nothing in this Convention shall create any rights in, or enable any rights to be enforced against, any vessel owned or operated by a State and used only on Government non-commercial service.

Article 14
Communication between States Parties

For the purpose of articles 3, 11 and 12, the competent authorities of the States Parties shall be authorized to correspond directly between themselves.

Article 15
Conflict of conventions

Nothing in this Convention shall affect the application of any international convention providing for limitation of liability or of national legislation giving effect thereto.

Article 16
Temporary change of flag

If a seagoing vessel registered in one State is permitted to fly temporarily the flag of another State, the following shall apply:

(a) For the purposes of this article, references in this Convention to the 'State in which the vessel is registered' or to the 'State of registration' shall be deemed to be references to the State in which the vessel was registered immediately prior to the change of flag, and references to 'the authority in charge of the register' shall be deemed to be references to the authority in charge of the register in that State.

(b) The law of the State of registration shall be determinative for the purpose of recognition of registered mortgages, 'hypothèques' and charges.

(c) The State of registration shall require a cross-reference entry in its register specifying the State whose flag the vessel is permitted to fly temporarily; likewise, the State whose flag the vessel is permitted to fly temporarily shall require that the authority in charge of the vessel's record specifies by a cross-reference in the record the State of registration.

(d) No State Party shall permit a vessel registered in that State to fly temporarily the flag of another State unless all registered mortgages, 'hypothèques' or charges on that vessel have been previously satisfied or the written consent of the holders of all such mortgages, 'hypothèques' or charges has been obtained.

(e) The notice referred to in article It shall be given also to the competent authority in charge of the vessel's record in the State whose flag the vessel is permitted to fly temporarily.

(f) Upon production of the certificate of deregistration referred to in article 12, paragraph 5, the competent authority in charge of the vessel's record in the State whose flag the vessel is permitted to fly temporarily shall, at the request of the purchaser, issue a certificate to the effect that the right to fly the flag of that State is revoked

(g) Nothing in this Convention is to be understood to impose any obligation on States Parties to permit foreign vessels to fly temporarily their flag or national vessels to fly temporarily a foreign flag.

Article 17
Depositary

This Convention shall be deposited with the Secretary-General of the United Nations.

Article 18
Signature, ratification, acceptance, approval and accession

1. This Convention shall be open for signature by any State at the Headquarters of the United Nations, New York, from 1 September 1993 to 31 August 1994 and shall thereafter remain open for accession.
2. States may express their consent to be bound by this Convention by:
   (a) Signature without reservation as to ratification, acceptance or approval; or
   (b) Signature subject to ratification, acceptance or approval, followed by ratification, acceptance or approval; or
   (c) Accession.
3. Ratification, acceptance, approval or accession shall be effected by the deposit of an instrument to that effect with the depositary.

Article 19
Entry into force

1. This Convention shall enter into force 6 months following the date on which 10 States have expressed their consent to be bound by it.
2. For a State which expresses its consent to be bound by this Convention after the conditions for entry into force thereof have been met, such consent shall take effect 3 months after the date of expression of such consent.

Article 20
Revision and amendment

1. A conference of States Parties for the purpose of revising or amending this Convention shall be convened by the Secretary-General of the United Nations at the request of one third of the States Parties.
2. Any consent to be bound by this Convention, expressed after the date of entry into force of an amendment to this Convention, shall be deemed to apply to the Convention, as amended.

Article 21
Denunciation

1. This Convention may be denounced by any State Party at any time after the date on which this Convention enters into force for that State.
2. Denunciation shall be effected by the deposit of an instrument of denunciation with the depositary.
3. A denunciation shall take effect one year, or such longer period as may be specified in the instrument of denunciation, after the receipt of the instrument of denunciation by the depositary.

Article 22
Languages

This Convention is established in a single original in the Arabic, Chinese, English, French, Russian and Spanish languages, each text being equally authentic.

Done at Geneva this sixth day of May, one thousand nine hundred and ninety-three.

In witness whereof the undersigned being duly authorized by their respective Governments for that purpose have signed this Convention.

TABLE OF STATE RATIFICATIONS

Total number of signatures not followed by ratifications: 0
Total number of ratifications/accessions: 5

Geneva, 6 May 1993
Not yet in force
(Condition: 10 ratifications)

State	Signature	Ratification	By	Entry into force
Monaco		28 March 1995	Accession	
Russian Federation		4 March 1999	Accession	
Saint Vincent and the Grenadines		11 March 1997	Accession	
Tunisia		2 February 1995	Ratification	
Vanuatu		10 August 1999	Accession	

(d) INTERNATIONAL CONVENTION ON ARREST OF SHIPS, 1999*

PREAMBLE

The States parties to this Convention,

Recognizing the desirability of facilitating the harmonious and orderly development of world seaborne trade,

Convinced of the necessity for a legal instrument establishing international uniformity in the field of arrest of ships which takes account of recent developments in related fields,

Have Agreed as follows:

For the purposes of this Convention:

Article 1
Definitions

For the purposes of this Convention:

1. 'Maritime Claim' means a claim arising out of one or more of the following:
   a. loss or damage caused by the operation of the ship;
   b. loss of life or personal injury occurring, whether on land or on water, in direct connection with the operation of the ship;
   c. salvage operations or any salvage agreement, including, if applicable, special compensation relating to salvage operations in respect of a ship which by itself or its cargo threatened damage to the environment;
   d. damage or threat of damage caused by the ship to the environment, coastline or related interests; measures taken to prevent, minimize, or remove such damage; compensation for such damage; costs of reasonable measures of reinstatement of the environment actually undertaken or to be undertaken; loss incurred or likely to be incurred by third parties in connection with such damage; and damage, costs, or loss of a similar nature to those identified in this subparagraph (d);
   e. costs or expenses relating to the raising, removal, recovery, destruction or the rendering harmless of a ship which is sunk, wrecked, stranded or abandoned, including anything that is or has been on board such ship, and costs or expenses relating to the preservation of an abandoned ship and maintenance of its crew;

---

* The United Nations is the author of the original material.

    f. any agreement relating to the use or hire of the ship, whether contained in a charter party or otherwise;

    g. any agreement relating to the carriage of goods or passengers on board the ship, whether contained in a charter party or otherwise;

    h. loss of or damage to or in connection with goods (including luggage) carried on board the ship;

    i. general average;

    j. towage;

    k. pilotage;

    l. goods, materials, provisions, bunkers, equipment (including containers) supplied or services rendered to the ship for its operation, management, preservation or maintenance;

    m. construction, reconstruction, repair, converting or equipping of the ship;

    n. port, canal, dock, harbour and other waterway dues and charges;

    o. wages and other sums due to the master, officers and other members of the ship's complement in respect of their employment on the ship, including costs of repatriation and social insurance contributions payable on their behalf;

    p. disbursements incurred on behalf of the ship or its owners;

    q. insurance premiums (including mutual insurance calls) in respect of the ship, payable by or on behalf of the shipowner or demise charterer;

    r. any commissions, brokerages or agency fees payable in respect of the ship by or on behalf of the shipowner or demise charterer;

    s. any dispute as to ownership or possession of the ship;

    t. any dispute between co-owners of the ship as to the employment or earnings of the ship;

    u. a mortgage or a 'hypothque' or a charge of the same nature on the ship;

    v. any dispute arising out of a contract for the sale of the ship.

2. 'Arrest' means any detention or restriction on removal of a ship by order of a Court to secure a maritime claim, but does not include the seizure of a ship in execution or satisfaction of a judgment or other enforceable instrument.

3. 'Person' means any individual or partnership or any public or private body, whether corporate or not, including a State or any of its constituent subdivisions.

4. 'Claimant' means any person asserting a maritime claim.

5. 'Court' means any competent judicial authority of a State.

Article 2
Powers of arrest

1. A ship may be arrested or released from arrest only under the authority of a Court of the State Party in which the arrest is effected.

2. A ship may only be arrested in respect of a maritime claim but in respect of no other claim.

3. A ship may be arrested for the purpose of obtaining security notwithstanding that, by virtue of a jurisdiction clause or arbitration clause in any relevant contract, or otherwise, the maritime claim in respect of which the arrest is effected is to be adjudicated in a State other than he State where the arrest is effected, or is to be arbitrated, or is to be adjudicated subject to the law of another State.

4. Subject to the provisions of this Convention, the procedure relating to the arrest of a ship or its release shall be governed by the law of the State in which the arrest was effected or applied for.

Article 3
Exercise of right of arrest

1. Arrest is permissible of any ship in respect of which a maritime claim is asserted if:
   a. the person who owned the ship at the time when the maritime claim arose is liable for the claim and is owner of the ship when the arrest is effected; or
   b. the demise chatterer of the ship at the time when the maritime claim arose is liable for the claim and is demise chatterer or owner of the ship when the arrest is effected; or
   c. the claim is based upon a mortgage or a 'hypothèque' or a charge of the same nature on the ship; or
   d. the claim relates to the ownership or possession of the ship; or
   e. the claim is against the owner, demise chatterer, manager or operator of the ship and is secured by a maritime lien which is granted or arises under the law of the State where the arrest is applied for.
2. Arrest is also permissible of any other ship or ships which, when the arrest is effected, is or are owned by the person who is liable for the maritime claim and who was, when the claim arose:
   a. owner of the ship in respect of which the maritime claim arose; or
   b. demise chatterer, time chatterer or voyage chatterer of that ship.
This provision does not apply to claims in respect of ownership or possession of a ship.
3. Notwithstanding the provisions of paragraphs 1 and 2 of this article, the arrest of a ship which is not owned by the person liable for the claim shall be permissible only if, under the law of the State where the arrest is applied for, a judgment in respect of that claim can be enforced against that ship by judicial or forced sale of that ship.

Article 4
Release from arrest

1. A ship which has been arrested shall be released when sufficient security has been provided in a satisfactory form, save in cases in which a ship has been arrested in respect of any of the in time claims enumerated in article 1, paragraphs I (s) and (t). In such cases, the Court an may permit the person in possession of the ship to continue trading the ship, upon such person providing sufficient security, or may otherwise deal with the operation of the ship during the period of the arrest.
2. In the absence of agreement between the parties as to the sufficiency and form of the security, the Court shall determine its nature and the amount thereof, not exceeding the value of the arrested ship.
3. Any request for the ship to be released upon security being provided shall not be construed as an acknowledgement of liability nor as a waiver of any defense or any right to limit liability.
4. If a ship has been arrested in a non-party State and is not released although security in respect of that ship has been provided in a State Party in respect of the same claim, that security shall be ordered to be released on application to the Court in the State Party.

5. If in a non-party State the ship is released upon satisfactory security in respect of that ship being provided, any security provided in a State Party in respect of the same claim shall be ordered to be released to the extent that the total amount of security provided in the two States exceeds:
   a. the claim for which the ship has been arrested, or
   b. the value of the ship,

whichever is the lower. Such release shall, however, not be ordered unless the security provided in the non-party State will actually be available to the claimant and will be freely transferable.

6. Where, pursuant to paragraph 1 of this article, security has been provided, the person providing such security may at any time apply to the Court to have that security reduced, modified, or cancelled.

Article 5
Right of rearrest and multiple arrest

1. Where in any State a ship has already been arrested and released or security in respect of that ship has already been provided to secure a maritime claim, that ship shall not thereafter be rearrested or arrested in respect of the same maritime claim unless:
   a. the nature or amount of the security in respect of that ship already provided in respect of the same claim is inadequate, on condition that the aggregate amount of security may not exceed the value of the ship; or
   b. the person who has already provided the security is not, or is unlikely to be, able to fulfil some or all of that person's obligations; or
   c. the ship arrested or the security previously provided was released either:
      i. upon the application or with the consent of the claimant acting on reasonable grounds, or
      ii. because the claimant could not by taking reasonable steps prevent the release.
2. Any other ship which would otherwise be subject to arrest in respect of the same maritime claim shall not be arrested unless:
   a. the nature or amount of the security already provided in respect of the same claim is inadequate; or
   b. the provisions of paragraph 1(b) or (c) of this article are applicable.
3. 'Release' for the purpose of this article shall not include any unlawful release or escape from arrest.

Article 6
Protection of owners and demise charterers of arrested ships

1. The Court may as a condition of the arrest of a ship, or of permitting an arrest already effected to be maintained, impose upon the claimant who seeks to arrest or who has procured the arrest of the ship the obligation to provide security of a kind and for an amount, and upon such terms, as may be determined by that Court for any loss which may be incurred by the defendant as a result of the arrest, and for which the claimant may be found liable, including but not restricted to such loss or damage as may be incurred by that defendant in consequence of:
   a. the arrest having been wrongful or unjustified; or
   b. excessive security having been demanded and provided.

2. The Courts of the State in which an arrest has been effected shall have jurisdiction to determine the extent of the liability, if any, of the claimant for loss or damage caused by the arrest of a ship, including but not restricted to such loss or damage as may be caused in consequence of:
   a. the arrest having been wrongful or unjustified, or
   b. excessive security having been demanded and provided.
3. The liability, if any, of the claimant in accordance with paragraph 2 of this article shall be determined by application of the law of the State where the arrest was effected.
4. If a Court in another State or an arbitral tribunal is to determine the merits of the case in accordance with the provisions of article 7, then proceedings relating to the liability of the claimant in accordance with paragraph 2 of this article may be stayed pending that decision.
5. Where pursuant to paragraph 1 of this article security has been provided, the person providing such security may at any time apply to the Court to have that security reduced, modified or cancelled.

Article 7
Jurisdiction on the merits of the case

1. The Courts of the State in which an arrest has been effected or security provided to obtain the release of the ship shall have jurisdiction to determine the case upon its merits, unless the parties validly agree or have validly agreed to submit the dispute to a Court of another State which accepts jurisdiction, or to arbitration.
2. Notwithstanding the provisions of paragraph 1 of this article, the Courts of the State in which an arrest has been effected, or security provided to obtain the release of the ship, may refuse to exercise that jurisdiction where that refusal is permitted by the law of that State and a Court of another State accepts jurisdiction.
3. In cases where a Court of the State where an arrest has been effected or security provided to obtain the release of the ship:
   a. does not have jurisdiction to determine the case upon its merits; or
   b. has refused to exercise jurisdiction in accordance with the provisions of paragraph 2 of this article,
   such Court may, and upon request shall, order a period of time within which the claimant shall bring proceedings before a competent Court or arbitral tribunal.
4. If proceedings are not brought within the period of time ordered in accordance with paragraph 3 of this article then the ship arrested or the security provided shall, upon request, be ordered to be released.
5. If proceedings are brought within the period of time ordered in accordance with paragraph 3 of this article, or if proceedings before a competent Court or arbitral tribunal in another State are brought in the absence of such order, any final decision resulting therefrom shall be recognized and given effect with respect to the arrested ship or to the security provided in order to obtain its release, on condition that:
   a. the defendant has been given reasonable notice of such proceedings and a reasonable opportunity to present the case for the defence; and
   b. such recognition is not against public policy (ordre public)
6. Nothing contained in the provisions of paragraph 5 of this article shall restrict any further effect given to a foreign judgment or arbitral award under the law of the State where the arrest of the ship was effected or security provided to obtain its release.

Article 8
Application

1. This Convention shall apply to any ship within the jurisdiction of any State Party, whether or not that ship is flying the flag of a State Party.
2. This Convention shall not apply to any warship, naval auxiliary or other ships owned or operates by a State and used, for the time being, only on government non-commercial service.
3. This Convention does not affect any rights, or powers vested in any Government or its departments, or in any public authority, or in any dock or harbour authority, under any international convention or under any domestic law or regulation, to detain or otherwise prevent from sailing any ship within their jurisdiction.
4. This Convention shall not affect the power of any State or Court to make orders affecting the totality of a debtor's assets.
5. Nothing in this Convention shall affect the application of international conventions providing for limitation of liability, or domestic law giving effect thereto, in the State where an arrest is effected. in this Convention shall affect.
6. Nothing in this Convention shall modify or affect the rules of law in force in the States Parties relating to the arrest of any ship physically within the jurisdiction of the State of its flag procured by a person whose habitual residence or principal place of business is in that State, or by any other person who has acquired a claim from such person by subrogation, assignment or otherwise.

Article 9
Non-creation of maritime liens

Nothing in this Convention shall be construed as creating a maritime lien.

Article 10
Reservations

1. Any State may, at the time of signature, ratification, acceptance, approval, or accession, or at any time thereafter, reserve the right to exclude the application of this Convention to any or all of the following:
   a. ships which are not seagoing;
   b. ships not flying the flag of a State Party;
   c. claims under article 1, paragraph 1(s).
2. A State may, when it is also a State Party to a specified treaty on navigation on inland waterways, declare when signing, ratifying, accepting, approving or acceding to this Convention, that rules on jurisdiction, recognition and execution of court decisions provided for in such treaties shall prevail over the rules contained in article 7 of this Convention.

Article 11
Depository

This Convention shall be deposited with the Secretary-General of the United Nations.

Article 12
Signature, ratification, acceptance, approval and accession

1. This Convention shall be open for signature by any State at the Headquarters of the United Nations, New York, from 1 September 1999 to 31 August 2000 and shall thereafter remain open for accession.
2. States may express their consent to be bound by this Convention by:
   a. signature without reservation as to ratification, acceptance or approval; or
   b. signature subject to ratification, acceptance or approval, followed by ratification, acceptance or approval; or
   c. accession.
3. Ratification, acceptance, approval or accession shall be effected by the deposit of an instrument to that effect with the depositary.

Article 13
States with more than one system of law

1. If a State has two or more territorial units in which different systems of law are applicable in relation to matters dealt with in this Convention, it may at the time of signature, ratification, acceptance, approval or accession declare that this Convention shall extend to all its territorial units or only to one or more of them and may modify this declaration by submitting another declaration at any time.
2. Any such declaration shall be notified to the depositary and shall state expressly the territorial units to which the Convention applies.
3. In relation to a State Party which has two or more systems of law with regard to arrest of ships applicable in different territorial units, references in this Convention to the Court of a State and the law of a State shall be respectively construed as referring to the Court of the relevant territorial unit within that State and the law of the relevant territorial unit of that State.

Article 14
Entry into force

1. This Convention shall enter into force six months following the date on which 10 States have expressed their consent to be bound by it.
2. For a State which expresses its consent to be bound by this Convention after the conditions for entry into force thereof have been met, such consent shall take effect three months after the date of expression of such consent.

Article 15
Revision and amendment

1. A conference of States Parties for the purpose of revising or amending this Convention shall be convened by the Secretary-General of the United Nations at the request of one-third of the States Parties.
2. Any consent to be bound by this Convention, expressed after the date of entry into force of an amendment to this Convention, shall be deemed to apply to the Convention, as amended.

Article 16
Denunciation

1. This Convention may be denounced by any State Party at any time after the date on which this Convention enters into force for that State.
2. Denunciation shall be effected by deposit of an instrument of denunciation with the depositary.
3. A denunciation shall take effect one year, or such longer period as may be specified in the instrument of denunciation, after the receipt of the instrument of denunciation by the depositary.

Article 17
Languages

This Convention is established in a single original in the Arabic, Chinese, English, French, Russian and: Spanish languages, each text being equally authentic.

Done at Geneva this twelfth day of March, one thousand nine hundred and ninety-nine.

In witness whereof the undersigned being duly authorized by their respective Governments far that purpose have signed this Convention.

TABLE OF STATE RATIFICATIONS

Total number of signatures not followed by ratifications: 0
Total number of ratifications/accessions: 2

Geneva, 12 March 1999
Not yet in force
(Condition: 10 ratifications)

State	Signature	Ratification	By	Entry into force
Bulgaria		27 July 2000	Ratification	
Estonia		11 May 2001	Accession	

(e) CONVENTION FOR THE UNIFICATION OF CERTAIN RULES RELATING TO THE PRECAUTIONARY ATTACHMENT OF AIRCRAFT 1933*

Article 1

The High Contracting Parties agree to take the necessary measures to give effect to the rules established by this Convention.

Article 2

(1) For the purposes of this Convention precautionary arrest includes every act, whatever its designation, whereby an aircraft is arrested, in pursuit of a private interest, by the agency of judicial or public administrative authorities, for the benefit either of a creditor, or of the owner or other person entitled to a right *in rem* over the aircraft, where the party on whose behalf the arrest is effected does not rely upon an immediately enforceable judgment already obtained by ordinary process, or upon any right of seizure equivalent thereto.

(2) Where the law governing the case gives a creditor, who takes or keeps possession of an aircraft without the consent of the operator, a right to retain it, the exercise of that right is, for the purposes of this Convention, assimilated to precautionary arrest and is subject to the rules contained in this Convention.

Article 3

(1) The following are exempt from precautionary arrest:
   (a) aircraft exclusively appropriated to a state service, including the postal service, but excluding commercial service;
   (b) aircraft actually in service on a regular line of public transport, together with the indispensable reserve aircraft;
   (c) every other aircraft appropriated to the carriage of persons or goods for reward, where such aircraft is ready to start on such carriage, unless the arrest is in respect of a contract debt incurred for the purposes of the journey which the aircraft is about to make, or of a claim which has arisen in the course of the journey.

---

* Reproduced with the kind permission of the United Nations.

(2) The provisions of this article do not apply to precautionary arrest on the part of an owner dispossessed of his aircraft by an unlawful act.

Article 4

(1) In all cases where arrest is not forbidden or where, although the aircraft is immune from arrest, the operator does not invoke such immunity, the giving of a sufficient security avoids precautionary arrest and gives a right to immediate release.
(2) A security is sufficient if it covers the amount of the debt and costs and if it is appropriated exclusively to the payment of the creditor, or if it covers the value of the aircraft if this value is smaller than the amount of the debt and costs.

Article 5

All claims for release from precautionary arrest shall be dealt with by summary and rapid procedure.

Article 6

(1) If an aircraft immune from arrest under the provisions of this Convention has been arrested, or if the debtor has been compelled to give security in order to prevent arrest or to obtain a release, the person effecting the arrest is liable in accordance with the provisions of the *lex fori*, for any damage which results therefrom to the operator or proprietor.
(2) The same rule applies in the case of a precautionary arrest effected without due cause.

Article 7

This Convention does not apply to precautionary steps taken in case of insolvency or of breach of customs, penal ox police regulations.

Article 8

Nothing in this Convention prejudices the application as between the High Contracting Parties of international conventions providing for a more extensive immunity.

Article 9

(1) The Convention is applicable in the territory of each of the High Contracting Parties to all aircraft registered in the territory of another High Contracting Party.
(2) The expression 'territory of a High Contracting Party' includes every territory under the sovereignty, suzerainty, protectorate, mandate or authority of that high Contracting Party in respect of which the latter is a party to the Convention.

Article 10

This Convention is drawn up in French in a single copy which shall remain deposited in the archives of the Ministry for Foreign Affairs of the Kingdom of Italy, and of which a certified true copy shall be transmitted by the Government of the Kingdom of Italy to each of the interested Governments.

Article 11

(1) This Convention shall be ratified. The instruments of ratification shall be deposited in the archives of the Ministry for Foreign Affairs of the Kingdom of Italy, which shall notify their deposit to each of the interested Governments.

(2) When five ratifications have been deposited, the Convention shall come into force between the High Contracting Parties who have ratified it ninety days after the deposit of the fifth ratification. Each ratification subsequently deposited shall take effect ninety days after deposit.

(3) The Government of the Kingdom of Italy shall notify each of the interested Governments of the date of the entry into force of the Convention.

Article 12

(1) This Convention after its entry into force shall be open to accession.

(2) Accession shall be effected by means of a notification addressed to the Government of the Kingdom of Italy, which will communicate it to each of the interested Governments.

(3) Accessions shall take effect ninety days after their notification to the Government of the Kingdom of Italy.

Article 13

(1) Each of the High Contracting Parties may denounce this Convention by means of a notification to be made to the Government of the Kingdom of Italy, which will at once inform each of the interested Governments thereof.

(2) Each denunciation shall take effect six months after notification and only in regard to the party making it.

Article 14

(1) The High Contracting Parties may at the time of signature, ratification or accession declare that their acceptance of this Convention does not apply to all or any part of their colonies, protectorates, overseas territories, territories under mandate, or any other territories under their sovereignty, authority or suzerainty.

(2) The High Contracting Parties may subsequently notify the Government of the Kingdom of Italy that they desire to render this Convention applicable to all or any part of their colonies, protectorates, overseas territories, territories under mandate, or any other territories under their sovereignty, authority or suzerainty thus excluded by their original declaration.

(3) The High Contracting Parties may at any moment notify the Government of the Kingdom of Italy that they desire to terminate the application of this Convention to all or any part of their colonies, protectorates, overseas territories, territories under mandate, or any other territories under their sovereignty, authority or suzerainty.

(4) The Government of the Kingdom of Italy shall inform each of the interested Governments of any notifications made in pursuance of the two preceding paragraphs.

Article 15

Each of the High Contracting Parties shall have the right, but not before two years from the entry into force of this Convention, to call for the assembling of a new international conference with the object of investigating the improvements which might be made in this Convention. For this purpose such High Contracting Party shall communicate with the Government of the French Republic, which will take the necessary steps to prepare for the conference.

TABLE OF STATE RATIFICATIONS

Total number of signatures not followed by ratifications: 11
Total number of ratifications/accessions: 31

Rome, 29 May 1933
Entered into force: 12 January 1937
(Condition: 5 ratifications)

State	Signature	Ratification	By
Algeria		21 July 1964	Accession
Angola		17 March 1998	Accession
Argentina		24 July 1985	Accession
Austria	29 May 1933		
Belgium		14 October 1936	Ratification
Brazil		6 March 1939	Ratification
Central African Republic		10 June 1969	Accession
Congo, Democratic Republic of		9 August 1962	Accession
Czechoslovakia	29 May 1933		
Denmark (excluding Greenland)		31 January 1939	Ratification
Egypt		7 June 1971	Accession
El Salvador	29 May 1933		
Finland		30 October 1953	Accession
France	29 May 1933		
Germany		22 February 1935	Ratification
Guatemala		6 July 1939	Ratification
Haiti		19 January 1961	Accession
Honduras	29 May 1933		
Hungary		15 May 1937	Ratification
India	29 May 1933		
Italy	29 May 1933	29 September 1936	Ratification
Ivory Coast		11 September 1965	Accession
Lebanon		5 March 1996	Accession
Mali		20 December 1961	Accession
Mauritania		26 July 1962	Accession
Netherlands (excluding colony)		28 January 1938	Ratification
Niger		23 September 1964	Accession
Norway		22 June 1939	Ratification
Poland		31 August 1937	Ratification
Romania		23 March 1935	Ratification
Rwanda		1 December 1964	Succession
San Marino	29 May 1933		
Senegal		1 September 1964	Accession
Spain (excluding colony)		28 June 1934	Ratification
Sweden		31 January 1939	Ratification
Switzerland		15 December 1949	Ratification
Tunisia		2 May 1966	Acession
Turkey	29 May 1933		
United Kingdom	29 May 1933		
United States of America	29 May 1933		
Yugoslavia	29 May 1933		
Zaire			Accession

Note. A list of reservations and declarations made by States has not been included in this volume.

531

(f) CONVENTION ON THE INTERNATIONAL RECOGNITION OF RIGHTS IN AIRCRAFT*

Signed at Geneva, on 19 June 1948

PREAMBLE

Whereas the International Civil Aviation Conference, held at Chicago in November-December 1944, recommended the early adoption of a Convention dealing with the transfer of title to aircraft,

Whereas it is highly desirable in the interest of the future expansion of international civil aviation that rights in aircraft be recognised internationally,

The undersigned, duly authorized, *HAVE AGREED*; on behalf of their respective Governments, *AS FOLLOWS*:

Article I

1. The Contracting States undertake to recognise:
   (a) rights of property in aircraft;
   (b) rights to acquire aircraft by purchase coupled with possession of the aircraft;
   (c) rights to possession of aircraft under leases of six months or more;
   (d) mortgages, hypothèques and similar rights in aircraft which are contractually created as security for payment of an indebtedness; provided that such rights
      (i) have been constituted in accordance with the law of the Contracting State in which the aircraft was registered as to nationality at the time of their constitution, and
      (ii) are regularly recorded in a public record of the Contracting State in which the aircraft is registered as to nationality.

The regularity of successive recordings in different Contracting States shall be determined in accordance with the law of the State where the aircraft was registered as to nationality at the time of each recording.

---

* The United Nations is the author of the original material.

2. Nothing in this Convention shall prevent the recognition of any rights in aircraft under the law of any Contracting State; but Contracting States shall not admit or recognise any right as taking priority over the rights mentioned in paragraph 1 of this Article.

Article II

1. All recordings relating to a given aircraft must appear in the same record.
2. Except as otherwise provided in this Convention, the effects of the recording of any right mentioned in Article I, paragraph 1, with regard to third parties shall be determined according to the law of the Contracting State where it is recorded.
3. A Contracting State may prohibit the recording of any right which cannot validly be constituted according to its national law.

Article III

1. The address of the authority responsible for maintaining the record must be shown on every aircraft's certificate of registration as to nationality.
2. Any person shall be entitled to receive from the authority duly certified copies or extracts of the particulars recorded. Such copies or extracts shall constitute *prima facie* evidence of the contents of the record.
3. If the law of a Contracting State provides that the filing of a document for recording shall have the same effect as the recording, it shall have the same effect for the purposes of this Convention. In that case, adequate provision shall be made to ensure that such document is open to the public.
4. Reasonable charges may be made for services performed by the authority maintaining the record.

Article IV

1. In the event that any claims in respect of:
   (a) compensation due for salvage of the aircraft, or
   (b) extraordinary expenses indispensable for the preservation of the aircraft give rise, under the law of the Contracting State where the operations of salvage or preservation were terminated, to a right conferring a charge against the aircraft, such right shall be recognised by Contracting States and shall take priority over all other rights in the aircraft.
2. The rights enumerated in paragraph 1 shall be satisfied in the inverse order of the dates of the incidents in connexion with which they have arisen.
3. Any of the said rights may, within three months from the date of the termination of the salvage or preservation operations, be noted on the record.
4. The said rights shall not be recognised in other Contracting States after expiration of the three months mentioned in paragraph 3 unless, within this period,
   (a) the right has been noted on the record in conformity with paragraph 3, and
   (b) the amount has been agreed upon or judicial action on the right has been commenced. As far as judicial action is concerned, the law of the forum shall determine the contingencies upon which the three months period may be interrupted or suspended.
5. This Article shall apply notwithstanding the provisions of Article I, paragraph 2.

Article V

The priority of a right mentioned in Article I, paragraph 1(d), extends to all sums thereby secured. However, the amount of interest included shall not exceed that accrued during the three years prior to the execution proceedings together with that accrued during the execution proceedings.

Article VI

In case of attachment or sale of an aircraft in execution, or of any right therein, the Contracting States shall not be obliged to recognise, as against the attaching or executing creditor or against the purchaser, any right mentioned in Article I, paragraph 1, or the transfer of any such right, if constituted or effected with knowledge of the sale or execution proceedings by the person against whom the proceedings are directed.

Article VII

1. The proceedings of a sale of an aircraft in execution shall be determined by the law of the Contracting State where the sale takes place.
2. The following provisions shall however be observed:
   (a) The date and place of the sale shall be fixed at least six weeks in advance.
   (b) The executing creditor shall supply to the Court or other competent authority a certified extract of the recordings concerning the aircraft. He shall give public notice of the sale at the place where the aircraft is registered as to nationality, in accordance with the law there applicable, at least one month before the day fixed, and shall concurrently notify by registered letter, if possible by air mail, the recorded owner and the holders of recorded rights in the aircraft and of rights noted on the record under Article IV, paragraph 3, according to their addresses as shown on the record.
3. The consequences of failure to observe the requirements of paragraph 2 shall be as provided by the law of the Contracting State where the sale takes place. However, any sale taking place in contravention of the requirements of that paragraph may be annulled upon demand made within six months from the date of the sale by any person suffering damage as the result of such contravention.
4. No sale in execution can be effected unless all rights having priority over the claim of the executing creditor in accordance with this Convention which are established before the competent authority, are covered by the proceeds of sale or assumed by the purchaser.
5. When injury or damage is caused to persons or property on the surface of the Contracting State where the execution sale takes place, by any aircraft subject to any right referred to in Article I held as security for an indebtedness, unless adequate and effective insurance by a State or an insurance undertaking in any State has been provided by or on behalf of the operator to cover such injury or damage, the national law of such Contracting State may provide in case of the seizure of such aircraft or any other aircraft owned by the same person and encumbered with any similar right held by the same creditor:
   (a) that the provisions of paragraph 4 above shall have no effect with regard to the person suffering such injury or damage or his representative if he is an executing creditor;

(b) that any right referred to in Article I held as security for an indebtedness encumbering the aircraft may not be set up against any person suffering such injury or damage or his representative in excess of an amount equal to 80% of the sale price.

In the absence of other limit established by the law of the Contracting State where the execution sale takes place, the insurance shall be considered adequate within the meaning of the present paragraph if the amount of the insurance corresponds to the value when new of the aircraft seized in execution.

6. Costs legally chargeable under the law of the Contracting State where the sale takes place, which are incurred in the common interest of creditors in the course of execution proceedings leading to sale, shall be paid out of the proceeds of sale before any claims, including those given preference by Article IV.

Article VIII

Sale of an aircraft in execution in conformity with the provisions of Article VII shall effect the transfer of the property in such aircraft free from all rights which are not assumed by the purchaser.

Article IX

Except in the case of a sale in execution in conformity with the provisions of Article VII, no transfer of an aircraft from the nationality register or the record of a Contracting State to that of another Contracting State shall be made, unless all holders of recorded rights have been satisfied or consent to the transfer.

Article X

1. If a recorded right in an aircraft of the nature specified in Article 1, and held as security for the payment of an indebtedness, extends, in conformity with the law of the Contracting State where the aircraft is registered, to spare parts stored in a specified place or places, such right shall be recognised by all Contracting States, as long as the spare parts remain in the place or places specified, provided that an appropriate public notice, specifying the description of the right, the name and address of the holder of this right and the record in which such right is recorded, is exhibited at the place where the spare parts are located, so as to give due notification to third parties that such spare parts are encumbered.

2. A statement indicating the character and the approximate number of such spare parts shall be annexed to or included in the recorded document. Such parts may be replaced by similar parts without affecting the right of the creditor.

3. The provisions of Article VII, paragraphs 1 and 4, and of Article VIII shall apply to a sale of spare parts in execution. However, where the executing creditor is an unsecured creditor, paragraph 4 of Article VII in its application to such a sale shall be construed so as to permit the sale to take place if a bid is received in an amount not less than two-thirds of the value of the spare parts as determined by experts appointed by the authority responsible for the sale. Further, in the distribution of the proceeds of sale, the competent authority may, in order to provide for the claim of the executing creditor, limit the amount payable to holders of prior rights to two-thirds of such proceeds of sale after payment of the costs referred to in Article VII, paragraph 6.

4. For the purpose of this Article the term 'spare parts' means parts of aircraft, engines, propellers, radio apparatus, instruments, appliances, furnishings, parts of any of the foregoing, and generally any other articles of whatever description maintained for installation in aircraft in substitution for parts or articles removed.

Article XI

1. The provisions of this Convention shall in each Contracting State apply to all aircraft registered as to nationality in another Contracting State.
2. Each Contracting State shall also apply to aircraft there registered as to nationality:
   (a) The provisions of Articles II, III, IX, and
   (b) The provisions of Article IV, unless the salvage or preservation operations have been terminated within its own territory.

Article XII

Nothing in this Convention shall prejudice the right of any Contracting State to enforce against an aircraft its national laws relating to immigration, customs or air navigation.

Article XIII

This Convention shall not apply to aircraft used in military, customs or police services.

Article XIV

For the purpose of this Convention, the competent judicial and administrative authorities of the Contracting States may, subject to any contrary provision in their national law, correspond directly with each other.

Article XV

The Contracting States shall take such measures as are necessary for the fulfilment of the provisions of this Convention and shall forthwith inform the Secretary General of the International Civil Aviation Organization of these measures.

Article XVI

For the purposes of this Convention the term 'aircraft' shall include the airframe, engines, propellers, radio apparatus, and all other articles intended or use in the aircraft whether installed therein or temporarily separated herefrom.

Article XVII

If a separate register of aircraft for purposes of nationality is maintained in any territory for whose foreign relations a Contracting State is responsible, references in this Convention to the law of the Contracting State shall be construed as references to the law of that territory.

Article XVIII

This Convention shall remain open for signature until it comes into force n accordance with the provisions of Article XX.

Article XIX

1. This Convention shall be subject to ratification by the signatory States.
2. The instruments of ratification shall be deposited in the archives of the International Civil Aviation Organization, which shall give notice of the date of deposit to each of the signatory and adhering States.

Article XX

1. As soon as two of the signatory States have deposited their instruments of ratification of this Convention, it shall come into force between them on the ninetieth day after the date of the deposit of the second instrument of ratification. It shall come into force, for each State which deposits its instrument of ratification after that date, on the ninetieth day after the deposit of its instrument of ratification.
2. The International Civil Aviation Organization shall give notice to each signatory State of the date on which this Convention comes into force.
3. As soon as this Convention comes into force, it shall be registered with the United Nations by the Secretary General of the International Civil Aviation Organization.

Article XXI

1. This Convention shall, after it has come into force, be open for adherence by non-signatory states.
2. Adherence shall be effected by the deposit of an instrument of adherence in the archives of the International Civil Aviation Organization, which shall give notice of the date of the deposit to each signatory and adhering State.
3. Adherence shall take effect as from the ninetieth day after the date of the deposit of the instrument of adherence in the archives of the International Civil Aviation Organization.

Article XXII

1. Any Contracting State may denounce this Convention by notification of denunciation to the International Civil Aviation Organization, which shall give notice of the date of receipt of such notification to each signatory and adhering State.
2. Denunciation shall take effect six months after the date of receipt by the International Civil Aviation Organization of the notification of denunciation.

Article XXIII

1. Any State may at the time of deposit of its instrument of ratification or adherence, declare that its acceptance of this Convention does not apply to any one or more of the territories for the foreign relations of which such State is responsible.
2. The International Civil Aviation Organization shall give notice of any such declaration to each signatory and adhering State.
3. With the exception of territories in respect of which a declaration has been made in accordance with paragraph 1 of this Article, this Convention shall apply to all territories for the foreign relations of which a Contracting State is responsible.
4. Any State may adhere to this Convention separately on behalf of all or any of the territories regarding which it has made a declaration in accordance with paragraph 1 of

this Article and the provisions of paragraphs 2 and 3 of Article XXI shall apply to such adherence.

5. Any Contracting State may denounce this Convention, in accordance with the provisions of Article XXII, separately for all or any of the territories for the foreign relations of which such State is responsible.

In witness whereof the undersigned Plenipotentiaries, having been duly authorized, have signed this Convention.

Done at Geneva, on the nineteenth day of the month of June of the year one thousand nine hundred and forty-eight in the English, French and Spanish languages, each text being of equal authenticity.

This Convention shall be deposited in the archives of the International Civil Aviation Organization where, in accordance with Article XVIII, it shall remain open for signature.

TABLE OF STATE RATIFICATIONS

Total number of signatures not followed by ratifications: 8
Total number of ratifications/accessions: 87

Geneva, 19 June 1948
Entered into force: 17 September 1953 (Condition: 2 ratifications)

State	Signature	Ratification	By	Entry into force
Algeria		10 August 1964	Accession	8 November 1964
Angola		24 February 1998	Accession	25 May 1998
Argentina	19 June 1948	31 January 1958		1 May 1958
Australia	9 June 1950			
Azerbaijan		23 March 2000	Accession	21 June 2000
Bahrain		3 March 1997	Accession	1 June 1997
Bangladesh		6 January 1988	Accession	5 April 1988
Belgium	19 June 1948	22 October 1993		20 January 1994
Bolivia		9 July 1998	Accession	7 October 1998
Bosnia and Herzegovina		7 March 1995	Succession	6 March 1992
Brazil	19 June 1948	3 July 1953		1 October 1953
Cameroon		23 July 1969	Accession	21 October 1969
Central African Republic		2 June 1969	Accession	31 August 1969
Chad		14 February 1974	Accession	15 May 1974
Chile	19 June 1948	19 December 1955		18 March 1956
China	19 June 1948	28 April 2000	Adherence	27 July 2000
Colombia	19 June 1948			
Congo		3 May 1982	Accession	1 August 1982
Côte d'Ivoire		23 August 1965	Accession	21 November 1965
Croatia		5 October 1993	Succession	3 January 1994
Cuba	20 June 1949	20 June 1961		18 September 1961
Czech Republic		24 August 1998	Accession	22 November 1998
Denmark	3 January 1949	18 January 1963		18 April 1963
Dominican Republic	19 June 1948			

State	Signature	Ratification	By	Entry into force
Ecuador		14 July 1958	Accession	12 October 1958
Egypt		10 September 1969	Accession	9 December 1969
El Salvador		14 August 1958	Accession	12 November 1958
Estonia		31 December 1993	Accession	31 March 1994
Ethiopia		7 June 1979	Accession	5 September 1979
France	19 June 1948	27 February 1964		27 May 1964
Gabon		14 January 1970	Accession	14 April 1970
Gambia		20 June 2000	Accession	18 September 2000
Germany		7 July 1959	Accession	5 October 1959
Ghana		15 July 1997	Accession	13 October 1997
Greece	19 June 1948	23 February 1971		24 May 1971
Grenada		28 August 1985	Accession	26 November 1985
Guatemala		9 August 1988	Accession	7 November 1988
Guinea		13 August 1980	Accession	11 November 1980
Haiti		24 March 1961	Accession	22 June 1961
Hungary		21 May 1993	Accession	19 August 1993
Iceland	19 June 1948	6 February 1967		7 May 1967
Iran (Islamic Republic of)	18 March 1950			
Iraq		12 January 1981	Accession	12 April 1981
Ireland	30 November 1948			
Italy	19 June 1948	6 December 1960		6 March 1961
Kenya		15 January 1997	Accession	15 April 1997
Kuwait		27 November 1979	Accession	25 February 1980
Kyrgyzstan		28 February 2000	Accession	28 May 2000
Lao People's Democratic Republic		4 June 1956	Accession	2 September 1956
Lebanon		11 April 1969	Accession	10 July 1969
Libyan Arab Jamahiriya		5 March 1973	Accession	4 June 1973
Luxembourg		16 December 1975	Accession	15 March 1976
Madagascar		9 January 1979	Accession	9 April 1979
Maldives		5 September 1995	Accession	4 December 1995
Mali		28 December 1961	Accession	28 March 1962
Mauritania		23 July 1962	Accession	21 October 1962
Mauritius		17 April 1991	Accession	16 July 1991
Mexico	19 June 1948	5 April 1950		17 September 1953
Monaco		14 December 1994	Accession	14 March 1995
Morocco		13 December 1993	Accession	13 March 1994
Netherlands	19 June 1948	1 September 1959		30 November 1959
Niger		27 December 1962	Accession	27 March 1963
Nigeria		10 May 2002	Accession	8 August 2002
Norway	3 January 1949	5 March 1954		3 June 1954
Oman		19 March 1992	Accession	17 June 1992
Pakistan	21 August 1951	19 June 1953		17 September 1953
Panama		26 October 1998	Accession	24 January 1999
Paraguay		26 September 1969	Accession	25 December 1969
Peru	19 June 1948			
Philippines		22 February 1978	Accession	23 May 1978
Portugal	19 June 1948	12 December 1985		12 March 1986
Romania		26 October 1994	Accession	24 January 1995
Rwanda		17 May 1971	Accession	15 August 1971

State	Signature	Ratification	By	Entry into force
Senegal		20 December 1995	Accession	19 March 1996
Serbia and Montenegro		6 September 2001	Succession	27 April 1992
Seychelles		16 January 1979	Accession	16 April 1979
Slovenia		9 April 1997	Accession	8 July 1997
South Africa		21 September 1998	Accession	20 December 1998
Sri Lanka		24 January 1994	Accession	24 April 1994
Surinam		27 March 2003	Accession	25 June 2003
Sweden	3 January 1949	16 November 1955		14 February 1956
Switzerland	19 June 1948	3 October 1960		1 January 1961
Tajikistan		20 March 1996	Accession	18 June 1996
Thailand		10 October 1967	Accession	8 January 1968
The former Yugoslav Republic of Macedonia		30 August 1994	Succession	17 September 1991
Togo		2 July 1980	Accession	30 September 1980
Tunisia		4 May 1966	Accession	2 August 1966
Turkmenistan		16 September 1993	Accession	15 December 1993
United Kingdom	19 June 1948			
United States	19 June 1948	6 September 1949		17 September 1953
Uruguay		21 August 1985	Accession	19 November 1985
Uzbekistan		8 May 1997	Accession	6 August 1997
Venezuela	19 June 1948			
Vietnam		18 June 1997	Accession	16 September 1997
Zimbabwe		6 February 1987	Accession	7 May 1987

Note. A list of reservations and declarations made by States has not been included in this volume. These can be obtained from http://www.icao.int/icao/en/leb/Genev.htm

(g) UNIDROIT CONVENTION ON INTERNATIONAL FINANCIAL LEASING*

(Ottawa, 28 May 1988)

PREAMBLE

The States parties to this Convention,

Recognising the importance of removing certain legal impediments to the international financial leasing of equipment, while maintaining a fair balance of interests between the different parties to the transaction,

Aware of the need to make international financial leasing more available,

Conscious of the fact that the rules of law governing the traditional contract of hire need to be adapted to the distinctive triangular relationship created by the financial leasing transaction,

Recognising therefore the desirability of formulating certain uniform rules relating primarily to the civil and commercial law aspects of international financial leasing,

Have agreed as follows:

CHAPTER I
SPHERE OF APPLICATION AND GENERAL PROVISIONS

Article 1

1. This Convention governs a financial leasing transaction as described in paragraph 2 in which one party (the lessor),
   (a) on the specifications of another party (the lessee), enters into an agreement (the supply agreement) with a third party (the supplier) under which the lessor acquires

---

* Reproduced with the kind permission of UNIDROIT.

plant, capital goods or other equipment (the equipment) on terms approved by the lessee so far as they concern its interests, and

    (b) enters into an agreement (the leasing agreement) with the lessee, granting to the lessee the right to use the equipment in return for the payment of rentals.

(2) The financial leasing transaction referred to in the previous paragraph is a transaction which includes the following characteristics:

    (a) the lessee specifies the equipment and selects the supplier without relying primarily on the skill and judgment of the lessor;

    (b) the equipment is acquired by the lessor in connection with a leasing agreement which, to the knowledge of the supplier, either has been made or is to be made between the lessor and the lessee; and

    (c) the rentals payable under the leasing agreement are calculated so as to take into account in particular the amortisation of the whole or a substantial part of the cost of the equipment.

(3) This Convention applies whether or not the lessee has or subsequently acquires the option to buy the equipment or to hold it on lease for a further period, and whether or not for a nominal price or rental.

(4) This Convention applies to financial leasing transactions in relation to all equipment save that which is to be used primarily for the lessee's personal, family or household purposes.

Article 2

In the case of one or more sub-leasing transactions involving the same equipment, this Convention applies to each transaction which is a financial leasing transaction and is otherwise subject to this Convention as if the person from whom the first lessor (as defined in paragraph 1 of the previous article) acquired the equipment were the supplier and as if the agreement under which the equipment was so acquired were the supply agreement.

Article 3

1. This Convention applies when the lessor and the lessee have their places of business in different States and:

    (a) those States and the State in which the supplier has its place of business are Contracting States; or

    (b) both the supply agreement and the leasing agreement are governed by the law of a Contracting State.

(2) A reference in this Convention to a party's place of business shall, if it has more than one place of business, mean the place of business which has the closest relationship to the relevant agreement and its performance, having regard to the circumstances known to or contemplated by the parties at any time before or at the conclusion of that agreement.

Article 4

1. The provisions of this Convention shall not cease to apply merely because the equipment has become a fixture to or incorporated in land.

2. Any question whether or not the equipment has become a fixture to or incorporated in land, and if so the effect on the rights *inter se* of the lessor and a person having real rights in the land, shall be determined by the law of the State where the land is situated.

Article 5

1. The application of this Convention may be excluded only if each of the parties to the supply agreement and each of the parties to the leasing agreement agree to exclude it.
2. Where the application of this Convention has not been excluded in accordance with the previous paragraph, the parties may, in their relations with each other, derogate from or vary the effect of any of its provisions except as stated in Articles 8(3) and 13(3)(b) and (4).

Article 6

1. In the interpretation of this Convention, regard is to be had to its object and purpose as set forth in the preamble, to its international character and to the need to promote uniformity in its application and the observance of good faith in international trade.
2. Questions concerning matters governed by this Convention which are not expressly settled in it are to be settled in conformity with the general principles on which it is based or, in the absence of such principles, in conformity with the law applicable by virtue of the rules of private international law.

CHAPTER II
RIGHTS AND DUTIES OF THE PARTIES

Article 7

1.—(a) The lessor's real rights in the equipment shall be valid against the lessee's trustee in bankruptcy and creditors, including creditors who have obtained an attachment or execution.
   (b) For the purposes of this paragraph 'trustee in bankruptcy' includes a liquidator, administrator or other person appointed to administer the lessee's estate for the benefit of the general body of creditors.
2. Where by the applicable law the lessor's real rights in the equipment are valid against a person referred to in the previous paragraph only on compliance with rules as to public notice, those rights shall be valid against that person only if there has been compliance with such rules.
3. For the purposes of the previous paragraph the applicable law is the law of the State which, at the time when a person referred to in paragraph 1 becomes entitled to invoke the rules referred to in the previous paragraph, is :
   (a) in the case of a registered ship, the State in which it is registered in the name of the owner (for the purposes of this sub-paragraph a bareboat charterer is deemed not to be the owner);
   (b) in the case of an aircraft which is registered pursuant to the Convention on International Civil Aviation done at Chicago on 7 December 1944, the State in which it is so registered;
   (c) in the case of other equipment of a kind normally moved from one State to another, including an aircraft engine, the State in which the lessee has its principal place of business;
   (d) in the case of all other equipment, the State in which the equipment is situated.

543

4. Paragraph 2 shall not affect the provisions of any other treaty under which the lessor's real rights in the equipment are required to be recognised.
5. This article shall not affect the priority of any creditor having:
    (a) a consensual or non-consensual lien or security interest in the equipment arising otherwise than by virtue of an attachment or execution, or
    (b) any right of arrest, detention or disposition conferred specifically in relation to ships or aircraft under the law applicable by virtue of the rules of private international law.

Article 8

1.—(a) Except as otherwise provided by this Convention or stated in the leasing agreement, the lessor shall not incur any liability to the lessee in respect of the equipment save to the extent that the lessee has suffered loss as the result of its reliance on the lessor's skill and judgment and of the lessor's intervention in the selection of the supplier or the specifications of the equipment.
    (b) The lessor shall not, in its capacity of lessor, be liable to third parties for death, personal injury or damage to property caused by the equipment.
    (c) The above provisions of this paragraph shall not govern any liability of the lessor in any other capacity, for example as owner.
2. The lessor warrants that the lessee's quiet possession will not be disturbed by a person who has a superior title or right, or who claims a superior title or right and acts under the authority of a court, where such title, right or claim is not derived from an act or omission of the lessee.
3. The parties may not derogate from or vary the effect of the provisions of the previous paragraph in so far as the superior title, right or claim is derived from an intentional or grossly negligent act or omission of the lessor.
4. The provisions of paragraphs 2 and 3 shall not affect any broader warranty of quiet possession by the lessor which is mandatory under the law applicable by virtue of the rules of private international law.

Article 9

1. The lessee shall take proper care of the equipment, use it in a reasonable manner and keep it in the condition in which it was delivered, subject to fair wear and tear and to any modification of the equipment agreed by the parties.
2. When the leasing agreement comes to an end the lessee, unless exercising a right to buy the equipment or to hold the equipment on lease for a further period, shall return the equipment to the lessor in the condition specified in the previous paragraph.

Article 10

1. The duties of the supplier under the supply agreement shall also be owed to the lessee as if it were a party to that agreement and as if the equipment were to be supplied directly to the lessee. However, the supplier shall not be liable to both the lessor and the lessee in respect of the same damage.
2. Nothing in this article shall entitle the lessee to terminate or rescind the supply agreement without the consent of the lessor.

Article 11

The lessee's rights derived from the supply agreement under this Convention shall not be affected by a variation of any term of the supply agreement previously approved by the lessee unless it consented to that variation.

Article 12

1. Where the equipment is not delivered or is delivered late or fails to conform to the supply agreement:
   (a) the lessee has the right as against the lessor to reject the equipment or to terminate the leasing agreement; and
   (b) the lessor has the right to remedy its failure to tender equipment in conformity with the supply agreement,

as if the lessee had agreed to buy the equipment from the lessor under the same terms as those of the supply agreement.

2. A right conferred by the previous paragraph shall be exercisable in the same manner and shall be lost in the same circumstances as if the lessee had agreed to buy the equipment from the lessor under the same terms as those of the supply agreement.
3. The lessee shall be entitled to withhold rentals payable under the leasing agreement until the lessor has remedied its failure to tender equipment in conformity with the supply agreement or the lessee has lost the right to reject the equipment.
4. Where the lessee has exercised a right to terminate the leasing agreement, the lessee shall be entitled to recover any rentals and other sums paid in advance, less a reasonable sum for any benefit the lessee has derived from the equipment.
5. The lessee shall have no other claim against the lessor for non-delivery, delay in delivery or delivery of non-conforming equipment except to the extent to which this results from the act or omission of the lessor.
6. Nothing in this article shall affect the lessee's rights against the supplier under Article 10.

Article 13

1. In the event of default by the lessee, the lessor may recover accrued unpaid rentals, together with interest and damages.
2. Where the lessee's default is substantial, then subject to paragraph 5 the lessor may also require accelerated payment of the value of the future rentals, where the leasing agreement so provides, or may terminate the leasing agreement and after such termination:
   (a) recover possession of the equipment; and
   (b) recover such damages as will place the lessor in the position in which it would have been had the lessee performed the leasing agreement in accordance with its terms.
3.—(a) The leasing agreement may provide for the manner in which the damages recoverable under paragraph 2(b) are to be computed.
   (b) Such provision shall be enforceable between the parties unless it would result in damages substantially in excess of those provided for under paragraph 2(b). The parties may not derogate from or vary the effect of the provisions of the present sub-paragraph.
4. Where the lessor has terminated the leasing agreement, it shall not be entitled to enforce a term of that agreement providing for acceleration of payment of future

rentals, but the value of such rentals may be taken into account in computing damages under paragraphs 2(b) and 3. The parties may not derogate from or vary the effect of the provisions of the present paragraph.

5. The lessor shall not be entitled to exercise its right of acceleration or its right of termination under paragraph 2 unless it has by notice given the lessee a reasonable opportunity of remedying the default so far as the same may be remedied.

6. The lessor shall not be entitled to recover damages to the extent that it has failed to take all reasonable steps to mitigate its loss.

Article 14

1. The lessor may transfer or otherwise deal with all or any of its rights in the equipment or under the leasing agreement. Such a transfer shall not relieve the lessor of any of its duties under the leasing agreement or alter either the nature of the leasing agreement or its legal treatment as provided in this Convention.

2. The lessee may transfer the right to the use of the equipment or any other rights under the leasing agreement only with the consent of the lessor and subject to the rights of third parties.

CHAPTER III
FINAL PROVISIONS

Article 15

1. This Convention is open for signature at the concluding meeting of the Diplomatic Conference for the Adoption of the Draft UNIDROIT Conventions on International Factoring and International Financial Leasing and will remain open for signature by all States at Ottawa until 31 December 1990.

2. This Convention is subject to ratification, acceptance or approval by States which have signed it.

3. This Convention is open for accession by all States which are not signatory States as from the date it is open for signature.

4. Ratification, acceptance, approval or accession is effected by the deposit of a formal instrument to that effect with the depositary.

Article 16

1. This convention enters into force on the first day of the month following the expiration of six months after the date of deposit of the third instrument of ratification, acceptance, approval or accession.

2. For each State that ratifies, accepts, approves, or accedes to this Convention after the deposit of the third instrument of ratification, acceptance, approval or accession, this Convention enters into force in respect of that State on the first day of the month following the expiration of six months after the date of the deposit of its instrument of ratification, acceptance, approval or accession.

Article 17

This Convention does not prevail over any treaty which has already been or may be entered into; in particular it shall not affect any liability imposed on any person by existing or future treaties.

Article 18

1. If a Contracting State has two or more territorial units in which different systems of law are applicable in relation to the matters dealt with in this Convention, it may, at the time of signature, ratification, acceptance, approval or accession, declare that this Convention is to extend to all its territorial units or only to one or more of them, and may substitute its declaration by another declaration at any time.
2. These declarations are to be notified to the depositary and are to state expressly the territorial units to which the Convention extends.
3. If, by virtue of a declaration under this article, this Convention extends to one or more but not all of the territorial units of a Contracting State, and if the place of business of a party is located in that State, this place of business, for the purposes of this Convention, is considered not to be in a Contracting State, unless it is in a territorial unit to which the Convention extends.
4. If a Contracting State makes no declaration under paragraph 1, the Convention is to extend to all territorial units of that State.

Article 19

1. Two or more Contracting States which have the same or closely related legal rules on matters governed by this Convention may at any time declare that the Convention is not to apply where the supplier, the lessor and the lessee have their places of business in those States. Such declarations may be made jointly or by reciprocal unilateral declarations.
2. A Contracting State which has the same or closely related legal rules on matters governed by this Convention as one or more non-Contracting States may at any time declare that the Convention is not to apply where the supplier, the lessor and the lessee have their places of business in those States.
3. If a State which is the object of a declaration under the previous paragraph subsequently becomes a Contracting State, the declaration made will, as from the date on which the Convention enters into force in respect of the new Contracting State, have the affect of a declaration made under paragraph 1, provided that the new Contracting State joins in such declaration or makes a reciprocal unilateral declaration.

Article 20

A Contracting State may declare at the time of signature, ratification, acceptance, approval or accession that it will substitute its domestic law for Article 8(3) if its domestic law does not permit the lessor to exclude its liability for its default or negligence.

Article 21

1. Declarations made under this Convention at the time of signature are subject to confirmation upon ratification, acceptance or approval.
2. Declarations and confirmations of declarations are to be in writing and to be formally notified to the depositary.
3. A declaration takes effect simultaneously with the entry into force of this Convention in respect of the State concerned. However, a declaration of which the depositary receives formal notification after such entry into force takes effect on the first day of the

month following the expiration of six months after the date of its receipt by the depositary. Reciprocal unilateral declarations under Article 19 take effect on the first day of the month following the expiration of six months after the receipt of the latest declaration by the depositary.

4. Any State which makes a declaration under this Convention may withdraw it at any time by a formal notification in writing addressed to the depositary. Such withdrawal is to take effect on the first day of the month following the expiration of six months after the date of the receipt of the notification by the depositary.

5. A withdrawal of a declaration made under Article 19 renders inoperative in relation to the withdrawing State, as from the date on which the withdrawal takes effect, any joint or reciprocal unilateral declaration made by another State under that article.

Article 22

No reservations are permitted except those expressly authorised in this Convention.

Article 23

This Convention applies to a financial leasing transaction when the leasing agreement and the supply agreement are both concluded on or after the date on which the Convention enters into force in respect of the Contracting States referred to in Article 3(1)(a), or of the Contracting State or States referred to in paragraph 1(b) of that article.

Article 24

1. This Convention may be denounced by any Contracting State at any time after the date on which it enters into force for that State.

2. Denunciation is effected by the deposit of an instrument to that effect with the depositary.

3. A denunciation takes effect on the first day of the month following the expiration of six months after the deposit of the instrument of denunciation with the depositary. Where a longer period for the denunciation to take effect is specified in the instrument of denunciation it takes effect upon the expiration of such longer period after its deposit with the depositary.

Article 25

1. This Convention shall be deposited with the Government of Canada.

2. The Government of Canada shall:

  (a) inform all States which have signed or acceded to this Convention and the President of the International Institute for the Unification of Private Law (UNIDROIT) of:

    (i) each new signature or deposit of an instrument of ratification, acceptance, approval or accession, together with the date thereof;

    (ii) each declaration made under Articles 18, 19 and 20;

    (iii) the withdrawal of any declaration made under Article 21(4);

    (iv) the date of entry into force of this Convention;

    (v) the deposit of an instrument of denunciation of this Convention together with the date of its deposit and the date on which it takes effect;

(b) transmit certified true copies of this Convention to all signatory States, to all States acceding to the Convention and to the President of the International Institute for the Unification of Private Law (UNIDROIT).

In witness whereof the undersigned plenipotentiaries, being duly authorised by their respective Governments, have signed this Convention.

Done at Ottawa, this twenty-eighth day of May, one thousand nine hundred and eighty-eight, in a single original, of which the English and French texts are equally authentic.

TABLE OF STATE RATIFICATIONS

Total number of signatures not followed by ratifications: 9
Total number of ratifications/accessions: 9

Entered into force: 1 May 1995
(Condition: 3 ratifications)

State	Signature	Ratification	By	Entry into force
Belarus		18 August 1998	Accession	1 March 1999
Belgium	21 December 1990			
Czechoslovakia	16 May 1990			
Finland	30 November 1990			
France	7 November 1989	23 September 1991		1 May 1995
Ghana	28 May 1988			
Guinea	28 May 1988			
Hungary		7 May 1996	Accession	1 December 1996
Italy	13 December 1990	29 November 1993		1 May 1995
Latvia		6 August 1997	Accession	1 March 1998
Morocco	4 July 1988			
Nigeria	28 May 1988	25 October 1994		1 May 1995
Panama	31 December 1990	26 March 1997		1 October 1997
Philippines	28 May 1988			
Republic of Uzbekistan		6 July 2000	Accession	1 February 2001
Russian Federation		3 June 1998	Accession	1 January 1999
United Republic of Tanzania	28 May 1988			
United States of America	28 December 1990			

Note. A list of reservations and declarations made by States has not been included in this volume. These can be obtained from http://www.unidroit.org/english/implement/i-88-l.htm.

(h) CONVENTION ON INTERNATIONAL INTERESTS IN MOBILE EQUIPMENT ON MATTERS SPECIFIC TO AIRCRAFT EQUIPMENT 2001*

* Reproduced with the kind permission of UNIDROIT.

PREAMBLE

The States parties to this Convention,

Aware of the need to acquire and use mobile equipment of high value or particular economic significance and to facilitate the financing of the acquisition and use of such equipment in an efficient manner,

Recognising the advantages of asset-based financing and leasing for this purpose and desiring to facilitate these types of transaction by establishing clear rules to govern them,

Mindful of the need to ensure that interests in such equipment are recognised and protected universally,

Desiring to provide broad and mutual economic benefits for all interested parties,

Believing that such rules must reflect the principles underlying asset-based financing and leasing and promote the autonomy of the parties necessary in these transactions,

Conscious of the need to establish a legal framework for international interests in such equipment and for that purpose to create an international registration system for their protection,

Taking into consideration the objectives and principles enunciated in existing Conventions relating to such equipment,

Have agreed upon the following provisions:

CHAPTER I
SPHERE OF APPLICATION AND GENERAL PROVISIONS

Article 1
Definitions

In this Convention, except where the context otherwise requires, the following terms are employed with the meanings set out below:

(a) 'agreement' means a security agreement, a title reservation agreement or a leasing agreement;

(b) 'assignment' means a contract which, whether by way of security or otherwise, confers on the assignee associated rights with or without a transfer of the related international interest;

(c) 'associated rights' means all rights to payment or other performance by a debtor under an agreement which are secured by or associated with the object;

(d) 'commencement of the insolvency proceedings' means the time at which the insolvency proceedings are deemed to commence under the applicable insolvency law;

(e) 'conditional buyer' means a buyer under a title reservation agreement;

(f) 'conditional seller' means a seller under a title reservation agreement;

(g) 'contract of sale' means a contract for the sale of an object by a seller to a buyer which is not an agreement as defined in (a) above;

(h) 'court' means a court of law or an administrative or arbitral tribunal established by a Contracting State;

(i) 'creditor' means a chargee under a security agreement, a conditional seller under a title reservation agreement or a lessor under a leasing agreement;

(j) 'debtor' means a chargor under a security agreement, a conditional buyer under a title reservation agreement, a lessee under a leasing agreement or a person whose interest in an object is burdened by a registrable non-consensual right or interest;

(k) 'insolvency administrator' means a person authorised to administer the reorganisation or liquidation, including one authorised on an interim basis, and includes a debtor in possession if permitted by the applicable insolvency law;

(l) 'insolvency proceedings' means bankruptcy, liquidation or other collective judicial or administrative proceedings, including interim proceedings, in which the assets and affairs of the debtor are subject to control or supervision by a court for the purposes of reorganisation or liquidation;

(m) 'interested persons' means:
   (i) the debtor;
   (ii) any person who, for the purpose of assuring performance of any of the obligations in favour of the creditor, gives or issues a suretyship or demand guarantee or a standby letter of credit or any other form of credit insurance;
   (iii) any other person having rights in or over the object;

(n) 'internal transaction' means a transaction of a type listed in Article 2(2)(a) to (c) where the centre of the main interests of all parties to such transaction is situated, and the relevant object located (as specified in the Protocol), in the same

Contracting State at the time of the conclusion of the contract and where the interest created by the transaction has been registered in a national registry in that Contracting State which has made a declaration under Article 50(1);

(o) 'international interest' means an interest held by a creditor to which Article 2 applies;

(p) 'International Registry' means the international registration facilities established for the purposes of this Convention or the Protocol;

(q) 'leasing agreement' means an agreement by which one person (the lessor) grants a right to possession or control of an object (with or without an option to purchase) to another person (the lessee) in return for a rental or other payment;

(r) 'national interest' means an interest held by a creditor in an object and created by an internal transaction covered by a declaration under Article 50(1);

(s) 'non-consensual right or interest' means a right or interest conferred under the law of a Contracting State which has made a declaration under Article 39 to secure the performance of an obligation, including an obligation to a State, State entity or an intergovernmental or private organisation;

(t) 'notice of a national interest' means notice registered or to be registered in the International Registry that a national interest has been created;

(u) 'object' means an object of a category to which Article 2 applies;

(v) 'pre-existing right or interest' means a right or interest of any kind in or over an object created or arising before the effective date of this Convention as defined by Article 60(2)(a);

(w) 'proceeds' means money or non-money proceeds of an object arising from the total or partial loss or physical destruction of the object or its total or partial confiscation, condemnation or requisition;

(x) 'prospective assignment' means an assignment that is intended to be made in the future, upon the occurrence of a stated event, whether or not the occurrence of the event is certain;

(y) 'prospective international interest' means an interest that is intended to be created or provided for in an object as an international interest in the future, upon the occurrence of a stated event (which may include the debtor's acquisition of an interest in the object), whether or not the occurrence of the event is certain;

(z) 'prospective sale' means a sale which is intended to be made in the future, upon the occurrence of a stated event, whether or not the occurrence of the event is certain;

(aa) 'Protocol' means, in respect of any category of object and associated rights to which this Convention applies, the Protocol in respect of that category of object and associated rights;

(bb) 'registered' means registered in the International Registry pursuant to Chapter V;

(cc) 'registered interest' means an international interest, a registrable non-consensual right or interest or a national interest specified in a notice of a national interest registered pursuant to Chapter V;

(dd) 'registrable non-consensual right or interest' means a non-consensual right or interest registrable pursuant to a declaration deposited under Article 40;

(ee) 'Registrar' means, in respect of the Protocol, the person or body designated by that Protocol or appointed under Article 17(2)(b);

(ff) 'regulations' means regulations made or approved by the Supervisory Authority pursuant to the Protocol;

(gg) 'sale' means a transfer of ownership of an object pursuant to a contract of sale;

(hh) 'secured obligation' means an obligation secured by a security interest;

(ii) 'security agreement' means an agreement by which a chargor grants or agrees to grant to a chargee an interest (including an ownership interest) in or over an object to secure the performance of any existing or future obligation of the chargor or a third person;

(jj) 'security interest' means an interest created by a security agreement;

(kk) 'Supervisory Authority' means, in respect of the Protocol, the Supervisory Authority referred to in Article 17(1);

(ll) 'title reservation agreement' means an agreement for the sale of an object on terms that ownership does not pass until fulfilment of the condition or conditions stated in the agreement;

(mm) 'unregistered interest' means a consensual interest or non-consensual right or interest (other than an interest to which Article 39 applies) which has not been registered, whether or not it is registrable under this Convention; and

(nn) 'writing' means a record of information (including information communicated by teletransmission) which is in tangible or other form and is capable of being reproduced in tangible form on a subsequent occasion and which indicates by reasonable means a person's approval of the record.

Article 2
The international interest

1. This Convention provides for the constitution and effects of an international interest in certain categories of mobile equipment and associated rights.

2. For the purposes of this Convention, an international interest in mobile equipment is an interest, constituted under Article 7, in a uniquely identifiable object of a category of such objects listed in paragraph 3 and designated in the Protocol:

   (a) granted by the chargor under a security agreement;

   (b) vested in a person who is the conditional seller under a title reservation agreement; or

   (c) vested in a person who is the lessor under a leasing agreement.

   An interest falling within sub-paragraph (a) does not also fall within sub-paragraph (b) or (c).

3. The categories referred to in the preceding paragraphs are:

   (a) airframes, aircraft engines and helicopters;

   (b) railway rolling stock; and

   (c) space assets.

4. The applicable law determines whether an interest to which paragraph 2 applies falls within sub-paragraph (a), (b) or (c) of that paragraph.

5. An international interest in an object extends to proceeds of that object.

Article 3
Sphere of application

1. This Convention applies when, at the time of the conclusion of the agreement creating or providing for the international interest, the debtor is situated in a Contracting State.

2. The fact that the creditor is situated in a non-Contracting State does not affect the applicability of this Convention.

Article 4
Where debtor is situated

1. For the purposes of Article 3(1), the debtor is situated in any Contracting State:
   (a) under the law of which it is incorporated or formed;
   (b) where it has its registered office or statutory seat;
   (c) where it has its centre of administration; or
   (d) where it has its place of business.
2. A reference in sub-paragraph (d) of the preceding paragraph to the debtor's place of business shall, if it has more than one place of business, mean its principal place of business or, if it has no place of business, its habitual residence.

Article 5
Interpretation and applicable law

1. In the interpretation of this Convention, regard is to be had to its purposes as set forth in the preamble, to its international character and to the need to promote uniformity and predictability in its application.
2. Questions concerning matters governed by this Convention which are not expressly settled in it are to be settled in conformity with the general principles on which it is based or, in the absence of such principles, in conformity with the applicable law.
3. References to the applicable law are to the domestic rules of the law applicable by virtue of the rules of private international law of the forum State.
4. Where a State comprises several territorial units, each of which has its own rules of law in respect of the matter to be decided, and where there is no indication of the relevant territorial unit, the law of that State decides which is the territorial unit whose rules shall govern. In the absence of any such rule, the law of the territorial unit with which the case is most closely connected shall apply.

Article 6
Relationship between the Convention and the Protocol

1. This Convention and the Protocol shall be read and interpreted together as a single instrument.
2. To the extent of any inconsistency between this Convention and the Protocol, the Protocol shall prevail.

CHAPTER II
CONSTITUTION OF AN INTERNATIONAL INTEREST

Article 7
Formal requirements

An interest is constituted as an international interest under this Convention where the agreement creating or providing for the interest:
   (a) is in writing;
   (b) relates to an object of which the chargor, conditional seller or lessor has power to dispose;

(c) enables the object to be identified in conformity with the Protocol; and

(d) in the case of a security agreement, enables the secured obligations to be determined, but without the need to state a sum or maximum sum secured.

CHAPTER III
DEFAULT REMEDIES

Article 8
Remedies of chargee

1. In the event of default as provided in Article 11, the chargee may, to the extent that the chargor has at any time so agreed and subject to any declaration that may be made by a Contracting State under Article 54, exercise any one or more of the following remedies:
   (a) take possession or control of any object charged to it;
   (b) sell or grant a lease of any such object;
   (c) collect or receive any income or profits arising from the management or use of any such object.

2. The chargee may alternatively apply for a court order authorising or directing any of the acts referred to in the preceding paragraph.

3. Any remedy set out in sub-paragraph (a), (b) or (c) of paragraph 1 or by Article 13 shall be exercised in a commercially reasonable manner. A remedy shall be deemed to be exercised in a commercially reasonable manner where it is exercised in conformity with a provision of the security agreement except where such a provision is manifestly unreasonable.

4. A chargee proposing to sell or grant a lease of an object under paragraph 1 shall give reasonable prior notice in writing of the proposed sale or lease to:
   (a) interested persons specified in Article 1(m)(i) and (ii); and
   (b) interested persons specified in Article 1(m)(iii) who have given notice of their rights to the chargee within a reasonable time prior to the sale or lease.

5. Any sum collected or received by the chargee as a result of exercise of any of the remedies set out in paragraph 1 or 2 shall be applied towards discharge of the amount of the secured obligations.

6. Where the sums collected or received by the chargee as a result of the exercise of any remedy set out in paragraph 1 or 2 exceed the amount secured by the security interest and any reasonable costs incurred in the exercise of any such remedy, then unless otherwise ordered by the court the chargee shall distribute the surplus among holders of subsequently ranking interests which have been registered or of which the chargee has been given notice, in order of priority, and pay any remaining balance to the chargor.

Article 9
Vesting of object in satisfaction; redemption

1. At any time after default as provided in Article 11, the chargee and all the interested persons may agree that ownership of (or any other interest of the chargor in) any object covered by the security interest shall vest in the chargee in or towards satisfaction of the secured obligations.

2. The court may on the application of the chargee order that ownership of (or any other interest of the chargor in) any object covered by the security interest shall vest in the chargee in or towards satisfaction of the secured obligations.

3. The court shall grant an application under the preceding paragraph only if the amount of the secured obligations to be satisfied by such vesting is commensurate with the value of the object after taking account of any payment to be made by the chargee to any of the interested persons.

4. At any time after default as provided in Article 11 and before sale of the charged object or the making of an order under paragraph 2, the chargor or any interested person may discharge the security interest by paying in full the amount secured, subject to any lease granted by the chargee under Article 8(1)(b) or ordered under Article 8(2). Where, after such default, the payment of the amount secured is made in full by an interested person other than the debtor, that person is subrogated to the rights of the chargee.

5. Ownership or any other interest of the chargor passing on a sale under Article 8(1)(b) or passing under paragraph 1 or 2 of this Article is free from any other interest over which the chargee's security interest has priority under the provisions of Article 29.

Article 10
Remedies of conditional seller or lessor

In the event of default under a title reservation agreement or under a leasing agreement as provided in Article 11, the conditional seller or the lessor, as the case may be, may:

(a) subject to any declaration that may be made by a Contracting State under Article 54, terminate the agreement and take possession or control of any object to which the agreement relates; or

(b) apply for a court order authorising or directing either of these acts.

Article 11
Meaning of default

1. The debtor and the creditor may at any time agree in writing as to the events that constitute a default or otherwise give rise to the rights and remedies specified in Articles 8 to 10 and 13.

2. Where the debtor and the creditor have not so agreed, 'default' for the purposes of Articles 8 to 10 and 13 means a default which substantially deprives the creditor of what it is entitled to expect under the agreement.

Article 12
Additional remedies

Any additional remedies permitted by the applicable law, including any remedies agreed upon by the parties, may be exercised to the extent that they are not inconsistent with the mandatory provisions of this Chapter as set out in Article 15.

Article 13
Relief pending final determination

1. Subject to any declaration that it may make under Article 55, a Contracting State shall ensure that a creditor who adduces evidence of default by the debtor may, pending final determination of its claim and to the extent that the debtor has at any time so

agreed, obtain from a court speedy relief in the form of such one or more of the following orders as the creditor requests:

(a) preservation of the object and its value;

(b) possession, control or custody of the object;

(c) immobilisation of the object; and

(d) lease or, except where covered by sub-paragraphs (a) to (c), management of the object and the income therefrom.

2. In making any order under the preceding paragraph, the court may impose such terms as it considers necessary to protect the interested persons in the event that the creditor:

(a) in implementing any order granting such relief, fails to perform any of its obligations to the debtor under this Convention or the Protocol; or

(b) fails to establish its claim, wholly or in part, on the final determination of that claim.

3. Before making any order under paragraph 1, the court may require notice of the request to be given to any of the interested persons.

4. Nothing in this Article affects the application of Article 8(3) or limits the availability of forms of interim relief other than those set out in paragraph 1.

Article 14
Procedural requirements

Subject to Article 54(2), any remedy provided by this Chapter shall be exercised in conformity with the procedure prescribed by the law of the place where the remedy is to be exercised.

Article 15
Derogation

In their relations with each other, any two or more of the parties referred to in this Chapter may at any time, by agreement in writing, derogate from or vary the effect of any of the preceding provisions of this Chapter except Articles 8(3) to (6), 9(3) and (4), 13(2) and 14.

CHAPTER IV
THE INTERNATIONAL REGISTRATION SYSTEM

Article 16
The International Registry

1. An International Registry shall be established for registrations of:

(a) international interests, prospective international interests and registrable non-consensual rights and interests;

(b) assignments and prospective assignments of international interests;

(c) acquisitions of international interests by legal or contractual subrogations under the applicable law;

(d) notices of national interests; and

(e) subordinations of interests referred to in any of the preceding sub-paragraphs.

2. Different international registries may be established for different categories of object and associated rights.

3. For the purposes of this Chapter and Chapter V, the term 'registration' includes, where appropriate, an amendment, extension or discharge of a registration.

Article 17
The Supervisory Authority and the Registrar

1. There shall be a Supervisory Authority as provided by the Protocol.
2. The Supervisory Authority shall:
   (a) establish or provide for the establishment of the International Registry;
   (b) except as otherwise provided by the Protocol, appoint and dismiss the Registrar;
   (c) ensure that any rights required for the continued effective operation of the International Registry in the event of a change of Registrar will vest in or be assignable to the new Registrar;
   (d) after consultation with the Contracting States, make or approve and ensure the publication of regulations pursuant to the Protocol dealing with the operation of the International Registry;
   (e) establish administrative procedures through which complaints concerning the operation of the International Registry can be made to the Supervisory Authority;
   (f) supervise the Registrar and the operation of the International Registry;
   (g) at the request of the Registrar, provide such guidance to the Registrar as the Supervisory Authority thinks fit;
   (h) set and periodically review the structure of fees to be charged for the services and facilities of the International Registry;
   (i) do all things necessary to ensure that an efficient notice-based electronic registration system exists to implement the objectives of this Convention and the Protocol; and
   (j) report periodically to Contracting States concerning the discharge of its obligations under this Convention and the Protocol.
3. The Supervisory Authority may enter into any agreement requisite for the performance of its functions, including any agreement referred to in Article 27(3).
4. The Supervisory Authority shall own all proprietary rights in the data bases and archives of the International Registry.
5. The Registrar shall ensure the efficient operation of the International Registry and perform the functions assigned to it by this Convention, the Protocol and the regulations.

CHAPTER V
OTHER MATTERS RELATING TO REGISTRATION

Article 18
Registration requirements

1. The Protocol and regulations shall specify the requirements, including the criteria for the identification of the object:
   (a) for effecting a registration (which shall include provision for prior electronic transmission of any consent from any person whose consent is required under Article 20);
   (b) for making searches and issuing search certificates, and, subject thereto;
   (c) for ensuring the confidentiality of information and documents of the International Registry other than information and documents relating to a registration.

2. The Registrar shall not be under a duty to enquire whether a consent to registration under Article 20 has in fact been given or is valid.
3. Where an interest registered as a prospective international interest becomes an international interest, no further registration shall be required provided that the registration information is sufficient for a registration of an international interest.
4. The Registrar shall arrange for registrations to be entered into the International Registry data base and made searchable in chronological order of receipt, and the file shall record the date and time of receipt.
5. The Protocol may provide that a Contracting State may designate an entity or entities in its territory as the entry point or entry points through which the information required for registration shall or may be transmitted to the International Registry. A Contracting State making such a designation may specify the requirements, if any, to be satisfied before such information is transmitted to the International Registry.

Article 19
Validity and time of registration

1. A registration shall be valid only if made in conformity with Article 20.
2. A registration, if valid, shall be complete upon entry of the required information into the International Registry data base so as to be searchable.
3. A registration shall be searchable for the purposes of the preceding paragraph at the time when:
   (a) the International Registry has assigned to it a sequentially ordered file number; and
   (b) the registration information, including the file number, is stored in durable form and may be accessed at the International Registry.
4. If an interest first registered as a prospective international interest becomes an international interest, that international interest shall be treated as registered from the time of registration of the prospective international interest provided that the registration was still current immediately before the international interest was constituted as provided by Article 7.
5. The preceding paragraph applies with necessary modifications to the registration of a prospective assignment of an international interest.
6. A registration shall be searchable in the International Registry data base according to the criteria prescribed by the Protocol.

Article 20
Consent to registration

1. An international interest, a prospective international interest or an assignment or prospective assignment of an international interest may be registered, and any such registration amended or extended prior to its expiry, by either party with the consent in writing of the other.
2. The subordination of an international interest to another international interest may be registered by or with the consent in writing at any time of the person whose interest has been subordinated.
3. A registration may be discharged by or with the consent in writing of the party in whose favour it was made.

4. The acquisition of an international interest by legal or contractual subrogation may be registered by the subrogee.
5. A registrable non-consensual right or interest may be registered by the holder thereof.
6. A notice of a national interest may be registered by the holder thereof.

Article 21
Duration of registration

Registration of an international interest remains effective until discharged or until expiry of the period specified in the registration.

Article 22
Searches

1. Any person may, in the manner prescribed by the Protocol and regulations, make or request a search of the International Registry by electronic means concerning interests or prospective international interests registered therein.
2. Upon receipt of a request therefor, the Registrar, in the manner prescribed by the Protocol and regulations, shall issue a registry search certificate by electronic means with respect to any object:
   (a) stating all registered information relating thereto, together with a statement indicating the date and time of registration of such information; or
   (b) stating that there is no information in the International Registry relating thereto.
3. A search certificate issued under the preceding paragraph shall indicate that the creditor named in the registration information has acquired or intends to acquire an international interest in the object but shall not indicate whether what is registered is an international interest or a prospective international interest, even if this is ascertainable from the relevant registration information.

Article 23
List of declarations and declared non-consensual rights or interests

The Registrar shall maintain a list of declarations, withdrawals of declaration and of the categories of non-consensual right or interest communicated to the Registrar by the Depositary as having been declared by Contracting States in conformity with Articles 39 and 40 and the date of each such declaration or withdrawal of declaration. Such list shall be recorded and searchable in the name of the declaring State and shall be made available as provided in the Protocol and regulations to any person requesting it.

Article 24
Evidentiary value of certificates

A document in the form prescribed by the regulations which purports to be a certificate issued by the International Registry is prima facie proof:
   (a) that it has been so issued; and
   (b) of the facts recited in it, including the date and time of a registration.

Article 25
Discharge of registration

1. Where the obligations secured by a registered security interest or the obligations giving rise to a registered non-consensual right or interest have been discharged, or where the conditions of transfer of title under a registered title reservation agreement have been fulfilled, the holder of such interest shall, without undue delay, procure the discharge of the registration after written demand by the debtor delivered to or received at its address stated in the registration.

2. Where a prospective international interest or a prospective assignment of an international interest has been registered, the intending creditor or intending assignee shall, without undue delay, procure the discharge of the registration after written demand by the intending debtor or assignor which is delivered to or received at its address stated in the registration before the intending creditor or assignee has given value or incurred a commitment to give value.

3. Where the obligations secured by a national interest specified in a registered notice of a national interest have been discharged, the holder of such interest shall, without undue delay, procure the discharge of the registration after written demand by the debtor delivered to or received at its address stated in the registration.

4. Where a registration ought not to have been made or is incorrect, the person in whose favour the registration was made shall, without undue delay, procure its discharge or amendment after written demand by the debtor delivered to or received at its address stated in the registration.

Article 26
Access to the international registration facilities

No person shall be denied access to the registration and search facilities of the International Registry on any ground other than its failure to comply with the procedures prescribed by this Chapter.

CHAPTER VI
PRIVILEGES AND IMMUNITIES OF THE SUPERVISORY AUTHORITY AND THE REGISTRAR

Article 27
Legal personality; immunity

1. The Supervisory Authority shall have international legal personality where not already possessing such personality.

2. The Supervisory Authority and its officers and employees shall enjoy such immunity from legal or administrative process as is specified in the Protocol.

3. (a) The Supervisory Authority shall enjoy exemption from taxes and such other privileges as may be provided by agreement with the host State.
   (b) For the purposes of this paragraph, 'host State' means the State in which the Supervisory Authority is situated.

4. The assets, documents, data bases and archives of the International Registry shall be inviolable and immune from seizure or other legal or administrative process.

5. For the purposes of any claim against the Registrar under Article 28(1) or Article 44, the claimant shall be entitled to access to such information and documents as are necessary to enable the claimant to pursue its claim.

6. The Supervisory Authority may waive the inviolability and immunity conferred by paragraph 4.

CHAPTER VII
LIABILITY OF THE REGISTRAR

Article 28
Liability and financial assurances

1. The Registrar shall be liable for compensatory damages for loss suffered by a person directly resulting from an error or omission of the Registrar and its officers and employees or from a malfunction of the international registration system except where the malfunction is caused by an event of an inevitable and irresistible nature, which could not be prevented by using the best practices in current use in the field of electronic registry design and operation, including those related to back-up and systems security and networking.

2. The Registrar shall not be liable under the preceding paragraph for factual inaccuracy of registration information received by the Registrar or transmitted by the Registrar in the form in which it received that information nor for acts or circumstances for which the Registrar and its officers and employees are not responsible and arising prior to receipt of registration information at the International Registry.

3. Compensation under paragraph 1 may be reduced to the extent that the person who suffered the damage caused or contributed to that damage.

4. The Registrar shall procure insurance or a financial guarantee covering the liability referred to in this Article to the extent determined by the Supervisory Authority, in accordance with the Protocol.

CHAPTER VIII
EFFECTS OF AN INTERNATIONAL INTEREST
AS AGAINST THIRD PARTIES

Article 29
Priority of competing interests

1. A registered interest has priority over any other interest subsequently registered and over an unregistered interest.

2. The priority of the first-mentioned interest under the preceding paragraph applies:
   (a) even if the first-mentioned interest was acquired or registered with actual knowledge of the other interest; and
   (b) even as regards value given by the holder of the first-mentioned interest with such knowledge.

3. The buyer of an object acquires its interest in it:
   (a) subject to an interest registered at the time of its acquisition of that interest; and
   (b) free from an unregistered interest even if it has actual knowledge of such an interest.
4. The conditional buyer or lessee acquires its interest in or right over that object:
   (a) subject to an interest registered prior to the registration of the international interest held by its conditional seller or lessor; and
   (b) free from an interest not so registered at that time even if it has actual knowledge of that interest.
5. The priority of competing interests or rights under this Article may be varied by agreement between the holders of those interests, but an assignee of a subordinated interest is not bound by an agreement to subordinate that interest unless at the time of the assignment a subordination had been registered relating to that agreement.
6. Any priority given by this Article to an interest in an object extends to proceeds.
7. This Convention:
   (a) does not affect the rights of a person in an item, other than an object, held prior to its installation on an object if under the applicable law those rights continue to exist after the installation; and
   (b) does not prevent the creation of rights in an item, other than an object, which has previously been installed on an object where under the applicable law those rights are created.

Article 30
Effects of insolvency

1. In insolvency proceedings against the debtor an international interest is effective if prior to the commencement of the insolvency proceedings that interest was registered in conformity with this Convention.
2. Nothing in this Article impairs the effectiveness of an international interest in the insolvency proceedings where that interest is effective under the applicable law.
3. Nothing in this Article affects:
   (a) any rules of law applicable in insolvency proceedings relating to the avoidance of a transaction as a preference or a transfer in fraud of creditors; or
   (b) any rules of procedure relating to the enforcement of rights to property which is under the control or supervision of the insolvency administrator.

CHAPTER IX
ASSIGNMENTS OF ASSOCIATED RIGHTS AND INTERNATIONAL INTERESTS; RIGHTS OF SUBROGATION

Article 31
Effects of assignment

1. Except as otherwise agreed by the parties, an assignment of associated rights made in conformity with Article 32 also transfers to the assignee:
   (a) the related international interest; and
   (b) all the interests and priorities of the assignor under this Convention.

2. Nothing in this Convention prevents a partial assignment of the assignor's associated rights. In the case of such a partial assignment the assignor and assignee may agree as to their respective rights concerning the related international interest assigned under the preceding paragraph but not so as adversely to affect the debtor without its consent.

3. Subject to paragraph 4, the applicable law shall determine the defences and rights of set-off available to the debtor against the assignee.

4. The debtor may at any time by agreement in writing waive all or any of the defences and rights of set-off referred to in the preceding paragraph other than defences arising from fraudulent acts on the part of the assignee.

5. In the case of an assignment by way of security, the assigned associated rights revest in the assignor, to the extent that they are still subsisting, when the obligations secured by the assignment have been discharged.

Article 32
Formal requirements of assignment

1. An assignment of associated rights transfers the related international interest only if it:
   (a) is in writing;
   (b) enables the associated rights to be identified under the contract from which they arise; and
   (c) in the case of an assignment by way of security, enables the obligations secured by the assignment to be determined in accordance with the Protocol but without the need to state a sum or maximum sum secured.

2. An assignment of an international interest created or provided for by a security agreement is not valid unless some or all related associated rights also are assigned.

3. This Convention does not apply to an assignment of associated rights which is not effective to transfer the related international interest.

Article 33
Debtor's duty to assignee

1. To the extent that associated rights and the related international interest have been transferred in accordance with Articles 31 and 32, the debtor in relation to those rights and that interest is bound by the assignment and has a duty to make payment or give other performance to the assignee, if but only if:
   (a) the debtor has been given notice of the assignment in writing by or with the authority of the assignor; and
   (b) the notice identifies the associated rights.

2. Irrespective of any other ground on which payment or performance by the debtor discharges the latter from liability, payment or performance shall be effective for this purpose if made in accordance with the preceding paragraph.

3. Nothing in this Article shall affect the priority of competing assignments.

Article 34
Default remedies in respect of assignment by way of security

In the event of default by the assignor under the assignment of associated rights and the related international interest made by way of security, Articles 8, 9 and 11 to 14 apply in the relations between the assignor and the assignee (and, in relation to associated rights, apply in so far as those provisions are capable of application to intangible property) as if references:

(a) to the secured obligation and the security interest were references to the obligation secured by the assignment of the associated rights and the related international interest and the security interest created by that assignment;

(b) to the chargee or creditor and chargor or debtor were references to the assignee and assignor;

(c) to the holder of the international interest were references to the assignee; and

(d) to the object were references to the assigned associated rights and the related international interest.

Article 35
Priority of competing assignments

1. Where there are competing assignments of associated rights and at least one of the assignments includes the related international interest and is registered, the provisions of Article 29 apply as if the references to a registered interest were references to an assignment of the associated rights and the related registered interest and as if references to a registered or unregistered interest were references to a registered or unregistered assignment.

2. Article 30 applies to an assignment of associated rights as if the references to an international interest were references to an assignment of the associated rights and the related international interest.

Article 36
Assignee's priority with respect to associated rights

1. The assignee of associated rights and the related international interest whose assignment has been registered only has priority under Article 35(1) over another assignee of the associated rights:

(a) if the contract under which the associated rights arise states that they are secured by or associated with the object; and

(b) to the extent that the associated rights are related to an object.

2. For the purposes of sub-paragraph (b) of the preceding paragraph, associated rights are related to an object only to the extent that they consist of rights to payment or performance that relate to:

(a) a sum advanced and utilised for the purchase of the object;

(b) a sum advanced and utilised for the purchase of another object in which the assignor held another international interest if the assignor transferred that interest to the assignee and the assignment has been registered;

(c) the price payable for the object;

(d) the rentals payable in respect of the object; or

(e) other obligations arising from a transaction referred to in any of the preceding sub-paragraphs.

3. In all other cases, the priority of the competing assignments of the associated rights shall be determined by the applicable law.

Article 37
Effects of assignor's insolvency

The provisions of Article 30 apply to insolvency proceedings against the assignor as if references to the debtor were references to the assignor.

Article 38
Subrogation

1. Subject to paragraph 2, nothing in this Convention affects the acquisition of associated rights and the related international interest by legal or contractual subrogation under the applicable law.
2. The priority between any interest within the preceding paragraph and a competing interest may be varied by agreement in writing between the holders of the respective interests but an assignee of a subordinated interest is not bound by an agreement to subordinate that interest unless at the time of the assignment a subordination had been registered relating to that agreement.

CHAPTER X
RIGHTS OR INTERESTS SUBJECT TO DECLARATIONS
BY CONTRACTING STATES

Article 39
Rights having priority without registration

1. A Contracting State may at any time, in a declaration deposited with the Depositary of the Protocol declare, generally or specifically:
   (a) those categories of non-consensual right or interest (other than a right or interest to which Article 40 applies) which under that State's law have priority over an interest in an object equivalent to that of the holder of a registered international interest and which shall have priority over a registered international interest, whether in or outside insolvency proceedings; and
   (b) that nothing in this Convention shall affect the right of a State or State entity, intergovernmental organisation or other private provider of public services to arrest or detain an object under the laws of that State for payment of amounts owed to such entity, organisation or provider directly relating to those services in respect of that object or another object.
2. A declaration made under the preceding paragraph may be expressed to cover categories that are created after the deposit of that declaration.
3. A non-consensual right or interest has priority over an international interest if and only if the former is of a category covered by a declaration deposited prior to the registration of the international interest.

4. Notwithstanding the preceding paragraph, a Contracting State may, at the time of ratification, acceptance, approval of, or accession to the Protocol, declare that a right or interest of a category covered by a declaration made under sub-paragraph (a) of paragraph 1 shall have priority over an international interest registered prior to the date of such ratification, acceptance, approval or accession.

Article 40
Registrable non-consensual rights or interests

A Contracting State may at any time in a declaration deposited with the Depositary of the Protocol list the categories of non-consensual right or interest which shall be registrable under this Convention as regards any category of object as if the right or interest were an international interest and shall be regulated accordingly. Such a declaration may be modified from time to time.

CHAPTER XI
APPLICATION OF THE CONVENTION TO SALES

Article 41
Sale and Prospective Sale

This Convention shall apply to the sale or prospective sale of an object as provided for in the Protocol with any modifications therein.

CHAPTER XII
JURISDICTION

Article
Choice of forum

1. Subject to Articles 43 and 44, the courts of a Contracting State chosen by the parties to a transaction have jurisdiction in respect of any claim brought under this Convention, whether or not the chosen forum has a connection with the parties or the transaction. Such jurisdiction shall be exclusive unless otherwise agreed between the parties.
2. Any such agreement shall be in writing or otherwise concluded in accordance with the formal requirements of the law of the chosen forum.

Article 43
Jurisdiction Under Article 13

1. The courts of a Contracting State chosen by the parties and the courts of the Contracting State on the territory of which the object is situated have jurisdiction to grant relief under Article 13(1)(a), (b), (c) and Article 13(4) in respect of that object.
2. Jurisdiction to grant relief under Article 13(1)(d) or other interim relief by virtue of Article 13(4) may be exercised either:
   (a) by the courts chosen by the parties; or

(b) by the courts of a Contracting State on the territory of which the debtor is situated, being relief which, by the terms of the order granting it, is enforceable only in the territory of that Contracting State.

2. A court has jurisdiction under the preceding paragraphs even if the final determination of the claim referred to in Article 13(1) will or may take place in a court of another Contracting State or by arbitration.

Article 44
Jurisdiction to Make Orders Against the Registrar

1. The courts of the place in which the Registrar has its centre of administration shall have exclusive jurisdiction to award damages or make orders against the Registrar.
2. Where a person fails to respond to a demand made under Article 25 and that person has ceased to exist or cannot be found for the purpose of enabling an order to be made against it requiring it to procure discharge of the registration, the courts referred to in the preceding paragraph shall have exclusive jurisdiction, on the application of the debtor or intending debtor, to make an order directed to the Registrar requiring the Registrar to discharge the registration.
3. Where a person fails to comply with an order of a court having jurisdiction under this Convention or, in the case of a national interest, an order of a court of competent jurisdiction requiring that person to procure the amendment or discharge of a registration, the courts referred to in paragraph 1 may direct the Registrar to take such steps as will give effect to that order.
4. Except as otherwise provided by the preceding paragraphs, no court may make orders or give judgments or rulings against or purporting to bind the Registrar.

Article 45
Jurisdiction in Respect of Insolvency Proceedings

The provisions of this Chapter are not applicable to insolvency proceedings.

CHAPTER XIII
RELATIONSHIP WITH OTHER CONVENTIONS

Article 45 *bis*
Relationship with the *United Nations Convention on the Assignment of Receivables in International Trade*

This Convention shall prevail over the *United Nations Convention on the Assignment of Receivables in International Trade,* opened for signature in New York on 12 December 2001, as it relates to the assignment of receivables which are associated rights related to international interests in aircraft objects, railway rolling stock and space assets.

Article 46
Relationship with the *UNIDROIT Convention on International Financial Leasing*

The Protocol may determine the relationship between this Convention and the *UNIDROIT Convention on International Financial Leasing*, signed at Ottawa on 28 May 1988.

CHAPTER XIV
FINAL PROVISIONS

Article 47
Signature, ratification, acceptance, approval or accession

1. This Convention shall be open for signature in Cape Town on 16 November 2001 by States participating in the Diplomatic Conference to Adopt a Mobile Equipment Convention and an Aircraft Protocol held at Cape Town from 29 October to 16 November 2001. After 16 November 2001, the Convention shall be open to all States for signature at the Headquarters of the International Institute for the Unification of Private Law (UNIDROIT) in Rome until it enters into force in accordance with Article 49.

2. This Convention shall be subject to ratification, acceptance or approval by States which have signed it.

3. Any State which does not sign this Convention may accede to it at any time.

4. Ratification, acceptance, approval or accession is effected by the deposit of a formal instrument to that effect with the Depositary.

Article 48
Regional Economic Integration Organisations

1. A Regional Economic Integration Organisation which is constituted by sovereign States and has competence over certain matters governed by this Convention may similarly sign, accept, approve or accede to this Convention. The Regional Economic Integration Organisation shall in that case have the rights and obligations of a Contracting State, to the extent that that Organisation has competence over matters governed by this Convention. Where the number of Contracting States is relevant in this Convention, the Regional Economic Integration Organisation shall not count as a Contracting State in addition to its Member States which are Contracting States.

2. The Regional Economic Integration Organisation shall, at the time of signature, acceptance, approval or accession, make a declaration to the Depositary specifying the matters governed by this Convention in respect of which competence has been transferred to that Organisation by its Member States. The Regional Economic Integration Organisation shall promptly notify the Depositary of any changes to the distribution of competence, including new transfers of competence, specified in the declaration under this paragraph.

3. Any reference to a 'Contracting State' or 'Contracting States' or 'State Party' or 'States Parties' in this Convention applies equally to a Regional Economic Integration Organisation where the context so requires.

Article 49
Entry into force

1. This Convention enters into force on the first day of the month following the expiration of three months after the date of the deposit of the third instrument of ratification, acceptance, approval or accession but only as regards a category of objects to which a Protocol applies:
   (a) as from the time of entry into force of that Protocol;
   (b) subject to the terms of that Protocol; and
   (c) as between States Parties to this Convention and that Protocol.
2. For other States this Convention enters into force on the first day of the month following the expiration of three months after the date of the deposit of their instrument of ratification, acceptance, approval or accession but only as regards a category of objects to which a Protocol applies and subject, in relation to such Protocol, to the requirements of sub-paragraphs (a), (b) and (c) of the preceding paragraph.

Article 50
Internal transactions

1. A Contracting State may, at the time of ratification, acceptance, approval of, or accession to the Protocol, declare that this Convention shall not apply to a transaction which is an internal transaction in relation to that State with regard to all types of objects or some of them.
2. Notwithstanding the preceding paragraph, the provisions of Articles 8(4), 9(1), 16, Chapter V, Article 29, and any provisions of this Convention relating to registered interests shall apply to an internal transaction.
3. Where notice of a national interest has been registered in the International Registry, the priority of the holder of that interest under Article 29 shall not be affected by the fact that such interest has become vested in another person by assignment or subrogation under the applicable law.

Article 51
Future Protocols

1. The Depositary may create working groups, in co-operation with such relevant non-governmental organisations as the Depositary considers appropriate, to assess the feasibility of extending the application of this Convention, through one or more Protocols, to objects of any category of high-value mobile equipment, other than a category referred to in Article 2(3), each member of which is uniquely identifiable, and associated rights relating to such objects.
2. The Depositary shall communicate the text of any preliminary draft Protocol relating to a category of objects prepared by such a working group to all States Parties to this Convention, all member States of the Depositary, member States of the United Nations which are not members of the Depositary and the relevant intergovernmental organisations, and shall invite such States and organisations to participate in intergovernmental negotiations for the completion of a draft Protocol on the basis of such a preliminary draft Protocol.
3. The Depositary shall also communicate the text of any preliminary draft Protocol prepared by such a working group to such relevant non-governmental organisations as

571

the Depositary considers appropriate. Such non-governmental organisations shall be invited promptly to submit comments on the text of the preliminary draft Protocol to the Depositary and to participate as observers in the preparation of a draft Protocol.

4. When the competent bodies of the Depositary adjudge such a draft Protocol ripe for adoption, the Depositary shall convene a diplomatic conference for its adoption.

5. Once such a Protocol has been adopted, subject to paragraph 6, this Convention shall apply to the category of objects covered thereby.

6. Article 45 *bis* of this Convention applies to such a Protocol only if specifically provided for in that Protocol.

Article 52
Territorial units

1. If a Contracting State has territorial units in which different systems of law are applicable in relation to the matters dealt with in this Convention, it may, at the time of ratification, acceptance, approval or accession, declare that this Convention is to extend to all its territorial units or only to one or more of them and may modify its declaration by submitting another declaration at any time.

2. Any such declaration shall state expressly the territorial units to which this Convention applies.

3. If a Contracting State has not made any declaration under paragraph 1, this Convention shall apply to all territorial units of that State.

4. Where a Contracting State extends this Convention to one or more of its territorial units, declarations permitted under this Convention may be made in respect of each such territorial unit, and the declarations made in respect of one territorial unit may be different from those made in respect of another territorial unit.

5. If by virtue of a declaration under paragraph 1, this Convention extends to one or more territorial units of a Contracting State:

   (a) the debtor is considered to be situated in a Contracting State only if it is incorporated or formed under a law in force in a territorial unit to which this Convention applies or if it has its registered office or statutory seat, centre of administration, place of business or habitual residence in a territorial unit to which this Convention applies;

   (b) any reference to the location of the object in a Contracting State refers to the location of the object in a territorial unit to which this Convention applies; and

   (c) any reference to the administrative authorities in that Contracting State shall be construed as referring to the administrative authorities having jurisdiction in a territorial unit to which this Convention applies.

Article 53
Determination of courts

A Contracting State may, at the time of ratification, acceptance, approval of, or accession to the Protocol, declare the relevant 'court' or 'courts' for the purposes of Article 1 and Chapter XII of this Convention.

Article 54
Declarations regarding remedies

1. A Contracting State may, at the time of ratification, acceptance, approval of, or accession to the Protocol, declare that while the charged object is situated within,

or controlled from its territory the chargee shall not grant a lease of the object in that territory.

2. A Contracting State shall, at the time of ratification, acceptance, approval of, or accession to the Protocol, declare whether or not any remedy available to the creditor under any provision of this Convention which is not there expressed to require application to the court may be exercised only with leave of the court.

Article 55
Declarations regarding relief pending final determination

A Contracting State may, at the time of ratification, acceptance, approval of, or accession to the Protocol, declare that it will not apply the provisions of Article 13 or Article 43, or both, wholly or in part The declaration shall specify under which conditions the relevant Article will be applied, in case it will be applied partly, or otherwise which other forms of interim relief will be applied.

Article 56
Reservations and declarations

1. No reservations may be made to this Convention but declarations authorised by Articles 39, 40, 50, 52, 53, 54, 55, 57, 58 and 60 may be made in accordance with these provisions.
2. Any declaration or subsequent declaration or any withdrawal of a declaration made under this Convention shall be notified in writing to the Depositary.

Article 57
Subsequent declarations

1. A State Party may make a subsequent declaration, other than a declaration authorised under Article 60, at any time after the date on which this Convention has entered into force for it, by notifying the Depositary to that effect.
2. Any such subsequent declaration shall take effect on the first day of the month following the expiration of six months after the date of receipt of the notification by the Depositary. Where a longer period for that declaration to take effect is specified in the notification, it shall take effect upon the expiration of such longer period after receipt of the notification by the Depositary.
3. Notwithstanding the previous paragraphs, this Convention shall continue to apply, as if no such subsequent declarations had been made, in respect of all rights and interests arising prior to the effective date of any such subsequent declaration.

Article 58
Withdrawal of declarations

1. Any State Party having made a declaration under this Convention, other than a declaration authorised under Article 60, may withdraw it at any time by notifying the Depositary. Such withdrawal is to take effect on the first day of the month following the expiration of six months after the date of receipt of the notification by the Depositary.

2. Notwithstanding the previous paragraph, this Convention shall continue to apply, as if no such withdrawal of declaration had been made, in respect of all rights and interests arising prior to the effective date of any such withdrawal.

Article 59
Denunciations

1. Any State Party may denounce this Convention by notification in writing to the Depositary.
2. Any such denunciation shall take effect on the first day of the month following the expiration of twelve months after the date on which notification is received by the Depositary.
3. Notwithstanding the previous paragraphs, this Convention shall continue to apply, as if no such denunciation had been made, in respect of all rights and interests arising prior to the effective date of any such denunciation.

Article 60
Transitional provisions

1. Unless otherwise declared by a Contracting State at any time, the Convention does not apply to a pre-existing right or interest, which retains the priority it enjoyed under the applicable law before the effective date of this Convention.
2. For the purposes of Article 1(v) and of determining priority under this Convention:
   (a) 'effective date of this Convention' means in relation to a debtor the time when this Convention enters into force or the time when the State in which the debtor is situated becomes a Contracting State, whichever is the later; and
   (b) the debtor is situated in a State where it has its centre of administration or, if it has no centre of administration, its place of business or, if it has more than one place of business, its principal place of business or, if it has no place of business, its habitual residence.
3. A Contracting State may in its declaration under paragraph 1 specify a date, not earlier than three years after the date on which the declaration becomes effective, when this Convention and the Protocol will become applicable, for the purpose of determining priority, including the protection of any existing priority, to pre-existing rights or interests arising under an agreement made at a time when the debtor was situated in a State referred to in sub-paragraph (b) of the preceding paragraph but only to the extent and in the manner specified in its declaration.

Article 61
Review Conferences, amendments and related matters

1. The Depositary shall prepare reports yearly or at such other time as the circumstances may require for the States Parties as to the manner in which the international regimen established in this Convention has operated in practice. In preparing such reports, the Depositary shall take into account the reports of the Supervisory Authority concerning the functioning of the international registration system.

2. At the request of not less than twenty-five per cent of the States Parties, Review Conferences of States Parties shall be convened from time to time by the Depositary, in consultation with the Supervisory Authority, to consider:
   (a) the practical operation of this Convention and its effectiveness in facilitating the asset-based financing and leasing of the objects covered by its terms;
   (b) the judicial interpretation given to, and the application made of the terms of this Convention and the regulations;
   (c) the functioning of the international registration system, the performance of the Registrar and its oversight by the Supervisory Authority, taking into account the reports of the Supervisory Authority; and
   (d) whether any modifications to this Convention or the arrangements relating to the International Registry are desirable.
3. Subject to paragraph 4, any amendment to this Convention shall be approved by at least a two-thirds majority of States Parties participating in the Conference referred to in the preceding paragraph and shall then enter into force in respect of States which have ratified, accepted or approved such amendment when ratified, accepted, or approved by three States in accordance with the provisions of Article 49 relating to its entry into force.
4. Where the proposed amendment to this Convention is intended to apply to more than one category of equipment, such amendment shall also be approved by at least a two-thirds majority of States Parties to each Protocol that are participating in the Conference referred to in paragraph 2.

Article 62
Depositary and its functions

1. Instruments of ratification, acceptance, approval or accession shall be deposited with the International Institute for the Unification of Private Law (UNIDROIT), which is hereby designated the Depositary.
2. The Depositary shall:
   (a) inform all Contracting States of:
       (i) each new signature or deposit of an instrument of ratification, acceptance, approval or accession, together with the date thereof;
       (ii) the date of entry into force of this Convention;
       (iii) each declaration made in accordance with this Convention, together with the date thereof;
       (iv) the withdrawal or amendment of any declaration, together with the date thereof; and
       (v) the notification of any denunciation of this Convention together with the date thereof and the date on which it takes effect;
   (b) transmit certified true copies of this Convention to all Contracting States;
   (c) provide the Supervisory Authority and the Registrar with a copy of each instrument of ratification, acceptance, approval or accession, together with the date of deposit thereof, of each declaration or withdrawal or amendment of a declaration and of each notification of denunciation, together with the date of notification thereof, so that the information contained therein is easily and fully available; and
   (d) perform such other functions customary for depositaries.

In witness whereof the undersigned Plenipotentiaries, having been duly authorised, have signed this Convention.

Done at Cape Town, this sixteenth day of November, two thousand and one, in a single original in the English, Arabic, Chinese, French, Russian and Spanish languages, all texts being equally authentic, such authenticity to take effect upon verification by the Joint Secretariat of the Conference under the authority of the President of the Conference within ninety days hereof as to the conformity of the texts with one another.

TABLE OF STATE RATIFICATIONS

Total number of signatures not followed by ratifications: 25
Total number of ratifications/accessions: 4

Entry into Force: 1 April 2004 but only as regards a category of objects to which a Protocol applies (art 49(1))
(Condition: 3 ratifications)

State	Signature	Ratification	By	Entry into force
Burundi	16 November 2001			
Canada	31 March 2004			
Chile	16 November 2001			
China	16 November 2001			
Congo	16 November 2001			
Cuba	16 November 2001			
Ethiopia	16 November 2001	21 November 2003	Ratification	1 April 2004
France	16 November 2001			
Germany	17 November 2003			
Ghana	16 November 2001			
Italy	6 December 2001			
Jamaica	16 November 2001			
Jordan	16 November 2001			
Kenya	16 November 2001			
Lesotho	16 November 2001			
Nigeria	16 November 2001	21 November 2003	Ratification	1 April 2004
Panama	11 September 2002	28 July 2003	Ratification	1 April 2004
Pakistan		22 January 2004	Accesion	1 April 2004
Saudi Arabia	12 March 2003			
Senegal	2 April 2002			
South Africa	16 November 2001			
Sudan	16 November 2001			
Switzerland	16 November 2001			
Tonga	16 November 2001			
Turkey	16 November 2001			
United Kingdom	16 November 2001			
United Republic of Tanzania	16 November 2001			
United States of America	9 May 2003			
Ukraine	3 March 2004			

Note. A list of reservations and declarations made by States at the time of signature has not been included in this volume. These can be obtained from http:/ /www.unidroit.org/english/implement/ i-2001-convention.htm.

(i) PROTOCOL
TO THE CONVENTION ON
INTERNATIONAL INTERESTS IN MOBILE EQUIPMENT ON
MATTERS SPECIFIC TO AIRCRAFT EQUIPMENT 2001*

* Reproduced with the kind permission of UNIDROIT.

The States parties to this Protocol,

Considering it necessary to implement the *Convention on International Interests in Mobile Equipment* (hereinafter referred to as 'the Convention') as it relates to aircraft equipment, in the light of the purposes set out in the preamble to the Convention,

Mindful of the need to adapt the Convention to meet the particular requirements of aircraft finance and to extend the sphere of application of the Convention to include contracts of sale of aircraft equipment,

Mindful of the principles and objectives of the *Convention on International Civil Aviation,* signed at Chicago on 7 December 1944,

Have agreed upon the following provisions relating to aircraft equipment:

CHAPTER I
SPHERE OF APPLICATION AND GENERAL PROVISIONS

Article I
Defined terms

1. In this Protocol, except where the context otherwise requires, terms used in it have the meanings set out in the Convention.
2. In this Protocol the following terms are employed with the meanings set out below:
    (a) 'aircraft' means aircraft as defined for the purposes of the Chicago Convention which are either airframes with aircraft engines installed thereon or helicopters;
    (b) 'aircraft engines' means aircraft engines (other than those used in military, customs or police services) powered by jet propulsion or turbine or piston technology and:
        (i) in the case of jet propulsion aircraft engines, have at least 1750 lb of thrust or its equivalent; and
        (ii) in the case of turbine-powered or piston-powered aircraft engines, have at least 550 rated take-off shaft horsepower or its equivalent,
        together with all modules and other installed, incorporated or attached accessories, parts and equipment and all data, manuals and records relating thereto;
    (c) 'aircraft objects' means airframes, aircraft engines and helicopters;
    (d) 'aircraft register' means a register maintained by a State or a common mark registering authority for the purposes of the Chicago Convention;
    (e) 'airframes' means airframes (other than those used in military, customs or police services) that, when appropriate aircraft engines are installed thereon, are type certified by the competent aviation authority to transport:
        (i) at least eight (8) persons including crew; or
        (ii) goods in excess of 2750 kilograms,
        together with all installed, incorporated or attached accessories, parts and equipment (other than aircraft engines), and all data, manuals and records relating thereto;

(f) 'authorised party' means the party referred to in Article XIII(3);

(g) 'Chicago Convention' means the *Convention on International Civil Aviation*, signed at Chicago on 7 December 1944, as amended, and its Annexes;

(h) 'common mark registering authority' means the authority maintaining a register in accordance with Article 77 of the Chicago Convention as implemented by the Resolution adopted on 14 December 1967 by the Council of the International Civil Aviation Organization on nationality and registration of aircraft operated by international operating agencies;

(i) 'de-registration of the aircraft' means deletion or removal of the registration of the aircraft from its aircraft register in accordance with the Chicago Convention;

(j) 'guarantee contract' means a contract entered into by a person as guarantor;

(k) 'guarantor' means a person who, for the purpose of assuring performance of any obligations in favour of a creditor secured by a security agreement or under an agreement, gives or issues a suretyship or demand guarantee or a standby letter of credit or any other form of credit insurance;

(l) 'helicopters' means heavier-than-air machines (other than those used in military, customs or police services) supported in flight chiefly by the reactions of the air on one or more power-driven rotors on substantially vertical axes and which are type certified by the competent aviation authority to transport:

    (i) at least five (5) persons including c0rew; or

    (ii) goods in excess of 450 kilograms, together with all installed, incorporated or attached accessories, parts and equipment (including rotors), and all data, manuals and records relating thereto;

(m) 'insolvency-related event' means:

    (i) the commencement of the insolvency proceedings; or

    (ii) the declared intention to suspend or actual suspension of payments by the debtor where the creditor's right to institute insolvency proceedings against the debtor or to exercise remedies under the Convention is prevented or suspended by law or State action;

(n) 'primary insolvency jurisdiction' means the Contracting State in which the centre of the debtor's main interests is situated, which for this purpose shall be deemed to be the place of the debtor's statutory seat or, if there is none, the place where the debtor is incorporated or formed, unless proved otherwise;

(o) 'registry authority' means the national authority or the common mark registering authority, maintaining an aircraft register in a Contracting State and responsible for the registration and de-registration of an aircraft in accordance with the Chicago Convention; and

(p) 'State of registry' means, in respect of an aircraft, the State on the national register of which an aircraft is entered or the State of location of the common mark registering authority maintaining the aircraft register.

Article II
Application of Convention as regards aircraft objects

1. The Convention shall apply in relation to aircraft objects as provided by the terms of this Protocol.
2. The Convention and this Protocol shall be known as the Convention on International Interests in Mobile Equipment as applied to aircraft objects.

Article III
Application of Convention to sales

The following provisions of the Convention apply as if references to an agreement creating or providing for an international interest were references to a contract of sale and as if references to an international interest, a prospective international interest, the debtor and the creditor were references to a sale, a prospective sale, the seller and the buyer respectively:

Articles 3 and 4;

Article 16(1)(a);

Article 19(4);

Article 20(1) (as regards registration of a contract of sale or a prospective sale);

Article 25(2) (as regards a prospective sale); and

Article 30.

In addition, the general provisions of Article 1, Article 5, Chapters IV to VII, Article 29 (other than Article 29(3) which is replaced by Article XIV(1) and (2)), Chapter X, Chapter XII (other than Article 43), Chapter XIII and Chapter XIV (other than Article 60) shall apply to contracts of sale and prospective sales.

Article IV
Sphere of application

1. Without prejudice to Article 3(1) of the Convention, the Convention shall also apply in relation to a helicopter, or to an airframe pertaining to an aircraft, registered in an aircraft register of a Contracting State which is the State of registry, and where such registration is made pursuant to an agreement for registration of the aircraft it is deemed to have been effected at the time of the agreement.
2. For the purposes of the definition of 'internal transaction' in Article 1 of the Convention:
   (a) an airframe is located in the State of registry of the aircraft of which it is a part;
   (b) an aircraft engine is located in the State of registry of the aircraft on which it is installed or, if it is not installed on an aircraft, where it is physically located; and
   (c) a helicopter is located in its State of registry,
at the time of the conclusion of the agreement creating or providing for the interest.
3. The parties may, by agreement in writing, exclude the application of Article XI and, in their relations with each other, derogate from or vary the effect of any of the provisions of this Protocol except Article IX (2)–(4).

Article V
Formalities, effects and registration of contracts of sale

1. For the purposes of this Protocol, a contract of sale is one which:
   (a) is in writing;
   (b) relates to an aircraft object of which the seller has power to dispose; and
   (c) enables the aircraft object to be identified in conformity with this Protocol.
2. A contract of sale transfers the interest of the seller in the aircraft object to the buyer according to its terms.

3. Registration of a contract of sale remains effective indefinitely. Registration of a prospective sale remains effective unless discharged or until expiry of the period, if any, specified in the registration.

Article VI
Representative capacities

A person may enter into an agreement or a sale, and register an international interest in, or a sale of, an aircraft object, in an agency, trust or other representative capacity. In such case, that person is entitled to assert rights and interests under the Convention.

Article VII
Description of aircraft objects

A description of an aircraft object that contains its manufacturer's serial number, the name of the manufacturer and its model designation is necessary and sufficient to identify the object for the purposes of Article 7(c) of the Convention and Article V(1)(c) of this Protocol.

Article VIII
Choice of law

1. This Article applies only where a Contracting State has made a declaration pursuant to Article XXX(1).
2. The parties to an agreement, or a contract of sale, or a related guarantee contract or subordination agreement may agree on the law which is to govern their contractual rights and obligations, wholly or in part.
3. Unless otherwise agreed, the reference in the preceding paragraph to the law chosen by the parties is to the domestic rules of law of the designated State or, where that State comprises several territorial units, to the domestic law of the designated territorial unit.

CHAPTER II
DEFAULT REMEDIES, PRIORITIES AND ASSIGNMENTS

Article IX
Modification of default remedies provisions

1. In addition to the remedies specified in Chapter III of the Convention, the creditor may, to the extent that the debtor has at any time so agreed and in the circumstances specified in that Chapter:
   (a) procure the de-registration of the aircraft; and
   (b) procure the export and physical transfer of the aircraft object from the territory in which it is situated.
2. The creditor shall not exercise the remedies specified in the preceding paragraph without the prior consent in writing of the holder of any registered interest ranking in priority to that of the creditor.

3. Article 8(3) of the Convention shall not apply to aircraft objects. Any remedy given by the Convention in relation to an aircraft object shall be exercised in a commercially reasonable manner. A remedy shall be deemed to be exercised in a commercially reasonable manner where it is exercised in conformity with a provision of the agreement except where such a provision is manifestly unreasonable.

4. A chargee giving ten or more working days' prior written notice of a proposed sale or lease to interested persons shall be deemed to satisfy the requirement of providing 'reasonable prior notice' specified in Article 8(4) of the Convention. The foregoing shall not prevent a chargee and a chargor or a guarantor from agreeing to a longer period of prior notice.

5. The registry authority in a Contracting State shall, subject to any applicable safety laws and regulations, honour a request for de-registration and export if:

   (a) the request is properly submitted by the authorised party under a recorded irrevocable de-registration and export request authorisation; and

   (b) the authorised party certifies to the registry authority, if required by that authority, that all registered interests ranking in priority to that of the creditor in whose favour the authorisation has been issued have been discharged or that the holders of such interests have consented to the de-registration and export.

6. A chargee proposing to procure the de-registration and export of an aircraft under paragraph 1 otherwise than pursuant to a court order shall give reasonable prior notice in writing of the proposed de-registration and export to:

   (a) interested persons specified in Article 1(m)(i) and (ii) of the Convention; and

   (b) interested persons specified in Article 1(m)(iii) of the Convention who have given notice of their rights to the chargee within a reasonable time prior to the de-registration and export.

Article X
Modification of provisions regarding relief pending final determination

1. This Article applies only where a Contracting State has made a declaration under Article XXX(2) and to the extent stated in such declaration.

2. For the purposes of Article 13(1) of the Convention, 'speedy' in the context of obtaining relief means within such number of working days from the date of filing of the application for relief as is specified in a declaration made by the Contracting State in which the application is made.

3. Article 13(1) of the Convention applies with the following being added immediately after sub-paragraph (d):

   '(e) if at any time the debtor and the creditor specifically agree, sale and application of proceeds therefrom',

   and Article 43(2) applies with the insertion after the words 'Article 13(1)(d)' of the words 'and (e)'.

4. Ownership or any other interest of the debtor passing on a sale under the preceding paragraph is free from any other interest over which the creditor's international interest has priority under the provisions of Article 29 of the Convention.

5. The creditor and the debtor or any other interested person may agree in writing to exclude the application of Article 13(2) of the Convention.

6. With regard to the remedies in Article IX(1):
   (a) they shall be made available by the registry authorioty and other administrative authorities, as applicable, in a Contracting State no later than five working days after the creditor notifies such authorities that the relief specified in Article IX(1) is granted or, in the case of relief granted by a foreign court, recognised by a court of that Contracting State, and that the creditor is entitled to procure those remedies in accordance with the Convention; and
   (b) the applicable authorities shall expeditiously co-operate with and assist the creditor in the exercise of such remedies in conformity with the applicable aviation safety laws and regulations.
7. Paragraphs 2 and 6 shall not affect any applicable aviation safety laws and regulations.

Article XI
Remedies on insolvency

1. This Article applies only where a Contracting State that is the primary insolvency jurisdiction has made a declaration pursuant to Article XXX(3).

Alternative A

2. Upon the occurrence of an insolvency-related event, the insolvency administrator or the debtor, as applicable, shall, subject to paragraph 7, give possession of the aircraft object to the creditor no later than the earlier of:
   (a) the end of the waiting period; and
   (b) the date on which the creditor would be entitled to possession of the aircraft object if this Article did not apply.
3. For the purposes of this Article, the 'waiting period' shall be the period specified in a declaration of the Contracting State which is the primary insolvency jurisdiction.
4. References in this Article to the 'insolvency administrator' shall be to that person in its official, not in its personal, capacity.
5. Unless and until the creditor is given the opportunity to take possession under paragraph 2:
   (a) the insolvency administrator or the debtor, as applicable, shall preserve the aircraft object and maintain it and its value in accordance with the agreement; and
   (b) the creditor shall be entitled to apply for any other forms of interim relief available under the applicable law.
6. Sub-paragraph (a) of the preceding paragraph shall not preclude the use of the aircraft object under arrangements designed to preserve the aircraft object and maintain it and its value.
7. The insolvency administrator or the debtor, as applicable, may retain possession of the aircraft object where, by the time specified in paragraph 2, it has cured all defaults other than a default constituted by the opening of insolvency proceedings and has agreed to perform all future obligations under the agreement. A second waiting period shall not apply in respect of a default in the performance of such future obligations.

8. With regard to the remedies in Article IX(1):
   (a) they shall be made available by the registry authority and the administrative authorities in a Contracting State, as applicable, no later than five working days after the date on which the creditor notifies such authorities that it is entitled to procure those remedies in accordance with the Convention; and
   (b) the applicable authorities shall expeditiously co-operate with and assist the creditor in the exercise of such remedies in conformity with the applicable aviation safety laws and regulations.
9. No exercise of remedies permitted by the Convention or this Protocol may be prevented or delayed after the date specified in paragraph 2.
10. No obligations of the debtor under the agreement may be modified without the consent of the creditor.
11. Nothing in the preceding paragraph shall be construed to affect the authority, if any, of the insolvency administrator under the applicable law to terminate the agreement.
12. No rights or interests, except for non-consensual rights or interests of a category covered by a declaration pursuant to Article 39(1), shall have priority in insolvency proceedings over registered interests.
13. The Convention as modified by Article IX of this Protocol shall apply to the exercise of any remedies under this Article.

Alternative B

2. Upon the occurrence of an insolvency-related event, the insolvency administrator or the debtor, as applicable, upon the request of the creditor, shall give notice to the creditor within the time specified in a declaration of a Contracting State pursuant to Article XXX(3) whether it will:
   (a) cure all defaults other than a default constituted by the opening of insolvency proceedings and agree to perform all future obligations, under the agreement and related transaction documents; or
   (b) give the creditor the opportunity to take possession of the aircraft object, in accordance with the applicable law.
3. The applicable law referred to in sub-paragraph (b) of the preceding paragraph may permit the court to require the taking of any additional step or the provision of any additional guarantee.
4. The creditor shall provide evidence of its claims and proof that its international interest has been registered.
5. If the insolvency administrator or the debtor, as applicable, does not give notice in conformity with paragraph 2, or when the insolvency administrator or the debtor has declared that it will give the creditor the opportunity to take possession of the aircraft object but fails to do so, the court may permit the creditor to take possession of the aircraft object upon such terms as the court may order and may require the taking of any additional step or the provision of any additional guarantee.
6. The aircraft object shall not be sold pending a decision by a court regarding the claim and the international interest.

Article XII
Insolvency assistance

1. This Article applies only where a Contracting State has made a declaration pursuant to Article XXX(1).
2. The courts of a Contracting State in which an aircraft object is situated shall, in accordance with the law of the Contracting State, co-operate to the maximum extent possible with foreign courts and foreign insolvency administrators in carrying out the provisions of Article XI.

Article XIII
De-registration and export request authorisation

1. This Article applies only where a Contracting State has made a declaration pursuant to Article XXX(1).
2. Where the debtor has issued an irrevocable de-registration and export request authorisation substantially in the form annexed to this Protocol and has submitted such authorisation for recordation to the registry authority, that authorisation shall be so recorded.
3. The person in whose favour the authorisation has been issued (the 'authorised party') or its certified designee shall be the sole person entitled to exercise the remedies specified in Article IX(1) and may do so only in accordance with the authorisation and applicable aviation safety laws and regulations. Such authorisation may not be revoked by the debtor without the consent in writing of the authorised party. The registry authority shall remove an authorisation from the registry at the request of the authorised party.
4. The registry authority and other administrative authorities in Contracting States shall expeditiously co-operate with and assist the authorised party in the exercise of the remedies specified in Article IX.

Article XIV
Modification of priority provisions

1. A buyer of an aircraft object under a registered sale acquires its interest in that object free from an interest subsequently registered and from an unregistered interest, even if the buyer has actual knowledge of the unregistered interest.
2. A buyer of an aircraft object acquires its interest in that object subject to an interest registered at the time of its acquisition.
3. Ownership of or another right or interest in an aircraft engine shall not be affected by its installation on or removal from an aircraft.
4. Article 29(7) of the Convention applies to an item, other than an object, installed on an airframe, aircraft engine or helicopter.

Article XV
Modification of assignment provisions

Article 33(1) of the Convention applies as if the following were added immediately after sub-paragraph (b):
> 'and (c)the debtor has consented in writing, whether or not the consent is given in advance of the assignment or identifies the assignee.'

Article XVI
Debtor provisions

1. In the absence of a default within the meaning of Article 11 of the Convention, the debtor shall be entitled to the quiet possession and use of the object in accordance with the agreement as against:

   (a) its creditor and the holder of any interest from which the debtor takes free pursuant to Article 29(4) of the Convention or, in the capacity of buyer, Article XIV(1) of this Protocol, unless and to the extent that the debtor has otherwise agreed; and

   (b) the holder of any interest to which the debtor's right or interest is subject pursuant to Article 29(4) of the Convention or, in the capacity of buyer, Article XIV(2) of this Protocol, but only to the extent, if any, that such holder has agreed.

2. Nothing in the Convention or this Protocol affects the liability of a creditor for any breach of the agreement under the applicable law in so far as that agreement relates to an aircraft object.

CHAPTER III
REGISTRY PROVISIONS RELATING TO
INTERNATIONAL INTERESTS IN AIRCRAFT OBJECTS

Article XVII
The Supervisory Authority and the Registrar

1. The Supervisory Authority shall be the international entity designated by a Resolution adopted by the Diplomatic Conference to Adopt a Mobile Equipment Convention and an Aircraft Protocol.

2. Where the international entity referred to in the preceding paragraph is not able and willing to act as Supervisory Authority, a Conference of Signatory and Contracting States shall be convened to designate another Supervisory Authority.

3. The Supervisory Authority and its officers and employees shall enjoy such immunity from legal and administrative process as is provided under the rules applicable to them as an international entity or otherwise.

4. The Supervisory Authority may establish a commission of experts, from among persons nominated by Signatory and Contracting States and having the necessary qualifications and experience, and entrust it with the task of assisting the Supervisory Authority in the discharge of its functions.

5. The first Registrar shall operate the International Registry for a period of five years from the date of entry into force of this Protocol. Thereafter, the Registrar shall be appointed or reappointed at regular five-yearly intervals by the Supervisory Authority.

Article XVIII
First regulations

The first regulations shall be made by the Supervisory Authority so as to take effect upon the entry into force of this Protocol.

Article XIX
Designated entry points

1. Subject to paragraph 2, a Contracting State may at any time designate an entity or entities in its territory as the entry point or entry points through which there shall or may be transmitted to the International Registry information required for registration other than registration of a notice of a national interest or a right or interest under Article 40 in either case arising under the laws of another State.

2. A designation made under the preceding paragraph may permit, but not compel, use of a designated entry point or entry points for information required for registrations in respect of aircraft engines.

Article XX
Additional modifications to Registry provisions

1. For the purposes of Article 19(6) of the Convention, the search criteria for an aircraft object shall be the name of its manufacturer, its manufacturer's serial number and its model designation, supplemented as necessary to ensure uniqueness. Such supplementary information shall be specified in the regulations.

2. For the purposes of Article 25(2) of the Convention and in the circumstances there described, the holder of a registered prospective international interest or a registered prospective assignment of an international interest or the person in whose favour a prospective sale has been registered shall take such steps as are within its power to procure the discharge of the registration no later than five working days after the receipt of the demand described in such paragraph.

3. The fees referred to in Article 17(2)(h) of the Convention shall be determined so as to recover the reasonable costs of establishing, operating and regulating the International Registry and the reasonable costs of the Supervisory Authority associated with the performance of the functions, exercise of the powers, and discharge of the duties contemplated by Article 17(2) of the Convention.

4. The centralised functions of the International Registry shall be operated and administered by the Registrar on a twenty-four hour basis. The various entry points shall be operated at least during working hours in their respective territories.

5. The amount of the insurance or financial guarantee referred to in Article 28(4) of the Convention shall, in respect of each event, not be less than the maximum value of an aircraft object as determined by the Supervisory Authority.

6. Nothing in the Convention shall preclude the Registrar from procuring insurance or a financial guarantee covering events for which the Registrar is not liable under Article 28 of the Convention.

CHAPTER IV
JURISDICTION

Article XXI
Modification of jurisdiction provisions

For the purposes of Article 43 of the Convention and subject to Article 42 of the Convention, a court of a Contracting State also has jurisdiction where the object is a helicopter, or an airframe pertaining to an aircraft, for which that State is the State of registry.

Article XXII
Waivers of sovereign immunity

1. Subject to paragraph 2, a waiver of sovereign immunity from jurisdiction of the courts specified in Article 42 or Article 43 of the Convention or relating to enforcement of rights and interests relating to an aircraft object under the Convention shall be binding and, if the other conditions to such jurisdiction or enforcement have been satisfied, shall be effective to confer jurisdiction and permit enforcement, as the case may be.
2. A waiver under the preceding paragraph must be in writing and contain a description of the aircraft object.

CHAPTER V
RELATIONSHIP WITH OTHER CONVENTIONS

Article XXIII
Relationship with the *Convention on the International Recognition of Rights in Aircraft*

The Convention shall, for a Contracting State that is a party to the *Convention on the International Recognition of Rights in Aircraft*, signed at Geneva on 19 June 1948, supersede that Convention as it relates to aircraft, as defined in this Protocol, and to aircraft objects. However, with respect to rights or interests not covered or affected by the present Convention, the Geneva Convention shall not be superseded.

Article XXIV
Relationship with the *Convention for the Unification of Certain Rules Relating to the Precautionary Attachment of Aircraft*

1. The Convention shall, for a Contracting State that is a Party to the *Convention for the Unification of Certain Rules Relating to the Precautionary Attachment of Aircraft*, signed at Rome on 29 May 1933, supersede that Convention as it relates to aircraft, as defined in this Protocol.
2. A Contracting State Party to the above Convention may declare, at the time of ratification, acceptance, approval of, or accession to this Protocol, that it will not apply this Article.

Article XXV
Relationship with the *UNIDROIT Convention on International Financial Leasing*

The Convention shall supersede the *UNIDROIT Convention on International Financial Leasing*, signed at Ottawa on 28 May 1988, as it relates to aircraft objects.

CHAPTER VI
FINAL PROVISIONS

Article XXVI
Signature, ratification, acceptance, approval or accession

1. This Protocol shall be open for signature in Cape Town on 16 November 2001 by States participating in the Diplomatic Conference to Adopt a Mobile Equipment

Convention and an Aircraft Protocol held at Cape Town from 29 October to 16 November 2001. After 16 November 2001, this Protocol shall be open to all States for signature at the Headquarters of the International Institute for the Unification of Private Law (UNIDROIT) in Rome until it enters into force in accordance with Article XXVIII.

2. This Protocol shall be subject to ratification, acceptance or approval by States which have signed it.

3. Any State which does not sign this Protocol may accede to it at any time.

4. Ratification, acceptance, approval or accession is effected by the deposit of a formal instrument to that effect with the Depositary.

5. A State may not become a Party to this Protocol unless it is or becomes also a Party to the Convention.

Article XXVII
Regional Economic Integration Organisations

1. A Regional Economic Integration Organisation which is constituted by sovereign States and has competence over certain matters governed by this Protocol may similarly sign, accept, approve or accede to this Protocol. The Regional Economic Integration Organisation shall in that case have the rights and obligations of a Contracting State, to the extent that that Organisation has competence over matters governed by this Protocol. Where the number of Contracting States is relevant in this Protocol, the Regional Economic Integration Organisation shall not count as a Contracting State in addition to its Member States which are Contracting States.

2. The Regional Economic Integration Organisation shall, at the time of signature, acceptance, approval or accession, make a declaration to the Depositary specifying the matters governed by this Protocol in respect of which competence has been transferred to that Organisation by its Member States. The Regional Economic Integration Organisation shall promptly notify the Depositary of any changes to the distribution of competence, including new transfers of competence, specified in the declaration under this paragraph.

3. Any reference to a 'Contracting State' or 'Contracting States' or 'State Party' or 'States Parties' in this Protocol applies equally to a Regional Economic Integration Organisation where the context so requires.

Article XXVIII
Entry into force

1. This Protocol enters into force on the first day of the month following the expiration of three months after the date of the deposit of the eighth instrument of ratification, acceptance, approval or accession, between the States which have deposited such instruments.

2. For other States this Protocol enters into force on the first day of the month following the expiration of three months after the date of the deposit of its instrument of ratification, acceptance, approval or accession.

Article XXIX
Territorial units

1. If a Contracting State has territorial units in which different systems of law are applicable in relation to the matters dealt with in this Protocol, it may, at the time of ratification, acceptance, approval or accession, declare that this Protocol is to extend to all its territorial units or only to one or more of them and may modify its declaration by submitting another declaration at any time.
2. Any such declaration shall state expressly the territorial units to which this Protocol applies.
3. If a Contracting State has not made any declaration under paragraph 1, this Protocol shall apply to all territorial units of that State.
4. Where a Contracting State extends this Protocol to one or more of its territorial units, declarations permitted under this Protocol may be made in respect of each such territorial unit, and the declarations made in respect of one territorial unit may be different from those made in respect of another territorial unit.
5. If by virtue of a declaration under paragraph 1, this Protocol extends to one or more territorial units of a Contracting State:
   (a) the debtor is considered to be situated in a Contracting State only if it is incorporated or formed under a law in force in a territorial unit to which the Convention and this Protocol apply or if it has its registered office or statutory seat, centre of administration, place of business or habitual residence in a territorial unit to which the Convention and this Protocol apply;
   (b) any reference to the location of the object in a Contracting State refers to the location of the object in a territorial unit to which the Convention and this Protocol apply; and
   (c) any reference to the administrative authorities in that Contracting State shall be construed as referring to the administrative authorities having jurisdiction in a territorial unit to which the Convention and this Protocol apply and any reference to the national register or to the registry authority in that Contracting State shall be construed as referring to the aircraft register in force or to the registry authority having jurisdiction in the territorial unit or units to which the Convention and this Protocol apply.

Article XXX
Declarations relating to certain provisions

1. A Contracting State may, at the time of ratification, acceptance, approval of, or accession to this Protocol, declare that it will apply any one or more of Articles VIII, XII and XIII of this Protocol.
2. A Contracting State may, at the time of ratification, acceptance, approval of, or accession to this Protocol, declare that it will apply Article X of this Protocol, wholly or in part. If it so declares with respect to Article X(2), it shall specify the time-period required thereby.
3. A Contracting State may, at the time of ratification, acceptance, approval of, or accession to this Protocol, declare that it will apply the entirety of Alternative A, or the entirety of Alternative B of Article XI and, if so, shall specify the types of insolvency proceeding, if any, to which it will apply Alternative A and the types of insolvency proceeding, if any,

to which it will apply Alternative B. A Contracting State making a declaration pursuant to this paragraph shall specify the time-period required by Article XI.

4. The courts of Contracting States shall apply Article XI in conformity with the declaration made by the Contracting State which is the primary insolvency jurisdiction.

5. A Contracting State may, at the time of ratification, acceptance, approval of, or accession to this Protocol, declare that it will not apply the provisions of Article XXI, wholly or in part. The declaration shall specify under which conditions the relevant Article will be applied, in case it will be applied partly, or otherwise which other forms of interim relief will be applied.

Article XXXI
Declarations under the Convention

Declarations made under the Convention, including those made under Articles 39, 40, 50, 53, 54, 55, 57, 58 and 60 of the Convention, shall be deemed to have also been made under this Protocol unless stated otherwise.

Article XXXII
Reservations and declarations

1. No reservations may be made to this Protocol but declarations authorised by Articles XXIV, XXIX, XXX, XXXI, XXXIII and XXXIV may be made in accordance with these provisions.

2. Any declaration or subsequent declaration or any withdrawal of a declaration made under this Protocol shall be notified in writing to the Depositary.

Article XXXIII
Subsequent declarations

1. A State Party may make a subsequent declaration, other than a declaration made in accordance with Article XXXI under Article 60 of the Convention, at any time after the date on which this Protocol has entered into force for it, by notifying the Depositary to that effect.

2. Any such subsequent declaration shall take effect on the first day of the month following the expiration of six months after the date of receipt of the notification by the Depositary. Where a longer period for that declaration to take effect is specified in the notification, it shall take effect upon the expiration of such longer period after receipt of the notification by the Depositary.

3. Notwithstanding the previous paragraphs, this Protocol shall continue to apply, as if no such subsequent declarations had been made, in respect of all rights and interests arising prior to the effective date of any such subsequent declaration.

Article XXXIV
Withdrawal of declarations

1. Any State Party having made a declaration under this Protocol, other than a declaration made in accordance with Article XXXI under Article 60 of the Convention, may withdraw it at any time by notifying the Depositary. Such withdrawal is to take effect on

the first day of the month following the expiration of six months after the date of receipt of the notification by the Depositary.

2. Notwithstanding the previous paragraph, this Protocol shall continue to apply, as if no such withdrawal of declaration had been made, in respect of all rights and interests arising prior to the effective date of any such withdrawal.

Article XXXV
Denunciations

1. Any State Party may denounce this Protocol by notification in writing to the Depositary.
2. Any such denunciation shall take effect on the first day of the month following the expiration of twelve months after the date of receipt of the notification by the Depositary.
3. Notwithstanding the previous paragraphs, this Protocol shall continue to apply, as if no such denunciation had been made, in respect of all rights and interests arising prior to the effective date of any such denunciation.

Article XXXVI
Review Conferences, amendments and related matters

1. The Depositary, in consultation with the Supervisory Authority, shall prepare reports yearly, or at such other time as the circumstances may require, for the States Parties as to the manner in which the international regime established in the Convention as amended by this Protocol has operated in practice. In preparing such reports, the Depositary shall take into account the reports of the Supervisory Authority concerning the functioning of the international registration system.
2. At the request of not less than twenty-five per cent of the States Parties, Review Conferences of the States Parties shall be convened from time to time by the Depositary, in consultation with the Supervisory Authority, to consider:
   (a) the practical operation of the Convention as amended by this Protocol and its effectiveness in facilitating the asset-based financing and leasing of the objects covered by its terms;
   (b) the judicial interpretation given to, and the application made of the terms of this Protocol and the regulations;
   (c) the functioning of the international registration system, the performance of the Registrar and its oversight by the Supervisory Authority, taking into account the reports of the Supervisory Authority; and
   (d) whether any modifications to this Protocol or the arrangements relating to the International Registry are desirable.
3. Any amendment to this Protocol shall be approved by at least a two-thirds majority of States Parties participating in the Conference referred to in the preceding paragraph and shall then enter into force in respect of States which have ratified, accepted or approved such amendment when it has been ratified, accepted or approved by eight States in accordance with the provisions of Article XXVIII relating to its entry into force.

Article XXXVII
Depositary and its functions

1. Instruments of ratification, acceptance, approval or accession shall be deposited with the International Institute for the Unification of Private Law (UNIDROIT), which is hereby designated the Depositary.
2. The Depositary shall:
   (a) inform all Contracting States of:
      (i) each new signature or deposit of an instrument of ratification, acceptance, approval or accession, together with the date thereof;
      (ii) the date of entry into force of this Protocol;
      (iii) each declaration made in accordance with this Protocol, together with the date thereof;
      (iv) the withdrawal or amendment of any declaration, together with the date thereof; and
      (v) the notification of any denunciation of this Protocol together with the date thereof and the date on which it takes effect;
   (b) transmit certified true copies of this Protocol to all Contracting States;
   (c) provide the Supervisory Authority and the Registrar with a copy of each instrument of ratification, acceptance, approval or accession, together with the date of deposit thereof, of each declaration or withdrawal or amendment of a declaration and of each notification of denunciation, together with the date of notification thereof, so that the information contained therein is easily and fully available; and
   (d) perform such other functions customary for depositaries.

In witness whereof the undersigned Plenipotentiaries, having been duly authorised, have signed this Protocol.

Done at Cape Town, this sixteenth day of November, two thousand and one, in a single original in the English, Arabic, Chinese, French, Russian and Spanish languages, all texts being equally authentic, such authenticity to take effect upon verification by the Joint Secretariat of the Conference under the authority of the President of the Conference within ninety days hereof as to the conformity of the texts with one another.

ANNEX
FORM OF IRREVOCABLE DE-REGISTRATION AND EXPORT REQUEST AUTHORISATION

Annex referred to in Article XIII

[Insert Date]

To: [Insert Name of Registry Authority]

Re: Irrevocable De-Registration and Export Request Authorisation

The undersigned is the registered [operator] [owner]* of the [insert the airframe/helicopter manufacturer name and model number] bearing manufacturers serial number

---

* Select the term that reflects the relevant nationality registration criterion.

[insert manufacturer's serial number] and registration [number] [mark] [insert registration number/mark] (together with all installed, incorporated or attached accessories, parts and equipment, the 'aircraft').

This instrument is an irrevocable de-registration and export request authorisation issued by the undersigned in favour of [insert name of creditor] ('the authorised party') under the authority of Article XIII of the Protocol to the Convention on International Interests in Mobile Equipment on Matters specific to Aircraft Equipment. In accordance with that Article, the undersigned hereby requests:

   (i) recognition that the authorised party or the person it certifies as its designee is the sole person entitled to:
      (a) procure the de-registration of the aircraft from the [insert name of aircraft register] maintained by the [insert name of registry authority] for the purposes of Chapter III of the *Convention on International Civil Aviation*, signed at Chicago, on 7 December 1944, and
      (b) procure the export and physical transfer of the aircraft from [insert name of country]; and
   (ii) confirmation that the authorised party or the person it certifies as its designee may take the action specified in clause (i) above on written demand without the consent of the undersigned and that, upon such demand, the authorities in [insert name of country] shall co-operate with the authorised party with a view to the speedy completion of such action.

The rights in favour of the authorised party established by this instrument may not be revoked by the undersigned without the written consent of the authorised party.

Please acknowledge your agreement to this request and its terms by appropriate notation in the space provided below and lodging this instrument in [insert name of registry authority].

[insert name of operator/owner]

Agreed to and lodged this	By: [insert name of signatory]
[insert date]	Its: [insert title of signatory]
[insert relevant notational details]	

TABLE OF STATE RATIFICATIONS

Total number of signatures not followed by ratifications: 25
Total number of ratifications/accessions: 4

Not yet in force
(Condition: 8 ratifications)

State	Signature	Ratification	By	Entry into force
Burundi	16 November 2001			
Chile	16 November 2001			
China	16 November 2001			
Congo	16 November 2001			
Cuba	16 November 2001			
Ethiopia	16 November 2001	21 November 2003	Ratification	

State	Signature	Ratification	By	Entry into force
France	16 November 2001			
Germany	17 September 2002			
Ghana	16 November 2001			
Italy	6 December 2001			
Jamaica	16 November 2001			
Jordan	16 November 2001			
Kenya	16 November 2001			
Lesotho	16 November 2001			
Nigeria	16 November 2001	16 December 2003	Ratification	
Panama	11 September 2002	28 July 2003	Ratification	
Saudi Arabia	12 March 2003			
Senegal	2 April 2002			
South Africa	16 November 2001			
Sudan	16 November 2001			
Switzerland	16 November 2001			
Tonga	16 November 2001			
Turkey	16 November 2001			
United Kingdom	16 November 2001			
United Republic of Tanzania	16 November 2001			
United States of America	9 May 2003			
Pakistan		22 January 2004	Accession	1 April 2004
Ukraine	3 March 2004			
Canada	31 March 2004			

Note. A list of reservations and declarations made by States at the time of signature has not been included in this volume. These can be obtained from http://www.unidroit.org/english/implement/i-2001-aircraftprotocol.htm.

(iii) International Receivables Financing

(a) UNIDROIT CONVENTION ON INTERNATIONAL FACTORING*

(Ottawa, 28 May 1988)

PREAMBLE

The States parties to this Convention,

Conscious of the fact that international factoring has a significant role to play in the development of international trade,

Recognising therefore the importance of adopting uniform rules to provide a legal framework that will facilitate international factoring, while maintaining a fair balance of interests between the different parties involved in factoring transactions,

Have agreed as follows:

CHAPTER I
SPHERE OF APPLICATION AND GENERAL PROVISIONS

Article 1

1. This Convention governs factoring contracts and assignments of receivables as described in this Chapter.
2. For the purposes of this Convention, 'factoring contract' means a contract concluded between one party (the supplier) and another party (the factor) pursuant to which:

---

* Reproduced with the kind permission of UNIDROIT.

(a) the supplier may or will assign to the factor receivables arising from contracts of sale of goods made between the supplier and its customers (debtors) other than those for the sale of goods bought primarily for their personal, family or household use;

(b) the factor is to perform at least two of the following functions:
   —finance for the supplier, including loans and advance payments;
   —maintenance of accounts (ledgering) relating to the receivables;
   —collection of receivables;
   —protection against default in payment by debtors;

(c) notice of the assignment of the receivables is to be given to debtors.

3. In this Convention references to 'goods' and 'sale of goods' shall include services and the supply of services.

4. For the purposes of this Convention:
   (a) a notice in writing need not be signed but must identify the person by whom or in whose name it is given;
   (b) 'notice in writing' includes, but is not limited to, telegrams, telex and any other telecommunication capable of being reproduced in tangible form;
   (c) a notice in writing is given when it is received by the addressee.

Article 2

1. This Convention applies whenever the receivables assigned pursuant to a factoring contract arise from a contract of sale of goods between a supplier and a debtor whose places of business are in different States and:
   (a) those States and the State in which the factor has its place of business are Contracting States; or
   (b) both the contract of sale of goods and the factoring contract are governed by the law of a Contracting State.

2. A reference in this Convention to a party's place of business shall, if it has more than one place of business, mean the place of business which has the closest relationship to the relevant contract and its performance, having regard to the circumstances known to or contemplated by the parties at any time before or at the conclusion of that contract.

Article 3

1. The application of this Convention may be excluded:
   (a) by the parties to the factoring contract; or
   (b) by the parties to the contract of sale of goods, as regards receivables arising at or after the time when the factor has been given notice in writing of such exclusion.

2. Where the application of this Convention is excluded in accordance with the previous paragraph, such exclusion may be made only as regards the Convention as a whole.

Article 4

1. In the interpretation of this Convention, regard is to be had to its object and purpose as set forth in the preamble, to its international character and to the need to promote uniformity in its application and the observance of good faith in international trade.

2. Questions concerning matters governed by this Convention which are not expressly settled in it are to be settled in conformity with the general principles on which it is

based or, in the absence of such principles, in conformity with the law applicable by virtue of the rules of private international law.

CHAPTER II
RIGHTS AND DUTIES OF THE PARTIES

Article 5

As between the parties to the factoring contract:

(a) a provision in the factoring contract for the assignment of existing or future receivables shall not be rendered invalid by the fact that the contract does not specify them individually, if at the time of conclusion of the contract or when they come into existence they can be identified to the contract;

(b) a provision in the factoring contract by which future receivables are assigned operates to transfer the receivables to the factor when they come into existence without the need for any new act of transfer.

Article 6

1. The assignment of a receivable by the supplier to the factor shall be effective notwithstanding any agreement between the supplier and the debtor prohibiting such assignment.

2. However, such assignment shall not be effective against the debtor when, at the time of conclusion of the contract of sale of goods, it has its place of business in a Contracting State which has made a declaration under Article 18 of this Convention.

3. Nothing in paragraph 1 shall affect any obligation of good faith owed by the supplier to the debtor or any liability of the supplier to the debtor in respect of an assignment made in breach of the terms of the contract of sale of goods.

Article 7

A factoring contract may validly provide as between the parties thereto for the transfer, with or without a new act of transfer, of all or any of the supplier's rights deriving from the contract of sale of goods, including the benefit of any provision in the contract of sale of goods reserving to the supplier title to the goods or creating any security interest.

Article 8

1. The debtor is under a duty to pay the factor if, and only if, the debtor does not have knowledge of any other person's superior right to payment and notice in writing of the assignment:

(a) is given to the debtor by the supplier or by the factor with the supplier's authority;

(b) reasonably identifies the receivables which have been assigned and the factor to whom or for whose account the debtor is required to make payment; and

(c) relates to receivables arising under a contract of sale of goods made at or before the time the notice is given.

2. Irrespective of any other ground on which payment by the debtor to the factor discharges the debtor from liability, payment shall be effective for this purpose if made in accordance with the previous paragraph.

Article 9

1. In a claim by the factor against the debtor for payment of a receivable arising under a contract of sale of goods the debtor may set up against the factor all defences arising under that contract of which the debtor could have availed itself if such claim had been made by the supplier.
2. The debtor may also assert against the factor any right of set-off in respect of claims existing against the supplier in whose favour the receivable arose and available to the debtor at the time a notice in writing of assignment conforming to Article 8(1) was given to the debtor.

Article 10

1. Without prejudice to the debtor's rights under Article 9, non-performance or defective or late performance of the contract of sale of goods shall not by itself entitle the debtor to recover a sum paid by the debtor to the factor if the debtor has a right to recover that sum from the supplier.
2. The debtor who has such a right to recover from the supplier a sum paid to the factor in respect of a receivable shall nevertheless be entitled to recover that sum from the factor to the extent that:
   (a) the factor has not discharged an obligation to make payment to the supplier in respect of that receivable; or
   (b) the factor made such payment at a time when it knew of the supplier's non-performance or defective or late performance as regards the goods to which the debtor's payment relates.

CHAPTER III
SUBSEQUENT ASSIGNMENTS

Article 11

1. Where a receivable is assigned by a supplier to a factor pursuant to a factoring contract governed by this Convention:
   (a) the rules set out in Articles 5 to 10 shall, subject to sub-paragraph (b) of this paragraph, apply to any subsequent assignment of the receivable by the factor or by a subsequent assignee;
   (b) the provisions of Articles 8 to 10 shall apply as if the subsequent assignee were the factor.
2. For the purposes of this Convention, notice to the debtor of the subsequent assignment also constitutes notice of the assignment to the factor.

Article 12

This Convention shall not apply to a subsequent assignment which is prohibited by the terms of the factoring contract.

CHAPTER IV
FINAL PROVISIONS

Article 13

1. This Convention is open for signature at the concluding meeting of the Diplomatic Conference for the Adoption of the Draft UNIDROIT Conventions on International Factoring and International Financial Leasing and will remain open for signature by all States at Ottawa until 31 December 1990.
2. This Convention is subject to ratification, acceptance or approval by States which have signed it.
3. This Convention is open for accession by all States which are not signatory States as from the date it is open for signature.
4. Ratification, acceptance, approval or accession is effected by the deposit of a formal instrument to that effect with the depositary.

Article 14

1. This Convention enters into force on the first day of the month following the expiration of six months after the date of deposit of the third instrument of ratification, acceptance, approval or accession.
2. For each State that ratifies, accepts, approves, or accedes to this Convention after the deposit of the third instrument of ratification, acceptance, approval or accession, this Convention enters into force in respect of that State on the first day of the month following the expiration of six months after the date of the deposit of its instrument of ratification, acceptance, approval or accession.

Article 15

This Convention does not prevail over any treaty which has already been or may be entered into.

Article 16

1. If a Contracting State has two or more territorial units in which different systems of law are applicable in relation to the matters dealt with in this convention, it may, at the time of signature, ratification, acceptance, approval or accession, declare that this Convention is to extend to all its territorial units or only to one or more of them, and may substitute its declaration by another declaration at any time.
2. These declarations are to be notified to the depositary and are to state expressly the territorial units to which the Convention extends.
3. If, by virtue of a declaration under this article, this Convention extends to one or more but not all of the territorial units of a Contracting State, and if the place of business of a party is located in that State, this place of business, for the purposes of this Convention, is considered not to be in a Contracting State, unless it is in a territorial unit to which the Convention extends.
4. If a Contracting State makes no declaration under paragraph 1, the Convention is to extend to all territorial units of that State.

Article 17

1. Two or more Contracting States which have the same or closely related legal rules on matters governed by this Convention may at any time declare that the Convention is not to apply where the supplier, the factor and the debtor have their places of business in those States. Such declarations may be made jointly or by reciprocal unilateral declarations.
2. A Contracting State which has the same or closely related legal rules on matters governed by this Convention as one or more non-Contracting States may at any time declare that the Convention is not to apply where the supplier, the factor and the debtor have their places of business in those States.
3. If a State which is the object of a declaration under the previous paragraph subsequently becomes a Contracting State, the declaration made will, as from the date on which the Convention enters into force in respect of the new Contracting State, have the effect of a declaration made under paragraph 1, provided that the new Contracting State joins in such declaration or makes a reciprocal unilateral declaration.

Article 18

A Contracting State may at any time make a declaration in accordance with Article 6(2) that an assignment under Article 6(1) shall not be effective against the debtor when, at the time of conclusion of the contract of sale of goods, it has its place of business in that State.

Article 19

1. Declarations made under this Convention at the time of signature are subject to confirmation upon ratification, acceptance or approval.
2. Declarations and confirmations of declarations are to be in writing and to be formally notified to the depositary.
3. A declaration takes effect simultaneously with the entry into force of this Convention in respect of the State concerned. However, a declaration of which the depositary receives formal notification after such entry into force takes effect on the first day of the month following the expiration of six months after the date of its receipt by the depositary. Reciprocal unilateral declarations under Article 17 take effect on the first day of the month following the expiration of six months after the receipt of the latest declaration by the depositary.
4. Any State which makes a declaration under this Convention may withdraw it at any time by a formal notification in writing addressed to the depositary. Such withdrawal is to take effect on the first day of the month following the expiration of six months after the date of the receipt of the notification by the depositary.
5. A withdrawal of a declaration made under Article 17 renders inoperative in relation to the withdrawing State, as from the date on which the withdrawal takes effect, any joint or reciprocal unilateral declaration made by another State under that Article.

Article 20

No reservations are permitted except those expressly authorised in this Convention.

Article 21

This Convention applies when receivables assigned pursuant to a factoring contract arise from a contract of sale of goods concluded on or after the date on which the Convention enters into force in respect of the Contracting States referred to in Article 2(1)(a), or the Contracting State or States referred to in paragraph 1(b) of that Article, provided that:
(a) the factoring contract is concluded on or after that date; or
(b) the parties to the factoring contract have agreed that the Convention shall apply.

Article 22

1. This Convention may be denounced by any Contracting State at any time after the date on which it enters into force for that State.
2. Denunciation is effected by the deposit of an instrument to that effect with the depositary.
3. A denunciation takes effect on the first day of the month following the expiration of six months after the deposit of the instrument of denunciation with the depositary. Where a longer period for the denunciation to take effect is specified in the instrument of denunciation it takes effect upon the expiration of such longer period after its deposit with the depositary.

Article 23

1. This Convention shall be deposited with the Government of Canada.
2. The Government of Canada shall:
   (a) inform all States which have signed or acceded to this Convention and the President of the International Institute for the Unification of Private Law (UNIDROIT) of:
      (i) each new signature or deposit of an instrument of ratification, acceptance, approval or accession, together with the date thereof;
      (ii) each declaration made under Articles 16, 17 and 18;
      (iii) the withdrawal of any declaration made under Article 19(4);
      (iv) the date of entry into force of this Convention;
      (v) the deposit of an instrument of denunciation of this Convention together with the date of its deposit and the date on which it takes effect;
   (b) transmit certified true copies of this Convention to all signatory States, to all States acceding to the Convention and to the President of the International Institute for the Unification of Private Law (UNIDROIT).

In witness whereof the undersigned plenipotentiaries, being duly authorised by their respective Governments, have signed this Convention.

Done at Ottawa, this twenty-eighth day of May, one thousand nine hundred and eighty-eight, in a single original, of which the English and French texts are equally authentic.

TABLE OF STATE RATIFICATIONS

Total number of signatures not followed by ratifications: 10
Total number of ratifications/accessions: 6

Entered into force: 1 May 1995

(Condition: 3 ratifications)

State	Signature	Ratification	By	Entry into force
Belgium	21 December 1990			
Czechoslovakia	16 May 1990			
Finland	30 November 1990			
France	7 November 1989	23 September 1991		1 May 1995
Germany	21 December 1990	20 May 1998		1 December 1998
Ghana	28 May 1988			
Guinea	28 May 1988			
Hungary		7 May 1996	Accession	1 December 1996
Italy	13 December 1990	29 November 1993		1 May 1995
Latvia		6 August 1997	Accession	1 March 1998
Morocco	4 July 1988			
Nigeria	28 May 1988	25 October 1994		1 May 1995
Philippines	28 May 1988			
United Kingdom	31 December 1990			
United Republic of Tanzania	28 May 1988			
United States of America	28 December 1990			

Note. A list of reservations and declarations made by States has not been included in this volume. These can be obtained from **http://www.unidroit.org/english/implement/i-88-f.htm.**

603

(b) UNITED NATIONS CONVENTION ON THE ASSIGNMENT OF RECEIVABLES IN INTERNATIONAL TRADE*

* Reproduced with the kind permission of UNCITRAL.

PREAMBLE

The Contracting States,

Reaffirming their conviction that international trade on the basis of equality and mutual benefit is an important element in the promotion of friendly relations among States,

Considering that problems created by uncertainties as to the content and the choice of legal regime applicable to the assignment of receivables constitute an obstacle to international trade,

Desiring to establish principles and to adopt rules relating to the assignment of receivables that would create certainty and transparency and promote the modernization of the law relating to assignments of receivables, while protecting existing assignment practices and facilitating the development of new practices,

Desiring also to ensure adequate protection of the interests of debtors in assignments of receivables,

Being of the opinion that the adoption of uniform rules governing the assignment of receivables would promote the availability of capital and credit at more affordable rates and thus facilitate the development of international trade,

Have agreed as follows:

CHAPTER I
SCOPE OF APPLICATION

Article 1
Scope of application

1. This Convention applies to:
   (a) Assignments of international receivables and to international assignments of receivables as defined in this chapter, if, at the time of conclusion of the contract of assignment, the assignor is located in a Contracting State; and
   (b) Subsequent assignments, provided that any prior assignment is governed by this Convention.

2. This Convention applies to subsequent assignments that satisfy the criteria set forth in paragraph 1(a) of this Article, even if it did not apply to any prior assignment of the same receivable.

3. This Convention does not affect the rights and obligations of the debtor unless, at the time of conclusion of the original contract, the debtor is located in a Contracting State or the law governing the original contract is the law of a Contracting State.

4. The provisions of chapter V apply to assignments of international receivables and to international assignments of receivables as defined in this chapter independently of paragraphs 1 to 3 of this article. However, those provisions do not apply if a State makes a declaration under article 39.

5. The provisions of the annex to this Convention apply as provided in article 42.

Article 2
Assignment of receivables

For the purposes of this Convention:

(a) 'Assignment' means the transfer by agreement from one person ('assignor') to another person ('assignee') of all or part of or an undivided interest in the assignor's contractual right to payment of a monetary sum ('receivable') from a third person ('the debtor'). The creation of rights in receivables as security for indebtedness or other obligation is deemed to be a transfer;

(b) In the case of an assignment by the initial or any other assignee ('subsequent assignment'), the person who makes that assignment is the assignor and the person to whom that assignment is made is the assignee.

Article 3
Internationality

A receivable is international if, at the time of conclusion of the original contract, the assignor and the debtor are located in different States. An assignment is international if, at the time of conclusion of the contract of assignment, the assignor and the assignee are located in different States.

Article 4
Exclusions and other limitations

1. This Convention does not apply to assignments made:
   (a) To an individual for his or her personal, family or household purposes;
   (b) As part of the sale or change in the ownership or legal status of the business out of which the assigned receivables arose.

2. This Convention does not apply to assignments of receivables arising under or from:
   (a) Transactions on a regulated exchange;
   (b) Financial contracts governed by netting agreements, except a receivable owed on the termination of all outstanding transactions;
   (c) Foreign exchange transactions;
   (d) Inter-bank payment systems, inter-bank payment agreements or clearance and settlement systems relating to securities or other financial assets or instruments;
   (e) The transfer of security rights in, sale, loan or holding of or agreement to repurchase securities or other financial assets or instruments held with an intermediary;

(f) Bank deposits;

(g) A letter of credit or independent guarantee.

3. Nothing in this Convention affects the rights and obligations of any person under the law governing negotiable instruments.

4. Nothing in this Convention affects the rights and obligations of the assignor and the debtor under special laws governing the protection of parties to transactions made for personal, family or household purposes.

5. Nothing in this Convention:

(a) Affects the application of the law of a State in which real property is situated to either:

  (i) An interest in that real property to the extent that under that law the assignment of a receivable confers such an interest; or

  (ii) The priority of a right in a receivable to the extent that under that law an interest in the real property confers such a right; or

(b) Makes lawful the acquisition of an interest in real property not permitted under the law of the State in which the real property is situated.

CHAPTER II
GENERAL PROVISIONS

Article 5
Definitions and rules of interpretation

For the purposes of this Convention:

(a) 'Original contract' means the contract between the assignor and the debtor from which the assigned receivable arises;

(b) 'Existing receivable' means a receivable that arises upon or before conclusion of the contract of assignment and 'future receivable' means a receivable that arises after conclusion of the contract of assignment;

(c) 'Writing' means any form of information that is accessible so as to be usable for subsequent reference. Where this Convention requires a writing to be signed, that requirement is met if, by generally accepted means or a procedure agreed to by the person whose signature is required, the writing identifies that person and indicates that person's approval of the information contained in the writing;

(d) 'Notification of the assignment' means a communication in writing that reasonably identifies the assigned receivables and the assignee;

(e) 'Insolvency administrator' means a person or body, including one appointed on an interim basis, authorized in an insolvency proceeding to administer the reorganization or liquidation of the assignor's assets or affairs;

(f) 'Insolvency proceeding' means a collective judicial or administrative proceeding, including an interim proceeding, in which the assets and affairs of the assignor are subject to control or supervision by a court or other competent authority for the purpose of reorganization or liquidation;

(g) 'Priority' means the right of a person in preference to the right of another person and, to the extent relevant for such purpose, includes the determination whether the right is a personal or a property right, whether or not it is a security right for indebtedness or other obligation and whether any requirements necessary to render the right effective against a competing claimant have been satisfied;

(h) A person is located in the State in which it has its place of business. If the assignor or the assignee has a place of business in more than one State, the place of business is that place where the central administration of the assignor or the assignee is exercised. If the debtor has a place of business in more than one State, the place of business is that which has the closest relationship to the original contract. If a person does not have a place of business, reference is to be made to the habitual residence of that person;

(i) 'Law' means the law in force in a State other than its rules of private international law;

(j) 'Proceeds' means whatever is received in respect of an assigned receivable, whether in total or partial payment or other satisfaction of the receivable. The term includes whatever is received in respect of proceeds. The term does not include returned goods;

(k) 'Financial contract' means any spot, forward, future, option or swap transaction involving interest rates, commodities, currencies, equities, bonds, indices or any other financial instrument, any repurchase or securities lending transaction, and any other transaction similar to any transaction referred to above entered into in financial markets and any combination of the transactions mentioned above;

(l) 'Netting agreement' means an agreement between two or more parties that provides for one or more of the following:
   (i) The net settlement of payments due in the same currency on the same date whether by novation or otherwise;
   (ii) Upon the insolvency or other default by a party, the termination of all outstanding transactions at their replacement or fair market values, conversion of such sums into a single currency and netting into a single payment by one party to the other; or
   (iii) The set-off of amounts calculated as set forth in subparagraph (l) (ii) of this Article under two or more netting agreements;

(m) 'Competing claimant' means:
   (i) Another assignee of the same receivable from the same assignor, including a person who, by operation of law, claims a right in the assigned receivable as a result of its right in other property of the assignor, even if that receivable is not an international receivable and the assignment to that assignee is not an international assignment;
   (ii) A creditor of the assignor; or
   (iii) The insolvency administrator.

Article 6
Party autonomy

Subject to Article 19, the assignor, the assignee and the debtor may derogate from or vary by agreement provisions of this Convention relating to their respective rights and obligations. Such an agreement does not affect the rights of any person who is not a party to the agreement.

Article 7
Principles of interpretation

1. In the interpretation of this Convention, regard is to be had to its object and purpose as set forth in the preamble, to its international character and to the need to promote uniformity in its application and the observance of good faith in international trade.
2. Questions concerning matters governed by this Convention that are not expressly settled in it are to be settled in conformity with the general principles on which it is based or, in the absence of such principles, in conformity with the law applicable by virtue of the rules of private international law.

CHAPTER III
EFFECTS OF ASSIGNMENT

Article 8
Effectiveness of assignments

1. An assignment is not ineffective as between the assignor and the assignee or as against the debtor or as against a competing claimant, and the right of an assignee may not be denied priority, on the ground that it is an assignment of more than one receivable, future receivables or parts of or undivided interests in receivables, provided that the receivables are described:
   (a) Individually as receivables to which the assignment relates; or
   (b) In any other manner, provided that they can, at the time of the assignment or, in the case of future receivables, at the time of conclusion of the original contract, be identified as receivables to which the assignment relates.
2. Unless otherwise agreed, an assignment of one or more future receivables is effective without a new act of transfer being required to assign each receivable.
3. Except as provided in paragraph 1 of this article, article 9 and article 10, paragraphs 2 and 3, this Convention does not affect any limitations on assignments arising from law.

Article 9
Contractual limitations on assignments

1. An assignment of a receivable is effective notwithstanding any agreement between the initial or any subsequent assignor and the debtor or any subsequent assignee limiting in any way the assignor's right to assign its receivables.
2. Nothing in this article affects any obligation or liability of the assignor for breach of such an agreement, but the other party to such agreement may not avoid the original contract or the assignment contract on the sole ground of that breach. A person who is not party to such an agreement is not liable on the sole ground that it had knowledge of the agreement.
3. This article applies only to assignments of receivables:
   (a) Arising from an original contract that is a contract for the supply or lease of goods or services other than financial services, a construction contract or a contract for the sale or lease of real property;
   (b) Arising from an original contract for the sale, lease or licence of industrial or other intellectual property or of proprietary information;
   (c) Representing the payment obligation for a credit card transaction; or

(d) Owed to the assignor upon net settlement of payments due pursuant to a netting agreement involving more than two parties.

Article 10
Transfer of security rights

1. A personal or property right securing payment of the assigned receivable is transferred to the assignee without a new act of transfer. If such a right, under the law governing it, is transferable only with a new act of transfer, the assignor is obliged to transfer such right and any proceeds to the assignee.
2. A right securing payment of the assigned receivable is transferred under paragraph 1 of this article notwithstanding any agreement between the assignor and the debtor or other person granting that right, limiting in any way the assignor's right to assign the receivable or the right securing payment of the assigned receivable.
3. Nothing in this article affects any obligation or liability of the assignor for breach of any agreement under paragraph 2 of this article, but the other party to that agreement may not avoid the original contract or the assignment contract on the sole ground of that breach. A person who is not a party to such an agreement is not liable on the sole ground that it had knowledge of the agreement.
4. Paragraphs 2 and 3 of this Article apply only to assignments of receivables:
   (a) Arising from an original contract that is a contract for the supply or lease of goods or services other than financial services, a construction contract or a contract for the sale or lease of real property;
   (b) Arising from an original contract for the sale, lease or licence of industrial or other intellectual property or of proprietary information;
   (c) Representing the payment obligation for a credit card transaction; or
   (d) Owed to the assignor upon net settlement of payments due pursuant to a netting agreement involving more than two parties.
5. The transfer of a possessory property right under paragraph 1 of this article does not affect any obligations of the assignor to the debtor or the person granting the property right with respect to the property transferred existing under the law governing that property right.
6. Paragraph 1 of this article does not affect any requirement under rules of law other than this Convention relating to the form or registration of the transfer of any rights securing payment of the assigned receivable.

CHAPTER IV
RIGHTS, OBLIGATIONS AND DEFENCES

SECTION I
ASSIGNOR AND ASSIGNEE

Article 11
Rights and obligations of the assignor and the assignee

1. The mutual rights and obligations of the assignor and the assignee arising from their agreement are determined by the terms and conditions set forth in that agreement, including any rules or general conditions referred to therein.

2. The assignor and the assignee are bound by any usage to which they have agreed and, unless otherwise agreed, by any practices they have established between themselves.

3. In an international assignment, the assignor and the assignee are considered, unless otherwise agreed, implicitly to have made applicable to the assignment a usage that in international trade is widely known to, and regularly observed by, parties to the particular type of assignment or to the assignment of the particular category of receivables.

Article 12
Representations of the assignor

1. Unless otherwise agreed between the assignor and the assignee, the assignor represents at the time of conclusion of the contract of assignment that;
   (a) The assignor has the right to assign the receivable;
   (b) The assignor has not previously assigned the receivable to another assignee; and
   (c) The debtor does not and will not have any defences or rights of set-off.

2. Unless otherwise agreed between the assignor and the assignee, the assignor does not represent that the debtor has, or will have, the ability to pay.

Article 13
Right to notify the debtor

1. Unless otherwise agreed between the assignor and the assignee, the assignor or the assignee or both may send the debtor notification of the assignment and a payment instruction, but after notification has been sent only the assignee may send such an instruction.

2. Notification of the assignment or a payment instruction sent in breach of any agreement referred to in paragraph 1 of this article is not ineffective for the purposes of article 17 by reason of such breach. However, nothing in this article affects any obligation or liability of the party in breach of such an agreement for any damages arising as a result of the breach.

Article 14
Right to payment

1. As between the assignor and the assignee, unless otherwise agreed and whether or not notification of the assignment has been sent:
   (a) If payment in respect of the assigned receivable is made to the assignee, the assignee is entitled to retain the proceeds and goods returned in respect of the assigned receivable;
   (b) If payment in respect of the assigned receivable is made to the assignor, the assignee is entitled to payment of the proceeds and also to goods returned to the assignor in respect of the assigned receivable; and
   (c) If payment in respect of the assigned receivable is made to another person over whom the assignee has priority, the assignee is entitled to payment of the proceeds and also to goods returned to such person in respect of the assigned receivable.

2. The assignee may not retain more than the value of its right in the receivable.

611

Article 15
Principle of debtor protection

1. Except as otherwise provided in this Convention, an assignment does not, without the consent of the debtor, affect the rights and obligations of the debtor, including the payment terms contained in the original contract.
2. A payment instruction may change the person, address or account to which the debtor is required to make payment, but may not change:
   (a) The currency of payment specified in the original contract; or
   (b) The State specified in the original contract in which payment is to be made to a State other than that in which the debtor is located.

Article 16
Notification of the debtor

1. Notification of the assignment or a payment instruction is effective when received by the debtor if it is in a language that is reasonably expected to inform the debtor about its contents. It is sufficient if notification of the assignment or a payment instruction is in the language of the original contract.
2. Notification of the assignment or a payment instruction may relate to receivables arising after notification.
3. Notification of a subsequent assignment constitutes notification of all prior assignments.

Article 17
Debtor's discharge by payment

1. Until the debtor receives notification of the assignment, the debtor is entitled to be discharged by paying in accordance with the original contract.
2. After the debtor receives notification of the assignment, subject to paragraphs 3 to 8 of this article, the debtor is discharged only by paying the assignee or, if otherwise instructed in the notification of the assignment or subsequently by the assignee in a writing received by the debtor, in accordance with such payment instruction.
3. If the debtor receives more than one payment instruction relating to a single assignment of the same receivable by the same assignor, the debtor is discharged by paying in accordance with the last payment instruction received from the assignee before payment.
4. If the debtor receives notification of more than one assignment of the same receivable made by the same assignor, the debtor is discharged by paying in accordance with the first notification received.
5. If the debtor receives notification of one or more subsequent assignments, the debtor is discharged by paying in accordance with the notification of the last of such subsequent assignments.
6. If the debtor receives notification of the assignment of a part of or an undivided interest in one or more receivables, the debtor is discharged by paying in accordance with the notification or in accordance with this article as if the debtor had not received

612

the notification. If the debtor pays in accordance with the notification, the debtor is discharged only to the extent of the part or undivided interest paid.

7. If the debtor receives notification of the assignment from the assignee, the debtor is entitled to request the assignee to provide within a reasonable period of time adequate proof that the assignment from the initial assignor to the initial assignee and any intermediate assignment have been made and, unless the assignee does so, the debtor is discharged by paying in accordance with this article as if the notification from the assignee had not been received. Adequate proof of an assignment includes but is not limited to any writing emanating from the assignor and indicating that the assignment has taken place.

8. This article does not affect any other ground on which payment by the debtor to the person entitled to payment, to a competent judicial or other authority, or to a public deposit fund discharges the debtor.

Article 18
Defences and rights of set-off of the debtor

1. In a claim by the assignee against the debtor for payment of the assigned receivable, the debtor may raise against the assignee all defences and rights of set-off arising from the original contract, or any other contract that was part of the same transaction, of which the debtor could avail itself as if the assignment had not been made and such claim were made by the assignor.

2. The debtor may raise against the assignee any other right of set-off, provided that it was available to the debtor at the time notification of the assignment was received by the debtor.

3. Notwithstanding paragraphs 1 and 2 of this article, defences and rights of set-off that the debtor may raise pursuant to Article 9 or 10 against the assignor for breach of an agreement limiting in any way the assignor's right to make the assignment are not available to the debtor against the assignee.

Article 19
Agreement not to raise defences or rights of set-off

1. The debtor may agree with the assignor in a writing signed by the debtor not to raise against the assignee the defences and rights of set-off that it could raise pursuant to Article 18. Such an agreement precludes the debtor from raising against the assignee those defences and rights of set-off.

2. The debtor may not waive defences:
   (a) Arising from fraudulent acts on the part of the assignee; or
   (b) Based on the debtor's incapacity.

3. Such an agreement may be modified only by an agreement in a writing signed by the debtor. The effect of such a modification as against the assignee is determined by Article 20, paragraph 2.

Article 20
Modification of the original contract

1. An agreement concluded before notification of the assignment between the assignor and the debtor that affects the assignee's rights is effective as against the assignee, and the assignee acquires corresponding rights.

2. An agreement concluded after notification of the assignment between the assignor and the debtor that affects the assignee's rights is ineffective as against the assignee unless:
   (a) The assignee consents to it; or
   (b) The receivable is not fully earned by performance and either the modification is provided for in the original contract or, in the context of the original contract, a reasonable assignee would consent to the modification.
3. Paragraphs 1 and 2 of this article do not affect any right of the assignor or the assignee arising from breach of an agreement between them.

Article 21
Recovery of payments

Failure of the assignor to perform the original contract does not entitle the debtor to recover from the assignee a sum paid by the debtor to the assignor or the assignee.

SECTION III

THIRD PARTIES

Article 22
Law applicable to competing rights

With the exception of matters that are settled elsewhere in this Convention and subject to articles 23 and 24, the law of the State in which the assignor is located governs the priority of the right of an assignee in the assigned receivable over the right of a competing claimant.

Article 23
Public policy and mandatory rules

1 The application of a provision of the law of the State in which the assignor is located may be refused only if the application of that provision is manifestly contrary to the public policy of the forum State.
2 The rules of the law of either the forum State or any other State that are mandatory irrespective of the law otherwise applicable may not prevent the application of a provision of the law of the State in which the assignor is located.
3 Notwithstanding paragraph 2 of this article, in an insolvency proceeding commenced in a State other than the State in which the assignor is located, any preferential right that arises, by operation of law, under the law of the forum State and is given priority over the rights of an assignee in insolvency proceedings under the law of that State may be given priority notwithstanding article 22. A State may deposit at any time a declaration identifying any such preferential right.

Article 24
Special rules on proceeds

1. If proceeds are received by the assignee, the assignee is entitled to retain those proceeds to the extent that the assignee's right in the assigned receivable had priority over the right of a competing claimant in the assigned receivable.
2. If proceeds are received by the assignor, the right of the assignee in those proceeds has priority over the right of a competing claimant in those proceeds to the same extent as

the assignee's right had priority over the right in the assigned receivable of that claimant if:

(a) The assignor has received the proceeds under instructions from the assignee to hold the proceeds for the benefit of the assignee; and

(b) The proceeds are held by the assignor for the benefit of the assignee separately and are reasonably identifiable from the assets of the assignor, such as in the case of a separate deposit or securities account containing only proceeds consisting of cash or securities.

3. Nothing in paragraph 2 of this Article affects the priority of a person having against the proceeds a right of set-off or a right created by agreement and not derived from a right in the receivable.

Article 25
Subordination

An assignee entitled to priority may at any time subordinate its priority unilaterally or by agreement in favour of any existing or future assignees.

CHAPTER V
AUTONOMOUS CONFLICT-OF-LAWS RULES

Article 26
Application of chapter V

The provisions of this chapter apply to matters that are:

(a) Within the scope of this Convention as provided in article 1, paragraph 4; and

(b) Otherwise within the scope of this Convention but not settled elsewhere in it.

Article 27
Form of a contract of assignment

1. A contract of assignment concluded between persons who are located in the same State is formally valid as between them if it satisfies the requirements of either the law which governs it or the law of the State in which it is concluded.

2. A contract of assignment concluded between persons who are located in different States is formally valid as between them if it satisfies the requirements of either the law which governs it or the law of one of those States.

Article 28
Law applicable to the mutual rights and obligations of the assignor and the assignee

1. The mutual rights and obligations of the assignor and the assignee arising from their agreement are governed by the law chosen by them.

2. In the absence of a choice of law by the assignor and the assignee, their mutual rights and obligations arising from their agreement are governed by the law of the State with which the contract of assignment is most closely connected.

Article 29
Law applicable to the rights and obligations of the assignee and the debtor

The law governing the original contract determines the effectiveness of contractual limitations on assignment as between the assignee and the debtor, the relationship between the assignee and the debtor, the conditions under which the assignment can be invoked against the debtor and whether the debtor's obligations have been discharged.

Article 30
Law applicable to priority

1. The law of the State in which the assignor is located governs the priority of the right of an assignee in the assigned receivable over the right of a competing claimant.
2. The rules of the law of either the forum State or any other State that are mandatory irrespective of the law otherwise applicable may not prevent the application of a provision of the law of the State in which the assignor is located.
3. Notwithstanding paragraph 2 of this Article, in an insolvency proceeding commenced in a State other than the State in which the assignor is located, any preferential right that arises, by operation of law, under the law of the forum State and is given priority over the rights of an assignee in insolvency proceedings under the law of that State may be given priority notwithstanding paragraph 1 of this article.

Article 31
Mandatory rules

1. Nothing in articles 27 to 29 restricts the application of the rules of the law of the forum State in a situation where they are mandatory irrespective of the law otherwise applicable.
2. Nothing in articles 27 to 29 restricts the application of the mandatory rules of the law of another State with which the matters settled in those Articles have a close connection if and insofar as, under the law of that other State, those rules must be applied irrespective of the law otherwise applicable.

Article 32
Public policy

With regard to matters settled in this chapter, the application of a provision of the law specified in this chapter may be refused only if the application of that provision is manifestly contrary to the public policy of the forum State.

CHAPTER VI
FINAL PROVISIONS

Article 33
Depositary

The Secretary-General of the United Nations is the depositary of this Convention.

Article 34
Signature, ratification, acceptance, approval, accession

1. This Convention is open for signature by all States at the Headquarters of the United Nations in New York until 31 December 2003.
2. This Convention is subject to ratification, acceptance or approval by the signatory States.
3. This Convention is open to accession by all States that are not signatory States as from the date it is open for signature.
4. Instruments of ratification, acceptance, approval and accession are to be deposited with the Secretary-General of the United Nations.

Article 35
Application to territorial units

1. If a State has two or more territorial units in which different systems of law are applicable in relation to the matters dealt with in this Convention, it may at any time declare that this Convention is to extend to all its territorial units or only one or more of them, and may at any time substitute another declaration for its earlier declaration.
2. Such declarations are to state expressly the territorial units to which this Convention extends.
3. If, by virtue of a declaration under this article, this Convention does not extend to all territorial units of a State and the assignor or the debtor is located in a territorial unit to which this Convention does not extend, this location is considered not to be in a Contracting State.
4. If, by virtue of a declaration under this article, this Convention does not extend to all territorial units of a State and the law governing the original contract is the law in force in a territorial unit to which this Convention does not extend, the law governing the original contract is considered not to be the law of a Contracting State.
5. If a State makes no declaration under paragraph 1 of this article, the Convention is to extend to all territorial units of that State.

Article 36
Location in a territorial unit

If a person is located in a State which has two or more territorial units, that person is located in the territorial unit in which it has its place of business. If the assignor or the assignee has a place of business in more than one territorial unit, the place of business is that place where the central administration of the assignor or the assignee is exercised. If the debtor has a place of business in more than one territorial unit, the place of business is that which has the closest relationship to the original contract. If a person does not have a place of business, reference is to be made to the habitual residence of that person. A State with two or more territorial units may specify by declaration at any time other rules for determining the location of a person within that State.

Article 37
Applicable law in territorial units

Any reference in this Convention to the law of a State means, in the case of a State which has two or more territorial units, the law in force in the territorial unit. Such a State may specify by declaration at any time other rules for determining the applicable law, including rules that render applicable the law of another territorial unit of that State.

Article 38
Conflicts with other international agreements

1. This Convention does not prevail over any international agreement that has already been or may be entered into and that specifically governs a transaction otherwise governed by this Convention.
2. Notwithstanding paragraph 1 of this Article, this Convention prevails over the UNIDROIT Convention on International Factoring ('the Ottawa Convention'). To the extent that this Convention does not apply to the rights and obligations of a debtor, it does not preclude the application of the Ottawa Convention with respect to the rights and obligations of that debtor.

Article 39
Declaration on application of chapter V

A State may declare at any time that it will not be bound by chapter V.

Article 40
Limitations relating to Governments and other public entities

A State may declare at any time that it will not be bound or the extent to which it will not be bound by articles 9 and 10 if the debtor or any person granting a personal or property right securing payment of the assigned receivable is located in that State at the time of conclusion of the original contract and is a Government, central or local, any subdivision thereof, or an entity constituted for a public purpose. If a State has made such a declaration, articles 9 and 10 do not affect the rights and obligations of that debtor or person. A State may list in a declaration the types of entity that are the subject of a declaration.

Article 41
Other exclusions

1. A State may declare at any time that it will not apply this Convention to specific types of assignment or to the assignment of specific categories of receivables clearly described in a declaration.
2. After a declaration under paragraph 1 of this Article takes effect:
   (a) This Convention does not apply to such types of assignment or to the assignment of such categories of receivables if the assignor is located at the time of conclusion of the contract of assignment in such a State; and
   (b) The provisions of this Convention that affect the rights and obligations of the debtor do not apply if, at the time of conclusion of the original contract, the debtor is located in such a State or the law governing the original contract is the law of such a State.
4. This article does not apply to assignments of receivables listed in article 9, paragraph 3.

Article 42
Application of the annex

1. A State may at any time declare that it will be bound by:
    (a) The priority rules set forth in section I of the annex and will participate in the international registration system established pursuant to section II of the annex;
    (b) The priority rules set forth in section I of the annex and will effectuate such rules by use of a registration system that fulfils the purposes of such rules, in which case, for the purposes of section I of the annex, registration pursuant to such a system has the same effect as registration pursuant to section II of the annex;
    (c) The priority rules set forth in section III of the annex;
    (d) The priority rules set forth in section IV of the annex; or
    (e) The priority rules set forth in articles 7 and 9 of the annex.
2. For the purposes of article 22:
    (a) The law of a State that has made a declaration pursuant to paragraph 1(a) or (b) of this Article is the set of rules set forth in section I of the annex, as affected by any declaration made pursuant to paragraph 5 of this article;
    (b) The law of a State that has made a declaration pursuant to paragraph 1(c) of this Article is the set of rules set forth in section III of the annex, as affected by any declaration made pursuant to paragraph 5 of this article;
    (c) The law of a State that has made a declaration pursuant to paragraph 1(d) of this Article is the set of rules set forth in section IV of the annex, as affected by any declaration made pursuant to paragraph 5 of this article; and
    (d) The law of a State that has made a declaration pursuant to paragraph 1(e) of this Article is the set of rules set forth in Articles 7 and 9 of the annex, as affected by any declaration made pursuant to paragraph 5 of this article.
3. A State that has made a declaration pursuant to paragraph 1 of this article may establish rules pursuant to which contracts of assignment concluded before the declaration takes effect become subject to those rules within a reasonable time.
4. A State that has not made a declaration pursuant to paragraph 1 of this article may, in accordance with priority rules in force in that State, utilize the registration system established pursuant to section II of the annex.
5. At the time a State makes a declaration pursuant to paragraph 1 of this article or thereafter, it may declare that:
    (a) It will not apply the priority rules chosen under paragraph 1 of this article to certain types of assignment or to the assignment of certain categories of receivables; or
    (b) It will apply those priority rules with modifications specified in that declaration.
6. At the request of Contracting or Signatory States to this Convention comprising not less than one third of the Contracting and Signatory States, the depositary shall convene a conference of the Contracting and Signatory States to designate the supervising authority and the first registrar and to prepare or revise the regulations referred to in section II of the annex.

Article 43
Effect of declaration

1. Declarations made under Articles 35, paragraph 1, 36, 37 or 39 to 42 at the time of signature are subject to confirmation upon ratification, acceptance or approval.

2. Declarations and confirmations of declarations are to be in writing and to be formally notified to the depositary.

3. A declaration takes effect simultaneously with the entry into force of this Convention in respect of the State concerned. However, a declaration of which the depositary receives formal notification after such entry into force takes effect on the first day of the month following the expiration of six months after the date of its receipt by the depositary.

4. A State that makes a declaration under Articles 35, paragraph 1, 36, 37 or 39 to 42 may withdraw it at any time by a formal notification in writing addressed to the depositary. Such withdrawal takes effect on the first day of the month following the expiration of six months after the date of the receipt of the notification by the depositary.

5. In the case of a declaration under articles 35, paragraph 1, 36, 37 or 39 to 42 that takes effect after the entry into force of this Convention in respect of the State concerned or in the case of a withdrawal of any such declaration, the effect of which in either case is to cause a rule in this Convention, including any annex, to become applicable:

   (a) Except as provided in paragraph 5(b) of this Article, that rule is applicable only to assignments for which the contract of assignment is concluded on or after the date when the declaration or withdrawal takes effect in respect of the Contracting State referred to in article 1, paragraph 1(a);

   (b) A rule that deals with the rights and obligations of the debtor applies only in respect of original contracts concluded on or after the date when the declaration or withdrawal takes effect in respect of the Contracting State referred to in article 1, paragraph 3.

6. In the case of a declaration under articles 35, paragraph 1, 36, 37 or 39 to 42 that takes effect after the entry into force of this Convention in respect of the State concerned or in the case of a withdrawal of any such declaration, the effect of which in either case is to cause a rule in this Convention, including any annex, to become inapplicable:

   (a) Except as provided in paragraph 6(b) of this article, that rule is inapplicable to assignments for which the contract of assignment is concluded on or after the date when the declaration or withdrawal takes effect in respect of the Contracting State referred to in article 1, paragraph 1(a);

   (b) A rule that deals with the rights and obligations of the debtor is inapplicable in respect of original contracts concluded on or after the date when the declaration or withdrawal takes effect in respect of the Contracting State referred to in article 1, paragraph 3.

7. If a rule rendered applicable or inapplicable as a result of a declaration or withdrawal referred to in paragraph 5 or 6 of this article is relevant to the determination of priority with respect to a receivable for which the contract of assignment is concluded before such declaration or withdrawal takes effect or with respect to its proceeds, the right of the assignee has priority over the right of a competing claimant to the extent that, under the law that would determine priority before such declaration or withdrawal takes effect, the right of the assignee would have priority.

Article 44
Reservations

No reservations are permitted except those expressly authorized in this Convention.

Article 45
Entry into force

1. This Convention enters into force on the first day of the month following the expiration of six months from the date of deposit of the fifth instrument of ratification, acceptance, approval or accession with the depositary.
2. For each State that becomes a Contracting State to this Convention after the date of deposit of the fifth instrument of ratification, acceptance, approval or accession, this Convention enters into force on the first day of the month following the expiration of six months after the date of deposit of the appropriate instrument on behalf of that State.
3. This Convention applies only to assignments if the contract of assignment is concluded on or after the date when this Convention enters into force in respect of the Contracting State referred to in article 1, paragraph 1(a), provided that the provisions of this Convention that deal with the rights and obligations of the debtor apply only to assignments of receivables arising from original contracts concluded on or after the date when this Convention enters into force in respect of the Contracting State referred to in article 1, paragraph 3.
4. If a receivable is assigned pursuant to a contract of assignment concluded before the date when this Convention enters into force in respect of the Contracting State referred to in article 1, paragraph 1(a), the right of the assignee has priority over the right of a competing claimant with respect to the receivable to the extent that, under the law that would determine priority in the absence of this Convention, the right of the assignee would have priority.

Article 46
Denunciation

1. A Contracting State may denounce this Convention at any time by written notification addressed to the depositary.
2. The denunciation takes effect on the first day of the month following the expiration of one year after the notification is received by the depositary. Where a longer period is specified in the notification, the denunciation takes effect upon the expiration of such longer period after the notification is received by the depositary.
3. This Convention remains applicable to assignments if the contract of assignment is concluded before the date when the denunciation takes effect in respect of the Contracting State referred to in article 1, paragraph 1(a), provided that the provisions of this Convention that deal with the rights and obligations of the debtor remain applicable only to assignments of receivables arising from original contracts concluded before the date when the denunciation takes effect in respect of the Contracting State referred to in article 1, paragraph 3.
4. If a receivable is assigned pursuant to a contract of assignment concluded before the date when the denunciation takes effect in respect of the Contracting State referred to in article 1, paragraph 1(a), the right of the assignee has priority over the right of a competing claimant with respect to the receivable to the extent that, under the law that would determine priority under this Convention, the right of the assignee would have priority.

621

Article 47
Revision and amendment

1. At the request of not less than one third of the Contracting States to this Convention, the depositary shall convene a conference of the Contracting States to revise or amend it.
2. Any instrument of ratification, acceptance, approval or accession deposited after the entry into force of an amendment to this Convention is deemed to apply to the Convention as amended.

ANNEX TO THE CONVENTION

SECTION I
PRIORITY RULES BASED ON REGISTRATION

Article 1
Priority among several assignees

As between assignees of the same receivable from the same assignor, the priority of the right of an assignee in the assigned receivable is determined by the order in which data about the assignment are registered under section II of this annex, regardless of the time of transfer of the receivable. If no such data are registered, priority is determined by the order of conclusion of the respective contracts of assignment.

Article 2
Priority between the assignee and the insolvency administrator or creditors of the assignor

The right of an assignee in an assigned receivable has priority over the right of an insolvency administrator and creditors who obtain a right in the assigned receivable by attachment, judicial act or similar act of a competent authority that gives rise to such right, if the receivable was assigned, and data about the assignment were registered under section II of this annex, before the commencement of such insolvency proceeding, attachment, judicial act or similar act.

SECTION II
REGISTRATION

Article 3
Establishment of a registration system

A registration system will be established for the registration of data about assignments, even if the relevant assignment or receivable is not international, pursuant to the regulations to be promulgated by the registrar and the supervising authority. Regulations promulgated by the registrar and the supervising authority under this annex shall be consistent with this annex. The regulations will prescribe in detail the manner in which the registration system will operate, as well as the procedure for resolving disputes relating to that operation.

622

Article 4
Registration

1. Any person may register data with regard to an assignment at the registry in accordance with this annex and the regulations. As provided in the regulations, the data registered shall be the identification of the assignor and the assignee and a brief description of the assigned receivables.
2. A single registration may cover one or more assignments by the assignor to the assignee of one or more existing or future receivables, irrespective of whether the receivables exist at the time of registration.
3. A registration may be made in advance of the assignment to which it relates. The regulations will establish the procedure for the cancellation of a registration in the event that the assignment is not made.
4. Registration or its amendment is effective from the time when the data set forth in paragraph 1 of this article are available to searchers. The registering party may specify, from options set forth in the regulations, a period of effectiveness for the registration. In the absence of such a specification, a registration is effective for a period of five years.
5. Regulations will specify the manner in which registration may be renewed, amended or cancelled and regulate such other matters as are necessary for the operation of the registration system.
6. Any defect, irregularity, omission or error with regard to the identification of the assignor that would result in data registered not being found upon a search based on a proper identification of the assignor renders the registration ineffective.

Article 5
Registry searches

1. Any person may search the records of the registry according to identification of the assignor, as set forth in the regulations, and obtain a search result in writing.
2. A search result in writing that purports to be issued by the registry is admissible as evidence and is, in the absence of evidence to the contrary, proof of the registration of the data to which the search relates, including the date and hour of registration.

SECTION III
PRIORITY RULES BASED ON THE TIME OF THE
CONTRACT OF ASSIGNMENT

Article 6
Priority among several assignees

As between assignees of the same receivable from the same assignor, the priority of the right of an assignee in the assigned receivable is determined by the order of conclusion of the respective contracts of assignment.

Article 7
Priority between the assignee and the insolvency administrator
or creditors of the assignor

The right of an assignee in an assigned receivable has priority over the right of an insolvency administrator and creditors who obtain a right in the assigned receivable by attachment, judicial act or similar act of a competent authority that gives rise to such right, if the receivable was assigned before the commencement of such insolvency proceeding, attachment, judicial act or similar act.

Article 8
Proof of time of contract of assignment

The time of conclusion of a contract of assignment in respect of articles 6 and 7 of this annex may be proved by any means, including witnesses.

SECTION IV

PRIORITY RULES BASED ON THE TIME OF

NOTIFICATION OF ASSIGNMENT

Article 9
Priority among several assignees

As between assignees of the same receivable from the same assignor, the priority of the right of an assignee in the assigned receivable is determined by the order in which notification of the respective assignments is received by the debtor. However, an assignee may not obtain priority over a prior assignment of which the assignee had knowledge at the time of conclusion of the contract of assignment to that assignee by notifying the debtor.

Article 10
Priority between the assignee and the insolvency administrator
or creditors of the assignor

The right of an assignee in an assigned receivable has priority over the right of an insolvency administrator and creditors who obtain a right in the assigned receivable by attachment, judicial act or similar act of a competent authority that gives rise to such right, if the receivable was assigned and notification was received by the debtor before the commencement of such insolvency proceeding, attachment, judicial act or similar act.

Done at New York, this 12th day of December two thousand one, in a single original, of which the Arabic, Chinese, English, French, Russian and Spanish texts are equally authentic.

In witness whereof the undersigned plenipotentiaries, being duly authorized by their respective Governments, have signed the present Convention.

TABLE OF STATE RATIFICATIONS

Total number of signatures not followed by ratifications:	3
Total number of ratifications/accessions:	0

Not yet in force
(Condition: 5 ratifications)

State	Signature	Ratification	By	Entry into force
Luxembourg	12 June 2002			
Madagascar	24 September 2003			
United States of America	30 December 2003			

8

CROSS-BORDER INSOLVENCY

A. Introductory Text

For many years States have laboured to produce a common legal framework to deal with insolvencies having an international element, in particular, issues of jurisdiction to open an insolvency proceeding, direct access of foreign insolvency administrators to local insolvency courts, recognition and enforcement in one State of insolvency orders made in another State, and the treatment of concurrent insolvencies in different States. Within the European Economic Community work started in the 1960s but for many years made no progress. The 1968 Brussels Jurisdiction and Judgments Convention[1] does not apply to insolvency proceedings[2] and the same is true of its successor, the Brussels Regulation.[3]

The 1990 Istanbul Convention,[4] produced by the Council of Europe, represented the first major breakthrough. However, with the conclusion of the 1995 EC Convention on Insolvency Proceedings interest in the Istanbul Convention waned

---

[1] Convention on Jurisdiction and Enforcement of Judgments in Civil and Commercial Matters.
[2] Article 1.
[3] Council Regulation (EC) No. 44/2001 of 22 December 2000 on jurisdiction and the recognition and enforcement of judgments in civil and commercial matters (generally known as Brussels I), Art 1(2)(b). See further p. 665.   [4] Convention on Certain International Aspects of Bankruptcy.

and it is unlikely ever to be brought into force. The EC Convention was signed by 14 of the 15 Member States but the United Kingdom refused to sign, partly because of an unconnected diplomatic dispute over British beef but primarily through failure to secure a clear statement that the Convention applied to Gibraltar. The Convention then lapsed. It is, however, reproduced in this volume because most of it is carried over into the Brussels Regulation and the Official Report on the Convention[5] can equally be used as an aid to interpretation of the regulation. In 1997 UNCITRAL produced its Model Law on Cross-Border Insolvency and three years later, following a decision to abandon the Convention method, the EC issued its Insolvency Regulation.[6] This introductory note is confined to the UNCITRAL Model Law and the EC Regulation.[7]

1. The UNCITRAL Model Law

Nature and purposes

As a Model Law the UNCITRAL text is not a legally operative instrument and is not open to ratification. States are free to reject it, to enact it in its entirety, or to select, amend, or add to particular provisions. The UNCITRAL Model Law has as its purpose the promotion of the objectives set out in its Preamble, which include cooperation between the courts and other competent authorities of the enacting State and foreign States, the fair and efficient administration of cross-border insolvencies, the protection and maximization of the debtor's assets and the facilitation of the rescue of troubled businesses.

Access and participation of foreign representatives and foreign creditors

The Model Law authorizes a foreign representative[8] to apply directly to the courts of the enacting State[9] and to institute or participate in an insolvency proceeding in that State.[10] Foreign creditors are given broadly the same rights as local creditors to commence and participate in such proceedings.[11]

Recognition of foreign proceedings and grant of relief

Subject to compliance with certain formalities a foreign representative may apply to the courts of the enacting State for recognition of foreign proceedings[12] and for urgent provisional relief to protect the assets of the debtor and the interests of creditors,[13] as by a stay of execution against the debtor's assets or the entrustment of the administration or realization of assets to the foreign representative.[14]

---

[5] See below, note 22.
[6] Council Regulation (EC) No. 1346/2000 of 29 May 2000 on insolvency proceedings.
[7] There are also a number of regional and bilateral treaties.
[8] Who may be compendiously described as the insolvency administrator.　　[9] Article 9.
[10] Articles 11 and 12.　　[11] Article 13.　　[12] Articles 15 and 16.
[13] Article 19. In order to reduce the risk of loss of assets, insolvency practitioners go to considerable trouble to synchronize proceedings for provisional relief in the different jurisdictions in which assets are situated.　　[14] Article 19.

Foreign main proceedings; concurrent proceedings

In general, the Model Law does not affect local jurisdiction rules. However, if the foreign proceeding has been recognized and is a foreign main proceeding,[15] individual proceedings in the enacting State and execution against the debtor's assets are stayed and the right to deal with the assets is suspended.[16] Further insolvency proceedings in the enacting State may be commenced only if the debtor has assets in that State and must be restricted to such assets.[17] In the case of concurrent proceedings in different States the relevant courts are required to seek cooperation and coordination under the provisions of the Model Law to the maximum extent possible.[18] There are also provisions restricting the right of an unsecured creditor to receive a payment in more than one insolvency proceeding until other creditors of the same class have received at least an equal *pro rata* payment.[19]

2. The EC Insolvency Regulation

The 2000 EC Regulation on Insolvency Proceedings adopts almost in its entirety the substance of the lapsed EC Convention, with various changes most of which are technical adaptations to reflect the direct effect of a regulation in Community law.

Nature of the regulation

The regulation is in essence a conflict of laws regulation which deals with insolvency jurisdiction, the applicable law, the effects of insolvency proceedings, and recognition across the Community of judgments by a court in a Member State having jurisdiction. Such substantive rules as there are deal principally with insolvency procedure and the duty of cooperation. The regulation does not, however, deal with substantive insolvency law, whether relating to the effect of insolvency on individual creditors, the assets comprising the estate, the avoidance of transactions, or otherwise. Substantive insolvency law remains within the exclusive competence of EC Member States. The conflict of laws position is complicated by the fact that in certain cases the regulation lays down the relevant conflict rule while in others it simply defers to the applicable law as determined by the conflict of laws rules of the forum where that is a court of a Member State which is not itself the insolvency State.

---

[15] That is, a foreign proceeding taking place in the State where the debtor has its main centre of interests (Art 2(b)).   [16] Article 20.   [17] Article 28.
[18] Article 29. Such cooperation and coordination had already evolved independently of the Model Law through the approval by the courts concerned of Protocols prepared and agreed by the insolvency administrators of their respective jurisdictions and by consultation between the judges with the knowledge of the parties.   [19] Article 32.

Types of proceeding to which the regulation applies

The regulation is confined to collective insolvency proceedings which entail the total or partial divestment of a debtor and the appointment of a liquidator.[20] Both corporate and individual insolvency are covered by the regulation, which applies not only to winding-up and bankruptcy proceedings but also to collective reorganization proceedings designed to rescue the undertaking or to improve the position of creditors in the event of an ensuing liquidation; and the term 'liquidator' is defined accordingly.[21]

Debtor's centre of main interests must be in a Member State

The regulation does not apply unless the centre of the debtor's main interests is situated within the territory of a Member State. This requirement applies equally to the opening of insolvency proceedings in that State ('main insolvency proceedings'), the opening of subsequent proceedings in another State where the debtor has an establishment ('secondary proceedings') and the opening of proceedings (helpfully labelled 'independent proceedings'[22]) in such other State when no main proceedings have yet been opened, which is permitted only in restricted circumstances. The label 'territorial proceedings' covers secondary proceedings and independent proceedings. Where the debtor is a company or legal person there is a rebuttable presumption that the place of its registered office is the centre of its main interests. This does not, however, provide any guide as to the concept of 'centre of main interests', though the official report on the equivalent provisions of the EC Convention stated that this phrase 'must be interpreted as the place where the debtor conducts the administration of his interests on a regular basis and is therefore ascertainable by third parties'.[23] This does, perhaps, need some refinement since there may be more than one such place within this definition. It is thought that what the phrase 'centre of main interests' seeks to convey is the place where the main decisions are taken, typically the head office or chief executive office.

Jurisdiction

Main insolvency proceedings affect all creditors, wherever situated, and all the debtor's assets on a worldwide basis[24] except assets within the territory of a Member State in which territorial insolvency proceedings have been properly instituted. Only the courts of the Member State where the debtor has its centre of main interests have jurisdiction to open main insolvency proceedings. The opening of main insolvency proceedings in a Member State does not preclude the opening of secondary proceedings in a Member State in the territory of which the debtor has an

---

[20] Article 1(1), 2(a). Excluded are insolvency proceedings concerning insurance undertakings, credit institutions, and investment undertakings (Art 1(2)).   [21] Article 2(b).
[22] *Virgos-Schmit Report on the Convention on Insolvency Proceedings* (July 1996), para 25.
[23] Ibid., para 75.
[24] This is implicit in para (11) of the Preamble and Arts 3(2) (contrasting the position in relation to secondary proceedings) and 16–8.

establishment but the effects are restricted to assets within that State.[25] Territorial insolvency proceedings may also be opened prior to the opening of main proceedings if (a) such opening is precluded by the law of the Member State where the debtor has its centre of main interests, or (b) the opening of the territorial proceedings is requested by a creditor that has its habitual residence, domicile or registered office in the Member State in which the debtor has its establishment.[26]

Law applicable

Subject to certain exceptions, the law applicable to insolvency proceedings and their effects is that of the Member State in which the proceedings are opened.[27] Under Article 4(2) the law of the insolvency thus determines the conditions for the opening of the proceedings, their conduct and their closure, and in particular the issues listed in paragraphs (a)–(l) of Article 4(2), including determination of the assets forming part of the estate, rights of set-off, the effect of the insolvency proceedings on current contracts, the rules governing the ranking of claims, and rules relating to the voidness, voidability, or unenforceability of legal acts detrimental to all the creditors. All the items listed are those which one would expect to be governed by the law of the insolvency. However, it is necessary to grasp certain key concepts.

(i) Relationship of insolvency law to the law governing pre-insolvency entitlements The starting position of insolvency law in most jurisdictions is respect for pre-insolvency entitlements. So security interests and other real rights validly created under the applicable law prior to insolvency are recognized in principle, but subject to rules of avoidance, for instance as transactions in fraud of creditors or as unfair preferences, and subject to insolvency rules as to the ranking of claims. By way of example, a secured creditor who outside insolvency would have priority over unsecured creditors may in given conditions find that his security is avoided as an unfair preference in his favour by an insolvent debtor or that his security interest ranks below the claims of preferential creditors for taxes or wages.

The regulation responds, though not in a wholly satisfactory manner, to this interplay between insolvency law and pre-insolvency entitlements through its provisions respecting third parties' rights *in rem,* reservation of title rights, and the like.

(ii) Third parties' rights in rem Article 5(1) provides that the opening of insolvency proceedings is not to affect the rights *in rem*[28] of creditors or third parties in respect of tangible or intangible movable or immovable assets—both specific assets and collections of indefinite assets as a whole which change from time to time[29]—belonging to the debtor which are situated within the territory of another Member

---

[25] Article 3(2).   [26] Article 3(4).   [27] Articles 4(1) and 28.

[28] In essence, rights in an asset of the debtor which are enforceable against third parties, including rights recorded in a public register. See Art 5(2). Reservation of title is treated separately, since it is not regarded as conferring an interest in an asset of the debtor but rather as deferring the transfer of ownership to the debtor.

[29] This part of Art 5(1) was specifically designed to protect the UK floating charge.

State at the time of the opening of proceedings. Article 5(1) does not exclude such assets from the universal scope of the insolvency proceedings, it merely prevents the insolvency law itself from interfering with the *in rem* rights in question. So if, for example, one such right is a security interest in a particular asset, the liquidator in the insolvency proceeding can treat the asset as part of the estate, subject, however, to the prior right of the secured creditor.

Article 5(1) does not itself prescribe the law applicable to determination of the *in rem* rights. That is a matter for the conflict of laws rules of the forum. Usually these will apply the *lex rei sitae*, that is the law of the place where the asset was located at the time of the disposition in question (or if more than one, then the last disposition), which may or may not be the *situs* of the asset at the time of the opening of the insolvency proceedings. Accordingly Article 5(1) should not be read as a conflict rule applying the *lex rei sitae* of the asset at the time of opening of the proceedings; the sole effect of Article 5(1) is to preserve whatever *in rem* rights may be given by the applicable law to assets situated in another Member State at the time of opening of the insolvency proceedings. In those cases where Article 5 does not apply—for example, where at the time of such opening the assets are situated in the insolvency State or in a State outside the European Community—the insolvency law is the law applicable, and it is that law, including its conflict of laws rules, that will determine to what extent pre-insolvency *in rem* rights created under the law of another State are to be respected.

(iii) Voidness, voidability, or unenforceability   The last of the items listed by Article 4(2) as governed by the insolvency law is expressed in paragraph (m) as 'the rules relating to the voidness, voidability or unenforceability of legal acts detrimental to all the creditors'. This is primarily aimed at transactions intended to defraud creditors or transactions entered into by an insolvent debtor which have the effect of diminishing the estate that would otherwise have been available to the general body of creditors. Bona fide transactions entered into by a debtor who is not insolvent or on the verge of insolvency are not normally detrimental to creditors, because *ex hypothesi* the debtor has enough assets to satisfy all claims.

Article 4(2)(m) is in any event subject to an important exception. It is not to be applied where the person benefiting from the act detrimental to all creditors proves that it is subject to the law of another Member State and that law does not allow any means of challenging it. So if the insolvency proceedings are opened in Member State A and a prior transaction which would be voidable as an unfair preference under the law of that State is proved to be governed by the law of State B, where it would not be open to challenge either under the general law of State B or under its insolvency law, it cannot be impeached. In effect, the party benefiting from the attacked transaction can rely either on the law of the insolvency or on the law of the other Member State, whichever is more favourable to the validity of the transaction.

(iv) Set-off   The opening of the insolvency proceedings does not affect a creditor's right of set-off where this is permitted by the law applicable to the insolvent

debtor's claim and is not avoided under the insolvency law as provided by Article 4(2)(m).[30]

(v) Reservation of title   Article 7 in substance applies to reservation of title the same rules as Article 5 does to *in rem* rights in the debtor's own asset. As under Article 5, the seller's rights based on reservation of title are determined by the applicable law rather than by the insolvency law where at the time of opening of the insolvency proceedings the asset is situated in another Member State. As under Articles 5 and 6, the application of Article 4(2)(m) is preserved.

(vi) Contracts relating to immovable property   The effects of insolvency proceedings on a contract conferring the right to acquire or make use of immovable property are governed solely by the *lex rei sitae* where the *situs* is that of a Member State. In other cases, it is governed by the insolvency law, including that law's conflicts rules, which in most States would apply the *lex rei sitae*.

(vii) Debtor's rights in immovable property, ships, and aircraft subject to registration in a public register   These are determined by the Member State under the authority of which the register is kept.[31] This provision is clearly confined to national registers and would not, for example, determine the effect of insolvency on the rights of a debtor who has granted an international interest in an aircraft object which has been registered in the international registry to be established under the 2001 Cape Town Convention on international interests in mobile equipment.[32]

(viii) Protection of third party rights under post-insolvency dispositions   In general, the rules preserving *in rem* rights discussed earlier are confined to rights acquired under dispositions made before the opening of the insolvency proceedings, after which the debtor in general ceases to have powers of disposition. Article 14 provides an exception to this as regards post-insolvency dispositions of an immovable asset, a ship, or aircraft subject to public registration or securities whose existence pre-supposes registration in a register laid down by law. In all these cases the validity of the act is determined by the *lex situs* of the immovable asset or the law of the State under the authority of which the register is kept.

Recognition of insolvency proceedings

Any judgment opening insolvency proceedings by a court of a Member State having jurisdiction under Article 3 is required to be recognized in all other Member States[33] and produces the same effects in those States as in the insolvency State without further formality.[34] In consequence the liquidator's powers are exercisable not only in the insolvency State but in all other Member States in which no separate

---

[30] Article 6.   [31] Article 11.   [32] See above, p. 550.

[33] Article 16(1). This does not, however, preclude the opening of secondary proceedings in another Member State (Art 16(2)) limited to assets in that State (Art 3(2)).

[34] Article 17.   [35] Articles 17 and 18.

insolvency proceedings have been opened.[35] However, recognition of insolvency proceedings opened in a Member State or the enforcement of a judgment in a Member State may be refused by another Member State where such recognition or enforcement would be manifestly contrary to that State's public policy, in particular its fundamental principles or the rights and liberties of the individual.[36] This provision is intended to apply only in exceptional cases.

Creditors' claims where concurrent proceedings

Where main insolvency proceedings are followed by secondary proceedings the liquidator in the one proceeding is required to lodge in the other proceeding claims lodged in the former where the interests of creditors in the insolvency proceedings in which the liquidator acts would thereby be served.[37] Moreover, the fact that secondary proceedings are confined to local assets does not mean that these are available only to local creditors. Creditors in the main proceedings may prove in the secondary proceedings and vice versa.[38]

Duty of liquidators to co-operate

The liquidator in the main proceedings and the liquidator in the secondary proceedings are duty bound to communicate information to each other and to cooperate with each other.[39]

---

[36] Article 26.   [37] Article 32.   [38] Ibid.   [39] Article 31.

B. Instruments

(i) UNCITRAL MODEL LAW ON CROSS-BORDER INSOLVENCY*

* Reproduced with the kind permission of UNCITRAL.

ANNEX

PREAMBLE

The purpose of this Law is to provide effective mechanisms for dealing with cases of cross-border insolvency so as to promote the objectives of:
- (a) Cooperation between the courts and other competent authorities of this State and foreign States involved in cases of cross-border insolvency;
- (b) Greater legal certainty for trade and investment;
- (c) Fair and efficient administration of cross-border insolvencies that protects the interests of all creditors and other interested persons, including the debtor;
- (d) Protection and maximization of the value of the debtor's assets; and
- (e) Facilitation of the rescue of financially troubled businesses, thereby protecting investment and preserving employment.

CHAPTER I
GENERAL PROVISIONS

Article 1
Scope of application

1. This Law applies where:
   - (a) Assistance is sought in this State by a foreign court or a foreign representative in connection with a foreign proceeding; or
   - (b) Assistance is sought in a foreign State in connection with a proceeding under *[identify laws of the enacting State relating to insolvency]*; or
   - (c) A foreign proceeding and a proceeding under *[identify laws of the enacting State relating to insolvency]* in respect of the same debtor are taking place concurrently; or
   - (d) Creditors or other interested persons in a foreign State have an interest in requesting the commencement of, or participating in, a proceeding under *[identify laws of the enacting State relating to insolvency]*.
2. This Law does not apply to a proceeding concerning *[designate any types of entities, such as banks or insurance companies, that are subject to a special insolvency regime in this State and that this State wishes to exclude from this Law]*.

Article 2
Definitions

For the purposes of this Law:
- (a) 'Foreign proceeding' means a collective judicial or administrative proceeding in a foreign State, including an interim proceeding, pursuant to a law relating to insolvency in which proceeding the assets and affairs of the debtor are subject to control or supervision by a foreign court, for the purpose of reorganization or liquidation;

(b) 'Foreign main proceeding' means a foreign proceeding taking place in the State where the debtor has the centre of its main interests;

(c) 'Foreign non-main proceeding' means a foreign proceeding, other than a foreign main proceeding, taking place in a State where the debtor has an establishment within the meaning of subparagraph *(f)* of this article;

(d) 'Foreign representative' means a person or body, including one appointed on an interim basis, authorized in a foreign proceeding to administer the reorganization or the liquidation of the debtor's assets or affairs or to act as a representative of the foreign proceeding;

(e) 'Foreign court' means a judicial or other authority competent to control or supervise a foreign proceeding;

(f) 'Establishment' means any place of operations where the debtor carries out a non-transitory economic activity with human means and goods or services.

Article 3
International obligations of this State

To the extent that this Law conflicts with an obligation of this State arising out of any treaty or other form of agreement to which it is a party with one or more other States, the requirements of the treaty or agreement prevail.

Article 4
[Competent court or authority][1]

The functions referred to in this Law relating to recognition of foreign proceedings and cooperation with foreign courts shall be performed by *[specify the court, courts, authority or authorities competent to perform those functions in the enacting State]*.

Article 5
Authorization of *[insert the title of the person or body administering reorganization or liquidation under the law of the enacting State]* to act in a foreign State

A *[insert the title of the person or body administering a reorganization or liquidation under the law of the enacting State]* is authorized to act in a foreign State on behalf of a proceeding under *[identify laws of the enacting State relating to insolvency]*, as permitted by the applicable foreign law.

Article 6
Public policy exception

Nothing in this Law prevents the court from refusing to take an action governed by this Law if the action would be manifestly contrary to the public policy of this State.

---

[1] A State where certain functions relating to insolvency proceedings have been conferred upon government-appointed officials or bodies might wish to include in article 4 or elsewhere in chapter I the following provision:

> Nothing in this Law affects the provisions in force in this State governing the authority of *[insert the title of the government-appointed person or body]*.

Article 7
Additional assistance under other laws

Nothing in this Law limits the power of a court or a *[insert the title of the person or body administering a reorganization or liquidation under the law of the enacting State]* to provide additional assistance to a foreign representative under other laws of this State.

Article 8
Interpretation

In the interpretation of this Law, regard is to be had to its international origin and to the need to promote uniformity in its application and the observance of good faith.

CHAPTER II
ACCESS OF FOREIGN REPRESENTATIVES AND CREDITORS TO COURTS IN THIS STATE

Article 9
Right of direct access

A foreign representative is entitled to apply directly to a court in this State.

Article 10
Limited jurisdiction

The sole fact that an application pursuant to this Law is made to a court in this State by a foreign representative does not subject the foreign representative or the foreign assets and affairs of the debtor to the jurisdiction of the courts of this State for any purpose other than the application.

Article 11
Application by a foreign representative to commence a proceeding under *[identify laws of the enacting State relating to insolvency]*

A foreign representative is entitled to apply to commence a proceeding under *[identify laws of the enacting State relating to insolvency]* if the conditions for commencing such a proceeding are otherwise met.

Article 12
Participation of a foreign representative in a proceeding under *[identify laws of the enacting State relating to insolvency]*

Upon recognition of a foreign proceeding, the foreign representative is entitled to participate in a proceeding regarding the debtor under *[identify laws of the enacting State relating to insolvency]*.

Article 13
Access of foreign creditors to a proceeding under *[identify laws of the enacting State relating to insolvency]*

1. Subject to paragraph 2 of this article, foreign creditors have the same rights regarding the commencement of, and participation in, a proceeding under *[identify laws of the enacting State relating to insolvency]* as creditors in this State.

2. Paragraph 1 of this article does not affect the ranking of claims in a proceeding under *[identify laws of the enacting State relating to insolvency]*, except that the claims of foreign creditors shall not be ranked lower than *[identify the class of general non-preference claims, while providing that a foreign claim is to be ranked lower than the general non-preference claims if an equivalent local claim (e.g. claim for a penalty or deferred-payment claim) has a rank lower than the general non-preference claims]*.[2]

Article 14
Notification to foreign creditors of a proceeding under *[identify laws of the enacting State relating to insolvency]*

1. Whenever under *[identify laws of the enacting State relating to insolvency]* notification is to be given to creditors in this State, such notification shall also be given to the known creditors that do not have addresses in this State. The court may order that appropriate steps be taken with a view to notifying any creditor whose address is not yet known.
2. Such notification shall be made to the foreign creditors individually, unless the court considers that, under the circumstances, some other form of notification would be more appropriate. No letters rogatory or other, similar formality is required.
3. When a notification of commencement of a proceeding is to be given to foreign creditors, the notification shall:
   (a) Indicate a reasonable time period for filing claims and specify the place for their filing;
   (b) Indicate whether secured creditors need to file their secured claims; and
   (c) Contain any other information required to be included in such a notification to creditors pursuant to the law of this State and the orders of the court.

CHAPTER III
RECOGNITION OF A FOREIGN PROCEEDING AND RELIEF

Article 15
Application for recognition of a foreign proceeding

1. A foreign representative may apply to the court for recognition of the foreign proceeding in which the foreign representative has been appointed.

---

[2] The enacting State may wish to consider the following alternative wording to replace paragraph 2 of article 13(2):

   2. Paragraph 1 of this article does not affect the ranking of claims in a proceeding under *[identify laws of the enacting State relating to insolvency]* or the exclusion of foreign tax and social security claims from such a proceeding. Nevertheless, the claims of foreign creditors other than those concerning tax and social security obligations shall not be ranked lower than *[identify the class of general non-preference claims, while providing that a foreign claim is to be ranked lower than the general non-preference claims if an equivalent local claim (e.g. claim for a penalty or deferred-payment claim) has a rank lower than the general non-preference claims]*.

2. An application for recognition shall be accompanied by:
   (a) A certified copy of the decision commencing the foreign proceeding and appointing the foreign representative; or
   (b) A certificate from the foreign court affirming the existence of the foreign proceeding and of the appointment of the foreign representative; or
   (c) In the absence of evidence referred to in subparagraphs (a) and (b), any other evidence acceptable to the court of the existence of the foreign proceeding and of the appointment of the foreign representative.
3. An application for recognition shall also be accompanied by a statement identifying all foreign proceedings in respect of the debtor that are known to the foreign representative.
4. The court may require a translation of documents supplied in support of the application for recognition into an official language of this State.

Article 16
Presumptions concerning recognition

1. If the decision or certificate referred to in paragraph 2 of article 15 indicates that the foreign proceeding is a proceeding within the meaning of subparagraph (a) of article 2 and that the foreign representative is a person or body within the meaning of subparagraph (d) of article 2, the court is entitled to so presume.
2. The court is entitled to presume that documents submitted in support of the application for recognition are authentic, whether or not they have been legalized.
3. In the absence of proof to the contrary, the debtor's registered office, or habitual residence in the case of an individual, is presumed to be the centre of the debtor's main interests.

Article 17
Decision to recognize a foreign proceeding

1. Subject to article 6, a foreign proceeding shall be recognized if:
   (a) The foreign proceeding is a proceeding within the meaning of subparagraph (a) of article 2;
   (b) The foreign representative applying for recognition is a person or body within the meaning of subparagraph (d) of article 2;
   (c) The application meets the requirements of paragraph 2 of article 15; and
   (d) The application has been submitted to the court referred to in article 4.
2. The foreign proceeding shall be recognized:
   (a) As a foreign main proceeding if it is taking place in the State where the debtor has the centre of its main interests; or
   (b) As a foreign non-main proceeding if the debtor has an establishment within the meaning of subparagraph (f) of article 2 in the foreign State.
3. An application for recognition of a foreign proceeding shall be decided upon at the earliest possible time.
4. The provisions of articles 15, 16, 17 and 18 do not prevent modification or termination of recognition if it is shown that the grounds for granting it were fully or partially lacking or have ceased to exist.

Article 18
Subsequent information

From the time of filing the application for recognition of the foreign proceeding, the foreign representative shall inform the court promptly of:

   (a) Any substantial change in the status of the recognized foreign proceeding or the status of the foreign representative's appointment; and

   (b) Any other foreign proceeding regarding the same debtor that becomes known to the foreign representative.

Article 19
Relief that may be granted upon application for recognition of a foreign proceeding

1. From the time of filing an application for recognition until the application is decided upon, the court may, at the request of the foreign representative, where relief is urgently needed to protect the assets of the debtor or the interests of the creditors, grant relief of a provisional nature, including:

   (a) Staying execution against the debtor's assets;

   (b) Entrusting the administration or realization of all or part of the debtor's assets located in this State to the foreign representative or another person designated by the court, in order to protect and preserve the value of assets that, by their nature or because of other circumstances, are perishable, susceptible to devaluation or otherwise in jeopardy;

   (c) Any relief mentioned in paragraph 1 (c), (d) and (g) of article 21.

2. *[Insert provisions (or refer to provisions in force in the enacting State) relating to notice.]*
3. Unless extended under paragraph 1 (f) of article 21, the relief granted under this article terminates when the application for recognition is decided upon.
4. The court may refuse to grant relief under this article if such relief would interfere with the administration of a foreign main proceeding.

Article 20
Effects of recognition of a foreign main proceeding

1. Upon recognition of a foreign proceeding that is a foreign main proceeding,

   (a) Commencement or continuation of individual actions or individual proceedings concerning the debtor's assets, rights, obligations or liabilities is stayed;

   (b) Execution against the debtor's assets is stayed; and

   (c) The right to transfer, encumber or otherwise dispose of any assets of the debtor is suspended.

2. The scope, and the modification or termination, of the stay and suspension referred to in paragraph 1 of this article are subject to *[refer to any provisions of law of the enacting State relating to insolvency that apply to exceptions, limitations, modifications or termination in respect of the stay and suspension referred to in paragraph 1 of this article].*
3. Paragraph 1 (a) of this article does not affect the right to commence individual actions or proceedings to the extent necessary to preserve a claim against the debtor.
4. Paragraph 1 of this article does not affect the right to request the commencement of a proceeding under *[identify laws of the enacting State relating to insolvency]* or the right to file claims in such a proceeding.

Article 21
Relief that may be granted upon recognition of a foreign proceeding

1. Upon recognition of a foreign proceeding, whether main or non-main, where necessary to protect the assets of the debtor or the interests of the creditors, the court may, at the request of the foreign representative, grant any appropriate relief, including:
   (a) Staying the commencement or continuation of individual actions or individual proceedings concerning the debtor's assets, rights, obligations or liabilities, to the extent they have not been stayed under paragraph 1 (a) of article 20;
   (b) Staying execution against the debtor's assets to the extent it has not been stayed under paragraph 1 (b) of article 20;
   (c) Suspending the right to transfer, encumber or otherwise dispose of any assets of the debtor to the extent this right has not been suspended under paragraph 1 *(c)* of article 20;
   (d) Providing for the examination of witnesses, the taking of evidence or the delivery of information concerning the debtor's assets, affairs, rights, obligations or liabilities;
   (e) Entrusting the administration or realization of all or part of the debtor's assets located in this State to the foreign representative or another person designated by the court;
   (f) Extending relief granted under paragraph 1 of article 19;
   (g) Granting any additional relief that may be available to *[insert the title of a person or body administering a reorganization or liquidation under the law of the enacting State]* under the laws of this State.
2. Upon recognition of a foreign proceeding, whether main or non-main, the court may, at the request of the foreign representative, entrust the distribution of all or part of the debtor's assets located in this State to the foreign representative or another person designated by the court, provided that the court is satisfied that the interests of creditors in this State are adequately protected.
3. In granting relief under this article to a representative of a foreign non-main proceeding, the court must be satisfied that the relief relates to assets that, under the law of this State, should be administered in the foreign non-main proceeding or concerns information required in that proceeding.

Article 22
Protection of creditors and other interested persons

1. In granting or denying relief under article 19 or 21, or in modifying or terminating relief under paragraph 3 of this article, the court must be satisfied that the interests of the creditors and other interested persons, including the debtor, are adequately protected.
2. The court may subject relief granted under article 19 or 21 to conditions it considers appropriate.
3. The court may, at the request of the foreign representative or a person affected by relief granted under article 19 or 21, or at its own motion, modify or terminate such relief.

Article 23
Actions to avoid acts detrimental to creditors

1. Upon recognition of a foreign proceeding, the foreign representative has standing to initiate *[refer to the types of actions to avoid or otherwise render ineffective acts detrimental*

to creditors that are available in this State to a person or body administering a reorganization or liquidation].

2. When the foreign proceeding is a foreign non-main proceeding, the court must be satisfied that the action relates to assets that, under the law of this State, should be administered in the foreign non-main proceeding.

Article 24
Intervention by a foreign representative in proceedings in this State

Upon recognition of a foreign proceeding, the foreign representative may, provided the requirements of the law of this State are met, intervene in any proceedings in which the debtor is a party.

CHAPTER IV
COOPERATION WITH FOREIGN COURTS AND FOREIGN REPRESENTATIVES

Article 25
Cooperation and direct communication between a court of this State and foreign courts or foreign representatives

1. In matters referred to in article 1, the court shall cooperate to the maximum extent possible with foreign courts or foreign representatives, either directly or through a *[insert the title of a person or body administering a reorganization or liquidation under the law of the enacting State].*
2. The court is entitled to communicate directly with, or to request information or assistance directly from, foreign courts or foreign representatives.

Article 26
Cooperation and direct communication between the *[insert the title of a person or body administering a reorganization or liquidation under the law of the enacting State]* and foreign courts or foreign representatives

1. In matters referred to in article 1, a *[insert the title of a person or body administering a reorganization or liquidation under the law of the enacting State]* shall, in the exercise of its functions and subject to the supervision of the court, cooperate to the maximum extent possible with foreign courts or foreign representatives.
2. The *[insert the title of a person or body administering a reorganization or liquidation under the law of the enacting State]* is entitled, in the exercise of its functions and subject to the supervision of the court, to communicate directly with foreign courts or foreign representatives.

Article 27
Forms of cooperation

Cooperation referred to in articles 25 and 26 may be implemented by any appropriate means, including:
  (a) Appointment of a person or body to act at the direction of the court;
  (b) Communication of information by any means considered appropriate by the court;

(c) Coordination of the administration and supervision of the debtor's assets and affairs;

(d) Approval or implementation by courts of agreements concerning the coordination of proceedings;

(e) Coordination of concurrent proceedings regarding the same debtor;

(f) *[The enacting State may wish to list additional forms or examples of cooperation].*

CHAPTER V
CONCURRENT PROCEEDINGS

Article 28
Commencement of a proceeding under *[identify laws of the enacting State relating to insolvency]* after recognition of a foreign main proceeding

After recognition of a foreign main proceeding, a proceeding under *[identify laws of the enacting State relating to insolvency]* may be commenced only if the debtor has assets in this State; the effects of that proceeding shall be restricted to the assets of the debtor that are located in this State and, to the extent necessary to implement cooperation and coordination under articles 25, 26 and 27, to other assets of the debtor that, under the law of this State, should be administered in that proceeding.

Article 29
Coordination of a proceeding under *[identify laws of the enacting State relating to insolvency]* and a foreign proceeding

Where a foreign proceeding and a proceeding under [identify laws of the enacting State relating to insolvency] are taking place concurrently regarding the same debtor, the court shall seek cooperation and coordination under articles 25, 26 and 27, and the following shall apply:

When the proceeding in this State is taking place at the time the application for recognition of the foreign proceeding is filed,

    (i) Any relief granted under article 19 or 21 must be consistent with the proceeding in this State; and

    (ii) If the foreign proceeding is recognized in this State as a foreign main proceeding, article 20 does not apply;

(b) When the proceeding in this State commences after recognition, or after the filing of the application for recognition, of the foreign proceeding,

    (i) Any relief in effect under article 19 or 21 shall be reviewed by the court and shall be modified or terminated if inconsistent with the proceeding in this State; and

    (ii) If the foreign proceeding is a foreign main proceeding, the stay and suspension referred to in paragraph 1 of article 20 shall be modified or terminated pursuant to paragraph 2 of article 20 if inconsistent with the proceeding in this State;

(c) In granting, extending or modifying relief granted to a representative of a foreign non-main proceeding, the court must be satisfied that the relief relates to assets that, under the law of this State, should be administered in the foreign non-main proceeding or concerns information required in that proceeding.

Article 30
Coordination of more than one foreign proceeding

In matters referred to in article 1, in respect of more than one foreign proceeding regarding the same debtor, the court shall seek cooperation and coordination under articles 25, 26 and 27, and the following shall apply:

(a) Any relief granted under article 19 or 21 to a representative of a foreign non-main proceeding after recognition of a foreign main proceeding must be consistent with the foreign main proceeding;

(b) If a foreign main proceeding is recognized after recognition, or after the filing of an application for recognition, of a foreign non-main proceeding, any relief in effect under article 19 or 21 shall be reviewed by the court and shall be modified or terminated if inconsistent with the foreign main proceeding;

(c) If, after recognition of a foreign non-main proceeding, another foreign non-main proceeding is recognized, the court shall grant, modify or terminate relief for the purpose of facilitating coordination of the proceedings.

Article 31
Presumption of insolvency based on recognition of a foreign main proceeding

In the absence of evidence to the contrary, recognition of a foreign main proceeding is, for the purpose of commencing a proceeding under *[identify laws of the enacting State relating to insolvency]*, proof that the debtor is insolvent.

Article 32
Rule of payment in concurrent proceedings

Without prejudice to secured claims or rights *in rem*, a creditor who has received part payment in respect of its claim in a proceeding pursuant to a law relating to insolvency in a foreign State may not receive a payment for the same claim in a proceeding under *[identify laws of the enacting State relating to insolvency]* regarding the same debtor, so long as the payment to the other creditors of the same class is proportionately less than the payment the creditor has already received.

ANNEX
GENERAL ASSEMBLY RESOLUTION 52/158 OF
15 DECEMBER 1997

52/158. MODEL LAW ON CROSS-BORDER INSOLVENCY OF
THE UNITED NATIONS COMMISSION ON INTERNATIONAL TRADE LAW

The General Assembly,

Recalling its resolution 2205 (XXI) of 17 December 1966, by which it created the United Nations Commission on International Trade Law with a mandate to further the progressive harmonization and unification of the law of international trade and in that respect to bear in mind the interests of all peoples, in particular those of developing countries, in the extensive development of international trade,

Noting that increased cross-border trade and investment leads to greater incidence of cases where enterprises and individuals have assets in more than one State,

Noting also that when a debtor with assets in more than one State becomes subject to an insolvency proceeding, there often exists an urgent need for cross-border cooperation and coordination in the supervision and administration of the insolvent debtor's assets and affairs,

Considering that inadequate coordination and cooperation in cases of cross-border insolvency reduce the possibility of rescuing financially troubled but viable businesses, impede a fair and efficient administration of cross-border insolvencies, make it more likely that the debtor's assets would be concealed or dissipated and hinder reorganizations or liquidations of debtors' assets and affairs that would be the most advantageous for the creditors and other interested persons, including the debtors and the debtors' employees,

Noting that many States lack a legislative framework that would make possible or facilitate effective cross-border coordination and cooperation,

Convinced that fair and internationally harmonized legislation on cross-border insolvency that respects the national procedural and judicial systems and is acceptable to States with different legal, social and economic systems would contribute to the development of international trade and investment,

Considering that a set of internationally harmonized model legislative provisions on cross-border insolvency is needed to assist States in modernizing their legislation governing cross-border insolvency,

1. Expresses its appreciation to the United Nations Commission on International Trade Law for completing and adopting the Model Law on Cross-Border Insolvency contained in the annex to the present resolution;
2. Requests the Secretary-General to transmit the text of the Model Law, together with the Guide to Enactment of the Model Law prepared by the Secretariat, to Governments and interested bodies;
3. Recommends that all States review their legislation on cross-border aspects of insolvency to determine whether the legislation meets the objectives of a modern and efficient insolvency system and, in that review, give favourable consideration to the Model Law, bearing in mind the need for an internationally harmonized legislation governing instances of cross-border insolvency;
4. Recommends also that all efforts be made to ensure that the Model Law, together with the Guide, become generally known and available.

72nd plenary meeting
15 December 1997

ADOPTIONS

Legislation based on the UNCITRAL Model Law on Cross-Border Insolvency has been adopted in Eritrea, Japan (2000), Mexico (2000), South Africa (2000), Montenegro (within Serbia and Montenegro) (2002), and Poland and Romania (2003).

(ii) EUROPEAN UNION CONVENTION ON INSOLVENCY PROCEEDINGS[1]

PREAMBLE

THE HIGH CONTRACTING PARTIES TO THIS CONVENTION, MEMBER STATES OF THE EUROPEAN UNION,

DESIRING to implement Article 220 of the Treaty establishing the European Community, by virtue of which they undertook to secure the simplification of formalities governing the reciprocal recognition and enforcement of the judgments of courts or tribunals,

ANXIOUS to strengthen in the Community the legal protection of persons therein established,

CONSIDERING that it is necessary for that purpose to determine the jurisdiction of their courts or authorities with regard to the intra-Community effects of insolvency proceedings, to create certain uniform conflict-of-laws rules for such proceedings, to ensure the recognition and enforcement of judgments given in such matters, to make provision for the possibility of opening secondary insolvency proceedings and to guarantee information for creditors and their right to lodge claims,

AWARE that this convention does not affect the application of the provisions of Community law which, in relation to particular matters, lay down rules relating to insolvency proceedings or of national law harmonized in implementation of such Community law,

MEETING WITHIN THE COUNCIL,

HAVE DECIDED AS FOLLOWS:

CHAPTER I
GENERAL PROVISIONS

Article 1
Scope

1. This Convention shall apply to collective insolvency proceedings which entail the partial or total divestment of a debtor and the appointment of a liquidator.
2. This Convention shall not apply to insolvency proceedings concerning insurance undertakings, credit institutions, investment undertakings which provide services involving the holding of funds or securities for third parties, or to collective investment undertakings.

Article 2
Definitions

For the purposes of this Convention:
  (a) 'insolvency proceedings' shall mean the collective proceedings referred to in Article 1(1). These proceedings are listed in Annex A, which shall form an integral part of this Convention.

---

[1] Text as open for signature between 23 November 1995 and 23 May 1996. See Chapter 6, at 6.1 and 6.4 above.

(b) 'liquidator' shall mean any person or body whose function is to administer or liquidate assets of which the debtor has been divested or to supervise the administration of his affairs. Those persons and bodies are listed in Annex C, which shall form an integral part of this Convention.

(c) 'winding-up proceedings' shall mean insolvency proceedings within the meaning of point (a) involving realizing the assets of the debtor, including where the proceedings have been closed by a composition or other measure terminating the insolvency, or closed by reason of the insufficiency of the assets. Those procedures are listed in Annex B, which shall form an integral part of this Convention.

(d) 'court' shall, with the exception of Articles 44 and 45, mean the judicial body or any other competent body of a Contracting State empowered to open insolvency proceedings or to take decisions in the course of such proceedings.

(e) 'judgment' in relation to the opening of insolvency proceedings or the appointment of a liquidator shall include the decision of any court empowered to open such proceedings or to appoint a liquidator.

(f) 'the time of the opening of proceedings' shall mean the time at which the judgment opening proceedings becomes effective, whether it is a final judgment or not.

(g) 'the Contracting State in which assets are situated' shall mean, in the case of:
   —tangible property, the Contracting State within the territory of which the property is situated;
   —property and rights ownership of or entitlement to which must be entered in a public register, the Contracting State under the authority of which the register is kept;
   —claims, the Contracting State within the territory of which the third party required to meet them has the centre of his main interests, as determined in Article 3(1).

(h) establishment' shall mean any place of operations where the debtor carries out a non-transitory economic activity with human means and goods.

Article 3
International jurisdiction

1. The courts of the Contracting State within the territory of which the centre of a debtor's main interests is situated shall have jurisdiction to open insolvency proceedings. In the case of a company or legal person, the place of the registered office shall be presumed to be the centre of its main interests in the absence of proof to the contrary.

2. Where the centre of a debtor's main interests is situated within the territory of a Contracting State, the courts of another Contracting State shall have jurisdiction to open insolvency proceedings against that debtor only if he possesses an establishment within the territory of that other Contracting State. The effects of those proceedings shall be restricted to the assets of the debtor situated in the territory of the latter Contracting State.

3. Where insolvency proceedings have been opened under paragraph 1, any proceedings opened subsequently under paragraph 2 shall be secondary proceedings. These latter proceedings must be winding-up proceedings.

4. Territorial insolvency proceedings referred to in paragraph 2 may be opened prior to the opening of main insolvency proceedings in accordance with paragraph 1 only:
   (a) where insolvency proceedings under paragraph 1 cannot be opened because of the conditions laid down by the law of the Contracting State within the territory of which the centre of the debtor's main interests is situated, or
   (b) where the opening of territorial insolvency proceedings is requested by a creditor who has his domicile, habitual residence or registered office in the Contracting State within the territory of which the establishment is situated, or whose claim arises from the operation of that establishment.

Article 4
Law applicable

1. Save as otherwise provided in this Convention, the law applicable to insolvency proceedings and their effects shall be that of the Contracting State within the territory of which such proceedings are opened, hereafter referred to as the 'State of the opening of proceedings'.

2. The law of the State of the opening of proceedings shall determine the conditions for the opening of those proceedings, their conduct and their closure. It shall determine in particular:
   (a) against which debtors insolvency proceedings may be brought on account of their capacity;
   (b) the assets which form part of the estate and the treatment of assets acquired by or devolving on the debtor after the opening of the insolvency proceedings;
   (c) the respective powers of the debtor and the liquidator;
   (d) the conditions under which set-offs may be invoked;
   (e) the effects of insolvency proceedings on current contracts to which the debtor is party;
   (f) the effects of the insolvency proceedings on proceedings brought by individual creditors, with the exception of lawsuits pending;
   (g) the claims which are to be lodged against the debtor's estate and the treatment of claims arising after the opening of insolvency proceedings;
   (h) the rules governing the lodging, verification and admission of claims;
   (i) the rules governing the distribution of proceeds from the realization of assets, the ranking of claims and the rights of creditors who have obtained partial satisfaction after the opening of insolvency proceedings by virtue of a right in rem or through a set-off;
   (j) the conditions for and the effects of closure of insolvency proceedings, in particular by composition;
   (k) creditors' rights after the closure of insolvency proceedings;
   (l) who is to bear the costs and expenses incurred in the insolvency proceedings;
   (m) the rules relating to the voidness, voidability or unenforceability of legal acts detrimental to all the creditors.

Article 5
Third parties' rights in rem

1. The opening of insolvency proceedings shall not affect the rights in rem of creditors or third parties in respect of tangible or intangible, movable or immovable assets belonging to the debtor which are situated within the territory of another Contracting State at the time of the opening of proceedings.
2. The rights referred to in paragraph 1 shall in particular mean:
    (a) the right to dispose of assets or have them disposed of and to obtain satisfaction from the proceeds of or income from those assets, in particular by virtue of a lien or a mortgage;
    (b) the exclusive right to have a claim met, in particular a right guaranteed by a lien in respect of the claim or by assignment of the claim by way of a guarantee;
    (c) the right to demand the assets from, and/or to require restitution by, anyone having possession or use of them contrary to the wishes of the party so entitled;
    (d) a right in rem to the beneficial use of assets.
3. The right, recorded in a public register and enforceable against third parties, under which a right in rem within the meaning of paragraph 1 may be obtained, shall be considered a right in rem.
4. Paragraph 1 shall not preclude the actions for voidness, voidability or unenforceability laid down in Article 4(2)(m).

Article 6
Set-off

1. The opening of insolvency proceedings shall not affect the right of creditors to demand the set-off of their claims against the claims of the debtor, where such a set-off is permitted by the law applicable to the insolvent debtor's claim.
2. Paragraph 1 shall not preclude the actions for voidness, voidability or unenforceability laid down in Article 4(2)(m).

Article 7
Reservation of title

1. The opening of insolvency proceedings against the purchaser of an asset shall not affect the seller's rights based on a reservation of title where at the time of the opening of proceedings the asset is situated within the territory of a Contracting State other than the State in which the proceedings were opened.
2. The opening of insolvency proceedings against the seller of an asset, after delivery of the asset, shall not constitute grounds for rescinding or terminating the sale and shall not prevent the purchaser from acquiring title where at the time of the opening of proceedings the asset sold is situated within the territory of a Contracting State other than the State of the opening of proceedings.
3. Paragraphs 1 and 2 shall not preclude the actions for voidness, voidability or unenforceability laid down in Article 4(2)(m).

651

Article 8
Contracts relating to immovable property

The effects of insolvency proceedings on a contract conferring the right to acquire or make use of immovable property shall be governed solely by the law of the Contracting State within the territory of which the immovable property is situated.

Article 9
Payment systems and financial markets

1. Without prejudice to Article 5, the effects of insolvency proceedings on the rights and obligations of the parties to a payment or settlement system or to a financial market shall be governed solely by the law of the Contracting State applicable to that system or market.
2. Paragraph 1 shall not preclude any action for voidness, voidability or unenforceability which may be taken to set aside payments or transactions under the law applicable to the relevant payment system or financial market.

Article 10
Contracts of employment

The effects of insolvency proceedings on employment contracts and relationships shall be governed solely by the law of the Contracting State applicable to the contract of employment.

Article 11
Effects on rights subject to registration

The effects of insolvency proceedings on the rights of the debtor in immovable property, a ship or an aircraft subject to registration in a public register shall be determined by the law of the Contracting State under the authority of which the register is kept.

Article 12
Community patents and trade marks

For the purposes of this Convention, a Community patent, a Community trade mark or any other similar right established by Community law may be included only in the proceedings referred to in Article 3(1).

Article 13
Detrimental acts

Article 4(2)(m) shall not apply where the person who benefited from a legal act detrimental to all the creditors provides proof that:
    —the said act is subject to the law of a Contracting State other than that of the State of the opening of proceedings, and
    —that law does not allow any means of challenging that act in the relevant case.

Article 14
Protection of third-party purchasers

Where, by an act concluded after the opening of insolvency proceedings, the debtor disposes, for consideration, of:

—an immovable asset or

—a ship or an aircraft subject to registration in a public register or

—securities whose existence presupposes registration in a register laid down by law,

the validity of that act shall be governed by the law of the State within the territory of which the immovable asset is situated or under the authority of which the register is kept.

Article 15
Effects of insolvency proceedings on lawsuits pending

The effects of insolvency proceedings on a lawsuit pending concerning an asset or a right of which the debtor has been divested shall be governed solely by the law of the Contracting State in which that lawsuit is pending.

CHAPTER II
RECOGNITION OF INSOLVENCY PROCEEDINGS

Article 16
Principle

1. Any judgment opening insolvency proceedings handed down by a court of a Contracting State which has jurisdiction pursuant to Article 3 shall be recognized in all the other Contracting States from the time that it becomes effective in the State of the opening of proceedings.

   This rule shall also apply where, on account of his capacity, insolvency proceedings cannot be brought against the debtor in other Contracting States.

2. Recognition of the proceedings referred to in Article 3(1) shall not preclude the opening of the proceedings referred to in Article 3(2) by a court in another Contracting State. The latter proceedings shall be secondary proceedings within the meaning of Chapter III.

Article 17
Effects of recognition

1. The judgment opening the proceedings referred to in Article 3(1) shall, with no further formalities, produce the same effects in any other Contracting State as under the law of the State of the opening of proceedings, unless the Convention provides otherwise and as long as no proceedings referred to in Article 3(2) are opened in that other Contracting State.

2. The effects of the proceedings referred to in Article 3(2) may not be challenged in other Contracting States. Any restriction of the creditors' rights, in particular a stay or

discharge, shall produce effects vis-à-vis assets situated within the territory of another Contracting State only in the case of those creditors who have given their consent.

Article 18
Powers of the liquidator

1. The liquidator appointed by a court which has jurisdiction pursuant to Article 3(1) may exercise all the powers conferred on him by the law of the State of the opening of proceedings in another Contracting State, as long as no other insolvency proceedings have been opened there nor any preservation measure to the contrary has been taken there further to a request for the opening of insolvency proceedings in that State. He may in particular remove the debtor's assets from the territory of the Contracting State in which they are situated, subject to Articles 5 and 7.

2. The liquidator appointed by a court which has jurisdiction pursuant to Article 3(2) may in any other Contracting State claim through the courts or out of court that movable property was removed from the territory of the State of the opening of proceedings to the territory of that other Contracting State after the opening of the insolvency proceedings. He may also bring any action to set aside which is in the interests of the creditors.

3. In exercising his powers, the liquidator shall comply with the law of the Contracting State within the territory of which he intends to take action, in particular with regard to procedures for the realization of assets. Those powers may not include coercive measures or the right to rule on legal proceedings or disputes.

Article 19
Proof of the liquidator's appointment

The liquidator's appointment shall be evidenced by a certified copy of the original decision appointing him or by any other certificate issued by the court which has jurisdiction.

A translation into the official language or one of the official languages of the Contracting State within the territory of which he intends to act may be required. No legalization or other similar formality shall be required.

Article 20
Return and imputation

1. A creditor who, after the opening of the proceedings referred to in Article 3(1) obtains by any means, in particular through enforcement, total or partial satisfaction of his claim on the assets belonging to the debtor situated within the territory of another Contracting State, shall return what he has obtained to the liquidator, subject to Articles 5 and 7.

2. In order to ensure equal treatment of creditors a creditor who has, in the course of insolvency proceedings, obtained a dividend on his claim shall share in distributions made in other proceedings only where creditors of the same ranking or category have, in those other proceedings, obtained an equivalent dividend.

Article 21
Publication

1. The liquidator may request that notice of the judgment opening insolvency proceedings and, where appropriate, the decision appointing him be published in any other Contracting State in accordance with the publication procedures provided for in that State. Such publication shall also specify the liquidator appointed and whether the jurisdiction rule applied is that pursuant to Article 3(1) or Article 3(2).

2. However, any Contracting State within the territory of which the debtor has an establishment may require mandatory publication. In such cases, the liquidator or any authority empowered to that effect in the Contracting State where the proceedings referred to in Article 3(1) are opened shall take all necessary measures to ensure such publication.

Article 22
Registration in a public register

1. The liquidator may request that the judgment opening the proceedings referred to in Article 3(1) be registered in the land register, the trade register and any other public register kept in the other Contracting States.

2. However, any Contracting State may require mandatory registration. In such cases, the liquidator or any authority empowered to that effect in the Contracting State where the proceedings referred to in Article 3(1) have been opened shall take all necessary measures to ensure such registration.

Article 23
Costs

The costs of the publication and registration provided for in Articles 21 and 22 shall be regarded as costs and expenses incurred in the proceedings.

Article 24
Honouring of an obligation to a debtor

1. Where an obligation has been honoured in a Contracting State for the benefit of a debtor who is subject to insolvency proceedings opened in another Contracting State, when it should have been honoured for the benefit of the liquidator in those proceedings, the person honouring the obligation shall be deemed to have discharged it if he was unaware of the opening of proceedings.

2. Where such an obligation is honoured before the publication provided for in Article 21 has been effected, the person honouring the obligation shall be presumed, in the absence of proof to the contrary, to have been unaware of the opening of insolvency proceedings; where the obligation is honoured after such publication has been effected, the person honouring the obligation shall be presumed, in the absence of proof to the contrary, to have been aware of the opening of proceedings.

Article 25
Recognition and enforceability of other judgments

1. Judgments handed down by a court whose judgment concerning the opening of proceedings is recognized in accordance with Article 16 and which concern the course and closure of insolvency proceedings, and compositions approved by that court shall also be recognized with no further formalities. Such judgments shall be enforced in accordance with Articles 31 to 51 of the Convention on Jurisdiction and the Enforcement of Judgments in Civil and Commercial Matters, with the exception of Article 34(2).

   The first subparagraph shall also apply to judgments deriving directly from the insolvency proceedings and which are closely linked with them, even if they were handed down by another court.

   The first subparagraph shall also apply to judgments relating to preservation measures taken after the request for the opening of insolvency proceedings.

2. The recognition and enforcement of judgments other than those referred to in paragraph 1 shall be governed by the Convention referred to in paragraph 1, provided that that Convention is applicable.

3. The Contracting States shall not be obliged to recognize or enforce a judgment referred to in paragraph 1 which might result in a limitation of personal freedom or postal secrecy.

Article 26
Public policy

Any Contracting State may refuse to recognize insolvency proceedings opened in another Contracting State or to enforce a judgment handed down in the context of such proceedings where the effects of such recognition or enforcement would be manifestly contrary to that State's public policy, in particular its fundamental principles or the constitutional rights and liberties of the individual.

CHAPTER III
SECONDARY INSOLVENCY PROCEEDINGS

Article 27
Opening of proceedings

The opening of the proceedings referred to in Article 3(1) by a court of a Contracting State and which is recognized in another Contracting State (main proceedings) shall permit the opening, in that other Contracting State a court of which has jurisdiction pursuant to Article 3(2), of secondary insolvency proceedings without the debtor's insolvency being examined in that other State. These latter proceedings must be among the proceedings listed in Annex B. Their effects shall be restricted to the assets of the debtor situated within the territory of that other Contracting State.

Article 28
Applicable law

Save as otherwise provided in this Convention, the law applicable to secondary proceedings shall be that of the Contracting State within the territory of which the secondary proceedings are opened.

Article 29
Right to request the opening of proceedings

The opening of secondary proceedings may be requested by:
- (a) the liquidator in the main proceedings;
- (b) any other person or authority empowered to request the opening of insolvency proceedings under the law of the Contracting State within the territory of which the opening of secondary proceedings is requested.

Article 30
Advance payment of costs and expenses

Where the law of the Contracting State in which the opening of secondary proceedings is requested requires that the debtor's assets be sufficient to cover in whole or in part the costs and expenses of the proceedings, the court may, when it receives such a request, require the applicant to make an advance payment of costs or to provide appropriate security.

Article 31
Duty to cooperate and communicate information

1. Subject to the rules restricting the communication of information, the liquidator in the main proceedings and the liquidators in the secondary proceedings shall be duty bound to communicate information to each other. They shall immediately communicate any information which may be relevant to the other proceedings, in particular the progress made in lodging and verifying claims and all measures aimed at terminating the proceedings.
2. Subject to the rules applicable to each of the proceedings, the liquidator in the main proceedings and the liquidators in the secondary proceedings shall be duty bound to cooperate with each other.
3. The liquidator in secondary proceedings shall give the liquidator in the main proceedings an early opportunity of submitting proposals on the liquidation or use of the assets in the secondary proceedings.

Article 32
Exercise of creditors' rights

1. Any creditor may lodge his claim in the main proceedings and in any secondary proceedings.

2. The liquidators in the main and any secondary proceedings shall lodge in other proceedings claims which have already been lodged in the proceedings for which they were appointed, provided that the interests of creditors in the latter proceedings are served thereby, subject to the right of creditors to oppose that or to withdraw the lodgement of their claims where the law applicable so provides.

3. The liquidator in the main or secondary proceedings shall be empowered to participate in other proceedings on the same basis as a creditor, in particular by attending creditors' meetings.

Article 33
Stay of liquidation

1. The court, which opened the secondary proceedings, shall stay the process of liquidation in whole or in part on receipt of a request from the liquidator in the main proceedings, provided that in that event it may require the liquidator in the main proceedings to take any suitable measure to guarantee the interests of the creditors in the secondary proceedings and of individual classes of creditors. Such a request from the liquidator may be rejected only if it is manifestly of no interest to the creditors in the main proceedings. Such a stay of the process of liquidation may be ordered for up to three months. It may be continued or renewed for similar periods.

2. The court referred to in paragraph 1 shall terminate the stay of the process of liquidation:
   —at the request of the liquidator in the main proceedings;
   —of its own motion, at the request of a creditor or at the request of the liquidator in the secondary proceedings if that measure no longer appears justified, in particular, by the interests of creditors in the main proceedings or in the secondary proceedings.

Article 34
Measures ending secondary insolvency proceedings

1. Where the law applicable to secondary proceedings allows for such proceedings to be closed without liquidation by a rescue plan, a composition or a comparable measure, the liquidator in the main proceedings shall be empowered to propose such a measure himself.

   Closure of the secondary proceedings by a measure referred to in the first sub-paragraph shall not become final without the consent of the liquidator in the main proceedings; failing his agreement, however, it may become final if the financial interests of the creditors in the main proceedings are not affected by the measure proposed.

2. Any restriction of creditors' rights arising from a measure referred to in paragraph 1 which is proposed in secondary proceedings, such as a stay of payment or discharge of debt, may not have effect in respect of the debtor's assets not covered by those proceedings without the consent of all the creditors having an interest.

3. During a stay of the process of liquidation ordered pursuant to Article 33, only the liquidator in the main proceedings or the debtor, with the former's consent, may

propose measures laid down in paragraph 1 of this Article in the secondary proceedings; no other proposal for such a measure shall be put to the vote or approved.

Article 35
Assets remaining in the secondary proceedings

If by the liquidation of assets in the secondary proceedings it is possible to meet all claims allowed under those proceedings, the liquidator appointed in those proceedings shall immediately transfer any assets remaining to the liquidator in the main proceedings.

Article 36
Subsequent opening of the main proceedings

Where the proceedings referred to in Article 3(1) are opened following the opening of the proceedings referred to in Article 3(2) in another Contracting State, Articles 31 to 35 shall apply to those opened first, in so far as the progress of those proceedings so permits.

Article 37
Conversion of earlier proceedings

The liquidator in the main proceedings may request that proceedings listed in Annex A previously opened in another Contracting State be converted into winding-up proceedings if this proves to be in the interests of the creditors in the main proceedings.

The court with jurisdiction under Article 3(2) shall order conversion into one of the proceedings listed in Annex B.

Article 38
Preservation measures

Where the court of a Contracting State which has jurisdiction pursuant to Article 3(1) appoints a temporary administrator in order to ensure the preservation of the debtor's assets, that temporary administrator shall be empowered to request any measures to secure and preserve any of the debtor's assets situated in another Contracting State, provided for under the law of that State, for the period between the request for the opening of insolvency proceedings and the judgment opening the proceedings.

CHAPTER IV
PROVISION OF INFORMATION FOR CREDITORS AND LODGEMENT OF THEIR CLAIMS

Article 39
Right to lodge claims

Any creditor who has his habitual residence, domicile or registered office in a Contracting State other than the State of the opening of proceedings, including the tax authorities and social security authorities of Contracting States, shall have the right to lodge claims in the insolvency proceedings in writing.

Article 40
Duty to inform creditors

1. As soon as insolvency proceedings are opened in a Contracting State, the court of that State having jurisdiction or the liquidator appointed by it shall immediately inform known creditors who have their habitual residences, domiciles or registered offices in the other Contracting States.
2. That information, provided by an individual notice, shall in particular include time limits, the penalties laid down in regard to those time limits, the body or authority empowered to accept the lodgement of claims and the other measures laid down. Such notice shall also indicate whether creditors whose claims are preferential or secured in rem need lodge their claims.

Article 41
Content of the lodgement of a claim

A creditor shall send copies of supporting documents, if any, and shall indicate the nature of the claim, the date on which it arose and its amount, as well as whether he alleges preference, security in rem or a reservation of title in respect of the claim and what assets are covered by the guarantee he is invoking.

Article 42
Languages

1. The information provided for in Article 40 shall be provided in the official language or one of the official languages of the State of the opening of proceedings. For that purpose a form shall be used bearing the heading 'Invitation to lodge a claim. Time limits to be observed' in all the official languages of the European Union.
2. Any creditor who has his habitual residence, domicile or registered office in a Contracting State other than the State of the opening of proceedings may lodge his claim in the official language or one of the official languages of that other State. In that event, however, the lodgement of his claim shall bear the heading 'Lodgement of claim' in the official language or one of the official languages of the State of the opening of proceedings. In addition, he may be required to provide a translation, into that language, of the lodgement of claim.

CHAPTER V
INTERPRETATION BY THE COURT OF JUSTICE

Article 43
Jurisdiction of the Court of Justice

1. The Court of Justice of the European Communities shall have jurisdiction to give rulings on the interpretation of this Convention, including the Annexes thereto, and

the Conventions on accession to this Convention by the States which become Members of the European Union after the date on which this Convention is closed for signature.

2. The Protocol on the Statute of the Court of Justice and the Rules of Procedure of the Court of Justice shall apply.

3. The Rules of Procedure of the Court of Justice shall, if necessary, be adjusted and supplemented in accordance with Article 188 of the Treaty establishing the European Community.

Article 44
Preliminary ruling proceedings

The following courts may request the Court of Justice to give a preliminary ruling on a question raised in a case pending before it and concerning interpretation of the provisions of the instruments referred to in Article 43(1) if that court considers that a decision on the question is necessary to enable it to give judgment:

(a) —in Belgium:
   la Cour de Cassation/het Hof van Cassatie and le Conseil d'Etat/de Raad van State;
—in Denmark:
   Højesteret;
—in the Federal Republic of Germany:
   die obersten Gerichtshöfe des Bundes;
—in Greece:
   'ΑρειοςΠάγος και Συμβούλιο της Επικρατείας;
—in Spain:
   el Tribunal Supremo;
—in France:
   la Cour de Cassation and le Conseil d'Etat;
—in Ireland:
   the Supreme Court;
—in Italy:
   la Corte suprema di cassazione and il Consiglio di Stato;
—in Luxembourg:
   la Court Supérieure de Justice, when sitting as Cour de Cassation;
—in Austria:
   = der Oberste Gerichtshof
   = der Verfassungsgerichtshof
   = der Verwaltungsgerichtshof;
—in the Netherlands:
   de Hoge Raad;
—in Portugal:
   o Supremo Tribunal de Justiça;
—in Finland:
   Korkein oikeus/Högsta domstolen;
—in Sweden:
   Högsta domstolen;

661

—in the United Kingdom:
the House of Lords and other courts from which no further appeal is possible;
(b) the courts of the Contracting States when acting as appeal courts.

Article 45
Proceedings brought by a competent authority

1. The competent authority of a Contracting State may request the Court of Justice to give a ruling on a question of interpretation of the instruments referred to in Article 43(1) if judgments given by courts of that State conflict with the interpretation given either by the Court of Justice or in a judgment of one of the courts of another Contracting State referred to in Article 44. The provisions of this paragraph shall apply only to judgments which have become *res judicata*.
2. The interpretation given by the Court of Justice in response to such a request shall not affect the judgments which gave rise to the request for interpretation.
3. The Procurators-General of the Supreme Courts of Appeal of the Contracting States, or any other authority designated by a Contracting State, shall be entitled to ask the Court of Justice to give a ruling on interpretation in accordance with paragraph 1.
4. The Registrar of the Court of Justice shall give notice of the request to the Contracting States, to the Commission and to the Council of the European Union; they shall then be entitled within two months of the notification to submit statements of case or written observations to the Court.
5. No fees shall be levied nor any costs or expenses awarded in respect of the proceedings provided for in this Article.

Article 46
Reservations

1. Any signatory State which is unable to apply Article 44 for constitutional reasons may enter a reservation on that Article at the time of signing this Convention.
2. Any signatory State which has entered a reservation pursuant to paragraph 1 may withdraw all or part of that reservation by notifying the depositary.
Withdrawal shall take effect from the date on which the depositary receives the notification.

CHAPTER VI
TRANSITIONAL AND FINAL PROVISIONS

Article 47
Applicability in time

The provisions of this Convention shall apply only to insolvency proceedings opened after its entry into force. Acts done by a debtor before the entry into force of this Convention shall continue to be governed by the law which was applicable to them at the time they were done.

Article 48
Relationship to other Conventions

1. When this Convention applies, it shall, in respect of the matters referred to therein, supersede, as between the States which are party to it, the following Conventions concluded between two or more of those States:
    — the Convention between Belgium and France on Jurisdiction an the Validity and Enforcement of Judgments, Arbitration Awards and Authentic Instruments, signed at Paris on 8 July 1899;
    — the Convention between Belgium and Austria on Bankruptcy, Winding-up, Arrangements, Compositions and Suspension of Payments (with Additional Protocol of 13 June 1973), signed at Brussels on 16 July 1969;
    — the Convention between Belgium and the Netherlands on Territorial Jurisdiction, Bankruptcy and the Validity and Enforcement of Judgments, Arbitration Awards and Authentic Instruments, signed at Brussels on 28 March 1925;
    — the Treaty between Germany and Austria on Bankruptcy, Winding-up, Arrangements and Compositions, signed at Vienna on 25 May 1979;
    — the Convention between France and Austria on Jurisdiction, Recognition and Enforcement of Judgments on Bankruptcy, signed at Vienna on 27 February 1979;
    — the Convention between France and Italy on the Enforcement of Judgments in Civil and Commercial Matters, signed at Rome on 3 June 1930;
    — the Convention between Italy and Austria on Bankruptcy, Winding-up, Arrangements and Compositions, signed at Rome on 12 July 1977;
    — the Convention between the Kingdom of the Netherlands and the Federal Republic of Germany on the Mutual Recognition and Enforcement of Judgments and other Enforceable Instruments in Civil and Commercial Matters, signed at The Hague on 30 August 1962;
    — the Convention between the United Kingdom and the Kingdom of Belgium providing for the reciprocal enforcement of judgments in civil and commercial matters, with Protocol, signed at Brussels on 2 May 1934;
    — the Convention between Denmark, Finland, Norway, Sweden and Iceland on Bankruptcy, signed at Copenhagen on 11 November 1933;
    — the European Convention on Certain International Aspects of Bankruptcy, signed at Istanbul on 5 June 1990.
2. The Conventions referred to in paragraph 1 shall continue to have effect with regard to proceedings opened before the entry into force of this Convention.
3. This Convention shall not apply:
    — in any Contracting State, to the extent that it is irreconcilable with the obligations arising in relation to bankruptcy from another convention concluded by that State with one or more non-contracting States before the entry into force of this Convention,
    — in the United Kingdom of Great Britain and Northern Ireland, to the extent that it is irreconcilable with the obligations arising in relation to bankruptcy and the winding-up of insolvent companies from any arrangements with the Commonwealth existing at the time this Convention enters into force.

Article 49
Signature, ratification and entry into force

1. The Secretary-General of the Council of the European Union shall be the depositary of this Convention.
2. This Convention shall be open from 23 November 1995 up to and including 23 May 1996 for signature by the Member States of the European Union.
3. This Convention shall not enter into force until it has been ratified, accepted or approved by all the Member States of the European Union as constituted on the date on which this Convention is closed for signature. It shall enter into force on the first day of the sixth month following that of the deposit of the instrument of ratification, acceptance or approval by the last Member State of the European Union to take that step.
4. The instruments of ratification, acceptance or approval shall be deposited with the depositary.

Article 50
Accession to the Convention

1. The Contracting States recognize that any State which becomes a member of the European Union shall be required to accept this Convention as a basis for the negotiations between the Contracting States and that State necessary to ensure the implementation of the last indent of Article 220 of the Treaty establishing the European Community in relations between the Contracting States and that State.
2. The necessary adjustments may be the subject of a special Convention between the Contracting States and the new Member State.

Article 51
Notification by the Depositary

The depositary shall notify the signatory States of:
(a) the deposit of each instrument of ratification, acceptance or approval;
(b) the date of entry into force of this Convention;
(c) any other act, notification or communication relating to this Convention.

Article 52
Duration of the Convention

This Convention is concluded for an unlimited period.

Article 53
Revision or evaluation of the Convention

Any Contracting State may request the holding of a conference for the revision or evaluation of this Convention. In that event, the President of the Council of the European Union shall convene the conference.

If, within ten years of the entry into force of this Convention, no Contracting State has requested the holding of a conference for the evaluation of the Convention, such a conference shall be convened at the initiative of the Council of the European Union.

Article 54
Amendment of the Annexes

The Contracting States may at any time address to the depositary a declaration containing any amendment it wishes to make to the Annexes.

The depositary shall notify the signatory States and the Contracting States of the content of any such declaration. The desired amendment shall be deemed accepted if none of the States thus notified raises objections within three months of the date of notification. The amendment shall enter into force on the first day of the following month.

Article 55
Deposit of the Convention

This Convention, drawn up in a single original in the Danish, Dutch, English, Finnish, French, German, Greek, Irish, Italian, Portuguese, Spanish and Swedish languages, all twelve texts being equally authentic, shall be deposited in the archives of the General Secretariat of the Council of the European Union.

The depositary shall transmit a certified copy to the Government of each signatory State.

In witness whereof, the undersigned Plenipotentiaries have hereunto set their hands.

ANNEX A

Belgique/België
—La faillite/Het faillissement
—Concordat judiciaire/Het gerechtelijk akkoord

Danmark
—Konkurs
—Tvangsakkord
—Betalingsstandsning
—Insolvensbehandling

Deutschland
—Das Konkursverfahren
—Das gerichtliche Vergleichsverfahren
—Das Gesamtvollstreckungsverfahren
—Das Insolvenzverfahren

ΕΛΛΑΣ
—Πτώχευση

—Η ειδική εκκαθάριση

—Η προσωρινή διαχείριση εταιρίας. Η διοίκηση και η διαχείριση των πιστωτών

—Η υπαγωγή επιχείρησηςς υπό επίτροπο με σκοπό τη σύναψη συμβιβασμού μετους πιστωτές

España
—Concurso de acreedores
—Quiebra
—Suspensión de pagos

France
—Liquidation judiciaire
—Redressement judiciaire avec nomination d'un administrateur

Eire/Ireland
— Foirceannadh éigeantach/Compulsory winding-up
— Féimheacht/Bankruptcy
—Eastát daoine a d'éag agus iad dócmhainneach a riaradh i bhféimheacht/The administration in bankruptcy of the estate of persons dying insolvent
—Foirceannadh comhpháirtíochta i bhféimheacht/Winding-up in bankruptcy of partnerships
—Foirceannadh deonach creidiúnaithe (le deimhniú Cúirte)/Creditors' voluntary winding-up (with confirmation of a Court)
—Socruithe faoi rialú na Cúirte, lena ngabhann dílsiú mhaoin an fhéichiúnaí go hiomlán nó go páirteach don Sannaí Oifigiúil lena réadú agus lena himdháileadh/Arrangements under the control of the Court, which involve the vesting of all or part of the property of the debtor in the Official Assignee for realisation and distribution
— Scrúdaitheoireacht chuideachta/Company examinership

Italia
—Fallimento
—Concordato preventivo
—Liquidazione coatta amministrativa
—Amministrazione straordinaria
—Amministrazione controllata

Luxembourg
—Faillite
—Gestion contrôlée
—Concordat préventif de faillite (par abandon d'actif)
—Régime spécial de liquidation du notariat

Nederland
—Het faillissement
—De surséance van betaling

Österreich
—das Konkursverfahren
—das Ausgleichsverfahren
—das Vorverfahren

Portugal
—O processo de falência
—Os processos especiais de recuperação de empresa, ou seja:
    = A concordata
    = O acordo de credores
    = A reestruturação financeira
    = A gestáo controlada

Suomi/Finland
—konkurssi/konkurs
—yrityssaneeraus/företagssanering

Sverige
—Konkurs
—Offentligt ackord
—Företagsrekonstruktion

United Kingdom
—Winding-up by the Court (Compulsory Winding-up)
—Bankruptcy (England and Wales, Northern Ireland)
—Administration of the insolvent estate of a deceased person (England and Wales, Northern Ireland)
—Administration by a Judicial Factor of the insolvent estate of a deceased person (Scotland)
—Sequestration (Scotland)
—Creditors' Voluntary winding-up (with confirmation by the Court)
—Administration
—Voluntary Arrangements under the Insolvency Act 1986 or the Insolvent Partnerships Order 1994

ANNEX B

Belgique/België
—La faillite/Het faillissement

Danmark
—Konkurs
—Likvidationsakkord
—Insolvensbehandling

Deutschland
—Das Konkursverfahren
—Das Gesamtvollstreckungsverfahren
—Das Insolvenzverfahren

ΕΛΛΑΣ
—Πτώχευση
—Η ειδική εκκαθώάριση

España
—Concurso de acreedores
—Quiebra
—Suspension de pagos basada en la insolvencia definitiva

France
—Liquidation judiciaire

Eire/Ireland
— Foirceannadh éigeantach/Compulsory winding-up
— Féimheacht/Bankruptcy
—Eastát daoine a d'éag agus iad dócmhainneach a riaradh i bhféimheacht/The administration in bankruptcy of the estate of persons dying insolvent
—Foirceannadh comhpháirtíochta i bhféimheacht/Winding-up in bankruptcy of partnerships
—Socruithe faoi rialú na Cúirte, lena ngabhann dílsiú mhaoin an fhéichiúnaí go hiomlán nó go páirteach don Sannaí Oifigiúil lena réadú agus lena himdháileadh/Arrangements under the control of the Court, which involve the vesting of all or part of the property of the debtor in the Official Assignee for realisation and distribution

Italia
—Fallimento
—Liquidazione coatta amministrativa

Luxembourg
—Faillite
—Régime spécial de liquidation du notariat

Nederland
—Het faillissement

Österreich
—das Konkursverfahren

Portugal
—O processo de falência

Suomi/Finland
—konkurssi/konkurs

664.4

Sverige
—Konkurs

United Kingdom
—Winding-up by the Court (Compulsory Winding-up)
—Bankruptcy (England and Wales, Northern Ireland)
—Administration of the insolvent estate of a deceased person (England and Wales, Northern Ireland)
—Administration by a Judicial Factor of the insolvent estate of a deceased person (Scotland)
—Sequestration (Scotland)

ANNEX C

Belgique/België
—Le curateur/De curator
—Le juge délégué/De rechter-commissaris

Danmark
—Kurator
—Midlertidig bestyrer
—Skifteretten
—Tilsyn
—Bobestyrer

Deutschland
—Konkursverwalter
—Vergleichsverwalter
—Sachwalter (nach der Vergleichsordnung)
—Verwalter
—Insolvenzverwalter
—Sachwalter (nach der Insolvenzordnung)
—Treuhänder

ΕΛΛΑΣ
—Σύνδικοσ
—Ο προσωρινός διαχειριστήσ. Η διοικούσαεπιτροπή των πιστωτών
—Ο ειδικόσεκκαθαριστής
—Ο επίτροπος

España
—Depositario-administrador
—Interventor o Interventores
—Síndicos
—Comisario

France
—Représentant des créanciers
—Mandataire liquidateur
—Administrateur judiciaire
—Commissaire à l'exécution de plan

Eire/Ireland
—Leachtaitheoir/Liquidator
—Sannaí Oifigiúil/Official Assignee
—Iontaobhaí i bhféimheacht/Trustee in bankruptcy
—Leachtaitheoir Sealadach/Provisional Liquidator
—Scrúdaitheoir/Examiner

Italia
—Curatore
—Commissario

Luxembourg
—Le curateur
—Le commissaire
—Le liquidateur
—Le conseil de gérance de la section d'assainissement du notariat

Nederland
—De curator in het faillissement
—De bewindvoerder in de surséance van betaling

Österreich
—Masseverwalter
—Ausgleichsverwalter
—Sachwalter
—Treuhänder
—Besonderer Verwalter
—Vorläufiger Verwalter
—das Konkursgericht

Portugal
—Gestor judicial
—Liquidatário judicial
—Comissáo de credores

Suomi/Finland
—pesänhoitaja/boförvaltare
—selvttäjä/utredare

Sverige
—Förvaltare
—God man
—Rekonstruktör

United Kingdom
—Liquidator (England and Wales, Scotland, Northern Ireland)
—Interim liquidator (Scotland)
—Official Receiver (England and Wales, Northern Ireland)
—Administrator (England and Wales, Scotland, Northern Ireland)
—Trustee (England and Wales, Scotland, Northern Ireland)
—Interim and Permanent Trustee in Sequestration (Scotland)
—Judicial Factor (Scotland)
—Supervisor of a voluntary arrangement

(iii) COUNCIL REGULATION (EC)
NO 1346/2000
OF 29 MAY 2000
ON INSOLVENCY PROCEEDINGS

PREAMBLE

THE COUNCIL OF THE EUROPEAN UNION,

Having regard to the Treaty establishing the European Community, and in particular Articles 61(c) and 67(1) thereof,

Having regard to the initiative of the Federal Republic of Germany and the Republic of Finland,

Having regard to the opinion of the European Parliament[1],

Having regard to the opinion of the Economic and Social Committee[2], Whereas:

(1) The European Union has set out the aim of establishing an area of freedom, security and justice.

(2) The proper functioning of the internal market requires that cross-border insolvency proceedings should operate efficiently and effectively and this Regulation needs to be adopted in order to achieve this objective which comes within the scope of judicial cooperation in civil matters within the meaning of Article 65 of the Treaty.

(3) The activities of undertakings have more and more cross-border effects and are therefore increasingly being regulated by Community law. While the insolvency of such undertakings also affects the proper functioning of the internal market, there is a need for a Community act requiring coordination of the measures to be taken regarding an insolvent debtor's assets.

(4) It is necessary for the proper functioning of the internal market to avoid incentives for the parties to transfer assets or judicial proceedings from one Member State to another, seeking to obtain a more favourable legal position (forum shopping).

(5) These objectives cannot be achieved to a sufficient degree at national level and action at Community level is therefore justified.

(6) In accordance with the principle of proportionality this Regulation should be confined to provisions governing jurisdiction for opening insolvency proceedings and judgments which are delivered directly on the basis of the insolvency proceedings and are closely connected with such proceedings. In addition, this Regulation should contain provisions regarding the recognition of those judgments and the applicable law which also satisfy that principle.

(7) Insolvency proceedings relating to the winding-up of insolvent companies or other legal persons, judicial arrangements, compositions and analogous proceedings are excluded from the scope of the 1968 Brussels Convention on Jurisdiction and the Enforcement of Judgments in Civil and Commercial Matters[3], as amended by the Conventions on Accession to this Convention[4].

---

[1] Opinion delivered on 2 March 2000 (not yet published in the Official Journal).

[2] Opinion delivered on 26 January 2000 (not yet published in the Official Journal).

[3] OJ L 299, 31.12.1972, p. 32.

[4] OJ L 204, 2.8.1975, p. 28; OJ L 304, 30.10.1978, p. 1; OJ L 388, 31.12.1982, p. 1; OJ L 285, 3.10.1989, p. 1; OJ C 15, 15.1.1997, p. 1.

(8) In order to achieve the aim of improving the efficiency and effectiveness of insolvency proceedings having cross-border effects, it is necessary, and appropriate, that the provisions on jurisdiction, recognition and applicable law in this area should be contained in a Community law measure which is binding and directly applicable in Member States.

(9) This Regulation should apply to insolvency proceedings, whether the debtor is a natural person or a legal person, a trader or an individual. The insolvency proceedings to which this Regulation applies are listed in the Annexes. Insolvency proceedings concerning insurance undertakings, credit institutions, investment undertakings holding funds or securities for third parties and collective investment undertakings should be excluded from the scope of this Regulation. Such undertakings should not be covered by this Regulation since they are subject to special arrangements and, to some extent, the national supervisory authorities have extremely wide-ranging powers of intervention.

(10) Insolvency proceedings do not necessarily involve the intervention of a judicial authority; the expression 'court' in this Regulation should be given a broad meaning and include a person or body empowered by national law to open insolvency proceedings. In order for this Regulation to apply, proceedings (comprising acts and formalities set down in law) should not only have to comply with the provisions of this Regulation, but they should also be officially recognised and legally effective in the Member State in which the insolvency proceedings are opened and should be collective insolvency proceedings which entail the partial or total divestment of the debtor and the appointment of a liquidator.

(11) This Regulation acknowledges the fact that as a result of widely differing substantive laws it is not practical to introduce insolvency proceedings with universal scope in the entire Community. The application without exception of the law of the State of opening of proceedings would, against this background, frequently lead to difficulties. This applies, for example, to the widely differing laws on security interests to be found in the Community. Furthermore, the preferential rights enjoyed by some creditors in the insolvency proceedings are, in some cases, completely different. This Regulation should take account of this in two different ways. On the one hand, provision should be made for special rules on applicable law in the case of particularly significant rights and legal relationships (e.g. rights *in rem* and contracts of employment). On the other hand, national proceedings covering only assets situated in the State of opening should also be allowed alongside main insolvency proceedings with universal scope.

(12) This Regulation enables the main insolvency proceedings to be opened in the Member State where the debtor has the centre of his main interests. These proceedings have universal scope and aim at encompassing all the debtor's assets. To protect the diversity of interests, this Regulation permits secondary proceedings to be opened to run in parallel with the main proceedings. Secondary proceedings may be opened in the Member State where the debtor has an establishment. The effects of secondary proceedings are limited to

the assets located in that State. Mandatory rules of coordination with the main proceedings satisfy the need for unity in the Community.

(13) The 'centre of main interests' should correspond to the place where the debtor conducts the administration of his interests on a regular basis and is therefore ascertainable by third parties.

(14) This Regulation applies only to proceedings where the centre of the debtor's main interests is located in the Community.

(15) The rules of jurisdiction set out in this Regulation establish only international jurisdiction, that is to say, they designate the Member State the courts of which may open insolvency proceedings. Territorial jurisdiction within that Member State must be established by the national law of the Member State concerned.

(16) The court having jurisdiction to open the main insolvency proceedings should be enabled to order provisional and protective measures from the time of the request to open proceedings. Preservation measures both prior to and after the commencement of the insolvency proceedings are very important to guarantee the effectiveness of the insolvency proceedings. In that connection this Regulation should afford different possibilities. On the one hand, the court competent for the main insolvency proceedings should be able also to order provisional protective measures covering assets situated in the territory of other Member States. On the other hand, a liquidator temporarily appointed prior to the opening of the main insolvency proceedings should be able, in the Member States in which an establishment belonging to the debtor is to be found, to apply for the preservation measures which are possible under the law of those States.

(17) Prior to the opening of the main insolvency proceedings, the right to request the opening of insolvency proceedings in the Member State where the debtor has an establishment should be limited to local creditors and creditors of the local establishment or to cases where main proceedings cannot be opened under the law of the Member State where the debtor has the centre of his main interest. The reason for this restriction is that cases where territorial insolvency proceedings are requested before the main insolvency proceedings are intended to be limited to what is absolutely necessary. If the main insolvency proceedings are opened, the territorial proceedings become secondary.

(18) Following the opening of the main insolvency proceedings, the right to request the opening of insolvency proceedings in a Member State where the debtor has an establishment is not restricted by this Regulation. The liquidator in the main proceedings or any other person empowered under the national law of that Member State may request the opening of secondary insolvency proceedings.

(19) Secondary insolvency proceedings may serve different purposes, besides the protection of local interests. Cases may arise where the estate of the debtor is too complex to administer as a unit or where differences in the legal systems concerned are so great that difficulties may arise from the extension of effects deriving from the law of the State of the opening to the other States where the assets are located. For this reason the liquidator in the main proceedings may request the opening of secondary proceedings when the efficient administration of the estate so requires.

(20) Main insolvency proceedings and secondary proceedings can, however, contribute to the effective realisation of the total assets only if all the concurrent

proceedings pending are coordinated. The main condition here is that the various liquidators must cooperate closely, in particular by exchanging a sufficient amount of information. In order to ensure the dominant role of the main insolvency proceedings, the liquidator in such proceedings should be given several possibilities for intervening in secondary insolvency proceedings which are pending at the same time. For example, he should be able to propose a restructuring plan or composition or apply for realisation of the assets in the secondary insolvency proceedings to be suspended.

(21) Every creditor, who has his habitual residence, domicile or registered office in the Community, should have the right to lodge his claims in each of the insolvency proceedings pending in the Community relating to the debtor's assets. This should also apply to tax authorities and social insurance institutions. However, in order to ensure equal treatment of creditors, the distribution of proceeds must be coordinated. Every creditor should be able to keep what he has received in the course of insolvency proceedings but should be entitled only to participate in the distribution of total assets in other proceedings if creditors with the same standing have obtained the same proportion of their claims.

(22) This Regulation should provide for immediate recognition of judgments concerning the opening, conduct and closure of insolvency proceedings which come within its scope and of judgments handed down in direct connection with such insolvency proceedings. Automatic recognition should therefore mean that the effects attributed to the proceedings by the law of the State in which the proceedings were opened extend to all other Member States. Recognition of judgments delivered by the courts of the Member States should be based on the principle of mutual trust. To that end, grounds for non-recognition should be reduced to the minimum necessary. This is also the basis on which any dispute should be resolved where the courts of two Member States both claim competence to open the main insolvency proceedings. The decision of the first court to open proceedings should be recognised in the other Member States without those Member States having the power to scrutinise the court's decision.

(23) This Regulation should set out, for the matters covered by it, uniform rules on conflict of laws which replace, within their scope of application, national rules of private international law. Unless otherwise stated, the law of the Member State of the opening of the proceedings should be applicable (lex concursus). This rule on conflict of laws should be valid both for the main proceedings and for local proceedings; the lex concursus determines all the effects of the insolvency proceedings, both procedural and substantive, on the persons and legal relations concerned. It governs all the conditions for the opening, conduct and closure of the insolvency proceedings.

(24) Automatic recognition of insolvency proceedings to which the law of the opening State normally applies may interfere with the rules under which transactions are carried out in other Member States. To protect legitimate expectations and the certainty of transactions in Member States other than that in which proceedings are opened, provisions should be made for a number of exceptions to the general rule.

(25) There is a particular need for a special reference diverging from the law of the opening State in the case of rights in rem, since these are of considerable

importance for the granting of credit. The basis, validity and extent of such a right in rem should therefore normally be determined according to the lex situs and not be affected by the opening of insolvency proceedings. The proprietor of the right in rem should therefore be able to continue to assert his right to segregation or separate settlement of the collateral security. Where assets are subject to rights in rem under the lex situs in one Member State but the main proceedings are being carried out in another Member State, the liquidator in the main proceedings should be able to request the opening of secondary proceedings in the jurisdiction where the rights in rem arise if the debtor has an establishment there. If a secondary proceeding is not opened, the surplus on sale of the asset covered by rights in rem must be paid to the liquidator in the main proceedings.

(26) If a set-off is not permitted under the law of the opening State, a creditor should nevertheless be entitled to the set-off if it is possible under the law applicable to the claim of the insolvent debtor. In this way, set-off will acquire a kind of guarantee function based on legal provisions on which the creditor concerned can rely at the time when the claim arises.

(27) There is also a need for special protection in the case of payment systems and financial markets. This applies for example to the position-closing agreements and netting agreements to be found in such systems as well as to the sale of securities and to the guarantees provided for such transactions as governed in particular by Directive 98/26/EC of the European Parliament and of the Council of 19 May 1998 on settlement finality in payment and securities settlement systems[5]. For such transactions, the only law which is material should thus be that applicable to the system or market concerned. This provision is intended to prevent the possibility of mechanisms for the payment and settlement of transactions provided for in the payment and set-off systems or on the regulated financial markets of the Member States being altered in the case of insolvency of a business partner. Directive 98/26/EC contains special provisions which should take precedence over the general rules in this Regulation.

(28) In order to protect employees and jobs, the effects of insolvency proceedings on the continuation or termination of employment and on the rights and obligations of all parties to such employment must be determined by the law applicable to the agreement in accordance with the general rules on conflict of law. Any other insolvency-law questions, such as whether the employees' claims are protected by preferential rights and what status such preferential rights may have, should be determined by the law of the opening State.

(29) For business considerations, the main content of the decision opening the proceedings should be published in the other Member States at the request of the liquidator. If there is an establishment in the Member State concerned, there may be a requirement that publication is compulsory. In neither case, however, should publication be a prior condition for recognition of the foreign proceedings.

(30) It may be the case that some of the persons concerned are not in fact aware that proceedings have been opened and act in good faith in a way that conflicts with the new situation. In order to protect such persons who make a payment to the debtor because they are unaware that foreign proceedings have been opened

---

[5] OJ L 166, 11.6.1998, p. 45.

when they should in fact have made the payment to the foreign liquidator, it should be provided that such a payment is to have a debt-discharging effect.

(31) This Regulation should include Annexes relating to the organisation of insolvency proceedings. As these Annexes relate exclusively to the legislation of Member States, there are specific and substantiated reasons for the Council to reserve the right to amend these Annexes in order to take account of any amendments to the domestic law of the Member States.

(32) The United Kingdom and Ireland, in accordance with Article 3 of the Protocol on the position of the United Kingdom and Ireland annexed to the Treaty on European Union and the Treaty establishing the European Community, have given notice of their wish to take part in the adoption and application of this Regulation.

(33) Denmark, in accordance with Articles 1 and 2 of the Protocol on the position of Denmark annexed to the Treaty on European Union and the Treaty establishing the European Community, is not participating in the adoption of this Regulation, and is therefore not bound by it nor subject to its application,

HAS ADOPTED THIS REGULATION:

CHAPTER I
GENERAL PROVISIONS

Article 1
Scope

1. This Regulation shall apply to collective insolvency proceedings which entail the partial or total divestment of a debtor and the appointment of a liquidator.
2. This Regulation shall not apply to insolvency proceedings concerning insurance undertakings, credit institutions, investment undertakings which provide services involving the holding of funds or securities for third parties, or to collective investment undertakings.

Article 2
Definitions

For the purposes of this Regulation:
   (a) 'insolvency proceedings' shall mean the collective proceedings referred to in Article 1(1). These proceedings are listed in Annex A;
   (b) 'liquidator' shall mean any person or body whose function is to administer or liquidate assets of which the debtor has been divested or to supervise the administration of his affairs. Those persons and bodies are listed in Annex C;
   (c) 'winding-up proceedings' shall mean insolvency proceedings within the meaning of point (a) involving realising the assets of the debtor, including where the proceedings have been closed by a composition or other measure terminating the insolvency, or closed by reason of the insufficiency of the assets. Those proceedings are listed in Annex B;
   (d) 'court' shall mean the judicial body or any other competent body of a Member State empowered to open insolvency proceedings or to take decisions in the course of such proceedings;

671

(e) 'judgment' in relation to the opening of insolvency proceedings or the appointment of a liquidator shall include the decision of any court empowered to open such proceedings or to appoint a liquidator;

(f) 'the time of the opening of proceedings' shall mean the time at which the judgment opening proceedings becomes effective, whether it is a final judgment or not;

(g) 'the Member State in which assets are situated' shall mean, in the case of:
   —tangible property, the Member State within the territory of which the property is situated,
   —property and rights ownership of or entitlement to which must be entered in a public register, the Member State under the authority of which the register is kept,
   —claims, the Member State within the territory of which the third party required to meet them has the centre of his main interests, as determined in Article 3(1);

(h) 'establishment' shall mean any place of operations where the debtor carries out a non-transitory economic activity with human means and goods.

Article 3
International jurisdiction

1. The courts of the Member State within the territory of which the centre of a debtor's main interests is situated shall have jurisdiction to open insolvency proceedings. In the case of a company or legal person, the place of the registered office shall be presumed to be the centre of its main interests in the absence of proof to the contrary.

2. Where the centre of a debtor's main interests is situated within the territory of a Member State, the courts of another Member State shall have jurisdiction to open insolvency proceedings against that debtor only if he possesses an establishment within the territory of that other Member State. The effects of those proceedings shall be restricted to the assets of the debtor situated in the territory of the latter Member State.

3. Where insolvency proceedings have been opened under paragraph 1, any proceedings opened subsequently under paragraph 2 shall be secondary proceedings. These latter proceedings must be winding-up proceedings.

4. Territorial insolvency proceedings referred to in paragraph 2 may be opened prior to the opening of main insolvency proceedings in accordance with paragraph 1 only:

(a) where insolvency proceedings under paragraph 1 cannot be opened because of the conditions laid down by the law of the Member State within the territory of which the centre of the debtor's main interests is situated; or

(b) where the opening of territorial insolvency proceedings is requested by a creditor who has his domicile, habitual residence or registered office in the Member State within the territory of which the establishment is situated, or whose claim arises from the operation of that establishment.

Article 4
Law applicable

1. Save as otherwise provided in this Regulation, the law applicable to insolvency proceedings and their effects shall be that of the Member State within the territory of which such proceedings are opened, hereafter referred to as the 'State of the opening of proceedings'.

2. The law of the State of the opening of proceedings shall determine the conditions for the opening of those proceedings, their conduct and their closure. It shall determine in particular:

   (a) against which debtors insolvency proceedings may be brought on account of their capacity;

   (b) the assets which form part of the estate and the treatment of assets acquired by or devolving on the debtor after the opening of the insolvency proceedings;

   (c) the respective powers of the debtor and the liquidator;

   (d) the conditions under which set-offs may be invoked;

   (e) the effects of insolvency proceedings on current contracts to which the debtor is party;

   (f) the effects of the insolvency proceedings on proceedings brought by individual creditors, with the exception of lawsuits pending;

   (g) the claims which are to be lodged against the debtor's estate and the treatment of claims arising after the opening of insolvency proceedings;

   (h) the rules governing the lodging, verification and admission of claims;

   (i) the rules governing the distribution of proceeds from the realisation of assets, the ranking of claims and the rights of creditors who have obtained partial satisfaction after the opening of insolvency proceedings by virtue of a right in rem or through a set-off;

   (j) the conditions for and the effects of closure of insolvency proceedings, in particular by composition;

   (k) creditors' rights after the closure of insolvency proceedings;

   (l) who is to bear the costs and expenses incurred in the insolvency proceedings;

   (m) the rules relating to the voidness, voidability or unenforceability of legal acts detrimental to all the creditors.

Article 5
Third parties' rights *in rem*

1. The opening of insolvency proceedings shall not affect the rights *in rem* of creditors or third parties in respect of tangible or intangible, moveable or immoveable assets—both specific assets and collections of indefinite assets as a whole which change from time to time—belonging to the debtor which are situated within the territory of another Member State at the time of the opening of proceedings.

2. The rights referred to in paragraph 1 shall in particular mean:

   (a) the right to dispose of assets or have them disposed of and to obtain satisfaction from the proceeds of or income from those assets, in particular by virtue of a lien or a mortgage;

(b) the exclusive right to have a claim met, in particular a right guaranteed by a lien in respect of the claim or by assignment of the claim by way of a guarantee;

(c) the right to demand the assets from, and/or to require restitution by, anyone having possession or use of them contrary to the wishes of the party so entitled;

(d) a right *in rem* to the beneficial use of assets.

3. The right, recorded in a public register and enforceable against third parties, under which a right *in rem* within the meaning of paragraph 1 may be obtained, shall be considered a right *in rem*.

4. Paragraph 1 shall not preclude actions for voidness, voidability or unenforceability as referred to in Article 4(2)(m).

Article 6
Set-off

1. The opening of insolvency proceedings shall not affect the right of creditors to demand the set-off of their claims against the claims of the debtor, where such a set-off is permitted by the law applicable to the insolvent debtor's claim.

2. Paragraph 1 shall not preclude actions for voidness, voidability or unenforceability as referred to in Article 4(2)(m).

Article 7
Reservation of title

1. The opening of insolvency proceedings against the purchaser of an asset shall not affect the seller's rights based on a reservation of title where at the time of the opening of proceedings the asset is situated within the territory of a Member State other than the State of opening of proceedings.

2. The opening of insolvency proceedings against the seller of an asset, after delivery of the asset, shall not constitute grounds for rescinding or terminating the sale and shall not prevent the purchaser from acquiring title where at the time of the opening of proceedings the asset sold is situated within the territory of a Member State other than the State of the opening of proceedings.

3. Paragraphs 1 and 2 shall not preclude actions for voidness, voidability or unenforceability as referred to in Article 4(2)(m).

Article 8
Contracts relating to immoveable property

The effects of insolvency proceedings on a contract conferring the right to acquire or make use of immoveable property shall be governed solely by the law of the Member State within the territory of which the immoveable property is situated.

Article 9
Payment systems and financial markets

1. Without prejudice to Article 5, the effects of insolvency proceedings on the rights and obligations of the parties to a payment or settlement system or to a financial market shall be governed solely by the law of the Member State applicable to that system or market.

2. Paragraph 1 shall not preclude any action for voidness, voidability or unenforceability which may be taken to set aside payments or transactions under the law applicable to the relevant payment system or financial market.

Article 10
Contracts of employment

The effects of insolvency proceedings on employment contracts and relationships shall be governed solely by the law of the Member State applicable to the contract of employment.

Article 11
Effects on rights subject to registration

The effects of insolvency proceedings on the rights of the debtor in immoveable property, a ship or an aircraft subject to registration in a public register shall be determined by the law of the Member State under the authority of which the register is kept.

Article 12
Community patents and trade marks

For the purposes of this Regulation, a Community patent, a Community trade mark or any other similar right established by Community law may be included only in the proceedings referred to in Article 3(1).

Article 13
Detrimental acts

Article 4(2)(m) shall not apply where the person who benefited from an act detrimental to all the creditors provides proof that:
—the said act is subject to the law of a Member State other than that of the State of the opening of proceedings, and
—that law does not allow any means of challenging that act in the relevant case.

Article 14
Protection of third-party purchasers

Where, by an act concluded after the opening of insolvency proceedings, the debtor disposes, for consideration, of:
—an immoveable asset, or
—a ship or an aircraft subject to registration in a public register, or
—securities whose existence presupposes registration in a register laid down by law, the validity of that act shall be governed by the law of the State within the territory of which the immoveable asset is situated or under the authority of which the register is kept.

Article 15
Effects of insolvency proceedings on lawsuits pending

The effects of insolvency proceedings on a lawsuit pending concerning an asset or a right of which the debtor has been divested shall be governed solely by the law of the Member State in which that lawsuit is pending.

CHAPTER II
RECOGNITION OF INSOLVENCY PROCEEDINGS

Article 16
Principle

1. Any judgment opening insolvency proceedings handed down by a court of a Member State which has jurisdiction pursuant to Article 3 shall be recognised in all the other Member States from the time that it becomes effective in the State of the opening of proceedings.

   This rule shall also apply where, on account of his capacity, insolvency proceedings cannot be brought against the debtor in other Member States.

2. Recognition of the proceedings referred to in Article 3(1) shall not preclude the opening of the proceedings referred to in Article 3(2) by a court in another Member State. The latter proceedings shall be secondary insolvency proceedings within the meaning of Chapter III.

Article 17
Effects of recognition

1. The judgment opening the proceedings referred to in Article 3(1) shall, with no further formalities, produce the same effects in any other Member State as under this law of the State of the opening of proceedings, unless this Regulation provides otherwise and as long as no proceedings referred to in Article 3(2) are opened in that other Member State.

2. The effects of the proceedings referred to in Article 3(2) may not be challenged in other Member States. Any restriction of the creditors' rights, in particular a stay or discharge, shall produce effects vis-à-vis assets situated within the territory of another Member State only in the case of those creditors who have given their consent.

Article 18
Powers of the liquidator

1. The liquidator appointed by a court which has jurisdiction pursuant to Article 3(1) may exercise all the powers conferred on him by the law of the State of the opening of proceedings in another Member State, as long as no other insolvency proceedings have been opened there nor any preservation measure to the contrary has been taken there further to a request for the opening of insolvency proceedings in that State. He may in particular remove the debtor's assets from the territory of the Member State in which they are situated, subject to Articles 5 and 7.

2. The liquidator appointed by a court which has jurisdiction pursuant to Article 3(2) may in any other Member State claim through the courts or out of court that moveable property was removed from the territory of the State of the opening of proceedings to the territory of that other Member State after the opening of the insolvency proceedings. He may also bring any action to set aside which is in the interests of the creditors.

3. In exercising his powers, the liquidator shall comply with the law of the Member State within the territory of which he intends to take action, in particular with regard to procedures for the realisation of assets. Those powers may not include coercive measures or the right to rule on legal proceedings or disputes.

Article 19
Proof of the liquidator's appointment

The liquidator's appointment shall be evidenced by a certified copy of the original decision appointing him or by any other certificate issued by the court which has jurisdiction.

A translation into the official language or one of the official languages of the Member State within the territory of which he intends to act may be required. No legalisation or other similar formality shall be required.

Article 20
Return and imputation

1. A creditor who, after the opening of the proceedings referred to in Article 3(1) obtains by any means, in particular through enforcement, total or partial satisfaction of his claim on the assets belonging to the debtor situated within the territory of another Member State, shall return what he has obtained to the liquidator, subject to Articles 5 and 7.
2. In order to ensure equal treatment of creditors a creditor who has, in the course of insolvency proceedings, obtained a dividend on his claim shall share in distributions made in other proceedings only where creditors of the same ranking or category have, in those other proceedings, obtained an equivalent dividend.

Article 21
Publication

1. The liquidator may request that notice of the judgment opening insolvency proceedings and, where appropriate, the decision appointing him, be published in any other Member State in accordance with the publication procedures provided for in that State. Such publication shall also specify the liquidator appointed and whether the jurisdiction rule applied is that pursuant to Article 3(1) or Article 3(2).
2. However, any Member State within the territory of which the debtor has an establishment may require mandatory publication. In such cases, the liquidator or any authority empowered to that effect in the Member State where the proceedings referred to in Article 3(1) are opened shall take all necessary measures to ensure such publication.

Article 22
Registration in a public register

1. The liquidator may request that the judgment opening the proceedings referred to in Article 3(1) be registered in the land register, the trade register and any other public register kept in the other Member States.
2. However, any Member State may require mandatory registration. In such cases, the liquidator or any authority empowered to that effect in the Member State where the proceedings referred to in Article 3(1) have been opened shall take all necessary measures to ensure such registration.

Article 23
Costs

The costs of the publication and registration provided for in Articles 21 and 22 shall be regarded as costs and expenses incurred in the proceedings.

Article 24
Honouring of an obligation to a debtor

1. Where an obligation has been honoured in a Member State for the benefit of a debtor who is subject to insolvency proceedings opened in another Member State, when it should have been honoured for the benefit of the liquidator in those proceedings, the person honouring the obligation shall be deemed to have discharged it if he was unaware of the opening of proceedings.
2. Where such an obligation is honoured before the publication provided for in Article 21 has been effected, the person honouring the obligation shall be presumed, in the absence of proof to the contrary, to have been unaware of the opening of insolvency proceedings; where the obligation is honoured after such publication has been effected, the person honouring the obligation shall be presumed, in the absence of proof to the contrary, to have been aware of the opening of proceedings.

Article 25
Recognition and enforceability of other judgments

1. Judgments handed down by a court whose judgment concerning the opening of proceedings is recognised in accordance with Article 16 and which concern the course and closure of insolvency proceedings, and compositions approved by that court shall also be recognised with no further formalities. Such judgments shall be enforced in accordance with Articles 31 to 51, with the exception of Article 34(2), of the Brussels Convention on Jurisdiction and the Enforcement of Judgments in Civil and Commercial Matters, as amended by the Conventions of Accession to this Convention.
   The first subparagraph shall also apply to judgments deriving directly from the insolvency proceedings and which are closely linked with them, even if they were handed down by another court.
   The first subparagraph shall also apply to judgments relating to preservation measures taken after the request for the opening of insolvency proceedings.
2. The recognition and enforcement of judgments other than those referred to in paragraph 1 shall be governed by the Convention referred to in paragraph 1, provided that that Convention is applicable.
3. The Member States shall not be obliged to recognise or enforce a judgment referred to in paragraph 1 which might result in a limitation of personal freedom or postal secrecy.

Article 26[6]
Public policy

Any Member State may refuse to recognise insolvency proceedings opened in another Member State or to enforce a judgment handed down in the context of such proceedings where the effects of such recognition or enforcement would be manifestly contrary to that State's public policy, in particular its fundamental principles or the constitutional rights and liberties of the individual.

---

[6] Note the Declaration by Portugal concerning the application of Articles 26 and 37 (OJ C 183, 30.6.2000, p. 1).

CHAPTER III
SECONDARY INSOLVENCY PROCEEDINGS

Article 27
Opening of proceedings

The opening of the proceedings referred to in Article 3(1) by a court of a Member State and which is recognised in another Member State (main proceedings) shall permit the opening in that other Member State, a court of which has jurisdiction pursuant to Article 3(2), of secondary insolvency proceedings without the debtor's insolvency being examined in that other State. These latter proceedings must be among the proceedings listed in Annex B. Their effects shall be restricted to the assets of the debtor situated within the territory of that other Member State.

Article 28
Applicable law

Save as otherwise provided in this Regulation, the law applicable to secondary proceedings shall be that of the Member State within the territory of which the secondary proceedings are opened.

Article 29
Right to request the opening of proceedings

The opening of secondary proceedings may be requested by:
(a) The liquidator in the main proceedings;
(b) any other person or authority empowered to request the opening of insolvency proceedings under the law of the Member State within the territory of which the opening of secondary proceedings is requested.

Article 30
Advance payment of costs and expenses

Where the law of the Member State in which the opening of secondary proceedings is requested requires that the debtor's assets be sufficient to cover in whole or in part the costs and expenses of the proceedings, the court may, when it receives such a request, require the applicant to make an advance payment of costs or to provide appropriate security.

Article 31
Duty to cooperate and communicate information

1. Subject to the rules restricting the communication of information, the liquidator in the main proceedings and the liquidators in the secondary proceedings shall be duty bound to communicate information to each other. They shall immediately communicate any information which may be relevant to the other proceedings, in particular the progress made in lodging and verifying claims and all measures aimed at terminating the proceedings.

2. Subject to the rules applicable to each of the proceedings, the liquidator in the main proceedings and the liquidators in the secondary proceedings shall be duty bound to cooperate with each other.

3. The liquidator in the secondary proceedings shall give the liquidator in the main proceedings an early opportunity of submitting proposals on the liquidation or use of the assets in the secondary proceedings.

Article 32
Exercise of creditors' rights

1. Any creditor may lodge his claim in the main proceedings and in any secondary proceedings.

2. The liquidators in the main and any secondary proceedings shall lodge in other proceedings claims which have already been lodged in the proceedings for which they were appointed, provided that the interests of creditors in the latter proceedings are served thereby, subject to the right of creditors to oppose that or to withdraw the lodgement of their claims where the law applicable so provides.

3. The liquidator in the main or secondary proceedings shall be empowered to participate in other proceedings on the same basis as a creditor, in particular by attending creditors' meetings.

Article 33
Stay of liquidation

1. The court, which opened the secondary proceedings, shall stay the process of liquidation in whole or in part on receipt of a request from the liquidator in the main proceedings, provided that in that event it may require the liquidator in the main proceedings to take any suitable measure to guarantee the interests of the creditors in the secondary proceedings and of individual classes of creditors. Such a request from the liquidator may be rejected only if it is manifestly of no interest to the creditors in the main proceedings. Such a stay of the process of liquidation may be ordered for up to three months. It may be continued or renewed for similar periods.

2. The court referred to in paragraph 1 shall terminate the stay of the process of liquidation:
   —at the request of the liquidator in the main proceedings,
   —of its own motion, at the request of a creditor or at the request of the liquidator in the secondary proceedings if that measure no longer appears justified, in particular, by the interests of creditors in the main proceedings or in the secondary proceedings.

Article 34
Measures ending secondary insolvency proceedings

1. Where the law applicable to secondary proceedings allows for such proceedings to be closed without liquidation by a rescue plan, a composition or a comparable measure, the liquidator in the main proceedings shall be empowered to propose such a measure himself.

   Closure of the secondary proceedings by a measure referred to in the first subparagraph shall not become final without the consent of the liquidator in the main proceedings; failing his agreement, however, it may become final if the financial interests of the creditors in the main proceedings are not affected by the measure proposed.

2. Any restriction of creditors' rights arising from a measure referred to in paragraph 1 which is proposed in secondary proceedings, such as a stay of payment or discharge of debt, may not have effect in respect of the debtor's assets not covered by those proceedings without the consent of all the creditors having an interest.

3. During a stay of the process of liquidation ordered pursuant to Article 33, only the liquidator in the main proceedings or the debtor, with the former's consent, may propose measures laid down in paragraph 1 of this Article in the secondary proceedings; no other proposal for such a measure shall be put to the vote or approved.

Article 35
Assets remaining in the secondary proceedings

If by the liquidation of assets in the secondary proceedings it is possible to meet all claims allowed under those proceedings, the liquidator appointed in those proceedings shall immediately transfer any assets remaining to the liquidator in the main proceedings.

Article 36
Subsequent opening of the main proceedings

Where the proceedings referred to in Article 3(1) are opened following the opening of the proceedings referred to in Article 3(2) in another Member State, Articles 31 to 35 shall apply to those opened first, in so far as the progress of those proceedings so permits.

Article 37[7]
Conversion of earlier proceedings

The liquidator in the main proceedings may request that proceedings listed in Annex A previously opened in another Member State be converted into winding-up proceedings if this proves to be in the interests of the creditors in the main proceedings.

The court with jurisdiction under Article 3(2) shall order conversion into one of the proceedings listed in Annex B.

Article 38
Preservation measures

Where the court of a Member State which has jurisdiction pursuant to Article 3(1) appoints a temporary administrator in order to ensure the preservation of the debtor's assets, that temporary administrator shall be empowered to request any measures to secure and preserve any of the debtor's assets situated in another Member State, provided for under the law of that State, for the period between the request for the opening of insolvency proceedings and the judgment opening the proceedings.

---

[7] Note the Declaration by Portugal concerning the application of Articles 26 and 37 (OJ C 183, 30.6.2000, p. 1).

CHAPTER IV
PROVISION OF INFORMATION FOR CREDITORS AND
LODGEMENT OF THEIR CLAIMS

Article 39
Right to lodge claims

Any creditor who has his habitual residence, domicile or registered office in a Member State other than the State of the opening of proceedings, including the tax authorities and social security authorities of Member States, shall have the right to lodge claims in the insolvency proceedings in writing.

Article 40
Duty to inform creditors

1. As soon as insolvency proceedings are opened in a Member State, the court of that State having jurisdiction or the liquidator appointed by it shall immediately inform known creditors who have their habitual residences, domiciles or registered offices in the other Member States.

2. That information, provided by an individual notice, shall in particular include time limits, the penalties laid down in regard to those time limits, the body or authority empowered to accept the lodgement of claims and the other measures laid down. Such notice shall also indicate whether creditors whose claims are preferential or secured in rem need lodge their claims.

Article 41
Content of the lodgement of a claim

A creditor shall send copies of supporting documents, if any, and shall indicate the nature of the claim, the date on which it arose and its amount, as well as whether he alleges preference, security in rem or a reservation of title in respect of the claim and what assets are covered by the guarantee he is invoking.

Article 42
Languages

1. The information provided for in Article 40 shall be provided in the official language or one of the official languages of the State of the opening of proceedings. For that purpose a form shall be used bearing the heading 'Invitation to lodge a claim. Time limits to be observed' in all the official languages of the institutions of the European Union.

2. Any creditor who has his habitual residence, domicile or registered office in a Member State other than the State of the opening of proceedings may lodge his claim in the official language or one of the official languages of that other State. In that event, however, the lodgement of his claim shall bear the heading 'Lodgement of claim' in the official language or one of the official languages of the State of the opening of

proceedings. In addition, he may be required to provide a translation into the official language or one of the official languages of the State of the opening of proceedings.

CHAPTER V
TRANSITIONAL AND FINAL PROVISIONS

Article 43
Applicability in time

The provisions of this Regulation shall apply only to insolvency proceedings opened after its entry into force. Acts done by a debtor before the entry into force of this Regulation shall continue to be governed by the law which was applicable to them at the time they were done.

Article 44
Relationship to Conventions

1. After its entry into force, this Regulation replaces, in respect of the matters referred to therein, in the relations between Member States, the Conventions concluded between two or more Member States, in particular:
   (a) the Convention between Belgium and France on Jurisdiction and the Validity and Enforcement of Judgments, Arbitration Awards and Authentic Instruments, signed at Paris on 8 July 1899;
   (b) the Convention between Belgium and Austria on Bankruptcy, Winding-up, Arrangements, Compositions and Suspension of Payments (with Additional Protocol of 13 June 1973), signed at Brussels on 16 July 1969;
   (c) the Convention between Belgium and the Netherlands on Territorial Jurisdiction, Bankruptcy and the Validity and Enforcement of Judgments, Arbitration Awards and Authentic Instruments, signed at Brussels on 28 March 1925;
   (d) the Treaty between Germany and Austria on Bankruptcy, Winding-up, Arrangements and Compositions, signed at Vienna on 25 May 1979;
   (e) the Convention between France and Austria on Jurisdiction, Recognition and Enforcement of Judgments on Bankruptcy, signed at Vienna on 27 February 1979;
   (f) the Convention between France and Italy on the Enforcement of Judgments in Civil and Commercial Matters, signed at Rome on 3 June 1930;
   (g) the Convention between Italy and Austria on Bankruptcy, Winding-up, Arrangements and Compositions, signed at Rome on 12 July 1977;
   (h) the Convention between the Kingdom of the Netherlands and the Federal Republic of Germany on the Mutual Recognition and Enforcement of Judgments and other Enforceable Instruments in Civil and Commercial Matters, signed at The Hague on 30 August 1962;
   (i) the Convention between the United Kingdom and the Kingdom of Belgium providing for the Reciprocal Enforcement of Judgments in Civil and Commercial Matters, with Protocol, signed at Brussels on 2 May 1934;
   (j) the Convention between Denmark, Finland, Norway, Sweden and Iceland on Bankruptcy, signed at Copenhagen on 7 November 1933;

    (k) the European Convention on Certain International Aspects of Bankruptcy, signed at Istanbul on 5 June 1990.

2. The Conventions referred to in paragraph 1 shall continue to have effect with regard to proceedings opened before the entry into force of this Regulation.

3. This Regulation shall not apply:

    (a) in any Member State, to the extent that it is irreconcilable with the obligations arising in relation to bankruptcy from a convention concluded by that State with one or more third countries before the entry into force of this Regulation;

    (b) in the United Kingdom of Great Britain and Northern Ireland, to the extent that is irreconcilable with the obligations arising in relation to bankruptcy and the winding-up of insolvent companies from any arrangements with the Commonwealth existing at the time this Regulation enters into force.

Article 45
Amendment of the Annexes

The Council, acting by qualified majority on the initiative of one of its members or on a proposal from the Commission, may amend the Annexes.

Article 46
Reports

No later than 1 June 2012, and every five years thereafter, the Commission shall present to the European Parliament, the Council and the Economic and Social Committee a report on the application of this Regulation. The report shall be accompanied if need be by a proposal for adaptation of this Regulation.

Article 47
Entry into force

This Regulation shall enter into force on 31 May 2002.

This Regulation shall be binding in its entirety and directly applicable in the Member States in accordance with the Treaty establishing the European Community.

Done at Brussels, 29 May 2000.

For the Council
The President
A. Costa

ANNEX A

Insolvency proceedings referred to in Article 2(a)

BELGIË-/BELGIQUE
—Het faillissement//La faillite
—Het gerechtelijk akkoord//Le concordat judiciaire
—De collectieve schuldenregeling//Le règlement collectif de dettes

DEUTSCHLAND
—Das Konkursverfahren
—Das gerichtliche Vergleichsverfahren
—Das Gesamtvollstreckungsverfahren
—Das Insolvenzverfahren

ÅëëÁÓ
—Ð ôÞ÷åõóç
—ÇåéäéêÞ åêêáèÜñéóç
—ÇðñïóùñéíÞ äéá÷;åßñéóç åôáéñßáò. Ç äéïßêçóç êáé ç äéá÷åßñéóç ôùí ðéóôùôÞí
—ÇõðáãùãÞ åðé÷åßñçóçò õðü åðßôñïðï ìå óêïðü ôç óýíáøç óõìâéâáóìïý ìå ôïõò ðéóôùôÝò

ESPAÑA
—Concurso de acreedores
—Quiebra
—Suspensión de pagos

FRANCE
—Liquidation judiciaire
—Redressement judiciaire avec nomination d'un administrateur

IRELAND
—Compulsory winding up by the court
—Bankruptcy
—The administration in bankruptcy of the estate of persons dying insolvent
—Winding—up in bankruptcy of partnerships
—Creditors' voluntary winding up (with confirmation of a Court)
—Arrangements under the control of the court which involve the vesting of all or part of the property of the debtor in the Official Assignee for realisation and distribution
—Company examinership

ITALIA
—Fallimento
—Concordato preventivo
—Liquidazione coatta amministrativa
—Amministrazione straordinaria
—Amministrazione controllata

LUXEMBOURG
—Faillite
—Gestion contrôlée

—Concordat préventif de faillite (par abandon d'actif)
—Régime spécial de liquidation du notariat

NEDERLAND
—Het faillissement
—De surséance van betaling
—De schuldsaneringsregeling natuurlijke personen

ÖSTERREICH
—Das Konkursverfahren
—Das Ausgleichsverfahren

PORTUGAL
—O processo de falência
—Os processos especiais de recuperação de empresa, ou seja:
— A concordata
—A reconstituição empresarial
—A reestruturação financeira
—A gestão controlada

SUOMI-/FINLAND
—Konkurssi//konkurs
—Yrityssaneeraus//företagssanering

SVERIGE
—Konkurs
—Företagsrekonstruktion

UNITED KINGDOM
—Winding up by or subject to the supervision of the court
—Creditors' voluntary winding up (with confirmation by the court)
—Administration
—Voluntary arrangements under insolvency legislation
—Bankruptcy or sequestration

ANNEX B
Winding up proceedings referred to in Article 2(c)

BELGIë-/BELGIQUE
—Het faillissement//La faillite

DEUTSCHLAND
—Das Konkursverfahren
—Das Gesamtvollstreckungsverfahren
—Das Insolvenzverfahren

ÅëëÁÓ
—Ð ôÞ÷åõóç
—Ç åéäéêÞ åêêáèÜñéóç

ESPAÑA
—Concurso de acreedores
—Quiebra
—Suspensión de pagos basada en la insolvencia definitiva

FRANCE
—Liquidation judiciaire

IRELAND
—Compulsory winding up
—Bankruptcy
—The administration in bankruptcy of the estate of persons dying insolvent
—Winding-up in bankruptcy of partnerships
—Creditors' voluntary winding up (with confirmation of a court)
—Arrangements under the control of the court which involve the vesting of all or part of the property of the debtor in the Official Assignee for realisation and distribution

ITALIA
—Fallimento
—Liquidazione coatta amministrativa

LUXEMBOURG
— Faillite
—Régime spécial de liquidation du notariat

NEDERLAND
—Het faillissement
—De schuldsaneringsregeling natuurlijke personen

ÖSTERREICH
—Das Konkursverfahren

PORTUGAL
—O processo de falência

SUOMI-/FINLAND
—Konkurssi//konkurs

SVERIGE
—Konkurs

UNITED KINGDOM
—Winding up by or subject to the supervision of the court
—Creditors' voluntary winding up (with confirmation by the court)
—Bankruptcy or sequestration

ANNEX C
Liquidators referred to in Article 2(b)

BELGIë-/BELGIQUE
—De curator//Le curateur
—De commissaris inzake opschorting//Le commissaire au sursis

—De schuldbemiddelaar//Le médiateur de dettes

DEUTSCHLAND
—Konkursverwalter
—Vergleichsverwalter
—Sachwalter (nach der Vergleichsordnung)
—Verwalter
—Insolvenzverwalter
—Sachwalter (nach der Insolvenzordnung)
—Treuhänder
—Vorläufiger Insolvenzverwalter

ÅëëÁÓ
—Ïóýíäééi
—Ïðñïóùñéíü äéá÷åéñéóôÞò. Ç äéïéêïýóá åðéôñïðÞ ôùí ðéóôùôÞí
—Ï äéäéêüò åêêáèáñéóôÞò
—ÏåðßôñïðïÏï

ESPAÑA
—Depositario-administrador
—Interventor o Interventores
—Síndicos
—Comisario

FRANCE
—Représentant des créanciers
—Mandataire liquidateur
—Administrateur judiciaire
—Commissaire à l'exécution de plan

IRELAND
—Liquidator
—Official Assignee
—Trustee in bankruptcy
—Provisional Liquidator
—Examiner

ITALIA
—Curatore
—Commissario

LUXEMBOURG
—Le curateur
—Le commissaire
—Le liquidateur
—Le conseil de gérance de la section d'assainissement du notariat

NEDERLAND
—De curator in het faillissement
—De bewindvoerder in de surséance van betaling

—De bewindvoerder in de schuldsaneringsregeling natuurlijke personen

ÖSTERREICH
—Masseverwalter
—Ausgleichsverwalter
—Sachwalter
—Treuhänder
—Besondere Verwalter
—Vorläufiger Verwalter
—Konkursgericht

PORTUGAL
—Gestor judicial
—Liquidatário judicial
—Comissão de credores

SUOMI-/FINLAND
—Pesänhoitaja//boförvaltare
—Selvittäjä//utredare

SVERIGE
—Förvaltare
—God man
—Rekonstruktör

UNITED KINGDOM
—Liquidator
—Supervisor of a voluntary arrangement
—Administrator
—Official Receiver
—Trustee
—Judicial factor

9

SECURITIES SETTLEMENT AND SECURITIES COLLATERAL

A. Introductory Text

1. EC Settlement Finality Directive

Introduction

The Settlement Finality Directive[1] is part of both the EC's prudential regulation regime and its internal-market insolvency regime. Settlement, i.e. the arrangement for delivery and payment after a trade has taken place, occurs mainly through settlement systems; parallel to the dematerialization of securities, settlement today hardly involves movement of paper but is carried out electronically through book entries (book entry transfer). Not all deliveries are however made against payment, e.g. because they are a transfer of securities collateral against a loan. The very nature of these settlement arrangements involves significant systemic risks. These are heightened in the context of transnational transactions in that the participation of foreign institutions in settlement systems entails that issues of property law, insolvency law, etc., are potentially governed by a multitude of domestic rules. The Directive is

---

[1] Directive 98/26/EC of the European Parliament and of the Council of 19 May 1998, on settlement finality in payment and securities settlement systems, OJ L 166, 11.6.1998, p.45.

designed to limit systemic risk and to ensure both the efficiency and the stability of dealings among participants in recognized clearing and settlement systems.

The Directive's objectives are firstly, to secure the finality of settlements in relation to transfer orders and netting;[2] secondly, to remove from attack under the general insolvency law of Member States the position of participants under the rules of a designated settlement system and; thirdly, to ensure the enforceability of security collateral.

Scope

The Directive applies to any system[3] governed by the law of a Member State operating in any currency, to all participants in such a system and to collateral security provided in connection with participation in a system or operations of Member States' central banks.[4]

A system is a formal arrangement between three or more participants[5] with common rules and standardized arrangements for the execution of transfer orders between the participants. The system must be governed by the law of a Member State chosen by the participants in which at least one of the participants has its head office. The system must be designated as a system and notified to the Commission by the Member State whose law is applicable.[6]

Participant means an institution,[7] a central counterparty, a settlement agent, or a clearing house[8] that is responsible for discharging the financial obligation arising from transfer orders within that system.[9]

Transfer orders, whose enforceability is the main concern of the Directive, are, firstly, instructions by a participant to place at the disposal of a recipient an amount of money[10] or which results in the assumption or discharge of a payment obligation or, secondly, to transfer the title to, or interest in, securities through a book entry on an account, a register, or otherwise.[11]

Settlement finality

Transfer orders and netting are binding on a third party and enforceable despite the insolvency of a participant, provided that transfer orders were entered into a system before the moment of opening of such insolvency proceedings.[12] Member States

---

[2] I.e. the conversion into one net claim or one net obligation of claims and obligations resulting from transfer orders that a participant or participants either issue to, or receive from, one or more other participants with the result that only a net claim can be demanded or a net obligation is owed, Art 2 (k).

[3] A term defined in Art 2(a).   [4] Article 1.

[5] A term defined in Art 2(f). A possible settlement agent, a possible central counter party, a possible clearing house, or a possible indirect participant are not counted.   [6] Article 2(a).

[7] I.e. certain credit institutions and investment firms etc., cf. Art 2(b).

[8] All further defined in Art 2(c)–(e).

[9] Article 2(f). See also Art 2(g) on 'indirect participants'.

[10] Through book entry on an account.   [11] Article 2(i).

[12] Article 3(1). Where the settlement system (the settlement agent, the central counterparty, or the clearing house) can prove that it was unaware of the opening of the proceedings, the transfer orders are binding also if they were entered after, but on the same day as the opening of the insolvency proceedings. For the latter, see Art 6(1).

may provide for the defaulting participant's assets to be used to meet its settlement obligations on the day of the opening of the insolvency.[13]

The moment of entry of a transfer order into a system is defined by the rules of that system which in turn must be in accordance with the national law governing that system.[14]

Collateral Security

The Directive defines collateral security as all realizable assets provided under a pledge, a repurchase, or similar agreement for the purposes of securing rights and obligations potentially arising in connection with a system, or provided to the central banks of Member States or the European Central Bank.[15] The insolvency of a collateral giver does not affect the collateral taker.[16] Thus, any restrictions imposed by domestic law on the enforcement of security while a petition for an administration order is pending or the order is in force do not apply in relation to a collateral security charge. The collateral security may be realized for the satisfaction of the collateral taker's rights.

Conflict of laws

The Directive also addresses the issue of which law governs the question of whether security, given in connection with participation in a system or to central banks, is valid and enforceable. The rule basically provides that, where securities are so provided and the right with respect to the securities is recorded in a register, account, or centralized deposit system located in a Member State, the rights of holders or the collateral are to be determined by the law of that Member State.[17] This conflict rule is likely to be amended in the light of the 2002 Hague Convention on the Law Applicable to Certain Rights in Respect of Securities Held with an Intermediary, discussed in Chapter 10.

2. EC Financial Collateral Directive

Introduction

This Directive[18] complements the Settlement Finality Directive as well as insolvency related EC law. It is however broader and more ambitious in its scope. The Directive addresses issues of legal risk associated with the taking of security in

---

[13] Article 4.   [14] Article 3(3).   [15] Article 2(m).
[16] Article 9(1).
[17] Article 9(2). See also the Directive's recitals 19–21. The Directive thus reflects the place of the relevant intermediary approach (PRIMA). The Hague Convention on the Law Applicable to Certain Rights in Respect of Securities Held with an Intermediary, below, p. 775, retains the concept of the relevant intermediary but substitutes the law selected to govern the account agreement for the place of the intermediary.
[18] Directive 2002/47/EC of the European Parliament and of the Council of 6 June 2002 on financial collateral arrangements, OJ L 168, 27.6.2002, p. 43.

financial collateral. It covers both directly held and indirectly held securities. The Directive requires Member States to disapply certain provisions of insolvency law with a view to achieving the necessary protection of the collateral taker.

The recitals are even more important for the understanding of this Directive than recitals usually are. They state the objective of establishing a 'Community regime...for the provision of securities and cash as collateral under both security interest and title transfer structures including repurchase agreements (repos). This will contribute to the integration and cost-efficiency of the financial market as well as to the stability of the financial system in the Community...'.[19]

Scope

The Directive covers financial collateral in the form of cash or financial instruments.[20] It focuses on bilateral financial collateral arrangements.[21]

The Directive applies only when the collateral has actually been provided and only where both the agreement for the provision of the collateral and the provision itself is evidenced in writing.[22] This aims at making the collateral identifiable through book entries or crediting to an account. Collateral is to be considered 'provided' only where there is some form of dispossession, i.e. it must have been transferred, held, registered, or otherwise designated so as to be in the possession or under the control of the collateral taker or a person acting on his behalf.[23]

Recognition of title transfer arrangements

There are two categories of financial collateral arrangements: title transfer arrangements and security ('book-entry') arrangements. Since the former, including repurchase agreements, were unknown under some domestic laws but widely used by the industry, the Directive requires Member States to ensure that a title transfer financial collateral arrangement takes effect in accordance with its terms.[24]

Reducing formal requirements

One of the Directive's purposes is to remove certain formal requirements[25] for the creation, validity, perfection, enforceability, or admissibility in evidence of a

---

[19] Recital (3).
[20] Article 1(4)(a). 'Financial instruments' is an all-embracing term defined in Art 2(1)(e).
[21] Recital (3).   [22] Article 1(5). See also Art 2(5) on the term 'writing'.
[23] Recitals (9), (10).
[24] Article 6. Title transfer financial collateral arrangements are arrangements, including repurchase agreements, under which a collateral provider transfers full ownership of the collateral to a collateral taker for the purpose of securing or otherwise covering the performance of relevant financial obligations (Art 2(1)(b)). Security financial collateral arrangements are those under which a collateral provider provides financial collateral by way of security in favour of, or to, a collateral taker and where full ownership of the financial collateral remains with the collateral provider when the security right is established (Art 2(1)(c)). Construed literally, the above definition fails to cover the case where the security takes the form of a transfer which leaves ownership divided between the collateral taker and the collateral provider (as in the case of the common law mortgage), but it must be assumed that the Directive was intended to cover this form of security.   [25] Listed in Recital 10.

financial collateral arrangement. Member States now may not any longer impose such requirements.[26]

Enforcement

On the occurrence of an enforcement event[27] the collateral taker must be able to realize, in the manner described in detail, the financial collateral provided under, and subject to the terms agreed upon in the collateral agreement,[28] i.e. sale, appropriation, or set–off.

Right of use

A right of use[29] is to be recognized,[30] even where the collateral has been provided in the form of a security interest. Where the collateral taker exercises this right of use, it is required to replace the original collateral or its equivalent.[31] This obligation, upon default, is set off against the collateralized obligation.[32]

Insolvency protection

The Directive provides for the protection of the provision of financial collateral against avoidance for insolvency. It requires Member States to ensure that a close-out netting provision[33] can take effect in accordance with its terms, notwithstanding the commencement or continuation of winding-up proceedings or reorganization measures in respect of either party.[34] The Directive further protects collateral arrangements from displacement under various rules of insolvency law, e.g. that the arrangement has come into existence, or the collateral has been provided, within a prescribed period prior to, and defined by reference to, the commencement of winding-up proceedings or reorganization measures.[35]

Conflict of laws

Article 9 of the Directive provides that the legal nature and proprietary effects of book entry securities collateral, including perfection requirements, priority rules, and steps required for realization or book entry securities collateral, are to be governed by the law of the country in which the relevant account is maintained. This provision is likely to be modified in the light of the 2002 Hague Convention on the Law Applicable to Certain Rights in Respect of Securities held with an Intermediary.[36]

---

[26] Article 3.
[27] Defined in Art 2(1)(l) as default of the collateral giver or any similar event as agreed upon between the parties. [28] Art 4.
[29] Defined in Art 2(1)(m) as the right of the collateral taker to use and dispose of financial collateral provided under a security financial collateral arrangement as the owner of it in accordance with the terms of the agreement. [30] Article 5(1).
[31] Article 5(2). [32] Article 5(5).
[33] Defined in Art 2(1)(n), *inter alia*, as a provision of a financial collateral arrangement or any statutory rule by which, in the case of default, the obligations are 'accelerated' so as to be immediately due.
[34] Art 7. [35] Art 8. [36] On which see p. 731 below.

B. Instruments

(i) DIRECTIVE 98/26/EC OF THE EUROPEAN PARLIAMENT AND OF THE COUNCIL OF 19 MAY 1998 ON SETTLEMENT FINALITY IN PAYMENT AND SECURITIES SETTLEMENT SYSTEMS

PREAMBLE

THE EUROPEAN PARLIAMENT AND THE COUNCIL OF THE EUROPEAN UNION,

Having regard to the Treaty establishing the European Community, and in particular Article 100a thereof,

Having regard to the proposal from the Commission,[1]

Having regard to the opinion of the European Monetary Institute,[2]

Having regard to the opinion of the Economic and Social Committee,[3]

Acting in accordance with the procedure laid down in Article 189b of the Treaty,[4]

(1) Whereas the Lamfalussy report of 1990 to the Governors of the central banks of the Group of Ten Countries demonstrated the important systemic risk inherent in payment systems which operate on the basis of several legal types of payment netting, in particular multilateral netting; whereas the reduction of legal risks associated with participation in real time gross settlement systems is of paramount importance, given the increasing development of these systems;

---

[1] OJ C 207, 18. 7. 1996, p. 13, and OJ C 259, 26. 8. 1997, p. 6.
[2] Opinion delivered on 21 November 1996.   [3] OJ C 56, 24. 2. 1997, p. 1.
[4] Opinion of the European Parliament of 9 April 1997 (OJ C 132, 28. 4. 1997, p. 74), Council Common Position of 13 October 1997 (OJ C 375, 10. 12. 1997, p. 34) and Decision of the European Parliament of 29 January 1998 (OJ C 56, 23. 2. 1998). Council Decision of 27 April 1998.

(2) Whereas it is also of the utmost importance to reduce the risk associated with participation in securities settlement systems, in particular where there is a close connection between such systems and payment systems;

(3) Whereas this Directive aims at contributing to the efficient and cost effective operation of cross-border payment and securities settlement arrangements in the Community, which reinforces the freedom of movement of capital in the internal market; whereas this Directive thereby follows up the progress made towards completion of the internal market, in particular towards the freedom to provide services and liberalization of capital movements, with a view to the realization of Economic and Monetary Union;

(4) Whereas it is desirable that the laws of the Member States should aim to minimise the disruption to a system caused by insolvency proceedings against a participant in that system;

(5) Whereas a proposal for a Directive on the reorganization and winding-up of credit institutions submitted in 1985 and amended on 8 February 1988 is still pending before the Council; whereas the Convention on Insolvency Proceedings drawn up on 23 November 1995 by the Member States meeting within the Council explicitly excludes insurance undertakings, credit institutions and investment firms;

(6) Whereas this Directive is intended to cover payment and securities settlement systems of a domestic as well as of a cross-border nature; whereas the Directive is applicable to Community systems and to collateral security constituted by their participants, be they Community or third country participants, in connection with participation in these systems;

(7) Whereas Member States may apply the provisions of this Directive to their domestic institutions which participate directly in third country systems and to collateral security provided in connection with participation in such systems;

(8) Whereas Member States should be allowed to designate as a system covered by this Directive a system whose main activity is the settlement of securities even if the system to a limited extent also deals with commodity derivatives;

(9) Whereas the reduction of systemic risk requires in particular the finality of settlement and the enforceability of collateral security; whereas collateral security is meant to comprise all means provided by a participant to the other participants in the payment and/or securities settlement systems to secure rights and obligations in connection with that system, including repurchase agreements, statutory liens and fiduciary transfers; whereas regulation in national law of the kind of collateral security which can be used should not be affected by the definition of collateral security in this Directive;

(10) Whereas this Directive, by covering collateral security provided in connection with operations of the central banks of the Member States functioning as central banks, including monetary policy operations, assists the European Monetary Institute in its task of promoting the efficiency of cross-border payments with a view to the preparation of the third stage of Economic and Monetary Union and thereby contributes to developing the necessary legal framework in which the future European central bank may develop its policy;

(11) Whereas transfer orders and their netting should be legally enforceable under all Member States' jurisdictions and binding on third parties;

(12) Whereas rules on finality of netting should not prevent systems testing, before the netting takes place, whether orders that have entered the system comply with the rules of that system and allow the settlement of that system to take place;

(13) Whereas nothing in this Directive should prevent a participant or a third party from exercising any right or claim resulting from the underlying transaction which they may have in law to recovery or restitution in respect of a transfer order which has entered a system, e.g. in case of fraud or technical error, as long as this leads neither to the unwinding of netting nor to the revocation of the transfer order in the system;

(14) Whereas it is necessary to ensure that transfer orders cannot be revoked after a moment defined by the rules of the system;

(15) Whereas it is necessary that a Member State should immediately notify other Member States of the opening of insolvency proceedings against a participant in the system;

(16) Whereas insolvency proceedings should not have a retroactive effect on the rights and obligations of participants in a system;

(17) Whereas, in the event of insolvency proceedings against a participant in a system, this Directive furthermore aims at determining which insolvency law is applicable to the rights and obligations of that participant in connection with its participation in a system;

(18) Whereas collateral security should be insulated from the effects of the insolvency law applicable to the insolvent participant;

(19) Whereas the provisions of Article 9(2) should only apply to a register, account or centralized deposit system which evidences the existence of proprietary rights in or for the delivery or transfer of the securities concerned;

(20) Whereas the provisions of Article 9(2) are intended to ensure that if the participant, the central bank of a Member State or the future European central bank has a valid and effective collateral security as determined under the law of the Member State where the relevant register, account or centralized deposit system is located, then the validity and enforceability of that collateral security as against that system (and the operator thereof) and against any other person claiming directly or indirectly through it, should be determined solely under the law of that Member State;

(21) Whereas the provisions of Article 9(2) are not intended to prejudice the operation and effect of the law of the Member State under which the securities are constituted or of the law of the Member State where the securities may otherwise be located (including, without limitation, the law concerning the creation, ownership or transfer of such securities or of rights in such securities) and should not be interpreted to mean that any such collateral security will be directly enforceable or be capable of being recognised in any such Member State otherwise than in accordance with the law of that Member State;

(22) Whereas it is desirable that Member States endeavour to establish sufficient links between all the securities settlement systems covered by this Directive with a view towards promoting maximum transparency and legal certainty of transactions relating to securities;

(23) Whereas the adoption of this Directive constitutes the most appropriate way of realizing the abovementioned objectives and does not go beyond what is necessary to achieve them,

HAVE ADOPTED THIS DIRECTIVE:

SECTION I

SCOPE AND DEFINITIONS

Article 1

The provisions of this Directive shall apply to:

(a) any system as defined in Article 2(a),governed by the law of a Member State and operating in any currency, the ecu or in various currencies which the system converts one against another;

(b) any participant in such a system;

(c) collateral security provided in connection with:

—oparticipation in a system, or

—operations of the central banks of the Member States in their functions as central banks.

Article 2

For the purpose of this Directive:

(a) 'system' shall mean a formal arrangement:

—between three or more participants, without counting a possible settlement agent, a possible central counterparty, a possible clearing house or a possible indirect participant, with common rules and standardised arrangements for the execution of transfer orders between the participants,

—governed by the law of a Member State chosen by the participants; the participants may, however, only choose the law of a Member State in which at least one of them has its head office, and

—designated, without prejudice to other more stringent conditions of general application laid down by national law, as a system and notified to the Commission by the Member State whose law is applicable, after that Member State is satisfied as to the adequacy of the rules of the system.

—Subject to the conditions in the first subparagraph, a Member State may designate as a system such a formal arrangement whose business consists of the execution of transfer orders as defined in the second indent of (i) and which to a limited extent executes orders relating to other financial instruments, when that Member State considers that such a designation is warranted on grounds of systemic risk.

—A Member State may also on a case-by-case basis designate as a system such a formal arrangement between two participants, without counting a possible settlement agent, a possible central counterparty, a possible clearing house or a possible indirect participant, when that Member State considers that such a designation is warranted on grounds of systemic risk;

(b) 'institution' shall mean:

—a credit institution as defined in the first indent of Article 1 of Directive 77/780/EEC[5] including the institutions set out in the list in Article 2(2) thereof, or

---

[5] First Council Directive 77/780/EEC of 12 December 1977 on the coordination of the laws, regulations and administrative provisions relating to the taking up and pursuit of the business of credit

—an investment firm as defined in point 2 of Article 1 of Directive 93/22/EEC[6] excluding the institutions set out in the list in Article 2(2)(a) to (k) thereof, or
—public authorities and publicly guaranteed undertakings, or
—any undertaking whose head office is outside the Community and whose functions correspond to those of the Community credit institutions or investment firms as defined in the first and second indent,
which participates in a system and which is responsible for discharging the financial obligations arising from transfer orders within that system.

If a system is supervised in accordance with national legislation and only executes transfer orders as defined in the second indent of (i), as well as payments resulting from such orders, a Member State may decide that undertakings which participate in such a system and which have responsibility for discharging the financial obligations arising from transfer orders within this system, can be considered institutions, provided that at least three participants of this system are covered by the categories referred to in the first subparagraph and that such a decision is warranted on grounds of systemic risk;

(c) 'central counterparty' shall mean an entity which is interposed between the institutions in a system and which acts as the exclusive counterparty of these institutions with regard to their transfer orders;

(d) 'settlement agent' shall mean an entity providing to institutions and/or a central counterparty participating in systems, settlement accounts through which transfer orders within such systems are settled and, as the case may be, extending credit to those institutions and/or central counterparties for settlement purposes;

(e) 'clearing house' shall mean an entity responsible for the calculation of the net positions of institutions, a possible central counterparty and/or a possible settlement agent;

(f) 'participant' shall mean an institution, a central counterparty, a settlement agent or a clearing house.
According to the rules of the system, the same participant may act as a central counterparty, a settlement agent or a clearing house or carry out part or all of these tasks.

(g) A Member State may decide that for the purposes of this Directive an indirect participant may be considered a participant if it is warranted on the grounds of systemic risk and on condition that the indirect participant is known to the system;

(h) 'indirect participant' shall mean a credit institution as defined in the first indent of (b) with a contractual relationship with an institution participating in a system executing transfer orders as defined in the first indent of (i) which enables the abovementioned credit institution to pass transfer orders through the system;

(i) 'securities' shall mean all instruments referred to in section B of the Annex to Directive 93/22/EEC;

---

institutions (OJ L 322, 17. 12. 1977, p. 30). Directive as last amended by Directive 96/13/EC (OJ L 66, 16. 3. 1996, p. 15).

[6] Council Directive 93/22/EEC of 10 May 1993 on investment services in the securities field (OJ L 141, 11. 6. 1993, p. 27). Directive as last amended by Directive 97/9/EC (OJ L 84, 26. 3. 1997, p. 22).

(j) 'transfer order' shall mean:
  —any instruction by a participant to place at the disposal of a recipient an amount of money by means of a book entry on the accounts of a credit institution, a central bank or a settlement agent, or any instruction which results in the assumption or discharge of a payment obligation as defined by the rules of the system, or
  —an instruction by a participant to transfer the title to, or interest in, a security or securities by means of a book entry on a register, or otherwise;

(j) 'insolvency proceedings' shall mean any collective measure provided for in the law of a Member State, or a third country, either to wind up the participant or to reorganise it, where such measure involves the suspending of, or imposing limitations on, transfers or payments;

(k) 'netting' shall mean the conversion into one net claim or one net obligation of claims and obligations resulting from transfer orders which a participant or participants either issue to, or receive from, one or more other participants with the result that only a net claim can be demanded or a net obligation be owed;

(l) 'settlement account' shall mean an account at a central bank, a settlement agent or a central counterparty used to hold funds and securities and to settle transactions between participants in a system;

(m) 'collateral security' shall mean all realizable assets provided under a pledge (including money provided under a pledge), a repurchase or similar agreement, or otherwise, for the purpose of securing rights and obligations potentially arising in connection with a system, or provided to central banks of the Member States or to the future European central bank.

SECTION II

NETTING AND TRANSFER ORDERS

Article 3

1. Transfer orders and netting shall be legally enforceable and, even in the event of insolvency proceedings against a participant, shall be binding on third parties, provided that transfer orders were entered into a system before the moment of opening of such insolvency proceedings as defined in Article 6(1).
   Where, exceptionally, transfer orders are entered into a system after the moment of opening of insolvency proceedings and are carried out on the day of opening of such proceedings, they shall be legally enforceable and binding on third parties only if, after the time of settlement, the settlement agent, the central counterparty or the clearing house can prove that they were not aware, nor should have been aware, of the opening of such proceedings.

2. No law, regulation, rule or practice on the setting aside of contracts and transactions concluded before the moment of opening of insolvency proceedings, as defined in Article 6(1) shall lead to the unwinding of a netting.

3. The moment of entry of a transfer order into a system shall be defined by the rules of that system. If there are conditions laid down in the national law governing the system as to the moment of entry, the rules of that system must be in accordance with such conditions.

Article 4

Member States may provide that the opening of insolvency proceedings against a participant shall not prevent funds or securities available on the settlement account of that participant from being used to fulfil that participant's obligations in the system on the day of the opening of the insolvency proceedings. Furthermore, Member States may also provide that such a participant's credit facility connected to the system be used against available, existing collateral security to fulfil that participant's obligations in the system.

Article 5

A transfer order may not be revoked by a participant in a system, nor by a third party, from the moment defined by the rules of that system.

SECTION III
PROVISIONS CONCERNING INSOLVENCY PROCEEDINGS

Article 6

1. For the purpose of this Directive, the moment of opening of insolvency proceedings shall be the moment when the relevant judicial or administrative authority handed down its decision.
2. When a decision has been taken in accordance with paragraph 1, the relevant judicial or administrative authority shall immediately notify that decision to the appropriate authority chosen by its Member State.
3. The Member State referred to in paragraph 2 shall immediately notify other Member States.

Article 7

nsolvency proceedings shall not have retroactive effects on the rights and obligations of a participant arising from, or in connection with, its participation in a system earlier than the moment of opening of such proceedings as defined in Article 6(1).

Article 8

In the event of insolvency proceedings being opened against a participant in a system, the rights and obligations arising from, or in connection with, the participation of that participant shall be determined by the law governing that system.

SECTION IV
INSULATION OF THE RIGHTS OF HOLDERS OF COLLATERAL SECURITY
FROM THE EFFECTS OF THE INSOLVENCY OF THE PROVIDER

Article 9

1. The rights of:
   — a participant to collateral security provided to it in connection with a system, and
   — central banks of the Member States or the future European central bank to collateral security provided to them,

shall not be affected by insolvency proceedings against the participant or counterparty to central banks of the Member States or the future European central bank which provided the collateral security. Such collateral security may be realised for the satisfaction of these rights.

2. Where securities (including rights in securities) are provided as collateral security to participants and/or central banks of the Member States or the future European central bank as described in paragraph 1, and their right (or that of any nominee, agent or third party acting on their behalf) with respect to the securities is legally recorded on a register, account or centralised deposit system located in a Member State, the determination of the rights of such entities as holders of collateral security in relation to those securities shall be governed by the law of that Member State.

SECTION V

FINAL PROVISIONS

Article 10

Member States shall specify the systems which are to be included in the scope of this Directive and shall notify them to the Commission and inform the Commission of the authorities they have chosen in accordance with Article 6(2).

The system shall indicate to the Member State whose law is applicable the participants in the system, including any possible indirect participants, as well as any change in them. In addition to the indication provided for in the second subparagraph, Member States may impose supervision or authorization requirements on systems which fall under their jurisdiction.

Anyone with a legitimate interest may require an institution to inform him of the systems in which it participates and to provide information about the main rules governing the functioning of those systems.

Article 11

1. Member States shall bring into force the laws, regulations and administrative provisions necessary to comply with this Directive before 11 December 1999. They shall forthwith inform the Commission thereof
   When Member States adopt these measures, they shall contain a reference to this Directive or shall be accompanied by such reference on the occasion of their official publication. The methods of making such a reference shall be laid down by the Member States.
2. Member States shall communicate to the Commission the text of the provisions of domestic law which they adopt in the field governed by this Directive. In this Communication, Member States shall provide a table of correspondence showing the national provisions which exist or are introduced in respect of each Article of this Directive.

Article 12

No later than three years after the date mentioned in Article 11(1), the Commission shall present a report to the European Parliament and the Council on the application of this Directive, accompanied where appropriate by proposals for its revision.

Article 13

This Directive shall enter into force on the day of its publication in the Official Journal of the European Communities.

Article 14

This Directive is addressed to the Member States.

Done at Brussels, 19 May 1998.

For the European Parliament
The President
J.M. Gil-Robles

For the Council
The President
G. Brown

(ii) DIRECTIVE 2002/47/EC OF THE EUROPEAN PARLIAMENT AND OF THE COUNCIL OF 6 JUNE 2002 ON FINANCIAL COLLATERAL ARRANGEMENTS

PREAMBLE

THE EUROPEAN PARLIAMENT AND THE COUNCIL OF THE EUROPEAN UNION,

Having regard to the Treaty establishing the European Community, and in particular Article 95 thereof,

Having regard to the proposal from the Commission,[1]

Having regard to the opinion of the European Central Bank,[2]

Having regard to the opinion of the Economic and Social Committee,[3]

Acting in accordance with the procedure laid down in Article 251 of the Treaty,[4]

Whereas:

(1) Directive 98/26/EC of the European Parliament and of the Council of 19 May 1998 on settlement finality in payment and securities settlement systems[5] constituted a milestone in establishing a sound legal framework for payment and securities settlement systems. Implementation of that Directive has demonstrated the importance of limiting systemic risk inherent in such systems stemming from the different influence of several jurisdictions, and the benefits of common rules in relation to collateral constituted to such systems.

(2) In its communication of 11 May 1999 to the European Parliament and to the Council on financial services: implementing the framework for financial markets: action plan, the Commission undertook, after consultation with

---

[1] OJ C 180 E, 26.6.2001, p. 312.   [2] OJ C 196, 12.7.2001, p. 10.
[3] OJ C 48, 21.2.2002, p. 1.
[4] Opinion of the European Parliament of 13 December 2001 (not yet published in the Official Journal), Council Common Position of 5 March 2002 (not yet published in the Official Journal) and Decision of the European Parliament of 15 May 2002.   [5] OJ L 166, 11.6.1998, p. 45.

market experts and national authorities, to work on further proposals for legislative action on collateral urging further progress in the field of collateral, beyond Directive 98/26/EC.

(3)   A Community regime should be created for the provision of securities and cash as collateral under both security interest and title transfer structures including repurchase agreements (repos). This will contribute to the integration and cost-efficiency of the financial market as well as to the stability of the financial system in the Community, thereby supporting the freedom to provide services and the free movement of capital in the single market in financial services. This Directive focuses on bilateral financial collateral arrangements.

(4)   This Directive is adopted in a European legal context which consists in particular of the said Directive 98/26/EC as well as Directive 2001/24/EC of the European Parliament and of the Council of 4 April 2001 on the reorganisation and winding up of credit institutions,[6] Directive 2001/17/EC of the European Parliament and of the Council of 19 March 2001 on the reorganisation and winding-up of insurance undertakings[7] and Council Regulation (EC) No 1346/2000 of 29 May 2000 on insolvency proceedings.[8] This Directive is in line with the general pattern of these previous legal acts and is not opposed to it. Indeed, this Directive complements these existing legal acts by dealing with further issues and going beyond them in connection with particular matters already dealt with by these legal acts.

(5)   In order to improve the legal certainty of financial collateral arrangements, Member States should ensure that certain provisions of insolvency law do not apply to such arrangements, in particular, those that would inhibit the effective realisation of financial collateral or cast doubt on the validity of current techniques such as bilateral close-out netting, the provision of additional collateral in the form of top-up collateral and substitution of collateral.

(6)   This Directive does not address rights which any person may have in respect of assets provided as financial collateral, and which arise otherwise than under the terms of the financial collateral arrangement and otherwise than on the basis of any legal provision or rule of law arising by reason of the commencement or continuation of winding-up proceedings or reorganization measures, such as restitution arising from mistake, error or lack of capacity.

(7)   The principle in Directive 98/26/EC, whereby the law applicable to book entry securities provided as collateral is the law of the jurisdiction where the relevant register, account or centralised deposit system is located, should be extended in order to create legal certainty regarding the use of such securities held in a cross-border context and used as financial collateral under the scope of this Directive.

(8)   The *lex rei sitae* rule, according to which the applicable law for determining whether a financial collateral arrangement is properly perfected and therefore good against third parties is the law of the country where the financial collateral is located, is currently recognized by all Member States. Without affecting the application of this Directive to directly-held securities, the location of book entry securities provided as financial collateral and held through one or more

---

[6] OJ L 125, 5.5.2001, p. 15.   [7] OJ L 110, 20.4.2001, p. 28.
[8] OJ L 160, 30.6.2000, p. 1.

intermediaries should be determined. If the collateral taker has a valid and effective collateral arrangement according to the governing law of the country in which the relevant account is maintained, then the validity against any competing title or interest and the enforceability of the collateral should be governed solely by the law of that country, thus preventing legal uncertainty as a result of other unforeseen legislation.

(9) In order to limit the administrative burdens for parties using financial collateral under the scope of this Directive, the only perfection requirement which national law may impose in respect of financial collateral should be that the financial collateral is delivered, transferred, held, registered or otherwise designated so as to be in the possession or under the control of the collateral taker or of a person acting on the collateral taker's behalf while not excluding collateral techniques where the collateral provider is allowed to substitute collateral or to withdraw excess collateral.

(10) For the same reasons, the creation, validity, perfection, enforceability or admissibility in evidence of a financial collateral arrangement, or the provision of financial collateral under a financial collateral arrangement, should not be made dependent on the performance of any formal act such as the execution of any document in a specific form or in a particular manner, the making of any filing with an official or public body or registration in a public register, advertisement in a newspaper or journal, in an official register or publication or in any other matter, notification to a public officer or the provision of evidence in a particular form as to the date of execution of a document or instrument, the amount of the relevant financial obligations or any other matter. This Directive must however provide a balance between market efficiency and the safety of the parties to the arrangement and third parties, thereby avoiding inter alia the risk of fraud. This balance should be achieved through the scope of this Directive covering only those financial collateral arrangements which provide for some form of dispossession, i.e. the provision of the financial collateral, and where the provision of the financial collateral can be evidenced in writing or in a durable medium, ensuring thereby the traceability of that collateral. For the purpose of this Directive, acts required under the law of a Member State as conditions for transferring or creating a security interest on financial instruments, other than book entry securities, such as endorsement in the case of instruments to order, or recording on the issuer's register in the case of registered instruments, should not be considered as formal acts.

(11) Moreover, this Directive should protect only financial collateral arrangements which can be evidenced. Such evidence can be given in writing or in any other legally enforceable manner provided by the law which is applicable to the financial collateral arrangement.

(12) The simplification of the use of financial collateral through the limitation of administrative burdens promotes the efficiency of the cross-border operations of the European Central Bank and the national central banks of Member States participating in the economic and monetary union, necessary for the implementation of the common monetary policy. Furthermore, the provision of limited protection of financial collateral arrangements from some rules of insolvency law in addition supports the wider aspect of the common monetary

policy, where the participants in the money market balance the overall amount of liquidity in the market among themselves, by cross-border transactions backed by collateral.

(13) This Directive seeks to protect the validity of financial collateral arrangements which are based upon the transfer of the full ownership of the financial collateral, such as by eliminating the so-called re-characterisation of such financial collateral arrangements (including repurchase agreements) as security interests.

(14) The enforceability of bilateral close-out netting should be protected, not only as an enforcement mechanism for title transfer financial collateral arrangements including repurchase agreements but more widely, where close-out netting forms part of a financial collateral arrangement. Sound risk management practices commonly used in the financial market should be protected by enabling participants to manage and reduce their credit exposures arising from all kinds of financial transactions on a net basis, where the credit exposure is calculated by combining the estimated current exposures under all outstanding transactions with a counterparty, setting off reciprocal items to produce a single aggregated amount that is compared with the current value of the collateral.

(15) This Directive should be without prejudice to any restrictions or requirements under national law on bringing into account claims, on obligations to set-off, or on netting, for example relating to their reciprocity or the fact that they have been concluded prior to when the collateral taker knew or ought to have known of the commencement (or of any mandatory legal act leading to the commencement) of winding-up proceedings or reorganisation measures in respect of the collateral provider.

(16) The sound market practice favoured by regulators whereby participants in the financial market use top-up financial collateral arrangements to manage and limit their credit risk to each other by mark-to-market calculations of the current market value of the credit exposure and the value of the financial collateral and accordingly ask for top-up financial collateral or return the surplus of financial collateral should be protected against certain automatic avoidance rules. The same applies to the possibility of substituting for assets provided as financial collateral other assets of the same value. The intention is merely that the provision of top-up or substitution financial collateral cannot be questioned on the sole basis that the relevant financial obligations existed before that financial collateral was provided, or that the financial collateral was provided during a prescribed period. However, this does not prejudice the possibility of questioning under national law the financial collateral arrangement and the provision of financial collateral as part of the initial provision, top-up or substitution of financial collateral, for example where this has been intentionally done to the detriment of the other creditors (this covers inter alia actions based on fraud or similar avoidance rules which may apply in a prescribed period).

(17) This Directive provides for rapid and non-formalistic enforcement procedures in order to safeguard financial stability and limit contagion effects in case of a default of a party to a financial collateral arrangement. However, this Directive balances the latter objectives with the protection of the collateral provider and third parties by explicitly confirming the possibility for Member States to keep or introduce in their national legislation an a posteriori control which the Courts

can exercise in relation to the realization or valuation of financial collateral and the calculation of the relevant financial obligations. Such control should allow for the judicial authorities to verify that the realisation or valuation has been conducted in a commercially reasonable manner.

(18) It should be possible to provide cash as collateral under both title transfer and secured structures respectively protected by the recognition of netting or by the pledge of cash collateral. Cash refers only to money which is represented by a credit to an account, or similar claims on repayment of money (such as money market deposits), thus explicitly excluding banknotes.

(19) This Directive provides for a right of use in case of security financial collateral arrangements, which increases liquidity in the financial market stemming from such reuse of 'pledged' securities. This reuse however should be without prejudice to national legislation about separation of assets and unfair treatment of creditors.

(20) This Directive does not prejudice the operation and effect of the contractual terms of financial instruments provided as financial collateral, such as rights and obligations and other conditions contained in the terms of issue and any other rights and obligations and other conditions which apply between the issuers and holders of such instruments.

(21) This Act complies with the fundamental rights and follows the principles laid down in particular in the Charter of Fundamental Rights of the European Union.

(22) Since the objective of the proposed action, namely to create a minimum regime relating to the use of financial collateral, cannot be sufficiently achieved by the Member States and can therefore, by reason of the scale and effects of the action, be better achieved at Community level, the Community may adopt measures, in accordance with the principle of subsidiarity as set out in Article 5 of the Treaty. In accordance with the principle of proportionality, as set out in that Article, this Directive does not go beyond what is necessary in order to achieve that objective,

HAVE ADOPTED THIS DIRECTIVE:

Article 1
Subject matter and scope

1. This Directive lays down a Community regime applicable to financial collateral arrangements which satisfy the requirements set out in paragraphs 2 and 5 and to financial collateral in accordance with the conditions set out in paragraphs 4 and 5.

2. The collateral taker and the collateral provider must each belong to one of the following categories:

   (a) a public authority (excluding publicly guaranteed undertakings unless they fall under points (b) to (e)) including:

      (i) public sector bodies of Member States charged with or intervening in the management of public debt, and

      (ii) public sector bodies of Member States authorised to hold accounts for customers;

   (b) a central bank, the European Central Bank, the Bank for International Settlements, a multilateral development bank as defined in Article 1(19) of Directive 2000/12/EC of the European Parliament and of the Council of 20 March 2000 relating to the taking up and pursuit of the business of credit institutions,[9] the International Monetary Fund and the European Investment Bank;

(c) a financial institution subject to prudential supervision including:

  (i) a credit institution as defined in Article 1(1) of Directive 2000/12/EC, including the institutions listed in Article 2(3) of that Directive;

  (ii) an investment firm as defined in Article 1(2) of Council Directive 93/22/EEC of 10 May 1993 on investment services in the securities field;[10]

  (iii) a financial institution as defined in Article 1(5) of Directive 2000/12/EC;

  (iv) an insurance undertaking as defined in Article 1(a) of Council Directive 92/49/EEC of 18 June 1992 on the coordination of laws, regulations and administrative provisions relating to direct insurance other than life assurance[11] and a life assurance undertaking as defined in Article 1(a) of Council Directive 92/96/EEC of 10 November 1992 on the coordination of laws, regulations and administrative provisions relating to direct life assurance[12];

  (v) an undertaking for collective investment in transferable securities (UCITS) as defined in Article 1(2) of Council Directive 85/611/EEC of 20 December 1985 on the coordination of laws, regulations and administrative provisions relating to undertakings for collective investment in transferable securities (UCITS)[13];

  (vi) a management company as defined in Article 1a(2) of Directive 85/611/EEC;

(d) a central counterparty, settlement agent or clearing house, as defined respectively in Article 2(c), (d) and (e) of Directive 98/26/EC, including similar institutions regulated under national law acting in the futures, options and derivatives markets to the extent not covered by that Directive, and a person, other than a natural person, who acts in a trust or representative capacity on behalf of any one or more persons that includes any bondholders or holders of other forms of securitised debt or any institution as defined in points (a) to (d);

(e) a person other than a natural person, includingunincorporated firms and partnerships, provided that the other party is an institution as defined in points (a) to (d).

3. Member States may exclude from the scope of this Directive financial collateral arrangements where one of the parties is a person mentioned in paragraph 2(e).

If they make use of this option Member States shall inform the Commission which shall inform the other Member States thereof.

4. (a) The financial collateral to be provided must consist of cash or financial instruments.

---

[9] OJ L 126, 26.5.2000, p. 1. Directive as amended by Directive 2000/28/EC (OJ L 275, 27.10.2000, p. 37).

[10] OJ L 141, 11.6.1993, p. 27. Directive as last amended by Directive 2000/64/EC of the European Parliament and of the Council (OJ L 290, 17.11.2000, p. 27).

[11] OJ L 228, 11.8.1992, p. 1. Directive as last amended by Directive 2000/64/EC of the European Parliament and of the Council.

[12] OJ L 360, 9.12.1992, p. 1. Directive as last amended by Directive 2000/64/EC of the European Parliament and of the Council.

[13] OJ L 375, 31.12.1985, p. 3. Directive as last amended by Directive 2001/108/EC of the European Parliament and of the Council. (OJ L 41, 13.2.2002, p. 35).

(b) Member States may exclude from the scope of this Directive financial collateral consisting of the collateral provider's own shares, shares in affiliated undertakings within the meaning of seventh Council Directive 83/349/EEC of 13 June 1983 on consolidated accounts[14], and shares in undertakings whose exclusive purpose is to own means of production that are essential for the collateral provider's business or to own real property.

5. This Directive applies to financial collateral once it has been provided and if that provision can be evidenced in writing.

The evidencing of the provision of financial collateral must allow for the identification of the financial collateral to which it applies. For this purpose, it is sufficient to prove that the book entry securities collateral has been credited to, or forms a credit in, the relevant account and that the cash collateral has been credited to, or forms a credit in, a designated account.

This Directive applies to financial collateral arrangements if that arrangement can be evidenced in writing or in a legally equivalent manner.

Article 2
Definitions

1. For the purpose of this Directive:
    (a) 'financial collateral arrangement' means a title transfer financial collateral arrangement or a security financial collateral arrangement whether or not these are covered by a master agreement or general terms and conditions;
    (b) 'title transfer financial collateral arrangement' means an arrangement, including repurchase agreements, under which a collateral provider transfers full ownership of financial collateral to a collateral taker for the purpose of securing or otherwise covering the performance of relevant financial obligations;
    (c) 'security financial collateral arrangement' means an arrangement under which a collateral provider provides financial collateral by way of security in favour of, or to, a collateral taker, and where the full ownership of the financial collateral remains with the collateral provider when the security right is established;
    (d) 'cash' means money credited to an account in any currency, or similar claims for the repayment of money, such as money market deposits;
    (e) 'financial instruments' means shares in companies and other securities equivalent to shares in companies and bonds and other forms of debt instruments if these are negotiable on the capital market, and any other securities which are normally dealt in and which give the right to acquire any such shares, bonds or other securities by subscription, purchase or exchange or which give rise to a cash settlement (excluding instruments of payment), including units in collective investment undertakings, money market instruments and claims relating to or rights in or in respect of any of the foregoing;
    (f) 'relevant financial obligations' means the obligations which are secured by a financial collateral arrangement and which give a right to cash settlement and/or delivery of financial instruments.

---

[14] OJ L 193, 18.7.1983, p. 1. Directive as last amended by Directive 2001/65/EC of the European Parliament and of the Council (OJ L 283, 27.10.2001, p. 28).

Relevant financial obligations may consist of or include:

(i) present or future, actual or contingent or prospective obligations (including such obligations arising under a master agreement or similar arrangement);

(ii) obligations owed to the collateral taker by a person other than the collateral provider; or

(iii) obligations of a specified class or kind arising from time to time;

(g) 'book entry securities collateral' means financial collateral provided under a financial collateral arrangement which consists of financial instruments, title to which is evidenced by entries in a register or account maintained by or on behalf of an intermediary;

(h) 'relevant account' means in relation to book entry securities collateral which is subject to a financial collateral arrangement, the register or account—which may be maintained by the collateral taker—in which the entries are made by which that book entry securities collateral is provided to the collateral taker;

(i) 'equivalent collateral':

(i) in relation to cash, means a payment of the same amount and in the same currency;

(ii) in relation to financial instruments, means financial instruments of the same issuer or debtor, forming part of the same issue or class and of the same nominal amount, currency and description or, where a financial collateral arrangement provides for the transfer of other assets following the occurrence of any event relating to or affecting any financial instruments provided as financial collateral, those other assets;

(j) 'winding-up proceedings' means collective proceedings involving realisation of the assets and distribution of the proceeds among the creditors, shareholders or members as appropriate, which involve any intervention by administrative or judicial authorities, including where the collective proceedings are terminated by a composition or other analogous measure, whether or not they are founded on insolvency or are voluntary or compulsory;

(k) 'reorganisation measures' means measures which involve any intervention by administrative or judicial authorities which are intended to preserve or restore the financial situation and which affect pre-existing rights of third parties, including but not limited to measures involving a suspension of payments, suspension of enforcement measures or reduction of claims;

(l) 'enforcement event' means an event of default or any similar event as agreed between the parties on the occurrence of which, under the terms of a financial collateral arrangement or by operation of law, the collateral taker is entitled to realisz or appropriate financial collateral or a close-out netting provision comes into effect;

(m) 'right of use' means the right of the collateral taker to use and dispose of financial collateral provided under a security financial collateral arrangement as the owner of it in accordance with the terms of the security financial collateral arrangement;

(n) 'close-out netting provision' means a provision of a financial collateral arrangement, or of an arrangement of which a financial collateral arrangement forms part, or, in the absence of any such provision, any statutory rule by which, on the occurrence of an enforcement event, whether through the operation of netting or set-off or otherwise:

(i) the obligations of the parties are accelerated so as to be immediately due and expressed as an obligation to pay an amount representing their estimated current value, or are terminated and replaced by an obligation to pay such an amount; and/or

(ii) an account is taken of what is due from each party to the other in respect of such obligations, and a net sum equal to the balance of the account is payable by the party from whom the larger amount is due to the other party.

2. References in this Directive to financial collateral being 'provided', or to the 'provision' of financial collateral, are to the financial collateral being delivered, transferred, held, registered or otherwise designated so as to be in the possession or under the control of the collateral taker or of a person acting on the collateral taker's behalf. Any right of substitution or to withdraw excess financial collateral in favour of the collateral provider shall not prejudice the financial collateral having been provided to the collateral taker as mentioned in this Directive.

3. References in this Directive to 'writing' include recording by electronic means and any other durable medium.

Article 3
Formal requirements

1. Member States shall not require that the creation, validity, perfection, enforceability or admissibility in evidence of a financial collateral arrangement or the provision of financial collateral under a financial collateral arrangement be dependent on the performance of any formal act.

2. Paragraph 1 is without prejudice to the application of this Directive to financial collateral only once it has been provided and if that provision can be evidenced in writing and where the financial collateral arrangement can be evidenced in writing or in a legally equivalent manner.

Article 4
Enforcement of financial collateral arrangements

1. Member States shall ensure that on the occurrence of an enforcement event, the collateral taker shall be able to realize in the following manners, any financial collateral provided under, and subject to the terms agreed in, a security financial collateral arrangement:

(a) financial instruments by sale or appropriation and by setting off their value against, or applying their value in discharge of, the relevant financial obligations;

(b) cash by setting off the amount against or applying it in discharge of the relevant financial obligations.

2. Appropriation is possible only

(a) this has been agreed by the parties in the security financial collateral arrangement; and

(b) the parties have agreed in the security financial collateral arrangement on the valuation of the financial instruments.

3. Member States which do not allow appropriation on 27 June 2002 are not obliged to recognize it.

If they make use of this option, Member States shall inform the Commission which in turn shall inform the other Member States thereof.

4. The manners of realizing the financial collateral referred to in paragraph 1 shall, subject to the terms agreed in the security financial collateral arrangement, be without any requirement to the effect that:

   (a) prior notice of the intention to realize must havebeen given;

   (b) the terms of the realization be approved by any court, public officer or other person;

   (c) the realization be conducted by public auction or in any other prescribed manner; or

   (d) any additional time period must have elapsed.

5. Member States shall ensure that a financial collateral arrangement can take effect in accordance with its terms notwithstanding the commencement or continuation of winding-up proceedings or reorganization measures in respect of the collateral provider or collateral taker.

6. This Article and Articles 5, 6 and 7 shall bewithout prejudice to any requirements under national law to the effect that the realization or valuation of financial collateral and the calculation of the relevant financial obligations must be conducted in a commercially reasonable manner.

Article 5
Right of use of financial collateral under security financial collateral arrangements

1. If and to the extent that the terms of a security financial collateral arrangement so provide, Member States shall ensure that the collateral taker is entitled to exercise a right of use in relation to financial collateral provided under the security financial collateral arrangement.

2. Where a collateral taker exercises a right of use, he thereby incurs an obligation to transfer equivalent collateral to replace the original financial collateral at the latest on the due date for the performance of the relevant financial obligations covered by the security financial collateral arrangement.

   Alternatively, the collateral taker shall, on the due date for the performance of the relevant financial obligations, either transfer equivalent collateral, or, if and to the extent that the terms of a security financial collateral arrangement so provide, set off the value of the equivalent collateral against or apply it in discharge of the relevant financial obligations.

3. The equivalent collateral transferred in discharge of an obligation as described in paragraph 2, first subparagraph, shall be subject to the same security financial collateral agreement to which the original financial collateral was subject and shall be treated as having been provided under the security financial collateral arrangement at the same time as the original financial collateral was first provided.

4. Member States shall ensure that the use of financial collateral by the collateral taker according to this Article does not render invalid or unenforceable the rights of the collateral taker under the security financial collateral arrangement in relation to the financial collateral transferred by the collateral taker in discharge of an obligation as described in paragraph 2, first subparagraph.

5. If an enforcement event occurs while an obligation as described in paragraph 2 first subparagraph remains outstanding, the obligation may be the subject of a close-out netting provision.

Article 6
Recognition of title transfer financial collateral arrangements

1. Member States shall ensure that a title transfer financial collateral arrangement can take effect in accordance with its terms.
2. If an enforcement event occurs while any obligation of the collateral taker to transfer equivalent collateral under a title transfer financial collateral arrangement remains outstanding, the obligation may be the subject of a close-out netting provision.

Article 7
Recognition of close-out netting provisions

1. Member States shall ensure that a close-out netting provision can take effect in accordance with its terms:
   (a) notwithstanding the commencement or continuation of winding-up proceedings or reorganisation measures in respect of the collateral provider and/or the collateral taker; and/or
   (b) notwithstanding any purported assignment, judicial or other attachment or other disposition of or in respect of such rights.
2. Member States shall ensure that the operation of a close-out netting provision may not be subject to any of the requirements that are mentioned in Article 4(4), unless otherwise agreed by the parties.

Article 8
Certain insolvency provisions disapplied

1. Memberr States shall ensure that a financial collateral arrangement, as well as the provision of financial collateral under such arrangement, may not be declared invalid or void or be reversed on the sole basis that the financial collateral arrangement has come into existence, or the financial collateral has been provided:
   (a) on the day of the commencement of winding-up proceedings or reorganization measures, but prior to the order or decree making that commencement; or
   (b) in a prescribed period prior to, and defined by reference to, the commencement of such proceedings or measures or by reference to the making of any order or decree or the taking of any other action or occurrence of any other event in the course of such proceedings or measures.
2. Member States shall ensure that where a financial collateral arrangement or a relevant financial obligation has come into existence, or financial collateral has been provided on the day of, but after the moment of the commencement of, winding-up proceedings or reorganization measures, it shall be legally enforceable and binding on third parties if the collateral taker can prove that he was not aware, nor should have been aware, of the commencement of such proceedings or measures.
3. Where a financial collateral arrangement contains:
   (a) an obligation to provide financial collateral or additional financial collateral in order to take account of changes in the value of the financial collateral or in the amount of the relevant financial obligations, or

715

(b) a right to withdraw financial collateral on providing, by way of substitution or exchange, financial collateral of substantially the same value,

Member States shall ensure that the provision of financial collateral, additional financial collateral or substitute or replacement financial collateral under such an obligation or right shall not be treated as invalid or reversed or declared void on the sole basis that:

 (i) such provision was made on the day of the commencement of winding-up proceedings or reorganization measures, but prior to the order or decree making that commencement or in a prescribed period prior to, and defined by reference to, the commencement of winding-up proceedings or reorganisation measures or by reference to the making of any order or decree or the taking of any other action or occurrence of any other event in the course of such proceedings or measures; and/or

 (ii) the relevant financial obligations were incurred prior to the date of the provision of the financial collateral, additional financial collateral or substitute or replacement financial collateral.

4. Without prejudice to paragraphs 1, 2 and 3, this Directive leaves unaffected the general rules of national insolvency law in relation to the voidance of transactions entered into during the prescribed period referred to in paragraph 1(b) and in paragraph 3(i).

Article 9
Conflict of laws

1. Any question with respect to any of the matters specified in paragraph 2 arising in relation to book entry securities collateral shall be governed by the law of the country in which the relevant account is maintained. The reference to the law of a country is a reference to its domestic law, disregarding any rule under which, in deciding the relevant question, reference should be made to the law of another country.

2. The matters referred to in paragraph 1 are:

 (a) the legal nature and proprietary effects of book entry securities collateral;

 (b) the requirements for perfecting a financial collateral arrangement relating to book entry securities collateral and the provision of book entry securities collateral under such an arrangement, and more generally the completion of the steps necessary to render such an arrangement and provision effective against third parties;

 (c) whether a person's title to or interest in such book entry securities collateral is overridden by or subordinated to a competing title or interest, or a good faith acquisition has occurred;

 (d) the steps required for the realization of book entry securities collateral following the occurrence of an enforcement event.

Article 10
Report by the commission

Not later than 27 December 2006, the Commission shall present a report to the European Parliament and the Council on the application of this Directive, in particular on the application of Article 1(3), Article 4(3) and Article 5, accompanied where appropriate by proposals for its revision.

Article 11
Implementation

Member States shall bring into force the laws, regulations and administrative provisions necessary to comply with this Directive by 27 December 2003 at the latest. They shall forthwith inform the Commission thereof.

When Member States adopt those provisions, they shall contain a reference to this Directive or be accompanied by such reference on the occasion of their official publication. Member States shall determine how such reference is to be made.

Article 12
Entry into force

This Directive shall enter into force on the day of its publication in the Official Journal of the European Communities.

Article 13
Addressees

This Directive is addressed to the Member States.

Done at Brussels, 6 June 2002

For the European Parliament
The President
P. Cox

For the Council
The President
A. M. Birulés Y Bertrán

10

CONFLICT OF LAWS

A. Introductory Text

1. Hague Convention on the Law Applicable to Agency 1978

Introduction

As is the case with the majority of instruments negotiated at the worldwide level, this Convention is very specific and limited in its scope. Moreover, an agency relationship is a means—or a vehicle—to the end of entering into other commercial transactions. This is why, in the analysis of this document, it is imperative not to lose sight of the many interfaces with, firstly, other regional and universal instruments on agency,[1] secondly, regional and universal instruments devoted to the conflict of laws in contracts[2] and to general substantive contracts law[3] and, thirdly, the many transnational instruments on specific types of contract. The Convention itself indicates[4] that it shall not affect 'any other international instrument containing provisions on matters governed by this Convention to which a Contracting State is, or becomes, a Party'. An important and as yet undecided issue is, whether EC Directives and Regulations are 'international instruments' in the sense of this provision.

The topic of agency in the conflict of laws requires making an important distinction between two separate relationships, namely that between principal and agent, and that between principal and any third party which may or may not come about as the result of the agent's activities. Finally, there may or may not come about a contractual relationship between the agent and the third party. The Convention is devoted to the first two legal relationships only.

Scope of application

The Convention determines the law applicable to relationships of an international character arising where a person, the agent, has the authority to act, acts, or purports to act on behalf of another person, the principal, in dealing with a third party.[5] It applies irrespective of whether the agent acts in his own name or in that of the principal[6] and whether he acts regularly or occasionally.[7]

The Convention itself excludes from its scope the capacity of the parties,[8] requirements as to form,[9] agency by operation of law in family law and the law of succession,[10] agency by virtue of a decision or subject to the control of a judicial authority,[11] representation in connection with judicial proceedings,[12] and the agency of a shipmaster acting in the exercise of his functions.[13] Since the Convention does not regard organs, officers, or partners of corporations, associations or partnerships acting in the exercise of their functions,[14] or trustees[15] as agents, this limits the scope still further. Moreover, the entire Chapter on relations between principal and agent[16] does not apply where the agreement creating the agency relationship is a contract of employment.[17] Finally, Contracting States may opt out

---

[1] For substantive rules on agency relationships, see Ch 5.

[2] See below, Art 1(2)(e)(f) of the Rome Convention on the Law Applicable to Contractual Obligations (hereafter 'Rome Convention'); Art 5(f), 15 of the Inter-American Convention on the Law Applicable to International Contracts 1994 (hereafter 'Inter-American Convention').

[3] See Ch 2   [4] Article 22.

[5] Article 1(1); this encompasses cases where the agent's function is receiving or communicating proposals or conducting negotiations, Art 1(2).

[6] The distinction between 'direct' and 'indirect' agency, important in some legal systems (above p. 291) is therefore irrelevant.   [7] Article 1(3).

[8] Article 2(a).   [9] Article 2(b).   [10] Article 2(c).   [11] Article 2(d).
[12] Artiicle 2(e).   [13] Article 2(f).   [14] Article 3(a).   [15] Article 3(b).
[16] Article 5–9.   [17] Article 10.

of the Convention's applicability to banking transactions, matters of insurance, and the acts of a public servant acting in the exercise of his functions as such on behalf of a private person.[18]

The law indicated by the Convention as applicable governs whether or not it is the law of a Contracting State.[19]

Relations between principal and agent

The point of departure is the autonomy of the parties. The principal and the agent may choose the law governing their relationship; this choice must be express or such that it may be inferred with reasonable certainty from their agreement and the circumstances.[20] Absent the parties' choice, the relationship is governed by the law of the State where the agent has his place of business or, if he has none, his habitual residence.[21] If the agent is primarily to act in one State and the principal has his business establishment in that State, that State's law governs.[22] Where either party has more than one business establishment, the establishment with which their relationship is most closely connected commands.[23]

Not infrequently, the creation of an agency relationship is but one purpose of an agreement among others. In these cases the law determined by the parties' choice or identified by reference to their business establishments etc. governs only if either the creation of the agency relationship was the principal purpose or the agency agreement is severable.[24]

The applicable law governs the formation and validity of the agency relationship, the obligations of the parties, the conditions of performance, the consequences of non-performance, and the extinction of those obligations.[25] This law governs in particular what for all practical purposes is the most important and overarching issue of the existence and extent of the authority of the agent, including modifications, termination, and the effects of any excess or abuse of his authority.[26]

Relations with the third party

Domestic rules on agency have to make a choice whether the main objective is protecting the principal's interests or the third party's interests. Accordingly, many autonomous conflict-of-laws rules opt either in favour of the applicability of the principal's or the third party's law. Some systems which, in principle, give preference to the latter inject a degree of 'principal protection' by stating that the law of

---

[18] Article 18.   [19] Article 4.   [20] Article 5.   [21] Article 6 (1).
[22] Article 6 (2). Again, failing a business establishment, the principal's habitual residence becomes the relevant connecting factor.   [23] Article 6(3).   [24] Article 7.
[25] Article 8. However, in regard to the *manner* of performance, the law of the place of performance is to be taken into consideration, Art 9.
[26] Article 8(a). The provision covers further details such as the authority to appoint substitutes (Art 8(b)), potential conflicts of interest (Art 8(c)), non-competition and *del credere* clauses (Art 8(d)), clientele allowances (*l'indemnité de clientèle*) (Art 8(e)) and the categories of recoverable damage (Art 8(f)).

the place where the agent *should have* used his authority to bring about a contract with the third party is applicable. In this perspective, the Convention's basic rule to have the law of the agent's business establishment etc. govern the agent's authority and the effects of his exercise or purported exercise of his authority,[27] comes as a surprise. This basic rule is somewhat refined, mainly in the third parties' interest, by providing for the applicability of the law of the State in which the agent has acted if the principal has his business establishment there and the agent acted in his name,[28] or the third party is located in that State,[29] or the agent acted at an exchange or auction,[30] or the agent has no business establishment.[31]

Where a party has more than one business establishment, the one with which the agent's acts are more closely connected determines the applicable law.[32]

In all these instances, where an agent in one State communicates with the third party in another by message, telegram, telex, telephone, 'or other similar means',[33] the agent is deemed to have acted at the place of his business establishment etc.[34]

Mandatory provisions and public policy

In applying the choice-of-law provisions of the Convention, a court may give effect to the mandatory rules of *any* State with which the situation has a significant connection, if and so far as, *that* State's law itself indicates that those rules must be applied whatever the law specified by *its*, i.e. that State's choice-of-law rules.[35] Following the 1980 Rome Convention,[36] this is one of the earliest examples of a universal instrument's recognition of the doctrine of 'règles d'application immédiate' and its equivalents. As is common, a court may—only—refuse the application of a law specified by the Convention where this would manifestly violate the forum's public policy.[37]

Territorial units

The Convention contains a detailed regime for States which comprise several territorial units each of which has its own rules in respect of agency.[38] In such a case, it is important to find out what declarations, if any, in respect of those territorial units have been made by the Contracting State.

---

[27] Article 11(1). For the purpose of this provision, where an agent acting under a contract of employment with his principal has no business establishment of his own, his principal's establishment is deemed to be his also.   [28] Article 11(2)(a).

[29] Article 11(2)(b).   [30] Article 11(2)(c).   [31] Article 11(2)(d).

[32] Article 11(3).

[33] It is submitted that, in accordance with the language that has recently amended or replaced the words 'in writing' (cf. above p. 000, this is to be construed so as to encompass electronic mail etc.

[34] Article 13.   [35] Article 16.   [36] More precisely, Art 7(1), below p. 757.

[37] Article 17.

[38] Article 19–21. Under Art 19, each territorial unit is to be considered as a State for the purpose of identifying the law applicable under the Convention.

2. Hague Convention on the Law Applicable to Contracts for the International Sale of Goods 1986[39]

Scope of application

The 1980 United Nations Convention on Contracts for the International Sale of Goods[40] ('the CISG') is devoted to creating uniform substantive rules on as broad as possible a range of issues. However, on a number of issues, the delegates to the 1980 Diplomatic Conference in Vienna either did not attempt to reach agreement or they were unable to reach such agreement. Moreover, until the second half of the 1980s, the extraordinary success of the CISG was not foreseeable. This is why it made sense to try to develop, at the worldwide level, an instrument devoted to determining the law applicable to international sales. It is noteworthy, however, that the 1986 Hague Convention specifically refers to and positions itself in relation to the CISG.[41]

The Convention itself determines the law applicable to contracts for the sale of goods between parties having their places of business[42] in different States[43] or in all other cases where foreign elements require that a choice of law be made. A Contracting State may declare that it will not be applied where such choice arises solely from the parties' stipulation as to the applicable law, even if accompanied by a choice of forum or arbitration clause;[44] those cases may be characterized as 'pseudo-international'.

Excluded are sales by way of execution or otherwise by authority of law,[45] sales of financial instruments[46] and consumer transactions.[47] The Convention's scope is wider than the scope of the CISG in that it includes the sale of ships, hovercraft, and aircraft as well as electricity.[48] Contracts for the supply of goods to be manufactured are contracts of sale unless the buyer himself supplies a substantial part of the material for such production.[49] Depending on whether the preponderant part of the obligations of the party who furnishes goods consists of the supply of labour or other services, a contract may not be considered a sales contract.[50]

---

[39] This Convention is not yet in force but as it is the most recent it is reproduced here with an explanatory comment. There are two earlier applicable law conventions, the 1955 Hague Convention on the law applicable to international sales of goods and the 1958 Hague Convention on the law governing transfer of title in international sales of goods. The first of these is in force, having been adopted by nine states (Belgium, Denmark, Finland, France, Italy, Luxembourg, Norway, Sweden, and Switzerland) but Belgium denounced the Convention on 19 February 1999, effective from 1 September 1999. There is no official English text of this Convention and it is not reproduced here. The 1958 Convention never entered into force, having been ratified only by Italy. Mention should also be made of the 1958 Hague Convention on the jurisdiction of the selected forum in the case of international sales of goods. No state has ratified this Convention and it is not reproduced. Information on the status of these and other Hague Conventions is available on the Hague Conference website, www.hcch.net.   [40] Above Ch 4   [41] Preamble, Arts 8(5), 23.
[42] As to the meaning of 'place of business', cf. Art 14.   [43] Article 1(a).
[44] Article 1(b) and Art 21(1)(a) providing for this reservation.   [45] Article 2(a).
[46] Article 2(b).   [47] Article 2(c).   [48] Article 3.   [49] Article 4(1).
[50] Article 4(2).

The Convention does not determine the law applicable to a whole range of incidental and connected issues, most importantly the capacity of the parties and the consequences flowing from incapacity[51] on the one hand and the transfer of ownership[52] on the other hand.

The law determined under the Convention applies whether it is the law of a Contracting State or not.[53]

In establishing its relationship with other international instruments, the Convention, under certain conditions, gives precedence to such other instruments.[54] Again, instruments emanating from the legislative procedures of regional economic integration organizations may merit particular attention in this regard.

Determination of the applicable law

The starting point is the parties' freedom to choose the governing law; this choice must be express or clearly implied in the terms of the agreement and the parties' conduct.[55] If the applicable law has not been chosen, the principal, objective, connecting factor is the seller's place of business.[56] The law of the buyer's place of business may however prevail in certain circumstances.[57] Finally, a manifestly closer connection of the contract with a law which is neither the buyer's nor the seller's may lead to the applicability of that third State's law.[58]

Transactions by auction or on exchanges, i.e. regulated markets, may be subjected by the parties' choice to a law other than the law of the place of that market or auction only to the extent permitted by the law of the exchange or the place of the auction.[59]

The existence and material validity of the consent as to the choice of law is governed by the law chosen or, if the choice was invalid, by the law indicated following an objective connecting factor.[60]

Issues of a contract's formal validity are essentially governed by the *lex causae* or the *lex loci actus*.[61]

Scope of the applicable law

The applicable law governs, as usual, the entire spectrum of issues regarding interpretation, performance, the consequences of non-performance etc.[62] Noteworthy are its governing the passing of risk from the seller to the buyer,[63] the validity and effects as between the parties of clauses reserving title to

---

[51] Article 5(a). [52] Article 5(c), but see also Art 12. [53] Article 6.
[54] Articles 22, 23. [55] Article 7(1). For the meaning of the term 'law' see Art 15.
[56] Article 8(1). For the meaning of the term, see Art 14. [57] Article 8(2).
[58] Article 8(3). But see also Art 8(4) and its reference to Art 21(1)(b) as well as Art 5(5) giving precedence to the CISG. [59] Article 9.
[60] Article 10. [61] Article 11. But see also Art 21(1)(c).
[62] Article 12. See however Art 13 on the modalities of the inspection of the goods.
[63] Article 12(d).

the goods,[64] and the various ways of extinguishing obligations, as well as pre-scription and limitation of actions.[65]

Mandatory provisions and public policy

Irrespective of the law determined under the Convention as applicable, the forum's mandatory provisions may prevail.[66] The application of a law specified by the Convention as applicable may be refused if that would be manifestly incompatible with—the forum's—public policy.[67]

Territorial units

Where a State comprises several territorial units, each of which has its own system of law or rules of law in respect of contracts for the sale of goods, references to the law of that State are to be construed as the law in force in the territorial unit in question.[68] Such a State is not bound to apply the Convention to conflicts between the laws in force in its territorial units.[69]

3. Rome Convention on the Law Applicable to Contractual Obligations 1980

Introduction

This most successful and most influential instrument in the area of conflict of laws (private international law) is about to change 'pillars' and become an EC Reg-ulation. Under (the Amsterdam version of) Article 65 EC, private international law and international civil procedure which have so far been dealt with in inter-governmental conventions[70] are now 'communitarized', and have become a branch of judicial cooperation. They therefore pass from the 'third pillar' to the 'first pillar', i.e. genuine Community legislation.[71]

The Brussels Protocol of 1988 on the interpretation of the Convention by the European Court of Justice did not enter into force. The ECJ's jurisdiction will shortly flow from the instrument's nature. For the time being, a provision of the Convention[72] and a very special document, the official report drawn up by Professors Giuliano and Lagarde and published with the Convention,[73] provide the glue which maintains a remarkable uniformity in the Con-vention's interpretation and application by the courts of the various Member States.

The Convention does not affect the application of provisions which, in relation to particular matters, lay down conflict of laws rules on contractual obligations and

---

[64] Article 12(e).   [65] Article 12(g). But see also Art 21(1)(d).   [66] Article 17.
[67] Article 18.   [68] Article 19.   [69] Article 20.
[70] Under Article 293 = ex Art 220 EC.   [71] Under Article 249(2) EC.
[72] Article 18.   [73] O.J. 1980 C 282, p.1.

which are contained in EC legislation or domestic law harmonized by EC legislation.[74]

As regards (other) international conventions to which a Contracting State of the Rome Convention is a party, the latter does not prejudice the application of the former.[75] In the future, however, the Member States' competence to conclude any such conventions will be curtailed.

Scope of application

The rules of the Convention, to the extent that they address an issue, determine the law that is applicable to contracts in all Contracting States. The rules of the Convention apply to contractual obligations in any situation involving a choice between the law of different countries.[76] Any law specified by the Convention's rules is to be applied whether or not it is the law of a Contracting State.[77] What constitutes a contractual obligation is to be ascertained in an autonomous and Convention-inherent manner. This need not coincide with what any domestic law characterizes as contractual. Excluded are questions of status, capacity, family law, and the law of succession.[78] More important in the context of commercial transactions is the exclusion[79] of certain obligations under negotiable instruments, arbitration agreements and choice-of-forum clauses, company law and the law of partnerships, authority of agents,[80] matters regarding trusts as well as evidence and procedure.[81] Insurance contracts covering risks situated in the EU territories are not encompassed whereas re-insurance contracts are not excluded.[82]

Renvoi is excluded since the Convention takes the position that reference to the law of a country is to be construed as a reference to that country's law other than its private international law.[83]

The Convention permits reservations only[84] to the provisions on the application of mandatory rules of 'third countries' laws,[85] and on the allocation of consequences of nullity of a contract to the applicable law.[86]

Determination of the applicable law

(i) Party autonomy and determination by virtue of objective connecting factors   The starting point is the parties' freedom to choose the law which is to govern their contract; the choice must be express or demonstrated with reasonable certainty by the contract's terms or the circumstances of the case.[87] The law chosen need not be a law which has a connection with the contract although in the majority of transactions that will be the case. Whether the provision in its present form would also permit the choice of non-state rules of law, restatements or similar such as the

---

[74] Article 20.   [75] Article 21.   [76] Article 1(1).   [77] Article 2.
[78] Article 1(2)(a)–(b).   [79] Article 1(2)(c)–(h).
[80] Article 1(2)(f). On agency, cf. the instruments presented above, Ch 5.
[81] But see below, Art 14.   [82] Article 1(3), (4).   [83] Article 15.
[84] Article 22.   [85] Article 7(1).   [86] Article 10(1)(e).   [87] Article 3(1).

UNIDROIT Principles of International Commercial Contracts or the Principles of European Contract Law has been the subject of some debate.[88] The Convention limits the freedom of choice when it states that, where all the other elements relevant to the situation are connected with one country only—usually a purely domestic case—the parties' choice shall not, even if combined with the choice of a foreign tribunal, prejudice the application of those rules which the law the situation is connected with considers as mandatory.[89]

To the extent that the parties have not chosen the applicable law, contracts are governed by the law of the country with which they are most closely connected.[90] There is a presumption that the contract is most closely connected with the country where the party who is to effect the 'characteristic performance'[91] has his habitual residence, central administration, or principal place of business.[92] This provision is to be disregarded if the characteristic performance cannot be determined. Where the subject matter of a contract is a right in immoveable property or a right to use such property the presumption is, however, that the contract is most closely connected with the country where the property is situated.[93] Finally, contracts for the carriage of goods are not subject to the basic presumption at all; here, it is the carrier's principal place of business which, provided other elements point to the same country, is the main connecting factor[94] and that country's law governs the contract. However, both presumptions regarding these specific contracts are to be disregarded if the circumstances as a whole indicate a closer connection with another country.[95]

(ii) Specific types of contract The Convention singles out only consumer contracts[96] and individual employment contracts[97] where the party identified from a socio-economic point of view as the 'weaker' party is protected by providing, for example, for the applicability of that party's law.

(iii) Mandatory rules and public policy The basic and—even before the Convention's entering into force—generally accepted principle is that a court is free to apply its own mandatory rules irrespective of the law otherwise applicable to the contract.[98] The innovation introduced by Article 7(2), previously known only from the case law in a few jurisdictions and rejected by way of a reservation in this respect entered by some Contracting States, is that effect may also be given to the mandatory rules of another country, i.e. a '*third country*' which is neither the forum nor the country whose law is otherwise applicable, provided the situation has a close connection with that country and under the law of *that* country—not in the

---

[88] The majority view being that this is not permissible (see above p. 40. It should, however, be noted that Art 3(1) does not refer—as Art 4(1) does—to the 'law of a country'.   [89] Article 1(3).
[90] Article 4(1).
[91] It is usually said that this is the 'typical', 'distinguishing', 'more complex', or non-payment performance.   [92] Article 4(2).
[93] Article 4(3).   [94] Article 4(4).   [95] Article 4(5).   [96] Article 5.
[97] Article 6.   [98] Article 7(2).

forum's view—those rules must be applied whatever the law applicable to the contract.[99]

Finally, a limit to the application of a rule of law specified by the Convention may be drawn if, and only if, the application is manifestly incompatible with the forum's public policy.[100]

Scope of the applicable law

(i) Material and formal validity; incapacity   The existence and validity of a contract or any term is determined by the law which would govern it under the Convention if the contract or term were valid.[101] However, as far as a party's conduct during the negotiation stage is concerned, that party may rely upon the law of his habitual residence to establish that it did not mean to consent.[102]

As regards formal validity, a contract concluded between persons who are in the same country is valid only if either the requirements of that country or of the law which governs the contract under the Convention (*lex contractus*) are met.[103] A contract concluded between persons who are in different countries is formally valid if it satisfies the requirements of either country or of the *lex contractus.*[104] Validation can, in an appropriate case, also be conferred by the law of the place where an act intended to have legal effect was done, the law of the country in which an agent acted, or the law of the country where immoveable property is situated.[105]

A natural person who concluded a contract while in the same country as the other contracting party may invoke his incapacity resulting from the law of another country only if the other party was aware or ought to have been aware of this incapacity.[106]

(ii) Specific issues   The law specified under the Convention governs in particular the interpretation, performance, the consequences of non-performance, the ways of extinguishing obligations, prescription and limitation of actions as well as the consequences of nullity of the contract.[107] However, in relation to the 'manner of performance' and the steps to be taken in the event of defective performance, regard shall be had to the law of the country where performance takes place.[108] To the extent that the burden of proof is dealt with in the law of contract these matters are also governed by the law applicable under the Convention.[109]

(iii) Voluntary assignment and subrogation   The mutual obligations of assignor and assignee are governed by the law applicable under the Convention to their contract.[110] The law governing the right to which the assignment relates determines its assignability, the relationship between assignee and debtor, the conditions under

---

[99] Article 7(1).   [100] Article 16.   [101] Article 8(1).   [102] Article 8(2).
[103] Article 9(1).   [104] Article 9(2).   [105] Article 3(3)–(6).   [106] Article 11.
[107] Article 10(1).   [108] Article 10(2).   [109] Article 14.   [110] Article 12(1).

which the assignment can be invoked against the debtor as well as the question whether the debtor's obligations have been discharged.[111]

The law which governs a third person's duty to satisfy a creditor determines whether and under which circumstances the third person is entitled to step 'into the creditor's shoes' as against the debtor.[112]

States with more than one legal system

Each territorial unit of a State which has its own contract law is to be considered as a country for the purpose of identifying the applicable law.[113] A State with such territorial units is not bound to apply the Convention to conflicts between the laws of those units.[114]

4. Inter-American Convention on the Law Applicable to International Contracts 1994

Introduction

This Convention, negotiated and concluded in the framework of the Organization of American States' Fifth Special Conference on Private International Law, on the one hand shows clearly the influence exercised by the Rome Convention but on the other hand demonstrates equally its own autonomy and, on some issues, its juxtaposition to the European solutions.

The application of other international conventions to which a Contracting State is a party and conventions concluded within 'the context of integration movements'[115] are not to be affected.

Scope of application

The definition of 'internationality'[116] is more elaborate than the one in the Rome Convention and therefore narrower. Contracts involving States or State agencies are, in principle, covered by the Convention, but a Contracting State may exclude them by declaration.[117]

The law designated by the Convention need not be the law of a Contracting State to be applicable.[118]

There are further provisions which, albeit somewhat vague, are interesting attempts apparently designed to make the instrument responsive to new technological developments.[119]

Excluded are matters of capacity, status, family law, succession, and, more importantly in our context, obligations deriving from securities and securities transactions, arbitration agreements, and choice of court agreements, as well as

---

[111] Article 12(2). [112] Article 13. [113] Article 19(1). [114] Article 19(2).
[115] Article 20. The reference is obviously to the MERCOSUR Treaty on International Jurisdiction in Disputes Relating to Contracts. [116] Article 1(2).
[117] Article 1(3), (4). [118] Article 2. [119] Article 3.

questions of company law.[120] Contracts governed by international instruments in force among Contracting States are equally excluded from the scope of this Convention.[121]

'Law' means the substantive domestic law designated, so that no renvoi can occur.[122]

The Convention surprisingly permits Contracting States to make reservations 'which are not incompatible with the effect and purpose of the Convention'.[123]

Determination of the applicable law

(i) Party autonomy and objective connecting factors The parties may choose the law governing their contract by express choice or implicitly, provided that the parties' conduct and the clauses of the contract in their entirety make it clear which law has been chosen.[124]

Absent parties' choice, the law of the State with which the contract has the closest ties governs.[125] However, the concept of 'characteristic performance' was deliberately not adopted. Instead, the court has to take all objective and subjective elements into account to establish those ties and their relative weight. Moreover, sets of rules of law such as the UNIDROIT Principles[126] may be applied since the court 'shall also take into account the general principles of international commercial law recognised by international organizations'.[127]

(ii) Mandatory provisions and public policy Mandatory rules of the forum are applied irrespective of the law governing the contract under the Convention.[128] It is for the forum to decide whether it applies mandatory rules of other States.[129] Application of the law designated as applicable by the Convention may be refused if this is manifestly contrary to the forum's public policy.[130]

Scope of the applicable law

(i) Existence and validity Both the existence and the validity of the contract, as well as the substantive validity of the parties' consent concerning the choice of the applicable law, are governed by the law which would govern if the contract and the choice of law were valid.[131] However, as under the Rome Convention, to establish whether a party has duly consented, the law of that party's habitual residence or place of business is taken into account.[132]

---

[120] Article 5.

[121] Art 6. For example, the Vienna Sales Convention (CISG) whose Art 1(1)(b) (on which see above) makes it clear that, in contrast to what Art 6 suggests, the specialized instrument does not have to be in force among all Contracting States to the Inter-American Convention.

[122] Article 17.   [123] Article 21.   [124] Article 7.   [125] Article 9(1).

[126] On which see further pp. 46–82 above.   [127] Article 9(2).

[128] Article 11(1).   [129] Article 11(2).   [130] Article 18.   [131] Article 12(1).

[132] Article 12(2).

Regarding formal validity, whether the parties are present in the same or in different States, the Convention takes the approach of favouring a contract's formal validity. A contract is valid if alternatively the requirements of the *lex contractus* under the Convention, the law(s) of the State(s) where the persons acted, or the law of the place of performance are satisfied.[133]

(ii) Specific issues   In this respect the Convention's solutions coincide largely with those proposed under the Rome Convention.[134] However, there are deviations: when deciding whether an agent had authority to bind his principal, this Convention refers also to customs, usages, and principles of international commercial law.[135] Secondly, the Convention contemplates contracts which are to be registered and designates in this respect the law of the State of the registry as governing.[136]

States with more than one legal system

The Convention's solutions[137] essentially coincide with those proposed by the Rome Convention.[138] In addition, it provides for the possibility that a Contracting State declares to which of its territorial unit(s) the Convention shall apply.[139]

5. Hague Convention on the Law Applicable to Certain Rights in Respect of Securities Held with an Intermediary

Introduction

The 2002 Hague Convention on the law applicable to certain rights in respect of securities held with an intermediary[140] is designed to accommodate a major market shift from direct holdings of investment securities (shares, bonds, etc.) from the issuer to indirect holdings through securities accounts with a bank, broker-dealer, or other securities intermediary. There may be several tiers of intermediary. Usually, where an intermediary holds a particular issue of securities for several of its customers these are held in a common (fungible) pool, or omnibus account, which is maintained by the intermediary with its own intermediary and does not identify any particular customer. Among the many advantages of these changes are that they enable huge volumes of transactions in securities to be processed without going through the books of the issuer, each investor having its relationship only with its own intermediary, and that pooled accounts give the intermediary much greater flexibility in dealings for customers.

But conflict of laws rules in most countries have yet to adapt to the change from direct to indirect holdings. The traditional conflict rule governing proprietary rights

---

[133] Article 13.
[134] Cf. Art 14, of the Inter-American Convention and Art 10 of the Rome Convention.
[135] Article 15, 10.   [136] Article 16.   [137] Article 22, 23.
[138] Cf. Art 19 of the Rome Convention.   [139] Article 24.
[140] Referred to hereafter as the PRIMA Convention, for reasons which will become apparent.

in investment securities is the *lex rei sitae* and in relation to registered securities the *situs* is considered to be the place of incorporation, or alternatively the place where the register is kept. But this is ill-suited to holdings with an intermediary, who may be based in a different country, and it subjects all holdings and dealings, at whatever level, to a single law which may have little or no connection with the account or the dealing in question.

The PRIMA approach

Given that each investor's relationship is solely with his own intermediary, a logical starting point, which was the initial focus of the draft Convention, is to adopt the law of the place of the relevant intermediary approach (PRIMA), so that the proprietary effects of a credit to a securities account and of dealings with that account are governed by the law of the place of the intermediary with whom the account is maintained. But that approach proved inadequate because in modern trading the function of maintaining accounts may be distributed among different offices of the intermediary situated in different countries or, indeed, may be centrally organized through an electronic system with no office at all. So though the concept of the relevant intermediary is retained, the primary rule is the law selected to govern the account agreement.

Scope of the Convention

The Convention is a pure conflict of laws Convention, having no rules of substantive law and no effect on substantive national laws. It is confined to issues listed in Article 2(1) ('the Article 2(1) issues') in respect of securities held with an intermediary, that is, the rights of an account holder resulting from a credit of securities to a securities account.[141] Thus in order for the Convention to apply (1) the rights must relate to securities as defined and (2) the securities must have entered the intermediated system by being credited to a securities account. It is important to note that the Convention has to be applied separately to each account and at each level. Each account holder's rights are determined by the law applicable to his holding with his own intermediary and with no one else.

(i) 'Securities' 'Securities' are defined as 'any shares, bonds or other financial instruments or financial assets (other than cash), or any interest therein'. The definition is deliberately framed in broad terms, avoiding detailed descriptions might exclude new categories of security developing from changing market practice. Cash is excluded from the definition, even if credited to a securities account, but the Convention law does determine whether a disposition carries with it an entitlement to dividends and other distributions.

---

141   See the definition of 'securities held with an intermediary' in Art 1(1)(f).

(ii) 'Held with an intermediary' Until securities have entered the intermediated system the Convention has no application. But once they come into the hands of a securities intermediary and are credited to a securities account the Convention comes into operation, not merely in relation to the account holder's rights but also in relation to those of transferees, at whatever level and whether or not there has been a credit to the account of the relevant transferee. This is because the Convention applies to dispositions of securities credited to a securities account. So if T purchases from A an interest in securities which A holds in an account with I, the law determined by the Convention in relation to A's holding will also apply to the transfer to T unless and until they are credited to an account in T's name, in which case T's rights become governed by the law applicable to his holding through his own account. There are various legal systems under which, although rights to securities can only be held or transferred across the books of an intermediary, the account holder is considered to hold directly from the issuer. Nevertheless they are treated as within the intermediated system for the purposes of the Convention because the account holder's rights depend on a credit to a securities account with an intermediary. Though the question whether and when securities are to be considered credited to a securities account is likely to arise only infrequently, it is implicit in the Convention that where it does arise the question will be determined by the Convention law.

In principle, the Convention law applies only to consensual interests, but by exception it extends to a lien by operation of law in favour of the account holder's intermediary in respect of any claim arising in connection with the maintenance and operation of the account.[142]

The Article 2(1) issues

Where the above conditions are satisfied the Convention determines the law applicable to all the Article 2(1) issues in relation to the securities themselves,[143] whether the entitlement to the securities is proprietary, co-proprietary, derived from a trust or fiduciary relationship, contractual or mixed, or indeed of any other character. Excluded are purely contractual or other purely personal rights which do not relate to the securities themselves as credited to a securities account but derive from the account agreement, such as the intermediary's standard of care in maintaining the account, the content and frequency of account statements, the time by which instructions must be given by the account holder in order to be carried out the same day, fees, and the like. This is the overall effect of the subordination of Article 2(3) to Article 2(2), though the wording of Article 2(3) and in particular its reference to rights resulting from a credit of securities to a securities account is not entirely felicitous.

---

[142] Article 1(2)(c).

[143] The law determined by the Convention means its law other than its choice of law rules; in other words, renvoi is excluded (Art 9).

The Article 2(1) issues cover virtually all of the situations likely in practice to affect securities held with an intermediary, including the legal nature and effects against the intermediary and third parties of rights resulting from the credit of securities to a securities account, the legal nature and effects of dispositions (including the grant of security interests), perfection requirements, priorities, and the duties of an intermediary faced with competing claims.

Internationality

The Convention applies in all cases involving a choice between the laws of different States,[144] and whether or not the applicable law is that of a Contracting State.[145] Thus the concept of internationality is given the widest scope, applying where one of the players (including for this purpose the issuer or any intermediary or account holder or a transferee) and any other player are located in different States, or where all the factors relevant to the situation are located in the same State but the law chosen by the parties is that of another State, or the proceedings are brought in another State. Moreover, the fact that the forum might not consider the foreign element relevant to the issue before it is immaterial to the applicability of the Convention.

The applicable law

The Convention lays down a primary rule for determining the applicable law and, where this does not apply, three fall-back rules are arranged in a cascade so that the first applicable fall-back rule is the one to be applied. In determining the applicable law Article 7 excludes from consideration the location of the issuer or of certificates to securities or of any intermediary other than the relevant intermediary, that is, the intermediary with whom the account holder in question has its account.

(i) The primary rule Article 4 lays down the primary rule, namely that the law applicable to all the issues specified in Article 2(1) is the law in force in the State[146] expressly agreed in the account agreement as the State whose law governs the account or such other law as the parties expressly agree.[147] This leaves the parties free to agree to choose a law to govern the Article 2(1) issues that is different from the law selected to govern the account agreement. In that case the validity of the choice of law to govern the account agreement will be governed not by the Convention but by the conflict rules of the forum.

But the parties do not have unlimited freedom of choice; it is necessary that the designated law satisfy the so-called 'Qualifying Office' test in being the law of a State in which the intermediary has an office that, whether alone or with others, is engaged in a business or other regular activity of maintaining securities accounts

---

[144] Article 3.   [145] Article 5.
[146] Where the parties have agreed on a territorial unit of a State, the reference is to the law of that territorial unit (Art 12).   [147] Article 4(1).

(though not necessarily the particular account in question) or is identified by an account number, bank code, or other specific means of identification as maintaining securities accounts in that State.

To allow parties to an account agreement to select the law governing not only their own relations but also proprietary effects as against third parties and even priorities is counter-intuitive and contrary to the traditional conflict of laws approach. However, it responds to market needs in subjecting all proprietary issues affecting the securities account to a single law, which a person intending to acquire an interest in the account can readily ascertain by enquiry of the intermediary and sight of the account agreement, and thereby avoids shopping for a forum whose conflict rules lead to the application of the law most favourable to the claimant. Experience under Article 8 of the American Uniform Commercial Code has shown the advantages of such a rule.

(ii) The fall-back rules These are laid down in Article 5. The first fall-back rule, which applies if the parties to the account agreement have not chosen the applicable law or if their choice does not satisfy the Qualifying Office test, looks to the law of the State in which is located the office of the intermediary expressly and unambiguously stated in a written account agreement as the office through which the intermediary entered into the agreement.[148] Failing such a statement, the intermediate fall-back rule is the law of the place where the intermediary is incorporated or otherwise organized[149] (e.g. as an unincorporated association given a legal status distinct from that of the individual members)—a law which in many cases has little connection with the account but has the merit of certainty and is likely to operate in only a small number of cases. If the intermediary is not incorporated or otherwise organized, the ultimate fall-back rule is to the law of its place of business or, if more than one, its principal place of business.[150]

(iii) Change in the applicable law The parties to the account agreement may agree to amend it so as to change the applicable law, in which case the new law, though not disturbing the existence and perfection of an interest under the old law and priority between pre-change dispositions or between a pre-change disposition and attachment by an attachment article (whether pre-change or post-change), will determine the priority effects of any re-perfection requirements and also a priority between a pre-change disposition and a post-change disposition.[151] Article 7 does not, however, apply to a new agreement between the same parties.

(iv) Insolvency Under Article 8 an insolvency court must respect the application of the Convention law to the Article 2(1) issues but this does not affect the application of the forum State's substantive or procedural insolvency rules, including those relating to the ranking of claims and the avoidance of a disposition

---

[148] Article 5(1).   [149] Article 5(2).   [150] Article 5(3).   [151] Article 7.

as a preference or a transfer in fraud of creditors. The effect of this is that the insolvency court cannot apply a different law (e.g. its own general law) to disturb the status, perfection, and priority of an interest in securities under the Convention law but, having respected the application of the Convention law to the Article 2(1) issues, the insolvency court then applies any special rules of its insolvency law providing for the avoidance or insolvency ranking of such an interest.

(v) Public policy and internationally mandatory rules   Article 11(1) provides that the application of the law determined under the Convention may be refused only if the effects of its application would be manifestly contrary to the public policy of the forum. This is intended to be of very limited application. Article 11(2) permits the application of internationally mandatory rules, that is, rules which apply regardless of the otherwise applicable law. The effect is thus not to displace the law applicable under the Convention but to superimpose rules designed to have international mandatory force. However, Article 11(3) precludes recourse to provisions of the *lex fori* imposing requirements with respect to perfection or relating to priorities between competing interests, unless the law of the forum is the applicable law under the Convention. The purpose of this provision is to ensure that the provisions of the Convention as to the law governing perfection and priorities, which lie at the heart of the Convention, cannot be undermined by recourse to rules of public policy or mandatory rules that would have the effect of supplanting or modifying the applicable law determined by the Convention.

Transition provisions

Chapter IV of the Convention contains two sets of transition provisions. The first, Article 15, provides that in a Contracting State the Convention law determines whether a person's interest acquired after the Convention entered into force for that State extinguishes or has priority over another person's interest acquired before the Convention entered into force for that State. This conforms to a general principle of private international law that in determining priorities one applies the law governing the last dealing or event, leaving it to that law to determine whether the later interest is overriding or whether it is dependent on the title of the transferor under earlier law. Article 16 has the broad effect of applying the Convention to pre-Convention account agreements.

Relationship between transferor's law and transferee's law

An account holder, A, pledges to P securities held by A in an account with Intermediary 1 in Ruritania. In conformity with Article 4(1) the account agreement specifies Ruritanian law as the governing law. A then fraudulently mortgages the same securities to T, the securities being transferred to a securities account held by T with Intermediary 2 in Urbania under an agreement validly expressed to be governed by Urbanian law. Under Urbanian law T acquires an overriding title. Under Ruritanian law the mortgage is ineffective to deprive P of its rights. Who

wins? Careful analysis showed that it was unnecessary for the Convention to provide for such case. As mentioned earlier, it is a well-established principle of the
conflict of laws that where there are competing dispositions governed by different
laws, the law to be applied is that governing the last disposition—in this case,
Urbanian law. If under that law T acquires an overriding title it is unnecessary to
consider whether under Ruritanian law the pledge to P precluded A from transferring an unencumbered title to T. If on the other hand the rule under Urbanian
law is that T cannot acquire a better right than A, then (assuming that T's interest
was acquired under a system which treated A as the direct transferor) a court
applying Urbanian law will hold that the validity of the pledge to P is governed by
Ruritanian law and that, if valid, that pledge will have priority over T's mortgage. It
should therefore not be possible for the situation to arise where T acquires an
overriding title without P losing its own interest. Even where T acquires an overriding title, Ruritanian law may still be relevant to P's rights, as where P, though
losing its interest in the securities transferred, is considered by Ruritanian law to
continue to hold a proportionate interest in the reduced pool of securities held by
Intermediary 1 for its various account holders.

B. Instruments

(i) CONVENTION ON THE LAW APPLICABLE TO AGENCY*
(Concluded March 14, 1978)

PREAMBLE

The States signatories to the present Convention,

Desiring to establish common provisions concerning the law applicable to agency,

Have resolved to conclude a Convention to this effect, and have agreed upon the following provisions—

CHAPTER I
SCOPE OF THE CONVENTION

Article 1

The present Convention determines the law applicable to relationships of an international character arising where a person, the agent, has the authority to act, acts or purports to act on behalf of another person, the principal, in dealing with a third party.

It shall extend to cases where the function of the agent is to receive and communicate proposals or to conduct negotiations on behalf of other persons.

The Convention shall apply whether the agent acts in his own name or in that of the principal and whether he acts regularly or occasionally.

---

* Reproduced with the kind permission of the Hague Conference on Private International Law.

Article 2

This Convention shall not apply to—
   a) the capacity of the parties;
   b) requirements as to form;
   c) agency by operation of law in family law, in matrimonial property regimes, or in the law of succession;
   d) agency by virtue of a decision of a judicial or quasi-judicial authority or subject to the direct control of such an authority;
   e) representation in connection with proceedings of a judicial character;
   f) the agency of a shipmaster acting in the exercise of his functions as such.

Article 3

For the purposes of this Convention—
   a) an organ, officer or partner of a corporation, association, partnership or other entity, whether or not possessing legal personality, shall not be regarded as the agent of that entity in so far as, in the exercise of his functions as such, he acts by virtue of an authority conferred by law or by the constitutive documents of that entity;
   b) a trustee shall not be regarded as an agent of the trust, of the person who has created the trust, or of the beneficiaries.

Article 4

The law specified in this Convention shall apply whether or not it is the law of a Contracting State.

CHAPTER II
RELATIONS BETWEEN PRINCIPAL AND AGENT

Article 5

The internal law chosen by the principal and the agent shall govern the agency relationship between them.

   This choice must be express or must be such that it may be inferred with reasonable certainty from the terms of the agreement between the parties and the circumstances of the case.

Article 6

In so far as it has not been chosen in accordance with Article 5, the applicable law shall be the internal law of the State where, at the time of formation of the agency relationship, the agent has his business establishment or, if he has none, his habitual residence.

   However, the internal law of the State where the agent is primarily to act shall apply if the principal has his business establishment or, if he has none, his habitual residence in that State.

   Where the principal or the agent has more than one business establishment, this Article refers to the establishment with which the agency relationship is most closely connected.

Article 7

Where the creation of the agency relationship is not the sole purpose of the agreement, the law specified in Articles 5 and 6 shall apply only if—
  a) the creation of this relationship is the principal purpose of the agreement, or
  b) the agency relationship is severable.

Article 8

The law applicable under Articles 5 and 6 shall govern the formation and validity of the agency relationship, the obligations of the parties, the conditions of performance, the consequences of non-performance, and the extinction of those obligations.
  This law shall apply in particular to—
  a) the existence and extent of the authority of the agent, its modification or termination, and the consequences of the fact that the agent has exceeded or misused his authority;
  b) the right of the agent to appoint a substitute agent, a sub-agent or an additional agent;
  c) the right of the agent to enter into a contract on behalf of the principal where there is a potential conflict of interest between himself and the principal;
  d) non-competition clauses and *del credere* clauses;
  e) clientele allowances (*l'indemnité de clientèle*);
  f) the categories of damage for which compensation may be recovered.

Article 9

Whatever law may be applicable to the agency relationship, in regard to the manner of performance the law of the place of performance shall be taken into consideration.

Article 10

This Chapter shall not apply where the agreement creating the agency relationship is a contract of employment.

CHAPTER III
RELATIONS WITH THE THIRD PARTY

Article 11

As between the principal and the third party, the existence and extent of the agent's authority and the effects of the agent's exercise or purported exercise of his authority shall be governed by the internal law of the State in which the agent had his business establishment at the time of his relevant acts.
  However, the internal law of the State in which the agent has acted shall apply if—
  a) the principal has his business establishment or, if he has none, his habitual residence in that State, and the agent has acted in the name of the principal; or
  b) the third party has his business establishment or, if he has none, his habitual residence in that State; or
  c) the agent has acted at an exchange or auction; or
  d) the agent has no business establishment.

Where a party has more than one business establishment, this Article refers to the establishment with which the relevant acts of the agent are most closely connected.

Article 12

For the purposes of Article 11, first paragraph, where an agent acting under a contract of employment with his principal has no personal business establishment, he shall be deemed to have his establishment at the business establishment of the principal to which he is attached.

Article 13

For the purposes of Article 11, second paragraph, where an agent in one State has communicated with the third party in another, by message, telegram, telex, telephone, or other similar means, the agent shall be deemed to have acted in that respect at the place of his business establishment or, if he has none, of his habitual residence.

Article 14

Notwithstanding Article 11, where a written specification by the principal or by the third party of the law applicable to questions falling within Article 11 has been expressly accepted by the other party, the law so specified shall apply to such questions.

Article 15

The law applicable under this Chapter shall also govern the relationship between the agent and the third party arising from the fact that the agent has acted in the exercise of his authority, has exceeded his authority, or has acted without authority.

CHAPTER IV
GENERAL PROVISIONS

Article 16

In the application of this Convention, effect may be given to the mandatory rules of any State with which the situation has a significant connection, if and in so far as, under the law of that State, those rules must be applied whatever the law specified by its choice of law rules.

Article 17

The application of a law specified by this Convention may be refused only where such application would be manifestly incompatible with public policy (*ordre public*).

Article 18

Any Contracting State may, at the time of signature, ratification, acceptance, approval or accession, reserve the right not to apply this Convention to—
(1) the agency of a bank or group of banks in the course of banking transactions;
(2) agency in matters of insurance;
(3) the acts of a public servant acting in the exercise of his functions as such on behalf of a private person.
No other reservation shall be permitted.

Any Contracting State may also, when notifying an extension of the Convention in accordance with Article 25, make one or more of these reservations, with its effect limited to all or some of the territories mentioned in the extension.

Any Contracting State may at any time withdraw a reservation which it has made; the reservation shall cease to have effect on the first day of the third calendar month after notification of the withdrawal.

Article 19

Where a State comprises several territorial units each of which has its own rules of law in respect of agency, each territorial unit shall be considered as a State for the purposes of identifying the law applicable under this Convention.

Article 20

A State within which different territorial units have their own rules of law in respect of agency shall not be bound to apply this Convention where a State with a unified system of law would not be bound to apply the law of another State by virtue of this Convention.

Article 21

If a Contracting State has two or more territorial units which have their own rules of law in respect of agency, it may, at the time of signature, ratification, acceptance, approval or accession, declare that this Convention shall extend to all its territorial units or to one or more of them, and may modify its declaration by submitting another declaration at any time.

These declarations shall be notified to the Ministry of Foreign Affairs of the Kingdom of the Netherlands, and shall state expressly the territorial units to which the Convention applies.

Article 22

The Convention shall not affect any other international instrument containing provisions on matters governed by this Convention to which a Contracting State is, or becomes, a Party.

CHAPTER V
FINAL CLAUSES

Article 23

The Convention is open for signature by the States which were Members of the Hague Conference on Private International Law at the time of its Thirteenth Session.

It shall be ratified, accepted or approved and the instruments of ratification, acceptance or approval shall be deposited with the Ministry of Foreign Affairs of the Kingdom of the Netherlands.

Article 24

Any other State may accede to the Convention.

The instrument of accession shall be deposited with the Ministry of Foreign Affairs of the Kingdom of the Netherlands.

Article 25

Any State may, at the time of signature, ratification, acceptance, approval or accession, declare that the Convention shall extend to all the territories for the international relations of which it is responsible, or to one or more of them. Such a declaration shall take effect at the time the Convention enters into force for that State.

Such declaration, as well as any subsequent extension, shall be notified to the Ministry of Foreign Affairs of the Kingdom of the Netherlands.

Article 26

The Convention shall enter into force on the first day of the third calendar month after the deposit of the third instrument of ratification, acceptance, approval or accession referred to in Articles 23 and 24.

Thereafter the Convention shall enter into force —

(1) for each State ratifying, accepting, approving or acceding to it subsequently, on the first day of the third calendar month after the deposit of its instrument of ratification, acceptance, approval or accession;

(2) for a territory to which the Convention has been extended in conformity with Articles 21 and 25, on the first day of the third calendar month after the notification referred to in those Articles.

Article 27

The Convention shall remain in force for five years from the date of its entry into force in accordance with the first paragraph of Article 26, even for States which subsequently have ratified, accepted, approved it or acceded to it.

If there has been no denunciation, it shall be renewed tacitly every five years.

Any denunciation shall be notified to the Ministry of Foreign Affairs of the Kingdom of the Netherlands at least six months before the expiry of the five year period. It may be limited to certain of the territories or territorial units to which the Convention applies.

The denunciation shall have effect only as regards the State which has notified it. The Convention shall remain in force for the other Contracting States.

Article 28

The Ministry of Foreign Affairs of the Kingdom of the Netherlands shall notify to the States Members of the Conference, and the States which have acceded in accordance with Article 24, the following —

(1) the signatures and ratifications, acceptances and approvals referred to in Article 23;

(2) the accessions referred to in Article 24;

(3) the date on which the Convention enters into force in accordance with Article 26;

(4) the extensions referred to in Article 25;

(5) the declarations referred to in Article 21;

(6) the reservations and the withdrawals of reservations referred to in Article 18;

(7) the denunciations referred to in Article 27.

In witness whereof the undersigned, being duly authorised thereto, have signed this Convention.

Done at The Hague, on the 14th day of March, 1978, in the English and French languages, both texts being equally authentic, in a single copy which shall be deposited in the archives of the Government of the Kingdom of the Netherlands, and of which a certified copy shall be sent, through the diplomatic channels, to each of the States Members of the Hague Conference on Private International Law at the date of its Thirteenth Session.

TABLE OF STATE RATIFICATION

Total number of signatures not followed by ratifications: 0
Total number of ratifications/accessions: 4

State	Signature	Ratification	By	Entry into force
Argentina	5 February 1992	5 February 1992		1 May 1992
France	14 March 1978	3 September 1985		1 May 1992
Netherlands (including Aruba)	11 September 1987	21 July 1992		1 October 1992
Portugal	26 May 1978	4 March 1982		1 May 1992

Entered into force: 1 May 1992

(Condition: 3 ratifications)

Note: A list of reservations and declarations made by States has not been included in the text. These can be obtained from http://www.hcch.net/e/status/stat27e.html.

(ii) CONVENTION ON THE LAW APPLICABLE TO CONTRACTS FOR THE INTERNATIONAL SALE OF GOODS*

(Concluded December 22, 1986)

PREAMBLE

The States Parties to the present Convention,

Desiring to unify the choice of law rules relating to contracts for the international sale of goods,

Bearing in mind the United Nations Convention on contracts for the international sale of goods, concluded at Vienna on 11 April 1980,

Have agreed upon the following provisions—

CHAPTER I
SCOPE OF THE CONVENTION

Article 1

This Convention determines the law applicable to contracts of sale of goods—
  a) between parties having their places of business in different States;

---

* Reproduced with the kind permission of the Hague Conference on Private International Law.

b) in all other cases involving a choice between the laws of different States, unless such a choice arises solely from a stipulation by the parties as to the applicable law, even if accompanied by a choice of court or arbitration.

Article 2

The Convention does not apply to—
a) sales by way of execution or otherwise by authority of law;
b) sales of stocks, shares, investment securities, negotiable instruments or money; it does, however, apply to the sale of goods based on documents;
c) sales of goods bought for personal, family or household use; it does, however, apply if the seller at the time of the conclusion of the contract neither knew nor ought to have known that the goods were bought for any such use.

Article 3

For the purposes of the Convention, 'goods' includes—
a) ships, vessels, boats, hovercraft and aircraft;
b) electricity.

Article 4

(1) Contracts for the supply of goods to be manufactured or produced are to be considered contracts of sale unless the party who orders the goods undertakes to supply a substantial part of the materials necessary for such manufacture or production.
(2) Contracts in which the preponderant part of the obligations of the party who furnishes goods consists of the supply of labour or other services are not to be considered contracts of sale.

Article 5

The Convention does not determine the law applicable to—
a) the capacity of the parties or the consequences of nullity or invalidity of the contract resulting from the incapacity of a party;
b) the question whether an agent is able to bind a principal, or an organ to bind a company or body corporate or unincorporate;
c) the transfer of ownership; nevertheless, the issues specifically mentioned in Article 12 are governed by the law applicable to the contract under the Convention;
d) the effect of the sale in respect of any person other than the parties;
e) agreements on arbitration or on choice of court, even if such an agreement is embodied in the contract of sale.

Article 6

The law determined under the Convention applies whether or not it is the law of a Contracting State.

CHAPTER II
APPLICABLE LAW

SECTION I
DETERMINATION OF THE APPLICABLE LAW

Article 7

(1) A contract of sale is governed by the law chosen by the parties. The parties' agreement on this choice must be express or be clearly demonstrated by the terms of the contract and the conduct of the parties, viewed in their entirety. Such a choice may be limited to a part of the contract.

(2) The parties may at any time agree to subject the contract in whole or in part to a law other than that which previously governed it, whether or not the law previously governing the contract was chosen by the parties. Any change by the parties of the applicable law made after the conclusion of the contract does not prejudice its formal validity or the rights of third parties.

Article 8

(1) To the extent that the law applicable to a contract of sale has not been chosen by the parties in accordance with Article 7, the contract is governed by the law of the State where the seller has his place of business at the time of conclusion of the contract.

(2) However, the contract is governed by the law of the State where the buyer has his place of business at the time of conclusion of the contract, if—
   a) negotiations were conducted, and the contract concluded by and in the presence of the parties, in that State; or
   b) the contract provides expressly that the seller must perform his obligation to deliver the goods in that State; or
   c) the contract was concluded on terms determined mainly by the buyer and in response to an invitation directed by the buyer to persons invited to bid (a call for tenders).

(3) By way of exception, where, in the light of the circumstances as a whole, for instance any business relations between the parties, the contract is manifestly more closely connected with a law which is not the law which would otherwise be applicable to the contract under paragraphs 1 or 2 of this Article, the contract is governed by that other law.

(4) Paragraph 3 does not apply if, at the time of the conclusion of the contract, the seller and the buyer have their places of business in States having made the reservation under Article 21, paragraph 1, sub-paragraph b).

(5) Paragraph 3 does not apply in respect of issues regulated in the United Nations Convention on contracts for the international sale of goods (Vienna, 11 April 1980) where, at the time of the conclusion of the contract, the seller and the buyer have their places of business in different States both of which are Parties to that Convention.

Article 9

A sale by auction or on a commodity or other exchange is governed by the law chosen by the parties in accordance with Article 7 to the extent to which the law of the State where the auction takes place or the exchange is located does not prohibit such choice. Failing a choice by the parties, or to the extent that such choice is prohibited, the law of the State where the auction takes place or the exchange is located shall apply.

Article 10

(1) Issues concerning the existence and material validity of the consent of the parties as to the choice of the applicable law are determined, where the choice satisfies the requirements of Article 7, by the law chosen. If under that law the choice is invalid, the law governing the contract is determined under Article 8.

(2) The existence and material validity of a contract of sale, or of any term thereof, are determined by the law which under the Convention would govern the contract or term if it were valid.

(3) Nevertheless, to establish that he did not consent to the choice of law, to the contract itself, or to any term thereof, a party may rely on the law of the State where he has his place of business, if in the circumstances it is not reasonable to determine that issue under the law specified in the preceding paragraphs.

Article 11

(1) A contract of sale concluded between persons who are in the same State is formally valid if it satisfies the requirements either of the law which governs it under the Convention or of the law of the State where it is concluded.

(2) A contract of sale concluded between persons who are in different States is formally valid if it satisfies the requirements either of the law which governs it under the Convention or of the law of one of those States.

(3) Where the contract is concluded by an agent, the State in which the agent acts is the relevant State for the purposes of the preceding paragraphs.

(4) An act intended to have legal effect relating to an existing or contemplated contract of sale is formally valid if it satisfies the requirements either of the law which under the Convention governs or would govern the contract, or of the law of the State where the act was done.

(5) The Convention does not apply to the formal validity of a contract of sale where one of the parties to the contract has, at the time of its conclusion, his place of business in a State which has made the reservation provided for in Article 21, paragraph 1, sub-paragraph c).

SECTION 2

SCOPE OF THE APPLICABLE LAW

Article 12

The law applicable to a contract of sale by virtue of Articles 7, 8 or 9 governs in particular—
    a) interpretation of the contract;
    b) the rights and obligations of the parties and performance of the contract;

748

c) the time at which the buyer becomes entitled to the products, fruits and income deriving from the goods;

d) the time from which the buyer bears the risk with respect to the goods;

e) the validity and effect as between the parties of clauses reserving title to the goods;

f) the consequences of non-performance of the contract, including the categories of loss for which compensation may be recovered, but without prejudice to the procedural law of the forum;

g) the various ways of extinguishing obligations, as well as prescription and limitation of actions;

h) the consequences of nullity or invalidity of the contract.

Article 13

In the absence of an express clause to the contrary, the law of the State where inspection of the goods takes place applies to the modalities and procedural requirements for such inspection.

CHAPTER III
GENERAL PROVISIONS

Article 14

(1) If a party has more than one place of business, the relevant place of business is that which has the closest relationship to the contract and its performance, having regard to the circumstances known to or contemplated by the parties at any time before or at the conclusion of the contract.

(2) If a party does not have a place of business, reference is to be made to his habitual residence.

Article 15

In the Convention 'law' means the law in force in a State other than its choice of law rules.

Article 16

In the interpretation of the Convention, regard is to be had to its international character and to the need to promote uniformity in its application.

Article 17

The Convention does not prevent the application of those provisions of the law of the forum that must be applied irrespective of the law that otherwise governs the contract.

Article 18

The application of a law determined by the Convention may be refused only where such application would be manifestly incompatible with public policy (*ordre public*).

Article 19

For the purpose of identifying the law applicable under the Convention, where a State comprises several territorial units each of which has its own system of law or its own rules of law in respect of contracts for the sale of goods, any reference to the law of that State is to be construed as referring to the law in force in the territorial unit in question.

Article 20

A State within which different territorial units have their own systems of law or their own rules of law in respect of contracts of sale is not bound to apply the Convention to conflicts between the laws in force in such units.

Article 21

(1) Any State may, at the time of signature, ratification, acceptance, approval or accession make any of the following reservations—
    a) that it will not apply the Convention in the cases covered by sub-paragraph b) of Article 1;
    b) that it will not apply paragraph 3 of Article 8, except where neither party to the contract has his place of business in a State which has made a reservation provided for under this sub-paragraph;
    c) that, for cases where its legislation requires contracts of sale to be concluded in or evidenced by writing, it will not apply the Convention to the formal validity of the contract, where any party has his place of business in its territory at the time of conclusion of the contract;
    d) that it will not apply sub-paragraph g) of Article 12 in so far as that sub-paragraph relates to prescription and limitation of actions.
(2) No other reservation shall be permitted.
(3) Any Contracting State may at any time withdraw a reservation which it has made; the reservation shall cease to have effect on the first day of the month following the expiration of three months after notification of the withdrawal.

Article 22

1) This Convention does not prevail over any convention or other international agreement which has been or may be entered into and which contains provisions determining the law applicable to contracts of sale, provided that such instrument applies only if the seller and buyer have their places of business in States Parties to that instrument.
2) This Convention does not prevail over any international convention to which a Contracting State is, or becomes, a Party, regulating the choice of law in regard to any particular category of contracts of sale within the scope of this Convention.

Article 23

This Convention does not prejudice the application—
    a) of the United Nations Convention on contracts for the international sale of goods (Vienna, 11 April 1980);
    b) of the Convention on the limitation period in the international sale of goods (New York, 14 June 1974), or the *Protocol* amending that Convention (Vienna, 11 April 1980).

Article 24

The Convention applies in a Contracting State to contracts of sale concluded after its entry into force for that State.

CHAPTER IV
FINAL CLAUSES

Article 25

(1) The Convention is open for signature by all States.
(2) The Convention is subject to ratification, acceptance or approval by the signatory States.
(3) The Convention is open for accession by all States which are not signatory States as from the date it is open for signature.
(4) Instruments of ratification, acceptance, approval and accession shall be deposited with the Ministry of Foreign Affairs of the Kingdom of the Netherlands, depositary of the Convention.

Article 26

(1) If a State has two or more territorial units in which different systems of law are applicable in relation to matters dealt with in this Convention, it may at the time of signature, ratification, acceptance, approval or accession declare that this Convention shall extend to all its territorial units or only to one or more of them and may modify this declaration by submitting another declaration at any time.
(2) Any such declaration shall be notified to the depositary and shall state expressly the territorial units to which the Convention applies.
(3) If a State makes no declaration under this Article, the Convention is to extend to all territorial units of that State.

Article 27

(1) The Convention shall enter into force on the first day of the month following the expiration of three months after the deposit of the fifth instrument of ratification, acceptance, approval or accession referred to in Article 25.
(2) Thereafter the Convention shall enter into force—
   a) for each State ratifying, accepting, approving or acceding to it subsequently, on the first day of the month following the expiration of three months after the deposit of its instrument of ratification, acceptance, approval or accession;
   b) for a territorial unit to which the Convention has been extended in conformity with Article 26 on the first day of the month following the expiration of three months after the notification referred to in that Article.

Article 28

For each State Party to the Convention on the law applicable to international sales of goods, done at The Hague on 15 June 1955, which has consented to be bound by this Convention and for which this Convention is in force, this Convention shall replace the said Convention of 1955.

Article 29

Any State which becomes a Party to this Convention after the entry into force of an instrument revising it shall be considered to be a Party to the Convention as revised.

Article 30

(1) A State Party to this Convention may denounce it by a notification in writing addressed to the depositary.
(2) The denunciation takes effect on the first day of the month following the expiration of three months after the notification is received by the depositary. Where a longer period for the denunciation to take effect is specified in the notification, the denunciation takes effect upon the expiration of such longer period after the notification is received by the depositary.

Article 31

The depositary shall notify the States Members of the Hague Conference on Private International Law and the States which have signed, ratified, accepted, approved or acceded in accordance with Article 25, of the following—

a) the signatures and ratifications, acceptances, approvals and accessions referred to in Article 25;
b) the date on which the Convention enters into force in accordance with Article 27;
c) the declarations referred to in Article 26;
d) the reservations and the withdrawals of reservations referred to in Article 21;
e) the denunciations referred to in Article 30.

In witness whereof the undersigned, being duly authorized thereto, have signed this Convention.

Done at The Hague, on the 22nd day of December, 1986, in the English and French languages, both texts being equally authentic, in a single copy which shall be deposited in the archives of the Government of the Kingdom of the Netherlands, and of which a certified copy shall be sent, through diplomatic channels, to each of the States Members of the Hague Conference on Private International Law as of the date of its Extraordinary Session of October 1985, and to each State which participated in that Session.

TABLE OF STATE RATIFICATIONS

Total number of signatures not followed by ratifications: 3
Total number of ratifications/accessions: 2

State	Signature	Ratification	By	Entry into force
Argentina	4 October 1991	4 October 1991		
Czech Republic	22 December 1986			
Moldova		24 December 1997	Accession	
Netherlands	2 February 1990			
Slovakia	22 December 1986			

The Hague, 22 December 1986

Not yet in force

(Condition: 5 ratifications)

Note: A list of reservations and declarations made by States has not been included in the text. These can be obtained from http://www.hcch.net/e/status/stat31e.html.

(iii) CONVENTION ON THE LAW APPLICABLE
TO CONTRACTUAL OBLIGATIONS
opened for signature in Rome on 19 June 1980 (80/934/EEC)[1]

PREAMBLE

The High Contracting Parties to the Treaty establishing the European Economic Community,

Anxious to continue in the field of private international law the work of unification of law which has already been done within the Community, in particular in the field of jurisdiction and enforcement of judgments,

Wishing to establish uniform rules concerning the law applicable to contractual obligations,

---

[1] Text as amended by the Convention of 10 April 1984 on the accession of the Hellenic Republic—hereafter referred to as the '1984 Accession Convention'—, by the Convention of 18 May 1992 on the accession of the Kingdom of Spain and the Portuguese Republic—hereafter referred to as the '1992 Accession Convention'—and by the Convention on the accession of the Republic of Austria, the Republic of Finland and the Kingdom of Sweden—hereafter referred to as the '1996 Accession Convention'.

Have agreed as follows:

TITLE I
SCOPE OF THE CONVENTION

Article 1
Scope of the Convention

1. The rules of this Convention shall apply to contractual obligations in any situation involving a choice between the laws of different countries.
2. They shall not apply to:
    (a) questions involving the status or legal capacity of natural persons, without prejudice to Article 11;
    (b) contractual obligations relating to:
        — wills and succession,
        — rights in property arising out of a matrimonial relationship,
        — rights and duties arising out of a family relationship, parentage, marriage or affinity, including maintenance obligations in respect of children who are not legitimate;
    (c) obligations arising under bills of exchange, cheques and promissory notes and other negotiable instruments to the extent that the obligations under such other negotiable instruments arise out of their negotiable character;
    (d) arbitration agreements and agreements on the choice of court;
    (e) questions governed by the law of companies and other bodies corporate or unincorporate such as the creation, by registration or otherwise, legal capacity, internal organization or winding up of companies and other bodies corporate or unincorporate and the personal liability of officers and members as such for the obligations of the company or body;
    (f) the question whether an agent is able to bind a principal, or an organ to bind a company or body corporate or unincorporate, to a third party;
    (g) the constitution of trusts and the relationship between settlors, trustees and beneficiaries;
    (h) evidence and procedure, without prejudice to Article 14.
3. The rules of this Convention do not apply to contracts of insurance which cover risks situated in the territories of the Member States of the European Economic Community. In order to determine whether a risk is situated in these territories the court shall apply its internal law.
4. The preceding paragraph does not apply to contracts of re-insurance.

Article 2
Application of law of non-contracting States

Any law specified by this Convention shall be applied whether or not it is the law of a Contracting State.

TITLE II
UNIFORM RULES

Article 3
Freedom of choice

1. A contract shall be governed by the law chosen by the parties. The choice must be expressed or demonstrated with reasonable certainty by the terms of the contract or the circumstances of the case. By their choice the parties can select the law applicable to the whole or a part only of the contract.
2. The parties may at any time agree to subject the contract to a law other than that which previously governed it, whether as a result of an earlier choice under this Article or of other provisions of this Convention. Any variation by the parties of the law to be applied made after the conclusion of the contract shall not prejudice its formal validity under Article 9 or adversely affect the rights of third parties.
3. The fact that the parties have chosen a foreign law, whether or not accompanied by the choice of a foreign tribunal, shall not, where all the other elements relevant to the situation at the time of the choice are connected with one country only, prejudice the application of rules of the law of that country which cannot be derogated from by contract, hereinafter called 'mandatory rules'.
4. The existence and validity of the consent of the parties as to the choice of the applicable law shall be determined in accordance with the provisions of Articles 8, 9 and 11.

Article 4
Applicable law in the absence of choice

1. To the extent that the law applicable to the contract has not been chosen in accordance with Article 3, the contract shall be governed by the law of the country with which it is most closely connected. Nevertheless, a severable part of the contract which has a closer connection with another country may by way of exception be governed by the law of that other country.
2. Subject to the provisions of paragraph 5 of this Article, it shall be presumed that the contract is most closely connected with the country where the party who is to effect the performance which is characteristic of the contract has, at the time of conclusion of the contract, his habitual residence, or, in the case of a body corporate or unincorporate, its central administration. However, if the contract is entered into in the course of that party's trade or profession, that country shall be the country in which the principal place of business is situated or, where under the terms of the contract the performance is to be effected through a place of business other than the principal place of business, the country in which that other place of business is situated.
3. Notwithstanding the provisions of paragraph 2 of this Article, to the extent that the subject matter of the contract is a right in immovable property or a right to use immovable property it shall be presumed that the contract is most closely connected with the country where the immovable property is situated.
4. A contract for the carriage of goods shall not be subject to the presumption in paragraph 2. In such a contract if the country in which, at the time the contract is concluded, the carrier has his principal place of business is also the country in which

the place of loading or the place of discharge or the principal place of business of the consignor is situated, it shall be presumed that the contract is most closely connected with that country. In applying this paragraph single voyage charter-parties and other contracts the main purpose of which is the carriage of goods shall be treated as contracts for the carriage of goods.

5. Paragraph 2 shall not apply if the characteristic performance cannot be determined, and the presumptions in paragraphs 2, 3 and 4 shall be disregarded if it appears from the circumstances as a whole that the contract is more closely connected with another country.

Article 5
Certain consumer contracts

1. This Article applies to a contract the object of which is the supply of goods or services to a person ('the consumer') for a purpose which can be regarded as being outside his trade or profession, or a contract for the provision of credit for that object.

2. Notwithstanding the provisions of Article 3, a choice of law made by the parties shall not have the result of depriving the consumer of the protection afforded to him by the mandatory rules of the law of the country in which he has his habitual residence:

   —if in that country the conclusion of the contract was preceded by a specific invitation addressed to him or by advertising, and he had taken in that country all the steps necessary on his part for the conclusion of the contract, or

   —if the other party or his agent received the consumer's order in that country, or

   —if the contract is for the sale of goods and the consumer travelled from that country to another country and there gave his order, provided that the consumer's journey was arranged by the seller for the purpose of inducing the consumer to buy.

3. Notwithstanding the provisions of Article 4, a contract to which this Article applies shall, in the absence of choice in accordance with Article 3, be governed by the law of the country in which the consumer has his habitual residence if it is entered into in the circumstances described in paragraph 2 of this Article.

4. This Article shall not apply to:

   (a) a contract of carriage;

   (b) a contract for the supply of services where the services are to be supplied to the consumer exclusively in a country other than that in which he has his habitual residence.

5. Notwithstanding the provisions of paragraph 4, this Article shall apply to a contract which, for an inclusive price, provides for a combination of travel and accommodation.

Article 6
Individual employment contracts

1. Notwithstanding the provisions of Article 3, in a contract of employment a choice of law made by the parties shall not have the result of depriving the employee of the protection afforded to him by the mandatory rules of the law which would be applicable under paragraph 2 in the absence of choice.

756

2. Notwithstanding the provisions of Article 4, a contract of employment shall, in the absence of choice in accordance with Article 3, be governed:

   (a) by the law of the country in which the employee habitually carries out his work in performance of the contract, even if he is temporarily employed in another country; or

   (b) if the employee does not habitually carry out his work in any one country, by the law of the country in which the place of business through which he was engaged is situated;

unless it appears from the circumstances as a whole that the contract is more closely connected with another country, in which case the contract shall be governed by the law of that country.

Article 7
Mandatory rules

1. When applying under this Convention the law of a country, effect may be given to the mandatory rules of the law of another country with which the situation has a close connection, if and in so far as, under the law of the latter country, those rules must be applied whatever the law applicable to the contract. In considering whether to give effect to these mandatory rules, regard shall be had to their nature and purpose and to the consequences of their application or non-application.

2. Nothing in this Convention shall restrict the application of the rules of the law of the forum in a situation where they are mandatory irrespective of the law otherwise applicable to the contract.

Article 8
Material validity

1. The existence and validity of a contract, or of any term of a contract, shall be determined by the law which would govern it under this Convention if the contract or term were valid.

2. Nevertheless a party may rely upon the law of the country in which he has his habitual residence to establish that he did not consent if it appears from the circumstances that it would not be reasonable to determine the effect of his conduct in accordance with the law specified in the preceding paragraph.

Article 9
Formal validity

1. A contract concluded between persons who are in the same country is formally valid if it satisfies the formal requirements of the law which governs it under this Convention or of the law of the country where it is concluded.

2. A contract concluded between persons who are in different countries is formally valid if it satisfies the formal requirements of the law which governs it under this Convention or of the law of one of those countries.

3. Where a contract is concluded by an agent, the country in which the agent acts is the relevant country for the purposes of paragraphs 1 and 2.

4. An act intended to have legal effect relating to an existing or contemplated contract is formally valid if it satisfies the formal requirements of the law which under this

Convention governs or would govern the contract or of the law of the country where the act was done.

5. The provisions of the preceding paragraphs shall not apply to a contract to which Article 5 applies, concluded in the circumstances described in paragraph 2 of Article. The formal validity of such a contract is governed by the law of the country in which the consumer has his habitual residence.

6. Notwithstanding paragraphs 1 to 4 of this Article, a contract the subject matter of which is a right in immovable property or a right to use immovable property shall be subject to the mandatory requirements of form of the law of the country where the property is situated if by that law those requirements are imposed irrespective of the country where the contract is concluded and irrespective of the law governing the contract.

Article 10
Scope of the applicable law

1. The law applicable to a contract by virtue of Articles 3 to 6 and 12 of this Convention shall govern in particular:
   (a) interpretation;
   (b) performance;
   (c) within the limits of the powers conferred on the court by its procedural law, the consequences of breach, including the assessment of damages in so far as it is governed by rules of law;
   (d) the various ways of extinguishing obligations, and prescription and limitation of actions;
   (e) the consequences of nullity of the contract.

2. In relation to the manner of performance and the steps to be taken in the event of defective performance regard shall be had to the law of the country in which performance takes place.

Article 11
Incapacity

In a contract concluded between persons who are in the same country, a natural person who would have capacity under the law of that country may invoke his incapacity resulting from another law only if the other party to the contract was aware of this incapacity at the time of the conclusion of the contract or was not aware thereof as a result of negligence.

Article 12
Voluntary assignment

1. The mutual obligations of assignor and assignee under a voluntary assignment of a right against another person ('the debtor') shall be governed by the law which under this Convention applies to the contract between the assignor and assignee.

2. The law governing the right to which the assignment relates shall determine its assignability, the relationship between the assignee and the debtor, the conditions under which the assignment can be invoked against the debtor and any question whether the debtor's obligations have been discharged.

Article 13
Subrogation

1. Where a person ('the creditor') has a contractual claim upon another ('the debtor'), and a third person has a duty to satisfy the creditor, or has in fact satisfied the creditor in discharge of that duty, the law which governs the third person's duty to satisfy the creditor shall determine whether the third person is entitled to exercise against the debtor the rights which the creditor had against the debtor under the law governing their relationship and, if so, whether he may do so in full or only to a limited extent.
2. The same rule applies where several persons are subject to the same contractual claim and one of them has satisfied the creditor.

Article 14
Burden of proof, etc.

1. The law governing the contract under this Convention applies to the extent that it contains, in the law of contract, rules which raise presumptions of law or determine the burden of proof.
2. A contract or an act intended to have legal effect may be proved by any mode of proof recognized by the law of the forum or by any of the laws referred to in Article 9 under which that contract or act is formally valid, provided that such mode of proof can be administered by the forum.

Article 15
Exclusion of renvoi

The application of the law of any country specified by this Convention means the application of the rules of law in force in that country other than its rules of private international law.

Article 16
'Ordre public'

The application of a rule of the law of any country specified by this Convention may be refused only if such application is manifestly incompatible with the public policy ('ordre public') of the forum.

Article 17
No retrospective effect

This Convention shall apply in a Contracting State to contracts made after the date on which this Convention has entered into force with respect to that State.

Article 18
Uniform interpretation

In the interpretation and application of the preceding uniform rules, regard shall be had to their international character and to the desirability of achieving uniformity in their interpretation and application.

Article 19
States with more than one legal system

1. Where a State comprises several territorial units each of which has its own rules of law in respect of contractual obligations, each territorial unit shall be considered as a country for the purposes of identifying the law applicable under this Convention.
2. A State within which different territorial units have their own rules of law in respect of contractual obligations shall not be bound to apply this Convention to conflicts solely between the laws of such units.

Article 20
Precedence of Community law

This Convention shall not affect the application of provisions which, in relation to particular matters, lay down choice of law rules relating to contractual obligations and which are or will be contained in acts of the institutions of the European Communities or in national laws harmonized in implementation of such acts.

Article 21
Relationship with other conventions

This Convention shall not prejudice the application of international conventions to which a Contracting State is, or becomes, a party.

Article 22
Reservations

1. Any Contracting State may, at the time of signature, ratification, acceptance or approval, reserve the right not to apply:
   (a) the provisions of Article 7 (1);
   (b) the provisions of Article 10 (1)(e).
2. ...[2]
3. Any Contracting State may at any time withdraw a reservation which it has made; the reservation shall cease to have effect on the first day of the third calendar month after notification of the withdrawal.

TITLE III
FINAL PROVISIONS

Article 23

1. If, after the date on which this Convention has entered into force for a Contracting State, that State wishes to adopt any new choice of law rule in regard to any particular category of contract within the scope of this Convention, it shall communicate its intention to the other signatory States through the Secretary-General of the Council of the European Communities.
2. Any signatory State may, within six months from the date of the communication made to the Secretary-General, request him to arrange consultations between signatory States in order to reach agreement.

---

[2] Paragraph deleted by Article 2(1) of the 1992 Accession Convention.

3. If no signatory State has requested consultations within this period or if within two years following the communication made to the Secretary-General no agreement is reached in the course of consultations, the Contracting State concerned may amend its law in the manner indicated. The measures taken by that State shall be brought to the knowledge of the other signatory States through the Secretary-General of the Council of the European Communities.

Article 24

1. If, after the date on which this Convention has entered into force with respect to a Contracting State, that State wishes to become a party to a multilateral convention whose principal aim or one of whose principal aims is to lay down rules of private international law concerning any of the matters governed by this Convention, the procedure set out in Article 23 shall apply. However, the period of two years, referred to in paragraph 3 of that Article, shall be reduced to one year.
2. The procedure referred to in the preceding paragraph need not be followed if a Contracting State or one of the European Communities is already a party to the multilateral convention, or if its object is to revise a convention to which the State concerned is already a party, or if it is a convention concluded within the framework of the Treaties establishing the European Communities.

Article 25

If a Contracting State considers that the unification achieved by this Convention is prejudiced by the conclusion of agreements not covered by Article 24 (1), that State may request the Secretary-General of the Council of the European Communities to arrange consultations between the signatory States of this Convention.

Article 26

Any Contracting State may request the revision of this Convention. In this event a revision conference shall be convened by the President of the Council of the European Communities.

Article 27[3]

. . .

Article 28

1. This Convention shall be open from 19 June 1980 for signature by the States party to the Treaty establishing the European Economic Community.
2. This Convention shall be subject to ratification, acceptance or approval by the signatory States. The instruments of ratification, acceptance or approval shall be deposited with the Secretary-General of the Council of the European Communities.[4]

---

[3] Article deleted by Article 2 (1) of the 1992 Accession Convention.
[4] Ratification of the Accession Conventions is governed by the following provisions of those conventions:

Article 29[5]

1. This Convention shall enter into force on the first day of the third month following the deposit of the seventh instrument of ratification, acceptance or approval.
2. This Convention shall enter into force for each signatory State ratifying, accepting or approving at a later date on the first day of the third month following the deposit of its instrument of ratification, acceptance or approval.

— as regards the 1984 Accession Convention, by Article 3 of that Convention, which reads as follows:
'Article 3
This Convention shall be ratified by the signatory States. The instruments of ratification shall be deposited with the Secretary-General of the Council of the European Communities.',
— as regards the 1992 Accession Convention, by Article 4 of that Convention, which reads as follows:
'Article 4
This Convention shall be ratified by the signatory States. The instruments of ratification shall be deposited with the Secretary-General of the Council of the European Communities.',
— as regards the 1996 Accession Convention, by Article 5 of that Convention, which reads as follows:
'Article 5
This Convention shall be ratified by the signatory States. The instruments of ratification shall be deposited with the Secretary-General of the Council of the European Union.'.

[5] The entry into force of the Accession Conventions is governed by the following provisions of those Conventions:
— as regards the 1984 Accession Convention, by Article 4 of that Convention, which reads as follows:
'Article 4
This Convention shall enter into force, as between the States which have ratified it, on the first day of the third month following the deposit of the last instrument of ratification by the Hellenic Republic and seven States which have ratified the Convention on the law applicable to contractual obligations.
This Convention shall enter into force for each Contracting State which subsequently ratifies it on the first day of the third month following the deposit of its instrument of ratification.',
— as regards the 1992 Accession Convention, by Article 5 of that Convention which reads as follows:
'Article 5
This Convention shall enter into force, as between the States which have ratified it, on the first day of the third month following the deposit of the last instrument of ratification by the Kingdom of Spain or the Portuguese Republic and by one State which has ratified the Convention on the law applicable to contractual obligations.
This Convention shall enter into force for each Contracting State which subsequently ratifies it on the first day of the third month following the deposit of its instrument of ratification.',
— as regards the 1996 Accession Convention, by Article 6 of that Convention, which reads as follows:
'Article 6
1. This Convention shall enter into force, as between the States which have ratified it, on the first day of the third month following the deposit of the last instrument of ratification by the Republic of Austria, the Republic of Finland or the Kingdom of Sweden and by one Contracting State which has ratified the Convention on the law applicable to contractual obligations.
2. This Convention shall enter into force for each Contracting State which subsequently ratifies it on the first day of the third month following the deposit of its instrument of ratification.'

Article 30

1. This Convention shall remain in force for 10 years from the date of its entry into force in accordance with Article 29(1), even for States for which it enters into force at a later date.
2. If there has been no denunciation it shall be renewed tacitly every five years.
3. A Contracting State which wishes to denounce shall, not less than six months before the expiration of the period of 10 or five years, as the case may be, give notice to the Secretary-General of the Council of the European Communities. Denunciation may be limited to any territory to which the Convention has been extended by a declaration under Article 27 (2).[6]
4. The denunciation shall have effect only in relation to the State which has notified it. The Convention will remain in force as between all other Contracting States.

Article 31[7]

The Secretary-General of the Council of the European Communities shall notify the States party to the Treaty establishing the European Economic Community of:
    (a) the signatures;
    (b) the deposit of each instrument of ratification, acceptance or approval;
    (c) the date of entry into force of this Convention;
    (d) communications made in pursuance of Articles 23, 24, 25, 26 and 30;[8]
    (e) the reservations and withdrawals of reservations referred to in Article 22.

Article 32

The Protocol annexed to this Convention shall form an integral part thereof.

---

[6] Phrase deleted by the 1992 Accession Convention.

[7] Notification concerning the Accession Convention is governed by the following provisions of those Conventions:
—as regards the 1984 Accession Convention, by Article 5 of that Convention, which reads as follows:
'Article 5
The Secretary-General of the Council of the European Communities shall notify Signatory States of:
(a) the deposit of each instrument of ratification;
(b) the dates of entry into force of this Convention for the Contracting States.',
—as regards the 1992 Accession Convention, by Article 6 of that Convention, which reads as follows:
'Article 6
The Secretary-General of the Council of the European Communities shall notify the signatory States of:
(a) the deposit of each instrument of ratification;
(b) the dates of entry into force of this Convention for the Contracting States.',
—as regards the 1996 Accession Convention, by Article 7 of that Convention, which reads as follows:
'Article 7
The Secretary-General of the Council of the European Union shall notify the signatory States of:
(a) the deposit of each instrument of ratification;
(b) the dates of entry into force of this Convention for the Contracting States.'

[8] Point (d) as amended by the 1992 Accession Convention.

Article 33[9]

This Convention, drawn up in a single original in the Danish, Dutch, English, French, German, Irish and Italian languages, these texts being equally authentic, shall be deposited in the archives of the Secretariat of the Council of the European Communities. The Secretary-General shall transmit a certified copy thereof to the Government of each signatory State.

---

[9] An indication of the authentic texts of the Accession Convention is to be found in the following provisions:

—as regards the 1984 Accession Convention, in Articles 2 and 6 of that Convention, which reads as follows:

'Article 2

The Secretary-General of the Council of the European Communities shall transmit a certified copy of the Convention on the law applicable to contractual obligations in the Danish, Dutch, English, French, German, Irish and Italian languages to the Government of the Hellenic Republic.

The text of the Convention on the law applicable to contractual obligations in the Greek language is annexed hereto. The text in the Greek language shall be authentic under the same conditions as the other texts of the Convention on the law applicable to contractual obligations.'

'Article 6

This Convention, drawn up in a single original in the Danish, Dutch, English, French, German, Greek, Irish and Italian languages, all eight texts being equally authentic, shall be deposited in the archives of the General Secretariat of the Council of the European Communities. The Secretary-General shall transmit a certified copy to the Government of each Signatory State.',

— as regards the 1992 Accession Convention, in Articles 3 and 7 of that Convention, which read as follows:

'Article 3

The Secretary-General of the Council of the European Communities shall transmit a certified copy of the Convention on the law applicable to contractual obligations in the Danish, Dutch, English, French, German, Greek, Irish and Italian languages to the Governments of the Kingdom of Spain and the Portuguese Republic.

The text of the Convention on the law applicable to contractual obligations in the Portuguese and Spanish languages is set out in Annexes I and II to this Convention. The texts drawn up in the Portuguese and Spanish languages shall be authentic under the same conditions as the other texts of the Convention on the law applicable to contractual obligations.'

'Article 7

This Convention, drawn up in a single original in the Danish, Dutch, English, French, German, Greek, Irish, Italian, Portuguese and Spanish languages, all texts being equally authentic, shall be deposited in the archives of the General Secretariat of the Council of the European Communities. The Secretary-General shall transmit a certified copy to the Government of each Signatory State.',

— as regards the 1996 Accession Convention, in Articles 4 and 8 of that Convention, which read as follows:

'Article 4

1. The Secretary-General of the Council of the European Union shall transmit a certified copy of the Convention of 1980, the Convention of 1984, the First Protocol of 1988, the Second Protocol of 1988 and the Convention of 1992 in the Danish, Dutch, English, French, German, Greek, Irish, Italian, Spanish and Portuguese languages to the Governments of the Republic of Austria, the Republic of Finland and the Kingdom of Sweden.

2. The text of the Convention of 1980, the Convention of 1984, the First Protocol of 1988, the Second Protocol of 1988 and the Convention of 1992 in the Finnish and Swedish languages

In witness whereof the undersigned, being duly authorized thereto, have signed this Convention.

Done at Rome on the nineteenth day of June in the year one thousand nine hundred and eighty.

PROTOCOL[10]

The High Contracting Parties have agreed upon the following provision which shall be annexed to the Convention:

'Notwithstanding the provisions of the Convention, Denmark, Sweden and Finland may retain national provisions concerning the law applicable to questions relating to the carriage of goods by sea and may amend such provisions without following the procedure provided for in Article 23 of the Convention of Rome. The national provisions applicable in this respect are the following:

—in Denmark, paragraphs 252 and 321(3) and (4) of the 'Sølov' (maritime law),

—in Sweden, Chapter 13, Article 2(1) and (2), and Chapter 14, Article 1(3), of 'sjölagen' (maritime law),

—in Finland, Chapter 13, Article 2(1) and (2), and Chapter 14, Article 1(3), of 'merilaki'/'sjölagen' (maritime law).'

In witness whereof the undersigned, being duly authorized thereto, have signed this Protocol.

Done at Rome on the nineteenth day of June in the year one thousand nine hundred and eighty.

[Signatures of the Plenipotentiaries]

JOINT DECLARATION

At the time of the signature of the Convention on the law applicable to contractual obligations, the Governments of the Kingdom of Belgium, the Kingdom of Denmark, the Federal Republic of Germany, the French Republic, Ireland, the Italian Republic, the Grand Duchy of Luxembourg, the Kingdom of the Netherlands and the United Kingdom of Great Britain and Northern Ireland,

---

shall be authentic under the same conditions as the other texts of the Convention of 1980, the Convention of 1984, the First Protocol of 1988, the Second Protocol of 1988 and the Convention of 1992.'

'Article 8

This Convention, drawn up in a single original in the Danish, Dutch, English, Finnish, French, German, Greek, Irish, Italian, Portuguese, Spanish and Swedish languages, all 12 texts being equally authentic, shall be deposited in the archives of the General Secretariat of the Council of the European Union. The Secretary-General shall transmit a certified copy to the Government of each signatory State.'

[10] Text as amended by the 1996 Accession Convention.

I.   anxious to avoid, as far as possible, dispersion of choice of law rules among several instruments and differences between these rules, express the wish that the institutions of the European Communities, in the exercise of their powers under the Treaties by which they were established, will, where the need arises, endeavour to adopt choice of law rules which are as far as possible consistent with those of this Convention;

II.   declare their intention as from the date of signature of this Convention until becoming bound by Article 24, to consult with each other if any one of the signatory States wishes to become a party to any convention to which the procedure referred to in Article 24 would apply;

III. having regard to the contribution of the Convention on the law applicable to contractual obligations to the unification of choice of law rules within the European Communities, express the view that any State which becomes a member of the European Communities should accede to this Convention.

In witness whereof the undersigned, being duly authorized thereto, have signed this Joint Declaration.

Done at Rome on the nineteenth day of June in the year one thousand nine hundred and eighty.

[Signatures of the Plenipotentiaries]

JOINT DECLARATION

The Governments of the Kingdom of Belgium, the Kingdom of Denmark, the Federal Republic of Germany, the French Republic, Ireland, the Italian Republic, the Grand Duchy of Luxembourg, the Kingdom of the Netherlands and the United Kingdom of Great Britain and Northern Ireland,
On signing the Convention on the law applicable to contractual obligations;
Desiring to ensure that the Convention is applied as effectively as possible;
Anxious to prevent differences of interpretation of the Convention from impairing its unifying effect;
Declare themselves ready:

1. to examine the possibility of conferring jurisdiction in certain matters on the Court of Justice of the European Communities and, if necessary, to negotiate an agreement to this effect;

2. to arrange meetings at regular intervals between their representatives.

In witness whereof the undersigned, being duly authorized thereto, have signed this Joint Declaration.

Done at Rome on the nineteenth day of June in the year one thousand nine hundred and eighty.

[Signatures of the Plenipotentiaries]

TABLE OF STATE RATIFICATIONS

Total number of signatures not followed by ratifications:
Total number of ratifications/accessions: 15

State	Signature	Ratification	By	Entry into force
Austria		29 November 1996	Accession	1 February 1997
Belgium		31 July 1987		1 April 1991
Denmark		7 January 1986		1 April 1991
Finland		29 November 1996	Accession	1 February 1997
France		3 October 1983		1 April 1991
Germany		8 January 1987		1 April 1991
Greece		29 September 1988	Accession	1 April 1991
Ireland		29 October 1991		1 January 1992
Italy		25 June 1985		1 April 1991
Luxembourg		1 October 1986		1 April 1991
Netherlands		21 June 1991		1 September 1991
Portugal		1 July 1994	Accession	1 October 1994
Spain		1 September 1993	Accession	1 December 1993
Sweden		29 November 1996	Accession	1 February 1997
United Kingdom		29 January 1991		1 April 1991

Entered into force: 1 April 1991

(Condition: 7 ratifications)

Note: A list of reservations and declarations made by States has not been included in the text. These can be obtained from http://www.rome-convention.org/.

(iv) INTER-AMERICAN CONVENTION ON THE LAW APPLICABLE TO INTERNATIONAL CONTRACTS*

Signed at Mexico, D.F., Mexico, on March 17, 1994,
at the Fifth Inter-American Specialized Conference on
Private International Law (CIDIP-V)

The States Parties to this Convention,

Reaffirming their desire to continue the progressive development and codification of private international law among member States of the Organization of American States;

Reasserting the advisability of harmonizing solutions to international trade issues;

Bearing in mind that the economic interdependence of States has fostered regional integration and that in order to stimulate the process it is necessary to facilitate international contracts by removing differences in the legal framework for them,

---

* Reproduced with the kind permission of the Organization of American States.

Have agreed to approve the following Convention:

CHAPTER I
SCOPE OF APPLICATION

Article 1

This Convention shall determine the law applicable to international contracts.

It shall be understood that a contract is international if the parties thereto have their habitual residence or establishments in different States Parties or if the contract has objective ties with more than one State Party.

This Convention shall apply to contracts entered into or contracts to which States or State agencies or entities are party, unless the parties to the contract expressly exclude it. However, any State Party may, at the time it signs, ratifies or accedes to this Convention, declare that the latter shall not apply to all or certain categories of contracts to which the State or State agencies and entities are party.

Any State Party may, at the time it ratifies or accedes to this Convention, declare the categories of contract to which this Convention will not apply.

Article 2

The law designated by the Convention shall be applied even if said law is that of a State that is not a party.

Article 3

The provisions of this Convention shall be applied, with necessary and possible adaptations, to the new modalities of contracts used as a consequence of the development of international trade.

Article 4

For purposes of interpretation and application of this Convention, its international nature and the need to promote uniformity in its application shall be taken into account.

Article 5

This Convention does not determine the law applicable to:
  a) questions arising from the marital status of natural persons, the capacity of the parties, or the consequences of nullity or invalidity of the contract as a result of the lack of capacity of one of the parties;
  b) contractual obligations intended for successional questions, testamentary questions, marital arrangements or those deriving from family relationships;
  c) obligations deriving from securities;
  d) obligations deriving from securities transactions;
  e) the agreements of the parties concerning arbitration or selection of forum;
  f) questions of company law, including the existence, capacity, function and dissolution of commercial companies and juridical persons in general

Article 6

The provisions of this Convention shall not be applicable to contracts which have autonomous regulations in international conventional law in force among the States Parties to this Convention.

CHAPTER 2
DETERMINATION OF APPLICABLE LAW

Article 7

The contract shall be governed by the law chosen by the parties. The parties' agreement on this selection must be express or, in the event that there is no express agreement, must be evident from the parties' behavior and from the clauses of the contract, considered as a whole. Said selection may relate to the entire contract or to a part of same.

Selection of a certain forum by the parties does not necessarily entail selection of the applicable law.

Article 8

The parties may at any time agree that the contract shall, in whole or in part, be subject to a law other than that to which it was previously subject, whether or not that law was chosen by the parties. Nevertheless, that modification shall not affect the formal validity of the original contract nor the rights of third parties.

Article 9

If the parties have not selected the applicable law, or if their selection proves ineffective, the contract shall be governed by the law of the State with which it has the closest ties.

The Court will take into account all objective and subjective elements of the contract to determine the law of the State with which it has the closest ties. It shall also take into account the general principles of international commercial law recognized by international organizations.

Nevertheless, if a part of the contract were separable from the rest and if it had a closer tie with another State, the law of that State could, exceptionally, apply to that part of the contract.

Article 10

In addition to the provisions in the foregoing articles, the guidelines, customs, and principles of international commercial law as well as commercial usage and practices generally accepted shall apply in order to discharge the requirements of justice and equity in the particular case.

Article 11

Notwithstanding the provisions of the preceding articles, the provisions of the law of the forum shall necessarily be applied when they are mandatory requirements.

It shall be up to the forum to decide when it applies the mandatory provisions of the law of another State with which the contract has close ties.

CHAPTER 3
EXISTENCE AND VALIDITY OF THE CONTRACT

Article 12

The existence and the validity of the contract or of any of its provisions, and the substantive validity of the consent of the parties concerning the selection of the applicable law, shall be governed by the appropriate rules in accordance with Chapter 2 of this Convention.

Nevertheless, to establish that one of the parties has not duly consented, the judge shall determine the applicable law, taking into account the habitual residence or principal place of business.

Article 13

A contract between parties in the same State shall be valid as to form if it meets the requirements laid down in the law governing said contract pursuant to this Convention or with those of the law of the State in which the contract is valid or with the law of the place where the contract is performed.

If the persons concerned are in different States at the time of its conclusion, the contract shall be valid as to form if it meets the requirements of the law governing it as to substance, or those of the law of one of the States in which it is concluded or with the law of the place where the contract is performed.

CHAPTER 4
SCOPE OF THE APPLICABLE LAW

Article 14

The law applicable to the contract in virtue of Chapter 2 of this Convention shall govern principally:
   a) its interpretation;
   b) the rights and obligations of the parties;
   c) the performance of the obligations established by the contract and the consequences of nonperformance of the contract, including assessment of injury to the extent that this may determine payment of compensation;
   d) the various ways in which the obligations can be performed, and prescription and lapsing of actions;
   e) the consequences of nullity or invalidity of the contract.

Article 15

The provisions of Article 10 shall be taken into account when deciding whether an agent can obligate its principal or an agency, a company or a juridical person.

Article 16

The law of the State where international contracts are to be registered or published shall govern all matters concerning publicity in respect of same.

Article 17

For the purposes of this Convention, 'law' shall be understood to mean the law current in a State, excluding rules concerning conflict of laws.

Article 18

Application of the law designated by this Convention may only be excluded when it is manifestly contrary to the public order of the forum.

CHAPTER 5
GENERAL PROVISIONS

Article 19

In a State Party, the provisions of this Convention shall apply to contracts concluded subsequent to its entry into force in that State.

Article 20

This Convention shall not affect the application of other international conventions to which a State Party to this Convention is or becomes a party, insofar as they are pertinent, or those concluded within the context of integration movements.

Article 21

When signing, ratifying or acceding to this Convention, States may formulate reservations that apply to one or more specific provisions and which are not incompatible with the effect and purpose of this Convention.

A State Party may at any time withdraw a reservation it has formulated. The effect of such reservation shall cease on the first day of the third calendar month following the date of notification of withdrawal.

Article 22

In the case of a State which has two or more systems of law applicable in different territorial units with respect to matters covered by the Convention:
   a) any reference to the laws of the State shall be construed as a reference to the laws in the territorial unit in question;
   b) any reference to habitual residence or place of business in that State shall be construed as a reference to habitual residence or place of business in a territorial unit of that State.

Article 23

A State within which different territorial units have their own systems of law in regard to matters covered by this Convention shall not be obliged to apply this Convention to conflicts between the legal systems in force in such units.

Article 24

If a State has two or more territorial units in which different systems of law apply in relation to the matters dealt with in this Convention, it may, at the time of signature, ratification or accession, declare that this Convention shall extend to all its territorial units or to only one or more of them.

Such declaration may be modified by subsequent declarations, which shall expressly indicate the territorial unit or units to which the Convention applies. Such subsequent declarations shall be transmitted to the General Secretariat of the Organization of American States, and shall take effect ninety days after the date of their receipt.

CHAPTER 6
FINAL CLAUSES

Article 25

This Convention shall be open to signature by the member States of the Organization of American States.

Article 26

This Convention shall be subject to ratification. The instruments of ratification shall be deposited with the General Secretariat of the Organization of American States.

Article 27

This Convention shall remain open for accession by any other State after it has entered into force. The instruments of accession shall be deposited with the General Secretariat of the Organization of American States.

Article 28

This Convention shall enter into force for the ratifying States on the thirtieth day following the date of deposit of the second instrument of ratification.

For each State ratifying or acceding to the Convention after the deposit of the second instrument of ratification, the Convention shall enter into force on the thirtieth day after deposit by such State of its instrument of ratification or accession.

Article 29

This Convention shall remain in force indefinitely, but any of the States Parties may denounce it. The instrument of denunciation shall be deposited with the General Secretariat of the Organization of American States. After one year from the date of deposit of the instrument of denunciation, the Convention shall no longer be in force for the denouncing State.

Article 30

The original instrument of this Convention, the English, French, Portuguese and Spanish texts of which are equally authentic, shall be deposited with the General Secretariat of the Organization of American States, which shall forward an authenticated copy of its text to

773

the Secretariat of the United Nations for registration and publication in accordance with Article 102 of its Charter. The General Secretariat of the Organization of American States shall notify the Member States of the Organization and the States that have acceded to the Convention of the signatures, deposits of instruments of ratification, accession and denunciation, as well as of reservations, if any, and of their withdrawal.

In witness whereof the undersigned Plenipotentiaries, being duly authorized thereto by their respective Governments, do hereby sign the present Convention.

Done at Mexico, D.F., Mexico, this seventeenth day of March, one thousand nine hundred and ninety-four.

TABLE OF STATE RATIFICATIONS

Total number of signatures not followed by ratifications:	3
Total number of ratifications/accessions:	2

Mexico, 17 March 1994
Entered into force: 15 December1996
(Condition: 2 ratifications)

State	Signature	Ratification	By	Entry into force
Bolivia	17 March 1994			
Brazil	17 March 1994			
Mexico	27 November 1995	15 November 1996		15 December 1996
Uruguay	17 March 1994			
Venezuela	17 March 1994	26 October 1995		15 December 1996

Source: http://www.oas.org/juridico/english/treaties.html

(v) CONVENTION ON THE LAW APPLICABLE TO CERTAIN RIGHTS IN RESPECT OF SECURITIES HELD WITH AN INTERMEDIARY*

PREAMBLE

The States signatory to the present Convention,

Aware of the urgent practical need in a large and growing global financial market to provide legal certainty and predictability as to the law applicable to securities that are now commonly held through clearing and settlement systems or other intermediaries,

Conscious of the importance of reducing legal risk, systemic risk and associated costs in relation to cross-border transactions involving securities held with an intermediary so as to facilitate the international flow of capital and access to capital markets,

Desiring to establish common provisions on the law applicable to securities held with an intermediary beneficial to States at all levels of economic development,

Recognising that the 'Place of the Relevant Intermediary Approach' (or PRIMA) as determined by account agreements with intermediaries provides the necessary legal certainty and predictability,

---

* Reproduced with the kind permission of the Hague Conference on Private International Law.

Have resolved to conclude a Convention to this effect, and have agreed upon the following provisions—

CHAPTER I
DEFINITIONS AND SCOPE OF APPLICATION

Article 1
Definitions and interpretation

1. In this Convention—
   a) 'securities' means any shares, bonds or other financial instruments or financial assets (other than cash), or any interest therein;
   b) 'securities account' means an account maintained by an intermediary to which securities may be credited or debited;
   c) 'intermediary' means a person that in the course of a business or other regular activity maintains securities accounts for others or both for others and for its own account and is acting in that capacity;
   d) 'account holder' means a person in whose name an intermediary maintains a securities account;
   e) 'account agreement' means, in relation to a securities account, the agreement with the relevant intermediary governing that securities account;
   f) 'securities held with an intermediary' means the rights of an account holder resulting from a credit of securities to a securities account;
   g) 'relevant intermediary' means the intermediary that maintains the securities account for the account holder;
   h) 'disposition' means any transfer of title whether outright or by way of security and any grant of a security interest, whether possessory or non-possessory;
   i) 'perfection' means completion of any steps necessary to render a disposition effective against persons who are not parties to that disposition;
   j) 'office' means, in relation to an intermediary, a place of business at which any of the activities of the intermediary are carried on, excluding a place of business which is intended to be merely temporary and a place of business of any person other than the intermediary;
   k) 'insolvency proceeding' means a collective judicial or administrative proceeding, including an interim proceeding, in which the assets and affairs of the debtor are subject to control or supervision by a court or other competent authority for the purpose of reorganisation or liquidation;
   l) 'insolvency administrator' means a person authorised to administer a reorganisation or liquidation, including one authorised on an interim basis, and includes a debtor in possession if permitted by the applicable insolvency law;
   m) 'Multi-unit State' means a State within which two or more territorial units of that State, or both the State and one or more of its territorial units, have their own rules of law in respect of any of the issues specified in Article 2(1);
   n) 'writing' and 'written' mean a record of information (including information communicated by teletransmission) which is in tangible or other form and is capable of being reproduced in tangible form on a subsequent occasion.

2. References in this Convention to a disposition of securities held with an intermediary include—
   a) a disposition of a securities account;
   b) a disposition in favour of the account holder's intermediary;
   c) a lien by operation of law in favour of the account holder's intermediary in respect of any claim arising in connection with the maintenance and operation of a securities account.
3. A person shall not be considered an intermediary for the purposes of this Convention merely because—
   a) it acts as registrar or transfer agent for an issuer of securities; or
   b) it records in its own books details of securities credited to securities accounts maintained by an intermediary in the names of other persons for whom it acts as manager or agent or otherwise in a purely administrative capacity.
4. Subject to paragraph (5), a person shall be regarded as an intermediary for the purposes of this Convention in relation to securities which are credited to securities accounts which it maintains in the capacity of a central securities depository or which are otherwise transferable by book entry across securities accounts which it maintains.
5. In relation to securities which are credited to securities accounts maintained by a person in the capacity of operator of a system for the holding and transfer of such securities on records of the issuer or other records which constitute the primary record of entitlement to them as against the issuer, the Contracting State under whose law those securities are constituted may, at any time, make a declaration that the person which operates that system shall not be an intermediary for the purposes of this Convention.

Article 2
Scope of the Convention and of the applicable law

1. This Convention determines the law applicable to the following issues in respect of securities held with an intermediary—
   a) the legal nature and effects against the intermediary and third parties of the rights resulting from a credit of securities to a securities account;
   b) the legal nature and effects against the intermediary and third parties of a disposition of securities held with an intermediary;
   c) the requirements, if any, for perfection of a disposition of securities held with an intermediary;
   d) whether a person's interest in securities held with an intermediary extinguishes or has priority over another person's interest;
   e) the duties, if any, of an intermediary to a person other than the account holder who asserts in competition with the account holder or another person an interest in securities held with that intermediary;
   f) the requirements, if any, for the realisation of an interest in securities held with an intermediary;
   g) whether a disposition of securities held with an intermediary extends to entitlements to dividends, income, or other distributions, or to redemption, sale or other proceeds.

2. This Convention determines the law applicable to the issues specified in paragraph (1) in relation to a disposition of or an interest in securities held with an intermediary even if the rights resulting from the credit of those securities to a securities account are determined in accordance with paragraph (1)(a) to be contractual in nature.

3. Subject to paragraph (2), this Convention does not determine the law applicable to—

   a) the rights and duties arising from the credit of securities to a securities account to the extent that such rights or duties are purely contractual or otherwise purely personal;

   b) the contractual or other personal rights and duties of parties to a disposition of securities held with an intermediary; or

   c) the rights and duties of an issuer of securities or of an issuer's registrar or transfer agent, whether in relation to the holder of the securities or any other person.

Article 3
Internationality

This Convention applies in all cases involving a choice between the laws of different States.

CHAPTER II
APPLICABLE LAW

Article 4
Primary rule

1. The law applicable to all the issues specified in Article 2(1) is the law in force in the State expressly agreed in the account agreement as the State whose law governs the account agreement or, if the account agreement expressly provides that another law is applicable to all such issues, that other law. The law designated in accordance with this provision applies only if the relevant intermediary has, at the time of the agreement, an office in that State, which—

   a) alone or together with other offices of the relevant intermediary or with other persons acting for the relevant intermediary in that or another State—

      i)   effects or monitors entries to securities accounts;

      ii) administers payments or corporate actions relating to securities held with the intermediary; or

      iii) is otherwise engaged in a business or other regular activity of maintaining securities accounts; or

   b) is identified by an account number, bank code, or other specific means of identification as maintaing securities accounts in that State.

2. For the purposes of paragraph (1)(a), an office is not engaged in a business or other regular activity of maintaining securities accounts—

   a) merely because it is a place where the technology supporting the bookkeeping or data processing for securities accounts is located;

   b) merely because it is a place where call centres for communication with account holders are located or operated;

    c) merely because it is a place where the mailing relating to securities accounts is organised or files or archives are located; or

    d) if it engages solely in representational functions or administrative functions, other than those related to the opening or maintenance of securities accounts, and does not have authority to make any binding decision to enter into any account agreement.

3. In relation to a disposition by an account holder of securities held with a particular intermediary in favour of that intermediary, whether or not that intermediary maintains a securities account on its own records for which it is the account holder, for the purposes of this Convention—

    a) that intermediary is the relevant intermediary;

    b) the account agreement between the account holder and that intermediary is the relevant account agreement;

    c) the securities account for the purposes of Article 5(2) and (3) is the securities account to which the securities are credited immediately before the disposition.

Article 5
Fall-back rules

1. If the applicable law is not determined under Article 4, but it is expressly and unambiguously stated in a written account agreement that the relevant intermediary entered into the account agreement through a particular office, the law applicable to all the issues specified in Article 2(1) is the law in force in the State, or the territorial unit of a Multi-unit State, in which that office was then located, provided that such office then satisfied the condition specified in the second sentence of Article 4(1). In determining whether an account agreement expressly and unambiguously states that the relevant intermediary entered into the account agreement through a particular office, none of the following shall be considered—

    a) a provision that notices or other documents shall or may be served on the relevant intermediary at that office;

    b) a provision that legal proceedings shall or may be instituted against the relevant intermediary in a particular State or in a particular territorial unit of a Multi-unit State;

    c) a provision that any statement or other document shall or may be provided by the relevant intermediary from that office;

    d) a provision that any service shall or may be provided by the relevant intermediary from that office;

    e) a provision that any operation or function shall or may be carried on or performed by the relevant intermediary at that office.

2. If the applicable law is not determined under paragraph (1), that law is the law in force in the State, or the territorial unit of a Multi-unit State, under whose law the relevant intermediary is incorporated or otherwise organised at the time the written account agreement is entered into or, if there is no such agreement, at the time the securities account was opened; if, however, the relevant intermediary is incorporated or otherwise organised under the law of a Multi-unit State and not that of one of its

territorial units, the applicable law is the law in force in the territorial unit of that Multi-unit State in which the relevant intermediary has its place of business, or, if the relevant intermediary has more than one place of business, its principal place of business, at the time the written account agreement is entered into or, if there is no such agreement, at the time the securities account was opened.

3. If the applicable law is not determined under either paragraph (1) or paragraph (2), that law is the law in force in the State, or the territorial unit of a Multi-unit State, in which the relevant intermediary has its place of business, or, if the relevant intermediary has more than one place of business, its principal place of business, at the time the written account agreement is entered into or, if there is no such agreement, at the time the securities account was opened.

Article 6
Factors to be disregarded

In determining the applicable law in accordance with this Convention, no account shall be taken of the following factors—

a) the place where the issuer of the securities is incorporated or otherwise organised or has its statutory seat or registered office, central administration or place or principal place of business;

b) the places where certificates representing or evidencing securities are located;

c) the place where a register of holders of securities maintained by or on behalf of the issuer of the securities is located; or

d) the place where any intermediary other than the relevant intermediary is located.

Article 7
Protection of rights on change of the applicable law

1. This Article applies if an account agreement is amended so as to change the applicable law under this Convention.

2. In this Article—

a) 'the new law' means the law applicable under this Convention after the change;

b) 'the old law' means the law applicable under this Convention before the change.

3. Subject to paragraph (4), the new law governs all the issues specified in Article 2(1).

4. Except with respect to a person who has consented to a change of law, the old law continues to govern—

a) the existence of an interest in securities held with an intermediary arising before the change of law and the perfection of a disposition of those securities made before the change of law;

b) with respect to an interest in securities held with an intermediary arising before the change of law—

   i) the legal nature and effects of such an interest against the relevant intermediary and any party to a disposition of those securities made before the change of law;

   ii) the legal nature and effects of such an interest against a person who after the change of law attaches the securities;

iii) the determination of all the issues specified in Article 2(1) with respect to an insolvency administrator in an insolvency proceeding opened after the change of law;

c) priority as between parties whose interests arose before the change of law.

5. Paragraph (4)(c) does not preclude the application of the new law to the priority of an interest that arose under the old law but is perfected under the new law.

Article 8
Insolvency

1. Notwithstanding the opening of an insolvency proceeding, the law applicable under this Convention governs all the issues specified in Article 2(1) with respect to any event that has occurred before the opening of that insolvency proceeding.
2. Nothing in this Convention affects the application of any substantive or procedural insolvency rules, including any rules relating to—
   a) the ranking of categories of claim or the avoidance of a disposition as a preference or a transfer in fraud of creditors; or
   b) the enforcement of rights after the opening of an insolvency proceeding.

CHAPTER III
GENERAL PROVISIONS

Article 9
General applicability of the Convention

This Convention applies whether or not the applicable law is that of a Contracting State.

Article 10
Exclusion of choice of law rules (renvoi)

In this Convention, the term 'law' means the law in force in a State other than its choice of law rules.

Article 11
Public policy and internationally mandatory rules

1. The application of the law determined under this Convention may be refused only if the effects of its application would be manifestly contrary to the public policy of the forum.
2. This Convention does not prevent the application of those provisions of the law of the forum which, irrespective of rules of conflict of laws, must be applied even to international situations.
3. This Article does not permit the application of provisions of the law of the forum imposing requirements with respect to perfection or relating to priorities between competing interests, unless the law of the forum is the applicable law under this Convention.

Article 12
Determination of the applicable law for Multi-unit States

1. If the account holder and the relevant intermediary have agreed on the law of a specified territorial unit of a Multi-unit State—
   a) the references to 'State' in the first sentence of Article 4(1) are to that territorial unit;
   b) the references to 'that State' in the second sentence of Article 4(1) are to the Multi-unit State itself.
2. In applying this Convention—
   a) the law in force in a territorial unit of a Multi-unit State includes both the law of that unit and, to the extent applicable in that unit, the law of the Multi-unit State itself;
   b) if the law in force in a territorial unit of a Multi-unit State designates the law of another territorial unit of that State to govern perfection by public filing, recording or registration, the law of that other territorial unit governs that issue.
3. A Multi-unit State may, at the time of signature, ratification, acceptance, approval or accession, make a declaration that if, under Article 5, the applicable law is that of the Multi-unit State or one of its territorial units, the internal choice of law rules in force in that Multi-unit State shall determine whether the substantive rules of law of that Multi-unit State or of a particular territorial unit of that Multi-unit State shall apply. A Multi-unit State that makes such a declaration shall communicate information concerning the content of those internal choice of law rules to the Permanent Bureau of the Hague Conference on Private International Law.
4. A Multi-unit State may, at any time, make a declaration that if, under Article 4, the applicable law is that of one of its territorial units, the law of that territorial unit applies only if the relevant intermediary has an office within that territorial unit which satisfies the condition specified in the second sentence of Article 4(1). Such a declaration shall have no effect on dispositions made before that declaration becomes effective.

Article 13
Uniform interpretation

In the interpretation of this Convention, regard shall be had to its international character and to the need to promote uniformity in its application.

Article 14 Review of practical operation of the Convention

The Secretary General of the Hague Conference on Private International Law shall at regular intervals convene a Special Commission to review the practical operation of this Convention and to consider whether any amendments to this Convention are desirable.

CHAPTER IV
TRANSITION PROVISIONS

Article 15
Priority between pre-Convention and post-Convention interests

In a Contracting State, the law applicable under this Convention determines whether a person's interest in securities held with an intermediary acquired after this Convention entered into force for that State extinguishes or has priority over another person's interest acquired before this Convention entered into force for that State.

Article 16
Pre-Convention account agreements and securities accounts

1. References in this Convention to an account agreement include an account agreement entered into before this Convention entered into force in accordance with Article 19(1). References in this Convention to a securities account include a securities account opened before this Convention entered into force in accordance with Article 19(1).

2. Unless an account agreement contains an express reference to this Convention, the courts of a Contracting State shall apply paragraphs (3) and (4) in applying Article 4(1) with respect to account agreements entered into before the entry into force of this Convention for that State in accordance with Article 19. A Contracting State may, at the time of signature, ratification, acceptance, approval or accession, make a declaration that its courts shall not apply those paragraphs with respect to account agreements entered into after the entry into force of this Convention in accordance with Article 19(1) but before the entry into force of this Convention for that State in accordance with Article 19(2). If the Contracting State is a Multi-unit State, it may make such a declaration with respect to any of its territorial units.

3. Any express terms of an account agreement which would have the effect, under the rules of the State whose law governs that agreement, that the law in force in a particular State, or a territorial unit of a particular Multi-unit State, applies to any of the issues specified in Article 2(1), shall have the effect that such law governs all the issues specified in Article 2(1), provided that the relevant intermediary had, at the time the agreement was entered into, an office in that State which satisfied the condition specified in the second sentence of Article 4(1). A Contracting State may, at the time of signature, ratification, acceptance, approval or accession, make a declaration that its courts shall not apply this paragraph with respect to an account agreement described in this paragraph in which the parties have expressly agreed that the securities account is maintained in a different State. If the Contracting State is a Multi-unit State, it may make such a declaration with respect to any of its territorial units.

4. If the parties to an account agreement, other than an agreement to which paragraph (3) applies, have agreed that the securities account is maintained in a particular State, or a territorial unit of a particular Multi-unit State, the law in force in that State or territorial unit is the law applicable to all the issues specified in Article 2(1), provided that the relevant intermediary had, at the time the agreement was entered into, an office in that State which satisfied the condition specified in the second sentence of Article 4(1). Such an agreement may be express or implied from the terms of the contract considered as a whole or from the surrounding circumstances.

CHAPTER V
FINAL CLAUSES

Article 17
Signature, ratification, acceptance, approval or accession

1. This Convention shall be open for signature by all States.

2. This Convention is subject to ratification, acceptance or approval by the signatory States.
3. Any State which does not sign this Convention may accede to it at any time.
4. The instruments of ratification, acceptance, approval or accession shall be deposited with the Ministry of Foreign Affairs of the Kingdom of the Netherlands, Depositary of this Convention.

Article 18
Regional Economic Integration Organisations

1. A Regional Economic Integration Organisation which is constituted by sovereign States and has competence over certain matters governed by this Convention may similarly sign, accept, approve or accede to this Convention. The Regional Economic Integration Organisation shall in that case have the rights and obligations of a Contracting State, to the extent that that Organisation has competence over matters governed by this Convention. Where the number of Contracting States is relevant in this Convention, the Regional Economic Integration Organisation shall not count as a Contracting State in addition to its Member States which are Contracting States.
2. The Regional Economic Integration Organisation shall, at the time of signature, acceptance, approval or accession, notify the Depositary in writing specifying the matters governed by this Convention in respect of which competence has been transferred to that Organisation by its Member States. The Regional Economic Integration Organisation shall promptly notify the Depositary in writing of any changes to the distribution of competence specified in the notice in accordance with this paragraph and any new transfer of competence.
3. Any reference to a 'Contracting State' or 'Contracting States' in this Convention applies equally to a Regional Economic Integration Organisation where the context so requires.

Article 19
Entry into force

1. This Convention shall enter into force on the first day of the month following the expiration of three months after the deposit of the third instrument of ratification, acceptance, approval or accession referred to in Article 17.
2. Thereafter this Convention shall enter into force—
   a) for each State or Regional Economic Integration Organisation referred to in Article 18 subsequently ratifying, accepting, approving or acceding to it, on the first day of the month following the expiration of three months after the deposit of its instrument of ratification, acceptance, approval or accession;
   b) for a territorial unit to which this Convention has been extended in accordance with Article 20(1), on the first day of the month following the expiration of three months after the notification of the declaration referred to in that Article.

Article 20
Multi-unit States

1. A Multi-unit State may, at the time of signature, ratification, acceptance, approval or accession, make a declaration that this Convention shall extend to all its territorial units or only to one or more of them.

2. Any such declaration shall state expressly the territorial units to which this Convention applies.
3. If a State makes no declaration under paragraph (1), this Convention extends to all territorial units of that State.

Article 21
Reservations

No reservation to this Convention shall be permitted.

Article 22
Declarations

For the purposes of Articles 1(5), 12(3) and (4), 16(2) and (3) and 20—
   a) any declaration shall be notified in writing to the Depositary;
   b) any Contracting State may modify a declaration by submitting a new declaration at any time;
   c) any Contracting State may withdraw a declaration at any time;
   d) any declaration made at the time of signature, ratification, acceptance, approval or accession shall take effect simultaneously with the entry into force of this Convention for the State concerned; any declaration made at a subsequent time and any new declaration shall take effect on the first day of the month following the expiration of three months after the date on which the Depositary made the notification in accordance with Article 24;
   e) a withdrawal of a declaration shall take effect on the first day of the month following the expiration of six months after the date on which the Depositary made the notification in accordance with Article 24.

Article 23
Denunciation

1. A Contracting State may denounce this Convention by a notification in writing to the Depositary. The denunciation may be limited to certain territorial units of a Multi-unit State to which this Convention applies.
2. The denunciation shall take effect on the first day of the month following the expiration of twelve months after the date on which the notification is received by the Depositary. Where a longer period for the denunciation to take effect is specified in the notification, the denunciation shall take effect upon the expiration of such longer period after the date on which the notification is received by the Depositary.

Article 24
Notifications by the Depositary

The Depositary shall notify the Members of the Hague Conference on Private International Law, and other States and Regional Economic Integration Organisations which have signed, ratified, accepted, approved or acceded in accordance with Articles 17 and 18, of the following—
   a) the signatures and ratifications, acceptances, approvals and accessions referred to in Articles 17 and 18;
   b) the date on which this Convention enters into force in accordance with Article 19;

c) the declarations and withdrawals of declarations referred to in Article 22;

d) the notifications referred to in Article 18(2);

e) the denunciations referred to in Article 23.

In witness whereof the undersigned, being duly authorised thereto, have signed this Convention.

Done at The Hague, on the ... day of ... 20 ..., in the English and French languages, both texts being equally authentic, in a single copy which shall be deposited in the archives of the Government of the Kingdom of the Netherlands, and of which a certified copy shall be sent, through diplomatic channels, to each of the Member States of the Hague Conference on Private International Law as of the date of its Nineteenth Session and to each State which participated in that Session.

STATE RATIFICATION

No State has, as yet, signed or ratified the Convention.

11

INTERNATIONAL CIVIL PROCEDURE

A. Introductory Text

1. European Convention on State Immunity

Introduction

Transnational commercial transactions and transnational commercial litigation do
not routinely involve issues of State immunity. However, foreign Governments and
foreign state-owned agencies or enterprises are often engaged in activities such as
the exploitation of natural resources, maritime and air transportation, construction
and operation of infrastructure projects, defence procurement, broadcasting, and
others. They are typically parties to concession and other joint-venture agreements,
and in many developing countries and economies in transition they are quite
generally the entry points for any foreign investment.

Next to the Vienna Convention on Treaties,[1] the European Convention on State
Immunity of 16 May 1972 is, therefore, the body of public international law rules
most relevant in the area of transnational commercial law. Any claim for breach of
contract, delictual conduct etc.—and in particular the initial (service) and the final
phases of judicial proceedings (recognition, attachment of property)—becomes
more complicated by the inclusion of a foreign sovereign.

Outside the scope of application of the Convention and prior to its entering
into force, general principles of public international law and their reception by both
case law and codified law[2] as well as a multitude of treaties for specific areas
governed the subject. All are expressions of the maxim *par in parem non habet
imperium*, meaning that the courts of one country will not by their process make a
foreign sovereign 'against his will a party to legal proceedings whether the proceedings involve process against his person or seek to recover from him specific
property or damages'.[3] The increase in state trading after the Second World War
had led many legislators and courts to move from the so-called 'absolute' theory to
the 'restrictive' theory according to which States were immune in respect of acts of
government (*acta jure imperii*) but not in respect of commercial acts (*acta jure
gestionis*).

---

[1] Above, p. 9.
[2] E.g. the UK State Immunity Act 1978, the US Foreign Sovereign Immunities Act 1976, the acts
on the organization of the judiciary, or the codes of civil procedure of many countries.
[3] *Compania Naviera Vascongado v S S Cristina* [1938] AC 485, *per* Lord Atkin at 490.

Scope of application

The Convention adopts a two-tiered approach. A Contracting State enjoys immunity in the courts of other Contracting States[4] unless a claim is based on any of the legal relationships enumerated in the provisions of the Convention itself.[5] These provisions reflect the negotiating States' minimalist consensus on what could be characterized as commercial acts. However, a Contracting State may opt into Chapter IV[6] designed to avoid petrification of the smallest common denominator and to allow for more advanced analysis. If it does, its courts may, in proceedings against another Contracting State, entertain an action even outside the limits set by Articles 4–11 and 14 if they would do so in proceedings against non-Contracting States unless *acta jure imperii* are concerned. Since the—often difficult—characterization is left to the forum, a declaration under Article 24(1) is nothing less than a reversal of the principle of immunity enshrined in Article 15. The extension by declaration has two consequences. Firstly, the declaring State assumes an obligation to recognize judgments entered against itself by the courts of other States under the optional regime. Secondly, the declaring State's property located in the forum State and serving exclusively commercial purposes loses its immunity[7] from the processes of execution.

Territorial units such as the member States of a federal State do not, in principle, enjoy State immunity under the Convention.[8] However, a Contracting State may declare[9] that its territorial units are entitled to State immunity.

Independent or, as the Convention terms it, 'distinct' *state enterprises* and similar '*entities*' are excluded from the Convention's scope of application.[10] However, if such entities exercise acts of government of their home State, they share their Governments' immunity in this respect.[11]

The Convention does not apply to proceedings relating to social security, damage caused by the use of nuclear energy, customs duties, taxes, and fines.[12] Claims falling within the scope of application of special treaties on the immunity of state-owned vessels, the acts of armed forces as well as diplomats are equally excluded from the Convention's scope.[13] A catch-all clause[14] provides for the precedence of the many treaties referred to above if any of these is to be characterized as *lex specialis*.

No State immunity ratione materiae

A State is not immune with respect to *contractual claims* if the obligation is to be performed in the forum State.[15] Of the three exceptions to this rule, one is of particular interest in transnational commercial law, and that is the parties' power to provide otherwise in their contract, e.g. in the context of an arbitration clause.[16]

---

[4] Article 15.   [5] Articles 4–11 and 14.   [6] Article 24–26.
[7] See below p. 791.   [8] Article 28(1).   [9] Article 28(2).   [10] Article 27(1).
[11] Article 27(2).   [12] Article 29.   [13] Articles 30–2.   [14] Article 33.
[15] Article 4(1).   [16] Article 4(2)(b).

No immunity can be claimed where a labour contract is concerned and the *locus laboris* is in the forum State[17] unless (a) the employee is a national of the employer State, (b) at the time when the contract was entered into, the employee was neither a national of nor habitually resident in the forum State or (c) the Parties have otherwise agreed in writing and the forum State does not have exclusive jurisdiction under its own laws.[18]

A State cannot claim immunity if it *participates* with private persons *in a company*, association, or other legal entity having its seat, registered office, or principal place of business on the territory of the forum State and where the proceedings concern the relationship between the State on the one hand and the entity or any other participant on the other hand.[19] Again, the parties may agree otherwise in writing.[20]

No immunity can be claimed by a State if it has on the territory of the forum State an *office, agency, or other establishment* through which it engages in an industrial, commercial, or financial activity to which the proceedings relate 'in the same manner as a private person'.[21] This is obviously a reference to acts *jure gestionis* and it raises the issues whether the acts have to be characterised in an autonomous manner or according to the *lex fori*.

In disputes concerning *intellectual property*, a State cannot claim State immunity.[22]

As had previously been widely accepted under customary public international law, a State cannot claim immunity from jurisdiction in proceedings related to *immovable property* situated in the forum State.[23] The same is true for its rights in moveable or immovable property arising by way of *succession, gift*, or *bona vacantia*.[24] In this respect, the Convention restricts immunity more than customary public international law did.

No claim of immunity can be raised under the Convention in proceedings which are related to *redress for personal injury* or *damage to tangible property* if the facts which occasioned the injury or damage occurred in the territory of the forum State and if the wrongdoer was present in that territory when those facts occurred.[25]

Noteworthy and at the time when the Convention was negotiated of even greater practical interest than today is Article 12 which provides that, where a State has agreed to submit a civil or commercial dispute to arbitration, it may not claim immunity from the jurisdiction of another Contracting State on the territory or according to the law of which the arbitration has taken place or will take place in respect of any proceedings relating to that arbitration.[26]

No State immunity by virtue of a State's own conduct

Customary public international law had no clear rules on how and under which circumstances a State may lose its privilege. However, it was and is undisputed that

---

[17] Article 5(1).   [18] Article 5(2).   [19] Article 6(1).   [20] Article 6(2).
[21] Article 7(1).   [22] Article 8.   [23] Article 9, but see also Art 14.
[24] Article 10, but see also Art 14.   [25] Article 11.   [26] Article 12.

a sovereign may waive its immunity. In countries adhering to the 'restrictive' theory,[27] this rule and the uncertainties surrounding its details are obviously not as important as in countries where the courts' practice is still based on the 'absolute' theory. Its principal sphere of application is the law of extra-contractual liability, i.e. the law of tort, in cases where the delictual conduct is an act *jure imperii*.

Under the Convention a State which institutes or intervenes in proceedings before a court of another State submits, for the purpose of those proceedings, to the jurisdiction of the latter.[28] However, this rule does not apply where the State asserts, in proceedings to which it is not a party, that it has a right or interest in property which is the subject-matter of the proceedings, and the circumstances are such that it would have been entitled to immunity had the proceedings been brought against it.[29] In respect of counterclaims, immunity from jurisdiction cannot be claimed if the counterclaim arises out of the same legal relationship or the same facts on which the principal claim is based and where that principal claim had been instituted by the State.[30] The same applies if, under the Convention, the State would not have been entitled to immunity in respect of that counterclaim had separate proceedings been brought against it.[31]

Finally, a State which makes a counterclaim in proceedings before the courts of another Contracting State submits to the jurisdiction of those courts also with respect to the principal claim.[32]

Apart from these very specific instances of implied waiver,[33] a State may of course submit expressly by (prior) agreement or consent given after the dispute has arisen.[34]

Procedure

When a question of immunity is raised, then the question of whether a State is or is not immune must be decided as a preliminary issue before the court can proceed. Unless any one of Articles 1 to 14 applies, the State shall be immune and the court seised shall decline to entertain such proceedings even if the State does not appear.[35]

To ascertain the relevant content of any rule on State immunity is usually much easier than to properly organize the practical steps in court proceedings against a State. In particular, service of documents creates not infrequently significant problems. According to Article 16(2) and (3), documents have to be served by the forum State through the diplomatic channels to the Ministry of Foreign Affairs of the defendant State, where appropriate, for onward transmission to the competent authority. That article makes detailed provision regarding languages, time-limits

---

[27] Above, p. 788.   [28] Article 1(1).   [29] Article 13.   [30] Article 1(2)(a).
[31] Article 1(2)(b).   [32] Article 1(3).
[33] Another one is the State 'taking steps' relating to the merits before claiming immunity, Art 3. If it appears only in order to assert immunity, it is not deemed to have waived it, Art 3(2).
[34] Article 2.   [35] Article 15. Cf. also Art 19.

etc. Of particular importance is paragraph (7) according to which default judgment may only be given if it is established that service has been effected in full conformity with Article 16.

Other provisions deal with States' exemption from paying bonds or security for costs or expenses[36] and certain limits on requiring the production of documentary evidence.[37]

Duty to comply with judgment and execution

Customary public international law distinguishes clearly between immunity from jurisdiction and immunity from execution. There is a general rule that, even if judgment against a State based on an act *jure gestionis* has been entered, measures of execution against that State's property may not be taken without the foreign State's consent if that property serves governmental purposes. Similarly, in the event of a State's waiving its immunity in the main proceedings the forum State cannot take measures of execution without prior and separate waiver of the immunity from execution.

Against this background Article 20 of the Convention establishes a State's duty to comply with the provisions of any judgment if given in accordance with Articles 1 to 13 and if it can no longer be set aside or if it is no longer subject to appeal or other form of review or annulment. This specific and innovative treaty obligation—which does not arise only in a few, precisely defined cases[38]—mirrors the Convention's general approach to grant jurisdiction—or exclude State immunity—only in circumstances which create a special link between the legal relationship at the basis of the dispute and the forum State.

If the State against whom a judgment has been given does not give effect thereto, the party seeking to invoke the judgment is entitled to have determined by the competent[39] court of the non-complying State whether effect should be given to the judgment.[40] That court may not review the merits of the judgment.

While—as a rule and absent express consent—no measures of execution or preventive measures may be taken against the property of a State in the territory of another State, Article 26 provides for an exception in case both States have made a declaration under Article 24 opting thereby into the 'advanced' or 'dynamic' regime under Chapter IV.[41] However, until the development of jurisprudence under Article 26 it is difficult to foresee its practical impact. One only has to think of agreements which the law of the State against whom judgment is given characterizes as 'administrative contracts'. In that case the judgment would not concern an activity in which the debtor State was engaged 'in the same manner as a private person' and execution would consequently not be available.

---

[36] Article 17.   [37] Article 18.   [38] Article 20(2) and (3).
[39] Article 21(4) states that court shall be designated by each Contracting State when depositing the instrument of ratification etc: [40] Article 21(1).
[41] Above, p. 789.

2. EC Regulation on Jurisdiction and Recognition and Enforcement of Judgments in Civil and Commercial Matters

Introduction

On 1 March 2002, the most successful instrument on international civil procedure of all time changed 'pillars': the Brussels Convention on Jurisdiction and Recognition and Enforcement of Judgments of 1968 (hereafter 'the Brussels Convention') became the EC Regulation 44/2001. It did so because, under (the Amsterdam version of) Article 65 EC, private international law and international civil procedure which had so far been dealt with in intergovernmental conventions[42] were 'communitarized' and so became a branch of judicial cooperation and passed from the 'third pillar' to the 'first pillar', i.e. genuine Community legislation.[43] By definition the Regulation entered into force without any further acts of implementation in all Member States[44] except Denmark. Since Denmark does not participate in the new regime, the Brussels Convention will remain in force with respect to that country. The Lugano Convention (the 'parallel convention' to Brussels) will continue to govern the relationship between EU Member States and the other Member States of the European Economic Area. Regulation 44/2001 is frequently referred to as 'Brussels I'.[45] The Regulation governs both the jurisdiction to adjudicate ('direct' jurisdiction) of Member States' courts and the recognition and enforceability of other Member States' courts' judgments. The Regulation's system is exclusive. Domestic rules on jurisdiction come into play only outside the Regulation's substantive scope of application or where the Regulation's provisions refer to them.[46]

Scope of application and relation with other instruments

(i) Civil and commercial matters There is no definition of these terms. Under principles established by the ECJ it is to be construed not according to any domestic criteria but in an autonomous manner and from a comparative perspective. Any specific branch of the judiciary where a matter is dealt with in a country does not determine a matter's nature. 'Administrative matters'[47] are understood to be matters arising out of the exercise of public or governmental authority. Where the public authority may choose between availing itself of contractual or other typically private-law forms of action and typically public-law forms then the chosen form of action determines its nature for the purposes of the Regulation.

Specifically *excluded* are, apart from revenue, customs and social security matters,[48] the following: *status* of natural persons, *family law* and *succession* related matters.[49]

---

[42] Under Art 293 = ex Art 220 EC.   [43] Under Art 249(2) EC.

[44] It is not in force in the British Channel Islands and the Isle of Man, Art 299(6)(b)–(c) EC.

[45] 'Brussels II' being the Regulation on Jurisdiction and Recognition and Enforcement in family-law matters.   [46] E.g. Art 4.

[47] Article 1(1).   [48] Article 1(1) and Art 1(2)(c),   [49] Article 1(2)(a).

In this respect, questions of legal capacity and the borderline between matrimonial property and assets of a family business may be raised in a commercial context. With respect to insolvency proceedings,[50] the EC Insolvency Regulation[51] now fills the gap. *Arbitration,*[52] which is also excluded from the scope of the Regulation, is to be construed broadly. Proceedings in State courts which are to serve or support the arbitral proceedings are equally excluded. Not excluded are provisional measures because they aim at securing claims not at the arbitral process.

(ii) Relation with other instruments The instruments whose position vis-à-vis the Regulation had to be clarified are Community instruments, bilateral recognition and enforcement treaties between Member States as well as national legislation to implement such instruments. Articles 67 to 72 make detailed provisions in this respect.

Jurisdiction

(i) General provisions; examination; lis alibi pendens; provisional measures Subject to specific provisions, persons domiciled in a Member State are to be sued in that State's courts.[53] The parties' and in particular the defendant's nationality is irrelevant. Who is a foreigner in the Member State of his domicile[54] is subject to that State's rules of jurisdiction applicable to its nationals. The characteristic closed system of the Regulation is further underlined by Article 3(1).[55] Lack of domicile in a Member State makes a person fully subject to the—autonomous—rules of jurisdiction of the Member States.[56]

There are further general provisions on how a person's domicile is to be determined, on certain peculiarities regarding specific groups of defendants, the meaning of the word 'court' and the position of defendants in civil claims brought in criminal proceedings.[57]

It is for the court seised[58] of a claim to examine whether it has jurisdiction and, where the courts of another Member State have jurisdiction, to decline to hear the case.[59] In cases of *lis (alibi) pendens* any court other than the first court seised must of its own motion stay the proceedings until such time as the first court's jurisdiction is established.[60] A court may stay its proceedings with a view to avoiding contradictory decisions where relevant actions are pending in different Member States.[61] *Provisional*, including protective, *measures* available under the law of any Member State may be applied for and granted even if another Member State's courts have jurisdiction as to the substance of the matter.[62] Again, the term

---

[50] Excluded by Art 1(2)(b).   [51] Above p. 665.   [52] Excluded by Art 1(2)(d).
[53] Article 2(1).   [54] E.g. a US citizen domiciled in France.
[55] Repeating that persons domiciled in a Member State may *only* be sued in other Member States by virtue of Arts 5 to 23. National rules of jurisdiction which are not to be applied are listed in Annex I, Art 3(2).   [56] Article 4. This is subject however to Arts 22 and 23.
[57] Articles 59 to 64.   [58] Cf. Art 30.   [59] Articles 25 and 26. See also Art 29.
[60] Article 27.   [61] Article 28.   [62] Article 31.

'provisional' is to be construed in an autonomous fashion so as to avoid limitations by technicalities under domestic law.

(ii) Specific bases for jurisdiction In commercial litigation the most important ground for a court to assume jurisdiction is that the place for performance of the *contractual obligation in dispute* is within its area of jurisdiction.[63] There is, subject to the parties agreeing otherwise, an irrebuttable presumption that, in the case of contracts for the sale of goods and contracts for services, the place of performance is where the goods are to be delivered or the services are to be provided.[64]

In disputes arising out of the operations of a *branch, agency, or other establishment*[65] the courts for the place in which the branch etc. is situated have jurisdiction. Again, the terms are to be construed broadly and from an autonomous and comparative perspective, not according to domestic law. What the courts are looking for is a certain degree of commercial organisation; a storage yard would not suffice. This ground is not so much a US-style 'doing business' connecting factor as a recognition that modern business enterprises are complex and articulate organizations. The outside party dealing with any one of their components is to be protected. The ECJ has developed the provision into an efficient judicial tool to address the phenomenon of groups of companies.

Other bases for jurisdiction which are particularly relevant in the commercial context are: in matters relating to *tort, delict, or quasi-delict*, the place where the harmful event occurred;[66] in matters relating to a *trust*, the trust's domicile;[67] in disputes concerning the payment of remuneration claimed in respect of the *salvage of a cargo or freight*, the place where the cargo or freight were or could have been arrested to secure payment.[68]

An entire section[69] is devoted to matters of *insurance*. While the insurer may be sued in the courts of his domicile or place of business, the courts of the policy holder's or the beneficiary's domicile, or in the courts of the place where the harm occurred, the insurer may bring proceedings only in the courts of the Member State where the defendant is domiciled. There is—limited—freedom for the parties to choose the forum.[70]

(iii) Exclusive jurisdiction In a number of cases[71] the Regulation provides for the exclusive jurisdiction of certain courts which are deemed to be close to the issues in question. Of particular interest in commercial litigation are the grounds for proceedings regarding *company law* where the courts at the company's seat are to hear the matter;[72] proceedings regarding the validity of entries in *public registries*[73] where the court of the registry is to be seised; and proceedings regarding *intellectual property*[74] where the place of the deposit or registration is the connecting factor for determining jurisdiction.

---

[63] Article 5(1)(a).   [64] Article 5(1)(b).   [65] Article 5(5).   [66] Article 5(3).
[67] Article 5(6).   [68] Article 5(7).   [69] Articles 8 to 14.   [70] Article 13a.
[71] Article 22.   [72] Article 22(2).   [73] Article 22(3).   [74] Article 22(4).

(iv) Choice of forum Another way for the parties to establish exclusive jurisdiction of the courts of a Member State is by prorogation. If at least one of them is domiciled in a Member State and they have agreed that such court or courts are to have jurisdiction to settle any disputes arising in connection with a particular legal relationship, this determination will be honoured in all Member States if the agreement is in writing or electronic form but of such a nature as to provide a durable record.[75] Many years of refinement of this provision[76] through the ECJ and the practice in national courts find expression in a formula according to which a form is treated as the equivalent of writing if it accords with practices which the parties have established between themselves[77] or, in international trade or commerce, a form which accords with a usage of which the parties are or ought to have been aware and which in that branch of business is known and observed.[78] This is a major development where the courts have cautiously but in a determined manner overcome legal formalism and adapted to living law merchant. In case neither party is domiciled in a Member State, the basic assumption[79] would not apply and the domestic, non-unified law of the court seised would govern the question whether that court has jurisdiction. However, the *derogating* effect is again 'communitarized' and the courts in all other Member States shall decline jurisdiction unless the chosen court has done so.[80]

There are special provisions for the prorogation contained in a trust instrument.[81]

The defendant's entering an appearance is treated as an agreement that the court has jurisdiction if he did not do so for the sole purpose of contesting the jurisdiction unless another court actually had exclusive jurisdiction.[82]

Recognition

Compared to its predecessor, the Brussels Convention, the Regulation has abolished a few more obstacles. Expeditious processing in the interest of the judgment creditor has been boosted to the detriment of the defendant's protection.

Judgments[83] given in a Member State are recognized in all other Member States without any special procedure being required.[84] This, along with decision to regulate the jurisdiction to adjudicate 'directly', i.e. not only in the ex-post perspective of whether one country gives effect to another country's court decisions, was the qualitative leap the Regulation and its predecessor made.[85] It creates a regional space for the free movement of judgments and the relevant provisions of the Regulation are therefore to be interpreted broadly and in a way favourable to recognition.

---

[75] Article 23(1)(a) and (2).   [76] The former Art 17 of the Brussels Convention.
[77] Article 23(1)(b).   [78] Article 23(1)(c).   [79] Of Art 23(1).   [80] Article 23(3).
[81] Article 23(4) and (5).   [82] Article 24. See above, p. 785.
[83] Meaning any decision given by a court or tribunal of a Member State irrespective of its name ('decree', 'order', 'writ of execution' as well as the determination of costs and expenses, Art 32).
[84] Article 33(1).   [85] From 1973 to 2002 under the the Brussels Convention.

Reasons justifying *non-recognition* are few and they are all and *exclusively* identified in the Regulation itself: firstly, manifest conflicts with *public policy* in the Member State where recognition is sought.[86] While there is unanimity that the language ('manifestly') should make sure that the application is an exceedingly rare event, the view is widely held that this 'safety net' is still needed. Moreover, the content of the public policy is thought to be national rather than European. However, it is for the ECJ to see to it that national courts do not overstep the boundaries and thwart the rationale of their duty to recognize. Secondly, where a *default judgment* was given, it shall not be recognised if the defendant was *not served* with the document which instituted the proceedings *in sufficient time* and *in a way that deprived him* of a fair chance to *arrange for his defence*.[87] The Brussels Convention had required that service be done 'properly', opening a whole range of potential inquiries to the detriment of expeditiousness in the judgment creditor's interest. Third, a judgment *irreconcilable* with a *judgment* given between the same parties in the Member State where recognition is sought.[88] Lastly, recognition may be refused if the judgment is irreconcilable with an earlier judgment given in another Member State or a third State involving the same cause of action and between the same parties, provided the earlier judgment fulfils the conditions for its recognition.[89]

Further grounds for refusing recognition are conflicts with selected[90] jurisdiction provisions of the Regulation.

Under no circumstances may a foreign judgment be reviewed on its merits.[91]

Enforcement

Again, the procedure has been simplified and accelerated in comparison to the situation under the Brussels Convention. A judgment in a Member State on the application of any interested party is declared enforceable in another Member State.[92] The Regulation deals in great detail with the procedural formalities of the application and the granting of that declaration.[93] For the purposes of this overview it is sufficient to point to four of them. First, the judgment is declared enforceable immediately without any review under the provisions governing the judgment's recognition.[94] Thus, even the protection of public-policy principles has been placed at the judgment debtor's disposal. He has to appeal the declaration. Second, the decision on the application for a declaration of enforceability may be appealed against by either party[95] and the appeal is governed by the procedural rules on contradictory matters. Third, the appellate court may refuse or revoke a declaration of enforceability only on one of the grounds on which a refusal of recognition can be based.[96] Fourth, the applicant for a declaration of recognition may avail himself of provisional, including protective, measures under the law of the State where

---

[86] Article 34(1).   [87] Article 34(2).   [88] Article 34(3).   [89] Article 34(4).
[90] Sections 3 (insurance), 4 (consumer contracts), 6 (exclusive jurisdiction, Art 22). Cf. also Art 72.
[91] Article 36.   [92] Article 38.   [93] Article 38 to 52 and 53 to 56.
[94] Article 41, 34, and 35.   [95] Article 43.   [96] Article 45, 34, and 35.

recognition is sought without a declaration of enforceability being required.[97] This again is a tool given to the judgment creditor which considerably strengthens his position and is a disincentive against delaying tactics at this second stage of proceedings to obtain a European title for execution.

Authentic instruments and court settlements

A document which has been formally drawn up[98] or registered as an authentic instrument and which is enforceable in one Member State is to be declared enforceable in another Member State upon application.[99]

The same applies to a settlement which has been approved by a court in the course of proceedings and is enforceable in the Member State in which it was concluded.[100]

3. The Las Leñas and Buenos Aires Protocols to the MERCOSUR Treaty

Introduction

A much more traditional approach than the one taken in the EC Regulation of 2000 is reflected in the Las Leñas Protocol of 1992 and the Buenos Aires Protocol of 5 August 1994 to the MERCOSUR Treaty. The starting point is—as it used to be in many pre-Brussels bilateral treaties on recognition of foreign judgments—a provision on the recognition and enforcement of judgments and arbitral awards in the Protocol of Las Leñas of 27 June 1992. That provision[101] establishes a number of, mostly formal, requirements for the 'extra-territorial effect' of judgments and arbitral awards in the Member States of the MERCOSUR.[102] Critical for our purposes is the substantive requirement that judgments are eligible for recognition if given 'by a court which, according to the rules on jurisdiction of the State where recognition is sought, was competent'.[103] This is the classic 'indirect' regulation of jurisdiction.

While there are many features which distinguish the South American from the European instrument and which cannot be discussed here, one fundamental difference must be mentioned: unlike under the EC Regulation there is, for the time being, no significant body of case law on the Buenos Aires Protocol and, more important still, no parallel to the ECJ's competence to interpret its provisions with binding force for the Member States' courts.

Scope of application

The *personal* scope of application is limited in that either both parties[104] must be domiciled or have their corporate headquarters[105] in different MERCOSUR

---

[97] Article 47.
[98] E.g. by a notary public, a governmental agency, a diplomatic or consular authority, in some cases documents drawn up by an attorney, etc.   [99] Article 57.
[100] Article 58.   [101] Article 20 LLP.   [102] Argentina, Brazil, Paraguay, and Uruguay.
[103] Article 20(c) LLP.   [104] Article 1 BAP envisages only 'private' parties.
[105] Domicile etc. are defined in Art 9 BAP.

Member States or, where only one party is domiciled or has its headquarters in a Member State, providing there is a 'reasonable connection'.[106] It is unclear from the language whether that connection has to exist with the chosen forum or with any Member State. It is submitted, however, that the former would appear to be more in line with the Protocol's conservative posture. A second query is raised by the provision's stating that that connection must exist 'in accordance with the rules on jurisdiction of this Protocol'.[107] This may refer to a hypothetical MERCOSUR domicile of the non-MERCOSUR party.

Limits *ratione materiae* flow from the instrument's excluding a whole range of potential matters and, beyond the exclusions familiar from the EC Regulation,[108] in particular, labour contracts, consumer sales contracts, transport contracts, insurance contracts, and property rights.[109]

Choice of forum

The Protocol's basic connecting factor to confer jurisdiction upon a court or arbitral tribunal is a written agreement by the parties to an international civil or commercial contract, provided that the agreement was not obtained abusively.[110] Such an agreement may be concluded from the time when the contract is signed.[111] The conclusion and the validity of the choice-of-forum clause is governed by the law of the Member State whose courts have jurisdiction under the Protocol. It is unclear what the consequences are where the parties' choice is the only possible ground for jurisdiction under the Protocol, e.g. because one party has no domicile or seat in a Member State. Again, a hypothetical domicile or corporate seat may provide a way out. If more than one national law potentially determines validity, then the most favourable applies.[112]

Irrespective of a valid agreement on jurisdiction of the courts of the State where the action is brought the choice is considered to be effective if the defendant recognizes the court's jurisdiction 'voluntarily, positively and not fictitiously'.[113] That requirement would appear to have been met when the defendant enters an appearance not only for the purpose of contesting the court's jurisdiction.

Subsidiary jurisdiction

Without a choice of forum, the plaintiff may choose one of the following fora: (a) the courts of the country where the contractual obligation at issue was to be performed;[114] (b) the courts of the country where the defendant is domiciled; (c) the

---

[106] Article 1(a) BAP. [107] Article 1(b) BAP.
[108] Above p. 665. In particular 'legal acts between bankrupt parties and their creditors or other similar proceedings, such as, in particular, the composition proceedings (rescheduling of payments)', cf. Art 2 nr 1 BAP.
[109] Given that financial service markets are not significantly developed, the Protocol seems therefore confined to commercial sales, contract for works, and services of modest scale and importance.
[110] Article 4 BAP. [111] Article 5(1) BAP. [112] Article 5(3) BAP.
[113] Article 6 BAP. [114] Article 7(a), 8(1) BAP.

courts of the plaintiff's domicile or corporate headquarters if the plaintiff proves that he discharged his own contractual obligations.[115]

The Protocol's provision defining the place of contractual performance distinguishes between specific and identified goods on the one hand and unidentified goods determined only by their nature or class on the other hand, between fungible and non-fungible goods.[116] As regards services, the place of performance is likewise determined according to a list of criteria.[117]

Specific bases for jurisdiction

The Protocol provides specifically for a forum for intra-corporate litigation,[118] juridical persons having entered into contracts in Member States other than the State of their seat,[119] multi-defendant disputes,[120] actions on a warranty or guarantee, or other third party proceedings.[121]

If a *counterclaim* is based on the same act or the same facts on which the principal claim is based the court that has jurisdiction to entertain the latter also has jurisdiction with respect to the former.[122]

Recognition and enforcement

A judgment (or arbitral award) given by a court (or tribunal) that had jurisdiction under the Buenos Aires Protocol is eligible for recognition under Article 20(c) of the Protocol of Las Leñas. The application for recognition is transmitted through the channels of judicial assistance and via the central authorities of the judgment State and the State where recognition is sought.[123]

The grounds on which recognition may be refused are, apart from lack of jurisdiction of the court of origin,[124] and a number of potential formal deficiencies the following: (1) the judgment debtor had not been served properly or had been unable to defend himself;[125] (2) the decision is not definitive or enforceable in its State of origin;[126] (3) the decision manifestly violates principles of public policy in the State where recognition is sought.[127] A judgment (or award) is not recognized if it is incompatible with a judgment (or award) between the same parties and concerning the same facts and cause of action.[128] The same applies if, before the action was brought, an action between the same parties, based on the same facts and

---

[115] This bears a resemblance to the German theory—extended to the Brussels Convention/EC Regulation—of 'double relevance' of facts which also constitutes the line of reasoning regarding jurisdiction under certain investment treaties: for the purposes of establishing the court's jurisdiction there has to take place some examination of the merits of the case. The solution advocated as a way out of this logical dilemma is that conclusive allegations on the plaintiff's part are sufficient to establish that the court has jurisdiction.   [116] Article 8(a)–(c) BAP.

[117] Article 8(d) BAP.   [118] Article 10 BAP.   [119] Article 11 BAP.
[120] Article 12(1) BAP.   [121] Article 12(2) BAP.   [122] Article 13 BAP.
[123] Article 19 LLP.

[124] Article 20(c) LLP, in clear contrast to the Brussels Convention/EC Regulation to be (re-)examined by the court of the recognition State.   [125] Article 20(d) LLP.
[126] Article 20(e) LLP.   [127] Article 20(f) LLP.   [128] Article 22(1) LLP.

concerning the same cause of action, was pending in the State where recognition is sought.

While there are no provisions explicitly addressing the issue of judicial review of the decision granting or refusing recognition, the general statement that recognition and enforcement proceedings are governed by the law of the State where the application is made[129] suggests that such decisions are subject to the general rules on appeal or other types of judicial review.

4. Hague Convention on the Service Abroad of Judicial and Extrajudicial Documents In Civil or Commercial Matters

Introduction

Service of process as well as other functions which are part of the conduct of transborder civil proceedings (judicial cooperation) are rooted in sharply diverging traditions. Civil law jurisdictions view service of a judicial document as an official act based on the State's sovereignty which consequently has to be effected by an official of the relevant authority. Common law jurisdictions, on the other hand, are historically used to the parties, more specifically the claimant, performing these functions directly or through agents. Both a significant number of bilateral civil procedure conventions and the Hague Convention of 1965 provide for institutional mechanisms aimed at bridging this divide.

Scope of application

The Convention applies in 'all cases, in civil and commercial matters, where a judicial document has to be transmitted and served abroad'.[130] There are no definitions of 'judicial document' or 'civil and commercial matters'. It is submitted that they may be construed broadly.[131]

Modes of service

(i) Through Central Authority

The Convention provides for the judicial documents to be sent to a designated Central Authority in the State in which service is required.[132] The documents are forwarded to that Authority by the competent judicial officer or Authority of the State in which the documents originate; they are attached to a model form of request annexed to the Convention, and the Convention excludes specifically any requirement of legislation or other formality.[133] The Central Authority examines the requests and informs the applicant promptly of any exception there may be with respect to formal compliance.[134] The Central Authority either provides for service

---

[129] Article 24 LLP.
[130] Article 1(1). It is, however, not applicable if the person's address is unknown, Art 1(2).
[131] Cf. also the blank space in the model request and certificate annexed to the Convention.
[132] Article 2.   [133] Article 3.   [134] Article 4.

according to its domestic law or by a particular method requested by the applicant unless such a method is incompatible with the law of the State addressed; the Convention also addresses language issues such as the requirement of a translation of the document to be transmitted.[135] The Central Authority or any Authority designated by it, upon service of the document, completes the model certificate of service annexed to the Convention.[136]

(ii) Alternative modes of transmission and service

The Convention preserves the possibility of serving through the traditional channels of transmission, i.e. diplomatic or consular agents,[137] to the extent that the mode chosen is compatible with the local law of the requested State. The Convention furthermore provides for service through the post, judicial authorities, or offices (e.g. huissiers) unless the State of destination objects to that mode of service.[138]

Hague Convention Mandatory?

The Convention states that it shall apply in '*all cases*' where a document has to be served abroad. There has, in particular in relation to cases originating in US courts, been much controversy as to whether the Convention is mandatory, excluding forms of service abroad not permitted by its provisions. The US Supreme Court[139] held that the provisions were mandatory for service abroad but that it was for the *lex fori* to determine when such service was required. If, for example, the *lex fori* permitted service on a wholly-owned subsidiary within the forum country of the foreign defendant resident abroad, the Convention did not preclude reliance on those provisions of the forum's law subject to that law's further qualification (due process).

Refusal to comply with request

Where a request for service complies with the terms of the Convention, the State addressed may refuse to comply only if it deems that compliance would infringe its sovereignty or security.[140] It may not refuse to comply solely on the ground that, under its internal law, it claims exclusive jurisdiction over the subject matter or that its law would not permit the action upon which the application is based.[141]

5. European Council Regulation on the Service in the Member States of Judicial and Extrajudicial Documents in Civil and Commercial Matters

Introduction

The Council Regulation (EC) No 1348/2000[142] entered into force on 31 May 2001. Member States are required to communicate to the Commission information regarding their respective implementation legislation.[143] For Member States of the

---

[135] Article 5.   [136] Article 6.   [137] Articles 8 and 9.   [138] Article 10.
[139] *Volkswagenwerk AG v Schlunk* 486 US 694 (1988).   [140] Article 13(1).
[141] Article 13(2).   [142] OJ L 160, 30.6.2000 p.37   [143] Article 23.

European Union, except Denmark, the Regulation replaces the Hague Convention of 1965 (or the Hague Convention on Civil Procedure of 1 March 1954).[144] The instrument simplifies and accelerates service procedures. Sovereign interests play a significantly reduced role. The grounds for refusal (*ordre public*)[145] have been abolished completely.

Scope of application

The Regulation applies where a document 'has to be transmitted' from one Member State to another for service there.[146] Whether that is the case (or whether fictitious service within the forum State as they are traditionally used in some Member States are sufficient) is for the *lex fori* to decide. The Regulation does, however, make it possible to mitigate the consequences where the law of the addressed State does not provide for such fictions.[147]

Modes of service

The Regulation provides basically for two modes of transmission: through direct transmission between agencies and 'other means of transmission'.

(i) Direct transmission between agencies While a number of Member States seek fully to take advantage of acceleration potential through direct and decentralized transmission at the operational level[148] others maintain the (Hague Convention) system of transmission through central bodies.[149] Another way of accelerating procedures is to permit transmission 'by any appropriate means' which includes fax and e-mail.[150] The receiving agency itself serves the document in accordance with the law of the Member State addressed or by a particular form requested by the transmitting agency.[151] In principle, no translation is required. Without the translation the addressee may, however, refuse to accept the document.[152] Unlike the Hague Convention the Regulation itself determines the date on which the document is served. The law of the Member State addressed governs the issue, but there are circumstances when the law of the State of origin has to be taken into account.[153]

(ii) Service by post, direct service, and traditional modes Service by post is permitted.[154] The Regulation does not interfere with the freedom of any person interested in a judicial proceeding to effect service of documents directly through the judicial officers or other competent persons of the Member State addressed.[155] Transmission through traditional modes (consular or diplomatic) continues to be provided for.[156]

---

[144] Article 20. [145] Cf. Art 13 Hague Convention. [146] Article 1(1).
[147] Article 19, 9. [148] Articles 2, 4–11. [149] Article 3.
[150] Article 4(2); cf. also Art 4(4). [151] Article 7(1). [152] Article 8.
[153] Article 9. [154] Articles 14, 23(1). [155] Articles 15, 23(1).
[156] Articles 12, 13.

6. Hague Convention on the Taking of Evidence Abroad in Civil or Commercial Matters

Introduction

The Convention establishes procedures designed to overcome the divide between, on the one hand, countries where the taking of evidence is viewed as part of the preparation of the trial and, therefore, a responsibility of the parties who may turn to their counsel and, on the other hand, countries who view the obtaining of evidence as a judicial act which may interfere with the sovereignty of the State where the evidence is to be obtained.

Letters of request

A judicial authority of a Contracting State may, in accordance with the law of that State, request the competent authority of another Contracting State, by means of a Letter of Request (hereafter 'LoR'), to obtain evidence, for use in judicial proceedings or to perform some other judicial act except service of judicial documents.[157] The request may be for a variety of forms of evidence, including oral testimony, witness statements, other documentary evidence, and the inspection of property.[158] The LoR is sent to a designated Central Authority in the country where evidence is to be taken.[159] The Convention does not prevent a Contracting State from obtaining evidence by other methods provided for under the domestic law of the State in which the evidence is sought.[160] The United States Supreme Court held that the Convention does not provide a mandatory or exclusive framework for obtaining evidence abroad. Only considerations of comity vis-à-vis the foreign State which may regard other ways as an infringement of its sovereignty were held to constitute limits.[161] A Contracting State may make a reservation to the effect that it will not execute LoR issued for the purpose of obtaining pre-trial discovery of documents as known in common law countries.[162] It has been said that this provision created more problems that it solved.

Taking of evidence by diplomatic officers, consular agents, and commissioners

Diplomatic officers, or consular agents of a Contracting State may, in the territory of another Contracting State, take evidence without compulsion of nationals of a State which represent in aid of proceedings commenced in the courts of a State they represent.[163] A Contracting State may declare that such taking of evidence requires permission by the declaring State.[164] Diplomats or consuls of a Contracting State may take evidence of other persons, i.e. nationals of the host State or third States, subject to prior permission unless the Contracting State concerned has waived that

---

[157] Article 1.   [158] Article 3(1)(f), (8).   [159] Article 2.   [160] Article 27(2).
[161] *Société Nationale Industrielle Aérospatiale v U.S. District Court for the Southern District of Iowa*, 482, U.S. 522 (1987).   [162] Article 23.
[163] Article 15(1).   [164] Article 15(2).

requirement.[165] The same applies where a commissioner is appointed to take any evidence.[166] A Contracting State may declare its willingness to make available appropriate assistance to obtain the evidence by compulsion.[167]

7. European Council Regulation on Cooperation between Courts of the Member States in the Taking of Evidence in Civil or Commercial Matters

Introduction

The Council Regulation (EC) No. 1206/2001[168] entered into force on 1 July 2001. It does not apply to Denmark. The words 'swift' and 'swiftest possible means', heavily employed in the text, reflect the policy objective. The basic idea of the Regulation No. 1348/2000 on service of documents,[169] i.e. the decentralized and direct communication between the requesting and the requested courts, is also at the heart of the procedure for taking evidence.[170] The central bodies designated by Member States have only support functions.[171]

Scope of Application

The Regulation applies to evidence which is intended for use in judicial proceedings in civil or commercial matters which have been commenced or are contemplated.[172] Since the Regulation explicitly refers to courts of Member States,[173] an arbitral tribunal may not directly participate in the procedure although it may certainly be the ultimate beneficiary.

Taking of evidence by the requested court

Chapter II of the Regulation deals, firstly, in detail with the transmission and execution of requests for the taking of evidence and the procedure for taking that evidence by the requested court.[174] The salient feature is the use of standardized forms that contemplate almost any conceivable procedural situation and are annexed to the Regulation. The request and all documents accompanying the request are exempted from authentication or any equivalent formality.[175] Within seven days of receipt of the request, the requested competent court must send an acknowledgement of receipt to the requesting court.[176] The requested court is also required to inform the requesting court without delay of any incompleteness of the request which renders the request incapable of being executed.[177] The actual procedure of the taking of evidence by the requested court is regulated with respect to time lines, the use of communication technology etc.[178] Generally speaking, the requested court executes the request in accordance with its *lex fori*.[179] The parties have, subject to the *lex fori*, the right to be present at the performance of the taking of evidence.[180] Subject to the law of the Member State of the requesting court,

---

[165] Article 16.   [166] Article 17.   [167] Article 18.
[168] L 174 27/06/2001 p. 1   [169] Above p. 802.   [170] Article 2.   [171] Article 3.
[172] Article 1.   [173] Article 1(1).   [174] Articles 4–16.   [175] Article 4(2).
[176] Article 7(1).   [177] Article 8.   [178] Article 10.   [179] Article 10(2).

representatives of the requesting court have equally the right to be present at the taking of evidence by the requested court.[181] Where necessary, the requested court is to apply the appropriate coercive measures in the instances and to the extent provided for by the law of the Member State of the requested court.[182] A request for the hearing of a person is not executed when the person concerned claims the right to refuse to give evidence or to be prohibited from giving evidence under either the law of the requested or the requesting court.[183]

Direct taking of evidence by the requesting court

Where a court requests to take evidence directly—a possibility provided for by the Hague Convention[184] by way of appointing commissioners—it must submit a request to the central body or any other competent authority.[185] Direct taking of evidence may only take place if it can be performed on a voluntary basis without the need for coercive measures.[186]

---

[180] Article 11.   [181] Article 12.   [182] Article 13.   [183] Article 14.
[184] Above p. 804   [185] Article 17(1).   [186] Article 17(2).

B. Instruments

(i) EUROPEAN CONVENTION ON STATE IMMUNITY*
Basle, 16.V.1972

PREAMBLE

The member States of the Council of Europe, signatory hereto,

Considering that the aim of the Council of Europe is to achieve a greater unity between its members;

Taking into account the fact that there is in international law a tendency to restrict the cases in which a State may claim immunity before foreign courts;

Desiring to establish in their mutual relations common rules relating to the scope of the immunity of one State from the jurisdiction of the courts of another State, and designed to ensure compliance with judgments given against another State;

---

* European Convention on State Immunity, ETS No. 74 is reproduced with the kind permission of the Council of Europe. Please note that the Council of Europe does not guarantee that documents published other than in the European Treaties series are exact reproductions of the officially adopted text.

Considering that the adoption of such rules will tend to advance the work of harmonisation undertaken by the member States of the Council of Europe in the legal field,

Have agreed as follows:

CHAPTER I
IMMUNITY FROM JURISDICTION

Article 1

1. A Contracting State which institutes or intervenes in proceedings before a court of another Contracting State submits, for the purpose of those proceedings, to the jurisdiction of the courts of that State.
2. Such a Contracting State cannot claim immunity from the jurisdiction of the courts of the other Contracting State in respect of any counterclaim:
   a. arising out of the legal relationship or the facts on which the principal claim is based;
   b. if, according to the provisions of this Convention, it would not have been entitled to invoke immunity in respect of that counterclaim had separate proceedings been brought against it in those courts.
3. A Contracting State which makes a counterclaim in proceedings before a court of another Contracting State submits to the jurisdiction of the courts of that State with respect not only to the counterclaim but also to the principal claim.

Article 2

A Contracting State cannot claim immunity from the jurisdiction of a court of another Contracting State if it has undertaken to submit to the jurisdiction of that court either:
   a. by international agreement;
   b. by an express term contained in a contract in writing; or
   c. by an express consent given after a dispute between the parties has arisen.

Article 3

1. A Contracting State cannot claim immunity from the jurisdiction of a court of another Contracting State if, before claiming immunity, it takes any step in the proceedings relating to the merits. However, if the State satisfies the Court that it could not have acquired knowledge of facts on which a claim to immunity can be based until after it has taken such a step, it can claim immunity based on these facts if it does so at the earliest possible moment.
2. A Contracting State is not deemed to have waived immunity if it appears before a court of another Contracting State in order to assert immunity.

Article 4

1. Subject to the provisions of Article 5, a Contracting State cannot claim immunity from the jurisdiction of the courts of another Contracting State if the proceedings

relate to an obligation of the State, which, by virtue of a contract, falls to be discharged in the territory of the State of the forum.

2. Paragraph 1 shall not apply:
   a. in the case of a contract concluded between States;
   b. if the parties to the contract have otherwise agreed in writing;
   c. if the State is party to a contract concluded on its territory and the obligation of the State is governed by its administrative law.

Article 5

1. A Contracting State cannot claim immunity from the jurisdiction of a court of another Contracting State if the proceedings relate to a contract of employment between the State and an individual where the work has to be performed on the territory of the State of the forum.

2. Paragraph 1 shall not apply where:
   a. the individual is a national of the employing State at the time when the proceedings are brought;
   b. at the time when the contract was entered into the individual was neither a national of the State of the forum nor habitually resident in that State; or
   c. the parties to the contract have otherwise agreed in writing, unless, in accordance with the law of the State of the forum, the courts of that State have exclusive jurisdiction by reason of the subject-matter.

3. Where the work is done for an office, agency or other establishment referred to in Article 7, paragraphs 2.a and b of the present article apply only if, at the time the contract was entered into, the individual had his habitual residence in the Contracting State which employs him.

Article 6

1. A Contracting State cannot claim immunity from the jurisdiction of a court of another Contracting State if it participates with one or more private persons in a company, association or other legal entity having its seat, registered office or principal place of business on the territory of the State of the forum, and the proceedings concern the relationship, in matters arising out of that participation, between the State on the one hand and the entity or any other participant on the other hand.

2. Paragraph 1 shall not apply if it is otherwise agreed in writing.

Article 7

1. A Contracting State cannot claim immunity from the jurisdiction of a court of another Contracting State if it has on the territory of the State of the forum an office, agency or other establishment through which it engages, in the same manner as a private person, in an industrial, commercial or financial activity, and the proceedings relate to that activity of the office, agency or establishment.

2. Paragraph 1 shall not apply if all the parties to the dispute are States, or if the parties have otherwise agreed in writing.

Article 8

A Contracting State cannot claim immunity from the jurisdiction of a court of another Contracting State if the proceedings relate:
  a. to a patent, industrial design, trade-mark, service mark or other similar right which, in the State of the forum, has been applied for, registered or deposited or is otherwise protected, and in respect of which the State is the applicant or owner;
  b. to an alleged infringement by it, in the territory of the State of the forum, of such a right belonging to a third person and protected in that State;
  c. to an alleged infringement by it, in the territory of the State of the forum, of copyright belonging to a third person and protected in that State;
  d. to the right to use a trade name in the State of the forum.

Article 9

A Contracting State cannot claim immunity from the jurisdiction of a court of another Contracting State if the proceedings relate to:
  a. its rights or interests in, or its use or possession of, immovable property; or
  b. its obligations arising out of its rights or interests in, or use or possession of, immovable property
and the property is situated in the territory of the State of the forum.

Article 10

A Contracting State cannot claim immunity from the jurisdiction of a court of another Contracting State if the proceedings relate to a right in movable or immovable property arising by way of succession, gift or *bona vacantia.*

Article 11

A Contracting State cannot claim immunity from the jurisdiction of a court of another Contracting State in proceedings which relate to redress for injury to the person or damage to tangible property, if the facts which occasioned the injury or damage occurred in the territory of the State of the forum, and if the author of the injury or damage was present in that territory at the time when those facts occurred.

Article 12

1. Where a Contracting State has agreed in writing to submit to arbitration a dispute which has arisen or may arise out of a civil or commercial matter, that State may not claim immunity from the jurisdiction of a court of another Contracting State on the territory or according to the law of which the arbitration has taken or will take place in respect of any proceedings relating to:
   a. the validity or interpretation of the arbitration agreement;
   b. the arbitration procedure;
   c. the setting aside of the award,
   unless the arbitration agreement otherwises provides.
2. Paragraph 1 shall not apply to an arbitration agreement between States.

Article 13

Paragraph 1 of Article 1 shall not apply where a Contracting State asserts, in proceedings pending before a court of another Contracting State to which it is not a party, that it has a right or interest in property which is the subject-matter of the proceedings, and the circumstances are such that it would have been entitled to immunity if the proceedings had been brought against it.

Article 14

Nothing in this Convention shall be interpreted as preventing a court of a Contracting State from administering or supervising or arranging for the administration of property, such as trust property or the estate of a bankrupt, solely on account of the fact that another Contracting State has a right or interest in the property.

Article 15

A Contracting State shall be entitled to immunity from the jurisdiction of the courts of another Contracting State if the proceedings do not fall within Articles 1 to 14; the court shall decline to entertain such proceedings even if the State does not appear.

CHAPTER II
PROCEDURAL RULES

Article 16

1. In proceedings against a Contracting State in a court of another Contracting State, the following rules shall apply.
2. The competent authorities of the State of the forum shall transmit
   - the original or a copy of the document by which the proceedings are instituted;
   - a copy of any judgment given by default against a State which was defendant in the proceedings,

   through the diplomatic channel to the Ministry of Foreign Affairs of the defendant State, for onward transmission, where appropriate, to the competent authority. These documents shall be accompanied, if necessary, by a translation into the official language, or one of the official languages, of the defendant State.
3. Service of the documents referred to in paragraph 2 is deemed to have been effected by their receipt by the Ministry of Foreign Affairs.
4. The time-limits within which the State must enter an appearance or appeal against any judgment given by default shall begin to run two months after the date on which the document by which the proceedings were instituted or the copy of the judgment is received by the Ministry of Foreign Affairs.
5. If it rests with the court to prescribe the time-limits for entering an appearance or for appealing against a judgment given by default, the court shall allow the State not less than two months after the date on which the document by which the proceedings are instituted or the copy of the judgment is received by the Ministry of Foreign Affairs.
6. A Contracting State which appears in the proceedings is deemed to have waived any objection to the method of service.

7. If the Contracting State has not appeared, judgment by default may be given against it only if it is established that the document by which the proceedings were instituted has been transmitted in conformity with paragraph 2, and that the time-limits for entering an appearance provided for in paragraphs 4 and 5 have been observed.

Article 17

No security, bond or deposit, however described, which could not have been required in the State of the forum of a national of that State or a person domiciled or resident there, shall be required of a Contracting State to guarantee the payment of judicial costs or expenses. A State which is a claimant in the courts of another Contracting State shall pay any judicial costs or expenses for which it may become liable.

Article 18

A Contracting State party to proceedings before a court of another Contracting State may not be subjected to any measure of coercion, or any penalty, by reason of its failure or refusal to disclose any documents or other evidence. However the court may draw any conclusion it thinks fit from such failure or refusal.

Article 19

1. A court before which proceedings to which a Contracting State is a party are instituted shall, at the request of one of the parties or, if its national law so permits, of its own motion, decline to proceed with the case or shall stay the proceedings if other proceedings between the same parties, based on the same facts and having the same purpose:
   a. are pending before a court of that Contracting State, and were the first to be instituted; or
   b. are pending before a court of any other Contracting State, were the first to be instituted and may result in a judgment to which the State party to the proceedings must give effect by virtue of Article 20 or Article 25.
2. Any Contracting State whose law gives the courts a discretion to decline to proceed with a case or to stay the the proceedings in cases where proceedings between the same parties, based on the same facts and having the same purpose, are pending before a court of another Contracting State, may, by notification addressed to the Secretary General of the Council of Europe, declare that its courts shall not be bound by the provisions of paragraph 1.

CHAPTER III
EFFECT OF JUDGMENT

Article 20

1. A Contracting State shall give effect to a judgment given against it by a court of another Contracting State:
   a. if, in accordance with the provisions of Articles 1 to 13, the State could not claim immunity from jurisdiction; and

b. if the judgment cannot or can no longer be set aside if obtained by default, or if it is not or is no longer subject to appeal or any other form of ordinary review or to annulment.

2. Nevertheless, a Contracting State is not obliged to give effect to such a judgment in any case:
   a. where it would be manifestly contrary to public policy in that State to do so, or where, in the circumstances, either party had no adequate opportunity fairly to present his case;
   b. where proceedings between the same parties, based on the same facts and having the same purpose:
      i. are pending before a court of that State and were the first to be instituted;
      ii. are pending before a court of another Contracting State, were the first to be instituted and may result in a judgment to which the State party to the proceedings must give effect under the terms of this Convention;
   c. where the result of the judgment is inconsistent with the result of another judgment given between the same parties:
      i. by a court of the Contracting State, if the proceedings before that court were the first to be instituted or if the other judgment has been given before the judgment satisfied the conditions specified in paragraph 1.b; or
      ii. by a court of another Contracting State where the other judgment is the first to satisfy the requirements laid down in the present Convention;
   d. where the provisions of Article 16 have not been observed and the State has not entered an appearance or has not appealed against a judgment by default.

3. In addition, in the cases provided for in Article 10, a Contracting State is not obliged to give effect to the judgment:
   a. if the courts of the State of the forum would not have been entitled to assume jurisdiction had they applied, *mutatis mutandis*, the rules of jurisdiction (other than those mentioned in the annex to the present Convention) which operate in the State against which judgment is given; or
   b. if the court, by applying a law other than that which would have been applied in accordance with the rules of private international law of that State, has reached a result different from that which would have been reached by applying the law determined by those rules.

   However, a Contracting State may not rely upon the grounds of refusal specified in sub-paragraphs a and b above if it is bound by an agreement with the State of the forum on the recognition and enforcement of judgments and the judgment fulfils the requirement of that agreement as regards jurisdiction and, where appropriate, the law applied.

Article 21

1. Where a judgment has been given against a Contracting State and that State does not give effect thereto, the party which seeks to invoke the judgment shall be entitled to have determined by the competent court of that State the question whether effect should be given to the judgment in accordance with Article 20. Proceedings may also be brought before this court by the State against which judgment has been given, if its law so permits.

2. Save in so far as may be necessary for the application of Article 20, the competent court of the State in question may not review the merits of the judgment.

3. Where proceedings are instituted before a court of a State in accordance with paragraph 1:
   a. the parties shall be given an opportunity to be heard in the proceedings;
   b. documents produced by the party seeking to invoke the judgment shall not be subject to legalisation or any other like formality;
   c. no security, bond or deposit, however described, shall be required of the party invoking the judgment by reason of his nationality, domicile or residence;
   d. the party invoking the judgment shall be entitled to legal aid under conditions no less favourable than those applicable to nationals of the State who are domiciled and resident therein.
4. Each Contracting State shall, when depositing its instrument of ratification, acceptance or accession, designate the court or courts referred to in paragraph 1, and inform the Secretary General of the Council of Europe thereof.

Article 22

1. A Contracting State shall give effect to a settlement to which it is a party and which has been made before a court of another Contracting State in the course of the proceedings; the provisions of Article 20 do not apply to such a settlement.
2. If the State does not give effect to the settlement, the procedure provided for in Article 21 may be used.

Article 23

No measures of execution or preventive measures against the property of a Contracting State may be taken in the territory of another Contracting State except where and to the extent that the State has expressly consented thereto in writing in any particular case.

CHAPTER IV
OPTIONAL PROVISIONS

Article 24

1. Notwithstanding the provisions of Article 15, any State may, when signing this Convention or depositing its instrument of ratification, acceptance or accession, or at any later date, by notification addressed to the Secretary General of the Council of Europe, declare that, in cases not falling within Articles 1 to 13, its courts shall be entitled to entertain proceedings against another Contracting State to the extent that its courts are entitled to entertain proceedings against States not party to the present Convention. Such a declaration shall be without prejudice to the immunity from jurisdiction which foreign States enjoy in respect of acts performed in the exercise of sovereign authority *(acta jure imperii)*.
2. The courts of a State which has made the declaration provided for in paragraph 1 shall not however be entitled to entertain such proceedings against another Contracting State if their jurisdiction could have been based solely on one or more of the grounds mentioned in the annex to the present Convention, unless that other Contracting State has taken a step in the proceedings relating to the merits without first challenging the jurisdiction of the court.

3. The provisions of Chapter II apply to proceedings instituted against a Contracting State in accordance with the present article.

4. The declaration made under paragraph 1 may be withdrawn by notification addressed to the Secretary General of the Council of Europe. The withdrawal shall take effect three months after the date of its receipt, but this shall not affect proceedings instituted before the date on which the withdrawal becomes effective.

Article 25

1. Any Contracting State which has made a declaration under Article 24 shall, in cases not falling within Articles 1 to 13, give effect to a judgment given by a court of another Contracting State which has made a like declaration:
   a. if the conditions prescribed in paragraph 1.b of Article 20 have been fulfilled; and
   b. if the court is considered to have jurisdiction in accordance with the following paragraphs.

2. However, the Contracting State is not obliged to give effect to such a judgment:
   a. if there is a ground for refusal as provided for in paragraph 2 of Article 20; or
   b. if the provisions of paragraph 2 of Article 24 have not been observed.

3. Subject to the provisions of paragraph 4, a court of a Contracting State shall be considered to have jurisdiction for the purpose of paragraph 1.b:
   a. if its jurisdiction is recognised in accordance with the provisions of an agreement to which the State of the forum and the other Contracting State are Parties;
   b. where there is no agreement between the two States concerning the recognition and enforcement of judgments in civil matters, if the courts of the State of the forum would have been entitled to assume jurisdiction had they applied, *mutatis mutandis*, the rules of jurisdiction (other than those mentioned in the annex to the present Convention) which operate in the State against which the judgment was given. This provision does not apply to questions arising out of contracts.

4. The Contracting States having made the declaration provided for in Article 24 may, by means of a supplementary agreement to this Convention, determine the circumstances in which their courts shall be considered to have jurisdiction for the purposes of paragraph 1.b of this article.

5. If the Contracting State does not give effect to the judgment, the procedure provided for in Article 21 may be used.

Article 26

Notwithstanding the provisions of Article 23, a judgment rendered against a Contracting State in proceedings relating to an industrial or commercial activity, in which the State is engaged in the same manner as a private person, may be enforced in the State of the forum against property of the State against which judgment has been given, used exclusively in connection with such an activity, if:
   a. both the State of the forum and the State against which the judgment has been given have made declarations under Article 24;
   b. the proceedings which resulted in the judgment fell within Articles 1 to 13 or were instituted in accordance with paragraphs 1 and 2 of Article 24; and
   c. the judgment satisfies the requirements laid down in paragraph 1.b of Article 20.

CHAPTER V
GENERAL PROVISIONS

Article 27

1. For the purposes of the present Convention, the expression 'Contracting State' shall not include any legal entity of a Contracting State which is distinct therefrom and is capable of suing or being sued, even if that entity has been entrusted with public functions.
2. Proceedings may be instituted against any entity referred to in paragraph 1 before the courts of another Contracting State in the same manner as against a private person; however, the courts may not entertain proceedings in respect of acts performed by the entity in the exercise of sovereign authority *(acta jure imperii)*.
3. Proceedings may in any event be instituted against any such entity before those courts if, in corresponding circumstances, the courts would have had jurisdiction if the proceedings had been instituted against a Contracting State.

Article 28

1. Without prejudice to the provisions of Article 27, the constituent States of a Federal State do not enjoy immunity.
2. However, a Federal State Party to the present Convention, may, by notification addressed to the Secretary General of the Council of Europe, declare that its constituent States may invoke the provisions of the Convention applicable to Contracting States, and have the same obligations.
3. Where a Federal State has made a declaration in accordance with paragraph 2, service of documents on a constituent State of a Federation shall be made on the Ministry of Foreign Affairs of the Federal State, in conformity with Article 16.
4. The Federal State alone is competent to make the declarations, notifications and communications provided for in the present Convention, and the Federal State alone may be party to proceedings pursuant to Article 34.

Article 29

The present Convention shall not apply to proceedings concerning:
   a. social security;
   b. damage or injury in nuclear matters;
   c. customs duties, taxes or penalties.

Article 30

The present Convention shall not apply to proceedings in respect of claims relating to the operation of seagoing vessels owned or operated by a Contracting State or to the carriage of cargoes and of passengers by such vessels or to the carriage of cargoes owned by a Contracting State and carried on board merchant vessels.

Article 31

Nothing in this Convention shall affect any immunities or privileges enjoyed by a Contracting State in respect of anything done or omitted to be done by, or in relation to, its armed forces when on the territory of another Contracting State.

Article 32

Nothing in the present Convention shall affect privileges and immunities relating to the exercise of the functions of diplomatic missions and consular posts and of persons connected with them.

Article 33

Nothing in the present Convention shall affect existing or future international agreements in special fields which relate to matters dealt with in the present Convention.

Article 34

1. Any dispute which might arise between two or more Contracting States concerning the interpretation or application of the present Convention shall be submitted to the International Court of Justice on the application of one of the parties to the dispute or by special agreement unless the parties agree on a different method of peaceful settlement of the dispute.
2. However, proceedings may not be instituted before the International Court of Justice which relate to:
   a. a dispute concerning a question arising in proceedings instituted against a Contracting State before a court of another Contracting State, before the court has given a judgment which fulfils the condition provided for in paragraph 1.b of Article 20;
   b. a dispute concerning a question arising in proceedings instituted before a court of a Contracting State in accordance with paragraph 1 of Article 21, before the court has rendered a final decision in such proceedings.

Article 35

1. The present Convention shall apply only to proceedings introduced after its entry into force.
2. When a State has become Party to this Convention after it has entered into force, the Convention shall apply only to proceedings introduced after it has entered into force with respect to that State.
3. Nothing in this Convention shall apply to proceedings arising out of, or judgments based on, acts, omissions or facts prior to the date on which the present Convention is opened for signature.

CHAPTER VI
FINAL PROVISIONS

Article 36

1. The present Convention shall be open to signature by the member States of the Council of Europe. It shall be subject to ratification or acceptance. Instruments of ratification or acceptance shall be deposited with the Secretary General of the Council of Europe.
2. The Convention shall enter into force three months after the date of the deposit of the third instrument of ratification or acceptance.

3. In respect of a signatory State ratifying or accepting subsequently, the Convention shall enter into force three months after the date of the deposit of its instrument of ratification or acceptance.

Article 37

1. After the entry into force of the present Convention, the Committee of Ministers of the Council of Europe may, by a decision taken by a unanimous vote of the members casting a vote, invite any non-member State to accede thereto.
2. Such accession shall be effected by depositing with the Secretary General of the Council of Europe an instrument of accession which shall take effect three months after the date of its deposit.
3. However, if a State having already acceded to the Convention notifies the Secretary General of the Council of Europe of its objection to the accession of another non-member State, before the entry into force of this accession, the Convention shall not apply to the relations between these two States.

Article 38

1. Any State may, at the time of signature or when depositing its instrument of ratification, acceptance or accession, specify the territory or territories to which the present Convention shall apply.
2. Any State may, when depositing its instrument of ratification, acceptance or accession or at any later date, by declaration addressed to the Secretary General of the Council of Europe, extend this Convention to any other territory or territories specified in the declaration and for whose international relations it is responsible or on whose behalf it is authorised to give undertakings.
3. Any declaration made in pursuance of the preceding paragraph may, in respect of any territory mentioned in such declaration, be withdrawn according to the procedure laid down in Article 40 of this Convention.

Article 39

No reservation is permitted to the present Convention.

Article 40

1. Any Contracting State may, in so far as it is concerned, denounce this Convention by means of notification addressed to the Secretary General of the Council of Europe.
2. Such denunciation shall take effect six months after the date of receipt by the Secretary General of such notification. This Convention shall, however, continue to apply to proceedings introduced before the date on which the denunciation takes effect, and to judgments given in such proceedings.

Article 41

The Secretary General of the Council of Europe shall notify the member States of the Council of Europe and any State which has acceded to this Convention of:
   a. any signature;
   b. any deposit of an instrument of ratification, acceptance or accession;

c. any date of entry into force of this Convention in accordance with Articles 36 and 37 thereof;

d. any notification received in pursuance of the provisions of paragraph 2 of Article 19;

e. any communication received in pursuance of the provisions of paragraph 4 of Article 21;

f. any notification received in pursuance of the provisions of paragraph 1 of Article 24;

g. the withdrawal of any notification made in pursuance of the provisions of paragraph 4 of Article 24;

h. any notification received in pursuance of the provisions of paragraph 2 of Article 28;

i. any notification received in pursuance of the provisions of paragraph 3 or Article 37;

j. any declaration received in pursuance of the provisions of Article 38;

k. any notification received in pursuance of the provisions of Article 40 and the date on which denunciation takes effect.

In witness whereof the undersigned, being duly authorised thereto, have signed this Convention.

Done at Basle, this 16th day of May 1972, in English and French, both texts being equally authoritative, in a single copy which shall remain deposited in the archives of the Council of Europe. The Secretary General of the Council of Europe shall transmit certified copies to each of the signatory and acceding States.

ANNEX

The grounds of jurisdiction referred to in paragraph 3, sub-paragraph a, of Article 20, paragraph 2 of Article 24 and paragraph 3, sub-paragraph b, of Article 25 are the following:

a. the presence in the territory of the State of the forum of property belonging to the defendant, or the seizure by the plaintiff of property situated there, unless:

- the action is brought to assert proprietary or possessory rights in that property, or arises from another issue relating to such property; or
- the property constitutes the security for a debt which is the subject-matter of the action;

b. the nationality of the plaintiff;

c. the domicile, habitual residence or ordinary residence of the plaintiff within the territory of the State of the forum unless the assumption of jurisdiction on such a ground is permitted by way of an exception made on account of the particular subject-matter of a class of contracts;

d. the fact that the defendant carried on business within the territory of the State of the forum, unless the action arises from that business;

e. a unilateral specification of the forum by the plaintiff, particularly in an invoice.

A legal person shall be considered to have its domicile or habitual residence where it has its seat, registered office or principal place of business.

ADDITIONAL PROTOCOL TO THE EUROPEAN CONVENTION ON STATE IMMUNITY

Basle, 16.V.1972

The member States of the Council of Europe, signatory to the present Protocol,

Having taken note of the European Convention on State Immunity—hereinafter referred to as 'the Convention'—and in particular Articles 21 and 34 thereof;

Desiring to develop the work of harmonisation in the field covered by the Convention by the addition of provisions concerning a European procedure for the settlement of disputes,

Have agreed as follows:

PART I

Article 1

1. Where a judgment has been given against a State Party to the Convention and that State does not give effect thereto, the party which seeks to invoke the judgment shall be entitled to have determined the question whether effect should be given to the judgment in conformity with Article 20 or Article 25 of the Convention, by instituting proceedings before either:
   a. the competent court of that State in application of Article 21 of the Convention; or
   b. the European Tribunal constituted in conformity with the provisions of Part III of the present Protocol, provided that that State is a Party to the present Protocol and has not made the declaration referred to in Part IV thereof.
   The choice between these two possibilites shall be final.
2. If the State intends to institute proceedings before its court in accordance with the provisions of paragraph 1 or Article 21 of the Convention, it must give notice of its intention to do so to the party in whose favour the judgment has been given; the State may thereafter institute such proceedings only if the party has not, within three months of receiving notice, instituted proceedings before the European Tribunal. Once this period has elapsed, the party in whose favour the judgment has been given may no longer institute proceedings before the European Tribunal.
3. Save in so far as may be necessary for the application of Articles 20 and 25 of the Convention, the European Tribunal may not review the merits of the judgment.

PART II

Article 2

1. Any dispute which might arise between two or more States parties to the present Protocol concerning the interpretation or application of the Convention shall be submitted, on the application of one of the parties to the dispute or by special agreement, to the

820

European Tribunal constituted in conformity with the provisions of Part III of the present Protocol. The States parties to the present Protocol undertake not to submit such a dispute to a different mode of settlement.

2. If the dispute concerns a question arising in proceedings instituted before a court of one State Party to the Convention against another State Party to the Convention, or a question arising in proceedings instituted before a court of a State Party to the Convention in accordance with Article 21 of the Convention, it may not be referred to the European Tribunal until the court has given a final decision in such proceedings.

3. Proceedings may not be instituted before the European Tribunal which relate to a dispute concerning a judgment which it has already determined or is required to determine by virtue of Part I of this Protocol.

Article 3

Nothing in the present Protocol shall be interpreted as preventing the European Tribunal from determining any dispute which might arise between two or more States parties to the Convention concerning the interpretation or application thereof and which might be submitted to it by special agreement, even if these States, or any of them, are not parties to the present Protocol.

PART III

Article 4

1. There shall be established a European Tribunal in matters of State Immunity to determine cases brought before it in conformity with the provisions of Parts I and II of the present Protocol.

2. The European Tribunal shall consist of the members of the European Court of Human Rights and, in respect of each non-member State of the Council of Europe which has acceded to the present Protocol, a person possessing the qualifications required of members of that Court designated, with the agreement of the Committee of Ministers of the Council of Europe, by the government of that State for a period of nine years.

3. The President of the European Tribunal shall be the President of the European Court of Human Rights.

Article 5

1. Where proceedings are instituted before the European Tribunal in accordance with the provisions of Part I of the present Protocol, the European Tribunal shall consist of a Chamber composed of seven members. There shall sit as *ex officio* members of the Chamber the member of the European Tribunal who is a national of the State against which the judgment has been given and the member of the European Tribunal who is a national of the State of the forum, or, should there be no such member in one or the other case, a person designated by the government of the State concerned to sit in the capacity of a member of the Chamber. The names of the other five members shall be chosen by lot by the President of the European Tribunal in the presence of the Registrar.

2. Where proceedings are instituted before the European Tribunal in accordance with the provisions of Part II of the present Protocol, the Chamber shall be constituted in

the manner provided for in the preceding paragraph. However, there shall sit as *ex officio* members of the Chamber the members of the European Tribunal who are nationals of the States parties to the dispute or, should there be no such member, a person designated by the government of the State concerned to sit in the capacity of a member of the Chamber.

3. Where a case pending before a Chamber raises a serious question affecting the interpretation of the Convention or of the present Protocol, the Chamber may, at any time, relinquish jurisdiction in favour of the European Tribunal meeting in plenary session. The relinquishment of jurisdiction shall be obligatory where the resolution of such question might have a result inconsistent with a judgment previously delivered by a Chamber or by the European Tribunal meeting in plenary session. The relinquishment of jurisdiction shall be final. Reasons need not be given for the decision to relinquish jurisdiction.

Article 6

1. The European Tribunal shall decide any disputes as to whether the Tribunal has jurisdiction.
2. The hearings of the European Tribunal shall be public unless the Tribunal in exceptional circumstances decides otherwise.
3. The judgments of the European Tribunal, taken by a majority of the members present, are to be delivered in public session. Reasons shall be given for the judgment of the European Tribunal. If the judgment does not represent in whole or in part the unanimous opinion of the European Tribunal, any member shall be entitled to deliver a separate opinion.
4. The judgments of the European Tribunal shall be final and binding upon the parties.

Article 7

1. The European Tribunal shall draw up its own rules and fix its own procedure.
2. The Registry of the European Tribunal shall be provided by the Registrar of the European Court of Human Rights.

Article 8

1. The operating costs of the European Tribunal shall be borne by the Council of Europe. States non-members of the Council of Europe having acceded to the present Protocol shall contribute thereto in a manner to be decided by the Committee of Ministers after agreement with these States.
2. The members of the European Tribunal shall receive for each day of duty a compensation to be determined by the Committee of Ministers.

PART IV

Article 9

1. Any State may, by notification addressed to the Secretary General of the Council of Europe at the moment of its signature of the present Protocol, or of the deposit of its

instrument of ratification, acceptance or accession thereto, declare that it will only be bound by Parts II to V of the present Protocol.

2. Such a notification may be withdrawn at any time.

PART V

Article 10

1. The present Protocol shall be open to signature by the member States of the Council of Europe which have signed the Convention. It shall be subject to ratification or acceptance. Instruments of ratification or acceptance shall be deposited with the Secretary General of the Council of Europe.
2. The present Protocol shall enter into force three months after the date of the deposit of the fifth instrument of ratification or acceptance.
3. In respect of a signatory State ratifying or accepting subsequently, the Protocol shall enter into force three months after the date of the deposit of its instrument of ratification or acceptance.
4. A member State of the Council of Europe may not ratify or accept the present Protocol without having ratified or accepted the Convention.

Article 11

1. A State which has acceded to the Convention may accede to the present Protocol after the Protocol has entered into force.
2. Such accession shall be effected by depositing with the Secretary General of the Council of Europe an instrument of accession which shall take effect three months after the date of its deposit.

Article 12

No reservation is permitted to the present Protocol.

Article 13

1. Any Contracting State may, in so far as it is concerned, denounce the present Protocol by means of a notification addressed to the Secretary General of the Council of Europe.
2. Such denunciation shall take effect six months after the date of receipt by the Secretary General of such notification. The Protocol shall, however, continue to apply to proceedings introduced in conformity with the provisions of the protocol before the date on which such denunciation takes effect.
3. Denunciation of the Convention shall automatically entail denunciation of the present Protocol.

Article 14

The Secretary General of the Council of Europe shall notify the member States of the Council and any State which has acceded to the Convention of:
  a. any signature of the present Protocol;
  b. any deposit of an instrument of ratification, acceptance or accession;

823

c. any date of entry into force of the present Protocol in accordance with Articles 10 and 11 thereof;

d. any notification received in pursuance of the provisions of Part IV and any withdrawal of any such notification;

e. any notification received in pursuance of the provisions of Article 13 and the date on which such denunciation takes effect.

In witness whereof the undersigned, being duly authorised thereto, have signed the present Protocol.

Done at Basle, this 16th day of May 1972, in English and French, both texts being equally authoritative, in a single copy which shall remain deposited in the archives of the Council of Europe. The Secretary General of the Council of Europe shall transmit certified copies to each of the signatory and acceding States.

TABLE OF STATE RATIFICATIONS

Total number of signatures not followed by ratifications: 1
Total number of ratifications/accessions: 8

Member States of the Council of Europe:

State	Signature	Ratification	Entry into force	Notes
Albania				
Andorra				
Armenia				
Austria	16 May 1972	10 July 1974	11 June 1976	Declaration; Authority
Azerbaijan				
Belgium	16 May 1972	27 October 1975	11 June 1976	Declaration; Authority
Bosnia and Herzegovina				
Bulgaria				
Croatia				
Cyprus	15 December 1975	10 March 1976	11 June 1976	
Czech Republic				
Denmark				
Estonia				
Finland				
France				
Georgia				
Germany	16 May 1972	15 May 1990	16 August 1990	Declaration; Authority; Territorial Application
Greece				
Hungary				
Iceland				
Ireland				

State	Signature	Ratification	Entry into force	Notes
Italy				
Latvia				
Liechtenstein				
Lithuania				
Luxembourg	16 May 1972	11 December 1986	12 March 1987	Declaration; Authority
Malta				
Moldova				
Netherlands	16 May 1972	21 February 1985	22 May 1985	Declaration; Authority; Territorial Application
Norway				
Poland				
Portugal	10 May 1979			
Romania				
Russia				
San Marino				
Serbia and Montenegro				
Slovakia				
Slovenia				
Spain				
Sweden				
Switzerland	16 May 1972	6 July 1982	7 October 1982	Declaration
The former Yugoslav Republic of Macedonia				
Turkey				
Ukraine				
United Kingdom	16 May 1972	3 July 1979	4 October 1979	Declaration; Authority; Territorial Application; Communication

Basel, 16 May 1972

Entered into force: 11 June 1976
(Condition: 5 ratifications)

(ii) COUNCIL REGULATION (EC) NO 44/2001 OF 22 DECEMBER 2000 ON JURISDICTION AND THE RECOGNITION AND ENFORCEMENT OF JUDGMENTS IN CIVIL AND COMMERCIAL MATTERS

PREAMBLE

THE COUNCIL OF THE EUROPEAN UNION,

Having regard to the Treaty establishing the European Community, and in particular Article 61(c) and Article 67(1) thereof,

Having regard to the proposal from the Commission[1],

Having regard to the opinion of the European Parliament[2],

Having regard to the opinion of the Economic and Social Committee[3],

Whereas:

(1) The Community has set itself the objective of maintaining and developing an area of freedom, security and justice, in which the free movement of persons is ensured. In order to establish progressively such an area, the Community should adopt, amongst other things, the measures relating to judicial cooperation in civil matters which are necessary for the sound operation of the internal market.

(2) Certain differences between national rules governing jurisdiction and recognition of judgments hamper the sound operation of the internal market. Provisions to unify the rules of conflict of jurisdiction in civil and commercial matters and to simplify the formalities with a view to rapid and simple recognition and enforcement of judgments from Member States bound by this Regulation are essential.

(3) This area is within the field of judicial cooperation in civil matters within the meaning of Article 65 of the Treaty.

(4) In accordance with the principles of subsidiarity and proportionality as set out in Article 5 of the Treaty, the objectives of this Regulation cannot be sufficiently achieved by the Member States and can therefore be better achieved by the Community. This Regulation confines itself to the minimum required in order

---

[1] OJ C 376, 28.12.1999, p. 1.
[2] Opinion delivered on 21 September 2000 (not yet published in the Official Journal).
[3] OJ C 117, 26.4.2000, p. 6.

to achieve those objectives and does not go beyond what is necessary for that purpose.

(5) On 27 September 1968 the Member States, acting under Article 293, fourth indent, of the Treaty, concluded the Brussels Convention on Jurisdiction and the Enforcement of Judgments in Civil and Commercial Matters, as amended by Conventions on the Accession of the New Member States to that Convention (hereinafter referred to as the 'Brussels Convention').[4] On 16 September 1988 Member States and EFTA States concluded the Lugano Convention on Jurisdiction and the Enforcement of Judgments in Civil and Commercial Matters, which is a parallel Convention to the 1968 Brussels Convention. Work has been undertaken for the revision of those Conventions, and the Council has approved the content of the revised texts. Continuity in the results achieved in that revision should be ensured.

(6) In order to attain the objective of free movement of judgments in civil and commercial matters, it is necessary and appropriate that the rules governing jurisdiction and the recognition and enforcement of judgments be governed by a Community legal instrument which is binding and directly applicable.

(7) The scope of this Regulation must cover all the main civil and commercial matters apart from certain well-defined matters.

(8) There must be a link between proceedings to which this Regulation applies and the territory of the Member States bound by this Regulation. Accordingly common rules on jurisdiction should, in principle, apply when the defendant is domiciled in one of those Member States.

(9) A defendant not domiciled in a Member State is in general subject to national rules of jurisdiction applicable in the territory of the Member State of the court seised, and a defendant domiciled in a Member State not bound by this Regulation must remain subject to the Brussels Convention.

(10) For the purposes of the free movement of judgments, judgments given in a Member State bound by this Regulation should be recognised and enforced in another Member State bound by this Regulation, even if the judgment debtor is domiciled in a third State.

(11) The rules of jurisdiction must be highly predictable and founded on the principle that jurisdiction is generally based on the defendant's domicile and jurisdiction must always be available on this ground save in a few well-defined situations in which the subject-matter of the litigation or the autonomy of the parties warrants a different linking factor. The domicile of a legal person must be defined autonomously so as to make the common rules more transparent and avoid conflicts of jurisdiction.

(12) In addition to the defendant's domicile, there should be alternative grounds of jurisdiction based on a close link between the court and the action or in order to facilitate the sound administration of justice.

---

[4] OJ L 299, 31.12.1972, p. 32.
OJ L 304, 30.10.1978, p. 1.
OJ L 388, 31.12.1982, p. 1.
OJ L 285, 3.10.1989, p. 1.
OJ C 15, 15.1.1997, p. 1.
For a consolidated text, see OJ C 27, 26.1.1998, p. 1.

(13) In relation to insurance, consumer contracts and employment, the weaker party should be protected by rules of jurisdiction more favourable to his interests than the general rules provide for.

(14) The autonomy of the parties to a contract, other than an insurance, consumer or employment contract, where only limited autonomy to determine the courts having jurisdiction is allowed, must be respected subject to the exclusive grounds of jurisdiction laid down in this Regulation.

(15) In the interests of the harmonious administration of justice it is necessary to minimise the possibility of concurrent proceedings and to ensure that irreconcilable judgments will not be given in two Member States. There must be a clear and effective mechanism for resolving cases of lis pendens and related actions and for obviating problems flowing from national differences as to the determination of the time when a case is regarded as pending. For the purposes of this Regulation that time should be defined autonomously.

(16) Mutual trust in the administration of justice in the Community justifies judgments given in a Member State being recognised automatically without the need for any procedure except in cases of dispute.

(17) By virtue of the same principle of mutual trust, the procedure for making enforceable in one Member State a judgment given in another must be efficient and rapid. To that end, the declaration that a judgment is enforceable should be issued virtually automatically after purely formal checks of the documents supplied, without there being any possibility for the court to raise of its own motion any of the grounds for non-enforcement provided for by this Regulation.

(18) However, respect for the rights of the defence means that the defendant should be able to appeal in an adversarial procedure, against the declaration of enforceability, if he considers one of the grounds for non-enforcement to be present. Redress procedures should also be available to the claimant where his application for a declaration of enforceability has been rejected.

(19) Continuity between the Brussels Convention and this Regulation should be ensured, and transitional provisions should be laid down to that end. The same need for continuity applies as regards the interpretation of the Brussels Convention by the Court of Justice of the European Communities and the 1971 Protocol[5] should remain applicable also to cases already pending when this Regulation enters into force.

(20) The United Kingdom and Ireland, in accordance with Article 3 of the Protocol on the position of the United Kingdom and Ireland annexed to the Treaty on European Union and to the Treaty establishing the European Community, have given notice of their wish to take part in the adoption and application of this Regulation.

(21) Denmark, in accordance with Articles 1 and 2 of the Protocol on the position of Denmark annexed to the Treaty on European Union and to the Treaty

---

[5] OJ L 204, 2.8.1975, p. 28.
OJ L 304, 30.10.1978, p. 1.
OJ L 388, 31.12.1982, p. 1.
OJ L 285, 3.10.1989, p. 1.
OJ C 15, 15.1.1997, p. 1.
For a consolidated text see OJ C 27, 26.1.1998, p. 28.

establishing the European Community, is not participating in the adoption of this Regulation, and is therefore not bound by it nor subject to its application.

(22) Since the Brussels Convention remains in force in relations between Denmark and the Member States that are bound by this Regulation, both the Convention and the 1971 Protocol continue to apply between Denmark and the Member States bound by this Regulation.

(23) The Brussels Convention also continues to apply to the territories of the Member States which fall within the territorial scope of that Convention and which are excluded from this Regulation pursuant to Article 299 of the Treaty.

(24) Likewise for the sake of consistency, this Regulation should not affect rules governing jurisdiction and the recognition of judgments contained in specific Community instruments.

(25) Respect for international commitments entered into by the Member States means that this Regulation should not affect conventions relating to specific matters to which the Member States are parties.

(26) The necessary flexibility should be provided for in the basic rules of this Regulation in order to take account of the specific procedural rules of certain Member States. Certain provisions of the Protocol annexed to the Brussels Convention should accordingly be incorporated in this Regulation.

(27) In order to allow a harmonious transition in certain areas which were the subject of special provisions in the Protocol annexed to the Brussels Convention, this Regulation lays down, for a transitional period, provisions taking into consideration the specific situation in certain Member States.

(28) No later than five years after entry into force of this Regulation the Commission will present a report on its application and, if need be, submit proposals for adaptations.

(29) The Commission will have to adjust Annexes I to IV on the rules of national jurisdiction, the courts or competent authorities and redress procedures available on the basis of the amendments forwarded by the Member State concerned; amendments made to Annexes V and VI should be adopted in accordance with Council Decision 1999/468/EC of 28 June 1999 laying down the procedures for the exercise of implementing powers conferred on the Commission[6],

HAS ADOPTED THIS REGULATION:

CHAPTER I
SCOPE

Article 1

1. This Regulation shall apply in civil and commercial matters whatever the nature of the court or tribunal. It shall not extend, in particular, to revenue, customs or administrative matters.

2. The Regulation shall not apply to:
   (a) the status or legal capacity of natural persons, rights in property arising out of a matrimonial relationship, wills and succession;
   (b) bankruptcy, proceedings relating to the winding-up of insolvent companies or other legal persons, judicial arrangements, compositions and analogous proceedings;

---

[6] OJ L 184, 17.7.1999, p. 23.

(c) social security;

(d) arbitration.

3. In this Regulation, the term 'Member State' shall mean Member States with the exception of Denmark.

CHAPTER II
JURISDICTION

SECTION I
GENERAL PROVISION

Article 2

1. Subject to this Regulation, persons domiciled in a Member State shall, whatever their nationality, be sued in the courts of that Member State.

2. Persons who are not nationals of the Member State in which they are domiciled shall be governed by the rules of jurisdiction applicable to nationals of that State.

Article 3

1. Persons domiciled in a Member State may be sued in the courts of another Member State only by virtue of the rules set out in Sections 2 to 7 of this Chapter.

2. In particular the rules of national jurisdiction set out in Annex I shall not be applicable as against them.

Article 4

1. If the defendant is not domiciled in a Member State, the jurisdiction of the courts of each Member State shall, subject to Articles 22 and 23, be determined by the law of that Member State.

2. As against such a defendant, any person domiciled in a Member State may, whatever his nationality, avail himself in that State of the rules of jurisdiction there in force, and in particular those specified in Annex I, in the same way as the nationals of that State.

SECTION 2
SPECIAL JURISDICTION

Article 5

A person domiciled in a Member State may, in another Member State, be sued:

1. (a) in matters relating to a contract, in the courts for the place of performance of the obligation in question;

(b) for the purpose of this provision and unless otherwise agreed, the place of performance of the obligation in question shall be:

—in the case of the sale of goods, the place in a Member State where, under the contract, the goods were delivered or should have been delivered,

—in the case of the provision of services, the place in a Member State where, under the contract, the services were provided or should have been provided,

(c) if subparagraph (b) does not apply then subparagraph (a) applies;

2. in matters relating to maintenance, in the courts for the place where the maintenance creditor is domiciled or habitually resident or, if the matter is ancillary to proceedings concerning the status of a person, in the court which, according to its own law, has jurisdiction to entertain those proceedings, unless that jurisdiction is based solely on the nationality of one of the parties;

3. in matters relating to tort, delict or quasi-delict, in the courts for the place where the harmful event occurred or may occur;

4. as regards a civil claim for damages or restitution which is based on an act giving rise to criminal proceedings, in the court seised of those proceedings, to the extent that that court has jurisdiction under its own law to entertain civil proceedings;

5. as regards a dispute arising out of the operations of a branch, agency or other establishment, in the courts for the place in which the branch, agency or other establishment is situated;

6. as settlor, trustee or beneficiary of a trust created by the operation of a statute, or by a written instrument, or created orally and evidenced in writing, in the courts of the Member State in which the trust is domiciled;

7. as regards a dispute concerning the payment of remuneration claimed in respect of the salvage of a cargo or freight, in the court under the authority of which the cargo or freight in question:
   (a) has been arrested to secure such payment, or
   (b) could have been so arrested, but bail or other security has been given;
   provided that this provision shall apply only if it is claimed that the defendant has an interest in the cargo or freight or had such an interest at the time of salvage.

Article 6

A person domiciled in a Member State may also be sued:
1. where he is one of a number of defendants, in the courts for the place where any one of them is domiciled, provided the claims are so closely connected that it is expedient to hear and determine them together to avoid the risk of irreconcilable judgments resulting from separate proceedings;

2. as a third party in an action on a warranty or guarantee or in any other third party proceedings, in the court seised of the original proceedings, unless these were instituted solely with the object of removing him from the jurisdiction of the court which would be competent in his case;

3. on a counter-claim arising from the same contract or facts on which the original claim was based, in the court in which the original claim is pending;

4. in matters relating to a contract, if the action may be combined with an action against the same defendant in matters relating to rights in rem in immovable property, in the court of the Member State in which the property is situated.

Article 7

Where by virtue of this Regulation a court of a Member State has jurisdiction in actions relating to liability from the use or operation of a ship, that court, or any other court substituted for this purpose by the internal law of that Member State, shall also have jurisdiction over claims for limitation of such liability.

SECTION 3
JURISDICTION IN MATTERS RELATING TO INSURANCE

Article 8

In matters relating to insurance, jurisdiction shall be determined by this Section, without prejudice to Article 4 and point 5 of Article 5.

Article 9

1. An insurer domiciled in a Member State may be sued:
   (a) in the courts of the Member State where he is domiciled, or
   (b) in another Member State, in the case of actions brought by the policyholder, the insured or a beneficiary, in the courts for the place where the plaintiff is domiciled,
   (c) if he is a co-insurer, in the courts of a Member State in which proceedings are brought against the leading insurer.
2. An insurer who is not domiciled in a Member State but has a branch, agency or other establishment in one of the Member States shall, in disputes arising out of the operations of the branch, agency or establishment, be deemed to be domiciled in that Member State.

Article 10

In respect of liability insurance or insurance of immovable property, the insurer may in addition be sued in the courts for the place where the harmful event occurred. The same applies if movable and immovable property are covered by the same insurance policy and both are adversely affected by the same contingency.

Article 11

1. In respect of liability insurance, the insurer may also, if the law of the court permits it, be joined in proceedings which the injured party has brought against the insured.
2. Articles 8, 9 and 10 shall apply to actions brought by the injured party directly against the insurer, where such direct actions are permitted.
3. If the law governing such direct actions provides that the policyholder or the insured may be joined as a party to the action, the same court shall have jurisdiction over them.

Article 12

1. Without prejudice to Article 11(3), an insurer may bring proceedings only in the courts of the Member State in which the defendant is domiciled, irrespective of whether he is the policyholder, the insured or a beneficiary.
2. The provisions of this Section shall not affect the right to bring a counter-claim in the court in which, in accordance with this Section, the original claim is pending.

Article 13

The provisions of this Section may be departed from only by an agreement:
1. which is entered into after the dispute has arisen, or

2. which allows the policyholder, the insured or a beneficiary to bring proceedings in courts other than those indicated in this Section, or

3. which is concluded between a policyholder and an insurer, both of whom are at the time of conclusion of the contract domiciled or habitually resident in the same Member State, and which has the effect of conferring jurisdiction on the courts of that State even if the harmful event were to occur abroad, provided that such an agreement is not contrary to the law of that State, or

4. which is concluded with a policyholder who is not domiciled in a Member State, except in so far as the insurance is compulsory or relates to immovable property in a Member State, or

5. which relates to a contract of insurance in so far as it covers one or more of the risks set out in Article 14.

Article 14

The following are the risks referred to in Article 13(5):

1. any loss of or damage to:
   (a) seagoing ships, installations situated offshore or on the high seas, or aircraft, arising from perils which relate to their use for commercial purposes;
   (b) goods in transit other than passengers' baggage where the transit consists of or includes carriage by such ships or aircraft;

2. any liability, other than for bodily injury to passengers or loss of or damage to their baggage:
   (a) arising out of the use or operation of ships, installations or aircraft as referred to in point 1(a) in so far as, in respect of the latter, the law of the Member State in which such aircraft are registered does not prohibit agreements on jurisdiction regarding insurance of such risks;
   (b) for loss or damage caused by goods in transit as described in point 1(b);

3. any financial loss connected with the use or operation of ships, installations or aircraft as referred to in point 1(a), in particular loss of freight or charter-hire;

4. any risk or interest connected with any of those referred to in points 1 to 3;

5. notwithstanding points 1 to 4, all 'large risks' as defined in Council Directive 73/239/EEC,[7] as amended by Council Directives 88/357/EEC[8] and 90/618/EEC[9], as they may be amended.

SECTION 4

JURISDICTION OVER CONSUMER CONTRACTS

Article 15

1. In matters relating to a contract concluded by a person, the consumer, for a purpose which can be regarded as being outside his trade or profession, jurisdiction

---

[7] OJ L 228, 16.8.1973, p. 3. Directive as last amended by Directive 2000/26/EC of the European Parliament and of the Council (OJ L 181, 20.7.2000, p. 65).

[8] OJ L 172, 4.7.1988, p. 1. Directive as last amended by Directive 2000/26/EC.

[9] OJ L 330, 29.11.1990, p. 44.

shall be determined by this Section, without prejudice to Article 4 and point 5 of Article 5, if:

(a) it is a contract for the sale of goods on instalment credit terms; or

(b) it is a contract for a loan repayable by instalments, or for any other form of credit, made to finance the sale of goods; or

(c) in all other cases, the contract has been concluded with a person who pursues commercial or professional activities in the Member State of the consumer's domicile or, by any means, directs such activities to that Member State or to several States including that Member State, and the contract falls within the scope of such activities.

2. Where a consumer enters into a contract with a party who is not domiciled in the Member State but has a branch, agency or other establishment in one of the Member States, that party shall, in disputes arising out of the operations of the branch, agency or establishment, be deemed to be domiciled in that State.

3. This Section shall not apply to a contract of transport other than a contract which, for an inclusive price, provides for a combination of travel and accommodation.

Article 16

1. A consumer may bring proceedings against the other party to a contract either in the courts of the Member State in which that party is domiciled or in the courts for the place where the consumer is domiciled.

2. Proceedings may be brought against a consumer by the other party to the contract only in the courts of the Member State in which the consumer is domiciled.

3. This Article shall not affect the right to bring a counter-claim in the court in which, in accordance with this Section, the original claim is pending.

Article 17

The provisions of this Section may be departed from only by an agreement:

1. which is entered into after the dispute has arisen; or

2. which allows the consumer to bring proceedings in courts other than those indicated in this Section; or

3. which is entered into by the consumer and the other party to the contract, both of whom are at the time of conclusion of the contract domiciled or habitually resident in the same Member State, and which confers jurisdiction on the courts of that Member State, provided that such an agreement is not contrary to the law of that Member State.

SECTION 5

JURISDICTION OVER INDIVIDUAL CONTRACTS OF
EMPLOYMENT

Article 18

1. In matters relating to individual contracts of employment, jurisdiction shall be determined by this Section, without prejudice to Article 4 and point 5 of Article 5.

2. Where an employee enters into an individual contract of employment with an employer who is not domiciled in a Member State but has a branch, agency or other establishment in one of the Member States, the employer shall, in disputes arising out of the operations of the branch, agency or establishment, be deemed to be domiciled in that Member State.

Article 19

An employer domiciled in a Member State may be sued:
1. in the courts of the Member State where he is domiciled; or
2. in another Member State:
   (a) in the courts for the place where the employee habitually carries out his work or in the courts for the last place where he did so, or
   (b) if the employee does not or did not habitually carry out his work in any one country, in the courts for the place where the business which engaged the employee is or was situated.

Article 20

1. An employer may bring proceedings only in the courts of the Member State in which the employee is domiciled.
2. The provisions of this Section shall not affect the right to bring a counter-claim in the court in which, in accordance with this Section, the original claim is pending.

Article 21

The provisions of this Section may be departed from only by an agreement on jurisdiction:
1. which is entered into after the dispute has arisen; or
2. which allows the employee to bring proceedings in courts other than those indicated in this Section.

SECTION 6

EXCLUSIVE JURISDICTION

Article 22

The following courts shall have exclusive jurisdiction, regardless of domicile:
1. in proceedings which have as their object rights in rem in immovable property or tenancies of immovable property, the courts of the Member State in which the property is situated.
   However, in proceedings which have as their object tenancies of immovable property concluded for temporary private use for a maximum period of six consecutive months, the courts of the Member State in which the defendant is domiciled shall also have jurisdiction, provided that the tenant is a natural person and that the landlord and the tenant are domiciled in the same Member State;
2. in proceedings which have as their object the validity of the constitution, the nullity or the dissolution of companies or other legal persons or associations of natural or legal persons, or of the validity of the decisions of their organs, the courts of the Member State in which the company, legal person or association has its seat. In order to determine that seat, the court shall apply its rules of private international law;
3. in proceedings which have as their object the validity of entries in public registers, the courts of the Member State in which the register is kept;
4. in proceedings concerned with the registration or validity of patents, trade marks, designs, or other similar rights required to be deposited or registered, the courts of

the Member State in which the deposit or registration has been applied for, has taken place or is under the terms of a Community instrument or an international convention deemed to have taken place.

Without prejudice to the jurisdiction of the European Patent Office under the Convention on the Grant of European Patents, signed at Munich on 5 October 1973, the courts of each Member State shall have exclusive jurisdiction, regardless of domicile, in proceedings concerned with the registration or validity of any European patent granted for that State;

5. in proceedings concerned with the enforcement of judgments, the courts of the Member State in which the judgment has been or is to be enforced.

SECTION 7

PROROGATION OF JURISDICTION

Article 23

1. If the parties, one or more of whom is domiciled in a Member State, have agreed that a court or the courts of a Member State are to have jurisdiction to settle any disputes which have arisen or which may arise in connection with a particular legal relationship, that court or those courts shall have jurisdiction. Such jurisdiction shall be exclusive unless the parties have agreed otherwise. Such an agreement conferring jurisdiction shall be either:
   (a) in writing or evidenced in writing; or
   (b) in a form which accords with practices which the parties have established between themselves; or
   (c) in international trade or commerce, in a form which accords with a usage of which the parties are or ought to have been aware and which in such trade or commerce is widely known to, and regularly observed by, parties to contracts of the type involved in the particular trade or commerce concerned.
2. Any communication by electronic means which provides a durable record of the agreement shall be equivalent to 'writing'.
3. Where such an agreement is concluded by parties, none of whom is domiciled in a Member State, the courts of other Member States shall have no jurisdiction over their disputes unless the court or courts chosen have declined jurisdiction.
4. The court or courts of a Member State on which a trust instrument has conferred jurisdiction shall have exclusive jurisdiction in any proceedings brought against a settlor, trustee or beneficiary, if relations between these persons or their rights or obligations under the trust are involved.
5. Agreements or provisions of a trust instrument conferring jurisdiction shall have no legal force if they are contrary to Articles 13, 17 or 21, or if the courts whose jurisdiction they purport to exclude have exclusive jurisdiction by virtue of Article 22.

Article 24

Apart from jurisdiction derived from other provisions of this Regulation, a court of a Member State before which a defendant enters an appearance shall have jurisdiction. This rule shall not apply where appearance was entered to contest the jurisdiction, or where another court has exclusive jurisdiction by virtue of Article 22.

Article 25

Where a court of a Member State is seised of a claim which is principally concerned with a matter over which the courts of another Member State have exclusive jurisdiction by virtue of Article 22, it shall declare of its own motion that it has no jurisdiction.

Article 26

1. Where a defendant domiciled in one Member State is sued in a court of another Member State and does not enter an appearance, the court shall declare of its own motion that it has no jurisdiction unless its jurisdiction is derived from the provisions of this Regulation.
2. The court shall stay the proceedings so long as it is not shown that the defendant has been able to receive the document instituting the proceedings or an equivalent document in sufficient time to enable him to arrange for his defence, or that all necessary steps have been taken to this end.
3. Article 19 of Council Regulation (EC) No 1348/2000 of 29 May 2000 on the service in the Member States of judicial and extrajudicial documents in civil or commercial matters[10] shall apply instead of the provisions of paragraph 2 if the document instituting the proceedings or an equivalent document had to be transmitted from one Member State to another pursuant to this Regulation.
4. Where the provisions of Regulation (EC) No 1348/2000 are not applicable, Article 15 of the Hague Convention of 15 November 1965 on the Service Abroad of Judicial and Extrajudicial Documents in Civil or Commercial Matters shall apply if the document instituting the proceedings or an equivalent document had to be transmitted pursuant to that Convention.

Article 27

1. Where proceedings involving the same cause of action and between the same parties are brought in the courts of different Member States, any court other than the court first seised shall of its own motion stay its proceedings until such time as the jurisdiction of the court first seised is established.
2. Where the jurisdiction of the court first seised is established, any court other than the court first seised shall decline jurisdiction in favour of that court.

Article 28

1. Where related actions are pending in the courts of different Member States, any court other than the court first seised may stay its proceedings.

---

[10] OJ L 160, 30.6.2000, p. 37.

2. Where these actions are pending at first instance, any court other than the court first seised may also, on the application of one of the parties, decline jurisdiction if the court first seised has jurisdiction over the actions in question and its law permits the consolidation thereof.
3. For the purposes of this Article, actions are deemed to be related where they are so closely connected that it is expedient to hear and determine them together to avoid the risk of irreconcilable judgments resulting from separate proceedings.

Article 29

Where actions come within the exclusive jurisdiction of several courts, any court other than the court first seised shall decline jurisdiction in favour of that court.

Article 30

For the purposes of this Section, a court shall be deemed to be seised:
1. at the time when the document instituting the proceedings or an equivalent document is lodged with the court, provided that the plaintiff has not subsequently failed to take the steps he was required to take to have service effected on the defendant, or
2. if the document has to be served before being lodged with the court, at the time when it is received by the authority responsible for service, provided that the plaintiff has not subsequently failed to take the steps he was required to take to have the document lodged with the court.

SECTION 10
PROVISIONAL, INCLUDING PROTECTIVE, MEASURES

Article 31

Application may be made to the courts of a Member State for such provisional, including protective, measures as may be available under the law of that State, even if, under this Regulation, the courts of another Member State have jurisdiction as to the substance of the matter.

CHAPTER III
RECOGNITION AND ENFORCEMENT

Article 32

For the purposes of this Regulation, 'judgment' means any judgment given by a court or tribunal of a Member State, whatever the judgment may be called, including a decree, order, decision or writ of execution, as well as the determination of costs or expenses by an officer of the court.

SECTION 1
RECOGNITION

Article 33

1. A judgment given in a Member State shall be recognised in the other Member States without any special procedure being required.

2. Any interested party who raises the recognition of a judgment as the principal issue in a dispute may, in accordance with the procedures provided for in Sections 2 and 3 of this Chapter, apply for a decision that the judgment be recognised.
3. If the outcome of proceedings in a court of a Member State depends on the determination of an incidental question of recognition that court shall have jurisdiction over that question.

Article 34

A judgment shall not be recognised:
1. if such recognition is manifestly contrary to public policy in the Member State in which recognition is sought;
2. where it was given in default of appearance, if the defendant was not served with the document which instituted the proceedings or with an equivalent document in sufficient time and in such a way as to enable him to arrange for his defence, unless the defendant failed to commence proceedings to challenge the judgment when it was possible for him to do so;
3. if it is irreconcilable with a judgment given in a dispute between the same parties in the Member State in which recognition is sought;
4. if it is irreconcilable with an earlier judgment given in another Member State or in a third State involving the same cause of action and between the same parties, provided that the earlier judgment fulfils the conditions necessary for its recognition in the Member State addressed.

Article 35

1. Moreover, a judgment shall not be recognised if it conflicts with Sections 3, 4 or 6 of Chapter II, or in a case provided for in Article 72.
2. In its examination of the grounds of jurisdiction referred to in the foregoing paragraph, the court or authority applied to shall be bound by the findings of fact on which the court of the Member State of origin based its jurisdiction.
3. Subject to the paragraph 1, the jurisdiction of the court of the Member State of origin may not be reviewed. The test of public policy referred to in point 1 of Article 34 may not be applied to the rules relating to jurisdiction.

Article 36

Under no circumstances may a foreign judgment be reviewed as to its substance.

Article 37

1. A court of a Member State in which recognition is sought of a judgment given in another Member State may stay the proceedings if an ordinary appeal against the judgment has been lodged.
2. A court of a Member State in which recognition is sought of a judgment given in Ireland or the United Kingdom may stay the proceedings if enforcement is suspended in the State of origin, by reason of an appeal.

Article 38

1. A judgment given in a Member State and enforceable in that State shall be enforced in another Member State when, on the application of any interested party, it has been declared enforceable there.
2. However, in the United Kingdom, such a judgment shall be enforced in England and Wales, in Scotland, or in Northern Ireland when, on the application of any interested party, it has been registered for enforcement in that part of the United Kingdom.

Article 39

1. The application shall be submitted to the court or competent authority indicated in the list in Annex II.
2. The local jurisdiction shall be determined by reference to the place of domicile of the party against whom enforcement is sought, or to the place of enforcement.

Article 40

1. The procedure for making the application shall be governed by the law of the Member State in which enforcement is sought.
2. The applicant must give an address for service of process within the area of jurisdiction of the court applied to. However, if the law of the Member State in which enforcement is sought does not provide for the furnishing of such an address, the applicant shall appoint a representative ad litem.
3. The documents referred to in Article 53 shall be attached to the application.

Article 41

The judgment shall be declared enforceable immediately on completion of the formalities in Article 53 without any review under Articles 34 and 35. The party against whom enforcement is sought shall not at this stage of the proceedings be entitled to make any submissions on the application.

Article 42

1. The decision on the application for a declaration of enforceability shall forthwith be brought to the notice of the applicant in accordance with the procedure laid down by the law of the Member State in which enforcement is sought.
2. The declaration of enforceability shall be served on the party against whom enforcement is sought, accompanied by the judgment, if not already served on that party.

Article 43

1. The decision on the application for a declaration of enforceability may be appealed against by either party.
2. The appeal is to be lodged with the court indicated in the list in Annex III.

3. The appeal shall be dealt with in accordance with the rules governing procedure in contradictory matters.
4. If the party against whom enforcement is sought fails to appear before the appellate court in proceedings concerning an appeal brought by the applicant, Article 26(2) to (4) shall apply even where the party against whom enforcement is sought is not domiciled in any of the Member States.
5. An appeal against the declaration of enforceability is to be lodged within one month of service thereof. If the party against whom enforcement is sought is domiciled in a Member State other than that in which the declaration of enforceability was given, the time for appealing shall be two months and shall run from the date of service, either on him in person or at his residence. No extension of time may be granted on account of distance.

Article 44

The judgment given on the appeal may be contested only by the appeal referred to in Annex IV.

Article 45

1. The court with which an appeal is lodged under Article 43 or Article 44 shall refuse or revoke a declaration of enforceability only on one of the grounds specified in Articles 34 and 35. It shall give its decision without delay.
2. Under no circumstances may the foreign judgment be reviewed as to its substance.

Article 46

1. The court with which an appeal is lodged under Article 43 or Article 44 may, on the application of the party against whom enforcement is sought, stay the proceedings if an ordinary appeal has been lodged against the judgment in the Member State of origin or if the time for such an appeal has not yet expired; in the latter case, the court may specify the time within which such an appeal is to be lodged.
2. Where the judgment was given in Ireland or the United Kingdom, any form of appeal available in the Member State of origin shall be treated as an ordinary appeal for the purposes of paragraph 1.
3. The court may also make enforcement conditional on the provision of such security as it shall determine.

Article 47

1. When a judgment must be recognised in accordance with this Regulation, nothing shall prevent the applicant from availing himself of provisional, including protective, measures in accordance with the law of the Member State requested without a declaration of enforceability under Article 41 being required.
2. The declaration of enforceability shall carry with it the power to proceed to any protective measures.
3. During the time specified for an appeal pursuant to Article 43(5) against the declaration of enforceability and until any such appeal has been determined, no measures of enforcement may be taken other than protective measures against the property of the party against whom enforcement is sought.

Article 48

1. Where a foreign judgment has been given in respect of several matters and the declaration of enforceability cannot be given for all of them, the court or competent authority shall give it for one or more of them.
2. An applicant may request a declaration of enforceability limited to parts of a judgment.

Article 49

A foreign judgment which orders a periodic payment by way of a penalty shall be enforceable in the Member State in which enforcement is sought only if the amount of the payment has been finally determined by the courts of the Member State of origin.

Article 50

An applicant who, in the Member State of origin has benefited from complete or partial legal aid or exemption from costs or expenses, shall be entitled, in the procedure provided for in this Section, to benefit from the most favourable legal aid or the most extensive exemption from costs or expenses provided for by the law of the Member State addressed.

Article 51

No security, bond or deposit, however described, shall be required of a party who in one Member State applies for enforcement of a judgment given in another Member State on the ground that he is a foreign national or that he is not domiciled or resident in the State in which enforcement is sought.

Article 52

In proceedings for the issue of a declaration of enforceability, no charge, duty or fee calculated by reference to the value of the matter at issue may be levied in the Member State in which enforcement is sought.

SECTION 3
COMMON PROVISIONS

Article 53

1. A party seeking recognition or applying for a declaration of enforceability shall produce a copy of the judgment which satisfies the conditions necessary to establish its authenticity.
2. A party applying for a declaration of enforceability shall also produce the certificate referred to in Article 54, without prejudice to Article 55.

Article 54

The court or competent authority of a Member State where a judgment was given shall issue, at the request of any interested party, a certificate using the standard form in Annex V to this Regulation.

843

Article 55

1. If the certificate referred to in Article 54 is not produced, the court or competent authority may specify a time for its production or accept an equivalent document or, if it considers that it has sufficient information before it, dispense with its production.
2. If the court or competent authority so requires, a translation of the documents shall be produced. The translation shall be certified by a person qualified to do so in one of the Member States.

Article 56

No legalisation or other similar formality shall be required in respect of the documents referred to in Article 53 or Article 55(2), or in respect of a document appointing a representative ad litem.

CHAPTER IV
AUTHENTIC INSTRUMENTS AND COURT SETTLEMENTS

Article 57

1. A document which has been formally drawn up or registered as an authentic instrument and is enforceable in one Member State shall, in another Member State, be declared enforceable there, on application made in accordance with the procedures provided for in Articles 38, et seq. The court with which an appeal is lodged under Article 43 or Article 44 shall refuse or revoke a declaration of enforceability only if enforcement of the instrument is manifestly contrary to public policy in the Member State addressed.
2. Arrangements relating to maintenance obligations concluded with administrative authorities or authenticated by them shall also be regarded as authentic instruments within the meaning of paragraph 1.
3. The instrument produced must satisfy the conditions necessary to establish its authenticity in the Member State of origin.
4. Section 3 of Chapter III shall apply as appropriate. The competent authority of a Member State where an authentic instrument was drawn up or registered shall issue, at the request of any interested party, a certificate using the standard form in Annex VI to this Regulation.

Article 58

A settlement which has been approved by a court in the course of proceedings and is enforceable in the Member State in which it was concluded shall be enforceable in the State addressed under the same conditions as authentic instruments. The court or competent authority of a Member State where a court settlement was approved shall issue, at the request of any interested party, a certificate using the standard form in Annex V to this Regulation.

CHAPTER V
GENERAL PROVISIONS

Article 59

1. In order to determine whether a party is domiciled in the Member State whose courts are seised of a matter, the court shall apply its internal law.
2. If a party is not domiciled in the Member State whose courts are seised of the matter, then, in order to determine whether the party is domiciled in another Member State, the court shall apply the law of that Member State.

Article 60

1. For the purposes of this Regulation, a company or other legal person or association of natural or legal persons is domiciled at the place where it has its:
   (a) statutory seat, or
   (b) central administration, or
   (c) principal place of business.
2. For the purposes of the United Kingdom and Ireland 'statutory seat' means the registered office or, where there is no such office anywhere, the place of incorporation or, where there is no such place anywhere, the place under the law of which the formation took place.
3. In order to determine whether a trust is domiciled in the Member State whose courts are seised of the matter, the court shall apply its rules of private international law.

Article 61

Without prejudice to any more favourable provisions of national laws, persons domiciled in a Member State who are being prosecuted in the criminal courts of another Member State of which they are not nationals for an offence which was not intentionally committed may be defended by persons qualified to do so, even if they do not appear in person. However, the court seised of the matter may order appearance in person; in the case of failure to appear, a judgment given in the civil action without the person concerned having had the opportunity to arrange for his defence need not be recognised or enforced in the other Member States.

Article 62

In Sweden, in summary proceedings concerning orders to pay (betalningsföreläggande) and assistance (handräckning), the expression 'court' includes the 'Swedish enforcement service' (kronofogdemyndighet).

Article 63

1. A person domiciled in the territory of the Grand Duchy of Luxembourg and sued in the court of another Member State pursuant to Article 5(1) may refuse to submit to the jurisdiction of that court if the final place of delivery of the goods or provision of the services is in Luxembourg.

2. Where, under paragraph 1, the final place of delivery of the goods or provision of the services is in Luxembourg, any agreement conferring jurisdiction must, in order to be valid, be accepted in writing or evidenced in writing within the meaning of Article 23(1)(a).
3. The provisions of this Article shall not apply to contracts for the provision of financial services.
4. The provisions of this Article shall apply for a period of six years from entry into force of this Regulation.

Article 64

1. In proceedings involving a dispute between the master and a member of the crew of a seagoing ship registered in Greece or in Portugal, concerning remuneration or other conditions of service, a court in a Member State shall establish whether the diplomatic or consular officer responsible for the ship has been notified of the dispute. It may act as soon as that officer has been notified.
2. The provisions of this Article shall apply for a period of six years from entry into force of this Regulation.

Article 65

1. The jurisdiction specified in Article 6(2), and Article 11 in actions on a warranty of guarantee or in any other third party proceedings may not be resorted to in Germany and Austria. Any person domiciled in another Member State may be sued in the courts:
   (a) of Germany, pursuant to Articles 68 and 72 to 74 of the Code of Civil Procedure (Zivilprozessordnung) concerning third-party notices,
   (b) of Austria, pursuant to Article 21 of the Code of Civil Procedure (Zivilprozessordnung) concerning third-party notices.
2. Judgments given in other Member States by virtue of Article 6(2), or Article 11 shall be recognised and enforced in Germany and Austria in accordance with Chapter III. Any effects which judgments given in these States may have on third parties by application of the provisions in paragraph 1 shall also be recognised in the other Member States.

CHAPTER VI
TRANSITIONAL PROVISIONS

Article 66

1. This Regulation shall apply only to legal proceedings instituted and to documents formally drawn up or registered as authentic instruments after the entry into force thereof.
2. However, if the proceedings in the Member State of origin were instituted before the entry into force of this Regulation, judgments given after that date shall be recognised and enforced in accordance with Chapter III,
   (a) if the proceedings in the Member State of origin were instituted after the entry into force of the Brussels or the Lugano Convention both in the Member State or origin and in the Member State addressed;

(b) in all other cases, if jurisdiction was founded upon rules which accorded with those provided for either in Chapter II or in a convention concluded between the Member State of origin and the Member State addressed which was in force when the proceedings were instituted.

CHAPTER VII
RELATIONS WITH OTHER INSTRUMENTS

Article 67

This Regulation shall not prejudice the application of provisions governing jurisdiction and the recognition and enforcement of judgments in specific matters which are contained in Community instruments or in national legislation harmonised pursuant to such instruments.

Article 68

1. This Regulation shall, as between the Member States, supersede the Brussels Convention, except as regards the territories of the Member States which fall within the territorial scope of that Convention and which are excluded from this Regulation pursuant to Article 299 of the Treaty.
2. In so far as this Regulation replaces the provisions of the Brussels Convention between Member States, any reference to the Convention shall be understood as a reference to this Regulation.

Article 69

Subject to Article 66(2) and Article 70, this Regulation shall, as between Member States, supersede the following conventions and treaty concluded between two or more of them:
— the Convention between Belgium and France on Jurisdiction and the Validity and Enforcement of Judgments, Arbitration Awards and Authentic Instruments, signed at Paris on 8 July 1899,
— the Convention between Belgium and the Netherlands on Jurisdiction, Bankruptcy, and the Validity and Enforcement of Judgments, Arbitration Awards and Authentic Instruments, signed at Brussels on 28 March 1925,
— the Convention between France and Italy on the Enforcement of Judgments in Civil and Commercial Matters, signed at Rome on 3 June 1930,
— the Convention between Germany and Italy on the Recognition and Enforcement of Judgments in Civil and Commercial Matters, signed at Rome on 9 March 1936,
— the Convention between Belgium and Austria on the Reciprocal Recognition and Enforcement of Judgments and Authentic Instruments relating to Maintenance Obligations, signed at Vienna on 25 October 1957,
— the Convention between Germany and Belgium on the Mutual Recognition and Enforcement of Judgments, Arbitration Awards and Authentic Instruments in Civil and Commercial Matters, signed at Bonn on 30 June 1958,
— the Convention between the Netherlands and Italy on the Recognition and Enforcement of Judgments in Civil and Commercial Matters, signed at Rome on 17 April 1959,

—the Convention between Germany and Austria on the Reciprocal Recognition and Enforcement of Judgments, Settlements and Authentic Instruments in Civil and Commercial Matters, signed at Vienna on 6 June 1959,

—the Convention between Belgium and Austria on the Reciprocal Recognition and Enforcement of Judgments, Arbitral Awards and Authentic Instruments in Civil and Commercial Matters, signed at Vienna on 16 June 1959,

—the Convention between Greece and Germany for the Reciprocal Recognition and Enforcement of Judgments, Settlements and Authentic Instruments in Civil and Commercial Matters, signed in Athens on 4 November 1961,

—the Convention between Belgium and Italy on the Recognition and Enforcement of Judgments and other Enforceable Instruments in Civil and Commercial Matters, signed at Rome on 6 April 1962,

—the Convention between the Netherlands and Germany on the Mutual Recognition and Enforcement of Judgments and Other Enforceable Instruments in Civil and Commercial Matters, signed at The Hague on 30 August 1962,

—the Convention between the Netherlands and Austria on the Reciprocal Recognition and Enforcement of Judgments and Authentic Instruments in Civil and Commercial Matters, signed at The Hague on 6 February 1963,

—the Convention between France and Austria on the Recognition and Enforcement of Judgments and Authentic Instruments in Civil and Commercial Matters, signed at Vienna on 15 July 1966,

—the Convention between Spain and France on the Recognition and Enforcement of Judgment Arbitration Awards in Civil and Commercial Matters, signed at Paris on 28 May 1969,

—the Convention between Luxembourg and Austria on the Recognition and Enforcement of Judgments and Authentic Instruments in Civil and Commercial Matters, signed at Luxembourg on 29 July 1971,

—the Convention between Italy and Austria on the Recognition and Enforcement of Judgments in Civil and Commercial Matters, of Judicial Settlements and of Authentic Instruments, signed at Rome on 16 November 1971,

—the Convention between Spain and Italy regarding Legal Aid and the Recognition and Enforcement of Judgments in Civil and Commercial Matters, signed at Madrid on 22 May 1973,

—the Convention between Finland, Iceland, Norway, Sweden and Denmark on the Recognition and Enforcement of Judgments in Civil Matters, signed at Copenhagen on 11 October 1977,

—the Convention between Austria and Sweden on the Recognition and Enforcement of Judgments in Civil Matters, signed at Stockholm on 16 September 1982,

—the Convention between Spain and the Federal Republic of Germany on the Recognition and Enforcement of Judgments, Settlements and Enforceable Authentic Instruments in Civil and Commercial Matters, signed at Bonn on 14 November 1983,

—the Convention between Austria and Spain on the Recognition and Enforcement of Judgments, Settlements and Enforceable Authentic Instruments in Civil and Commercial Matters, signed at Vienna on 17 February 1984,

—the Convention between Finland and Austria on the Recognition and Enforcement of Judgments in Civil Matters, signed at Vienna on 17 November 1986, and

—the Treaty between Belgium, the Netherlands and Luxembourg in Jurisdiction, Bankruptcy, and the Validity and Enforcement of Judgments, Arbitration Awards and Authentic Instruments, signed at Brussels on 24 November 1961, in so far as it is in force.

Article 70

1. The Treaty and the Conventions referred to in Article 69 shall continue to have effect in relation to matters to which this Regulation does not apply.
2. They shall continue to have effect in respect of judgments given and documents formally drawn up or registered as authentic instruments before the entry into force of this Regulation.

Article 71

1. This Regulation shall not affect any conventions to which the Member States are parties and which in relation to particular matters, govern jurisdiction or the recognition or enforcement of judgments.
2. With a view to its uniform interpretation, paragraph 1 shall be applied in the following manner:
   (a) this Regulation shall not prevent a court of a Member State, which is a party to a convention on a particular matter, from assuming jurisdiction in accordance with that convention, even where the defendant is domiciled in another Member State which is not a party to that convention. The court hearing the action shall, in any event, apply Article 26 of this Regulation;
   (b) judgments given in a Member State by a court in the exercise of jurisdiction provided for in a convention on a particular matter shall be recognised and enforced in the other Member States in accordance with this Regulation.

   Where a convention on a particular matter to which both the Member State of origin and the Member State addressed are parties lays down conditions for the recognition or enforcement of judgments, those conditions shall apply. In any event, the provisions of this Regulation which concern the procedure for recognition and enforcement of judgments may be applied.

Article 72

This Regulation shall not affect agreements by which Member States undertook, prior to the entry into force of this Regulation pursuant to Article 59 of the Brussels Convention, not to recognise judgments given, in particular in other Contracting States to that Convention, against defendants domiciled or habitually resident in a third country where, in cases provided for in Article 4 of that Convention, the judgment could only be founded on a ground of jurisdiction specified in the second paragraph of Article 3 of that Convention.

CHAPTER VIII
FINAL PROVISIONS

Article 73

No later than five years after the entry into force of this Regulation, the Commission shall present to the European Parliament, the Council and the Economic and Social

Committee a report on the application of this Regulation. The report shall be accompanied, if need be, by proposals for adaptations to this Regulation.

Article 74

1. The Member States shall notify the Commission of the texts amending the lists set out in Annexes I to IV. The Commission shall adapt the Annexes concerned accordingly.
2. The updating or technical adjustment of the forms, specimens of which appear in Annexes V and VI, shall be adopted in accordance with the advisory procedure referred to in Article 75(2).

Article 75

1. The Commission shall be assisted by a committee.
2. Where reference is made to this paragraph, Articles 3 and 7 of Decision 1999/468/EC shall apply.
3. The Committee shall adopt its rules of procedure.

Article 76

This Regulation shall enter into force on 1 March 2002.

This Regulation is binding in its entirety and directly applicable in the Member States in accordance with the Treaty establishing the European Community.

Done at Brussels, 22 December 2000.

For the Council
The President
C. Pierret

ANNEX I
RULES OF JURISDICTION REFERRED TO IN
ARTICLE 3(2) AND ARTICLE 4(2)

The rules of jurisdiction referred to in Article 3(2) and Article 4(2) are the following:
  —in Belgium: Article 15 of the Civil Code (Code civil/Burgerlijk Wetboek) and Article 638 of the Judicial Code (Code judiciaire/Gerechtelijk Wetboek);
  —in Germany: Article 23 of the Code of Civil Procedure (Zivilprozessordnung),
  —in Greece, Article 40 of the Code of Civil Procedure (Êþäéêáò Ðïëéôéê̂Ðò Äéêïíïìßáò);
  —> in France: Articles 14 and 15 of the Civil Code (Code civil),
  —in Ireland: the rules which enable jurisdiction to be founded on the document instituting the proceedings having been served on the defendant during his temporary presence in Ireland,
  —in Italy: Articles 3 and 4 of Act 218 of 31 May 1995,

—in Luxembourg: Articles 14 and 15 of the Civil Code (Code civil),

—in the Netherlands: Articles 126(3) and 127 of the Code of Civil Procedure (Wetboek van Burgerlijke Rechtsvordering),

—in Austria: Article 99 of the Court Jurisdiction Act (Jurisdiktionsnorm),

—in Portugal: Articles 65 and 65A of the Code of Civil Procedure (Código de Processo Civil) and Article 11 of the Code of Labour Procedure (Código de Processo de Trabalho),

—in Finland: the second, third and fourth sentences of the first paragraph of Section 1 of Chapter 10 of the Code of Judicial Procedure (oikeudenkäymiskaari/ rättegångsbalken),

—in Sweden: the first sentence of the first paragraph of Section 3 of Chapter 10 of the Code of Judicial Procedure (rättegångsbalken),

—in the United Kingdom: rules which enable jurisdiction to be founded on:

    (a) the document instituting the proceedings having been served on the defendant during his temporary presence in the United Kingdom; or

    (b) the presence within the United Kingdom of property belonging to the defendant; or

    (c) the seizure by the plaintiff of property situated in the United Kingdom.

ANNEX II

The courts or competent authorities to which the application referred to in Article 39 may be submitted are the following:

—in Belgium, the 'tribunal de première instance' or 'rechtbank van eerste aanleg' or 'erstinstanzliches Gericht',

—in Germany, the presiding judge of a chamber of the 'Landgericht',

—in Greece, the 'ÌïíïìåëÝò Ðñùôïäéêåßï',

—in Spain, the 'Juzgado de Primera Instancia',

—in France, the presiding judge of the 'tribunal de grande instance',

—in Ireland, the High Court,

—in Italy, the 'Corte d'appello',

—in Luxembourg, the presiding judge of the 'tribunal d'arrondissement',

—in the Netherlands, the presiding judge of the 'arrondissementsrechtbank';

—in Austria, the 'Bezirksgericht',

—in Portugal, the 'Tribunal de Comarca',

—in Finland, the 'käräjäoikeus/tingsrätt',

—in Sweden, the 'Svea hovrätt',

—in the United Kingdom:

    (a) in England and Wales, the High Court of Justice, or in the case of a maintenance judgment, the Magistrate's Court on transmission by the Secretary of State;

    (b) in Scotland, the Court of Session, or in the case of a maintenance judgment, the Sheriff Court on transmission by the Secretary of State;

    (c) in Northern Ireland, the High Court of Justice, or in the case of a maintenance judgment, the Magistrate's Court on transmission by the Secretary of State;

(d) in Gibraltar, the Supreme Court of Gibraltar, or in the case of a maintenance judgment, the Magistrates' on transmission by the Attorney General of Gibraltar.

ANNEX III

The courts with which appeals referred to in Article 43(2) may be lodged are the following:
— in Belgium,
(a) as regards appeal by the defendant: the 'tribunal de première instance' or 'rechtbank van eerste aanleg' or 'erstinstanzliches Gericht',
(b) as regards appeal by the applicant: the 'Cour d'appel' or 'hof van beroep',
— in the Federal Republic of Germany, the 'Oberlandesgericht',
— in Greece, the 'Åöåôåßi',
— in Spain, the 'Audiencia Provincial',
— in France, the 'cour d'appel',
— in Ireland, the High Court,
— in Italy, the 'corte d'appello',
— in Luxembourg, the 'Cour supérieure de Justice' sitting as a court of civil appeal,
— in the Netherlands:
(a) for the defendant: the 'arrondissementsrechtbank',
(b) for the applicant: the 'gerechtshof',
— in Austria, the 'Bezirksgericht',
— in Portugal, the 'Tribunal de Relação',
— in Finland, the 'hovioikeus/hovrätt',
— in Sweden, the 'Svea hovrätt',
— in the United Kingdom:
(a) in England and Wales, the High Court of Justice, or in the case of a maintenance judgment, the Magistrate's Court;
(b) in Scotland, the Court of Session, or in the case of a maintenance judgment, the Sheriff Court;
(c) in Northern Ireland, the High Court of Justice, or in the case of a maintenance judgment, the Magistrate's Court;
(d) in Gibraltar, the Supreme Court of Gibraltar, or in the case of a maintenance judgment, the Magistrates' Court.

ANNEX IV

The appeals which may be lodged pursuant to Article 44 are the following:
— in Belgium, Greece, Spain, France, Italy, Luxembourg and the Netherlands, an appeal in cassation,
— in Germany, a 'Rechtsbeschwerde',
— in Ireland, an appeal on a point of law to the Supreme Court,
— in Austria, a 'Revisionsrekurs',
— in Portugal, an appeal on a point of law,
— in Finland, an appeal to the 'korkein oikeus/högsta domstolen',
— in Sweden, an appeal to the 'Högsta domstolen',
— in the United Kingdom, a single further appeal on a point of law.

ANNEX V
CERTIFICATE REFERRED TO IN ARTICLES 54 AND 58 OF THE REGULATION ON JUDGMENTS AND COURT SETTLEMENTS

(English, inglés, anglais, inglese, . . .)
1. Member State of origin
2. Court or competent authority issuing the certificate
   2.1 Name
   2.2 Address
   2.3 Tel./fax/e-mail
3. Court which delivered the judgment/approved the court settlement*
   3.1 Type of court
   3.2 Place of court
4. Judgment/court settlement*
   4.1 Date
   4.2 Reference number
   4.3 The parties to the judgment/court settlement*
       4.3.1 Name(s) of plaintiff(s)
       4.3.2 Name(s) of defendant(s)
       4.3.3 Name(s) of other party(ies), if any
   4.4 Date of service of the document instituting the proceedings where judgment was given in default of appearance
   4.5 Text of the judgment/court settlement* as annexed to this certificate
5. Names of parties to whom legal aid has been granted

The judgment/court settlement* is enforceable in the Member State of origin (Articles 38 and 58 of the Regulation) against:

Name:
Done at . . . , date . . .
Signature and/or stamp . . .

ANNEX VI
CERTIFICATE REFERRED TO IN ARTICLE 57(4) OF THE REGULATION ON AUTHENTIC INSTRUMENTS

(English, inglés, anglais, inglese . . . .)
1. Member State of origin
2. Competent authority issuing the certificate
   2.1 Name
   2.2 Address
   2.3 Tel./fax/e-mail
3. Authority which has given authenticity to the instrument

*Delete as appropriate.

3.1 Authority involved in the drawing up of the authentic instrument (if applicable)
    3.1.1 Name and designation of authority
    3.1.2 Place of authority
3.2 Authority which has registered the authentic instrument (if applicable)
    3.1.1 Type of authority
    3.1.2 Place of authority
4. Authentic instrument
    4.1 Description of the instrument
    4.2 Date
        4.2.1 on which the instrument was drawn up
        4.2.2 if different: on which the instrument was registered
    4.3 Reference number
    4.4 Parties to the instrument
        4.4.1 Name of the creditor
        4.4.2 Name of the debtor
5. Text of the enforceable obligation as annexed to this certificate

The authentic instrument is enforceable against the debtor in the Member State of origin (Article 57(1) of the Regulation)

Done at ..., date ...
Signature and/or stamp ...

(iii) MERCOSUR/CMC/DEC NO. 05/92

VISTO

El Tratado de Asunción suscripto el 26 de marzo de 1991 y el 'Protocolo de Cooperación y Asistencia Jurisdiccional en materia Civil, Comercial, Laboral y Administrativa', refrendado por los Ministros de Justicia de los Estados Partes y

Considerando:

Que es necesario establecer un marco jurídico que permita a los ciudadanos y residentes permanentes acceder a la Justicia de los Estados Partes en igualdad de condiciones;

Que resulta necesario simplificar y allanar las tramitaciones jurisdiccionales, en materia civil, comercial, laboral y administrativa entre los Estados Partes;

EL CONSEJO MERCADO COMUN DECIDE:

Articulo 1ro. Aprobar el 'Protocolo de Cooperación y Asistencia Jurisdiccional en materia Civil, Comercial, Laboral y Administrativa', anexo a la presente.

Articulo 2do. Elevar el Protocolo a sus respectivos Gobiernos para que inicien los trámites internos pertinentes para su ratificación, a fin de su pronta entrada en vigencia.

PROTOCOLO DE COOPERACION Y ASISTENCIA JURISDICCIONAL EN MATERIA CIVIL, COMERCIAL, LABORAL Y ADMINISTRATIVA

Los Gobiernos de la *Republica Argentina, de la Republica Federativa del Brasil, de la Republica del Paraguay y de la Republica Oriental del Uruguay,*

Considerando que el Mercado Común del Sur (MERCOSUR) previsto en el Tratado de Asunción implica el compromiso de los Estados Partes de armonizar sus legislaciones en las áreas pertinentes, para lograr el fortalecimiento del proceso de integración;

Deseosos de promover e intensificar la cooperación jurisdiccional en materia civil, comercial, laboral y administrativa, a fin de contribuir de este modo al desarrollo de sus relaciones de integración en base a los principios de respeto a la soberanía nacional y a la igualdad de derechos e intereses recíprocos;

Convencidos de que este Protocolo coadyuvará al trato equitativo de los ciudadanos y residentes permanentes de los Estados Partes del Tratado de Asunción y les facilitará el libre acceso a la jurisdicción en dichos Estados para la defensa de sus derechos e intereses;

Consciente de la importancia que reviste para el proceso de integración de los Estados Partes la adopción de instrumentos comunes que consoliden la seguridad jurídica y tengan como finalidad alcanzar los objetivos del Tratado de Asunción, suscripto el 26 de marzo de 1991.

ACUERDAN

CAPITULO I
COOPERACION Y ASISTENCIA JURISDICCIONAL

ARTICULO 1

Los Estados Partes se comprometen a prestarse asistencia mutua y amplia cooperación jurisdiccional en materia civil, comercial, laboral y administrativa. La asistencia jurisdiccional se extenderá a los procedimientos administrativos en los que se admitan recursos ante los tribunales.

CAPITULO II
AUTORIDADES CENTRALES

ARTICULO 2

A los efectos del presente Protocolo cada Estado Parte designará una Autoridad Central encargada de recibir y tramitar los pedidos de asistencia jurisdiccional en materia civil, comercial, laboral y administrativa. A tal fin, dichas Autoridades Centrales se comunicarán directamente entre ellas, dando intervención a las respectivas autoridades competentes, cuando sea necesario.

Los Estados Partes, al depositar el instrumento de ratificación al presente Protocolo, comunicarán dicha designación al Gobierno depositario, el cual lo pondrá en conocimiento de los demás Estados Partes.

La Autoridad Central podrá ser cambiada en cualquier momento, debiendo el Estado Parte comunicarlo en el menor tiempo posible al Gobierno depositario del presente Protocolo, a fin de que ponga en conocimiento de los demás Estados Partes el cambio efectuado.

CAPITULO III
IGUALDAD DE TRATO PROCESAL

ARTICULO 3

Los ciudadanos y los residentes permanentes de uno de los Estados Partes gozarán, en las mismas condiciones que los ciudadanos y residentes permanente de otro Estado Parte, del libre acceso a la jurisdicción en dicho Estado para la defensa de sus derechos e intereses.

El párrafo precedente se aplicará a las personas jurídicas constituídas, autorizadas o registradas de acuerdo a las leyes de cualquiera de los Estados Partes.

ARTICULO 4

Ninguna caución o depósito, cualquiera sea su denominación, podrá ser impuesta en razón de la calidad de ciudadano o residente permanente de otro Estado Parte.

El párrafo precedente se aplicará a las personas jurídicas constituídas, autorizadas o registradas de acuerdo a las leyes de cualquiera de los Estados Partes.

CAPITULO IV
COOPERACION EN ACTIVIDADES DE MERO TRAMITE Y PROBATORIAS

ARTICULO 5

Cada Estado Parte deberá enviar a las autoridades jurisdiccionales del otro Estado, según la vía prevista en el artículo 2, los exhortos en materia civil, comercial, laboral o administrativa, cuando tengan por objeto:
   a) diligencias de mero trámite, tales como citaciones, intimaciones, emplazamientos, notificaciones u otras semejantes;
   b) recepción u obtención de pruebas.

ARTICULO 6

Los exhortos deberán contener:
   a) denominación y domicilio del órgano jurisdiccional requirente;
   b) individualización del expediente con especificación del objeto y naturaleza del juicio y de nombre y domicilio de las partes;

c) copia de la demanda y transcripción de la resolución que ordena la expedición del exhorto;

d) nombre y domicilio del apoderado de la parte solicitante en el Estado requerido, si lo hubiere;

e) indicación del objeto del exhorto precisando el nombre y domicilio del destinatario de la medida;

f) información del plazo de que disponen la persona afectada por la medida para cumplirla;

g) descripción de las formas o procedimientos especiales con que ha de cumplirse la cooperación solicitada;

h) cualquier otra información que facilite el cumplimiento del exhorto.

ARTICULO 7

Si se solicitare la recepción de pruebas, el exhorto deberá además contener:

a) una descripción del asunto que facilite la diligencia probatoria;

b) nombre y domicilio de testigos u otras personas o instituciones que deban intervenir;

c) texto de los interrogatorios y documentos necesarios.

ARTICULO 8

La ejecución de los exhortos deberá ser diligenciada de oficio por la autoridad jurisdiccional competente del Estado requerido y sólo podrá denegarse cuando la medida solicitada, por su naturaleza, atente contra los principios de orden público del Estado requerido.

Dicha ejecución no implicará un reconocimiento de la jurisdicción internacional del juez del cual emana.

ARTICULO 9

La autoridad jurisdiccional requerida tendrá competencia para conocer de las cuestiones que se susciten con motivo del cumplimiento de la diligencia solicitada.

Si la autoridad jurisdiccional requerida se declarare incompetente para proceder a la tramitación del exhorto, remitirá de oficio los documentos y antecedentes del caso a la autoridad jurisdiccional competente de su Estado.

ARTICULO 10

Los exhortos y los documentos que los acompañen deberán redactarse en el idioma de la autoridad requirente y ser acompañados de una traducción al idioma de la autoridad requerida.

ARTICULO 11

La autoridad requirente podrá solicitar de la autoridad requerida se le informe el lugar y la fecha en que la medida solicitada se hará efectiva, a fin de permitir que la autoridad requirente, las partes interesadas o sus respectivos representantes puedan comparecer y ejercer las facultades autorizadas por la legislación de la Parte requerida.

Dicha comunicación deberá efectuarse con la debida antelación por intermedio de las Autoridades Centrales de los Estados Partes.

ARTICULO 12

La autoridad jurisdiccional encargada de la ejecución de un exhorto aplicará su ley interna en lo que a los procedimientos se refiere.

Sin embargo, podrá accederse, la solicitud de la autoridad requirente a otorgar al exhorto una tramitación especial o aceptarse el cumplimiento de formalidades adicionales en la diligencia del exhorto, siempre que ello no sea incompatible con el orden público del Estado requerido.

La ejecución del exhorto deberá llevarse a cabo sin demora.

ARTICULO 13

Al ejecutar el exhorto, la autoridad requerida aplicará las medidas coercitivas previstas en su legislación interna, en los casos y con el alcance en que deba hacerlo para ejecutar un exhorto de las autoridades de su propio Estado o un pedido presentado a este efecto por una parte interesada.

ARTICULO 14

Los documentos en los que conste la ejecución del exhorto serán comunicados por intermedio de las Autoridades Centrales.

Cuando el exhorto no haya sido ejecutado en todo o en parte, este hecho, así como las razones que determinaron el incumplimiento, deberán ser comunicados de inmediato a la autoridad requirente, utilizando el medio señalado en párrafo precedente.

ARTICULO 15

La ejecución del exhorto no podrá dar lugar al reembolso de ningún tipo de gasto, excepto cuando se soliciten medios probatorios que ocasionen erogaciones especiales o se designen profesionales para intervenir en el diligenciamiento.

En tales casos, se deberá consignar en el cuerpo del exhorto los datos de la persona que en el Estado requerido procederá a dar cumplimiento al pago de los gastos y honorarios devengados.

ARTICULO 16

Cuando los datos relativos al domicilio del destinatario del acto o de la persona citada están incompletos o sean inexactos, la autoridad requerida deberá votar los medios para satisfacer el pedido. Al efecto, podrá también solicitar al Estado requirente los datos complementarios que permitan la identificación y la localización de la referida persona.

ARTICULO 17

Los trámites pertinentes para hacer efectivo el cumplimiento del exhorto no requerirán necesariamente la intervención de parte interesada, debiendo ser practicados de oficio por la autoridad jurisdiccional competente del Estado requerido.

CAPITULO V
RECONOCIMIENTO Y EJECUCION DE SENTENCIAS Y LAUDOS ARBITRALES

ARTICULO 18

Las disposiciones del presente Capítulo serán aplicables al reconocimiento y ejecución de las sentencias y laudos arbitrales pronunciados en las jurisdicciones de los Estados Partes en materia civil, comercial, laboral y administrativa.Lasmismas serán igualmente aplicables a las sentencias en materia de reparación de datos y restitución de bienes pronunciadas en jurisdicción penal.

ARTICULO 19

La solicitud de reconocimiento y ejecución de sentencias y laudos arbitrales por parte de las autoridades jurisdiccionales se tramitará por vía de exhortos y por intermedio de la Autoridad Central.

ARTICULO 20

Las sentencias y laudos arbitrales a que se refiere el artículo precedente, tendrán eficacia extraterritorial en los Estados Partes si reúnen las siguientes condiciones:
   a) que vengan revestidos de las formalidades externas necesarias para que sean considerados auténticos en el Estado de donde proceden;
   b) que estos y los documentos anexos que fueren necesarios, estén debidamente traducidos al idioma oficial del Estado en el que se solicita su reconocimiento y ejecución;
   c) que estos emanen de un órgano jurisdiccional o arbitral competente, según las normas del Estado requerido sobre jurisdicción internacional;
   d) que la parte contra la que se pretende ejecutar la decisión haya sido debidamente citada y se haya garantizado el ejercicio de su derecho de defensa;
   e) que la decisión tenga fuerza de cosa juzgada y/o ejecutoria en el Estado en el que fue dictada;
   f) que no contraríen manifiestamente los principios de orden público del Estado en el que se solicitare el reconocimiento y/o la ejecución.
Los requisitos de los incisos a), c), d), e) y f) deben surgir del testimonio de la sentencia o laudo arbitral.

ARTICULO 21

La parte que en un juicio invoque una sentencia o un laudo arbitral de alguno de los Estados Partes, deberá acompañar un testimonio de la sentencia o laudo arbitral con los requisitos del artículo precedente.

ARTICULO 22

Cuando se tratare de una sentencia o laudo arbitral entre las mismas partes, fundadas en los mismos hechos y que tuviere el mismo objeto que el de otro proceso jurisdiccional o arbitral en el Estado requerido, su reconocimiento y ejecutoriedad dependerán de que la decisión no sea incompatible con otro pronunciamiento anterior o simultáneo recaído en tal proceso en el Estado requerido.

Asimismo, no se reconocerá ni se procederá a la ejecución, cuando se hubiere iniciado un procedimiento entre las mismas partes, fundado en los mismos hechos y sobre el mismo objeto, ante cualquier autoridad jurisdiccional de la Parte requerida con anterioridad a la presentación de la demanda ante la autoridad jurisdiccional que hubiere pronunciado la resolución de la que se solicite el reconocimiento.

ARTICULO 23

Si una sentencia o laudo no pudiere tener eficacia en su totalidad, la autoridad jurisdiccional competente en el Estado requerido podrá admitir su eficacia parcial mediante solicitud de parte interesada.

ARTICULO 24

Los procedimientos, incluso la competencia de los respectivos órganos jurisdiccionales, a los efectos de reconocimiento y ejecución de las sentencias o laudos arbitrales, se regirán por la ley del Estado requerido.

CAPITULO VI
DE LOS INSTRUMENTOS PUBLICOS Y OTROS DOCUMENTOS

ARTICULO 25

Los instrumentos públicos emanados de un Estado Parte tendrán en el otro la misma fuerza probatoria que sus propios instrumentos públicos.

ARTICULO 26

Los documentos emanados de autoridades jurisdiccionales u otras autoridades de uno de los Estados Partes, así como las escrituras públicas y los documentos que certifiquen la validez, la fecha y la veracidad de la firma o la conformidad con el original, que sean tramitados por intermedio de la Autoridad Central, quedan exceptuados de toda legislación, apostilla u otra formalidad análoga cuando deban ser presentados en el territorio de otro Estado Parte.

ARTICULO 27

Cada Estado Parte remitir, a través de la Autoridad Central, a solicitud de otro y para fines exclusivamente públicos, los certificados de las actas de los registros de estado civil, sin cargo alguno.

CAPITULO VII
INFORMACION DEL DERECHO EXTRANJERO

ARTICULO 28

Las Autoridades Centrales de los Estados Partes se suministrarán, en concepto de cooperación judicial, y siempre que no se opongan a las disposiciones de su orden público, informes en materia civil, comercial, laboral, administrativa y de derecho internacional privado, sin gasto alguno.

ARTICULO 29

La información a que se refiere el artículo anterior podrá también efectuarse ante la jurisdicción del otro Estado, a través de informes suministrados por las autoridades diplomáticas o consulares del Estado Parte de cuyo derecho se trate.

ARTICULO 30

El Estado que brinde los informes sobre el sentido y alcance legal de su derecho, no ser responsable por la opinión emitida ni está obligado a aplicar su derecho según la respuesta proporcionada.

El Estado que reciba dichos informes no estar obligado ha aplicar o hacer aplicar el derecho extranjero según el contenido de la respuesta recibida.

CAPITULO VIII
CONSULTAS Y SOLUCION DE CONTROVERSIAS
ARTICULO 31

Las Autoridades Centrales de los Estados Partes celebrarán consultas en las oportunidades que convengan mutuamente con el fin de facilitar la aplicación del presente Protocolo.

ARTICULO 32

Las dificultades derivadas de la aplicación del presente Protocolo serán solucionadas por la vía diplomática.

Los procedimientos previstos en el Protocolo de Brasilia para la Solución de Controversias se aplicarán cuando, éste entre en vigor y hasta tanto se adopte un Sistema Permanente de Solución de Controversias para el Mercado Común del Sur.

CAPITULO IX
DISPOSICIONES FINALES
ARTICULO 33

El presente Protocolo, parte integrante del Tratado de Asunción, entrar en vigor TREINTA (30) días después de la fecha de depósito del segundo instrumento de ratificación, y se aplicará provisionalmente a partir de la fecha de su firma.

ARTICULO 34

La adhesión por parte de un Estado al Tratado de Asunción, implicará Ipso iure la adhesión al presente Protocolo.

ARTICULO 35

El Gobierno de la República del Paraguay será el depositario del presente Protocolo y de los instrumentos de ratificación y enviará copias debidamente autenticadas de los mismos a los Gobiernos de los demás Estados Partes.

Asimismo, el Gobierno de la República del Paraguay notificará a los Gobiernos de los demás Estados Partes la fecha de entrada en vigor del presente Protocolo y la fecha de depósito de los instrumentos de ratificación.

Hecho en a los días del mes de mayo de 1992, en un original en los idiomas español y portugués, siendo ambos textos igualmente auténticos.

STATE RATIFICATIONS

DEC No. 5/92 Protocolo de Cooperación y Asistencia Jurisdiccional en Materia Civil, Comercial, Laboral y Administrativa. (Protocolo de las Leñas).

Argentina: Ley No. 24.578 del 25/10/95 y promulgada el 22/11/95, publicada en el BO el 27/11/95.
Brasil: Decreto Legislativo 55, Publicado no DOU, 19/4/95.- Promulgado por el Decreto Federal No. 2067 del 12/11/96, publicado en el DOU el 13/11/96.
Paraguay: Ley No. 270/93 del 12/9/95, publicado en la GO, el 16/3/96.
Uruguay: Ley No. 16.971 del 15/06/98, D. O. el 02/07/98.

Note. Please note this instrument is only available in Spanish and Portuguese. Visit www.redmercosur.org.uy/portal/mercosur.html for more information.

(iv) MEROSUR/CMC/DEC. NO. 07/02
ENMIENDA AL PROTOCOLO DE COOPERACIÓN Y ASISTENCIA JURISDICCIONAL EN MATERIA CIVIL, COMERCIAL, LABORAL Y ADMINISTRATIVA ENTRE LOS ESTADOS PARTES DEL MERCOSUR

VISTO

El Tratado de Asunción, el Protocolo de Ouro Preto y las Decisiones No. 5/92 y 5/97 del Consejo del Mercado Común.

Considerando:

Que es voluntad de los Estados Partes del MERCOSUR buscar soluciones jurídicas que ayuden a fortalecer los esquemas de integración que los vinculan;

Que la Decisión CMC N° 5/92 aprobó el Protocolo de Cooperación y Asistencia Jurisdiccional en Materia Civil, Comercial, Laboral y Administrativa, alcanzado por la Reunión de Ministros de Justicia del MERCOSUR.

EL CONSEJO DEL MERCADO COMÚN DECIDE:

Art. 1—Aprobar la 'Enmienda al Protocolo de Cooperación y Asistencia Jurisdiccional en Materia Civil, Comercial, Laboral y Administrativa entre los Estados Partes del MERCOSUR', que consta como Anexo y forma parte de la presente Decisión.

Art. 2 – Por la presente Decisión se sustituyen los Artículos 1, 3, 4, 5, 10, 14, 19 y 35 del 'Protocolo de Las Leñas sobre Cooperación y Asistencia Jurisdiccional en Materia Civil, Comercial, Laboral y Administrativa', Decisión CMC No 5/92.

XXII CMC BUENOS AIRES, 5 VII/02

ANEXO

ENMIENDA AL PROTOCOLO DE COOPERACIÓN Y ASISTENCIA JURISDICCIONAL EN MATERIA CIVIL, COMERCIAL, LABORAL Y ADMINISTRATIVA ENTRE LOS ESTADOS PARTES DEL MERCOSUR

Los Gobiernos de la República Argentina, de la República Federativa del Brasil, de la República del Paraguay y de la República Oriental del Uruguay, en adelante 'Estados Partes';

Teniendo en cuenta el Protocolo de Cooperación y Asistencia Jurisdiccional en Materia Civil, Comercial, Laboral y Administrativa, suscrito entre los Estados Partes del MERCOSUR en el Valle de Las Leñas, República Argentina, el 27 de junio de 1992;

Considerando el Acuerdo de Cooperación y Asistencia Jurisdiccional en Materia Civil, Comercial, Laboral y Administrativa entre los Estados Partes del MERCOSUR y la República de Bolivia y la República de Chile, firmado en la XVII Reunión de Ministros de Justicia de los Estados Partes del MERCOSUR;

Conscientes de la necesidad de armonizar ambos textos.

ACUERDAN:

ARTÍCULO I

Modificar los artículos 1, 3, 4, 5, 10, 14, 19 y 35 del Protocolo de Cooperación y Asistencia Jurisdiccional en Materia Civil, Comercial, Laboral y Administrativa entre los Estados Partes del MERCOSUR, conforme a la siguiente redacción:

'ARTÍCULO 1.– Los Estados Partes se comprometen a prestarse asistencia mutua y amplia cooperación jurisdiccional en materia civil, comercial, laboral y administrativa. La asistencia jurisdiccional en materia administrativa se referirá, según el derecho interno de cada Estado, a los procedimientos contencioso-administrativos en los que se admitan recursos ante los tribunales'.

'ARTÍCULO 3.– Los nacionales, ciudadanos y residentes permanentes o habituales de uno de los Estados Partes gozarán, en las mismas condiciones que los nacionales, ciudadanos y residentes permanentes o habituales de otro Estado Parte, del libre acceso a la jurisdicción en dicho Estado para la defensa de sus derechos e intereses.

El párrafo precedente se aplicará a las personas jurídicas constituidas, autorizadas o registradas de acuerdo a las leyes de cualquiera de los Estados Partes'.

'ARTÍCULO 4.– Ninguna caución o depósito, cualquiera sea su denominación, podrá ser impuesta en razón de la calidad de nacional, ciudadano o residente permanente o habitual de otro Estado Parte.

El párrafo precedente se aplicará a las personas jurídicas constituidas, autorizadas o registradas de acuerdo a las leyes de cualquiera de los Estados Partes'.

'ARTÍCULO 5.– Cada Estado Parte deberá enviar a las autoridades jurisdiccionales del otro Estado Parte, según las vías previstas en los artículos 2 y 10, los exhortos en materia civil, comercial, laboral o administrativa, cuando tengan por objeto:

a) diligencias de mero trámite, tales como citaciones, intimaciones o apercibimientos, emplazamientos, notificaciones u otras semejantes;
b) recepción u obtención de pruebas'.

'ARTÍCULO 10.–Los exhortos podrán ser transmitidos por vía diplomática o consular, por intermedio de la respectiva Autoridad Central o por las partes interesadas, conforme al derecho interno.

Si la transmisión del exhorto fuere efectuada por intermedio de las Autoridades Centrales o por vía diplomática o consular, no se exigirá el requisito de la legalización.

Si se transmitiere por intermedio de la parte interesada, deberá ser legalizado ante los agentes diplomáticos o consulares del Estado requerido, salvo que entre los Estados requirente y requerido se hubiere suprimido el requisito de la legalización o sustituido por otra formalidad.

Los exhortos y los documentos que los acompañen deberán redactarse en el idioma de la autoridad requirente y ser acompañados de una traducción al idioma de la autoridad requerida'.

'ARTÍCULO 14.–Los documentos en los que conste el cumplimiento del exhorto serán devueltos por los medios y en la forma prevista en el artículo 10.

Cuando el exhorto no haya sido cumplido en todo o en parte, este hecho, así como las razones que determinaron el incumplimiento, deberán ser comunicados de inmediato a la autoridad requirente, utilizando los medios referidos en el párrafo precedente'.

'ARTÍCULO 19.–El reconocimiento y ejecución de sentencias y laudos arbitrales solicitado por las autoridades jurisdiccionales podrá tramitarse por vía de exhortos y transmitirse por intermedio de la Autoridad Central o por conducto diplomático o consular, conforme al derecho interno.

No obstante lo señalado en el párrafo anterior, la parte interesada podrá tramitar directamente el reconocimiento o ejecución de la sentencia. En tal caso, la sentencia deberá estar debidamente legalizada de acuerdo con la legislación del Estado en que se pretenda su eficacia, salvo que entre el Estado de origen del fallo y el Estado donde es invocado, se hubiere suprimido el requisito de la legalización o sustituido por otra formalidad'.

'ARTÍCULO 35.–El presente Acuerdo no restringirá las disposiciones de las Convenciones que sobre la misma materia, hubieran sido suscriptas anteriormente entre los Estados Partes', en tanto sean más beneficiosas para la cooperación'.

ARTÍCULO II

Corregir los artículos 11 y 22 del texto en portugués del Protocolo de Cooperación y Asistencia Jurisdiccional en Materia Civil, Comercial, Laboral y Administrativa entre los Estados Partes del MERCOSUR, a los efectos de armonizar su redacción con los respectivos artículos 11 y 22 del texto en español que poseen la siguiente redacción:

'ARTÍCULO 11.–La autoridad requirente podrá solicitar de la autoridad requerida se le informe el lugar y la fecha en que la medida solicitada se hará efectiva, a fin de permitir que la autoridad requirente, las partes interesadas o sus respectivos representantes puedan comparecer y ejercer las facultades autorizadas por la legislación de la Parte requerida.

Dicha comunicación deberá efectuarse con la debida antelación por intermedio de las Autoridades Centrales de los Estados Partes'.

'ARTÍCULO 22.– Cuando se tratare de una sentencia o de un laudo arbitral entre las mismas partes, fundadas en los mismos hechos y que tuviere el mismo objeto que el de otro proceso jurisdiccional o arbitral en el Estado requerido, su reconocimiento y ejecutoriedad dependerán de que la decisión no sea incompatible con otro pronunciamiento anterior o simultáneo recaído en tal proceso en el Estado requerido.

Asimismo, no se reconocerá ni se procederá a la ejecución, cuando se hubiere iniciado un procedimiento entre las mismas partes, fundado en los mismos hechos y sobre el mismo objeto, ante cualquier autoridad jurisdiccional de la Parte requerida con anterioridad a la presentación de la demanda ante la autoridad jurisdiccional que hubiere pronunciado la resolución de la que se solicite el reconocimiento'.

En el texto original en portugués dice :

'Artigo 11: A autoridade requerida poderá, atendendo a solicitação da autoridade requerente, informar o lugar e a data em que a medida solicitada será cumprida, a fim de permitir que a autoridade requerente, as partes interessadas ou seus respectivos representantes possam comparecer e exercer as faculdades autorizadas pela legislação da Parte requerida.

A referida comunicação deverá efetuar-se, com a devida antecedência, por intermédio das Autoridades Centrais dos Estados Partes'.

Debe decir:

'ARTIGO 11: A autoridade requerente poderá solicitar da autoridade requerida informação quanto ao lugar e a data em que a medida solicitada será cumprida, a fim de permitir que a autoridade requerente, as partes interessadas ou seus respectivos representantes, possam comparecer e exercer as faculdades autorizadas pela legislação da Parte requerida.

A referida comunicação deverá efetuar-se, com a devida antecedência, por intermédio das Autoridades Centrais dos Estados Partes'.

En el texto original en portugués dice:

'Artigo 22: Quando se tratar de uma sentença ou de um laudo arbitral entre as mesmas partes, fundamentado nos mesmos fatos, e que tenha o mesmo objeto de outro processo judicial ou arbitral no Estado requerido, seu reconhecimento e sua executoriedade dependerão de que a decisão não seja incompatível com outro pronunciamento anterior ou simultâneo proferido no Estado requerido.

Do mesmo modo não se reconhecerá nem se procederá à execução, quando se houver iniciado um procedimento entre as mesmas partes, fundamentado nos mesmos fatos e sobre o mesmo objeto, perante qualquer autoridade jurisdicional da Parte requerida, anteriormente à apresentação da demanda perante a autoridade jurisdicional que teria pronunciado a decisão da qual haja solicitação de reconhecimento'.

Debe decir:

'ARTIGO 22: Quando se tratar de uma sentença ou de um laudo arbitral entre as mesmas partes, fundamentado nos mesmos fatos, e que tenha o mesmo objeto de outro processo judirisdicional ou arbitral no Estado requerido, seu reconhecimento e sua executoriedade dependerão de que a decisão não seja incompatível com outro pronunciamento anterior ou simultâneo proferido nesse processo no Estado requerido.

Do mesmo modo não se reconhecerá nem se procederá à execução, quando se houver iniciado um procedimento entre as mesmas partes, fundamentado nos mesmos fatos e sobre o mesmo objeto, perante qualquer autoridade jurisdicional do Estado requerido, anteriormente à apresentação da demanda perante a autoridade jurisdicional que teria pronunciado a decisão da qual haja solicitação de reconhecimento'.

ARTÍCULO III

La presente Enmienda entrará en vigor treinta (30) días después de la fecha del depósito del cuarto instrumento de ratificación.

El Gobierno de la República del Paraguay será el depositario de la presente Enmienda y de los instrumentos de ratificación, y enviará copias debidamente autenticadas de los mismos a los Gobiernos de los demás Estados Partes.

Hecho en la ciudad de Buenos Aires, República Argentina, a los cinco (5) días del mes de julio de 2002, en un ejemplar original, en los idiomas español y portugués, siendo ambos textos igualmente auténticos.

Note. Please note this instrument is only available in Spanish and Portuguese. Visit www.redmercosur.org.uy/portal/mercosur.html for more information.

(v) BUENOS AIRES PROTOCOL ON INTERNATIONAL JURISDICTION IN CONTRACTUAL MATTERS

PREAMBLE

The Governments of the Argentine Republic, the Federative Republic of Brazil, the Republic of Paraguay, and the Oriental Republic of Uruguay,

Whereas: The Treaty of Asunción, signed on 26 March 1991, establishes the commitment of the State Parties to reconcile their legislations in the pertinent areas;

Reaffirming the desire of the State Parties to agree upon common legal solutions to reinforce the integration process;

Underscoring the need to provide the States Parties' private sector with a framework of legal security that will guarantee just solutions and international harmony in judicial and arbitration related decisions associated with contracting in the context of the Treaty of Asunción;

Convinced of the importance of adopting common rules on international jurisdiction in contractual matters, for the purpose of promoting the development of economic relations among the State Parties' private sectors;

Aware that, in the area of international business, contracting is the legal format of the commerce that takes place in connection with the integration process;

Agree:

TITLE I
SCOPE OF APPLICATION

Article 1

This Protocol shall be applied to the international adjudicatory jurisdiction relating to international contracts of a civil or commercial nature entered into between private, natural or juridical persons:

    a. with domicile or corporate headquarters in different State Parties to the Treaty of Asunción;

    b. when at least one of the parties to the contract has its domicile or corporate headquarters in a State Party of the Treaty of Asunción, and an agreement also has been made on selection of venue in favor of a judge of a State Party, and there is a reasonable connection, according to the rules of jurisdiction of this Protocol.

Article 2

The scope of application of this Protocol excludes:

1. legal negotiations between the bankrupt and their creditors, and other analogous procedures, especially agreements between insolvents and their creditors;
2. agreements in the area of family and inheritance law;
3. social security contracts;
4. administrative contracts;
5. labor contracts;
6. contracts for sale to the consumer;
7. transportation contracts;
8. insurance contracts;
9. rights *in rem*.

TITLE II
INTERNATIONAL JURISDICTION

Article 3

The procedural requirement of international jurisdiction in contractual matters shall be considered fulfilled when the jurisdictional body of a State Party assumes jurisdiction according to the stipulations of this Protocol.

CHAPTER I
SELECTION OF JURISDICTION

Article 4

1. In disputes that arise in international contracts concerning civil or commercial matters, the courts of the State Party to whose jurisdiction the contracting parties have agreed in writing to submit, shall have jurisdiction, provided that this agreement has not been obtained abusively.
2. Opting in favor of arbitration courts may be agreed upon.

Article 5

1. The agreement on selection of jurisdiction may be made at the time that the contract is entered into, during its effective period, or when the dispute has arisen.
2. The validity and effects of the agreement on selection of venue shall be governed by the law of the State Parties that would have jurisdiction according to the provisions of this Protocol.
3. In all cases, the law most favorable to the validity of the agreement shall be applied.

Article 6

Whether or not jurisdiction has been selected, it shall be understood as extended in favor of the State Party in which the suit has been brought when the respondent, after it has been filed its answer, accepts it voluntarily, positively, and not falsely.

CHAPTER II
ANCILLARY JURISDICTION

Article 7

In the absence of an agreement, those having jurisdiction at the plaintiffs selection are:
   a. The judges of the location for fulfillment of the contract;
   b. The judges of the respondent's domicile;
   c. The judges of plaintiff's domicile or corporate headquarters when it demonstrates that it has fulfilled its obligation.

Article 8

1. For purposes of Article 7, letter a), location for fulfillment of the contract shall be interpreted as the State Party in which the obligation serving as a basis for the claim has been or should be fulfilled.
2. Fulfillment of the claimed obligation shall be:
   a. For contracts on certain, individualized things: the location at which they existed at the time that they were entered into;
   b. For contracts on things determined by their type: the location of the debtor's domicile at the time that they were entered into;
   c. For contracts involving fungibles, the location of debtor's domicile at the time the contract was entered into;
   d. In contracts dealing with provision of services:
      1. If they affect things: the location where they existed at the time that the contract was entered into;
      2. If their effectiveness is related to any special location: the one in which the effects must necessarily occur;
      3. Apart from these cases: the location of the debtor's domicile at the time that the contract was entered into.

Article 9

1. For purposes of Article 7, letter b), the domicile of the respondent shall be interpreted as:

a. When natural persons are involved:
  1. Their usual residence;
  2. Subsidiarily, the principal center of their business;
  3. In the absence of these circumstances, the location of the simple residence.
  b. When juridical persons are involved: the principal administrative headquarters.
2. If the juridical person has branches, establishments, agencies, or any kind of representation, it shall be considered domiciled in the location where it operates and is subject to the jurisdiction of local authorities, in matters concerning the operations conducted there. This description is not an obstacle to the plaintiff's right to file suit in the courts where its principal administrative headquarters are located.

Article 10

The judges of the principal administrative headquarters are competent to hear litigation that arises between partners in their capacity as such.

Article 11

Juridical persons with headquarters in one State Party that enter into contracts in another State Party may be sued before judges of the latter.

Article 12

If there are several respondents, the State Party of the domicile of any of them shall have jurisdiction.

Suits based on obligations involving a guaranty of a personal nature, or for the intervention of third parties, may be filed in the court that is hearing the principal suit.

CHAPTER III
COUNTERCLAIM

Article 13

If a counterclaim is founded upon the act or deed on which the principal suit was based, the judges who heard the principal suit shall also have jurisdiction for hearing the counter-claims.

TITLE III
JURISDICTION AS A REQUIREMENT FOR RECOGNITION AND EXECUTION OF ARBITRATION JUDGMENTS AND DECISIONS

Article 14

The international jurisdiction regulated by Article 20, letter c) of the Las Leñas Protocol on Jurisdictional Cooperation and Assistance in Civil, Commercial, Labor, and Administrative Matters shall be subject to the provisions of this Protocol.

TITLE IV
CONSULTATIONS AND RESOLUTIONS OF CONTROVERSIES

Article 15

1. Controversies that may arise among the State Parties in connection with the application, interpretation, or non-fulfillment of the provisions contained in this Protocol shall be resolved through direct diplomatic negotiations.
2. If an agreement cannot be reached through such negotiations, or if the controversy is only partly resolved, the procedures called for in the System for Solution of Controversies in effect among the Parties to the Treaty of Asunción shall be applied.

TITLE V
FINAL PROVISIONS

Article 16

1. This Protocol, an integral part of the Treaty of Asunción, shall go into effect thirty (30) days after the deposit of the second ratification instrument in relation to the first two States that ratify it.
2. For the other signatories, it shall go into effect on the thirtieth (30) day after the deposit of the respective ratification instrument, in the order in which the ratifications were deposited.

Article 17

Accession to the Treaty of Asunción on the part of a State shall imply, ipso jure, accession to this Protocol.

Article 18

1. The Government of the Republic of Paraguay shall be the depositary of this Protocol and of the ratification instruments, and shall send duly authenticated copies thereof to the Governments of the other State Parties.
2. The Government of the Republic of Paraguay shall notify the Governments of the other State Parties of the date on which this Protocol goes into effect, and the date of deposit of the ratification instruments.

Executed in the city of Buenos Aires, on the fifth of August of 1994, in an original in the Spanish and Portuguese languages, both texts being equally authentic.

(vi) CONVENTION ON THE SERVICE ABROAD OF JUDICIAL AND EXTRAJUDICIAL DOCUMENTS IN CIVIL OR COMMERCIAL MATTERS*

(Concluded November 15, 1965)

PREAMBLE

The States signatory to the present Convention,

Desiring to create appropriate means to ensure that judicial and extrajudicial documents to be served abroad shall be brought to the notice of the addressee in sufficient time,

Desiring to improve the organisation of mutual judicial assistance for that purpose by simplifying and expediting the procedure,

Have resolved to conclude a Convention to this effect and have agreed upon the following provisions:

Article 1

The present Convention shall apply in all cases, in civil or commercial matters, where there is occasion to transmit a judicial or extrajudicial document for service abroad.

---

* Reproduced with the kind permission of the Hague Conference on Private International Law.

This Convention shall not apply where the address of the person to be served with the document is not known.

CHAPTER I
JUDICIAL DOCUMENTS

Article 2

Each Contracting State shall designate a Central Authority which will undertake to receive requests for service coming from other Contracting States and to proceed in conformity with the provisions of Articles 3 to 6.

Each State shall organise the Central Authority in conformity with its own law.

Article 3

The authority or judicial officer competent under the law of the State in which the documents originate shall forward to the Central Authority of the State addressed a request conforming to the model annexed to the present Convention, without any requirement of legalisation or other equivalent formality.

The document to be served or a copy thereof shall be annexed to the request. The request and the document shall both be furnished in duplicate.

Article 4

If the Central Authority considers that the request does not comply with the provisions of the present Convention it shall promptly inform the applicant and specify its objections to the request.

Article 5

The Central Authority of the State addressed shall itself serve the document or shall arrange to have it served by an appropriate agency, either—
   a) by a method prescribed by its internal law for the service of documents in domestic actions upon persons who are within its territory, or
   b) by a particular method requested by the applicant, unless such a method is incompatible with the law of the State addressed.
Subject to sub-paragraph *(b)* of the first paragraph of this Article, the document may always be served by delivery to an addressee who accepts it voluntarily.

If the document is to be served under the first paragraph above, the Central Authority may require the document to be written in, or translated into, the official language or one of the official languages of the State addressed.

That part of the request, in the form attached to the present Convention, which contains a summary of the document to be served, shall be served with the document.

Article 6

The Central Authority of the State addressed or any authority which it may have designated for that purpose, shall complete a certificate in the form of the model annexed to the present Convention.

The certificate shall state that the document has been served and shall include the method, the place and the date of service and the person to whom the document was delivered. If the document has not been served, the certificate shall set out the reasons which have prevented service.

The applicant may require that a certificate not completed by a Central Authority or by a judicial authority shall be countersigned by one of these authorities.

The certificate shall be forwarded directly to the applicant.

Article 7

The standard terms in the model annexed to the present Convention shall in all cases be written either in French or in English. They may also be written in the official language, or in one of the official languages, of the State in which the documents originate.

The corresponding blanks shall be completed either in the language of the State addressed or in French or in English.

Article 8

Each Contracting State shall be free to effect service of judicial documents upon persons abroad, without application of any compulsion, directly through its diplomatic or consular agents.

Any State may declare that it is opposed to such service within its territory, unless the document is to be served upon a national of the State in which the documents originate.

Article 9

Each Contracting State shall be free, in addition, to use consular channels to forward documents, for the purpose of service, to those authorities of another Contracting State which are designated by the latter for this purpose.

Each Contracting State may, if exceptional circumstances so require, use diplomatic channels for the same purpose.

Article 10

Provided the State of destination does not object, the present Convention shall not interfere with —
a) the freedom to send judicial documents, by postal channels, directly to persons abroad,
b) the freedom of judicial officers, officials or other competent persons of the State of origin to effect service of judicial documents directly through the judicial officers, officials or other competent persons of the State of destination,
c) the freedom of any person interested in a judicial proceeding to effect service of judicial documents directly through the judicial officers, officials or other competent persons of the State of destination.

Article 11

The present Convention shall not prevent two or more Contracting States from agreeing to permit, for the purpose of service of judicial documents, channels of transmission other than those provided for in the preceding Articles and, in particular, direct communication between their respective authorities.

Article 12

The service of judicial documents coming from a Contracting State shall not give rise to any payment or reimbursement of taxes or costs for the services rendered by the State addressed.

The applicant shall pay or reimburse the costs occasioned by-

a) the employment of a judicial officer or of a person competent under the law of the State of destination,

b) the use of a particular method of service.

Article 13

Where a request for service complies with the terms of the present Convention, the State addressed may refuse to comply therewith only if it deems that compliance would infringe its sovereignty or security.

It may not refuse to comply solely on the ground that, under its internal law, it claims exclusive jurisdiction over the subject-matter of the action or that its internal law would not permit the action upon which the application is based.

The Central Authority shall, in case of refusal, promptly inform the applicant and state the reasons for the refusal.

Article 14

Difficulties which may arise in connection with the transmission of judicial documents for service shall be settled through diplomatic channels.

Article 15

Where a writ of summons or an equivalent document had to be transmitted abroad for the purpose of service, under the provisions of the present Convention, and the defendant has not appeared, judgment shall not be given until it is established that—

a) the document was served by a method prescribed by the internal law of the State addressed for the service of documents in domestic actions upon persons who are within its territory, or

b) the document was actually delivered to the defendant or to his residence by another method provided for by this Convention,

and that in either of these cases the service or the delivery was effected in sufficient time to enable the defendant to defend.

Each Contracting State shall be free to declare that the judge, notwithstanding the provisions of the first paragraph of this Article, may give judgment even if no certificate of service or delivery has been received, if all the following conditions are fulfilled—

a) the document was transmitted by one of the methods provided for in this Convention,

b) a period of time of not less than six months, considered adequate by the judge in the particular case, has elapsed since the date of the transmission of the document,

c) no certificate of any kind has been received, even though every reasonable effort has been made to obtain it through the competent authorities of the State addressed.

Notwithstanding the provisions of the preceding paragraphs the judge may order, in case of urgency, any provisional or protective measures.

Article 16

When a writ of summons or an equivalent document had to be transmitted abroad for the purpose of service, under the provisions of the present Convention, and a judgment has been entered against a defendant who has not appeared, the judge shall have the power to relieve the defendant from the effects of the expiration of the time for appeal from the judgment if the following conditions are fulfilled—

    a) the defendant, without any fault on his part, did not have knowledge of the document in sufficient time to defend, or knowledge of the judgment in sufficient time to appeal, and

    b) the defendant has disclosed a *prima facie* defence to the action on the merits.

An application for relief may be filed only within a reasonable time after the defendant has knowledge of the judgment.

Each Contracting State may declare that the application will not be entertained if it is filed after the expiration of a time to be stated in the declaration, but which shall in no case be less than one year following the date of the judgment.

This Article shall not apply to judgments concerning status or capacity of persons.

CHAPTER II
EXTRAJUDICIAL DOCUMENTS

Article 17

Extrajudicial documents emanating from authorities and judicial officers of a Contracting State may be transmitted for the purpose of service in another Contracting State by the methods and under the provisions of the present Convention.

CHAPTER III
GENERAL CLAUSES

Article 18

Each Contracting State may designate other authorities in addition to the Central Authority and shall determine the extent of their competence.

The applicant shall, however, in all cases, have the right to address a request directly to the Central Authority.

Federal States shall be free to designate more than one Central Authority.

Article 19

To the extent that the internal law of a Contracting State permits methods of transmission, other than those provided for in the preceding Articles, of documents coming from abroad, for service within its territory, the present Convention shall not affect such provisions.

Article 20

The present Convention shall not prevent an agreement between any two or more Contracting States to dispense with—

    a) the necessity for duplicate copies of transmitted documents as required by the second paragraph of Article 3,

b) the language requirements of the third paragraph of Article 5 and Article 7,
c) the provisions of the fourth paragraph of Article 5,
d) the provisions of the second paragraph of Article 12.

Article 21

Each Contracting State shall, at the time of the deposit of its instrument of ratification or accession, or at a later date, inform the Ministry of Foreign Affairs of the Netherlands of the following—
a) the designation of authorities, pursuant to Articles 2 and 18,
b) the designation of the authority competent to complete the certificate pursuant to Article 6,
c) the designation of the authority competent to receive documents transmitted by consular channels, pursuant to Article 9.
Each Contracting State shall similarly inform the Ministry, where appropriate, of—
a) opposition to the use of methods of transmission pursuant to Articles 8 and 10,
b) declarations pursuant to the second paragraph of Article 15 and the third paragraph of Article 16,
c) all modifications of the above designations, oppositions and declarations.

Article 22

Where Parties to the present Convention are also Parties to one or both of the Conventions on civil procedure signed at The Hague on 17th July 1905, and on 1st March 1954, this Convention shall replace as between them Articles 1 to 7 of the earlier Conventions.

Article 23

The present Convention shall not affect the application of Article 23 of the Convention on civil procedure signed at The Hague on 17th July 1905, or of Article 24 of the Convention on civil procedure signed at The Hague on 1st March 1954.

These Articles shall, however, apply only if methods of communication, identical to those provided for in these Conventions, are used.

Article 24

Supplementary agreements between Parties to the Conventions of 1905 and 1954 shall be considered as equally applicable to the present Convention, unless the Parties have otherwise agreed.

Article 25

Without prejudice to the provisions of Articles 22 and 24, the present Convention shall not derogate from Conventions containing provisions on the matters governed by this Convention to which the Contracting States are, or shall become, Parties.

Article 26

The present Convention shall be open for signature by the States represented at the Tenth Session of the Hague Conference on Private International Law.

It shall be ratified, and the instruments of ratification shall be deposited with the Ministry of Foreign Affairs of the Netherlands.

Article 27

The present Convention shall enter into force on the sixtieth day after the deposit of the third instrument of ratification referred to in the second paragraph of Article 26.

The Convention shall enter into force for each signatory State which ratifies subsequently on the sixtieth day after the deposit of its instrument of ratification.

Article 28

Any State not represented at the Tenth Session of the Hague Conference on Private International Law may accede to the present Convention after it has entered into force in accordance with the first paragraph of Article 27. The instrument of accession shall be deposited with the Ministry of Foreign Affairs of the Netherlands.

The Convention shall enter into force for such a State in the absence of any objection from a State, which has ratified the Convention before such deposit, notified to the Ministry of Foreign Affairs of the Netherlands within a period of six months after the date on which the said Ministry has notified it of such accession.

In the absence of any such objection, the Convention shall enter into force for the acceding State on the first day of the month following the expiration of the last of the periods referred to in the preceding paragraph.

Article 29

Any State may, at the time of signature, ratification or accession, declare that the present Convention shall extend to all the territories for the international relations of which it is responsible, or to one or more of them. Such a declaration shall take effect on the date of entry into force of the Convention for the State concerned.

At any time thereafter, such extensions shall be notified to the Ministry of Foreign Affairs of the Netherlands.

The Convention shall enter into force for the territories mentioned in such an extension on the sixtieth day after the notification referred to in the preceding paragraph.

Article 30

The present Convention shall remain in force for five years from the date of its entry into force in accordance with the first paragraph of Article 27, even for States which have ratified it or acceded to it subsequently.

If there has been no denunciation, it shall be renewed tacitly every five years.

Any denunciation shall be notified to the Ministry of Foreign Affairs of the Netherlands at least six months before the end of the five year period.

It may be limited to certain of the territories to which the Convention applies.

The denunciation shall have effect only as regards the State which has notified it. The Convention shall remain in force for the other Contracting States.

Article 31

The Ministry of Foreign Affairs of the Netherlands shall give notice to the States referred to in Article 26, and to the States which have acceded in accordance with Article 28, of

the following—
   a) the signatures and ratifications referred to in Article 26;
   b) the date on which the present Convention enters into force in accordance with the first paragraph of Article 27;
   c) the accessions referred to in Article 28 and the dates on which they take effect;
   d) the extensions referred to in Article 29 and the dates on which they take effect;
   e) the designations, oppositions and declarations referred to in Article 21;
   f) the denunciations referred to in the third paragraph of Article 30.

In witness whereof the undersigned, being duly authorised thereto, have signed the present Convention.

Done at The Hague, on the 15th day of November, 1965, in the English and French languages, both texts being equally authentic, in a single copy which shall be deposited in the archives of the Government of the Netherlands, and of which a certified copy shall be sent, through the diplomatic channel, to each of the States represented at the Tenth Session of the Hague Conference on Private International Law.

(N.B. On 25 October 1980 the Fourteenth Session adopted a *Recommendation on information to accompany judicial and extrajudicial documents to be sent or served abroad in civil or commercial matters (Actes et documents de la Quatorzième session (1980)*, Tome I, *Matières diverses*, p. I-67; *idem*, Tome IV, *Entraide judiciaire*, p. 339; *Practical Handbook on the Operation of the Hague Convention of 15 November 1965 on the Service Abroad of Judicial and Extrajudicial Documents in Civil or Commercial Matters).*

FORMS (REQUEST AND CERTIFICATE)
SUMMARY OF THE DOCUMENT TO BE SERVED
(ANNEXES PROVIDED FOR ARTICLES 3, 5, 6 AND 7)

ANNEX TO THE CONVENTION
FORMS
REQUEST FOR SERVICE ABROAD OF JUDICIAL OR
EXTRAJUDICIAL DOCUMENTS

CONVENTION ON THE SERVICE ABROAD OF JUDICIAL
AND EXTRAJUDICIAL DOCUMENTS IN CIVIL OR
COMMERCIAL MATTERS, SIGNED AT THE HAGUE,
THE 15TH OF NOVEMBER 1965.

Identity and address of the applicant	Address of receiving authority

The undersigned applicant has the honour to transmit—in duplicate—the documents listed below and, in conformity with Article 5 of the above-mentioned Convention, requests prompt service of one copy thereof on the addressee, *i.e,*
(identity and address).. .

....

   a) in accordance with the provisions of sub-paragraph *(a)* of the first paragraph of Article 5 of the Convention*.

   b) in accordance with the following particular method (sub-paragraph *(b)* of the first paragraph of Article 5)*:

....

....

   c) by delivery to the addressee, if he accepts it voluntarily (second paragraph of Article 5)*.

The authority is requested to return or to have returned to the applicant a copy of the documents—and of the annexes*—with a certificate as provided on the reverse side.

List of documents

....

....

....

....

....

....

....

....

....

Done at . . . ., the . . . .
Signature and/or stamp.

*Delete if inappropriate.

Reverse of the request

CERTIFICATE

The undersigned authority has the honour to certify, in conformity with Article 6 of the Convention,

1) that the document has been served*
   - the (date)

....

   - at (place, street, number)

....

....

   — in one of the following methods authorised by Article 5:
     a) in accordance with the provisions of sub-paragraph *(a)* of the first paragraph of Article 5 of the Convention*.
     b) in accordance with the following particular method*:

....

....

     c) by delivery to the addressee, who accepted it voluntarily*

The documents referred to in the request have been delivered to:
   - (identity and description of person)

....

....

   - relationship to the addressee (family, business or other):

....

....

....

2) that the document has not been served, by reason of the following facts*:

....

....

....

In conformity with the second paragraph of Article 12 of the Convention, the applicant is requested to pay or reimburse the expenses detailed in the attached statement*.

Annexes
Documents returned:

....

....

....

In appropriate cases, documents establishing the service:

....

....

....

....

....

Done at . . . ., the . . . .
Signature and/or stamp.

*Delete if inappropriate.

SUMMARY OF THE DOCUMENT TO BE SERVED

CONVENTION ON THE SERVICE ABROAD OF JUDICIAL AND EXTRAJUDICIAL
DOCUMENTS IN CIVIL OR COMMERCIAL MATTERS,
SIGNED AT THE HAGUE, THE 15TH OF NOVEMBER 1965.
(ARTICLE 5, FOURTH PARAGRAPH)

Name and address of the requesting authority:

....

....

....

....

Particulars of the parties*:

....

....

....

....

JUDICIAL DOCUMENT**

Nature and purpose of the document:

....

....

....

....

Nature and purpose of the proceedings and, where appropriate, the amount in dispute:

....

....

....

Date and place for entering appearance**:

....

....

Court which has given judgment**:

....

....

Date of judgment**:

....

Time-limits stated in the document**:

....

....

EXTRAJUDICIAL DOCUMENT**

Nature and purpose of the document:

....

....

....

....

Time-limits stated in the document**:

....

....

....

....

*If appropriate, identity and address of the person interested in the transmission of the document.

** Delete if inappropriate.

TABLE OF STATE RATIFICATIONS

Total number of signatures not followed by ratifications: 0

Total number of ratifications/accessions: 53

State	Signature	Ratification, Acceptance or Approval	By Accession	Entry into force	Expiry date under Article 28***
Antigua and Barbuda		17 May 1985 (date of declaration to be bound by the Convention as per date of independence		1 November 1981	
Argentina			2 February 2001	1 December 2001	15 November 2001
Bahamas			17 June 1997	1 February 1998	1 January 1998
Barbados			10 February 1969	1 October 1969	27 September 1969
Belarus			6 June 1997	1 February 1998	1 January 1998
Belgium	19 November 1970			18 January 1971	
Botswana			10 February 1969	1 September 1969	28 August 1969
Bulgaria			23 November 1999	1 August 2000	31 July 2000
Canada		26 September 1988		1 May 1989	10 April 1989

State	Signature	Ratification, Acceptance or Approval	By Accession	Entry into force	Expiry date under Article 28***
People's Republic of China			6 May 1991	1 January 1992	1 December 1991
China, Hong Kong SAR		1 July 1997 (date on which the UK restored Hong Kong to China)			
China, Macao SAR		20 December 1999 (date on which Portugal restored Macao to China)		12 April 1999	
Cyprus			26 October 1982	1 June 1983	15 May 1983
Czech Republic			23 September 1981	1 June 1982	9 May 1982
Denmark		2 August 1969		1 October 1969	
Egypt		12 December 1968		10 February 1969	
Estonia			2 February 1996	1 October 1996	15 September 1996
Finland		11 September 1969		10 November 1969	
France		3 July 1972		1 September 1972	
Germany		27 April 1979		26 June 1979	
Greece		20 July 1983		18 September 1983	
Ireland		5 April 1994		4 June 1994	
Israel		14 August 1972		13 October 1972	
Italy		25 November 1981		24 January 1982	
Japan		28 May 1970		27 July 1970	
Republic of Korea			13 January 2000	1 August 2000	31 July 2000
Kuwait			8 May 2002	1 December 2002	21 November 2002
Latvia			28 March 1995	1 November 1995	15 October 1995
Lithuania			2 August 2000	1 June 2001	15 May 2001
Luxembourg		9 July 1975		7 September 1975	
Malawi			24 April 1972	1 December 1972	25 November 1972
Mexico			2 November 1999	1 June 2000	30 May 2000
Netherlands *		3 November 1975		2 January 1976	
Norway		2 August 1969		1 October 1969	

State	Signature	Ratification, Acceptance or Approval	By Accession	Entry into force	Expiry date under Article 28***
Pakistan			7 December 1988	1 August 1999	6 July 1989
Poland			13 February 1996	1 September 1996	29 August 1996
Portugal		27 December 1973		25 February 1974	
Romania			21 August 2003	1 April 2004	1 March 2004
Russian Federation			1 May 2001	1 December 2001	15 November 2001
San Marino			15 April 2002	1 November 2002	25 October 2002
Seychelles			18 November 1980	1 July 1981	18 June 1981
Slovakia			23 September 1981	1 June 1982	9 May 1982
Slovenia			18 September 2000	1 June 2001	15 May 2001
Spain	4 June 1987			3 August 1987	
Sri Lanka			31 August 2000	1 June 2001	15 May 2001
Sweden		2 August 1969		1 October 1969	
Switzerland		2 November 1994		1 January 1995	
Turkey		28 February 1972		28 April 1972	
Ukraine			1 February 2001	1 December 2001	15 November 2001
United Kingdom**		17 November 1967		10 February 1969	
United States of America		24 August 1967		10 February 1969	
Venezuela			29 October 1993	1 July 1994	15 June 1994

*For extensions made by the Netherlands, please consult the full status report on the web-site.

**For extensions made by the UK, please consult the full status report on the web-site.

***In accordance with Article 28 of the Convention, the accession has effect only in the absence of any objection from a State, which has ratified the Convention before such deposit, notified to the Ministry of Foreign Affairs of the Netherlands within a period of six months after the date on which the said Ministry has notified it of such accession. The date specified here is the expiry date of that six-month period

Note: A list of reservations and the details of accessions made by States has not been included in the text. These can be obtained from http://www.hcch.net/e/status/stat14e.html.

The Hague, 15 November 1965
(Entry into force on 10 February 1969)

(vii) COUNCIL REGULATION (EC) NO. 1348/2000 OF 29 MAY 2000 ON THE SERVICE IN THE MEMBER STATES OF JUDICIAL AND EXTRAJUDICIAL DOCUMENTS IN CIVIL OR COMMERCIAL MATTERS

PREAMBLE

THE COUNCIL OF THE EUROPEAN UNION,

Having regard to the Treaty establishing the European Community, and in particular Article 61(c) and Article 67(1) thereof,
Having regard to the proposal from the Commission[1],
Having regard to the opinion of the European Parliament[2],
Having regard to the opinion of the Economic and Social Committee[3],

---

[1] OJ C 247 E, 31.8.1999, p. 11.
[2] Opinion of 17 November 1999 (not yet published in the Official Journal).
[3] OJ C 368, 20.12.1999, p. 47.

Whereas:

(1) The Union has set itself the objective of maintaining and developing the Union as an area of freedom, security and justice, in which the free movement of persons is assured. To establish such an area, the Community is to adopt, among others, the measures relating to judicial cooperation in civil matters needed for the proper functioning of the internal market.

(2) The proper functioning of the internal market entails the need to improve and expedite the transmission of judicial and extrajudicial documents in civil or commercial matters for service between the Member States.

(3) This is a subject now falling within the ambit of Article 65 of the Treaty.

(4) In accordance with the principles of subsidiarity and proportionality as set out in Article 5 of the Treaty, the objectives of this Regulation cannot be sufficiently achieved by the Member States and can therefore be better achieved by the Community. This Regulation does not go beyond what is necessary to achieve those objectives.

(5) The Council, by an Act dated 26 May 1997[4], drew up a Convention on the service in the Member States of the European Union of judicial and extrajudicial documents in civil or commercial matters and recommended it for adoption by the Member States in accordance with their respective constitutional rules. That Convention has not entered into force. Continuity in the results of the negotiations for conclusion of the Convention should be ensured. The main content of this Regulation is substantially taken over from it.

(6) Efficiency and speed in judicial procedures in civil matters means that the transmission of judicial and extrajudicial documents is to be made direct and by rapid means between local bodies designated by the Member States. However, the Member States may indicate their intention of designating only one transmitting or receiving agency or one agency to perform both functions for a period of five years. This designation may, however, be renewed every five years.

(7) Speed in transmission warrants the use of all appropriate means, provided that certain conditions as to the legibility and reliability of the document received are observed. Security in transmission requires that the document to be transmitted be accompanied by a pre-printed form, to be completed in the language of the place where service is to be effected, or in another language accepted by the Member State in question.

(8) To secure the effectiveness of this Regulation, the possibility of refusing service of documents is confined to exceptional situations.

(9) Speed of transmission warrants documents being served within days of reception of the document. However, if service has not been effected after one month has elapsed, the receiving agency should inform the transmitting agency. The expiry of this period should not imply that the request be returned to the transmitting agency where it is clear that service is feasible within a reasonable period.

(10) For the protection of the addressee's interests, service should be effected in the official language or one of the official languages of the place where it is to be

---

[4] OJ C 261, 27.8.1997, p. 1. On the same day as the Convention was drawn up the Council took note of the explanatory report on the Convention which is set out on page 26 of the aforementioned Official Journal.

effected or in another language of the originating Member State which the addressee understands.

(11) Given the differences between the Member States as regards their rules of procedure, the material date for the purposes of service varies from one Member State to another. Having regard to such situations and the possible difficulties that may arise, this Regulation should provide for a system where it is the law of the receiving Member State which determines the date of service. However, if the relevant documents in the context of proceedings to be brought or pending in the Member State of origin are to be served within a specified period, the date to be taken into consideration with respect to the applicant shall be that determined according to the law of the Member State of origin. A Member State is, however, authorised to derogate from the aforementioned provisions for a transitional period of five years, for appropriate reasons. Such a derogation may be renewed by a Member State at five-year intervals due to reasons related to its legal system.

(12) This Regulation prevails over the provisions contained in bilateral or multilateral agreements or arrangements having the same scope, concluded by the Member States, and in particular the Protocol annexed to the Brussels Convention of 27 September 1968[5] and the Hague Convention of 15 November 1965 in relations between the Member States party thereto. This Regulation does not preclude Member States from maintaining or concluding agreements or arrangements to expedite or simplify the transmission of documents, provided that they are compatible with the Regulation.

(13) The information transmitted pursuant to this Regulation should enjoy suitable protection. This matter falls within the scope of Directive 95/46/EC of the European Parliament and of the Council of 24 October 1995 on the protection of individuals with regard to the processing of personal data and on the free movement of such data[6], and of Directive 97/66/EC of the European Parliament and of the Council of 15 December 1997 concerning the processing of personal data and the protection of privacy in the telecommunications sector[7].

(14) The measures necessary for the implementation of this Regulation should be adopted in accordance with Council Decision 1999/468/EC of 28 June 1999 laying down the procedures for the exercise of implementing powers conferred on the Commission[8].

(15) These measures also include drawing up and updating the manual using appropriate modern means.

(16) No later than three years after the date of entry into force of this Regulation, the Commission should review its application and propose such amendments as may appear necessary.

(17) The United Kingdom and Ireland, in accordance with Article 3 of the Protocol on the position of the United Kingdom and Ireland annexed to the Treaty on European Union and the Treaty establishing the European Community, have

---

[5] Brussels Convention of 27 September 1968 on Jurisdiction and the Enforcement of Judgments in Civil and Commercial Matters (OJ L 299, 13.12.1972, p. 32; consolidated version, OJ C 27, 26.1.1998, p. 1).
[6] OJ L 281, 23.11.1995, p. 31.   [7] OJ L 24, 30.1.1998, p. 1.
[8] OJ L 184, 17.7.1999, p. 23.

given notice of their wish to take part in the adoption and application of this Regulation.

(18) Denmark, in accordance with Articles 1 and 2 of the Protocol on the position of Denmark annexed to the Treaty on European Union and the Treaty establishing the European Community, is not participating in the adoption of this Regulation, and is therefore not bound by it nor subject to its application,

HAS ADOPTED THIS REGULATION:

CHAPTER I
GENERAL PROVISIONS

Article 1
Scope

1. This Regulation shall apply in civil and commercial matters where a judicial or extrajudicial document has to be transmitted from one Member State to another for service there.
2. This Regulation shall not apply where the address of the person to be served with the document is not known.

Article 2
Transmitting and receiving agencies

1. Each Member State shall designate the public officers, authorities or other persons, hereinafter referred to as 'transmitting agencies', competent for the transmission of judicial or extrajudicial documents to be served in another Member State.
2. Each Member State shall designate the public officers, authorities or other persons, hereinafter referred to as 'receiving agencies', competent for the receipt of judicial or extrajudicial documents from another Member State.
3. A Member State may designate one transmitting agency and one receiving agency or one agency to perform both functions. A federal State, a State in which several legal systems apply or a State with autonomous territorial units shall be free to designate more than one such agency. The designation shall have effect for a period of five years and may be renewed at five-year intervals.
4. Each Member State shall provide the Commission with the following information:
    (a) the names and addresses of the receiving agencies referred to in paragraphs 2 and 3;
    (b) the geographical areas in which they have jurisdiction;
    (c) the means of receipt of documents available to them; and
    (d) the languages that may be used for the completion of the standard form in the Annex.
Member States shall notify the Commission of any subsequent modification of such information.

Article 3
Central body

Each Member State shall designate a central body responsible for:
    (a) supplying information to the transmitting agencies;

(b) seeking solutions to any difficulties which may arise during transmission of documents for service;

(c) forwarding, in exceptional cases, at the request of a transmitting agency, a request for service to the competent receiving agency.

A federal State, a State in which several legal systems apply or a State with autonomous territorial units shall be free to designate more than one central body.

CHAPTER II
JUDICIAL DOCUMENTS

SECTION I

TRANSMISSION AND SERVICE OF JUDICIAL DOCUMENTS

Article 4
Transmission of documents

1. Judicial documents shall be transmitted directly and as soon as possible between the agencies designated on the basis of Article 2.

2. The transmission of documents, requests, confirmations, receipts, certificates and any other papers between transmitting agencies and receiving agencies may be carried out by any appropriate means, provided that the content of the document received is true and faithful to that of the document forwarded and that all information in it is easily legible.

3. The document to be transmitted shall be accompanied by a request drawn up using the standard form in the Annex. The form shall be completed in the official language of the Member State addressed or, if there are several official languages in that Member State, the official language or one of the official languages of the place where service is to be effected, or in another language which that Member State has indicated it can accept. Each Member State shall indicate the official language or languages of the European Union other than its own which is or are acceptable to it for completion of the form.

4. The documents and all papers that are transmitted shall be exempted from legalisation or any equivalent formality.

5. When the transmitting agency wishes a copy of the document to be returned together with the certificate referred to in Article 10, it shall send the document in duplicate.

Article 5
Translation of documents

1. The applicant shall be advised by the transmitting agency to which he or she forwards the document for transmission that the addressee may refuse to accept it if it is not in one of the languages provided for in Article 8.

2. The applicant shall bear any costs of translation prior to the transmission of the document, without prejudice to any possible subsequent decision by the court or competent authority on liability for such costs.

Article 6
Receipt of documents by receiving agency

1. On receipt of a document, a receiving agency shall, as soon as possible and in any event within seven days of receipt, send a receipt to the transmitting agency by the swiftest possible means of transmission using the standard form in the Annex.
2. Where the request for service cannot be fulfilled on the basis of the information or documents transmitted, the receiving agency shall contact the transmitting agency by the swiftest possible means in order to secure the missing information or documents.
3. If the request for service is manifestly outside the scope of this Regulation or if non-compliance with the formal conditions required makes service impossible, the request and the documents transmitted shall be returned, on receipt, to the transmitting agency, together with the notice of return in the standard form in the Annex.
4. A receiving agency receiving a document for service but not having territorial jurisdiction to serve it shall forward it, as well as the request, to the receiving agency having territorial jurisdiction in the same Member State if the request complies with the conditions laid down in Article 4(3) and shall inform the transmitting agency accordingly, using the standard form in the Annex. That receiving agency shall inform the transmitting agency when it receives the document, in the manner provided for in paragraph 1.

Article 7
Service of documents

1. The receiving agency shall itself serve the document or have it served, either in accordance with the law of the Member State addressed or by a particular form requested by the transmitting agency, unless such a method is incompatible with the law of that Member State.
2. All steps required for service of the document shall be effected as soon as possible. In any event, if it has not been possible to effect service within one month of receipt, the receiving agency shall inform the transmitting agency by means of the certificate in the standard form in the Annex, which shall be drawn up under the conditions referred to in Article 10(2). The period shall be calculated in accordance with the law of the Member State addressed.

Article 8
Refusal to accept a document

1. The receiving agency shall inform the addressee that he or she may refuse to accept the document to be served if it is in a language other than either of the following languages:
   (a) the official language of the Member State addressed or, if there are several official languages in that Member State, the official language or one of the official languages of the place where service is to be effected; or
   (b) a language of the Member State of transmission which the addressee understands.
2. Where the receiving agency is informed that the addressee refuses to accept the document in accordance with paragraph 1, it shall immediately inform the transmitting agency by means of the certificate provided for in Article 10 and return the request and the documents of which a translation is requested.

Article 9
Date of service

1. Without prejudice to Article 8, the date of service of a document pursuant to Article 7 shall be the date on which it is served in accordance with the law of the Member State addressed.
2. However, where a document shall be served within a particular period in the context of proceedings to be brought or pending in the Member State of origin, the date to be taken into account with respect to the applicant shall be that fixed by the law of that Member State.
3. A Member State shall be authorised to derogate from the provisions of paragraphs 1 and 2 for a transitional period of five years, for appropriate reasons.
   This transitional period may be renewed by a Member State at five-yearly intervals due to reasons related to its legal system. That Member State shall inform the Commission of the content of such a derogation and the circumstances of the case.

Article 10
Certificate of service and copy of the document served

1. When the formalities concerning the service of the document have been completed, a certificate of completion of those formalities shall be drawn up in the standard form in the Annex and addressed to the transmitting agency, together with, where Article 4(5) applies, a copy of the document served.
2. The certificate shall be completed in the official language or one of the official languages of the Member State of origin or in another language which the Member State of origin has indicated that it can accept. Each Member State shall indicate the official language or languages of the European Union other than its own which is or are acceptable to it for completion of the form.

Article 11
Costs of service

1. The service of judicial documents coming from a Member State shall not give rise to any payment or reimbursement of taxes or costs for services rendered by the Member State addressed.
2. The applicant shall pay or reimburse the costs occasioned by:
   (a) the employment of a judicial officer or of a person competent under the law of the Member State addressed;
   (b) the use of a particular method of service.

SECTION 2
OTHER MEANS OF TRANSMISSION AND SERVICE OF JUDICIAL DOCUMENTS

Article 12
Transmission by consular or diplomatic channels

Each Member State shall be free, in exceptional circumstances, to use consular or diplomatic channels to forward judicial documents, for the purpose of service, to those agencies of another Member State which are designated pursuant to Article 2 or 3.

Article 13
Service by diplomatic or consular agents

1. Each Member State shall be free to effect service of judicial documents on persons residing in another Member State, without application of any compulsion, directly through its diplomatic or consular agents.
2. Any Member State may make it known, in accordance with Article 23(1), that it is opposed to such service within its territory, unless the documents are to be served on nationals of the Member State in which the documents originate.

Article 14
Service by post

1. Each Member State shall be free to effect service of judicial documents directly by post to persons residing in another Member State.
2. Any Member State may specify, in accordance with Article 23(1), the conditions under which it will accept service of judicial documents by post.

Article 15
Direct service

1. This Regulation shall not interfere with the freedom of any person interested in a judicial proceeding to effect service of judicial documents directly through the judicial officers, officials or other competent persons of the Member State addressed.
2. Any Member State may make it known, in accordance with Article 23(1), that it is opposed to the service of judicial documents in its territory pursuant to paragraph 1.

CHAPTER III
EXTRAJUDICIAL DOCUMENTS

Article 16
Transmission

Extrajudicial documents may be transmitted for service in another Member State in accordance with the provisions of this Regulation.

CHAPTER IV
FINAL PROVISIONS

Article 17
Implementing rules

The measures necessary for the implementation of this Regulation relating to the matters referred to below shall be adopted in accordance with the advisory procedure referred to in Article 18(2):

    (a) drawing up and annually updating a manual containing the information provided by Member States in accordance with Article 2(4);

    (b) drawing up a glossary in the official languages of the European Union of documents which may be served under this Regulation;

    (c) updating or making technical amendments to the standard form set out in the Annex.

Article 18
Committee

1. The Commission shall be assisted by a committee.
2. Where reference is made to this paragraph, Articles 3 and 7 of Decision 1999/468/EC shall apply.
3. The Committee shall adopt its rules of procedure.

Article 19
Defendant not entering an appearance

1. Where a writ of summons or an equivalent document has had to be transmitted to another Member State for the purpose of service, under the provisions of this Regulation, and the defendant has not appeared, judgment shall not be given until it is established that:
   (a) the document was served by a method prescribed by the internal law of the Member State addressed for the service of documents in domestic actions upon persons who are within its territory; or
   (b) the document was actually delivered to the defendant or to his residence by another method provided for by this Regulation;
   (c) and that in either of these cases the service or the delivery was effected in sufficient time to enable the defendant to defend.
2. Each Member State shall be free to make it known, in accordance with Article 23(1), that the judge, notwithstanding the provisions of paragraph 1, may give judgment even if no certificate of service or delivery has been received, if all the following conditions are fulfilled:
   (a) the document was transmitted by one of the methods provided for in this Regulation;
   (b) a period of time of not less than six months, considered adequate by the judge in the particular case, has elapsed since the date of the transmission of the document;
   (c) no certificate of any kind has been received, even though every reasonable effort has been made to obtain it through the competent authorities or bodies of the Member State addressed.
3. Notwithstanding paragraphs 1 and 2, the judge may order, in case of urgency, any provisional or protective measures.
4. When a writ of summons or an equivalent document has had to be transmitted to another Member State for the purpose of service, under the provisions of this Regulation, and a judgment has been entered against a defendant who has not appeared, the judge shall have the power to relieve the defendant from the effects of the expiration of the time for appeal from the judgment if the following conditions are fulfilled:
   (a) the defendant, without any fault on his part, did not have knowledge of the document in sufficient time to defend, or knowledge of the judgment in sufficient time to appeal; and
   (b) the defendant has disclosed a prima facie defence to the action on the merits.
   An application for relief may be filed only within a reasonable time after the defendant has knowledge of the judgment.

Each Member State may make it known, in accordance with Article 23(1), that such application will not be entertained if it is filed after the expiration of a time to be stated by it in that communication, but which shall in no case be less than one year following the date of the judgment.

Paragraph 4 shall not apply to judgments concerning status or capacity of persons.

Article 20
Relationship with agreements or arrangements to which Member States are Parties

1. This Regulation shall, in relation to matters to which it applies, prevail over other provisions contained in bilateral or multilateral agreements or arrangements concluded by the Member States, and in particular Article IV of the Protocol to the Brussels Convention of 1968 and the Hague Convention of 15 November 1965.
2. This Regulation shall not preclude individual Member States from maintaining or concluding agreements or arrangements to expedite further or simplify the transmission of documents, provided that they are compatible with this Regulation.
3. Member States shall send to the Commission:
   (a) a copy of the agreements or arrangements referred to in paragraph 2 concluded between the Member States as well as drafts of such agreements or arrangements which they intend to adopt;
   and
   (b) any denunciation of, or amendments to, these agreements or arrangements.

Article 21
Legal aid

This Regulation shall not affect the application of Article 23 of the Convention on Civil Procedure of 17 July 1905, Article 24 of the Convention on Civil Procedure of 1 March 1954 or Article 13 of the Convention on International Access to Justice of 25 October 1980 between the Member States Parties to these Conventions.

Article 22
Protection of information transmitted

1. Information, including in particular personal data, transmitted under this Regulation shall be used by the receiving agency only for the purpose for which it was transmitted.
2. Receiving agencies shall ensure the confidentiality of such information, in accordance with their national law.
3. Paragraphs 1 and 2 shall not affect national laws enabling data subjects to be informed of the use made of information transmitted under this Regulation.
4. This Regulation shall be without prejudice to Directives 95/46/EC and 97/66/EC.

Article 23
Communication and publication

1. Member States shall communicate to the Commission the information referred to in Articles 2, 3, 4, 9, 10, 13, 14, 15, 17(a) and 19.
2. The Commission shall publish in the Official Journal of the European Communities the information referred to in paragraph 1.

Article 24
Review

No later than 1 June 2004, and every five years thereafter, the Commission shall present to the European Parliament, the Council and the Economic and Social Committee a report on the application of this Regulation, paying special attention to the effectiveness of the bodies designated pursuant to Article 2 and to the practical application of point (c) of Article 3 and Article 9. The report shall be accompanied if need be by proposals for adaptations of this Regulation in line with the evolution of notification systems.

Article 25
Entry into force

This Regulation shall enter into force on 31 May 2001.
This Regulation shall be binding in its entirety and directly applicable in the Member States in accordance with the Treaty establishing the European Community.

Done at Brussels, 29 May 2000.

For the Council
The President
A. Costa

ANNEX

REQUEST FOR SERVICE OF DOCUMENTS

(Article 4(3) of Council Regulation (EC) No 1348/2000 on the service in the Member States of judicial and extrajudicial documents in civil or commercial matters ([1]))

Reference No: ...

1. TRANSMITTING AGENCY
   - 1.1. Identity:
   - 1.2. Address:
     - 1.21. Street and number/PO box:
     - 1.22. Place and code:
     - 1.23. County:
   - 1.3. Tel:
   - 1.4. Fax(*):
   - 1.5. E-main (*)

2. RECEIVING AGENCY
   - 2.1. Identity:
   - 2.2. Address:
     - 2.21. Street and number/PO box:
     - 2.22. Place and code:
     - 2.23. County:
   - 2.3. Tel:
   - 2.4. Fax(*):
   - 2.5. E-mail(*):

3. APPLICANT
   - 3.1. Identity:
   - 3.2. Address:
     - 3.21. Street and number/PO box:
     - 3.22. Place and code:
     - 3.23. Country:
   - 3.3. Tel(*):
   - 3.4. Fax(*):
   - 3.5. E-mail(*):

4. ADDRESSEE
   - 4.1. Identity:
   - 4.2. Address:
     - 4.2.1. Street and number/PO box:
     - 4.2.2. Place and code:
     - 4.2.3. Country:

([1]) OJL 160, 30.6.2000,p. 37.   (*) This item is optional.

4.3. Tel(*):

4.4. Fax(*):

4.5. E-mail(*):

4.6. Identification number/social number/organisation number/or equivalent(*):

5. METHOD OF SERVICE
   5.1. In accordance with the law of the Member State addressed
   5.2. By the following particular method:
      5.2.1. If this method is incompatible with the law of the Member State addressed, the document(s) should be served in accordance with the law:
         5.2.1.1. yes
         5.2.1.2. no

6. DOCUMENT TO BE SERVED
   (a) 6.1. Nature of the document
      6.1.1. judicial
         6.1.1.1. writ of summons
         6.1.1.2. judgment
         6.1.1.3. appeal
         6.1.1.4. other
      6.1.2. extrajudicial
   (b) 6.2. Date or time limit stated in the document(*):
   (c) 6.3. Language of document:
      6.3.1. original DE, EN, DK, EL, FI, FR, GR, IT, NL, PT, SV, others:
      6.3.2. translation (*) DE, EN, DK, ES, FI, FR, EL, IT, NL, PT, SV, others:
   6.4. Number of enclosures:

7. A COPY DOCUMENT TO BE RETURNED WITH THE CERTIFICATE OF SERVICE (Article 4(5) of the Regulation)
   7.1. Yes (in this case send two copies of the document to be served)
   7.2. No

---

1. You are required by Article 7(2) of the Regulation to effect all steps required for service of the document as soon as possible. In any event, if it is not possible for you to effect service within one month of receipt, you must inform this agency by means of the certificate provided for in point 13.

2. If you cannot fulfil this request for service on the basis of the information or documents transmitted, you are required by Article 6(2) of the Regulation to contact this agency by the swiftest possible means in order to secure the missing information or document.

Done at:

Date:

Signature and/or stamp:

(*) This item is optional.   (*) This item is optional.

Reference No of the receiving agency:

ACKNOWLEDGEMENT OF RECEIPT

(Article 6(1) of Council Regulation (EC) No 1348/2000)

This acknowledgement must be sent by the swiftest possible means of transmission as soon as possible after receipt of the document and in any event within seven days of receipt.

---

8. DATE OF RECEIPT:

Done at:

Date:

NOTICE OF RETURN OF REQUEST AND DOCUMENT

(Article 6(3) of Council Regulation (EC) No 1348/2000)

The request and document must be returned on receipt.

Signature and/or stamp:

9. REASON FOR RETURN:
    9.1. The request is manifestly outside the scope of the Regulation:
        9.1.1. the document is not civil or commercial
        9.1.2. the service is not from one Member State to another Member State
    9.2. Non-compliance with formal conditions required makes service impossible:
        9.2.1. the document is not easily legible
        9.2.2. the language used to complete the form is incorrect
        9.2.3. the document received is not a true and faithful copy
        9.2.4. other (please give details):
    9.3. The method of service is incompatible with the law of that Member State (Article 7(1) of the Regulation)

Done at:

Date:

Signature and/or stamp:

NOTICE OF RETRANSMISSION OF REQUEST AND DOCUMENT TO THE APPROPRIATE RECEIVING AGENCY

(Article 6(4) of Council Regulation (EC) No 1348/2000)

The request and document were forwarded on to the following receiving agency, which has territorial jurisdiction to serve it:

10.1. Indentity:
10.2. Address:
    10.2.1. Street and number/PO box:
    10.2.2. Place and Code:
    10.2.3. Country:
10.3. Tel:
10.4. Fax(*):
10.5. E-mail (*):

Done at:

Date:

Signature and/or stamp:

Reference No of the appropriate agency:

NOTICE OF RECEIPT BY THE APPROPRIATE RECEIVING AGENCY HAVING TERRITORIAL JURISDICTION TO THE TRANSMITTING AGENCY

(Article 6(4) of Council Regulation (EC) No 1348/2000)

This notice must be sent by the swiftest possible means of transmission as soon as possible after receipt of the document and in any event within seven days of receipt.

---

11. DATE OF RECEIPT:

Done at:

Date:

Signature and/or stamp:

904

CERTIFICATE OF SERVICE OR NON-SERVICE OF DOCUMENTS

(Article 10 of Council Regulation (EC) No 1348/2000)

The service shall be effected as soon as possible. In any event, if it has not been possible to effect service within one month of receipt, the receiving agecy shall inform the transmitting agency (according to Article 7(2) of the Regulation)

---

12. COMPLETION OF SERVICE
    (a) 12.1. Date and address of service:
    (b) 12.2. The document was
        (A) 12.2.1. served in accordance with the law of the Member State addressed, namely
            12.2.1.1. handed to
                12.2.1.1.1. the addressee in person
                12.2.1.1.2. another person
                    12.2.1.1.2.1. Name:
                    12.2.1.1.2.2. Address:
                        12.2.1.1.2.2.1. Street and number/PO box:
                        12.2.1.1.2.2.2. Place and code:
                        12.2.1.1.2.2.3. Country:
                    12.2.1.1.2.3. Relation to the addressee:
                    family   employee
                12.2.1.1.3. the addressee's address
            12.2.1.2. served by post
                12.2.1.2.1. without acknowledgement of receipt
                12.2.1.2.2. with the enclosed acknowledgement of receipt
                    12.2.1.2.2.1. from the addressee
                    12.2.1.2.2.2. another person
                        12.2.1.2.2.2.1. Name:
                        12.2.1.2.2.2.2. Address
                            12.2.1.2.2.2.2.1. Street and number/PO box:
                            12.2.1.2.2.2.2.2. Place and code:
                            12.2.1.2.2.2.2.3. Country:
                        12.2.1.2.2.2.3. Relation to the Address
                    family   employee   others
            12.2.1.3. Other method (please say how):
        (B) 12.2.2. served by the following particular method (please say how):
    (c) 12.3. The addressee of the document was informed (orally) (in writing) that he or she may refuse to accept it if it was not in an official language of the place of service or in an official language of the state of transmission which he or she understands.
13. INFORMATION IN ACCORDANCE WITH ARTICLE 7(2)
    It was not possible to effect service within one month of receipt.

14. REFUSAL OF DOCUMENT

The addressee redused to accept the document on account of the language used. The documents are annexed to this certificate.

15. REASON FOR NON-SERVICE OF DOCUMENT

   15.1. Address unknown

   15.2. Addressee cannot be located

   15.3. Document could not be served before the date or time limit stated in point 6.2.

   15.4. Others (please specify):

The documents are annexed to this certificate.

Done at:

Date:

Signature and/or stamp:

(viii) CONVENTION ON THE TAKING OF EVIDENCE ABROAD IN CIVIL OR COMMERCIAL MATTERS*

(Concluded March 18, 1970)

PREAMBLE

The States signatory to the present Convention,
Desiring to facilitate the transmission and execution of Letters of Request and to further the accommodation of the different methods which they use for this purpose,

Desiring to improve mutual judicial co-operation in civil or commercial matters,

Have resolved to conclude a Convention to this effect and have agreed upon the following provisions:

CHAPTER I
LETTERS OF REQUEST

Article 1

In civil or commercial matters a judicial authority of a Contracting State may, in accordance with the provisions of the law of that State, request the competent authority of another Contracting State, by means of a Letter of Request, to obtain evidence, or to perform some other judicial act.

---

* Reproduced with the kind permission of the Hague Convention on Private International Law.

A Letter shall not be used to obtain evidence which is not intended for use in judicial proceedings, commenced or contemplated.

The expression 'other judicial act' does not cover the service of judicial documents or the issuance of any process by which judgments or orders are executed or enforced, or orders for provisional or protective measures.

Article 2

A Contracting State shall designate a Central Authority which will undertake to receive Letters of Request coming from a judicial authority of another Contracting State and to transmit them to the authority competent to execute them. Each State shall organize the Central Authority in accordance with its own law.

Letters shall be sent to the Central Authority of the State of execution without being transmitted through any other authority of that State.

Article 3

A Letter of Request shall specify—
  a) the authority requesting its execution and the authority requested to execute it, if known to the requesting authority;
  b) the names and addresses of the parties to the proceedings and their representatives, if any;
  c) the nature of the proceedings for which the evidence is required, giving all necessary information in regard thereto;
  d) the evidence to be obtained or other judicial act to be performed.
Where appropriate, the Letter shall specify, *inter alia*—
  e) the names and addresses of the persons to be examined;
  f) the questions to be put to the persons to be examined or a statement of the subject-matter about which they are to be examined;
  g) the documents or other property, real or personal, to be inspected;
  h) any requirement that the evidence is to be given on oath or affirmation, and any special form to be used;
  i) any special method or procedure to be followed under Article 9.
A Letter may also mention any information necessary for the application of Article 11.

No legalization or other like formality may be required.

Article 4

A Letter of Request shall be in the language of the authority requested to execute it or be accompanied by a translation into that language.

Nevertheless, a Contracting State shall accept a Letter in either English or French, or a translation into one of these languages, unless it has made the reservation authorized by Article 33.

A Contracting State which has more than one official language and cannot, for reasons of internal law, accept Letters in one of these languages for the whole of its territory, shall, by declaration, specify the language in which the Letter or translation thereof shall be expressed for execution in the specified parts of its territory. In case of failure to comply with this declaration, without justifiable excuse, the costs of translation into the required language shall be borne by the State of origin.

A Contracting State may, by declaration, specify the language or languages other than those referred to in the preceding paragraphs, in which a Letter may be sent to its Central Authority.

Any translation accompanying a Letter shall be certified as correct, either by a diplomatic officer or consular agent or by a sworn translator or by any other person so authorized in either State.

Article 5

If the Central Authority considers that the request does not comply with the provisions of the present Convention, it shall promptly inform the authority of the State of origin which transmitted the Letter of Request, specifying the objections to the Letter.

Article 6

If the authority to whom a Letter of Request has been transmitted is not competent to execute it, the Letter shall be sent forthwith to the authority in the same State which is competent to execute it in accordance with the provisions of its own law.

Article 7

The requesting authority shall, if it so desires, be informed of the time when, and the place where, the proceedings will take place, in order that the parties concerned, and their representatives, if any, may be present. This information shall be sent directly to the parties or their representatives when the authority of the State of origin so requests.

Article 8

A Contracting State may declare that members of the judicial personnel of the requesting authority of another Contracting State may be present at the execution of a Letter of Request. Prior authorization by the competent authority designated by the declaring State may be required.

Article 9

The judicial authority which executes a Letter of Request shall apply its own law as to the methods and procedures to be followed.

However, it will follow a request of the requesting authority that a special method or procedure be followed, unless this is incompatible with the internal law of the State of execution or is impossible of performance by reason of its internal practice and procedure or by reason of practical difficulties.

A Letter of Request shall be executed expeditiously.

Article 10

In executing a Letter of Request the requested authority shall apply the appropriate measures of compulsion in the instances and to the same extent as are provided by its internal law for the execution of orders issued by the authorities of its own country or of requests made by parties in internal proceedings.

Article 11

In the execution of a Letter of Request the person concerned may refuse to give evidence in so far as he has a privilege or duty to refuse to give the evidence—
   a) under the law of the State of execution; or

909

b) under the law of the State of origin, and the privilege or duty has been specified in the Letter, or, at the instance of the requested authority, has been otherwise confirmed to that authority by the requesting authority.

A Contracting State may declare that, in addition, it will respect privileges and duties existing under the law of States other than the State of origin and the State of execution, to the extent specified in that declaration.

Article 12

The execution of a Letter of Request may be refused only to the extent that—
  a) in the State of execution the execution of the Letter does not fall within the functions of the judiciary; or
  b) the State addressed considers that its sovereignty or security would be prejudiced thereby.

Execution may not be refused solely on the ground that under its internal law the State of execution claims exclusive jurisdiction over the subject-matter of the action or that its internal law would not admit a right of action on it.

Article 13

The documents establishing the execution of the Letter of Request shall be sent by the requested authority to the requesting authority by the same channel which was used by the latter.

In every instance where the Letter is not executed in whole or in part, the requesting authority shall be informed immediately through the same channel and advised of the reasons.

Article 14

The execution of the Letter of Request shall not give rise to any reimbursement of taxes or costs of any nature.

Nevertheless, the State of execution has the right to require the State of origin to reimburse the fees paid to experts and interpreters and the costs occasioned by the use of a special procedure requested by the State of origin under Article 9, paragraph 2.

The requested authority whose law obliges the parties themselves to secure evidence, and which is not able itself to execute the Letter, may, after having obtained the consent of the requesting authority, appoint a suitable person to do so. When seeking this consent the requested authority shall indicate the approximate costs which would result from this procedure. If the requesting authority gives its consent it shall reimburse any costs incurred; without such consent the requesting authority shall not be liable for the costs.

CHAPTER II
TAKING OF EVIDENCE BY DIPLOMATIC OFFICERS, CONSULAR AGENTS AND COMMISSIONERS

Article 15

In civil or commercial matters, a diplomatic officer or consular agent of a Contracting State may, in the territory of another Contracting State and within the area where he exercises his functions, take the evidence without compulsion of nationals of a State which he represents in aid of proceedings commenced in the courts of a State which he represents.

A Contracting State may declare that evidence may be taken by a diplomatic officer or consular agent only if permission to that effect is given upon application made by him or on his behalf to the appropriate authority designated by the declaring State.

Article 16

A diplomatic officer or consular agent of a Contracting State may, in the territory of another Contracting State and within the area where he exercises his functions, also take the evidence, without compulsion, of nationals of the State in which he exercises his functions or of a third State, in aid of proceedings commenced in the courts of a State which he represents, if—

    a) a competent authority designated by the State in which he exercises his functions has given its permission either generally or in the particular case, and

    b) he complies with the conditions which the competent authority has specified in the permission.

A Contracting State may declare that evidence may be taken under this Article without its prior permission.

Article 17

In civil or commercial matters, a person duly appointed as a commissioner for the purpose may, without compulsion, take evidence in the territory of a Contracting State in aid of proceedings commenced in the courts of another Contracting State, if—

    a) a competent authority designated by the State where the evidence is to be taken has given its permission either generally or in the particular case; and

    b) he complies with the conditions which the competent authority has specified in the permission.

A Contracting State may declare that evidence may be taken under this Article without its prior permission.

Article 18

A Contracting State may declare that a diplomatic officer, consular agent or commissioner authorized to take evidence under Articles 15, 16 or 17, may apply to the competent authority designated by the declaring State for appropriate assistance to obtain the evidence by compulsion. The declaration may contain such conditions as the declaring State may see fit to impose.

If the authority grants the application it shall apply any measures of compulsion which are appropriate and are prescribed by its law for use in internal proceedings.

Article 19

The competent authority, in giving the permission referred to in Articles 15, 16 or 17, or in granting the application referred to in Article 18, may lay down such conditions as it deems fit, *inter alia,* as to the time and place of the taking of the evidence. Similarly it may require that it be given reasonable advance notice of the time, date and place of the taking of the evidence; in such a case a representative of the authority shall be entitled to be present at the taking of the evidence.

Article 20

In the taking of evidence under any Article of this Chapter persons concerned may be legally represented.

Article 21

Where a diplomatic officer, consular agent or commissioner is authorized under Articles 15, 16 or 17 to take evidence—

 a) he may take all kinds of evidence which are not incompatible with the law of the State where the evidence is taken or contrary to any permission granted pursuant to the above Articles, and shall have power within such limits to administer an oath or take an affirmation;

 b) a request to a person to appear or to give evidence shall, unless the recipient is a national of the State where the action is pending, be drawn up in the language of the place where the evidence is taken or be accompanied by a translation into such language;

 c) the request shall inform the person that he may be legally represented and, in any State that has not filed a declaration under Article 18, shall also inform him that he is not compelled to appear or to give evidence;

 d) the evidence may be taken in the manner provided by the law applicable to the court in which the action is pending provided that such manner is not forbidden by the law of the State where the evidence is taken;

 e) a person requested to give evidence may invoke the privileges and duties to refuse to give the evidence contained in Article 11.

Article 22

The fact that an attempt to take evidence under the procedure laid down in this Chapter has failed, owing to the refusal of a person to give evidence, shall not prevent an application being subsequently made to take the evidence in accordance with Chapter I.

CHAPTER III
GENERAL CLAUSES

Article 23

A Contracting State may at the time of signature, ratification or accession, declare that it will not execute Letters of Request issued for the purpose of obtaining pre-trial discovery of documents as known in Common Law countries.

Article 24

A Contracting State may designate other authorities in addition to the Central Authority and shall determine the extent of their competence. However, Letters of Request may in all cases be sent to the Central Authority.

Federal States shall be free to designate more than one Central Authority.

Article 25

A Contracting State which has more than one legal system may designate the authorities of one of such systems, which shall have exclusive competence to execute Letters of Request pursuant to this Convention.

Article 26

A Contracting State, if required to do so because of constitutional limitations, may request the reimbursement by the State of origin of fees and costs, in connection with the execution of Letters of Request, for the service of process necessary to compel the appearance of a person to give evidence, the costs of attendance of such persons, and the cost of any transcript of the evidence.

Where a State has made a request pursuant to the above paragraph, any other Contracting State may request from that State the reimbursement of similar fees and costs.

Article 27

The provisions of the present Convention shall not prevent a Contracting State from—
   a) declaring that Letters of Request may be transmitted to its judicial authorities through channels other than those provided for in Article 2;
   b) permitting, by internal law or practice, any act provided for in this Convention to be performed upon less restrictive conditions;
   c) permitting, by internal law or practice, methods of taking evidence other than those provided for in this Convention.

Article 28

The present Convention shall not prevent an agreement between any two or more Contracting States to derogate from—
   a) the provisions of Article 2 with respect to methods of transmitting Letters of Request;
   b) the provisions of Article 4 with respect to the languages which may be used;
   c) the provisions of Article 8 with respect to the presence of judicial personnel at the execution of Letters;
   d) the provisions of Article 11 with respect to the privileges and duties of witnesses to refuse to give evidence;
   e) the provisions of Article 13 with respect to the methods of returning executed Letters to the requesting authority;
   f) the provisions of Article 14 with respect to fees and costs;
   g) the provisions of Chapter II.

Article 29

Between Parties to the present Convention who are also Parties to one or both of the Conventions on Civil Procedure signed at The Hague on the 17th of July 1905 and the 1st of March 1954, this Convention shall replace Articles 8–16 of the earlier Conventions.

Article 30

The present Convention shall not affect the application of Article 23 of the Convention of 1905, or of Article 24 of the Convention of 1954.

Article 31

Supplementary Agreements between Parties to the Conventions of 1905 and 1954 shall be considered as equally applicable to the present Convention unless the Parties have otherwise agreed.

Article 32

Without prejudice to the provisions of Articles 29 and 31, the present Convention shall not derogate from conventions containing provisions on the matters covered by this Convention to which the Contracting States are, or shall become Parties.

Article 33

A State may, at the time of signature, ratification or accession exclude, in whole or in part, the application of the provisions of paragraph 2 of Article 4 and of Chapter II. No other reservation shall be permitted.

Each Contracting State may at any time withdraw a reservation it has made; the reservation shall cease to have effect on the sixtieth day after notification of the withdrawal.

When a State has made a reservation, any other State affected thereby may apply the same rule against the reserving State.

Article 34

A State may at any time withdraw or modify a declaration.

Article 35

A Contracting State shall, at the time of the deposit of its instrument of ratification or accession, or at a later date, inform the Ministry of Foreign Affairs of the Netherlands of the designation of authorities, pursuant to Articles 2, 8, 24 and 25.

A Contracting State shall likewise inform the Ministry, where appropriate, of the following—
   a) the designation of the authorities to whom notice must be given, whose permission may be required, and whose assistance may be invoked in the taking of evidence by diplomatic officers and consular agents, pursuant to Articles 15, 16 and 18 respectively;
   b) the designation of the authorities whose permission may be required in the taking of evidence by commissioners pursuant to Article 17 and of those who may grant the assistance provided for in Article 18;
   c) declarations pursuant to Articles 4, 8, 11, 15, 16, 17, 18, 23 and 27;
   d) any withdrawal or modification of the above designations and declarations;
   e) the withdrawal of any reservation.

Article 36

Any difficulties which may arise between Contracting States in connection with the operation of this Convention shall be settled through diplomatic channels.

Article 37

The present Convention shall be open for signature by the States represented at the Eleventh Session of the Hague Conference on Private International Law.

It shall be ratified, and the instruments of ratification shall be deposited with the Ministry of Foreign Affairs of the Netherlands.

Article 38

The present Convention shall enter into force on the sixtieth day after the deposit of the third instrument of ratification referred to in the second paragraph of Article 37.

The Convention shall enter into force for each signatory State which ratifies subsequently on the sixtieth day after the deposit of its instrument of ratification.

Article 39

Any State not represented at the Eleventh Session of the Hague Conference on Private International Law which is a Member of this Conference or of the United Nations or of a specialized agency of that Organization, or a Party to the Statute of the International Court of Justice may accede to the present Convention after it has entered into force in accordance with the first paragraph of Article 38.

The instrument of accession shall be deposited with the Ministry of Foreign Affairs of the Netherlands.

The Convention shall enter into force for a State acceding to it on the sixtieth day after the deposit of its instrument of accession.

The accession will have effect only as regards the relations between the acceding State and such Contracting States as will have declared their acceptance of the accession. Such declaration shall be deposited at the Ministry of Foreign Affairs of the Netherlands; this Ministry shall forward, through diplomatic channels, a certified copy to each of the Contracting States.

The Convention will enter into force as between the acceding State and the State that has declared its acceptance of the accession on the sixtieth day after the deposit of the declaration of acceptance.

Article 40

Any State may, at the time of signature, ratification or accession, declare that the present Convention shall extend to all the territories for the international relations of which it is responsible, or to one or more of them. Such a declaration shall take effect on the date of entry into force of the Convention for the State concerned.

At any time thereafter, such extensions shall be notified to the Ministry of Foreign Affairs of the Netherlands.

The Convention shall enter into force for the territories mentioned in such an extension on the sixtieth day after the notification indicated in the preceding paragraph.

Article 41

The present Convention shall remain in force for five years from the date of its entry into force in accordance with the first paragraph of Article 38, even for States which have ratified it or acceded to it subsequently.

If there has been no denunciation, it shall be renewed tacitly every five years.

Any denunciation shall be notified to the Ministry of Foreign Affairs of the Netherlands at least six months before the end of the five year period.

It may be limited to certain of the territories to which the Convention applies.

The denunciation shall have effect only as regards the State which has notified it. The Convention shall remain in force for the other Contracting States.

Article 42

The Ministry of Foreign Affairs of the Netherlands shall give notice to the States referred to in Article 37, and to the States which have acceded in accordance with Article 39, of the following—

a) the signatures and ratifications referred to in Article 37;
b) the date on which the present Convention enters into force in accordance with the first paragraph of Article 38;
c) the accessions referred to in Article 39 and the dates on which they take effect;
d) the extensions referred to in Article 40 and the dates on which they take effect;
e) the designations, reservations and declarations referred to in Articles 33 and 35;
f) the denunciations referred to in the third paragraph of Article 41.

In witness whereof the undersigned, being duly authorized thereto, have signed the present Convention.

Done at The Hague, on the 18th day of March, 1970, in the English and French languages, both texts being equally authentic, in a single copy which shall be deposited in the archives of the Government of the Netherlands, and of which a certified copy shall be sent, through the diplomatic channel, to each of the States represented at the Eleventh Session of the Hague Conference on Private International Law.

TABLE OF STATE RATIFICATIONS

Total number of signatures not followed by ratifications: 0
Total number of ratifications/accessions: 42

The Convention applies in the following States or territories as a result of ratification, acceptance or approval:	Entry into force:
CHINA, HONG KONG Special Administrative Region only	22 August 1978
CHINA, MACAU Special Administrative Region only	14 December 1999
CZECH REPUBLIC	11 July 1976
DENMARK	7 October 1972
FINLAND	6 June 1976
FRANCE (for all the territories of the French Republic)	6 October 1974
GERMANY	26 June 1979
ISRAEL	17 September 1979
ITALY	21 August 1982
LUXEMBOURG	24 September 1977
NETHERLANDS (for the Kingdom in Europe)	7 June 1981
Aruba	27 July 1986
NORWAY	7 October 1972
PORTUGAL	11 May 1975
SLOVAKIA	11 July 1976
SPAIN	21 July 1987
SWEDEN	1 July 1975
SWITZERLAND	1 January 1995

The Convention applies in the following States or territories as a result of ratification, acceptance or approval:	Entry into force:
UNITED KINGDOM*	14 September 1976
Gibraltar	20 January 1979
Sovereign Base Areas of Akrotiri and Dhekelia in the Island of Cyprus	24 August 1979
Falkland Islands and Dependencies	25 January 1980
Isle of Man	15 June 1980
Cayman Islands	15 November 1980
Guernsey	18 January 1986
Anguilla	1 September 1986
Jersey	7 March 1987
UNITED STATES OF AMERICA	7 October 1972
Guam, Puerto Rico, Virgin Islands	10 April 1973

*By a Note dated 9 February 1995 and received on 21 February 1995, the Embassy of the United Kingdom of Great Britain and Northern Ireland informed the Ministry of Foreign Affairs of the Kingdom of the Netherlands that, unless otherwise stated, in future the acceptance by the United Kingdom of the accession of any State to the Convention shall also be acceptance in respect of all the territories for the international relations of which the United Kingdom is responsible and to which the application of the Convention has been extended.

The Convention applies in the following States or territories as a result of accession:	Entry into force:
Argentina	7 July 1987
Australia	22 December 1992
Barbados	4 May 1981
Belarus	6 October 2001
Bulgaria	22 January 2000
China	6 February 1998
Cyprus	14 March 1983
Estonia	2 April 1996
Kuwait	7 July 2002
Latvia	27 May 1995
Lithuania	1 October 2000
Mexico	25 September 1989
Monaco	18 March 1986
Poland	13 April 1996
Romania	20 October 2003
Russian Federation	30 June 2001
Seychelles	7 March 2004
Singapore	26 December 1978
Slovenia	17 November 2000
South Africa	6 September 1997
Sri Lanka	30 October 2000
Ukraine	1 April 2001
Venezuela	31 December 1993

*In accordance with the Joint Declaration of the Government of the People's Republic of China and the Government of the United Kingdom of Great Britain and Northern Ireland on the Question of Hong Kong signed on 19 December 1984, the People's Republic of China has resumed the exercise of sovereignty over Hong Kong with effect from 1 July 1997. For more information, please consult the full status report of this Convention.

Note. A list of reservations and the details of accessions made by States has not been included in the text. These can be obtained from http://www.hcch.net/e/status/stat20e.html.

The Hague, 18 November 1970
(Entry into force on 7 October 1972)

(ix) COUNCIL REGULATION (EC) NO. 1206/2001 OF 28 MAY 2001 ON COOPERATION BETWEEN THE COURTS OF THE MEMBER STATES IN THE TAKING OF EVIDENCE IN CIVIL OR COMMERCIAL MATTERS

PREAMBLE

THE COUNCIL OF THE EUROPEAN UNION,

Having regard to the Treaty establishing the European Community, and in particular Article 61(c) and Article 67(1) thereof,
Having regard to the initiative of the Federal Republic of Germany,[1]
Having regard to the opinion of the European Parliament,[2]
Having regard to the opinion of the Economic and Social Committee,[3]
Whereas:

(1) The European Union has set itself the objective of maintaining and developing the European Union as an area of freedom, security and justice in which the free movement of persons is ensured. For the gradual establishment of such an area,

the Community is to adopt, among others, the measures relating to judicial co-operation in civil matters needed for the proper functioning of the internal market.

(2) For the purpose of the proper functioning of the internal market, cooperation between courts in the taking of evidence should be improved, and in particular simplified and accelerated.

(3) At its meeting in Tampere on 15 and 16 October 1999, the European Council recalled that new procedural legislation in cross-border cases, in particular on the taking of evidence, should be prepared.

(4) This area falls within the scope of Article 65 of the Treaty.

(5) The objectives of the proposed action, namely the improvement of cooperation between the courts on the taking of evidence in civil or commercial matters, cannot be sufficiently achieved by the Member States and can therefore be better achieved at Community level. The Community may adopt measures in accordance with the principle of subsidiarity as set out in Article 5 of the Treaty. In accordance with the principle of proportionality, as set out in that Article, this Regulation does not go beyond what is necessary to achieve those objectives.

(6) To date, there is no binding instrument between all the Member States concerning the taking of evidence. The Hague Convention of 18 March 1970 on the taking of evidence abroad in civil or commercial matters applies between only 11 Member States of the European Union.

(7) As it is often essential for a decision in a civil or commercial matter pending before a court in a Member State to take evidence in another Member State, the Community's activity cannot be limited to the field of transmission of judicial and extrajudicial documents in civil or commercial matters which falls within the scope of Council Regulation (EC) No 1348/2000 of 29 May 2000 on the serving in the Member States of judicial and extrajudicial documents in civil or commercial matters[4]. It is therefore necessary to continue the improvement of cooperation between courts of Member States in the field of taking of evidence.

(8) The efficiency of judicial procedures in civil or commercial matters requires that the transmission and execution of requests for the performance of taking of evidence is to be made directly and by the most rapid means possible between Member States' courts.

(9) Speed in transmission of requests for the performance of taking of evidence warrants the use of all appropriate means, provided that certain conditions as to the legibility and reliability of the document received are observed. So as to ensure the utmost clarity and legal certainty the request for the performance of taking of evidence must be transmitted on a form to be completed in the language of the Member State of the requested court or in another language accepted by that State. For the same reasons, forms should also be used as far as possible for further communication between the relevant courts.

(10) A request for the performance of the taking of evidence should be executed expeditiously. If it is not possible for the request to be executed within 90 days of receipt by the requested court, the latter should inform the requesting court accordingly, stating the reasons which prevent the request from being executed swiftly.

(11) To secure the effectiveness of this Regulation, the possibility of refusing to execute the request for the performance of taking of evidence should be confined to strictly limited exceptional situations.

(12) The requested court should execute the request in accordance with the law of its Member State.

(13) The parties and, if any, their representatives, should be able to be present at the performance of the taking of evidence, if that is provided for by the law of the Member State of the requesting court, in order to be able to follow the proceedings in a comparable way as if evidence were taken in the Member State of the requesting court. They should also have the right to request to participate in order to have a more active role in the performance of the taking of evidence. However, the conditions under which they may participate should be determined by the requested court in accordance with the law of its Member State.

(14) The representatives of the requesting court should be able to be present at the performance of the taking of evidence, if that is compatible with the law of the Member State of the requesting court, in order to have an improved possibility of evaluation of evidence. They should also have the right to request to participate, under the conditions laid down by the requested court in accordance with the law of its Member State, in order to have a more active role in the performance of the taking of evidence.

(15) In order to facilitate the taking of evidence it should be possible for a court in a Member State, in accordance with the law of its Member State, to take evidence directly in another Member State, if accepted by the latter, and under the conditions determined by the central body or competent authority of the requested Member State.

(16) The execution of the request, according to Article 10, should not give rise to a claim for any reimbursement of taxes or costs. Nevertheless, if the requested court requires reimbursement, the fees paid to experts and interpreters, as well as the costs occasioned by the application of Article 10(3) and (4), should not be borne by that court. In such a case, the requesting court is to take the necessary measures to ensure reimbursement without delay. Where the opinion of an expert is required, the requested court may, before executing the request, ask the requesting court for an adequate deposit or advance towards the costs.

(17) This Regulation should prevail over the provisions applying to its field of application, contained in international conventions concluded by the Member States. Member States should be free to adopt agreements or arrangements to further facilitate cooperation in the taking of evidence.

(18) The information transmitted pursuant to this Regulation should enjoy protection. Since Directive 95/46/EC of the European Parliament and of the Council of 24 October 1995 on the protection of individuals with regard to the processing of personal data and on the free movement of such data[5], and Directive 97/66/EC of the European Parliament and of the Council of 15 December 1997 concerning the processing of personal data and the protection of privacy in the telecommunications sector[6], are applicable, there is no need for specific provisions on data protection in this Regulation.

(19) The measures necessary for the implementation of this Regulation should be adopted in accordance with Council Decision 1999/468/EC of 28 June 1999[7] laying down the procedures for the exercise of implementing powers conferred on the Commission.

(20) For the proper functioning of this Regulation, the Commission should review its application and propose such amendments as may appear necessary.

(21) The United Kingdom and Ireland, in accordance with Article 3 of the Protocol on the position of the United Kingdom and Ireland annexed to the Treaty on the European Union and to the Treaty establishing the European Community, have given notice of their wish to take part in the adoption and application of this Regulation.

(22) Denmark, in accordance with Articles 1 and 2 of the Protocol on the position of Denmark annexed to the Treaty on European Union and to the Treaty establishing the European Community, is not participating in the adoption of this Regulation, and is therefore not bound by it nor subject to its application,

HAS ADOPTED THIS REGULATION:

CHAPTER I
GENERAL PROVISIONS

Article 1
Scope

1. This Regulation shall apply in civil or commercial matters where the court of a Member State, in accordance with the provisions of the law of that State, requests:
   (a) the competent court of another Member State to take evidence; or
   (b) to take evidence directly in another Member State.
2. A request shall not be made to obtain evidence which is not intended for use in judicial proceedings, commenced or contemplated.
3. In this Regulation, the term 'Member State' shall mean Member States with the exception of Denmark.

Article 2
Direct transmission between the courts

1. Requests pursuant to Article 1(1)(a), hereinafter referred to as 'requests', shall be transmitted by the court before which the proceedings are commenced or contemplated, hereinafter referred to as the 'requesting court', directly to the competent court of another Member State, hereinafter referred to as the 'requested court', for the performance of the taking of evidence.
2. Each Member State shall draw up a list of the courts competent for the performance of taking of evidence according to this Regulation. The list shall also indicate the territorial and, where appropriate, the special jurisdiction of those courts.

Article 3
Central body

1. Each Member State shall designate a central body responsible for:
   (a) supplying information to the courts;
   (b) seeking solutions to any difficulties which may arise in respect of a request;
   (c) forwarding, in exceptional cases, at the request of a requesting court, a request to the competent court.

2. A federal State, a State in which several legal systems apply or a State with autonomous territorial entities shall be free to designate more than one central body.

3. Each Member State shall also designate the central body referred to in paragraph 1 or one or several competent authority(ies) to be responsible for taking decisions on requests pursuant to Article 17.

CHAPTER II
TRANSMISSION AND EXECUTION OF REQUESTS

SECTION I
TRANSMISSION OF THE REQUEST

Article 4
Form and content of the request

1. The request shall be made using form A or, where appropriate, form I in the Annex. It shall contain the following details:
   (a) the requesting and, where appropriate, the requested court;
   (b) the names and addresses of the parties to the proceedings and their representatives, if any;
   (c) the nature and subject matter of the case and a brief statement of the facts;
   (d) a description of the taking of evidence to be performed;
   (e) where the request is for the examination of a person:
      —the name(s) and address(es) of the person(s) to be examined,
      —the questions to be put to the person(s) to be examined or a statement of the facts about which he is (they are) to be examined,
      —where appropriate, a reference to a right to refuse to testify under the law of the Member State of the requesting court,
      —any requirement that the examination is to be carried out under oath or affirmation in lieu thereof, and any special form to be used,
      —where appropriate, any other information that the requesting court deems necessary;
   (f) where the request is for any other form of taking of evidence, the documents or other objects to be inspected;
   (g) where appropriate, any request pursuant to Article 10(3) and (4), and Articles 11 and 12 and any information necessary for the application thereof.

2. The request and all documents accompanying the request shall be exempted from authentication or any equivalent formality.

3. Documents which the requesting court deems it necessary to enclose for the execution of the request shall be accompanied by a translation into the language in which the request was written.

Article 5
Language

The request and communications pursuant to this Regulation shall be drawn up in the official language of the requested Member State or, if there are several official languages in that Member State, in the official language or one of the official languages of the place where the requested taking of evidence is to be performed, or in another language which the requested Member State has indicated it can accept. Each Member State shall indicate the official language or languages of the institutions of the European Community other than its own which is or are acceptable to it for completion of the forms.

Article 6
Transmission of requests and other communications

Requests and communications pursuant to this Regulation shall be transmitted by the swiftest possible means, which the requested Member State has indicated it can accept. The transmission may be carried out by any appropriate means, provided that the document received accurately reflects the content of the document forwarded and that all information in it is legible.

SECTION 2
RECEIPT OF REQUEST

Article 7
Receipt of request

1. Within seven days of receipt of the request, the requested competent court shall send an acknowledgement of receipt to the requesting court using form B in the Annex. Where the request does not comply with the conditions laid down in Articles 5 and 6, the requested court shall enter a note to that effect in the acknowledgement of receipt.
2. Where the execution of a request made using form A in the Annex, which complies with the conditions laid down in Article 5, does not fall within the jurisdiction of the court to which it was transmitted, the latter shall forward the request to the competent court of its Member State and shall inform the requesting court thereof using form A in the Annex.

Article 8
Incomplete request

1. If a request cannot be executed because it does not contain all of the necessary information pursuant to Article 4, the requested court shall inform the requesting court thereof without delay and, at the latest, within 30 days of receipt of the request using form C in the Annex, and shall request it to send the missing information, which should be indicated as precisely as possible.
2. If a request cannot be executed because a deposit or advance is necessary in accordance with Article 18(3), the requested court shall inform the requesting court thereof without delay and, at the latest, within 30 days of receipt of the request using form C in the Annex and inform the requesting court how the deposit or advance should be made. The requested Court shall acknowledge receipt of the deposit or advance without delay, at the latest within 10 days of receipt of the deposit or the advance using form D.

Article 9
Completion of the request

1. If the requested court has noted on the acknowledgement of receipt pursuant to Article 7(1) that the request does not comply with the conditions laid down in Articles 5 and 6 or has informed the requesting court pursuant to Article 8 that the request cannot be

executed because it does not contain all of the necessary information pursuant to Article 4, the time limit pursuant to Article 10 shall begin to run when the requested court received the request duly completed.

2. Where the requested court has asked for a deposit or advance in accordance with Article 18(3), this time limit shall begin to run when the deposit or the advance is made.

SECTION 3

TAKING OF EVIDENCE BY THE REQUESTED COURT

Article 10
General provisions on the execution of the request

1. The requested court shall execute the request without delay and, at the latest, within 90 days of receipt of the request.
2. The requested court shall execute the request in accordance with the law of its Member State.
3. The requesting court may call for the request to be executed in accordance with a special procedure provided for by the law of its Member State, using form A in the Annex. The requested court shall comply with such a requirement unless this procedure is incompatible with the law of the Member State of the requested court or by reason of major practical difficulties. If the requested court does not comply with the requirement for one of these reasons it shall inform the requesting court using form E in the Annex.
4. The requesting court may ask the requested court to use communications technology at the performance of the taking of evidence, in particular by using videoconference and teleconference.

    The requested court shall comply with such a requirement unless this is incompatible with the law of the Member State of the requested court or by reason of major practical difficulties.

    If the requested court does not comply with the requirement for one of these reasons, it shall inform the requesting court, using form E in the Annex.

    If there is no access to the technical means referred to above in the requesting or in the requested court, such means may be made available by the courts by mutual agreement.

Article 11
Performance with the presence and participation of the parties

1. If it is provided for by the law of the Member State of the requesting court, the parties and, if any, their representatives, have the right to be present at the performance of the taking of evidence by the requested court.
2. The requesting court shall, in its request, inform the requested court that the parties and, if any, their representatives, will be present and, where appropriate, that their participation is requested, using form A in the Annex. This information may also be given at any other appropriate time.
3. If the participation of the parties and, if any, their representatives, is requested at the performance of the taking of evidence, the requested court shall determine, in accordance with Article 10, the conditions under which they may participate.

4. The requested court shall notify the parties and, if any, their representatives, of the time when, the place where, the proceedings will take place, and, where appropriate, the conditions under which they may participate, using form F in the Annex.

5. Paragraphs 1 to 4 shall not affect the possibility for the requested court of asking the parties and, if any their representatives, to be present at or to participate in the performance of the taking of evidence if that possibility is provided for by the law of its Member State.

Article 12
Performance with the presence and participation of representatives of the requesting court

1. If it is compatible with the law of the Member State of the requesting court, representatives of the requesting court have the right to be present in the performance of the taking of evidence by the requested court.

2. For the purpose of this Article, the term 'representative' shall include members of the judicial personnel designated by the requesting court, in accordance with the law of its Member State. The requesting court may also designate, in accordance with the law of its Member State, any other person, such as an expert.

3. The requesting court shall, in its request, inform the requested court that its representatives will be present and, where appropriate, that their participation is requested, using form A in the Annex. This information may also be given at any other appropriate time.

4. If the participation of the representatives of the requesting court is requested in the performance of the taking of evidence, the requested court shall determine, in accordance with Article 10, the conditions under which they may participate.

5. The requested court shall notify the requesting court, of the time when, and the place where, the proceedings will take place, and, where appropriate, the conditions under which the representatives may participate, using form F in the Annex.

Article 13
Coercive measures

Where necessary, in executing a request the requested court shall apply the appropriate coercive measures in the instances and to the extent as are provided for by the law of the Member State of the requested court for the execution of a request made for the same purpose by its national authorities or one of the parties concerned.

Article 14
Refusal to execute

1. A request for the hearing of a person shall not be executed when the person concerned claims the right to refuse to give evidence or to be prohibited from giving evidence,

   (a) under the law of the Member State of the requested court; or

   (b) under the law of the Member State of the requesting court, and such right has been specified in the request, or,

   if need be, at the instance of the requested court, has been confirmed by the requesting court.

2. In addition to the grounds referred to in paragraph 1, the execution of a request may be refused only if:

(a) the request does not fall within the scope of this Regulation as set out in Article 1; or

(b) the execution of the request under the law of the Member State of the requested court does not fall within the functions of the judiciary; or

(c) the requesting court does not comply with the request of the requested court to complete the request pursuant to Article 8 within 30 days after the requested court asked it to do so; or

(d) a deposit or advance asked for in accordance with Article 18(3) is not made within 60 days after the requested court asked for such a deposit or advance.

3. Execution may not be refused by the requested court solely on the ground that under the law of its Member State a court of that Member State has exclusive jurisdiction over the subject matter of the action or that the law of that Member State would not admit the right of action on it.

4. If execution of the request is refused on one of the grounds referred to in paragraph 2, the requested court shall notify the requesting court thereof within 60 days of receipt of the request by the requested court using form H in the Annex.

Article 15
Notification of delay

If the requested court is not in a position to execute the request within 90 days of receipt, it shall inform the requesting court thereof, using form G in the Annex. When it does so, the grounds for the delay shall be given as well as the estimated time that the requested court expects it will need to execute the request.

Article 16
Procedure after execution of the request

The requested court shall send without delay to the requesting court the documents establishing the execution of the request and, where appropriate, return the documents received from the requesting court. The documents shall be accompanied by a confirmation of execution using form H in the Annex.

SECTION 4

DIRECT TAKING OF EVIDENCE BY THE REQUESTING COURT

Article 17

1. Where a court requests to take evidence directly in another Member State, it shall submit a request to the central body or the competent authority referred to in Article 3(3) in that State, using form I in the Annex.

2. Direct taking of evidence may only take place if it can be performed on a voluntary basis without the need for coercive measures.
   Where the direct taking of evidence implies that a person shall be heard, the requesting court shall inform that person that the performance shall take place on a voluntary basis.

3. The taking of evidence shall be performed by a member of the judicial personnel or by any other person such as an expert, who will be designated, in accordance with the law of the Member State of the requesting court.

4. Within 30 days of receiving the request, the central body or the competent authority of the requested Member State shall inform the requesting court if the request is accepted and, if necessary, under what conditions according to the law of its Member State such performance is to be carried out, using form J.

In particular, the central body or the competent authority may assign a court of its Member State to take part in the performance of the taking of evidence in order to ensure the proper application of this Article and the conditions that have been set out. The central body or the competent authority shall encourage the use of communications technology, such as videoconferences and teleconferences.

5. The central body or the competent authority may refuse direct taking of evidence only if:
   (a) the request does not fall within the scope of this Regulation as set out in Article 1;
   (b) the request does not contain all of the necessary information pursuant to Article 4; or
   (c) the direct taking of evidence requested is contrary to fundamental principles of law in its Member State.

6. Without prejudice to the conditions laid down in accordance with paragraph 4, the requesting court shall execute the request in accordance with the law of its Member State.

SECTION 5
COSTS

Article 18

1. The execution of the request, in accordance with Article 10, shall not give rise to a claim for any reimbursement of taxes or costs.
2. Nevertheless, if the requested court so requires, the requesting court shall ensure the reimbursement, without delay, of:
   —the fees paid to experts and interpreters, and
   —the costs occasioned by the application of Article 10(3) and(4).
   The duty for the parties to bear these fees or costs shall be governed by the law of the Member State of the requesting court.
3. Where the opinion of an expert is required, the requested court may, before executing the request, ask the requesting court for an adequate deposit or advance towards the requested costs. In all other cases, a deposit or advance shall not be a condition for the execution of a request.
   The deposit or advance shall be made by the parties if that is provided for by the law of the Member State of the requesting court.

CHAPTER III
FINAL PROVISIONS

Article 19
Implementing rules

1. The Commission shall draw up and regularly update a manual, which shall also be available electronically, containing the information provided by the Member States in

accordance with Article 22 and the agreements or arrangements in force, according to Article 21.
2. The updating or making of technical amendments to the standard forms set out in the Annex shall be carried out in accordance with the advisory procedure set out in Article 20(2).

Article 20
Committee

1. The Commission shall be assisted by a Committee.
2. Where reference is made to this paragraph, Articles 3 and 7 of Decision 1999/468/EC shall apply.
3. The Committee shall adopt its Rules of Procedure.

Article 21
Relationship with existing or future agreements or arrangements between Member States

1. This Regulation shall, in relation to matters to which it applies, prevail over other provisions contained in bilateral or multilateral agreements or arrangements concluded by the Member States and in particular the Hague Convention of 1 March 1954 on Civil Procedure and the Hague Convention of 18 March 1970 on the Taking of Evidence Abroad in Civil or Commercial Matters, in relations between the Member States party thereto.
2. This Regulation shall not preclude Member States from maintaining or concluding agreements or arrangements between two or more of them to further facilitate the taking of evidence, provided that they are compatible with this Regulation.
3. Member States shall send to the Commission:
   (a) by 1 July 2003, a copy of the agreements or arrangements maintained between the Member States referred to in paragraph 2;
   (b) a copy of the agreements or arrangements concluded between the Member States referred to in paragraph 2 as well as drafts of such agreements or arrangements which they intend to adopt; and
   (c) any denunciation of, or amendments to, these agreements or arrangements.

Article 22
Communication

By 1 July 2003 each Member State shall communicate to the Commission the following:
   (a) the list pursuant to Article 2(2) indicating the territorial and, where appropriate, the special jurisdiction of the courts;
   (b) the names and addresses of the central bodies and competent authorities pursuant to Article 3, indicating their territorial jurisdiction;
   (c) the technical means for the receipt of requests available to the courts on the list pursuant to Article 2(2);
   (d) the languages accepted for the requests as referred to in Article 5.
Member States shall inform the Commission of any subsequent changes to this information.

Article 23
Review

No later than 1 January 2007, and every five years thereafter, the Commission shall present to the European Parliament, the Council and the Economic and Social Committee a report on the application of this Regulation, paying special attention to the practical application of Article 3(1)(c) and 3, and Articles 17 and 18.

Article 24
Entry into force

1. This Regulation shall enter into force on 1 July 2001.
2. This Regulation shall apply from 1 January 2004, except for Articles 19, 21 and 22, which shall apply from 1 July 2001.

This Regulation shall be binding in its entirety and directly applicable in the Member States in accordance with the Treaty establishing the European Community.

Done at Brussels, 28 May 2001.
For the Council
The President
T. Bodström

ANNEX

FORM A

Request for the taking of evidence

(Article 4 of Council Regulation (EC) No 1206/2001 of 28 May 2001 on cooperation between the courts of the Member States in the taking of evidence in civil or commercial matters (OJ L 174, 27.6.2001, p. 1))

1. Reference of the requesting court:

2. Reference of the requested court:

3. Requesting court:
   3.1. Name:
   3.2. Address:
       3.2.1. Street and No/PO box:
       3.2.2. Place and postcode:
       3.2.3. Country:
   3.2. Tel.
   3.3. Fax
   3.4. E-mail:

4. Requested court:
   4.1. Name:
   4.2. Address:
       4.2.1. Street and No/PO box:
       4.2.2. Place and postcode:
       4.2.3. Country:
   4.3. Tel.
   4.4. Fax
   4.5. E-mail:

5. In the case brought by the claimant/petitioner:
   5.1. Name:
   5.2. Address:
       5.2.1. Street and No/PO box:
       5.2.2. Place and postcode:
       5.2.3. Country:
   5.3. Tel.
   5.4. Fax
   5.5. E-mail:

6. Representatives of the claimant/petitioner:
   6.1. Name:

931

6.2. Address:
    6.2.1. Street and No/PO box:
    6.2.2. Place and postcode:
    6.2.3. country:
6.3. Tel.
6.4. Fax
6.5. E-mail:

7. Against the defendant/respondent:
    7.1. Name:
    7.2. Address:
        7.2.1. Street and No/PO box:
        7.2.2. Place and postcode:
        7.2.3. country:
    7.3. Tel.
    7.4. Fax
    7.5. E-mail:

8. Representatives of defendant/respondent:
    8.1. Name:
    8.2. Address:
        8.2.1. Street and No/PO box:
        8.2.2. Place and postcode:
        8.2.3. Country:
    8.3. Tel:
    8.4. Fax:
    8.5. E-mail:

9. Presence and participation of the parties:
    9.1. Parties and, if any, their representatives will be present at the taking of evidence: ☐
    9.2. Participation of the parties and, if any, their representatives is requested: ☐

10. Presence and participation of the representatives of the requesting court:
    10.1. Representatives will be present at the taking of evidence: ☐
    10.2. Participation of the representatives is requested: ☐
        10.2.1. Name:
        10.2.2. Title:
        10.2.3. Function:
        10.2.4. Task:

11. Nature and subject matter of the case and a brief statement of the facts (in annex, where appropriate):

12. Taking of evidence to be performed
    12.1. Description of the taking of evidence to be performed (in annex, where appropriate):
    12.2. Examination of witnesses:
        12.2.1. Name and surname:
        12.2.2. Address:

12.2.3. Tel.

12.2.4. Fax

12.2.5. E-mail:

12.2.6. Questions to be put to the witness or a statement of the facts about which they are to be examined (in annex, where appropriate):

12.2.7. Right to refuse to testify under the law of the Member State of the requesting court (in annex, where appropriate):

12.2.8. Please examine the witness:

    12.2.8.1. under oath: ☐

    12.2.8.2. On affirmation: ☐

12.2.9. Any other information that the requesting court deems necessary (in annex, where appropriate):

12.3. Other taking of evidence:

    12.3.1. Documents to be inspected and a description of the requested taking of evidence (in annex, where appropriate):

    12.3.2. Objects to be inspected and description of the requested taking of evidence (in annex, where appropriate):

13. Please execute the request

    13.1. In accordance with a special procedure (Article 10(3)) provided for by the law of the Member State of the requesting court and/or by the use of communications technology (Article 10(4)) described in annex:

    13.2. Following information is necessary for the application thereof:

Done at:

Date:

Notification of forwarding the request

Article 7(2) of Council Regulation (EC) No 1206/2001 of 28 May 2001 on cooperation between the courts of the Member States in the taking of evidence in civil or commercial matters (OJ L 174, 27.6.2001, p. 1).

---

14. The request does not fall within the jurisdiction of the court indicated in point 4 above and was forwarded to

    14.1. Name of the competent court:

    14.2. Address:

        14.2.1. Street and No/PO box:

        14.2.2. Place and postcode:

        14.2.3. Country:

    14.3. Tel.

    14.4. Fax

    14.5. E-mail:

Done at:

Date:

FORM B

> Acknowledgement of receipt of a request for the taking of evidence
>
> Article 7(1) of Council Regulation (EC) No 1206/2001 of 28 May 2001 on cooperation between the courts of the Member States in the taking of evidence in civil or commercial matters (OJ L 174, 27.6.2001, p. 1))

1. Reference of the requesting court:
2. Reference of the requested court:
3. Name of the requesting court:
4. Requested court:
   4.1. Name:
   4.2. Address:
      4.2.1. Street and No/PO box:
      4.2.2. Place and postcode:
      4.2.3. Country:
   4.3. Tel.
   4.4. Fax
   4.5. E-mail:
5. The request was received on ... (date of receipt) by the court indicated in point 4 above.
6. The request cannot be dealt with because:
   6.1. The language used to complete the form is not acceptable (Article 5): ☐
      6.1.1. Please use one the following languages:
   6.2. The document is not legible (Article 6): ☐

Done at:

Date:

FORM C

> Request for additional information for the taking of evidence
>
> (Article 8 of Council Regulation (EC) No 1206/2001 of 28 May 2001 on cooperation between the courts of the Member States in the taking of evidence in civil or commercial matters (OJ L 174, 27.6.2001, p. 1))

1. Reference of the requested court:
2. Reference of the requesting court:
3. Name of the requesting court:

4. Name of the requested court:
5. The request cannot be executed without the following additional information:
6. The request cannot be executed before a deposit or advance is made in accordance with Article 18(3). The deposit or advance should be made in the following way:

Done at:

Date:

FORM D

Acknowledgement of receipt of the deposit or advance

(Article 8(2) of Council Regulation (EC) No 1206/2001 of 28 May 2001 on cooperation between the courts of the Member States in the taking of evidence in civil or commercial matters (OJ L 174, 27.6.2001, p.1))

1. Reference of the requesting court:
2. Reference of the requested court:
3. Name of the requesting court:
4. Name of the requested court:
5. The deposit or advance was received on ... (date of receipt) by the court indicated in point 4 above.

Done at:

Date:

FORM E

Notification concerning the request for special procedures and/or for the use of communications technologies

(Article 10(3) and (4) of Council Regulation (EC) No 1206/2001 of 28 May 2001 on cooperation between the courts of the Member States in the taking of evidence in civil or commercial matters
(OJ L 174, 27.6.2001, p.1))

1. Reference of the requested court:
2. Reference of the requesting court:
3. Name of the requesting court:
4. Name of the requested court:
5. The requirement for execution of the request according to the special procedure indicated in point 13.1 of the request (Form A) could not be complied with because:

5.1. the required procedure is incompatible with the law of the Member State of the requested court: ☐

5.2. the performance of the requested procedure is not possible by reason of major practical difficulties: ☐

6. The requirement for execution of the request for the use of communications technologies indicated in point 13.1 of the request (Form A) could not be complied with because:

6.1. The use of communications technology is incompatible with the law of the Member State of the requested court ☐

6.2. The use of the communications technology is not possible by reason of major practical difficulties ☐

Done at:

Date:

FORM F

Notification of the date, time, place of performance of the taking of evidence and the conditions for participation

(Articles 11(4) and 12(5) of Council Regulation (EC) No 1206/2001 of 28 May 2001 on cooperation between the courts of the Member States in the taking of evidence in civil or commercial matters
(OJ L 174, 27.6.2001, p. 1))

---

1. Reference of the requesting court:
2. Reference of the requested court:
3. Requesting court
   3.1. Name:
   3.2. Address:
       3.2.1. Street and No/PO box:
       3.2.2. Place and postcode:
       3.2.3. Country:
   3.3. Tel.
   3.4. Fax
   3.5. E-mail:
4. Requested court
   4.1. Name:
   4.2. Address:
       4.2.1. Street and No/PO box:
       4.2.2. Place and postcode:
       4.2.3. Country:
   4.3. Tel.
   4.4. Fax
   4.5. E-mail:

5. Date and time of the performance of the taking of evidence:
6. Place of the performance of the taking of evidence, if different from that referred to in point 4 above:
7. Where appropriate, conditions under which the parties and, if any, their representatives may participate:
8. Where appropriate, conditions under which the representatives of the requesting court may participate:

Done at:
Date:

FORM G

Notification of delay

(Article 15 of Council Regulation (EC) No 1206/2001 of 28 May 2001 on cooperation between the courts of the Member States in the taking of evidence in civil or commercial matters (OJ L 174, 27.6.2001,p. 1))

1. Reference of the requested court:
2. Reference of the requesting court:
3. Name of the requesting court:
4. Name of the requested court:
5. The request can not be executed within 90 days of receipt for the following reasons:
6. It is estimated that the request will be executed by ... (indicate an estimated date)

Done at:

Date:

FORM H

(Articles 14 and 16 of Council Regulation (EC) No 1206/2001 of 28 May 2001 on cooperation between the courts of the Member States in the taking of evidence in civil or commercial matters
(OJ L 174, 27.6.2001, p. 1))

1. Reference of the requested court:
2. Reference of the requesting court:
3. Name of the requesting court:
4. Name of the requested court:
5. The request has been executed.
   The documents establishing execution of the request are attached: ☐

6. Execution of the request has been refused because:
    6.1. the person to be examined has claimed the right to refuse to give evidence or has claimed to be prohibited from giving evidence:
        6.1.1. under the law of the Member State of the requested court: ☐
        6.1.2. under the law of the Member State of the requesting court: ☐
    6.2. The request does not fall within the scope of this Regulation   ☐
    6.3. Under the law of the Member State of the requested court, the execution of the request does not fall within the functions of the judiciary: ☐
    6.4. The requesting court has not complied with the request for additional information from the requested court dated ... (date of the request):   ☐
    6.5. A deposit or advance asked for in accordance with Article 18(3) has not been made: ☐

Done at:

Date:

FORM I

> Request for direct taking of evidence
> (Article 17 of Council Regulation (EC) No 1206/2001 of 28 May 2001 on cooperation between the courts of the Member States in the taking of evidence in civil or commercial matters (OJ L 174, 27.6.2001, p.1))

1. Reference of the requesting court:
2. Reference of the central body/competent authority:
3. Requesting court:
    3.1. Name:
    3.2. Address:
        3.2.1. Street and No/PO box:
        3.2.2. Place and postcode:
        3.2.3. Country:
    3.3. Tel.
    3.4. Fax
    3.5. E-mail:
4. Central body/competent authority of the requested State:
    4.1. Name:
    4.2. Address:
        4.2.1. Street and No/PO box:
        4.2.2. Place and postcode:
        4.2.3. Country:
    4.1. Tel.
    4.2. Fax
    4.3. E-mail:

5. In the case brought by the claimant/petitioner:
    5.1. Name:
    5.2. Address:
        5.2.1. Street and No/PO box:
        5.2.2. Place and postcode:
        5.2.3. Country:
    5.1. Tel.:
    5.2. Fax
    5.3. E-mail:
6. Representatives of the claimant/petitioner:
    6.1. Name:
    6.2. Address:
        6.2.1. Street and No/PO box:
        6.2.2. Place and postcode:
        6.2.3. Country:
    6.3. Tel.
    6.4. Fax
    6.5. E-mail:
7. Against the defendant/respondent:
    7.1. Name:
    7.2. Address:
        7.2.1. Street and No/PO box:
        7.2.2. Place and postcode:
        7.2.3. Country:
    7.3. Tel.
    7.4. Fax
    7.5. E-mail:
8. Representatives of defendant/respondent:
    8.1. Name:
    8.2. Address:
        8.2.1. Street and No/PO box:
        8.2.2. Place and postcode:
        8.2.3. Country:
    8.3. Tel.
    8.4. Fax
    8.5. E-mail:
9. The taking of evidence shall be performed by:
    9.1. Name:
    9.2. Title:
    9.3. Function:
    9.4. Task:
10. Nature and subject matter of the case and a brief statement of the facts (in annex, where appropriate):
11. Taking of evidence to be performed:
    11.1. Description of the taking of evidence to be performed (in annex, where appropriate):
    11.2. Examination of witnesses:

11.2.1. First names and surname:

11.2.2. Address:

11.2.3. Tel.

11.2.4. Fax

11.2.5. E-mail:

11.2.6. Questions to be put to the witness or a statement of the facts about which they are to be examined (in the annex, where appropriate):

11.2.7. Right to refuse to testify under the law of the Member State of the requesting court (in annex, where appropriate):

11.3. Other taking of evidence (in annex, where appropriate):

12. The requesting court requests to take evidence directly by use of the following communications technology (in annex, where appropriate):

Done at:

Date:

FORM J

> Information from the central body/competent authority
> (Article 17 of Council Regulation (EC) No 1206/2001 of 28 May 2001 on cooperation between the courts of the Member States in the taking of evidence in civil or commercial matters (OJ L 174, 27.6.2001, p.1))

1. Reference of the requesting court:
2. Reference of the central body/competent authority:
3. Name of the requesting court:
4. Central body/competent authority:
   4.1. Name:
   4.2. Address:
       4.2.1. Street and No/PO box:
       4.2.2. Place and postcode:
       4.2.3. Country:
   4.3. Tel.
   4.4. Fax
   4.5. E-mail:
5. Information from the central body/competent authority:
   5.1. Direct taking of evidence in accordance with the request is accepted: ☐
   5.2. Direct taking of evidence in accordance with the request is accepted under the following conditions (in annex, where appropriate): ☐
   5.3. Direct taking of evidence in accordance with the request is refused for the following reasons: ☐

5.3.1. The request does not fall within the scope of this Regulation: ☐

5.3.2. The request does not contain all of the necessary information pursuant to Article 4: ☐

5.3.3. The direct taking of evidence requested for is contrary to fundamental principles of law of the Member State of the central body/competent authority: ☐

Done at:

Date:

12

INTERNATIONAL COMMERCIAL ARBITRATION

A. Introductory Text

Arbitration is a widely used alternative to litigation in cross-border commercial disputes and a number of international and regional instruments have been devoted to it.[1] These together encompass three distinct matters: substantive arbitration law, arbitration procedure, and the recognition and enforcement of foreign arbitral awards. The 1985 UNCITRAL Model Law on international commercial arbitration is devoted to substantive arbitration law. It has been widely adopted, albeit

---

[1] In addition, many national arbitral laws also cover international commercial arbitrations.

with modifications from jurisdiction to jurisdiction. The 1958 New York Convention on the recognition and enforcement of foreign arbitral awards is one of the world's most successful conventions, and also one of the shortest. It deals exclusively with the conditions in which an award given in one jurisdiction must be recognized and may be enforced in another. The remaining rules reproduced in this section are procedural rules which deal with such matters as the initiation of the arbitration, the establishment of the arbitral tribunal, the conduct of the proceedings, and the payment of costs. Three sets of rules have been produced by international organizations, namely the 1976 UNCITRAL Arbitration Rules, the ICC Rules of Arbitration (current edition 1998), and the rules of the International Centre for the Settlement of Investment Disputes (ICSID) established under the 1965 Washington Convention. The first two of these are given effect by incorporation into contracts.[2] The ICSID rules, which are not reproduced in this volume, deal with investment disputes between a Contracting State and a national of another Contracting State and apply where the parties have agreed to submit their dispute to ICSID. The Inter-American Convention on International Commercial Arbitration (otherwise known as the OAS or Panama Convention) is a regional convention designed in particular for disputes between nationals of a State within the Organization of American States and provides for arbitrations to be conducted in accordance with the rules of procedure of the Inter-American Commercial Arbitration Commission (IACAC). The 1998 Mercosur Agreement on International Commercial Arbitration is equally devoted to substantive arbitration law with direct impact on all proceedings in the four Member States.

1. The New York Convention

The purpose of the New York Convention is to ensure that courts enforce agreements to arbitrate and to facilitate the recognition and enforcement in a State of arbitral awards made in another State or otherwise constituting non-domestic awards. This facility provides a powerful inducement to use arbitration as a dispute resolution mechanism, since there is no comparable convention for the recognition and enforcement of court judgments and work on a projected Hague Convention, which almost collapsed, has now been narrowed down to issues of choice of forum.

The Convention applies to the recognition and enforcement in one State of an arbitral award made in another, but, or alternatively, treated by the law of the State of enforcement as non-domestic.[3] So the courts of a State may apply the

---

[2] In the case of the UNCITRAL Rules this may be done either directly by express incorporation into the contract between the parties or because the arbitration rules by which disputes between the parties are governed themselves incorporate the UNCITRAL Rules. Thus the 1983 Rules of the Iran-US Claims Tribunal adopt the UNCITRAL Arbitration Rules with some modifications.

[3] Article I (1).

Convention to the enforcement in that State of an award made in the same State where its arbitration law treats the arbitration as non-domestic, as it might do, for example, if both parties were foreigners.[4]

In order for the Convention to apply, various conditions must be satisfied. The award must be an arbitral award, not a court judgment, a determination by an expert, an interim adjudication, or a non-binding award in a mediation or other form of alternative dispute resolution. The parties must have agreed to refer their differences to arbitration, and these must arise from a defined legal relationship. The arbitration agreement must be in writing, a requirement the meaning of which has given rise to much discussion but is generally taken to include an electronic record capable of being reproduced on a subsequent occasion. The subject-matter of the dispute must be capable of settlement by arbitration in the Contracting State where recognition and enforcement are sought.[5] Finally, a Contracting State may declare that it will apply the Convention only on the basis of reciprocity and only to differences arising out of legal relationships considered commercial under its law.[6]

At the request of one of the parties the court of a Contracting State is obliged to refer the parties to arbitration in a dispute falling within the scope of the Convention unless it finds that the agreement to arbitrate is null and void, inoperative, or incapable of being performed.[7] Subject to compliance with the requisite formalities[8] the courts of a Contracting State are obliged to recognize and enforce an arbitral award unless the party against whom relief is sought furnishes proof of the existence of one of the grounds of refusal set out in Article V.[9] Though recognition and enforcement may only be refused if one or other of the above grounds exist, the Convention does not preclude enforcement even where such a ground does exist and even where an award has been set aside by a court in the country of origin.[10]

---

[4] The Convention extends not only to arbitral tribunals appointed for each case but also to permanent arbitral tribunals to whom the parties have submitted.

[5] The courts of a number of States now accept that issues capable of settlement by arbitration include not only matters of private law but also questions relating to securities, intellectual property rights, and competition law, including European Community law where applicable. Questions that are obviously not capable of settlement by arbitration include the criminal law and questions of status such as marriage and divorce. [6] Article I(3). [7] Article II(3). [8] See Art IV.

[9] These are: (1) incapacity of a party or invalidity of the arbitration agreement; (2) failure to give a party proper notice of the appointment of the arbitrator or of the arbitration proceedings or inability of a party to present his case; (3) the inclusion within the award of matters outside the terms of reference of the arbitral tribunal; (4) composition of the arbitral tribunal otherwise than in accordance with the agreement of the parties or, failing such agreement, the *lex loci arbitri*; (5) the fact that the award has not yet become binding or has been set aside or suspended by a competent authority of the country in which or under the law of which it was made; (6) the non-arbitrability of the dispute under the law of the country of intended recognition and enforcement; and (7) the fact that such enforcement would be contrary to the public policy of that country.

[10] This follows from the fact that Art V merely restricts the grounds of refusal to enforce, not the grounds of enforcement, and is reinforced by Art VII, which allows the party seeking enforcement to invoke a more generous approach given by the law of the country in which enforcement is sought. In a few countries the courts have ignored orders of foreign courts setting aside arbitral awards on the

2. The Inter-American Convention on International Commercial Arbitration

Introduction

In 1975, the Organization of American States (OAS) promulgated this Convention, also known as The Panama Convention, with a view to achieving greater uniformity of law and practice in the Western Hemisphere. Many OAS Member States have ratified both the Panama and the New York Convention of 1958 which is in many respects mirrored by this instrument. The scope of the Panama Convention is slightly wider in that it explicitly addresses certain issues relevant during the pre-recognition stages of the arbitral process on which the parties may seek guidance.

Arbitration Agreement

The Convention states that an agreement in which the parties undertake to submit to dispute resolution by arbitration any differences that may arise or have arisen between them with respect to a commercial transaction is valid if set forth in an instrument signed by the parties, or in the form of exchange of letters, telegrams or telex communications.[11]

Appointment of Arbitrators

Under the Convention, arbitrators are to be appointed in the manner agreed upon by the parties. The parties may delegate their appointing power to a third party which may be a juridical or a natural person. In its regional context it was seen as important that the provision[12] goes on by stating expressly that the arbitrators may be nationals[13] or foreigners.

Arbitral Proceedings

Article 3 provides that, in the absence of an express agreement between the parties, the arbitration is conducted in accordance with the rules of procedure of the Inter-American Commercial Arbitration Commission. This is a very distinct feature of this Convention. While it leaves the parties the freedom to design their own procedural framework or to agree upon the applicability of the arbitration rules of the ICC, any of the other arbitration institutions,[14] or the UNCITRAL Rules of Arbitration,[15] it provides a fall back solution: the Rules of Procedure of the Inter-American Commercial Arbitration Commission (IACAC).[16]

---

ground that, the awards being international and therefore stateless, such orders were of no significance in the country of enforcement.   [11] Article 1.

[12] Article 2.

[13] It is submitted that this may be construed as a reference to the countries of origin of the parties, the country of the seat of the arbitration, and any court seised of the matter at any stage.

[14] See below, p. 997.   [15] See below, p. 982.

[16] Adopted on 1 July 2000, in force on 1 April 2002.

Finality of Award

An arbitral award which is not subject to judicial review under the applicable law or rules of arbitration has the force of a final judicial decision.[17] Its execution or recognition may be ordered in the same manner as that of decisions tendered by national or foreign courts in accordance with the country where it is to be executed, including provisions of international treaties.

Recognition and Enforcement

Article 5 of the Convention which sets forth the grounds on which recognition and enforcement of an award may be refused emulates Article V of the New York Convention.[18] The same applies with respect to Article 6 of this Convention and Article VI of the New York Convention.[19]

3. The UNCITRAL Model Law

The 1985 UNCITRAL Model Law is designed to make available to national legislatures a set of principles and rules that can be adopted to provide or improve national laws governing international commercial arbitration, and in so doing to bring such laws into closer harmony with each other. The Model Law covers all stages of the arbitral process, from the agreement to arbitrate to recognition and enforcement and the judicial review of arbitral awards. On procedural issues there is considerable overlap between the Model Law and the UNCITRAL Rules of Arbitration, but the former is given effect by legislation, the latter by agreement of the parties. The Law applies to international commercial arbitration.[20] The principal test of internationality is that at the time of conclusion of an arbitration agreement the parties to it have their places of business in different States.[21] A note to Article 1(1) indicates that the term 'commercial' is to be given a wide meaning.

In defining an arbitration agreement and prescribing its form Article 7 of the Model tracks the New York Convention, while setting out more fully what constitutes an agreement in writing so as to capture electronic records. Article 8 follows Article II of the New York Convention in imposing a duty to refer the parties to arbitration in the absence of one of the applicable exceptions. Chapter III deals with the composition of arbitral tribunals and covers such matters as the number of arbitrators, their appointment, the grounds and procedure for challenges, and the appointment of a substitute arbitrator where an arbitrator's mandate comes to an end.

The Model Law adopts two already well-established principles of arbitration law affecting jurisdiction. The first is that the arbitral tribunal may rule on its own

---

[17] Article 4.   [18] Above, p. 945, note 9.
[19] Dealing with the situation that the award is not yet binding on the parties or has been annulled or suspended by a competent authority of the State where the arbitration took place.
[20] Article 1(1).   [21] Article 1(3)(a).

jurisdiction,[22] the second, that an arbitration clause forming part of a contract is to be treated as an independent agreement, with the result that a decision by the arbitral tribunal that the contract is null and void does not *ipso jure* entail the invalidity of the arbitration clause.[23] The tribunal may rule on jurisdiction, either in a preliminary award or in an award on the merits. If it rules as a preliminary question that it has jurisdiction, a party can apply to a court to decide the matter.[24] A party to an arbitration who wishes to challenge the arbitral tribunal's jurisdiction has a choice. He may take part in the arbitration but challenge the jurisdiction and, if the ruling goes against him either in an interim award or in an award on the merits, apply to the court to have the award set aside; or he may decline to take part in the proceedings and challenge any resulting award.[25]

Chapter V of the Model law contains provisions for the conduct of the proceedings. The arbitral tribunal is required to decide the dispute in accordance with such rules of law as are chosen by the parties as applicable to the substance of the dispute or, failing such choice, by the law determined by the conflict of laws rules which it considers applicable.[26]

A basic objective of the Model Law is to secure the finality of arbitral awards. To that end Article 5 starkly provides that 'in matters governed by this Law, no court shall intervene except where so provided in this Law'. Accordingly, the grounds on which an award may be set aside in the country of origin or refused recognition in another country are limited[27] and closely follow Article V of the New York Convention.[28]

4. MERCOSUR Agreement 1998

Scope of application

This Agreement applies to the organization and the conduct of the proceedings as well as to arbitral awards if there is one of the following connecting factors:[29] (a) the arbitration agreement was entered into between parties domiciled or having their

---

[22] Article 16(1). This is the principle of Kompetenz-Kompetenz.   [23] Ibid.

[24] Article 16(3). Curiously there is no express provision for recourse to the court if as a preliminary question the tribunal decides it has no jurisdiction.

[25] Under Art 34(2)(a). This procedure is not without danger, for if the court dismisses the challenge the party concerned is bound by the award unless there are independent grounds on which to have it set aside.

[26] Article 28(1), (2). The reference to 'rules of law' enables effect to be given to rules chosen by the parties which are not part of a national legal system, for example, the *lex mercatoria* or 'general principles of law'. But in the absence of party choice the tribunal is required to apply 'the law' determined by the conflict of laws, that is, the rules of a national legal system, though it is free to decide which conflict rules to apply, and in particular what should be the connecting factor.

[27] See Arts 34 and 35.

[28] Thus they do not include such matters as failure to conduct the arbitration in accordance with the procedure agreed by the parties, failure of the award to state reasons, procurement of the award by fraud, corruption, or bias on the part of an arbitrator or wilful disregard of the applicable law.

[29] Article 3.

corporate seats, subsidiaries, branch offices, or agencies in more than one Member State; (b) the underlying contract has any legal or economic connecting factor with more than one member State; (c) the underlying contract is so connected and the arbitral tribunal has its seat in a Member State and parties do not indicate otherwise; (d) the underlying contract is so connected without the tribunal having its seat in a Member State but the parties have indicated their intention to be subject to this Agreement; (e) the underlying contract is not in any way connected with any Member State but the parties have chosen a tribunal which has its seat in a Member State and have explicitly indicated their intention to be subject to this Agreement.

Equal treatment and good faith

An arbitration agreement, even if part of standard terms, must guarantee that the parties will be treated fairly and not abusively and is generally governed by good faith.[30] An arbitration clause in a contract has to be placed prominently and be readable.[31]

Independence of contract and form of arbitration agreement

An arbitration agreement is independent of the underlying contract. The latter's non-existence does not entail nullity of the former.[32]

The agreement has to be in writing and it is the law of the State where the agreement was executed which governs formal validity.[33] The exchange of letters or faxes with proof of receipt may create a valid agreement. Communication by fax, e-mail, etc. 'must be confirmed by original documents'.[34] An agreement between persons not physically present in the same place becomes effective at the time and in the State where the declaration is received 'through the means chosen and confirmed by the original document'.[35]

Law governing the arbitration agreement

The parties' capacity is governed by the laws of their respective domicile. Validity and effects of the arbitration agreement are governed by the law of the Member State where the arbitral tribunal has its seat.[36]

Jurisdiction of the arbitral tribunal

The arbitral tribunal decides ex officio whether the arbitration agreement is valid and whether it has jurisdiction.[37]

---

[30] Article 4(1).   [31] Article 4(2).   [32] Article 5.   [33] Article 6(1), (2).
[34] Article 6(3). This is subject to Article 6(5), see note 35.
[35] Article 6(4). However, formal validity according to the law of any of the States having substantial contacts with the underlying contract 'saves' an agreement even if the requirements of the place of its execution are not met, Art 6(5).   [36] Article 7.
[37] Article 8.

Amiable compositeur

The parties may authorise the tribunal to act as *amiable compositeur ex aequo et bono*, that is to say, to decide this dispute on the basis of equity and fairness rather than by the application of legal rules. Without any such authorization it has to apply the law.[38]

Applicable law

The parties are free to determine the law governing the merits of the dispute on the basis of the rules of private international law and its principles as well as the law of international commerce. Failing such agreement the tribunal has to decide according to the same sources.[39]

Ad hoc arbitration and institutional arbitration: general principles

Starting with a statement that arbitrators have to follow the principles of adversarial proceedings, act fairly and impartially, and decide according to their free conviction,[40] the Agreement describes the characteristics of both ways to conduct arbitrations. Where the parties in an *ad hoc* arbitration have not determined otherwise and to the extent compatible with the Agreement, the rules of the Inter-American Commission for Commercial Arbitration (IACCA)[41] govern the procedure subject to the general principles in Article 11.

Arbitral tribunal and proceedings

The Agreement reflects generally accepted principles regarding the commencement of the proceedings,[42] communications,[43] composition of the arbitral tribunal,[44] determination of the tribunal's jurisdiction,[45] and conservatory and protective measures.[46] Regarding appointment, challenge, and replacement of arbitrators in ad hoc arbitrations, the Agreement refers to the rules of procedure of the IACCA.[47]

Arbitral awards

While majority decisions are the rule, the Agreement allows for decisions taken by the chairman alone where there is no majority.[48] Dissenting opinions may be submitted.[49] There is a detailed provision on corrections and amendments to the award.[50]

Action to set aside; refusal or recognition

Article 22 provides for the award being subject to an action to set it aside which may be brought only in the courts of the arbitral tribunal's seat. The grounds on which an award may be set aside in the country of origin are limited but they are both

---

[38] Article 9.   [39] Article 10.   [40] Article 11(2), in the second sentence.
[41] Based on the Inter-American Convention on International Commercial Arbitration of 1975.
[42] Article 15.   [43] Article 14.   [44] Article 16.   [45] Article 18.
[46] Article 19.   [47] Above p. 946.   [48] Article 20(2).   [49] Article 20(3).
[50] Article 21.

more numerous and wider than those under Article V of the New York Convention.[51] They do, for example, include failure to conduct the arbitration in accordance with the procedure agreed to by the parties[52] or the—quite generally worded—failure to conduct the proceedings 'in accordance with the principles of proper procedure'.[53]

The *recognition* and the *enforcement* of foreign arbitral awards is, to the extent applicable, governed by the Inter-American Convention on International Commercial Arbitration of 1975 and the MERCOSUR Protocol of Las Leñas of 1992.[54]

5. Rules of Arbitration as Party-Determined Framework for Dispute Settlement through Arbitration

Ad hoc *arbitration and institutional arbitration*

(i) General There are two principal ways to take a dispute to arbitration: the parties either organize the proceedings *ad hoc* themselves or with minimal outside assistance. Alternatively, they use the services of an institution that specializes in the administration of arbitration proceedings. There is no one-size-fits-all rule whether one or the other is more advisable because faster, less expensive, or 'better' on other accounts. While parties and counsel will have to establish a set of rules governing their *ad hoc* proceedings, arbitration institutions offer standardized proceedings under their respective rules.

In 1976, the General Assembly of the United Nations adopted the UNCITRAL Arbitration Rules, a landmark in the modernization of international commercial arbitration. They have become very popular in regulating *ad hoc* proceedings. Moreover, they acquired benchmark status for the development of many rules of leading arbitral institutions.

(ii) Major arbitration institutions and their rules There is a large number of arbitration institutions. Major ones whose published rules may be easily consulted and on whose case load there is accurate statistical information are: American Arbitration Association (AAA), Austrian Federal Economic Chamber Vienna, China International Economic and Trade Arbitration Commission (CIETAC), Court of International Arbitration of the Chamber of Commerce and Industry of the Russian Federation, Moscow, German Arbitration Institution (DIS), Hong Kong International Arbitration Centre (HKIAC), International Chamber of Commerce (ICC), London Court of International Arbitration (LCIA), Singapore International Arbitration Centre (SIAC), Stockholm Chamber of Commerce Arbitration Institute (SCC).

---

[51] Article 22(2).   [52] Article 22(2)(c).   [53] Article 22(2)(d).   [54] Above, p. 855.

The International Court of Arbitration of the International Chamber of Commerce (ICC) is the arbitration body attached to the ICC. The Court's members are appointed by the World Council of the ICC. The Court does not itself settle disputes but has the function of ensuring the application of the ICC Rules of Arbitration.[55] The Secretariat of the Court under the direction of its Secretary General is the executive arm of the Court in charge of the actual day-to-day administration of the proceedings.

UNCITRAL Rules and ICC Rules

(i) Commencing the arbitration   The party initiating recourse to arbitration (claimant), under the UNCITRAL Rules, gives to the other party (respondent) a 'notice of arbitration',[56] containing information such as the parties' names and contact details, the arbitration agreement, the nature of the contract or other legal relationship giving rise to the dispute, the claim, the relief sought, particulars concerning the arbitral tribunal etc.[57] In ICC arbitrations, it is the Secretariat of the institution to whom the 'request for arbitration' is sent and who transmits this request to the respondent[58] for the respondent to reply by an 'answer to the request' which contains similar information, comments and, as the case may be, counterclaims.[59] The involvement of the institution's organization in setting up the arbitral tribunal etc. requires that the parties make advance payments on administrative expenses.[60]

Where the parties have agreed to submit to arbitration under the ICC Rules[61] and the respondent does not file an answer or a party raises doubts concerning the existence, validity, or scope of the arbitration agreement, the Court decides whether to proceed applying a *prima facie* test, and it is then for the arbitral tribunal to decide whether it has jurisdiction.[62] It may actually have jurisdiction by virtue of a valid arbitration agreement even though the contract as such may be non-existent.[63] A party's refusal or failure to take part in the proceedings does not stop them; the arbitration proceeds.[64]

(ii) Arbitral Tribunal   The number of arbitrators—one or three—and who is to serve in the specific case is either agreed upon by the parties or has to be determined in a procedure involving outsiders. Under the UNCITRAL Rules it is the so-called

---

[55] Article 1(2) ICC Rules.   [56] Article 3(1) UNCITRAL Rules.
[57] Article 3(3), (4) UNCITRAL Rules.   [58] Article 4(5) ICC Rules.
[59] Article 5 ICC Rules.   [60] Article 4(4), (5), 30 ICC Rules.
[61] There is a standard clause recommended by the ICC: 'All disputes arising out of or in connection with the present contract shall be finally settled under the Rules of Arbitration of the International Chamber of Commerce by one or more arbitrators appointed in accordance with the said Rules'.   [62] Article 6 ICC Rules.
[63] Article 6(4) ICC Rules.   [64] Article 6(3) ICC Rules.
[65] Articles 6(1)(b), (2)–(4), 7(2), (3), 8 UNCITRAL Rules.

'appointing authority', an individual or an institution either agreed upon by the parties or designated by the Secretary-General of the Permanent Court of Arbitration at The Hague.[65] Under the ICC Rules it is, in the absence of an agreement, the Court who decides whether a sole arbitrator or a panel of three are to hear a case and who appoints, in the absence of party nominations, the arbitrator(s).[66] Arbitrators nominated by the parties have to be confirmed by the Court or the Secretary-General.[67]

A sole arbitrator or the chairman of an arbitral tribunal chosen not by the parties—or, in the case of the chairman, by the arbitrators nominated by the parties—but by the appointing authority (UNCITRAL) or the Court (ICC) will normally be of a nationality other than those of the parties.[68]

Every arbitrator must be and remain independent of the parties involved in the arbitration.[69] A prospective arbitrator must disclose any circumstances likely to give rise to doubts as to his independence or impartiality. The same applies once the arbitrator has been chosen. While the UNCITRAL Rules frame this as a general duty vis-à-vis 'those who approach' the prospective arbitrator or the parties,[70] the ICC Rules provide for a formal screening on the basis of declarations of independence submitted by the prospective arbitrator and input from the parties.[71] The Court decides whether to appoint or confirm or replace an arbitrator who has been successfully challenged.[72]

Both sets of rules provide for a very detailed framework for challenging arbitrators if circumstances exist that give rise to doubts as to their impartiality or independence.[73] While the UNCITRAL Rules envisage that this will primarily be discussed among and decided upon by the parties and the challenged arbitrator and will involve the appointing authority in appropriate cases only as a last resort, in ICC proceedings a challenge is immediately to be submitted to the Secretariat and the Court decides on its admissibility and merits.[74]

An arbitrator may have to be replaced upon his death, the acceptance of his resignation or a challenge, or in the event of the impossibility of his performing his functions. The ICC Rules confer significant powers—even of an investigative nature—upon the Court.[75] The UNCITRAL Rules apply the provisions regarding appointments fully to replacements.[76] Under the ICC Rules the Court has discretion to decide whether or not to follow the original procedure.[77]

---

[66] Articles 8(2)–(4), 9(3)–(6), 10(2) ICC Rules.   [67] Article 9(1)–(2) ICC Rules.
[68] Article 6(4) UNCITRAL Rules; Art 9(5) ICC Rules.
[69] Article 7(1) ICC Rules.   [70] Article 9 UNCITRAL Rules.
[71] Article 7(2) ICC Rules. Arbitrators are also required to immediately inform the Secretariat of circumstances arising during the arbitration, Art 7(3).   [72] Article 7(4) ICC Rules.
[73] Articles 10–12 UNCITRAL Rules; Article 11 ICC Rules. Article 11(1) also indicates other potential grounds for challenge.   [74] Article 11 ICC Rules.
[75] Article 12(2), (3) ICC Rules.   [76] Article 12(2) UNCITRAL Rules.
[77] Article 12(4) ICC Rules.

(iii) Arbitral proceedings Provided that the parties are treated with equality and fairly and that at any stage of the proceedings each party is given a full opportunity of presenting his case[78] both sets of rules give the parties and the tribunal much leeway for determining the procedure. Where the parties do not agree, under the UNCITRAL Rules the arbitral tribunal will make the necessary decisions.[79] The ICC Rules leave some procedural issues to the ICC Court.[80]

As to the law or rules of law to be applied by the tribunal to the merits of the dispute, the parties are free to agree upon those rules. In the absence of any such agreement the tribunal applies the law or the rules of law which it determines to be appropriate (ICC) or the law determined by the conflict of laws rules which it considers applicable (UNCITRAL).[81] Only if authorized by the parties may the arbitral tribunal assume the powers of an *amiable compositeur* or decide *ex aequo et bono*.[82]

A distinctive feature of ICC arbitrations is a document ('Terms of Reference') to be drawn up by the arbitral tribunal as soon as it receives the file from the Secretariat. In particular, it includes: a summary of the parties' respective claims and the relief sought, a list of the issues to be determined, the place of the arbitration as well as the particulars of the applicable procedural rules, the names and the contact details of the parties and the members of the tribunal.[83] Signed by the parties and the tribunal, the document is submitted to the Court for approval and constitutes a programme and a 'road map' for the proceedings.[84] Moreover, the tribunal has to communicate a provisional timetable to the Court and the parties.[85]

Both the UNCITRAL Rules and the ICC Rules leave it basically to the arbitral tribunal and the parties how best to establish the facts of the case. Usually a full statement of claim and a full statement of defence state the facts supporting the respective claims, the points at issue, the relief and the remedies sought.[86] Evidence may be submitted in documents, written witness statements and expert reports, or by oral testimony.[87] Of its own motion or at the request of either party the tribunal holds a hearing[88] where the parties, witnesses, and (tribunal appointed)[89] experts appear to give evidence.

---

[78] Article 15(1) UNCITRAL Rules; Art 15(1), (2) ICC Rules.
[79] E.g. regarding the place of arbitration (Art 16), and the language (Art 17).
[80] E.g. to fix the place of the arbitration. (Art 14[1] ICC Rules).
[81] Article 33(1) UNCITRAL Rules; Art 17(1) ICC Rules.
[82] Article 33(2) UNCITRAL Rules (which require also that the law applicable to the procedure consent); Art 17(3) ICC Rules.   [83] Article 18 ICC Rules.
[84] New claims which fall outside its limits have to be authorized by the tribunal, Art 19 ICC Rules. By contrast, Art 20 UNCITRAL Rules envisages amendments to the claim and defence as being the rule.
[85] Article 18(4) ICC Rules. Subsequent modifications are also to be communicated.
[86] Articles 18, 19 UNCITRAL Rules; Art 20 ICC Rules.
[87] Articles 24, 25, 27 UNCITRAL Rules; Art 20 ICC Rules.
[88] Articles 15(2), 25, 27(4) UNCITRAL Rules; Art 20(2)–(5), 21 ICC Rules.
[89] Article 27(1) UNCITRAL Rules, Art 20(4) ICC Rules.

When the arbitral tribunal is satisfied that the parties have had a reasonable opportunity to present their cases it declares the proceedings closed.[90]

Both the UNCITRAL Rules and the ICC Rules provide for conservatory and interim measures.[91]

(iv) Arbitral awards Normally, an award is given by a majority decision.[92] The ICC Rules provide also for an award to be made by the chairman alone if there is no majority.[93] The award is to state the reasons upon which it is based.[94]

ICC arbitrations are charcterized by two additional features. Firstly, there are time limits—fixed by the Rules or the Court—within which the tribunal must render its final award.[95] Secondly, before signing an award, an ICC tribunal must submit it in draft form to the Court. The Court may lay down modifications as to the form and, without affecting the tribunal's liberty of decision, may also draw its attention to points of substance. No award is rendered until the Court has approved it as to its form.[96]

Both sets of rules set forth details regarding notification of the award to the parties, deposit, interpretation, and correction of the award.[97]

The parties undertake to carry out the award without delay.[98]

(v) Costs Both sets of rules contain detailed provisions regarding the costs of the arbitration. The arbitral tribunal fixes the costs of the arbitration and decides which of the parties bears them or in what proportion they are borne by the parties.[99] However, the UNCITRAL Rules state that, in principle, the costs shall be borne by the unsuccessful party.[100]

While, under the UNCITRAL Rules, it is the tribunal which makes decisions regarding advance payments (deposits) for costs,[101] it is the ICC Court which makes the relevant decisions in arbitrations administered by this institution.[102]

---

[90] Article 29 UNCITRAL Rules; Art 22 ICC Rules.
[91] Article 28 UNCITRAL rules; Art 23 ICC Rules.
[92] Article 31(1) UNCITRAL Rules; Art 25(1) ICC Rules.
[93] Article 25(1). The UNCITRAL Rules provide only for the chairman's making decisions on issues of procedure, Art 31(2).
[94] Article 36(3) UNCITRAL Rules; Art 25(3) ICC Rules.
[95] Article 24 ICC Rules.   [96] Article 27 ICC Rules.
[97] Articles 32(6), (7), 35, 36 UNCITRAL Rules; Arts 28, 29 ICC Rules.
[98] Article 32(2) UNCITRAL Rules; Art 28(6) ICC Rules.
[99] Article 38 UNCITRAL Rules; Art 31(3) ICC Rules.
[100] Article 40(1) UNCITRAL Rules.   [101] Article 41 UNCITRAL Rules.
[102] Article 30 ICC Rules.

B. Instruments

(i) CONVENTION ON THE RECOGNITION AND ENFORCEMENT OF FOREIGN ARBITRAL AWARDS*

Article I

1. This Convention shall apply to the recognition and enforcement of arbitral awards made in the territory of a State other than the State where the recognition and enforcement of such awards are sought, and arising out of differences between persons, whether physical or legal. It shall also apply to arbitral awards not considered as domestic awards in the State where their recognition and enforcement are sought.
2. The term 'arbitral awards' shall include not only awards made by arbitrators appointed for each case but also those made by permanent arbitral bodies to which the parties have submitted.
3. When signing, ratifying or acceding to this Convention, or notifying extension under article X hereof, any State may on the basis of reciprocity declare that it will apply the Convention to the recognition and enforcement of awards made only in the territory of another Contracting State. It may also declare that it will apply the Convention only to differences arising out of legal relationships, whether contractual or not, which are considered as commercial under the national law of the State making such declaration.

Article II

1. Each Contracting State shall recognize an agreement in writing under which the parties undertake to submit to arbitration all or any differences which have arisen or which may arise between them in respect of a defined legal relationship, whether contractual or not, concerning a subject matter capable of settlement by arbitration.
2. The term 'agreement in writing' shall include an arbitral clause in a contract or an arbitration agreement, signed by the parties or contained in an exchange of letters or telegrams.
3. The court of a Contracting State, when seized of an action in a matter in respect of which the parties have made an agreement within the meaning of this article, shall, at the request of one of the parties, refer the parties to arbitration, unless it finds that the said agreement is null and void, inoperative or incapable of being performed.

---

* Reproduced with the kind permission of UNCITRAL.

Article III

Each Contracting State shall recognize arbitral awards as binding and enforce them in accordance with the rules of procedure of the territory where the award is relied upon, under the conditions laid down in the following articles. There shall not be imposed substantially more onerous conditions or higher fees or charges on the recognition or enforcement of arbitral awards to which this Convention applies than are imposed on the recognition or enforcement of domestic arbitral awards.

Article IV

1. To obtain the recognition and enforcement mentioned in the preceding article, the party applying for recognition and enforcement shall, at the time of the application, supply:
   (a) The duly authenticated original award or a duly certified copy thereof;
   (b) The original agreement referred to in article II or a duly certified copy thereof.
2. If the said award or agreement is not made in an official language of the country in which the award is relied upon, the party applying for recognition and enforcement of the award shall produce a translation of these documents into such language. The translation shall be certified by an official or sworn translator or by a diplomatic or consular agent.

Article V

1. Recognition and enforcement of the award may be refused, at the request of the party against whom it is invoked, only if that party furnishes to the competent authority where the recognition and enforcement is sought, proof that:
   (a) The parties to the agreement referred to in article II were, under the law applicable to them, under some incapacity, or the said agreement is not valid under the law to which the parties have subjected it or, failing any indication thereon, under the law of the country where the award was made; or
   (b) The party against whom the award is invoked was not given proper notice of the appointment of the arbitrator or of the arbitration proceedings or was otherwise unable to present his case; or
   (c) The award deals with a difference not contemplated by or not falling within the terms of the submission to arbitration, or it contains decisions on matters beyond the scope of the submission to arbitration, provided that, if the decisions on matters submitted to arbitration can be separated from those not so submitted, that part of the award which contains decisions on matters submitted to arbitration may be recognized and enforced; or
   (d) The composition of the arbitral authority or the arbitral procedure was not in accordance with the agreement of the parties, or, failing such agreement, was not in accordance with the law of the country where the arbitration took place; or
   (e) The award has not yet become binding, on the parties, or has been set aside or suspended by a competent authority of the country in which, or under the law of which, that award was made.
2. Recognition and enforcement of an arbitral award may also be refused if the competent authority in the country where recognition and enforcement is sought finds that:
   (a) The subject matter of the difference is not capable of settlement by arbitration under the law of that country; or

(b) The recognition or enforcement of the award would be contrary to the public policy of that country.

Article VI

If an application for the setting, aside or suspension of the award has been made to a competent authority referred to in article V (1) *(e)*, the authority before which the award is sought to be relied upon may, if it considers it proper, adjourn the decision on the enforcement of the award and may also, on the application of the party claiming enforcement of the award, order the other party to give suitable security.

Article VII

1. The provisions of the present Convention shall not affect the validity of multilateral or bilateral agreements concerning the recognition and enforcement of arbitral awards entered into by the Contracting States nor deprive any interested party of any right he may have to avail himself of an arbitral award in the manner and to the extent allowed by the law or the treaties of the country where such award is sought to be relied upon.
2. The Geneva Protocol on Arbitration Clauses of 1923 and the Geneva Convention on the Execution of Foreign Arbitral Awards of 1927 shall cease to have effect between Contracting States on their becoming bound and to the extent that they become bound, by this Convention.

Article VIII

1. This Convention shall be open until 31 December 1958 for signature on behalf of any Member of the United Nations and also on behalf of any other State which is or hereafter becomes a member of any specialized agency of the United Nations, or which is or hereafter becomes a party to the Statute of the International Court of Justice, or any other State to which an invitation has been addressed by the General Assembly of the United Nations.
2. This Convention shall be ratified and the instrument of ratification shall be deposited with the Secretary-General of the United Nations.

Article IX

1. This Convention shall be open for accession to all States referred to in article VIII.
2. Accession shall be effected by the deposit of an instrument of accession with the Secretary-General of the United Nations.

Article X

1. Any State may, at the time of signature, ratification or accession, declare that this Convention shall extend to all or any of the territories for the international relations of which it is responsible. Such a declaration shall take effect when the Convention enters into force for the State concerned.
2. At any time thereafter any such extension shall be made by notification addressed to the Secretary-General of the United Nations and shall take effect as from the ninetieth day after the day of receipt by the Secretary-General of the United Nations of this

notification, or as from the date of entry into force of the Convention for the State concerned, whichever is the later.

3. With respect to those territories to which this Convention is not extended at the time of signature, ratification or accession, each State concerned shall consider the possibility of taking the necessary steps in order to extend the application of this Convention to such territories, subject, where necessary for constitutional reasons, to the consent of the Governments of such territories.

Article XI

In the case of a federal or non-unitary State, the following provisions shall apply:

(a) With respect to those articles of this Convention that come within the legislative jurisdiction of the federal authority, the obligations of the federal Government shall to this extent be the same as those of Contracting States which are not federal States;

(b) With respect to those articles of this Convention that come within the legislative jurisdiction of constituent states or provinces which are not, under the constitutional system of the federation, bound to take legislative action, the federal Government shall bring such articles with a favourable recommendation to the notice of the appropriate authorities of constituent states or provinces at the earliest possible moment;

(c) A federal State Party to this Convention shall, at the request of any other Contracting State transmitted through the Secretary-General of the United Nations, supply a statement of the law and practice of the federation and its constituent units in regard to any particular provision of this Convention, showing the extent to which effect has been given to that provision by legislative or other action.

Article XII

1. This Convention shall come into force on the ninetieth day following the date of deposit of the third instrument of ratification or accession.

2. For each State ratifying or acceding to this Convention after the deposit of the third instrument of ratification or accession, this Convention shall enter into force on the ninetieth day after deposit by such State of its instrument of ratification or accession.

Article XIII

1. Any Contracting State may denounce this Convention by a written notification to the Secretary-General of the United Nations. Denunciation shall take effect one year after the date of receipt of the notification by the Secretary-General.

2. Any State which has made a declaration or notification under article X may, at any time thereafter, by notification to the Secretary-General of the United Nations, declare that this Convention shall cease to extend to the territory concerned one year after the date of the receipt of the notification by the Secretary-General.

3. This Convention shall continue to be applicable to arbitral awards in respect of which recognition or enforcement proceedings have been instituted before the denunciation takes effect.

Article XIV

A Contracting State shall not be entitled to avail itself of the present Convention against other Contracting States except to the extent that it is itself bound to apply the Convention.

Article XV

The Secretary-General of the United Nations shall notify the States contemplated in article VIII of the following:
  (a) Signatures and ratifications in accordance with article VIII;
  (b) Accessions in accordance with article IX;
  (c) Declarations and notifications under articles I, X and XI;
  (d) The date upon which this Convention enters into force in accordance with article XII;
  (e) Denunciations and notifications in accordance with article XIII.

Article XVI

1. This Convention, of which the Chinese, English, French, Russian and Spanish texts shall be equally authentic, shall be deposited in the archives of the United Nations.
2. The Secretary-General of the United Nations shall transmit a certified copy of this Convention to the States contemplated in article VIII.

TABLE OF STATE RATIFICATIONS

Total number of signatures not followed by ratifications: 1
Total number of ratifications/accessions: 134

Entered into force: 7 June 1959
(Condition: 3 ratifications)

State	Signature	Ratification	By	Entry into force
Albania		27 June 2001	Accession	25 September 2001
Algeria		7 February 1989	Accession	8 May 1989
Antigua and Barbuda		2 February 1989	Accession	3 May 1989
Argentina	26 August 1958	14 March 1989		12 June 1989
Armenia		29 December 1997	Accession	29 March 1998
Australia		26 March 1975	Accession	24 June 1975
Austria		2 May 1961	Accession	31 July 1961
Azerbaijan		29 February 2000	Accession	29 May 2000
Bahrain		6 April 1988	Accession	5 July 1988
Bangladesh		6 May 1992	Accession	4 August 1992
Barbados		16 March 1993	Accession	14 June 1993
Belarus	29 December 1958	15 November 1960		13 February 1961
Belgium	10 June 1958	18 August 1975		16 November 1975
Benin		16 May 1974	Accession	14 August 1974
Bolivia		28 April 1995	Accession	27 July 1995
Bosnia and Herzegovina		1 September 1993	Succession	6 March 1992
Botswana		20 December 1971	Accession	19 March 1972
Brazil		7 June 2002	Accession	5 September 2002

State	Signature	Ratification	By	Entry into force
Brunei Darussalam		25 July1996	Accession	23 October 1996
Bulgaria	17 December 1958	10 October 1961		8 January 1962
Burkina Faso		23 March 1987	Accession	21 June 1987
Cambodia		5 January 1960	Accession	4 April 1960
Cameroon		19 February 1988	Accession	19 May 1988
Canada		12 May 1986	Accession	10 August 1986
Central African Republic		15 October 1962	Accession	13 January 1963
Chile		4 September 1975	Accession	3 December 1975
China		22 January 1987	Accession	22 April 1987
Colombia		25 September 1979	Accession	24 December 1979
Costa Rica	10 June 1958	26 October 1987		24 January 1988
Côte d'Ivoire		1 February 1991	Accession	2 May 1991
Croatia		26 July 1993	Succession	8 October 1991
Cuba		30 December 1974	Accession	30 March 1975
Cyprus		29 December 1980	Accession	29 March 1981
Czech Republic		30 September 1993	Succession	1 January 1993
Denmark		22 December 1972	Accession	22 March 1973
Djibouti		14 June 1983	Succession	27 June 1977
Dominica		28 October 1988	Accession	26 January 1989
Dominican Republic		11 April 2002	Accession	10 July 2002
Ecuador	17 December 1958	3 January 1962		3 April 1962
Egypt		9 March 1959	Accession	7 June 1959
El Salvador	10 June 1958	26 February 1998		27 May 1998
Estonia		30 August 1993	Accession	28 November 1993
Finland	29 December 1958	19 January 1962		19 April 1962
France	25 November 1958	26 June 1959		24 September 1959
Georgia		2 June 1994	Accession	31 August 1994
Germany	10 June 1958	30 June 1961		28 September 1961
Ghana		9 April 1968	Accession	8 July 1968
Greece		16 July 1962	Accession	14 October 1962
Guatemala		21 March 1984	Accession	19 June 1984
Guinea		23 January 1991	Accession	23 April 1991
Haiti		5 December 1983	Accession	4 March 1984
Holy See		14 May 1975	Accession	12 August 1975
Honduras		3 October 2000	Accession	1 January 2001
Hungary		5 March 1962	Accession	3 June 1962
Iceland		24 January 2002	Accession	24 April 2002
India	10 June 1958	13 July 1960		11 October 1960
Indonesia		7 October 1981	Accession	5 January 1982
Iran (Islamic Rep of)		15 October 2001	Accession	13 January 2002
Ireland		12 May 1981	Accession	10 August 1981
Israel	10 June 1958	5 January 1959		7 June 1959
Italy		31 January 1969	Accession	1 May 1969
Jamaica		10 July 2002	Accession	8 October 2002
Japan		20 June 1961	Accession	18 September 1961
Jordan	10 June 1958	15 November 1979		13 February 1980
Kazakhstan		20 November 1995	Accession	18 February 1996
Kenya		10 February 1989	Accession	11 May 1989
Kuwait		28 April 1978	Accession	27 July 1978
Kyrgyzstan		18 December 1996	Accession	18 March 1997
Lao People's Democratic Republic		17 June 1998	Accession	15 September 1998

State	Signature	Ratification	By	Entry into force
Latvia		14 April 1992	Accession	13 July 1992
Lebanon		11 August 1998	Accession	9 November 1998
Lesotho		13 June 1989	Accession	11 September 1989
Lithuania		14 March 1995	Accession	12 June 1995
Luxembourg	11 November 1958	9 September 1983		8 December 1983
Madagascar		16 July 1962	Accession	14 October 1962
Malaysia		5 November 1985	Accession	3 February 1986
Mali		8 September 1994	Accession	7 December 1994
Malta		22 June 2000	Accession	20 September 2000
Mauritania		30 January 1997	Accession	30 April 1997
Mauritius		19 June 1996	Accession	17 September 1996
Mexico		14 April 1971	Accession	13 July 1971
Monaco	31 December 1958	2 June 1982		31 August 1982
Mongolia		24 October 1994	Accession	22 January 1995
Morocco		12 February 1959	Accession	7 June 1959
Mozambique		11 June 1998	Accession	9 September 1998
Nepal		4 March 1998	Accession	2 June 1998
Netherlands	10 June 1958	24 April 1964		23 July 1964
New Zealand		6 January 1983	Accession	6 April 1983
Nicaragua		24 September 2003	Accession	23 December 2003
Niger		14 October 1964	Accession	12 January 1965
Nigeria		17 March 1970	Accession	15 June 1970
Norway		14 March 1961	Accession	12 June 1961
Oman		25 February 1999	Accession	26 May 1999
Pakistan	30 December 1958			
Panama		10 October 1984	Accession	8 January 1985
Paraguay		8 October 1997	Accession	6 January 1998
Peru		7 July 1988	Accession	5 October 1988
Philippines	10 June 1958	6 July 1967		4 October 1967
Poland	10 June 1958	3 October 1961		1 January 1962
Portugal		18 October 1994	Accession	16 January 1995
Qatar		30 December 2002	Accession	30 March 2003
Republic of Korea		8 February 1973	Accession	9 May 1973
Republic of Moldova		18 September 1998	Accession	17 December 1998
Romania		13 September 1961	Accession	12 December 1961
Russian Federation	29 December 1958	24 August 1960		22 November 1960
Saint Vincent and the Grenadines		12 September 2000	Accession	11 December 2000
San Marino		17 May 1979	Accession	15 August 1979
Saudi Arabia		19 April 1994	Accession	18 July 1994
Senegal		17 October 1994	Accession	15 January 1995
Serbia and Montenegro		12 March 2001	Succession	27 April 1992
Singapore		21 August 1986	Accession	19 November 1986
Slovakia		28 May 1993	Succession	1 January 1993
Slovenia		6 July 1992	Succession	25 June 1991
South Africa		3 May 1976	Accession	1 August 1976
Spain		12 May 1977	Accession	10 August 1977
Sri Lanka	30 December 1958	9 April 1962		8 July 1962
Sweden	23 December 1958	28 January 1972		27 April 1972
Switzerland	29 December 1958	1 June 1965		30 August 1965
Syrian Arab Republic		9 March 1959	Accession	7 June 1959
Thailand		21 December 1959	Accession	20 March 1960

State	Signature	Ratification	By	Entry into force
The former Yugoslav Republic of Macedonia		10 March 1994	Succession	17 September 1991
Trinidad and Tobago		14 February 1966	Accession	15 May 1966
Tunisia		17 July 1967	Accession	15 October 1967
Turkey		2 July 1992	Accession	30 September 1992
Uganda		12 February 1992	Accession	12 May 1992
Ukraine	29 December 1958	10 October 1960		8 January 1961
United Kingdom of Great Britain and Northern Ireland		24 September 1975	Accession	23 December 1975
United Republic of Tanzania		13 October 1964	Accession	12 January 1965
United States of America		30 September 1970	Accession	29 December 1970
Uruguay		30 March 1983	Accession	28 June 1983
Uzbekistan		7 February 1996	Accession	7 May 1996
Venezuela		8 February 1995	Accession	9 May 1995
Vietnam		12 September 1995	Accession	11 December 1995
Zambia		14 March 2002	Accession	12 June 2002
Zimbabwe		29 September 1994	Accession	28 December 1994

Source: http://www.uncitral.org/en-index.htm

(ii) INTER-AMERICAN CONVENTION ON INTERNATIONAL COMMERCIAL ARBITRATION*

The Governments of the Member States of the Organization of American States desirous of concluding a convention on international commercial arbitration, have agreed as follows:

Article 1

An agreement in which the parties undertake to submit to arbitral decision any differences that may arise or have arisen between them with respect to a commercial transaction is valid. The agreement shall be set forth in an instrument signed by the parties, or in the form of an exchange of letters, telegrams, or telex communications.

Article 2

Arbitrators shall be appointed in the manner agreed upon by the parties. Their appointment may be delegated to a third party, whether a natural or juridical person.

Arbitrators may be nationals or foreigners.

Article 3

In the absence of an express agreement between the parties, the arbitration shall be conducted in accordance with the rules of procedure of the Inter-American Commercial Arbitration Commission.

Article 4

An arbitral decision or award that is not appealable under the applicable law or procedural rules shall have the force of a final judicial judgment. Its execution or recognition may be ordered in the same manner as that of decisions handed down by national or foreign ordinary courts, in accordance with the procedural laws of the country where it is to be executed and the provisions of international treaties.

Article 5

1. The recognition and execution of the decision may be refused, at the request of the party against which it is made, only if such party is able to prove to the competent authority of the State in which recognition and execution are requested:
   a. That the parties to the agreement were subject to some incapacity under the applicable law or that the agreement is not valid under the law to which the parties

---

* Reproduced with the kind permission of the Organization of American States.

have submitted it, or, if such law is not specified, under the law of the State in which the decision was made; or

b. That the party against which the arbitral decision has been made was not duly notified of the appointment of the arbitrator or of the arbitration procedure to be followed, or was unable, for any other reason, to present his defense; or

c. That the decision concerns a dispute not envisaged in the agreement between the parties to submit to arbitration; nevertheless, if the provisions of the decision that refer to issues submitted to arbitration can be separated from those not submitted to arbitration, the former may be recognized and executed; or

d. That the constitution of the arbitral tribunal or the arbitration procedure has not been carried out in accordance with the terms of the agreement signed by the parties or, in the absence of such agreement, that the constitution of the arbitral tribunal or the arbitration procedure has not been carried out in accordance with the law of the State where the arbitration took place; or

e. That the decision is not yet binding on the parties or has been annulled or suspended by a competent authority of the State in which, or according to the law of which, the decision has been made.

2. The recognition and execution of an arbitral decision may also be refused if the competent authority of the State in which the recognition and execution is requested finds:

a. That the subject of the dispute cannot be settled by arbitration under the law of that State; or

b. That the recognition or execution of the decision would be contrary to the public policy ('ordre public') of that State.

Article 6

If the competent authority mentioned in Article 5. 1. e has been requested to annul or suspend the arbitral decision, the authority before which such decision is invoked may, if it deems it appropriate, postpone a decision on the execution of the arbitral decision and, at the request of the party requesting execution, may also instruct the other party to provide appropriate guaranties.

Article 7

This Convention shall be open for signature by the Member States of the Organization of American States.

Article 8

This Convention is subject to ratification. The instruments of ratification shall be deposited with the General Secretariat of the Organization of American States.

Article 9

This Convention shall remain open for accession by any other State. The instruments of accession shall be deposited with the General Secretariat of the Organization of American States.

Article 10

This Convention shall enter into force on the thirtieth day following the date of deposit of the second instrument of ratification.

For each State ratifying or acceding to the Convention after the deposit of the second instrument of ratification, the Convention shall enter into force on the thirtieth day after deposit by such State of its instrument of ratification or accession.

Article 11

If a State Party has two or more territorial units in which different systems of law apply in relation to the matters dealt with in this Convention, it may, at the time of signature, ratification or accession, declare that this Convention shall extend to all its territorial units or only to one or more of them.

Such declaration may be modified by subsequent declarations, which shall expressly indicate the territorial unit or units to which the Convention applies. Such subsequent declarations shall be transmitted to the General Secretariat of the Organization of American States, and shall become effective thirty days after the date of their receipt.

Article 12

This Convention shall remain in force indefinitely, but any of the States Parties may denounce it. The instrument of denunciation shall be deposited with the General Secretariat of the Organization of American States. After one year from the date of deposit of the instrument of denunciation, the Convention shall no longer be in effect for the denouncing State, but shall remain in effect for the other States Parties.

Article 13

The original instrument of this Convention, the English, French, Portuguese and Spanish texts of which are equally authentic, shall be deposited with the General Secretariat of the Organization of American States. The Secretariat shall notify the lumber States of the Organization of American States and the States that have acceded to the Convention of the signatures, deposits of instruments of ratification, accession, and denunciation as well as of reservations, if any. It shall also transmit the declarations referred to in Article 11 of this Convention.

In witness where of the undersigned Plenipotentiaries, being duly authorized thereto by their respective Governments, have signed this Convention.

Done At Panama City, Republic of Panama, this thirtieth day of January one thousand nine hundred and seventy-five.

TABLE OF STATE RATIFICATIONS

Total number of signatures not followed by ratifications: 2
Total number of ratifications/accessions: 17

Entered into force: 16 June 1976
(Condition: 2 ratifications)

State	Signature	Ratification	By	Entry into force
Argentina	15 March 1991	5 January 1995		4 February 1995
Bolivia	2 August 1983	29 April 1999		29 May 1999
Brazil	30 January 1975	27 November 1995		27 December 1995
Chile	30 January 1975	17 May 1976		16 June 1976
Colombia	30 January 1975	29 December 1986		28 January 1987
Costa Rica	30 January 1975	20 January 1978		19 February 1978
Dominican Republic	18 April 1977			30 January 2000
Ecuador	30 January 1975	23 October 1991		22 November 1991
El Salvador	30 January 1975	11 August 1980		10 September 1980
Guatemala	30 January 1975	20 August 1986		19 September 1986
Honduras	30 January 1975	22 March 1979		21 April 1979
Mexico	27 October 1977	27 March 1978		26 April 1978
Nicaragua	30 January 1975			30 January 2000
Panama	30 January 1975	17 December 1975		16 June 1976
Paraguay	26 August 1975	15 December 1976		14 January 1977
Peru	21 April 1988	22 May 1989		21 June 1989
United States	9 June 1978	27 September 1990		27 October 1990
Uruguay	30 January 1975	25 April 1977		25 May 1977
Venezuela	30 January 1975	16 May 1985		15 June 1985

Source: http://www.sice.oas.org/Disputee.asp

(iii) UNCITRAL MODEL LAW ON INTERNATIONAL COMMERCIAL ARBITRATION*

(United Nations document A/40/17, annex I)

(As adopted by the United Nations Commission on International Trade Law on 21 June 1985)

* Reproduced with the kind permission of UNCITRAL.

CHAPTER I
GENERAL PROVISIONS

Article 1
Scope of application[1]

(1) This Law applies to international commercial[2] arbitration, subject to any agreement in force between this State and any other State or States.

(2) The provisions of this Law, except articles 8, 9, 35 and 36, apply only if the place of arbitration is in the territory of this State.

(3) An arbitration is international if:

    (a) the parties to an arbitration agreement have, at the time of the conclusion of that agreement, their places of business in different States; or

    (b) one of the following places is situated outside the State in which the parties have their places of business:

        (i) the place of arbitration if determined in, or pursuant to, the arbitration agreement;

        (ii) any place where a substantial part of the obligations of the commercial relationship is to be performed or the place with which the subject-matter of the dispute is most closely connected; or

    (c) the parties have expressly agreed that the subject-matter of the arbitration agreement relates to more than one country.

(4) For the purposes of paragraph (3) of this article:

    (a) if a party has more than one place of business, the place of business is that which has the closest relationship to the arbitration agreement;

    (b) if a party does not have a place of business, reference is to be made to his habitual residence.

(5) This Law shall not affect any other law of this State by virtue of which certain disputes may not be submitted to arbitration or may be submitted to arbitration only according to provisions other than those of this Law.

Article 2
Definitions and rules of interpretation

For the purposes of this Law:

    (a) 'arbitration' means any arbitration whether or not administered by a permanent arbitral institution;

    (b) 'arbitral tribunal' means a sole arbitrator or a panel of arbitrators;

---

[1] Article headings are for reference purposes only and are not to be used for purposes of interpretation.

[2] The term 'commercial' should be given a wide interpretation so as to cover matters arising from all relationships of a commercial nature, whether contractual or not. Relationships of a commercial nature include, but are not limited to, the following transactions: any trade transaction for the supply or exchange of goods or services; distribution agreement; commercial representation or agency; factoring; leasing; construction of works; consulting; engineering; licensing; investment; financing; banking; insurance; exploitation agreement or concession; joint venture and other forms of industrial or business co-operation; carriage of goods or passengers by air, sea, rail or road.

(c) 'court' means a body or organ of the judicial system of a State;
(d) where a provision of this Law, except article 28, leaves the parties free to determine a certain issue, such freedom includes the right of the parties to authorize a third party, including an institution, to make that determination;
(e) where a provision of this Law refers to the fact that the parties have agreed or that they may agree or in any other way refers to an agreement of the parties, such agreement includes any arbitration rules referred to in that agreement;
(f) where a provision of this Law, other than in articles 25(a) and 32(2)(a), refers to a claim, it also applies to a counter-claim, and where it refers to a defence, it also applies to a defence to such counter-claim.

Article 3
Receipt of written communications

(1) Unless otherwise agreed by the parties:
    (a) any written communication is deemed to have been received if it is delivered to the addressee personally or if it is delivered at his place of business, habitual residence or mailing address; if none of these can be found after making a reasonable inquiry, a written communication is deemed to have been received if it is sent to the addressee's last-known place of business, habitual residence or mailing address by registered letter or any other means which provides a record of the attempt to deliver it;
    (b) the communication is deemed to have been received on the day it is so delivered.
(2) The provisions of this article do not apply to communications in court proceedings.

Article 4
Waiver of right to object

A party who knows that any provision of this Law from which the parties may derogate or any requirement under the arbitration agreement has not been complied with and yet proceeds with the arbitration without stating his objection to such non-compliance without undue delay or, if a time-limit is provided therefore, within such period of time, shall be deemed to have waived his right to object.

Article 5
Extent of court intervention

In matters governed by this Law, no court shall intervene except where so provided in this Law.

Article 6
Court or other authority for certain functions of arbitration assistance and supervision

The functions referred to in articles 11(3), 11(4), 13(3), 14, 16(3) and 34(2) shall be performed by ... [Each State enacting this model law specifies the court, courts or, where referred to therein, other authority competent to perform these functions.]

CHAPTER II
ARBITRATION AGREEMENT

Article 7
Definition and form of arbitration agreement

(1) 'Arbitration agreement' is an agreement by the parties to submit to arbitration all or certain disputes which have arisen or which may arise between them in respect of a defined legal relationship, whether contractual or not. An arbitration agreement may be in the form of an arbitration clause in a contract or in the form of a separate agreement.

(2) The arbitration agreement shall be in writing. An agreement is in writing if it is contained in a document signed by the parties or in an exchange of letters, telex, telegrams or other means of telecommunication which provide a record of the agreement, or in an exchange of statements of claim and defence in which the existence of an agreement is alleged by one party and not denied by another. The reference in a contract to a document containing an arbitration clause constitutes an arbitration agreement provided that the contract is in writing and the reference is such as to make that clause part of the contract.

Article 8
Arbitration agreement and substantive claim before court

(1) A court before which an action is brought in a matter which is the subject of an arbitration agreement shall, if a party so requests not later than when submitting his first statement on the substance of the dispute, refer the parties to arbitration unless it finds that the agreement is null and void, inoperative or incapable of being performed.

(2) Where an action referred to in paragraph (1) of this article has been brought, arbitral proceedings may nevertheless be commenced or continued, and an award may be made, while the issue is pending before the court.

Article 9
Arbitration agreement and interim measures by court

It is not incompatible with an arbitration agreement for a party to request, before or during arbitral proceedings, from a court an interim measure of protection and for a court to grant such measure.

CHAPTER III
COMPOSITION OF ARBITRAL TRIBUNAL

Article 10
Number of arbitrators

(1) The parties are free to determine the number of arbitrators.

(2) Failing such determination, the number of arbitrators shall be three.

Article 11
Appointment of arbitrators

(1) No person shall be precluded by reason of his nationality from acting as an arbitrator, unless otherwise agreed by the parties.

(2) The parties are free to agree on a procedure of appointing the arbitrator or arbitrators, subject to the provisions of paragraphs (4) and (5) of this article.

(3) Failing such agreement,

    (a) in an arbitration with three arbitrators, each party shall appoint one arbitrator, and the two arbitrators thus appointed shall appoint the third arbitrator; if a party fails to appoint the arbitrator within thirty days of receipt of a request to do so from the other party, or if the two arbitrators fail to agree on the third arbitrator within thirty days of their appointment, the appointment shall be made, upon request of a party, by the court or other authority specified in article 6;

    (b) in an arbitration with a sole arbitrator, if the parties are unable to agree on the arbitrator, he shall be appointed, upon request of a party, by the court or other authority specified in article 6.

(4) Where, under an appointment procedure agreed upon by the parties,

    (a) a party fails to act as required under such procedure, or

    (b) the parties, or two arbitrators, are unable to reach an agreement expected of them under such procedure, or

    (c) a third party, including an institution, fails to perform any function entrusted to it under such procedure,

any party may request the court or other authority specified in article 6 to take the necessary measure, unless the agreement on the appointment procedure provides other means for securing the appointment.

(5) A decision on a matter entrusted by paragraph (3) or (4) of this article to the court or other authority specified in article 6 shall be subject to no appeal. The court or other authority, in appointing an arbitrator, shall have due regard to any qualifications required of the arbitrator by the agreement of the parties and to such considerations as are likely to secure the appointment of an independent and impartial arbitrator and, in the case of a sole or third arbitrator, shall take into account as well the advisability of appointing an arbitrator of a nationality other than those of the parties.

Article 12
Grounds for challenge

(1) When a person is approached in connection with his possible appointment as an arbitrator, he shall disclose any circumstances likely to give rise to justifiable doubts as to his impartiality or independence. An arbitrator, from the time of his appointment and throughout the arbitral proceedings, shall without delay disclose any such circumstances to the parties unless they have already been informed of them by him.

(2) An arbitrator may be challenged only if circumstances exist that give rise to justifiable doubts as to his impartiality or independence, or if he does not possess qualifications agreed to by the parties. A party may challenge an arbitrator appointed by him, or in whose appointment he has participated, only for reasons of which he becomes aware after the appointment has been made.

Article 13
Challenge procedure

(1) The parties are free to agree on a procedure for challenging an arbitrator, subject to the provisions of paragraph (3) of this article.

(2) Failing such agreement, a party who intends to challenge an arbitrator shall, within fifteen days after becoming aware of the constitution of the arbitral tribunal or after becoming aware of any circumstance referred to in article 12(2), send a written statement of the reasons for the challenge to the arbitral tribunal. Unless the challenged arbitrator withdraws from his office or the other party agrees to the challenge, the arbitral tribunal shall decide on the challenge.

(3) If a challenge under any procedure agreed upon by the parties or under the procedure of paragraph (2) of this article is not successful, the challenging party may request, within thirty days after having received notice of the decision rejecting the challenge, the court or other authority specified in article 6 to decide on the challenge, which decision shall be subject to no appeal; while such a request is pending, the arbitral tribunal, including the challenged arbitrator, may continue the arbitral proceedings and make an award.

Article 14
Failure or impossibility to act

(1) If an arbitrator becomes *de jure* or *de facto* unable to perform his functions or for other reasons fails to act without undue delay, his mandate terminates if he withdraws from his office or if the parties agree on the termination. Otherwise, if a controversy remains concerning any of these grounds, any party may request the court or other authority specified in article 6 to decide on the termination of the mandate, which decision shall be subject to no appeal.

(2) If, under this article or article 13(2), an arbitrator withdraws from his office or a party agrees to the termination of the mandate of an arbitrator, this does not imply acceptance of the validity of any ground referred to in this article or article 12(2).

Article 15
Appointment of substitute arbitrator

Where the mandate of an arbitrator terminates under article 13 or 14 or because of his withdrawal from office for any other reason or because of the revocation of his mandate by agreement of the parties or in any other case of termination of his mandate, a substitute arbitrator shall be appointed according to the rules that were applicable to the appointment of the arbitrator being replaced.

CHAPTER IV
JURISDICTION OF ARBITRAL TRIBUNAL

Article 16
Competence of arbitral tribunal to rule on its jurisdiction

(1) The arbitral tribunal may rule on its own jurisdiction, including any objections with respect to the existence or validity of the arbitration agreement. For that purpose, an

arbitration clause which forms part of a contract shall be treated as an agreement independent of the other terms of the contract. A decision by the arbitral tribunal that the contract is null and void shall not entail *ipso jure* the invalidity of the arbitration clause.

(2) A plea that the arbitral tribunal does not have jurisdiction shall be raised not later than the submission of the statement of defence. A party is not precluded from raising such a plea by the fact that he has appointed, or participated in the appointment of, an arbitrator. A plea that the arbitral tribunal is exceeding the scope of its authority shall be raised as soon as the matter alleged to be beyond the scope of its authority is raised during the arbitral proceedings. The arbitral tribunal may, in either case, admit a later plea if it considers the delay justified.

(3) The arbitral tribunal may rule on a plea referred to in paragraph (2) of this article either as a preliminary question or in an award on the merits. If the arbitral tribunal rules as a preliminary question that it has jurisdiction, any party may request, within thirty days after having received notice of that ruling, the court specified in article 6 to decide the matter, which decision shall be subject to no appeal; while such a request is pending, the arbitral tribunal may continue the arbitral proceedings and make an award.

Article 17
Power of arbitral tribunal to order interim measures

Unless otherwise agreed by the parties, the arbitral tribunal may, at the request of a party, order any party to take such interim measure of protection as the arbitral tribunal may consider necessary in respect of the subject-matter of the dispute. The arbitral tribunal may require any party to provide appropriate security in connection with such measure.

CHAPTER V
CONDUCT OF ARBITRAL PROCEEDINGS

Article 18
Equal treatment of parties

The parties shall be treated with equality and each party shall be given a full opportunity of presenting his case.

Article 19
Determination of rules of procedure

(1) Subject to the provisions of this Law, the parties are free to agree on the procedure to be followed by the arbitral tribunal in conducting the proceedings.

(2) Failing such agreement, the arbitral tribunal may, subject to the provisions of this Law, conduct the arbitration in such manner as it considers appropriate. The power conferred upon the arbitral tribunal includes the power to determine the admissibility, relevance, materiality and weight of any evidence.

Article 20
Place of arbitration

(1) The parties are free to agree on the place of arbitration. Failing such agreement, the place of arbitration shall be determined by the arbitral tribunal having regard to the circumstances of the case, including the convenience of the parties.

(2) Notwithstanding the provisions of paragraph (1) of this article, the arbitral tribunal may, unless otherwise agreed by the parties, meet at any place it considers appropriate for consultation among its members, for hearing witnesses, experts or the parties, or for inspection of goods, other property or documents.

Article 21
Commencement of arbitral proceedings

Unless otherwise agreed by the parties, the arbitral proceedings in respect of a particular dispute commence on the date on which a request for that dispute to be referred to arbitration is received by the respondent.

Article 22
Language

(1) The parties are free to agree on the language or languages to be used in the arbitral proceedings. Failing such agreement, the arbitral tribunal shall determine the language or languages to be used in the proceedings. This agreement or determination, unless otherwise specified therein, shall apply to any written statement by a party, any hearing and any award, decision or other communication by the arbitral tribunal.

(2) The arbitral tribunal may order that any documentary evidence shall be accompanied by a translation into the language or languages agreed upon by the parties or determined by the arbitral tribunal.

Article 23
Statements of claim and defence

(1) Within the period of time agreed by the parties or determined by the arbitral tribunal, the claimant shall state the facts supporting his claim, the points at issue and the relief or remedy sought, and the respondent shall state his defence in respect of these particulars, unless the parties have otherwise agreed as to the required elements of such statements. The parties may submit with their statements all documents they consider to be relevant or may add a reference to the documents or other evidence they will submit.

(2) Unless otherwise agreed by the parties, either party may amend or supplement his claim or defence during the course of the arbitral proceedings, unless the arbitral tribunal considers it inappropriate to allow such amendment having regard to the delay in making it.

Article 24
Hearings and written proceedings

(1) Subject to any contrary agreement by the parties, the arbitral tribunal shall decide whether to hold oral hearings for the presentation of evidence or for oral argument, or whether the proceedings shall be conducted on the basis of documents and other materials. However, unless the parties have agreed that no hearings shall be held, the arbitral tribunal shall hold such hearings at an appropriate stage of the proceedings, if so requested by a party.

(2) The parties shall be given sufficient advance notice of any hearing and of any meeting of the arbitral tribunal for the purposes of inspection of goods, other property or documents.

(3) All statements, documents or other information supplied to the arbitral tribunal by one party shall be communicated to the other party. Also any expert report or evidentiary document on which the arbitral tribunal may rely in making its decision shall be communicated to the parties.

Article 25
Default of a party

Unless otherwise agreed by the parties, if, without showing sufficient cause,

(a) the claimant fails to communicate his statement of claim in accordance with article 23(1), the arbitral tribunal shall terminate the proceedings;

(b) the respondent fails to communicate his statement of defence in accordance with article 23(1), the arbitral tribunal shall continue the proceedings without treating such failure in itself as an admission of the claimant's allegations;

(c) any party fails to appear at a hearing or to produce documentary evidence, the arbitral tribunal may continue the proceedings and make the award on the evidence before it.

Article 26
Expert appointed by arbitral tribunal

(1) Unless otherwise agreed by the parties, the arbitral tribunal

(a) may appoint one or more experts to report to it on specific issues to be determined by the arbitral tribunal;

(b) may require a party to give the expert any relevant information or to produce, or to provide access to, any relevant documents, goods or other property for his inspection.

(2) Unless otherwise agreed by the parties, if a party so requests or if the arbitral tribunal considers it necessary, the expert shall, after delivery of his written or oral report, participate in a hearing where the parties have the opportunity to put questions to him and to present expert witnesses in order to testify on the points at issue.

Article 27
Court assistance in taking evidence

The arbitral tribunal or a party with the approval of the arbitral tribunal may request from a competent court of this State assistance in taking evidence. The court may execute the request within its competence and according to its rules on taking evidence.

CHAPTER VI
MAKING OF AWARD AND TERMINATION OF PROCEEDINGS

Article 28
Rules applicable to substance of dispute

(1) The arbitral tribunal shall decide the dispute in accordance with such rules of law as are chosen by the parties as applicable to the substance of the dispute. Any

designation of the law or legal system of a given State shall be construed, unless otherwise expressed, as directly referring to the substantive law of that State and not to its conflict of laws rules.

(2) Failing any designation by the parties, the arbitral tribunal shall apply the law determined by the conflict of laws rules which it considers applicable.

(3) The arbitral tribunal shall decide *ex aequo et bono* or as *amiable compositeur* only if the parties have expressly authorized it to do so.

(4) In all cases, the arbitral tribunal shall decide in accordance with the terms of the contract and shall take into account the usages of the trade applicable to the transaction.

Article 29
Decision making by panel of arbitrators

In arbitral proceedings with more than one arbitrator, any decision of the arbitral tribunal shall be made, unless otherwise agreed by the parties, by a majority of all its members. However, questions of procedure may be decided by a presiding arbitrator, if so authorized by the parties or all members of the arbitral tribunal.

Article 30
Settlement

(1) If, during arbitral proceedings, the parties settle the dispute, the arbitral tribunal shall terminate the proceedings and, if requested by the parties and not objected to by the arbitral tribunal, record the settlement in the form of an arbitral award on agreed terms.

(2) An award on agreed terms shall be made in accordance with the provisions of article 31 and shall state that it is an award. Such an award has the same status and effect as any other award on the merits of the case.

Article 31
Form and contents of award

(1) The award shall be made in writing and shall be signed by the arbitrator or arbitrators. In arbitral proceedings with more than one arbitrator, the signatures of the majority of all members of the arbitral tribunal shall suffice, provided that the reason for any omitted signature is stated.

(2) The award shall state the reasons upon which it is based, unless the parties have agreed that no reasons are to be given or the award is an award on agreed terms under article 30.

(3) The award shall state its date and the place of arbitration as determined in accordance with article 20(1). The award shall be deemed to have been made at that place.

(4) After the award is made, a copy signed by the arbitrators in accordance with paragraph (1) of this article shall be delivered to each party.

Article 32
Termination of proceedings

(1) The arbitral proceedings are terminated by the final award or by an order of the arbitral tribunal in accordance with paragraph (2) of this article.

(2) The arbitral tribunal shall issue an order for the termination of the arbitral proceedings when:

   (a) the claimant withdraws his claim, unless the respondent objects thereto and the arbitral tribunal recognizes a legitimate interest on his part in obtaining a final settlement of the dispute;

   (b) the parties agree on the termination of the proceedings;

   (c) the arbitral tribunal finds that the continuation of the proceedings has for any other reason become unnecessary or impossible.

(3) The mandate of the arbitral tribunal terminates with the termination of the arbitral proceedings, subject to the provisions of articles 33 and 34(4).

Article 33
Correction and interpretation of award; additional award

(1) Within thirty days of receipt of the award, unless another period of time has been agreed upon by the parties:

   (a) a party, with notice to the other party, may request the arbitral tribunal to correct in the award any errors in computation, any clerical or typographical errors or any errors of similar nature;

   (b) if so agreed by the parties, a party, with notice to the other party, may request the arbitral tribunal to give an interpretation of a specific point or part of the award.

(2) If the arbitral tribunal considers the request to be justified, it shall make the correction or give the interpretation within thirty days of receipt of the request. The interpretation shall form part of the award.

(3) The arbitral tribunal may correct any error of the type referred to in paragraph (1)(a) of this article on its own initiative within thirty days of the date of the award.

(4) Unless otherwise agreed by the parties, a party, with notice to the other party, may request, within thirty days of receipt of the award, the arbitral tribunal to make an additional award as to claims presented in the arbitral proceedings but omitted from the award. If the arbitral tribunal considers the request to be justified, it shall make the additional award within sixty days.

(5) The arbitral tribunal may extend, if necessary, the period of time within which it shall make a correction, interpretation or an additional award under paragraph (1) or (3) of this article.

(6) The provisions of article 31 shall apply to a correction or interpretation of the award or to an additional award.

CHAPTER VII
RECOURSE AGAINST AWARD

Article 34
Application for setting aside as exclusive recourse against arbitral award

(1) Recourse to a court against an arbitral award may be made only by an application for setting aside in accordance with paragraphs (2) and (3) of this article.

(2) An arbitral award may be set aside by the court specified in article 6 only if:

   (a) the party making the application furnishes proof that:

      (i) a party to the arbitration agreement referred to in article 7 was under some incapacity; or the said agreement is not valid under the law to which the parties have subjected it or, failing any indication thereon, under the law of this State; or

  (ii) the party making the application was not given proper notice of the appointment of an arbitrator or of the arbitral proceedings or was otherwise unable to present his case; or

  (iii) the award deals with a dispute not contemplated by or not falling within the terms of the submission to arbitration, or contains decisions on matters beyond the scope of the submission to arbitration, provided that, if the decisions on matters submitted to arbitration can be separated from those not so submitted, only that part of the award which contains decisions on matters not submitted to arbitration may be set aside; or

  (iv) the composition of the arbitral tribunal or the arbitral procedure was not in accordance with the agreement of the parties, unless such agreement was in conflict with a provision of this Law from which the parties cannot derogate, or, failing such agreement, was not in accordance with this Law; or

(b) the court finds that:

  (i) the subject-matter of the dispute is not capable of settlement by arbitration under the law of this State; or

  (ii) the award is in conflict with the public policy of this State.

(3) An application for setting aside may not be made after three months have elapsed from the date on which the party making that application had received the award or, if a request had been made under article 33, from the date on which that request had been disposed of by the arbitral tribunal.

(4) The court, when asked to set aside an award, may, where appropriate and so requested by a party, suspend the setting aside proceedings for a period of time determined by it in order to give the arbitral tribunal an opportunity to resume the arbitral proceedings or to take such other action as in the arbitral tribunal's opinion will eliminate the grounds for setting aside.

CHAPTER VIII
RECOGNITION AND ENFORCEMENT OF AWARDS

Article 35
Recognition and enforcement

(1) An arbitral award, irrespective of the country in which it was made, shall be recognized as binding and, upon application in writing to the competent court, shall be enforced subject to the provisions of this article and of article 36.

(2) The party relying on an award or applying for its enforcement shall supply the duly authenticated original award or a duly certified copy thereof, and the original arbitration agreement referred to in article 7 or a duly certified copy thereof. If the award or agreement is not made in an official language of this State, the party shall supply a duly certified translation thereof into such language.[3]

---

[3] The conditions set forth in this paragraph are intended to set maximum standards. It would, thus, not be contrary to the harmonization to be achieved by the model law if a State retained even less onerous conditions.

Article 36
Grounds for refusing recognition or enforcement

(1) Recognition or enforcement of an arbitral award, irrespective of the country in which it was made, may be refused only:

  (a) at the request of the party against whom it is invoked, if that party furnishes to the competent court where recognition or enforcement is sought proof that:

    (i) a party to the arbitration agreement referred to in article 7 was under some incapacity; or the said agreement is not valid under the law to which the parties have subjected it or, failing any indication thereon, under the law of the country where the award was made; or

    (ii) the party against whom the award is invoked was not given proper notice of the appointment of an arbitrator or of the arbitral proceedings or was otherwise unable to present his case; or

    (iii) the award deals with a dispute not contemplated by or not falling within the terms of the submission to arbitration, or it contains decisions on matters beyond the scope of the submission toarbitration, provided that, if the decisions on matters submitted to arbitration can be separated from those not so submitted, that part of the award which contains decisions on matters submitted to arbitration may be recognized and enforced; or

    (iv) the composition of the arbitral tribunal or the arbitral procedure was not in accordance with the agreement of the parties or, failing such agreement, was not in accordance with the law of the country where the arbitration took place; or

    (v) the award has not yet become binding on the parties or has been set aside or suspended by a court of the country in which, or under the law of which, that award was made; or

  (b) if the court finds that:

  (c) the subject-matter of the dispute is not capable of settlement by arbitration under the law of this State; or

  (d) the recognition or enforcement of the award would be contrary to the public policy of this State.

(2) If an application for setting aside or suspension of an award has been made to a court referred to in paragraph (1)(a)(v) of this article, the court where recognition or enforcement is sought may, if it considers it proper, adjourn its decision and may also, on the application of the party claiming recognition or enforcement of the award, order the other party to provide appropriate security.

DERIVATIVE LEGISLATION

Legislation based on the *UNCITRAL Model Law on International Commercial Arbitration* has been enacted in:

Australia	Lithuania
Azerbaijan	Macau Special Administrative Region of China
Bahrain	Madagascar
Bangladesh	
Belarus	Malta

Australia	Lithuania
Bermuda	Mexico
Bulgaria	New Zealand
Canada	Nigeria
Croatia	Oman
Cyprus	Paraguay
Egypt	Peru
Germany	Republic of Korea
Greece	Russian Federation
Guatemala	Singapore
	Spain
Hong Kong Special Administrative Region of China	Sri Lanka
	Thailand
Hungary	Tunisia
India	Ukraine
Iran (Islamic Republic of)	Within the United Kingdom of Great Britain and Northern Ireland: Scotland
Ireland	Within the United States: California, Connecticut, Illinois, Oregon and Texas
Jordan	Zambia
Kenya	Zimbabwe

(iv) UNCITRAL ARBITRATION RULES*

RESOLUTION 31/98 ADOPTED BY THE GENERAL
ASSEMBLY ON 15 DECEMBER 1976

31/98. Arbitration Rules of the United Nations Commission on International Trade Law

The General Assembly, Recognizing the value of arbitration as a method of settling disputes arising in the context of international commercial relations,

Being convinced that the establishment of rules for ad hoc arbitration that are acceptable in countries with different legal, social and economic systems would significantly contribute to the development of harmonious international economic relations,

Bearing in mind that the Arbitration Rules of the United Nations Commission on International Trade Law have been prepared after extensive consultation with arbitral institutions and centres of international commercial arbitration,

---

* Reproduced with the kind permission of UNCITRAL.

Noting that the Arbitration Rules were adopted by the United Nations Commission on International Trade Law at its ninth session[1] after due deliberation,

1. *Recommends* the use of the Arbitration Rules of the United Nations Commission on International Trade Law in the settlement of disputes arising in the context of international commercial relations, particularly by reference to the Arbitration Rules in commercial contracts;
2. *Requests* the Secretary-General to arrange for the widest possible distribution of the Arbitration Rules.

SECTION I
INTRODUCTORY RULES

Scope of Application
Article 1

1. Where the parties to a contract have agreed in writing[2] that disputes in relation to that contract shall be referred to arbitration under the UNCITRAL Arbitration Rules, then such disputes shall be settled in accordance with these Rules subject to such modification as the parties may agree in writing.
2. These Rules shall govern the arbitration except that where any of these Rules is in conflict with a provision of the law applicable to the arbitration from which the parties cannot derogate, that provision shall prevail.

Notice, Calculation of Periods of Time
Article 2

1. For the purposes of these Rules, any notice, including a notification, communication or proposal, is deemed to have been received if it is physically delivered to the addressee or if it is delivered at his habitual residence, place of business or mailing address, or, if none of these can be found after making reasonable inquiry, then at the addressee's last-known residence or place of business. Notice shall be deemed to have been received on the day it is so delivered.
2. For the purposes of calculating a period of time under these Rules, such period shall begin to run on the day following the day when a notice, notification, communication or proposal is received. If the last day of such period is an official holiday or a non-business day at the residence or place of business of the addressee, the period is extended until the first business day which follows. Official holidays or non-business days occurring during the running of the period of time are included in calculating the period.

---

[1] *Official Records of the General Assembly, Thirty-first Session, Supplement No. 17* (A31/17), chap. V, sect. V.

[2] *MODEL ARBITRATION CLAUSE*

Any dispute, controversy or claim arising out of or relating to this contract, or the breach, termination or invalidity thereof, shall be settled by arbitration in accordance with the UNCITRAL Arbitration Rules as at present in force.

Note—Parties may wish to consider adding:
(a) The appointing authority shall be ... (name of institution or person);
(b) The number of arbitrators shall be ... (one or three);
(c) The place of arbitration shall be ... (town or country);
(d) The language(s) to be used in the arbitral proceedings shall be ...

Notice of Arbitration
Article 3

1. The party initiating recourse to arbitration (hereinafter called the 'claimant') shall give to the other party (hereinafter called the 'respondent') a notice of arbitration.
2. Arbitral proceedings shall be deemed to commence on the date on which the notice of arbitration is received by the respondent.
3. The notice of arbitration shall include the following:
   (a) A demand that the dispute be referred to arbitration;
   (b) The names and addresses of the parties;
   (c) A reference to the arbitration clause or the separate arbitration agreement that is invoked;
   (d) A reference to the contract out of or in relation to which the dispute arises;
   (e) The general nature of the claim and an indication of the amount involved, if any;
   (f) The relief or remedy sought;
   (g) A proposal as to the number of arbitrators (i.e. one or three), if the parties have not previously agreed thereon.
4. The notice of arbitration may also include:
   (a) The proposals for the appointments of a sole arbitrator and an appointing authority referred to in article 6, paragraph 1;
   (b) The notification of the appointment of an arbitrator referred to in article 7;
   (c) The statement of claim referred to in article 18.

Representation and Assistance
Article 4

The parties may be represented or assisted by persons of their choice. The names and addresses of such persons must be communicated in writing to the other party; such communication must specify whether the appointment is being made for purposes of representation or assistance.

SECTION II

COMPOSITION OF THE ARBITRAL TRIBUNAL

Numbers of Arbitrators
Article 5

If the parties have not previously agreed on the number of arbitrators (i.e. one or three), and if within fifteen days after the receipt by the respondent of the notice of arbitration the parties have not agreed that there shall be only one arbitrator, three arbitrators shall be appointed.

Appointment of Arbitrators (Articles 6 to 8)
Article 6

1. If a sole arbitrator is to be appointed, either party may propose to the other:
   (a) The names of one or more persons, one of whom would serve as the sole arbitrator; and

(b) If no appointing authority has been agreed upon by the parties, the name or names of one or more institutions or persons, one of whom would serve as appointing authority.

2. If within thirty days after receipt by a party of a proposal made in accordance with paragraph 1 the parties have not reached agreement on the choice of a sole arbitrator, the sole arbitrator shall be appointed by the appointing authority agreed upon by the parties. If no appointing authority has been agreed upon by the parties, or if the appointing authority agreed upon refuses to act or fails to appoint the arbitrator within sixty days of the receipt of a party's request therefor, either party may request the Secretary-General of the Permanent Court of Arbitration at The Hague to designate an appointing authority.

3. The appointing authority shall, at the request of one of the parties, appoint the sole arbitrator as promptly as possible. In making the appointment the appointing authority shall use the following list-procedure, unless both parties agree that the list-procedure should not be used or unless the appointing authority determines in its discretion that the use of the list-procedure is not appropriate for the case:

   (a) At the request of one of the parties the appointing authority shall communicate to both parties an identical list containing at least three names;

   (b) Within fifteen days after the receipt of this list, each party may return the list to the appointing authority after having deleted the name or names to which he objects and numbered the remaining names on the list in the order of his preference;

   (c) After the expiration of the above period of time the appointing authority shall appoint the sole arbitrator from among the names approved on the lists returned to it and in accordance with the order of preference indicated by the parties;

   (d) If for any reason the appointment cannot be made according to this procedure, the appointing authority may exercise its discretion in appointing the sole arbitrator.

4. In making the appointment, the appointing authority shall have regard to such considerations as are likely to secure the appointment of an independent and impartial arbitrator and shall take into account as well the advisability of appointing an arbitrator of a nationality other than the nationalities of the parties.

Article 7

1. If three arbitrators are to be appointed, each party shall appoint one arbitrator. The two arbitrators thus appointed shall choose the third arbitrator who will act as the presiding arbitrator of the tribunal.

2. If within thirty days after the receipt of a party's notification of the appointment of an arbitrator the other party has not notified the first party of the arbitrator he has appointed:

   (a) The first party may request the appointing authority previously designated by the parties to appoint the second arbitrator; or

   (b) If no such authority has been previously designated by the parties, or if the appointing authority previously designated refuses to act or fails to appoint the arbitrator within thirty days after receipt of a party's request therefor, the first party may request the Secretary-General of the Permanent Court of Arbitration at The Hague to designate the appointing authority. The first party may then request the appointing authority so designated to appoint the second arbitrator.

In either case, the appointing authority may exercise its discretion in appointing the arbitrator.

3. If within thirty days after the appointment of the second arbitrator the two arbitrators have not agreed on the choice of the presiding arbitrator, the presiding arbitrator shall be appointed by an appointing authority in the same way as a sole arbitrator would be appointed under article 6.

Article 8

1. When an appointing authority is requested to appoint an arbitrator pursuant to article 6 or article 7, the party which makes the request shall send to the appointing authority a copy of the notice of arbitration, a copy of the contract out of or in relation to which the dispute has arisen and a copy of the arbitration agreement if it is not contained in the contract. The appointing authority may require from either party such information as it deems necessary to fulfil its function.

2. Where the names of one or more persons are proposed for appointment as arbitrators, their full names, addresses and nationalities shall be indicated, together with a description of their qualifications.

Challenge of Arbitrators (Articles 9 to 12)
Article 9

A prospective arbitrator shall disclose to those who approach him in connexion with his possible appointment any circumstances likely to give rise to justifiable doubts as to his impartiality or independence. An arbitrator, once appointed or chosen, shall disclose such circumstances to the parties unless they have already been informed by him of these circumstances.

Article 10

1. Any arbitrator may be challenged if circumstances exist that give rise to justifiable doubts as to the arbitrator's impartiality or independence.

2. A party may challenge the arbitrator appointed by him only for reasons of which he becomes aware after the appointment has been made.

Article 11

1. A party who intends to challenge an arbitrator shall send notice of his challenge within fifteen days after the appointment of the challenged arbitrator has been notified to the challenging party or within fifteen days after the circumstances mentioned in articles 9 and 10 became known to that party.

2. The challenge shall be notified to the other party, to the arbitrator who is challenged and to the other members of the arbitral tribunal. The notification shall be in writing and shall state the reasons for the challenge.

3. When an arbitrator has been challenged by one party, the other party may agree to the challenge. The arbitrator may also, after the challenge, withdraw from his office. In

neither case does this imply acceptance of the validity of the grounds for the challenge. In both cases the procedure provided in article 6 or 7 shall be used in full for the appointment of the substitute arbitrator, even if during the process of appointing the challenged arbitrator a party had failed to exercise his right to appoint or to participate in the appointment.

Article 12

1. If the other party does not agree to the challenge and the challenged arbitrator does not withdraw, the decision on the challenge will be made:
   (a) When the initial appointment was made by an appointing authority, by that authority;
   (b) When the initial appointment was not made by an appointing authority, but an appointing authority has been previously designated, by that authority;
   (c) In all other cases, by the appointing authority to be designated in accordance with the procedure for designating an appointing authority as provided for in article 6.
2. If the appointing authority sustains the challenge, a substitute arbitrator shall be appointed or chosen pursuant to the procedure applicable to the appointment or choice of an arbitrator as provided in articles 6 to 9 except that, when this procedure would call for the designation of an appointing authority, the appointment of the arbitrator shall be made by the appointing authority which decided on the challenge.

Replacement of an Arbitrator
Article 13

1. In the event of the death or resignation of an arbitrator during the course of the arbitral proceedings, a substitute arbitrator shall be appointed or chosen pursuant to the procedure provided for in articles 6 to 9 that was applicable to the appointment or choice of the arbitrator being replaced.
2. In the event that an arbitrator fails to act or in the event of the *de jure* or *de facto* impossibility of his performing his functions, the procedure in respect of the challenge and replacement of an arbitrator as provided in the preceding articles shall apply.

Repetition of Hearings in the Event of the Replacement of an Arbitrator

Article 14

If under articles 11 to 13 the sole or presiding arbitrator is replaced, any hearings held previously shall be repeated; if any other arbitrator is replaced, such prior hearings may be repeated at the discretion of the arbitral tribunal.

SECTION III
ARBITRAL PROCEEDINGS

General Provisions
Article 15

1. Subject to these Rules, the arbitral tribunal may conduct the arbitration in such manner as it considers appropriate, provided that the parties are treated with equality

and that at any stage of the proceedings each party is given a full opportunity of presenting his case.

2. If either party so requests at any stage of the proceedings, the arbitral tribunal shall hold hearings for the presentation of evidence by witnesses, including expert witnesses, or for oral argument. In the absence of such a request, the arbitral tribunal shall decide whether to hold such hearings or whether the proceedings shall be conducted on the basis of documents and other materials.

3. All documents or information supplied to the arbitral tribunal by one party shall at the same time be communicated by that party to the other party.

Place of Arbitration
Article 16

1. Unless the parties have agreed upon the place where the arbitration is to be held, such place shall be determined by the arbitral tribunal, having regard to the circumstances of the arbitration.

2. The arbitral tribunal may determine the locale of the arbitration within the country agreed upon by the parties. It may hear witnesses and hold meetings for consultation among its members at any place it deems appropriate, having regard to the circumstances of the arbitration.

3. The arbitral tribunal may meet at any place it deems appropriate for the inspection of goods, other property or documents. The parties shall be given sufficient notice to enable them to be present at such inspection.

4. The award shall be made at the place of arbitration.

Language
Article 17

1. Subject to an agreement by the parties, the arbitral tribunal shall, promptly after its appointment, determine the language or languages to be used in the proceedings. This determination shall apply to the statement of claim, the statement of defence, and any further written statements and, if oral hearings take place, to the language or languages to be used in such hearings.

2. The arbitral tribunal may order that any documents annexed to the statement of claim or statement of defence, and any supplementary documents or exhibits submitted in the course of the proceedings, delivered in their original language, shall be accompanied by a translation into the language or languages agreed upon by the parties or determined by the arbitral tribunal.

Statement of Claim
Article 18

1. Unless the statement of claim was contained in the notice of arbitration, within a period of time to be determined by the arbitral tribunal, the claimant shall communicate his statement of claim in writing to the respondent and to each of the arbitrators. A copy of the contract, and of the arbitration agreement if not contained in the contract, shall be annexed thereto.

2. The statement of claim shall include the following particulars:
   (a) The names and addresses of the parties;
   (b) A statement of the facts supporting the claim;
   (c) The points at issue;
   (d) The relief or remedy sought.
3. The claimant may annex to his statement of claim all documents he deems relevant or may add a reference to the documents or other evidence he will submit.

Statement of Defence
Article 19

1. Within a period of time to be determined by the arbitral tribunal, the respondent shall communicate his statement of defence in writing to the claimant and to each of the arbitrators.
2. The statement of defence shall reply to the particulars *(b)*, *(c)* and *(d)* of the statement of claim (article 18, para. 2). The respondent may annex to his statement the documents on which he relies for his defence or may add a reference to the documents or other evidence he will submit.
3. In his statement of defence, or at a later stage in the arbitral proceedings if the arbitral tribunal decides that the delay was justified under the circumstances, the respondent may make a counter-claim arising out of the same contract or rely on a claim arising out of the same contract for the purpose of a set-off.
4. The provisions of article 18, paragraph 2, shall apply to a counter-claim and a claim relied on for the purpose of a set-off.

Amendments to the Claim or Defence
Article 20

During the course of the arbitral proceedings either party may amend or supplement his claim or defence unless the arbitral tribunal considers it inappropriate to allow such amendment having regard to the delay in making it or prejudice to the other party or any other circumstances. However, a claim may not be amended in such a manner that the amended claim falls outside the scope of the arbitration clause or separate arbitration agreement.

Pleas as to the Jurisdiction of the Arbitral Tribunal
Article 21

1. The arbitral tribunal shall have the power to rule on objections that it has no jurisdiction, including any objections with respect to the existence or validity of the arbitration clause or of the separate arbitration agreement.
2. The arbitral tribunal shall have the power to determine the existence or the validity of the contract of which an arbitration clause forms a part. For the purposes of article 21, an arbitration clause which forms part of a contract and which provides for arbitration under these Rules shall be treated as an agreement independent of the other terms of the contract. A decision by the arbitral tribunal that the contract is null and void shall not entail *ipso jure* the invalidity of the arbitration clause.

3. A plea that the arbitral tribunal does not have jurisdiction shall be raised not later than in the statement of defence or, with respect to a counter-claim, in the reply to the counter-claim.

4. In general, the arbitral tribunal should rule on a plea concerning its jurisdiction as a preliminary question. However, the arbitral tribunal may proceed with the arbitration and rule on such a plea in their final award.

Further Written Statements
Article 22

The arbitral tribunal shall decide which further written statements, in addition to the statement of claim and the statement of defence, shall be required from the parties or may be presented by them and shall fix the periods of time for communicating such statements.

Periods of Time
Article 23

The periods of time fixed by the arbitral tribunal for the communication of written statements (including the statement of claim and statement of defence) should not exceed forty-five days. However, the arbitral tribunal may extend the time-limits if it concludes that an extension is justified.

Evidence and Hearings (Articles 24 and 25)
Article 24

1. Each party shall have the burden of proving the facts relied on to support his claim or defence.

2. The arbitral tribunal may, if it considers it appropriate, require a party to deliver to the tribunal and to the other party, within such a period of time as the arbitral tribunal shall decide, a summary of the documents and other evidence which that party intends to present in support of the facts in issue set out in his statement of claim or statement of defence.

3. At any time during the arbitral proceedings the arbitral tribunal may require the parties to produce documents, exhibits or other evidence within such a period of time as the tribunal shall determine.

Article 25

1. In the event of an oral hearing, the arbitral tribunal shall give the parties adequate advance notice of the date, time and place thereof.

2. If witnesses are to be heard, at least fifteen days before the hearing each party shall communicate to the arbitral tribunal and to the other party the names and addresses of the witnesses he intends to present, the subject upon and the languages in which such witnesses will give their testimony.

3. The arbitral tribunal shall make arrangements for the translation of oral statements made at a hearing and for a record of the hearing if either is deemed necessary by the tribunal under the circumstances of the case, or if the parties have agreed thereto and have communicated such agreement to the tribunal at least fifteen days before the hearing.

4. Hearings shall be held *in camera* unless the parties agree otherwise. The arbitral tribunal may require the retirement of any witness or witnesses during the testimony of other witnesses. The arbitral tribunal is free to determine the manner in which witnesses are examined.

5. Evidence of witnesses may also be presented in the form of written statements signed by them.

6. The arbitral tribunal shall determine the admissibility, relevance, materiality and weight of the evidence offered.

Interim Measures of Protection
Article 26

1. At the request of either party, the arbitral tribunal may take any interim measures it deems necessary in respect of the subject-matter of the dispute, including measures for the conservation of the goods forming the subject-matter in dispute, such as ordering their deposit with a third person or the sale of perishable goods.

2. Such interim measures may be established in the form of an interim award. The arbitral tribunal shall be entitled to require security for the costs of such measures.

3. A request for interim measures addressed by any party to a judicial authority shall not be deemed incompatible with the agreement to arbitrate, or as a waiver of that agreement.

Experts
Article 27

1. The arbitral tribunal may appoint one or more experts to report to it, in writing, on specific issues to be determined by the tribunal. A copy of the expert's terms of reference, established by the arbitral tribunal, shall be communicated to the parties.

2. The parties shall give the expert any relevant information or produce for his inspection any relevant documents or goods that he may require of them. Any dispute between a party and such expert as to the relevance of the required information or production shall be referred to the arbitral tribunal for decision.

3. Upon receipt of the expert's report, the arbitral tribunal shall communicate a copy of the report to the parties who shall be given the opportunity to express, in writing, their opinion on the report. A party shall be entitled to examine any document on which the expert has relied in his report.

4. At the request of either party the expert, after delivery of the report, may be heard at a hearing where the parties shall have the opportunity to be present and to interrogate the expert. At this hearing either party may present expert witnesses in order to testify on the points at issue. The provisions of article 25 shall be applicable to such proceedings.

Default
Article 28

1. If, within the period of time fixed by the arbitral tribunal, the claimant has failed to communicate his claim without showing sufficient cause for such failure, the arbitral tribunal shall issue an order for the termination of the arbitral proceedings. If, within

the period of time fixed by the arbitral tribunal, the respondent has failed to communicate his statement of defence without showing sufficient cause for such failure, the arbitral tribunal shall order that the proceedings continue.

2. If one of the parties, duly notified under these Rules, fails to appear at a hearing, without showing sufficient cause for such failure, the arbitral tribunal may proceed with the arbitration.

3. If one of the parties, duly invited to produce documentary evidence, fails to do so within the established period of time, without showing sufficient cause for such failure, the arbitral tribunal may make the award on the evidence before it.

Closure of Hearings
Article 29

1. The arbitral tribunal may inquire of the parties if they have any further proof to offer or witnesses to be heard or submissions to make and, if there are none, it may declare the hearings closed.

2. The arbitral tribunal may, if it considers it necessary owing to exceptional circumstances, decide, on its own motion or upon application of a party, to reopen the hearings at any time before the award is made.

Waiver of Rules
Article 30

A party who knows that any provision of, or requirement under, these Rules has not been complied with and yet proceeds with the arbitration without promptly stating his objection to such non-compliance, shall be deemed to have waived his right to object.

SECTION IV

THE AWARD

Decisions
Article 31

1. When there are three arbitrators, any award or other decision of the arbitral tribunal shall be made by a majority of the arbitrators.

2. In the case of questions of procedure, when there is no majority or when the arbitral tribunal so authorizes, the presiding arbitrator may decide on his own, subject to revision, if any, by the arbitral tribunal.

Form and Effect of the Award
Article 32

1. In addition to making a final award, the arbitral tribunal shall be entitled to make interim, interlocutory, or partial awards.

2. The award shall be made in writing and shall be final and binding on the parties. The parties undertake to carry out the award without delay.

3. The arbitral tribunal shall state the reasons upon which the award is based, unless the parties have agreed that no reasons are to be given.

4. An award shall be signed by the arbitrators and it shall contain the date on which and the place where the award was made. Where there are three arbitrators and one of them fails to sign, the award shall state the reason for the absence of the signature.

5. The award may be made public only with the consent of both parties.

6. Copies of the award signed by the arbitrators shall be communicated to the parties by the arbitral tribunal.

7. If the arbitration law of the country where the award is made requires that the award be filed or registered by the arbitral tribunal, the tribunal shall comply with this requirement within the period of time required by law.

Applicable Law, Amiable Compositeur
Article 33

1. The arbitral tribunal shall apply the law designated by the parties as applicable to the substance of the dispute. Failing such designation by the parties, the arbitral tribunal shall apply the law determined by the conflict of laws rules which it considers applicable.

2. The arbitral tribunal shall decide as *amiable compositeur* or *ex aequo et bono* only if the parties have expressly authorized the arbitral tribunal to do so and if the law applicable to the arbitral procedure permits such arbitration.

3. In all cases, the arbitral tribunal shall decide in accordance with the terms of the contract and shall take into account the usages of the trade applicable to the transaction.

Settlement of Other Grounds for Termination
Article 34

1. If, before the award is made, the parties agree on a settlement of the dispute, the arbitral tribunal shall either issue an order for the termination of the arbitral proceedings or, if requested by both parties and accepted by the tribunal, record the settlement in the form of an arbitral award on agreed terms. The arbitral tribunal is not obliged to give reasons for such an award.

2. If, before the award is made, the continuation of the arbitral proceedings becomes unnecessary or impossible for any reason not mentioned in paragraph 1, the arbitral tribunal shall inform the parties of its intention to issue an order for the termination of the proceedings. The arbitral tribunal shall have the power to issue such an order unless a party raises justifiable grounds for objection.

3. Copies of the order for termination of the arbitral proceedings or of the arbitral award on agreed terms, signed by the arbitrators, shall be communicated by the arbitral tribunal to the parties. Where an arbitral award on agreed terms is made, the provisions of article 32, paragraphs 2 and 4 to 7, shall apply.

Interpretation of the Award
Article 35

1. Within thirty days after the receipt of the award, either party, with notice to the other party, may request that the arbitral tribunal give an interpretation of the award.

2. The interpretation shall be given in writing within forty-five days after the receipt of the request. The interpretation shall form part of the award and the provisions of article 32, paragraphs 2 to 7, shall apply.

Correction of the Award
Article 36

1. Within thirty days after the receipt of the award, either party, with notice to the other party, may request the arbitral tribunal to correct in the award any errors in computation, any clerical or typographical errors, or any errors of similar nature. The arbitral tribunal may within thirty days after the communication of the award make such corrections on its own initiative.
2. Such corrections shall be in writing, and the provisions of article 32, paragraphs 2 to 7, shall apply.

Additional Award
Article 37

1. Within thirty days after the receipt of the award, either party, with notice to the other party, may request the arbitral tribunal to make an additional award as to claims presented in the arbitral proceedings but omitted from the award.
2. If the arbitral tribunal considers the request for an additional award to be justified and considers that the omission can be rectified without any further hearings or evidence, it shall complete its award within sixty days after the receipt of the request.
3. When an additional award is made, the provisions of article 32, paragraphs 2 to 7, shall apply.

Costs (Articles 38 to 40)
Article 38

The arbitral tribunal shall fix the costs of arbitration in its award. The term 'costs' includes only:
  (a) The fees of the arbitral tribunal to be stated separately as to each arbitrator and to be fixed by the tribunal itself in accordance with article 39;
  (b) The travel and other expenses incurred by the arbitrators;
  (c) The costs of expert advice and of other assistance required by the arbitral tribunal;
  (d) The travel and other expenses of witnesses to the extent such expenses are approved by the arbitral tribunal;
  (e) The costs for legal representation and assistance of the successful party if such costs were claimed during the arbitral proceedings, and only to the extent that the arbitral tribunal determines that the amount of such costs is reasonable;
  (f) Any fees and expenses of the appointing authority as well as the expenses of the Secretary-General of the Permanent Court of Arbitration at The Hague.

Article 39

1. The fees of the arbitral tribunal shall be reasonable in amount, taking into account the amount in dispute, the complexity of the subject-matter, the time spent by the arbitrators and any other relevant circumstances of the case.

2. If an appointing authority has been agreed upon by the parties or designated by the Secretary-General of the Permanent Court of Arbitration at The Hague, and if that authority has issued a schedule of fees for arbitrators in international cases which it administers, the arbitral tribunal in fixing its fees shall take that schedule of fees into account to the extent that it considers appropriate in the circumstances of the case.

3. If such appointing authority has not issued a schedule of fees for arbitrators in international cases, any party may at any time request the appointing authority to furnish a statement setting forth the basis for establishing fees which is customarily followed in international cases in which the authority appoints arbitrators. If the appointing authority consents to provide such a statement, the arbitral tribunal in fixing its fees shall take such information into account to the extent that it considers appropriate in the circumstances of the case.

4. In cases referred to in paragraphs 2 and 3, when a party so requests and the appointing authority consents to perform the function, the arbitral tribunal shall fix its fees only after consultation with the appointing authority which may make any comment it deems appropriate to the arbitral tribunal concerning the fees.

Article 40

1. Except as provided in paragraph 2, the costs of arbitration shall in principle be borne by the unsuccessful party. However, the arbitral tribunal may apportion each of such costs between the parties if it determines that apportionment is reasonable, taking into account the circumstances of the case.

2. With respect to the costs of legal representation and assistance referred to in article 38, paragraph *(e)*, the arbitral tribunal, taking into account the circumstances of the case, shall be free to determine which party shall bear such costs or may apportion such costs between the parties if it determines that apportionment is reasonable.

3. When the arbitral tribunal issues an order for the termination of the arbitral proceedings or makes an award on agreed terms, it shall fix the costs of arbitration referred to in article 38 and article 39, paragraph 1, in the text of that order or award.

4. No additional fees may be charged by an arbitral tribunal for interpretation or correction or completion of its award under articles 35 to 37.

Deposit of Costs
Article 41

1. The arbitral tribunal, on its establishment, may request each party to deposit an equal amount as an advance for the costs referred to in article 38, paragraphs *(a)*, *(b)* and *(c)*.

2. During the course of the arbitral proceedings the arbitral tribunal may request supplementary deposits from the parties.

3. If an appointing authority has been agreed upon by the parties or designated by the Secretary-General of the Permanent Court of Arbitration at The Hague, and when a party so requests and the appointing authority consents to perform the function, the arbitral tribunal shall fix the amounts of any deposits or supplementary deposits only after consultation with the appointing authority which may make any comments to the arbitral tribunal which it deems appropriate concerning the amount of such deposits and supplementary deposits.

4. If the required deposits are not paid in full within thirty days after the receipt of the request, the arbitral tribunal shall so inform the parties in order that one or another of them may make the required payment. If such payment is not made, the arbitral tribunal may order the suspension or termination of the arbitral proceedings.

5. After the award has been made, the arbitral tribunal shall render an accounting to the parties of the deposits received and return any unexpended balance to the parties.

(v) RULES OF ARBITRATION OF THE INTERNATIONAL CHAMBER OF COMMERCE, 1998*

A. INTRODUCTORY PROVISIONS

Article 1
International Court of Arbitration

(1) The International Court of Arbitration (the 'Court') of the International Chamber of Commerce (the 'ICC') is the arbitration body attached to the ICC. The statutes of the Court are set forth in Appendix I. Members of the Court are appointed by the Council of the ICC. The function of the Court is to provide for the settlement by arbitration of business disputes of an international character in accordance with the Rules of Arbitration of the International Chamber of Commerce (the 'Rules'). If so empowered by an arbitration agreement, the Court shall also provide for the settlement by arbitration in accordance with these Rules of business disputes not of an international character.

---

* ICC Publication No. 808(E)–ISBN 92.842.1302.0 Published in its official English version by the International Chamber of Commerce, Paris. Copyright ©1997, 2001.

(2) The Court does not itself settle disputes. It has the function of ensuring the application of these Rules. It draws up its own Internal Rules (Appendix II).

(3) The Chairman of the Court or, in the Chairman's absence or otherwise at his request, one of its Vice-Chairmen shall have the power to take urgent decisions on behalf of the Court, provided that any such decision is reported to the Court at its next session.

(4) As provided for in its Internal Rules, the Court may delegate to one or more committees composed of its members the power to take certain decisions, provided that any such decision is reported to the Court at its next session.

(5) The Secretariat of the Court (the 'Secretariat') under the direction of its Secretary General (the 'Secretary General') shall have its seat at the headquarters of the ICC.

Article 2
Definitions

In these Rules:

   i)   'Arbitral Tribunal' includes one or more arbitrators.
   ii) 'Claimant' includes one or more claimants and 'Respondent' includes one or more respondents.
   iii) 'Award' includes, *inter alia*, an interim, partial or final Award.

Article 3
Written Notifications or Communications; Time Limits

(1) All pleadings and other written communications submitted by any party, as well as all documents annexed thereto, shall be supplied in a number of copies sufficient to provide one copy for each party, plus one for each arbitrator, and one for the Secretariat. A copy of any communication from the Arbitral Tribunal to the parties shall be sent to the Secretariat.

(2) All notifications or communications from the Secretariat and the Arbitral Tribunal shall be made to the last address of the party or its representative for whom the same are intended, as notified either by the party in question or by the other party. Such notification or communication may be made by delivery against receipt, registered post, courier, facsimile transmission, telex, telegram or any other means of telecommunication that provides a record of the sending thereof.

(3) A notification or communication shall be deemed to have been made on the day it was received by the party itself or by its representative, or would have been received if made in accordance with the preceding paragraph.

(4) Periods of time specified in, or fixed under the present Rules, shall start to run on the day following the date a notification or communication is deemed to have been made in accordance with the preceding paragraph. When the day next following such date is an official holiday, or a non-business day in the country where the notification or communication is deemed to have been made, the period of time shall commence on the first following business day. Official holidays and non-business days are included in the calculation of the period of time. If the last day of the relevant period of time granted is an official holiday or a non-business day in the country where the notification or communication is deemed to have been made, the period of time shall expire at the end of the first following business day.

B. COMMENCING THE ARBITRATION

Article 4
Request for Arbitration

(1) A party wishing to have recourse to arbitration under these Rules shall submit its Request for Arbitration (the 'Request') to the Secretariat, which shall notify the Claimant and Respondent of the receipt of the Request and the date of such receipt.

(2) The date when the Request is received by the Secretariat shall, for all purposes, be deemed to be the date of the commencement of the arbitral proceedings.

(3) The Request shall, *inter alia*, contain the following information:

   (a) the name in full, description and address of each of the parties;

   (b) a description of the nature and circumstances of the dispute giving rise to the claims;

   (c) a statement of the relief sought, including, to the extent possible, an indication of any amount(s) claimed;

   (d) the relevant agreements and, in particular, the arbitration agreement;

   (e) all relevant particulars concerning the number of arbitrators and their choice in accordance with the provisions of Articles 8, 9 and 10, and any nomination of an arbitrator required thereby; and,

   (f) any comments as to the place of arbitration, the applicable rules of law and the language of the arbitration.

(4) Together with the Request, the Claimant shall submit the number of copies thereof required by Article 3(1) and shall make the advance payment on administrative expenses required by Appendix III ('Arbitration Costs and Fees') in force on the date the Request is submitted. In the event that the Claimant fails to comply with either of these requirements, the Secretariat may fix a time limit within which the Claimant must comply, failing which the file shall be closed without prejudice to the right of the Claimant to submit the same claims at a later date in another Request.

(5) The Secretariat shall send a copy of the Request and the documents annexed thereto to the Respondent for its Answer to the Request once the Secretariat has sufficient copies of the Request and the required advance payment.

(6) When a party submits a Request in connection with a legal relationship in respect of which arbitration proceedings between the same parties are already pending under these Rules, the Court may, at the request of a party, decide to include the claims contained in the Request in the pending proceedings provided that the Terms of Reference have not yet been signed or approved by the Court. Once the Terms of Reference have been signed or approved by the Court, claims may only be included in the pending proceedings subject to the provisions of Article 19.

Article 5
Answer to the Request; Counterclaims

(1) Within 30 days from the receipt of the Request from the Secretariat, the Respondent shall file an Answer (the 'Answer') which shall, *inter alia*, contain the following information:

   (a) its name in full, description and address;

(b) its comments as to the nature and circumstances of the dispute giving rise to the claim(s);

(c) its response as to the relief sought;

(d) any comments concerning the number of arbitrators and their choice in light of the Claimant's proposals and in accordance with the provisions of Articles 8, 9 and 10, and any nomination of an arbitrator required thereby; and,

(e) any comments as to the place of arbitration, the applicable rules of law and the language of the arbitration.

(2) The Secretariat may grant the Respondent an extension of the time for filing the Answer, provided the application for such an extension contains the Respondent's comments concerning the number of arbitrators and their choice, and, where required by Articles 8, 9 and 10, the nomination of an arbitrator. If the Respondent fails so to do, the Court shall proceed in accordance with these Rules.

(3) The Answer shall be supplied to the Secretariat in the number of copies specified by Article 3(1).

(4) A copy of the Answer and the documents annexed thereto shall be communicated by the Secretariat to the Claimant.

(5) Any counterclaim(s) made by the Respondent shall be filed with its Answer and shall provide:

(a) a description of the nature and circumstances of the dispute giving rise to the counterclaim(s); and,

(b) a statement of the relief sought, including, to the extent possible, an indication of any amount(s) counterclaimed.

(6) The Claimant shall file a Reply to any counterclaim within 30 days from the date of receipt of the counterclaim(s) communicated by the Secretariat. The Secretariat may grant the Claimant an extension of time for filing the Reply.

Article 6
Effect of the Arbitration Agreement

(1) Where the parties have agreed to submit to arbitration under the Rules, they shall be deemed to have submitted *ipso facto* to the Rules in effect on the date of commencement of the arbitration proceedings, unless they have agreed to submit to the Rules in effect on the date of their arbitration agreement.

(2) If the Respondent does not file an Answer, as provided by Article 5, or if any party raises one or more pleas concerning the existence, validity or scope of the arbitration agreement, the Court may decide, without prejudice to the admissibility or merits of the plea or pleas, that the arbitration shall proceed if it is *prima facie* satisfied that an arbitration agreement under the Rules may exist. In such a case, any decision as to the jurisdiction of the Arbitral Tribunal shall be taken by the Arbitral Tribunal itself. If the Court is not so satisfied, the parties shall be notified that the arbitration cannot proceed. In such a case, any party retains the right to ask any court having jurisdiction whether or not there is a binding arbitration agreement.

(3) If any of the parties refuses or fails to take-part in the arbitration or any stage thereof, the arbitration shall proceed notwithstanding such refusal or failure.

(4) Unless otherwise agreed, the Arbitral Tribunal shall not cease to have jurisdiction by reason of any claim that the contract is null and void or allegation that it is non-existent, provided that the Arbitral Tribunal upholds the validity of the arbitration

agreement. The Arbitral Tribunal shall continue to have jurisdiction to determine the respective rights of the parties and to adjudicate upon their claims and pleas even though the contract itself may be non-existent or null and void.

C. THE ARBITRAL TRIBUNAL

Article 7
General Provisions

(1) Every arbitrator must be and remain independent of the parties involved in the arbitration.
(2) Before appointment or confirmation, a prospective arbitrator shall sign a statement of independence and disclose in writing to the Secretariat any facts or circumstances which might be of such a nature as to call into question the arbitrator's independence in the eyes of the parties. The Secretariat shall provide such information to the parties in writing and fix a time-limit for any comments from them.
(3) An arbitrator shall immediately disclose in writing to the Secretariat and to the parties any facts or circumstances of similar nature which may arise during the arbitration.
(4) The decisions of the Court as to the appointment, confirmation, challenge or replacement of an arbitrator shall be final and the reasons for such decisions shall not be communicated.
(5) By accepting to serve, every arbitrator undertakes to carry out his responsibilities in accordance with these Rules.
(6) Insofar as the parties shall not have provided otherwise, the Arbitral Tribunal shall be constituted in accordance with the provisions of Articles 8, 9 and 10.

Article 8
Number of Arbitrators

(1) The disputes shall be decided by a sole arbitrator or by three arbitrators.
(2) Where the parties have not agreed upon the number of arbitrators, the Court shall appoint a sole arbitrator, save where it appears to the Court that the dispute is such as to warrant the appointment of three arbitrators. In such case, the Claimant shall nominate an arbitrator within a period of 15 days from the receipt of the notification of the decision of the Court, and the Respondent shall nominate an arbitrator within a period of 15 days from the receipt of the notification of the nomination made by the Claimant.
(3) Where the parties have agreed that the dispute shall be settled by a sole arbitrator, they may, by agreement, nominate the sole arbitrator for confirmation. If the parties fail so to nominate a sole arbitrator within 30 days from the date when the Claimant's Request for Arbitration has been received by the other party, or within such additional time as may be allowed by the Secretariat, the sole arbitrator shall be appointed by the Court.
(4) Where the dispute is to be referred to three arbitrators, each party shall nominate in the Request and the Answer, respectively, one arbitrator for confirmation. If a party fails to nominate an arbitrator, the appointment shall be made by the Court. The third arbitrator, who will act as chairman of the Arbitral Tribunal, shall be appointed by the Court, unless the parties have agreed upon another procedure for such

appointment, in which case the nomination will be subject to confirmation pursuant to Article 9. Should such procedure not result in a nomination within the time-limit fixed by the parties or the Court, the third arbitrator shall be appointed by the Court.

Article 9
Appointment and Confirmation of the Arbitrators

(1) In confirming or appointing arbitrators, the Court shall consider the prospective arbitrator's nationality, residence and other relationships with the countries of which the parties or the other arbitrators are nationals and the prospective arbitrator's availability and ability to conduct the arbitration in accordance with these Rules. The same shall apply where the Secretary General confirms arbitrators pursuant to Article 9(2).

(2) The Secretary General may confirm as co-arbitrators, sole arbitrators and chairmen of Arbitral Tribunals persons nominated by the parties or pursuant to their particular agreements, provided they have filed a statement of independence without qualification or a qualified statement of independence has not given rise to objections. Such confirmation shall be reported to the Court at its next session. If the Secretary General considers that a co-arbitrator, sole arbitrator or chairman of an Arbitral Tribunal should not be confirmed, the matter shall be submitted to the Court.

(3) Where the Court is to appoint a sole arbitrator or the chairman of an Arbitral Tribunal, it shall make the appointment upon a proposal of a National Committee of the ICC that it considers to be appropriate. If the Court does not accept the proposal made, or if the National Committee fails to make the proposal requested within the time-limit fixed by the Court, the Court may repeat its request or may request a proposal from another National Committee that it considers to be appropriate.

(4) Where the Court considers that the circumstances so demand, it may choose the sole arbitrator or the chairman of the Arbitral Tribunal from a country where there is no National Committee, provided that neither of the parties objects within the time-limit fixed by the Court.

(5) The sole arbitrator or the chairman of the Arbitral Tribunal shall be of a nationality other than those of the parties. However, in suitable circumstances and provided that neither of the parties objects within the time-limit fixed by the Court, the sole arbitrator or the chairman of the Arbitral Tribunal may be chosen from a country of which any of the parties is a national.

(6) Where the Court is to appoint an arbitrator on behalf of a party which has failed to nominate one, it shall make the appointment upon a proposal of the National Committee of the country of which that party is a national. If the Court does not accept the proposal made, or if the National Committee fails to make the proposal requested within the time-limit fixed by the Court, or if the country of which the said party is a national has no National Committee, the Court shall be at liberty to choose any person whom it regards as suitable. The Secretariat shall inform the National Committee, if one exists, of the country of which such person is a national.

Article 10
Multiple Parties

(1) Where there are multiple parties, whether as Claimant or as Respondent, and where the dispute is to be referred to three arbitrators, the multiple Claimants, jointly, and

the multiple Respondents, jointly, shall nominate an arbitrator for confirmation pursuant to Article 9.

(2) In the absence of such a joint nomination and where all parties are unable to agree to a method for the constitution of the Arbitral Tribunal, the Court may appoint each member of the Arbitral Tribunal and shall designate one of them to act as chairman. In such case, the Court shall be at liberty to choose any person whom it regards as suitable to act as arbitrator, applying Article 9 when it considers this appropriate.

Article 11
Challenge of Arbitrators

(1) A challenge of an arbitrator, whether for an alleged lack of independence or otherwise, shall be made by the submission to the Secretariat of a written statement specifying the facts and circumstances on which the challenge is based.

(2) For a challenge to be admissible, it must be sent by a party either within 30 days from receipt by that party of the notification of the appointment or confirmation of the arbitrator, or within 30 days from the date when the party making the challenge was informed of the facts and circumstances on which the challenge is based if such date is subsequent to the receipt of such notification.

(3) The Court shall decide on the admissibility and, at the same time, if necessary, on the merits of a challenge after the Secretariat has afforded an opportunity for the arbitrator concerned, the other party or parties and any other members of the Arbitral Tribunal to comment in writing within a suitable period of time. Such comments shall be communicated to the parties and to the arbitrators.

Article 12
Replacement of Arbitrators

(1) An arbitrator shall be replaced upon his death, upon the acceptance by the Court of the arbitrator's resignation, upon acceptance by the Court of a challenge or upon the request of all the parties.

(2) An arbitrator shall also be replaced on the Court's own initiative when it decides that he is prevented *de jure* or *de facto* from fulfilling his functions, or that he is not fulfilling his functions in accordance with the Rules or within the prescribed time limits.

(3) When, on the basis of information that has come to its attention, the Court considers applying Article 12(2), it shall decide on the matter after the arbitrator concerned, the parties and any other members of the Arbitral Tribunal have had an opportunity to comment in writing within a suitable period of time. Such comments shall be communicated to the parties and to the arbitrators.

(4) When an arbitrator is to be replaced, the Court has discretion to decide whether or not to follow the original nominating process. Once reconstituted, and after having invited the parties to comment, the Arbitral Tribunal shall determine if and to what extent prior proceedings shall be repeated before the reconstituted Arbitral Tribunal.

(5) Subsequent to the closing of the proceedings, instead of replacing an arbitrator who has died or been removed by the Court pursuant to Articles 12(1) and 12(2), the Court may decide, when it considers it appropriate, that the remaining arbitrators shall continue the arbitration. In making such determination, the Court shall take

into account the views of the remaining arbitrators and of the parties and such other matters that it considers appropriate in the circumstances.

D. THE ARBITRAL PROCEEDINGS

Article 13
Transmission of the File to the Arbitral Tribunal

The Secretariat shall transmit the file to the Arbitral Tribunal as soon as it has been constituted, provided the advance on costs requested by the Secretariat at this stage has been paid.

Article 14
Place of the Arbitration

(1) The place of the arbitration shall be fixed by the Court, unless agreed upon by the parties.
(2) The Arbitral Tribunal may, after consultation with the parties, conduct hearings and meetings at any location it considers appropriate unless otherwise agreed by the parties.
(3) The Arbitral Tribunal may deliberate at any location it considers appropriate.

Article 15
Rules Governing the Proceedings

(1) The proceedings before the Arbitral Tribunal shall be governed by these Rules and, where these Rules are silent, by any rules which the parties or, failing them, the Arbitral Tribunal may settle on, whether or not reference is thereby made to the rules of procedure of a national law to be applied to the arbitration.
(2) In all cases, the Arbitral Tribunal shall act fairly and impartially and ensure that each party has a reasonable opportunity to present its case.

Article 16
Language of the Arbitration

In the absence of an agreement by the parties, the Arbitral Tribunal shall determine the language or languages of the arbitration, due regard being given to all relevant circumstances, including the language of the contract.

Article 17
Applicable Rules of Law

(1) The parties shall be free to agree upon the rules of law to be applied by the Arbitral Tribunal to the merits of the dispute. In the absence of any such agreement, the Arbitral Tribunal shall apply the rules of law which it determines to be appropriate.
(2) In all cases the Arbitral Tribunal shall take account of the provisions of the contract and the relevant trade usages.
(3) The Arbitral Tribunal shall assume the powers of an *amiable compositeur* or decide *ex aequo et bono* only if the parties have agreed to give it such powers.

Article 18
Terms of Reference; Procedural Timetable

(1) As soon as it has received the file from the Secretariat, the Arbitral Tribunal shall draw up, on the basis of documents or in the presence of the parties and in the light of their most recent submissions, a document defining its Terms of Reference. This document shall include the following particulars:

    (a) the full names and descriptions of the parties;

    (b) the addresses of the parties to which notifications and communications arising in the course of the arbitration may be made;

    (c) a summary of the parties' respective claims and of the relief sought by each party, with an indication to the extent possible of the amounts claimed or counter-claimed;

    (d) unless the Arbitral Tribunal considers it inappropriate, a list of issues to be determined;

    (e) the full names, descriptions and addresses of the arbitrators;

    (f) the place of the arbitration; and,

    (g) particulars of the applicable procedural rules and, if such is the case, reference to the power conferred upon the Arbitral Tribunal to act as *amiable compositeur* or to decide *ex aequo et bono*.

(2) The Terms of Reference shall be signed by the parties and the Arbitral Tribunal. Within two months of the date when the file has been transmitted to it, the Arbitral Tribunal shall transmit to the Court the Terms of Reference signed by it and by the parties. The Court may extend this time limit, pursuant to a reasoned request from the Arbitral Tribunal or on its own initiative if it decides it is necessary to do so.

(3) If any of the parties refuses to take part in the drawing up of the Terms of Reference or to sign the same, they shall be submitted to the Court for approval. When the Terms of Reference are signed in accordance with Article 18(2) or approved by the Court, the arbitration shall proceed.

(4) When drawing up the Terms of Reference, or as soon as possible thereafter, the Arbitral Tribunal, after having consulted the parties, shall establish in a separate document a provisional timetable that it intends to follow for the conduct of the arbitration and shall communicate it to the Court and the parties. Any subsequent modifications of the provisional timetable shall be communicated to the Court and the parties.

Article 19
New Claims

After the Terms of Reference have been signed or approved by the Court, no party shall make new claims or counter-claims which fall outside the limits of the Terms of Reference unless it has been authorised to do so by the Arbitral Tribunal, which shall consider the nature of such new claims or counterclaims, the stage of the arbitration and other relevant circumstances.

Article 20
Establishing the Facts of the Case

(1) The Arbitral Tribunal shall proceed within as short a time as possible to establish the facts of the case by all appropriate means.

(2) After studying the written submissions of the parties and all documents relied upon, the Arbitral Tribunal shall hear the parties together in person if any of them so requests or, failing such a request, it may of its own motion decide to hear them.

(3) The Arbitral Tribunal may decide to hear witnesses, experts appointed by the parties or any other person, in the presence of the parties, or in their absence provided they have been duly summoned.

(4) The Arbitral Tribunal, after having consulted the parties, may appoint one or more experts, define their terms of reference and receive their reports. At the request of a party, the parties shall be given the opportunity to question at a hearing any such expert appointed by the Tribunal.

(5) At any time during the proceedings, the Arbitral Tribunal may summon any party to provide additional evidence.

(6) The Arbitral Tribunal may decide the case solely on the documents submitted by the parties unless any of the parties requests a hearing.

(7) The Arbitral Tribunal may take measures for protecting trade secrets and confidential information.

Article 21
Hearings

(1) When a hearing is to be held, the Arbitral Tribunal, giving reasonable notice, shall summon the parties to appear before it on the day and at the place fixed by it.

(2) If any of the parties, although duly summoned, fails to appear without valid excuse, the Arbitral Tribunal shall have the power to proceed with the hearing.

(3) The Arbitral Tribunal shall be in full charge of the hearings, at which all the parties shall be entitled to be present. Save with the approval of the Arbitral Tribunal and the parties, persons not involved in the proceedings shall not be admitted.

(4) The parties may appear in person or through duly authorised representatives. In addition, they may be assisted by advisers.

Article 22
Closing of the Proceedings

(1) When it is satisfied that the parties have had a reasonable opportunity to present their cases, the Arbitral Tribunal shall declare the proceedings closed. Thereafter, no further submission or argument may be made or evidence produced, unless requested or authorised by the Arbitral Tribunal.

(2) When the Arbitral Tribunal has declared the proceedings closed, it shall indicate to the Secretariat an approximate date by which the draft Award will be submitted to the Court for approval pursuant to Article 27. Any postponement of that date shall be communicated to the Secretariat by the Arbitral Tribunal.

Article 23
Conservatory and Interim Measures

(1) Unless the parties have otherwise agreed, as soon as the file has been transmitted to it, the Arbitral Tribunal may, at the request of a party, order any interim or conservatory

measure it deems appropriate. The Arbitral Tribunal may make the granting of any such measure subject to appropriate security being furnished by the requesting party. Any such measure shall take the form of an order, giving reasons, or of an Award, as the Arbitral Tribunal considers appropriate.

(2) Before the file is transmitted to the Arbitral Tribunal, and in appropriate circumstances even thereafter, the parties may apply to any competent judicial authority for interim or conservatory measures. The application of a party to a judicial authority for such measures or for the implementation of any such measures ordered by an Arbitral Tribunal shall not be deemed to be an infringement or a waiver of the arbitration agreement and shall not affect the relevant powers reserved to the Arbitral Tribunal. Any such application and any measures taken by the judicial authority must be notified without delay to the Secretariat. The Secretariat shall inform the Arbitral Tribunal thereof.

E. AWARDS

Article 24
Time Limit for the Award

(1) The time limit within which the Arbitral Tribunal must render its final Award is six months. Such time limit shall start to run from the date of the last signature by the Arbitral Tribunal or by the parties of the Terms of Reference, or, in the case of application of Article 18(3), the date of the notification to the Arbitral Tribunal by the Secretariat of the approval of the Terms of Reference by the Court.

(2) The Court may extend this time-limit, pursuant to a reasoned request from the Arbitral Tribunal or on its own initiative if it decides it is necessary to do so.

Article 25
Making of the Award

(1) When the Arbitral Tribunal is composed of more than one arbitrator, an Award is given by a majority decision. If there be no majority, the Award shall be made by the chairman of the Arbitral Tribunal alone.

(2) The Award shall state the reasons upon which it is based.

(3) The Award shall be deemed to be made at the place of the arbitration and on the date stated therein.

Article 26
Award by Consent

If the parties reach a settlement alter the file has been transmitted to the Arbitral Tribunal in accordance with Article 13, the settlement shall be recorded in the form of an Award made by consent of the parties if so requested by the parties and the Arbitral Tribunal agrees to do so.

Article 27
Scrutiny of the Award by the Court

Before signing any Award, the Arbitral Tribunal shall submit it in draft form to the Court. The Court may lay down modifications as to the form of the Award and, without affecting the Arbitral Tribunal's liberty of decision, may also draw its attention to points of substance. No Award shall be rendered by the Arbitral Tribunal until it has been approved by the Court as to its form.

Article 28
Notification, Deposit and Enforceability of the Award

(1) Once an Award has been made, the Secretariat shall notify to the parties the text signed by the Arbitral Tribunal, provided always that the costs of the arbitration have been fully paid to the ICC by the parties or by one of them.
(2) Additional copies certified true by the Secretary General shall be made available on request and at any time to the parties, but to no one else.
(3) By virtue of the notification made in accordance with Paragraph 1 of this Article, the parties waive any other form of notification or deposit on the part of the Arbitral Tribunal.
(4) An original of each Award made in accordance with the present Rules shall be deposited with the Secretariat.
(5) The Arbitral Tribunal and the Secretariat shall assist the parties in complying with whatever further formalities may be necessary.
(6) Every Award shall be binding on the parties. By submitting the dispute to arbitration under these Rules, the parties undertake to carry out any Award without delay and shall be deemed to have waived their right to any form of recourse insofar as such waiver can validly be made.

Article 29
Correction and Interpretation of the Award

(1) On its own initiative, the Arbitral Tribunal may correct a clerical, computational or typographical error, or any errors of similar nature contained in an Award, provided such correction is submitted for approval to the Court within 30 days of the date of such Award.
(2) Any application of a party for the correction of an error of the kind referred to in Article 29(1), or for the interpretation of an Award, must be made to the Secretariat within 30 days of the receipt of the Award by such party, in a number of copies as stated in Article 3(1). After transmittal of the application to the Arbitral Tribunal, the latter shall grant the other party a short time limit, normally not exceeding 30 days, from the receipt of the application by that party, to submit any comments thereon. If the Arbitral Tribunal decides to correct or interpret the Award, it shall submit its decision in draft form to the Court not later than 30 days following the expiration of the time limit for the receipt of any comments from the other party or within such other period as the Court may decide.
(3) The decision to correct or to interpret the Award shall take the form of an addendum and shall constitute part of the Award. The provisions of Articles 25, 27 and 28 shall apply *mutatis mutandis.*

F. COSTS

Article 30
Advance to Cover the Costs of the Arbitration

(1) After receipt of the Request, the Secretary General may request the Claimant to pay a provisional advance in an amount intended to cover the costs of arbitration until the Terms of Reference have been drawn up.

(2) As soon as practicable, the Court shall fix the advance on costs in an amount likely to cover the fees and expenses of the arbitrators and the ICC administrative costs for the claims and counterclaims which have been referred to it by the parties. This amount may be subject to readjustment at any time during the arbitration. Where, apart from the claims, counterclaims are submitted, the Court may fix separate advances on costs for the claims and the counterclaims.

(3) The advance on costs fixed by the Court shall be payable in equal shares by the Claimant and the Respondent. Any provisional advance paid on the basis of Article 30(1) will be considered as a partial payment thereof. However, any party shall be free to pay the whole of the advance on costs in respect of the principal claim or the counterclaim should the other party fail to pay its share. When the Court has set separate advances on costs in accordance with Article 30(2), each of the parties shall pay the advance on costs corresponding to its claims.

(4) When a request for an advance on costs has not been complied with, and after consultation with the Arbitral Tribunal, the Secretary General may direct the Arbitral Tribunal to suspend its work and set a time limit, which must be not less than 15 days, on the expiry of which the relevant claims, or counterclaims, shall be considered as withdrawn. Should the party in question wish to object to this measure, it must make a request within the aforementioned period for the matter to be decided by the Court. Such party shall not be prevented on the ground of such withdrawal from reintroducing the same claims or counterclaims at a later date in another proceeding.

(5) If one of the parties claims a right to a set-off with regard to either claims or counterclaims, such set-off shall be taken into account in determining the advance to cover the costs of arbitration in the same way as a separate claim insofar as it may require the Arbitral Tribunal to consider additional matters.

Article 31
The Costs of the Arbitration

(1) The costs of the arbitration shall include the fees and expenses of the arbitrators and the ICC administrative costs fixed by the Court, in accordance with the scale in force at the time of the commencement of the arbitral proceedings, as well as the fees and expenses of any experts appointed by the Arbitral Tribunal and the reasonable legal and other costs incurred by the parties for the arbitration.

(2) The Court may fix the fees of the arbitrators at a figure higher or lower than that which would result from the application of the relevant scale should this be deemed necessary due to the exceptional circumstances of the case. Decisions on costs other than those fixed by the Court may be taken by the Arbitral Tribunal at any time during the proceedings.

(3) The final Award shall fix the costs of the arbitration and decide which of the parties shall bear them or in what proportions they shall be borne by the parties.

G. MISCELLANEOUS

Article 32
Modified Time Limits

(1) The parties may agree to shorten the various time limits set out in these Rules. Any such agreement entered into subsequent to the constitution of an Arbitral Tribunal shall become effective only upon the approval of the Arbitral Tribunal.

(2) The Court, on its own initiative, may extend any time limit which has been modified pursuant to Article 32(1) if it decides that it is necessary to do so in order that the Arbitral Tribunal or the Court may fulfil their responsibilities in accordance with these Rules.

Article 33
Waiver

A party which proceeds with the arbitration without raising its objection to a failure to comply with any provisions of these Rules, or of any other rules applicable to the proceedings, any direction given by the Arbitral Tribunal, or any requirement under the arbitration agreement relating to the constitution of the Arbitral Tribunal, or to the conduct of the proceedings, shall be deemed to have waived its right to object.

Article 34
Exclusion of Liability

Neither the arbitrators, nor the Court and its members, nor the ICC and its employees, nor the ICC National Committees shall be liable to any person for any act or omission in connection with the arbitration.

Article 35
General Rule

In all matters not expressly provided for in these Rules, the Court and the Arbitral Tribunal shall act in the spirit of these Rules and shall make every effort to make sure that the Award is enforceable at law.

(vi) MERCOSUR/CMC/NO. 03/98
ACUERDO SOBRE ARBITRAJE COMERCIAL INTERNACIONAL DEL MERCOSUR*

(Buenos Aires, 23 de julio de 1998)

La República Argentina, la República Federativa del Brasil, la República del Paraguay y la República Oriental del Uruguay, en adelante los 'Estados Partes';

Considerando el Tratado de Asunción suscripto el 26 de marzo de 1991 entre la República Argentina, la República Federativa del Brasil, la República del Paraguay y la República Oriental del Uruguay, y el Protocolo de Ouro Preto suscripto el 17 de diciembre de 1994 entre los mismos Estados;

---

* Ref: MERCOSUR/CMC/no 3/98. Adopted by the *Consejo del Mercado Común* on 23 July 1998/ *Adopté par le* Consejo del Mercado Común *le 23 juillet 1998* (XIV CMC Buenos Aires, 23/VII/98).

The *'Acuerdo sobre arbitraje comercial internacional entre el Mercosur, la República de Bolivia y la República de Chile'* (MERCOSUR/CMC/DEC No 4/98), adopted by the *Consejo del Mercado Común* on 23 July 1998 (XIV CMC—Buenos Aires, 23/VII/98), contains the same provisions as the *Acuerdo sobre arbitraje comercial internacional del Mercosur* reproduced above, with appropriate adjustments to enable their application in the MERCOSUR countries, Bolivia and Chile. / L''Acuerdo sobre arbitraje comercial internacional entre el Mercosur, la República de Bolivia y la República de Chile' (MERCOSUR/CMC/DEC No 4/98), *adopté par le* Consejo del Mercado Común *le 23 juillet 1998* (XIV CMC—Buenos Aires, 23/VII/98), *reprend les dispositions* de l' Acuerdo sobre arbitraje comercial internacional del MERCOSUR *ici reproduit, avec les adaptations nécessaires pour les rendre applicables aux pays du Mercosur, á la Bolivie et au Chili.*

Recordando que los instrumentos fundacionales del MERCOSUR establecen el compromiso de los Estados Partes de armonizar sus legislaciones en las áreas pertinentes;

Reafirmando la voluntad de los Estados Partes del MERCOSUR de acordar soluciones jurídicas comunes para el fortalecimiento del proceso de integración del MERCOSUR;

Destacando la necesidad de proporcionar al sector privado de los Estados Partes del MERCOSUR métodos alternativos para la resolución de controversias surgidas de contratos comerciales internacionales concluidos entre personas físicas o jurídicas de derecho privado;

Convencidos de la necesidad de uniformar la organización y funcionamiento del arbitraje internacional en los Estados Partes para contribuir a la expansión del comercio regional e internacional;

Deseosos de promover e incentivar la solución extrajudicial de controversias privadas por medio del arbitraje en el MERCOSUR, práctica acorde con las peculiaridades de las transacciones internacionales;

Considerando que fueron aprobados en el MERCOSUR protocolos que prevén la elección del foro arbitral y el reconocimiento y la ejecución de laudos o sentencias arbitrales extranjeros;

Teniendo en cuenta la Convención Interamericana sobre Arbitraje Comercial Internacional del 30 de enero de 1975, concluida en la ciudad de Panamá, la Convención Interamericana sobre Eficacia Extraterritorial de las Sentencias y Laudos Arbitrales Extranjeros del 8 de mayo de 1979, concluida en Montevideo y la Ley Modelo sobre Arbitraje Comercial Internacional de la Comisión de las Naciones Unidas para el Derecho Mercantil Internacional, del 21 de junio de 1985;

ACUERDAN:

Artículo 1
Objeto

El presente Acuerdo tiene por objeto regular el arbitraje como medio alternativo privado de solución de controversias, surgidas de contratos comerciales internacionales entre personas físicas o jurídicas de derecho privado.

Artículo 2
Definiciones

A los fines de la aplicación del presente Acuerdo se entiende por:
   a) 'arbitraje': medio privado –*institucional o 'ad hoc'*- para la solución de controversias;
   b) 'arbitraje internacional': medio privado para la solución de controversias relativas a contratos comerciales internacionales entre particulares, personas físicas o jurídicas;
   c) 'autoridad judicial': órgano del sistema judicial estatal;
   d) 'contrato base': acuerdo que origina las controversias sometidas a arbitraje;
   e) 'convención arbitral': acuerdo por el que las partes deciden someter a arbitraje todas o algunas controversias que hayan surgido o puedan surgir entre ellas respecto de

relaciones contractuales. Podrá adoptar la forma de una cláusula compromisoria incluida en un contrato o la de un acuerdo independiente;

f) 'domicilio de las personas físicas': su residencia habitual y subsidiariamente el centro principal de sus negocios;

g) 'domicilio de las personas jurídicas o sede social': lugar principal de la administración o el asiento de sucursales, establecimientos o agencias;

h) 'laudo o sentencia arbitral extranjera': resolución definitiva de la controversia por el tribunal arbitral con sede en el extranjero;

i) 'sede del tribunal arbitral': Estado elegido por los contratantes o en su defecto por los árbitros, a los fines de los arts. 3, 7, 13, 15, 19 y 22 de este Acuerdo, sin perjuicio del lugar de la actuación del tribunal;

j) 'tribunal arbitral': órgano constituido por uno o varios árbitros.

Artículo 3
Ambito material y espacial de aplicación

El presente Acuerdo se aplicará al arbitraje, su organización y procedimientos, y a las sentencias o laudos arbitrales, si mediare alguna de las siguientes circunstancias:

a) la convención arbitral fuere celebrada entre personas físicas o jurídicas que en el momento de su celebración, tengan ya sea su residencia habitual, el centro principal de sus negocios, la sede, sucursales, establecimientos o agencias, en más de un Estado Parte del MERCOSUR.

b) el contrato base tuviere algún contacto objetivo –jurídico o económico- con más de un Estado Parte del MERCOSUR.

c) las partes no expresaren su voluntad en contrario y el contrato base tuviere algún contacto objetivo –jurídico o económico- con un Estado Parte, siempre que el tribunal tenga su sede en uno de los Estados Partes del MERCOSUR.

d) el contrato base tuviere algún contacto objetivo—jurídico o económico—con un Estado Parte y el tribunal arbitral no tuviere su sede en ningún Estado Parte del MERCOSUR, siempre que las partes declaren expresamente su intención de someterse al presente Acuerdo.

e) el contrato base no tuviere ningún contacto objetivo –jurídico o económico- con un Estado Parte y las partes hayan elegido un tribunal arbitral con sede en un Estado Parte del MERCOSUR, siempre que las partes declaren expresamente su intención de someterse al presente Acuerdo.

Artículo 4
Tratamiento equitativo y buena fe

1. La convención arbitral dará un tratamiento equitativo y no abusivo a los contratantes, en especial en los contratos de adhesión, y será pactada de buena fe.

2. La convención arbitral inserta en un contrato deberá ser claramente legible y estar ubicada en un lugar razonablemente destacado.

Artículo 5
Autonomía de la convención arbitral

La convención arbitral es autónoma respecto del contrato base. La inexistencia o invalidez de éste no implica la nulidad de la convención arbitral.

Artículo 6
Forma y derecho aplicable a la validez formal de la convención arbitral

1. La convención arbitral deberá constar por escrito.
2. La validez formal de la convención arbitral se regirá por el derecho del lugar de celebración.
3. La convención arbitral celebrada entre ausentes podrá instrumentarse por el intercambio de cartas o telegramas con recepción confirmada. Las comunicaciones realizadas por telefax, correo electrónico o medio equivalente, deberán ser confirmadas por documento original, sin perjuicio de lo establecido en el numeral cinco.
4. La convención arbitral realizada entre ausentes se perfecciona en el momento y en el Estado en el que se recibe la aceptación por el medio elegido, confirmado por el documento original.
5. Si no se hubieren cumplido los requisitos de validez formal exigidos por el derecho del lugar de celebración, la convención arbitral se considerará válida si cumpliere con los requisitos formales del derecho de alguno de los Estados con el cual el contrato base tiene contactos objetivos de acuerdo a lo establecido en el art.3 literal b).

Artículo 7
Derecho aplicable a la validez intrínseca de la convención arbitral

1. La capacidad de las partes de la convención arbitral se regirá por el derecho de sus respectivos domicilios.
2. La validez de la convención arbitral en cuanto al consentimiento, objeto y causa será regida por el derecho del Estado Parte sede del tribunal arbitral.

Artículo 8
Competencia para conocer sobre la existencia y validez de la convención arbitral

Las cuestiones relativas a la existencia y validez de la convención arbitral serán resueltas por el tribunal arbitral, de oficio o a solicitud de partes.

Artículo 9
Arbitraje de derecho o de equidad

Por disposición de las partes, el arbitraje podrá de ser de derecho o de equidad. En ausencia de disposición será de derecho.

Artículo 10
Derecho aplicable a la controversia por el tribunal arbitral

Las partes podrán elegir el derecho que se aplicará para solucionar la controversia en base al derecho internacional privado y sus principios, así como al derecho del comercio internacional. Si las partes nada dispusieren en esta materia, los árbitros decidirán conforme a las mismas fuentes.

Artículo 11
Tipos de arbitraje

Las partes podrán libremente someterse a arbitraje institucional o 'ad hoc'.

En el procedimiento arbitral serán respetados los principios del contradictorio, de la igualdad de las partes, de la imparcialidad del árbitro y de su libre convencimiento.

Artículo 12
Normas generales de procedimiento

1. En el arbitraje institucional:
   a) el procedimiento ante las instituciones arbitrales se regirá por su propio reglamento;
   b) sin perjuicio de lo dispuesto en el literal anterior, los Estados incentivarán a las entidades arbitrales asentadas en sus territorios para que adopten un reglamento común;
   c) las instituciones arbitrales podrán publicar para su conocimiento y difusión las listas de árbitros, nómina y composición de los tribunales y reglamentos organizativos.
2. En el arbitraje 'ad hoc':
   a) las partes podrán establecer el procedimiento arbitral. En el momento de celebrar la convención arbitral las partes, preferentemente, podrán acordar la designación de los árbitros y, en su caso, los árbitros sustitutos, o establecer la modalidad por la cual serán designados;
   b) si las partes o el presente Acuerdo nada hubiesen previsto, se aplicarán las normas de procedimiento de la Comisión Interamericana de Arbitraje Comercial (CIAC)—conforme a lo establecido en el art. 3 de la Convención Interamericana sobre Arbitraje Comercial Internacional de Panamá de 1975—vigentes al momento de celebrarse la convención arbitral.
   c) todo lo no previsto por las partes, por el Acuerdo y por las normas de procedimiento de la CIAC, será resuelto por el tribunal arbitral atendiendo a los principios establecidos en el artículo 11.

Artículo 13
Sede e idioma

1. Las partes podrán designar a un Estado Parte como sede del tribunal arbitral. En caso que no lo hicieren, el tribunal arbitral determinará el lugar del arbitraje en alguno de esos Estados, atendidas las circunstancias del caso y la conveniencia de las partes.
2. A falta de estipulación expresa de las partes, el idioma será el de la sede del tribunal arbitral.

Artículo 14
Comunicaciones y notificaciones

1. Las comunicaciones y notificaciones practicadas para dar cumplimiento a las normas del presente Acuerdo, se considerarán debidamente realizadas, salvo disposición en contrario de las partes:
   a) cuando hayan sido entregadas personalmente al destinatario, o se hayan recibido por carta certificada, telegrama colacionado o medio equivalente dirigidos a su domicilio declarado;

b) si las partes no hubieren establecido un domicilio especial y si no se conociere el domicilio después de una indagación razonable, se considerará recibida toda comunicación y notificación escrita que haya sido remitida a la última residencia habitual o al último domicilio conocido de sus negocios.

2. La comunicación y la notificación se considerarán recibidas el día en que se haya realizado la entrega según lo establecido en el literal a) del numeral anterior.

3. En la convención arbitral podrá establecerse un domicilio especial distinto al domicilio de las personas físicas o jurídicas, con el objeto de recibir las comunicaciones y notificaciones. También podrá designarse una persona a dichos efectos.

Artículo 15
Inicio del procedimiento arbitral

1. En el arbitraje institucional el procedimiento se iniciará conforme a lo que disponga el reglamento al cual las partes se hayan sometido. En el arbitraje 'ad hoc' la parte que pretenda iniciar el procedimiento arbitral intimará a la otra en la forma establecida en la convención arbitral.

2. En la intimación constará necesariamente:
   a) el nombre y domicilio de las partes;
   b) la referencia al contrato base y a la convención arbitral;
   c) la decisión de someter el asunto a arbitraje y designar los árbitros;
   d) el objeto de la controversia y la indicación del monto, valor o cuantía comprometida.

3. No existiendo una estipulación expresa en cuanto a los medios de hacer efectiva la intimación, ésta será practicada conforme a lo establecido en el artículo 14.

4. La intimación para iniciar un arbitraje 'ad hoc' o el acto procesal equivalente en el arbitraje institucional será válido, incluso a los fines del reconocimiento o ejecución de los laudos o sentencias arbitrales extranjeras, cuando hubieren sido efectuados de acuerdo a lo establecido en la convención arbitral, en las disposiciones de este Acuerdo o, en su caso, en el derecho del Estado sede del tribunal arbitral. En todos los supuestos se asegurará a la parte intimada un plazo razonable para ejercer el derecho de defensa.

5. Efectuada la intimación en el arbitraje 'ad hoc' o el acto procesal equivalente en el arbitraje institucional según lo dispuesto en el presente artículo, no podrá invocarse una violación al orden público para cuestionar su validez, sea en el arbitraje institucional o en el 'ad hoc'.

Artículo 16
Arbitros

1. Podrá ser árbitro cualquier persona legalmente capaz y que goce de la confianza de las partes.

2. La capacidad para ser árbitro se rige por el derecho de su domicilio.

3. En el desempeño de su función, el árbitro deberá proceder con probidad, imparcialidad, independencia, competencia, diligencia y discreción.

4. La nacionalidad de una persona no será impedimento para que actúe como árbitro, salvo acuerdo en contrario de las partes. Se tendrá en cuenta la conveniencia de designar personas de nacionalidad distinta a las partes en el conflicto. En el arbitraje 'ad hoc' con más de un árbitro, el tribunal no podrá estar compuesto únicamente por

árbitros de la nacionalidad de una de las partes, salvo acuerdo expreso de éstas, en el que se manifiesten las razones de dicha selección, que podrán constar en la convención arbitral o en otro documento.

Artículo 17
Nombramiento, recusación y sustitución de los árbitros

En el arbitraje 'ad hoc' a falta de previsión de las partes, las normas de procedimiento de la Comisión Interamericana de Arbitraje Comercial (CIAC), vigentes al momento de la designación de los árbitros, regirán su nombramiento, recusación y sustitución.

Artículo 18
Competencia del tribunal arbitral

1. El tribunal arbitral está facultado para decidir acerca de su propia competencia y, conforme lo establece el art. 8, de las excepciones relativas a la existencia y validez de la convención arbitral.
2. La excepción de incompetencia del tribunal fundada en la inexistencia de materia arbitrable o en la inexistencia, nulidad o caducidad de la convención arbitral en las instituciones arbitrales se rige por su propio reglamento.
3. En el arbitraje 'ad hoc' la excepción de incompetencia por las causales anteriores deberá oponerse hasta el momento de presentar la contestación a la demanda o en el caso de la reconvención, hasta la réplica a la misma. Las partes no están impedidas de oponer esta excepción por el hecho de que hayan designado un árbitro o participado en su designación.
4. El tribunal arbitral podrá decidir las excepciones relativas a su competencia como cuestión previa; empero, también podrá seguir adelante con sus actuaciones y reservar la decisión de las excepciones para el laudo o sentencia final.

Artículo 19
Medidas cautelares

Las medidas cautelares podrán ser dictadas por el tribunal arbitral o por la autoridad judicial competente. La solicitud de cualquiera de las partes a la autoridad judicial no se considerará incompatible con la convención arbitral ni implicará una renuncia al arbitraje.

1. En cualquier estado del proceso, a petición de parte, el tribunal arbitral, podrá disponer por sí las medidas cautelares que estime pertinentes, resolviendo en su caso sobre la contracautela.
2. Dichas medidas cuando fueren dictadas por el tribunal arbitral se instrumentarán por medio de un laudo provisional o interlocutorio.
3. El tribunal arbitral podrá solicitar, de oficio o a petición de parte, a la autoridad judicial competente la adopción de una medida cautelar.
4. Las solicitudes de cooperación cautelar internacional dispuestas por el tribunal arbitral de un Estado Parte serán remitidas al juez del Estado de la sede del tribunal arbitral a efectos de que dicho juez la trasmita para su diligenciamiento al juez competente del Estado requerido, por las vías previstas en el Protocolo de Medidas Cautelares del MERCOSUR, aprobado por Decisión del Consejo del Mercado Común N°27/94. En

este supuesto, los Estados podrán declarar en el momento de ratificar este Acuerdo o con posterioridad que, cuando sea necesaria la ejecución de dichas medidas en otro Estado, el tribunal arbitral podrá solicitar el auxilio de la autoridad judicial competente del Estado en el que deba ejecutarse la medida, por intermedio de las respectivas autoridades centrales o, en su caso, de las autoridades encargadas del diligenciamiento de la cooperación jurisdiccional internacional.

Artículo 20
Laudo o sentencia arbitral

1. El laudo o sentencia arbitral será escrito, fundado, y decidirá completamente el litigio. El laudo o sentencia será definitivo y obligatorio para las partes y no admitirá recursos, excepto los establecidos en los artículos 21 y 22.
2. Cuando los árbitros fueren varios, la decisión será tomada por mayoría. Si no hubiere acuerdo mayoritario, decidirá el voto del presidente.
3. El árbitro que disienta con la mayoría podrá emitir y fundar su voto separadamente.
4. El laudo o sentencia será firmado por los árbitros y contendrá:
   a) la fecha y lugar en que se dictó;
   b) los fundamentos en que se basa, aún si fuera por equidad;
   c) la decisión acerca de la totalidad de las cuestiones sometidas a arbitraje;
   d) las costas del arbitraje.
5. En caso de que uno de los árbitros no firme el laudo o sentencia, se indicará el motivo por el cual no ha firmado, debiendo el presidente del tribunal arbitral certificar tal supuesto.
6. El laudo o sentencia será debidamente notificado a las partes por el tribunal arbitral.
7. Si en el curso del arbitraje las partes llegaren a un acuerdo en cuanto al litigio, el tribunal arbitral, a pedido de las partes, homologará tal hecho mediante un laudo o sentencia que contenga los requisitos del numeral 4 del presente artículo.

Artículo 21
Solicitud de rectificación y ampliación

1. Dentro de los treinta (30) días siguientes a la notificación del laudo o sentencia arbitral, salvo que las partes hayan acordado otro plazo, cualquiera de ellas podrá solicitar al tribunal que:
   a) rectifique cualquier error material;
   b) precise el alcance de uno o varios puntos específicos;
   c) se pronuncie sobre alguna de las cuestiones materia de la controversia que no haya sido resuelta.
2. La solicitud de rectificación será debidamente notificada a la otra parte por el tribunal arbitral.
3. Salvo lo dispuesto por las partes, el tribunal arbitral decidirá respecto de la solicitud, en un plazo de veinte (20) días y les notificará su resolución.

Artículo 22
Petición de nulidad del laudo o sentencia arbitral

1. El laudo o sentencia arbitral sólo podrá impugnarse ante la autoridad judicial del Estado sede del tribunal arbitral mediante una petición de nulidad.

2. El laudo o sentencia podrá ser impugnado de nulidad cuando:
   a) la convención arbitral sea nula;
   b) el tribunal se haya constituido de modo irregular;
   c) el procedimiento arbitral no se haya ajustado a las normas de este Acuerdo, al reglamento de la institución arbitral o a la convención arbitral, según corresponda;
   d) no se hayan respetado los principios del debido proceso;
   e) se haya dictado por una persona incapaz para ser árbitro;
   f) se refiera a una controversia no prevista en la convención arbitral;
   g) contenga decisiones que excedan los términos de la convención arbitral.
3. En los casos previstos en los literales a), b), d) y e) del numeral 2 la sentencia judicial declarará la nulidad absoluta del laudo o sentencia arbitral.

En los casos previstos en los literales c), f) y g) la sentencia judicial determinará la nulidad relativa del laudo o sentencia arbitral.

En el caso previsto en el literal c), la sentencia judicial podrá declarar la validez y prosecución del procedimiento en la parte no viciada y dispondrá que el tribunal arbitral dicte laudo o sentencia complementaria.

En los casos de los literales f) y g) se dictará un nuevo laudo o sentencia arbitral.
4. La petición, debidamente fundada, deberá deducirse dentro del plazo de 90 días corridos desde la notificación del laudo o sentencia arbitral o, en su caso, desde la notificación de la decisión a que se refiere el art. 21.
5. La parte que invoca la nulidad deberá acreditar los hechos en que se funda la petición.

Artículo 23
Ejecución del laudo o sentencia arbitral extranjero

Para la ejecución del laudo o sentencia arbitral extranjero se aplicarán, en lo pertinente, las disposiciones de la Convención Interamericana sobre Arbitraje Comercial Internacional de Panamá de 1975; el Protocolo de Cooperación y Asistencia Jurisdiccional en Materia Civil, Comercial, Laboral y Administrativa del MERCOSUR, aprobado por Decisión del Consejo del Mercado Común N° 5/92, y la Convención Interamericana sobre Eficacia Extraterritorial de las Sentencias y Laudos Arbitrales Extranjeros de Montevideo de 1979.

Artículo 24
Terminación del arbitraje

El arbitraje terminará cuando sea dictado el laudo o sentencia definitivo, o cuando sea ordenada la terminación del arbitraje por el tribunal arbitral si:
   a) las partes están de acuerdo en terminar el arbitraje;
   b) el tribunal arbitral compruebe que el procedimiento arbitral se tornó, por cualquier razón, innecesario o imposible.

Artículo 25
Disposiciones Generales

1. La aplicación de las normas de procedimiento de la Comisión Interamericana de Arbitraje Comercial (CIAC) para el arbitraje 'ad hoc', conforme a lo previsto en el art.12, numeral 2, literal b), no implicará que el arbitraje se considere institucional.

2. Salvo disposición en contrario de las partes o del tribunal arbitral, los gastos resultantes del arbitraje serán solventados por igual entre las partes.

3. Para las situaciones no previstas por las partes, por el presente Acuerdo, por las reglas de procedimiento de la Comisión Interamericana de Arbitraje Comercial Internacional, ni por las convenciones y normas a los que este Acuerdo se remite, se aplicarán los principios y reglas de la Ley Modelo sobre Arbitraje Comercial Internacional de la Comisión de las Naciones Unidas para el Derecho Mercantil Internacional, del 21 de junio de 1985.

Artículo 26
Disposiciones finales

El presente Acuerdo entrará en vigor, con relación a los dos primeros Estados Partes que lo ratifiquen, treinta días después que el segundo país proceda al depósito de su instrumento de ratificación.

1. Para los demás Estados ratificantes, entrará en vigor el trigésimo día posterior al depósito de su respectivo instrumento de ratificación.

2. El presente Acuerdo no restringirá las disposiciones de las convenciones vigentes sobre la misma materia entre los Estados Partes, en tanto no las contradigan.

3. La República del Paraguay será depositaria del presente Acuerdo y de los instrumentos de ratificación y enviará copias debidamente autenticadas a los demás Estados Partes.

4. De la misma forma, la República del Paraguay notificará a los demás Estados Partes la fecha de entrada en vigor del presente Acuerdo y la fecha de depósito de los instrumentos de ratificación.

Hecho en Buenos Aires, República Argentina, a los 23 días del mes de julio de 1998, en un original en los idiomas español y portugués, siendo ambos textos igualmente auténticos.

Note: Please note this instrument is only available in Spanish and Portuguese visit www. redmercosur.org.uy/portal/mercosur.html for more information.

INDEX

Page references in *italics* indicate introductory text.